THE NEW AMERICAN COMMENTARY

An Exegetical and Theological
Exposition of Holy Scripture

THE NEW AMERICAN COMMENTARY

Volume
2

EXODUS

Douglas K. Stuart

BROADMAN & HOLMAN PUBLISHERS
Nashville, Tennessee

ISBN 10: 0-8054-0102-4
ISBN 13: 978-0-8054-0102-8
Dewey Decimal Classification: 222
Subject Heading: BIBLE. O.T. EXODUS
Printed in the United States of America
14 13 12 11 10 09 08 07 06 10 9 8 7 6 5 4 3 2 1

To

John Pressey

gifted pastor and evangelist
enthusiastic student of Exodus

Editors' Preface

God's Word does not change. God's world, however, changes in every generation. These changes, in addition to new findings by scholars and a new variety of challenges to the gospel message, call for the church in each generation to interpret and apply God's Word for God's people. Thus, THE NEW AMERICAN COMMENTARY is introduced to bridge the twentieth and twenty-first centuries. This new series has been designed primarily to enable pastors, teachers, and students to read the Bible with clarity and proclaim it with power.

In one sense THE NEW AMERICAN COMMENTARY is not new, for it represents the continuation of a heritage rich in biblical and theological exposition. The title of this forty-volume set points to the continuity of this series with an important commentary project published at the end of the nineteenth century called AN AMERICAN COMMENTARY, edited by Alvah Hovey. The older series included, among other significant contributions, the outstanding volume on Matthew by John A. Broadus, from whom the publisher of the new series, Broadman Press, partly derives its name. The former series was authored and edited by scholars committed to the infallibility of Scripture, making it a solid foundation for the present project. In line with this heritage, all NAC authors affirm the divine inspiration, inerrancy, complete truthfulness, and full authority of the Bible. The perspective of the NAC is unapologetically confessional and rooted in the evangelical tradition.

Since a commentary is a fundamental tool for the expositor or teacher who seeks to interpret and apply Scripture in the church or classroom, the NAC focuses on communicating the theological structure and content of each biblical book. The writers seek to illuminate both the historical meaning and contemporary significance of Holy Scripture.

In its attempt to make a unique contribution to the Christian community, the NAC focuses on two concerns. First, the commentary emphasizes how each section of a book fits together so that the reader becomes aware of the theological unity of each book and of Scripture as a whole. The writers, however, remain aware of the Bible's inherently rich variety. Second, the NAC is produced with the conviction that the Bible primarily belongs to the church. We believe that scholarship and the academy provide an indispensable foundation for biblical understanding and the service of Christ, but the editors and authors of this series have attempted to communicate the findings of their research in a manner that will build up the whole body of Christ. Thus, the commentary concentrates on theological exegesis while providing practical, applicable exposition.

THE NEW AMERICAN COMMENTARY's theological focus enable

the reader to see the parts as well as the whole of Scripture. The biblical books vary in content, context, literary type, and style. In addition to this rich variety, the editors and authors recognize that the doctrinal emphasis and use of the biblical books differs in various places, contexts, and cultures among God's people. These factors, as well as other concerns, have led the editors to give freedom to the writers to wrestle with the issues raised by the scholarly community surrounding each book and to determine the appropriate shape and length of the introductory materials. Moreover, each writer has developed the structure of the commentary in a way best suited for expounding the basic structure and the meaning of the biblical books for our day. Generally, discussions relating to contemporary scholarship and technical points of grammar and syntax appear in the footnotes and not in the text of the commentary. This format allows pastors and interested laypersons, scholars and teachers, and serious college and seminary students to profit from the commentary at various levels. This approach has been employed because we believe that all Christians have the privilege and responsibility to read and seek to understand the Bible for themselves.

Consistent with the desire to produce a readable, up-to-date commentary, the editors selected the *New International Version* as the standard translation for the commentary series. The selection was made primarily because of the NIV's faithfulness to the original languages and its beautiful and readable style. The authors, however, have been given the liberty to differ at places from the NIV as they develop their own translations from the Greek and Hebrew texts.

The NAC reflects the vision and leadership of those who provide oversight for Broadman Press, who in 1987 called for a new commentary series that would evidence a commitment to the inerrancy of Scripture and a faithfulness to the classic Christian tradition. While the commentary adopts an "American" name, it should be noted some writers represent countries outside the United States, giving the commentary an international perspective. The diverse group of writers includes scholars, teachers, and administrators from almost twenty different colleges and seminaries, as well as pastors, missionaries, and a layperson.

The editors and writers hope that THE NEW AMERICAN COMMENTARY will be helpful and instructive for pastors and teachers, scholars and students, for men and women in the churches who study and teach God's Word in various settings. We trust that for editors, authors, and readers alike, the commentary will be used to build up the church, encourage obedience, and bring renewal to God's people. Above all, we pray that the NAC will bring glory and honor to our Lord who has graciously redeemed us and faithfully revealed himself to us in his Holy Word.

SOLI DEO GLORIA
The Editors

Author's Preface

The commentary format is only one way for scholars to address biblical research, but it continues to be a popular one. As a result, more and more commentaries continue to appear, along with other books and a wealth of periodical literature, from all points of the theological spectrum, on every part of Scripture. So much is this the case that no commentary can now do justice to all the published viewpoints or even to summarizing all the published approaches to the issues in a given text, without actually risking losing the opportunity to speak to the reader in a focused, coherent, helpful fashion. It has been a real joy for me to be able to contribute to the New American Commentary. It is a scholarly endeavor, with the highest standards, but it doesn't leave the reader bewildered with so much interaction with secondary, critical literature that the chance to learn from what's going on in the inspired text ends up becoming what is secondary. In this volume I have tried not to avoid, but to subordinate purely interscholarly interests to the far more important interests of the pastors, missionaries, evangelists, and other workers who will, I hope, find this book a helpful guide to their use of Exodus in Christian ministry.

I am very grateful to the dozens of students in my advanced Hebrew classes at Gordon-Conwell Theological Seminary over the years, whom I forced to plow through the original text of Exodus and its textual variants during the writing of this commentary. They are great scholars in their own right and were rigorous in helping me seek to arrive at the linguistic precision necessary for understanding many passages.

In addition I am very grateful to many dozens of students in my Exodus class at First Church, Boxford, Massachusetts, who spent an hour every Sunday with me for many years studying Exodus. Some Sundays we spent several weeks on a single verse, and other Sundays we actually sped up enough to make it through two or three verses! Their relentless questions and well-pondered insights are reflected in various ways throughout this commentary.

By now my wife and eight children are very used to all the time I put into writing books, and even my grandchildren are now getting used to it. Gayle, my wife, encourages me in all the things I do, even though she could do many of them better than I. Her own amazing productivity in God's work is always an inspiration to me, as I know it is to others as well.

It is also a pleasure to thank Ray Clendenen and all the team involved in the production of the NAC. That a world-class scholar like Ray should put so much time and energy into helping those of us who produce these commentaries to get them into the best shape, and do it with such an encouraging and supportive spirit, is an evidence of God's goodness.

Bradford, Massachusetts
Easter, 2006

Abbreviations

Bible Books

Gen	Isa	Luke
Exod	Jer	John
Lev	Lam	Acts
Num	Ezek	Rom
Deut	Dan	1, 2 Cor
Josh	Hos	Gal
Judg	Joel	Eph
Ruth	Amos	Phil
1, 2 Sam	Obad	Col
1, 2 Kgs	Jonah	1, 2 Thess
1, 2 Chr	Mic	1, 2 Tim
Ezra	Nah	Titus
Neh	Hab	Phlm
Esth	Zeph	Heb
Job	Hag	Jas
Ps (pl. Pss)	Zech	1, 2 Pet
Prov	Mal	1, 2, 3 John
Eccl	Matt	Jude
Song	Mark	Rev

Commonly Used Sources

AASOR	Annual of the American Schools of Oriental Research
AB	Anchor Bible
ABD	*Anchor Bible Dictionary*
ABW	*Archaeology and the Biblical World*
AC	An American Commentary, ed. A. Hovey
AcOr	*Acta orientalia*
AEL	M. Lichtheim, *Ancient Egyptian Literature*
AJSL	*American Journal of Semitic Languages and Literature*
Akk	Akkadian
AnBib	Analecta Biblica
ANET	J. B. Pritchard, ed., *Ancient Near Eastern Texts*
AOAT	Alter Orient und Altes Testament

AOTS	*Archaeology and Old Testament Study,* ed. D. W. Thomas
ArOr	Archiv orientální
ATD	Das Alte Testament Deutsch
ATR	*Anglican Theological Review*
Aug	*Augustinianum*
AusBR	*Australian Biblical Review*
BA	*Biblical Archaeologist*
BAGD	W. Bauer, W. F. Arndt, F. W. Gingrich, and F. W. Danker, *Greek-English Lexicon of the New Testament*
BARev	*Biblical Archaeology Review*
BASOR	*Bulletin of the American Schools of Oriental Research*
BDB	F. Brown, S. R. Driver, and C. A. Briggs, *Hebrew and English Lexicon of the Old Testament*
BETL	Bibliotheca ephemeridum theologicarum lovaniensium
BFT	Biblical Foundations in Theology
BHS	*Biblia hebraica stuttgartensia*
Bib	*Biblica*
BKAT	Biblischer Kommentar: Altes Testament
BO	*Bibliotheca orientalis*
BRev	*Bible Review*
BSac	*Bibliotheca Sacra*
BSC	Bible Study Commentary
BT	*Bible Translator*
BurH	*Buried History*
BV	*Biblical Viewpoint*
BZ	*Biblische Zeitschrift*
BZAW	Beihefte zur ZAW
CAD	*The Assyrian Dictionary of the Oriental Institute of the University of Chicago*
CAH	*Cambridge Ancient History*
CBSC	Cambridge Bible for Schools and Colleges
CBC	Cambridge Bible Commentary
CBQ	*Catholic Biblical Quarterly*
CHAL	*Concise Hebrew and Aramic Lexicon,* ed. W. L. Holladay
CTR	*Criswell Theological Review*
DOTT	*Documents from Old Testament Times,* ed. D. W. Thomas
DSS	Dead Sea Scrolls
EBC	Expositor's Bible Commentary
Ebib	Etudes bibliques

EstBib	*Estudios biblicos*
ETL	*Ephermerides theologicae lovanienses*
Exeg	*Exegetica* (Japanese)
FB	Forschung zur Bibel
FOTL	Forms of Old Testament Literature
GKC	Gesenius' Hebrew Grammar, ed. E. Kautzsch, tr. A. E. Cowley
GTJ	*Grace Theological Journal*
HAR	Hebrew Annual Review
HAT	Handbuch zum Alten Testament
HBT	*Horizons in Biblical Theology*
HDR	Harvard Dissertations in Religion
Her	Hermeneia
HKAT	Handkommentar zum Alten Testament
HSM	Harvard Semitic Monographs
HT	Helps for Translators
HTR	*Harvard Theological Review*
HUCA	*Hebrew Union College Annual*
IB	*Interpreter's Bible*
IBC	Interpretation: A Bible Commentary for Teaching and Preaching
ICC	International Critical Commentary
IDB	*Interpreter's Dictionary of the Bible,* ed. G. A. Buttrick et al.
IDBSup	IDB Supplementary Volume
IBHS	B. K. Waltke and M. O'Connor, *Introduction to Biblical Hebrew Syntax*
IEJ	*Israel Exploration Journal*
IES	Israel Exploration Society
Int	*Interpretation*
ITC	International Theological Commentary
IOS	*Israel Oriental Society*
ISBE	*International Standard Bible Encyclopedia,* rev. ed. G. W. Bromiley
IJT	*Indian Journal of Theology*
ITC	International Theological Commentary
JANES	*Journal of Ancient Near Eastern Society*
JAOS	*Journal of the American Oriental Society*
JBL	*Journal of Biblical Literature*
JBR	*Journal of Bible and Religion*
JCS	*Journal of Cuneiform Studies*
JEA	*Journal of Egyptian Archaeology*

JETS	*Journal of the Evangelical Theological Society*
JJS	*Journal of Jewish Studies*
JNES	*Journal of Near Eastern Studies*
JNSL	*Journal of Northwest Semitic Languages*
JPOS	*Journal of Palestine Oriental Society*
JSJ	*Journal for the Study of Judaism in the Persian, Hellenistic, and Roman Period*
JSOR	*Journal of the Society for Oriental Research*
JSOT	*Journal for the Study of the Old Testament*
JSOTSup	JSOT—Supplement Series
JSS	*Journal of Semitic Studies*
JTS	*Journal of Theological Studies*
JTSNS	*Journal of Theological Studies, New Series*
KAT	Kommentar zum Alten Testament
KB	Koehler and W. Baumgartner, *Lexicon in Veteris* Testamenti libros
LCC	Library of Christian Classics
LLAVT	*Lexicon Linguae Aramaicae Veteris Testamenti*
LTQ	*Lexington Theological Quarterly*
MT	Masoretic Text
NAC	New American Commentary
NCBC	New Century Bible Commentary
NICOT	New International Commentary on the Old Testament
NJPS	*Tanakh: The Holy Scriptures: The New JPS Translation according to the Traditional Hebrew Text*
NKZ	*Neue kirchliche Zeitschrift*
NovT	*Novum Testamentum*
NTS	*New Testament Studies*
Or	*Orientalia*
OTE	*Old Testament Essays*
OTL	Old Testament Library
OTS	*Oudtestamentische Studiën*
OTWSA	*Ou-Testamentiese Werkgemeenskap in Suid-Afrika*
PaVi	*Parole di Vita*
PCB	*Peake's Commentary on the Bible*, ed. M. Black and H. H. Rowley
PEQ	*Palestine Exploration Quarterly*
POTT	*Peoples of Old Testament Times*, ed. D. J. Wiseman
RA	Revue d'assyriologie et d'archéologie orientale
RB	*Revue biblique*
ResQ	*Restoration Quarterly*
RevExp	*Review and Expositor*

RivB	*Revista biblica italiana*
RSR	Recherches de science religieuse
SANE	Sources from the Ancient Near East
SBLDS	Society of Biblical Literature Dissertation Series
SBLSCS	Society of Biblical Literature Septuagint and Cognate Studies
SBT	Studies in Biblical Theology
ScrB	*Scripture Bulletin*
SJT	*Scottish Journal of Theology*
SP	Samaritan Pentateuch
SR	Studies in Religion/Sciences religieuses
ST	*Studia theologica*
STJD	Studies on the Texts of the Desert of Judah
SwJT	*Southwestern Journal of Theology*
Syr	Syriac
TDOT	*Theological Dictionary of the Old Testament,* ed. G. J. Botterweck and H. Ringgren
Tg	Targum
TrinJ	*Trinity Journal*
TLZ	*Theologische Literaturzeitung*
TOTC	Tyndale Old Testament Commentaries
TS	*Theological Studies*
TWAT	*Theologisches Wörterbuch zum Alten Testament,* ed. G. J. Botterweck and H. Ringgren
TWOT	*Theological Wordbook of the Old Testament*
TynBul	*Tyndale Bulletin*
TZ	*Theologische Zeitung*
UF	*Ugarit-Forschungen*
Vg	Vulgate
VT	*Vetus Testamentum*
VTSup	Vetus Testamentum, Supplements
WBC	Word Biblical Commentaries
WEC	Wycliffe Exegetical Commentary
WTJ	*Westminster Theological Journal*
WMANT	Wissenschaftliche Monographien zum Alten und Neuen Testament
ZABR	*Zeitschrift für altorientalische und biblische Rechtsgeschichte*
ZAW	*Zeitschrift für die alttestamentliche Wissenschaft*
ZDMG	*Zeitschrift der deutschen morgenländischen Gesellschaft*
ZDPV	*Zeitschrift des deutschen Palätina-Vereing*
ZTK	*Zeitschrift für katholische Theologie*

Contents

Exodus

INTRODUCTION OUTLINE

INTRODUCTION

1. Structure

The book of Exodus is bifid in composition, meaning that its material is presented to the reader in two main parts. A first part tells the story of God's rescue of the people of Israel from Egypt and his bringing them to Mount Sinai (chaps. 1–19), and a second part describes his covenant with them, made as they encamped at Mount Sinai (chaps. 20–40). Many possible subdivisions are found within these two major halves of the book (as, indeed, this commentary takes note of), but it is hard to miss the basic division of stories of Israel *on their way* to Sinai and accounts of God's covenant provision for them (including confirmations of and threats to that covenant relationship) *after* they are there.[1] Exodus may thus be divided into two broad topics: (1) deliverance of a group of people from submission to their oppressors to submission to God and (2) the constitution of that group as a people of God. Put another way, Exodus is about rescue from human bondage and rescue from sin's bondage.[2] Yet another way to think of the two parts of the book is through the idea of servitude: in Egypt, Israel was the servant of pharaoh; at Sinai they became God's servants.

An important qualification must be made to any statement about the structure of Exodus: the book itself is not a separate, independent work but a subsection of what has virtually always been understood as a five-part work, the Pentateuch.[3] Exodus follows closely on Genesis, so that Exodus 1 constitutes not the beginning of an entirely new work but the beginning of a new section of a larger work that has yet other sections. Likewise, Exodus 40

---

[1] Thus chaps. 1–19 deal with the gathering of a people not only *out of* Egypt but also *to* a place promised in the divine call as proof to Moses of God's purpose (the divine sign; see comments on 3:12a). Chaps. 20–40 deal with what 3:12b predicts: the establishment of a people who know how to worship the one true God because chaps. 20–40 explain in covenant legal terms how it's done. Many scholars have chosen other dividing points, including especially the great Song of the Sea in chap. 15. Because this song is poetry, and poems sometimes are located at or near the end of narrative books or sections of narrative books as if to conclude them (e.g., Deut 32–33, ignoring or redefining Deut 34 as an added transition to Joshua; 2 Sam 22–23, with the same sort of exception applied to 2 Sam 24. Even Genesis 49 is sometimes said to fit this pattern as if Genesis 50 were not a decisively concluding chapter to Genesis). This approach in the case of Exodus has the merit of considering a division of the book to be indicated by the placement of a poem at a key point somewhat near the middle of the otherwise prose material, i.e, of taking the change of literary form as an indication of structural design. I don't think this approach is convincing. In too many places—many dozens of places—in the narrative portions of the OT as well as in predominantly narrative blocks of material within OT prophetical books, poems have been placed by their authors simply because those poems contribute forcefully to the impact of the narrative (a parade example being that of the Song of Lamech in Gen 4:23–24, a poem within prose that brings nothing to a conclusion in terms of the overall structure of Genesis). Moses placed several poems within Genesis, without any indication of an intention that they should be taken as dividing portions of the book. Accordingly, having established a pattern of using poems wherever they would appropriately supplement his prose narrative and without regard to a structural formatting purpose, Moses could be expected to continue that approach and have no structural formatting purpose for the victory song he composed and incorporated into the narrative of Exodus at chap. 15.

[2] These themes are important not merely for Exodus but for the rest of Scripture, as are so many of the other subthemes in Exodus. R. Clifford suggests that Exodus so richly embodies the most basic themes of the Bible that it can usefully be employed as an organizing lens for the appreciation of much of the rest of Scripture, including the NT ("The Exodus in the Christian Bible: The Case for 'Figural' Reading," *TS* 63 [2002]: 345–62).

[3] We are thus taking the predominant scholarly position that there is no Hexateuch per se and that Joshua is the beginning of the Deuteronomy History rather than the ending of the Mosaic books.

hardly brings to a conclusion the major written enterprise Moses had in mind for his audience but concludes only the portion that brings the reader to the point that the tabernacle is built and ready for use as Israel's worship center. When we speak of the structure of Exodus, therefore, we must remember that it is a substructure—the bigger picture is that of the first five books of the Bible, one integral part of which is the section we call Exodus.[4]

Bifid composition of books is a rather common biblical phenomenon. Sometimes the two parts of a book are organized so that they contain almost the same amount of material, as in the close balance between Ezekiel 1–24, which deals with predictions of the fall of Judah and Jerusalem, and Ezekiel 25–48, which reveals God's plans for the future after that great turning point in Israel's history. In other places the division may be more for convenience, allowing the approximate halving of the length of an otherwise substantial scroll (as in 1, 2 Samuel, 1, 2 Kings, 1, 2 Chronicles, and possibly even Ezra-Nehemiah). Bifid books are also sometimes divided into a first part that establishes some sort of situation and then a second part that shows the consequence of what has been established. This is exemplified in the bifid book of Joshua. It contains in chaps. 1–12 the story of the conquest of the land of Canaan (establishing general control of the promised land), and in chaps. 13–24, the story of the division of that land among the tribes (a consequence of being able to control the land). This is somewhat parallel to the situation in Exodus, where the first part (chaps. 1–19) establishes the freedom from human enemies by God's gracious deliverance, and the second part (chaps. 20–40) provides the consequence of that freedom: the opportunity to become God's people and adhere to his covenant requirements.

Other examples of bifid composition may also be noted. Isaiah is arranged with a more chronological focus in that its first part (chaps. 1–33) contains mainly oracles intended to explain the coming demise of Israel and Judah up to 586 BC, whereas chaps. 40–66 present the more distant focus of hope for a renewed relationship with God after the unleashing of the covenant curses by way of the great Babylonian exile. This, too, is at least partly parallel to the organization of Exodus, since the focus of the first part of Exodus precedes chronologically the focus of the second part.[5] Even New

---

[4] And by all means, Exodus is a subunit of a greater literary work, still, that is, the whole of Scripture. See G. D. Fee and D. K. Stuart, *How to Read the Bible Book by Book* (Grand Rapids: Zondervan, 2002), 34–42, esp. 42.

[5] Isaiah, however, differs from Exodus in that its first part does not describe historical events that set the scene for the second part. It is like Exodus in another way, however: all its material was written at the same time (by Isaiah the prophet) even though its topics cover a substantial span of time—this being parallel to the way Moses wrote about events taking more than eighty years (in Exodus alone; if Genesis is included, the span is far greater indeed), yet he did the writing in a relatively short space of time.

Testament epistles are often bifid; in fact, all of Paul's are, to one extent or another. He tended to write his letters beginning with theological exposition and ending with paraenesis, or put more simply, beginning with doctrine and ending with duty, and the two sections are usually roughly balanced.[6]

By no means is bifid composition a wooden method. It is simply a general organizing principle, useful in a primarily oral culture, where the grouping of materials into two discernible blocks helped people keep that material in mind by associating the various contents within either "half" of the book with like contents in that same half. There is no reason to think that bifid composition has some sort of great advantage over other patterns (such as the prologue-dialogue-epilogue structure of Job, or the acrostic-chiastic structure of Lamentations, or the threefold woe-weal pattern of Micah, or the six disputations of Malachi). Like those alternative patterns, bifid composition is just a convenient structural device. Within the broad parameters of a bifid biblical book, any number of subcategories and special, particular elements may be found. Thus Isaiah may include several prophecies in chaps. 1–33 that point toward the time after the fall of Jerusalem, prophecies that could, in other words, have been placed in chaps. 40–66; and he can also include (although we cannot tell if the decision was his or that of an inspired editor) descriptions of his interaction with Jerusalem and its king in chaps. 34–39 as a kind of hinge linking the two main parts of the bifid structure. In Exodus, Moses included some narrative within the mainly legal/covenant "half" (e.g., the story of the ratification of the covenant in chap. 24 or the story of the breaking of the covenant in chap. 32) when so doing suits the purpose of informing the reader of how important or how difficult it was for the Israelites fully to agree to and to honor the covenant they had been graciously provided by their God. Moses also included some law within the earlier, pre-Sinai covenant part of the book, since it pleased God to start revealing that law (e.g., regarding the Passover) at the time of the first occasion of observing it (see comments on chap. 12).

Getting out of Egypt and to Sinai safely constitutes the first great theme of the book, found in the first section of the two-part work. Getting to know God's covenant will makes for the second great theme, including the revelation of how he wishes to be worshiped, as indicated especially by the tabernacle focus of chaps. 25–40.

---

[6] We find a certain amount of mixing of the two categories in Paul's letters, but in all of them doctrine *predominates* in the first half, and application/paraenesis/duty *predominate* in the second.

2. Historical Issues

In the case of most matters described in Exodus, scant corroborating evidence exists[7] by which a historian, regardless of his or her bias, could confirm or deny the historicity of the biblical accounts.[8] For example, the pharaoh under whose (probably distant and perhaps ever unwitting) protection Moses was raised,[9] the pharaoh who sought to kill Moses, and the

[7] Quite possibly by design on the part of the ancient Egyptians. G. Wheeler has argued persuasively that the ancient Egyptian mind-set would have found it almost impossible to record for posterity anything about the exodus, the plagues that led up to them, or other events that showed the weakness of Egypt, its leaders, or its people. This is because Egyptians believed that writing was an act of the creation of reality—that written words actually brought into being the things they described. From the Egyptian point of view, writing had the power to control the forces of the cosmos, to make them become what the words described. Therefore, they thought, to put into writing the story of the domination of Yahweh over the gods of Egypt and the killing of the firstborn, as well as other details of the plagues and the "ruin" of the country (Exod 10:7), would be to fix them in reality and give them a currency and a continuation that would be harmful for the future of Egypt (G. Wheeler, "Ancient Egypt's Silence about the Exodus," *AUSS* 40 [2002]: 257–64).

[8] J. I. Durham, (*Exodus*, WBC [Waco: Word, 1987], puts the case rather extremely, but his comments are not without considerable value in reference to many data of the book that cannot specifically be confirmed either by archaeology or by contemporary written sources: "We can present archaeological data to support more than one set of dates for the wilderness wandering and the conquest/settlement, as shown by such studies as those of de Vaux (291–472), Herrmann (1–91), Nicholson (xiii–xv, 1–90) and Bimson (7–324). We can make a case for three or four excellent Egyptian *Sitze im Leben* that would fit the sojourn-exodus narratives and Genesis and Exodus (Thompson). *What we cannot do, without more specific data than we have, however, is provide historical confirmation for anything or anybody mentioned in the Book of Exodus* [italics mine]. No one yet has given any convincing extra-biblical hint, much less proof, of any single part of the Exodus narrative. Apart from Pharaoh's store-cities, Pithom and Ra'amses, which can be generally located, and the oasis of Kadesh-Barnea, which can be certainly located, we cannot fix with any degree of certainty one single place of the many mentioned in the Book of Exodus, not even Mount Sinai itself (Coats, Walsh, Davies, Zenger). This is not of course to say that the events and persons referred to by Exodus are not historical, only that we have no historical proof of them" (*Exodus*, WBC [Waco: Word, 1987], xxv). By contrast, K. Kitchen, a renowned Egyptologist, is far more sanguine about the historicity of the book ("Egyptians and Hebrews from Raises to Jericho," in *The Origin of Early Israel* [Beer-Sheva: Ben-Gurion University of the Negev Press, 1998], 65–131). Kitchen argues at length for the historical reasonableness of the biblical stories of how the Israelites got into Egypt, how they lasted there for four centuries, and how they left. The Exodus commentary by J. Currid, cited repeatedly in our commentary, as well as his *Ancient Egypt and the Old Testament* (Grand Rapids: Baker, 1997) and J. Hoffmeier's *Israel in Egypt* (New York: Oxford University Press, 1997) provide many cogent lines of evidence for a greater confidence in the factuality of the historical data in Exodus than Durham is willing to concede.

[9] Moses said nothing about any personal contact with the pharaoh who was the father of the woman who took him as her son. She made decisions on her own in the story. In the ancient world it was a normal practice for a king to give one of his daughters to another king as wife (and vice versa) upon the conclusion of a treaty. Having many of daughters was considered a desirable asset—certainly for a pharaoh who had numerous contacts with a great many other kings, many of whom ruled only small regions around small cities, as evidenced in the Amarna letters from, generally, the time of Moses. Having many wives was regarded as indicating personal prowess and general influence. The pharaoh described in chap. 1 of the book probably had many daughters, most of whom probably saw him mainly at a distance. Private conversations between father and daughter likely were rare and in some cases may never have occurred in a lifetime.

pharaoh of the exodus are not named. This may be a literary device on Moses' part, a way of reducing the greatest man in the greatest national power of the day to a mere office via a somewhat generic title.[10] Similarly, we cannot (at least not convincingly for most people) pinpoint the date of the exodus by reference to firmly established evidence from Egypt. Moreover, the route of the exodus, including the location of Mount Sinai itself, remains debatable. In this commentary we have accepted the evidence, debated as it is, for a fifteenth-century exodus[11] and the location of Mount Sinai as Jebel-Musa, in the modern Sinai Peninsula, rather than, as others have argued, for a thirteenth-century exodus and, in the opinion of some, a strictly Midianite (northwest Saudi Arabian) location for Mount Sinai. We don't argue the case for any of these conclusions definitively (as if anyone could); we rest our case on the careful arguments of others, comforted by the fact that our ignorance of the exact modern locations for places mentioned in Exodus does not in itself change either the message of the book or the confidence we may have in its historical reliability.[12]

We also take seriously the description of the rapid increase of the Israelite population in northeast Egypt,[13] the Egyptian population control plan that involved killing male infants, the descriptions of Moses' access to Pharaoh in spite of his being a mere slave-class representative from the Egyptian point of view, the plagues, the national (and international[14]) escape from Egypt followed by a determined pursuit of chariot-mounted Egyptian troops, and the miraculously enabled encampment of the people at Mount Sinai, a place that otherwise did not have (and to this day does not have) a water supply capable of supporting so many thousands, let alone an active

---

[10] "Pharaoh" is Egyptian for "big house" (*pr* = house, *ʿh* = big) so that reference to the pharaoh in Exodus is somewhat like using the term "the White House" in modern times, as in "The White House said today that no new legislation would be proposed." It refers generally to the government and national leader, but only from the point of view of the office and not the man. In Exodus, Moses used "Pharaoh" more often than his other generic term for the same person, "king of Egypt," but interchanged the two terms without any obvious intentional pattern. Hence, we have chosen to refer to the king by his title "the pharaoh."

[11] The more specific evidence for this date is actually found in 1 Kgs 6:1, not Exodus itself. Arguments for either a fifteenth-century exodus or a thirteenth-century exodus abound, and there exists as well an intriguing and carefully presented argument for a fourteenth-century exodus, in 1312 BC, during the reign of Pharaoh Horemheb (J. Adler, "Dating the Exodus: A New Perspective," *JBQ* 23 [1995]: 44–51). For one of the recent articulations of the evidence for and plausibility of the fifteenth-century date, see S. Horn, "What We Don't Know about Moses and the Exodus," *BAR* 3 (1977): 22–31. Horn also argues for the traditional southern route of the exodus and the traditional Jebel-Musa as Mount Sinai, positions we agree do not need to be abandoned.

[12] Cf. A. R. Millard, "How Reliable Is Exodus?" *BAR* 26 (2000): 50–57.

[13] See J. M. Cohen, "The Fertility of the Early Israelites," *JBQ* 27 (1999): 195–98.

[14] See comments on 12:38.

volcano.[15] All of these events, and others, have been thought unlikely or impossible by various writers and commentators, but in this commentary we seek consistently to show their reasonableness and, indeed, likelihood, albeit without as much outside evidence from beyond the text of Exodus as we would find it convenient to possess were it to exist or eventually be discoverable.[16]

Our position is that the pharaoh "who did not know about Joseph" (see comments on 1:8) was a native Egyptian Pharaoh newly in power sometime after the overthrow of the Hyksos occupiers, the Hyksos having been the Asiatic conquerors of Egypt under whose domain the Israelite Joseph, another Asiatic, had been promoted to prominence.[17] In Genesis, Moses preserved the Joseph story in considerable detail, in part, we surmise, because it explains so much of the history of the people he had been called by God to lead to the promised land, the people who constituted his original audience for Genesis as well as Exodus.[18] The kinds of data assembled and analyzed especially by Hoffmeier and Currid have validity, we judge, and their general approach has, accordingly, influenced the outlook of this commentary.[19] Nevertheless, it is the overall believability of Moses' narrative, surviving all these years and inspiring and encouraging people with great power still today, that will convince the reader, we expect, of the general historicity of

---

[15] In our opinion it is highly unlikely that the glory cloud atop Mount Sinai would have been merely the smoke from a volcano active at the time the Israelites came to the mountain. It seems to us that this really does no justice to the many accounts of Moses' entering that cloud personally—or for that matter the Israelites' elders entering it (24:9–11). Not a few persons looking for the location of biblical Mount Sinai have, however, insisted that the starting point for their search had to be the list of volcanic mountains in the general region likely to have been active in biblical times, as if the biblical account were actually a rather wildly distorted fantasy built up from what was originally nothing more than a natural event. If one has that low a view of the historicity of the biblical account, what is the point of spending a lot of energy looking for the original location that generated such a skewed history? Why not merely conclude that the whole account is nonsense or that a few thunderstorms or a few foggy days would do just as well or better than a volcano for the source of the Mount Sinai "folklore"?

[16] On the unlikelihood that any written Egyptian evidence of this sort would ever be discovered, since it wouldn't ever have existed by reason of the religious design of Egyptian historical writing, see Wheeler, "Ancient Egypt's Silence," 257–64.

[17] This is not to say that it would have been impossible for native Egyptian pharaohs to feel warmly toward Israelites. In general, the Bible presents a picture of Egyptian-Israelite relations that are for the most part friendly or at least not regularly hostile, and the frequency with which Israelites sought refuge in Egypt as described in various biblical stories tends to confirm this (as do such passages as Isa 19:23–25). See M. T. McHatten, "Israel and Egypt during the Exodus," *BT* 40 (2002): 141–47.

[18] Cf. D. Garrett, *Rethinking Genesis: The Sources and Authorship of the First Book of the Bibl*e (Fearn: Mentor, 2000).

[19] Hoffmeier, *Israel in Egypt*; Currid, *Ancient Egypt and the Old Testament.*

the book and specifically of the events described in it.[20] Our purpose in this commentary has been less to repeat the arguments of those who have taken up the challenge to defend the historical accuracy of Exodus as to show the reasonableness of everything in the account—explaining as best we are able the cogency of the presentation and the historically realistic nature of the actions and speeches as they unfold. The reader will be our judge as to whether or not or to what extent we have succeeded in this.

3. Text

The text of the book of Exodus is on the whole rather well preserved in the Masoretic tradition, which is the tradition that all modern English translations are based primarily on. In all likelihood, the reason for this good state of preservation textually is the work of Ezra. He quite probably brought back from Babylon to Jerusalem in 458 BC a carefully preserved and well-edited copy of at least the Pentateuch and Former Prophets, if not many or most other parts of the Old Testament in Hebrew.[21] For Ezra, as for many generations of Israelites before him, Exodus was revered as holy Scripture, and the care with which it was preserved stems from this reverence.[22] The book's text was, of course, copied many dozens of times thereafter before it came into the form now known as the MT (Masoretic Text)[23] and exemplified by the most commonly used manuscript from that tradition, the Leningrad Codex of AD 1008.[24]

---

[20] In other words, a truly thoughtful analysis of Exodus ought to demonstrate that if someone or some group had wanted to fabricate the story of how the Israelites came into existence, they would, in all probability, not have produced the book of Exodus that we have today. Fiction writers can produce lovely, balanced, "smooth," and, so-to-speak, problem-free narratives because they can make up everything and simply cause it all to fit together nicely. History writers must write what happened—warts and all, embarrassments and all, behavior oddities and all, unexplainable developments and all, and many accounts that they may well wish they didn't have to tell because those accounts make either their subjects or themselves (or both) look bad. Exodus is the latter sort of narrative; it reads throughout like a true history from ancient times, not like a fiction.

[21] For an expansion on this approach taking into account the entire theory of "local texts" and the special nature of the Pentateuch and Former Prophets from the point of view of ancient copyists, see F. M. Cross Jr., *The Ancient Library of Qumran and Modern Biblical Studies*, rev. ed. (Grand Rapids: Baker, 1980).

[22] A parade example of this reverence in action may be found in Neh 8.

[23] The Masoretes, medieval Jewish scribes dedicated to preserving the text of the SC and providing vocalizations that would help medieval worshipers to chant it accurately in synagogue worship services, began their enterprise around 600 BC and were active into the time of the Renaissance.

[24] All modern translations work primarily from the Leningrad Codex, which forms the basis even for the latest BH5 or Quinta edition of the Hebrew because the LC is the earliest *complete* MT manuscript. It is unlikely that an earlier complete and well-preserved text will ever surface.

The Septuagint (LXX) confirms the vast majority of MT readings, and in a relatively few places, also some longer readings. This comports with what can generally be said of the Pentateuch and Former Prophets: the LXX of these books is not expansionistic, but rather the MT of these books tends now and again to be haplographic, that is, characterized by omissions that shorten the overall text slightly. Most of these omissions are minor; none has, in our opinion, any significant meaning-changing bearing on the interpretation of the book of Exodus or any full passage therein. Sometimes the Qumran (Dead Sea Scrolls, also called Q or DSS) evidence helps resolve textual questions, but in only about fifty places[25] are the Qumran readings lengthy enough and at the same time different from the MT to make possible the use of the Qumran readings as legitimate comparison texts in establishing the theoretical original wording of Exodus. Rarely, evidence from Jerome's Vulgate or the Syriac Peshitta or the Aramaic Targum of Exodus will shed significant, independent light on a text option, though these often enough do add some weight to what the LXX and/or Qumran readings will already have brought to the attention of the textual analyst.

We have not hesitated in this commentary to bring to the reader's attention textual issues as they bear, even theoretically, upon the interpretation of a given passage. But we also have not hesitated to omit mention of routine textual matters, the resolution of which simply would reinforce an MT reading or cannot be definitively resolved against an MT reading. Where a variant reading in one of the ancient versions might be thought important, we have tried to evaluate the importance thereof but have, again, done so selectively so as not to expand the commentary into something that it is not, that is, a technical-critical commentary giving constant attention to textual issues large and small, consequential and inconsequential.[26] All in all, happily, the text of Exodus is rather well preserved.

---

[25] Cf. J. Fitzmeyer, *The Dead Sea Scrolls: Major Publications and Tools for Study* (Missoula: Scholars Press, 1977), 153ff.

[26] This volume, like most others in the NAC series, addresses text-critical matters when they actually do or might affect the interpretation of the text rather than wherever a variant—major or minor—is attested. The reader should also know that the author of this volume is the very opposite of a "Masoretic fundamentalist." Our approach throughout is that whatever reading can be shown to reflect the likely original text ought to be accepted, regardless of whether or not it agrees with the MT.

4. Authorship[27]

Moses had nearly thirty-nine years to write Exodus. When he did so during that time period between the Israelites' departure from Sinai and his death and exactly how many days or weeks he spent doing so is impossible to reconstruct. We may reasonably conjecture that the first audience for whom he wrote was the second postexodus generation, the one that had grown up in the wilderness during the days described in the book of Numbers. He would have written the book for them as that generation was preparing to enter the promised land as a reminder of who they were and what their origins (i.e., the events and instructions their parents had experienced) had been and what was required of them in the covenant God had made with their parents. If these conjectures are correct, Exodus would have been produced in writing sometime near the end of the forty-year period after the Israelites left Egypt and before they entered Canaan, that is, when Moses himself was nearing the end of his life.[28] Exodus describes events that took place mainly over a period of about eighty-one years (i.e., starting with the time from Moses' birth as described in 2:1ff. to the time of the completion of the tabernacle as described in 40:1–35, when Moses was about eighty-one years old). It also gives the background of the Israelites' sojourn in Egypt, reviewing the story of how the Israelites settled in Egypt more than four centuries before Moses' birth, and provides as well a small bit of "foreground," in 40:36–38, describing how the glory cloud of God moved spatially relative to the tabernacle to lead the Israelites through the wilderness, something that could have taken only a few weeks or months to establish as a pattern but a

[27] A commentary such as this, which recognizes and discusses the Mosaic authorship of Exodus throughout, could seem rather extreme to some of those embracing the Documentary Hypothesis. Some source critics hold their views with great tenacity. Some, we expect (perhaps even some of our own much-valued friends in the nonevangelical camp), may assume that a commentary espousing Mosaic authorship cannot possibly be entirely erudite. Most scholars are more open-minded than that, however, whatever their personal views, and would not disallow a commentary's usefulness merely because it rejects source criticism as neither convincing nor useful in the study of the Pentateuch. Additionally, we are well aware that even evangelical scholars who hold to Mosaic authorship often soft-pedal that fact so that readers of their works are hardly aware of their commitment to it. We have done just the opposite, seeking openly and repeatedly to analyze Moses' style and authorial purposes wherever they might be discerned since behind them lies God's design for the reader, something we have been eager to try to discover to the extent possible.

[28] One reason for the description of Moses as still possessing all his faculties up to the time of his death (Deut 34:7) may have been the assurance it would give to readers of the Pentateuch that he was fully capable of sophisticated, accurate authorship and reliable remembrance of the events that constitute the subject matter of the five books to which Deuteronomy provides the conclusion.

phenomenon that was in fact experienced by the people all during the wilderness wanderings of that roughly forty-year period.[29]

Style Variety and Source Analysis

A substantial philosophical and methodological distance lies between those following the traditional approach, who regard Moses as the author of Exodus, and those who believe that the book was produced partly after the introduction of the monarchy in Israel (i.e., not until at least the tenth-ninth centuries), partly another century or so thereafter (i.e., sometime in the ninth or eighth century) and partly after the Judean exile (i.e., essentially during the late sixth and/or fifth century BC).[30] Since this gulf affects basic issues in the interpretation of the book, a brief review of some aspects of the difference may be in order here. It will hardly serve the reader's purpose for us to give more than an overview of the older antitraditional approach, especially since many scholars have moved away from it and there are now a variety of competing viewpoints on the authorship of the Pentateuch.[31]

One popular school of biblical scholarship holds to the "Documentary Hypothesis," the theory that the book of Exodus is the product of three very different authors: "J," a theological genius who produced most of the narrative portion of Exodus sometime around the ninth century BC in Judah, "E," a northern theologian who added to this narrative from sources and perspectives available to him when he wrote sometime around the eighth century, and "P," a school of priests writing after the Judean exile, that is, mainly in the sixth and/or fifth century BC in Judah, who generated most of the legal materials that dominate the second half of the book. Many different theories

---

[29] Nothing in 40:36–38 requires the conclusion that Moses penned the book toward the end of his life, i.e., toward the end of the forty years in the wilderness since the wording "during all their travels" (40:38) could effectively mean "all their travels to this point," meaning the point at which Moses wrote the book. On the other hand, nothing prohibits the possibility that he wrote some of Exodus, or at least the last few verses of it, while in Moab during the time he was preparing to preach Deuteronomy to the people in anticipation of their entering the promised land. As Garrett has argued in *Rethinking Genesis,* the Pentateuch shows no knowledge of later Israelite experience over the centuries in the promised land of Canaan; all its five books are consistently anticipatory, looking forward to occupying the promised land just as they at points look back to bondage in Egypt—but they are always in between Egypt and Canaan in their perspective.

[30] These dates are simply those commonly (but not exclusively) theorized for the so-called J source, the E source, and the P source, respectively.

[31] See, e.g., G. Wenham, "Pentateuchal Studies Today," *Themelios* 22 (1996): 3–13; D. L. Peterson, "The Formation of the Pentateuch," in *Old Testament Interpretation: Past, Present, and Future* (Nashville: Abingdon, 1995), 31–45; R. N. Whybray, *Introduction to the Pentateuch* (Grand Rapids: Eerdmans, 1995), 12–28.

exist as to who put these sources together, but just as the sources themselves are anonymous, so is (are) their editor(s).

The arguments for and against this hypothesis and its reliance on what is typically called either "source criticism" or "source analysis" are many and have been widely published. One consideration that has not been much discussed, however, is the interrelationship between the preference for style variation in ancient Israelite writing and the criterion of vocabulary preference that has been a foundational means of differentiating sources by those who hold to the Documentary Hypothesis.

Source analysis rests in considerable measure on perceived vocabulary differences among the three major sources since style cannot be discerned except by the analysis, in one way or another, of vocabulary.[32] For example, the theoretical "J source" is alleged to use exclusively or virtually exclusively the proper name "Yahweh" for God, whereas the "E source" uses Elohim instead. This is only one example. In fact, a considerable variety of vocabulary words are alleged to be pointers to their respective sources. But are these sorts of vocabulary variations really what source critics think they are? Was it the case that a given ancient author—or copyist—would have used a single given word for a single given concept consistently, without variation, whenever he or she wrote about that concept? If such were the case, the Documentary Hypothesis might at least try to claim some credence since it could indeed be said to have measurable means of tracing the marks of its various sources. But did such consistency actually occur? Did ancient Israelite writers have such limited vocabularies that they were incapable of routinely employing synonyms (variant vocabulary) for a given concept? Or did they perhaps have such a commitment to rigidity of verbal expression that they were prevented from using alternative vocabulary words as a matter of policy?

In fact, the contrary situation appears to be true. In ancient Israel there were four demonstrable indications of a preference for variety in written expression rather than of desire for stylistic consistency. (1) If there were two different ways of spelling a word, the Israelites chose to preserve both spellings as valid and to include both of them frequently in any document. Thus with regard to spelling (orthography), ancient Israelites had no commitment to consistency of style but rather the free use of alternative spellings was regarded as not only proper but desirable.[33] (2) In the case of

---

[32] This qualification applies even to issues of religious concept. One can claim to discern that a supposed anonymous literary "source" is different from another supposed anonymous literary "source" only by working from their vocabulary. It is not that words and concepts are the same thing but that words are the only way to convey concepts in written materials.

[33] This is evident in the preservation of spellings that differ. E.g., David's name is spelled either דָּוִד or דָּוִיד; Daniel's is either דָּנִאֵל or דָּנִיֵּאל—and such variations can take place in a single verse, not merely in a single book in a single MS.

common expressions, a similar phenomenon can be observed. Where variation was possible, it apparently was not avoided but preferred. Alternative ways of forming a given multiword expression were employed commonly so that both alternatives were preserved. Thus in the case of repeated phraseology in prose contexts, there was no commitment to consistency of style but rather the free use of alternative formulations was regarded as not only proper but desirable.[34] (3) With regard to variation in grammatical forms, a similar phenomenon is observed. If there existed two different ways of saying something, even in the case of a common verb form, both ways were used so as to preserve both in the common discourse.[35] Again the preference clearly appears to have been for inclusion of variety rather than for consistency of one form if two existed. (4) The Masoretic system of *Kethib-Qere* represents a fourth indicator of the tendency in past times to preserve variants rather than to select one option and to employ it consistently—a tendency that extended into the medieval period when the Masoretes worked. This system arose from a desire to include, not merely side-by-side but actually within the same word, two variant readings rather than to select one. The Masoretes provided the consonants of one text option and the vowels of another. They indicated their preferred reading but did not omit the reading they regarded as inferior—they simply did not vocalize it.

A first question that must be answered by a source critic is this: If these various indications of a preference for preservation of variety rather than of consistency existed in the ancient world, is not variety of vocabulary an instance of the same phenomenon rather than an indication of multiple authorship? Indeed, might it not follow that the expectation of a

[34] As an illustration of this point, consider the two phrases "Daughter Zion" (בַּת־צִיּוֹן) and "Daughter Jerusalem" (בַּת יְרוּשָׁלָם). These are obviously synonyms, as indicated by their occurrences together in poetic parallelism (e.g., 2 Kgs 19:21 = Isa 37:22; Zeph 3:14), but they also vary unpredictably in otherwise source-unified contexts (as in Lam 2:15,18).

[35] One of the many examples of this is that of the variation exemplified by the difference between וַיֹּאמֶר לוֹ and וַיֹּאמֶר אֵלָיו, "he said to him." Such variation occurs in places where variant sources have never been suggested and is a variation Moses also used, crossing the boundaries usually thought to indicate separate literary sources (both אמר ל and אמר אל are actually used together in eighteen verses in the OT, none of which is commonly considered to be source-composite; e.g., Gen 44:4; Exod 3:13; Judg 17:9; 1 Sam 2:16; 9:27; 2 Sam 1:3,8; 13:5; Isa 36:7; Ezek 28:2; 33:10). Another parade example is found in Ezra 5, where the Aramaic *peal* infinitive for "to build" is written twice as לְמִבְנֵא (vv. 2,17), twice as לִבְנֵא (vv. 3,13), and once as לְמִבְנְיָה (v. 9). These three variant forms existed in the language, and the writer of Ezra 5 did not select one but used all three in a concentric or chiastic pattern of distribution. There are many other examples of the same sort of phenomena, by which scribes are simply writing in the "high style" that favored the inclusion of vocabulary and grammatical variations within single passages rather than settling on one option and ignoring others. It is this high style that Moses used—and that looked to scholars unaware of it in former centuries as if it were somehow the product of redactors weaving together fragments of separate sources.

commitment—by reason of vocabulary paucity or vocabulary rigidity—to consistent vocabulary usage in "sources" was in fact only apparent and not real since it would run counter to the demonstrated tendency for variety and against consistency in these other analogous components of ancient Hebrew literary style? A second question would be: Why do source critics routinely attribute remarkable consistency to their theorized sources in the use of style and vocabulary and then attribute almost complete inconsistency to their theorized redactors, to whom are ascribed the tendency to combine portions of material from their sources freely and, to be blunt, sloppily?[36]

Our conclusion, then, is that Moses was following the popular tendency of ancient literary convention in employing varying vocabulary forms and orthography. Clearly he was not preserving variant textual readings since these would not have existed until after the manuscript copying and recopying had produced over time variants of his autograph of the five-book grand epic of Israel's early history and law that he wrote under God's controlling inspiration.[37]

At several points in the Pentateuch, Moses described himself in the third person[38] as the author of what he had written. For example, he mentioned how he was told by God to write down the story of the Israelite encounter with the Amalekites at Rephidim (Exod 17:14). He also described at various points his being instructed to write down the law as given him from God (Exod 24:4; 34:1,27–28; Deut 31:9,24). He mentioned as well his requirement from God to write down at God's dictation the so-called Song of Moses (Deut 31:19–22, referring to the song in chap. 32). These references

[36] Although advocates of the Documentary Hypothesis do not normally employ the adjective "sloppy" to describe what they suggest ancient redactors did with their sources, we would contend that this is in fact a fair summary of what they are suggesting. Source critics are able, it seems, to discern the piecing together of sources only when that piecing together is awkward, amateurish, and obviously tendentious. Otherwise, there would be no way, at this far-removed point in time, to detect the cobbling of sources into a composite that is not consistent enough to hide the original sources. Source critics invariably have a high view of the quality and consistency of their supposed sources and a low view of the quality and consistency of their supposed source redactors. P. Enns makes a similar observation: "Too often, appeal is made to a theory of a 'mindless redactor,' who evidently is not bothered by such tensions as the presence of the name Yahweh in the immediate context of [Exodus 3:14–15], where that name is supposedly introduced for the first time. In my view, it has never been adequately explained why, according to source criticism, *authors* are assumed to be consistent in their use of names for God and other terms, but redactors are perfectly happy to bring these sources together in seemingly contradictory ways" (*Exodus*, NIV Application Commentary [Grand Rapids: Zondervan, 2002], 105, n. 29).

[37] Assuming that few readers of this commentary obtained it in order to be tutored at length on the fine points of the Documentary Hypothesis and our opinion of its weaknesses, we say no more at this point on the topic.

[38] Third-person description of one's actions, thoughts, and words, is, of course, widely attested in all sorts of ANE literature.

to Mosaic authorship are substantial. Deuteronomy 31:24 says, for example, that Moses wrote "in a book the words of this law from beginning to end." This can mean nothing less than a claim that he wrote all of Deuteronomy, though it may very well imply all of the law from Exodus 20 onward.[39]

We could not reasonably expect Moses to say any more by way of authorship claims than he said.[40] In the ancient world, authors did not normally make any statement within their works of their authorship of those works, just as is almost always the case in the modern world.[41] The fact that Moses actually stretched the boundaries of this practice and referred to his authorship within the works we call the books of the Pentateuch probably represents a special attempt to lend authority to those works from within rather than merely via a title or superscription. Moses wrote during the wilderness years after the exodus from Egypt for the benefit of all Israelites who needed to know the full story of their national history—especially the new generation born in the wilderness as well as those from other ethnic groups (Exod

---

[39] Moses never claimed, either by word or action, kingship of any sort, even though it was usually and normally the prerogative of a king to issue laws. In this sense Moses is constantly, if implicitly, characterized over against the usual ANE legal corpus's orientation toward monarchical law. See J. W. Watts, "The Legal Characterization of Moses in the Rhetoric of the Pentateuch," *JBL* 117 (1998): 415–26. What Moses did claim to be was a sort of amanuensis to the eternal, heavenly King, a scribe with no authority of his own to issue a single word of law but one who must always get everything he wrote down from the direct revelation of Yahweh. Typical examples of this are found in Num 15, where the case of a man gathering wood on the Sabbath requires an inquiry of God for an answer of how to proceed by way of punishment, and Num 27, where the case of the daughters of Zelophehad required Moses to go to God for an answer about their claim to inheritance—he had no authority to issue an answer himself.

[40] Indeed, though Moses is necessarily a huge presence in the book of Exodus, he carefully presented himself in a literarily impersonal way—portraying himself as slightly aloof even when he was a character involved in many of the issues and developments, with the result that the person and presence of Yahweh and Yahweh's covenant law, rather than Moses, take center stage (Moses decreased so that Yahweh and the covenant may increase). See P. Machinist, "The Man Moses," *BR* 26 (2000): 18–19, 53. (While we believe Machinist's analysis helps provide a perspective that aides in explaining why Moses presented himself as he did, Machinist himself does not regard the downplaying/distancing of the role of Moses as the result of Moses' own writing but as the product of anonymous sources and their anonymous editing.)

[41] Where, e.g., in modern literature will the name of the author of a history, or a novel, or a set of poems, or virtually any type of literary production appear after the title page—except perhaps when one is referring to oneself in an autobiography (and even then the reader cannot usually tell who the "I" in an autobiography refers to if the title page is not known)? Thus to expect that Moses would somehow try to claim authorship every so often within the pages of what he wrote is simply naïve. On the other hand, the NT statements about Moses' authorship of the law are fairly comprehensive (Matt 8:4; 19:7; 22:24ff.; Mark 7:10). Note especially Jesus' statement about Exodus (at least) in Mark 12:26: "Now about the dead rising—have you not read in the book of Moses, in the account of the bush, how God said to him, 'I am the God of Abraham, the God of Isaac, and the God of Jacob'?" as well as Jesus' characterization of the entire Pentateuch as "Moses" in Luke 16:29,31; 24:27,44. Cf. John 5:46; 7:19,22–23; Acts 3:22; esp. 6:11.

12:38) who joined Israel as a result of the plagues and who would have been virtually ignorant of most of Israelite history.

5. The Theology of Exodus

In Exod 6:6–8 God lays before the Israelites an outline of what he is doing for them and a definition of how they are to think of themselves in relation to him:[42]

> Therefore, say to the Israelites: "I am the LORD, and I will bring you out from under the yoke of the Egyptians. I will free you from being slaves to them, and I will redeem you with an outstretched arm and with mighty acts of judgment. I will take you as my own people, and I will be your God. Then you will know that I am the LORD your God, who brought you out from under the yoke of the Egyptians. And I will bring you to the land I swore with uplifted hand to give to Abraham, to Isaac and to Jacob. I will give it to you as a possession. I am the LORD."

These three verses can be understood to more or less sum up the theological message that Moses was required to relay to the Israelites, and, we submit, that the reader is expected to recognize as the principal statement of the theology of the book. We will review each of these themes briefly below and then introduce some subthemes as well.

---

[42] E. Martens, in *God's Design: A Focus on Old Testament Theology*, 3d. ed. (N. Richland Hills, Tex.: Bibal, 1998), takes his outline of a comprehensive OT/biblical theology from Exod 6:6–8 in a manner that we consider generally convincing. In this commentary we naturally limit ourselves largely to the theology of Exodus, which includes subthemes of particular emphasis in Exodus as opposed to the entire OT. Nevertheless, for either Exodus itself or for the Bible as a whole, Martens' identification of four great theological topics (salvation, knowledge of God, covenant relationship, and promised land) as *together* constituting a kind of fourfold, multidimensional theological framework for the revelation of God commends itself as right-minded and appropriately variegated. Most OT theologies have tried to find a single theme under which to subordinate all other issues (so von Rad, with the idea of confession; Eichrodt, with the idea of covenant; Hanson, with the idea of people; and so on). Martens instead argues that one needs to respect the fact that God himself reveals four great themes—not just one—in his initial explanation of himself and his plan to the Israelites in Exod 6:6–8. A homespun sort of analogy might be that of the choice of God to reveal his Son to readers of the NT in four Gospels, none of which can be considered superior to the others and none of which can be omitted as unnecessary to the gospel story. Likewise, the four great theological truths—of God as savior, God as one who can be known personally, God as covenant benefactor but also covenant enforcer, and God as owner of a wonderful land of promise for his people where he himself will dwell with them—need not be arranged hierarchically but can be viewed as complimentary and logically interconnected, providing a fuller, more accurate sense of the theology of the Bible, and of Exodus in particular, than exclusive focus on any single theme could successfully do.

(1) Theology of Exodus: Salvation, Freedom from Bondage

"I am the LORD, and I will bring you out from under the yoke of the Egyptians. I will free you from being slaves to them, and I will redeem you with an outstretched arm and with mighty acts of judgment" (Exod 6:6).

So-called liberation theology often misunderstands Exodus.[43] The book is not about liberation in general or about political and religious freedom in particular, but about deliverance from bad servitude to good servitude. The Israelites served *(ʾābad)* Pharaoh but were called by God to serve (again, *ʾābad*) him instead.[44] It was not a question of needing freedom from being under the control of a national leader; it was a question of a good, divine national (and universal) leader rescuing his chosen people from a bad, human national leader. The threat of bondage to a hostile great power is one of the curses of the Old Testament. Once the Israelites arrived at Sinai, they were reminded of the horrors of servitude to those who would oppress them if they failed to keep Yahweh's covenant.[45] The generation that followed the exodus likewise faced the prospect that disobedience to the rules graciously and protectively revealed in the divine covenant would lead to oppression under enemies who would conquer and enslave the chosen nation.[46]

In the New Covenant, bondage to the greatest power, sin, and its consequence, death, constitutes the "last enemy."[47] But this is not merely a New Covenant concept. Sin is whatever offends God, and sin is an enslaver. But this slavery can be escaped—not by skill or cunning but by changing masters from sin to God.[48] This comes about not by human initiative but by God's gift, to which humans can only respond.[49] In Exodus, likewise, freedom from bondage is accomplished only by God. The Israelites are portrayed as having no chance whatever to save themselves. God must make the demands ("Let my people go!"); the people on their own, with or without Moses, would never have dared even asked. Moreover, God makes those demands through his chosen representative Moses so that the people cannot take credit for having thought up the idea themselves. Not only so, but when

---

[43] Liberation theology often misunderstands many other things as well, including the basics of objective biblical interpretation, but it especially fails exegetically when it tries to suggest that the book of Exodus—exemplaristically—provides a template of sorts for justifying violence in the name of political deliverance.

[44] See comments on 4:23ff. Since *ʾābad* can mean both "serve" and "worship," it is always challenging for the translator to render the nuance(s) appropriately in any given context. I would love to have been able to write "serve/worship" instead of one or the other at many, many points in my Exodus translation draft for the HCSB.

[45] E.g., Lev 26:16–17,32,34,36–38,41.

[46] E.g., Deut 28:25,31,38,48,68.

[47] 1 Cor 15:26.

[48] So Paul's comprehensive teaching in Rom 6:11,13,17,20–22; 7:25.

[49] E.g., Rom 5:6; 8:3.

the people were reconfronted with the possibility of being opposed by the Egyptians, they became afraid. Indeed, later in the wilderness, when the going became hard, some of them actually rationalized their way to thinking that they were better off in Egypt than free from it.[50] People need both a Savior and a Lord. They cannot do without either. Exodus reveals God as for Israel and for all who will join Israel, as many did upon seeing his mighty acts unleashed against the Egyptian oppressors.[51]

(2) Theology of Exodus: Real Knowledge of God

"Then you will know that I am the LORD your God, who brought you out from under the yoke of the Egyptians. . . . I am the LORD" (Exod 6:7–8).

The repetition of the statement "I am the LORD" is unmistakably a way of God's repeatedly emphasizing his self-disclosure to his people. How can they obey and be benefited by a God whom they only vaguely understand, whose characteristics and will for them are clouded by ignorance on their part? But if his people can actually understand him, that is, be fully aware of his covenant stipulations and therefore know what to do to please him and receive his favor, they can actually live in relationship with him so that their own lives are influenced directly and constantly by his. A whole new order of existence beckons from this divine promise.

Most often the people in Exodus have contact with God by representative only; it is Moses who has the personal connection to and interaction with God, not the Israelite people, but he does so on their behalf, not his own. Exodus also shows how the high priest will represent the people in his actions of worship ritual so they can be assured of access to the (limited) presence of God and the benefits of that close proximity to eternal and universal sovereignty.[52] Sometimes in Exodus, God shows his personal interest in his people through more than just one representative, as instanced by the way the elders confirmed the Sinai covenant in his presence (24:9–11). At other times they are known "by name" to him, as the ephod's breastpiece bears their tribal names, symbolic of their membership in his family, before him. And individual Israelites can be singled out for service[53] by way of example, suggesting a personal knowledge by God of the people and a personal, not just corporate, knowledge of each of the people by God.

---

[50] Num 11.

[51] Exod 12:38. For Moses, Elijah, and Jesus to describe Jesus' work on the cross as *his exodus* (τὴν ἔξοδον αὐτοῦ, Luke 9:31, unfortunately translated as "departure" in the NIV) is yet one more way in the NT that Jesus is identified as God. Yahweh accomplished the exodus in the OT; Jesus, the exodus in the NT.

[52] See esp. comments on 28:6–30.

[53] As in the case of Bezalel and Oholiab in chaps. 31; 35–38.

What does a knowledge of God provide? The reformer Melanchthon said it well: *"Hoc est Christum cognoscere: beneficia euis cognoscere"* ("To know Christ is to know his benefits"). It is not an emotive matter; it is a reception into a family whose paterfamilias is God himself, loving and benefiting in all full appropriateness the people he has made his own in covenant.[54] That is what gets underway in the book of Exodus, not by anything Israel can do for itself but because of God's kindly seeking to adopt to himself a people, consistent with his oft-repeated earlier promises.[55]

(3) Theology of Exodus: A Covenant People

"I will take you as my own people, and I will be your God" (Exod 6:7).

When God first demanded that the Egyptian Pharaoh let Israel leave Egypt, he referred to Israel as "my . . . people." Again and again he said those famous words to Pharaoh, *Let my people go*.[56] Pharaoh may not have known who Yahweh was,[57] but Yahweh certainly knew Israel. He knew them not just as a nation needing rescue but as his own people needing to be closely bound to him by the beneficent covenant he had in store for them once they reached the place he was taking them to himself, out of harm's way, and into his sacred space.[58]

To be in the image of God is to have a job assignment. God's "image"[59] is supposed to represent him on earth and accomplish his purposes here. Reasoning from a degenerate form of this truth, pagan religions thought that an image (idol) in the form of something they fashioned would convey to its worshipers the presence of a god or goddess. But the real purpose of the heavenly decision described in 1:26 was not to have a humanlike statue as a representative of God on earth but to have humans do his work here, as the Lord's Prayer asks ("your will be done on earth as it is in heaven," Matt 6:10).

Although the fall of humanity as described in Genesis 3 corrupted the ability of humans to function properly in the image of God, the divine plan of redemption was hardly thwarted. It took the form of the calling of

---

[54] The essence of covenant is kinship, as we will remind the reader at various points throughout the commentary; a covenant confers a relationship that either mimics or in fact creates the sort of interpersonal closeness and obligation that exists in a family. The purpose of God's covenant with his people in Exodus is just the start of the divine plan to redeem a family for himself to join him in heaven forever, becoming part of his eternal household and living where he himself has always lived in delight and glory forever.

[55] E.g., Gen 12:7; 13:15–16; 21:12; 22:18; 24:7; 26:4; 28:14.

[56] Exod 5:1; 7:16; 8:1,20–21; 9:1,13; 10:3.

[57] See comments on 5:2.

[58] Exod 3:2 et passim.

[59] Hb. צֶלֶם, a standard word for "idol" both in Hebrew and in its Semitic cognate languages.

Abraham and the promises to him of a special people. In both Exod 6:6–8 and 19:4–6 God reiterates his plan to develop a people that will be his very own, a special people that, in distinction from all other peoples of the earth, will belong to him and accomplish his purposes, being as Exod 19:6 says "a kingdom of priests and a holy nation." Since the essence of holiness is belonging to God, by belonging to God this people became holy, reflecting the character of their Lord as well as being obedient to his purposes. No other nation in the ancient world ever claimed Yahweh as its God, and Yahweh never claimed any other nation as his people. This is not to say that he did not love and care for other nations[60] but only to say that he chose Israel as the focus of his plan of redemption for the world.

In the New Testament, Israel becomes all who will place faith in Jesus Christ—not an ethnic or political entity at all but now a spiritual entity, a family of God. Thus the New Testament speaks of the true Israel as defined by conversion to Christ in rebirth and not by physical birth at all. But in the Old Covenant, the true Israel was the people group that, from the various ethnic groups that gathered at Sinai, agreed to accept God's covenant and therefore to benefit from this abiding presence among them (see comments on Exod 33:12–24:28). Exodus is the place in the Bible where God's full covenant with a nation—as opposed to a person or small group—emerges, and the language of Exod 6:7, "I will take you as my own people, and I will be your God," is language predicting that covenant establishment.[61]

(4) Theology of Exodus: A Promised Land

"I will bring you to the land I swore with uplifted hand to give to Abraham, to Isaac and to Jacob. I will give it to you as a possession. I am the LORD" (Exod 6:8).

Since the time of the Patriarchs it had been the hope of Israel to occupy a land of its own—not because the idea had occurred to Abraham and his family and then had taken on a life of its own but because God revealed it as his intention and reiterated it to each successive generation.[62] In Exodus that divine promise becomes the basis for an expectation of deliverance from Egypt,[63] which constitutes the beginning of a great journey undertaken by a whole people with all their possessions, including their livestock, to relocate to that new land, one described metaphorically as "flowing with milk and honey,"[64] so right and proper would it be for them.

---

[60] So Gen 17:20 of the Ishmaelites/Arabs.

[61] As seen also in different but related wording in such contexts as Gen 17:7; Lev 26:12; Deut 7:6; 14:2; 27:9; 28:9; 29:13; Jer 11:4.

[62] Gen 12:7; 15:7; 15:18; 17:8; 24:7; 26:3; 28:15; 48:3; 50:24.

[63] Exod 3:8ff.

[64] Exod 3:8,17; 13:5; 33:3.

In Egypt the Israelites were a noncitizen gang of slaves without any land of their own or any human hope of having one. But God had not abandoned his covenant plans for them[65] and led them forth by a mighty hand from the domination of the earth's greatest superpower, not merely to a wilderness existence but to a place of permanent settlement, hymned predictively by Moses in 15:13–17. Thus already at Sinai, lest they become complacent there, God ordered them well in advance to prepare to leave;[66] and they, in turn, pleaded repeatedly with him to accompany them on the journey, lest it be a journey without blessing to a place without rest.[67] One very big part of their preparation for the trip was the construction of the tabernacle. Without it they would not have had proper housing for the symbols of God's (limited) presence among them or a place to gather for the corporate worship he told them he would accept from them when they rendered it. Thus most of chaps. 25–40, more than a third of the book of Exodus, is occupied by accounts of the tabernacle. It had to be made just right, and that included being made fully portable so that it could be broken down and transported whenever God led his people on a new leg of their journey toward his promised land. It likewise had to be easy enough to set up that they could erect it and use it for worship promptly upon arriving at a stopping place anywhere in the wilderness. The tabernacle was therefore a tent, not a temple, a portable worship center, not a fixed emplacement for worship. The Israelites of Exodus were a people on the go, not a people who had yet arrived at their ultimate destination.

They knew that they would eventually be given a land they did not deserve, where none of them had in fact ever lived, a land seen by their distant ancestors but not by any of the people of Israel alive at the time of the Exodus. Yet the place had been designed by God to be their home. To occupy it they would have to dispossess the people groups that currently lived there, a task far beyond their own abilities unless God should deign to take upon himself the task of driving out the inhabitants. This is exactly what he promised to do,[68] and until the validity of that promise was absolutely certain via reiteration after the great covenant-breaking sin of chap. 32, the Israelites were genuinely afraid to invade the promised land.[69] It was

---

[65] See comments on 2:23–25.

[66] Note the command already in 33:1, not fulfilled until Num 10:11. The lack of immediate compliance was not a fault of Israel's. There was still much to be done before departing Sinai, but the early command reminded the people that they were destined for a very different, quite distant place and needed to regard their stay at Mount Sinai as purely temporary.

[67] See comments on 33:12–23; 34:8–16.

[68] See comments on 23:23–28; 33:2; 34:11.

[69] See comments on 33:4–6,12–13,14–16; 34:8–9.

the land of their dreams, but it made sense to go there only if it was also Yahweh's land, where he would abide in their midst.

(5) Theology of Exodus: The Limited Presence of God in Israel's Midst

"'Do not come any closer,' God said. 'Take off your sandals, for the place where you are standing is holy ground'" (Exod 3:5).

"Put limits for the people around the mountain and tell them, 'Be careful that you do not go up the mountain or touch the foot of it. Whoever touches the mountain shall surely be put to death'" (Exod 19:12).

"Aaron and his sons must wear them whenever they enter the Tent of Meeting or approach the altar to minister in the Holy Place, so that they will not incur guilt and die. This is to be a lasting ordinance for Aaron and his descendants" (Exod 28:43).

Almost all commentaries, Bible dictionary articles, and study Bibles speak at least generally of the theme of the presence of God as a hallmark of Exodus. But the idea of God's presence is often articulated at least somewhat inaccurately in such sources. What most of them fail to note adequately, if at all, is that Exodus carefully presents not so much the concept of the *presence* of God as that of the *limited presence* of God.

The situation may be summarized this way: God shows himself to his covenant people by *symbols behind barriers*. He does not fully disclose himself in the manner that New Covenant believers look forward to as one of the great joys of heaven. Rather, he puts *symbols* of himself (a visible brilliance associated with his glory; the gold-surfaced ark of the covenant) behind *barriers* that keep his people from direct access even to those symbols, let alone to the very God of gods that they symbolize. These barriers include such things as distance (God normally comes to the top of Mount Sinai while the people are strictly forbidden to go anywhere above the base of the mountain), darkness (God usually "appears" within a thick, dark cloud that conceals most of his glory and through which no human eyes can penetrate), and the tabernacle itself (with its layers of thick curtains and hide covers, its special floor-to-ceiling curtain shielding the ark from view by everyone, even priests). When the tabernacle was disassembled and its component parts carried, the ark was elaborately wrapped in its shielding curtain so that it could not be seen by anyone.[70] What this means is that, with the exception

[70] Num 4:5 can be read to indicate that the high priest and his sons may have seen the ark uncovered as they performed the act of covering it for transport. But it is just as likely that they were expected, starting from within the holy place of the tabernacle, to take the curtain that divided the holy of holies from the holy place and, with it between themselves and the ark, approach the ark and drape it over the ark and then wrap the ark within it, so that they in fact never did see the ark uncovered at all. The annual anointing of the ark as described in Exod 30:26 is another matter. Surely the high priest saw the ark uncovered in that instance.

of the high priest annually,[71] no Israelite saw the ark once it had been constructed and placed in the tabernacle. The Israelites believed there was an ark on faith: what they saw carried as they traveled was something wrapped in layers of curtain and hide out of which poles protruded; they never saw the ark or its contents under any conditions. God *symbolized* his presence by that most holy object, the ark, but he kept it hidden from his people by barriers at all times.

It is usual for commentators to point out that the tabernacle design provides a way of thinking about three levels of the presence of God—as indicated by the closest (the holy of holies and the ark within it), the next closest (the holy place), and the third closest (the tabernacle courtyard). To these may be added the "level" of Israel as a whole. At this fourth level, the presence of God continues to be an important, sometimes dominant, issue: God is regularly with the whole people, protecting them (the pillar of cloud/fire was a benefit of divine presence to them but a danger for the Egyptians); he is their covenant God in a way he is not to other nations (Exod 19); the people can worship him even when they are in the camp (so 33:7–11); and his willingness to go with them (or not) in their wilderness travel and conquest of the promised land becomes the dominant question for the nation (chaps. 33–34) after the sin of idolatry described in chap. 32. Thus Israel in general, as a people, constitute a fourth region of presence to Yahweh, not as intense as the other three represented by the tabernacle design or shown in Moses' close encounters with Yahweh either at the Tent of Meeting or at the tabernacle or atop Mount Sinai. Indeed, one could also speak of a fifth level of the presence of Yahweh, outside Israel, when Yahweh made himself known to other people in their own territories, as he did with the Egyptians in his encounters with them, or in Canaan, when he attacked and drove out the inhabitants of the land in accordance with his promise to do so in Gen 15. Note that Exod 15 speaks of his sanctuary, which can be Zion but seems in the context to refer generally to all of the promised land—certainly a fifth level of presence from the point of view of the levels of presence experienced at Sinai. These five levels are not described per se in the book or delineated and explained generally in the Bible. Recognizing them is merely a matter of convenience for us as we try to understand the logic of the issue of the divine presence—a human way of categorizing the material of the book of Exodus. It is not a revealed pattern or system inherent in the pages of the text itself.

What must be kept in mind is that holiness does not happen because God's people are gathered all together in one place but occurs because God is in a place, regardless of whether his people are there also. The ancient

[71] Heb 9:25.

pagan notion of the presence of gods derived from the assumption in paganism that the gods could (collectively, not individually) do virtually anything but feed themselves. Therefore it was generally thought that unless people were regularly feeding a god (i.e., bringing food offerings to shrines devoted to him), that god would not hang around those people; in other words, gods gravitated to those places, and only those places, where food was "sent up" to them via sacrifice.[72] In the New Covenant, however, it is possible to say that wherever God's people are gathered, he is in fact present there in a special way. This is the result not of the ability of God's people to create a setting of holiness but of God's gracious promise to inhabit his people—each one and all of them—so that where any sort of gathering of two or more Christian believers occurs, their Lord is present.[73]

(6) Theology of Exodus: Representing an Invisible God by Visible Symbols

"Place the cover on top of the ark and put in the ark the Testimony, which I will give you. There, above the cover between the two cherubim that are over the ark of the Testimony, I will meet with you and give you all my commands for the Israelites" (Exod 25:21–22).

"Seeing is believing," we say. But how can you see an invisible God? Idolatry tried to solve this challenge by means of the creation of statues and other depictions that were thought to represent a god or goddess. Even the Israelites tried it, though to their great dismay.[74] The limitations of idolatry are evident in the fact that as soon as worshipers reduce God to association with/depiction by/inhabitation of a manufactured object, they have limited his greatness. Part of the genius of invisibility is that it does not place limits on God's greatness. Indeed, it prohibits even the depiction of limitation of him by forbidding any likeness at all.

If God is omnipresent, he should not be given a shape that can be thought to confine him or concentrate him somewhere. Thus, for example, the ark of the covenant is introduced in Exodus as a place above which God may be met,[75] but it is never said to be God's footstool or throne or any such

[72] E.g., Jonah may have had a sufficiently imperfect theology that he thought he could run away from Yahweh's presence westward on the Mediterranean to some place where no one was worshiping Yahweh via food offerings and therefore where Yahweh would simply not have bothered to be located.

[73] Matt 18:20. Note that the terminology of "two or three" is used directly after "two or three witnesses" as referenced in 18:16 via the quote of the law from Deut 19:15. Christ's presence is witnessed to by his people when they gather—it has to be so, for otherwise they would not be his people. Witnessing to his presence should happen automatically if believers are following their Lord in thought, speech, and behavior.

[74] Exod 32, esp. 32:1,4, showing that the Israelites regarded the idol Aaron made at their request as some sort of representation, however forbidden and polytheistic, of Yahweh.

[75] So 25:22, "There, above the cover between the two cherubim that are over the ark of the Testimony, I will meet with you and give you all my commands for the Israelites." Cf. Num 7:89; 1 Sam 4:4; 2 Sam 6:2.

thing.[76] That would place a kind of limitation on God that would be false and misleading theologically.

Moreover, if God is omnipotent, he should not be depicted as smaller than any part of his creation. There is obviously no way that an idol can be as large as God is, and therefore any idol must automatically suggest something of a smallness in God—a limitation of some sort to his stature. If a statue (and the ones we have from the ancient Near East were virtually always smaller in size than a typical human is) could depict God with any degree of accuracy at all, even a faint degree of accuracy, then it would suggest, however faintly, that he was smaller than his creation. For polytheistic pagans the implications of the size of idols was in fact no problem. None of them thought of any of their gods as being bigger than creation, or for that matter anywhere near that size. A large number of gods and goddesses occupied only parts of the earth and sky (as the pagans understood things), so of course no single god could dominate all things, and the depicting of a god or goddess on a small scale had the rational advantage of corresponding to the belief that all of them were smaller than the world as a whole.

If God is omniscient, he is obviously aware of all events by being able to observe all events and should not be portrayed as having only one set of humanlike eyes or one pair of ears or one mouth to speak in one direction to one group of people. When Zechariah (3:9; 4:10) and John (Rev 5:6) spoke of God's many eyes, they were symbolizing the fact that God's omniscience means that he cannot be depicted accurately or helpfully by a typical idol. His easy awareness of all things at once, unlike any idol, makes him a subject for which idolatry is completely inappropriate.

If God is the only wise God, he should not be shown in the same manner as the whole panoply of other gods and goddesses are shown in pagan idolatry. Idolatry as practiced by ancient people failed, at any rate, to understand how God was properly to be represented on earth, that is, represented by humans.[77] Exodus begins the biblical process of helping us to understand how it might be that God could be symbolized, though never properly idolized.

---

[76] David thought he might somehow make the temple a *footstool* for God, but his speech in that case (1 Chr 28:2) seems mainly metaphorical, intended to suggest an appropriate humility of scope for the temple in comparison to the greatness of God.

[77] This is precisely the meaning of Gen 1:26, "Let us make man in our image," which would be better translated, "Let us create humans as our idol" or, "Let us create humans as our representative." Note that this statement is immediately followed by the details of the job assignment, i.e., to rule over animal life on earth. Being in God's image is not an ontological statement but a description of how humans are supposed to do God's will on earth as his representatives. It describes a function, not an essence.

In objection to what has been said thus far, it might be argued that the ark of the covenant that stood in the holy of holies of the tabernacle was, in fact, essentially an idol. After all, the Philistines certainly thought they had encountered a "god" (i.e., an idol representing a god or gods) when they encountered the ark in battle among the Israelites (1 Sam 4:5–8). But theirs was a grave error in analysis. The genius of God's self-disclosure via the tabernacle and its most precious content, the ark, is that the ark, like the tabernacle itself, was a *container*. It was not itself a representation of anything or anyone but was a place for containing the tablets and eventually some manna and Aaron's staff, items that represented not a single person but a relationship between persons—between God and his people. This was signified primarily by the two *tablets of the Testimony*, or *covenant*, and thus the term *the ark of the covenant* is regularly employed. It was what was in the ark, not the ark itself, that revealed God to his people—and that was his word. Humans know God via his revealed truth, which, if believed and kept, has the power to solidify a relationship, essentially a family relationship,[78] that will last forever.

(7) Theology of Exodus: The Necessity of Law

"Now if you obey me fully and keep my covenant, then out of all nations you will be my treasured possession. . . . Do not be afraid. God has come to test you, so that the fear of God will be with you to keep you from sinning" (Exod 19:5; 20:20).

God is a guide, and his Law gives guidance. Human law gives guidance for living peacefully and productively within a community. Divine law does this as well but goes far beyond it, to give guidance as to how to be holy within a covenant (kinship) relationship with a holy God. The fruit of this guidance—if it is kept—is far more than a happy life on earth. It is nothing short of an eternal relationship that begins to take a person out of the limits of temporal living for temporal pleasures and leads that person to eternal life in a setting where all the highest and noblest desires of life are actually provided instead of merely dreamed about. It makes that person, and his or her community (to the extent that community also truly obeys God's covenant) into a part of the family of God.

---

[78] See F. M. Cross Jr., "Kinship and Covenant in Ancient Israel" in *From Epic to Canon: History and Literature in Ancient Israel* (Baltimore: Johns Hopkins University Press, 1998), 3–21. Cross argues that covenants are not mere contracts but arrangements that bring the parties to the covenant into actual kinship relationships, including the sorts of obligations and arrangements that families have. Cf. S. Ackerman, "The Personal Is Political: Covenantal and Affectionate Love: (*'AHEB, 'AHeBAH*) in the Hebrew Bible," *VT* 52 (2002): 437–58. Note also the importance of the phrase *ark of the testimony* and its parallel *ark of the covenant*. What relationship with God is there apart from the truth of his word?

Pagan idolatry was attractive to the ancients because, among other things, it was based on an assumption that frequency and generosity of worship (bringing a lot of food to an idol's shrine) would establish a good relationship with one's god or goddess. Ethical living was not required. By contrast, Israel's God insisted on obedience to his law, comprehensively stated in many commandments, but especially and magisterially revealed in the Ten Words/Commandments[79] of the Decalogue in chap. 20. No Israelite could draw near to God without accepting the responsibility to live ethically, according to the revealed standard of ethics found in the Law. This did not mean that the Law by itself saved—only that it provided the standards by which someone saved by faith could know how to respond to the new Master he or she had taken in becoming an Israelite, an Israelite not merely of the flesh but of faith.[80]

Exodus provides divine law in a covenant framework, starting with the Ten Words that summarize everything, followed by the so-called Covenant Code (chaps. 21–23) giving much more detail and dozens of examples of how the Law was to be performed and enforced. Exodus then devotes the greatest amount of "legal content" space to worship, the ongoing, basic responsibility of the believing, covenant people of God, as manifested in the instructions for the design, manufacture, and erection of the tabernacle (chaps. 25–40). By no means, however, is the totality of the Mosaic covenant limited to Exodus. Leviticus and Numbers complete the "Sinai" part of the Mosaic covenant, and Deuteronomy completes the rest via renewal of the covenant for a new generation. The Law begins in Exodus; it certainly doesn't end there.

Israel had no option but to obey the covenant revealed first in the pages of Exodus if Israel wished to enjoy God's favor. Exodus never presents the Law as an option. Assent was required from all the people.[81] In this regard, Exodus demonstrates the biblical principle that God does not relate savingly to his people without expecting of them proof of loyalty via the keeping of his commands. His family has household rules; his people are not honorary citizens but real citizens of a kingdom that has laws that must be kept. They are vassals of a sovereign who has required obedience of them for their benefit. The laws of Exodus spell out both the obligations and the benefits.

---

[79] They are never actually called "commandments" but always referred to in the Hebrew as "words." See comments on Exod 20:1.

[80] Cf. Rom 2:27–29.

[81] See 19:8; 24:3,7.

(8) Theology of Exodus: The Necessity of Following God

"In all the travels of the Israelites, whenever the cloud lifted from above the tabernacle, they would set out; but if the cloud did not lift, they did not set out—until the day it lifted. So the cloud of the LORD was over the tabernacle by day, and fire was in the cloud by night, in the sight of all the house of Israel during all their travels" (Exod 40:36–38).

These are the final words of the book of Exodus. They cap a long story of following God. The book begins with a brief review of the way the Israelites got into Egypt in the first place, the result of God's provision through Joseph, who had issued the invitation to follow him into residency in Egypt as the result of God's giving him the inclination to make such an invitation.[82] But that journey involved a few dozen people. Four centuries later, the greatly expanded nation of Israel listened to another call to migrate from where they were to a new land. First, Moses had to follow God's call to lead the Israelites out of Egypt,[83] and then the Israelite elders had to follow that call as well, difficult as it proved for them to do in light of the oppression they had been placed under by the Egyptians.[84]

Nevertheless, as Moses followed God's commands, the people followed Moses.[85] They followed God directly too as he led them via the special manifestation of his presence, the glory cloud that appeared dark in the day and fiery at night.[86] More specifically with regard to their covenant relationship with him, they also followed him by following his instructions (16:4). Once they had broken his covenant by a reversion to the idolatry of their past life in Egypt (chap. 32), they feared they could no longer follow him. His willingness (offered rhetorically to test them rather than as a final offer) to do less than actually go with them, leading them through the wilderness personally, was, fortunately, something they understood as not enough. Wisely, they respectfully insisted through Moses that if God himself would not go with them they would not go at all.[87]

In this they were thinking rightly, however imperfectly their actions sometimes compromised what would have been best for them. Exodus dem-

---

[82] Gen 45:8–9: "So then, it was not you who sent me here, but God. He made me father to Pharaoh, lord of his entire household and ruler of all Egypt. Now hurry back to my father and say to him, 'This is what your son Joseph says: God has made me lord of all Egypt. Come down to me; don't delay.'" Gen 45:18: "Bring your father and your families back to me. I will give you the best of the land of Egypt and you can enjoy the fat of the land."

[83] See comments on chaps. 3–4.

[84] See comments on 4:29–31; 5:6–23.

[85] See esp. 11:8.

[86] So 13:21–22; 14:9,20,24; 16:10.

[87] See comments on 33:15ff. Moses was speaking in that context, but his speech was not on behalf of himself but of the nation, so the pronouns are plural.

onstrates that it can never be considered advisable to take one's own direction if God is available to lead. Israel is taught in the book of Exodus, and certainly thereafter throughout the wilderness wanderings as described in Numbers and reviewed in Deuteronomy, that its proper role before God is that of follower—not because God desired to denigrate his people but because following the right leader is good for the followers. Although Moses was that leader proximately, God was that leader ultimately. Clearly, it was hard for the Israelites to follow Moses consistently, especially when they could not discern how a circumstance or location that looked dangerous or inhospitable could possibly turn out to be beneficial.[88] But Exodus demonstrates that what God had in mind for them, even if it were not apparent to them at first, was nothing short of a path full of reward and blessing, not the least part of which was God's own character and glory revealed as the people stayed with him and kept obeying faithfully.[89] The Israelites made it to Sinai by following God. They would be able to leave there (33:1) and make it to the promised land only in the same way—by following the only One who could make the little, insecure and vulnerable, newly formed people into a great nation occupying their own land and centered around the only true God.

(9) Theology of Exodus: Only One God Has Any Real Power

"I will bring judgment on all the gods of Egypt. I am the LORD" (Exod 12:12).

The Egyptians, like virtually all ancients, were polytheists, pantheists, and syncretists.[90] That is, they believed in many different gods, that all aspects of nature partook of the divine and were in some sense coterminous with it, and that exclusivism in religion was foolish—the wise person tried to understand and benefit from all the worship he could manage of as many gods as he could get to know.

The Israelites in Egypt at the time of the exodus had lived in this sort of cultural milieu for more than four centuries. From a human point of view it would seem virtually impossible that they could fully break free of such a

---

[88] See, e.g., comments on 15:24ff.; 16:2–12; 17:3ff.

[89] As 33:12–23 portrays, God's presence with the Israelites was not merely a matter of providing accurate directions and a safe trip to the promised land but was a source of something far more powerfully rewarding: knowing God personally, knowing his favor (33:12), understanding his character and will (33:13), being certain of his establishment as a people in their own land (33:14), knowing his special election (33:16), being aware of his personal interest and favor (33:13,17), and sensing his glory (33:18ff.) and the goodness/mercy/compassion associated with that glorious presence (33:19).

[90] See J. A. Wilson, "Egypt," in *Before Philosophy: The Intellectual Adventure of Ancient Man* (Baltimore: Penguin, 1949), 39–133.

powerful, long-term enculturation and come to believe in and serve only one true God, and certainly it would seem impossible that such a conversion could be accomplished quickly. Yet that is exactly what the only God had in mind for his chosen people: to show them that all other gods were false and that he alone was true and held in himself all the power they had been attributing to the various gods and goddesses of their mythopoeic belief system. It was his plan that they should see his absolute sovereignty so visibly that they would be able to convert to the truth, leave Egypt, and become his covenant people at Sinai—all in the space of a few months. He planned to show them that the gods of Egypt were empty nothings.[91]

By definition, gods are supposed to be powerful. Gods are worshiped precisely because they have power. A powerless god would be, in fact, no god at all. Why would anyone even bother to learn about, tell about, pray to, or otherwise honor a being who had no effect on anything? Among the ancients, certainly, there was no interest in ineffective gods, no theoretical interest in the doings of feckless existences. Therefore, if a believed-in god, a supposed deity, could be shown powerless not just in some area tangential to his or her reputed main strength but in the very realm where he or she was considered the power among all the powers of the universe, it would swiftly undermine belief in that god or goddess.

That is exactly what the only true God, Yahweh, does in the book of Exodus. Easily, comprehensively, impressively, dramatically, publicly, decisively—he demonstrates his total control over all aspects of the physical world that were thought by the Egyptians to be the province of "the gods of Egypt." He shows that the supposed gods of the Nile, or the sun, or the wind, or of various other parts or players in the world[92] have no strength, no will, no effectiveness of any kind. Their power was illusory. They couldn't even help the Egyptians prevail against well-subjugated slaves; they couldn't control the phenomena of nature that they were supposed to be coterminous with and supposed to inhabit uniquely through their pantheistic divinity.

In this regard, as part of their religion, the Egyptians maintained a superior view of themselves and their land.[93] They hated foreigners.[94] They con-

---

[91] "Empty nothings" is our literal translation of the expression הַבְלֵי־שָׁוְא, used of idols in Jonah 2:8, usually translated didactically as something like "worthless idols." Jonah, like Moses, was called to preach the word of God in a hostile, pagan place, but he handled his assignment rather less aptly and willingly than did Moses.

[92] Z. Zevit, "Three Ways to Look at the Ten Plagues," *BibRev* 6 (1990): 16–23, 42, 44; D. P. Silverman, "Divinities and Deities in Ancient Egypt," in *Religion in Ancient Egypt: Gods, Myths and Personal Practice* (Ithaca: Cornell University Press, 1991).

[93] M. Greenberg, *Understanding Exodus* (New York: Behrman, 1969), 20.

[94] Thus the Egyptian queen Hatshepsut says in her xenophobic boast about helping drive out the Asiatic Hyksos, "I have made distant those whom the gods abominate" (*ANET* 231a). Likewise, Pharaoh Ka-Mose, in planning to attack the Hyksos, says contemptuously, "[Here] I sit associated with an Asiatic and a Negro!" and "My wish is to save Egypt and smite the Asiatics!" (*ANET* 232).

sidered themselves the greatest of all peoples and their country the greatest place on the earth. Some of that was natural; even today most people tend to be patriotic, loving what is familiar politically and geographically and identifying with their own neighbors and countrymen. The Egyptians went beyond this. They considered that no place on earth had the advantages of the united Upper and Lower Egypts and that this was the result of nothing less than the combined favor of the gods upon them. They had the best and the most powerful gods, who had long loved Egypt above other places, and their religious faithfulness to these gods had long been paying off, they thought, in the superior prosperity, military might, and culture that Egypt enjoyed.[95]

Yahweh, a God previously unknown to the Egyptians, overturned all that. By the time the plagues were completed, the Egyptians—including Pharaoh himself—were begging the Israelites to leave Egypt.[96] Their gods had failed miserably in the face of the only real power in Egypt: the God of the Hebrews, who had sent his servant Moses to announce his demands for the deliverance of his people to him. Thereafter, this Yahweh brought his people to Mount Sinai, where he graciously gave them a covenant relationship with himself and promised them his dwelling in their very midst. No other god surfaces in Exodus.[97] Even the golden young bull of chap. 32 is a depiction, however distorted and foolish, of the one who delivered the Israelites from Egypt, that is, Yahweh. The book closes with a description of the way God reminded the Israelites by day and by night of his glory (40:35–38). No non-gods, Egyptian or otherwise, could share it.

---

[95] To this might be raised immediately the objection that the Hyksos military conquest of Egypt that had occurred prior to Moses' birth (roughly 1725–1575 BC) obviously would have disproved to any thoughtful Egyptians that their gods were, in fact, weak as compared to those of the Hyksos. But two factors kept this from happening. First, it appears that the Hyksos may have rather rapidly accommodated themselves religiously to Egyptian beliefs and practices. Compare the way the Hyksos Pharaoh Apophis is described in a post-Hyksos document: "Then King Apophis . . . made himself Seth as lord, and he would not serve any God who was in the land except Seth" (*ANET* 231), demonstrating Apophis's determination to take a "when-in-Rome . . ." approach to the local religion. Adopting Egyptian religion would have been something their own syncretistic inclinations would have suggested to the Hyksos. Second, the Egyptians routinely rationalized their being conquered by Asiatics as the result of the wrath of their own Egyptian gods against them, thus saving face for their religion.

[96] Exod 10:7; 12:31–33.

[97] Indeed, Jethro's words in 18:11 are decisive: "Now I know that the LORD is greater than all other gods, for he did this to those who had treated Israel arrogantly." Moses had already indicated the sole glorious power of Yahweh in 15:11's poetic interrogative, "Who among the gods is like you, O LORD? / Who is like you—majestic in holiness, awesome in glory, working wonders?" The covenant then outlawed polytheism decisively (20:3,23; 23:13,24,32–33; 34:15–16).

OUTLINE OF THE BOOK

I. Israel's Egyptian Oppression and God's Choice of a Deliverer (1:1–2:25)
   1. Opening Genealogy, Connecting the Story with Genesis (1:1–6)
   2. How Israel Came under Egyptian Bondage (1:7–14)
   3. A New Pharaoh's Initiative: Genocide as Population Control (1:15–22)
   4. Moses' Birth and God's Provision (2:1–10)
   5. Moses' Own Exile/Exodus: Midian and Marriage (2:11–22)
   6. Summative Reminder: Severity of the Oppression and God's Concern (2:23–25)

II. Moses' Call, Commission, and Challenge (3:1–7:7)
   1. Moses' Call: The Burning Bush Theophany (3:1–12)
   2. Revelation of the Name Yahweh (3:13–15)
   3. Summary of Commission and Prediction of Acceptance by Israelites (3:16–22)
   4. Moses' Special Signs of His Believability (4:1–9)
   5. Moses' Ritual and Actual Protests and Divine Reassurance (4:10–18)
   6. A Shaky Start but Initial Acceptance: Moses Returns to Egypt (4:19–31)
   7. First Audience with Pharaoh: Harsh Results (5:1–14)
   8. Negative Reaction of the Israelite Foremen (5:15–20)
   9. Moses' Complaint and God's Covenant Assurance (5:22–6:12)
   10. Genealogy of Moses and Aaron (6:13–27)
   11. Divine Reassurance of Moses' Call, Commission, Challenge (6:28–7:7)

III. Eleven Signs of Yahweh's sovereignty: The Ten Plagues: Judgment on the gods of Egypt (7:8–11:10)
   1. First Sign: An Opening Miracle before Pharaoh: Aaron's Staff Becomes a Snake (7:8–13)
   2. Second Sign: First Plague: Water to Blood (7:14–24)
   3. Third Sign: Second Plague: Frogs (7:25–8:15) [Hb. 7:25–8:11]
   4. Fourth Sign: Third Plague: Mosquitoes or Gnats (8:16–19) [Hb. 8:12–15]
   5. Fifth Sign: Fourth Plague: Swarms of Flies (8:20–32) [Hb. 8:16–28]
   6. Sixth Sign: Fifth Plague: Death of Livestock (9:1–7)
   7. Seventh Sign: Sixth Plague: Festering Boils (9:8–12)
   8. Eighth Sign: Seventh Plague: Hail (9:13–35)
   9. Ninth Sign: Eighth Plague: Locusts (10:1–20)

10. Tenth Sign: Ninth Plague: Darkness (10:21–29)
11. The Great Sign of Sovereignty Announced: Tenth Plague Predicted: Death of Firstborn (11:1–10)

IV. The Passover and the Exodus (12:1–13:16)
1. God's Instructions for Passover including the Use of the Blood (12:1–13)
2. God's Instructions for Passover Memorial of Unleavened Bread (12:14–20)
3. Moses and the Israelites Follow the Passover Instructions (12:21–28)
4. The Tenth Plague Strikes: Death of the Firstborn (12:29–30)
5. The Exodus Is Permitted, Under God's Vigil (12:31–36)
6. The Exodus Begins (12:37–42)
7. Summation: The Passover Statute and Its Connection to the Exodus (12:43–51)
8. Exodus Memorials: Consecration/Redemption of Firstborn, Eating Unleavened Bread (13:1–16)

V. The Wilderness Journey to Sinai (13:17–19:25)
1. Reasons for an Irregular Route (13:17–14:4)
2. Attack of the Egyptian Army and Israelite Panic (14:5–14)
3. Parting of the Red Sea and Drowning of the Egyptians (14:15–32)
4. Victory Hymn of Moses (15:1–18)
5. Prose Summation and Miriam's Reprise of the Hymn (15:19–21)
6. Grumbling Begins: Water at Marah and Elim and God's Promise of Healing (15:22–27)
7. More Grumbling: About Food (16:1–9)
8. God Sends Quail and Manna from Heaven (16:10–36)
9. More Grumbling and Water at Massah-Meribah (17:1–7)
10. Battle against the Amalekites at Rephidim and the Curse on Amalek (17:8–16)
11. The Visit and Conversion of Jethro (18:1–12)
12. Jethro Advises Implementing a Hierarchical Court System (18:13–27)
13. Arrival at Sinai and Call to Holiness (19:1–8)
14. Consecration in Preparation for Meeting God (19:9–15)
15. Meeting God on the Mountain (19:16–25)

VI. Covenant Law (20:1–31:18) [Continued in the Book of Leviticus]
1. The Ten Words and Their Significance (20:1–17)
2. The Covenant Code and Its Ratification (21:1–24:18)
3. Laws on the Means of Worship (25:1–31:18)

VII. Rebellion, Renewal, and Fulfillment of God's Instructions for the Tabernacle (32:1–40:38)

1. Rebellion, Covenant Breaking, God's Mercy, and Covenant Renewal (32:1–34:35)
2. Fulfillment of the Laws on the Means of Worship (35:1–40:38)

DIVISION OUTLINE

I. ISRAEL'S EGYPTIAN OPPRESSION AND GOD'S CHOICE OF A DELIVERER (1:1–2:25)
   1. Opening Genealogy, Connecting the Story with Genesis (1:1–6)[1]
   2. How Israel Came under Egyptian Bondage (1:7–14)
   3. A Pharaoh's Initiative: Genocide as Population Control (1:15–22)
   4. Moses' Birth and God's Provision (2:1–10)
   5. Moses' Own Exile/Exodus: Midian and Marriage (2:11–22)
   6. Summative Reminder: Severity of the Oppression and God's Concern (2:23–25)

I. ISRAEL'S EGYPTIAN OPPRESSION AND GOD'S CHOICE OF A DELIVERER (1:1–2:25)

From all appearances, Moses intended this block of narrative to function as a transitional introduction to the entire book of Exodus. It provides a sense of continuity to some of the main themes of his first book, with the result that the reader of Exodus senses a natural fit with the ongoing story of God's plan of redemption, that is, that story which begins to develop so eloquently in Genesis.[2] Many in the original audience would not have known most of the details found in these first two chapters of Exodus any more than they would have known many of the details of their spiritual and/or ethnic backgrounds as narrated in Genesis. These were, after all, people who had spent hundreds of years in pagan surroundings, most of whom probably needed reintroduction even to the very identity of Yahweh (the LORD) himself.[3] Garrett has carefully argued the position that Moses

---

[1] Although most commentators consider vv. 1–7 to be the first literary unit of the book, we believe that v. 7 more naturally introduces the next unit than concludes this one.

[2] Cf. C. Isbell, "Exodus 1–2 in the Context of Exodus 1–14: Story Lines and Key Words," in *Art and Meaning: Rhetoric in Biblical Literature* (Sheffield: JSOT Press, 1982), 37–61. From a different perspective, cf. G. F. Davies, *Israel in Egypt: Reading Exodus 1–2,* JSOT 135 (Sheffield: Sheffield Academic Press, 1992); and D. W. Wicke, "The Literary Structure of Exodus 1:2–2:10," *JSOT* 24 (1982): 99–107.

[3] See comments on 3:6ff. and cf. O. Eissfeldt, "Jakobs Begegnung mit El und Moses Begegnung mit Jahweh," *Kleine Schriften,* Vol. 4 (Tübingen: Mohr, 1968), 92–98. Our position differs considerably from that of Eissfeldt in that we conclude that the revelation of the name and identity of Yahweh to the Israelites was not new but a rerevelation and confirmation of prior revelations to the patriarchs (see comments on chap. 3), but we nevertheless appreciate that for many individuals, including the non-Israelites who joined in the exodus (see comments on 12:38) virtually nothing of Yahweh was known, even if his name was "an old name from the past" or the like.

most likely composed these materials during the years of the wilderness wanderings for the benefit of the second-generation Israelites who were growing up during that thirty-nine-year period, as well as for the benefit of those who came to join with Israel either spiritually or ethnically.[4]

We should remember that a considerable proportion of the people who actually arrived at Mount Sinai, after fleeing Egypt to meet with the only true and living God, were not originally Israelites at all.[5] They had seen the plagues, had come to believe that the Israelites were indeed a people to join with, and had taken advantage of the discomfiture of the Egyptians on the night of the Passover to join the Israelite ranks and seek freedom. Of course, as they traveled with the Israelites, they would begin to pick up bits and pieces of the history they were officially to adopt as their own at Sinai, but Moses' authoritative and systematic version was what they especially required if they were to be spiritually at one with the new people God was creating for himself in the process of the exodus.

This transitional-introductory material in chaps. 1–2 is composed of six component parts:[6] (1) First comes an opening genealogy (1:1–6) of the twelve tribes of Israel, featuring the twelve sons of Jacob and thus connecting the story of the exodus with the patriarchal narratives that comprise the bulk (chaps. 12–50) of Genesis.[7] The fact that this opening genealogy mentions the descent of Jacob's family into Egypt is part of its transitional character.[8] (2) Next comes a brief section describing how the descendants of Jacob grew into a large nation and eventually came under Egyptian bondage (1:7–14).[9] This information informs the alert reader that the promises of great growth to Abraham's descendants—restated, as carefully noted in

---

[4] D. Garrett, *Rethinking Genesis: The Sources and Authorship of the First Book of the Pentateuch* (Grand Rapids: Baker, 1991). Garrett's analysis of the purpose of composition and of the likely original audience applies to Exodus in some ways almost as much as to Genesis. Cf. also M. Woudstra, "Calvin Interprets What 'Moses Reports': Observations on Calvin's Commentary on Exodus 1–19," *Calvin Theological Journal* 21 (1986): 151–74. Obviously, our approach to the authorship of Exodus is quite distant from that reflected in, e.g., H. W. Wolff, "The Elohistic Fragments in the Pentateuch," in *The Vitality of Old Testament Traditions* (Atlanta: John Knox, 1975), 41–82, 138–40; or O. Eissfeldt, "Die Komposition von Exodus 1–12. Eine Rettung des Elohisten," *Kleine Schriften*, Vol. 2 (Tübingen: Mohr, 1963), 160–70.

[5] Cf. P. Trible, Bringing Miriam out of the Shadows," *BibRev* 5 (1989): 14–25, 34.

[6] For other ways of describing the structure of these chapters, see D. W. Wicke, "The Literary Structure of Exodus 1:2–2:10," *JSOT* 24 (1982): 99–107 and C. Isbell, "Exodus 1–2 in the Context of Exodus 1–14: Story Lines and Key Words," in *Art and Meaning: Rhetoric in Biblical Literature* (Sheffield: JSOT Press, 1982), 37–61.

[7] Cf. B. Gosse, "Transitions redactionnelles de l'histoire des Clans a l'histoire des Peuples en Ex 1, 7; 2, 24b," *EstBib* 51 (1993): 163–70. Cf. also Noth, *Die israelitischen Personnennamen im Rahmen der gemeinsemitischen Namengebung*.

[8] Cf. G. W. Coats, "A Structural Transition in Exodus," *VT* 22 (1972): 129–42.

[9] Cf. M. Goldberg, "Exodus 1:13–14." *Int* 37 (1983): 389–91.

Genesis (e.g., 26:3–4; 46:3) to both Abraham's son and grandson—are in active process of fulfillment. It also orients the reader to how it could come about that the people of Israel should be subject to such extreme loathing that (3) they would become, as described in the following section (1:5–22), the targets of a vicious genocidal campaign by the new pharaoh, with the goal of controlling the population of the Israelites through male infanticide.[10] (4) At the beginning of chap. 2 (2:1–10) Moses described his birth[11] and, more importantly for the salvation theme that dominates the entire first half of the book, the unusual circumstances that led to his being found by one of the Egyptian princesses and raised as an Egyptian yet nursed by his own mother and well aware of the plight of his own ethnic people.[12] (5) The fifth element (2:16–22) is the story of Moses' own exodus/exile from Egypt, in which he was forced to flee for his life as a criminal sought for murder because he sided with his people over against his office as an Egyptian princeling. This covers a forty-year period, during which Moses got married, settled in Midianite territory in the Sinai wilderness, and assumed the life of a shepherd within the overall estate of his father-in-law. By this turn of events, Moses was allowed to understand both the experience of fleeing Egypt and a great deal about survival in the Sinai wilderness, knowledge that constituted part of God's preparation of him to assume the position of leader of God's deliverance. (6) A brief summative reminder (2:23–25) then draws the first two chapters to a close.[13] These concluding three verses remind the reader of two things especially: the severity of the oppression the Israelites endured for many decades and the fact that in spite of their long sojourn in foreign territory and their long period of suffering, God had not forgotten them but was indeed deeply concerned for the plight of his people.

In all of this portion of the book (1:1–2:25), Moses carefully avoided mention of the divine name Yahweh (the LORD) which he does not reintroduce until 3:2, even though he used it 175 times throughout Genesis. His

[10] See K. Kitchen, "From the Brickfields of Egypt," *TynBul* 27 (1976): 137–47.

[11] On the significance of this part of the narrative in its own right, see, e.g., B. Childs, "The Birth of Moses," *JBL* 84 (1965): 109–22; I. Willi-Plein, "Ort und literarische Funktion der Geburtsgeschichte des Mose," *VT* 41 (1991): 110–18; J. Ackerman, "The Literary Context of the Moses Birth Story," in *Literary Interpretations of Biblical Narratives* (Nashville: Abingdon, 1974), 74–119; A. Kenk, "Moses and Jesus: The Birth of the Savior," *Jud* 42 (1993): 43–49; J. Macchi, "La Naissance de Moise (Exode 2/1–10)," *ETR* 69 (1994): 397–403.

[12] See J. Feather, "The Princess Who Rescued Moses: Who Was She?" *ExpTim* (1931–32): 423–425; W. W. Feilchenfeldt, "Die Entpersonlichung Moses in der Bibel und ihre Bedeutung." *ZAW* 64 (1952): 156–78.

[13] See J. Cunchillos, "La dynamique de l'histoire du salut-liberation, Exode 2, 23–25," in *La Bible. Premiere lecture de l'Ancien Testament -I,* Le point théologique, II (Paris: Beauchesne, 1974), 97–107.

purpose for this is almost certainly a desire to heighten for the reader the significance of the rerevelation of the divine name to the people of God, the centerpiece of chap. 3)[14] and the focus of the covenantal theology that dominates the rest of the Pentateuch.

1. Opening Genealogy: Connecting the Story with Genesis (1:1–6)

[1]These are the names of the sons of Israel who went to Egypt with Jacob, each with his family: [2]Reuben, Simeon, Levi and Judah; [3]Issachar, Zebulun and Benjamin; [4]Dan and Naphtali; Gad and Asher. [5]The descendants of Jacob numbered seventy in all; Joseph was already in Egypt. [6]Now Joseph and all his brothers and all that generation died,

These opening verses provide an obvious connection to what Moses said in the latter chapters of Genesis, in that they contain a brief recapitulation of the story of how Jacob and his sons entered Egypt and were reunited with Joseph (esp. Gen 46) as well as the death of Joseph in the context of his association with his brothers (Gen 50:22–26; note how vv. 25–26 implicitly reflect the concept of "all that generation" in Exod 1:6). Thus there is a conscious concern here to be sure the reader understands that Exodus is not strictly a self-contained narrative but a segment of a narrative on a grander

[14] Moses also omitted the name Yahweh in most of the Joseph narrative in Genesis (37–50) for a presumably similar reason. In fact, the name Yahweh does not occur between Gen 32:9 and 38:7, as well as between Gen 39:23 and 49:18. The former section of narrative concerns relationships with non-Yahwists, including Esau, the Shechemites, and the like. The latter section is about the Israelite sojourn in Egypt, where Yahweh was likewise unknown. In both instances Moses' avoidance of the divine proper name is an effective literary device to convey a realistic impression of situations in which Yahweh was largely or entirely unknown. D. Patrick has provided an observation in connection with the Decalogue that may have relevance here as well ("The First Commandment in the Structure of the Pentateuch," *VT* 45 [1995]: 107–18). He contends that a careful examination of the entirety of Genesis and Exodus up to Exodus 20 demonstrates that Yahweh, with a few minor exceptions that are easily explained, is portrayed as the only god that has any direct effect on human affairs or activities and the only god that receives worship from human beings. In other words, for all practical purposes, the Pentateuch up to Exodus 20 is implicitly monotheistic and in effect ignores the existence (at least the efficacy) of other gods and goddesses besides Yahweh. Then, with the introduction of the prohibition against having other gods than Yahweh in the first commandment of the Ten Words/Commandments (Exod 20:3–6 by his enumeration), the Pentateuch immediately addresses the dangers both of idolatry and of apostasy, and the reader sees thereafter many instances of Israelite interaction with belief in other gods than Yahweh. Patrick suggests that behind this structure is the concept that people are not responsible to keep a law and will not be punished for not doing what it says until that law is actually made public as a commandment. We simply take what Patrick contends is a pattern brought about by "the authors" of the Pentateuch as in fact the author Moses' purposeful stylistic device for employing the name of Yahweh along the lines we have discussed above.

scale, that is, the full Pentateuch. In other words, the story continues smoothly from Genesis into Exodus.

1:1 The book begins by introducing to the reader a list of names. Accordingly, following the common *incipit* naming system[15] of ancient times, the name of the book of Exodus in Hebrew is "These are the Names" *(ʾēlleh šĕmôt).*[16] To a modern reader such an opening might not seem consistent with high literary style. It was, however, not only good style but entirely welcome in the ancient setting, where a group of refugees of mixed ethnic origin, many of whom were young enough to be learning their national traditions for the first time, were being reminded of God's plan through a people descended from Abraham and heirs to the promises first made to him. These promises had four main components: (1) vast population increase for his descendants (Gen 12:2); (2) a long and important family lineage (the meaning of "make your name great" in Gen 12:2); (3) a worldwide blessing through his offspring[17] (Gen 12:2–3), and (4) the eventual granting of unearned citizenship in a special land of God's choosing (implied in Gen 12:1; explicit in Gen 15:18–21). The fact that several biblical books begin with a genealogy (e.g., 1 Chr 1–9) or end with one (e.g., Ruth) is a reflection of the importance ancient Israelites placed on being able to trace their lineage, as part of understanding who they were and what their purpose was on earth.

An even more basic reason for beginning the book with a list of names, however, was the desire to ensure that the reader understood Exodus as a direct continuation of Genesis, accomplished from the outset by making the first six words in the Hebrew of Exodus ("These are the names of the sons of Israel who went . . ."[18]) identical to the first six words of Gen 46:8.[19] The latter context contained a promise to Jacob about his sons and their place in

---

[15] The incipit is the first few words of any piece of literature used as its title. That this system for naming pieces prevailed in ancient times is evident not only from the Hebrew names of biblical books but also from the way psalm titles are mentioned in OT narratives, as, e.g., in 2 Chr 5:13; Jer 33:11 referring to Ps 106.

[16] The MT, followed by the other ancient versions except the LXX and Vg., has *wĕʾēlleh,* i.e., "And these are the names of the sons of Israel." The failure of the NIV to realize that the first words of Exod 1:1 are purposely identical to the first words of Gen 46:8 led them to omit translating the we ("and") even though the syntax is disjunctive, thus obscuring Moses' purpose in linking Exodus to Genesis.

[17] The Hb. for "offspring," *zeraʿ*, is richly ambiguous and may be either singular or plural, so that Paul's explanation of how the original is best understood as singular (offspring = Christ, Gal 3:16) is grammatically sophisticated.

[18] Either "entered" or "went [to]" would be acceptable, but "came," a normal rendering for Hb. *bāʾ,* may be the best translation here to convey the perspective of Moses and his audience, who thought of Egypt as their primary place of residence and saw their ancestors as having *come* to where they themselves had accordingly lived.

[19] J. I Durham, (*Exodus,* WBC [Waco: Word, 1987]).

God's plan. The book of Exodus opens with a description of Jacob's grown family in Egypt (1:1, "who went [came] to Egypt with Jacob, each with his family") that shows clearly how God was beginning to move that plan onto its next stage.[20] Genesis had already introduced the theme of the fertility of Abraham's descendants in the patriarchal promises, as noted above, and had developed those promises in such passages as Gen 47:6–12,27; 48:3–7. The next stage also is anticipated in the use of *yiśrā'ēl* here as "sons of [the man] Israel" in contrast to its next usage in 1:7, where the same phrase, *bĕnê yiśrā'ēl,* will have its usual post-Genesis meaning, "Israelites," that is, the nation, not merely an extended family.[21]

1:2–4 It is possible to make either too much or too little of this list of eleven names. It would be a mistake to make too much of their order. There appears to have been no established order for the names in Israelite tradition, as shown by the way the order varies among Gen 46:8–27; 49:3–27; Deut 33:2–29; and the present passage. Likewise, the way they are grouped is of no special importance. The verse divisions are medieval so irrelevant to Moses' original purpose. The placement of the conjunction "and" seems to be[22] as follows: n,n,n and n . . . n, n and n . . . n, and n . . . n and n. In other words, the pattern reflects a simple descending order of number of names grouped before a copula is inserted (four names, three names, two names, two names): a pattern for convenience, but not otherwise meaningful.

But what about the meaning of the individual names? Hebrew names were known to be given to children according to events or concepts present at the time of their birth.[23] Should the reader therefore hear in the recitation of these names some sort of echo of their original significance? We think not. By this point in the narrative that began with Genesis, there is no hint that the names carry any symbolic meaning. They are simply names for identification as all names are, simply functioning to remind us that the tribes of Israel were named after the sons of Jacob, that is, that the organiza-

[20] Durham, *Exodus,* puts it, this linkage of Exod 1:1 and Gen 46:8 "is a clear rhetorical indication of the continuity intended not only in the narrative, but in the underlying theological assertion" (*Exodus,* WBC [Waco: Word, 1987], 3).

[21] Cf. A. Besters, "'Israel' et 'fils d'Israel' dans les livres historiques (Genese-II Rois)," *RB* 74 (1967): 5–23; id., "L'expression 'fils d'Israel' en Ex. I–XIV," *RB* 74 (1967): 321–55.

[22] The copula placement may be only apparent since textual corruption in the process of copying the list over the years may have altered its original "punctuation." Hebrew *wĕ* ("and") is not always well preserved in copying. See F. M. Cross and D. N. Freedman, "Table: The Evidence for the Use of the Conjunction at the Beginning of Cola, in the Hebrew Text and the Principal Versions," in *Studies in Ancient Yahwistic Poetry* (Grand Rapids: Eerdmans/Dove, 1997).

[23] For a summary of how the naming process worked in ancient Israel, see D. Stuart, "Names, Proper," *ISBE* 3.483–88.

tion of the people of Israel could be traced back to the original family of the patriarch Israel.[24]

1:5 Here the Hebrew literally says, "Thus the full offspring of the loins of Jacob was seventy souls in all," but the NIV translation renders the Hebrew well into idiomatic English—the main point of the first part of the verse being simply to inform the reader that the great nation of Israel that came out of Egypt numbering many tens of thousands had gone into Egypt numbering only seventy. The first readers of the book were people who belonged to the huge exodus nation, for whom Moses composed the narrative. This little detail was a reminder of the faithfulness of God to his promises. The background of this great host was traceable to a single man's family.

The mention that "Joseph was already in Egypt" is a required detail since otherwise Moses' narrative might seem to imply either that Joseph was not counted in the seventy or that he was among those who went to Egypt with Jacob.[25] However, it also leads nicely to the next point, made by the next verse, that is, that the special influence of Joseph that had made Jacob's family privileged guests in Egypt was linked to Joseph's person and position and would not continue after his death (a point made clear in v. 8).

1:6 The book of Genesis ends (50:26) with the death of Joseph. The summary in this verse of how the Israelites settled in Egypt ends likewise. Genesis 50:26 also notes that Joseph died at age 110, suggesting that he might have been the last of all the brothers to die. He was the next to youngest son,[26] and 110 years is a very long life, presenting the likelihood that he outlived his brothers. Accordingly, it appears that at the very end of this verse Moses begins to take the reader beyond the Genesis story by noting the end of the entire original patriarchal generation, thus paving the way for

---

[24] When an ancient reader/listener encountered any of these names this far along in the narrative and without any explanatory wording to suggest that their original meaning should be brought to mind, it is no more likely that he or she thought, e.g., "Aha! Reuben means 'Behold a son'" than he or she would have thought every time the name Moses was mentioned, "Aha! Moses sounds like 'draw out'" or, in fact, any more than a modern reader seeing the name Carol in a story would say, "Aha! The name Carol means 'song.'" It is unfortunately common for both commentators and preachers to insist on informing their audience of the literal meaning of biblical names as if this somehow makes biblical passages or books more meaningful. In fact, it is usually misleading because the mention of a name in any culture functions primarily to identify a person, not to call attention every time the name is mentioned to the original thinking process employed by the naming parents.

[25] In the LXX here and Gen 46:27 (cf. 4QEx[a]) the number given is seventy-five, almost surely not original but a later insertion based on the desire to include in the total all the immediate descendants of Ephraim and Manasseh, which were not yet separate tribes at the time Moses composed this. Indeed, the fact that Moses did not think here in terms of the later history of Ephraim and Manasseh, the Joseph tribes, is one earmark of the early date of the material.

[26] Cf. Gen 30:1–24; 35:24; 37:3.

the next part of the narrative, which will discuss what happened once post-patriarchal Israel was permanently ensconced in Egypt.[27] It is possible that this verse is composed in what may have been a somewhat standardized or formulaic pattern for the passing of a great leader and his contemporaries or that the verse set the pattern for the formula that later was repeated.[28]

2. How Israel Came under Egyptian Bondage (1:7–14)

[7]but the Israelites were fruitful and multiplied greatly and became exceedingly numerous, so that the land was filled with them.

**[8]Then a new king, who did not know about Joseph, came to power in Egypt.
[9]"Look," he said to his people, "the Israelites have become much too numerous for us. [10]Come, we must deal shrewdly with them or they will become even more numerous and, if war breaks out, will join our enemies, fight against us and leave the country."**

[11]So they put slave masters over them to oppress them with forced labor, and they built Pithom and Rameses as store cities for Pharaoh. [12]But the more they were oppressed, the more they multiplied and spread; so the Egyptians came to dread the Israelites [13]and worked them ruthlessly. [14]They made their lives bitter with hard labor in brick and mortar and with all kinds of work in the fields; in all their hard labor the Egyptians used them ruthlessly.

These eight verses function as a unit in the narrative by reason of their common topic: a summary of how the Israelites went from favor to disgrace, from a protected people with government connections at the highest level to a gang of slaves laboring under severe oppression. The common reason throughout this explanatory section is their numerical growth.[29]

Of course, this represents an irony. Their rapid growth was a glorious blessing of God, in faithful fulfillment of his creation decrees (see below) and patriarchal promises (see vv. 1–7). How then could it get them in so much trouble? The short answer is that in a fallen world, the blessings of God are often so in conflict with the prevailing corrupt values of this world's culture that they function as a threat to those who are not aligned with God's will. The parade example of this phenomenon is the rejection of Jesus. He

[27] Grammatically, the second part of the verse ("Joseph was already in Egypt") is in the Hb. a circumstantial noun clause, with a well-known grammatical parallel in Gen 1:2 ("the earth being formless and empty"). It could thus be translated either "Joseph being already in Egypt" or "including Joseph, who was already in Egypt." Cf. R. J. Williams, *Hebrew Syntax: An Outline,* 2d ed. (Toronto: University of Toronto Press, 1976), par. 495; König, *Lehrgebäude* III, 302a, 362k.

[28] Cf. esp. the close parallels in Josh 5:4,6; 1 Sam 31:6; 1 Chr 10:6. The case for a formulaic structure has been argued by T. Vriezen in "Exodusstudien, Exodus I," *VT* 17 (1967): 334–36.

[29] For a discussion of the issues involved see J. M. Cohen, "The Fertility of the Israelites," *JBQ* 27 (1999): 195–98.

was the purest example of good that the world has seen, and yet God could send him to earth with the certain knowledge that he would be put to death by people who thought they were doing the world a favor.

So Moses holds the population factor clearly before the reader, as both a good thing from a righteous person's point of view and also as the cause of much evil because of the reaction of evil people to it. In addition, he points out a further irony: the fact that the oppression of the people and their population growth increased together (v. 12). And he does not word it as might be expected, that is, that as their growth increased, they naturally experienced more oppression; rather, it was as they experienced more oppression that their growth increased. This has the effect of "dramatizing the need of Israel, and thus increasing the reader's concern that something must be done."[30] If God caused their original growth and then accelerated it in correspondence with their suffering, surely in his plan there must be a means of resolution—some way to bring good out of the current unfairness. This unit of the narrative thus alerts us to expect divine intervention.

That divine intervention would be the result is also heightened by the careful avoidance of any mention of God in these verses and, indeed, in the narrative so far. This helps convey the sense that presumably prevailed among the Israelites in those days: it seemed as though God wasn't around and that unless he showed up, things were not going to get better.

1:7 Most of the vocabulary of this verse hearkens to the Genesis creation story, showing that Israel was in itself a fulfillment of the creation commands ("Be fruitful . . . increase [multiply] . . . fill," Gen 1:22,28). This language continues at many points in Genesis (e.g., 8:17; 9:1,7; 17:20; 28:3; 35:11; 47:27; 48:4) as the creation theme unfolds in the narrative. The common but incorrect notion that the creation story is to be found only in the first chapters of Genesis misses the fact that the biblical picture of creation is one of ongoing creation, starting with Adam and Eve, continuing with human society in general, continuing further with Noah and the patriarchs, then with the nation Israel and many of its institutions (even Jerusalem; cf. Exod 15:17; Isa 65:18), and culminating in the new creation (Isa 65:17) in which all who truly place faith in Christ are recreated (2 Cor 5:17; Eph 2:10). In support of this theme of ongoing creation relative to Israel in Egypt, Moses packed into the verse about every possible way of saying that the Israelites rapidly increased in number. The Hebrew literally reads, "As for the Israelites, they grew, they were fruitful, they swarmed, they increased, they got powerful more and more, and the land was filled with them."[31]

---

[30] Durham, *Exodus*, 6.

[31] The grammar is disjunctive, but not necessarily strongly contrastive; therefore we would prefer the translation "As for the Israelites, they were fruitful and . . ." to indicate that a new topic is the subject of vv. 7–14, namely, the way the Israelites' population growth led to their being oppressed.

The point made by such language is twofold: (1) that Israel's amazing population growth was the result of God's original design and ongoing care[32] and (2) that Israelites were living, at least in small colonies or scattered families, in sufficient numbers as to dominate the population of one part of Egypt at the time of the persecution, that is, just in the eastern Nile delta area of Goshen, even if they were not the sole inhabitants of that general area.[33] Their population growth was taking place in a land where the Israelites were resident aliens, and therefore what follows—the hostility of the Egyptians—is hardly a total surprise. "Land" here refers almost certainly not to the entirety of Egypt, nor to the earth in general, but to the land of Goshen.[34] For any land or major portion thereof to be filled with people of external origin and allegiance is bound to threaten those who regard themselves as its rightful citizens. In a fallen world, hostility to foreigners is unfortunately a common human sin.

1:8 In this brief sentence is contained reference to a vast political and ideological shift in Egypt. Joseph almost certainly rose to power (Gen 41–42) during the time of the Hyksos pharaohs, outsiders who had invaded and conquered Egypt. After the expulsion of the Hyksos, an accomplishment much celebrated in Egyptian history,[35] it is quite understandable that feeling against foreigners would run high. It is also understandable that a pharaoh who had expelled—or whose ancestors had expelled—hated foreign oppres-

[32] This sort of perspective on the text is evidenced even in the work of those who regard the numbers and general population descriptions as fictional (e.g., M. Gruber, "The Exaggerated Number of the Israelites in Egypt," *BMik* 33 [1987/1988]: 171–75 [Hebrew].

[33] Cf. H. Cazelles, "le pays de Goshen," *MDB* 41 (1985): 45.

[34] See comments on 8:22 ("the land of Goshen, where my people live") and 9:26 ("the land of Goshen, where the Israelites were"). Goshen was well established already in the Genesis narrative as the place of sojourn for the Israelites (Gen 47:4,6,27; 50:8).

[35] The expulsion of the Hyksos is chronicled in some detail in the Thebes inscription of Ahmose, the founder of the Eighteenth Dynasty. After building up and gathering to himself a powerful army, he began threatening the Hyksos, whose capital was Avaris (biblical Zoan, in the northeast Delta). After a successful siege of Avaris, he chased the Hyksos entirely out of Egypt and pursued them as far as Sharuhen in southern Palestine. Not only did the Egyptians drive the Hyksos out of Egypt proper upon the founding of the Eighteenth Dynasty, but they reasserted their influence in Syria and Palestine (Egyptian "Retjenu") as a matter of imperial policy for that dynasty. E.g., the inscriptions of Thutmose III (1483–1450 BC) in the temple of Amon-Re at Karnak and elsewhere (*ANET,* 234–41) indicate that he conducted no fewer than seventeen military campaigns in Syria-Palestine in his first twenty years as independent king (i.e., no longer co-regent). His first campaign, in which his forces decisively defeated a coalition of nations at Megiddo, was perhaps the most decisive, paving the way for the continued assertion of Egyptian influence in Asia thereafter. His eighth campaign went all the way to the Euphrates, where his forces crushed Mitanni, the united Hurrian nation, and thus secured control of Syria for Egypt. His successors in the Eighteenth Dynasty also boasted often in their own inscriptions of their prowess against Asiatics in such a way that it is obvious they continued to take seriously the lessons learned during the humiliation of Hyksos domination of Egypt during the Second Intermediate Period.

sors would have had no sympathy for or even interest in honoring the memory of a foreigner who had served as Egypt's prime minister during the reign of one of those Hyksos pharaohs. In other words, the Israelites were now foreigners in a country whose government hated foreigners, under a pharaoh who was surely determined to prevent what he saw as the miseries of the past from returning, and who would have had not the slightest sense of loyalty to any agreements his Hyksos predecessors worked out with Joseph. The functional implication of "did not know about Joseph" is therefore "refused to honor any prior arrangements protecting the status of the Israelites."[36] By implication, the Israelites are going to be in trouble, their former assurances[37] of acceptance as foreigners in Egypt now being useless.

1:9 It is possible that Moses heard these words when they were first spoken, since as an Egyptian princeling during his first forty years of life he presumably attended at least some of the royal court sessions. This sounds like a summary of a major policy initiative speech given by the pharaoh to the sort of large assembly that would have included the lesser members of the royal family. Much depends, however, on whether or not the pharaoh of the oppression is this same pharaoh who initiated the campaign against Israel, that is, how many years went by between vv. 9 and 12. Nevertheless, even if Moses served under a later pharaoh than the one who initiated this policy, it is likely that Moses heard these words often referred to, since it appears that the policy was endorsed and adopted as a national goal for the long term rather than for the duration of a single administration. It became, in other words, the policy of a dynasty rather than of a single pharaoh.

A subtlety in the pharaoh's language is not reflected in the NIV translation: what he literally said was that "the nation of the Israelites has become so numerous as to be stronger than we are." With regard to the first part of this statement, the normal way of referring to the Israelites was simply as "the Israelites" *(bĕnê yiśrāʾēl)*. To refer to "the nation of the Israelites" *(ʿam bĕnê yiśrāʾēl)* is more pejorative. First, it dehumanizes the Israelites somewhat by focusing on their category rather than their humanity (slightly akin to speaking of "the Mongol hordes" rather than simply "the Mongols"); second, it identifies them as a separate nation/people (*ʿam* tends to refer to entire, major, ethnic-political groups). Thus the pharaoh was undoubtedly using language, a bit of which is preserved here to give its flavor, that

---

[36] B. Jacob's translation (in his commentary, *Das Zweite Buch Mose,* also titled *Das Zweite Buch der Torah*, pub. in Eng. as *Exodus*, trans. W. Jakob [Hoboken, Holland: KTAV, 1992]), "chose/decided not to know Joseph," is plausible but has the disadvantage of going beyond the simple meaning of the more neutral Hb., which says nothing about motive or will—only that the new king, whether by reason of ignorance, disinterest, or determination, did not honor the original promises made through Joseph to the Israelites as recorded in Gen 47:11.

[37] Gen 45:10–11; 47:1–12.

identified Israel as a nation within a nation, something not innocuous. This language drew attention to the fact that the Egyptians now had to contend not merely with a minor group of people living in a region of a great country but a full foreign nation within their midst.

The second part of the statement, while surely an exaggeration intended to frighten rather than to present the facts accurately, plays on the universal xenophobic tendency of peoples to fear losing their jobs, their wealth, their land, and their political control to foreigners in their midst. It is no accident that all major countries of the modern world have immigration laws including numerical restrictions on the influx of foreigners and that many have restrictions on foreign investment within their borders as well. It is likewise no accident that the constitution of the United States, for example, requires the president to be born in America. Nations throughout history have tended to be afraid of losing their power to "outsiders," so the Egyptian mentality at this point can easily be understood. What the pharaoh did was to sound the alarmist note, calculated to get approval from the masses for his planned campaign of oppression, that the Egyptians had fallen behind the foreigners in their midst, and would need to act quickly to regain control. To portray his own people as somehow a minority, potentially dominated by the outsider majority, was a clever way to engender popular support for his plan. All oppressive regimes use the threat of some great danger, real or imagined, to justify violations of human rights. The pharaoh was simply following this well-attested course of action.

1:10 Here the pharaoh's proposal for action is summarized. He called for population control of the Israelites. The *shrewd* dealing he suggested is intended to prevent their becoming "more numerous." That became the centerpiece of all further Egyptian strategy with regard to the Israelites. It was their *further* growth that was portrayed as the threat, one that could not be tolerated. As well, the excusing threat that will justify violating the Israelites' rights is now more precisely defined: in the event of war, the Israelites would side with the enemy and not with Egypt, thus producing an intolerable defensive situation: the enemy both within and without in force.[38] This sort of propaganda has worked countless times in history. If a regime wishes to be given freedom to oppress a given group within a nation, it defines that group as an undermining force, a real danger, and potentially the agent of overthrow of the established order. The pharaoh was spouting ethnic hate propaganda of the sort still widely employed in the modern world to justify ethnic persecution and eventually genocide.

---

[38] A more precise translation of וְהָיָה כִּי־תִקְרֶאנָה מִלְחָמָה וְנוֹסַף גַּם־הוּא עַל־שֹׂנְאֵינוּ would be, "If war breaks out, they too will join our enemies." The Hb. demonstrates that the pharaoh was concerned with active international enmity and that Egypt was feeling threatened and potentially outnumbered—even if the argument made by the pharaoh was based on exaggeration of the facts (see comments on 12:37).

Like most propaganda, it was a distortion of the truth rather than entirely false. The Israelites were foreigners, as the hated Hyksos had been, and they were, like the Hyksos, "mountain people" (the literal meaning of the Egyptian from which the Greek *hyksos* is corrupted), that is, from mountainous Canaan. Moreover, in the ancient world ethnic loyalties were usually stronger than political ones,[39] and the pharaoh's reasoning had a general ring of truth. History was also, in a sense, on his side. Foreigners had recently ruled Egypt as a result of war. Was this not what history taught—that you had to be suspicious of the motives of foreigners toward Egypt and its desirable, famine-proof[40] land?

The final words in the pharaoh's speech appear to comprise a relatively rare Hebrew idiom that may not mean what it has seemed to mean to most translators. The NIV translation "and leave the country" renders contextually what the more traditional English translations have rendered as "and go up from the land" or "and escape from the land," or the like. But this specific combination of Hebrew words[41] has a semantic value different from what either a literal or typical dynamic equivalence reading might seem to suggest (i.e., simply "go up from the land" or some similar wording of the same concept of "leaving"). The idiom to which we refer appears only in the following three texts, each of which has to do either with water rising or people rising up over land, that is, overcoming, overwhelming, or dominating it:

> Gen 2:6: But a flow of water would *come over* the earth, and water the whole surface of the earth.
>
> Exod 1:10: Come, let us deal shrewdly with them, or they will increase and, in the event of war, join our enemies and fight against us and *take possession of* the land. [author translation]
>
> Hos 1:11: The people of Judah and the people of Israel shall be gathered together, and they shall appoint for themselves one head; and they shall *take possession of* the land, for great shall be the day of Jezreel. [NRSV, italics mine]

The NRSV correctly recognizes the idiom's meaning in Hos 1:11 ("take possession of the land"), but none of the best-known translations[42]

---

[39] As exemplified in the way the Benjamites sided with their own Gibeathites against the will of the nation and the rule of law in Israel (Judg 19–20).

[40] The huge Nile always flowed and supplied abundant water for the irrigation canals into the rich fields along its banks. Accordingly, Egypt could relatively well withstand any drought, the major cause of famine in the ancient world. Even today over 90 percent of the population of Egypt lives within five miles of the Nile, the key to Egyptian prosperity in a land with minimal rainfall.

[41] ו [*wāw* conversive] + עלה [*qal* perfect, "go up,"] + מִן [from/over] + ה [the] + ארץ [land].

[42] A commendable exception is found in the Torah (NJPS version), which translates "gain ascendancy over the land." In further support thereof, see H. M. Orlinsky, *Notes on the New Translation* (New York: JPS, 1969), 149.

recognize the idiom here in Exod 1:10, where we believe it should also be translated "take possession of the land." The idiom is implicitly discernible in Gen 2:6 even in the unsatisfactory traditional translations because what is depicted in that verse is a flow of water that covers the land and thus waters it—it "rises over" or "comes over" or "overwhelms" or "overflows" or "takes possession of" the land—the sort of thing the pharaoh was suggesting in Exod 1:10 that the Israelites might do in Egypt.

With the proper translation of Exod 1:10, the pharaoh's speech makes sense; without it, it does not.[43] What sort of threat would it be to the Egyptians if the Israelites were to "leave the country" during a war waged by foreigners against Egypt? Indeed, an Israelite departure during war might well be the best possible development from an Egyptian point of view since it would eliminate the enemy threat in their midst. But if the pharaoh is warning about actually being overtaken/overwhelmed/dispossessed from within by the foreign element already resident in Egypt, his speech would have the sort of impact on the collective consciousness that would help justify a full-scale campaign of oppression against a people previously accepted and treated decently.

1:11 Moses' wording of this verse implies that the pharaoh's proposal was accepted and its implementation begun fairly rapidly—at least rapidly enough that Moses felt no need to describe any intervening developments between the proposal and its implementation. It obviously was an incremental policy of population control designed to suppress gradually the Israelites' will and ability to resist.[44]

The first step was to reorder the Israelites' position in Egyptian society.[45] No longer would they be an independent people but would instead be a slave caste under the control of slave masters, and their main purpose in life would be to perform forced labor assigned to them by the Egyptians. Their original identity had been as shepherds and contract herders in the grazing lands of northeast Egypt (Gen 46:34; 47:4–6,27) with official recognition by the government in this role (Gen 47:6).[46] Now the government redefined

---

[43] In other words, regardless of the exact wording chosen for the translation, the Hb. idiom employed must mean the equivalent of "gain control over the land" rather than "leave the country."

[44] Those familiar with the way the Nazis gradually placed more and more restrictive and then oppressive and then finally mortal strictures on the Jews, gypsies, and other "internal enemies" during the period from 1937 to 1945 will recognize a similar progression in the case of the Israelites in Egypt at this time.

[45] See J. S. Croatto, *Exodus: A Hermeneutics of Freedom* (Maryknoll, N.Y.: Orbis, 1981), 17; D. B. Redford, "Ex. 1,11," *VT* 13 (1963): 401–18; W. G. Plaut, "The Israelites in Pharaoh's Egypt—A Historical Reconstruction," *Judaism* 27 (1978): 40–46.

[46] It is especially instructive to note that the third-century BC Egyptian historian Manetho described the pharaohs of the Hyksos period as the "Shepherd Kings" (as cited by Josephus, *C. Ap.* 1.14, 75–82), suggesting that shepherding, a practice loathsome to native Egyptians (Gen 46:34), was in fact officially encouraged during the Hyksos rule.

them as conscript construction laborers[47] and, as the reader soon learns, forced them to do general labor and especially to make bricks (Exod 1:14; 5:7–19). The lower a group is on the social-economic scale, the less likely it is to be able to organize itself in opposition to those in authority.[48] Thus the Egyptian program had its first achievement: the Israelite population was reduced in influence, less likely to be a threat to native Egyptian sovereignty.

Next would come, gradually, a reduction also in numbers. This would be the expected natural result of the combination of poverty and extremely hard work the Israelites were forced to endure.[49] The text does not overtly report that the pharaoh said, "Let's kill off some of the Israelites with hard labor" because he probably never announced publicly any such wording, but that is surely the implication of his plan.

Moses mentioned the fact that during this time the Israelites were the group used to build two entire cities, Pithom and Rameses, which he described as "store cities." Pithom has been commonly identified with Egyptian *prtm*, that is, "house of 'Tum" [= house of the god Atum], a city known to have been located somewhere to the east of Wadi Tumilat and thus likely where either Tel el-Maskutah or Tel er-Ratabah are known today, and possibly at or near Heliopolis. The city of Rameses, on the other hand, is commonly thought to bear in its name the Hebrew reflex of Egyptian "house of Ramses," but it may in fact have derived originally from *riʿamsēs,* meaning "Re created it/him." It was a royal city the pharaohs of the Nineteenth and Twentieth Dynasties occupied, that is, the royal residence of the Ramessides in the delta region from about 1300 to about 1100 BC. In Gen 47:11 "Rameses" seems to function as a metonymy for the entire land of Goshen. Many scholars have thus assumed that the region is given that name somewhat anachronistically, based on the later Israelite knowledge of the chief city of the region, the place mentioned in Exod 12:37 and Num 33:3–5 as the departure point for the exodus. By this understanding, it would eventually have replaced "Avaris" in the biblical text for the convenience of later readers, much as "New York" eventually replaced the original "New Amsterdam" in the evolving nomenclature of colonial America. However, there is no reason to rule out the possibility that the city that Ramses later "constructed" and perhaps called "house of Ramses," was

[47] On the general idea of a system of conscripted labor, see I. Mendelsohn, "On Corvée Labor in Ancient Canaan and Israel," *BASOR* 167 (1962): 31–35; cf. Plaut, "The Israelites in Pharaoh's Egypt," 40–46.

[48] For exactly that reason the Babylonians left only the common folk, the "poorest people of the land," in Judah after the exile of Jehoiachin in 598 BC (2 Kgs 24:14).

[49] T. Fretheim puts it succinctly: "History has shown that such cruelties result not only in tighter controls over the community but in many deaths" (*Exodus*, Interpretation: A Bible Commentary for Teaching and Preaching [Louisville: Westminster John Knox, 1991], 28).

in fact a rebuilding and expansion of the earlier *riʿamsēs*. This would be consistent with Ramses' extensive building and rebuilding efforts in many parts of Egypt, and the way that new dynasties often rebuilt cities to their liking and/or to new strategic uses, so that many cities show evidence of several major and many minor reconstructions over their history. This description raises two questions, the answers to which remain somewhat speculative.

First, where were the two cities located? It is reasonable to speculate that they were built near the land of Goshen, that is, in the eastern Delta, close to the Sinai peninsula, since this was the heart of the Israelite territory and the place where the largest concentration of Israelite slave workers could be found.[50] The answer to the second question is that while they certainly were "store" or even "treasure" cities in the sense of being places where valuable assets of various sorts from the point of view of the kingdom were kept, they were also *de facto* probably *military* store cities by reason of being built in the northeast corner of the country at the area where invasion would first come from Asia, that is, the direction of the earlier invasion that had taken place under the Asiatic Hyksos[51]—the direction of Egypt's most feared

[50] The exact location remains in dispute. Both Tanis (biblical Zoan, Num 13:22, also known as Avaris, modern San el-Hagar) and Qantir (modern Tel el-Dab´a, located about twelve miles southwest of Tanis) have been thought appropriate sites for ancient Rameses. Egyptian annals and other records seem to agree that between the end of the eighteenth century BC and 1318 BC there was no royal residence in the eastern Delta. Because Ramses II (1304–1227) made the decision to build a royal residence at *[pr] rʿ-ms-sw* early in his reign, this has naturally led to the assumption that he would have been the actual pharaoh of the oppression, and therefore his son, Merneptah, would have been the pharaoh of the exodus. See the Introduction, however, for options to this later-date scenario. There are arguments for and against any identification of the exact location. The identification with Qantir seems to have the most support among recent scholars, including M. Hamza (Annales du service des antiquités de l'Égypte 30 [1930]: 31–68); K. A. Kitchen (*The Bible in Its World* [Exeter: Paternoster, 1977], 76–79); J. Baines and J. Málek (*Atlas of Ancient Egypt* [Oxford: Phaedon, 1980], 28, 46–48, 84, 166, 175–77, 212–13); and C. F. Aling ("The Biblical City of Ramses," *JETS* 25 [1982]: 129–38). E. P. Uphill's assessment at the conclusion of his especially thorough study of the problem is representative: "It may therefore be suggested that the biblical account is in substantial agreement with the known evidence which can be gleaned from Egypt, if Per Atum is accepted as being the capital city of Heliopolis, and Per Ramesses the other great administrative center—the royal residence at or in the Qantir district" ("Pithom and Raamses: Their Location and Significance," *JNES* 27[1968]: 291–316; 28 [1969]: 15–39). See also the discussion of the arguments for and against Tanis/Zoan and Qantir in J. Van Seters, *The Hyksos: A New Investigation* (New Haven: Yale, 1966), 127–51. Cp. also M. Bietak, "Du nuveau dans l'archaeologie biblique: la ville de Pi-Ramses," *MDB* 41 (1985): 39–44.

[51] The ancient sources (e.g., the Rhind Papyrus, Josephus) do not agree on the length of the Hyksos rule, and early dates in Egyptian history are hard to fix with accuracy, but the usual dates from the beginning of their conquest to their expulsion from Egypt are thought to be roughly 1725–1575 (by the earlier chronology) or 1700–1550 (by the later chronology)—i.e., about 150 years. These dates fit well with the prospect of a post-Hyksos Pharaoh launching a systematic pogrom against the Israelites prior to Moses' birth (ca. 1520 BC).

potential enemies. Today we would call these "royal garrison cities" or "fortified border settlements." They presumably contained not only quarters, provisions, and weaponry for the limited number of troops and their dependents and civilian support population that occupied them during peacetime but also additional facilities to accommodate and equip troops that could be rushed to them in war or the threat thereof. The Israelites were therefore assigned the monumental task of building entire special areas of cities from the ground up, supplying not only the labor but also the materials.[52]

This took individual Hebrews away from their families for long periods of time—men from wives and children, mothers from children. Such separations obviously cut down on the time both to conceive children and also to nurture them. The Egyptian plan would have assumed that in both ways the Israelite population would begin to decrease. Additionally, agriculture would have suffered greatly since one can't easily be a productive farmer and a slave laborer at the same time. Again the presumption of the Egyptian strategy was that many Israelites would now starve for lack of adequate attention to their herds, flocks, and plots. Finally, any slave labor system worthy of the name does not tolerate ill health. People are worked daily, endlessly, regardless of their physical condition, until many of them simply die of one of the many complications of malnourishment and maltreatment and overwork. This again would be a third means of reducing the Israelite population.

Of statistical interest, but of no semantic importance and likewise of no source-critical value, is that this verse is the first point in Exodus at which Moses called the king of Egypt "Pharaoh." He used the term regularly in Genesis, including the immediately prior chapter, Gen 50, and interchanged these terms somewhat randomly hereafter except in the plagues stories, where he used Pharaoh almost exclusively for reasons discussed in the commentary at that point. Sometimes he even combined the two terms (e.g., 14:8, "Pharaoh king of Egypt"). "Pharaoh" derives from an Egyptian circumlocution, lit., "big house," which increasingly over time was used to refer to the king, becoming eventually a title.[53] Simple stylistic variation in vocabulary is the purpose here and elsewhere in the narrative.

---

[52] Those who prefer the late date for the exodus usually propose associating the construction of these two cities with the extensive building programs of the Nineteenth Dynasty in the Nile delta region. The fact that one of the cities is named Rameses, possibly after Ramses II, is usually assumed to support this. On the other hand, the name of the city known eventually as Rameses is identified in the LXX as "On, which is Heliopolis," a place that is more likely the site of Pithom (Pr-Atum) than of Rameses; see the reference to the work of Uphill, above, and S. Horn, "What We Don't Know about Moses and the Exodus," *BAR* 3 (1977): 22–31.

[53] Cf. A. H. Gardiner, *Egyptian Grammar* (Oxford: Griffith Institute, 1969), 75.

1:12–13 The oppression policy backfired. Instead of a reduced Israelite population, the Egyptians saw an Israelite population growth parallel to the intensity of the persecution.[54] This implies that as the early years of the attrition program went by and the population of the Israelites did not decline, the Egyptians stepped up the oppression, assuming that it needed to be more severe in order to work effectively. But the results were the opposite of what common sense expected. Over the generations the greater the oppression, the greater the growth. If one analyzes this result as the Egyptians did, apart from the eyes of faith, one has no real explanation for how it could happen. On the other hand, the reader who knows the God of Israel as savior is not mystified for a moment but cheered and reinforced in his or her faith: obviously, God was turning the Egyptians' oppression policy against them. However, the Israelites were certainly not enjoying it. Cruel oppression is *ipso facto* horrible to endure, and one can hardly imagine any of them saying, in effect, "We don't mind this extreme suffering because, after all, we're growing numerically."

Population growth virtually always results in spatial spread, and the note that "they multiplied and spread" (v. 12) confirms this. It should be remembered that the xenophobic Egyptians were naturally suspicious of the Israelites as outsider practitioners of the mountain farming skills and representatives of foreign, Asiatic culture (Gen 46:34; cf. Gen 43:32). Israelite dress and manners[55] were different from those of the Egyptians, and therefore as the Israelites kept spreading out into areas where they had not previously lived, Egyptian resentment would have increased accordingly. Having bought into the national policy first enunciated by the "new king" in vv. 9–10 and continued since,[56] Egyptians in general could and would come "to dread the Israelites."[57]

What remedy did they have? To work the Israelites even harder (v. 13). If hard work had failed to curtail the Israelite growth so far, harder work should be used to try to stem the tide. "Worked them ruthlessly"[58] is the first of five different expressions in vv. 13–14 to describe how extreme the Israelite workload became.

---

[54] On the translation of כַּאֲשֶׁר . . . כֵּן as "the more . . . the more" see Williams, *Hebrew Syntax* #264.

[55] For a useful summary of the attitudes of Egyptians to foreigners, see A. Dollinger, "Egyptians and Foreigners: The Egyptian View of the World," http://nefertiti.iwebland.com/ people.foreigners.htm and the bibliography provided there. Cf. also Leiden Papyrus 344; D. O'Connor, *Ancient Nubia: Egypt's Rivals in Africa* (Philadelphia: University of Pennsylvania Museum of Archaeology and Anthropology, 1993), passim.

[56] In other words, "the Pharaoh's propaganda campaign worked" (Durham, *Exodus*, 8).

[57] "The Egyptians" is a logically supplied subject in the NIV, as in the LXX, Vg., and Tg.; the MT has just the verb form (= "they came to dread").

[58] וַיַּעֲבִדוּ בְּפָרֶךְ.

1:14 Moses made sure the reader cannot miss Israel's desperate need for deliverance. "Lives bitter," "hard labor," "all kinds of work," "hard labor," and "used them ruthlessly" follow after "worked them ruthlessly" at the end of v. 13 to hammer home the point that the situation was intolerable.[59] The reader is expected to identify with the unfairness of this.[60] For Moses this was not merely historical reporting. He had witnessed it all firsthand, and its severity had eventually become too much even for him, raised an Egyptian, to witness (2:11–12). The severity of the workload was, of course, integral to the population control plan. If people are going to die under a workload, it has to be hard enough to kill people, making weak and sick those who were previously strong and terminating the lives of those who were already weak and/or sick. Someone in the Egyptian leadership possibly also assumed that this sort of oppressive labor might keep husbands and wives away from each other for long periods of time or render them too tired to procreate, but nothing in the text per se suggests that this reasoning was part of the strategy. The workload itself was supposed to be sufficiently hard as to be fatal to enough people to bring the population under control.

This verse contains an important repetition of the Hebrew verbal root *ʿābad*, the significance of which the English reader will simply miss unless it is pointed.[61] This word has a range of meaning in Hebrew much broader than the range of meaning of any word in English available to translate it. In its verb usages it can mean, depending on the context, "work, serve, labor" and also "perform, do, make" and also "worship, live for, be under the control of." In its noun usages it can mean, depending on the context, "work, service, labor," "performance, effort, accomplishment, task" and "worship, obligation, ministry." Later in Exodus, Moses will use the word frequently to refer to Israel's desire to "worship/live for/be under the control of" Yahweh. At this point in the narrative, Israel was involuntarily having to "serve/work for/live for/be under the control of" Pharaoh. What Israel needed was not independence from Pharaoh and Egypt per se but a shift of dependency,

---

[59] Cf. M. Goldberg, "Exodus 1:13–14," *Int* 37 (1983): 389–91.

[60] Fretheim, *Exodus,* 30: "The recalling of oppression is to lead to an identification with those who suffer."

[61] Fretheim (*Exodus,* 30) considers v. 14 a chiasm that is built on the repetition of the root עבד:

So they made the people *serve* with rigor,
  and made their lives bitter with backbreaking *service* in mortar and brick
    and with every kind of *service* in the field;
  with every kind of *service*
they made them *serve* with vigor.

However, this works easily only with the English and not the Hebrew, the latter having more of a vocabulary variation than Fretheim's English translation might suggest. The supposed chiasm would not have been visible to an ancient Hebrew reader. Nevertheless, there is in this verse an unmistakable repetition of this crucial term occurring in all ninety-seven times in the book.

a switching of masters from Pharaoh and the Egyptians to the true and living God. They needed to get out from under an oppressive leader so as to be under a beneficent one, no longer "serving" *[ʿābad]* Pharaoh but "serving" *[ʿābad]* God. The richness of this vocabulary ambiguity and the overtones it creates are a part of the book's stylistic impact on the reader and yet constitute a frequent problem for the translator. Nevertheless, we will do our best to point out the contextual nuances of this central vocabulary term when they occur in ways the reader might not recognize.

Brickwork apparently was the main assignment of most Israelites, in light of its prominence here and in 5:7–19. Nevertheless, wherever Israelites worked, they were treated cruelly by national design[62] so that those engaged in "all kinds of work in the fields" were no less miserable than those directly involved in building Pithom and Rameses.

3. A New Pharaoh's Initiative: Genocide as Population Control (1:15–22)

15The king of Egypt said to the Hebrew midwives, whose names were Shiphrah
and Puah, 16"When you help the Hebrew women in childbirth and observe them
on the delivery stool, if it is a boy, kill him; but if it is a girl, let her live." 17The
midwives, however, feared God and did not do what the king of Egypt had told
them to do; they let the boys live. 18Then the king of Egypt summoned the mid-
wives and asked them, "Why have you done this? Why have you let the boys live?"

19The midwives answered Pharaoh, "Hebrew women are not like Egyptian women; they are vigorous and give birth before the midwives arrive."

20So God was kind to the midwives and the people increased and became even
more numerous. 21And because the midwives feared God, he gave them families
of their own.

22Then Pharaoh gave this order to all his people: "Every boy that is born you must throw into the Nile, but let every girl live."

Now begins the penultimate stage of the forced population control program—directly killing Israelites. It is not quite the ultimate stage because the pharaoh was at this point trying to get Israelites themselves (i.e., midwives) to kill Israelites (i.e., male newborns) subtly, whereas the ultimate state comes with v. 22, where children are killed openly by Egyptians themselves.

However much time has elapsed, it is obvious the Egyptians concluded that mere oppressive labor would not reduce the Israelites' numbers. The propaganda campaign against Israel had long since been accepted into the

[62] The syntax of the last clause in the verse is somewhat unusual in Hebrew. Cf. J. Blau, "Zum angeblichen Gebrauch vom *'et* vor dem Nominativ," *VT* 4 (1954): 7–19, *ad loc*; and P. P. Saydon, "Meanings and Uses of the Particle *'et*," *VT* 14 (1964): 192–210, esp. 201. The sense is rather obvious, and therefore all the modern translations capture the sense in approximately the same way.

general consciousness, and the government had reason to think that the citizenry would tolerate this escalation.[63]

The story of the midwives is a story of heroic resistance. So noteworthy was their courage that their personal names are recorded, in contrast to any of the elders of Israel (3:16,18; 4:29) and even the pharaoh. Thus these two midwives' names, along with the names of Jacob's children and Moses' family, are the only names actually mentioned in the early chapters of the book. But again, the Egyptian plan backfires. This strategy also yielded nothing but more Israelite population growth—even within the families of the midwives, where it would not have been expected.[64]

In part this section of the book is also implicitly about Moses. Like any male Hebrew child, he was endangered by the escalation of population control to actual genocide of male children. His preservation was also a defiance of the pharaoh's orders. But it would be a mistake to take this section as mainly related to Moses' birth[65] because this was still the stage at which Israelites were *not* dying. This stage was still focusing on Israel as a people, not Moses, and the only heroes in sight were the midwives, from the human point of view, and God, who kept growing his people in spite of the best Egyptian attempts to retard their growth.[66]

Some recent scholarship has focused especially on the gender issues raised by the fact that the pharaoh's instructions both to the Hebrew midwives (v. 16) and later to the Egyptians in general (v. 22) allowed females to live but required males to be put to death.[67] This was, however, simply a commonsense approach

---

[63] This progression is all too familiar to anyone cognizant of genocidal oppressions throughout history, including those of modern times.

[64] See comments on v. 21.

[65] As a great many scholars have done, interpreting it especially as part of the background for the story of Moses' call; e.g., Childs, *Exodus,* 4–26; "The Birth of Moses," 109–22; G. von Rad, "Beobachtungen an der Moseerzählung Exodus 1–14," *EvT* 31 (1972): 579–88; F. V. Winnett, *The Mosaic Tradition* (Toronto: University of Toronto Press, 1949); O. Eissfeldt, "Die Komposition von Exodus 1–12. Eine Rettung des Elohisten," *Kleine Schriften*, Vol. 2 (Tübingen: Mohr, 1963), 160–70; cf. J. S. Hommes, "Die Geburtsgeschichte des Mose innerhalb des Erzahlzusammenhangs von Exodus i and ii," *VT* 42 (1992): 398–404; D. W. Wicke, "The Literary Structure of Exodus 1:2–2:10," *JSOT* 24 (1982): 99–107; Willi-Plein, "Ort und literarische Funktion der Geburtsgeschichte des Mose," 110–18; J. D. Macchi, "La Naissance de Moise (Exod 2/1–10)," *ETR* 60 (1994): 397–403.

[66] Cf. 1 Cor 3:6, which though it states the biblical principle of church growth ("God gave the increase" NKJV) could just as well be considered a statement of the principle behind Exod 1.

[67] Cf. J. C. Exum, "'You Shall Let Every Daughter Live': A Study of Exodus 1:8–2:10," *Semeia* 28 (1983): 63–82; "Second Thoughts about Secondary Characters: Women in Exodus 1.8–2.10," in *A Feminist Companion to Exodus and Deuteronomy* (Sheffield: Sheffield Academic Press, 1994): 75–87; J. S. Hommes, *Laat de dochters leven! De literaire architectuur van Exodus 1 en 2 als toegang tot de interpretatie* (Kampen: Kok, 1993); "Hebreeuwse vrouwen brengen 'leven' voort (Exodus 1:19)," *ACEBT* 11 (1992): 23–34; "Twelve Women in Exodus 1 and 2," *ACEBT* 9 (1988): 47–58; B. Weber, "'. . . Jede Tochter aber sollt ihr am Leben Lassen!'—Beobachtungen zu Ex 1, 15–2, 10 und seinem Kontext aus literaturrwissenschaftlicher Perspektive," *BN* 55 (1990): 47–76; R. J. Weems, "The Hebrew Women Are Not Like the Egyptian Women: The Ideology of Race, Gender and Sexual Reproduction in Exodus 1," *Semeia* 59 (1992): 25–34.

in the ancient situation and not driven by gender-focused biases, so the reader should be careful not to reinterpret the story through the eyes of sociopolitical interests that were not issues in the original context.

1:15 This verse is partly introductory, leading to the horrific genocidal command of v. 16, and its significance can thus be easily missed. Its special contribution to this section of the book is its careful naming of the two Hebrew midwives and the implications thereof. Four questions are raised by the verse: Why name the midwives? Are their names symbolic? Were there only two? Would the pharaoh actually deal personally with two women of such relatively low political status?

The NIV treats this verse as a sentence fragment, but in the overall grammatical structure of the passage in Hebrew it is just as likely an independent statement than an introductory clause containing a parenthesis. In other words, the Hebrew construction is not just mentioning the women's names in passing but actually focusing on them. It could even be said that Moses virtually stretched out the wording employed in identification of their names for emphasis. The Hebrew literally says, "The king of Egypt said/spoke/gave instructions for the Hebrew midwives,[68] one who was named Shiphrah, and the other who was named Puah." There are more compact ways in Hebrew to give names. This way, however, is typical of how a narrator might choose carefully to identify prominent characters at the beginning of an account. Moses chose to be sure the reader has a good chance to remember both names.

Why name them so overtly? The answer would appear to be that they were to be regarded as heroes in Israel's early history—so noteworthy for their bravery in choosing to obey God rather than Pharaoh that they deserved to be remembered so that others might follow their example. The honor thus given is all the more evident when one realizes that neither Pharaoh nor his magicians nor the elders of Israel nor any other characters save those in

---

[68] Some commentators, at least as early as the medieval Jewish commentator Rashi, have made much of the fact that although the MT here has the wording מְיַלְּדֹת הָעִבְרִיֹּת, lit., "Hebrew midwives," the LXX has ταῖς μαίαις τῶν Εβραίων, lit., "the midwives of the Hebrews," and have suggested that the LXX wording implies that the midwives were Egyptian women who served as midwives to the Hebrew women. This is unlikely on two counts: first, such interracial midwifery would outrageously contradict the established Egyptian loathing of Hebrews (Gen 43:32; 46:34; Exod 8:26); second, grammatically it would be more natural for the dative to be employed in such a case ("midwives *to* the Hebrews") rather than the genitive as the LXX has it ("midwives *of/from* the Hebrews"). The natural way to read the LXX is simply as equal to the Hebrew, using a genitival construction rather than an adjectival construction. The Rashi argument also depends partly on taking the *piel* participle normally translated nominally as "midwives" and construing it as a causative ("those who did midwifery for") in contradiction to the obvious nominal meaning of the *piel* participle of the same root in Gen 35:17. Cf. J. Cohen, "To the Hebrew Midwives," *Leshonenu* 55 (1991): 195–97 (Hebrew).

Jacob's and Moses' families are named in the first five chapters of Exodus. An instructive parallel is that of Jesus' words in Matt 26:13 and parallels about the Mary who anointed him: "I tell you the truth, wherever this gospel is preached throughout the world, what she has done will also be told, in memory of her." Mary's faith in understanding the need for Jesus to die earned her a special place in the gospel story; the midwives' faith in protecting the Israelites earned them a special place in the exodus story.

Are their names symbolic? The answer is almost surely no. They are typical feminine personal names from the second half of the second millennium BC with no indication of symbolic value in the story. "Shiphrah" means something like "Dawn" or "Fair" and appears on a list of Semitic slaves in Egyptian possession as *sp-ra*.[69] "Puah" means something like "Fragrant" or, perhaps, "Splendid."[70] Both meanings connect in no way with the events described in the context. The women were named because of the power of their example in what they did for Israel in faithfulness to God, not what their names symbolize.[71]

Were there only two Hebrew midwives? The importance of this question relates to its implications for the size of the Israelite nation. If one imagines that a busy midwife could attend perhaps as many as (but not likely more than) ten births a week, that is, about five hundred per year, this would mean that two midwives might attend one thousand births per year (without even considering the problem of physically getting to all the homes; the Israelites had "spread," vv. 7,12).[72] In that era if one-third of the children born actually survived to adulthood, one could imagine an average annually surviving population of about three hundred thirty-four, which, multiplied by seventy-

---

[69] See Albright, "Northwest-Semitic Names," 222–33, and n. 11 above. Albright points out that the name Shiphrah appears in nearly the same form in the Egyptian Slave List (line 21) as it does in Exod 1:15 and that both Shiphrah and Puah are normal Northwest Semitic names of women from the first half of the second millennium BC. "There is no reason to consider them as not authentic in their appearance about the end of the 14th century B.C. in Hebrew tradition" (p. 233).

[70] The sometimes-suggested cognate connection to Ug. *pqt*, "girl," seems speculative in light of the difficulty of associating Ug. *q* with Hb. *ayin;* this can happen, but it is hardly automatic. Moreover, if the Hb. spelling represents an originally Egyptian name (even a name that was borrowed from Egyptian into Northwest Semitic), the connection would be suspect since the Egyptian consonants would have an entirely different meaning.

[71] On the biblical concept of renown as a reminder to do—or avoid—some sort of behavior or as an honor for accomplishment, thus also instructive by example, or as a point of helpful identification not to be ignored, cf. Gen 6:4; 12:2; Deut 32:7; Judg 13:17; 2 Sam 7:9; Prov 22:1; Ezek 26:17; Zech 13:2; Rev 21:12; and esp. Heb 11:1–40. Judg 13:17 is especially illustrative of the concept: "Then Manoah inquired of the angel of the LORD, 'What is your name, so that we may honor you when your word comes true?' "

[72] Our obvious problem in all of this is that we simply do not have data from ancient times allowing us to know with any certainty what sort of schedule midwives kept and how much attention they gave to each of their patients at or around the time of delivery.

five years[73] yields about twenty-five thousand Israelites.[74] Any apparent result of Israelite population calculation in this manner is obviated, however, by the way these two midwives spoke of other, unnamed midwives in v. 19. Shiphrah and Puah were almost surely the senior midwives, functioning as the leaders, or administrators, over an indefinite number of others. There are two reasons for concluding this: first, in a culture that honored age, older women would naturally be viewed as appropriate leaders within their group. Second, v. 21 (q.v.) is worded in such a way as to indicate that it was a special act of God for the two midwives in question to have children. Accordingly, we presume they had been childless into old age, and without typical family responsibility they were suitable candidates for long-term, dedicated, full-time midwifery among the Israelites. It was to these two senior midwives that Pharaoh gave instructions.

But did he speak to them directly? Here the text is somewhat ambiguous but may be read naturally to indicate that he probably did not at first. The verb *ʾāmar* used to describe the king's communication to the two midwives can mean "speak to" but also can simply mean "communicate to" or "give instructions for."[75] It can reasonably be assumed that at first the king passed on the deadly instructions of v. 16 to the midwives via his officials, and only later actually summoned them and spoke directly to them (v. 18) after much time had gone by and there were no apparent results from his latest escalation of the population-control plan. It cannot be ruled out, however, that he spoke to them personally from the start in order to impress upon them the urgency of their assignment or to make them realize that the consequences would be grave if they failed to obey. Perhaps it was a strategy to divert the midwives' loyalty from the women they served to the government and thus to help diminish their effectiveness and keep the population controlled.

1:16 Here we find the announcement of the penultimate stage in the murderous population control plan. Male Israelite children are to be killed at birth and, indeed, by their own midwives. Did the pharaoh think this would be agreed to? Apparently he did, being used to obedience without question and presumably being experienced enough to know that in most circles there is no sort of evil that people will not do if there is adequate personal gain for doing it (cf. 1 Tim 6:10). Moses' narration declines to delineate all the terms of the pharaoh's proposed deal with the midwives, but unless he were a truly

---

[73] It is common for people to confuse full lifespan, which is mainly genetically influenced and was about seventy-five years in ancient Israel according to Ps 90:10, with average lifespan, which may vary enormously depending on mortality rates from disease and other causes.

[74] On the reasonableness of this number see the excursus at 12:37.

[75] For the meaning "communicate to" cf., e.g., Gen 22:3; 43:17; Exod 32:13; for "give instructions" cf., e.g., Gen 3:3; Exod 17:10; Esth 1:17.

incompetent administrator, the king surely proposed both a carrot and stick. The carrot would be the promise of financial reward, and the stick would be the threat of death or the like for noncompliance. No mention is made of who came up with the idea of using midwives to accomplish the infanticide. Perhaps it was the idea of a male official unable to appreciate the sort of dedication to the preservation of infant life usually found among midwives, at least in ancient times; perhaps it was suggested by Egyptian midwives already feeling the discomfort of being judged less productive than their Israelite counterparts.

At any rate, it was certainly true that Israelite midwives were in an ideal position to kill babies. They attended the birth and had time at any of various points of looking after an emerging or just-delivered child to suffocate or strangle him. Perhaps the pharaoh believed this could be done without most mothers even realizing it, assuming as he might arrogantly have done that women in the throes of childbirth would not be sufficiently alert to spot such a felony if it were subtly practiced.[76]

There is nothing about delivery stools (or birth stones or birth stools or the like) in this verse. What the Hebrew says is probably quite simple: "When you help the Hebrew women to give birth, look at the genitals."[77] "If it is a boy, put him to death. If a girl, let her live." There is no evidence that ancient Israelites or Egyptians used any sort of stones for supporting a mother during childbirth.[78] It is hard to imagine that kneeling on stones to

[76] V. 19 helps confirm that the pharaoh expected the males to be killed immediately, right at the appearance of the child from the womb, thus simulating stillbirth, in light of its language about "letting the boys live." Once a child had been alive for a few minutes (i.e., 'let live"), the likelihood of fooling the parents would diminish rapidly.

[77] וראית על האבנים, lit., "look at the stones." Already in 1931 the American Translation of the Bible adopted "genitals" here, but unfortunately only a few others have followed.

[78] The Hb. words here do not mean "delivery stool," nor does the grammar of the sentence encourage the usual translation; the NIV, along with several other versions, is thus quite misleading. An ingenious solution is proposed by S. Morschauer ("Potter's Wheels and Pregnancies: A Note on Exodus 1:16," *JBL* 122 [2003], 731–33), who thinks the "stones" in this verse may reflect a metaphorical use of a putative Egyptian expression "on the potters' wheel" (Egyptian *ḥr nḥp*), referring to "in utero, not yet born," so that the command to the midwives to "look on the stones" means "undertake a prenatal examination." He suggests on the basis of claims made in ancient Egyptian medical texts (as published by H. Grapow in *Kranker, Krankheiten und Artz: Grundriss der Medizin der Alten Ägypter III* [Berlin: Akademie Verlag, 1956, 11–17]) that Egyptian midwives actually could determine the gender of a child before it was born, while still in utero. The obvious problem with this approach is that Egyptian medical texts contain a mixture of spurious diagnostic techniques, formulas for potions supposedly effective in all sorts of illnesses, and other prescriptions for things that are far from scientific, and the mere fact that one or more of such texts claim to advise how to determine the gender of an unborn child hardly means that it could actually be done. In addition, the idioms "on the pottery wheel" (Eg.) and "on the stones" (Hb.) are not provably related.

give birth, the usual explanation of this misunderstood language, would really have been practiced.[79]

Here and in v. 15 Moses used the term "Hebrew" instead of "Israelite" to refer to the midwives. This is consistent with the general pattern in the Old Testament when Israelites are dealing with non-Israelites: people of other cultures tended to lump the Israelites together with other, related ethnic groups and refer to them via the more broadly generic term "Hebrew."[80] On occasion the Israelites called themselves "Hebrews" when dealing with non-Hebrew peoples. Just as someone from Nebraska probably would not say when introducing himself in Uganda, "I'm a Nebraskan" but rather, "I'm an American," so ancient Israelites often politely referred to themselves as "Hebrews," in accordance with the terminology others were best acquainted with. Moses reflected the flavor of this terminological practice here and, as appropriate, elsewhere in the Pentateuch in the context of Israelite–non-Israelite interaction.

But why kill only the boys? Would that not deprive the pharaoh of a workforce? Not if the pharaoh's plan had any level of sophistication to it—and undoubtedly it did in light of all the years he had to think it through. He would surely have reasoned that (1) there had to be a simple criterion for killing children,[81] and the obvious choice was between males and females. (2) Males are those who fight in wars, and the fear of losing in a war was the official public reason for the population control policy, so it could hardly be girls who were killed. (3) If enough boys were killed, women, who were dependent on men in Bible times for survival, would eventually decline in numbers. (4) In agrarian societies people are used to the idea of killing the male animals and keeping alive the females, whereas killing females is simply not a normal practice.[82] (5) If the policy were successful and the Israelite numbers were reduced sufficiently, it could simply be suspended at any

[79] Cf. H. A. Brongers and A. S. van der Woude, "Wat Is De Bekentnis van *'Abanayim* in Exodus 1:16?" *NedTT* 20 (1965–66): 241–54. The LXX has καὶ ὦσιν πρὸς τῷ τίκτειν, "when they are about to give birth." This is followed by the NAB, even though it is merely a contextual guess on the part of the LXX translator. Pictures of supposed Egyptian "birthstones" are published in A. Erman, *Die Religion der Ägypter* (Berlin: 1934), 55, but these are not stones and their actual identity and use is debated. Common sense must prevail here. The gender of a baby is established very simply—by looking at its genitals, which is what the command to the midwives specified since their assignment from Pharaoh was to differentiate the fate of girls from that of boys.

[80] Cf. J. Lewy, "Origin and Signification of the Biblical Term 'Hebrew,'" *HUCA* 28 (1957): 1–13; J. Bottero, *Le probleme des Habiru a la 4e recontre assyriologique internationale,* Cahiers de la Société Asiatique XII (Paris: Imprimerie Nationale, 1954).

[81] A criterion such as "kill all the healthy ones" or "kill all the bigger ones" would have been subject to such loose interpretation as to be bound to fail.

[82] This is a theme reflected in various literary contexts in the ancient world; cf. Weber, "'. . . Jede Tochter aber sollt ihr am Leben Lassen!'—Beobachtungen zu Ex 1, 15–2,10 un seinem Kontext aus literaturwissenschaftlicher Perspektive," 47–76.

time. Males would not die off suddenly. Since all males already above infancy age were to be allowed to live and grow up to adult slavery, this was obviously a long-term policy of population control. Its impact would be primarily psychological at first, and only as years went by and boys who would have lived did not reach fighting age would it begin to have real effect on the internal security situation—that is, about twenty years later.[83] It could, of course, be modified to any extent and at any point as its outcomes became measurable and were judged to have succeeded or not.

1:17 Here the great heroism of the midwives is lauded. They sided with God over against the pharaoh and flatly refused to carry out their foul assignment. They did not kill any boys.

"Feared God" does not imply "believed in the true God, the God of Israel." It also does not carry the connotation of the New Testament language in which "feared God" had come to mean "was a Gentile convert to Judaism." In the Pentateuch "fear God" tends to mean "to be honest, faithful, trustworthy, upright, and, above all, religious."[84] The midwives may not have had great knowledge of the traditions of the Patriarchs (limited in their ethical content as those traditions necessarily were at any rate) and like all their contemporary Israelites certainly did not yet have what we would call "scriptural" knowledge, but they did understand that right and wrong are not human inventions but part of a divinely created order. This is the perspective of many proverbs from all over the ancient world, not merely those of the Old Testament, which reflect the idea that the fear of God is the most important orienting truth available in the world. To fear God does not mean being afraid of him in general but being afraid of the consequences of disobeying him. Since death was the presumed consequence of disobeying the pharaoh, this verse is one of many in the Bible that implicitly witnesses to a belief in life after death and a final judgment. These women clearly feared what God could do to them after death more than the death the pharaoh could put them to.

At this point the reader knows that the midwives are in trouble. They must answer to the king of Egypt. Can there be any hope for them—that is, apart from God's protection?

1:18 Several, perhaps many, years may have elapsed between the king's decree to the midwives (v. 16) and his angry summoning of the disobedient midwives as described here. How could such a long time elapse? Why wouldn't it have taken just a few months for news to reach the king that newborn baby boys were appearing as frequently as ever among the Israelite

---

[83] Based on the consistent OT pattern of military service beginning at age twenty, it is not likely that teenagers were normally involved in military service at any period in Israel's history. Cf. Exod 38:26; Lev 27 (passim); Num 1 (passim); 14:29; 26 (passim); 32:11

[84] See Gen 22:12; 42:18; Exod 18:21; cf. Job 1:1,8; 2:3; Eccl 8:13; 12:13; Luke 18:2,4.

families? The answer is that in ancient Israelite society, as in most societies prior to modern times and machine-made clothing, little boys and girls were often dressed alike and had similar hair lengths, so they could easily be confused. The pharaoh's command envisioned a secretive killing of infants done by midwives at birth, and therefore he could hardly order Egyptian soldiers openly to go into Israelite tents and houses to forcibly examine the gender of young children in order to see if the program were working. That would make public what he had sought to keep private. Thus it must be assumed that only years later, as older children's groups seemed obviously to have as many boys as girls among them, the midwives were summoned to appear before the pharaoh to give account of why they had not carried out his loathsome mandate.

The king's question was surely not dispassionate. His clearly stated will had been defied, and he wanted an answer as to why he had not been obeyed, presumably as a prelude to executing the midwives. The two questions presumably are representative excerpts of the king's words to the midwives, effectively providing a summary of what the king more fully said.

1:19 The midwives had years to prepare their answer, since they certainly knew from the start of their defiance of the pharaoh's command that he might eventually demand an explanation (the other option being that he would simply kill them without even giving them a chance to explain).

A theological issue is raised by the midwives' answer: Was it a lie that God then rewarded (v. 20)?[85] In other words, were they telling the truth to claim that the Egyptian women were slow to deliver children and the Israelite women fast, to the extent that one group actually bore babies before the midwives could get to them while the other group, like all other known groups, experienced a normally long labor for many hours before delivery? Or is there some other meaning to the midwives' reply? To some extent the answer hinges on the meaning of the hapax legomenon *ḥayôt,* translated in the NIV as "vigorous" and by others as "robust" (i.e., both essentially translations that suggest the difference was physiological) but perhaps best translated as "more active" or "more involved" (i.e., suggesting that the difference was sociological). The most probable concept behind the meaning of *ḥayôt*, derived as it is from the verbal root *ḥyh* ("to live") would be that of a greater level of activity in connection with childbirth. In other words, the midwives' reply may well testify not to any genetic difference

[85] A frequent approach of more skeptical commentators is to conclude that this is essentially a folk story portraying the midwives as having tricked a slow-witted, evil Pharaoh by a clever lie that he would have difficulty checking up on and that negatively describes the Egyptians in such a way as to delight the later Israelite audience (so, with various nuances, Childs, Durham, Fretheim). We suggest that a more convincing approach is to see this as a serious historical narrative of a deadly situation in and through which God worked for his glory, as he always does.

between Egyptians and Israelites that shortened the delivery time for Israelite babies but to a cultural difference in the way Israelite women chose to have their babies as opposed to how Egyptian women did. The first part of their answer, "Hebrew women are not like Egyptian women," could be true in several ways that are not necessarily specified. It is a conjecture, to be sure, but a reasonable one that the actual difference between the two groups was a matter of family style rather than of physiology. It is possible that at the time of the exodus, Egyptian women—at least of the classes that Pharaoh would be familiar with and that the midwives were referring to in 1:19—took a minimal role in delivering their own children. They may well have mainly lain back with their eyes closed during and perhaps immediately after childbirth and let midwives do all the rest. If this were so,[86] it would certainly fit with the pharaoh's original expectation that a midwife could easily kill a baby at the point of emergence from the womb without a mother's realizing it since the mother's role was usually so passive.[87]

By contrast, it may well have been the practice in Israel for women to play an active role in the delivery of their own children. The role assigned to midwives may have been minimal at any event, and if there were any sort of nationwide collusion designed to limit that role further, it would all the more heighten the contrast between the "more active/involved" Israelite women and the presumably much less active Egyptian women relative to self-involvement in childbirth.[88]

The final part of the verse, "they . . . give birth before the midwives arrive," could thus be perfectly true, perhaps in part because of a purposely

[86] The uncertainty stems from the fact that we simply do not have any literary data from the ancient world to tell us whether or not this conjecture, however reasonable, is really accurate.

[87] As Durham points out, the midwives' characterization of the Egyptian women may even be somewhat pejorative, i.e., suggesting to the pharaoh that the Egyptians were lazier and/or less fit than they should be, such a thinly disguised criticism thereby enhancing the brave defiance of the midwives (*Exodus,* 12). But the text can also be well understood to suggest that the midwives were polite and respectful and gave an answer that so confounded the pharaoh (as God worked on his mind, of course) that he found himself unable to justify putting them to death.

[88] In light of its parallels to the Egyptian-Israelite contrast, the twentieth century in most of the Western world saw a huge change from women's passive role in childbirth to a much more active involvement, all based on cultural judgment, not on physiology. As recently as 1950 the common practice in American hospitals was for women to be kept sedated during and after delivery, for them to be allowed out of bed only briefly beginning on the second day, and to go home from the hospital with full access to their babies only after five to seven days. Babies often were denied access to their mothers for several hours after birth, being fed sugar water instead of breast milk on the basis of theories of newborn metabolism now known to be harmful but at the time thought to be scientific. Sick babies were actually kept from their mothers, who usually were not allowed to be with them in the hospital at all. By contrast modern "natural "childbirth emphasizes the mother's own role at all points and sometimes involves a physician in the picture only after the baby has been born (if at all).

slow arrival of the midwives as part of a quiet, widespread plot among Israelites to fool the Egyptians. Indeed, one can imagine the midwives, as part of this strategy, regularly informing Israelite women to do "everything possible to give birth before we are summoned to your home. We'll take it from there. But whatever you do, don't call for us before the baby actually comes."

1:20–21 These verses complete the story of the midwives; and, more importantly for the overall story, they contain once again the report that nothing could stop the divinely ordained growth of the people of Israel. In the particular way it translates v. 20, the NIV gives the impression of a causal connection between God's kindness to the midwives and the people's growth, but this is unintended. It might better be rendered: "So God was kind to the midwives; moreover, the people increased."[89] Verse 21 actually specifies how God was kind to, that is, rewarded, the midwives: implicitly he protected them from the pharaoh's potential wrath by allowing their explanation about not killing the Hebrew boys to prevail; explicitly, he allowed them to conceive and bear children ("gave them families of their own"[90]).

Did Israelite midwives normally not have children? Apparently they did not. The evidence from the ancient world is sketchy, but these verses are worded in such a way as to suggest strongly that most midwives were women who had not been blessed with children of their own, thus enabling them to spend the required long hours out of the house both day and night that would otherwise have been difficult for women with children.

An implicit moral imperative to "fear God" is in these verses, especially in light of the resumption of the Hebrew expression *yārēʾ ʾĕlōhîm* ("fear God") from v. 17. But what does it mean to fear God? We have already suggested that fearing God is "to be honest, faithful, trustworthy, upright, and, above all, religious."[91] In short, "fearing God" is commonly in Scripture a virtual abbreviation for "believing in God, and therefore fearing the consequence of not pleasing him, thus being a person of moral conviction and righteous actions"[92]—although in Hebrew it is surely not per se an abbreviation but an idiom. A variety

[89] The SP, some versions of the Syr., and *Tg. J.* assume the ambiguous Hb. consonants to represent the *hiphil,* thus, "So God was kind to the midwives and increased the people and they became even more numerous." In the absence of the direct object marker, however, the Hb. syntax is more naturally read with the MT's pointed *qal* verb form and translated as the NIV has it.

[90] The LXX and *Tg. J.* read the plural of the verb here (יעשׂו), which would yield the sense "they [the midwives] got families" [lit., "they made families for themselves"], but this reading is no more likely than that of the MT. On the concept and wording, cf. S. M. Paul, "'To Found a Family'—A Biblical and Akkadian Idiom," *Maarav* 8 (1992): 139–42.

[91] See comments at 1:17.

[92] See G. A. Lee, "Fear," *ISBE* 2:289–92; J. Becker, *Gottesfurcht im Alten Testament*, AnBib 25 (Rome: Pontifical Biblical Institute, 1965); H. A. Brongers, "La Crainte du Segneur," *OTS* 5 (1948): 151–73. Cf. also T. Römer, "Les sages-femmes du Pharaoh," *ETR* 69 (1994): 265–70.

of Hebrew vocabulary words are translated by English "fear," but the expression *yārēʾ ʾĕlōhîm* ("fear God") as used here is the most common. Moses employed it six times in the Pentateuch, in each instance with the meaning indicated above.[93] Inasmuch as the "fear of the LORD is the beginning of wisdom,"[94] the midwives' fear of God was what helped them avoid acting out of self-interest; instead, they bravely in defied the unquestioned leader of the greatest nation of their day, risking everything to do what was right instead of what was easy.[95]

1:22 At this point the pogrom plan reached its final stage. There was no more subterfuge, no limitation on involvement: all Egyptians were expected to join in killing all Israelite newborn boys.[96] The process of persecution that had begun modestly and had escalated in steps had reached its zenith, a full-blown, open, national policy of large-scale genocide against a particular ethnic group.

Why throw the boys into the Nile? Why not just kill them with knives or rocks or by dashing them on the ground[97] or the like? There are two good reasons why an Egyptian pharaoh would have suggested this approach. First, it was a convenient and "clean" sort of way to kill infants. It was convenient in that virtually the entire population of Egypt lived essentially on the banks of the Nile, the arable land in ancient Egypt being limited mainly to that area that was served by the Nile directly or via irrigation canals drawing from it. Accordingly, the Nile served not only as the nation's source of water and therefore wealth but like many great rivers, as its nation's sewer, its relentless current taking away anything that was not wanted. Throwing a baby into the Nile was a lot easier and quicker, involving no cleanup and leaving no evidence, than almost any other means of killing. The child would simply fall into the water and disappear—out of sight and hopefully, from the Egyptian point of view, out of mind. Second, it shifted some of the blame because of the way the pantheistic Egyptians viewed the Nile as a god.[98] If the Nile

---

[93] Gen 22:12; 42:18; Exod 1:17,21; 18:21; Deut 25:18. Especially helpful is Gen 20:11, where Abraham is afraid to be in Gerar because "there is no fear of God in this place," i.e., the place is lawless, immoral, unrighteous.

[94] Prov 1:7; 9:10, wisdom being ability to make the right choices in life.

[95] Looking at the overall structure of Exod 1, G. dell'Orto regards vv. 1–7 as setting up a kind of creation blessing of the nation of Israel, vv. 8–14 as setting up a kind of curse via the opposition of the pharaoh, and the blessing of the midwives in v. 21 as a sort of reversal of the curse, at least in microcosm ("Soggiorno e schiavitù degli Ebrei in Egitto," *PaVi* 42 [1997]: 10–15). That Moses might have organized the material of Exod 1 in a conscious parallel to the organization of the first few chapters of Genesis is not at all impossible, though dell'Orto fails to show that the structure of Exod 1 is obviously intended to be recognized by readers as a creation blessing-curse-curse reversal motif.

[96] See comments on v. 16 for the discussion of why boys rather than girls.

[97] Cf. 2 Kgs 8:12; Isa 13:16; Nah 3:10; Ps 137:9.

[98] On Egyptian pantheistic religion that made the Nile a god, see the excellent descriptions by H. Frankfort in *Ancient Egyptian Religion* (New York: Harper & Row, 1961) and / or H. Frankfort and H. A. Frankfort, J. Wilson, T. Jacobsen, *Before Philosophy: The Intellectual Adventure of Ancient Man* (Baltimore: Penguin, 1967), originally published with the title *The Intellectual Adventure of Ancient Man* (Chicago: University of Chicago Press, 1946). See also W. LaSor, "Nile," *ISBE* 3:536–37.

were to "receive" the infant, it would at least to some degree represent the god Nile's judgment rather than that of the individual who carried out the pharaoh's order. The Nile was viewed both as a giver and taker of life. If the Nile were to take a baby's life, that was the Nile's decision, was it not? While the narrative is appropriately terse at this point, it is easy to imagine that the pharaoh's messengers, in bringing his command to the people, were instructed to inform them that by throwing babies into the Nile they were doing the will of the gods and giving the Nile its proper due among the gods.

A proleptic irony follows from this approach to killing the Israelite baby boys. Later God would kill large numbers of grown-up boys, that is, Egyptian soldiers, by drowning them in the Red Sea (e.g., Exod 15:4: "Pharaoh's chariots and his army he has hurled into the sea./The best of Pharaoh's officers are drowned in the Red Sea"; Heb 11:29: "By faith the people passed through the Red Sea as on dry land; but when the Egyptians tried to do so, they were drowned").

4. Moses' Birth and God's Provision (2:1–10)

1Now a man of the house of Levi married a Levite woman, 2and she became
pregnant and gave birth to a son. When she saw that he was a fine child, she hid
him for three months. 3But when she could hide him no longer, she got a papyrus
basket for him and coated it with tar and pitch. Then she placed the child in it
and put it among the reeds along the bank of the Nile. 4His sister stood at a dis-
tance to see what would happen to him.

5Then Pharaoh's daughter went down to the Nile to bathe, and her attendants
were walking along the river bank. She saw the basket among the reeds and sent
her slave girl to get it. 6She opened it and saw the baby. He was crying, and she
felt sorry for him. "This is one of the Hebrew babies," she said.

7Then his sister asked Pharaoh's daughter, "Shall I go and get one of the
Hebrew women to nurse the baby for you?"

8"Yes, go," she answered. And the girl went and got the baby's mother.
9Pharaoh's daughter said to her, "Take this baby and nurse him for me, and I will
pay you." So the woman took the baby and nursed him. 10When the child grew
older, she took him to Pharaoh's daughter and he became her son. She named
him Moses, saying, "I drew him out of the water."

Names provide the inclusio that sets this section off as a unit. Verse 1 names the house (tribe) of Levi as the genealogical locus for the story, and v. 10 ends with the naming of Moses and an explanation of his name's meaning. On one hand, the story concerns a baby born a humble Israelite but, surprisingly, adopted as a royal Egyptian. On the other hand, it forms part of a cheering story of God's careful provision of a deliverer for his people. Of course, at this preliminary point in the book the reader has not yet learned formally that Moses will function in the role of deliverer of God's people. But that is of little consequence since the earliest readers were already familiar with Moses, who wrote this story only after he had become Israel's divinely-designated leader. The story of his birth is thus both a prelude to his call and, in part, an indication of his call.[99]

Although this portion of the overall narrative features Moses, it is also the story of how God used three women to save a baby from death. It features two mothers and two daughters, with the daughter of Pharaoh in two roles, initially that of daughter and eventually also of adoptive mother. Moses' biological mother[100] also figures prominently in these events as the one who not only did everything she could to preserve the life of her child, but also as the woman who ended up being able to nurse and thus substantially rear (see vv. 7–10) her own little boy. The final major figure is this woman's daughter, that is, Moses' sister, who will be identified later as Miriam, one of the leaders of the exodus.[101] Miriam's oversight of Moses as he floated among the rushes of the Nile and her quick thinking in proposing an Israelite nurse for the baby (knowing full well she would "recruit" his own mother) helped preserve Moses for her family and for Israel's salvation.[102] The motives of all these women appear to have been pure and appropriate. God used them to do what they were good at and what their culture especially honored in women: preserving and raising a child. Their faithfulness to that noble role parallels in no small degree the faithfulness of the Israelite midwives to theirs as described in the prior chapter. In each instance children were preserved from the death the pharaoh had decreed by women who defied his repugnant command. Pharaoh's daughter could do so by reason of her privileged status; Moses' mother and sister, by reason of their wit and fortitude and—though it is only implicit at this point in the narrative—their faith.

2:1 This verse might seem at first glance to provide only incidental and minor information to the reader, but it does more. It demonstrates that Moses was a chosen child from the only proper tribe for his future calling, fully in compliance with the law that God had not yet revealed to Israel but would reveal within Moses' lifetime. In other words, the verse assures the

---

[99] Cf. P. E. Hughes, "Moses' Birth Story: A Biblical Matrix for Prophetic Messianism," in *Eschatology, Messianism and the Dead Sea Scrolls* (Grand Rapids: Eerdmans, 1997), 10–22. Moses was careful not to make himself the main figure in Exodus—God is by all means the focus, not him. But he also showed the way in the early chapters of the book that he was used by God, even from the very beginning of his life, in a manner that would link his own fate and that of Israel. See L. Boadt, "Divine Wonders Never Cease: The Birth of Moses in God's Plan of Exodus," in *Preaching Biblical Texts* (Grand Rapids: Eerdmans, 1995), 46–61.

[100] Later identified as Jochebed in Exod 6:20 and Num 26:59.

[101] Miriam is first named in Exod 15:20–21 as the leader of the Israelite women singing the battle victory song recorded in that chapter; she is identified as a leader of Israel in Mic 6:4 ("I sent Moses to lead you, also Aaron and Miriam").

[102] Cf. P. Trible, "Bringing Miriam out of the Shadows," *BibRev* 5 (1989): 14–25, 34.

reader that Moses was prequalified for the service God later gave him, even in advance of the revelation that would make that qualification necessary.

The verse pointedly tells the reader that Moses was fully a Levite, that is, from Levite stock on both his father's and his mother's side. This means that he was unquestionably of the tribe that would soon be specially designated by God to provide the religious and spiritual leadership for the people of Israel (Exod 32:26–29; Num 3:12; 8:6–26; Deut 10:8–9)—the tribe that showed itself readily loyal to Yahweh (e.g., Exod 32:26), the tribe that would supply the priests to bridge the holiness gap between God and Israel (Exod 28–30) and the tribe selected to provide most of Israel's regular court judges (Deut 21:5). That the Levites were destined during Moses' lifetime to become the "clergy" tribe for all Israel was well known even to the first readers of the book of Exodus, since the writing of the book postdated the appointment of the Levites to their sacred tasks.

The Scriptures describe other prequalifications of persons called to play a role in the divine plan of redemption. Abraham's prequalification involved his family's willingness to settle in Canaan, which then led to the revelation of his position as the father of many nations (Gen 11:31; 12:1). Aaron, Moses' brother, had to be a Levite and witness of God's theophany if he were to be a priest and the leader and progenitor of all subsequent priests (Exod 4:14; 19:24; 28:1). Samson was set aside from birth as a Nazirite to become a deliverer of his people from the Philistines (Judg 13:2–25). Samuel's prequalification came in the form of a divine call of endearment[103] early in life (1 Sam 3:2–21). David' s early anointing (1 Sam 16:13) and precocious military skills (1 Sam 17) established his prequalification. Paul's descendancy from Jews on both sides of his family gave his mission to the Gentiles the credibility of his impeccable Hebrew lineage. And, of course, Jesus was prequalified in every conceivable way, from his eternality (John 1:1) to his descendancy from David (Matt 1; Luke 3:23–38) to his Nazarene citizenship (Matt 2:23).

2:2 No special significance attaches to the expression "she became pregnant and gave birth to." It is standard hendiadys in Hebrew narrative for describing a baby coming into a family.[104] Special significance should, however, be noted in the pattern of its usage: this is the sixteenth and final time that Moses used the expression in the Pentateuch. He had used it fifteen times throughout Genesis to describe important births.[105] The sixteenth usage describes his own. Thereafter the expression ceases in his writings,[106]

---

[103] On the phenomenon of endearment as signalled in speech, see on 3:4.

[104] The idiom "became pregnant and gave birth to" (ילד + הרה) occurs over thirty times in the OT.

[105] From 4:1 (the birth of Cain to Adam and Eve) to 38:4 (the birth of the first two sons to Judah and Shua).

[106] In only two other places in the Pentateuch are the הרה "become pregnant") and ילד ("give birth") found. Exod 21:22 is a law about injuring a pregnant woman; Num 11:12, a hortatory context metaphorically comparing God's creation of his people to his conceiving and birthing them. Neither is historical narrative, as all the others are, and neither employs the pattern so standard in all the others.

suggesting that he understood himself to be the final figure in a long line of persons through whom God had been preserving and preparing the formation of the nation—not merely the family—of Israel. In other words, once the reader reaches the story of the birth of Moses here, he or she has come to the last required special mention of a birth story in the Pentateuch.

The women's role in rescuing Moses[107] continues with the actions of his mother, later identified as Jochebed.[108] This should not be understood to mean that Moses' father, Amram,[109] was not in agreement or was deceived. As Heb 11:23 makes clear, "By faith Moses' parents hid[110] him for three months after he was born, because they saw he was no ordinary child, and they were not afraid of the king's edict."[111] It is simply the case in the Exodus description that the mother's primary role is emphasized. Amram would have been expected to work as a slave, away from home those daily long hours; Jochebed was the one who had to carry out the risky and innovative preservation plan.[112]

The NIV translation "she saw that he was a fine child" can be improved upon. The Hebrew idiom used here, *rāʾāh + [noun or pronoun] + kî ṭôb,* actually means "to care about," "to be fond of," or "to want [to have or to keep]."[113] The verse is better translated: "She became pregnant and gave

[107] Here see also the careful analysis by C. Exum, "'You shall let every daughter live': A Study of Exodus 1:8–2:10," *Semeia* 28 (1983): 63–82.

[108] Exod 6:20; Num 26:59.

[109] Ibid.

[110] The Hb. for "hid" (צפן) actually has the fuller sense of "hid for safekeeping" and usually is applied to situations of hiding something of great value, i.e., "treasuring away." Thus it might be possible to translate here "she hid him like a treasure" or even "she kept her little treasure secret."

[111] The NIV of Heb 11:23 is somewhat misleadingly translated in its middle clause ("because they saw that he was no ordinary child") because it is a simple calque of the Hebrew, thus lit. "because they saw their child to be special" [to them]. Also important for appreciating the present context in Exodus is the ending of Heb 11:23 ("were not afraid"), which does not imply that Moses' parents didn't take Pharaoh's edict seriously, only that it didn't scare them into doing the wrong thing, i.e., letting their child be killed. The risk, in other words, was apparent in their plan.

[112] There is no evidence that women were forced to perform slave labor during the Israelite oppression as the men were. But even if this were the expectation, the fact that Israelite women were allowed to carry and bear female children under either of the pharaoh's edicts (1:16; 1:22) meant that they may have been exempted from their slave labor during at least the latter stages of pregnancy and the first months of child rearing. It is, however, hard to imagine that any ancient society would actually have tried to deny women the right to bear and raise children at home, and thus de facto women with families were surely exempted at some times and to some degree from forced labor programs.

[113] Elsewhere in the Pentateuch this Hb. idiom occurs in Gen 1:4,10,12,18,21,25 describing God's love for the world he had made; in Gen 3:18 describing Eve's attraction to the forbidden fruit of the garden; in Gen 6:2 describing how the "sons of God" were attracted to the "daughters of men"; in Gen 40:16 to describe Pharaoh's baker's being drawn to Joseph's interpretation of his dream; and in Jacob's blessing in Gen 49:15 to describe being attracted to a resting place. An analogy in English would be, "This one looks good to me," meaning "I am attracted to it," or "I like it," or I want it." Cp. W. F. Albright's discussion of the idiom in *Mélanges bibliques rédigés en l'honneur de André Robert,* Travaux de l'Institut catholique de Paris, 4 (Paris: Bloud et Gay, 1956), 22–32; and the analysis of T. J. Meek, "New Bible Translation," *JBL* 82 (1963): 265–71, esp. 268.

birth to a son. Longing to have/keep him, she hid him—for three months." This is not to suggest that Jochebed cared about her son more than other Israelite women did for theirs, or that many other women were not doing the same thing—hiding their newborns as long as possible—but only that Moses here credits his mother with doing what any responsible, caring mother would have done, loving her baby and trying to keep it alive.

"For three months" may be a somewhat rounded or approximate figure, indicating the period of time when a newborn could be expected to sleep extensively. He would be small enough to be hidden easily in the home, would not move around much, and usually could be kept from crying by nursing or rocking. Thereafter, it would become harder to hide a baby from prying eyes and ears, so the actions of v. 3 represent the logical next step taken by Jochebed.

2:3 The term used here for what Moses' mother[114] put him in is *tēbāh,* found elsewhere in the Bible only in the flood story in Genesis 6–8, where it is translated "ark."[115] Moses apparently was consciously drawing the reader's attention to the fact that God, through Moses' mother's actions, was graciously protecting him from death by a small ark, just as God had protected Noah and the animals by a great ark in the days of the great flood. Indeed, it is hard to imagine that Moses was not keenly aware of the obvious comparison between himself and Noah. They both were deliverers/rescuers who were called by God to lead people and animals through and out of danger into a new location where those people and animals would become dominant in establishing a new stage of God's unfolding plan of redemption of the world.

This ark was made of papyrus (as perhaps were many items of furniture in Egypt since virtually all of the population lived close to the Nile, where papyrus grew abundantly; wood was very costly, available mainly by importation by sea). It may have been a piece of storage furniture that Moses' parents already owned or that they bought for this new, special purpose. Jochebed's special contribution was sealing it with tar (bitumen/asphalt, abundant in many places in Egypt) and pitch (a term used for various sorts of tar mixtures and tarry substances, possibly plant sap, though less likely actual tree sap in light of the pau-

---

[114] Since both the LXX and SP read the equivalent of "his mother" rather than simply "she" here (i.e., "his mother got a papyrus basket for him and coated it"), a haplography of אמו ("his mother") likely occurred at an early stage in the text's transmission—a loss that fortunately has little effect on meaning or readability.

[115] Here the NIV translators not only inadvertently missed the significance of the Hb. word *tēbāh* ("ark") and its connection to Gen 6–8 but by choosing "basket" to render it unintentionally gave the possible impression that it might be some sort of open, flimsy container since most baskets are open topped and light in construction. In fact, it was almost surely a covered papyrus box (possibly modified for the baby with air holes and/or insect netting), giving protection from insects and the sun much better than a typical basket would. Because v. 6 describes the need to "open" the ark, it had a secured lid. From the flood story in Gen 6–8 it is evident that the special characteristic of a *tēbāh* was its provision of protection—thus the term "chest" in some of the lexicons and translations, but certainly not "basket."

city of larger trees in Egypt). Nothing in the text suggests that this was an especially brilliant or especially desperate method of attempting to hide a baby—only that Moses' mother was doing her best to protect him. This involved concealment in perhaps the best place to hide something outdoors in Egypt and not actually bury it, but still be able to watch it and care for it—the reeds along the Nile. Here Jochebed would be able to retrieve her baby to nurse him[116] and give him love when no Egyptian police/soldiers were around. But here she also could quickly place him where, should he cry, his cries would be muffled by the enclosure of the ark, the thickness of the reeds, the general outdoor noises, the nearby sound of the Nile waters [he would not have been out in the current itself, of course], and at such a distance from where police/soldiers would normally be likely to walk that they likely could not hear him.

The general parallel between Moses' "exposure" in his ark and that of Sargon in the Legend of Sargon of Akkad[117]—in which Sargon is put into a river in a container made of reeds sealed with pitch, rescued by a water-drawer, cared for and raised, and eventually becomes a legendary hero and then king—may or may not have any relation to these events. If Jochebed knew that legend, it might have encouraged her to try the technique once again. On the other hand, she is much more likely to have known the Genesis flood story in some form[118] with its own parallels of rescue on water in a pitch-sealed container.[119]

---

[116] Under no conditions in ancient times would a three-month-old baby yet be able to survive without nursing. See M. I. Gruber, "Breast-feeding Practices in Biblical Israel and in Old Babylonian Mesopotamia," *JANES* 19 (1989): 61–83.

[117] *ANET*, 119.

[118] The Israelites in Egypt did not necessarily have a fully accurate "biblical faith" after so many centuries of exposure to the pagan influences of Egypt, and among the reasons Moses wrote Genesis was presumably to help the exodus generation gain some sense of their ethnic and spiritual history: the sort of thing each generation has to learn afresh in any culture.

[119] In particular B. Childs' form-critical analysis, concluding that Exod 2:1–10 is a wisdom-style reworking of the exposed child motif known from many stories in the ANE follows this line of reasoning ("The Birth of Moses," 109–22; see also D. B. Redford, "The Literary Motif of the Exposed Child," *Numen* 14 [1967]: 209–28). The problems with this approach include the fact that it programmatically subordinates history to genre. Also in the ancient world, for various reasons, many children had precarious infancies, and many were threatened with death or left to die, so the motif likely would be common in the literature of the cultures. Today a parallel might be the many stories in books, movies, and television programs involving adopted children, none of which can properly be adduced to call into question the historical fact that large numbers of children are in reality adopted, some from desperate circumstances into loving, nurturing environments. As is usually the case, social realities give birth to literary motifs, not the other way around. What happened to Moses (being "exposed" to save his life) was the sort of thing that has happened, regrettably, often in history. In current days many states in the US even have laws expressly allowing for the exposing of a child (laws that provide for no legal penalty if an unwanted child is dropped off at a hospital, police station, or other such legally recognized location). Thus Durham (*Exodus,* 13) is right in saying: "As intriguing as these parallels certainly are, however, too strict a dependence upon them as *Vorlagen* must be avoided. . . . For one thing, there is not even a suggestion here of the divine rescuer so essential in the exposure-of-the-infant-hero motif. For another, the exposure of Moses by a *Hebrew* woman, and by his own mother at that, would turn a positive story, in this context, into negative nonsense."

It need not be assumed that the baby Moses would have been in his ark virtually around the clock. Egyptian sweeps for babies in Israelite settlements were presumably occasional rather than constant, lest the whole Egyptian local force be occupied with little else. Such sweeps were almost surely conducted by day, since at night in ancient times torches and larger (search) lamps were not easily brought into houses (Pharaoh had not, after all, ordered Israelite houses burned down, either purposely or accidentally). The Israelites also may have developed warning systems that gave at least a few minutes' notice to mothers. The ark had always to be ready, so especially during periods of the day when Egyptians were around, Moses would be secreted there.

2:4 This short verse provides several useful bits of information. First, unless this sister is one who is otherwise unknown and unmentioned in the narrative, it introduces Miriam (whose name will be provided first at 15:20) as an important person in Moses' life.[120] Second, it shows that the family was together involved in protecting Moses, as would be expected. Third, it suggests that Miriam was older even than Aaron (who was already three years old at this time; cf. Exod 7:7), but not so old that she would be expected to be working as the young women did at home and field tasks. In other words, she was old enough for the responsibility of watching her little brother in his ark and to have the ability to do so without drawing attention to his presence, but not old enough that her lingering for long periods of time along the Nile would raise questions about an older girl doing no work. Thus she was perhaps between six and twelve years old. Her presence of mind and capable conversation with the daughter of Pharaoh in vv. 7–8 suggest she may have been closer to the upper limit of this age range. She was not merely watching to see what happened but was on guard so as to know anything that would happen and be able to act accordingly.[121]

2:5–6 There was surely no attempt to place Moses in his little ark at a location where he was likely to be discovered. The whole intent was just the opposite. Yet he was discovered—and by an Egyptian! In the story's surprising twist, however, the discovery by an Egyptian, under other conditions likely to lead to the boy's death, leads instead to a perfect protection of his life. This is God at work, providing deliverance in an unanticipated yet wonderful way.

Pharaoh's daughter is described as going "down" to the Nile simply because that was always necessary, all housing being built on higher ground as protection against the Nile's overflowing its banks annually. We have no

---

[120] Cf. R. Le Déault, "Miryam, soeur de Moise et Marie, Mere du Messie," *Bib* 45 (1964): 198–219.

[121] The Hb. should be translated not merely "to see what would happen to him" (NIV), which could imply an expectation of something going wrong or a change in the situation, but more contextually and idiomatically it should be "to be aware of it if anything happened to him."

way of knowing how many daughters this pharaoh had, but there may have been dozens,[122] and the popular idea that Moses was one of just a few favored grandchildren of the pharaoh lacks the merit of realism. Nevertheless, to be found and then cared for by one so highly placed could result at least in protection from the pogrom against the Hebrews and guarantee at least a fine opportunity for survival. That the princess would choose to bathe in the Nile as opposed to a bathtub reflects the esteem of the pantheistic Egyptians for the sacredness of that river, an issue only hinted at here but of great importance to the later aspects of the story (chaps. 4; 7).

The attendants were on guard, thus not bathing; the princess alone was in the water and able to spot the little ark from her angle. Again the better translation is "ark" rather than "basket"; almost any ancient Israelite would catch the significance of the use of *tēbāh* here, regardless of whether the story was read or heard. Sending a servant girl to retrieve it merely reflects the fact that the ark would have been placed where it could be reached from the shore, and the princess did not choose to wade through several feet of reed to get it herself when it could be easily pulled from the water by one of those already on shore. The fact that the boy was crying when the princess opened the lid may be a clue to how she noticed the ark in the first place; she may have heard the crying and then looked for its source. At any rate, here was not a woman inclined toward her father's cold-blooded population control program. She simply felt concern for a little boy who was crying. One imagines, in fact, Moses' adoptive mother telling him the story of his rescue many times—and how precious he seemed to her the first moment she set eyes on him.[123] Her recognition that Moses was a Hebrew boy (*yeled,* which the NIV unfortunately neuters both times in this verse to "baby"[124]) probably was predicated on four things at least: the general physical differences between Hebrews and Egyptians, the type of baby clothes used, the fact that her discovery occurred in an Israelite settlement area, and the general situation (the need to hide Israelite baby boys but not Egyptian baby boys).

2:7–8 Moses must have heard this part of the story many times, and not merely from his adoptive mother but from Jochebed and, indeed, from

[122] Treaty intermarriage was a common practice in the ANE. Kings forming alliances would each give the other a daughter as a wife so that each king would be the other king's son-in-law and father-in-law, thus providing the added surety of a family relationship to the political alliance. This practice was the primary reason Solomon, e.g., had so many wives. Cf. also J. Feather, "The Princess Who Rescued Moses: Who Was She?" *ExpTim* (1931–1932): 423–25.

[123] The princess's reaction is entirely realistic. The author's family includes four adopted children. Any adoptive parent can testify to the almost instantaneous love that wells up inside us upon seeing a child who needs care, when we know that we are in a position to give it.

[124] The Hb. reminds the reader that this was not just a child but a *boy*—the gender of baby that was supposed to be killed. Cf. D. Barthélemy et al., *Preliminary and Interim Report on the Hebrew Old Testament Text Project: The Pentateuch* (London: United Bible Societies, 1974), 89–90.

Miriam herself. Miriam controlled the action: she apparently didn't run when the Egyptian women arrived but remained at her post and affected curiosity when the baby was found. She must have gotten close enough to the action to overhear the princess's various expressions of concern for the boy (e.g., "He's crying!" "He must be hungry!" "I can't leave him like this!"), and Miriam wisely volunteered a wet nurse she knew well (her own mother). The turning point of the story is contained in a one-word command, that of the princess: "Go"![125] With that decision of the king's daughter, Moses' protection was assured. It goes without saying that Miriam knew Egyptian well enough to converse with the princess; most Hebrews probably knew Egyptian relatively well, in light of their long history in the country, notwithstanding their partial geographical confinement.[126]

It may have been difficult for Jochebed to process what she first heard from Miriam, breathlessly arriving at the home to summon her. Egyptians—the enemy—had found the baby she had so carefully hidden! But Miriam was obviously able to convince her mother that there was no harm—at least not yet—in following through with the offer to become her baby's nurse. After all, that immediately legitimized her caring openly for her own child and eliminated the need to hide him any longer. So the determined mother met the daughter of the source of her worst fears, God having turned the circumstances toward hope and salvation.

2:9–10 In this concluding portion of the passage, God's special provision for Moses cannot be missed. The baby boy once in grave peril received royal protection, his own mother raised him in his early years, she was actually paid to care for him, and the princess formally adopted him as evidenced by her giving him an Egyptian name. The rejoicing in Amram and Jochebed's home would be tempered only by the realization that eventually their son would be transferred to another home; but he was alive, and now he had every chance to survive into adulthood. On the other hand, we can only speculate on the level of risk involved for Pharaoh's daughter, but there must have been so little that it did not occur to her to worry about the fact that she was technically violating her father's order relative to Hebrew boys. Without consulting anyone else, she made the decision to keep the baby she found and concluded the negotiation for a wet nurse before leaving the Nile to return to her home.

The nursing contract described in v. 9 presumably took a standard form in which the wet nurse was compensated for caring for a child but the legal

---

[125] What the NIV justifiably in the context renders as "Yes, go" is a single word in the Hb., לְכִי.

[126] It is also possible that the princess knew enough Hebrew/Canaanite to converse with Miriam rather than the other way around, and there is also a third option: that a translator existed among the princess's retinue because she was located at the time, for whatever reason, in Hebrew country.

possession remained with the one making the payment.[127] Because in ancient times children were nursed for three or four years before being weaned,[128] the princess realized that she would have actual physical custody of the boy only later. It presumably would not have been thinkable that a Hebrew wet nurse would reside in the royal housing as a full-time caregiver; and most wet nurses would have families to care for at any rate. So the princess does not say "Come with me" but "Take this boy away" (the literal meaning of the Hb. *hiphil* of *hālak*).

Though giving up her little boy when the time came to turn him over to the princess must have been heartwrenching for Jochebed, we should not assume that Moses never had contact thereafter with his family. The descriptions of his later reuniting with his brother Aaron as described in chap. 4 assume that they knew each other all along, and the importance of Miriam's role in the exodus leadership suggests that she and Moses were hardly strangers. The emphasis of v. 10 rests on the adoption, with requisite Egyptian name. "Moses" follows the typical pattern of ancient naming in which a name (usually an existing, known name) was not selected prior to birth, as in modern Western practice, but only after birth and suggested by some sort of circumstance or speech experienced or heard at the time of birth[129]—in this case at the time of the child's discovery. So a relatively common Egyptian name, meaning "son" or "to beget a son,"[130] is chosen as appropriate because it sounds something like *mōšēh,* the active participle of the verb *māšāh,* "draw out," which connects to the circumstances of Moses' discovery and being "drawn out" of the water. Through this name, the princess both consciously honors the Hebrew origins of her son and also makes him legitimately Egyptian with a name in her own language that emphasizes that she is adopting a son.

5. Moses' Own Exile/Exodus: Midian and Marriage (2:11–22)

[11]One day, after Moses had grown up, he went out to where his own people were and watched them at their hard labor. He saw an Egyptian beating a Hebrew, one of his own people. [12]Glancing this way and that and seeing no one, he killed the Egyptian and hid him in the sand. [13]The next day he went out and

---

[127] Childs reviews the evidence for ancient wet nursing contracts in "The Birth of Moses," 109–22.

[128] Cf. Gruber, "Breast-feeding Practices in Ancient Israel," 61–83; Stuart, *Hosea-Jonah,* 32; some of the key evidence comes from *2 Macc* 7:27 and 1 Sam 1:23, as well as from the Egyptian "Instructions of Ani" (*ANET,* 420).

[129] See Stuart, "Names, Proper," 3.483–88.

[130] As in the names Ahmose and Thutmose; cf. J. G. Griffiths, "The Egyptian Derivation of the Name Moses," *JNES* 12 (1953): 225–31.

saw two Hebrews fighting. He asked the one in the wrong, "Why are you hitting your fellow Hebrew?"

[14]The man said, "Who made you ruler and judge over us? Are you thinking of killing me as you killed the Egyptian?" Then Moses was afraid and thought, "What I did must have become known."

[15]When Pharaoh heard of this, he tried to kill Moses, but Moses fled from
Pharaoh and went to live in Midian, where he sat down by a well. [16]Now a priest
of Midian had seven daughters, and they came to draw water and fill the troughs
to water their father's flock. [17] Some shepherds came along and drove them
away, but Moses got up and came to their rescue and watered their flock.

[18]When the girls returned to Reuel their father, he asked them, "Why have you returned so early today?"

[19]They answered, "An Egyptian rescued us from the shepherds. He even drew water for us and watered the flock."

[20]"And where is he?" he asked his daughters. "Why did you leave him? Invite him to have something to eat."

[21]Moses agreed to stay with the man, who gave his daughter Zipporah to
Moses in marriage. [22]Zipporah gave birth to a son, and Moses named him Ger-
shom, saying, "I have become an alien in a foreign land."

This portion of the narrative takes the story of Moses from his own childhood to that of his (first) child, from living as a foreigner in an urban Egyptian royal household to living as a foreigner in a rural Midianite priestly household, and from the privilege of a princeling of the greatest nation of his world to the obscurity of criminal exile in the Sinai wilderness. It also brings the reader to the point of preparation for the exodus, with its concluding declaration by Moses of being "an alien in a foreign land" (v. 22).

2:11–12 The narrative now jumps ahead[131] approximately thirty-six years,[132] skipping completely over Moses' later childhood, adolescence, and early adulthood. This sort of leap from infancy/childhood to later adulthood is not only efficient for purposes of getting to the heart of the story but apparently was preferred often in ancient times, when the story of an important person's birth might be recounted if it had special significance but his "biography" in effect began with the first truly prominent actions he undertook. The New Testament Gospels illustrate both options: Mark and John describe Jesus first at age thirty; Matthew and Luke tell about his birth and

[131] What the NIV renders as "one day" is lit. "and it was in those days," a standard Hb. idiomatic means of indicating the passage of an indefinite period of time. A translation such as "Years later" might better convey the sense of the original.

[132] This assumes Moses was about four years old when fully weaned, forty when he killed the Egyptian and fled to Midian (cf. Acts 7:23–30), and eighty when he began the encounters with Pharaoh that led to the exodus (Exod 7:7). *Jub* 47:1 and 48:1 both assert that Moses was forty-two when he fled to Midian, though the reason for the additional two years remains unexplained.

then jump to his life at age thirty—though Luke adds as well a brief story about him at age twelve, an exception to the usual approach.

These two verses explain how Moses had by this time identified with the Israelites over against the Egyptians and how his zeal against the oppression of his people got him into trouble.[133] This was his first attempt at delivering his people—acting alone and in secret and relying on his own strength and wisdom—and though it failed miserably, it certainly shows the strength of Moses' sentiments on behalf of his people. Twice in v. 11 the phrase *ʾeḥāyw,* "his own people" (lit., "his brothers"), serves to orient the reader to the fact that Moses saw himself by this point as an Israelite, not an Egyptian. It is possible that the wording of v. 11 intends us to understand that Moses had heard increasingly of the severity of Israelite servitude[134] and finally decided to monitor it for himself, thus for the first time being in a position to become fully enraged at how his "brothers" were being treated. It is equally possible that he had often witnessed his own people at their slave labor but that this time the extent of the cruelty was greater, and a long-smoldering fire of resentment was kindled into a white-hot rage that led him to murder.

Verse 12 does not necessarily suggest that the beating Moses observed was done in an isolated location. These statements are brief summaries, and although the beating was widely witnessed, perhaps Moses waited until the Egyptian who had given the beating was alone (i.e., perhaps he followed him) and killed him then. There appears to be thus some degree of premeditation in Moses' act, as indicated in the statement that "he looked this way and that" (NIV "glancing" gives the incorrect impression that Moses did the whole thing on the spur of the moment). Hiding the man in the sand would be a rather natural thing to do since burying a body is the fastest, best way to conceal it in a part of the world characterized by little foliage, a largely flat terrain, and plenty of sand.

Of all the possible events in Moses' life that Stephen might have chosen to include in his apologetic speech for Christ, he included in considerable detail the story of Moses' slaying the Egyptian (Acts 7:23–29). The special theme of Stephen's speech functions as an indictment of the Jews to whom he was speaking for thinking they were following Moses when in fact they

[133] Biblical narratives are honest about the failures and weaknesses of their characters, in contrast to most ANE literature, in which the heroes of stories—especially national heroes—are commonly portrayed in an unrealistically good light. So blunt is the criticism that Moses brought on himself as he wrote about his murdering the Egyptian that some critical scholars have even identified 2:11–15 as representative of an Israelite tradition hostile to Moses (cf. T. Butler, "An Anti-Moses Tradition," *JSOT* 12 [1979]: 9–15). Cf. also B. Childs, "Moses' Slaying in the Theology of the Two Testaments," in *Biblical Theology in Crisis* (Philadelphia: Westminster, 1970), 164–83.

[134] The Hb. term employed here for "[their] hard labor" (סִבְלֹת) is the same as that used already in 1:11, where the "slave masters" are also mentioned. It is therefore well within reason to conclude that it probably was a slave master that Moses killed.

were missing the implications of his teaching—indeed, stubbornly so. In other words, Stephen apparently recounted these events from Moses' pre-Midianite days not because they are more important than others but because they are the beginning of the story of the adult Moses. In effect, Stephen was saying: "Do you really understand who Moses was and what he was teaching? Let me remind you of some parts of the story in detail as a way of reminding you that the whole of what Moses did and taught points in one way or another to the importance of Jesus Christ, which you are missing."[135]

Hebrews 11:24 provides another perspective on these verses that might easily be missed in a rapid read through of the Old Testament story:

> By faith Moses, when he had grown up, refused to be known as the son of Pharaoh's daughter. He chose to be mistreated along with the people of God rather than to enjoy the pleasures of sin for a short time.

Moses might easily have so enjoyed the perquisites of power and wealth that were his as an Egyptian princeling that he would have proudly identified himself throughout his life as an Egyptian. Instead, in spite of his outward appearance as established by his dress and hairstyle (which was clearly Egyptian; cf. 2:19), he eschewed all the privileges of Egyptian rank and sided with an oppressed people. He thus guaranteed himself mistreatment along with them. Nevertheless, he recognized that the Egyptian stance was sinful and that the right life was to be found with the lowly Hebrews, who in spite of their poverty and affliction were God's people and chosen for great purposes

2:13–14 These two verses provide the reason why Moses had to flee Egypt and in the process give further emphasis to the fact that he had identified with the hardship of the Hebrews as over against the superior status of the Egyptians, even though it cost him dearly (cf. Heb 11:24–26).[136] Here is

---

[135] For a different though very thoughtfully presented angle on this, see Childs, "Moses' Slaying in the Theology of the Two Testaments," 164–83; and *Exodus,* 33–46. As Childs points out, most commentators throughout history have tended to see Moses' murder of the oppressing Egyptian as a relatively noble deed, though Childs himself seems more inclined to see it in a less positive light. We would suggest that the best way to interpret the act biblically is that it was indeed a rash act of violence, even if altruistically motivated, and therefore not excusable ethically in itself. But the God who understands all thoughts and actions in the universe used it, without approving it, as a means to extricate Moses from Egypt and to make sure he would never again identify with the Egyptians and their gods but only with the chosen people and their God. At the same time, God was making sure Moses would learn that however well intentioned his motives were, he could not expect acceptance or success to come automatically but could expect misunderstanding and opposition even from his own people. To state this principally: When a believer is willing to be sorry for and to learn from his sins, there is no telling what good God may bring thereafter, transforming the consequences of what was ill-conceived and wrongly done into that which will honor God and bless his people, but this process does not guarantee freedom from subsequent trial and tribulation.

[136] Moses' upbringing contributed to this attitude: he was the only Israelite who "needed nothing." He had no vested interest in getting something for himself by throwing off Egyptian power, and, free from ambition for personal gain, he could be used by Yahweh to take the risks necessary to promote the just cause of the Israelites. See E. Neufeld, "Why Moses?" *JBQ* 20 (1991–1992): 271–73.

God at work in a way that Moses surely did not recognize at the time, just as we can virtually never understand how our own miseries and emergencies, at the time we are experiencing them, might end up leading to blessing. Moses had gotten himself in terrible trouble and was afraid, and at least one of his fellow Hebrews was voicing what many others felt: in spite of their own plight,[137] they did not welcome Moses' newfound conversion from Egyptian to Hebrew identity. In hindsight Moses could admit to weakness: not only the weakness of being afraid, but also the weakness of being rejected by the man who said, "Who made you ruler and judge[138] over us?"—clearly an expression of resentment against this johnny-come-lately styling himself as a defender of the Hebrews.[139] It is not difficult to imagine why Moses was disliked or why the news about his murderous act had spread so far so fast:[140] an Egyptian overseer was missing, an investigation probably was underway or soon would be, and there was every likelihood that the Hebrews would be blamed and severely punished for the overseer's murder. Such a situation would become the talk of the community and would easily surface someone's admission, "I saw who did it!" What Moses had tried to do had, from his people's point of view, backfired. He had taken matters into his own hands, and his arrogance in doing so probably was going to get a lot of people in trouble.

From Moses' point of view, he had tried to act in secret to help one of his people, and he thought he had succeeded. Now that in the process of his further intervention to try to help another of his people he had learned that his deed of the day before was known, the whole course he had set himself on was suddenly leading in the wrong direction. In both cases Moses had acted out of altruism.[141] The Hebrew who in this instance spoke back to him, however, in effect anticipated the later attitude of the leaders of the

---

[137] The act that the one Hebrew was doing to the other was serious, and the NIV translation, "Why are you hitting?" might be rendered a bit more precisely, "[Why are you] attacking [or beating]" (*hiphil* of נכה).

[138] Two separate terms are used in the Hb.: אִישׁ שַׂר and שֹׁפֵט עָלֵינוּ, which mean respectively "official/man in charge" and "judge/leader over us." The use of two discrete terms emphasizes the sarcasm, in a manner similar to what would be intended if someone said in English, "Who do you think you are—the chief of police? the judge?"

[139] Hb. לָרָשָׁע, lit., "the guilty one," probably is a normal legal term, our equivalent of "the guilty party." The NIV translation "the one in the wrong" captures the sense fairly well, although not reflecting the juridical overtone.

[140] The LXX, Acts 7:28, and *Jub* 47:12 all have one form or another of ἐχθὲς, "yesterday," after the equivalent of "Are you thinking of killing me as you killed the Egyptian?" suggesting the strong possibility of a haplography of an original Hb. אֶתְמוֹל ["yesterday"], so that Moses was hearing just a day later that the news had spread generally already.

[141] A. Zivotofsky argues that this narrative about Moses' willingness to oppose injustice and to demonstrate compassion gives some insight into why God called him (as opposed to anyone else he might have called) to lead the Israelites out of Egypt and to oversee God's people for a generation ("The Leadership Qualities of Moses," *Judaism* 43 [1994]: 258–69). Cf. J. M. Cohen, "The Call of Moses," *JBQ* 20 (1991–1992): 256–61.

Hebrews, who would repeatedly look at what Moses was trying to do as damaging to their interests, in spite of the fact that Moses would intend it as deliverance (5:19–21; Exod 17:3; Num 14:2; Deut 1:27). This is in the nature of leadership: the best attempts to help are sometimes faulty in themselves, yet even when proper and magnanimous, they can provoke the resentment of those who fail to appreciate how they are being led. As would often be the case with Jesus, Moses was here not recognized/accepted readily by his own people. He eagerly wanted to help them; they were suspicious that he represented trouble.

2:15 Moses was in danger of death at various times by various persons. The earlier story of his rescue as a baby reflects a general attempt to kill Israelite male children, Moses included. Now he is sought for murder by a presumably enraged Pharaoh, since testimony during the investigation of the crime must have pointed directly to Moses, and the king could hardly have been unmoved by the implications of a turncoat Hebrew-raised-as-an-Egyptian now killing Egyptian work supervisors! Later, Moses would be threatened with death from his own people (e.g., Exod 17:4), and his firstborn son, threatened by God himself (see comments on 4:24–26).

But it is all part of a great plan. Moses was now clearly separated from his Egyptian ties and could not even remain in the country. Where, then, could he go that would be relatively safe from Egyptian influence, relatively hospitable to an Israelite (speaking a related language and sharing some customs), and relatively easy to get to from northeast Egypt, where his flight originated? Even in the short time Moses probably had to gather his things and flee, the answer must have seemed obvious to him: Midian. The Midianites were descended from Abraham through his wife Keturah (Gen 25:2) and occupied sparsely (i.e., to the extent that such regions can support population) portions of the central and northern Sinai peninsula in addition to their main location, northwestern Arabia, so that Midianites could be encountered in that day from the Arabian gulf in the south to the plains of Moab in the north.[142] Though the Midianites in most of their history were enemies of the Israelites (as were most other Semitic groups as well), a single Israelite on the run from Egypt, a country that had often tried to dominate the Midianites, would not necessarily represent a threat but perhaps even something of a kindred spirit. Moreover, the relatively independent and isolated Midianites were just the sort of people to seek refuge among for a fugitive like Moses.[143]

The final clause, "where he sat down by a well,"[144] brings the story to a specific location, where the fugitive, looking for some place to settle, will

[142] Thus most of what was biblical Midian was included in what we call northwestern Saudi Arabia today, even though the Midianites did not have what would today be considered fixed boundaries to their "nation."

[143] Cf. G. W. Coats, "Moses in Midian," *JBL* 92 (1973): 3–10.

[144] Hb. הַבְּאֵר, lit., "the well," a typical instance of proleptic definition; perhaps best translated "a certain well."

have yet another opportunity to intervene in a dispute on behalf of the oppressed and in so doing will also begin to meet those with whom he will live and work for the next forty years. In the largely barren Sinai wilderness, a well was a necessity for human and domesticated animal life, a meeting place, a community center; roads led to it, and travelers sought it out. For Moses, "a certain well" would be the beginning point of a new life.

2:16–19 The account of the encounter at the well in Midian in vv. 16–19 tells several things about Moses' character: his flight from Egypt had not blunted his instinct for intervening against injustice and righting wrongs; he was quick to act against oppression, even alone, isolated, and with the odds against him; he was sufficiently imposing and/or assertive to intimidate several shepherds; he was physically vigorous enough to chase off a group of shepherds and then do work that seven girls were planning to do;[145] he was not easily cowed himself; he was generous and helpful to people he hardly knew, acting from principle rather than merely from personal loyalty; and he did not ask for a personal reward for what he had done. All of these characteristics are seen again in various ways as Moses responded to God's call to deliver the Israelites from Egypt. In other words, the Moses we see here is basically the same Moses we have already seen as an adult in Egypt and whom we will see again throughout the Pentateuch—a figure whom God continued to prepare for a great and daunting task yet for whom such a task, however potentially dispiriting, would not be something inimical to his basic nature.

These verses tell us a bit more about Moses as well. He was, though surely not yet romantically, attracted to the daughters of Reuel,[146] the priest of Midian.

[145] Some commentators have inferred that the shepherds drove the girls away after they had drawn the water (e.g., Childs, *Exodus*, 31), but the most direct reading of the text suggests that the shepherds arrived after the girls, simply refused to wait their turn, and attempted to take advantage of their strength as opposed to that of the girls to take over access to the well. Moses then drew the water that the girls had been planning to draw.

[146] The sisters' father, eventually Moses' father-in-law, is usually called Jethro (3:1; 4:18; 18:1), but he also appears to bear the name (depending on the way the text is translated) of Reuel here and also Hobab (Judg 4:11). From Num 10:29 Hobab is sometimes thought to be identified as Zipporah's grandfather. W. F. Albright solved the confusion in his article, "Jethro, Hobab and Reuel in Early Hebrew Tradition," *CBQ* 25 (1963): 1–11, essentially as follows: Jethro was the man's usual name, with the variant Jether (Exod 4:18); Reuel was his clan name (what we might call his "last" name today); whereas Hobab was Moses' son-in-law. The vowels of "son-in-law" and "father-in-law" are choices of Masoretic pointing for the consonants חתן, which both words share. Thus the confusion about Hobab is simply the result of a misunderstanding by the medieval Masorete who first pointed Num 10:29 as "father-in-law" rather than the proper "son-in-law." Cf. G. F. Moore, *Judges*, ICC (Edinburgh: T&T Clark, 1895), 32–33; M. Greenberg, *Understanding Exodus* (New York: Behrman, 1969), 47. A number of critical scholars, however, regard the name differentiation as evidence of different sources. Cf. M. Noth, *A History of Pentateuchal Traditions* (Chico, Cal.: Scholars Press, 1981), 183–84; R. F. Johnson, "Jethro," *IDB* 2:896; G. Widengren, "What Do We Know about Moses?" in *Proclamation and Presence* (Macon: Mercer University Press), 28–30. Yet another approach is taken by J. D. Hays ("Moses: The Private Man Behind the Public Leader," *BR* 16 [2000]: 16–26, 60–63), who suggests that Reuel was Zipporah's father-in-law and Jethro her brother and thus Moses' brother-in-law (with the word חתן meaning generally "in-law"). None of the three names (Reuel, Jethro, Hobab) has any special symbolic meaning for the narrative.

Something about their looks and/or demeanor awakened his interest and concern. Perhaps, in light of his extensive education already in Egypt, he was well aware of the family connection between Midian and Israel and thus was warmly predisposed toward a group of Midianite women. He obviously knew that he was in Midianite territory and might already have been looking for a place to settle down. Additionally, it should not be surprising in light of his eventual betrothal and marriage to one of Jethro's daughters that he should be inspired to include in the narrative the details of how he met his wife. He was also recognizably dressed and presumably tonsured like an Egyptian; otherwise the girls would not have described him so readily as "an Egyptian."[147] Although these Midianite women may not have spoken any Egyptian, it would not have surprised them that an Egyptian might speak a recognizable form of Semitic. The Egyptians, whose Hamitic tongue was not cognate to Hebrew or Midianite, had over the centuries sent armies, occupation forces, diplomatic representatives, and traders into Midianite regions, and thus the women would know what an Egyptian looked like and would not have been surprised that one would know their language. In addition to this, the opportunity was once again presenting itself for Moses to benefit from the intervention of women on his behalf, as the following verses indicate. He had rescued them; they in turn provided hospitality for him, eventually a living arrangement and marriage, and later one of them would save his son's life put in danger by his own neglect (4:24–26).

2:20–22 These three verses provide a fast summary that takes the reader through Jethro's invitation to dinner, Moses' settling down as part of Jethro's household, Moses' marriage to Zipporah, and the birth and naming of their first child. Thus Moses had become a permanent resident (emphasized by the last statement in v. 22) among the Midianites and an exile both from the land, Egypt, and the people of his birth, Israel.

Jethro's three questions represent a sufficiently extensive emphasis in this otherwise short account that he must have felt that his daughters had forgotten their manners in their excitement at having been paid such favorable attention by a prominent stranger. Jethro is shown here in a typically favorable light,[148] as a

---

[147] Egyptian art depictions of foreigners indicate different dress and hair styles for various ethnic groups, and it would have been important for people in ancient times to know the differences since there were so many enmities between the various groups. Cf. J. Osing, "Les populations asiatiques," *MDB* 41 (1985): 22–24.

[148] One must not rush to paint Jethro in too favorable a religious light—such as has commonly been done by advocates of the "Kenite Hypothesis," the theory that Moses must have picked up his ideas about Yahweh from Jethro and his Midianite/Kenite culture, then shaped them as he applied his understanding of Yahwism to the situation he eventually confronted in Egypt. By this theory, Jethro's influence as a priest (i.e., of Yahweh) and as Moses' benefactor and father-in-law would have provided the opportunity for Moses' indoctrination into Yahwism. The whole theory is highly speculative, looking at OT religion as a thing of human origin, not as a body of truth and practice revealed to humans. Cf. R. de Vaux, "Sur l'origine kenite ou madianite du Yahvisme," *Eretz-Israel* 9; W. F. Albright Volume (Jerusalem: Israel Exploration Society, 1969), 28–32; G. W. Coats, "Moses in Midian," *JBL* 92 (1973): 3–10; H. J. Gunneweg, "Mose in Midian," *ZTK* 61 (1964): 1–9; J. C. S. Hommes, "Moses-'vreemdeling' in Midjan," *ACEBT* 10 (1989): 16–20.

gracious and diplomatic individual who found in Moses someone he could appreciate. When in chap. 18 Jethro's conversion is described (no small matter in light of his being a priest of another religion), his delight at Moses' role in his life is also obvious. The fact that Zipporah's name occurs twice is also no accident, inasmuch as the reader is now introduced to the woman who will have a prominent role in God's plans for Moses. It is not entirely incidental that this prominent attention is paid to Moses' marrying a non-Israelite; contrary to popular impression, the composition of the Israelites was simply not genetically/ethnically monolithic but rather a matter of faith as opposed to flesh.[149]

The naming of Gershom in v. 22 represents another instance of homophonous naming of a child (cf. 2:10), the name in this case suggested by its being similar in sound to the explanation Moses provided: *gēr* ("alien") and *šōm* (close in sound to *šām*, "there"[150]) combining to suggest the approximate meaning "an alien there." The name itself probably was preexisting[151] and thus not a new name but one carefully chosen in light of Moses' circumstances. These circumstances are not entirely positive. From Moses' point of view, he was now permanently separated both from what he regarded as his homeland, Egypt, and also from the people he now identified with as his own, Israel. Consider, then, the spiritual challenge that was his. He was a failure as a deliverer of his people, a failure as a citizen of Egypt, unwelcome among either of the nations he might have called his own, a wanted man, a now-permanent resident of an obscure place, alone and far from his origins, and among people of a different religion (however much or little Midianite religion may have shared some features with whatever unwritten Israelite religion existed at this time). His character, as we have seen, was clearly that of a deliverer. His circumstances, however, offered no support for any calling appropriate to that character. It would surely require an amazing supernatural action of a sovereign God for this washed-up exile to play any role in Israel's future. Moses knew this, and his

[149] This is emphasized in 12:38 and developed in its theological implications in such great passages as Rom 2:28–29.

[150] The Hb. short *o* and long *a* were indicated by the same vowel marker *(qamets)* by the time of the medieval Masoretes, a phenomenon that may reflect the closeness of long *a* and *o* in earlier times; the so-called Canaanite vowel shift also presumably was occasioned in part by the virtual allophonic closeness of *a* and *o* in northwest Semitic pronunciation during OT times.

[151] The name Gershom is, however, actually attested only later, in Judg 18:30; 1 Chr 6:1; and Ezra 8:2, and may derive from גרשׁ ("drive out/expel"). As pointed out earlier in connection with Moses' own name, Hebrew names often were not strictly etymological but were chosen because existing names were suggested by circumstances or words that attended or surrounded the birth. See Stuart, "Names, Proper," 3.483–88; cf. R. Nogah, "The Explanation of the Names 'Gershom' and 'Eliezer,'" *BMik* 35 (1989–1990): 257–60 [Hebrew]. For a somewhat different approach, cf. also J. Fichter, *VT* 6 (1956): 372; B. O. Long, *The Problem of Etiological Narrative in the Old Testament*, *BZAW* 108 (Berlin: Töpelmann, 1968), 4ff.

statement, "I have become an alien in a foreign land," resignedly confirms it.[152]

6. Summative Reminder: Severity of the Oppression and God's Concern (2:23–25)

[23]During that long period, the king of Egypt died. The Israelites groaned in their slavery and cried out, and their cry for help because of their slavery went up to God. [24]God heard their groaning and he remembered his covenant with Abraham, with Isaac and with Jacob. [25]So God looked on the Israelites and was concerned about them.

2:23–25 Now that Moses' situation has been summarized, these verses conclude the entire large section of introduction to the exodus story (1:1–2:25) by returning the reader's attention to Egypt, where God's people are trapped in crushing slavery and where he will on their behalf unleash his mighty deliverance. This little "postscript" prepares us to expect that God will now take action. Five important assertions are made, each bearing implications for the events that follow.

First, the pharaoh who sought Moses' life had died. This would make possible Moses' return to deal with the Egyptian leadership no longer as a criminal fugitive (cf. this assurance in 4:19) but as a prophet of the true God.

Second, the change in government produced no relief for the Israelites, whose painful slavery continued unabated. Their misery is emphasized noticeably by four terms, two of them verbs ("groaned," "cried out")[153] and two nouns ("cry," "groaning"),[154] constituting four different vocabulary words in the Hebrew, even though represented in the NIV by what would seem to be only two terms ("groan," "cry"). The double use of the expression "because of their slavery"[155] reinforces this, with the intention that the reader must not miss the severity of Israel's miserable situation.

Third, the people of Israel began to pray. That is the point made by the language in v. 23 ("cried out . . . their cry . . . went up to God")[156] and v. 24

---

[152] On the significance of the name Gershom as a kind of marker in the narrative of Moses' past and future countries, see J. C. Siebert-Hommes, "Mozes—vreemdeling in Midjan," *Amsterdamse Cahiers voor Exegese van de Bijbel en zijn Tradities* 10 (1989): 16–20.

[153] As they appear in the text, וַיֵּאָנְחוּ ("they groaned") and וַיִּזְעָקוּ ("they cried out") respectively.

[154] As inflected in the text, שַׁוְעָתָם ("their cry") and נַאֲקָתָם ("their groaning") respectively.

[155] Twice in this verse the same expression, מִן־הָעֲבֹדָה ("because of their slavery"), is used to emphasize the burden of forced work. This emphasis through repetition is lost in the NIV by the needlessly confusing variation between the translation "in their slavery" ("groaned because of their slavery") and "because of their slavery" ("their cry for help because of their slavery went up to God").

[156] On this idiom, which occurs in a variety of related wordings, cf., e.g., 1 Sam 5:12 ("the cry of the city went up to heaven"); Jonah 1:2 (lit., "their trouble has come up to me"); Jer 16:2.

("God heard their groaning"). This description of their prayer is central. However little they may have known about the true God at this stage in their emerging corporate theological education, they were during this time earnestly praying to him for help; and God, faithful both to his nature and to his past promises, heard them. Later, in Deut 26:7, Moses summarized: "Then we cried out to the LORD, the God of our fathers, and the LORD heard our voice and saw our misery, toil and oppression." The exodus did not come about simply because people were in trouble; it was the result of a prayer of lament for rescue to the only one who could actually do something about it. As Jesus taught, the one who knows all needs before they are prayed for nevertheless expects them to be prayed for (Matt 6:5–8,32).

Fourth, God "remembered his covenant." The word *bĕrîṯ* ("covenant") occurs twenty-five times in Genesis; this is its first occurrence in Exodus. The covenant in question is usually referred to as the "Abrahamic covenant" because it was made initially to Abraham and then simply renewed, without change in essentials, to both Isaac and Jacob. Here the statement "remembered his covenant with Abraham, with Isaac and with Jacob" is worded in such a way as to emphasize that renewal to each subsequent generation (likewise the wordings, though slightly varied, in Lev 26:42 and 2 Kgs 13:23). In fact, after Genesis the Abrahamic covenant is never again referred to by simply including the name of Abraham but always in some manner that brings in as well the other patriarchs (1 Chr 16:16; Ps 105:9; Acts 3:25; 7:8) so as to remind the reader that it is an ongoing covenant fully applicable to the generations that followed Abraham. In covenantal language the term "remember" *(zākar)* should not be misunderstood to suggest that God was somehow unaware or unconcerned previously.[157] The Bible consistently portrays him as intervening at various times for various purposes, though rarely as soon as humans, self-centeredly, would like. Indeed, this particular *remembering* comes at the end of no less than 430 years of captivity (12:40)! Thus the emphasis is on ongoing covenant: God's promises never stopped being valid, however seldom most Israelites may have called upon him to honor his promises in the past. The average Israelite likely knew at least something about the Abrahamic covenant, and it may be useful for the modern reader to realize that the term *zākar,* "remember," is idiomatic for covenant *application* rather than *recollection* (cf. Gen 9:15; Exod 6:5; Lev 26:42,45; 1 Chr 16:15; Pss 105:8; 106:45; 111:5; Jer 14:21; Ezek 16:60; Luke 1:72). In other words, to say "God remembered his covenant" is to say "God decided to honor the terms of his covenant at this time."[158] What were

[157] Cf. W. Schottroff, *Gedenken im Alten Orient und im Alten testament*, WMANT 15 (Neukirchen-Vluyn: Neukirchener Verlag, 1964).

[158] Thus the idiom never implies that anything was in fact forgotten or pushed to the back of God's mind.

those terms? They were, from Gen 12:2–3, the general promises of greatness (already largely achieved) and blessing—including protection (now needing to be addressed); and from Gen 15:13–16, the specific promises of punishment of the nation that oppressed Israel in slavery and deliverance with great possessions (esp. Gen 15:14).

Fifth, God was closely interested in his people and in the process of making himself known to them. Moses now mentioned God again for the first time since the account of the midwives in 1:17–20—not because God had been disinterested or irrelevant but as a way of heightening the fact that God alone was the Israelite's hope in this situation. The best reading of the original, "God looked on them and made himself known to them,"[159] sets the scene for what follows. God was initiating the process of deliverance, and the circumstances of both Moses and Israel were about to change. Implicitly, the theological issue here is not whether or how people suffer; the issue is: does suffering go unnoticed? If it does not—and indeed the one doing the noticing is the true, omnipotent, and loving covenant God—his people can properly surmise that their suffering may well be part of a plan, that it is a suffering with a distinct beginning and end, a hardship understood by and watched over by a sovereign who will not let it continue without good purpose and result.

---

[159] The NIV "was concerned about them" is a possible meaning of the MT Hb. (cf. D. W. Thomas, "A Note on וַיֵּדַע אֱלֹהִים in Exod. II.25," *JTS* 49 [1948]: 143–44), though ידע in the sense of "be concerned about/care about" normally takes a direct object (cf. Gen 39:6) rather than either no object at all (as the MT reading would be construed) or a preposition (here, MT אל). More likely, as the LXX (ἐγνώσθη αὐτοῖς) attests, the reading should be ויודע אליהם ("became known/revealed himself to them" reading the *niphal* ידע and the preposition אל with 3mpl suffix), the MT representing a simple scribal corruption in which the unpointed *niphal* was misread as the *qal* and "to them" was then misread as the similar "God." The supposedly comparable construction in Ps 31:8 (so Thomas) is neither sufficiently grammatically parallel nor textually secure. Cf. also C. Carniti, "*wajjēdaʿ ʾelohîm* (Es 2, 25): 'e Dio li riconobbe'?" *Greg* 73 (1992): 337–38. As a possible alternative to the NIV reading, the NRSV does a good job with the translation of the MT ("God looked upon the Israelites, and God took notice of them").

DIVISION OUTLINE

II. MOSES' CALL, COMMISSION, CHALLENGE (3:1–7:7)
1. Moses' Call: The Burning Bush Theophany (3:1–12)
   - Excursus: The Theophany Structure of Exodus 3–4
   - Excursus: The Angel of the Lord
   - Excursus: Fire Theophany
2. Revelation of the Name Yahweh (3:13–15)
3. Summary of Commission and Prediction of Acceptance by Israelites (3:16–22)
4. Moses' Special Signs of His Believability (4:1–9)
   - Excursus: The Nile as a God
5. Moses' Ritual and Actual Protests and Divine Reassurance (4:10–18)
   - Excursus: Moses' Staff
6. A Shaky Start but Initial Acceptance: Moses Returns to Egypt (4:19–31)
   - Excursus: The Hardening of Pharaoh's Heart
7. First Audience with Pharaoh: Harsh Results (5:1–14)
8. Negative Reaction of the Israelite Foremen (5:15–21)
9. Moses' Complaint and God's Covenant Assurance (5:22–6:12)
10. Genealogy of Moses and Aaron (6:13–27)
11. Divine Reassurance of Moses' Call, Commission, Challenge (6:28–7:7)

II. MOSES' CALL, COMMISSION, CHALLENGE (3:1–7:7)

This block of narrative moves the exodus story from the obscurity of one man's quiet, isolated life in Midian to the decisive challenges of a nation demanding its freedom—in the name of Yahweh—from the vastly superior Egyptians. The (re-)revelation of the name Yahweh (3:1–15) is central to the direction of Moses' call, described in 3:1–12 and reinforced in 4:10–18: if he is to be accepted by the Israelites (anticipated in 3:16–22), it is because he comes in the name of their true, historic, only God. Armed with initial miraculous signs to underscore his credibility (4:1–9), he gains a hearing from the Israelite leadership in spite of his own personal failures (4:19–31). The need for perseverance and reassurance (5:22–6:12) becomes obvious as both the pharaoh (5:1–14) and the Israelite work supervisors (5:15–20) react negatively to Moses' message. Clearly, Moses is God's chosen representative,[1] with Aaron as his partner. Not only is their role highlighted by the inclusion of their genealogy (6:13–27), but Moses' call and the significance of his assignment once again receive special divine approbation (6:28–7:7) on the verge of the campaign of plagues that will demonstrate God's total superiority to the "gods" of Egypt (cf. 12:12).

1. Moses' Call: The Burning Bush Theophany (3:1–12)

1Now Moses was tending the flock of Jethro his father-in-law, the priest of Midian, and he led the flock to the far side of the desert and came to Horeb, the mountain of God. 2There the angel of the LORD appeared to him in flames of fire from within a bush. Moses saw that though the bush was on fire it did not burn up. 3So Moses thought, "I will go over and see this strange sight—why the bush does not burn up."

4When the LORD saw that he had gone over to look, God called to him from within the bush, "Moses! Moses!" And Moses said, "Here I am."

5"Do not come any closer," God said. "Take off your sandals, for the place where you are standing is holy ground." 6Then he said, "I am the God of your father, the God of Abraham, the God of Isaac and the God of Jacob." At this, Moses hid his face, because he was afraid to look at God.

7The LORD said, "I have indeed seen the misery of my people in Egypt. I have heard them crying out because of their slave drivers, and I am concerned about their suffering. 8So I have come down to rescue them from the hand of the Egyptians and to bring them up out of that land into a good and spacious land, a land flowing with milk and honey—the home of the Canaanites, Hittites, Amorites, Perizzites, Hivites and Jebusites. 9And now the cry of the Israelites has reached me, and I have seen the way the Egyptians are oppressing them. 10So now, go. I am sending you to Pharaoh to bring my people the Israelites out of Egypt."

11But Moses said to God, "Who am I, that I should go to Pharaoh and bring the Israelites out of Egypt?"

12And God said, "I will be with you. And this will be the sign to you that it is I who have sent you: When you have brought the people out of Egypt, you will worship God on this mountain."

Excursus: The Theophany Structure of Exodus 3–4

Chapters 3 and 4 of Exodus follow a literary pattern well attested both in the Bible and in other literature of the ancient Near East: the theophany form. This form was apparently long established in the culture of Moses and the Israelites for whom he wrote the Pentateuch, and it is not surprising therefore that he

[1] Although, just as clearly, the recognition of Moses' stature with God and the Israelites did not come at once but by reason of a combination of his faithfulness to God's call (sometimes reluctantly at first) and God's correction and guidance through a series of events. Cf. E. Neufeld, "The Redemption of Moses," *Jud* 42 (1993): 50–58.

would employ it repeatedly as he wrote. Beginning with the work of H. Gunkel, who identified this form in general terms in the stories of the patriarchs in Genesis[2] (i.e., Moses had already employed this form several times before his use of it to describe his own initial theophany story here), a number of scholars[3] have advanced the study of the form and its component parts. Kuntz[4] has described the theophany form as having, in its full representation, ten component parts. This approach is refined and exhaustively documented by Niehaus, who demonstrates particularly well the usefulness of the form for understanding the many Old Testament theophany accounts.[5]

Kuntz's description, slightly modified by Niehaus, of the general structure of a typical full theophany account is as follows:

1. Introductory description in the third person
2. Deity's utterance of the name of the (mortal) addressee
3. Response of the addressee
4. Deity's self-asseveration
5. His quelling of human fear
6. Assertion of his gracious presence
7. The *hieros logos*[6] addressed to the particular situation
8. Inquiry or protest by the addressee
9. Continuation of the *hieros logos* with perhaps some repetition of elements 4, 5, 6, 7, and/or 8
10. Concluding description in the third person

Here is how the structure plays out in Exodus 3 and 4[7]:

1.	Introductory description in the third person	3:1–4a
2.	Deity's utterance of the name of the (mortal) addressee	3:4b
3.	Response of the addressee	3:4c
4.	Deity's self-asseveration	3:5–6
5.	His quelling of human fear	3:7
6.	Assertion of his gracious presence	3:8
7.	The *hieros logos* addressed to the particular situation	3:9–10
8.	Inquiry or protest by the addressee	3:11

---

[2] H. Gunkel, *Genesis*, 6th ed. (Göttingen: Vandenhoeck & Ruprecht, 1964).

[3] See esp. J. Morgenstern, "Biblical Theophanies," *ZA* 25 (1911): 139–93; *ZA* 28 (1913): 15–60; E. Norden, *Agnostos Theos: Untersuchungen zur Formgeschichtliche religiöser Rede* (Leipzig/Berlin: B. G. Tuebner, 1913); J. Jeremias, *Theophanie: die Geschichte einer alttestamentlichen Gattung*, WMANT (Neukirchen-Vluyn: Neukirchener Verlag, 1965).

[4] J. K. Kuntz, *The Self-Revelation of God* (Philadelphia: Westminster, 1965), esp. 73–102.

[5] J. J. Niehaus, *God at Sinai* (Grand Rapids: Zondervan, 1995), 30–42 *et passim.*

[6] *Hieros logos* means "holy word," a revelatory message from God to humans.

[7] We have here followed closely Niehaus (*God at Sinai*, 186–87) with minor modifications as to how elements 4–7 and 10 are distributed among the verses of the biblical text.

9. Continuation of the *hieros logos* with perhaps some repetition of elements 4, 5, 6, 7, and/or 8:

hieros logos	3:12
protest	3:13
hieroi logoi[8]	3:14–22
protest	4:1
hieroi logoi	4:2–9
protest	4:10
hieros logos	4:11–12
protest	4:13
hieroi logoi	4:14–17

10. Concluding description in the third person 4:18

In these two chapters we will refer to this structure and its individual elements regularly. An awareness of the prominence of the theophany form in this section of Exodus not only clarifies the purposes of the various details in the narrative but also confirms the unity of the entire passage.[9]

3:1 The main purpose of this first verse in the third-person description (theophany form element 1) of Moses' life-changing encounter with God is to provide a brief explanation for how Moses came to be located far from normal Midianite haunts, at Sinai, where God would reveal himself to him. Important subsidiary information, however, is revealed in the process. We learn, for example, that Moses' identification with his own ethnic people was now so strong that he was willing to serve in the occupation of shepherd, an assignment that no one who still thought of himself as an Egyptian would ever have taken on, so loathsome was shepherding to Egyptians.[10] In other words, it is apparent that should he ever return to Egypt, he would go as an Israelite, not as an Egyptian. Additionally, we learn that he did not have his own flock but tended that of his father-in-law, suggesting that he had not come into substantial means of his own.[11] In contrast to his days as an Egyptian princeling, he was now, even if in a favored way, at least in some sense a household worker. We also learn that Jethro continued to be a Midianite priest, perhaps even chief priest of that people.[12]

---

[8] *Hieroi logoi* is the plural of *hieros logos*, meaning "holy words," i.e., more than a single revelatory statement.

[9] Source critics assign various parts of Exod 3–4 to various sources (J, E, P). Their delicate labors are rendered void by the realization that the theophany form explains all the elements, with nothing left over to assign to multiple sources. Cf. also E. J. Young, "The Call of Moses," *WTJ* 29 (1966–67): 117–35; and *WTJ* 30 (1967–68): 1–23.

[10] Cf. Gen 36:32–34; 37:1–6.

[11] Contrast, e.g., Jacob, who had accumulated a great deal in fourteen years (Gen 30:25–43); Moses apparently had accumulated little in forty years.

[12] The grammar of the Hb. construct, כֹּהֵן מִדְיָן, a common noun in construct to a proper noun, is correctly reflected in the NIV, "the priest of Midian." If Moses had intended to convey "a priest of Midian," the wording would have been כהן למדין with the preposition ל breaking up the construct. In contrast to the grammatical situation at the end of 2:15 (see comments on 2:15), there is no likelihood of proleptic definiteness here.

Of significance for the story of the exodus is the placing of Horeb (Mount Sinai)[13] west of/to the far side of the desert from Midian. Various theories have been advanced in favor of locating Mount Sinai somewhere in Midian, but this verse is part of the contrary evidence. Moses apparently had gone with the flock from Midianite territory (located mainly east of the east fork of the Red Sea) westward past Elat/Ezion-geber and then southwest into the Sinai wilderness—weeks away from home, taking advantage of the available high grassy slopes whose value to feeding the sheep was worth the great distance required for him to traverse. The special distance may even have been occasioned by poor grass conditions in Midian itself that year. At any rate, Moses had gone no small distance toward Egypt in his cattle drive.

3:2–3 Suddenly a supernatural encounter of great consequence took place, continuing the third-person description (i.e., still theophany form element 1). Nothing prior to this in the book is demonstrably supernatural, in the sense of the miraculous suspension of the usual laws of nature. Now, however, God, in the form of the "Angel of the LORD" (see excursus below, "The Angel of the Lord") appeared in a fire theophany (see excursus below, "Fire Theophany") to Moses, a special personal appearance of God to an aging exile working as a shepherd, to initiate the divine call for this unlikely candidate to be his prophet for the purpose of delivering the Israelites from Egypt.

Moses' understanding of what was happening to him unfolds in stages described in the remainder of chaps. 4 and 5. These two verses describe the encounter both in summary form from the point of view of the reader, who is told immediately that what Moses began to see was in fact an appearance of the Angel of the Lord, and also from Moses' point of view, recounted in vv. 2a–3, which makes clear that at first he had no idea what he was seeing beyond the fact that it was a bush on fire that kept burning steadily. The term used for this bush, *sěneh,* denotes a relatively small (at most a few feet in diameter) thorny bush/shrub. Moses, knowing how to keep warm on cold nights in the wilderness, would have been well aware of how quickly bushes burn and would thus have been struck by two factors: first, a single bush on a hillside without anyone else around it was on fire; and second, instead of burning up it burned on and on. Moses was naturally attracted to this unusual phenomenon and chose to try to understand it by getting closer. God

---

[13] Source critics tend to link the name "Horeb" to their theorized E (Elohist) source, which produces some embarrassment for the Documentary Hypothesis at this point since this part of Exodus is supposed to be J (Yahwist) material; e.g., J. I. Durham can offer no better explanation than: "At the end of v. 1, most of which can be assigned to the Yahwist, Horeb, the Elohist's name for the mount of the theophany is used" (*Exodus,* WBC [Waco: Word, 1987], 29). Cf. also G. I. Davies, "Hagar, El-Hagra and the Location of Mount Sinai," *VT* 22 (1972): 152–63.

thus used this burning bush, as he so often uses various sorts of circumstances, to begin to bring someone closer to himself.

But why a bush? It may only be because God's likely choice was between rocks and bushes—the two sorts of objects that can typically be found sticking out of the ground in that terrain—and he simply chose a bush. But it may also be that the similarity between the sounds of *sĕneh*, "bush," and *sînāy*, "Sinai," fit his purposes. Indeed, so close are the two words that in Deut 33:16 the expression *šōkĕnî sĕneh*, "the one who resided in the bush," sometimes has been emended to *šōkēn sînāy*, "the one who dwells on Sinai" (e.g., NRSV). At any rate, it is certainly conceivable that the mention of the bush, *sĕneh*, was designed also to become a reminder of its location, *sînāy*. Because in biblical culture bushes or trees can symbolize people or groups, the use of a bush on fire to gain Moses' attention would not have been outside of his cognition: he could have adapted quickly, as he did to the idea that an angel/the angel of the Lord/the Lord himself had manifested himself (to get Moses' attention) within that bush. Not only so, but later, as he told and retold the story of his call, others would also be able to relate to the idea that a burning bush could in fact represent Israel's God.[14]

Excursus: The Angel of the Lord[15]

The term *mal'āk yahweh*, usually translated "the Angel of the LORD," appears sixty-seven times in the Old Testament. Exodus 3:2 is its only occurrence in Exodus, though it was already prominent in both Gen 16, the story of Hagar, and Gen 22, the story of Abraham's near sacrifice of Isaac.[16] Grammatically, *mal'āk yahweh* is a construct (also called bound form, genitive construction) and according to the rule of constructs, both elements must be either definite or indefinite. Since the proper noun "Yahweh" is intrinsically definite, the noun that precedes it musts also be definite; so the phrase cannot therefore mean "an angel of the Lord" but must connote greater definiteness, in other words, "the Angel of the LORD." But can it mean something more precise even than this? This question may be answered in part by asking what sort of construct the phrase is most likely to represent. Of the dozen or so types of constructs typically recognized by Hebrew grammarians, the most likely type involved here is the appositional construct (also called definitional construct, genitive of apposition, genitive of definition, genitive of association), that is, the form of the con-

---

[14] J. G. Janzen, ". . . And the Bush Was Not Consumed," *Enc* 63 (2002): 117–27.

[15] R. Ficker (*THAT* 1:906–8) lists five major theories of who the Angel of Yahweh is, from simply any angel Yahweh happens to use to manifest himself to the approach we take here. See also W. Baumgartner, "Zum Problem des Jahwe-Engels," in *Zum Alten Testament und Seiner Umwelt* (Leiden: Brill, 1959), 240–46.

[16] See, e.g., J. O. Akao, "Yahweh and *Mal'ak* in the Early Traditions of Israel: A Study of the Underlying Traditions of Yahweh/Angel Theophany in Exodus 3," *IBS* 12 (1990): 72–85. We take the historicity of the present account more seriously than does Akao.

struct that uses the second word to identify the first.[17] A useful analogy is found in the well-known expression *nĕhar pĕrāt,* [the] River Euphrates, also an appositional construct in which the second noun is intrinsically definite by reason of being a proper noun. Consider the nature of the River Euphrates: it was not *a* river *in* or *of* Euphrates; rather, all of [the] Euphrates was the river, that is, the River Euphrates or [the] Euphrates River.

Likewise, *mal'āk yahweh* is grammatically appositional and best translated as "the angel that is Yahweh"[18] or "the Angel Yahweh" or "Angel Yahweh." But what does this imply ontologically? Are we to conclude that Yahweh is merely an angel or, perhaps, *sometimes* merely an angel? Or is there a certain angel who on occasion takes the identity of Yahweh for certain purposes, such as special revelatory encounters with humans in Old Testament times? In a number of Old Testament passages an individual described as an angel (*mal'āk;* not always specifically *mal'āk yahweh,* "Angel of the LORD") is either called "the LORD" (e.g., Gen 12:7; 17:1; 18:1) or becomes recognized as the Lord (e.g., Gen 16:13: "She gave this name to the LORD who spoke to her: 'You are the God who sees me,' for she said, 'I have now seen the One who sees me' "; Gen 48:15–16: "May the God before whom my fathers Abraham and Isaac walked, / the God who has been my shepherd all my life to this day, / the Angel who has delivered me from all harm") or actually calls himself the Lord or God (e.g., Gen 31:11–13: "The angel of God said to me . . . I am the God of Bethel").[19]

Sometimes an angel is described in terms that can refer only to God, as in the case of Exod 23:20–23:

> See, I am sending an angel ahead of you to guard you along the way and to bring you to the place I have prepared. Pay attention to him and listen to what he says. Do not rebel against him; he will not forgive your rebellion, since my Name is in him. If you listen carefully to what he says and do all that I say, I will be an enemy to your enemies and will oppose those who oppose you. My

---

[17] On this type of construct see the explanations and examples in R. J. Williams, *Hebrew Syntax: An Outline,* 2d ed. (Toronto: University of Toronto Press, 1976), 42, and *IBHS* §9.5.3h ("genitive of association"); and esp. W. F. Stinespring, "No Daughter of Zion: A Study of the Appositional Genitive in Hebrew Grammar," *Enc* 26 (1965): 133–41; and "Daughter of Zion," in *IDBSup* (Nashville: Abingdon, 1976), 985; cf. A. Fitzgerald, "*BTWLT* and *BT* as Titles for Capital Cities," *CBQ* 37 (1975): 167–83. Most languages, in fact, have some sort of appositional genitives. NT Gk. has dozens of examples (thus the genitive of apposition/definition is recognized as a standard NT Gk. category by A. T. Robertson, *A Grammar of the Greek New Testament: In Light of Historical Research* (Nashville: Broadman, 1934), 498–99.

[18] Cf. G. von Rad's statement that Yahweh and the Angel of Yahweh are "one and the same" as well as his emphasis on the Angel of Yahweh as "the personification of Yahweh's assistance to Israel" (*TDNT* 1:77–78).

[19] Akao concludes that "it is an impossible task to differentiate between the *Mal'ak* and Yahweh Himself. This is because the one who speaks or acts, Yahweh or *Mal'ak*, is obviously one and the same person"—even though Akao believes that there were two original theophany traditions behind Exod 3, one related to *Mal'ak* and the other related to Yahweh ("Yahweh and *Mal'ak* in the Early Traditions of Israel," 72–85).

angel will go ahead of you and bring you into the land of the Amorites, Hittites, Perizzites, Canaanites, Hivites and Jebusites, and I will wipe them out.

This passage presumes that the angel would bring Israel into the promised land, had the power to forgive or not forgive sins, spoke teachings and commands that must be obeyed, had within him God's Name, and was the judge and destroyer of Israel's enemies—all attributes clearly associated with God alone many times elsewhere.[20] Strikingly, in Exod 3 the "Angel of the LORD" said to be "in flames of fire from within a bush" (v. 2) is in v. 4 called both Yahweh [LORD] and God: "When the LORD saw that he had gone over to look, God called to him from within the bush." Indeed, Exod 3 is perhaps the strongest of all passages for identifying the "Angel of the LORD" as the Lord himself, for it continually refers to the individual first identified as the "Angel of the Lord" as both Lord [Yahweh] (vv. 2,4,7, 5,16,18) and God (vv. 4–6,11–16,18).

These and other passages indicate that the Angel of the Lord is the Lord God himself and not merely one of heaven's angels standing in for God or speaking with his authority. What reason, therefore, would there be for God to take the form of an angel in so many instances? Why not just show up in person, as it were? The answer, we suggest, is most probably to be found particularly in two attributes of God: his omnipresence and his holiness. These two great doctrines would require enormous space for anything approaching an adequately full statement of their reflection in Scripture, but we can at least summarize how they relate to the appropriateness of God's manifesting himself in angelic form.

Because of his omnipresence, God is not limited to any space. Therefore, when he occupies a small space for purposes of revelation, he typically does so by representation. He has made humans his representatives to do his will (Gen 1:26; Matt 6:10) on the little space in the universe that we call the earth, and he has chosen angels as his representatives from heaven to earth (Heb 1:14). But he sometimes has specially represented himself in human form, such as through the angel who could be called Angel Yahweh and most brilliantly and importantly of all through his own Son in human likeness. Such appearances have the advantage of giving people something to look at and listen to, since looking and listening are so basic to relating. Since Pentecost, both the Son and the Father are represented by the Spirit within believers—an extremely personal and significant representation that goes beyond even the benefits of visibility and voice provided by an angel.

God's holiness does not tolerate evil. Throughout the Bible we trace the pattern of God's beneficent distance from sinful humans; were he to place himself fully and precisely in our presence prior to the elimination of all evil through the final judgment, we would have to die because his holiness would not abide our present sin (see 33:20). This was a reason for the expulsion of the first humans from the Garden after they sinned, a reason for God's dwelling among his people

---

[20] As R. North puts it, מַלְאַךְ יהוה "is in some cases an expression for God himself" ("Separated Spiritual Substances in the Old Testament," *CBQ* 29 [1967]: 419–49).

by indirect representation in the tabernacle/temple and in Zion/Jerusalem, and through his occasional appearance in visible and audible form as the Angel Yahweh. The Angel Yahweh was not all there was to God but was a true and real representation of him, much as a videoconferencing call brings a valuable sense of the presence of an individual into a room through a video screen and speaker—visibility and voice—even though the individual is not actually *fully* present thereby.[21]

Excursus: Fire Theophany

The term "theophany" ("appearance of God") is normally used to refer to instances recorded in Scripture where God appears in some way to humans. As described in prior excursus, God's appearances do not represent his totality or the fullness of his essence. They instead are occasions in which he is visible *in some fashion*—normally, through a shape that is not exactly natural (i.e., he does not look like a human); but he can nevertheless be looked at and focused on by a human, an appearance often accompanied by fire. A pot of fire is thus how God represented himself in his covenant with Abraham in Gen 15:17. To lead the Israelites through the wilderness, he showed himself as a pillar of fire (Exod 13:21 and thereafter). At Sinai he "descended in fire" (Exod 19:18 and thereafter) to meet with Israel and reveal his Law. Later, again at Sinai, he accompanied his visit to Elijah with fire (1 Kgs 19:6). He often is actually identified as fire (e.g., Deut 4:24) and his coming as accompanied by fire (e.g., Ps 50:3). Ezekiel saw him as a fiery shape (Ezek 1; 8); Daniel, as one sitting on a throne of fire (Dan 9:7); John, as one with eyes of fire (Rev 1:14; 2:18; 19:12). Often his judgment is described as coming in the form of destructive fire (e.g., Num 11:1–3; 16:35; 2 Kgs 1:12–14; Job 1:16; Amos 1:4–2:5), as was the baptism of Christ, which resulted in judgment against sin (Matt 3:11), and the second death, in the fire that consumes fully and cannot be quenched in any way (e.g., Matt 18:8–9; 2 Pet 3:7; Jude 7; Rev 20:14).

The present passage, Exod 3, thus provides one of the many instances in the Bible of God's representation of himself in a fire theophany. Of course, not all fires indicated God's presence (indeed Exod 3:3 indicates that initially Moses made no such assumption about the origin of the fire that kept the bush burning), and a number of other phenomena also are used to indicate his theophanic presence (storms, wind, clouds, smoke, blazing light)—with or without any accompanying fire.

3:4–5 After God's method of attracting Moses closer to the bush worked, as of course he knew it would, God then began to reveal himself (v. 4) from within the theophanic fire by addressing Moses through a speech pattern ("Moses! Moses!") that may be called "repetition of endearment." In ancient Semitic culture, addressing someone by saying his or her name

[21] For a summary of a common alternative view, namely that the Angel of the Lord is actually the preincarnate Christ, see W. C. Kaiser Jr. et al., *Hard Sayings of the Bible* (Downers Grove: InterVarsity, 1996), 191–92.

twice was a way of expressing endearment, that is, affection and friendship.[22] Thus Moses would have understood immediately that he was being addressed by someone who loved him and was concerned about him. Moses' reply, *hinnēnî* ("Here I am"), has no special meaning beyond being the standard way in Hebrew of replying "Yes?" when one is called.[23]

Without yet identifying himself, God began to teach Moses about the holy nature of his presence (v. 5). The theme of the divine Presence is a major topic of Exodus. It often is emphasized by commands requiring distance from God so as not to intrude too far on his holiness, proximity to which carries with it danger to the person not properly prepared (sanctified). This passage, with its come-no-further command, is remarkably parallel to that of Exod 19:9–25, where a series of conditions of sanctification (procedures that confer holiness) and distance (e.g., 19:23, "Put limits around the mountain and set it apart as holy") are imposed upon the Israelites. Thus what God's people would eventually have to learn from God through him, Moses now began to learn from God. Moses must do two things: keep a proper distance away from the bush (i.e., from God manifest in the fire) and take off his sandals. There are many references in the Bible to taking off or putting on sandals, but none has any connection with holiness except this one. Presumably, taking off shoes was done when entering the presence of a superior person, which usually would occur formally when one was at the

---

[22] Repetition of endearment is found in a variety of OT and NT passages, including the following prominent examples. Note that in Matt 7:21–22; Luke 6:46 Jesus used the repetition-of-endearment pattern to refer to people who claimed to be close to him but who were not his friends because of their disobedience to his will. In the case of 1 Sam 3; 10 and the Acts passages, the repetition of endearment is used also in call narratives, somewhat in parallel to the present call narrative in Exod 3:

1 Sam 3:4: Then the LORD called Samuel. Samuel answered, "Here I am."

1 Sam 3:10: The LORD came and stood there, calling as at other times, "Samuel! Samuel!"

2 Sam 18:33: The king was shaken. He went up to the room over the gateway and wept. As he went, he said, "O my son Absalom! My son, my son Absalom! If only I had died instead of you—O Absalom, my son, my son!"

2 Sam 19:4: The king covered his face and cried aloud, "O my son Absalom! O Absalom, my son, my son!"

Matt 27:46: About the ninth hour Jesus cried out in a loud voice, "Eloi, Eloi, lama sabachthani?" which means, "My God, my God, why have you forsaken me?"

Matt 7:21: Not everyone who says to me, "Lord, Lord," will enter the kingdom of heaven, but only he who does the will of my Father who is in heaven.

Matt 7:22: Many will say to me on that day, "Lord, Lord, did we not prophesy in your name, and in your name drive out demons and perform many miracles?"

Luke 6:46: Why do you call me, "Lord, Lord," and do not do what I say?

Acts 9:4: He fell to the ground and heard a voice say to him, "Saul, Saul, why do you persecute me?"

Acts 22:7: I fell to the ground and heard a voice say to me, 'Saul! Saul! Why do you persecute me?'

Acts 26:14: We fell to the ground, and I heard a voice saying to me in Aramaic, "Saul, Saul, why do you persecute me? It is hard for you to kick against the goads."

[23] Gen 22:1; 22:7; 22:11; 27:1; 27:18; 31:11; 37:13; 46:2; 1 Sam 3:4–6,8,16; 22:12; Isa 58:9; 65:1; cf. Acts 9:10. Note that *hinnēnî* can be said by equals to equals, superiors to inferiors, or inferiors to superiors—it simply means "Yes?" and does not have special theological or spiritual connotations. Moses said what any person would normally say when called by someone else.

superior person's house, palace, or tent. Thus Sinai/Horeb is here implicitly identified as "Yahweh's place." Thus the very *ground* is holy—something said of no other location in the Bible.[24]

3:6 This verse is noteworthy for the precise designation of whom Moses is talking to, that is, who the true God is, as well as of the history of divine relationships with the descendants of Abraham that Moses now joins. No special significance should be read into the fact that "the God of" is repeated. Greek can avoid the repetition by stringing out genitives (thus, "the God of Abraham, Isaac and Jacob"), but strings of genitives (i.e., the governing words in construct phrases) are much less common in Hebrew.[25] The normal way to indicate what in English would be "the *w* of *x, y,* and *z*" is to say "the *w* of *x*, the *w* of *y,* and the *w* of *z,*" as in this verse.[26] Moses was being told straightforwardly that he was speaking with the God of his father[27] and of the great patriarchs.[28]

This need not imply, however, that Amram, Moses' biological father, was somehow of equal importance to the patriarchs or that Amram knew the true God as closely as they. God's mention of Amram was more likely a means of assuring Moses (1) that he was now in the Israelite tradition of faith[29] and had

---

[24] Acts 7:33 repeats even this detail of the call of Moses, suggesting that the topic of holy ground is integral to the apostolic understanding of the essence of the story. Cf. also J. Dunford, "Holy Ground," *ExpTim* 91 (1979): 45–46.

[25] Although they do occur, especially when the genitives are closely related, as in Gen 14:19; 28:5; Deut 10:18. But three genitives in a row would be unusual.

[26] On the textually questionable pattern in 3:16, see comments on that verse.

[27] The fact that God identified himself to Moses through the expression "the God of your father" is part of the evidence that Yahweh was a name known to the patriarchs and not newly revealed at this time (see comments on 6:3). But the common view remains that this is the point of the invention or introduction of the name Yahweh into Israelite religion. Cf. J. P. Hyatt, "YHWH as the 'God of My Father,'" *VT* 5 (1955): 130–36; J. G. Janzen, "What's in a Name? 'Yahweh' in Exodus 3 and the Wider Biblical Context," *Int* 33 (1979): 227–39; C. D. Isbell, "The Divine Name *'hyh* as a Symbol of Presence in Israelite Tradition," *HAR* 2 (1978): 101–18; C. R. Seitz, "The Call of Moses and the 'Revelation' of the Divine Name: Source-Critical Logic and its Legacy," in C. Seitz et al. eds., *Theological Exegesis: Essays in Honor of Brevard S. Childs* (Grand Rapids: Eerdmans, 1999), 145–61.

[28] Jesus reminded his listeners (Matt 22:32 and parallels) that the rich ambiguity of this formula, employing the verbless nominative construction אני אלהי ("I am the God of") allows it to refer not merely to history (as היתי אלהי, "I was the God of" would) but to the present. Thus Moses would have understood God to be saying that he was at the present time still the God of the four persons named, i.e., that they had not ceased to exist even though they were no longer among the living on earth.

[29] What cannot convincingly be asserted, however, is that Moses learned only as of 3:6 that he was a Hebrew/Israelite, as if he had no knowledge thereof prior to the burning bush revelation. Neufeld ("The Redemption of Moses," 50–58) has argued exactly that—i.e., that Moses first learned he was an Israelite by the special revelation granted him at the burning bush, a position that certainly is theoretically possible but that seems to us to disregard the implications of the clear understanding of his Egyptian princess stepmother about his ancestry (see comments on 1:6), the length of time that Moses' Hebrew mother cared for him (see comments on 1:9–10), the strength of his identification with Israelites as described in 2:11–14, the hostility of Pharaoh toward him in 2:15, and the ease with which he fit into Jethro's family both linguistically and socially (2:15–22). The fact that Jethro's daughters at first mistook him for an Egyptian (2:19) was surely more related to his dress and hairstyle than his innate physical characteristics or speech and was at any rate a first impression by strangers, not a definitive indicator of Moses' self-awareness of his origins.

the opportunity to know the true God just as his father and all who preceded him since Abraham had; (2) God's faithful provision over all the many generations since Abraham, according to the promises made him in Gen 12; 15, was beginning to come to fruition (cf. 1:7). It had never been suspended and was at work even in God's provision for Moses' immediate family, the family of Amram. Accordingly, this verse constitutes one of the strongest, most overt link to the themes of the book of Genesis so far encountered in Exodus.

Moses' fear of seeing God has various parallels and represents a general assumption in ancient Near Eastern culture that if one were actually to look at a god (except in the form of an idol, according to pagan notions of the concept), he or she might be in great danger because gods—and certainly the one true God—guarded their full presence from humans (cf. John 1:18; 6:46; 1 John 4:12). Especially relevant parallels are Gen 32:30, "So Jacob called the place Peniel, saying, "It is because I saw God face to face, and yet my life was spared"; and Judg 13:22, "We are doomed to die!" he said to his wife. "We have seen God!" Accordingly, being able to see God is always wondrous (even figuratively; cf. 3 John 11) and in its fullness is reserved for a future state (e.g., Matt 5:8, "Blessed are the pure in heart, for they will see God"; cf. Heb 12:14). Though Moses' theology was hardly fully formed at this point, he nevertheless well understood something of the potential power of God's holiness. Later, his being allowed to see God in part (Exod 24:1–2; 33:21–23) would constitute an extremely unusual privilege and credential. The fact that God eventually made himself visible *in human form* represents the highest earthly experience of seeing God (John 14:9), far surpassing even Moses' unusual opportunity.

3:7–10 What the reader has already learned from mention of the patriarchal covenant in 2:23–25 (and which was implicit in the reference to Abraham, Isaac, and Jacob in 3:6) Moses now heard spelled out explicitly: Yahweh cared about his people and planned to deliver them from Egypt to Canaan. In 2:23–25 the exodus was already adumbrated by the reference to remembering the covenant with Abraham and his descendants, the terms of which included both their slavery and their deliverance to Canaan (Gen 15:13–16).

Two great challenges to Moses' faith appear here implicitly, at either end of these verses. The first (v. 7) is a challenge shared by all believers: to trust that God has always and continues to be concerned about their suffering since in the present fallen world, God allows suffering. That the Israelites had been suffering oppression such a long time without rescue begs the question of God, "If you are willing to help now, why didn't you help earlier?" The Bible provides clear answers in principle to such a question,[30] but

[30] E.g., Rom 5:3; 8:17; Phil 1:29; 2 Thess 1:5; 1 Pet 1:6; 3:17; 4:19.

individuals or groups cannot normally know why their particular suffering is so severe or has gone on as long as it has.[31] The second challenge (v. 10) involves Moses' past: how could one who tried and failed to help his fellow Israelites on an individual scale forty years before (2:11–14) now, in his late years, be God's choice as deliverer of the whole nation?

Verse 7 summarizes the plight of the Israelites in their forced labor with four terms: "misery . . . crying out . . . slave drivers . . . suffering."[32] With three verbs God announced his compassion: "I have indeed seen . . . I have heard them . . . I am concerned."[33] The first of these, "I have indeed seen" *(rāʾōh rāʾîtî)* involves the Hebrew infinitive absolute construction, which connotes the sense "I have carefully watched" or "I have paid very close attention to," thus by itself indicating the intensity of God's interest in the misery of his people. Note also that God called Israel "my people," echoing but also more grandly superseding Moses' reference to "his own people" in 2:11.

Verse 8 declares God's rescue plan. The wording "I have come down [descended]" is characteristic of many biblical passages related to theophany and divine rescue of humans[34] and should not be understood as suggesting a primitive view of God within a three-tiered universe. He promised to bring them to a place ample in both size[35] and nourishment[36] for them. By mentioning the six (or seven) Canaanite-Amorite groups,[37] God both

---

[31] Thus the model of Job, who was not allowed to be aware that his suffering greatly honored God and humiliated Satan, as the suffering of the righteous invariably does whether or not they are aware of it.

[32] All four terms (עני, "misery"; צעקה, "crying out"; נגש, "slave driver"; מכאב, "suffering") are used here in Exodus for the first time, even though Israel's suffering has already been referred to in various ways in chaps. 1–2, suggesting that this verse is programmatic for many following references to Israel's suffering under Egyptian bondage.

[33] In contrast to the nouns cited above, the three verbs are all resumptive of vocabulary used in 2:24–25.

[34] E.g., Gen 11:5; Exod 19:20; 34:5; Num 11:25; 12:5; Neh 9:13; Ps 18:9; Isa 64:3; Luke 3:22; John 6:41,51; Eph 4:9; cf. Kuntz, *The Self-Revelation of God*, 42; Niehaus, *God at Sinai*, 187.

[35] On the term "spacious land" cf. Judg 18:10; 2 Sam 18:20/Ps 18:19; 1 Chr 4:40; Neh 9:35.

[36] The term "flowing with milk and honey," grammatically unusual because it involves a participle constructed to a compound noun, became nevertheless the standard term for describing the goodness of God's provision for his people in Canaan (cf. 3:17; 13:5). The expression is apt for the land of promise, where flocks thrived and where honey bees were abundant but where some other types of agriculture, such as vegetable cultivation (note the wistful reference in Num 11:5), were more difficult.

[37] On the identity of these groups, sometimes listed in the OT in a group of six or seven (and not always with the same names or order whether six or seven), all of which can be generally summarized with the term "Canaanites," see H. A. Hoffner, "The Hittites and Hurrians"; M. Liverani, "The Amorites"; A. R. Millard, "The Canaanites"; and D. J. Wiseman, "Introduction," in *Peoples of Old Testament Times* (Oxford: Clarendon Press, 1973), 29–52. Note especially that the biblical "Hittites" were not the great nation of ancient Anatolia (which would be indicated by *ḥattî* rather than *ḥittî* in the OT) but a local Palestinian group possibly related in some way to the Hurrians.

clarified for Moses exactly which territories he planned to give his people and proleptically identified the future enemies in the war of conquest fought by Joshua.

Verse 9 reiterates both 3:7 and 2:23–25, providing yet another occasion to remind the reader, and in this case Moses in the situation of his call, that God had not forgotten his people, was deeply concerned for them, and would act on their behalf. Nevertheless, as the ensuing portions of the narrative make clear, it was not easy for Moses to hear the command of v. 10, with its demand that he *go* as God's prophet ("I am sending you"[38]) to Pharaoh to *bring* Israel out of Egypt. Not only was Moses to be involved in the exodus but he was to lead it, in defiance of the greatest potentate on earth, the Egyptian Pharaoh.

3:11–12 In these verses appear, respectively, element 8 of the theophany form (inquiry or protest by the addressee, v. 11) and part of element 9 (continuation of the *hieros logos* with perhaps some repetition of previous elements [v. 12 is one of the *hieros logos* statements]). The two verses together constitute the first of several patterns of *hieros logos* followed by Moses' protest—pairs of elements that take the narrative all the way to 4:17. Moses' protest in v. 11 conforms to the usual pattern in such cases: being called to a task by God, he properly and respectfully expressed his humility at being given such an important assignment. In other words, Moses' question, "Who am I?" is a *pro forma* question, not an expression of actual lack of self-confidence. At this point, at least, he was not trying to get out of the job Yahweh was calling him to perform but was being mannerly according to the dictates of his culture.[39] The exact expression, "Who am I" *(mîʾānōḵî)* occurs two other times in the Old Testament, in each instance as part of expressing polite *acceptance* of an honor rather than as an attempt to decline it.[40] From the wording of his response, it is clear that Moses understood the nature of his assignment.

God's reply (v. 12) contains two key elements: a promise of help and guidance ("I will be with you") and a fulfillment sign. For God to "be with" someone means that he provides that person direct, special help and guidance[41] that, in turn, can cause people to recognize that person's worth and/or authority in given situations.[42] A fulfillment sign is a confirmation that a

---

[38] On *sending* as a concept identifying prophets, cf., e.g., Judg 6:8; 2 Chr 24:19; Jer 7:25; 14:15; 23:21; Zech 7:12; Mal 4:5; Matt 23:37 and par; Acts 7:37.

[39] See comments on 4:10 for actual examples of ritual protests in call narratives.

[40] 1 Sam 18:18: "David said to Saul, 'Who am I, and what is my family or my father's clan in Israel, that I should become the king's son-in-law?' "; 2 Sam. 7:18: "Then King David went in and sat before the LORD, and he said, "Who am I, O Sovereign LORD, and what is my family, that you have brought me this far?"

[41] Cp. the same idiom in Gen 26:28; 39:2,21,23; Deut 32:12; Josh 1:17; 3:7. Cf. H. D. Preuss, "Ich will mit dir sein," *ZAW* 80 (1968): 139–73.

[42] E.g., Gen 26:28; Josh 3:7; 6:27; 1 Sam 3:19; 18:12; 2 Chr 15:9; cf. Acts 11:21; 2 Thess 3:1.

prophet or leader has completed a key part of a task assigned him by God. The fulfillment sign for Moses' call was a successful exodus followed by arrival at Mount Sinai and worship there by all the people ("you will worship" is plural). This is significant because it is not merely measurable by the movement of the people from one place to another but also by their movement from one faith to another. They would get to Sinai, but more importantly they would get to saving belief in the only true and living God. Fulfillment signs require faith since they promise proof to follow after an interval of time rather than immediately; in doing so they encourage faith.[43] This one is no exception. It would be fulfilled three months after the start of the exodus (Exod 19:1) but would continue to provide its retrospective reassurance for forty more years.

2. Revelation of the Name Yahweh (3:13–15)

[13]Moses said to God, "Suppose I go to the Israelites and say to them, 'The God of your fathers has sent me to you,' and they ask me, 'What is his name?' Then what shall I tell them?"

[14]God said to Moses, "I AM WHO I AM. This is what you are to say to the Israelites: 'I AM has sent me to you.'"

[15]God also said to Moses, "Say to the Israelites, 'The LORD, the God of your fathers—the God of Abraham, the God of Isaac and the God of Jacob—has sent me to you.' This is my name forever, the name by which I am to be remembered from generation to generation.

These verses include Moses' first protest (v. 13) and the beginning of God's first group of *hieroi logoi* responses; that is, they represent part of the continuation of element 9 in the theophany structure of Exod 3–4. Knowing the name of God would be for Moses both a comfort and a credential in his dealing with the Israelites, and for the Israelites in turn it would become a first means of designating true faith and worship.

3:13 Moses' protest *at this point* is appropriate for someone willing to respond favorably to a call of God, particularly in light of the culture he and his fellow Israelites lived in. Theirs was a polytheistic, pantheistic, and

---

[43] Fulfillment signs are of various types and durations, some more easily measurable or quantifiable than others (e.g., Exod 8:28: "I will make a distinction between my people and your people. This miraculous sign will occur tomorrow") and some broad and general (e.g., Ezek 33:33: "When all this comes true—and it surely will—then they will know that a prophet has been among them"). The grandest fulfillment sign of all is found in Jesus' teaching in Matt 24:3–31, a long, compound-complex fulfillment sign encouraging faith for a long duration of human history. Other fulfillment sign references in the OT include the following, in which it will be evident that one of Ezekiel's distinctives is the frequent employment of fulfillment sign language: Jer 44:27–29; 2 Kgs 19:29 [=Isa 37:30]; 1 Kgs 13:3; Jer 16:21; Ezek 6:14; 7:27; 12:16; 25:11; 25:17; 26:6; 28:23–24; 28:26; 29:9,16,21; 30:8,25; 32:15; 33:29; 34:30; 35:15; 36:38; 38:23; 39:28.

syncretistic world in which all people groups and nations—there are no known exceptions—believed that there were many gods, that all nature partook to some degree of divinity, and that all religions had at least some validity no matter how many or what sort of gods or goddesses those religions worshiped and regardless of the contradictions a modern person can immediately see between any two such religions.[44]

Moses therefore wondered *Which God am I speaking to?* since "the God of your fathers" (a summation of v. 6) might have different meanings to different Israelites. Having lived in the midst of pagan cultures all their lives, all Israelites were at risk for heterodox beliefs and/or the distortion of whatever correct beliefs they may theoretically have inherited.[45] Moreover, since the true God was known by various names and titles in the patriarchal era (e.g., *El Elyon,* "God Most High" in Gen 14:18–22; *Pahad Yitṣḥaq,* "Fear of Isaac" in Gen 31:42, 53; *El Shaddai,* "God Almighty" in Gen 17:1; 28:3; 35:11; 43:14; 48:3; *El Roʾi,* "The God Who Sees Me" in Gen 16:13; *El Bethel,* "God of Bethel" in Gen 31:13)[46] specificity was desirable. Perhaps most importantly, however, was the assumption in that culture that to call on a god—that is, to pray to and worship him—involved calling on his name, specifically naming him in prayer and worship (cf. 1 Kgs 18:24–26).

3:14 Here appears God's rerevelation of his actual proper name. *Yahweh* was already known by early generations (Gen 4:26) and used thereafter by the patriarchs (Noah, Gen 9:26; Abraham, Gen 12:8; Isaac, Gen 26:25; Jacob, Gen 28:16; Laban, Gen 30:27)—but it was not used, or not prominently used, by any of the children of Jacob, at least in terms of what is in the biblical record. Thus it appears that Moses, as he had constructed the narrative we now call the book of Genesis, intended that we realize that the generation after Jacob and all subsequent generations up to his own had lost at least a measure—and probably, over time, a greater and greater measure—of the knowledge of the true God and therefore, presumably, of the practice of praying to him and worshiping him regularly and properly, by his name. An analogy is found in the way the book of Esther is written: God is not mentioned in any manner in that book, not because he was not involved in the events of the story but as a stylistic device to provide for the reader the constant, ongoing, didactic impression that the Jews of Esther's day had

[44] For understanding the ancient myth-making religious mind and its threefold commitment to polytheism, pantheism, and syncretism, nothing surpasses H. Frankfort et al., *Before Philosophy: The Intellectual Adventure of Ancient Man* (New York: Penguin, 1967).

[45] A possible analogy to the likelihood of the Israelites' having fully correct doctrine before learning such at Mount Sinai would be the likelihood of the average European peasant's having fully correct doctrine in the ninth century AD.

[46] See also comments on Exod 6:3, "I appeared to Abraham, to Isaac and to Jacob as God Almighty, but by my name [Yahweh] the LORD I did not make myself known to them." Various place names (e.g., "The LORD Will Provide" in Gen 22:14; "God of Bethel" in Gen 35:7) are commonly but incorrectly described in popular literature as names of God even though they are clearly identified in the biblical text as names of localities, not the deity.

become largely paganized. Moses carefully avoided any mention of the name *Yahweh* until now for a presumably similar reason in this narrative.

Here the rerevelation of the name *Yahweh* is first given in its first-person form, *ʾahyeh,* later vocalized by the medieval Masoretes and also understood by the translators of the LXX as the simple imperfect tense of the verb "to be" (in the earliest Hb. *hwh,* later *hyh*), thus *ʾehyeh,* I am," rather than the early Canaanite causative (what later became the *hiphil* in Hb.), which means "I cause to be." The name should thus be understood as referring to Yahweh's being the creator and sustainer of all that exists and thus the Lord of both creation and history, all that is and all that is happening—a God active and present in historical affairs. The well-established vocalization of the third-person form of the divine name, *yahweh,* clearly a causative, strongly points to the original vocalization of the first-person form of the name here as *ʾahyeh,* also a causative. It is possible that the language of this verse is a summation of a lengthier explanation, which included both the noncausative *(qal)* sense of the root, that is, "I AM" (the "explanation" that became dominant in Jewish and Christian tradition, a tradition Jesus capitalized on in his "I AM" declarations in the Gospel of John) and the causative *(hiphil)* sense "I create/sustain." At any rate, the causative was obviously at least one of the intended understandings since the causative *Yahweh*—not the simple verb "to be" form, which would be *Yihw/yeh* ("I am/will be")—became the form thereafter employed, as in 13:15 and subsequently. By this reasoning, what the NIV necessarily translates as "I AM WHO I AM" probably was actually heard by Moses as "I CAUSE TO BE because I cause to be."[47]

---

[47] On the divine name and issues of vocalization, see W. F. Albright, "Contributions to Biblical Archaeology and Philology: 2. The Divine Name," *JBL* 43 (1924): 370–78; F. M. Cross Jr., "Yahweh and the God of the Patriarchs," *HTR* 55 (1962): 225–59; D. N. Freedman, "The Name of the God of Moses," *JBL* 79 (1960): 151–56; W. H. Brownlee, "The Ineffable Name of God," *BASOR* 226 (1977): 39–46. Brownlee argues particularly strongly for the concept of Yahweh as a creator God, even to the point of suggesting that *yahweh ṣĕbāʾôṭ* should be translated "He who creates [and therefore commands] the Divine Host" or "He who [uses the Divine Assembly of His creation, and thereby] brings things to pass." His preferred translation of *yahweh ʾĕlōhîm* would be "He creates gods" or "He creates the members of the Divine Assembly." Though these retranslations may go beyond the evidence by failing to see how early the name became frozen rather than merely the first element in a sentence name, the strength of Brownlee's position is its emphasis on the fact that the "ineffable name" was an affirmation of Israel's God as creator of all that exists, including the host of heaven/divine assembly. For various contrasting views see J. P. Hyatt, "Was Yahweh Originally a Creator Deity?" *JBL* 86 (1967): 369–77; D. J. McCarthy, "Exod 3:14: History, Philology and Theology," *CBQ* 40 (1978): 311–22; R. Abba, "The Divine Name Yahweh," *JBL* 80 (1961): 320–28; O. Eissfeldt, "Neue Zeugnisse für die Aussprache des Tetragramms als Jahwe," *ZAW* 53 (1935): 59–76; id., "'*ʾehyeh ʾašer ʾehyeh*ʾ and ' *ʾel ʿolam*' " in *Kleine Schriften,* Vol. 4 (Tübingen: Mohr, 1969), 193–98; S. D. Goitein, "YHWH the Passionate: The Monotheistic Meaning and Origin of the Name YHWH," *VT* 6 (1956): 1–9; E. C. B. MacLaurin, "YHWH: The Origin of the Tetragrammaton," *VT* 12 (1962): 439–63; S. Mowinckel, "The Name of the God of Moses," *HUCA* 32 (1961): 121–33; N. D. Osborn, "This Is My Name Forever: 'I Am' or 'Yahweh,'" *BT* 39 (1989): 410–15; C. Noce, "Il nome di Dio: Origine e l'interpretazione dell'Es. 3, 14," *Div* 21 (1977): 23–50; R. de Vaux, "La revelation du nom divin," in *Histoire ancienne d'Israël, Vol. 1: Des origine à l'installation en Canaan* (Paris: Gabalda, 1971), 48–75. On *ʾăšer* as "because/for as much as/in that/since" rather than "who," in the present context see any standard Hb. lexicon; and B. Albrektson, "On the Syntax of אהיה אשר אהיה in Exodus 3:14," in *Words and Meaning* (Cambridge: Cambridge University Press, 1968), 15–28; B. N. Wambacq, "*ʾehyeh ʾăšer ʾehyeh,*" *Bib* 59 (1978): 317–38.

By authorizing Moses to say, "I AM/CAUSE TO BE" has sent me to you," God made Moses his ambassadorial representative, that is, prophet, assigned to speak on his behalf to the Israelites. They would have recognized, if they perceived the situation correctly, that what he said was not of his own making but was the word of Yahweh, the God of their forefathers.

3:15 What had just been revealed in terms of the divine name was now reiterated with connection to the Patriarchs, so that the Israelites in Egypt would be able properly to draw the conclusion that Moses was not coming to them in the name of a new god but the true God of old, the God their own ancestors worshiped, and thus the God who should logically be their national deliverer. God also made clear that the third-person form of his name, *Yahweh,* was to be employed immediately (since no human could use it properly in the first-person form) and would identify him to his people for the generations thereafter.[48]

3. Summary of Commission and Prediction of Acceptance by Israelites (3:16–22)

16"Go, assemble the elders of Israel and say to them, 'The LORD, the God of your fathers—the God of Abraham, Isaac and Jacob—appeared to me and said: I have watched over you and have seen what has been done to you in Egypt. 17And I have promised to bring you up out of your misery in Egypt into the land of the Canaanites, Hittites, Amorites, Perizzites, Hivites and Jebusites—a land flowing with milk and honey.'

18"The elders of Israel will listen to you. Then you and the elders are to go to the king of Egypt and say to him, 'The LORD, the God of the Hebrews, has met with us. Let us take a three-day journey into the desert to offer sacrifices to the LORD our God.' 19But I know that the king of Egypt will not let you go unless a mighty hand compels him. 20So I will stretch out my hand and strike the Egyptians with all the wonders that I will perform among them. After that, he will let you go.

21"And I will make the Egyptians favorably disposed toward this people, so that when you leave you will not go empty-handed. 22Every woman is to ask her neighbor and any woman living in her house for articles of silver and gold and for clothing, which you will put on your sons and daughters. And so you will plunder the Egyptians."

As regards the theophany form that structures Exod 3–4, these verses bring to a conclusion the group of *hieroi logoi* that began in v. 14 with the revelation of the divine name. Here God's assurances include the revelation

[48] I.e., as long as the Old Covenant endures. Name changes in the Bible signify changes of status, and with the New Covenant comes the supremacy of the name Jesus, replacing Yahweh (cf. Phil 2:10; 1 John 3:23, and the frequent, obviously intentional emphasis on the efficacy of the "name of Jesus" in the book of Acts).

of the divine name to the leaders of Israel (v. 16), a prediction of the fulfillment of the homeland promise originally given to Abraham (v. 17), the Israelite strategy for requesting freedom (v. 18), prediction of the Egyptian resistance (v. 19), and the power of God on behalf of his people over the various powers of Egypt and its people (vv. 20–22).

3:16–17 God assigned Moses to report on his theophany to the Israelite[49] leaders so they could share with him the knowledge that the God of their ancestors[50] would help them out of their suffering as well as an understanding of what a wonderful future God had planned for them in the land he promised centuries prior to Abraham. Thus the promises to Abraham in Gen 12 and 15, of covenant relationship with him and his descendants and the gift of a permanent homeland of abundance, figure prominently here as they do throughout the Scriptures. We should not miss the significance of *pāqōd pāqadtî* ("I have been carefully watching over you"),[51] which is an instance of a biblical semantic idiom in which when God said that he had noticed/seen/known/remembered/watched over/paid attention to/understood or the like what he meant was not merely that he was aware but that *he was going to do something about it.* This is, for example, the implicit meaning of "I have seen" and "has reached me" in 3:9 and "[God] remembered" in 2:24 (cf. 6:5). The different wordings are all variations of an idiom that is essentially a synecdoche—a part for the whole—in which because of God's nature, his own overt mention of his being *aware* automatically implies additionally his determination to *act.* Thus God's announcement of awareness of a problem was at the same time an announcement that he would attend to that problem—because it could not be solved by human means, not even "by a mighty hand" (v. 19).

Verses 16–17 repeat much of the language used in vv. 7–9, and v. 17 in particular repeats almost verbatim the end of v. 8. This was not a failure on Moses' part to vary his vocabulary in telling his story (the sort of thing a modern writer might do) but part of the ancient, well-established narrative

---

[49] Based on the evidence of the SP, LXX, and Vg., the likely original wording here was בְּנֵי יִשְׂרָאֵל "[elders of] the Israelites" rather than merely יִשְׂרָאֵל "[elders of] Israel," reflecting Moses' original intention of describing the Israelites at this point as still a people group rather than as a unified nation, providing something of a transition from the literal "sons of Israel" in 1:1 to simply "Israel," the term that will dominate in Exodus hereafter.

[50] The strong evidence from the LXX and Vg. indicates that the original wording here in reference to the patriarchs was "the God of Abraham, the God of Isaac and the God of Jacob," i.e., the expected and well-attested pattern, reflecting the tendency in Hb. to avoid composing the genitive/nomen regens of a construct chain out of compound nouns. Cf. 2:24; 3:6.

[51] The sense of פָּקֹד פָּקַדְתִּי *(pāqōd pāqadtî)* is stronger than the NIV renders it. A better translation would be "I have been carefully watching over you," thus emphasizing that God had at all times been concerned and involved and had not decided just recently to become interested in and/or do something about his people's plight.

method known as "command-fulfillment style" in which the narrator tells what was commanded and then, using entirely or largely the same vocabulary, tells either how it was to be fulfilled or how it actually was fulfilled. Later in Exodus, Moses employed command-fulfillment style on a grand scale in describing the command to build the tabernacle and thereafter its implementation.[52]

3:18 As part of the continuing *hieroi logoi* of this section (3:14–22), God here assures Moses of success—not yet success at bringing the people out of Egypt but success at convincing the leaders[53] of his own people to believe in Yahweh and to join Moses and Aaron in confronting Pharaoh with God's demands. Even though the Israelites were in desperately hard conditions, it could not have been easy for them to rally to a former Egyptian criminal, whose help previously had been spurned (2:14), to accept on faith his report that Yahweh (to many of them a name from the distant past or a new name entirely) had appeared to him as their representative (thus the language "has met with *us*") and to demand from the great king the right to leave Egypt.

According to God's instruction, the elders were to identify themselves as Hebrews rather than Israelites, thus using terminology Pharaoh would understand.[54] They also were to speak in the name of Yahweh (because the demand was his, not theirs) in spite of the fact that this name might be completely new to Pharaoh, as it indeed proved to be (5:2). Moreover, they were to ask to leave Egypt.

This latter request is easily misunderstood because of its wording here and in several subsequent locations in the story. "Let us take a three-day journey into the wilderness [NIV desert]" seems like a modest enough request. It actually implied, however, full and permanent departure from Egypt, yet without seeming to do so, and thus requires some explanation.

First, we must appreciate the way people in many Eastern societies, including those of the ancient Near East, have preferred to use suggestive, gentle, restrained, and limited ways of making requests as opposed to simply coming right out and asking for what they wanted. There are few analogies in North American/Western culture, but the following might be illustrative: "Would you please hand me the remote?" is actually a way of saying, "I'm going to control what we watch, if you don't mind." Likewise,

---

[52] Thus much of Exod 35–40 repeats verbatim the wording of much of Exod 25–31, with verbs and adverbs changed to reflect that the latter chapters describe how the Israelites *did* what in the earlier chapters they were *told to do*.

[53] *zāqēn* actually implies nothing about a person's age but instead conveys almost precisely what the word "leader" does in English.

[54] Indeed, terminology Moses himself had used when he was still more an Egyptian princeling than a true Israelite (2:13).

"Dad, can I have the keys to the car?" usually means, "Dad, may I use the car for the next several hours, with no one else being able to use it?" Also, "How much money do you have on you?" is actually a way of indicating, "I'm planning to borrow some money from you." In particular, English-speaking cultures do this sort of thing with requests for time; "Have you got a second?" is not literal at all but really is a way of saying, "I'd like to take an indefinite amount of your time," and "He'll be with you in a moment" is not literally true but can mean "Keep waiting; he'll be free whenever he's free." In these expressions the amount of time literally stated is minuscule compared to the amount of time actually expected.

This is how "Let us take a three-day journey" functions in the speech Moses and the elders of Israel were to make to Pharaoh. The time requested is minuscule compared to the time actually expected. "Three-day journey" was an idiom in the ancient world for "a major trip with formal consequences."[55] Pharaoh would have heard it that way and would also have heard it as meaning "We want to leave Egypt for however long we choose." Moreover, the demand for the people to "offer sacrifices to the LORD our God" was yet another way of implying—without quite saying so in so many words—that the people would leave Egypt since, as develops later in the actual event (10:25–26) the Israelites expected to worship Yahweh far from Egypt at Mount Sinai, completely out of and free from any Egyptian oversight, having taken all their possessions with them. Pharaoh's continuing resistance to the demands of Yahweh must be read in this light. He knew from the start that the Israelites were not merely asking for three days off from work; they were asking to migrate from Egypt. Thus his resistance: what they were asking for was the very sort of thing that could create the situation his predecessor feared, namely, an Israelite movement of separate national identity, dissociating itself from Egypt and heading out into Asiatic reaches where the Israelites might join with anti-Egyptian forces and become effective enemies of Pharaoh and his people (see comments on 1:10).

3:19–20 These verses constitute a summation of the upcoming plague account. No human threat (the "mighty hand" here refers to human power, not to God's mighty "hand,"[56] which is introduced immediately thereafter

---

[55] See D. Stuart in connection with Jonah's "three day journey" to Nineveh (*Hosea-Jonah,* WBC [Waco: Word, 1987], 483–88), and D. J. Wiseman, "Jonah's Nineveh," *TynBul* 30 (1979): 38; cf. Gen 30:36 and the general idiom "three days," which occurs dozens of times in the OT and often means "a while" or "quite some time" (e.g., 2 Kgs 2:17); it can also be used in parallelism with "four" so that many events are described as taking 'three days" and then having resolution on the "fourth day," the exact numbers being nonliteral. See also S. Gevirtz, "Patterns in the Early Poetry of Israel" (Chicago: University of Chicago Press, 1963), 15–30.

[56] On "hand" as a common synecdoche for "power," cf., e.g., Exod 7:4: Deut 3:24; Josh 4:24; 1 Sam 7:13; Job 6:8.

by way of contrast)[57] can intimidate the most powerful potentate in the known world of that day—something Moses, with his experience of living near Egyptian power, could understand well. Here God showed his full knowledge of people's character and thinking processes by predicting that Pharaoh would remain stubborn, thus also anticipating the "hardness of heart" theme that recurs in the plague stories (4:21 and commonly in chaps. 7–14).

The solution for what otherwise would be an impasse was divine intervention against the Egyptians, those who were oppressing God's people, through his "miracles" (*niplĕʾôṭay,* "my miracles," which the NIV obscures slightly with its rendering "all *the* wonders"). He would not perform these miracles merely for display but as punishments, and thus he would strike/strike down (*hiphil* of *nkh*) the Egyptians with supernatural acts. "Stretch out my hand and strike" is effectively a hendiadys for "unleash my destruction" or "powerfully strike down." God did not yet reveal to Moses how many plagues and of what sort he would employ, but clearly there would be a variety, and they would be impressively destructive. Divinely unleashed plagues, not any human persuasion, would cause Pharaoh to let the people go.[58] The "you" at the end of v. 20 is plural because God here assigned Moses what he was to say to the leaders of the Israelites and what they were therefore to expect.

3:21–22 Moses is the only Old Testament writer to use the precise idiom *nāṭan+ ḥēn + bĕʿênê,* "make favorably disposed toward" (lit., "give favor in the sight of"). He employed this wording previously (Gen 39:21) to describe Joseph's being in the good graces of the chief jailer at his prison, that is, in narrating the reversing of an expected hostility. Hereafter he used it only twice more (Exod 11:3; 12:36), both times in contexts similar to the present one. God here predicted that he would reverse the attitude of the Egyptians, which had been so anti-Israelite that the Egyptian people in general could be expected voluntarily to help kill Israelite children (1:22), so great was their dread of the Israelites (1:12). Now God would engineer events so that Egyptians would willingly give valuables and clothing to Israelites. Clearly, the women in an ancient family, as often in modern cultures,

---

[57] The Hb. expression וְלֹא בְּ has been misunderstood by the NIV translators of this verse. It does not mean "unless" (which is typically rendered by כִּי אִם) in any of its twenty occurrences in the OT but "and not by" or "not even by." Cf. Zech 4:6 for a parade example of its meaning "and not by" or "not even by." Thus the verse should be translated, "But I know that the king of Egypt will not let you go, not even by a mighty hand (cf. Durham, *Exodus,* 35–36). God would, of course, supply another sort of "mighty hand"—his own, as predicted in 6:1, which *would* make Pharaoh do his bidding.

[58] Some commentators (e.g., Durham, *Exodus,* 40) have suggested that the *piel* of שִׁלַּח, used here, should mean "drive out" or "hurl out," but its normal meaning is simply "let go," as it has most often been translated and as the NIV correctly renders it.

were normally the custodians of clothing, jewelry, and similar family valuables. By introducing the term "plunder" *(nṣl, piel),* a term otherwise associated with gathering up the spoils after battle, God brought to the people's attention through Moses the concept that they would be involved in a holy war against the Egyptians.[59] But what a war! Instead of having to defeat their enemies in bloody combat to obtain the plunder, it would simply be theirs for the (peaceful) asking. Why? Because God would fight on behalf of his people, defeating and disheartening the enemy and rendering the enemy's women—who would not be combatants in any case—all too willing to give the Israelites anything that might help them on their journey.[60] Here again God's beneficent foreknowledge was operating: he knew that their sojourn in the wilderness would be very long and that a poor group hardly could expect to survive without supplies and financial reserves. So from their former persecutors he would supply those needs, further demonstrating his power and control over all people and circumstances.

Assumed in the language of these two verses are two further concepts: (1) In some cases Egyptians and Israelites lived together in the same household ("any woman living in her house"), not necessarily because Egyptians were tenants of Israelites but more often probably because Israelites were household workers in Egyptian homes (cf. Gen 39:2; Prov 31:15). (2) The "sons and daughters" would need clothing and other valuables because God knew that their generation would grow up in the wilderness; this is the first focus in the narrative on the second generation to whom Moses would eventually preach what we call Deuteronomy.

With this promise ends the section of *hieroi logoi* that began in 3:14. It was time for Moses to protest again.

4. Moses' Special Signs of His Believability (4:1–9)

[1]Moses answered, "What if they do not believe me or listen to me and say, 'The LORD did not appear to you'?"

[2]Then the LORD said to him, "What is that in your hand?"

"A staff," he replied.

[3]The LORD said, "Throw it on the ground."

---

[59] Cf. G. W. Coats, "Despoiling the Egyptians," *VT* 18 (1968): 450–57; Y. T. Radday, "The Spoils of Egypt," *ASTI* 12 (19983): 125–47.

[60] See P. Galpaz-Feller, "וְנָתַתִּי אֶת־הָעָם הַזֶּה בְּעֵינֵי מִצְרָיִם" ["And I Will Give This People Favor in the Sight of the Egyptians (Exod 3:22)"], *BMik* 47 (2002): 133–42. Galpaz-Feller takes the willingness of the Egyptians to give valuables to the Israelites as an instance of a practice in ancient Egyptian culture that provided for the receiving of silver, gold, and garments as tokens of the achievement of a new status in society. Galpaz-Feller assumes that the Exodus account was written later, rather than close to the time of the exodus, but nevertheless thinks it preserves with general accuracy the practice of giving and receiving such gifts as status change indicators.

Moses threw it on the ground and it became a snake, and he ran from it. 4Then the LORD said to him, "Reach out your hand and take it by the tail." So Moses reached out and took hold of the snake and it turned back into a staff in his hand. 5"This," said the LORD, "is so that they may believe that the LORD, the God of their fathers—the God of Abraham, the God of Isaac and the God of Jacob—has appeared to you."

6Then the LORD said, "Put your hand inside your cloak." So Moses put his hand into his cloak, and when he took it out, it was leprous, like snow.

7"Now put it back into your cloak," he said. So Moses put his hand back into his cloak, and when he took it out, it was restored, like the rest of his flesh.

8Then the LORD said, "If they do not believe you or pay attention to the first miraculous sign, they may believe the second. 9But if they do not believe these two signs or listen to you, take some water from the Nile and pour it on the dry ground. The water you take from the river will become blood on the ground."

In this section of the theophany narrative of chaps. 3 and 4, Moses' third formal protest of his call (v. 1) elicits God's third direct response of encouragement to him, this time in a series of three *hieroi logoi* (vv. 2–5,6–8,9) that grant him three miraculous divine signs at his disposal to convince others of his authority to represent God. Now that he had told the story of how Yahweh revealed his name to him, Moses employed the name throughout, with the more generic title "God" *(Elohim)* appearing only in v. 5 as necessary to identify Yahweh as "the God of . . ."[61]

The three miraculous signs all involved changing something into something else. In the case of the first two (staff to snake, normal hand to leprous hand) what got changed was immediately changed back into what it was at first, so that the change was only temporarily frightening. In the case of the third (water to blood), what got changed stayed changed—and the consequences were far more widespread and life threatening.

4:1 Moses' first two protests (3:11,13) were of the formal sort, properly expressing humility before such a great assignment, but here his words revealed the presence of uncertainty in his mind. God had already assured him in unmistakable language that the Israelite leaders would listen to him (3:18): now he wondered if he could be sure that this would happen—that they would believe[62] his claim that the Lord[63] had appeared to him and do what he said ("obey me";

[61] With the possible exception also of v. 1; see n. 50.

[62] Or "trust" him. Here the *hiphil* of אמן is used for the first of five times in this passage (vv. 1,5,8,9) with the nuance in each case referring not merely to the Israelites' believing something theoretically but of trusting themselves to Moses; thus the appositional employment also of שׁמע + קול + ב, "obey"), filling out the sense of "believe/trust."

[63] Here instead of "Yahweh" (the LORD) the LXX has ὁ θεός, "God," which may conceivably be original since Moses might have assumed in his protest that at first it would be difficult for the elders to refer to the brand-new name Yahweh.

NIV "listen to me").[64] This sort of timidity did not constitute the sort of disobedience that the outright plea for relief from the task that he would express in his fifth and final protest (4:13), but it clearly represented at least an initial concern for how easily others would accept God's promise at face value. Moses was not doubting God's promise, but he certainly was afraid the Israelites would doubt it. Fortunately, God was prepared to reassure him with three signs he could use to overcome the doubt he was bound to encounter.

4:2–5 Moses appeared to welcome this sign, by responding promptly and obediently to each command, even when he had to take hold of a snake he had just run from. The fact that his common wooden shepherd's staff could become a snake and vice versa would, in the absence of trickery, be a perfectly convincing demonstration of divine power in itself. Although it is not specifically so stated, the presumption here is that this sign could be done over and over again, for various groups of Israelites as they were encountered, because Moses would routinely have had his staff with him. There is, however, a greater import to the use of the staff than derives merely from its availability: this is the beginning of the development of the concept that Moses' staff symbolized Yahweh's power, a concept that culminates in Moses' holding up the staff at the Battle of Rephidim as a symbol of God's throne (see comments on 17:16). The ability to perform this miracle at will would function as a credential for Moses, giving his report of a theophanic commission by the God of the patriarchs credibility with the oppressed and wary Egyptian Israelites.

Snakes are frightening to most people when suddenly encountered, and it is fully understandable that Moses should run from one that sprung to life from his staff. Nothing in the text suggests that this snake was poisonous, and nothing links it with the Gen 3 account of Satan in the form of the serpent in the Garden of Eden.[65] Moses simply did what most people would do in the same circumstance—ran from a snake that suddenly appeared in front of him until he could get far enough away to see whether or not it was poisonous.[66] The purpose was

[64] A better translation of the verse than that found in the NIV might be: Moses answered: "What if they don't believe me and don't obey me? What if they say, 'The LORD did not appear to you'?" It should also be noted that the best LXX MSS reflect an original LXX reading here of *māh ʾōmar ʾĕlêhem*, "What shall I say to them," the three words also found at the end of 3:13. But it is difficult to decide whether these words were lost from the MT by haplography or whether they were added here from 3:13 in the LXX *Vorlage* through conflation.

[65] In Gen 3:1–14 the same term, נָחָשׁ *nāḥāš,* is used; but such is the case also in Gen 49:17, which is also not a referent of this story. Interestingly, נָחָשׁ is translated "snake" or "serpent" variably and inconsistently in almost all modern Eng. translations.

[66] F. Bodenheimer (*IDB* 4:289) suggests that in the ANE "probably, as is often the case, all serpents were thought to be poisonous." Moses may have known better in light of his extensive experience outdoors as a shepherd, but he was certainly sensible enough to treat a newly encountered snake as potentially dangerous. Moreover, there are no simple rules for distinguishing poisonous snakes from nonpoisonous snakes; one has to learn which is which in each locality. Additionally, nothing in the text tells us that Moses' staff turned into an easily identifiable (common) snake in the region; indeed, its appearance may have been somewhat unique and its potential for harm may have been entirely uncertain, thus making Moses' willingness to catch it by the tail truly an obedient act of faithful response to Yahweh's command.

not to scare him or anyone else; the purpose was to help introduce Yahweh as the true God to people who didn't know him yet but who desperately needed his salvation. Yahweh's control of something as frightening as a snake, including his ability to make it materialize from a piece of wood, was evidence of his powerful reality.[67]

4:6–8 Now comes a backup miracle. God's words in v. 8 ("if they do not believe . . . they may believe") indicate that he knew how hard it would be for the Israelite elders to trust Moses. For them to join Moses in making demands on Pharaoh, who was persecuting them so severely and before whose power they had previously always succumbed, would indeed take some convincing. This second miracle is generally similar to the first in that it involved the changing of something harmless into something harmful and then changing it back, and again, would be something Moses could do repeatedly (putting his hand inside his garment to his chest[68] and pulling it out again) to convince various groups of people at various times that God was with him.

The skin diseases lumped under the English translation "leprous" *(mĕṣōraʿat)* here would include not only actual leprosy but also a variety of serious infectious skin diseases that were likewise feared in biblical times.[69] Elaborate precautions were taken to avoid contact with persons so infected (Lev 13–14; Num 5:2; Deut 24:8–9; 2 Kgs 15:5; 2 Chr 26:2; Luke 17:12), and immediate cures,

---

[67] A variety of snakes are found in Egypt, where this sign was to be employed, and several of the varieties are poisonous. Thus it should not be surprising that a number of Egyptian incantations are devoted to the attempt to gain power over snakes and snakebites (e.g., "The Repulsing of the Dragon" and "The God and His Unknown Name of Power," both translated by J. A. Wilson, *ANET,* 11–14; and "Charms against Snakes," *ANET,* 326). For Moses to be able to demonstrate this power at will would have been a truly impressive sign for his fellow Hebrews to observe.

[68] The Hb. says, lit., "to your chest/bosom." No mention of Moses' garment is made in the story, but the easiest way for most translators to convey the sense is by the rendering, "Put your hand inside your cloak."

[69] See E. V. Hulse, "The Nature of Biblical 'Leprosy' and the Use of Alternative Medical Terms in Modern Translations of the Bible," *PEQ* 107 (1975): 87–105. Hulse argues that the best explanation for biblical leprosy probably would be modern-day psoriasis; but he contends that due to the difficulty of understanding the terminology and symptoms fully, the best actual translation for צרעת (Gk. λεπτα) might be "a repulsive, scaly skin disease." Among other things, Hulse suggests that biblical "leprosy" was "compared to snow, not because the skin was white ('white as snow' is a mistranslation) but because the most characteristic sign of the disease was the presence of scales which rubbed off the surface of the skin like flakes of snow. This interpretation is confirmed by the comparison of Miriam's condition to that of a macerated foetus." With regard to the diagnostic advice in Lev 13, Hulse states that the purpose of the descriptions there "is not to provide a description of צרעת but to guide the priest in . . . distinguishing צרעת from diseases which superficially might resemble it." For a medical overview of the subject, see R. Jackson, C. McMaster, eds., *Morphological Diagnosis of Skin Disease* (Lewiston, N.Y.: Manticore, 1999). Cf. also J. F. A. Sawyer, "A Note on the Etymology of *Ṣāraʿat*," *VT* 26 (1976): 241–45; and with regard to the LXX's λεπτα, C. Houtman, "A Note on the LXX Version of Exodus 4,6," *ZAW* 97 (1985): 253–54.

like that in this demonstration miracle, were never expected.[70] But could this miracle convince people who had not been convinced by the first—as the wording of v. 8 implies? The answer is yes. There was a strong association in ancient thinking of disease with the power of the gods, specifically their judgment/punishment power. A major function in ancient religion, as in modern, was that of offering sacrifices in worship to various gods and goddesses to appeal to their ability to withdraw disease from a supplicant. For Moses to say, in effect, "Look what Yahweh can do with disease!" was virtually to ask, "Can any god you've been worshiping heal like this?"

4:9 This third proof-of-commission sign is of a grander sort: it anticipate the first plague (7:14–24) in which water—mainly from the Nile in the case of the plague—is turned into blood,[71] hinting at the fact that God had in store some serious threats to unleash upon the Egyptians, which he would first demonstrate, through this sample, to his own people. The third sign, in other words, was not so much about Moses as it was about Egypt, and specifically the Nile. For God's servant Moses to demonstrate through this simple act God's power over the Nile would be to demonstrate God's power generally over Egypt and the Egyptians *a fortiori*.

Excursus: The Nile as a God

The primary physical source of all life in Egypt is the Nile, and the vast majority of the population has always lived near it, making Egypt the most densely populated country in the modern world and almost certainly also in the ancient world, if one excludes the vast barren regions from the density calculation. Comparatively little water is available in Egypt aside from the deep aquifers (not penetrable in ancient times) except through the Nile, its branches and canals, or shore wells that tap its seepage. Since at all times ancient Egypt, including the Egypt of Moses' day, was pantheistic, it is hardly surprising that at all times the Nile was worshiped as a great god.

In early Egyptian the name of the Nile, vocalized Hapi, is exactly the same as the name of the Nile-god, the two being indistinguishable in the pantheistic thinking of that era. Hapi was represented in Egyptian iconography as a male-female deity, a hermaphrodite, capable thus of both fertilizing that land (the male aspect) and also nourishing it (the female aspect).[72] For most of its history, Egypt

[70] Durham (*Exodus,* 45) suggests that because Miriam's "leprosy" (Num 12) was clearly a token of divine judgment, that this might generally have been the way such diseases were viewed in the ancient world (citing Hulse), thus inferring that this sign might have carried with it a sort of implicit overtone that to refuse to believe and continue to resist would be met by divine judgment.

[71] On the significance of water-blood for virtually outlining the plagues in general and the ironic symbolism of blood, otherwise life-giving but in the case of this sign a deadly substitute for water, see comments on 7:17ff.

[72] A picture of the statue of Hapi constitutes the first plate in R. Patrick, ed., *All Color Book of Egyptian Mythology* (London: Octopus, 1972). On this and some of the other matters summarized here, see W. S. LaSor, "Nile," *ISBE* 3.536–37.

was the scene of annual religious festivities marking the onset of the yearly flooding of the Nile. Some religious texts praise the Nile for its provision of life for the land and its people. One, the famous *Hymn to Aton,* praises the Nile as the water source par excellence, the source of rain from heaven for all lands as well as the underground source of water for all Egypt:

Thou makest a Nile in the underworld,
Thou bringest it forth as thou desirest
To maintain the people (of Egypt) . . .

All distant foreign countries, thou makest their life (also),
For thou hast set a Nile in heaven,
That it may descend for them and make waves upon the mountains,
Like the great green sea,
To water the fields in their towns.
How effective they are, thy plans, O Lord of eternity!
The Nile in heaven, it is for the foreign peoples
And for the beasts of every desert, that go upon (their) feet;
(While the true) Nile comes from the underworld for Egypt.[73]

Hapi, the Nile-god, had a temple (*Per-Hapi,* "House of Hapi") near what is now known as Old Cairo, and no less a potentate than Pharaoh Ramses III recorded offering gifts to him-her there, among many other places where he-she was worshiped. The expected response of Hapi was, of course, to flood the Nile basin once again, bringing the annual abundance for the king and people.

Osiris is also identified as the god of the Nile since in Egyptian mythology Hapi apparently was his child, and there also is evidence that both the crocodile-god Subek and the dead king Unis (appearing as Subek after his death) were considered the gods responsible for the annual flooding. For these various gods to be identified as "god of the Nile" is to modern thinking evidence of a somewhat contradictory theology, but such is typical of the ancient Egyptian mythopoeic religion, which was not concerned for what modern people would regard as the need for truth to be consistent.[74]

When Moses later struck the Nile with his staff and demonstrated God's power over it (7:20), he was showing God's superiority to and predicting God's victory over the Nile-god and as well, by extension, "all the gods of Egypt" (12:12). Later, when the prophets Ezekiel and Zechariah described God's sovereignty over Egypt, they did so in part by a prediction of the drying up of the Nile (Ezek 29:9; 30:12; Zech 10:11), which would, of course, completely desolate Egypt.

---

[73] Wilson, *ANET,* 369–71. It is important to appreciate that the Egyptians did not believe their own country was "rainless," as some have argued, but rather that all rain in other lands was simply the Nile flowing from the sky for those lands, whereas in Egypt it flowed from the earth. In other words, they saw the Nile as the source of all fresh water. Cf. Frankfort, *Before Philosophy* , 46–47.

[74] See H. Frankfort, *Ancient Egyptian Religion* (New York: Harper & Row, 1961), 1–29; note his explanation that "the Egyptian interpreted the non-human as superhuman" (p. 13).

5. Moses' Ritual and Actual Protests and Divine Reassurance (4:10–18)

[10]Moses said to the LORD, "O Lord, I have never been eloquent, neither in the past nor since you have spoken to your servant. I am slow of speech and tongue."

[11]The LORD said to him, "Who gave man his mouth? Who makes him deaf or mute? Who gives him sight or makes him blind? Is it not I, the LORD? [12]Now go; I will help you speak and will teach you what to say."

[13]But Moses said, "O Lord, please send someone else to do it."

[14]Then the LORD's anger burned against Moses and he said, "What about your brother, Aaron the Levite? I know he can speak well. He is already on his way to meet you, and his heart will be glad when he sees you. [15]You shall speak to him and put words in his mouth; I will help both of you speak and will teach you what to do. [16]He will speak to the people for you, and it will be as if he were your mouth and as if you were God to him. [17]But take this staff in your hand so you can perform miraculous signs with it."

[18]Then Moses went back to Jethro his father-in-law and said to him, "Let me go back to my own people in Egypt to see if any of them are still alive."

Jethro said, "Go, and I wish you well."

This section of the overall theophany pattern of chaps. 3 and 4 contains two of Moses' protests (vv. 10 and 13 respectively) as well as, in response to each, a brief *hieros logos* in vv. 11–12 and a somewhat longer group of *hieroi logoi* in 4:4–17. His first protest (4:10) is still of the "ritual" sort, mannerly and emphasizing his need for divine help. The second (4:13), however, represents a blatant attempt to be excused from the assignment itself and draws God's immediate anger (4:14–17, and later is probably part of the background for God's continuing anger relative to another instance of Moses' resistance to carrying out God's instructions [4:24–26]). The concluding description in the third person (4:18) will mark the end of the current two-chapter literary form.

4:10 Moses' statement in this verse has generated much misunderstanding on the part of those who have not recognized it as a ritual protest, and it has thus often been taken literally, as if Moses actually either had a speech defect or was incompetent as a public speaker or had forgotten his Egyptian. In fact, Moses did a huge amount of speaking in the remainder of the Pentateuchal narrative and law, yet nowhere did he reveal the slightest speech hesitancy or inability to make himself understood. Why, then, did he make the claim to be "slow of speech and tongue"?[75] The answer lies not in physiology but in culture—in the

---

[75] Lit., "I have a heavy mouth and a heavy tongue." Cf. D. Gewalt, "Der Sprachfehler Moses," *DBAT* 27 (1991): 8–16; J. Tigay, "'Heavy of Mouth' and 'Heavy of Tongue': On Moses' Speech Difficulty," *BASOR* 231 (1978): 57–67. Tigay's survey of the possible meanings of Moses' ritual protest rules out the idea that he was trying to claim that he had forgotten his Hebrew and affirms that "slow of speech and tongue" can certainly mean having a speech defect—but it does not literally need to mean that. Moses did not start his ritual protests with the claim to have a speech problem, which, if real, might have been a genuine cause (at least in his mind) for disqualification from the assignment to which he was being called. It was in fact the fourth excuse/objection (after 3:11,13; 4:1) he raised, showing that he was once again "reaching" for yet another way to "object" (again, we contend, formally only, for purposes of modesty) to the call.

style of ancient Near Eastern "exaggerated humility," often employed in situations where one is appealing for help or mercy from someone else or showing one's mannerly self-deprecation at being given a great assignment. The following are among the parade examples of this style in the Bible:

Gen 18:26: I have been so bold as to speak to the Lord, though I am nothing but dust and ashes. (Abraham)

Exod 4:10: I have never been eloquent . . . I am slow of speech and tongue. (Moses)

1 Sam 9:21: Saul answered, "But am I not a Benjamite, from the smallest tribe of Israel, and is not my clan the least of all the clans of the tribe of Benjamin? Why do you say such a thing to me?"

1 Sam 18:23: David said, "Do you think it is a small matter to become the king's son-in-law? I'm only a poor man and little known."

1 Sam 24:14: "Against whom has the king of Israel come out? Whom are you pursuing? A dead dog? A flea?

1 Sam 26:20: Now do not let my blood fall to the ground far from the presence of the LORD. The king of Israel has come out to look for a flea—as one hunts a partridge in the mountains."

2 Sam 9:8: Mephibosheth bowed down and said, "What is your servant, that you should notice a dead dog like me?"

2 Kgs 8:13: Hazael said, "How could your servant, a mere dog, accomplish such a feat?"

1 Kgs 3:7: You have made your servant king . . . I am only a little child and do not know how to carry out my duties. (Solomon)

Isa 6:5: Woe is me! . . . For I am a man of unclean lips. (Isaiah)

Isa 56:3: And let not any [official] complain, "I am only a dry tree."

Jer 1:6: Ah, Sovereign LORD, . . . I do not know how to speak; I am only a child. (Jeremiah)

1 Cor 2:3: I came to you in weakness and fear, and with much trembling. (Paul)

Eph 3:8: Although I am less than the least of all God's people, this grace was given me. (Paul)

1 Tim 1:15: Christ Jesus came into the world to save sinners—of whom I am the worst. (Paul)

Heb 13:22: Brothers, I urge you to bear with my word of exhortation, for I have written you only a short letter.

Of particular interest for their close parallels with Exod 4:10 are Saul's claim to be obscure in origin when he was in fact from a prominent family (1 Sam 9:21); David's claim to be a nobody when in fact he was already a popular war hero (1 Sam 18:23); Hazael's claim to be no better than a dog when he was in fact already a major leader in Syria (2 Kgs 8:13); Solomon's assertion that he was only a child when in fact he probably was at least thirty years old at the time he became king (1 Kgs 3:7); and Paul's claim to be the lowest of the low among God's people (Eph 3:8; 1 Tim 1:15) when in fact he was an influential apostle. The closest parallel of all is that of Jeremiah's protest (Jer 1:6), in which he claimed to be unable to talk, something he then did quite eloquently for the next forty-one years.

All of these parallels point to the simple fact that Moses was not speaking literally here but figuratively, responding to a great assignment[76] with the proper sort of exaggerated humility and self-effacement expected and valued in his culture. There is no evidence anywhere in the Bible that he had any lack of skill in speech, public or private—and overwhelming evidence to the contrary.

4:11–12 This *hieros logos* might seem to be tailored to the ritual protest Moses had just made, in that God referred to his control over human ability to speak. However, the fact that God also cited his control over human ability to hear and to see (v. 11)—issues not in dispute since Moses did not claim to have any hearing or vision problem—shows that it is more a general encouragement for Moses, his protest having been figurative rather than literal. The promise of help in knowing what to say and how to say it (v. 12) is relevant to any prophetic call since what prophets do above all things is *say* what God teaches them to say.[77] The NIV's "I will help you speak" (*ʾānōkî ʾehyeh ʿim pîkā,* v. 12) means literally "I will be with your mouth" and is exactly what God promised to both Moses and Aaron in v. 15. In light of the absence of any concern about Aaron's ability to speak publicly, this is simply further evidence that Moses likewise had no speech defect.[78] As the giver of all gifts, God knows people's gifts and calls them to his service—and supports them in it—accordingly.

---

[76] Cf. J. Cohen, "The Call of Moses" *JBQ* 20 (1991–1992): 256–61; H. Schmid, "Die Berufung des Mose," in *Mose: Uberlieferung und Geschichte*, BZAW 110 (Berlin: Töpelmann, 1966), 27–38, and esp. Gewalt, "Der 'Sprachfehler' des Mose," 8–16. Gewalt shows how the interpretation that Moses had a speech defect developed throughout history even though nothing about a speech defect is indicated in the text.

[77] In several other prominent prophetic call narratives, the prophet is also given explicit assurance of God's control over speech and of help for the prophet's speaking per se; e.g., "I will make your tongue stick to the roof of your mouth so that you will be silent and unable to rebuke them, though they are a rebellious house. But when I speak to you, I will open your mouth and you shall say to them, 'This is what the Sovereign LORD says.' Whoever will listen let him listen" (Ezek 3:26–27); "Then the LORD reached out his hand and touched my mouth and said to me, 'Now, I have put my words in your mouth'" (Jer 1:9).

[78] As Childs (*Exodus*, 70) points out, the verb "to speak" *(dbr)* and the noun "mouth" *(peh)* each occur seven times in the immediate context as a necessary function of the subject matter rather than as a contrived pattern.

4:13 The NIV idiomatically renders Moses' request here, which is literally, "[He said][79] 'Please, my lord, send by you will send,' "[80] a somewhat elliptical expression unattested elsewhere in the Bible and one apparently designed to mean, "I don't want to do it" but worded as neutrally and non-offensively as possible. The same sort of sense might be implied in English by: "With all due respect, sir, you must know someone who's available to send."

This final protest of Moses represents a dramatic departure from all four of his previous protests (3:11,13; 4:1,10), which had the style of ritual, non-literal demurrers. If Moses were to continue that pattern he would here say something else about his unworthiness and/or the magnitude of the challenge. He did not. Instead, he actually asked that God send someone else to do the job—in other words, he tried to refuse to accept the call. Among the various call narratives in the Bible[81] there is only one other in which a prophet attempted to refuse to accept a call from God: that of Jonah. In Jonah's case the pattern is similar to that found here in Exod 4:

God calls prophet to preach in a foreign land	Exod 3:4–10	Jonah 1:1–2
Prophet tries to refuse	Exod 4:13	Jonah 1:3
Divine death penalty nearly imposed during travels	Exod 4:24	Jonah 1:4–15
Prophet learns his lesson	Exod 4:25	Jonah 2:1–10 [also 1:12]
God spares him	Exod 4:26	Jonah 1:17
God renews the call	Exod 4:27–28	Jonah 3:1
Prophet finally cooperates with calling	Exod 4:29–30 et passim	Jonah 3:3–4
Call comes to successful fruition	Exod 4:31 et passim	Jonah 3:5–10

Jonah is a much smaller book than Exodus, and it is therefore understandable that the pattern would be rather more compactly presented in Jonah

[79] The NIV supplies "Moses" here for clarity.

[80] בִּי אֲדֹנָי שְׁלַח־נָא בְּיַד־תִּשְׁלָח.

[81] Cf. N. Habel, "The Form and the Significance of the Call Narratives," *ZAW* 77 (1965): 297–323.

than in Exodus, where various more grand issues are also in play. It need not be assumed that the story of Jonah is modeled on that of Moses; rather, each story proceeds logically from the facts: if God is determined to use a prophet he will indeed do so, and woe to the prophet who tries to avoid his calling.[82]

4:14–17 The NIV has made translation assumptions in v. 14 that are only one set of possibilities for accurately representing the sense of the original. In fact, the first part of the verse probably is better translated: "Even though[83] the LORD was angry with Moses, he said, 'Is not Aaron your Levite brother?[84] I know . . .'" In other words, the verse appears to assert that Moses' protest in v. 13 was not acceptable to God but rather aroused his anger, and yet the verse does not necessarily go on to assert that the provision of Aaron his "Levite brother" was the result of anger but rather that it was the result of grace.

This is, again, not unlike the situation of Jonah, whose refusal to obey God's command to preach repentance to Nineveh aroused God's anger but who nevertheless experienced God's grace in the form of the large fish that unexpectedly appeared to keep him from drowning. Here Moses' brother Aaron is provided unexpectedly as a helper to Moses (so Zipporah, as well, in another sense helped Moses continue his ministry [4:24–26]). Moses presumably had no way of knowing before this that Aaron had set out to find him, but the idea that Aaron would do at least some of the speaking once they were in Egypt, so that the hostility generated by that speaking would not fall exclusively on Moses, must have been welcome encouragement indeed. In other words, Aaron was provided as a cospeaker for Moses, not because Moses could not speak well but because of the encouragement

---

[82] Cf., e.g., "But if I say, 'I will not mention him or speak any more in his name,' / his word is in my heart like a fire, a fire shut up in my bones. / I am weary of holding it in; indeed, I cannot" (Jer 20:9); "But I am full of the wrath of the LORD, and I cannot hold it in" (Jer 6:11); "I am compelled to preach. Woe to me if I do not preach the gospel" (1 Cor 9:16); "I must preach the good news of the kingdom of God to the other towns also, because that is why I was sent" (Luke 4:43).

[83] On simple prostactic juxtaposition of clauses as a means of representing the concessive ("even though, although, even if"), cf., e.g., וַיַּכֵּר יוֹסֵף אֶת־אֶחָיו וְהֵם לֹא הִכִּרֻהוּ ("Although Joseph recognized his brothers, they did not recognize him," Gen 42:8); וָאֲדַבֵּר אֲלֵיכֶם וְלֹא שְׁמַעְתֶּם ("So I told you, but you would not listen," Deut 1:43); וּבְנֵי יִשְׂרָאֵל נִשְׁבְּעוּ לָהֶם וַיְבַקֵּשׁ שָׁאוּל לְהַכֹּתָם ("Although the people of Israel had sworn to spare them, Saul had tried to wipe them out," 2 Sam 21:2 NRSV).

[84] The NIV "What about your brother, Aaron the Levite?" assumes from the context that the question must be equivalent to "Have you thought about your brother, Aaron the Levite?" But this fails to recognize that the question in the Hb. has all the earmarks of a simple "polar" interrogative (see *IBHS* §40.3), that Moses did not use הלא elsewhere in the Pentateuch to mean "what about" or the like, and, moreover, that the Hb. word order does not allow for the translation "Aaron the Levite." Indeed, the Hb. word order, הֲלֹא אַהֲרֹן אָחִיךָ הַלֵּוִי, separates "Aaron" from "the Levite" so that unless an audacious instance of hypallage be alleged, the meaning must be "Is not Aaron your Levite brother?"

Aaron would bring to Moses in the daunting task of facing the hostility of the pharaoh of Egypt.[85]

Verse 15 makes clear that both Moses and Aaron would speak for God, and this was in fact the case. Moses eventually did the vast majority of the speaking, with virtually no mention made of Aaron's public speaking beyond the early chapters of Exodus—but at first Aaron was either speaking for him or with him (4:30; 5:1). Presumably, as Moses' courage and faith increased, the need for Aaron's close collegial support and/or public representation of his brother lessened. Verses 15 and 16 together also suggest that, from the first, Moses was the true prophet (the one into whose mind God placed his words with the intent that they be passed on to others) and that Aaron was Moses' spokesperson rather than a direct recipient of God's revelation. Thus God was the revealer; Moses, the prophet; and Aaron, the public repeater, an arrangement not unlike that in the modern church involving God, the Scriptures as the location of his word, and the preacher as the public repeater. Although at first Aaron primarily would have repeated verbatim what God had said to Moses and would not have exposited upon it as does the modern preacher, the role of priest certainly involved teaching in the sacred assembly, as a number of subsequent texts demonstrate.[86]

Verse 17 highlights the importance of Moses' staff, an object that plays a significant role in the exodus story. The staff is the ultimate immediate reassurance, in this final set of *hieroi logoi*, of God's presence with Moses as he enters upon the challenging task to which he has been called.

Excursus: Moses' Staff

In ancient Palestinian-Israelite society, one's staff was an essential personal possession, a means of protection and identification and even a symbol of one's power.[87] Various Hebrew terms are translated "staff." It is possible to use them rather interchangeably here in light of their semantic overlap and render them all

---

[85] Cf. Jesus' sending the disciples and apostles out two-by-two rather than all alone (Mark 6:7; Luke 10:1).

[86] E.g., 2 Kgs 17:27 NRSV: "Then the king of Assyria commanded, "Send there one of the priests whom you carried away from there; let him go and live there, and teach them the law of the god of the land"; 2 Chr 15:3 NRSV: "For a long time Israel was without the true God, and without a teaching priest, and without law; Ezek 22:26 NRSV: "Its priests have done violence to my teaching and have profaned my holy things; they have made no distinction between the holy and the common, neither have they taught the difference between the unclean and the clean, and they have disregarded my sabbaths, so that I am profaned among them"; Mic 3:11 NRSV: "Its rulers give judgment for a bribe, its priests teach for a price."

[87] J. Currid derives the Hb. word for "staff" used most often in the present context (מַטֶּה) from the Egyptian word for staff *(mdw)* and supports his etymological contention by showing that both words have essentially the same range of meaning: shepherd's staff, walking stick, and symbolic indication of power (either magical power or the power of a divinity; "The Rod of Moses," *BurH* 33 [1997]: 107–14).

with the English word "staff" just as "rod," "staff," "big stick," and "walking stick" can all be used largely interchangeably in English. From the point of view of identifying oneself, a staff was in certain ways the equivalent in ancient culture of what a passport, wallet, or driver's license would be today.[88] From the point of view of protection, it was the ancient equivalent of what a sidearm would be today. From the point of view of its function as a symbol of one's personal power, a modern analogy might be one's photo ID pass or even, in some situations, one's parking pass. It is likely that women often carried staffs; however, as it happens, the only references to staffs in the Bible involve men.

A staff was so basic and prized a possession that it might be the mentioned metaphorically as the only thing a person possessed, or the first thing in a short list of very basic possessions, as reflected in Gen 32:10 ("I had only my staff when I crossed this Jordan, but now I have become two groups) or Luke 9:3 ("Take nothing for the journey—no staff, no bag, no bread, no money").

In many cases a person's staff apparently was carefully carved with various markings and/or words to make it uniquely identifiable both by the owner and by others who might be familiar with the owner.[89] An example of this practice is reflected in Gen 38:18 ("He said, 'What pledge should I give you?' 'Your seal and its cord, and the staff in your hand,' she answered"; cf. Num 17:2, 9; 2 Kgs 4:29).

The habit of carrying a staff may have originated in connection with its usefulness as both a weapon and a tool, that is, as a weapon against wild animals and human foes and as a tool for keeping animals under one's control or manipulating objects:

> Num 22:27: When the donkey saw the angel of the LORD, she lay down under Balaam, and he was angry and beat her with his staff.
>
> 1 Sam 14:27: But Jonathan . . . reached out the end of the staff that was in his hand and dipped it into the honeycomb. He raised his hand to his mouth.
>
> 1 Sam 17:40: Then [David] took his staff in his hand . . . and, with his sling in his hand, approached the Philistine.
>
> Mark 15:19: Again and again they struck him on the head with a staff and spit on him.
>
> Ps 23:4: Even though I walk through the valley of the shadow of death, / I will fear no evil, for you are with me; / your rod and your staff, they comfort me.

---

[88] Thus misuse of a staff was a serious offense, akin to but potentially worse than forgery, depending on the circumstance, as Moses learned when he used God's staff without authorization in Num 20:1–13 (see J. Kok, *The Sin of Moses and the Staff of God: A Narrative Approach* [Assen: Van Gorcum, 1997]).

[89] In this regard a staff could function somewhat in the manner that a seal did, under certain conditions (cf. Exod 28:11,21; 1 Kgs 21:8; Neh 9:38; L. G. Herr, "Seal," *ISBE* 4.369–75.

Staffs also could be used as crutches. Although the modern style of crutch, with a padded support under the arm and a place to grip with the hand, was unknown in Bible times, one's staff provided a workable substitute, as seen in Gen 47:31 ("Israel worshiped as he leaned on the top of his staff") and Exod 21:19 ("the one who struck the blow will not be held responsible if the other gets up and walks around outside with his staff"; cf. Isa 36:6; Ezek 29:6).

For those with a degree of societal power, a staff was an accoutrement that shared by association, and thus represented, their authority:

> Gen 49:10: The scepter will not depart from Judah, nor the ruler's staff from between his feet, until he comes to whom it belongs and the obedience of the nations is his.
>
> Num 17:2–3,7,10: Speak to the Israelites and get twelve staffs from them, one from the leader of each of their ancestral tribes. Write the name of each man on his staff. On the staff of Levi write Aaron's name, for there must be one staff for the head of each ancestral tribe . . . Moses placed the staffs before the LORD in the Tent of the Testimony . . . The LORD said to Moses, "Put back Aaron's staff in front of the Testimony, to be kept as a sign to the rebellious."
>
> Num 21:18: Nobles with scepters and staffs . . .
>
> Judg 5:14: From Makir captains came down, from Zebulun those who bear a commander's staff.
>
> Matt 27:29: And then twisted together a crown of thorns and set it on his head. They put a staff in his right hand and knelt in front of him.
>
> Jer 48:17: How broken is the mighty scepter, how broken the glorious staff!

In Zech 11 the prophet exploits two common uses of the staff—the practice of using a staff to control sheep and the function of a staff to signal authority—to symbolize God's judgment for covenant-breaking (Zech 11:7–14: "Then I took two staffs and called one Favor and the other Union, and I pastured the flock. . . . I took my staff called Favor and broke it, revoking the covenant I had made with all the nations. . . . Then I broke my second staff called Union, breaking the brotherhood between Judah and Israel").

Although Moses' staff had potentially all the uses categorized above, it had yet another that elevated its importance far beyond that of any other staff. By divine designation it became not merely Moses' staff but God's. In Exod 4 this fact becomes progressively evident, beginning with the first mention of the staff as something to which God called special attention (Exod 4:2, "Then the LORD said to him, 'What is that in your hand?' ") and continuing through the account of how God invested the staff with supernatural power (beginning with 4:4; but esp. 4:17, "But take this staff in your hand so you can perform miraculous signs with it") to the climactic description of the staff as "the staff of God" [worded more naturally, "God's staff"] in 4:20.

At God's command the staff functioned integrally in Moses' first miracle-making encounter with Pharaoh (7:9ff.; note especially the ambiguity of Moses' language when he said in 7:17, "This is what the LORD says: By this you will know that I am the LORD: With the staff that is in my hand I will strike the water of the Nile, and it will be changed into blood"—almost as if Moses stood for God not merely in speech but also in body). The staff figures prominently in the initiation of various plagues (9:23; 10:13), the miracle at the Red Sea (14:16), and the miraculous provision of water in the wilderness near Sinai (17:5). Moses on one other occasion called his staff "God's staff" [NIV "the staff of God"], that is, in 17:9 ("Moses said to Joshua, 'Choose some of our men and go out to fight the Amalekites. Tomorrow I will stand on top of the hill with the staff of God in my hands'"). Since in the context Moses himself was speaking to Joshua of the staff as "God's staff" rather than "my staff," it would seem possible that this term *(maṭṭēh hāʾĕlōhîm)* may have become the term the leaders themselves used to refer to the staff.

Moses was hardly the only Israelite leader, however, who carried a staff. Indeed, we must inquire about the significance of "Aaron's staff," which is also mentioned in the Pentateuchal narrative on a number of occasions, particularly Exod 7–8 and Num 20. A careful examination of all references to this staff indicates that it too functioned as "God's staff," that both Aaron and Moses used it at various times, and that when Moses used it the staff could be called "his [Moses'] staff," suggesting that Moses and Aaron functioned so closely as a team that their roles vis-à-vis the staff are not distinct enough to require much differentiation in the narrative. Thus Aaron's staff could become a snake in the same manner that Moses' staff could (Exod 7:8–13) and was employed in the initiation of the first plague (7:14–24, mentioned four times; note that "the staff that was changed into a snake" in v. 15 is technically ambiguous as to ownership; it could refer to the immediately preceding story, involving Aaron's staff, or to the story of chap. 4, involving Moses' staff). Not all the other plague stories mention the use of a staff, but among those that do, Aaron's staff was used to initiate plagues two (8:5) and three (8:16–17), whereas Moses' was used in plagues seven (9:23) and eight (10:13).

The account in Num 20:1–13 of water from the rock at Meribah mentions Moses' taking "the staff from the LORD's presence" (v. 9), also simply called "his [Moses'] staff" (20:11), and using it in the miraculous production of water. This staff is surely the same one that had been put specially in the Lord's presence, that is, Aaron's staff[90] as featured in the story of Num 17. Aaron's staff was used to demonstrate God's favor on both the house of Levi and Aaron's leadership, and it was put "in front of the Testimony to be kept as a sign" (Num 17:10). The fact that it is called "his [Moses'] staff" three chapters later (Num 20:11) seems to show the lack of concern to differentiate the staffs of Moses and Aaron, which may well stem from the fact that either staff was ultimately God's so that

[90] Thus the reference in Heb 9:4, "Which had the golden altar of incense and the gold-covered ark of the covenant. This ark contained the gold jar of manna, Aaron's staff that had budded, and the stone tablets of the covenant."

the human owner or user matters little. Both Isaiah and Micah refer to Moses' staff, in its role as God's staff, in their prophecies (Isa 10:26: "The LORD Almighty will lash them with a whip, as when he struck down Midian at the rock of Oreb; and he will raise his staff over the waters, as he did in Egypt"; Mic 7:14: "Shepherd your people with your staff, the flock of your inheritance, which lives by itself in a forest, in fertile pasturelands. Let them feed in Bashan and Gilead as in days long ago").

A noteworthy parallel to the miracle-working staff of Moses/Aaron is that of the angel's staff in Judg 6:21 ("With the tip of the staff that was in his hand, the angel of the LORD touched the meat and the unleavened bread. Fire flared from the rock, consuming the meat and the bread"). Thus is portrayed for the reader the fact that even an angel, when he assumed human form, carried a staff, as virtually all male humans did, and could use it much as God's prophets did. Much later, Elisha employed his staff in a similarly miraculous way to effect a healing, even at a distance (2 Kgs 4:29, "Elisha said to Gehazi, 'Tuck your cloak into your belt, take my staff in your hand and run. . . . Lay my staff on the boy's face'"). This use of a staff as a healing token finds a parallel in some Akkadian incantation texts, where the "staff" is sometimes mentioned as an instrument by which are exorcised *asakku* demons, who cause fevers and other diseases.[91]

Did Moses' staff have power in itself? Not at all. Its power, and every aspect of its effectiveness, came from God's use of the staff in Moses' (or Aaron's) hand as a symbol of the divine authority, supremacy, and presence. The miraculous staff was designated to convince Moses and Aaron, then the Israelite leadership, and in turn Pharaoh, and finally the nation of Israel of God's sovereign control in his plan to liberate his people from their bondage. It becomes progressively clear that the staff was not really Moses' or Aaron's (or anyone else's) but God's.

4:18 With this verse the theophany structure becomes complete via the expected concluding third-person description. Here Moses indicated his initial assent to the theophanic call of God by formally indicating to Jethro that he would be leaving for Egypt, and he received his first human approbation in the form of Jethro's willingness to see him depart. It may seem from the wording that Moses, a grown man, required permission from his father-in-law for the journey. This is only partially true. What he really sought was blessing—a happy departure rather than a forced one. As an employee of Jethro (3:1) he would need release from his job, something he would prefer to accomplish amicably. As a son-in-law he would desire the blessing of his wife's father, both because he was taking Zipporah with him (4:20) and because he owed decades of hospitality to this Midianite priest. Otherwise, Moses' language was more a matter of politely informing Jethro of his intentions ("let me go back to my own people in Egypt") and providing a socially appropriate reason ("to see if any of them are still alive"). It should

---

[91] J. H. Walton, V. H. Matthews, and M. W. Chavalas, *The IVP Bible Background Commentary: Old Testament* (Downers Grove: InterVarsity, 2000).

be noted that Moses would use essentially the same form in speaking to Pharaoh, requesting release from Egypt for Israel. Before Pharaoh he made his request politely and offered an acceptable reason for the need to leave, but this does not mean that he saw himself as actually *requiring* permission to go as if it could rightly be denied him (see comments on 5:3).

This is the last mention of Jethro[92] until chap. 18, where he and Moses are reunited and where the stories of his conversion and his valuable leadership advice to Moses demonstrate both the quality of his piety and his wisdom.[93] That Jethro wished Moses well is apparently a pro forma send-off in goodwill, and it does not imply in itself anything specific about Jethro's agreement with Moses' new theology or the exact terms of his calling.[94]

6. A Shaky Start but Initial Acceptance: Moses' Return to Egypt (4:19–31)

[19]Now the LORD had said to Moses in Midian, "Go back to Egypt, for all the men who wanted to kill you are dead." [20]So Moses took his wife and sons, put them on a donkey and started back to Egypt. And he took the staff of God in his hand.

[21]The LORD said to Moses, "When you return to Egypt, see that you perform before Pharaoh all the wonders I have given you the power to do. But I will harden his heart so that he will not let the people go. [22]Then say to Pharaoh, 'This is what the LORD says: Israel is my firstborn son, [23]and I told you, "Let my son go, so he may worship me." But you refused to let him go; so I will kill your firstborn son.'"

[24]At a lodging place on the way, the LORD met [Moses] and was about to kill him. [25]But Zipporah took a flint knife, cut off her son's foreskin and touched [Moses'] feet with it. "Surely you are a bridegroom of blood to me," she said. [26]So the LORD let him alone. (At that time she said "bridegroom of blood," referring to circumcision.)

---

[92] The MT spells Jethro two different ways in the verse: first as יֶתֶר and then as the more usual יִתְרוֹ. The other versions all have the usual spelling in both places, so the aberration seems likely to be the result of a simple copyist's error before the days of the Masoretes, who were then forced to vocalize the shortened name as best they could.

[93] Nothing in either place, however, provides real evidence for the so-called "Kenite hypothesis," an older theory, never widely held, that Moses got his monotheistic religion from Jethro (identified as a Kenite in Judg 1:16; the Kenites were a branch of the Midianites). As we argue in chap. 18, it was Jethro who (eventually) got his religion from Moses, not the other way around.

[94] Indeed, a more literal translation would be, "And Jethro said to Moses 'Go in peace.'" לֵךְ לְשָׁלוֹם, a simple gracious departure formula, as seen in Judg 18:6; 1 Sam 1:17; 20:24; and 2 Kgs 5:19; and in its parallel form לֵךְ בְּשָׁלוֹם in 1 Sam 29:7 and 2 Sam 15:9; *pace* J. I. Durham, "שָׁלוֹם and the Presence of God," in *Proclamation and Presence* (Macon: Mercer University Press, 1983), 272–93; and id., *Exodus*, 53, n. 18.b.

[27]The LORD said to Aaron, "Go into the desert to meet Moses." So he met Moses at the mountain of God and kissed him. [28]Then Moses told Aaron everything the LORD had sent him to say, and also about all the miraculous signs he had commanded him to perform.

[29]Moses and Aaron brought together all the elders of the Israelites, [30]and Aaron told them everything the LORD had said to Moses. He also performed the signs before the people, [31]and they believed. And when they heard that the LORD was concerned about them and had seen their misery, they bowed down and worshiped.

In this part of the narrative Moses takes us from the time of his departure from Midian (v. 19) to the initial meeting with the Israelite elders, who were converted to the true God based on Moses' testimony and the miraculous signs he performed (vv. 30–31). This account is in part both resumptive (harkening back to Moses' call in Midian, thus the NIV's entirely proper translation in v. 22 with pluperfect verb, "The LORD had said to Moses in Midian") and proleptic (thus the prediction in v. 23 of how Moses would eventually announce the tenth and final plague, that of the death of the Egyptian firstborn, thereby broadly anticipating events up through chap. 11). Here again the staff of God figures prominently (v. 20), and here for the first time in the Bible God's people are described collectively as his "son" (vv. 22–23). The threat to Pharaoh (v. 23) is followed by a laconic story about Moses' son Gershom nearly being put to death by God for long-term disobedience (vv. 24–26, q.v.) and then by far more cheerful circumstances: his reuniting with Aaron (vv. 27–28) and the meeting with and initial success in convincing the Israelite elders, undertaken by Moses and Aaron together (vv. 29–31).

4:19–20 Verse 19 begins with one of the several simple resumptions found in Exodus, placed to help the reader (much more often in the ancient world, however, the listener) keep the overall story in mind. The long, compound-complex theophany call account that concluded in 4:18 had excluded a crucial detail of divine reassurance, and that detail Moses now placed before the reader in a way that nicely ties his departure for Egypt with the divine reassurance elements in the *hieroi logoi* of the theophany: Moses' life would not be in danger upon arrival in Egypt. He was no longer sought as a fugitive criminal. It was common practice in the ancient world, as it is in the modern, for a new government to cancel criminal penalties imposed by a previous government, thus granting general amnesty to prisoners and those sought by the law.[95] Thus for God to say to Moses "all the men who wanted to kill you are dead" would likely represent news that the pharaoh in power

[95] Israel practiced the same sort of change-of-administration amnesty in connection with the cities of refuge laws, which specify that the death of the high priest would nullify previous charges against fugitives (Num 35:25,28,32; Josh 20:6).

when Moses killed an Egyptian (2:15) was now himself dead, along with any others, such as immediate survivors of the deceased who might have had both the legal standing and the desire to press the case.

Verse 20 contributes an important emphasis: Moses was not merely returning to Egypt personally to accomplish a short-term task; he was relocating to Egypt to become an Israelite and thus moved his family with him.[96] His sons are later identified in 18:4 and 1 Chr 23:15,17. On the importance of the note that he took with him God's staff, see "Excursus: Moses' Staff" after the comments on 4:14–17.

4:21–23 In 3:10, at the conclusion of the formal statement of his call to deliver Israel from Egypt, the Lord had told Moses: "So now, go. I am sending you to Pharaoh." The present verses allude to and expand upon that instruction, with special added emphasis that takes into purview the plagues, comprehending all of them with mention of the final and most lethal, the plague of death upon the Egyptian firstborn—here personalized to include Pharaoh's own firstborn. Note, then, that Moses did not have instructions to go merely to Egyptians or Israelites but must appear before and issue commands in the name of the Lord to Pharaoh himself, likely the most ardent opponent of any exodus (see on 1:10) and the one with the most power at his disposal to prevent it. Moses' instructions required that he actually confront Pharaoh in person; to do so was therefore not merely a strategy he happened to choose.

Moses learned how to do three miracles (4:1–9) as preparation for being believed by his own people, the Israelites in Egypt (4:1,8–9); indeed, he eventually did perform them before the Israelites (4:30). But are these same three signs the ones that are indicated by the words "perform before Pharaoh all the wonders I have given you the power to do" in v. 21? Moses certainly did perform two of them before Pharaoh, that is, the first (changing his staff into a snake) and the third (changing water into blood), according to 7:8–24. But he did not perform the second miracle at all (changing his hand from healthy to leprous) before Pharaoh. This suggests that the three proof-of-calling signs are not coterminous with "all the wonders" that, as the narrative unfolds, turn out to be the ten plagues, the exodus itself, and the crossing of the Red Sea. The third of the proof signs, in other words, is only the first of many great signs of God's power.

---

[96] The reference to their being placed on "a donkey" [ass] does not necessarily mean that the children were very small and therefore rode with their mother Zipporah; it is normal, optional style in Hb. to use the singular to indicate things distributively owned or used by different people (e.g., Isa 6:10, לֶב־הָעָם הַזֶּה, "the mind of this people"; 2 Chr 25:5, בֵּית־אָבוֹת, "house of fathers" = paternal estates; 1 Kgs 12:31, בֵּית בָּמוֹת, "the place of high places" = high place locations). Additionally, חֲמוֹר, the word for donkey, is often used collectively, as in Gen 32:6, וַיְהִי־לִי שׁוֹר וַחֲמוֹר, "I have cattle and donkeys."

Verses 22–23 link the concept of Yahweh's "firstborn son," Israel, with Pharaoh's (and by implication every Israelite's) "firstborn son" (see comments on 11:1–10). The firstborn son in the ancient world was the one specially favored with inheritance, the one who would represent the father in many ways as he came into maturity and the father gave him more and more responsibility. Moreover, in ancient Israelite society the firstborn son, as the firstfruits of a marriage, was devoted to God—he belonged specially to God and could not even be taken and raised by his parents without the payment of a special redemption or "buy back" fee that symbolized the family's recognition that the son was by rights Yahweh's and not theirs (see comments on 13:2,13). Until entering into his special, double inheritance (Deut 21:17), the firstborn son "served" his father. The verb in 4:23 of the NIV translated as "worship" ("Let my son go that he may worship me") is *ʿābad*, normally translated as "work, serve" elsewhere. The Israelites had been serving Pharaoh; now God told Pharaoh that the Israelites were going to serve *him*. Their liberation came not in being freed from having to work but in being freed from working for the wrong master.[97]

With the statement in v. 21, "I will harden his heart so that he will not let the people go," God introduced a new detail into the assignment, that of his own divine causation of Pharaoh's stubbornness, but not a new expectation. He had already warned Moses that Pharaoh would be highly resistant (3:19–20). The reader might at first blush think that God was here announcing to Moses that he was going to frustrate Moses' efforts. In fact, it was just the opposite. By indicating that he would control Pharaoh's resistance to the exodus, God assured Moses that he was totally in control of Pharaoh in every way, able to make him resist as long as necessary even during a buildup of increasingly painful plagues and then make him give up and let the Israelites go at the moment of God's choosing (which was already the essential message of 3:19–20).[98]

Excursus: The Hardening of Pharaoh's Heart

Three different terms are employed in Exodus to describe God's making Pharaoh (and, as is sometimes overtly stated, his officials[99] and/or the Egyptians in general[100]) stubborn so that he would not allow the Israelites to leave Egypt. His purpose in preventing Pharaoh from giving in too easily and too early was, as

---

[97] Everyone is supposed to work (Gen 2:15). The question is: for whom? Those not servants to God will be servants to sin (Rom 6:16–22) in one way or another. The Israelites were being offered a chance to work for the one who could make their work a blessing—and to be liberated from the one who made it a curse. See A. Ahuviah, "I Will Bring You Up from Egyptian Affliction (Exod 17)," *BMik* 23 (1978): 301–3.

[98] See J. Currid, "Why Did God Harden Pharaoh's Heart?" *BibRev* 9 (1993): 46–51.

[99] Exod 9:34; 10:1.

[100] Exod 14:7

will be seen in subsequent parts of the narrative, to allow himself fully to demonstrate his sovereignty over Pharaoh,[101] the Egyptians, the land of Egypt itself, and the gods in which Pharaoh and the Egyptians trusted. It should not be surprising that portraying such a significant purpose—one of the main issues of the entire exodus story—would, in the course of the narrative, eventually involve all the different ways of describing in Hebrew the act of making someone stubborn.

All three terms essentially function synonymously in Exodus, and although all three are typically rendered in most English translations as one variation or another on "harden the heart," that is, following the KJV literalistic wording, their meaning in normal modern English is simply "be/make stubborn."

The most common way of the three to speak of "making stubborn/being stubborn" is the combination *ḥāzaq* + *lēb,* the term used in the present verse. In these cases the causative is expressed through the Hebrew *piel* (as in 4:21) and the simple descriptive through the Hebrew *qal* (as in 7:13):

> Exod 4:21: The LORD said to Moses, "When you return to Egypt, see that you perform before Pharaoh all the wonders I have given you the power to do. But I will harden his heart so that he will not let the people go."
>
> Exod 7:13: Yet Pharaoh's heart became hard and he would not listen to them, just as the LORD had said.
>
> Exod 7:22: But the Egyptian magicians did the same things by their secret arts, and Pharaoh's heart became hard; he would not listen to Moses and Aaron, just as the LORD had said.
>
> Exod 8:19: The magicians said to Pharaoh, "This is the finger of God." But Pharaoh's heart was hard and he would not listen, just as the LORD had said.
>
> Exod 9:12: But the LORD hardened Pharaoh's heart and he would not listen to Moses and Aaron, just as the LORD had said to Moses.
>
> Exod 9:35: So Pharaoh's heart was hard and he would not let the Israelites go, just as the LORD had said through Moses.
>
> Exod 10:20: But the LORD hardened Pharaoh's heart, and he would not let the Israelites go.
>
> Exod 10:27: But the LORD hardened Pharaoh's heart, and he was not willing to let them go.

[101] See W. Brueggemann, "Pharaoh as Vassal: A Study of Political Metaphor," *CBQ* 57 (1995): 27–51. Brueggemann contends rather persuasively that Exod 1–15 portrays the pharaoh as a sort of reluctant, obstreperous vassal whom Yahweh, the great sovereign, puts in his place. We would add that in 6:10 and similar places, Moses is effectively presented with the commission to function as the sovereign's messenger to the vassal, a paradigm for all future prophets and their relationship as mediators between Yahweh and Israel or any other vassal.

Exod 11:10: Moses and Aaron performed all these wonders before Pharaoh, but the LORD hardened Pharaoh's heart, and he would not let the Israelites go out of his country.

Exod 14:4: And I will harden Pharaoh's heart, and he will pursue them. But I will gain glory for myself through Pharaoh and all his army, and the Egyptians will know that I am the LORD." So the Israelites did this.

Exod 14:8: The LORD hardened the heart of Pharaoh king of Egypt, so that he pursued the Israelites, who were marching out boldly.

Exod 14:17: I will harden the hearts of the Egyptians so that they will go in after them. And I will gain glory through Pharaoh and all his army, through his chariots and his horsemen.[102]

The next term of the three to appear in Moses' Exodus narrative is *qāšāh* + *lēb,* "harden one's heart," that is, "be determined / stubborn." In the single instance employed in Exodus, the causative *(hiphil)* form of the verb is used:

Exod 7:3: But I will harden Pharaoh's heart, and though I multiply my signs and wonders in Egypt, . . .[103]

The third of the three terms to appear in Moses' vocabulary in Exodus is *kābēd* + *lēb,* which likewise means "be stubborn, be unbending." With this term the simple descriptive employs the Hebrew *qal* stative (e.g., 7:14), whereas the causative is indicated by the *hiphil* (whether referring to Pharaoh's hardening his own heart, as in 8:15 [Eng. 8:11], or God's doing so, as in 10:1).

Exod 7:14: Then the LORD said to Moses, "Pharaoh's heart is unyielding; he refuses to let the people go."

Exod 8:15: But when Pharaoh saw that there was relief, he hardened his heart and would not listen to Moses and Aaron, just as the LORD had said.

Exod 8:32: But this time also Pharaoh hardened his heart and would not let the people go.

Exod 9:7: Pharaoh sent men to investigate and found that not even one of the animals of the Israelites had died. Yet his heart was unyielding and he would not let the people go.

Exod 9:34: When Pharaoh saw that the rain and hail and thunder had stopped, he sinned again: He and his officials hardened their hearts.

[102] The same idiom, i.e., חזק + לב meaning "be stubborn," occurs also in Ezek 2:4; 3:7.

[103] This term (קשׁה + לב) also appears in 1 Sam 25:3; Ezek 2:4; 3:7; and Prov 28:14. In each the meaning is likewise "be/make stubborn," and the appearance in Ezek 2:4 and 3:7 of both this idiom and the previous one (חזק + לב) in parallel proves their synonymy.

Exod 10:1: Then the LORD said to Moses, "Go to Pharaoh, for I have hardened his heart and the hearts of his officials so that I may perform these miraculous signs of mine among them."

Exod 14:4: "And I will harden Pharaoh's heart, and he will pursue them. But I will gain glory for myself through Pharaoh and all his army, and the Egyptians will know that I am the LORD." So the Israelites did this.[104]

Most often God himself made Pharaoh stubborn. In some places, however, the wording of most translations properly describes Pharaoh's making himself stubborn ("hardening his own heart"), as in 8:15,32; 9:34. Additionally, some wordings suggest a neutral situation, that is, that Pharaoh's heart simply "was/became hard" (7:13–14,22; 8:19; 9:7,35). Based on the way these various wordings for "be/make stubborn" seem to occur in no particular pattern, are routinely used synonymously, and clearly refer to the same essential phenomenon (i.e., God's keeping Pharaoh from letting the Israelites leave Egypt until a time of God's choosing), it is not likely that any real semantic difference is intended by the three wordings. Rather, they represent the sort of variation found in all good writing, in which a concept repeatedly mentioned is referred to with various wordings rather than the same wording each time. This would seem to be the operating principle also in 9:34, which explicitly states that Pharaoh "sinned again: He and his officials hardened their hearts," a wording that would seem to indicate that Pharaoh's action was truly voluntary since it is not normal for us to think that God would cause anyone to sin. This, however, is more likely the result either of the greater range of meaning of the Hebrew word for sin *(ḥṭʾ)* or else of the way the two concepts (sinning and being stubborn) are mentioned together in the verse without any intention that they should be understood as coterminous in meaning (see the commentary on 9:34).

Was Pharaoh a sinner? Most assuredly. Indeed, one of the reasons for God's choice of the term "harden the heart" in the revelation of his plan to Moses in 4:21 may have been that to an Egyptian (as Moses had been by adoption) or to those who understood the basics of Egyptian culture (as most of the Hebrews surely did, even if imperfectly) the concept of hardening someone's heart would call to mind that person's sinfulness. Egyptian religious texts speak often of the *ʾib* (Egyptian for "heart") as the representation of a person's basic essence, the place where a person's guilt and innocence, motives and general righteousness are to be found. In Egyptian thinking, the weighing/evaluating of the *ʾib* by the gods at the time of a person's death was a means of determining whether or not one is a sinner and therefore whether or not one can go to the Egyptian equivalent of heaven. The Egyptian Pharaoh was supposed to be a pure person, a divine manifestation of the gods, and one whose sovereignty over the people was credentialized in part by the purity of his *ʾib*. The idea that Yahweh could do whatever he wanted with Pharaoh's heart, and specifically could "harden" it, therefore, was both an evidence of Yahweh's control of all things including the

[104] The same idiom is found also in 1 Sam 6:6 and Isa 6:10.

mightiest monarch of the day and also evidence that Yahweh had done what the Egyptians thought the "gods" would usually do—weigh the heart and decide whether its owner was worthy of eternal life or not. In effect, then, each time Yahweh is described as hardening Pharaoh's heart, the alert reader is reminded that Yahweh had, as it were, weighed Pharaoh and found him wanting.[105] Thus God disgraced Pharaoh. In terms of the comparison between what the Egyptians would have expected to happen to Pharaoh's heart after death and God's hardening of it during Pharaoh's life is not that Pharaoh was condemned to be denied eternal life (something the text cannot be read to mean) but that God had reduced the supposedly divine Pharaoh to the level of a mere mortal, easily manipulated and possessing no divine "purity" at all.

In terms of the classical theological-philosophical issue of free will versus determinism, none of the references to the hardening of Pharaoh's heart is decisive. That is because God's causing Pharaoh to be stubborn is simply not presented in the narrative as a general permanent phenomenon (eternal election or rejection) but rather as an ad hoc action of God, temporary in nature (i.e., Pharaoh's mind was not permanently made stubborn so that he had no ability to repent later in life) and limited to the special purpose of humiliating the Egyptians and their false religion.[106]

In vv. 22–23 Moses was instructed to be prepared to announce to Pharaoh the close and tender protected relationship of Israel to God, as firstborn son to father, and to contrast it to the deadly fate that awaited the firstborn of Egypt, individualized in Pharaoh's son. God had chosen Israel for election to a special status, that of firstborn son, with the implication of inheritance that went with it.[107] Israel's coming inheritance certainly included the promised land of Canaan but included also the special relationship of God's presence.[108] God was not only promising to protect his son over against Pha-

---

[105] See Currid, "Why Did God Harden Pharaoh's Heart?" 46–51.

[106] So, we could contend, is the perspective of Paul's point in Rom 9:17–18. The Exodus narrative cannot properly be read as teaching determinism (so P. Gilbert, "Libre arbitre et déterminisme: une réflexion sur la figure de Pharaon," *Theoforum* 32 [2001]: 5–21). For alternate approaches see G. K. Beale, "An Exegetical and Theological Consideration of the Hardening of Pharaoh's Heart in Exodus 4–14 and Romans 9," *TJ* 5 (1984): 129–54; R. Dietzfelbinger, "Ego Indurabo cor Pharaonis: Ammerkungen zu einer crux interpretum," in *Philologia Sacra,* Vol. 1 (Freiburg: Herder, 1993), 16–35; D. Gunn, "The 'Hardening of Pharaoh's Heart': Plot, Character and Theology in Exodus 1–14," in *Art and Meaning: Rhetoric in Biblical Literature* (Sheffield: JSOT, 1982), 72–96.

[107] In Israelite society the firstborn was the favored son and special heir, who received twice the portion of inherited property from the father than that received by the other heirs, a fact that leads to various metaphorical and/or symbolic references to "double portion" and other theological inheritance analogies (e.g., 2 Kgs 2:9; Isa 61:7; Deut 32:9; Gal 4:7; Heb 1:2).

[108] T. Fretheim (*Exodus*, Interpretation: A Bible Commentary for Teaching and Preaching [Louisville: Westminster John Knox, 1991], 77): "A central question for Exodus has been, Whose child is Israel? God's claim: Israel is *my* firstborn (not only) child, not Pharaoh's (see 3:10). Israel is here "brought into the closest and dearest relation to God" (quoting S. R. Driver, *Exodus, The Cambridge Bible* [(Cambridge: Cambridge University Press, 1911], 31).

raoh's son and to use his awesome power to do so, but he was announcing that the one must die so that the other may be liberated from bondage. Although this is certainly not explicitly a reference to Christ's sacrifice of his life on the cross, it is an early biblical instance of the concept of substitutionary death in the human sphere.

Additionally, it adumbrates the concept of the Messiah's embodiment of Israel, the same connection made, for example, in the "servant songs" in Isaiah (esp. Isa 53) and by Matthew (2:15, identifying the fulfillment of Hos 11:1). Note as well that God's purpose in rescuing his son was that his son might worship him, a role Jesus fulfilled in his own faithful worship of the Father and a role God's people are expected to fulfill as their most basic response to his deliverance of their lives. The request to leave Egypt to "worship" the true God repeatedly characterizes Moses' exodus demands before Pharaoh in the ensuing chapters.[109] Implicit in God's close identification of himself with his "son" was his concern for the son's suffering. This sort of empathetic attention of God to Israel also appears three times in Jeremiah (Jer 3:19; 31:9 ["I am Israel's father, and Ephraim [Israel] is my firstborn son"]; 31:20).

The announcement of the tenth plague in advance is something the NIV translation of Exod 11:1 properly highlights by its translation with the English pluperfect ("the LORD had said"). In other words, Moses entered into the process of fulfilling God's commands with the prior understanding[110] that the mighty acts of God in the form of the plagues would build in intensity until they culminated in the death of the Egyptian firstborn—touching even Pharaoh himself.[111]

---

[109] Cf. 7:16; 8:1,20; 9:1,13; 10:3,7.

[110] As Cassuto *(Exodus),* Childs (*Exodus,* 102), and others have pointed out, the mention of what Moses would say later is not irregular chronologically but is characteristic of Hb. narrative style (cf. Gen 28:10–22; Jonah 4:5–11, which logically precedes 3:10–4:4; 1 Sam 16 vs. 17.

[111] M. Noth's theory on the development of the plague stories was that they arose over time as folkloristic addenda to a single original plague, that of the death of the firstborn (*A History of Pentateuchal Traditions* [Englewood Cliffs, N.J.: Prentice-Hall, 1972], 66–70). Noth's theory fails to understand the mention of the death of the firstborn here as a synecdoche by which all the plagues are essentially included.

4:24–26 This unusual story has engendered many different interpretations and attempts at explanation.[112] The following assertions are important for understanding such a seemingly enigmatic story, which contains many events and assumptions that tend to be foreign to modern Western ears:

a. Whether one follows the MT Hebrew of v. 24 ("Yahweh met up with him and sought to kill him") or the likely original LXX/Tg. of v. 24 ("The Angel of the Lord[113] met up with him and sought to kill him"), the same essential point is made: God was not going to allow someone (Gershom—

---

[112] To review all of them fairly would require scores of pages. The reader interested in digesting the full range of theories and their supporting argumentation takes on a major task. A brief review is provided by G. Vermes, "Baptism and Jewish Exegesis: New Light from Ancient Sources," *NTS* 4 (1958): 309–18 and in more detail by J. Morgenstern, "The 'Bloody Husband' (?) Once Again," *HUCA* 34 (1963): 35–70. We draw with appreciation on Durham's succinct and lucid overview (*Exodus,* 57) in this summary: Some scholars (Kosmala, Morgenstern, Schmid et al.) have suggested that these verses were originally part of an older Kenite or Midianite story that was not about Moses at all. The Hb. of vv. 24–26 does not mention Moses; his name is supplied in both cases in the NIV. Such a view requires that the mention of Zipporah and "her son" be regarded as an interpolation into the story on the part of a narrator to make it apply to Moses. Others (Gressman, Meyer et al.) have concluded that Yahweh was not the one who sought to attack Moses in the original version of this story; it was instead a demon, and the story was eventually adapted to refer to Yahweh as the attacker rather than a demon. Vriezen argues instead that Yahweh's seeking to kill Moses was actually an act of grace whereby he stopped Moses in his tracks and gave him the sign of grace, i.e., the covenant of circumcision. Others (Aurerbach, Beer, Beltz) have sought to identify the reason for the inclusion of the story at this point in terms of its being an early etiology for circumcision; according to this line of reasoning, the story teaches how circumcision first came about and makes Gershom's circumcision something of a model for that of all future children. A variation on this (Buber, Gunkel et al.) concludes that the story is an etiology explaining how circumcision shifted from being a premarital rite to a childhood or puberty rite. Against this approach, Childs and Durham, among others, argue (correctly in our opinion) that the story is far too specifically linked to Moses and Zipporah and their family to be a general etiology for circumcision in Israel (which is in fact provided not by this passage but by Gen 17:10–27). The differences between the Hb. and the Gk. translation of the LXX are variously explained as the result of a different Hb. *Vorlage* (e.g., Hehn) or a different understanding of circumcision (e.g., Junker) or a conscious rewording of the text by a mystified LXX translator (a far more common circumstance than might be realized). Such scholars as Cassuto and Fohrer consider Yahweh's attack to have been aimed mainly at Gershom because he had not been circumcised (the "him" in v. 24 is taken, rightly, we think, to refer to Gershom, not Moses), while Hyatt and many others opine that it was Moses himself who had not yet been circumcised and was therefore the target of Yahweh's wrath. The following are well worthy of examination by anyone interested in the various approaches to the passage, though they are hardly the only sources: J. Derby, "Why Did God Want to Kill Moses?" *JBQ* 18 (1989–1990): 222–29; D. Gelernter, "Tsipporah's Bloodgroom: A Biblical Breaking Point," *Orim* 3 (1988): 46–55; L. H. Fink, "The Incident at the Lodging House," *JBQ* 21 (1993): 236–241; G. W. Ashby, "The Bloody Bridegroom: The Interpretation of Exodus 4:24–26," *ExpTim* 106 (1995): 203–5; W. Dumbrell, "Exodus 4:24–26: A Textual Re-examination," *HTR* 65 (1972): 285–90; C. Houtman, "Exodus 4:24–26 and Its Interpretation," *JNSL* 11 (1983): 81–105; T. Lescow, "Ex 4,24–26: Ein archaisher Bundesschlussritus," *ZAW* 105 (1993): 19–26; A. S. Maller, "The Bridegroom of Blood," *JBQ* 21 (1993): 94–98; B. P. Robinson, "Zipporah to the Rescue: A Contextual Study of Exodus IV 24–26," *VT* 36 (1986): 447–62; W. H. Propp, "That Bloody Bridegroom (Exodus iv 24–26)," *VT* 43 (1993): 495–518.

[113] Cf. "Excursus: The Angel of the Lord" after 3:2–3. The Angel of the Lord would hardly act independently of Yahweh's will.

not Moses: the text of 4:24–26 never mentions Moses!)[114] to get to Egypt alive without a decisive change in their circumcision status.[115] The fact that this story follows immediately the warning of Yahweh about the potential death of Pharaoh's firstborn son provides a spatial setting in the text: we now read a story about the potential death of Moses' firstborn son, upon whose fate the focus of the pericope should naturally fall. The NIV, in inserting the name Moses at two points in the story via brackets, merely misleads the reader into thinking that Moses, not Gershom, was the subject of what Zipporah said and did.

b. Zipporah, who had grown up in the household of a Midianite (high?) priest, surely understood how circumcision was done and what its significance was—including the proper words to say in connection with a circumcision ceremony. Many people groups in the ancient world practiced circumcision, including, the Midianites; it was hardly unknown outside of Israelite circles.

c. The Egyptians practiced a partial circumcision, involving cutting only a small amount of the foreskin, a practice considered so illegitimate by the Israelites that it could be called "the reproach of Egypt" (Josh 5:9).[116] If Moses had followed this sort of approach in circumcising Gershom, thinking that it fulfilled Yahweh's expectations, he would have been quite mistaken and still would have been in defiance of Yahweh's will, even if he himself had been fully and properly circumcised prior to his marriage to Zipporah.[117]

---

[114] The Hb. grammar of the passage uses proleptic pronouns to refer to Gershom at first and never names Moses at all. Gershom is referred to in v. 25 finally as *her son*, which tells the reader who it was that God threatened to kill. The choice of the NIV to include the name of Moses twice (in brackets each time) is just that: a translator's choice, not a matter of literal translation. Its effect is to skew the reader's attention to Moses rather than the actual referent of the pronouns, "her son." T. J. Lehane takes the threat of the prior verse (4:23), "so I will kill your firstborn son," as referring not only to Pharaoh but to Moses ("Zipporah and the Passover," *JBQ* 24 [1996]: 46–50). This seems to us impossible to justify from the grammar of the verse, but Lehane otherwise rightly shows that 4:23 naturally leads into 4:24–26 by the connection of the concept of the threat of killing a firstborn son. The wording of v. 23, in other words, primes the reader for the referent of the laconic vv. 24–26—the "son," not the father, is the one whose life was in danger in each case.

[115] The simplest and clearest translation of v. 24 perhaps would be: "Where they spent the night while on the road, Yahweh made contact with him [Gershom, not Moses] and was intending to kill him."

[116] See J. M. Sasson, "Circumcision in the Ancient Near East," *JBL* 85 (1966): 473–76; "Circumcision in Egypt," *ANET*, 326; D. Dunham, *Naga-ed-Der Stelae of the First Intermediate Period* (London, 1937), Plate xxxvii, No. 84, 102–4.

[117] Because Moses' parents, Amram and Jochebed, would likely not have circumcised him at birth in order to avoid the automatic identification of him as a Hebrew/Israelite baby if he were found by Egyptians, his adoptive mother, the daughter of Pharaoh, might have been the one to have had him circumcised but in the Egyptian manner, the partial circumcision condemned in Josh 5:9. It is very likely that prior to his marriage to a Midianite priest's daughter Moses would have been circumcised fully, so the issue of disobedience to God that occasions Yahweh's wrath here does not relate to Moses' own circumcision at this point in his life.

d. Moses probably had undergone this partial Egyptian circumcision either upon his adoption by Pharaoh's daughter or perhaps later in life.[118] His biological parents may have avoided having him circumcised at birth for fear it would identify him as an Israelite and/or make him cry more and thus be detected by Egyptians seeking to kill the infant boys at that time (1:22–2:2), if indeed circumcision was even consistently practiced among the Israelites in Egypt in those days. This may have predisposed him not to circumcise Gershom, whom he was bringing along—uncircumcised—on the trip.

e. The expression "relative of blood," or more naturally, "blood relative" *(ḥăṭan dāmîm)* found in both vv. 25 and 26, is key to understanding what Zipporah was thinking and doing: she was not necessarily using language about Moses as her husband (which would be expressed by the word *ʾîš*) or necessarily language she or someone else might have used at the time of their marriage, long prior to this event, when he was still (or still about to become) her bridegroom (which can be but is not the only meaning of *ḥăṭan*). It may well be that the language she used here is the sort that she would naturally have used about any male relative, since *ḥăṭan* simply means "relative." Among the Midianites full circumcision was presumably practiced early in a male child's life, although it is possible that some men probably were circumcised a few weeks prior to marriage rather than earlier in life.[119] Zipporah said what she understood to be the proper language—which was her best attempt and apparently was a sufficient attempt—to show that the circumcision she performed was official and pious. When she said "you are a blood relative to me" (our translation), she presumably was speaking to Gershom, not to Moses.[120]

f. The flint knife probably was the proper, traditional instrument for performing a circumcision (cf. Josh 5:2–9).

g. Zipporah touched[121] the foreskin of Gershom to Gershom's *genitals* from which it had just been removed. "Feet" *(rĕgālîm)* is one of several Hebrew euphemisms for "genitals" (cf. Isa 6:2; 7:20; Ezek 16:25; Deut

---

[118] Sasson suggests that the Egyptians circumcised only adults, which is almost certainly correct. All known references to Egyptian circumcision describe only the circumcision of adults, often in large groups ("Circumcision in Egypt," *ANET,* 326, mentions a group circumcision of 120 adult males).

[119] Cf. Gen 34:14–24.

[120] Alternatively, she could have been speaking to Moses as a sign that she had just acted on his behalf, but such an idea does not need to be forced on the passage.

[121] The *hiphil* of נגע does not normally mean "make *X* touch *Y*" but simply "touch / reach." Ashby argues that the similarities between Exod 4:24–26 and Gen 32:23–32 (where the wrestling angel touches Jacob's "thigh") are instructive: each story represents "a close physical encounter between Yahweh and his chosen person" ("The Bloody Bridegroom," 203–5). He also suggests that circumcision is inherently connected conceptually to blood sacrifice and that "blood has a power of holiness: as life, it belongs to God and it either exercises witness *against* (as with Cain and Abel) or *for* (as in the Passover blood-touching)." Accordingly, Ashby views Exod 4:24–26 as foreshadowing the Passover in the following parallel particulars: the touching of blood, involvement of the firstborn son, the intention of God initially to kill, but then not killing because of the blood sacrifice.

28:57; others include "hand," "knee," "stones [see comments on 1:16"]). She thus had physically circumcised Gershom; then immediately she symbolically used the removed foreskin to touch Gershom's genitals and said the "right words" (the ones she understood to be godly and proper at a circumcision) in an effort perhaps to legitimize the previously neglected and now emergency circumcision. (Again, it was not Moses God sought to kill, nor was Moses likely to have been the person whose genitals were touched by the foreskin. An actual circumcision of Moses would have prevented his traveling for a number of days.[122] Since from this point on in the narrative neither Zipporah nor Moses' sons are mentioned until their reuniting in 18:2–6, it is likely that they did not travel farther than this camping place (*mālōn,* v. 24) and, after Gershom had healed, returned to Midian.

h. The expression "relative of blood" is not negative but positive, an endearing reference[123] to a husband's and wife's joining to become one flesh/blood and thus producing offspring that are their own flesh and blood so that Gershom was clearly Zipporah's "blood relative." Quite possibly Zipporah, in saying this, was not merely repeating words Midianites said at circumcisions but was using these words to link herself closely to Gershom; so her act on his behalf would suffice instead of Moses' actually doing Gershom's circumcision.[124] Accordingly, v. 26 is perhaps best translated, "The Lord let him [Gershom] alone since[125] she said 'blood relative' in connection with the circumcision."

i. Moses may have failed God in two ways: he had not himself been fully circumcised according to the expectations implicit in Gen 17:10–14 until such time as his marriage to Zipporah, but far more importantly, he had not circumcised or at least not adequately circumcised one of his sons, likewise in violation of those expectations—both very serious sins of omission.

j. The consequence of failure to be circumcised is "to be cut off" from the holy people (Gen 17:14). This is just what God threatened to make happen in Gershom's case according to v. 24. Fortunately, Zipporah saved her son from such a fate by saying and doing the right thing, as best she knew how.

k. The fact that Zipporah had time to do the right thing and remove the danger shows that somehow she was warned and given time to act. The

---

[122] See Gen 34:25.

[123] The entire phrase can be translated "my blood relative"; לִי does not necessarily mean "to me" but can simply mean "my" in the context. Ashby suggests that "you are a bridegroom of blood" (his translation) is not a rebuke but in fact a "triumphant statement" ("The Bloody Bridegroom," 204) expressing the celebration of the fact that Moses was now fully a part of the covenant community and accordingly was finally worthy to be leader of that covenant community (Israel). This assumes, of course, that Moses was the person Zipporah spoke of as the "blood relative."

[124] Since the term חָתָן can connote any relative (e.g. husband, son, son-in-law), her words may have had something of the effect of "since we are related, I can do this on your behalf."

[125] אָז can indeed mean "since" or "in as much as," even though the more common word statistically in such constructions would be כִּי.

specifics of that warning are not provided in the narrative, but the grace of God is implied clearly in the fact that by acting, Zipporah prevented a serious consequence. Thereby, the result was that Moses' family was consistent with the practices God required of his covenant people, and thus the story ends happily with the will of God accomplished, even if by threat, and the blessing of God retained by Moses and his family.

k. For all its laconic style and seemingly dramatic mood, this story is actually fully consistent with other evidence for Moses' tendency to resist the call of God to such a daunting assignment as delivering the Israelites from Egypt against Pharaoh's wishes, a tendency that began in 4:13 with his attempt to refuse the call. Even as he headed toward Egypt, he still did not have all aspects of his life (in this case his family life) in order. This is therefore one of several stories Moses told about himself in the Pentateuch that demonstrate his less than perfect obedience to God's commands at various times (cf. esp. Deut 32:51–52).

By way of summarizing our view of the pericope: Exod 4:24–26 is a story showing how Zipporah, by performing as officially as she could a circumcision on her son—whom his father had failed so far to conform to the covenant requirements of Gen 17:10–14—saved him from the punishment required by the Abrahamic covenant of circumcision. Nothing can thwart God's plan of redemption. Since Moses had not yet done his part in regard to Gershom's circumcision, God accepted Zipporah's decisive and pious actions in circumcising her son as an appropriate substitute so that God's chosen, yet reluctant and headstrong, prophet could continue his assignment to lead the Israelites out of bondage. God often relents if people repent. Right words and actions, if they show the true intent of the heart, demonstrate right repentance. Moses might have lost his own firstborn son, just as Pharaoh would later lose his (predicted immediately prior to the present passage, in 4:23). Zipporah's intervention prevented that from happening.

4:27–28 The three individual narratives at the end of chap. 4 are all brief—the prior story of God's seeking to kill Moses (vv. 24–26), this story of Moses' reuniting with Aaron (vv. 27–28), and the concluding story of Moses' and Aaron's arrival and acceptance in Egypt (vv. 29–31). The terse narrative style serves Moses' purpose as narrator: he wanted to move the story focus on to Egypt, and he obviously therefore had chosen not to belabor the events that took place between his call at Sinai and his arrival in Egypt. The details of such events might fascinate us, but they would contribute little to the progress of the plan of redemption of God's people, which was Moses' concern.

Verse 27 begins resumptively,[126] referring back to the call of Aaron. This is important in helping the reader understand that Aaron was genuinely, fully

[126] Thus the verse could as easily begin in translation, "The LORD had said to Aaron" with the converted imperfect functioning in the pluperfect mode. (Not all scholars of Hb. recognize a pluperfect semantic option for the converted imperfect, but the author agrees with the NIV translators that such an option is indeed a common part of the semantic range of the converted imperfect.)

committed to the exodus plan; we now learn that he had been explicitly sent by God to join forces with Moses—that is, that the events described in 4:14 ("What about your brother Aaron? . . . He is already on his way") came about not merely by reason of a desire on Aaron's part to have a family visit with Moses but by a call of God, parallel to but apparently not as extensive as that of Moses' own. Aaron's key role as Moses' supporter and spokesman was previously arranged in 4:14–16.

The location of the "mountain of God" (Sinai) is here implied not to be in Midian but somewhere between Midian and Egypt, in light of the fact that both Aaron, going from Egypt toward Midian, and Moses, going from Midian toward Egypt, were well into their journeys when they met. Perhaps Aaron already knew by reputation where the mountain was; or, just as likely, they were guided to their meeting by God, who had directly called both to the meeting and arranged the timing so that they would encounter one another. At any rate, this meeting of family long separated parallels to some degree the meeting of Moses and Jethro at the same location in chap. 18—demonstrating the importance, and presumably the fame, of Mount Sinai.

The message of v. 28 is simple and direct: Aaron knew everything and agreed with everything in the plan to confront Pharaoh and demand the release of the Israelites. The repeated object pronoun in v. 28 ("him") is technically ambiguous but is placed in syntactical context in a way that suggests that it must refer to Moses and not to Aaron. In other words, the wording still makes Moses the preeminent spokesman and miracle worker. He was not simply handing over those tasks to Aaron.

4:29–31 The time elapsed between Moses' leaving Jethro (v. 18) and the Israelites' worship of Yahweh (v. 31) may have been as little as a few weeks or perhaps as long as many months. Nonetheless, it is summarized rapidly. These verses do not even mention the arrival of Moses and Aaron in Egypt but get right to the point that they gathered the elders, performed the signs, and saw the people believe.

There is an underlying assumption in this part of the story of a special aspect of Aaron's role: his ability to provide immediate credibility with his fellow Israelite elders[127] in Egypt. Moses was an outsider, someone most of them probably had never met, even if they had heard of him, and someone they may even have been afraid of, based on the tenor of the incident described in 2:11–14. Aaron, on the other hand, was almost surely an Israelite elder himself (how else would he have had the means and the freedom to leave

---

[127] "The Israelite elders" (זִקְנֵי בְּנֵי יִשְׂרָאֵל) were the leaders of the people, and their number included many who were not necessarily advanced in age (so that "elder" really means simply "leader"). The people obviously were already organized by clan leaders, tribal leaders, and so on, as is born out later in the narrative and as would be consistent with the organization of tribal societies in general. Cf. J. L. McKenzie, "The Elders in the Old Testament," *Bib* 48 (1959): 522–40.

Egypt and take a trip to meet Moses while most of the people were working seven days a week?), in a position to introduce Moses to the leadership of the people much as Barnabas did for Saul (Acts 9:26–28). Thus Aaron did the talking, told the whole story of Moses' call, and performed at least two of the three signs (4:1–9) before the people (v. 30). He may have needed to perform only two signs, the staff-to-a snake and the leprous hand, since v. 31 says that the people *believed* (the Hb. making it clear that the *people,* not merely the elders, believed[128]) whereas 4:9 would seem to imply that the changing of water to blood was a backup sign in case of *refusal* to believe.

Verse 31 describes the Israelites' conversion to faith in Yahweh, evidenced by the posture of bowing before God (not Moses) as the people's sign that they believed in and accepted the demands of his words and promises for them.[129] They likely had no knowledge of his name prior to this (any more than Moses had had before his encounter at Sinai) and no previous idea that he was their national God who had chosen them as his people (which is what "was concerned about them and had seen their misery" implies). In the terse style of Old Testament[130] (and usually NT[131]) conversion accounts, Moses tells the reader in v. 31 that the Israelites trusted in Yahweh for their salvation. This trust was soon to be sorely tested.

7. First Audience with Pharaoh: Harsh Results (5:1–14)

1Afterward Moses and Aaron went to Pharaoh and said, "This is what the LORD, the God of Israel, says: 'Let my people go, so that they may hold a festival to me in the desert.'"

2Pharaoh said, "Who is the LORD, that I should obey him and let Israel go? I do not know the LORD and I will not let Israel go."

3Then they said, "The God of the Hebrews has met with us. Now let us take a three-day journey into the desert to offer sacrifices to the LORD our God, or he may strike us with plagues or with the sword."

4But the king of Egypt said, "Moses and Aaron, why are you taking the people away from their labor? Get back to your work!" 5Then Pharaoh said, "Look, the people of the land are now numerous, and you are stopping them from working."

---

[128] To "believe" is no less important in the OT than in the NT, and there is a rich vocabulary associated with this concept. See, e.g., E. Pfeiffer, "Glaube im Alten Testament," *ZAW* 71 (1959): 151–64; A. Jepsen, אמן, *TDOT* I.

[129] See also comments on 12:37–38. For a liberationist-focused comparison of the spiritual inclinations of the Israelites as opposed to those of the Egyptians, see L. A. S. Rossi, "Espiritualidade dos hebreus versus espiritualidade do Farao," *EBib* 30 (1991): 26–31. Rossi suggests that the Israelites' spirituality was one that naturally inclined them to action, resulting ultimately in their willingness to participate in the exodus, as opposed to that of the Egyptians, which ultimately inclined them to inaction.

[130] Cf. 18:11–12; Ruth 1:16.

[131] Cf. Acts 2:47; 5:14; 11:21; 13:48; John 1:37; 4:39.

[6]That same day Pharaoh gave this order to the slave drivers and foremen in charge of the people: [7]"You are no longer to supply the people with straw for making bricks; let them go and gather their own straw. [8]But require them to make the same number of bricks as before; don't reduce the quota. They are lazy; that is why they are crying out, 'Let us go and sacrifice to our God.' [9]Make the work harder for the men so that they keep working and pay no attention to lies."

[10]Then the slave drivers and the foremen went out and said to the people, "This is what Pharaoh says: 'I will not give you any more straw. [11]Go and get your own straw wherever you can find it, but your work will not be reduced at all.'" [12]So the people scattered all over Egypt to gather stubble to use for straw. [13]The slave drivers kept pressing them, saying, "Complete the work required of you for each day, just as when you had straw." [14]The Israelite foremen appointed by Pharaoh's slave drivers were beaten and were asked, "Why didn't you meet your quota of bricks yesterday or today, as before?"

With Chapter 5 the encounters with Pharaoh begin. Three key themes of those encounters are included already in these verses (5:1–14): the demand made by Yahweh, and quoted prophetically by Moses and Aaron, that "my people" be allowed to leave Egypt to worship "me" in the wilderness (vv. 1,3); Pharaoh's resistance, showing no sufficient fear of Yahweh (vv. 2,4); and Pharaoh's stubbornness, shown in either doing nothing or doing the opposite of what Yahweh demanded (vv. 4–14, in this case resulting in even harsher conditions for the Israelites). These themes, represented in various explicit and implicit ways, and with varying degrees of emphasis, persist through chap. 11. Thus at this point in Moses' narrative, the reader is exposed only to Pharaoh's *initial* resistance and stubbornness, which, fierce from the start, did not abate even as the plagues were unleashed and grew ever more severe. Nothing less than the tenth plague, the already-predicted (4:22–23) death of the firstborn (chap. 12) would break the intransigence of Pharaoh, his advisors, and the Egyptians in general. Until then, as this pericope invites us to appreciate, the Israelites not only would not make progress toward freedom, but they would actually suffer more harsh oppression as a result of their God's demands on their behalf.

The reader must not lose sight of the identity of the combatants. It is easy to assume that the contest for Israelite deliverance was between Moses and Pharaoh, or between Israel and Pharaoh, or between Israel and Egypt. It was none of these. Rather, it was between Yahweh and Egypt's gods,[132] the pharaoh being a devotee of, representative of, and human focal point for those gods.

---

[132] A point summed up in 12:12, at the very high point of announcing the punishment of Egypt as predicted in 4:22–23. We do not mean to suggest that Egypt's gods were real but rather that their "gods"—the whole false faith system and worldview of the Egyptians that eventuated in their religion and general behavior—were a dreadful enemy of saving truth that Yahweh showed worthless in his display of power on behalf of Israel.

5:1 "Afterward" *(wĕʾaḥar)* is a simple way to cover the indeterminate time Moses wishes to bridge in order to get right to the story of the initial encounter with Pharaoh. Mark's frequent "right afterward" *(euthus)* has the same sort of narrative purpose.

It might be thought unusual that Moses and Aaron would have the right to see the great king personally. After all, they were members of a hated and suppressed people group. The reason probably was not related to Moses' long-past status as an Egyptian princeling but rather to a right of audience with a monarch in the traditional legal system of much of the ancient world. Kings were seen as expected to be available to the lowliest and greatest alike, a requirement that Israel's prophets used regularly, often in highly critical, confrontational ways and sometimes even with the purpose of denouncing the king's own personal behavior.[133] Here is the first actual use in the Bible of the prophetic messenger speech formula "Thus says the LORD" (*kōh ʾāmar yahweh,* here translated by the NIV as "This is what the LORD . . . says"). In 4:22 Moses was taught this form in advance of the requirement to use it; now he and Aaron did indeed use it. In this instance "the God of Israel" is added in definitional apposition to explain to Pharaoh who Yahweh was. Later prophets also added the term, following in the footsteps of Moses, the paradigm prophet. Pharaoh would surely have recognized the messenger speech form, judging from its regular use in the Amarna Letters.[134] Without the addition of "the God of Israel" he might at first have assumed that "Yahweh" was some minor king or leader of the Israelites rather than their God since the name was otherwise new to him. Moses used the messenger speech formula "Thus says the LORD" regularly in his confrontations with Pharaoh during the plague stories[135] but otherwise only one other time in Exodus, when God through him commanded the Levites to attack Israelite idolaters (32:27). The formula is never found in the Pentateuch outside of Exodus.[136]

---

[133] 2 Sam 12:1–14 provides an early example in Israel. Isaiah's frequent, easy access to Hezekiah is a later instance. A modern example is the Arabic *majlis* ("court meeting") whereby *any* patient citizen can expect eventually to have an opportunity to present his problem personally to the king.

[134] The Amarna Letters, mainly copies of correspondence to and from the pharaohs and various minor Near Eastern kings during the period roughly 1400–1360 BC, contain in many cases the expression "Thus says [name of king]," which the king's messenger would read before the pharaoh. A messenger formula makes the point that the person speaking the words is not making them up, but simply repeating them verbatim on behalf of the one who sent him to deliver his or her message.

[135] As in 5:1; 7:17; 8:1,20; 9:1,13; 10:3; 11:4.

[136] The limitation of this messenger speech formula to confrontation situations in Exodus has a kind of statistical parallel in the Prophets. They use messenger speech formula (the other common ones are "says the LORD," *nĕʾūm yahweh,* and just *ʾāmar yahweh,* "the LORD said") much more frequently when they are confronting hostile opposition than when speaking to a group of relatively willing listeners. See D. Stuart, "The Old Testament Prophets' Self-Understanding of Their Prophecy," *Themelios* (1980/81): 9–14.

God's demand that his people be allowed to "hold a festival" *(ḥgg)* to him in the wilderness (NIV "desert") recalls 3:18 (q.v.). In the style of Near Eastern requesting favors, the initial request was purposefully stated in a modest way, although what was really being sought was much more: full permanent departure.[137]

5:2 The theme of Pharaoh's not knowing Yahweh follows a certain progression, especially from this point to the end of the plague accounts. Pharaoh started out not knowing who Yahweh was in the sense of not recognizing the name Yahweh, and then thereafter he obviously recognized the name but did not realize who Yahweh *really* was, and then finally, before it was all over, he knew very well who Yahweh was and was sorry that he had to find out the hard way. In other words, there are two meanings to "Who is the LORD?" (1) "Who are you talking about? I don't recognize that name." (2) "What makes you think I would care about obeying Yahweh?" The latter usage is found, for example, in Prov 30:9 ("Or I shall be full, and deny you, and say, 'Who is the LORD?' / or "I shall be poor, and steal, and profane the name of my God" [NRSV]). Thus when Pharaoh said further, "I do not know the LORD" *(lōʾ yādaʿtî ʾet-yahweh),* he was employing *in concept* the second sense of "Who is the LORD?" namely, "to take the LORD seriously").[138] In comparison to the pharaoh who did not know Joseph (1:8), we now read of a pharaoh who did not know Yahweh. Moses and Aaron had received their first refusal, as God had predicted, and there would be many more.[139]

5:3–5 In saying, "The God of the Hebrews has met with us" (v. 3), Moses and Aaron used "Hebrews" rather than "Israelites" in accordance with the common practice of identifying themselves to foreigners.[140] Most of what they said to Pharaoh was word for word what they were told to say in 3:18, with the added statement "or he may strike us with plagues or with the sword," presumably their way of assuring Pharaoh that they were deadly serious about obeying the Lord and that obedience was not something about

---

[137] In bargaining one usually asks for more than is desired, on the expectation that the bargaining process will reduce the amount to what one can actually obtain. Sometimes in asking for favor or permission, however (something to which one is not actually entitled), the process may involve initiating the bargaining with euphemistic understatement. See the discussion on 3:18. An example of the bargaining style that begins with an understatement and eventually openly states the full content of what is desired is found in Gen 23, where Abraham began his negotiation with Ephron for his cave and field by first not even speaking directly to Ephron (vv. 7–8) and then by asking only for the cave (v. 9) and then, finally, by asking for the field including the cave (v. 13), which was the real goal all along. There is no deception intended in such bargaining (God was not instructing Moses to try to trick the pharaoh). It was an accepted and respected style of negotiation in some cultures, including that of ancient Canaan and Egypt.

[138] I.e., "know the LORD," ידע את־יהוה, often has the sense of "pay attention to/care about/take seriously the LORD"; cf. Judg 2:10; 1 Sam 2:12; 3:7; Jer 31:34; Hos 2:20; 6:3; or what is often conveyed by the alternative wording "fear the LORD" (ירא את־יהוה).

[139] See M. P. V. Barrett, "Tests, Tests, and More Tests: Theme Through Several Chapters: Exodus 5,14–17, 32," *BV* 25 (1991): 29–40.

[140] See comments on 1:16.

which in their minds there was any option. Ironically, it was the Egyptians, not the Israelites, who would eventually be struck with plagues (the ten) and the sword ("sword" being a standard OT synecdoche for defeat and death in battle, which the Egyptians experienced at the Red Sea [chaps. 14–15]). "Plague" and "sword" are two of the famous three expressions summarizing all the various curses of God against his enemies.[141]

It is possible that by his statement "Why are you taking the people away from their labor?"[142] the king[143] meant to suggest only that Israelites had been shirking work ever since, or at least recently as a result of, being organized by Moses and Aaron into the beginnings of a resistance movement. Reports had surely reached him of Israelite work stoppages and slowdowns (some of which may have been related to their newfound worship of the true God as referred to in 4:31). However, since the Hebrew imperfect verb form employed here *(taprîʿû)* in context can convey not merely "why are you taking the people away?" but equally as likely "why would you take the people away?" it is probable that Pharaoh also was verbalizing the implications of what he understood they were asking for in the name of their God—an actual physical departure from the site of work. At any rate, it is clear from v. 5 ("the people of the land[144] are now numerous, and you are stopping them from working") that most or all Israelites may at that moment not only have stopped work but amassed somewhere to await the report from the encounter at the palace and perhaps to pray for the immediate success of that encounter, an optimistic expectation in light of the more arduous process we know God was planning (cf. 3:19; 4:21).

Pharaoh's language in v. 5 carries an overtone of the Egyptian xenophobic paranoia described in 1: 9–14, where the dangerously large population of the

---

[141] The usual full expression is "sword, famine and plague" as often in Jeremiah and Ezekiel and also in Rev 6:8.

[142] What the NIV translates here as "[their] labor" (סִבְלֹתָם) more accurately translates as "hard labor" in 2:18. In other words, Pharaoh had no problem admitting that the Israelite labor was "hard labor"—something the NIV translators may have incorrectly assumed he would not have been inclined to acknowledge.

[143] The variation between "king" and "Pharaoh" is stylistic only, and vv. 4–5 here represent an instance of the way the variation holds no special implications for meaning.

[144] The SP wording, "they are now more numerous than the people of the land," interprets עם הארץ ("people of the land") to refer to the native Egyptians rather than the Israelites in accordance with the most common way Moses himself used the term elsewhere (e.g., Gen 23:7,12; 42:6; Num 14:9). But Moses also used עם הארץ to refer to the "common people" or "ordinary people" of the Israelites (as in Lev 4:27); and this is its meaning in many other OT contexts (e.g., 2 Kgs 11:14; 24:14; Jer 37:2; Ezek 7:27). Moses may well have used the term here to translate what Pharaoh had actually said to him in Egyptian, i.e., to refer to the subservient Israelites in contrast to their masters, the Egyptians. Durham captures the sense in his "land-people, working-people, and so in the translation [here], 'peasants.'" See also S. Zeitlin, "The Am haaretz," *JQR* 23 (1932): 45–61 (who sees the term as referring basically to farmers); L. Rost confines the term mainly to free citizens (i.e., not nobility and not slaves; "Die Bezeichnungen für Land und Folk im Alten Testament," in *Das Kleine Credo und Andere Studien zum Alten Testament* [Heidelberg: Quelle und Meyer, 1965], 76–101). By contrast, S. Daiches takes the term to refer more often to leaders among the population (by reason of their land ownership; "The Meaning of עם הארץ in the Old Testament," *JTS* 30 [1929]: 245–49). The reason for these differing analyses is that the term can be used in different ways, as we have noted, depending on context.

Israelites (as seen from the Egyptian point of view) resulted in a long-term plan to suppress them by heavy labor. Here the population, even larger (1:12), must—according to the logic of that long-term Egyptian plan—be even more suppressed by even more labor. Accordingly, Pharaoh took control, as his office and training dictated, and next proposed a workload increase that made perfect sense from the point of view of the agreed-upon Egyptian remedy for a large, potentially hostile Israelite population (see comments on 1:11–14).

5:6–9 The remedy proposed by the king was predictable: if work was the way to *keep* the Israelites quiet and obedient (a method that had worked well for decades), more work was the way to *restore* quiet and obedience. According to 1:14, the forced labor burden on the Israelites was related mainly to brick making ("brick and mortar and with all kinds of work in the fields").[145] Presumably the "work in the fields" was not originally focused on gathering the straw for the bricks but on planting, tending, and harvesting crops. The Egyptians must have used some other group for the straw. Now, ratcheting up the workload, Pharaoh ordered the Israelites to gather their own straw.[146] From the reader's point of view, however, if the old attempt to keep down the Israelite population growth and aspirations for freedom failed (1:12), there was little chance that this greater oppression would turn the tide in favor of Egypt and against Israel.

The "slave drivers" (*nōgĕśîm,* probably a synonym for the term "slave masters," *śārê missîm,* used in 1:11) were likely Egyptian; the "foremen" were clearly Israelite[147] (cf. 5:14–15,19). Thus immediately ("that same

---

[145] In spite of his contention that the OT preserves the overall gist of the story of the Israelite oppression with much accuracy, J. Heller ("Ziegel oder Steine?" in *Prophetie und geschichtliche Wirklichkeit im alten Israel: Festschrift für Siegfried Herrmann zum 65* [Stuttgart: Kohlhammer, 1991], 165–70) opines that the author of this part of Exodus changed the actual material the Israelites had to work with (stone) to "bricks" and "straw" because the real facts (the Israelites were employed cutting stones in quarries and transporting them to building locations) were less useful to the theme of the narrative than the substituted ideas (bricks and straw function metaphorically to indicate that whatever was done in Egypt was temporary, bound to fade and dissolve). Although it is certainly true that stone endures longer than brick, properly made brick lasts for millennia and can be far more readily obtained and shaped in some locations than stone can. Not only so, but the narrative makes no overt claim whatever that the Israelites were producing for the Egyptians something merely temporal that would in time fade away. Egyptian historical records do indeed report that many indentured people groups worked in Egypt as stone cutters, but that hardly requires the conclusion that all of them did. If anything, the text may suggest that the Israelites had the less glamorous and perhaps harder assignment of brick making as opposed to other foreigners in servitude in Egypt, who had higher-status stonecutting jobs.

[146] תֶּבֶן, "cut/chopped straw," of the sort specially prepared by others and previously supplied ready-to-use to the Israelites (see C. F. Nims, "Bricks Without Straw?" *BA* 13 [1950]: 22–28). As iron bars ("rebars") strengthen concrete in modern building techniques, keeping the material from cracking and splitting, straw did the same for ancient clay bricks, making it possible to use sun drying rather than exclusively kiln baking in their manufacture, and thus saving energy and money in Egyptian construction. Egypt was fully deforested in ancient times, and its firewood had to be imported (see, e.g., "A Trip to Lebanon for Cedar," *ANET,* 243). Being able to make bricks without firewood-intensive kiln baking was therefore essential, and the use of reinforcing straw was therefore essential as well.

[147] See A. Erman, *Life in Ancient Egypt* (London: Macmillan, 1894), 123–29.

day") upon hearing Yahweh's demands on him on behalf of his people, Pharaoh showed his contempt by making *his* demands on Yahweh's people—the same brick output as previously, with a greatly increased supply problem relative to the straw.

In 3:18 and 5:3 the Israelites are quoted as asking for permission to "offer sacrifices to [Yahweh] the LORD." Here Pharaoh characterized their request as a desire to "sacrifice to our God," leaving out the name Yahweh. He had not forgotten the divine name, which he used in v. 2 and would mention readily again until 8:8, when in desperation he needed Moses' prayer to Yahweh to relieve the plague of the frogs. Rather, this omission subtly and efficiently conveys the impression of Pharaoh's disdain for Yahweh—who was to him in effect merely "the god these people worship." To him, Yahweh's words were not valid; they were just *lies*. This is ever the view of the nonbeliever: God's words are *lies* that keep you from conforming to the expectations of the world you live in and from enjoying life on your own terms (a concept that began early in human history, according to Gen 3:4).

5:10–14 The Israelites had believed in the Lord, and Moses and Aaron had faithfully spoken his word to Pharaoh, but things got worse rather than better. Surely this relatively detailed[148] account of the increased workload and the suffering it engendered makes a principal point: God's people must not assume that carrying out his commands will increase their own comfort.[149] Of course, Moses had been forewarned that Pharaoh would be resistant (3:19; 4:21), but the severity and breadth of the suffering his resistance would cause the Israelites was not explicitly stated; it is likely that Moses, Aaron, the Israelite foremen, and the Israelites in general were caught unprepared for a punitive workload increase.

What Pharaoh required was not simply that the Israelites themselves start gathering and chopping straw, a job previously done by others.[150] Rather, "I will give you no straw" means that they could not have any or grow any of their own—no straw *(teben)* at all was to be provided them—not by others, not by their own hand (v. 10). What they then had to do, according to v. 12, was go everywhere[151] looking for stubble *(qaš)* to serve as a substitute for

---

[148] Comparing the degree of detail to 4:27–31.

[149] This concept is so well represented in the NT and so strong in the teachings of Jesus that Paul claimed that the proof of his being chosen as a disciple was the amount of suffering he was forced to undergo. See S. J. Hafemann, *Suffering and Ministry in the Spirit: Paul's Defense of His Ministry in II Corinthians 2:14–3:3* (Carlisle, Cumbria: Paternoster, 2000).

[150] Chopping straw is necessary to make it most effective in brick making so that it does not protrude from the surfaces of the brick, works into the clay, and is distributed most evenly.

[151] The Hb. wording of v. 12 is somewhat ambiguous. It can be translated "the people scattered throughout all the land of Egypt" or "the people throughout all the land of Egypt scattered." It seems unlikely that Israelites would have been given free reign to go anywhere in Egypt they chose to find chaff. Rather, as the second translation option suggests (which we prefer), every Israelite available, whatever his or her location in Egypt, was pressed into service to help find chaff.

straw *(teben)*. Straw is preserved plant stalks from the more rigid long-stalk grains and vegetables. Straw comes from those plants that are harvested but whose stalks are inedible to humans and/or animals. Stubble is the very short remaining stalks of plants after harvesting: the bit between the root and where the reaping scythe or sickle cut the plant. It was only a relatively poor substitute for straw, making the process of producing suitable bricks much harder, but it also was much harder to gather from harvested fields even when the season is right (requiring careful, tedious hand pulling and cutting) as compared to the purposely preserved (and usually bundled) straw and was almost hopelessly difficult to gather in the off season.[152] As Job said, referring to a fruitless endeavor, "Will you frighten a windblown leaf and pursue dry chaff?" (Job 13:25 NRSV). The fact that the Israelites under the new rules simply could not meet their brick quotas is not surprising: Pharaoh had made the task virtually impossible. When the foremen, even under the penalty of being beaten, could not get the people to produce any more bricks (vv. 13–14), the situation was obviously intolerable. It is not surprising that an anguished appeal to Pharaoh for relief followed (vv. 15–16), even though such an appeal was essentially an act of desperation, presumably having little chance of success.

8. Negative Reaction of the Israelite Foreman (5:15–21)

15Then the Israelite foremen went and appealed to Pharaoh: "Why have you treated your servants this way? 16Your servants are given no straw, yet we are told, 'Make bricks!' Your servants are being beaten, but the fault is with your own people."

17Pharaoh said, "Lazy, that's what you are—lazy! That is why you keep saying, 'Let us go and sacrifice to the LORD.' 18Now get to work. You will not be given any straw, yet you must produce your full quota of bricks."

19The Israelite foremen realized they were in trouble when they were told, "You are not to reduce the number of bricks required of you for each day."
20When they left Pharaoh, they found Moses and Aaron waiting to meet them,
21and they said, "May the LORD look upon you and judge you! You have made us a stench to Pharaoh and his officials and have put a sword in their hand to kill us."

[152] The relatively dry climate of most parts of the Near East produces dusty soil in the nonrainy seasons, and such soil does not hold stubble easily. It tends to wither, dislodge from the soil, and blow away (cf. Isa 41:2; Jer 13:24; Ps 83:13). In the words of Isa 40:24 (NRSV), "Scarcely are they planted, scarcely sown, scarcely has their stem taken root in the earth, / when he blows upon them, and they wither, and the tempest carries them off like stubble." Stubble also was burned easily, sometimes on purpose, to create more tillable land and to eliminate weeds (e.g., Exod 15:7; Isa 5:24; 47:14; Joel 2:5; Obad 1:18; Mal 4:1).

5:15–21 This section of the story contains several repetitions of information already known from prior verses in the chapter. The repeated material reinforces the severity of the problem confronting the Israelites. Its special emphasis lies in its focus on the rejection of the appeal and the hopelessness of the Israelites: when Pharaoh said, "'You will not be given any straw, yet you must produce your full quota of bricks,' the Israelite foremen realized they were in trouble" (vv. 18–19).

Thus the situation had transformed from one of hopefulness and faith (4:31) to resentment and doubt. Why? Because of Pharaoh's intransigence. He clearly is portrayed here as unyielding, determined to put the Israelites in their place, suggesting that the Israelites were going to need something much stronger than words to convince him to change his mind. As v. 20 indicates, Moses and Aaron did not attempt to return to the royal court to handle this appeal, suggesting that they saw no hope in it or realized that they would not have been welcome. Pharaoh was the final court of appeal, the equivalent of the supreme court of his country. Thus his final verdict had been rendered to Moses and Aaron already, and they may even have been barred from seeing him so soon again on essentially the same issue. Someone else, however, might have had the opportunity to address the king on the topic of the impossibility of fulfilling a royal edict (making a full quota of bricks without straw) under the court rules of that time (assuming the ancient Near Eastern general right of access; see comments on 5:1), and it was perhaps thus that the Israelite foremen tried themselves to appeal the penalty assigned in response to Moses' and Aaron's representation of Yahweh's demand.

When the bad news was delivered and the foremen had left the court and found Moses and Aaron outside (by all appearances, waiting in order to be supportive), the resentment and frustration engendered by their defeat at court boiled over into an angry accusation at the two brother leaders ("You have made us a stench[153] to Pharaoh and his officials and have put a sword in their hand[154] to kill us," v. 21). It is noteworthy that the foremen did not state that they had lost faith in Yahweh. Apparently they had not actually overthrown their newfound faith. They apparently thought, however, that

[153] The exact wording of the idiom הִבְאַשְׁתֶּם אֶת־רֵיחֵנוּ בְּעֵינֵי ("to make odious to") is unique here, but several close parallels exist confirming the sense (Gen 34:30; 1 Sam 13:4; 27:12; 2 Sam 10:6; 16:21; Isa 30:5; 1 Chr 19:6).

[154] Ezekiel used this imagery of God's putting a sword in a monarch's hand for judgment *against* Egypt in what appears to be a conscious ironic echo of the present passage: "I will strengthen the arms of the king of Babylon and put my sword in his hand, but I will break the arms of Pharaoh, and he will groan before him like a mortally wounded man. I will strengthen the arms of the king of Babylon, but the arms of Pharaoh will fall limp. Then they will know that I am the LORD, when I put my sword into the hand of the king of Babylon and he brandishes it against Egypt" [Ezek 30:24–25]).

Moses and Aaron could not have properly represented the case or handled it well and thus had disobeyed Yahweh ("May the LORD look upon you and judge you!"[155]). Behind this rebuke appears to be the conviction that Moses and Aaron needed judgment because the nation's God, Yahweh, would not have let such a thing happen without his will having been thwarted by these leaders. The presumption that a good God never lets dangerous or harmful events happen to his people, false as it has always been, is a very old belief.[156]

9. Moses' Complaint and God's Covenant Assurance (5:22–6:12)

22Moses returned to the LORD and said, "O Lord, why have you brought trou-
ble upon this people? Is this why you sent me? 23Ever since I went to Pharaoh to
speak in your name, he has brought trouble upon this people, and you have not
rescued your people at all."

1Then the LORD said to Moses, "Now you will see what I will do to Pharaoh:
Because of my mighty hand he will let them go; because of my mighty hand he will
drive them out of his country." 2God also said to Moses, "I am the LORD. 3I
appeared to Abraham, to Isaac and to Jacob as God Almighty, but by my name the
LORD I did not make myself known to them. 4I also established my covenant with
them to give them the land of Canaan, where they lived as aliens. 5Moreover, I have
heard the groaning of the Israelites, whom the Egyptians are enslaving, and I have
remembered my covenant. 6"Therefore, say to the Israelites: 'I am the LORD, and I
will bring you out from under the yoke of the Egyptians. I will free you from being
slaves to them, and I will redeem you with an outstretched arm and with mighty
acts of judgment. 7I will take you as my own people, and I will be your God. Then
you will know that I am the LORD your God, who brought you out from under the
yoke of the Egyptians. 8And I will bring you to the land I swore with uplifted hand
to give to Abraham, to Isaac and to Jacob. I will give it to you as a possession. I am
the LORD.'" 9Moses reported this to the Israelites, but they did not listen to him
because of their discouragement and cruel bondage. 10Then the LORD said to
Moses, 11 "Go, tell Pharaoh king of Egypt to let the Israelites go out of his country."
12But Moses said to the LORD, "If the Israelites will not listen to me, why would
Pharaoh listen to me, since I speak with faltering lips?"

---

[155] The wording here, involving the jussives of ראה and of שׁפט ("look . . . and judge") has a relatively close parallel in 1 Sam 24:15 (NRSV): "May the LORD therefore be judge, and give sentence between me and you. May he see to it, and plead my cause, and vindicate me against you." It is clearly a call for divine punishment for wrongdoing, not merely a request for God to decide who's right and who's wrong in a given disagreement.

[156] The prophetical books reflect repeatedly the idea that Israelites expected the Day of Yahweh, the time of God's great, decisive intervention on behalf of good and against evil, to be fully beneficial to them since they were, after all, God's chosen people. The idea that the day would actually be a day of judgment *against* them because of their covenant violations was hard for them to understand (cf. esp. Amos 5:18–24).

5:22–23 The wording "Moses returned to the LORD" is not a reference to his going to any particular location (as if there were already some sort of tent of meeting erected or as if he went back to Sinai) but to Moses' leaving the scene of the encounter with the furious foremen and taking his own discouragement privately to God in prayer. The wording could also be translated "Moses *turned* to the LORD," which is the more common translation of *šûb* in descriptions of prayer (e.g., 2 Kgs 23:25; 2 Chr 15:4; Ps 78:34; Dan 9:3; cf. Acts 9:35; 11:21).

His repeated refrain, "brought trouble upon this people," is attributed to God as the ultimate cause and Pharaoh as the immediate cause. The foremen had blamed Moses and Aaron; Moses now blamed God.[157] Moses apparently was genuinely dismayed by what had happened. He had been told to anticipate pharaoh's stubbornness, but he had not anticipated cruel retribution against the Israelites themselves as a result of his mission ("Is this why you sent me?").[158] "Ever since I went to Pharaoh" suggests what 5:10–14 implies: that a considerable time had elapsed between Pharaoh's rejection of the request to leave Egypt and this point in time—time taken by the publication of the new, harder requirement, by the desperate attempts to meet it, by the failures, by the process of beatings that followed the failures, and by the foremen's appeal.[159]

By concluding his prayer with "you have not rescued your people at all," Moses showed what he had actually been thinking: that God's promised deliverance would occur relatively quickly and would not involve setbacks or disappointments. From a literary point of view, Moses was telling this story on himself. That is, writing for the wilderness generation and beyond (see Introduction), Moses included a detail that shows how he himself was unreasonably impatient for God's deliverance. The wilderness generation—and all that had

[157] His words are bold, but not as bold as those of Jeremiah in his famous "complaint" (Jer 20:7–18, a lament psalm over the hardship of being rejected and ridiculed for his preaching) in which Jeremiah accused God of "deceiving" him in calling him and then allowing him so little success in his preaching. Neither prophet was actually charging God with wrongdoing; both were employing language that they wished they had been allowed to understand what they were in for at the time of their call.

[158] The rhetorical question is often a device in Hb. discourse for asking for action or making a point. Thus Moses was not so much expressing his puzzlement here as stating his objection to God's approach. Cp., e.g., Gen 32:29: "Jacob said, 'Please tell me your name.' But he replied, 'Why do you ask my name?'" [meaning "Don't ask my name!"]; Gen 42:1: "When Jacob learned that there was grain in Egypt, he said to his sons, 'Why do you just keep looking at each other?'" [meaning "Don't just keep looking at each other!"]; and Gen 47:15: "When the money of the people of Egypt and Canaan was gone, all Egypt came to Joseph and said, 'Give us food. Why should we die before your eyes?'" [meaning "Don't let us die before your eyes!"].

[159] For Moses the agony of dealing with Pharaoh was in part compounded by the fact that he was in the middle of a contest between Yahweh and Pharaoh and had the responsibility as a prophetic messenger of not only taking Yahweh's word to Pharaoh but of formally taking Pharaoh's word back to Yahweh (cf. A. Nicacci, "Yahweh e il Faraone: Teologia biblica ed egiziana a confronto," *BN* 38/39 [1987]: 85–102).

succeeded it—had a similar tendency, and what Moses eventually learned, all believers have had to learn for themselves: God's timing only sometimes coincides with our expectations, and his idea of the hardships we need to go through only sometimes coincides with our idea of how much we can take.

6:1 Using "by a mighty hand" (NRSV; *bĕyād hĕzāqāh)* twice[160] in this verse, God answered Moses' complaint not by addressing its component parts each in turn or by explaining why he had chosen to allow things to be so difficult for Moses and the Israelites.[161] Rather, he answered by reference back to his original promise in 3:19 that it would take something greater than human power to move Pharaoh to let the Israelites go. The NIV translation "because of my mighty hand" is grammatically inexplicable; no pronoun appears in the Hebrew in either place the expression occurs in the verse. The language is an idiom connoting "by force,"[162] and the NIV routinely translates it in other contexts (though not consistently so) as "by a mighty hand" rather than "because of my mighty hand." God here promised Moses that he would force Pharaoh to let the Israelites go—not just for a three-day festival[163] but he would "drive them out of his country." What God was planning for and reassuring Moses about was nothing less than the full exodus.

6:2–5 God's reassurance to Moses continues with covenant language, reminding him that he is Yahweh (v. 2), the God of the patriarchs, that the patriarchs worshiped him by that name,[164] and that the patriarchal promises included their descendants' possession of Canaan. To possess Canaan required leaving Egypt, and therefore the patriarchal covenant was always,

---

[160] The LXX and Syr. substitute "and with uplifted arm" for the second "by a mighty hand," which probably is the result of translating from a *Vorlage* that had already adjusted the reading by conflation from the many other places where "by a mighty hand" is paired with "and with an uplifted arm" rather than repeated.

[161] So with Job: he never found out that his suffering was a means of humiliating Satan and bringing glory to God in a contest initiated by God. God, in fact, silenced Job by convincing him that he was far superior to Job in his ways and in his knowledge (Job 38–41) but did not reveal the purpose he had in making Job suffer so much. The soldier in God's army is expected to obey orders whether or not his role in the overall battle strategy is shared with him by the Commander in Chief.

[162] Cf. Exod 13:9; 32:11; Num 20:20; Deut 4:34; 5:15; 6:21; 7:8; 9:26; 26:8; Ezek 20:33–34; Ps 136:12; Dan 9:15. The NIV translators may have confused this with the phenomenon of possessive use of the article, whereby body parts are sometimes referred to literally as, e.g., "the feet" to be translated "my feet," but the construction here is not definite and does not fit that pattern.

[163] Which, as we have already argued, was never the literal intent in the wording of 3:18; 5:3.

[164] The most likely translation of 6:3 is not that of the NIV ("but by my name the LORD I did not make myself known to them") but rather a question, "and by my name Yahweh, did I not make myself known to them?" In Hb. interrogatives are only sometimes marked by the so-called interrogative particle. The construction used here is common enough for interrogatives beginning with "is it not" or "did he not" or the like that require a positive answer ("is it not the case that *x* is *y*?" interrogatives). The disjunctive structure of the clause lends itself to the emphasis indicated by the interrogative, namely that Moses was supposed to understand that "my name Yahweh" was indeed already a proto-Israelite divine name. For similar constructions (interrogatives that begin with Hb. לֹא but without the so-called interrogative particle), cf. Num 23:19; 2 Sam 23:5; 2 Kgs 5:26; Jer 18:6; Jonah 4:11; Job 11:11; 30:25 et al.

implicitly, also an exodus promise. This is the first time in Exodus that God says "I am Yahweh" (NIV "I am the LORD").[165] He had said these words *('ănî yahweh)* only twice before, in Gen 15:7 to Abraham and in Gen 28:13 to Jacob, each time in connection with the promise of the land to their descendants. Again here the promise of the land follows. On the theological significance of this statement, see comments on v. 8.

In v. 3 God explains to Moses something else that up to this point had been only implicit: He, Yahweh, was the *El Shaddai* ("God the Mountain One"[166]; the NIV, following LXX tradition, *God Almighty*) referred to in the patriarchal stories (Gen 17:1; 28:3; 35:11; 43:14; 48:3; cf. also the early use of the name in Job 8:5; 13:3; 15:25, and the later use in Ezek 10:5). Thus Moses should assume full continuity between the promises to the patriarchs and the need for confidence in the present difficulties. Those promises held central the eventual gift of the land to the descendants of Abraham after their being enslaved in a foreign land and mistreated but liberated and enriched in the process—in other words, the whole exodus story in a very compact form:

> Then the LORD said to him, "Know for certain that your descendants will be strangers in a country not their own, and they will be enslaved and mistreated four hundred years. But I will punish the nation they serve as slaves, and afterward they will come out with great possessions. You, however, will go to your fathers in peace and be buried at a good old age. In the fourth generation your descendants will come back here, for the sin of the Amorites has not yet reached its full measure." (Gen 15:13–16)

What the patriarchs trusted would one day happen was now underway, and God encouraged Moses here to believe that fact.

Verse 5 recalls 2:24, including much of its vocabulary. "I have heard"[167] and "I have remembered"[168] are both idiomatic ways of saying "I will

---

[165] Accordingly, not a few scholars approaching Exodus from a source-critical viewpoint have assumed that 6:2–9 is the account of Moses' call and the revelation of the divine name from a separate source from that which produced 3:1–4,17. This is too narrow a stance. The present passage differs from the earlier one in chap. 3 because it describes what the name means and implies, whereas the chap. 3 account describes how Moses came to be chosen to know the name. See C. Seitz, "The Call of Moses and the 'Revelation' of the Divine Name: Source-Critical Logic and Its Legacy," in *Theological Exegesis: Essays in Honor of Brevard S. Childs* (Grand Rapids: Eerdmans, 1999), 145–67.

[166] Cf. J. Felton, "El Shaddai," *DD* 16 (1987/88): 186–91; R. D. Wilson, "Critical Note on Exodus VI 3," *PTR* 22 (1924): 108–19; E. C. B. MacLaurin, "Shaddai," *AbrN* 3 (1961–62): 99–118.

[167] When God says "I have heard," it most often has or leads to the sense of "I am going to respond favorably to your prayers and meet your needs" (e.g., Gen 17:20; Exod 3:7; 1 Kgs 9:3; 19:20; 20:5; 2 Kgs 22:19; 2 Chr 7:12; 34:27; Isa 38:5; cf. Acts 7:34).

[168] In the wording of the Hb. perfect, "I have remembered," the divine statement about "remembering" is used only here; otherwise the more common wording, that of the Hb. imperfect "I will remember," is used in divine speech almost always to indicate the sense of "I will honor the terms of my covenant" (as in Gen 9:15; Lev 26:42,45; Ezek 16:60). See comments on 2:24.

respond to your prayers and am now going into action relative to my earlier promises."

6:6–8 God had just reassured Moses. Next he gave Moses the words with which to reassure the Israelites, words that represent an expansion on his reassurance to Moses—similar in some ways to it but adding some important particulars as well. These words summarize God's plan for his people.[169]

The prophetic speech to the Israelites will also begin with *I am Yahweh* (see above on v. 2). The language of freedom from the "yoke" (v. 6) is language idiomatic of freedom from servitude (Gen 27:40; Lev 26:13; Deut 28:48; 1 Kgs 12:4). The reference to "an outstretched arm"[170] and "with mighty acts of judgment"[171] in that same verse connotes the upcoming plagues that would force Pharaoh to do what he otherwise never would have done and would serve as a *judgment* against Egypt. Egypt had unfairly oppressed the Israelites—they were never a real threat, they never would actually have joined with Asiatic enemies to try to take over Egypt (1:10), and they were therefore illegally placed in servitude. Accordingly, God would not merely rescue his people from the Egyptians but would also overtly punish the Egyptians in the process.

Verse 7 contains a special declaration of divine covenantal election of Israel in the words "I will take you as my own[172] people, and I will be your God." Similar statements modeled on this one, often with somewhat varied wording but always with "my people" and "your God" as the key vocabulary, are found in later contexts referring to this covenant promise (e.g., Jer 7:23; 11:4); or to the breaking of the covenant (e.g., Ps 50:7; Hos 1:9); or to

---

[169] Cf. E. Martens, *God's Design: A Focus on Old Testament Theology*, 3d ed. (Richland Hills, Tex.: Bibal, 1998). The present context (usually the entire 6:2–8) has long been recognized as programmatic for all of Exodus, if not for the OT generally. See P. Auffret, "The Literary Structure of Exodus 6.2–8," *JSOT* 27 (1983): 46–54; id., "Remarks on J. Magonet's Interpretation of Exodus 6. 2–8," *JSOT* 27 (1983): 69–71; B. Gosse, "Le livre d'Ezéchiel et Ex 6, 2–8 dans le cadre du Pentateuch," *BN* 104 (2000): 20–25; J. Magonet, "The Rhetoric of God: Exodus 6. 2–8," *JSOT* 27 (1983): 56–67; J.-L. Ska, "La place d'Ex 6:2–8 dans la narration de l'exode," *ZAW* 94 (1982): 530–48; I. B. Gottlieb, "Law, Love, and Redemption: Legal Connotations in the Language of Exodus 6:6–8," *JANES* 26 (1998): 47–57.

[170] The expression "outstretched arm" is used commonly in the OT to indicate God's decisive use of his power (Exod 6:6; Deut 4:34; 5:15; 7:19; 9:29; 11:2; 26:8; 1 Kgs 8:42; 2 Kgs 17:36; 2 Chr 6:32; Ps 136:12; Jer 27:5; 32:17,21; Ezek 20:33–34). K. Martens describes the expression as "the fundamental metaphor of the Old Testament traditions of the exodus" and shows how it refers throughout the OT and NT to the exodus. She notes that the use of "arm" in this and other expressions often has a military connotation ("With a Strong Hand and an Outstretched Arm," *SJOT* 15 (2001): 123–42.

[171] Although the Psalms four times refer to God's "mighty acts" (Pss 71:16; 106:2; 145:4,12), the longer term "mighty acts of judgment" is written only by Moses (here and in 7:4).

[172] The NIV "my *own* people" is an ad hoc translation choice; the Hb. does not necessarily emphasize the concept suggested by the use of "own." The NIV also uses "my *own* people" subjectively to translate a variety of other Hb. wordings (as in אחי, Exod 4:18; עמי, Ruth 1:16; מולדתי, Num 10:30).

keeping the Mosaic covenant in general (e.g., Lev 26:12); or to postcurse restoration of covenant blessings (e.g., Isa 40:1; Jer 30:22; Ezek 36:28). By these words God assured Israel of a special status: they were, corporately, his own people in a way that no other people were. The actual gift of the covenant at Sinai would flesh out the blessings and responsibilities associated with this election. For the time being, he assured them of his particular interest in them and of the coming ratification (at Sinai) of this promise of election.[173]

When would he "take" them as his people? That question is actually answered immediately in v. 7: "Then you will know that I am the LORD your God, who brought you out from under the yoke of the Egyptians." The expression "then you will know . . ." is found commonly in prophetical passages, where "proof by fulfillment" is a type of incentivizing to encourage the people to believe and act upon the divine word. Here what God was saying was, in effect: "Trust me that I will bring you out from under the yoke of the Egyptians. What is the proof? I won't give you any yet, but when you are out of Egypt and at the place where I will take you as my own people (which any reader understands to be Sinai since Moses wrote Exodus after Sinai), you will be able to look back on what has happened and see that I accomplished everything that I promised you." Only at Sinai, with its occasion of full ratification of the covenant, would God fully *take* Israel as his own people. The process began here, however, with their assent in faith to the promise that he would do so *after* having rescued them from Egyptian bondage.

Verse 8 hearkens back to the repeated forward-looking formal assurances given by God to the patriarchs that he would bring their descendants back to Canaan (Gen 15:13–20; 24:7; 26:2–5; 28:15; 35:12; 48:4). The solemnity of the promises is signaled in the wording "I swore with uplifted hand," an idiom for "I formally promised."[174] In saying "I will give it to you as a possession," God indicated that he would not merely let the Israelites live in Canaan but would actually let them own Canaan. They had never owned land—thus making Abraham's purchase of land to bury Sarah an exceptional event worthy of a special story in Genesis (Gen 23:3–20). But now they would have the land where the patriarchs resided as resident aliens given to them as a gift from God. Here was an incentive to follow Yahweh indeed!

The words "I am the LORD" that appear at the end of v. 8 had also opened this section of divine response to Moses' complaint (vv. 2–8), forming an inclusio for the entire divine speech. These two words (in Hb. just *ʾănî yahweh*) have profound significance theologically in two different

---

[173] On the importance of corporate election (rather than individual election) for biblical theology and the NT doctrine of election, see W. Klein, *The New Chosen People: A Corporate View of Election* (Grand Rapids: Academie Books, 1990).

[174] Cp. Num 14:30; Neh 9:15; Ps 106:26; Ezek 20:5,15,23,42; 36:7; 44:12; 47:14.

ways. First, they function as a synecdoche to bring to mind God's impending covenant because identification of the giver of a covenant is part of the preamble (identification of the parties to the covenant), that is, the initial content of a typical ancient Near Eastern covenant. Thus "I am the LORD" is almost tantamount to saying, "I am Yahweh, your covenant God." Second, "I am the LORD" is a statement of identity—not just theoretical identity but relational identity.[175] It invites the hearer to say: "I have a connection to him. I know him personally. He is not just any god. He is mine." This direct relationship, so crucial to our Christian sense of conversion and salvation from sin, is signaled in God's identifying himself personally.[176]

6:9–12 Optimism is often dashed by suffering, especially ongoing suffering. Faith is often diminished by hardship because emotions play a powerful part in most human thinking, and thinking can become increasingly pessimistic when any sort of pain continues unabated. Accordingly, it is understandable that the Israelites would not listen (v. 9) to Moses' latest message of divine reassurance, even though they had previously welcomed Yahweh's words (4:29–31). Pharaoh's strategy (5:7–9) had proved remarkably successful. The people were overcome by impatience[177] for relief and by hard slavery (NIV "discouragement and cruel bondage").

This presented an obvious tactical problem for Moses, which he voiced in v. 12. If the Israelites, who would be his natural allies and who stood to gain from the message he was speaking on God's behalf, would not listen, how could he ever expect to meet success by carrying on with the task of demanding freedom from Pharaoh, who was his natural enemy in this situation and who stood to lose hugely from an Israelite exodus? Nevertheless, God assigned him to confront Pharaoh once again and demand Israel's exodus (vv. 10–11). The wording of the request reflects less of the previous "opening bargaining style" now. In 5:1 the request was stated as "let my people go, so that they may hold a festival to me in the desert." Now it is less modest in scope: Pharaoh was to "let the Israelites go out of his country"—using the more blunt, full-exodus language that God had first used with Moses in connection with the exodus demand he was eventually to deliver (3:10).

At the end of v. 12 Moses reverted to his earlier protest mode (as seen in chaps. 3 and 4, esp. in 4:10–13), still seeking release from the difficult assignment. He employed here a variation on his earlier description of himself as

---

[175] Martens' book *God's Design* takes Exod 5:22–6:8 as a principal text for OT theology and argues persuasively that knowledge of God is one of the four great themes of biblical theology. The others, salvation, covenant community, and land, also are represented in Exod 5:22–6:8.

[176] Cf. esp. Gal 4:8–9; 1 Thess 4:5; 2 Thess 1:8; Titus 1:16; 1 John 4:8.

[177] "Impatience" is the basic sense of קצר רוח rather than the NIV "discouragement" or NRSV "broken spirit"; cf. Mic 2:7; Job 21:4; Prov 14:29.

"never . . . eloquent . . . slow of speech and tongue" (4:10). The NIV "I speak with faltering lips" misses the connection with 4:24–26 that the more literal translation "My lips are uncircumcised" *(ănî ʿăral śĕpātāyim)* would suggest. Moses was not saying that he had a speech impediment ("faltering lips"); he was rather saying (disingenuously) that he was "not ready for public speaking," using the metaphorical language of circumcision. Did Moses think that since God was willing to kill him for failing to circumcise his children and perhaps himself (see comments on 4:24–26) he would now be willing to dismiss him as a prophet for being unwilling to speak to speak to Pharaoh again—claiming lack of skill even if not lack of physical ability? This seems indeed likely. In other words, Moses was still desperate and desperately discouraged and pessimistic. He wanted out. God, however, knew better.

10. Genealogy of Moses and Aaron (6:13–27)

13Now the LORD spoke to Moses and Aaron about the Israelites and Pharaoh king of Egypt, and he commanded them to bring the Israelites out of Egypt.

14These were the heads of their families:

The sons of Reuben the firstborn son of Israel were Hanoch and Pallu, Hezron and Carmi. These were the clans of Reuben.

15The sons of Simeon were Jemuel, Jamin, Ohad, Jakin, Zohar and Shaul the son of a Canaanite woman. These were the clans of Simeon.

16These were the names of the sons of Levi according to their records: Gershon, Kohath and Merari. Levi lived 137 years.

17The sons of Gershon, by clans, were Libni and Shimei.

18The sons of Kohath were Amram, Izhar, Hebron and Uzziel. Kohath lived 133 years.

19The sons of Merari were Mahli and Mushi.

These were the clans of Levi according to their records.

20Amram married his father's sister Jochebed, who bore him Aaron and Moses. Amram lived 137 years.

21The sons of Izhar were Korah, Nepheg and Zicri.

22The sons of Uzziel were Mishael, Elzaphan and Sithri.

23Aaron married Elisheba, daughter of Amminadab and sister of Nahshon, and she bore him Nadab and Abihu, Eleazar and Ithamar.

24The sons of Korah were Assir, Elkanah and Abiasaph. These were the Korahite clans.

25Eleazar son of Aaron married one of the daughters of Putiel, and she bore him Phinehas.

These were the heads of the Levite families, clan by clan.

26It was this same Aaron and Moses to whom the LORD said, "Bring the Israelites out of Egypt by their divisions." 27They were the ones who spoke to Pharaoh king of Egypt about bringing the Israelites out of Egypt. It was the same Moses and Aaron.

In the style of ancient Near Eastern writing and according to the concerns of ancient Near Eastern culture, a genealogy here is neither out of place nor stylistically intrusive but welcome and perfectly placed. At the end of 6:12, the ongoing narrative stops[178] for a moment: right at the point where Moses said, in effect, "I can't do it." This would be the ideal point for a commercial in a modern TV dramatic presentation, the point just before the resolution of the suspense, since the viewer's interest level is held by the emotional interest in story resolution. Most ancient narratives had no concern for preservation of suspense per se. But neither did it hurt to place a review and retrospective, which is what 6:13–27 functions as in Exodus, at a location just prior to a major story resolution, the final, great divine reassurance of Moses' call, commission, and challenge (6:28–7:7) equipping him for the launching of the plagues (7:8 and following).

The reader has already been learning about the importance of Moses and Aaron. They obviously were going to be featured as the two key Israelite figures of the exodus story. Now is the time that the reader finds out what he has already been wondering (if he is an Israelite, attuned to his culture's high interest in family connections, as the original readers of Exodus were) just who Moses and Aaron really were in terms of their familial links within the sociological structure of their people.

This portion of the book is composed of a genealogical list (vv. 14–25, the first and last verses of which are linked in an inclusio by "These were the heads of . . . families") surrounded by a prose introduction (v. 13) and prose conclusion (vv. 26–27) that likewise make extensive use of shared themes and vocabulary, vv. 26–27 being essentially an expanded rewording of v. 13. The genealogical list itself has at least seven particular purposes: (1) It begins with Reuben, Jacob's firstborn son, and thus traces the lineage of Aaron and Moses back to *Israel* the man, linking them with the very beginnings of their people, as a proper Israelite genealogy was expected to do. (2) It ends with Aaron's grandson (Phinehas, v. 25) and thus brings the genealogy into the time of the book of Judges (Judg 20:28), providing a way for successive generations to link these leaders with their own place in time. (3) It honors Aaron and the true priesthood, one of Moses' special concerns in Exodus. (4) It shows the reader where Korah, the leader of the wilderness rebellion (Num 16:1–49) founded his claim to credentials of leadership. (5) It reminds the reader that Moses was from a priestly family and tribe, thus qualified and called to perform priestly—not merely

[178] Some scholars (e.g., Durham, *Exodus,* 71–79) have taken 6:13 as the conclusion to the section that begins with 6:1 or 6:2 and therefore regard the placement of the genealogy of 6:14–27 as a separate section inserted here as occasioned by the mention of Aaron in 6:13. The priestly interest of the supposed P source in Aaron's lineage sometimes is cited as a likely reason. This theory fails not only to see the structural unity of vv. 13–27 but misses Moses' literary motives in selecting the genealogical material.

prophetic—duties from time to time (including his directing the building of the tabernacle, his right to enter it, and his offering the ordination sacrifice in Lev 8:28–29). (6) It reminds the reader that the Israelites were not ethically pure,[179] by specifically mentioning the Canaanite woman in v. 15. (7) By reason of calling special attention to several women in the priestly family lineage (vv. 20,23,25), it reminds the reader of the importance attached to proper, godly marriage for priests, a theme also reflected later, in the laws.[180]

Virtually all Old Testament genealogical lists are selective.[181] That is, they normally name prominent or necessary persons in a genetic line, but not by any means always every person in that line. They can skip several generations at a time and/or can leave off at any point in the rundown of a particular line. They can include some lines from a given set of brothers and not others and/or can take the line of one brother all the way to a final point, while taking the line of another brother only part of the way and then abandoning further listing. Moses' listing of his and Aaron's ancestry has, typically, gaps. It mentions Moses and Aaron in the fourth generation after Jacob, although Aaron's wife Elisheba (v. 23) seems to fit in the sixth generation after Jacob according to the data in the lists in 1 Chr 2:4–10 and Ruth 4:18–20. By mentioning only the generations of Levi, Kohath, Amram, and Aaron/Moses (vv. 16–20), it could seem to give the impression that there were in fact only four generations from the entrance into Egypt until the exodus—a period of 430 years (cf. Exod 12:20). This is theoretically possible in light of the long lives of Levi, Kohath, and Amram and the fact that Moses was eighty when the exodus began, but it would require that each father in this group had the son named in this group at about age one hundred.[182] Where other selectivity is evident, we point this out in the comments below.

[179] Cf. 12:38.

[180] Marriage purity was especially important for priests; e.g., Lev 21:7,14; 22:12–13.

[181] Likewise, Matthew's NT genealogy of Jesus (Matt 1:1–17) is an instructive example: in order to help his readers follow and remember the names in Jesus' human lineage, Matthew divided them into three groups of fourteen names each, in the process leaving out a considerable number of names, and thus generations, well known from OT genealogies. This produces a typically selective genealogy but one with the memory-enhancing merit of listing fourteen generations in each block of time between Adam, David, the exile, and Jesus (1:17). If this means that, e.g., the kings of Judah between Jehoram (who died in 841 BC) and Uzziah (who came to the throne in 791 BC) are left out, Matthew expected his readers not to mind because Ahaziah (841 BC) and Joash (835–796 BC)—as well as wicked Queen Athaliah (841–835 BC)—were not so important to Matthew's purposes that he felt he must mention them simply because they were kings of Judah in the lineage of David.

[182] U. Cassuto in his *Commentary of the Book of Exodus* (London: ET, 1967) suggests that the time span and the number of generations can be harmonized by assuming that the time mentioned in 12:20 is a conversion to a decimal system from an original sexigesimal system, thus increasing it by a factor of roughly two-thirds. It seems to us much simpler to recognize that this genealogy, like most in the OT, selectively skips some generations.

6:14 The phrase "the heads of their families" is standard in genealogies. Reuben, Jacob's firstborn son, is mentioned first, in the manner of normal genealogical preference. His listing, however, goes only to his immediate children and then stops because Moses and Aaron were not descended from him.

6:15 Simeon, Jacob's second-born, is listed next, as is proper; but his listing likewise stops at the second generation because Aaron and Moses were not descended from him either. The mention of "a Canaanite woman" as the father of Shaul has two purposes: it contrasts to the line of Levi, which is purer Israelite as appropriate for the tribe of the priests, and it reminds the reader that some prominent matriarchs in Israel were not Israelite by birth, a theme consistent with 12:38.

6:16 Here begins the lineage that will be traced down to Aaron's grandson (v. 25) because it is the lineage of the tribe of Levi, Jacob's third son. Had Levi been the twelfth son, the verses prior to this one might have been more, to accommodate the listing of all brothers prior to Levi. Conveniently for the reader, this was not necessary. So far the list corresponds to the one Moses had already written in Gen 46:8–11. Hereafter, however, it diverges because there is no further interest in naming sons of Jacob and their offspring; all the attention is now on Levites. Levi's long life span (137 years) is typical of those of the patriarchs—part of the reason Israel could multiply so rapidly in Egypt.

6:17–19 Levi's sons Gershon, Kohath, and Merari are all named here with a second generation given for each, but only Kohath's age is given since he was the one from whom Aaron and Moses were descended. Hebron is named as a son of Kohath in v. 18, but his lineage is not brought further—not even to a second generation, as is the case with the other sons of Kohath. Unless he died childless but was nevertheless so prominent that leaving out his name would seem improper, this is simply another example of selective genealogizing.

6:20 Amram, Moses' and Aaron's father, is now mentioned for the first time by name. Moses mentioned him only as "a man of the house of Levi" in 2:1, where giving further detail about him was not useful in the narrative. Of special note is the remark Moses adds as this point: Amram married his aunt [NIV "father's sister"] Jochebed. This apparently was so bothersome to the LXX translator that he rendered it "married the daughter of his father's brother," a translation for which there is no justification otherwise. Why the concern? Later incest laws (e.g., Lev 18:12, "Do not have sexual relations with your father's sister; she is your father's close relative") prohibit marriage to any close relative (Lev 18:6). But a cousin is technically not a close relative according to Lev 18, and the LXX translator of this passage apparently felt that something that violated the later law could not have occurred in the immediate lineage of the lawgiver Moses and thus came up with his translation. This, however, is a true genealogy of Moses and Aaron, antedating the Sinai law, simply stating a fact about who Moses' mother really was. Amram had violated no law; there did not yet exist one to violate.[183] Further on the positive side, Jochebed was thus clearly a Levite herself, making Moses' and Aaron's parentage Levite on both sides.

6:21–22 The sons of Kohath unimportant for the lineage of Moses and Aaron are mentioned, with their children, in all but one case for a single further generation. Note, however, the name "Korah" in v. 21, a cousin of Moses and Aaron. His importance will emerge in the rebellion narrated in Num 16. From the point of view of strict genealogical prestige, he was the equal of Moses and Aaron and could lay his claim to Israelite leadership accordingly. Thus his lineage is further described in v. 24.

6:23 Aaron married a Judahite woman, Elisheba, whose father and brother were ancestors of Jesus Christ,[184] a small but not insignificant connection of two threads of salvation history in the biblical text. His four sons have roles in various future narratives because of their importance in the priestly lineage. Once God established the priesthood as an inherited office, the descendancy of a priest became a nonnegotiable credential.

6:24 Korah's lineage, on the other hand, may have had an ominous overtone for future readers for whom the story of the great rebellion in the wilderness (Num 16) led by Korah was history. "The Korahites," ignoble as their ancestor's actions were, nevertheless were a powerful clan among the Levites and fully worthy of mention here even if only for that reason.

6:25 Moses ended his and Aaron's Levite genealogy with Phinehas. By the time Moses wrote this genealogy, Aaron's first two sons, Nadab and Abihu, were dead by reason of illegal activity (Lev 10:1–2). In a later genealogy, in Numbers, Moses explained that Aaron's other two sons, Eleazar and Ithamar, continued as priests.[185] Why, then, mention only Eleazar and his son Phinehas here? After all, Ithamar had children and was the ancestor of a huge division of priests in his own right.[186] The answer is simply that here again we have an interrupted/selective genealogy in which Moses had chosen to mention only a single grandson of Aaron: the most famous one. Phinehas had such a prominent role in ending the cultic prostitution scandal

---

[183] An obvious parallel is that of Abram's marrying his half-sister (see Gen 20:12).

[184] Cf. Num 1:7; 2:3; 7:12,17; 10:14; Ruth 4:17; Matt 1:4; Luke 3:33.

[185] Num 3:2–4: The names of the sons of Aaron were Nadab the firstborn and Abihu, Eleazar and Ithamar . . . who were ordained to serve as priests. . . . Nadab and Abihu, however, fell dead before the LORD when they made an offering with unauthorized fire before him in the Desert of Sinai. They had no sons; so only Eleazar and Ithamar served as priests during the lifetime of their father Aaron.

[186] Num 4:28,33; 7:8; 1 Chr 24:1–6; Ezra 8:2.

at Baal-Peor in Num 25 that it is understandable that he should be mentioned here as opposed to his own relatively less-known brothers and the relatively less-known children of Ithamar.[187] The statement "these were the heads of the Levite families, clan by clan" brings the Levite genealogy to a formal conclusion through its slightly expanded resumption of the opening words of the genealogy ("these were the heads of their families") in v. 14.

6:26–27 These two verses are slightly expanded inclusio resumptions of v. 13, parallel to the way the end of v. 25 is a slightly expanded resumption of the beginning of v. 14. The names are repeated for emphasis so that "it was Moses and Aaron" (NIV "it was this same Aaron and Moses") unmistakably links the two brothers with both the genealogy and the exodus. Otherwise the only really new information added to v. 13 is the expression "by armies" (*ʿal-ṣĕbāʾôt;* NIV "by their divisions"). In English translations "divisions" can refer to various sorts of divisions, including clan divisions (e.g. Gen 36:30) and priestly divisions (e.g., 1 Chr 28:13), but here the wording of the Hebrew is focused on the theme of Israel's organization as an *army* of God, the main referent for the language of *divisions* in the Pentateuch.[188] This verse thus adumbrates the fighting role of Israel in the exodus and conquest, which will first be tested in 17:8–16 at Rephidim, near Sinai.

11. Divine Reassurance of Moses' Call, Commission, Challenge (6:28–7:7)

28 Now when the LORD spoke to Moses in Egypt, 29 he said to him, "I am the
LORD. Tell Pharaoh king of Egypt everything I tell you."
30 But Moses said to the LORD, "Since I speak with faltering lips, why would
Pharaoh listen to me?"

1 Then the LORD said to Moses, "See, I have made you like God to Pharaoh,
and your brother Aaron will be your prophet. 2 You are to say everything I com-
mand you, and your brother Aaron is to tell Pharaoh to let the Israelites go out of
his country. 3 But I will harden Pharaoh's heart, and though I multiply my mirac-
ulous signs and wonders in Egypt, 4 he will not listen to you. Then I will lay my
hand on Egypt and with mighty acts of judgment I will bring out my divisions,

---

[187] Phinehas continued in notable exploits in his old age as the high priest during the days of Joshua and at least the early days of the Judges (Num 31:6; Josh 22:13,30–32; 24:33; Judg 20:28), confirming the sort of leadership skills that already caused Moses to include him and end the Levite genealogy with him here. If Phinehas was indeed a black African, as some scholars think (see comments on 12:38; cf. J. D. Hays, "Moses: The Private Man Behind the Public Leader," *BR* 16 [2000]: 16–26, 60–63), this would be strong evidence of the lack of racism in early Israel and one more divine endorsement of the necessity of a nonracist attitude.

[188] All fourteen times that עַל־צִבְאֹתָם occurs in the Pentateuch it has this same emphasis: Israel was organized as God's army; cf. Num 1:3, "You and Aaron are to number by their divisions all the men in Israel twenty years old or more who are able to serve in the army."

my people the Israelites. [5]And the Egyptians will know that I am the LORD when I stretch out my hand against Egypt and bring the Israelites out of it."

[6]Moses and Aaron did just as the LORD commanded them. [7]Moses was eighty years old and Aaron eighty-three when they spoke to Pharaoh.

Exodus 6:28–7:7 is largely summational material, reminding the hearer/reader of key issues in the story so far, with a focus on the confrontation with Pharaoh and Egypt. The plagues are about to begin, and this is an appropriate place in the narrative to be sure that the hearer has the key characters and the essential themes in mind in preparation for the great conflict story. Such a reminder has value to hearers, however, who must keep everything in mind because they cannot go back and look at it in print. Ancient readers were few, full literacy was relatively rare, and even partial literacy the exception, so many readers probably read haltingly and benefited from the reorientation a passage such as the present one provided to them.

The passage concentrates especially on Moses' need for reassurance. The hero of the story, in other words, is Yahweh, not Moses. Moses openly admitted repeatedly in Exodus that he lacked confidence in his ability to carry out God's orders and reminded us in each case that God sustained him through the entire process.[189] Even the note about his and Aaron's age in 7:7 is instructive: The two of them were called upon to lead a great movement at an age when most people have already died (Ps 90:10). Their contribution to the exodus was not their genius or their experience (what experience had they in leading an exodus?) or their credentials (Moses' were essentially negative as far as most Israelites were concerned) or their vitality, or any such thing. What made them successful leaders was the fact that they "did just as the LORD commanded them" (7:6)

6:28–30 All that was required of Moses was that he should function as God's spokesman. He was not required to be inventive or a clever organizer or a gifted persuader. He was simply required to pass on to Pharaoh king of Egypt[190] what God told him to say—to fulfill the role of a prophet. His protest, "Why would Pharaoh listen to me, since I speak with faltering lips?" is

---

[189] Durham's observation is insightful on this point: "We have allowed centuries of the glorification of Moses (surveyed in detail by Cazelles, Gelin et al., *Moïse, l'homme de l'alliance*, and more briefly by Daiches, *Moses*, 233–56), begun even in the biblical period, to cover overmuch our interpretation of the Exodus narratives. We need to note with more precision the amount of attention really given to Moses, how flawed a hero he actually is, how often his involvement is a kind of spring board for an emphasis on the activity of real consequence—the activity of Yahweh—and how at every crucial point, the presence of Moses is either forgotten or at least obscured by the Presence of Yahweh" (Durham, *Exodus*, 86).

[190] "Pharaoh king of Egypt" occurs in twenty-three verses in the Bible, in Exodus only in chaps. 6 and 14; whereas "king of Egypt" is more common (forty-four verses) and simply "Pharaoh" the most common of all (197 verses). Such terminological variations are common to good style when a figure or concept is mentioned frequently.

mentioned here by way of linkage with 6:12, the point at which the narrative left off and the intervening genealogy began. It is not, in other words, a second protest using the same words but simply a reminder to the reader of what Moses had said previously.

7:1–2 This is also summative material, essentially repeating the main concepts, in somewhat different words, of 4:14–16. The largest difference is that in contrast to 4:14–16 the emphasis here is not on Aaron's speaking to "the people" (4:16) but to *Pharaoh,* and the goal is not merely to get the people to accept God's plan but to get the king to do Yahweh's will. The purpose of these words was, once again, to remove from Moses any reason for resistance. As we have already noted, Moses would, in the event, actually do most of the talking; but the promise that Aaron could be the spokesperson was a reassurance that took away the ground of Moses' *pro forma* objection about his speaking skill. The reference to Egypt as "his country," that is, Pharaoh's country, is not new: it occurred in 6:1,11 and occurs again in 11:10, always in the exact wording "out of his country." It is only a detail of diction in the narrative, but it underscores the fact that Moses and the Israelites were to think of Egypt as someone else's country, not theirs. "Your land" is the term given to Canaan, the land of Israel's promise in Exodus (23:26,33; 34:24) and thereafter repeatedly in the Pentateuch.

7:3–6 These verses also contain much that is summative. In v. 3 the prediction of the hardening of Pharaoh's heart recalls 4:21 (q.v.), and although the use of the expression "signs and wonders" is new here to Exodus, the empowerment of Moses and Aaron with proof *signs* had already appeared as a significant theme (4:9,17–18,30), and the promise of *wonders* in 3:20 and 4:21 uses much of the same language as appears here. What is somewhat new in v. 3 is the intention of God to *multiply* his signs and wonders—an adumbration of the multiple plagues that will successively humiliate Egypt and her gods and increasingly demonstrate that Yahweh alone controls the supernatural world.[191] The concept of "mighty acts of judgment" in v. 4 recalls 6:6, and departure by *armies* (NIV "divisions") recalls 6:26. God's designation of the Israelites as "my people" has been seen already in 3:7,10; 5:1; 6:7.

Verse 5 contains something of a transformation of a previously encountered theme. In 6:7 ("then you will know that I am the LORD your God, who brought you out from under the yoke of the Egyptians") God predicted a promise fulfillment in the sense of the Israelites' eventually realizing who he really was and how great was his power. Now that language is applied to the

[191] The all-too-common notion that Satan is independent of God and not under his control has no basis in the biblical text, which consistently presents Satan as answerable to God (e.g., Job 1:6; Zech 3:1; Rom 16:20; Rev 20:2,7).

Egyptians. It is one thing when a people acknowledges the greatness of their own God. It is yet another when grudgingly yet inescapably a pagan people acknowledges the supremacy of a god they previously had never even heard of. The remainder of v. 5 closely links to what was already said in 3:20.

Our repeatedly calling attention to ways in which the language of the present passage relates to what has already been introduced in the narrative should not be misunderstood. These are all great themes, and the fact that they are repeated here does not diminish their significance but rather enhances it. The current passage is a powerful review of the truly big issues—the very opposite of a needless tautology.

7:6–7 It is possible that v. 6 is referring only to the past, that is, to the fact that Moses and Aaron had, in their one encounter with Pharaoh so far (5:1–5), been fully faithful in delivering God's message to Pharaoh. It is even more likely, however, that both vv. 6 and 7 are intended to lead into the entire set of stories that describe encounters with Pharaoh, especially in light of the immediately following account (7:8–13) in which v. 10 once again says that Moses and Aaron "did just as the Lord commanded"—referring to their overall faithfulness during the remainder of their service in Egypt. That is, because v. 7 describes their ages "when they spoke to Pharaoh," and since they spoke to Pharaoh on many subsequent occasions, we take these verses as programmatic for the entire following set of encounters with Pharaoh, namely chaps. 7–12.

The figure given for Moses' age is confirmed by Deut 34:7, Moses' death coming forty years later than the present events, at age one hundred and twenty. That Aaron was the older brother is confirmed in part by the (culturally proper) precedence given to Aaron within the genealogy (6:20) and as well in its wrap-up sentence (6:26). Aaron's age at death is given in Num 33:39 ("Aaron was a hundred and twenty-three years old when he died on Mount Hor"), a figure that is, again, consistent with what is stated here. That Aaron's death (cf. also Num 10:28; Deut 10:6) and Miriam's death (Num 20:1) came somewhat before that of Moses is also consistent with the evidence that they were the older siblings.

DIVISION OUTLINE

III. ELEVEN SIGNS OF YAHWEH'S SOVEREIGNTY: THE TEN PLAGUES: JUDGMENT ON THE GODS OF EGYPT (7:8–11:10)

Excursus: The Progression and Structure of the Ten Plagues

Excursus: Were the Plagues Merely Natural Events?

1. First Sign: An Opening Miracle before Pharaoh: Aaron's Staff Becomes a Snake (7:8–13)
2. Second Sign: First Plague: Water to Blood (7:14–24)
3. Third Sign: Second Plague: Frogs (7:25–8:15) [Hb. 7:25–8:11]
4. Fourth Sign: Third Plague: Mosquitoes or Gnats (8:16–19) [Hb. 8:12–15]
5. Fifth Sign: Fourth Plague: Swarms of Flies (8:20–32) [Hb. 8:16–28]
   (1) Announcement of the Plague (8:20–23) [Hb. 8:16–19]
   (2) The Plague and Its Devastation (8:24) [Hb. 8:20]
   (3) Pharaoh's first Concession: An Offer of a Religious Holiday, But Only Inside Egypt (8:25) [Hb. 8:21]
   (4) Moses' Rejection of Pharaoh's First Offer (8:26–27) [Hb. 8:22–23]
   (5) Pharaoh's Second Concession: Permission for a Temporary Trip into the Wilderness (8:28–29) [Hb. 8: 24–25]
   (6) Removal of the Plague, Followed by Pharaoh's Reneging on His Promise (8:30–32) [Hb. 8:26–28]
6. Sixth Sign: Fifth Plague: Death of Livestock (9:1–7)
   (1) Announcement of the Plague (9:1–4)
   (2) The Plague and Its Devastation (9:5–6)
   (3) Pharaoh's Investigation of Israelite Animals and His Continuing Refusal (9:7)
7. Seventh Sign: Sixth Plague: Festering Boils (9:8–12)
   Excursus: Did Anthrax Cause the Fifth and Sixth Plagues?
   (1) Announcement of the Plague (9:8–9)
   (2) The Plague and Its Devastation (9:10–12)
8. Eighth Sign: Seventh Plague: Hail (9:13–35)
   (1) Announcement of the Plague (9:13–19)
   (2) Compliance by Some; Disdain by Others (9:20–21)
   (3) The Plague and Its Devastation (9:22–25)
   (4) Pharaoh's Partial Repentance and Concession (9:27–28)
   (5) Moses' Agreement to Stop the Plague, Though Not Convinced by Pharaoh's Words (9:29–30)

(6) Assessment of the Damage to Crops (9:31–32)
(7) Removal of the Plague, Followed by Pharaoh's Reneging on His Promise (9:33–35)

9. Ninth Sign: Eighth Plague: Locusts (10:1–20)
   (1) Summons, Instruction, and Encouragement (10:1–2)
   (2) Announcement of the Plague (10:3–6)
   (3) Pharaoh Tries Again to Bargain, Without Success (10:7–11)
   (4) The Plague and Its Consequences (10:12–20)
10. Tenth Sign: Ninth Plague: Darkness (10:21–29)
   (1) Announcement, Plague, and Consequences (10:21–23)
   (2) Pharaoh's Most Substantial Concession So Far (10:24)
   (3) Moses' Insistence on a Full Exodus (10:25–26)
   (4) Pharaoh's Refusal and Moses' Prophetic Play on His Words (10:27–29)
11. The Great Sign of Sovereignty Announced: Tenth Plague Predicted: Death of Firstborn (11:1–10)
   (1) Review of the Plans for the Final Plague and the Enrichment of the Israelites by the Egyptians (11:1–3)
   (2) Announcement of the Final, Decisive Plague to Pharaoh (11:4–8)
   (3) Review of Pharaoh's Prior History of Resistance to the Exodus (11:9–10)

III. ELEVEN SIGNS OF YAHWEH'S SOVEREIGNTY: THE TEN PLAGUES: JUDGMENT ON THE GODS OF EGYPT (7:8–11:10)

The term "the ten plagues" is a traditional, but not strictly biblical, expression. It derives both from the translation "plague" for a variety of Hebrew words[1] such as *deber* in 5:3 and *negaʿ* in 11:1 and from God's reference in 15:26 to "the diseases I brought on the Egyptians." Even though the expression "ten plagues" refers in summary fashion to both disease plagues and non-disease signs of sovereignty, as does "diseases" in 15:26[2], the term "plague" is not a misleading term as long as it is understood properly in the context of Exodus. The Hebrew term most often used in what we call the plague accounts, however, is *ʾot,* a word usually connoting "miraculous sign." What Moses recorded in the book of Exodus is actually a series of *eleven* miraculous signs having in common their indication of God's sovereignty over

[1] None of which need be translated "plague," though some of them can be and have been.

[2] See the commentary on 15:22–27.

Egypt,[3] the Egyptians, and their Pharaoh—the final one in the series being an especially great sign both of his sovereignty and of judgment: the imposition of death upon the firstborn of people and animals among the Egyptians. Of these eleven signs of sovereignty, the first (7:8–13) is a *demonstration* rather than a *plague* since the only harm it involved was the loss of a small number of things, that is, the loss of magicians' staffs and the death of some snakes (7:12), not a general annoyance or harm to the human or animal population as a whole. Nevertheless, it, like the other ten, was designed to show Pharaoh and the Egyptians Yahweh's superiority to them and their gods through the miraculous transformation of an inanimate object (staff) into a living being (snake) and the superiority of that snake to any others. The last ten, on the other hand, were both signs of sovereignty and, in the terminology commonly but loosely employed for them, *plagues*. They caused death (mainly of animals until the tenth) or miseries of various sorts (on both people and animals in most plagues) even if some of them had nothing to do with illness per se (notably nos. seven [hail], eight [locusts], and nine [darkness]).

All eleven signs humiliated the Egyptians and proved Yahweh's power over them.[4] All shared certain formal features and a basically similar outline, moving from a very simple first sign account (7:8–13) through closely related (similar to one another) sign accounts (the first nine *plagues*), which vary in length but build in intensity of misery caused, to culmination in a compound-complex account of the death of the firstborn that is much longer and much more a matter of final judgment than any of the others (11:1–12:30). All eleven signs led inexorably to the great mighty act of God around which the book of Exodus centers, the exodus from Egypt, which also involved a great sovereign act of humiliation of the Egyptians, the destruction of the Egyptian army in the Red Sea.[5] Thus the signs of sovereignty must not be understood as ends in themselves but as lead-ins to God's

---

[3] On the general OT concept of Yahweh's sovereignty over all other powers, see C. J. Labuschagne, *The Incomparability of Yahweh in the Old Testament*, POS 5 (Leiden: Brill, 1966).

[4] E. L. Greenstein ("The Firstborn Plague and the Reading Process," in *Pomegranates and Golden Bells* [Winona Lake: Eisenbrauns, 1995], 555–68) makes the important point that seeing the plagues as merely divine punishment for the Egyptians' mistreatment of the Hebrews misses their real significance. They were, rather, a means of making sure that everyone, whether Egyptian or Hebrew, understood that it was Yahweh to whom worship and loyalty was due (they were, in other words, what we have called "signs of sovereignty"). In particular, Greenstein suggests that the final plague, the death of the firstborn, should be regarded in terms of the requirements of the Passover as delineated in chaps. 13–14, where the firstborn of all living things belongs to Yahweh by right. Taking the firstborn of the Egyptians (cf. 4:23) is a major theme of Exodus: it shows God's sovereignty over them as a matter of his right as a sovereign.

[5] Note that this event is also characterized by the hardening of Pharaoh's heart (and the hearts of the Egyptians), a theme found consistently in the sovereign sign stories that lead up to it (cf. 14:4,8,17).

great deliverance of his people from bondage to the greatest superpower of their day, a deliverance that was completed only when the Egyptian army was destroyed and Pharaoh's power broken (14:21–31; 15:1–21).

The overall 1:9:1 pattern of the eleven signs of Yahweh's sovereignty may be schematized as follows. Note how the first sign already contains most of the typical elements that will be found in the remaining sign stories.

First Sign of Sovereignty: Staff to Snake (7:8–13)

Elements, also typical[6] of all eleven accounts: God's instruction to Moses (and Aaron) before they encounter Pharaoh; the encounter with Pharaoh itself "just as the LORD commanded"; a symbolic action (throwing down the staff); resulting action taking place in the presence of Pharaoh (and his officials); duplication of the sign by Egyptian magicians (first three sign accounts only; magicians' impotence described in two other sign accounts as well); Pharaoh hardens his heart and does not give in, "just as the LORD had said."

Second through Tenth Signs of Sovereignty: Plagues One through Nine (7:14–10:29)[7]

Typical elements: God's instruction to Moses (and Aaron) before they encounter Pharaoh; the encounter with Pharaoh itself "just as the LORD commanded"; a symbolic action taking place in the presence of Pharaoh (often: "and his officials"); duplication of the sign by Egyptian magicians (first three sign accounts only); resulting action (plague); Pharaoh hardens his heart and does not give in, "just as the LORD had said."

Eleventh Sign of Sovereignty: Tenth Plague, Death of Firstborn (11:1–12:31)

Elements: God announces this plague as final; how the Israelites are to become enriched at the expense of the Egyptians; announcement of plague itself; provision for a permanent memorial of the event in the Passover regulations; celebration of the first Passover; resulting plague (death of firstborn of humans and animals); Pharaoh does not harden his heart but rather gives in.

The first sign is introductory, limited in its effect and audience, and duplicates the final of the three earlier faith signs already shown to the Israelites (not any Egyptians) so that they might trust Yahweh.[8] The last sign is by far

[6] The sign accounts are not woodenly constructed, so even though they all share certain characteristics, some other characteristics are shared by fewer than the eleven for the sake of variety and brevity.

[7] Note that 10:29 concludes the first ten sign accounts (i.e., everything leading up to the death of the firstborn) in a unique way, with Moses' declaration that he would not (need to) appear formally before Pharaoh again because the request phase was over; now Yahweh would simply *make* the exodus happen (see commentary on 10:21–29).

[8] The fact that the Israelites placed their faith in Yahweh as a result of the three signs shown to them (4:29–31) contrasts obviously with the fact that the Egyptians did not, in spite of the eleven signs shown to them.

the most severe, is specially memorialized, and represents a culmination of God's acts of humiliation and judgment of the Egyptians. In between are the first nine *plagues,* displaying a special, rather elaborate [sub] pattern of their own, discussed in the following excursus.

Excursus: The Progression and Structure of the Ten Plagues

This section of narrative (7:8–11:10) focuses on one of the great confrontations of history: the reigning human power on earth, Egypt—and particularly its autocratic head, Pharaoh—versus the God who promised to rescue his people from that power and the miseries it had imposed on them.

The plagues built in intensity. The early plagues (blood, frogs, biting insects) were relatively brief in duration, did not cause death, and affected mainly people's patience and convenience—though certainly severely. The Egyptian magicians were able to duplicate the first two plagues (though presumably on a very small scale only; see comments on 7:14–25; 8:1–15), but they could not duplicate the third, evidence that the "quality," not just the quantity, of the plagues was becoming more intense. None of the first three plagues produced a lasting willingness on the part of Pharaoh to let the Israelites go. Plagues four, five, and six (swarming insects, animal disease, and skins sores[9]) were much more harmful. The fifth killed off many livestock, and the sixth brought serious disease upon humans. Even so, these plagues were not enough to result in Pharaoh's relenting from his resistance to Israelite demands for freedom. The seventh, eighth, and ninth plagues (hail, locusts, and darkness) were even more severe since the seventh plague resulted in the destruction of both animals and certain crops, the locusts ruined what crops remained, and the darkness plague was so frightening and debilitating during its three-day duration that Pharaoh was actually willing—at first—to allow all Israelites to depart if only they would leave their animals behind as surety of their eventual return (10:24).

Although the plagues built in intensity, the increase was not equally incremental. There was a quantum leap in severity to the culmination of all plagues in the tenth plague, that of the death of the firstborn,[10] which actually launched the exodus and which was seen as a supreme act of judgment against Egypt, in particular against the gods of Egypt.[11] Accordingly, the tenth plague received the greatest attention in the narrative, to the extent of its being separately and uniquely predicted and prepared for by the Israelites as described rather elaborately in the closing pericope of this section (11:1–10). Although it might be argued that the full story of the tenth plague should be included here along with the prior nine, our judgment is that Moses intentionally structured his narrative so as to highlight the actual imposition of the tenth and final plague as the

---

[9] See commentary on 9:1–12 and the remarks below on Hort's theory on the question of whether or not plagues five and six may have been anthrax.

[10] As 4:22–23 already anticipates by prediction of the tenth plague only as *the* punishment on Pharaoh and Egypt.

[11] Thus Exod 12:12, "On that same night I will pass through Egypt and strike down every firstborn—both men and animals—and I will bring judgment on all the gods of Egypt. I am the LORD."

beginning of the exodus itself (in 12:1 and following). He did this in part by placing the rules for the Passover in chap. 12 as an introduction to what follows, that is, a distinctly new and separate block of narrative that concentrates on and links together the Passover and the exodus (12:1–13:16) since it can already be anticipated that the exodus would and should be remembered for all generations to come.

It cannot be accidental that God used ten plagues to teach the Egyptians that he is sovereign and that their gods were of no account. At the time of the exodus, both the Israelites and the Egyptians used a decimal counting system, which meant that the number ten tended to connote a full, complete, sufficient quantity of anything being explicitly enumerated.[12] A run-through of the whole decimal list from one to ten provided more than enough demonstration of God's power over Egypt for anyone to get the message.[13]

God brought about the plagues with a structure to their occurrences designed to hammer home to the Egyptians that he is firmly in control of the entire process, and of them and their nation, even to the extent of controlling their environment, which they so completely admired and worshiped in their pantheism. The following chart[14] shows how the first nine plagues had certain features that appear in groupings of three, with variety provided in the length of the plague accounts to keep them from becoming tedious reading:[15]

In sharp contrast to the first nine, the tenth plague caused death to humans, was preannounced long before it or any of the others occurred through various adumbrations going back as far as the call of Moses at the burning bush (4:23), was interwoven with the initiation of the Passover memorial feast, functioned as the actual supreme judgment of God on Egypt and its gods, and produced the result originally predicted: full permission—indeed an official requirement!—that the Israelites leave Egypt. Thus it does not itself "fit" within the chart but is rather the culmination to which the plagues that do fit within the chart all point.

It may be noted that the structure of the plague accounts provides telling evidence against the theory known as the Documentary Hypothesis as applied to

---

[12] Cf. A. M. Cartun, "'Who Knows Ten?' The Structural and Symbolic Use of Numbers in the Ten Plagues: Exodus 7:14–13:16," *USQR* 45 (1991): 65–119; S. E. Loewenstamm, "The Number of Plagues in Psalm 105," *Bib* 50 (1969): 34–38; A. Barucq, "Plaies d'Egypte," *Supplément au Dictionnaire de la Bible,* Vol. 7 (Paris: Letouzey et Ane, 1928–1970), col. 6–18. The Ten Commandments are another example of this method of producing a full yet easily remembered coverage of data. One might also compare the modern "Ten Ways to . . ." and "Ten Reasons Why . . ." lists in magazine articles, and self-help books, and lists of "Top Ten" this or that popular in current culture.

[13] Since the average human can remember a list of only six or seven items, a list of ten vivid demonstrations of any fact is "more than enough" for almost anyone's mind to be convinced.

[14] The chart is an expansion, rearrangement, and modification of a helpful chart provided by F. W. Bush in his article "Plagues of Egypt," *ISBE,* 878–80.

[15] The variety in length of the accounts is not random but clearly patterned by threes, i.e., long-long-short; then long-short-short; then, again replicating the first pattern, long-long-short. The nine plague accounts are presaged by the first sign, which is very short, and followed by the final sign and tenth plague, which is very long. Thus there are never more than two long accounts or two short accounts in a row among all eleven sign accounts.

Method of introduction	**Plague cycle**	**Plague number and relative length**	**Plague type**	**Plague number and relative length**	**Plague type**	**Plague number and relative length**	**Plague type**
Outdoor morning confrontation with Pharaoh	First cycle (1, 4, 7)	1 long	Nile water becomes blood	4 long	swarming insects	7 long	hail and thunder-storms
Indoor (court) confrontation with Pharaoh	Second cycle (2, 5, 8)	2 long	frogs	5 short	animal disease (anthrax?)	8 long	locusts
Outdoor symbolic action (limited confrontation with Pharaoh)	Third cycle (3, 6, 9)	3 short	biting insects (mosquitoes?)	6 short	skin sores (anthrax?)	9 short	darkness

this part of the book of Exodus. This hypothesis, still well entrenched in some circles of biblical scholarship, holds that the plague accounts as they appear in Exodus are an amalgam of stories from the J (tenth-ninth century BC "Yahwistic") source and the P (fifth century BC "Priestly") source, with portions reflecting also the E (ninth-eighth centuries BC "Elohistic") source. In the way the theory is most often asserted, J supposedly accounts for seven of the plagues and P for three, with some—though not all—scholars also seeing strong evidence of the E source in various parts of the plague accounts, even though generally the E source is seen as supplemental to the J source rather than as independent of it in the material as it stands. Childs, for example, suggests that the sources used to compose the plague narratives are distributed as follows (references marked with an asterisk represent parts of verses in which wording from two sources has in Childs' view been carefully blended rather than merely combined by juxtaposition).[16]

The J Source:
7:14–15a,16–17a,17b*,18, 21a, 24–25,26–29, 8:4–11a,16–28; 9:1–7,13,17–18, 23b,24a*,24b,25b,26–30,33–34; 10:1a, 3–11,13b, 14b,15a*,15b–19,24–26, 28–29; 11:4–8

[16] B. S. Childs (*The Book of Exodus: A Critical-Theological Commentary* [Louisville: Westminster John Knox, 1974], 130–51) provides a careful, remarkably detailed analysis of the theories of sources for the plague narratives, following generally the analysis of J. Wellhausen (who was in turn followed with only modest modifications by Holzinger, Bacon, Bäntsch, and Gressman) and especially the restatement of Wellhausen's view (with further argumentation and some modifications) by G. Fohrer.

The E Source:
7:15b,17b*,20b, 23; 9:22–23a,24a*,25a,35a; 10:12–13a,15a*,15b,20,21–23, 27; 11:1–3

The P Source:
7:1–7,8–13,19–20a,21b–22; 8:1–3,11b,12–15; 9:8–12,35b; 11:9–10

Later additions:
9:14–16,19–21,31–32; 10:1b–2*

This entire scheme is carefully hypothesized from the narrative on the basis of supposed vocabulary and theological tendencies of the three different theorized sources. It is obviated by the reality to which the chart above points: the plague stories have a unified structure, are not strung together from a variety of sources whose disparate nature can be discerned by the choppiness resulting from juxtaposition of source materials in the narrative (since the narrative is in fact not choppy at all), and are part of a carefully described progression of events (because the events were carefully arranged by God), suggesting a single author's consistent composition rather than a hybrid composition from at least three (indeed, four, when the "additions" are included) disparate sources.[17] The fact that these nine are centered within the carefully structured 1:9:1 pattern of signs of Yahweh's sovereignty over the powers of Egypt that precede the exodus is merely further evidence of their careful, rather than cut-and-paste, composition.

---

[17] Other patterns in the plague narrative also demonstrate its tightly structured integrity. T. Fretheim, in spite of his own commitment to the Documentary Hypothesis, including the notion that the J source originally had only seven plagues, dutifully draws attention to certain unavoidably obvious unifying patterns (*Exodus,* Interpretation: A Bible Commentary for Teaching and Preaching [Louisville: Westminster John Knox, 1991], 105–6). These include the general progression of severity so that the plagues "become increasingly more serious and unpleasant, more and more a threat to Egypt's well-being, beginning with annoyances, moving to disease and damage and finally to darkness (= uncreation) and death." He also points out that the plagues are effectively grouped in five blocks of two plagues each (two relating closely to the Nile, two relating to insects, two that bring disease, two describing damage on the land, and two that bring darkness/death). Moreover, if one thinks of the plague accounts particularly as *demonstrations* of God's sovereignty over Egypt, Pharaoh, and their gods, one can include as the first *demonstration* the account of how Aaron's staff became a snake in the presence of Pharaoh (7:8–13). The following pattern emerges: "Aaron's staff becomes the instrument in the first four, Moses' hand/staff in the last four, and God more directly in the middle two." Finally, among what Fretheim calls the plagues' "complex interrelationships," he mentions the elaborate pattern visible in connection with the agency of the plagues: "God is explicitly active in only six plagues (1, 4, 5, 7, 8, 10). Aaron/Moses are involved in three of these in a dual role (1, 7, 8) and alone in plagues 2, 3, 6, and 9 (see 7:1!). In the summary, however, only the agency of Moses and Aaron is acknowledged (11:10; cf. 4:17), as only God's was in the introduction (7:3). In the four cases where a plague is removed (plagues 2, 4, 7, 8), a dual role is again evident as God did 'according to the word of Moses' (8:13). In the eighth plague, a third agency (wind) is active in both execution and removal."

Excursus: Were the Plagues Merely Natural Events?

A widely held understanding of the plagues must also be addressed here. the view that the plagues are natural ecological events. This view, most eloquently espoused and documented by G. Hort,[18] has gained favor in many circles and seemingly has much to commend it. We will summarize it here but address some of its particulars in connection with the commentary on the various plagues. Hort argues that the plagues are in fact all natural phenomena, occurring in the order that such phenomena would occur in nature, with some of the plagues being the result of well-known periodic or seasonal Egyptian phenomena and some being the result of immediately prior plagues, with anthrax figuring prominently in several. The following schema summarizes her approach.

Thus according to Hort's thesis, the plagues were all natural phenomena that could and did otherwise occur in Egypt but were extremely harsh just prior to the exodus due to extraordinary rainfall at the headwaters of the Nile and the resultant environmental-biological effects. Hort's thesis still leaves many questions unanswered, which she simply does not address in any detail. These include the following questions, which may roughly describe in rhetorical fashion the range of views relative to whether or not the plagues were real historical events: (1) Were the plagues merely natural phenomena later embellished by tradition and attributed by storytellers to supernatural power summoned by the actions of Moses and Aaron? (2) Were the plagues natural phenomena that God foresaw and then gave Moses and Aaron instructions on how to be seen as summoning them by various symbolic actions? (3) Were the plagues "natural" phenomena brought about fully by supernatural means and timed directly by God (i.e., God

---

[18] G. Hort, "The Plagues of Egypt," *ZAW* 69 (1957): 84–103; *ZAW* 70 (1958): 48–59. Hort's approach is irenic to the basic historicity of the biblical story: "If it thus can be shown that the salient features of each plague are also the salient features of one specific phenomenon, and that the plagues follow upon each other in the Bible in the sequence which such phenomena would have in nature, then it must be said that the historical nucleus in the "saga" of the plagues is so great as to give us an almost complete picture of the events which lead up to the Exodus of the Israelites from Egypt," *ZAW* 69, 85). Cf. also p. 100, "Again we see how accurate the essential facts in the biblical account are." Cf. Z. Zevit, "Three Ways to Look at the Ten Plagues," *BibRev* 6 (1990): 16–23, 42, 44; D. J. McCarthy, "Plagues and Sea of Reeds: Exodus 4–14," *JBL* 85 (1966): 137–58; T. E. Fretheim, "The Plagues as Ecological Signs of Historical Disaster," *JBL* 110 (1991): 385–96. Further, on the medical possibilities without direct analysis of the supernatural nature of the overall event, cf. H. M. D. Hoyte, "The Plagues of Egypt: What Killed the Animals and the Firstborn?" *The Medical Journal of Australia* 158 (1993): 706–8. Hoyte, a university parasitologist, follows the general line of thinking offered by Hort and offers this summation of his own conclusions as to the disease process operating through the plagues: "A bloom of red dinoflagellates killed the fish in the Nile; dehydration then killed the frogs; the people were attacked first by swarms of culicine mosquitoes, then by swarms of stable flies; these flies initiated an epidemic of surra in the farm animals while their bites caused an epidemic of ecthyma in the people. Next, there was a hail storm, a swarm of locusts and a sandstorm, and as the final plague, an epidemic of typhoid fever that killed, among many others, Pharaoh's eldest child. Internal evidence indicates that the plagues started in summer and ended in the summer of the following year, and were localized in the Nile delta (or parts of it), not affecting the whole of Egypt."

Plague	Cause	Effect
Plague 1 (Nile becomes blood)	Unusually heavy rainfall in the upper Nile headwaters (Blue Nile sources)	The flooding dissolves and brings red dirt characteristic of the Abyssinian and Ethiopian plateau at the headwaters of the Blue Nile all the way into lower Egypt. Added to the reddish color of the dirt is the reddish color of certain microorganisms known as flagellates, which are always present in the Nile but because of the flooding and the nutrients brought with it and which multiply in abundance, making the Nile red in color, undrinkable, and poison to the fish.
Plague 2 (frogs leave Nile and go into houses)	Polluted Nile and rotting fish, which in turn breed bacillus anthracis (anthrax)	Frogs leave the uninhabitable Nile and invade homes, but then die off suddenly because they are killed by the anthrax.
Plague 3 (mosquitoes, not the usually postulated gnats or lice)	Perfect breeding conditions in pooled stagnant water along the Nile as floodwaters recede	Huge swarms of mosquitoes biting humans and animals[a]
Plague 4 (flies, particularly the stomoxis calcitrans, carrier of anthrax)	Perfect breeding conditions in pooled stagnant water along the Nile as floodwaters recede	Ingestion during grazing by animals, and biting of humans, causing plagues 5 (cattle anthrax) and 6 (human skin anthrax).
Plague 5 (animal death)	Anthrax from ingestion of grasses growing out of soil where frogs had died and where the bacilli anthracis spores were left in the soil. (Later, anthrax was cleansed from the soil by spring rain squalls.)	Nonstabled cattle (those allowed to graze "in the field") die.
Plague 6 (human skin sores)	Skin anthrax from bite of stomoxis calcitrans fly, which had picked up the spores from feeding on dead frogs	Severe skin sores, but no fatalities, as is characteristic generally of cutaneous anthrax
Plague 7 (hail and thunderstorms)	Extreme weather conditions not unknown for the time of year	Destruction of flax and barley, but not wheat and spelt, which were not yet up
Plague 8 (locusts)	Ideal breeding conditions from previously mentioned heavy rains and resultant wet grounds	Destruction of wheat and spelt and all other crops
Plague 9 (palpable darkness)	Extreme desert sandstorm from the south	"Darkness that can be felt" (10:21)

a. Hort (*ZAW* 69, 98): "This plague consists simply in a heightening of the customary phenomenon of mosquitoes which bite men and animals indifferently."

initiated all the plagues as natural phenomena under his control and put them in a timed sequence also under his control)? (4) Were the plagues genuine miracles intended to replicate in extreme fashion natural phenomena that can and do occur in Egypt so as to demonstrate that God controlled both the environment and the "gods" the Egyptians thought produced the environment and that God could do with it/them whatever he wills?

Bush[19] cogently summarizes the weaknesses of Hort's thesis as follows: The biblical account describes the plagues as the result of commands given by Moses and Aaron and as commencing instantaneously by a gesture rather than coming gradually with the seasons (e.g., the Nile turned to blood "in the presence of Pharaoh" according to 7:20, and ashes thrown into the air "before Pharaoh" produced skin sores according to 9:10). The extremity of the plagues goes beyond what mere flooding of the Nile, no matter how unprecedented, would justify (e.g., the frogs "covered the land" according to 8:6; the very dust of the ground turns into biting insects according to 8:17). Moreover, since the Egyptian magicians could and did duplicate the phenomena of the first two plagues of blood and frogs, they obviously were reacting to what they and Pharaoh perceived as "magic" on the part of Moses and Aaron—not some gradually occurring environmental phenomenon already well known to them as natives of Egypt. In other words, if native Egyptian magicians could tell that the plagues were not natural phenomena, why should moderns, a millennium and a half later, try to overrule the opinion of observers on site at the time?

To Bush's summary of weaknesses in Hort's approach one might add that the magicians saw the third, irreproducible plague as "the finger of God" (8:19) rather than as something that normally happens in Egypt, even if on a lesser scale. Moreover, their ability to duplicate the plagues failed completely thereafter, and they gave up trying to duplicate what obviously was something beyond their experience. Additionally, Pharaoh's reactions to each plague suggest genuine surprise and dismay—hardly likely if the plagues were merely normal environmental phenomena experienced to a severe degree. Further, the plagues differentially affected the Egyptians but left the Israelites unscathed, so that "natural "phenomena were respecting political-ethnic boundaries, something hardly explained by recourse to the outworkings of mere natural processes. Perhaps most significantly, the final plague, that of the death of the firstborn, has no natural explanation at all. It was a special judgment of God (how could any natural disease strike only firstborn children and not harm others?) and is so obviously so that because of it Pharaoh insisted on the exodus of the Israelites in sudden and direct contrast to the determined prior policy not to let them go.

The view that best takes account of all the data may be summarized as follows: The first nine plagues were special, divinely produced manifestations of God's sovereignty over Egypt—its king, its people, its environment, and its gods—accomplished by imitations on a huge and destructive scale of phenomena thought by the Egyptians to be the province of their gods. God turned things believed to be the specialty of "the gods of Egypt"[20] against the Egyptians, and showed himself in control of all events and powers they would have attributed to the objects of their faith. The tenth plague, on the other hand, was in no way a magnified imitation of a natural phenomenon but stood apart from the first nine

[19] *ISBE* 3.880.

[20] So, in 12:12, is the summational purpose of the plagues and exodus stated.

as a decisive imposition of the death penalty on the nation that tried to enslave and mortally oppress God's special people, his "firstborn son."

1. First Sign: An Opening Miracle before Pharaoh: Aaron's Staff Becomes a Snake (7:8–13)

[8]The LORD said to Moses and Aaron, [9]"When Pharaoh says to you, 'Perform a miracle,' then say to Aaron, 'Take your staff and throw it down before Pharaoh,' and it will become a snake."

[10]So Moses and Aaron went to Pharaoh and did just as the LORD commanded. Aaron threw his staff down in front of Pharaoh and his officials, and it became a snake. [11]Pharaoh then summoned wise men and sorcerers, and the Egyptian magicians also did the same things by their secret arts: [12]Each one threw down his staff and it became a snake. But Aaron's staff swallowed up their staffs. [13]Yet Pharaoh's heart became hard and he would not listen to them, just as the LORD had said.

7:8–13 This account describes Aaron's enactment of one of the signs Moses had been given to convince the Israelites of his call from God (4:5, "that they may believe") and also one of the signs that would demonstrate God's power to Pharaoh (4:21, "See that you perform before Pharaoh all the wonders I have given you the power to do"). The text seems clearly to say, however, that the Egyptian magicians summoned by Pharaoh were able to duplicate this staff-to-snake miracle, and the reader may well wonder any of the following: "What sort of miracle is it that can be duplicated by *all* the magicians ("each one," v. 12) in a group of pagans? Are we to assume that they too had supernatural powers? Or did God give Moses and Aaron nothing more than a simple magic trick (i.e., not a *miracle* at all) that other magicians could also perform? Was Satan perhaps helping the magicians; was that the source of their ability to replicate a miracle? Did God actually think that a low-quality "miracle"[21] that was so easily replicated would convince Pharaoh to let the Israelites go?"

Four considerations provide the resolution to these questions. First, Moses and Aaron were not magicians. What God did through them was genuine—turning a piece of wood into an animal. The Egyptians, on the other hand, *were* magicians,[22] and the simplest reading of the text is one that

---

[21] The Hb. term in v. 9, מוֹפֵת, occurs thirty-six times in the OT and clearly means "miracle" or "supernatural wonder" or "portent" or the like.

[22] The wording of v. 11 appears to indicate that although Pharaoh had summoned all his practitioners of occult arts, "wise men and sorcerers" (לַחֲכָמִים וְלַמְכַשְּׁפִים), it was the Egyptian "magicians" (חַרְטֻמֵּי מִצְרַיִם) who imitated Aaron's actions. It would be grammatically possible to read the verse in the manner of the NRSV ("Then Pharaoh summoned the wise men and the sorcerers; and they also, the magicians of Egypt, did the same") as if the wise men and sorcerers were all magicians, but this option effectively equates groups that are not coterminous.

assumes they *imitated* by magical deception what Aaron had done by divine power.[23] For a Pharaoh eager not to be persuaded to believe in a foreigner's God, their ability to produce snakes from staffs (perhaps using boxes and curtains, in the usual manner of magicians doing substitution tricks) would be enough to allow him to follow his predilections and doubt Moses and Aaron—and thus disregard their God. Second, the text states that the magicians accomplished their imitation "by their secret arts"[24] ("trickery," v. 11) rather than by any sort of supernatural means or with the help of Satan or any other similar nonworldly mechanism.[25] Third, the end of v. 12 states that Aaron's staff swallowed theirs, a performance they could not and apparently did not even try to duplicate. They were at that point trumped because a substitution trick is nothing compared to causing one snake to eat a group of other snakes.[26] Clearly, the power of the God of Moses and Aaron was vastly superior to their ability.[27] Fourth, it was God's purpose to start small. This preplague miraculous portent was *intentionally* a simple, small-scale miracle to test the will of Pharaoh and to show Moses and Aaron what they were up against.[28] It was one thing to use these sorts of miracles to convince the Israelites (4:31); it was very much another to use them to convince Pharaoh. Egypt's king, as predicted (3:19; 4:21), was not going to be so easy to impress, and that fact was clearly part of the divine plan. Impressed though the Egyptian magicians themselves may actually have been once Aaron's rod ate theirs, Pharaoh, his mind made stubborn by God, now had an excuse

---

[23] S. B. Noege offers a study of the way the various references to Egyptian magic in Exodus are all polemical—all are aimed at showing Egyptian magic as something to avoid and condemn ("Moses and Magic: Notes on the Book of Exodus," *JANES* 24 [1996]: 45–59).

[24] בְּלַהֲטֵיהֶם. The meaning of the word used here, the plural of לֹהט, is open to debate since it is a hapax legomenon in the OT. It need not refer to any nonhuman "powers" but may mean simply "trickery" or "sleight-of-hand magic" or the like.

[25] Cf. Y. van Koening, "Le Magie égyptienne," *MDB* 41 (1985): 13–14.

[26] We are translating here *tannîn* as "snake," as to nearly all modern translations. P. Galpaz-Feller suggests that the term refers rather to the crocodile, an animal that in ancient Egyptian religion was understood as a voracious devourer and one that could devour magical spells ("Egyptological Motifs in the Sign of the Serpent (Exod 4:2–5; 7:8–14)," *BMik* 47 [2002]: 322–35). By this reasoning Aaron's staff's devouring of the other staffs was no accident but a symbol of the impending demise of the Egyptian power in the face of Yahweh's.

[27] That a simple shepherd's staff should be superior in power to a magician's staff is the sort of thing no Egyptian would have expected. It demonstrated Yahweh's control over everything Egyptian (J. Currid, "The Rod of Moses," *BurH* 33 [1997]: 107–14).

[28] As Childs notes: "The narrative does not suggest for a moment that Moses thought up the sign himself, and was therefore to be blamed for an unlikely choice. Rather, . . . it was God's choice of a sign . . . that was duplicated by the magicians [and] . . . the author makes it clear that the witness of the plague stories does not lie just in a naïve display of supernatural fireworks" (*Exodus*, 152).

for resisting, even if a lame one; he could for the time being content himself with the comforting belief that what Aaron had done was just a magic trick.

2. Second Sign: First Plague: Water to Blood (7:14–24)

**[14]Then the LORD said to Moses, "Pharaoh's heart is unyielding; he refuses to
let the people go. [15]Go to Pharaoh in the morning as he goes out to the water.
Wait on the bank of the Nile to meet him, and take in your hand the staff that was
changed into a snake. [16]Then say to him, 'The LORD, the God of the Hebrews,
has sent me to say to you: Let my people go, so that they may worship me in the
desert. But until now you have not listened. [17]This is what the LORD says: By this
you will know that I am the LORD: With the staff that is in my hand I will strike
the water of the Nile, and it will be changed into blood. [18]The fish in the Nile will
die, and the river will stink; the Egyptians will not be able to drink its water.'"**

[19]The LORD said to Moses, "Tell Aaron, 'Take your staff and stretch out your hand over the waters of Egypt—over the streams and canals, over the ponds and all the reservoirs'—and they will turn to blood. Blood will be everywhere in Egypt, even in the wooden buckets and stone jars."

**[20]Moses and Aaron did just as the LORD had commanded. He raised his staff
in the presence of Pharaoh and his officials and struck the water of the Nile, and
all the water was changed into blood. [21]The fish in the Nile died, and the river
smelled so bad that the Egyptians could not drink its water. Blood was everywhere in Egypt.**

**[22]But the Egyptian magicians did the same things by their secret arts, and
Pharaoh's heart became hard; he would not listen to Moses and Aaron, just as
the LORD had said. [23]Instead, he turned and went into his palace, and did not
take even this to heart. [24]And all the Egyptians dug along the Nile to get drinking
water, because they could not drink the water of the river.**

Prominent in the structure of this first plague account is the emphasis on God's involvement in Pharaoh's stubbornness.[29] Verses 14 and 22–23 function as something of an inclusio for the passage, reminding the reader that Moses knew directly from God that Pharaoh would be resistant (v. 14) and that he would not be moved easily, even by things supernatural (vv. 22–23). The last verse of the pericope (v. 24), something of a postscript, briefly answers the reader's logical question, "How then could the Egyptians survive since their drinking water came from the Nile?" By reason of that final verse, the first plague is shown to be a severe annoyance more than a life-threatening disaster, reflecting the sort of severity level one might expect of the opening plague—a shot fired across Egypt's bow, as it were.

The Nile is mentioned six times by name here and also referred to by terms like "water" and "river," in addition to the description in v. 19 of "the

[29]The only other plague that opened with an advance reminder of Pharaoh's stubbornness is the eighth, the locust plague (cf. 10:1).

waters of Egypt," then delineated in that verse to be sure that the reader realizes that every surface source of water was affected by the plague in the same manner as was the Nile. Thus "blood was everywhere in Egypt" (v. 21), and no Egyptian could escape the effect of this plague. No longer were the mighty acts of God confined to demonstrations for a private audience. Now all the citizens of the nation began to feel the effect of God's wrath, and the pressure began to ratchet up on Pharaoh. It was one thing for him to ignore a display intended to convince him of God's power but another to ignore the cries of his people for one of their most basic needs, water to drink.

In considering the story of the first plague, it is important to bear in mind that the Egyptians understood the Nile to be a god.[30] Their pantheistic view of the universe considered all things to be partakers of the divine, and things that moved to be obviously divine in their essence.[31] The ultimate victory of the only true God, Yahweh, over the many false gods of the Egyptians ("judgment on the gods of Egypt," 12:12) began with the humiliation of the Nile. The nation's great waterway and source of life was turned odious and made into a source of death (7:18), demonstrating the sovereign power of the God of Israel and the subordinate impotence of the Nile.

7:14 In the NIV translation ("Pharaoh's heart is unyielding; he refuses") this verse might almost seem to be suggesting that Yahweh was "learning" or "finding out" how Pharaoh reacted to the sign Aaron had just performed (7:8–13). The thrust of the Lord's statement is, however, that Moses must not be surprised by the resistance just encountered or by the further resistance that he was about to encounter, which the Lord knew well in advance. In other words, the Lord informed Moses here that nothing had changed or would in his control of Pharaoh's inclinations. The verse could also be translated: "Pharaoh [still] has a hard heart/is stubborn,[32] refusing to let the people go."

7:15 As noted above, plagues one, four, and seven each begin with an outdoor morning confrontation with Pharaoh, as opposed to a court confrontation with him in plagues two, five, and eight and no confrontation at all in plagues three, six, and nine. That this first "plague confrontation" should take place along the banks of the Nile is highly appropriate in light of this

---

[30] Cf. the Excursus: The Nile as a God," at 4:9.

[31] See esp. J. A. Wilson, "Egypt: The Nature of the Universe," in *Before Philosophy: The Intellectual Adventure of Ancient Man* (New York: Penguin, 1949). On Egyptian pantheistic religion see also H. Frankfort, *Ancient Egyptian Religion* (New York: Harper & Row, 1961) and W. LaSor, "Nile," *ISBE* 3:536–37.

[32] The Hb. translated by the NIV as "unyielding" is simply כָּבֵד, one of the normal ways for saying "stubborn" (see at 4:23 "Excursus: The Hardening of Pharaoh's Heart") and does not have any special nuance of "unyielding."

plague's nature: a demonstration of God's sovereignty over the river that was Egypt's greatest landmark and special source of life.

There is no evidence that people bathed in rivers frequently in Bible times; few ancients could swim and were therefore not as at home in or near deep water as might be the case in modern times, and bathing regularly is in general a luxury of modernity. Moses had already noted, however, that Pharaoh's daughter bathed in the Nile (2:5ff.), and members of the royal family may well have bathed frequently or even daily, something their privileged lifestyle allowed them to do.[33] Though we cannot be sure of it, the most likely meaning of "as he goes out to the water" is "as he goes to take a bath in the water." Since Moses would make the Nile immediately odious, this plague would have an instant effect on Pharaoh, preventing him from doing what he was directly on his way to do before meeting up with Moses and Aaron. In other words, Pharaoh could not ignore this plague, even though he might have resisted its implications.[34]

The special mention of the staff relates to its special nature, already seen in the book and often to be seen again. This is the staff that partly represents God and his power; that it should end up in the ark of the covenant[35] is testimony to its growing significance in the story.

7:16–18 The speech God here gave Moses to say to Pharaoh clearly describes who Moses represented (Yahweh, "the God of the Hebrews," v. 16), what Yahweh was demanding ("let my people go,"[36] v. 16), the reason a plague-punishment was warranted ("until now you have not listened," v. 16), the fact that Yahweh was determined to teach Pharaoh who he, Yahweh, was—meaning his greatness and exclusive power, not merely his name

---

[33] It need not be assumed that God's prediction of the location at which Moses could find Pharaoh the next day was predicated on a regular, daily schedule Pharaoh kept. Even if Pharaoh rarely went to the Nile, God's foreknowledge of his actions meant that he knew that one of those rare trips would take place the very next morning. It is even possible that we should take this prediction as the virtual equivalent of saying, "I'll cause Pharaoh to decide to take a bath tomorrow morning in the Nile, so you can plan to encounter him then, on his way."

[34] The precise prediction of where the encounter would take place is consistent with a number of other instructions to prophets to be at a certain place at a certain time (e.g., 1 Kgs 17:3; 21:18; 2 Kgs 1:3; Isa 7:3; cf. Exod 4:27; 1 Sam 10:2–8). God controls both the present and the future, and his prophets can have confidence that even the spatial and temporal parameters of their actions will be part of his plan.

[35] Num 17:10: "The LORD said to Moses, 'Put back Aaron's staff in front of the Testimony, to be kept as a sign"; Heb 9:4: "This ark contained the gold jar of manna, Aaron's staff that had budded, and the stone tablets of the covenant." See also "Excursus: Moses' Staff" at 4:14–17.

[36] "Let my people go" is worded so that Moses would clearly represent Yahweh as his spokesman, i.e., prophet, and became the standard message to Pharaoh—the one demand that must be fulfilled without compromise. As the narrative of the plagues progressed, Pharaoh tried to let the Israelites "go" in various limited ways, each somewhat less limiting than the next, until as a result of the tenth plague he finally let—indeed insisted that—Israel go unconditionally. But the divine demand itself is *from the start* essentially unconditional. The various purpose clauses attached to it as part of the eastern bargaining style ("so that they may hold a festival to me" and the like) should not be read as indicating that Yahweh ever expected anything less than a full, permanent exodus of his people from Egypt.

("by this you will know that I am the LORD," v. 17), the mechanism for bringing about the punishment ("with the staff that is in my hand I will strike the water of the Nile," v. 17), and what the punishment would be ("it will be changed into blood. The fish . . . will die, and the river will stink; the Egyptians will not be able to drink its water, vv. 17–18). Such precision made sure that Pharaoh could not misunderstand the purpose of the plague and the power of the God who caused it. Pharaoh needed to understand that Moses was merely an instrument of God; his adversary was the King of the universe, not a former Egyptian princeling. He must also understand that his refusal to allow the Israelites to leave Egypt would be "rubbed into his face" by divine design. And, as well, he must understand that the Egyptian people in general would share in the misery that his cruel stubbornness, with their complicity, would bring upon them in retribution.

"By this you will know that I am the LORD" (v. 17) is very important to this message. Previously the announcement "I am the LORD" had been spoken to the patriarchs (Gen 15:7; 28:13), to Moses (6:2,29), and to the Israelites (6:6–8); but this is the first time it is to be spoken to a non-Israelite. In effect, it was part of the very early announcement of the gospel to the Gentiles since, as we have already noted, it was not a mere statement of identification but a declaration of the application of saving power. Here it is used in a manner consistent with its usage in the prediction earlier in 7:5 ("And the Egyptians will know that I am the LORD when I stretch out my hand against Egypt and bring the Israelites out of it") and, even more importantly, with its usage in the central locus of explanation for the plagues ("I will bring judgment on all the gods of Egypt. I am the LORD," Exod 12:12).

7:19–21 In these verses is described the actual first plague, the changing of all surface water in Egypt (nearly all of it being in or from the Nile) to blood. Six considerations should be kept in mind in the analysis of this plague: (1) "Blood" is a color in Hebrew as well as a substance, just as in English, and no firm data exist for the interpreter to differentiate in this story between the possibility that the Nile and other surface water turned to actual blood[37] from the possibility that the waters turned—for whatever reason—"blood" in color.[38] (2) No special theological overtone is present relative to

[37] And, further, what type of blood—fish? animal? human? No explanation is provided, in part presumably because none could be; the ability to differentiate blood types was not available in ancient times.

[38] It has often been suggested that the Hb. word for "blood," *dām,* is actually a biform of the Hb. word for red/be red, *ʾādām*. "Blood" can also refer to juice (as in Deut 32:14, the "blood" of grapes) and frequently has the derived meanings "death" (Eng. parallel: "bloodshed") or "bloodguilt." The word's use in connoting the color (dark) red is found in Joel 2:30–31[Hb. 3:3–4]: "I will show wonders in the heavens and on the earth, blood and fire and billows of smoke. / The sun will be turned to darkness and the moon to blood before the coming of the great and dreadful day of the LORD"; and in 2 Kgs 3:22–23: "When they got up early in the morning, the sun was shining on the water. To the Moabites across the way, the water looked red—like blood. [אֲדֻמִּים כַּדָּם] 'That's blood!' they said. 'Those kings must have fought and slaughtered each other. Now to the plunder, Moab!' "

the "blood" here; it is not a foreshadowing of "the blood of Christ that flows" or any such thing. (3) The important punishment element in the plague is neither the substance nor the color but the pollution of the water, rendering it not merely undrinkable for humans but deadly to fish. (4) Yahweh's implied control over "Nile" (the Nile river god) could hardly have been missed by any thoughtful Egyptian considering the meaning of this plague.[39] (5) Aaron's staff was not merely a simple visual device but a symbolic reminder that God, not Aaron or Moses, was actually performing the miracle of the plague.[40] (6) The plague may well have imitated a natural phenomenon by which some parts of the Nile sometimes turned reddish, but it does not appear to have been merely a natural phenomenon in light of the immediacy of the result and its extent.

In the implementation of this miracle, Moses by his words directed Aaron, who did the actual motion with the staff in accordance with the general pattern of responsibility predicted in 4:15–17, which specifically indicated that Moses would teach Aaron "what to do" (4:16) and that the staff would be the device for performing "miraculous signs" (4:17). Thus we see here Moses and Aaron working together in accordance with the revealed pattern, as the opening words of v. 20 also imply. The mention of "streams . . . canals . . . ponds . . . reservoirs" (v. 19) delineates all the sorts of bodies of surface water in Egypt and therefore forms an explicative apposition to the phrase "the waters of Egypt." The extension of the plague even to "the wooden buckets and stone jars" is especially informative: it tends to confirm the comprehensiveness of the plague and its instantaneous nature.[41]

As the following verse (7:25) indicates, the plague of blood lasted only seven days. Virtually all commentators have observed that the plagues appear to have increased in intensity from first to last.[42] How, then, could

[39] See "Excursus: The Nile as a God" at 4:9.

[40] See "Excursus: Moses' Staff" at 4:17.

[41] Of course, if one wished to remain skeptical of the biblical account, it would be possible to regard the detail of the bloody water in buckets and jars not as proof that all the water in Egypt was suddenly turned bloody, even though it had been drawn and stored previously, but as a later folk-story embellishment or a consequence of the gradual natural reddening of the water of the Nile via microorganism reproduction (which then would make water drawn from the Nile gradually turn red as the microorganisms continued to multiply in the stored water) not properly understood and therefore told by later generations as an all-at-once miraculous development. But cf. B. Lemellijn, "The Phrase *wb'sm wb'bnym* in Exodus 7,19," *Bib* 80 (1999): 264–68. Lemellijn concludes that the meaning of the last two words in 7:19 connects to Egyptian idolatry (even the idols' holy water was affected, or the like). Cf. C. Houtman, "On the Meaning of *uba'esim ub'abanim* in Exodus vii 19," *VT* 36 (1986): 347–52; M. H. Pope, "Mid Rock and Scrub, A Ugaritic Parallel to Exodus 7:19," in *Biblical and Near Eastern Studies: Essays in Honor of William Sanford LaSor* (Grand Rapids: Eerdmans, 1978), 146–50.

[42] In two Psalter references to the first plague (Pss 78:44; 105:29) the progression from the more modest plagues to the most serious one, that of the death of the firstborn, also is evident.

this plague be regarded as the least threatening of the ten? The answer is that this plague involved not the changing of water into *real* blood (which would be so huge an environmental pollution of Egypt that its effects would be far more threatening to life than some of the later plagues) but the temporary reddening and contamination of the Nile and other surface water in a way that made the Nile undrinkable and killed its fish. This plague functioned more as a severe frustration for Egyptians than as a threat to life.[43] Fish died from this plague, but humans and other animals did not. We have already argued that this divine tainting of Egypt's water was, however, not merely an especially strong version of the seasonal reddening of the Nile. That it may have looked like and perhaps, to skeptical Egyptians, seemed to be merely a very severe manifestation of a known natural phenomenon would be consistent with the way that comforting self-deception works in general. If one is

[43] Some commentators have cited as a parallel to the biblical account of the first plague a portion of an Egyptian text from around the nineteenth or twentieth dynasties (1350–1100 BC) known as the Admonitions of Ipu-Wer, to suggest that the reddening of the Nile was a known occurrence to Egyptians. Taken out of context, the this portion seems, indeed, to be quite parallel:

> Why really the River is blood. If one drinks of it, one rejects (it) as human and thirsts for water. (*ANET,* 441, ii 10)

But the context is not that of a description of actual events. It is rather a long list of hyperbolic portrayals of the breakdown of normal life in Egypt during the first intermediate period (the period between the Old and Middle Kingdoms, ca. 2300–2050 BC) that Ipu-Wer, an Egyptian "prophet," is purported to have lamented in the royal Egyptian court, attacking the feckless leadership of an unnamed [prior?] pharaoh. The following excerpts will suffice to give a feel for the obviously nonliteral nature of Ipu-Wer's cries of doom:

> Why really, the Nile is in flood, (but) no one plows for himself, (because) every man says: "We do not know what may happen throughout the land!"
> Why really, women are dried up, and none can conceive. Knum cannot fashion mortals because of the state of the land.
> Why really, the land spins around as a potter's wheel does.
> Why really, crocodiles [sink] down because of what they have carried off, (for) men go to them of their own accord.
> Why really, the children of nobles are abandoned in the streets.
> Behold, the owners of robes are (now) in rags. (But) he who never wove for himself is (now) the owner of fine linen.
> Behold, he who knew not the lyre is (now) the owner of a harp. He who never sang for himself (now) praises the goddess of music . . .
> Behold, the bald-headed man who had no oil has become the owner of jars of sweet myrrh.

All these statements are stylized, imagistic, nonliteral ways of saying that Pharaoh needed to intervene to make things better for the Egyptian people because the times were bad. Some of the images speak of economic troubles (e.g., "the owners of robes are now in rags"); some seem to describe impossible geographic change (e.g., "the land spins around as a potter's wheel does"). The economic descriptions probably were the real focus of Ipu-Wer's concerns. The geographical descriptions, including that of the Nile River as blood are to be taken as metaphors for the unusual times. Cf. 2 Kgs 21:13; Pss 97:5; 114:4,6; Isa 40:4.

predisposed to doubt God, one will always be attracted to "natural" explanations for all of the Bible's supernatural phenomena, from creation *ex nihilo* to the resurrection of Jesus.

7:22–24 It is again likely that what was meant by the statement "the Egyptian magicians did the same things by their secret arts" (v. 22) was that the magicians were able to duplicate on a small scale, by simple trickery, the changing of water into reddish water. Such a duplication (or, more technically, *imitation*) would have required only the ability to add something that would dye some water red through slight of hand. It is noteworthy that the magicians did not attempt to undo the havoc wrought upon the Nile or other large bodies of water—for the obvious reason that they could not do so. But the work of the magicians had its effect on Pharaoh. He could comfort himself with the thought that somehow the trickery of Moses and Aaron (or the power of their God, if he thought that it was real divine power by which his magicians worked) was simply the same sort of thing his people could do, and on short notice at that. Thus, as with the changing of Aaron's staff into a snake, magic undermined the credibility of reality, and Pharaoh had an excuse to yield nothing to the Israelites and the demands of their God. The only thing Pharaoh had lost in this encounter was the opportunity to have his bath (v. 23).

The Egyptian people, however, had to scramble to get water, which was available only from new wells. Subsurface water had not been affected; the miracle of the first plague was limited in its lethality to fish—people were merely greatly inconvenienced. Nevertheless, the superiority of Israel's God to the god of the Nile was obvious. Verse 24 provides a postscript similar to that which accompanied the account of the staff-to-snake miracle (cf. 7:12), the purpose of which was to clarify that what the magicians could do was limited. In the case of the staff-to-snake miracle, they could imitate one aspect of the miracle, but they could not duplicate the action of the superior snake. In the case of the water-to-blood plague, they could imitate the changing of clear water to red water, but they could not reverse the curse, so the general population suffered. What Moses and Aaron had done was no trick; anyone desperately digging a well to get pure water knew that.

3. Third Sign: Second Plague: Frogs (7:25–8:15) [Hb. 7:25–8:11]

**25 Seven days passed after the LORD struck the Nile. 1 Then the LORD said to
Moses, "Go to Pharaoh and say to him, 'This is what the LORD says: Let my peo-
ple go, so that they may worship me. 2 If you refuse to let them go, I will plague
your whole country with frogs. 3 The Nile will teem with frogs. They will come up
into your palace and your bedroom and onto your bed, into the houses of your
officials and on your people, and into your ovens and kneading troughs. 4 The
frogs will go up on you and your people and all your officials.'"**

[5]Then the LORD said to Moses, "Tell Aaron, 'Stretch out your hand with your staff over the streams and canals and ponds, and make frogs come up on the land of Egypt.'"

[6]So Aaron stretched out his hand over the waters of Egypt, and the frogs came up and covered the land. [7]But the magicians did the same things by their secret arts; they also made frogs come up on the land of Egypt.

[8]Pharaoh summoned Moses and Aaron and said, "Pray to the LORD to take the frogs away from me and my people, and I will let your people go to offer sacrifices to the LORD."

[9]Moses said to Pharaoh, "I leave to you the honor of setting the time for me to pray for you and your officials and your people that you and your houses may be rid of the frogs, except for those that remain in the Nile."

[10]"Tomorrow," Pharaoh said. Moses replied, "It will be as you say, so that you may know there is no one like the LORD our God. [11]The frogs will leave you and your houses, your officials and your people; they will remain only in the Nile."

[12]After Moses and Aaron left Pharaoh, Moses cried out to the LORD about the frogs he had brought on Pharaoh. [13]And the LORD did what Moses asked. The frogs died in the houses, in the courtyards and in the fields. [14]They were piled into heaps, and the land reeked of them. [15]But when Pharaoh saw that there was relief, he hardened his heart and would not listen to Moses and Aaron, just as the LORD had said.

7:25–8:3 The second plague encounter took place, as also did the fifth and the eighth, at Pharaoh's court, as may be inferred from the command, "Go [in][44] to Pharaoh and say to him . . ." (8:1). It took place just a week after the first[45] (7:25), but otherwise its relationship to the first plague, if any, remains unstated. Could the frog epidemic have occurred in part as a predictable result of the pollution of the Nile, since whatever killed the fish likely would have driven the frogs as well from the river, even if not accounting for their enormous multiplication?[46] We are not told. Or had the

---

[44] The verb בּוֹא connotes going *in* to a place; the NIV obscured this to keep faith with normal Eng. idiom, but the Hb. explicitly indicates Moses went *in* to where Pharaoh was, i.e., the palace.

[45] This detail presumably is to indicate to the reader that there was little, if any, "let-up" in the pressure God exerted on the Egyptians with the sequencing of the plagues. This timing detail probably was intended to be programmatic: to function as an indicator that the reader should assume that *all* the plagues came one after another in relatively rapid succession, rather than being strung out over a period of repeated seasons or years. That the plagues should have lasted the better part of one year, however, is not at all impossible to imagine based on the evidence.

[46] This, of course, is generally the view of G. Hort, "The Plagues of Egypt," *ZAW* 69 (1957): 84–103; and *ZAW* 70 (1958): 48–59 (see "Excursus: The Progression and Structure of the Ten Plagues," above) although Hort appears to assume that story-telling tradition has at least somewhat exaggerated the extent of the frog plague. But note that the wording of 8:3 predicts that "the Nile will teem with frogs," which would seem to suggest that the frogs were not driven out of the Nile by rotting fish and polluted water but by miraculous overpopulation. Huge numbers of frogs were incubated in the Nile itself until the Nile simply could not contain them. This would seem to argue against Hort's thesis, although the paucity of detail ought to cause us to hold cautiously any view of the mechanisms of any of the plagues.

pollution by this time (perhaps gradually) abated so that the Egyptians could once again manage to drink water from the Nile? Moses did not say. Although one might argue theoretically that having the answers to these questions would help support biblical history apologetically, no such concern appears to have occupied Moses' mind. He was writing, after all, for an audience who had personally lived through the plagues (or whose parents had) and among whom there was ample experiential certainty that the plagues occurred and a strong memory of how and when. Moses' purpose seems rather to center on producing a relatively succinct summary of all the plagues together as a permanent *reminder* for all generations of their cumulative impact and, in the case of the first nine, as a compound-complex lead-in to the great final and decisive plague, that of the death of the firstborn. Too much detail about the timing and mechanism of the individual plagues would actually undermine that purpose.

The first plague produced great inconvenience, requiring the digging of (shallow) wells along the Nile as opposed to the easy access to drinking water that the Nile usually afforded, and it also produced the death of large quantities of fish. Spatially, it was limited to places where water was visible on the surface of the ground. This second plague announcement presaged greater problems, though still none was remotely life threatening. The frogs would go everywhere—without virtually any limitation—including the interior of the palace (mentioned first to be sure Pharaoh knew he would not be immune), bedrooms, beds,[47] and cooking utensils (mentioned as well to complete the picture of a gross manifestation of all places where humans lived). It is one thing for someone to be required work harder to get potable water for his family or neighborhood; it is quite another to have undesirable animals infesting all the lower surfaces of one's living areas. Thus the plague of frogs has traditionally, with good reason, been judged a more discomforting plague than the one that preceded it.

Psalms 78 and 105 both mention the frogs, as expected in these historical psalms covering the plagues. Psalm 78:45 describes the "frogs that devastated them," and Ps 105:30 summarizes the Exodus account, "Their land teemed with frogs, which went up into the bedrooms of their rulers." Both of these represent independent compositions reflecting the consistency of the plagues tradition in later Israelite times.

With regard to the thematic progression evident in the plague accounts, in 8:1 the demand of Yahweh is to "let my people go so that they may worship me." This wording reflects the more comprehensive, less restricted language

---

[47] "Beds" in Bible times refers to mats on floors, not elevated beds of modern times in Western countries. The frogs would have no trouble getting into anything near floor level, including the cooking utensils (there was not a lot of what we would call "shelving" in Bible times in nonforested Egypt—or anywhere else in the ancient world—to keep food utensils elevated).

originally revealed to Moses at Mount Sinai in 4:23 ("Let my son go, so he may worship me") and does not include the phrase "in the desert" that had been included in 7:16. This may seem a minor point, but it serves as part of a pattern that progresses from a request initially expressed in modest, limited wording to the full request (the point all along in actual fact) for complete, permanent freedom from Egypt.

7:25 The brief note that a full week had transpired between the onset of the first plague and God's announcement of the second might seem trivial, or even awkwardly placed. Most plague accounts do not contain similar descriptions of timing, and this note does not seem to bear directly on the significance of the plague of frogs per se (i.e., what is there about a frog plague that makes specifying the days until it happened any more meaningful to the reader than would be the case with any other plague?). Rather than being incidental, however, the information in v. 1 is almost surely programmatic: the reader is expected to reason that if there was at least a week between the first and second plagues (eight days, in fact, when the delay of one day between the announcement and the initiation is added, according to 8:9) there probably were comparable spaces of time between most of the other plagues. In the style typical of ancient Near Eastern narrative, stating something early on in a compound story or repetitive sequence is one way of saying implicitly *that it kept happening like this in the other cases too*.[48] By this device, Moses signaled the reader/listener that the duration of the entire period of plagues was *at least* a good many weeks, that is, several months.

This short verse has a second function in the narrative. By specifying that "the LORD struck the Nile," using the same verb for "strike" *(nkh)* that had been employed twice to describe what Moses and Aaron had done in the first plague, *striking* the Nile (7:17,20), the verse reinforces in the reader's mind that the actions of Moses and Aaron were symbolic; the real mover of the miracles was Yahweh himself. They went through the motions; he made it happen.

8:1–4 [Hb. 7:26–29] The demand of Yahweh ("Let my people go, so that they may worship me") will be repeated verbatim again in 8:1,20;

---

[48] Cf. Josh 7, where Israel's defeat in one small conquest battle is understood by Joshua and the Israelites to be programmatic of what might be coming in the future, in such a way that the writer of Joshua could allow it to serve as his sole detailed example of disobedience resulting in a partial conquest, even though the partial conquest as a result of disobedience theme is important to his whole account. Cf. also Exod 20:12, in which the promise of living long in the land is added only to the first of the "horizontal" Commandments (honor father and mother) even though it logically applies to the remaining Commandments as well. The most immediate parallel is found within the account of the fourth plague ("flies"). In 8:22–23 much is made of the distinction between the effect on the Egyptians and the absence of any effect on the Israelites, a way of using a detail in one plague account to suggest that it was similarly the case in all the plagues, thus relieving the narrator of the need to keep mentioning the obvious.

9:1,13; 10:3. It is the standard expression of God's demand to Pharaoh through Moses, and a slight but significant variation on the previous wordings (5:1, "Let my people go, so that they may hold a festival to me in the desert,") and 7:16, "Let my people go, so that they may worship me in the desert." At this point, the bargaining-style reference to holding a festival/ worship in the wilderness ceases, and the demand is thus more nearly explicitly one of full, permanent release. The Hb. verb translated "worship" by the NIV *(ʿbd)* could as easily be translated "serve," reminding Pharaoh that the God of the people he had forced to serve him as slaves was demanding their release to serve freely and permanently a new master, himself.

In this second plague account is sounded the first actual note of warning ("If you refuse to let them go, . . ." vv. 2–4). Warnings would accompany most of the demands hereafter. The warning itself refers to a consequence that was mainly offensive rather than truly dangerous. What was actually threatened was the ugliness of having slimy, unsanitary, unpleasant to the touch amphibians everywhere and the constant annoyance of having to listen to them croak and peep throughout all parts of people's houses. Implied is the disgust that would occur when people stepped on the frogs (as far as we know, Egyptians did not wear shoes indoors), when they rolled over on them in bed (again, people slept on mats on the floor, not in elevated beds as Westerners think of "beds"), and when they were surprised by them in various places thought otherwise to be clean (feeding troughs, ovens). Of particular significance to Pharaoh was the promise that this plague would affect him to the same degree that it affected all other Egyptians. The first plague was presumably of little personal hardship for him; others brought him water from the freshly dug wells, so all he missed was his usual bath in the Nile. Now, however, he would quite possibly encounter just as many frogs and be just as repulsed by them as anyone else (except the Israelites, who were always implicitly and sometimes explicitly exempted from the plagues). The progression of status implied in the mention of Pharaoh, then his officials, then the people in general in v. 3 is partly reversed in v. 4 (where it is Pharaoh ["you"], the people, and the officials, respectively). This double listing with different order of elements is a way of emphasizing that no one would escape the effects of this plague; indeed the point of the descriptions of vv. 2–4 is to make clear that virtually no person, place, or thing would be immune from the frog infestation. If kneading troughs and even bake ovens—places where frogs would never normally be found—were to be infested, surely little else would be free from the plague.[49]

[49] A modern parallel might be: "There will be frogs everywhere—in people's shoes, in desk drawers, in pets' water bowls, perched on computer keyboards, in bathrobe pockets."

Although we may assume that this speech to Pharaoh was delivered by Moses as instructed, the delivery per se is not mentioned. This is part of the variation in the plague accounts that keeps them from being overly formulaic. The hearer/reader simply assumes the repetition in the presence of Pharaoh. An element in this portion of the narrative that may also have occurred to the alert hearer/reader is the repetition of the term "teem" *(šrṣ)* in v. 3, quite possibly intended to evoke comparison with the *teeming* of Israelites in 1:7, the only other time the verb occurs in the book.

8:5–7 [Hb. 8:1–3] This portion of the story describes the command-fulfillment pattern of the frog plague as it relates to Moses' and Aaron's roles and the fact that the Egyptian magicians could in some manner replicate this feat as well as the prior two (staff to snake and Nile water turned red).

Had it been Moses' desire in the other plague accounts to provide the sort of detail he gave here as to his and Aaron's precise roles, the other stories might also have delineated his command to Aaron and Aaron's fulfillment thereof, as well as the fact that both hand and staff were involved. Later, the apparent difference between *hand and staff* in some of the plague accounts will be obviated by recognition that this plague account shows the distinction to be literary, that is, stylistic rather than materially consequential.[50] Thus there is no special differentiation intended by the mention of *staff* as opposed to *hand* or vice versa. Similarly, no contradiction exists between what is said in v. 5 about the source of the frogs ("streams and canals and ponds") as opposed to v. 3 ("the Nile will teem with frogs") since the Nile was the actual source of virtually all surface water in Egypt, channeling the water that fills the streams, canals, and ponds.

Two characteristics of this plague make it more than a mere natural result of the pollution of the Nile as described in the first plague: the number of frogs was enormous beyond all natural explanation, and they did not merely leave the Nile and its related bodies of water and then stay nearby (as might be expected if they were simply driven temporarily out of polluted water); they *covered the land.* The reaction of Pharaoh in v. 8 is logical in light of this: he begged for relief. Additionally, the cleanup described in vv. 13–14 makes sense only if the frog plague was something far beyond just a displacement of the number of frogs usually found in Egyptian bodies of water. But how are we to understand the ability of the Egyptian magicians to replicate what God had done (v. 7)? The answer must be essentially the same as it was in the case of the prior two portents: the magicians duplicated by magic, on a small scale, what God had done on a nationwide scale. Their

---

[50] The essential equivalency of "stretch out your hand" with "stretch out your staff" can be seen also in 9:22–23, where Yahweh said to Moses, "Stretch out your hand . . . " (נְטֵה אֶת־יָֽדְךָ, v. 23), and then of Moses it is immediately said in fulfillment that he "stretched out his staff . . ." (וַיֵּט מֹשֶׁה אֶת־מַטֵּהוּ).

efforts could provide some comfort for persons wanting to doubt the exclusive power of Yahweh to control events but could do little more than represent a token imitation, by deception, of what divine power could do.[51]

8:8–11 [Hb. 8:4–7] A special focus of this portion of the frog story is Pharaoh's opportunity to choose the time of the frogs' removal. Giving the Egyptian king this power of timing is from a human point of view apologetically brilliant on God's part: if the king could say when the frogs would go away, he would *personally* know that the timing was not due to the simple consequences of natural processes or a fiat of the gods of the Egyptians but the sovereignty of the God of Israel. Theologically, therefore, this plague was the point by which Pharaoh should have been able to admit that there was a true, powerful God behind the demands voiced by Moses. His refusal to believe even then is a paradigm for all people who, though confronted with the reasonableness of biblical truth, nevertheless refuse to believe by reason of factors other than the believability of the evidence.

In v. 8 it is already evident that Pharaoh placed little stock in the apparent ability of the magicians to replicate the production of frogs on a small scale since getting rid of them, rather than producing more of them, was what Pharaoh was driven to seek. His request to Moses to "pray to the LORD to take the frogs away from me and my people" implies as well that he by now knew that Yahweh existed and could control parts of nature the Egyptians previously thought were the sole province of their own gods. What Pharaoh was offering in return was still, of course, merely the chance to "offer sacrifices to the LORD," a privilege far short of what he by now also surely understood was the Israelite demand: full freedom from Egypt.

The literal translation of the idiomatic Hebrew of the first part of v. 9 is, "Honor yourself over me[52] as to the time for me to pray for you." The NIV rendering captures the sense nicely. Note here also the significance of what Moses was offering: the words "pray for you and your officials and your

---

[51] A possible scenario for what the Egyptian magicians did to imitate the frog plague would be the following: They would gather a large number of frogs in containers (easily done because there were frogs everywhere) suitably placed around, say, a courtyard. Then they would temporarily clear the courtyard of all frogs to the satisfaction of onlookers. Then, using curtains or incense smoke or any similar opaquing device, they would release their captured frogs from the containers, out of sight of the onlookers, so that the frogs would seem to appear suddenly and in abundance just as had been the case after Moses and Aaron brought them out in the first place. The onlookers were then, if so inclined, able to say, "Those Israelites aren't doing anything that our own magicians can't also do." Of course, the magicians had to hope the onlookers did not spend too much time analyzing why it was the magicians chose only to duplicate the production of frogs on a small scale and did not choose to use their "powers" to eliminate frogs on a large scale. That is where the remainder of the frog story, in fact, leaves the magicians—they are not mentioned in connection with duplicating the removal of the frogs because, of course, they could not.

[52] הִתְפָּאֵר עָלַי.

people" may be summarized by Jesus' words in Matt 5:44 ("Pray for those who persecute you") and Luke 6:28 ("Pray for those who mistreat you"). Prayer for one's enemies is thus not a concept initiated in the New Testament but is in fact first encountered in the Old Testament.[53] The wording of the final part of v. 9 ("except for those that remain in the Nile") is ambiguous as to whether there were frogs in the Nile that never came out onto the land in the first place or whether some frogs would return to the Nile as the rest died. Here the NIV translation differs from the NIV of v. 11, even though both verses end identically in the Hebrew. A clearer translation might end the prior sentence with "your officials and your people" and then make the final words of the verse a new clause or sentence (e.g., "they will remain only in the Nile,"[54] as in v. 11). Although it is an unlikely scenario in the context, according to the grammar of the Hebrew one could reach the conclusion that there had been frogs all along up to this point in the Nile and thus infer that the reddening of the Nile that killed the fish did not kill the frogs as well. Far more likely is the scenario that some frogs returned to the Nile after the frog plague ended.

One might ask why Pharaoh did not say "Today!" instead of "Tomorrow" in v. 10. After all, why not get rid of a nuisance as soon as possible? Since the quoted parts of the conversation between Moses and Pharaoh represent only a small portion of the total dialogue that surely took place between them, it may be assumed that Pharaoh understood that Moses' offer in v. 9 of "setting the time" was understood to mean "set the day." Moreover, v. 12 implies that Moses prayed earnestly for a period of time in intercession the next day; our modern style of quick prayers tends to blind us to how normal and common lengthy intercessory prayer was in Bible times,[55] so both Pharaoh and Moses may well have assumed that at least a day would be needed for intercession with God—and therefore Pharaoh had in fact requested the earliest possible moment for relief from the frogs. Moses practiced here a form of what today is called in some quarters prayer evangelism. In saying that he would pray for a result "so that you may know there is no one like the LORD our God," he was offering Pharaoh, even though in the context of an adversarial relationship, the opportunity to understand the uniqueness of the true God. Knowing this God as he did, he could be confident of his prediction in v. 11 that his prayers would indeed be answered. After all, he was already well aware that the confrontation with Pharaoh would end in the death of the Egyptian firstborn (cf. 4:23) and not simply by means of a relatively preliminary plague such as that of the teeming frogs.

---

[53] There are many other examples, including Job's prayer at God's behest for his "comforters," [NIV "friends] who became his persecutors in the course of the dialogues (Job 42:8).

[54] רַק בַּיְאֹר תִּשָּׁאַרְנָה.

[55] Cf. Ezra 10:1; Neh 1:4; 9:3; Luke 2:37; 6:12; Acts 1:14; 12:12; 1 Tim 5:5.

8:12–15 [Hb. 8:8–11] This final section of the story of the second plague demonstrates God's gracious willingness to respond to Moses' intercessory prayer (vv. 12–13), reminds the hearer/reader of the enormity of the plague (vv. 13–14), and affirms that all happened consistent with God's control of Pharaoh's actions, as predicted by God in the first place (v. 15).

The NIV translation of v. 12 might seem to suggest that the Hb. implies that Moses prayed "as soon as" he was away from the Egyptian court. In fact, the verse probably should be translated without the interpretive temporal clause but with the Hb. idiom *śām* + *lě* rendered "agreed," thus: "Moses and Aaron went out from Pharaoh, and Moses cried out for help[56] to the LORD concerning the frogs, as he had agreed with Pharaoh." Similarly, in v. 15 the NIV provides the names "Moses and Aaron" as if the use of the proper names carried special emphasis, whereas the original simply has the pronoun "them."

These verses describe the power of prayer, when a faithful servant of the one true God prays in accordance with his Master's will. Moses might have had good reason to assume that the frogs would eventually go away on their own, but he had certainly not been notified by God that they would die off on the day Pharaoh specified. Accordingly, he prayed earnestly for a result that from his point of view, at least, was not guaranteed but in faith that the Lord would do what he asked if his prayer were proper. It was, and the frogs died off suddenly enough that they could be gathered in heaps to decompose and smell,[57] as v. 14 indicates. According to God's already announced plan, this plague was not what would cause Pharaoh to release the Israelites. It would in fact meet with no success in light of God's making Pharaoh stubborn (7:3–5; 4:21–23), so v. 15 reminds the reader, in effect, that "there's much more to come before God is finished with Egypt and its king."[58]

4. Fourth Sign: Third Plague: Mosquitoes or Gnats (8:16–19) [Hb. 8:12–15]

[16]Then the LORD said to Moses, "Tell Aaron, 'Stretch out your staff and strike the dust of the ground,' and throughout the land of Egypt the dust will become gnats." [17]They did this, and when Aaron stretched out his hand with the staff and struck the dust of the ground, gnats came upon men and animals. All the dust throughout the land of Egypt became gnats. [18]But when the magicians tried to

---

[56] וַיִּצְעַק מֹשֶׁה אֶל (Moses cried out for help to . . .) reflects the idiom צעק ל/אל, which routinely connotes appealing in prayer for help.

[57] The Hb. says simply "the land smelled" or "the land stank"; the NIV "of them" is interpretive.

[58] See also D. J. McCarthy, "Moses' Dealings with Pharaoh: Ex 7,8–10,27," *CBQ* 27 (1965): 336–47; and Zevit, "Three Ways to Look at the Ten Plagues," 16–23, 42, 44.

produce gnats by their secret arts, they could not. And the gnats were on men and animals.

[19]The magicians said to Pharaoh, "This is the finger of God." But Pharaoh's heart was hard and he would not listen, just as the LORD had said.

8:16–19 The term "gnats" in English is properly used technically to describe virtually any two-winged biting insects, including mosquitoes, and therefore several of the English versions, including the NIV, have justifiably employed the broader term *gnats* in translating the Hb. *kinnîm*. Popular parlance, however, tends to speak of "gnats" as mainly annoying, tiny biting insects including some types of flies and "mosquitoes" as the far more commonly encountered blood-sucking, disease-spreading insect almost universally distributed—and loathed.[59] The brief description in this account does not allow us to be sure which type of "gnat" actually plagued the Egyptians (and it is not out of the question that more than one type was involved). Our discussion uses the term "mosquitoes" for the most part, on the theory that they usually are the most hated and troublesome branch of the gnat family.[60]

In some ways this plague is like that of the frogs that preceded it: both involve the miraculous production of a massive superabundance of an animal, with the effect of annoying and disturbing the Egyptians but without serious devastation otherwise. Likewise, this plague was caused by striking something with the staff of God in Aaron's hand—previously water, this time the ground, so that God's sovereignty over "land and sea"[61] was clearly evidenced. And, again, the magicians set out to duplicate this plague as well. What is notably *different* about the third plague is the failure of the magicians. They had been able to make it look as if they could change water into blood and produce frogs by their magical arts. But what magician has ever done a trick with trained mosquitoes? The magicians may have tried long and hard to duplicate the miracle (v. 18), but capturing enough mosquitoes to make an impressive display when released, keeping them alive and confined until the right time, and being able to release them in such a way that they would promptly and visibly swarm on people and animals in significant numbers would surely have proved too complicated.

---

[59] Most people, if asked, "Have you ever been bitten by a gnat?" would probably reply, "I suppose so. I'm not really sure" or the like. If asked, "Have you ever been bitten by a mosquito?" however, they probably would reply, "Of course. Who hasn't?" or the like. In other words, the range of meaning of the term "gnat" is vague in popular English.

[60] Hort ("The Plagues of Egypt," *ZAW* 69:84–103; *ZAW* 70:48–59) argues that they definitely were mosquitoes, based on her hypothesis that the most of the plagues relate to unusually severe upper Nile rainfall. Flooding of the lower Nile banks would create the sort of stagnant pools ideally suited to breeding mosquito larvae. On the problem of identifying the insects described in the third and fourth plagues, see I. Himbaza, "*La troisième et la quatrième plaies d'Égypte*," *BN* 94 (1998): 68–78.

[61] Cf. Isa 40:12; Jer 17:13; Pss 95:5; 106: 22; Jonah 1:9; Rev 7:1; 10:2,5,8.

What happened, then, was that the magicians confessed publicly that this plague (and by implication the others so far) was not a trick but a miracle. The expression "this is the finger of God," in light of its usage in Exod 31:18 and Deut 9:10, would seem to mean something like "a supernatural act of God" rather than literally referring to God's hand or figuratively conveying a sense such as "something easy enough for him to do with just a finger." The magicians were not confessing to their own conversion to true faith; they were simply saying that the plague was divine in origin, not human.[62]

5. Fifth Sign: Fourth Plague: Swarms of Flies (8:20–32) [Hb. 8:16–28]

As the earlier chart[63] displayed, the fourth plague replicates some features of the first, including the way it begins: with an outdoor morning confrontation with Pharaoh. Moses here also issued a warning to Pharaoh as in the case of the second plague. But a special emphasis in this plague account is not mentioned in any of the earlier ones: the differentiation between what happened to the Egyptians and what happened to the Israelites. As we have already argued, this differentiation is implicit in the earlier plagues as well, but at this point Moses chose to make it explicit. It will appear as a feature in some of the subsequent plague accounts as well (nos. five, seven, nine, ten), but not in all of them—indicating that the cases where the distinction is overtly described are intended to suggest to the reader the general pattern that prevailed in all ten plagues.[64]

Another important feature of this fourth plague account is Pharaoh's partial capitulation to Moses' demands: in v. 25 Pharaoh expressed willingness to let the Israelites have a special religious holiday as long as they held it within the land of Egypt; and in v. 28 he went so far as to authorize a brief departure from the land into the wilderness—on which he subsequently reneged (v. 32). These concessions, however brief and partial, represent the first cracks in the stone of the official Egyptian government resistance, demonstrating that the plagues were beginning to affect the king's resolve. Moses' account does not differentiate between the two most likely causes for Pharaoh's wavering, the growing intensity of the plagues and their over-

---

[62] Childs (*Exodus,* 156): "This is the first explicit indication of how the author settles the question of the true and false miracle. The true overwhelms the false, and the magicians themselves bear testimony to the fact." Cf. also G. L. Klingbeil, "The Finger of God in the Old Testament," *ZAW* 112 (2000): 409–15; B. Couroyer, "Le 'doigt de Dieu' (Exode 8:15, 19)," *RB* 63 (1956): 481–95.

[63] See p. 192.

[64] It is again worth stating that if all the common features the reader is expected to take as *assumed* in all the plague accounts were actually listed each time, the accounts themselves would be overly long for Moses' purposes and unwieldy stylistically as a matter of literary composition. To repeat obvious facts ten times over is not consistent with good narrative writing. Common facts must be mentioned *sometimes* for the reader's benefit but should not be mentioned *every* time.

all cumulative effect. Presumably, both causes worked to influence Pharaoh's decision toward compromise. As plagues kept coming, as their severity kept increasing, and as it became ever more obvious that they were not mere tricks but real, divinely instigated acts of judgment against Egypt, the king began searching for ways to end them without ending Egyptian domination over Israel. This plague account thus represents a way station on the road from imperious disdain for anything the God of Israel was asking for to the eventual complete capitulation that will follow the tenth and final plague, the death of the Egyptian firstborn.

(1) Announcement of the Plague (8:20–23) [Hb. 8:16–19]

20Then the LORD said to Moses, "Get up early in the morning and confront Pharaoh as he goes to the water and say to him, 'This is what the LORD says: Let my people go, so that they may worship me. 21If you do not let my people go, I will send swarms of flies on you and your officials, on your people and into your houses. The houses of the Egyptians will be full of flies, and even the ground where they are.

22"'But on that day I will deal differently with the land of Goshen, where my people live; no swarms of flies will be there, so that you will know that I, the LORD, am in this land. 23I will make a distinction between my people and your people. This miraculous sign will occur tomorrow.'"

8:20 [Hb. 8:16] The wording of this verse is essentially a condensation of the wording of the opening verses of the first plague account (water to blood, 7:14–16). This is appropriate since by now Moses was experienced in the process of confronting Pharaoh, and there would be no advantage to God's repeating to Moses his instructions in the same degree of detail. Thus the instructions were limited to the time and place of the confrontation and the more broad, less qualified demand, "Let my people go, so that they may worship me." The initial formal bargaining-style qualifier "in the desert" is no longer used[65] as it was in 7:16, and Moses referred to God simply as Yahweh [NIV "the LORD"] rather than "Yahweh, the God of the Hebrews," as in 7:16 since Pharaoh too had been learning from these encounters and was far more fully aware—to his great displeasure—of who Yahweh was and of his awesome power. The first plague encounter with Pharaoh was at the Nile, "as he goes out to the water" (7:15), and involved turning the Nile's water into blood. It cannot have been lost on Pharaoh, when he saw Moses waiting for him on the bank of the Nile in fulfillment of this command from God, that he was once again in the place and situation where the plagues had

[65] The LXX does add here the phrase ἐν τῇ ἐρήμῳ ("in the wilderness") as in 7:16, but it is far more likely that it does so via conflation—not as likely its own conflation as conflation already present in its Hb. *Vorlage*.

started. The cycle of encounter locations and patterns[66] is presumably intended to have this effect on Pharaoh: to cause him as the pattern begins to repeat itself to think, in effect, "Oh, no! Not again!"

8:21 [Hb. 8:17] The rather brief account of the third plague (gnats/mosquitoes) in 8:16–19 omitted any reference to a spoken threat as a warning of what would happen if Pharaoh did not comply with God's demand. Here, in a longer plague account, the threat component is again explicitly stated (as in the second plague, 8:2–4). The Egyptians were threatened with a huge infestation of swarming insects, so enormous that the insects would be everywhere, indoors and out, and constantly on everyone, including Pharaoh and his officials. The description "and even the ground where they are" literally refers to the ground where the houses were located, as a way of emphasizing that the swarms would be concentrated on inhabited areas and is comparable to saying "to the extent that you won't even be able to put a foot down without stepping on lots of them." What the NIV translates as "swarms of flies" is *ʿārōb,* a single word designating insects in swarms. Although it is likely that the insects in swarms were in this case mostly various sorts of flies, it is not certain that they would have been limited to what English speakers normally think of when they hear the word "flies." A translation such as "various kinds of annoying biting and nonbiting insects in huge swarms," cumbersome though it would be, might actually give a somewhat clearer sense of the threat to the Egyptians.[67]

8:22–23 [Hb. 8:18–19] Especially significant in this fourth plague account, and indeed an inherent part of the threat, is the stress on the fact that God would not do to his own people what he would do to the Egyptians, their oppressors. To one extent or another, all the plagues anticipated and progressively led up to the final, ultimate judgment of God in the form of the tenth plague, the death of the firstborn.[68] In that climactic event, much

[66] See the chart on p. 192.

[67] In early times the Hb. word עָרֹב (*ʿārōb*) was not uniformly understood as referring to "flies." In fact, the *Tg. Ps.-J.* to the Pentateuch (Jerusalem Targum I) translates the word in the present context as "wild animals." This is surely not correct but nevertheless serves as a reminder that the term is defined in most modern Eng. translations mainly from context rather than via sure etymology. Philo, perhaps following haggadic legend (so J. I. Durham, (*Exodus,* WBC [Waco: Word, 1987], 114), and L. Ginzberg, *Legends of the Jews* [New York: Simon & Schuster, 1961], 335–36), said that the fourth plague was made up of "a mixed horde of wild animals, lions, bears, wolves, and panthers, and . . . many birds of prey." Some of his reasoning may have been influenced by the wording of Ps 78:45, which says, "He sent swarms of flies that devoured them," a wording that might seem (though it need not) to describe people being eaten by wild animals. In fact, the common Eng. expressions "I'm being eaten up by these [insects]!" and "They're [the insects] eating me alive!" are parallel to what Ps 78 intends to describe. Surely, some of the flies that were part of the swarms were biting flies, but it must be kept in mind that אכל, "eat/devour," has many metaphorical uses, and thus many sorts of things are said to "eat/devour," such as the sword (Deut 32:42), fire (Num 16:35; cf. Holladay, *Lexicon,* 14).

[68] I.e., 11:1–12:30.

emphasis is placed on the distinction made between the Egyptians and the Israelites, a distinction that follows from the willingness of God's people to act in faith by marking their homes with the sign of the blood of the lamb.[69] Here God's distinction[70] between his own and those who do not belong to him is shown by his control of nature: although flies and other swarming insects cannot naturally discriminate by nationality or political boundaries[71] in deciding on whom they will land and whose skin they will bite, nationality/political boundary was exactly the basis for the plaguing or nonplaguing by the swarming insects. Here, then, is brought overtly to the reader's attention the fact that the plagues, far from being natural phenomena naturally produced, were nature turned on its head: nature ordered by its Creator to act in abnormal ways that were ominously frightening for the Egyptians, wonderfully reassuring for the Israelites, and clearly evidential (in this plague, even to Pharaoh) of a divine mighty act in service of a divine demand.

(2) The Plague and Its Devastation (8:24) [Hb. 8:20]

[24]And the LORD did this. Dense swarms of flies poured into Pharaoh's palace and into the houses of his officials, and throughout Egypt the land was ruined by the flies.

8:24 The window screen did not exist in ancient times; windows were simply openings in walls (and ceilings). It would have been possible for some of the wealthier Egyptians to fix cloth at doorways and windows to keep out the insect swarms, but this would have produced an almost intolerable lack of airflow in a perennially hot climate, making life indoors essentially unbearable, so it is unlikely that any Egyptians even considered such a

[69] See the commentary on chap. 12, esp. vv. 7–13,21–30.

[70] The NIV translation "make a distinction" is properly based on a textual decision to read the presumed Hb. nominal form פדרת from the root פרד, thus following the LXX διαστολὴν, "distinction," Vg. *divisionem* ("distinction"), rather than the MT reading פדת, "redemption." Although it is conceivable that the original wording is in fact represented by the MT so that 8:23 would read, "I will provide a redemption between my people and your people," the MT wording is so unusual and nonidiomatic and so classically an example of the accidental substitution by a copyist of a familiar word for a rarer one (thus inviting virtually all text critics to identify here the need for application of the principle of *lectio difficilior probabilior*) that the NIV choice is virtually assured as correct. The point of vv. 22–23 is consistent differentiation between Egypt in general and Goshen in particular and thus between the Egyptians and the Israelites, not the broader concept of divine redemption. Goshen was not *redeemed* in this plague account; it was simply *spared* swarms that ruined the quality of life elsewhere in Egypt.

[71] Accordingly, the LXX addition, "[This miraculous sign will occur tomorrow] upon the land," ἐπὶ τῆς γῆς, appears to be more likely a partial dittography from the end of v. 22 than a preservation of an actual original wording.

move.[72] Thus the swarms of flies were allowed access to everyone whether indoors or outdoors, and once the plague began, the Egyptians were living (or trying to live) covered with flies. Flies of various sorts were nothing new to the Egyptians. There were plenty of flies in Egypt in Bible times, just as there are in modern times. The devastation here described was not the result of something new but of something well known and usually tolerable as an annoyance becoming multiplied thousands of times over by God's special action[73] so as to constitute an intolerable pestilence, to the extent that "the land was ruined by the flies." The ruin here described was not topological but rather referred to the quality of life.[74] People couldn't eat without ingesting flies; they couldn't sleep without flies covering their bodies; they couldn't work for having to swat flies and/or because they couldn't see well through the swarms; their skin was welted with fly bites.

(3) Pharaoh's First Concession: An Offer of a Religious Holiday but Only inside Egypt (8:25) [Hb. 8:21]

[25]Then Pharaoh summoned Moses and Aaron and said, "Go, sacrifice to your God here in the land."

8:25 This is the point at which Pharaoh began to weaken. We are not told how many days had gone by, how many complaints and expressions of panic he had received from his advisors and from the Egyptian people in general, and how severely he and his own family had been driven to distraction by the insect swarms, but we *are* told that he was now so bothered by the flies that he called Moses and Aaron to the palace and offered the Israelites a partial accession to their God's demands. In one sense this concession goes beyond that of 8:8 by reason of its specificity: Pharaoh was offering a real, clearly defined option to the Israelites in exchange for relief from the flies. Nevertheless, the reader is well advised to bear in mind that Pharaoh knew from the beginning that the Israelites were expecting much more than

---

[72] In many areas of the world today, screens are eschewed even by people who can easily afford them because they restrict airflow through houses that are not designed with multiple windows and doors, as Western/northern hemisphere houses usually are. Windows in dwellings in biblical times were few, as were doors. Most houses were built so as to share common walls and had back or inner rooms that were typically dark and windowless, thus isolated from the house's courtyard (cf. Judg 3:24; 1 Kgs 20:30; 22:25; 2 Kgs 9:2; Matt 24:26; Luke 12:3). Putting cloth over the outer windows would have been regarded as an unacceptable alternative, in spite of the insect threat.

[73] Both the SP and *Tg. Onq.* read in place of "dense swarms of flies poured into . . ." the equivalent of "he [Yahweh] brought dense swarms of flies into . . ." This appears to be a translation decision rather than a manuscript reading difference, owing to the obvious fact that the ancient translators of these two versions knew instinctively that the swarms of insects would not have acted as they did without special divine control.

[74] Thus "land" here is essentially personified, referring in fact to the people of the land, as in, e.g., Lev 18:25,27; 19:29; 20:22; 26:34–35; Job 31:38; Jer 51:47; Amos 8:8; Zech 12:12.

he was now offering. They were asking for nothing else than to leave Egypt permanently,[75] and the language used thus far by Moses and Aaron in demanding the right to leave permanently, modified by such phrases as "into the wilderness" and "to offer sacrifices to our God" and "three days," simply reflects ancient/modern Eastern bargaining style; so the modifying phrases were never meant to be taken literally and never were. Now Pharaoh, from his perspective, was bargaining too and offering terms he wanted the Israelites to settle for: an Israelite national holiday to sacrifice to Yahweh *within Egypt*. From Pharaoh's point of view as a bargainer, this might gain him the end of the plagues while ceding little to Israel: only a short time off from work. Pharaoh would retain Israel under Egyptian domination and continue to prevent their being able to organize alliances with other peoples or nations in any way that would be threatening to Egypt (cf. 1:10). Pharaoh may have genuinely thought this concession would work; in a bargaining culture, neither side can necessarily be sure at the outset what the minimum or maximum price of the other side really is until the bargaining proceeds further or is completed.

(4) Moses' Rejection of Pharaoh's First Offer (8:26–27) [Hb. 8:22–23]

[26]But Moses said, "That would not be right. The sacrifices we offer the LORD our God would be detestable to the Egyptians. And if we offer sacrifices that are detestable in their eyes, will they not stone us? [27]We must take a three-day journey into the desert to offer sacrifices to the LORD our God, as he commands us."

8:26–27 Moses, of course, would not think of settling for a mere in-country religious holiday. He well knew that God's promise to Israel was "to rescue them from the hand of the Egyptians and to bring them up out of that land into a good and spacious land, a land flowing with milk and honey—the home of the Canaanites, Hittites, Amorites, Perizzites, Hivites and Jebusites . . . to bring my people the Israelites out of Egypt" (3:8,10). He did not, however, reply to Pharaoh as a modern Westerner might:[76] "No, sorry, we will accept nothing less than permanent emigration from Egypt to Canaan, never again to be under your domination." He continued in bargaining-style mode, with an appropriately gentle response argument[77] that made

[75] See comments on 5:1.

[76] An exception would be modern international diplomatic negotiation, in which countless hours can be spent in subtly hinting at desired outcomes while rehearsing well-known stances through seemingly endless repetition of the facts—a process often exasperating to the novice diplomat but nevertheless all too often standard procedure.

[77] Part of the bargaining transaction process is to bring the other person to see your point of view; if this can be accomplished without insulting or defying the other person, the final results normally are superior to those obtained by coming across as unbending and uncompromising throughout the negotiation process.

three reasonable assertions, all of which were ways of saying "that's not what we will accept" yet in a manner calculated to sound as nondemanding and nonthreatening as possible. These assertions are: (1) Israelite animal sacrifices were abominable to Egyptians. This was certainly true. The Egyptians, as typical pantheists, still made animal sacrifices even though they identified many of their gods with them. What they detested was anything related to mountain-dwelling peoples' habits and preferences, including the raising of sheep and goats (Gen 46:34). (2) In light of Egyptian animosity toward Israelites, it made little sense to perform openly, among Egyptians, what was so repugnant to them and merely invited active resentment and attack.[78] This language, too, was part of the bargaining; we have no knowledge that would lead us to conclude that all Egyptians throughout the land would, if they saw an Israelite goat or lamb sacrifice, automatically react by stoning those who made it. (3) God had not called for a minor sort of religious holiday but a *formal* national act of worship *in a different location* to identify the Israelites as his people.

The term "a three-day journey" is not to be taken literally; it is an idiom for "an official, formal, foreign visit."[79] Moses again used this phrase, just as it was dictated to him in 3:18 and as he had employed it in 5:3, to remind Pharaoh that no mere simple, informal, brief, or local religious observance could substitute for what the God of Israel was demanding of Egypt's king. "Three-day journey" can also carry the overtone of "far from here" or "very far away" as in Gen 30:36 ("Then he put a three-day journey between himself and Jacob"). Pharaoh obviously understood it this way since his counterbargaining reply in the next verse asked that the Israelites "not go very far," in a vain attempt somehow to save face by suggesting that they would actually not make a full, permanent departure from Egypt.

(5) Pharaoh's Second Concession: Permission for a Temporary Trip into the Wilderness (8:28–29) [Hb. 8:24–25]

[28]Pharaoh said, "I will let you go to offer sacrifices to the LORD your God in the desert, but you must not go very far. Now pray for me."

---

[78] Rather than the negative interrogative wording of the MT (*And if we offer sacrifices that are detestable in their eyes, will they not stone us*?) the LXX, Syriac Peshitta and Vulgate all read a declarative sentence ("And if we offer sacrifices that are detestable in their eyes, they will stone us!), which probably reflects the actual original wording. There are various grammatical and contextual reasons why a declarative translation is better in English, as long as one recognizes the probability that what the Masoretes vocalized as *lōʾ* ("no") was actually a misunderstood asseverative *lamedh*, literally "indeed" or "definitely." See F. Nötscher, "Zum emphatischen lamedh" (*VT* 3 [1953]: 372–80), esp. p. 375.

[79] See the comments on 3:18; 5:3; and cf. Jonah 3:3: "Jonah obeyed the word of the LORD and went to Nineveh. Now Nineveh was a very important city—a visit required three days." Further see D. Stuart, *Hosea-Jonah*, WBC (Waco: Word, 1987), 483–88.

[29]Moses answered, "As soon as I leave you, I will pray to the LORD, and tomorrow the flies will leave Pharaoh and his officials and his people. Only be sure that Pharaoh does not act deceitfully again by not letting the people go to offer sacrifices to the LORD."

8:28–29 Pharaoh now offered to let the Israelites leave Egypt, and Moses apparently accepted his offer as a genuine capitulation to Yahweh's demands. True, Pharaoh placed restrictions on his offer ("I will let you go [only] to offer sacrifices . . . you must not go very far"), and Moses remained suspicious and wary, as indicated by his words in rejoinder ("Only be sure that Pharaoh does not act deceitfully again by not letting the people go"). Nevertheless, this interchange raises a question: Did Moses really think he had won, and if so, wasn't he mistaken? The most likely answer would seem to be: He did not know for sure whether or not he (or more precisely, Yahweh) had won, but he regarded it as a real possibility—that is, that now the exodus could get underway. The main reason for this is to be found, once again, in the implications of the bargaining style. The style allows many unspoken transactions to be subsumed under that which is actually stated. Moses could well have understood Pharaoh's spoken restrictions as mere face-saving devices for allowing the exodus to take place without having to say, "Okay, you win. I give up. You can have your exodus." It is important to bear in mind that Moses had never been told how many plagues there would be and could well have wondered if this fourth plague, having several similarities to the first, might indicate by its somewhat resumptive nature that the pattern was starting again, so that means we've come full circle and this part of the sequence was coming to a conclusion. He also did not have to assume that the predicted death of the Egyptian firstborn (4:23) was no longer a valid expectation. That event could still happen, after the plague of swarming insects abated and during or after the time the Israelites left Egypt. In other words, there was nothing in what Moses had so far been led to expect that would automatically cause him to think he was as yet far from the time of the exodus and that many more plagues would be needed before he could begin to lead the Israelites into the wilderness. Moses was operating on faith as regards God's timing throughout the entire sequence of the plagues.

Pharaoh's words, "now pray for me,"[80] in v. 28 suggest that this plague had touched him personally to an extent that the prior three had not. Moses' promise

[80] The LXX adds πρός κύριον so that the final sentence of v. 28 reads, "Now pray *to Yahweh* for me." This is as likely as not an interpretive translation on the part of the LXX translator, who wanted to be sure his audience realized what is implicit in the context—that Pharaoh was not just asking for prayers to any god but specifically to Israel's God. Conversely, and less easily explained, the LXX reads [I will pray] πρὸς τὸν θεόν ("to God") rather than [I will pray] πρὸς κύριον ("to Yahweh") in the next verse (8:29). It may be that the LXX translator tried to blend the translation of the two verses with regard to the recipient of Moses' prayers so as equalize his compromises: since he had made explicit what was implicit in v. 28, he reversed the process in v. 29 as a way of "averaging out" his previous translation liberty.

to pray immediately after departing the palace ("as soon as I leave you," v. 29) may be another indication of the way people were being "driven crazy" by the swarms of flies: it was the sort of thing one might say if during the encounter with Pharaoh there had been many expressions of desire for relief from what had become intolerable. Moses' promise of quick rather than gradual relief ("tomorrow the flies will leave") appears as well to fit with this scenario.

(6) Removal of the Plague, Followed by Pharaoh's Reneging on His Promise (8:30–32) [Hb. 8:26–28]

[30]Then Moses left Pharaoh and prayed to the LORD, [31]and the LORD did what Moses asked: The flies left Pharaoh and his officials and his people; not a fly remained. [32]But this time also Pharaoh hardened his heart and would not let the people go.

8:30–32 These three verses closely parallel 8:12–15, the concluding statements of the plague of frogs account, immediately preceding. Each of the two successive plague accounts (nos. three and four) thus ends with mention of Moses' departure from Pharaoh, his prayer, assurance of Yahweh's full response (what Moses asked), complete relief from the plague, and Pharaoh's stubborn refusal to honor his promise.

By this time it should be obvious to the reader that one of the things that Yahweh accomplished by making Pharaoh's heart hard (i.e., making him stubborn) was to cause Pharaoh to become someone whose word simply could not be trusted. This is adumbrated by Moses' verbalized concern that Pharaoh must not renege on his agreement to let the Israelites go (8:29), which sets the stage all the more visibly for the reader to notice unreliability in Pharaoh. With regard to the bigger picture of Pharaoh's overall humiliation in the plagues-exodus-Red Sea narrative, the reader is already able to ask the question, "If Pharaoh cannot keep his word with regard to things clearly within his power to accomplish, can he be trusted even remotely to keep his word [or boast] with regard to things about which there might be doubt as to his power—or willingness—to perform (e.g., his afterthought attempt to destroy Israel after the exodus had taken place; 14:5–15:21)?

6. Fifth Plague: Death of Livestock (9:1–7)

This plague account is one of the shorter ones, only slightly longer than plagues two and six but long enough to provide the basic elements necessary to inform the reader of the particulars: it would kill livestock, but only Egyptian animals; it was a further humiliation of Pharaoh directly tied to his continuing refusal to release the Israelites; its differentiation between the Egyptians and the Israelites was validated by formal investigation; and when it was over, it still didn't move Pharaoh to allow the exodus.

(1) Announcement of the Plague (9:1–4)

[1]Then the LORD said to Moses, "Go to Pharaoh and say to him, 'This is what the LORD, the God of the Hebrews, says: "Let my people go, so that they may worship me." [2]If you refuse to let them go and continue to hold them back, [3]the hand of the LORD will bring a terrible plague on your livestock in the field—on your horses and donkeys and camels and on your cattle and sheep and goats. [4]But the LORD will make a distinction between the livestock of Israel and that of Egypt, so that no animal belonging to the Israelites will die."'

9:1–2 This account begins similarly to plagues two and eight, with Moses being sent to Pharaoh indoors, presumably at his court,[81] with both a demand and a warning, "Let my people go, so that they may worship[82] me. If you refuse to let them go, . . ." In this account v. 2 adds "and continue to hold them back," a wording that is not found in the other plague accounts but might have been included in almost any of them; it has the effect of reminding Pharaoh—and the reader—that there was an impetus to the Israelite cause that Pharaoh was restraining. He was *holding back* people who belonged somewhere else.

9:3 Part of the evidence leading to the conclusion that the plagues increased in severity as they progressed is found in the words of v. 3, "The hand of the LORD will bring a terrible plague." None of the prior plagues was announced by Moses as the work of "the hand of the LORD." It is, of course, the case that the Egyptian magicians used a similar expression in the third plague account to explain to Pharaoh that the plague of biting insects was supernatural in origin ("This is the finger of God," 8:19), but now God himself announced a plague as coming directly from himself, implicitly referring to its severity. He had, of course, caused all the others; but now he

[81] In much of the Near East, the custom of the *majlis,* or "open court," has survived even to modern times, a custom by which even the lowliest citizen in a monarchy is afforded the right to have a face-to-face meeting with the monarch of his country, providing an opportunity for redress of grievances or meeting of special needs. For biblical examples of this sort of access to the leader of a nation or empire in ancient times, whether in person or by proxy, cf. Exod 18:13–16; 2 Sam 12:1–6; 1 Kgs 3:16–28; Acts 25:10–12. Moses and Aaron were taking advantage of this right when they appeared at Pharaoh's court and were allowed an audience with him. But we have no idea what sort of schedule applied to opportunities to confront Pharaoh at court, so we cannot be sure how many days Moses and Aaron may have had to wait to see Pharaoh once they had been told by God to do so. On the other hand, by this point, in light of the pressures placed on Egypt and Pharaoh by the plagues, Pharaoh may have given standing orders that Moses and Aaron were allowed access to him at virtually any time. Alternatively, their requests to see him may have been acceded to virtually immediately even without standing orders of any sort.

[82] It bears repeating that "worship" is only one possible translation of עבד, which can also mean "serve," or "work for." The Hb. easily shows this constant interplay between the Israelites' current status of *serving* Pharaoh and their God's demand that they be free to *serve* him, Yahweh, instead—a theme unfortunately lost in translation.

warned Pharaoh that he would make this one happen, in effect, in a big way. The NIV "will bring a terrible plague" is a finessed conceptual rendering of the Hebrew,[83] but it captures some of the sense of the final three words in the original, which may literally be translated "a very severe plague."[84]

9:4 Verse 4 not only emphasizes once again[85] the differentiation between the Egyptians and the Israelites with regard to the destructive effects of the plague but announces death for the first time. It was not yet the death of people, but it was far greater than, say, the dying off of the frogs mentioned in the second plague story (8:13–14). Domesticated animals were treasured as enormously valuable assets in Bible times (as in any time prior to the industrial revolution, or any place even today where farming predominates). Moreover, they were seen as closely interrelated to the welfare of humans, a fact reflected even in the Bible's creation accounts.[86] The pantheistic Egyptians revered all animals but birds and livestock more than fish and amphibians. For them to have lost livestock would constitute a serious blow indeed. For them to have lost livestock while the Israelites retained all theirs represented a nationwide humiliation.

(2) The Plague and Its Devastation (9:5–6)

5The LORD set a time and said, "Tomorrow the LORD will do this in the land." 6And the next day the LORD did it: All the livestock of the Egyptians died, but not one animal belonging to the Israelites died.

9:5 God's verbally setting a time for a localized event (not merely a plague) to happen has no parallel elsewhere in Scripture, and the mention here of the expression "the LORD set a time" presumably is included as a contrast with the wording in the second plague account (7:25–8:15), where Moses specifically allowed Pharaoh to set the time ("I leave to you the honor of setting the time," 8:9). This implicit connection of the wording of the fifth plague to that of the sec-

---

[83] Especially of interest is the unusual use of the participle הֹוָיָה from the verb היה. On the grammar see G. S. Ogden, "Notes on the Use of *hwyh* in Exodus IX 3," *VT* 17 (1967): 483–84.

[84] V. 3 constitutes an unusual sentence in Hb., one that has for its key verb the feminine singular participle הויה of the verb היה, a hapax legomenon in the OT. Why would Moses employ what is to modern scholars and may even have been to his first readers such an unusual form? Ogden (ibid.) has cogently argued that the participle appears here as part of a macropattern in the plague accounts, in which participles are used regularly (7:17,27; 9:3; 10:4).

[85] Cf. 8:22–23.

[86] Considerable significance follows from the fact that both humans and potentially domesticatable animals were created on the same day (Gen 1:24–26). The respective worths of both human workers and animal workers (usually translated, respectively, "slaves" and "livestock") are often regarded in parallel (e.g., Gen 20:14; Exod 9:20–21; Job 1:2). Note also that the plague on the firstborn extends to the firstborn of the cattle as well (Exod 11:5). God himself definitively reminded Jonah of the value of livestock life on its own merits in Jonah 4:11. Cf. also the common phrase "men and animals" used in contexts where the focus of God is on the higher elements of his creation (e.g., esp. Jer 21:6; 31:27; 32:43; 33:10,12; 36:29; 50:3; Ezek 14:21; 25:13; 29:8; 36:11).

ond is yet further evidence that the plague stories are highly integrated, composed as a unit, and therefore expect the reader to be thinking of the elements of all of them as he or she reads any particular one. Specifically, the cyclic nature of the composition of the first nine plague accounts means that the reader is presumed to have especially in mind what happened in the second plague, the initial plague of the "second cycle" when reading the account of the fifth plague, the next account in that cycle.[87] The fact that Pharaoh was given a chance to set the time for relief from the second plague, and did so but was not able to learn from the result that he should have let the Israelites go, means that now there was no point in giving him other chances. So God named the date. The way God spoke of himself in the third person in v. 5 is paralleled by many other instances in Scripture, particularly in the prophetical books. Moses was throughout Exodus and the following Pentateuchal books speaking of himself in the first person as well. Both are examples of a phenomenon normal to Hebrew narrative style. "The land" refers to Egypt, again highlighting the supernatural nature of the plague, since a naturally occurring plague would not limit itself by political boundaries.

9:6 Verse 6 describes the actuation of what had been warned and predicted previously. God fulfilled his word and the timing he had announced, and the Egyptian livestock died, with Israelite livestock being untouched. The verse also contains a translation choice in the NIV that creates a possible misimpression for the reader. The NIV translation "all the livestock of the Egyptians died" would seem to suggest that no Egyptian livestock survived the plague, especially when this statement is followed by the (correctly translated) statement "but not one animal belonging to the Israelites died." Yet when one reads on to the account of the seventh plague, it is clear that there were plenty of Egyptian livestock still alive, since they are mentioned as being in danger of being killed by the next plague, that of ferocious hail (9:19–21). Moreover, Egyptian livestock are described as alive at the advent of the account of the final plague, that of the death of the firstborn (12:29). This apparent contradiction is not due to inconsistency among the plague accounts, multiple contradictory sources for them, or any similar cause. It is due simply to the fact that the Hebrew word *kol,* usually translated "all," can mean "all sorts of"[88] or

[87] See the chart on p 189 and the accompanying discussion.

[88] That כול/כל can mean "all sorts of" or the like is well known. E.g., it is usually translated either "all sorts of" or "all kinds of" in modern Eng. translations in the following sampling of contexts from early and late biblical Hebrew: Gen 4:22; 24:10; 40:17; Exod 35:22; Lev 19:23; Deut 6:11; 2 Kgs 8:9; 1 Chr 18:10; 22:15; 29:2; 2 Chr 2:14; 32:27–28; Neh 9:25; 13:15; 13:20; Ps 45:13; Prov 1:13; Eccl 2:5; Ezek 8:10; 27:22; 39:20; 47:12. The semantic range of NT Gk. πας is similar: more often than not it means "all," but in a wide variety of contexts it means "all sorts of" or "all kinds of," one of the most important being in 1 Tim 6:10, which does not say that the love of money is the root of all evil but the root of all sorts of evil. Plenty of evil has nothing to do with the love of money; but there are few evils that people will not resort to if the money for doing them is great enough.

"from all over" or "all over the place."[89] In this verse the better translation of the full expression would be "all sorts of Egyptian livestock died" or "Egyptian livestock died all over the place."

(3) Pharaoh's Investigation of Israelite Animals and His Continuing Refusal (9:7)

[7]Pharaoh sent men to investigate and found that not even one of the animals of the Israelites had died. Yet his heart was unyielding and he would not let the people go.

9:7 Now that so many Egyptian cattle had died, representing an economic disaster for the Egyptians, Pharaoh decided to find out for himself whether or not the same sort of thing had happened to the Israelites. All over Egypt the bodies of cows, horses, and other animals were rotting in the sun. If a similar situation were found in Goshen, the Israelite enclave, it would prove that the plague had been natural or—perhaps better yet—that Yahweh had somehow turned against his own people as well. Of course, this plague does not represent the first time that God had differentiated between his people Israel and the Egyptians. But in the case of the other plagues, the results would have been somewhat harder to verify or the difference easier to hide on the part of the Israelites if they were given to deception, as Pharaoh, if paranoid enough, might have wishfully thought.

Presumably he sent enough investigators that they could cover the whole land of Goshen quickly, but no evidence of any death of livestock was found there. Egyptian taskmasters and military personnel stationed at or near Goshen may also have confirmed to the investigators what they could discern with their own eyes: not a single Israelite animal had died. God had spared Israel and devastated Egypt. Nevertheless, Pharaoh's heart was unyielding, and he would not give the Israelites their freedom. God was controlling Pharaoh in a manner leading progressively to Pharaoh's and Egypt's complete humiliation and tragic defeat. Continuing to resist was the most foolish thing Pharaoh could do, and that was exactly what God was making him do.

7. Seventh Sign: Sixth Plague: Festering Boils (9:8–12)

Although this sixth plague account mentions no overt verbal confrontation with Pharaoh (no catching him as he headed somewhere or spoken warning directly to him, or the like), both he and his magicians were required to witness the symbolic action that presumably took place out-

---

[89] So commonly in the Hb. expression "all Israel," which in many contexts refers only to representatives (e.g., 1 Sam 12:1; 1 Kgs 18:19; 1 Chr 11:1; 15:3) or soldiers (Josh 8:24) or leaders from all segments of the nation (2 Chr 1:2) or the like, not literally to "every single Israelite."

doors.[90] This is, by a slight margin, the shortest of the plague accounts, and yet its severity is clearly indicated in the words of v. 11, "The magicians could not stand before Moses because of the boils that were on them." Nothing that had yet happened to the Egyptians had been so debilitating that it prevented their mobility. Here was a plague that no one could ignore or easily explain away as trivial.

Excursus: Did Anthrax Cause the Fifth and Sixth Plagues?

A number of commentators and even some medical specialists have raised the possibility that plagues five and six both represent the effects of anthrax.[91] The arguments in favor of this theory may be summarized with the following scenario:

Plague one, the turning of water to "blood," killed many or most of the fish in the Nile. Since anthrax can at least theoretically breed in dead and rotting fish, the huge quantity of rotting fish in and along the banks of the river could have provided a fertile medium for the multiplication of the *bacillus anthracis*. The frogs that had been in the Nile and were now driven from it by its pollution (plague two) carried the anthrax infection as they spread out over the land along the Nile. Since virtually all of Egypt's population in both ancient and modern times was/is located very close to the Nile, the frogs were spreading the anthrax bacillus to much of the inhabited area of Egypt, including the locations where the Egyptian cattle grazed. What killed the frogs where they were—all over Egypt and in huge quantities[92]—was anthrax.[93] As the dead frog bodies rotted in the sun,

---

[90] It is actually not possible from the brevity of detail in this account to discern whether or not the action "in the presence of Pharaoh" (vv. 8,10) was done within the court or outdoors. In favor of an indoor setting would be the lack of any directions to Moses and Aaron to meet up with Pharaoh outdoors and the concomitant realization that the normal place to "stand before Pharaoh" (v. 10) and to encounter his magicians would be the court. Strongly favoring an outdoor setting is the nature of the symbolic action: throwing dust "into the sky" (the literal translation of what the NIV renders in vv. 8,10 somewhat puzzlingly as "into the air").

[91] This is not to suggest that only the fifth and sixth plagues have been considered attributable to anthrax. Nevertheless, in terms of descriptions of symptoms, it is only the fifth and six plague accounts that actually contain the descriptions that have led to the anthrax theory of their etiology.

[92] Cf. 8:13–14.

[93] Bacillus anthracis takes the form of a quite large, gram-positive, spore forming rod. Anthrax is easily cultivated via an ordinary nutrient medium [thus it was the first bacterium to be cultivated and shown to be the cause of a disease, by Dr. R. Koch in 1878] and multiplies best aerobically, although it can multiply anaerobically as well. As regards its genotype and phenotype, it is similar to *bacillus cereus,* also easily isolated from soil. The disease caused by the anthrax bacillus is also known simply as "anthrax" and attacks mainly domesticated and wild animals—but especially herbivorous animals. How, then, do humans become infected with anthrax? This happens usually when they somehow come into contact with diseased animals either by touching their hide or hair or by touching their droppings. Fortunately, in humans the disease is considered rare, with the risk of infection being only about one in one hundred thousand in the general population. The form of the disease humans are most likely to succumb to is cutaneous anthrax, and the medium of infection in that case is normally injured skin or mucous membranes. Any sort of breach in the skin, such as a cut or scratch on one's face, neck, or arms, can be infected by spores from soil, from the surface of an infected live animal, or from the carcass of an animal that has died of anthrax. As the anthrax spores germinate in the skin lesion, a gelatinous edema forms as cells multiply. From this

anthrax was released in large quantities into the soil, where it could remain dormant almost indefinitely. But a long dormancy was not required in this case. Even after the smell of the frogs (cf. 8:14) was gone because their bodies were desiccated, the anthrax was alive and well in the soil and was beginning to spread to the grasses as they grew from the soil where the frogs had died.[94] When cattle grazed over these grasses, plague five, the death of the cattle, was caused by anthrax as it multiplied without check in the bodies of the cattle.

Meanwhile, the breeding conditions for various sorts of flies (plague four) (and, incidentally, mosquitoes, plague three) were ideal since the Nile as well as the various stagnant pools of water along the Nile contained large amounts of rotting fish that were anthrax-infected. The rotting carcasses of frogs likewise contained anthrax, as would the rotting carcasses of dead cattle. From any and all of these sources, the various flies, but particularly the *stomoxis calcitrans*, fed and multiplied, becoming carriers of anthrax. Anthrax spores that are inhaled or ingested by humans in large quantities can cause death as anthrax overwhelms the immune system. Cutaneous anthrax (skin anthrax), however, is not usually fatal. It causes festering sores on the skin, which are painful and debilitating, but most people recover fully from skin anthrax eventually. The description of what the Egyptians were suffering in plague six (9:9–10) would seem to comport with an epidemic infestation of anthrax.[95]

The problems with the theory that anthrax caused the fifth and sixth plagues, however, are several. First, the theory reflects a normal human tendency to reduce the supernatural to what the natural can comprehend. In effect, people tend to read the brief and rather general descriptions of the effects of the plague(s)

---

develops an anthrax papule, twelve to thirty-six hours after infection. The papule eventually becomes a vesicle, and subsequently a malignant pustule, and finally a necrotic ulcer. The infected area then oozes further infection, resulting typically in septicemia. In a week or less, lymph glands begin to swell as the immune system becomes increasingly affected. What really causes the symptoms of the disease is tissue poisoning from the toxic waste given off from the bacteria as they multiply, not the volume of the bacteria or their mechanical interference with any typical metabolical processes. If the infection reaches the bloodstream in sufficient mass, the disease can be fatal, but this is not normally the course of the cutaneous form of the disease. Cf. K. J. Roche, M. W. Chang, and H. Lazarus, "Cutaneous Anthrax Infection," *New England Journal of Medicine* (29 Nov 2001); R. A. Gardner, "Anthrax (Bacillus Anthracis)," *Cambridge Scientific Abstracts* (Cambridge University, 2001); T. Ingaldsby, M.D. et al., "Anthrax as a Biological Weapon: Medical and Public Health Management," *Journal of the American Medical Association*, Vol. 281, No. 18 (12 May 1999), 1735–45; www.bact.wisc.edu/Bact330; www.drlera.com.

[94] Anthrax that causes cattle deaths is almost always soil-derived, as cattle graze over infected areas and are exposed either directly via the vegetation growing on those infected areas or via exposure of broken skin, cuts, bruises to the soil. Moreover, a certain amount of soil attaches to the vegetation in the form of dust (especially in dry climates of the sort found in Egypt), which can then be ingested directly by the cattle.

[95] Virtually all of the above scenario is to one degree or another consistent with the ideas advanced by Hort in "The Plagues of Egypt," *ZAW* 69:84–103 and *ZAW* 70:48–59.

and—sometimes quite unconsciously—ask "what *natural* event that I *do* understand would come closest to being an explanation for this biblical event, the origin and characteristics of which otherwise I do *not* understand? The desire to understand an event tends to make a naturalistic explanation enticingly attractive and a supernatural explanation off-putting. If the Bible mentions a divinely caused disease, many people immediately search for whatever known disease seems to come closest to what the Bible describes and assume that to be what the disease must actually have been. Likewise with disasters, floods, the glory/fire atop Sinai, the empty tomb, and so on. It is always tempting to "demythologize" biblical miracles. Second, the fifth and sixth plagues do not fit a key criterion for natural epidemics or disasters because they do not develop naturally, that is, gradually and inconsistently from person to person or animal to animal. They come about virtually instantaneously and uniformly, according to timing that is not controlled by nature but overtly by God. One reason for specifically granting Pharaoh the choice of time for ending the plague of frogs (8:9) was surely so that those who followed the plague stories closely would be reminded of their supernatural origin and conclusion. Third, as the biblical text itself makes clear (12:12), the plagues were not mere natural developments but were *supernatural developments related to the natural sphere*—purposeful evidences of divine control over the natural world of Egypt designed to show the one true God's superiority over the natural world as it was (pantheistically) conceived by the Egyptians. In other words, the plagues *imitated* nature in certain ways as a means of showing God's control over nature (and its "gods")—ways that can make it easy for a reader mistakenly to think that the plagues were *merely* natural. Fourth, with regard specifically to the sixth plague, the cause of the disease does not appear to be consistent with its type. Fine particles or airborne dust normally would be associated more with a dust storm (in extreme form a "sand storm") than with anthrax, and contact with airborne particulates would be likely to cause the inhaled form of the disease at least as frequently if not more commonly than the skin form, producing death in great numbers rather than simply festering sores.[96] Finally, it is not entirely clear that the fifth and sixth plagues were a single disease, whatever the type. Many things can cause cattle to die; many things can give animals and humans skin lesions. The most convincing, contextually based understanding of the fifth and sixth plagues, in fact, is that they were somewhat epidemic-like supernatural events intended to humiliate the gods of Egypt, the Egyptians in general, and Pharaoh in particular and show the objective observer that there was only one God in whom faith should be placed.

Were there any objective observers to benefit from the demonstration of true divine power inherent in the plagues? The answer is yes. The "great mixed multitude" (12:38; NIV "many other people") of non-Egyptian, non-Israelite people living in Egypt along with the Israelites had no reason to identify either with the Egyptians or with the Israelites in analyzing the plagues. They simply saw them for what they were: proof that the God of Israel was supreme over Egypt and the

---

[96] The inhaled form of anthrax is nearly always fatal, even when treated aggressively with modern medical measures; the dermal form is nearly always survivable.

Egyptians and one whose people they ought to join with if they wished to enjoy a redeemed future. For them the plagues showed the way to salvation by forcibly calling their attention to the God who saves. Accordingly, they seized the chance to leave Egypt when the Israelites did.

(1) Announcement of the Plague (9:8–9)

[8]Then the LORD said to Moses and Aaron, "Take handfuls of soot from a furnace and have Moses toss it into the air in the presence of Pharaoh. [9]It will become fine dust over the whole land of Egypt, and festering boils will break out on men and animals throughout the land."

9:8–9 This plague is brought about by a transformation of one substance into another, as was the case with the initial signs God gave Moses as proof of his being a true prophet. Two of the three were the transformation of his staff into a snake and the transformation of his healthy hand into a diseased one (4:1–8), and one served also as the first plague (the transformation of water into "blood"; 4:9; 7:14–24). The transformation in this case involved filling his cupped hands[97] full of soot [98]from a furnace and throwing it skyward in the sight of Pharaoh.[99] What started as a small amount of soot was changed and vastly multiplied by divine fiat into a huge amount of fine dust, covering Egypt and causing festering boils[100] on both humans and animals.

(2) The Plague and Its Devastation (9:10–12)

[10]So they took soot from a furnace and stood before Pharaoh. Moses tossed it into the air, and festering boils broke out on men and animals. [11]The magicians could not stand before Moses because of the boils that were on them and on all the Egyptians. [12]But the LORD hardened Pharaoh's heart and he would not listen to Moses and Aaron, just as the LORD had said to Moses.

---

[97] מְלֹא חָפְנֵיכֶם, lit., "the fullness of your cupped hands." The NIV (also NRSV) "handfuls of" is sufficiently ambiguous, suggesting multiple handfuls, that it can mislead the reader.

[98] פִּיחַ from the root פוח ("blow" or "puff"), which presumably has the sense of (fine, powdery) "soot" rather than "ash." Cf. also C. J. Singer et al. eds., *A History of Technology* (Oxford: Clarendon Press, 1954–84), 1:391–97; R. W. Funk, "Brickkiln," *IDB* 1:446); id., "Furnace," *IDB* 2:330). But the word is a hapax legomenon from this context only, and those who prefer the translation "ash" cannot be proved wrong.

[99] The LXX adds "and in sight of his servants." It is difficult to assess whether or not this represents an original reading lost by haplography from the MT or a conflation in the LXX *Vorlage*. Obviously, Pharaoh would have had his servants with him in any case.

[100] The Hb. uses a compound of terms to be sure the reader understands that these were not mere boils or skin eruptions but what are sometimes in English called angry boils and/or putrefying sores and/or skin ulcers.

9:10–11 Verse 10 summarizes the fulfillment of the events that the plague announcement predicted and it understandably contains, therefore, nothing truly surprising. An element of the story that could be considered somewhat unpredictable, however, is the mention of the magicians in v. 11. They were last mentioned in 8:19 at the end of the third plague (gnats/biting insects) where they admitted their inability to replicate the miraculous in that situation with the words, "This is the finger of God!" This present plague account is the last in which they appear; they are not mentioned again in Exodus or the entire Pentateuch for that matter. Why, then, are they brought into the narrative here? Presumably for two reasons. The first is to help the reader appreciate the fact that Pharaoh probably used the magicians as advisors in dealing with the various plagues. To the Egyptians the magical, the medicinal, and the miraculous were all closely linked,[101] and anything the magicians could do to alleviate the effects of a given plague or to show it to be something that they themselves could also do (on a small scale) would help bolster Pharaoh's resistance to the demands made by Yahweh. The second is that if the physicians could not heal themselves (i.e., the magicians could not make themselves well from the boils) then the power of God over the powers resorted to by Pharaoh was obvious. The magicians need not be mentioned again. They had been proved impotent in the face of real power. The boils were obviously debilitating; so sick and in pain were the Egyptians from them that they were not physically able to be available for any sort of confrontation with Moses of the sort seen in the first three miracle accounts.

9:12 Verse 12 closes out the brief plague account with yet another, by now predictable, statement that Pharaoh remained unyielding. It is clear that Moses did not want the reader to forget that God caused this, according to the plan he had announced to Moses and Aaron from the start,[102] for the reader has been reminded by the same words "just as the LORD had said to Moses" at the end of the story of Aaron's rod changing into a snake (7:13), the first plague (7:22), the second plague (8:15), and the third plague (8:19). Thus these words are resumed here and will be again, with slightly different wording, at the conclusion of the next plague account (9:35).

---

[101] Indeed, magic in most of the ancient world usually was an aspect of the practice of religion. Cf. B. Brier, *Ancient Egyptian Magic* (New York: Morrow, 1980); E. A. W. Budge, *Egyptian Magic* (New York: B. Blom, 1971); T. W. Davies, *Magic, Divination and Demonology among the Hebrews and Their Neighbors* (New York: Ktav, 1969); W. J. Goode, *Religion among the Primitives* (Chicago: Bolchazy-Carducci, 1951); D. Aune, "Magic, Magician," *IDB* 3:213–19. Thus Daniel, a prophet of God, was naturally regarded as among the "wise men, enchanters, magicians and diviners" of Babylon (Dan 2:10–13) and effectively identified himself with them compassionately in the process of seeking their exoneration even while showing the true God's sole superiority (5:24–27).

[102] I.e., 3:19; 4:21–23; 7:3–5.

8. Eighth Sign: Seventh Plague: Hail (9:13–35)

Is hail worse than anthrax? That is the way the question of whether or not the plagues increased steadily in severity is sometimes posed, though the wording betrays two questionable assumptions: that the sixth plague was in fact anthrax-caused and that the hail involved was simply a minor, short-lived type of crystallized rain. What the biblical record indicates, however, is that the sixth plague caused nonfatal skin sores that were temporarily debilitating but eventually healed, whereas the plague of hail was far worse than typical hail, to the extent that it killed unprotected humans and animals (v. 21) and obliterated major crops (vv. 25,31).[103] This unprecedented frozen downpour represented "the full force of my plagues" (v. 14) and produced a momentary, albeit insincere repentance of Pharaoh (vv. 27–28, "This time I have sinned, . . . I will let you go; you don't have to stay any longer"). Of course, it is also easy to tell when hail stopped falling—and once the hail ceased, Pharaoh sinned yet further by again refusing to do what he had promised to do during the hailstorm. Israel remained confined to Egypt.

(1) Announcement of the Plague (9:13–19)

13Then the LORD said to Moses, "Get up early in the morning, confront Pharaoh and say to him, 'This is what the LORD, the God of the Hebrews, says: Let my people go, so that they may worship me, 14or this time I will send the full force of my plagues against you and against your officials and your people, so you may know that there is no one like me in all the earth. 15For by now I could have stretched out my hand and struck you and your people with a plague that would have wiped you off the earth. 16But I have raised you up for this very purpose, that I might show you my power and that my name might be proclaimed in all the earth. 17You still set yourself against my people and will not let them go. 18Therefore, at this time tomorrow I will send the worst hailstorm that has ever fallen on Egypt, from the day it was founded till now. 19Give an order now to bring your livestock and everything you have in the field to a place of shelter, because the hail will fall on every man and animal that has not been brought in and is still out in the field, and they will die.'"

Benefiting the interests of timeless readability, Moses varied the accounts of the signs of Yahweh's sovereignty in detail and overall length, even as he managed at the same time to hold before the reader the fact that all eleven signs had key similarities and shared repeated features.[104] In the case of the

---

[103] A careful argument that the seventh plague (hail) was the second most serious of all the plagues is offered by S. Noegel, "The Significance of the Seventh Plague," *Bib* 76 (1995): 532–39.

[104] The variety in length of the accounts is not random but falls into patterns of threes, i.e., long-long-short; then long-short-short; then, again, long-long-short. The first nine plague accounts, following their own internal pattern, are also part of the pattern of the eleven sign accounts, with the first sign being very short as an introduction to all eleven and the final sign and tenth plague being very long as a conclusion to all eleven. Accordingly, there are never more than two long accounts or two short accounts in a row among all eleven sign accounts, thus keeping the reader from a sense of tedium.

first six plagues, the pattern in terms of relative length was long-long-short, followed by long-short-short. Now come two accounts, the seventh and eighth, that are both long; indeed, they are the longest two of the central nine signs (i.e., "plagues" one to nine). Grouped with the ninth plague account, which is short, they complete the repetition of the starting pattern, long-long-short.

9:13–17 The words of 9:13 are not new; they comport closely with the wordings already seen at the beginning of plague accounts one and four. In particular the wording of the command, "This is what the LORD, the God of the Hebrews, says: Let my people go, so that they may worship me," represents the relatively full form of the way the command in the various plague accounts is given: Yahweh is identified, his people are identified, the call for release is made, and its purpose is described. Those who had been forced to serve *(ʿābad)* Pharaoh must now be allowed to worship/serve *(ʿābad)* Yahweh. Most of the concepts in 9:14–16 are quite new, however, and it is likely that 9:14–16 plays a special role in the entire narrative of the plague account in two ways. First, it appears as an *apologia* for the plagues as a group. In other words, this is the point in the narrative about the plagues at which God had certainly gotten Pharaoh's attention and that of the Egyptians in general. Now he issued his explanation for *all* the plagues that he had sent and would send against[105] them.[106] At the same time, it represents a point of intensification so that the reader is aware that the prior plagues, troublesome as they were, were essentially preliminary and that now a series of developments that would really do damage to Egypt—including actually taking of human life—was underway in the form of the final four plagues.[107] If Pharaoh retained any doubts about the purpose of the plagues to this point, he had no reason to be uncertain any longer. The explanation given him in these verses is clear and simple: Pharaoh must learn that Yahweh alone is supreme, the implication being that the gods in whom Pharaoh had trusted and whom he represented[108] were essentially nothing (9:14); the earlier plagues, hard as

---

[105] In 9:14 "against" is represented by *ʾel* (to/towards/against,) in the MT but *ʿal* (unambiguously meaning *against*) in the SP. But *ʾel* / *ʿal* confusion is common in the Qumran texts because of the way the two prepositions had become pronounced alike by that time; so the SP reading could be the result of an aural confusion as a scribe read to a group of copying scribes, rather than a preservation of the original. The same contrast of prepositions occurs in v. 21 between the MT and SP.

[106] Note that 9:14 represents the only place in the Old Testament where the plural of *maggēpāh*, "plague," appears. Cf. also J. P. Hyatt, *Exodus,* NCB (London: Oliphants, 1971), 118.

[107] So U. Cassuto, *A Commentary on the Book of Exodus* (Jerusalem: Magnes Press, 1967), 115–16.

[108] Bear in mind that Pharaoh was regarded as at least semidivine, being the "son of the gods" and their representative on earth. But this does not mean that Pharaoh was considered an incarnation of deity. Rather, he was a god by reason of his office rather than his essence. Cf. J. G. Griffiths, *JEA* 49 (1963): 189–92; G. Posener, *De la Divinité du Pharaon* (1960).

they were on the Egyptians, were actually examples of restraint since God already could have sent at any time a fully destructive plague to eliminate the Egyptian population entirely (9:15). Pharaoh himself had come to power and was acting as he was under God's control,[109] the result being not only that he, the king of the world's greatest superpower at that time, would see true divine power but that all who learned of the exodus story in all generations thereafter would give the true God credit for that power (9:16).

Note that the word "earth" *('ereṣ)* appears in three verses (9:14–16). In all three it surely means "the earth," that is, the planet, not merely "the [local] land," as it can also mean in many contexts. This passage is something of a *proto-evangelium*, a call to the whole world (even though it is addressed specifically to Pharaoh[110]) to appreciate what the plagues ultimately showed, that there is one God in control of all things and that he alone can save. The world needs to recognize that "there is no one like me in all the earth" (v. 14) and that the will of God is "that my name might be proclaimed in all the earth" (v. 16).

The irony of God's upbraiding of Pharaoh in v. 17 is that Pharaoh could not help himself (any longer) and yet well deserved the criticism he received. It was both his natural inclination to keep the Israelites suppressed and localized (cf. 1:9–10) and the attitude subsequently fixed in him by God as a humiliation and punishment. Pharaoh's behavior mirrors the phenomenon described by Paul in Rom 1:18–32, that of people being fixed by God in the sinful behavior patterns that would eventually bring about their destruction as a punishment for those very behavior patterns. In other words, one of the ways God punishes sin is to allow the sin to continue and therefore to allow it to take its natural, destructive course. Behind this is the biblical truth that people cannot rescue themselves from their own sin; they always need help to break the patterns of sin in their lives. If God withholds that help, they become fixed in those patterns, will see the harmful effects increasingly during their lives, and will die in those sins. Pharaoh had long ago "set [him]self against [God's] people and [would] not let them go," and

---

[109] This must have been all the more galling to him since as the representative of the gods on earth according to Egyptian religion, he was supposed to be responsible for everything that took place in the land of Egypt, including the well-being of the Nile River itself (cf. S. Morenz, *Egyptian Äegypten* [Berlin: Akodemie Verlag, 1964], 42).

[110] All the second person forms (you/your) are second person *singulars* in the Hb.; Pharaoh was the direct audience for these words, although obviously all in his retinue would also hear what was said. This fits the chronological pattern described by F. H. Cryer, *Divination in Ancient Israel and Its Near Eastern Environment* (Sheffield: JSOT, 1994), 217–20, i.e., that Egyptian oracles were delivered to and focused on Pharaoh and his court in the early centuries of the New Kingdom and that only after the Amarna period did oracles also focus on legal matters, with direct address to the judiciary, and by the Greco-Roman period they applied to various people and areas of everyday life. Cf. J. D. Currid, *Ancient Egypt and the Old Testament* (Grand Rapids: Baker, 1997), 220–21.

he was still doing the same. God's hardening of Pharaoh's heart—making him remain stubborn—serves as a punishment although the action itself is also a sin.

9:18 The expression employed in v. 18, "from the day it was founded till now," is apparently a Hebrew reflex of a common Egyptian expression usually translated "since/from the founding of Egypt."[111] The Egyptians were enormously proud of their long history as a nation and thought of all other peoples as newcomers, johnny-come-latelys—automatically inferior to themselves, whom they viewed as the original and central civilization of the earth. Accordingly, when God spoke through Moses here about the severity of the coming plague, using an expression well known and commonly used by the Egyptians (and certainly well known to Moses) that would have meant to the average Egyptian something like "since the beginning of time," he was powerfully emphasizing what a terrible plague it would indeed be. Note that what God announced was not simply hail but a hailstorm *(mamṭîr . . . . bārād),* with the implication that some of the damage and danger, as well as some of the frightening power of the storm, would be contained in its wind, rain, thunder, and lightning and not merely in the hailstones themselves. The description of the storm in vv. 23–24 and vv. 32–33 and of Pharaoh's reaction in v. 28 all support this: it was the storm *in toto* that demonstrated God's awesome control of nature.

9:19 With the order recorded in v. 19 to Pharaoh,[112] God tested the Egyptians. In effect there were now three categories of persons in the story: those who derided or ignored Yahweh's word, those who had by now become sufficiently convinced of his existence and power that they would be

[111] B. Couroyer, "Un égyptianisme biblique: 'depuis la fondation de l'Égypte,'" *RB* 67 (1960): 42–48. Couroyer's argument is that the phrase is a standard one at all historical stages of Egyptian literature, whereas reference to the founding of a nation is not a feature of any OT texts except at this point. Thus Moses was inspired by God to put the challenge to the Egyptians in a wording familiar to them. Moses, we may assume, was speaking Egyptian, not Hebrew, in all his conversations with Pharaoh. He had, after all, used Egyptian for the first forty years of his life. It is less clear what language God used in speaking to Moses; it is quite possible that God generally addressed Moses in Hebrew but gave him verbatim speeches in Egyptian for relay to Pharaoh and his advisors. It is likely that Moses was fluently bilingual in both Hebrew (learned from infancy via exposure to his family's speech while he was cared for by his own mother) and Egyptian (learned from infancy via exposure to his adoptive Egyptian royal family). He must also have known Akkadian, the *lingua franca* of the ancient world of his day as evidenced by the fact the international correspondence to and from Egypt was primarily in Akkadian, but how well he knew his Akkadian is not known. It is possible that he knew it very well since his knowledge of a Semitic cognate, Hebrew, would have made its acquisition easier than would have been the case for the typical Egyptian. (Egyptian is a Hamitic language, with virtually no significant similarities to Semitic languages.) Of course, he also knew Midianite, but how close it was to Hebrew/Canaanite is not known.

[112] The order is given in the singular imperative, lit., "send [out the command]."

willing to take advantage of a warning from him to save human and animal life, and the Israelites, who not merely believed in his power but, as his people, actually worshiped him (cf. 4:31). In other words, it would be going beyond the evidence to say that any of the Egyptians had actually come to full faith in Israel's God, including ascribing to him sole divinity, but it was clearly the case that many Egyptians had decided that Yahweh was at least a powerful deity among deities and that he could deliver on any threats he made. The generally promulgated order to "bring your livestock and everything you have in the field to a place of shelter" implicitly includes not only animals but also human field workers, as the further wording, "because the hail will fall on every man and animal that has not been brought in," implies. An even better translation than that of the NIV would be, "Bring your livestock and everyone[113] you have in the field." The latter wording, "in the field," is a simple idiom for "outdoors" or "out-of-doors" and does not refer only to actual farm fields. People and animals could be killed in courtyards as well as pastures and crop areas. This is the first plague announcement in which the prediction is made that Egyptian lives would actually be lost. Those who would die would be those who failed to hear the warning; thus the biblical principle that people's *choices* do them harm—not merely what they cannot control.

(2) Compliance by Some; Disdain by Others (9:20–21)

[20]Those officials of Pharaoh who feared the word of the LORD hurried to bring their slaves and their livestock inside. [21]But those who ignored the word of the LORD left their slaves and livestock in the field.

9:20–21 The wording "those officials of Pharaoh who feared the word of the LORD" is carefully composed. Had Moses written "those officials of Pharaoh who feared the LORD . . .," he would have indicated that Egyptian court officials had actually converted to faith in Yahweh.[114] Instead, he used the hapax legomenon *yārēʾ ʾet-dābār* ("fear the word of") because of the uniqueness of the situation, that is, belief short of conversion, people's belief in something they had been told but not saving faith in the one who revealed it to them. It was, however, a belief sufficient to cause some Egyptians to act immediately, based on their experience of the sudden onset of prior plagues. As Moses' words in v. 30 indicate, he knew well that Pharaoh and his officials did not actually "fear the LORD." They had plenty of allies, as v. 21

[113] כָּל is ambiguous as to its human, animal, or material referent.

[114] ירא את־יהוה, "fear the LORD") is a very important expression not only later in Exodus (14:31) to indicate real full faith in Yahweh but a central requirement in the law of Deuteronomy differentiating the Israelites from other peoples who were polytheistic. (Deut 6:2,13,24; 10:12,20; 31:12–13) and a major theme throughout the OT.

makes clear, who in spite of all the plagues that had occurred so far were hardly able to overcome their lifelong training in Egyptian ways of thinking, a mind-set that told them they need not fear Israel's God. They simply went on doing as they had done, working their fields and grazing their cattle. Why miss a single day of work, especially at harvest time?[115]

These verses seem to indicate that Pharaoh, however reluctantly or disdainfully, had actually carried out God's command given to him in v. 19 to warn the people of the impending danger. If he himself did not believe it would amount to anything, he may still have acceded to the pleas of some of his officials (those who did believe God's warning, presumably) to allow *them* to spread the word of what was about to happen. He may even have gladly promulgated the order to bring cattle indoors, a difficult and complicated thing for many people to do,[116] on the theory that it would simply arouse greater resentment against Israel, something he could use to his advantage, and would make the Israelites look foolish if the hailstorm were simply that—a typical hailstorm. It is hard to imagine that many Egyptians were not saying something like: "Hail? We've seen plenty of hailstorms. So what? They never last long."

(3) The Plague and Its Devastation (9:22–26)

22Then the LORD said to Moses, "Stretch out your hand toward the sky so that hail will fall all over Egypt—on men and animals and on everything growing in the fields of Egypt." 23When Moses stretched out his staff toward the sky, the LORD sent thunder and hail, and lightning flashed down to the ground. So the LORD rained hail on the land of Egypt; 24hail fell and lightning flashed back and forth. It was the worst storm in all the land of Egypt since it had become a nation. 25Throughout Egypt hail struck everything in the fields—both men and animals;

[115] On the timing of the plague, see comments on vv. 31–32.

[116] Although it is normal to provide barns for cattle in modern times in northern climes, it was not common in Bible times and certainly not in places like Egypt, just as it is not common today in perennially warmer parts of the world. Barns were for storing grain, not animals. There is evidence of stabling of war horses in Egypt and Israel, but not with certainty cattle. Indeed, the typical assumption that Jesus was born in a "stable" is highly unlikely; he would have been born in the courtyard of the inn where Joseph and Mary had sought lodging and laid in the (outdoor) manger of that courtyard. Animals were often kept in courtyards at night, except for sheep and goats, which were kept in the fields and hills. Some of those courtyards had pillar and roof shelters, but many did not. Accordingly, the only way most Egyptians could have put their cattle under cover would have been to bring them right into their living spaces or into grain storage barns, where there may have been some empty space in light of the time of year (just before the first spring harvests were to be collected). Cf. J. S. Holladay, "The Stables of Ancient Israel," in *The Archaeology of Jordan and Other Studies* (Berrien Springs, Mich.: Andrews University Press, 1986), 103–65; L. E. Stager, "The Archaeology of the Family in Ancient Israel," *BASOR* 260 (1985): 1–35; P. J. King and L. E. Stager, *Life in Biblical Israel* (Louisville: Westminster John Knox, 2001).

it beat down everything growing in the fields and stripped every tree. 26The only place it did not hail was the land of Goshen, where the Israelites were.

Moses' hands holding the staff in the air again signaled the start of a plague. The staff[117] (v. 23) in his outstretched hands was the staff of God, representing divine power and presence.[118] The plague wrought its devastation on humans, animals, and crops "all over Egypt" (vv. 22,25) except in "the land of Goshen," which once again escaped from the terrors being unleashed on the rest of Egypt. The hail, part of a massive nationwide thunderstorm, was accompanied by extensive lightning[119] and large quantities of wind and rain that also could and would have caused extensive damage in their own right. Note that 9:23 emphasizes that even though Moses made the motions, it was God who sent the plague ("the LORD sent . . ."). This was a killer storm, with huge hailstones destined to do damage of all sorts, including destroying humans, animals, and crops.

Verse 24 confirms what God had predicted in v. 18: this was the worst hailstorm in the history of Egypt. Since Egypt became a nation sometime around 3200 BC and these events took place sometime in the second half of the second millennium BC, it could be said that the storm was the worst in almost two millennia. As already noted, however, the expression "since [Egypt] had become a nation" is actually an idiomatic way of saying "since the earliest times," and the actual sense of the final statement in v. 24 is that this hailstorm was "worst [ever] in all the land of Egypt."[120] Verse 25 delineates the damage and in the usual order of relative worth: humans first, then animals, then plants. Nothing alive in the open could have remained undamaged. Humans and animals were killed, at least in large numbers,[121] anything growing in fields was beaten down. Although trees might have lost

---

[117] Instead of "staff" the LXX reads "hand" (χεῖρά) here, a difference probably due more to careless copying under the influence of the prior verse than a preservation of the actual original sense. In 10:12–13 is a similar sequence: God commanded Moses to stretch out his "hand" (10:12), but in fact the narrative immediately states that he stretched out his "staff" (10:13). There is no contradiction. The combination of statements represents a kind of shorthand for saying that Moses stretched out his hand (or both hands—the idiom could allow for either arrangement) with the staff of God in it (them) as a symbolic gesture to bring about the plague.

[118] See at 4:14–17 "Excursus: Moses' Staff."

[119] In 9:23 "lightning flashed down to the ground" renders, lit., "fire was going to the earth." In 9:24 "lightning flashed back and forth" translates, lit., "fire was fetching all around." In other words, the lightning mentioned was typically viewed as *fire,* not without significance in terms of its ability, by starting fires on the ground, to contribute to the damage caused and not merely to the display seen.

[120] In 9:24 where the MT has "in all the land of Egypt," the LXX and SP have simply "in Egypt," which may therefore be the more original; the concept is unaffected.

[121] Some humans possibly did manage to save their lives by getting under trees or by running to nearby buildings, but most likely they were caught without enough protection to survive, too far from a durable shelter to make it to safety before being knocked down and knocked out by the hail.

smaller branches but survived alive, their fruit would have been knocked off (thus "stripped every tree") and smashed on the ground under the force of the falling hailstones. Again, as v. 26 states, Goshen was spared, as is stated in several of the prior plague accounts and by extrapolation may be assumed to have been the case in all of the instances of prior plagues.

There is nothing in this account that does not comport with what is known scientifically about the lethal power of a severe hailstorm. Fatal hailstorms occur often around the world still today. The largest tend to occur in northeast India (in 1888 two hundred and forty people were killed and hundreds more injured by hail in Moradabad), but hundreds of destructive hailstorms occur every year and in virtually all parts of the globe. For example, a single hailstorm killed or injured four hundred people in Germany in 1984, and a storm in China's Henan province killed twenty-two people and injured two hundred on July 22, 2002. In modern times hailstones as large as one kilogram have been measured. Hail falls at more than fifty meters per second, and hailstorms can devastate entire crop fields in just minutes. Hail damage is often an aspect of tornado complexes, and thus it cannot be ruled out that there was a degree of tornado activity present in the storm described in this account.

(4) Pharaoh's Partial Repentance and Concession (9:27–28)

27Then Pharaoh summoned Moses and Aaron. "This time I have sinned," he said to them. "The LORD is in the right, and I and my people are in the wrong. 28Pray to the LORD, for we have had enough thunder and hail. I will let you go; you don't have to stay any longer."

9:27–28 Was Pharaoh here saying that he was actually sorry for his sins—was he taking the first step of genuine repentance by acknowledging himself to be a sinner ("this time I have sinned") and, indeed, recognizing the truth of God's ways ("the LORD is in the right, and I and my people are in the wrong") and praying for forgiveness, at least through Moses ("pray to the LORD,[122] for we have had enough thunder[123] and hail"[124])? At first blush this certainly seems to be the closest Pharaoh had so far come to expressing belief in Yahweh's power and the closest he had come to any sort of repentance,

122 The LXX reads here "pray therefore to the LORD for me" instead of merely "pray to the LORD," i.e., it employs, probably by simple conflation, the same wording it uses in 8:4,24. In other words, there is no convincing basis for emending the MT on the basis of the LXX witness.

123 The Hb. has קֹלֹת אֱלֹהִים, lit.," thunders of God," probably an idiomatic use of אֱלֹהִים, "God," in superlative expressions; cf. D. W. Thomas, *VT* 3 (1953): 210, who translates "mighty thunderings." The NRSV translates somewhat more literally but contrary to the actual syntax of the original, "God's thunder and hail."

124 After "thunder and hail" the LXX reads "and fire," which may conceivably be a preservation in translation of the original wording, but it is more likely conflation in light of the LXX's tendency to be conflationary in this context.

accompanied by a concession that had the ring of finality to it, as if he really had surrendered to Yahweh's will ("I will let you go; you don't have to stay any longer"). If so, why did Moses remain so skeptical, as indicated by his words in v. 30? Part of the answer is to be found in the range of meaning of the Hebrew *ḥāṭā'tî* (NIV and most Eng. versions: "I have sinned"). The root *ḥṭ'* has a semantic field that includes "to miss" or "to err" (Judg 20:16; Prov 8:35–36; 19:2; Job 5:24) as well as "to offend" someone of close relationship (e.g., Gen 4:22; 50:17), or "to rebel" against a superior (Gen 40:1; 1 Sam 24:11; 26:21; 2 Kgs 18:14), or "to abuse/mistreat" (1 Sam 19:4). Indeed, with regard to the closest usage of the root to the present context, the NRSV translates *ḥṭ'* as "be unjust" in Exod 5:16 ("you are unjust to your own people"). In other words, a translation such as "I have acted unjustly" or "I have been unfair" would be equally possible in Exod 9:27 for what Pharaoh said in Egyptian to Moses, who rendered it accurately in Hebrew but whose rendering is somewhat misleadingly represented in English by "I have sinned."[125] That is, nothing in what Pharaoh said need lead us to believe that he actually was sorry for his sins and seeking forgiveness from the God of Israel. Rather, he was, at most, admitting to being wrong for having treated the Israelites as he had—and doing so temporarily under the pressure of the worst, most damaging plague he and the Egyptians had yet encountered.

Pharaoh's words in v. 28 represent a further concession beyond what he had already said when reeling from the effects of the plague of flies.[126] Even if implicitly he was still hoping or assuming the Israelites would not permanently leave Egypt but would be gone only temporarily to offer sacrifices in the wilderness, he did not qualify his words here to any such effect. It is possible to read his remarks as virtually allowing the exodus to begin. "We have had enough" is tantamount to saying "we can't stand it any more." The point of his request "pray to the LORD" is, however, not significantly different from that of the similar request in 8:28. What Pharaoh wanted was for the horrible hailstorm to stop—nothing more. He was not asking for a closer relationship to the true God or for any other blessing per se.

(5) Moses' Agreement to Stop the Plague (9:29–30)

[29]Moses replied, "When I have gone out of the city, I will spread out my hands in prayer to the LORD. The thunder will stop and there will be no more hail, so

[125] See K. Koch, "חטא *chaṭa'*," *TDOT* 4.309–19; cf. A. Barucq, "Péché et innocence dans les psaumes bibliques et les textes réligieux de l'Égypte du Nouvel Empire," in *Études de critique et d'histoire réligiouses: Festschrift L. Vaganay* (Lyon, 1948), 111–37; "Péché, I. Dans l'A. T.," in *Dictionnaire de la Bible, Supplément* (Paris: 1966), 7:407–71; N. Lade, "The Concept of Sin in the Law," *ABR* 7 (1959): 54–57; G. Robinson, "A Terminological Study of the Concept of Sin in the OT," *IJT* 18 (1969): 12–123.

[126] Cf. esp. 8:25,28.

you may know that the earth is the LORD's. [30]But I know that you and your officials still do not fear the LORD God."

9:29 In the only two previous plague narratives that mention a prayer to bring an end to the misery experienced by the Egyptians, Moses followed a pattern of praying for the end of a plague only after he had gone out from the presence of Pharaoh (frogs, 8:12; flies, 8:29–30). This time he indicated that he would pray only after he had gone "out of the city," a phrase repeated in v. 33. There is nothing especially idiomatic about the phrase. It does not seem to connote "away from pagan influence" or any such thing. So why would Moses use it twice? The answer would appear to be that by going out of the city into the open (the "field") to pray while the unprecedented hailstorm continued unabated during his journey, Moses showed his complete trust that the hail could not harm him. He not only could travel through the hail but could stand and pray for the end to the hail in the very location—exposed, out of doors—that was otherwise fatal to people and animals; he could go into the area of danger and remain unharmed. His action of going "out of the city" was, in other words, a further demonstration of Yahweh's differentiation between the Israelites and the Egyptians, a theme of this and several other plague accounts overtly and implicitly a theme of all of them.

The NIV translation "I will spread out my hands in prayer" can be misunderstood; a less ambiguous rendering would be "I will reach out my hands in prayer," indicating that the actual posture was one of reaching heavenward, not of holding one's hands open or out to either side of the body as "spread out" can imply.[127] Moses' posture would have been analogous to that described in Exod 18:9–16 (q.v.)—hands lifted up overhead, holding the staff of God, looking to heaven and praying. Note that Yahweh, the LORD, is mentioned three times in the two verses that make up this part of the pericope. Moses stated not merely that he would pray but made clear that his prayer would be to Yahweh, the one true God that Pharaoh and his people needed to learn to fear (v. 29). He asserted that the purpose of his prayer, bringing to a conclusion the plague, would be to help convince Pharaoh (and presumably the Egyptians also since they were included in v. 30, though "you may know" is singular in the Hb.) that Yahweh owns the world.[128] And it was Yahweh the leaders of the land needed to learn to fear, even though it

[127] Cf. 1 Kgs 8:22,38,54; Isa 1:15; Ps 143:6; Job 11:13. It is not that פרשׂ cannot mean "spread" or "spread out" but rather that when used with "hands" in a description of prayer, it tends more to have the meaning "stretch out."

[128] Although technically ארץ can refer to "land" (i.e., the land of Egypt) and does not need to connote "earth" in the sense of "the world," for an Egyptian to believe that Yahweh owned Egypt and not the rest of the world would make little sense; if he owned Egypt, the center of the world, he surely would be supreme in the rest as well.

is clear from Moses' words in v. 30 that they still did not fear him. This is what "no more hail"[129] should have produced; it did not.

9:30 Exodus 9:30 contains the first usage in the Bible of the term "fear the LORD" *(yārēʾ ʾet-yahweh),* a wording that designates an enormously important theological concept. The fear of the Lord is enjoined throughout Scripture, demanding that God's people stand always in awe of him, appreciate his supremacy and greatness, fear the consequences of disobeying his will, and not treat lightly any aspect of their covenant relationship with him, lest the consequences be severe or even fatal. Attempts on the part of some in modern times to define fearing the Lord as merely respecting him distort the biblical evidence.[130] Pharaoh and the Egyptians may have moved much closer to capitulation to the Israelites' God in the bargaining process, and may have been much more disposed to granting some sort of serious concessions, but they (the verb at the end of v. 30 is plural) had not actually come to the point of religious faith in Yahweh.

(6) Assessment of the Damage to Crops (9:31–32)

31(The flax and barley were destroyed, since the barley had headed and the flax was in bloom. 32The wheat and spelt, however, were not destroyed, because they ripen later.)

9:31–32 Why this aside? The answer is presumably that most readers throughout history, and certainly in ancient times among the original audience, were farmers[131] who would have a keen interest in what sort of damage to crops had been caused by the hail. Although it is possible to get cattle under cover and thus protect them from hail, it is not normally possible to get crops under cover, so typical readers would wonder about them most. As for the Egyptians themselves, they were not known for large scale cattle farming but more for crop farming, so the latter was of far greater significance to them than the former, and a hailstorm was a far greater threat to their economy than it would have been for some other peoples.

---

[129] After "no more hail" the LXX adds "and rain," an addition that appears to be more likely conflationary than necessarily reflective of the original wording.

[130] Cf. A. Alt, *The God of the Fathers* (Oxford: Oxford University, 1966); J. Becker, *Gottesfurcht im Alten Testament* (Rome: Pontifical Biblical Institute,1965); J. Bunyan, *A Treatise on the Fear of God* (Morgan, Penn.: Soli Deo Gloria, 1999); L. Desrousseaux, *La Crainte de Dieu dans L'Ancien Testament* (Paris: Éditions du Cerf, 1970); D. New and R. Peterson, *How to Fear God without Being Afraid of Him* (Wheaton: Victor, 1994); R. Otto, *The Idea of the Holy* (New York: Oxford, 1950); G. B. Funderburk, "Fear," *ZPEB* 2:518–521; G. A. Lee, "Fear," *ISBE* 2.289–92; E. Puech, "The Fear of Isaac," *ABD* 3:779–80; M. van Pelt and W. C. Kaiser Jr., ירא, *NIDOTTE* 2:527–533.

[131] Prior to the Industrial Revolution, the world's economy was largely agrarian, and the vast majority of people in all societies were farmers.

In Egypt flax and barley were harvested in February-March, a fact that provides a clear time-of-year date for this part of the story at least. Wheat and spelt, however, were harvested in March-April, a full month later, that is, at the time of the tenth plague and exodus itself; they were too small at this time to be permanently damaged by the hailstorm. Though the wheat and spelt shoots were up and growing, and surely were smashed down by the hail, they were able to recover and continue to grow fairly normally. This does not mean that the Egyptians were spared disaster because in God's plan the locusts were on the way to dispose of the last remaining hope (via the plague immediately following, 10:1–20), so that even those Egyptians who may have said, "Well, at least we can eat wheat and spelt and make it through until next year" were quite mistaken.

Also with regard to timing: since the time of year of the exodus is known, it becomes evident that there could not have been more than a month or so of time between this plague and the tenth and final plague. This overall time frame comports well with the "benchmark" one-week duration of the first plague (7:25) and the general reckoning that the plagues took place over the duration of a few months within a single year, perhaps from winter to early spring.

(7) Removal of the Plague, Followed by Pharaoh's Reneging on His Promise (9:33–35)

33Then Moses left Pharaoh and went out of the city. He spread out his hands toward the LORD; the thunder and hail stopped, and the rain no longer poured down on the land. 34When Pharaoh saw that the rain and hail and thunder had stopped, he sinned again: He and his officials hardened their hearts. 35So Pharaoh's heart was hard and he would not let the Israelites go, just as the LORD had said through Moses.

9:33–35 This conclusion to the seventh plague account resumes the theme of Pharaoh's "sin" that had been introduced by Pharaoh himself in v. 27. As already argued in connection with v. 27, this "sin," referring to Pharaoh's willful intent to disobey what he knew to be the will of God, can also be understood as "doing the wrong thing"; and the second clause in v. 34 could be translated "he did the wrong thing again."[132] Moses, on the other hand, did exactly what he said he would do, and God responded faithfully to Moses' prayer (v. 33); the plague came to an abrupt halt—not merely the hail but the entire storm, including "the rain and hail and thunder" (v. 34). Both Pharaoh, however, and his officials

---

[132] In other words, there is no warrant in the text for concluding that God purposely caused Pharaoh to sin and unfairly prevented him from righteousness. God punished Pharaoh (and the Egyptians) by causing him to do what was harmful to himself (and to the Egyptians); but that is not the equivalent of saying that God forced Pharaoh to be a sinner. The distinction is delicate but real.

resumed their stubborn stance against any compromise with the Israelites (vv. 34–35a). All had happened "just as the LORD had said through Moses."[133] The "sinful" tendency that had first motivated Egypt to enslave Israel (1:9–14) was being used by God to subjugate not Israel now but Egypt. The alert reader cannot escape the conclusion that Pharaoh and his advisors were simply not in control of their own destinies but were being forced to repeat stupid actions to their own disadvantage as punishments. The wise course of action for them would have been to let the Israelites leave and prevent further divine destruction of their land and possessions. But they were no longer able to take wise courses of action; their inclinations and intellectual capacities were subject to frustration by the only wise God, who was making fools out of them.[134] As he ratcheted up the severity of the plagues, he kept them from responding accordingly. Using their pride, their willfulness, their cultural assumptions, their emotional tendencies, and any and all other characteristics under his control, he simply made them do what would be to their disadvantage: he made them resist yet further.

9. Ninth Sign: Eighth Plague: Locusts (10:1–20)

The eighth plague account, the second longest of the nine that lead up to the final and decisive tenth plague,[135] shares various features with the other "second cycle" plague accounts (frogs and animal disease) including the fact that it involved an indoor (court) confrontation between Moses and Pharaoh. In contrast to prior plague accounts, however, this one describes Pharaoh's reaction before the plague as well as after it. Moreover, Pharaoh's partial concession to allow adult Israelite males to leave Egypt temporarily was given even before the plague began, that is, merely on the basis of the warning. By this time in the overall story, Pharaoh could not help but realize that a severe harm was coming and wished to head it off before it occurred.

This account helps identify the real nature of the demand made by Yahweh on the Egyptian king and his people: full, permanent exodus from Egypt by the Israelites. It is evident that Pharaoh understood this, for he tried to hold Moses to a literalistic interpretation of the demand by suggesting, contrary to fact, that if Moses' bargaining language were taken at face value, that is, if Moses were demanding only a three-day festival, only men would be required; he hardly would need to take the whole population along. Of course, Pharaoh was thinking according to the Egyptian style, that women and children need not be involved directly in worship, something very different from what God had in mind for his people. Israelite worship

---

[133] See comments on 8:12.

[134] The covenant curses included the category of psychological afflictions (e.g., Deut 28:20,28, 34,65–67; cf. Hos 4:14) whereby people were unable to do what would be rational and sensible in a given situation.

[135] The longest, that of the destructive hail, preceded it immediately (9:13–35).

was to be a full family affair. The men played a key role in the actual offering of the sacrifice by the priests, but the women and children also participated, both by observation and by eating the meal after it was prepared through the sacrifice process. Accordingly, Moses could only regard Pharaoh's offer as too little too late, and he reacted accordingly.

(1) Summons, Instruction, and Encouragement (10:1–2)

[1]Then the LORD said to Moses, "Go to Pharaoh, for I have hardened his heart and the hearts of his officials so that I may perform these miraculous signs of mine among them [2]that you may tell your children and grandchildren how I dealt harshly with the Egyptians and how I performed my signs among them, and that you may know that I am the LORD."

10:1–2 In the prior two plague accounts in this cycle (two and five) God said to Moses, "Go to Pharaoh and say to him . . ." This time, instead, God followed his command to go to Pharaoh with an explanation that was for the benefit of Moses and the Israelites in general, throughout their generations. He reminded Moses (and at the same time all future audiences of Moses' writing) that the reason for Pharaoh's intransigence was his (Yahweh's) own doing—he had been making it happen for a purpose. What was that purpose? It was an evangelistic purpose, stated in the final clause of v. 2, "that you may know that I am the LORD." The prior purpose mentioned in v. 2, "that you may tell your children and grandchildren[136] how I [humiliated] the Egyptians and how I performed my signs among them," is intermediate: Moses and successive Israelites had been provided with irresistibly interesting stories to tell their children and grandchildren, not for the sake of the entertainment value they held but so that their children and grandchildren would understand who God really is and how important it is to be rightly in covenant with him—the meaning of "know that I am the LORD."[137]

---

[136]Lit., "your son and your son's son," or "your child and your child's child." It conveys the sense of "all coming generations."

[137]"Know that I am the LORD" is a sort of shorthand in OT language for "understand that I am the one true God who is faithful to those who keep his covenant and the judge of those who don't." As would be expected, the expression is not found in Genesis since God did not have the same sort of full covenant relationship with a people before the exodus and Sinai covenant events as after. It first occurred in Exod 6:7, in God's instructions to Moses concerning the basic truths he was to reveal to the Israelites to encourage them to wait patiently for his deliverance: ("I will take you as my own people, and I will be your God. Then you will know that I am [Yahweh] the LORD your God, who brought you out from under the yoke of the Egyptians"). It has already been repeated twice, in 7:5,17, in reference to the Egyptians' coming to understand that Yahweh [the LORD] is supreme over them and their "gods" (e.g., 7:5: "And the Egyptians will know that I am [Yahweh] the LORD when I stretch out my hand against Egypt and bring the Israelites out of it"). After the present passage it occurs again in 14:4,18 (in relation to the Egyptians' learning who Yahweh really is because of being defeated in the exodus); 16:12 (in relation to the Israelites' understanding the significance of being miraculously fed by quail); 29:46 (Israel understanding God's presence via the tabernacle); and 31:13 (Israelites appreciating the Sabbath as a reminder of their holy God who makes them holy).

The NIV translation of the second clause of v. 2 ("how I dealt harshly with the Egyptians") takes the least likely option among the possibilities for translating the verb in question, *ʿll, hithpael* + preposition *b.*[138] The verb in this conjugational form can mean "abuse" or "mistreat" but in the sense of "humiliate" rather than in the sense of "be tough on" or "deal harshly with." It sometimes also connotes "making a fool of" or "making a spectacle of"[139] (the latter being translations that have been proposed for the present text).[140] In light of what is going on in the entire corpus of plague accounts, summarized here, it seems best to render the verb as "humiliated." What God did to Pharaoh, the Egyptians in general, and to Egypt's gods was to show them powerless and helpless, to expose their pride as empty arrogance, and to shame them forever in the process—that is, to humiliate them.

(2) Announcement of the Plague (10:3–6)

3So Moses and Aaron went to Pharaoh and said to him, "This is what the LORD, the God of the Hebrews, says: 'How long will you refuse to humble yourself before me? Let my people go, so that they may worship me. 4If you refuse to let them go, I will bring locusts into your country tomorrow. 5They will cover the face of the ground so that it cannot be seen. They will devour what little you have left after the hail, including every tree that is growing in your fields. 6They will fill your houses and those of all your officials and all the Egyptians—something neither your fathers nor your forefathers have ever seen from the day they settled in this land till now.'" Then Moses turned and left Pharaoh.

10:3 Although God's instructions were issued specifically to Moses (10:1), Aaron was involved routinely in the plague stories, and his name thus surfaces again here in v. 3, as it frequently does in the "middle" of various other accounts.[141] The introduction to their speech to Pharaoh ("this is what the LORD, the God of the Hebrews, says") is not new (cf. 3:18; 7:16; 9:1,13), nor is the wording of the demand itself at the end of v. 3 ("let my people go, so that they may worship me"; cf. 7:16; 8:1,20; 9:1,13), but the rhetorical question that appears between these familiar phrases ("how long will you refuse to humble yourself before me?") is unique to the plague accounts and, indeed, to the entire Old Testament. When individuals or groups willingly acknowledge God's sovereignty—not in general but over

---

[138] It is important to appreciate that the full term is the verb plus preposition, which occurs exclusively in the sense of "humiliate" or "make a fool of" and only in Exod 10:2; Num 22:29; Judg 19:25; 1 Sam 6:6 (referring back to the present passage); 31:4; Jer 38:19; and 1 Chr 10:4.

[139] Cf. the NRSV "how I have made fools of the Egyptians"; Durham, "How I amused myself aggravating the Egyptians" (*Exodus,* 131).

[140] It is also used euphemistically in Judg 19:25 in the sense of "humiliated sexually" by a mob, i.e., "gang-raped."

[141] E.g., 7:20,22; 8:5–6,8; 8:25; 9:27.

them—they assume their proper position and role in the created order. When people do not acknowledge the one true God as their own Lord, however, they are in rebellion against their very nature[142] and eventually must be forcibly taught who is boss. The Bible teaches that everyone will eventually acknowledge the lordship of the only God;[143] the Egyptians were required to acknowledge it, however reluctantly, through the plagues, before Yahweh ("before me"). They could not simply in the privacy of their minds admit to themselves that Yahweh was impressive. They had to demonstrate their humility to him, which is what "humble yourself before me" requires. This is the import of the full rhetorical question, "How long will you refuse to humble yourself before me?" Arrogance and pride, not humility and deference, had characterized the Egyptian attitude toward Israel since the time of the "king who did not know about Joseph" (1:8). Because of God's determination to be acknowledged by his creation and by reason of his power to accomplish that acknowledgment, the Egyptians didn't stand a chance of holding on to their prideful stance in oppressing the Israelites. The only question was how long they would resist. Since they had been unwilling to be humble, they would now have to be humbled, that is, humiliated, directly by Yahweh.

10:4–6 These verses describe the severity of the coming plague for the benefit of Pharaoh and his court advisors. The prior plague of hail and the coming plague of locusts together constituted a "one-two punch" to knock out the Egyptian agrarian economy. Introduced by a rhetorical conditional "if you refuse to let them go," which God knew would certainly be fulfilled since he had already so determined and was within his power to do so, the description envisions complete devastation of remaining crops through a blanket of locusts covering Egypt so thickly as virtually to prevent the ground itself from being visible. This vast, border-to-border[144] swarm[145] would not only devour any crops left after the hail but would annoy humans by invading houses in great numbers. With wording relatively similar to that used to describe the unprecedented nature of the earlier hail[146] ("something neither your fathers nor your forefathers have ever seen from the day they

---

[142] The meaning of "creation in the image of God" is not primarily ontological (we are somehow in our nature like God) but vocational (we have a job to do that God has given us—do his will on earth as it is in heaven).

[143] E.g., Isa 2:12; 45:23; Ps 147:6; Zeph 3:11–12; Rom 14:11; Phil 2:10; Jas 4:6; 1 Pet 5:5.

[144] Cf. v. 14.

[145] "Locust swarm" is in fact the precise meaning of the term (אַרְבֶּה) translated "locusts" by the NIV. There is no "dense swarm" in the original of v. 14 as the NRSV translates אַרְבֶּה, nor is there any wording "plague of locusts" in that verse as the NIV translates it. The term אַרְבֶּה is used throughout.

[146] I.e., that of 9:24.

settled in this land till now"), the Egyptians were told that this plague would be without parallel in Egypt's history.[147]

Verse 6 concludes with a unique wording, "Then Moses turned and left Pharaoh." This is the only time in the accounts of Moses' encounters with Pharaoh that he is described as turning and leaving Pharaoh. Otherwise, the common expression is simply "left Pharaoh."[148] The reason for this detail in the narrative presumably is a desire to call the reader's attention to this particular leave taking, which is the first of two in this narrative and the one from which Moses (and Aaron) would be recalled as soon as the plague actually comes about. "Turned and left" *(pnh + yṣʾ),* a hapax legomenon pairing, almost certainly connotes leaving in opposition, without a happy resolution of an encounter. A more unambiguous translation might be "turned around and left" or "turned his back and left" or even "turned on his heels and left."

(3) Pharaoh Tries Again to Bargain, without Success (10:7–11)

[7]Pharaoh's officials said to him, "How long will this man be a snare to us? Let the people go, so that they may worship the LORD their God. Do you not yet realize that Egypt is ruined?"

[8]Then Moses and Aaron were brought back to Pharaoh. "Go, worship the LORD your God," he said. "But just who will be going?"

[9]Moses answered, "We will go with our young and old, with our sons and daughters, and with our flocks and herds, because we are to celebrate a festival to the LORD."

[10]Pharaoh said, "The LORD be with you—if I let you go, along with your women and children! Clearly you are bent on evil. [11]No! Have only the men go; and worship the LORD, since that's what you have been asking for." Then Moses and Aaron were driven out of Pharaoh's presence.

10:7 The court officials who advised Pharaoh became rather blunt in their assessment for Pharaoh's benefit of the problem that faced Egypt. Using the expression "to become a snare *[môqēš]* to *X,*" they identified Moses[149] as a

[147] Hb. uses a class of expressions, usually translatable by English expressions using the words "ever" or "never" (as in "ever/never heard of" or "ever/never seen") to indicate events without parallel. These expressions are not mere hyperbole but ways of indicating the uniqueness of something (cf. Exod 11:6; Deut 4:32; 5:26; Isa 66:8; 1 Kgs 10:20; 2 Chr 9:11,19; Jer 2:10; 18:13; Dan 9:12). Joel 1:12 provides an especially noteworthy parallel to the present context by reason of its reference to a locust plague in Joel's day. There is no contradiction involved; Joel was not suggesting that his plague was worse than the eighth plague in Egypt of Moses' day but merely that for Palestine, it was the worst ever. On the similarities as well as the possibility that what Joel was describing was metaphorically a locust plague but in fact an invasion by the Babylonians, see Stuart, *Hosea-Jonah*, 240–46. Cf. B. S. Childs, "A Study of the Formula, 'Until this Day,'" *JBL* 82 (1963): 279–92.

[148] Exod 5:20; 8:12,30; 9:33; 10:18; 11:8.

[149] But the Hb. is ambiguous, so it is not certain that the זֶה (lit., just "this") of the text means "this person [Moses]." It could as well mean "this situation." Cf. Durham, "Just how long is this impasse to bring ruin upon us?" (*Exodus*, 131).

snare to "us," presumably meaning all Egyptians, not just the governmental leadership. The same expression occurs repeatedly throughout the Old Testament and within the corpus of Moses' writings is used elsewhere (but not in this context; i.e., in Exod 23:3; 34:12; Deut 7:16) to refer to the way that worshiping idols would be a snare to the Israelites, that is, a means of entrapping them and enslaving them. A snare *(môqēš)* is simply a type of trap attached to or made from a cord that either pierces and holds or binds and holds its prey (cf. Amos 3:5; Job 40:24). Thus what the Egyptian officials were saying with this metaphor was that Moses had become a means by which the Egyptians were denied their freedom and trapped in a situation they did not want to be in. The irony is apparent: those who had enslaved the Israelites, keeping them trapped and denying them their freedom, were now "getting a taste of their own medicine;" they were themselves being held against their wills by their opponent. Of course, the reader should not for a minute think they had focused on the real source of their trouble. It was not Moses who had troubled them but God, and as a punishment for their own "snaring" of the Israelites.[150]

From the point of view of the officials, the only—and obvious—course was to give in to Yahweh's demands and let his people go to worship/serve *(ʿbd)* him. They were not motivated toward this position by a sense of justice or by compassion; they simply recognized what Pharaoh was slower to grasp—that Egypt was being ruined[151] and that relief from the trials was needed on an emergency basis. Pharaoh's splendid isolation and elaborately pampered care undoubtedly had shielded him from most of the pain associated with the plagues thus far. But the advisors in his court, though still materially well-off, were far more likely to have seen the extent of the hardships the nation was experiencing and more likely as well to have heard the escalating complaints of the citizenry. It may not have been easy for them to speak to Pharaoh in terms of a "ruin" of Egypt, but they had come to the point where there was no option for them but to help him understand just how far things had deteriorated. The attitude of Pharaoh at this point, however, was still very much like that of imperious leaders throughout history who failed to see the severity of what confronted them and their impending demise. Powerful leaders can get so used to having their will carried out that they find it hard to grasp the fact that the opposite might become the case.[152]

---

[150] Cf. 1 Kgs 18:17–18, where King Ahab called Elijah the "troubler of Israel," and Elijah turned the attack back immediately on Ahab by saying: "I have not made trouble for Israel, . . . but you and your father's family have. You have abandoned the LORD's commands and have followed the Baals."

[151] It is possible to translate אָבְדָה מִצְרָיִם not only as "Egypt is ruined" but as "Egypt has been getting ruined" or the like, i.e., as the past progressive use of the perfect.

[152] Among the many historical parallels, one could cite the attitude of Hitler in his last days, still thinking he could force a favorable peace with the Allies, or the Roman emperors who presided with misplaced confidence over their empire's decline, or Belshazzar and his nobles, drinking away the night as their armies fled from the Persians at the outskirts of Babylon (Dan 5). Powerful people can learn to love power so much that they refuse even to consider the possibility of having to give it up.

10:8 The wording of v. 8 assumes a partial capitulation of Pharaoh to the advice of his court officials, at least to the extent of a partial agreement to let the people go so they could worship the Lord their God. His words "go worship the LORD your God" so precisely parallel those of his advisors that this clearly was the reason for their being called back to his presence. Messengers were obviously sent out to find Moses and Aaron, who, upon request, reappeared at the court. Pharaoh, however, had not actually agreed without reservation to the advice to release the Israelites since he introduced a limitation in his question, "But just who will be going?" That was not a question he would bother to ask unless he were still bargaining, still trying to restrict the outright emigration permission sought by the Israelites.

10:9 The short wording for Moses' answer could have been, "Every Israelite will leave Egypt" because that was what he meant by his carefully worded response indicating that all ages, all genders, all relatives, and all moveable possessions of the Israelites would "celebrate a festival to the LORD," that is, leave the country.[153] Moses thus continued to stick to his own bargaining position, including the bargaining style and language that went with it, which consistently used "gentle" ways of saying that nothing less than a complete exodus would do.

10:10 The part of Pharaoh's response recorded in the first clauses of v. 10 ("the LORD be with you—if I let you go, along with your women and children!"), though not actually ambiguous in the original,[154] has been translated variously by modern versions. For example, "The LORD indeed will be with you, if ever I let your little ones go with you!" (NRSV); "Very well then; take your dependants with you when you go; and the Lord be with you" (NEB); "The LORD help you if . . ." (NAB). None of these, in our judgment, renders the Hebrew adequately because all are trying—somewhat misleadingly—to help the reader realize that Pharaoh was not actually giving permission for the exodus. In fact, what Pharaoh said was literally: "Let it be so![155] Yahweh will be with you when I let you and your family members go!" His words, however, were not intended literally but sarcastically, as the critical and negative final statement in the verse ("clearly you are bent on evil") makes clear. Were Pharaoh speaking modern colloquial English, he might have said something like: "Oh, sure, that's fine. And it would certainly prove that Yahweh was with you if I actually allowed all your family members to go with you, but, look, it's obvious you have evil in mind."[156]

[153] Moses had, of course, already defined the celebration of the festival as requiring leaving Egypt (8:25–28).

[154] יְהִי כֵן יְהוָה עִמָּכֶם כַּאֲשֶׁר אֲשַׁלַּח אֶתְכֶם וְאֶת־טַפְּכֶם.

[155] This is the simple meaning of יְהִי כֵן. Cf. the past-tense usage of the same idiom by Moses repeatedly in Gen 1 ("and it was so"); Judg 6:38; and the almost identical construction in Amos 5:14.

10:11 At this point Pharaoh said what he meant without sarcasm, the opposite of his earlier (lit.) "let it be so," that is, "not so!" (NIV "No!"). The NIV rightly separates the first clause from the second by a semicolon. Pharaoh's reference to "what you have been asking for" applies only to his command, "worship the LORD," not to "have only the men go." Moses and Aaron had been asking for the former but certainly not for the restrictive limitations of the latter.[157] What Pharaoh may not have been able to anticipate about Israelite worship was its relatively gender-blind nature. Of course, there could be no full "Israelite" worship until the Israelites received God's law and built the tabernacle and installed the priests, but God's demands to Pharaoh were given in anticipation of bringing the *whole* nation out of Egypt to serve him (and stop serving Pharaoh). Once it became constituted in the Law, Israelite worship did insist upon the full participation of women. Women were required to attend the designated worship feasts (Deut 16:11,14) and, in parallel from the point of view of prohibitions applying to them, were appropriately banned from participating in pagan rituals (Deut 17:2–7), even though it was the special responsibility of the man of the house, not the woman, to provide the actual offering materials (Deut 16:16–17).[158] Pharaoh certainly did not accept Moses' demand, and it apparently also was the case that he saw immediately from Moses' response that Moses would not accept a men-only sacrifice departure scenario. Since Pharaoh could not get his way, that is, could not keep the Israelites trapped in Egypt by means of allowing only a partial and temporary leave taking, he required in anger that Moses and Aaron be expelled from his presence. Did his advisors join him in feeling that Moses was being unreasonable? It is possible that they did, in light of the plural verb form (lit., "they drove them out") of the original.[159]

---

[156] The final clause of the verse would lit. be translated, "Look, indeed, evil is before your face." The only close parallel to the final two words (נֶגֶד פְּנֵיכֶם lit., "before your face") is found in Isa 5:21,where the third person reflex of the expression נֶגֶד פְּנֵיכֶם is usually translated "[clever] in their own eyes/sight." A translation such as, "Look, you've obviously got evil in sight/mind" would capture the sense of what Pharaoh was saying.

[157] On the grammar see R. Weiss, "A Note on *ʾotah* in Ex 10,11," *ZAW* 76 (1964): 188.

[158] Such passages as 2 Kgs 23:7; Ezek 9:6; Judg 16:27 (Canaanite mixed worship) make clear that men and women worshiped together, at least outside of Egypt. They would have stood in different parts of the tabernacle/temple, as they also later sat separately in the NT church sanctuaries where to ask their husbands a question meant shouting it across an aisle (1 Cor 14:35). Cf. also Neh 4:23; Luke 2:36–37.

[159] The MT reading, וַיְגָרֶשׁ אֹתָם מֵאֵת פְּנֵי פַרְעֹה, "he drove [them] out from the presence of Pharaoh," is unlikely in light of the evidence from other versions, namely the SP, the LXX, and the Syr., that the verb was plural in the original, lit., "they [indef. third person] drove them out from Pharaoh's presence." The NIV translation is well worded, however, since the best way to translate many indefinite third person verbs from Hb. and Aram. to Eng. is with a passive construction.

(4) The Plague and Its Consequences (10:12–20)

**[12]And the LORD said to Moses, "Stretch out your hand over Egypt so that
locusts will swarm over the land and devour everything growing in the fields,
everything left by the hail."**
**[13]So Moses stretched out his staff over Egypt, and the LORD made an east
wind blow across the land all that day and all that night. By morning the wind
had brought the locusts; [14]they invaded all Egypt and settled down in every area
of the country in great numbers. Never before had there been such a plague of
locusts, nor will there ever be again. [15]They covered all the ground until it was
black. They devoured all that was left after the hail—everything growing in the
fields and the fruit on the trees. Nothing green remained on tree or plant in all the
land of Egypt.**
**[16]Pharaoh quickly summoned Moses and Aaron and said, "I have sinned
against the LORD your God and against you. [17]Now forgive my sin once more and
pray to the LORD your God to take this deadly plague away from me."**
**[18]Moses then left Pharaoh and prayed to the LORD. [19]And the LORD
changed the wind to a very strong west wind, which caught up the locusts and
carried them into the Red Sea. Not a locust was left anywhere in Egypt. [20]But
the LORD hardened Pharaoh's heart, and he would not let the Israelites go.**

10:12 As in the case of the prior plague account (see 9:22–23), the command from God was for Moses to stretch out his "hand" (10:12), but the narrative states that he stretched out his "staff" (10:13). Again there is no contradiction. The combination of statements is a shorthand way of saying that he stretched out his hand or hands with the staff of God in it/them and brought about the plague. The command to perform this gesture contains a metaphorical element: God told Moses to stretch out his hand *over Egypt,* something he obviously could not literally do because of the length of his arm relative to the size of Egypt. What is meant by the obvious ellipsis of speech is that Moses was to hold up God's staff and either face various directions or perhaps slowly turn a complete circle to symbolize for any onlookers the pan-national extent of the coming plague. Moses' staff actually was elevated over only a tiny bit of Egypt; the plague, however, would affect it all, save for the Israelites' lands in Goshen.[160] The NIV wording "everything growing in the fields" represents an odd and potentially misleading translation choice, one that would imply that the locusts were to devour merely planted crops rather than all vegetation. The NRSV represents the majority of modern versions in its translation "every plant in the land," which is in fact the simple, literal translation of the Hebrew.[161] Here also the SP and the LXX preserve the added wording "and all the fruit of the trees,"

[160] Again implicitly assumed to be exempt, as stated in a representative sampling of plague accounts rather than tediously in all of them.

[161] אֶת־כָּל־עֵשֶׂב הָאָרֶץ.

which is likely original, having been lost from the MT by haplography. The parallel wording in v. 15 supports its inclusion as well. Accordingly, the end of the verse should be regarded as having read originally "every plant in the land and all the fruit of the trees—everything that the hail had left." The NIV translation also morphs the simple literal meaning of the third clause, "let them come up over the land of Egypt,"[162] into "so that locusts will swarm over the land," attenuating the meaning beyond what the rules of a dynamic equivalency translation call for.

10:13–15 Again Moses undertook the symbolic action and God undertook the miracle. The miraculous in this case included the control and use of the natural order. God did not manufacture locusts by fiat but instead caused already existing locusts to leave a location where they had bred and matured in abundance somewhere to the east, take flight, and be borne by a special wind so as to be dispersed in a pattern precisely covering the territory of Egypt. Locusts are merely grasshoppers that have hatched and grown under ideal conditions in the sandy soil where grasshopper eggs are deposited. Instead of a survival rate of a few per thousand, they survive by the hundreds per thousand. In the larval stage they rub together so frequently as to produce the characteristic brown exterior pigmentation, as opposed to the green color associated with grasshoppers that hatch in relatively greater isolation.[163] Where did the locusts originate? This is almost impossible to identify with certainty. One cannot assume simply that the specially controlled east wind that brought the locusts blew for, say, twenty-four hours at twenty miles per hour, and thus calculate that the locusts came from a location roughly four hundred and eighty miles east of Egypt. The beginning of the east wind simply may have *reached* Egypt so as to be felt at the time Moses was led to make his gesture, having actually originated far to the east at an earlier time; the wind may have preceded the locusts many hours before they flew into it and with it; or some other combination of wind and locusts may have been used by God to accomplish the plague. The general impression given by the wording of the original in vv. 13–14 is that on the morning after Moses raised God's staff, the locusts simply began to arrive and over a period of time gradually spread over Egypt rather than that they blanketed

[162] וְיַעַל עַל־אֶרֶץ מִצְרָיִם.

[163] See M. F. Leheta and M. S. Hassanein, *Developments in Applied Research and Control Techniques of the Desert Locust in the Arabian Peninsula* (Cairo, General Organisation for Government Printing Offices, 1963); R. A. Farrow, *The African Migratory Locust in Its Main Outbreak Area of the Middle Niger: Quantitative Studies of Solitary Populations in Relation to Environmental Factors* (Bamako, République du Mali: Organisation Internationale Contre le Criquet Migrateur Africain, 1975); United Nations Development Programme, *Desert Locust Project; Final Report* (Rome: Food and Agriculture Organization of the United Nations, 1968); C. Gillott, *Entomology*, 2d ed. (New York: Plenum Press, 1995).

Egypt instantly. Since nearly all the crops of Egypt are grown within sight of the Nile or its irrigation canals, one may presume that the locusts were especially concentrated near the Nile, so that "every area of the country" in v. 14 refers more to "every area where there were plants to eat" rather than "equally over the whole land mass."

The wording in v. 15, "they covered all the ground until it was black" has sometimes been questioned, partly because locusts are brown rather than black and partly because the LXX translator rendered it otherwise.[164] But the wording in this case represents not only a translation decision but a figure of speech, dramatically highlighting this plague in its own right but also foreshadowing the plague of darkness that followed immediately. An alternative translation would be "[until] the land was darkened";[165] the verb is from the same root as the term for darkness used in the following plague story. Locusts have voracious appetites and can eat virtually any type of plant. No crop vegetable or fruit stood a chance against this unprecedented, unduplicated[166] plague. What the hail had started the locusts finished. Soon Egypt would have no food—a remarkable reversal of what happened during Joseph's day (Gen 41:49).[167]

---

[164] The LXX has καὶ ἐφθάρη ἡ γῆ, "and the land was ruined," presumably a contextual guess on the LXX translator's part on the analogy of 10:7. It is not difficult to imagine that a translator might have concluded that there was no connection between locusts and darkness and thus mistakenly assumed that the obvious translation could not have been the right one.

[165] וַתֶּחְשַׁךְ הָאָרֶץ could even be translated "[until] the land had the appearance of darkness."

[166] Joel's language (Joel 1:2–3: "Has anything like this ever happened in your days or in the days of your forefathers? / Tell it to your children, and let your children tell it to their children, and their children to the next generation") might seem to suggest that the disaster of which he was speaking was at least as great as the Exodus locust plague. But whether Joel was speaking of an actual locust plague or metaphorically of the Babylonian invasion, it is likely he was modeling his language to speak of the extent of the attack after Exod 10:2 ("that you may tell your children and grandchildren") and 10:6 ("something neither your fathers nor your forefathers have ever seen").

[167] In the summer of 2004 a number of areas in West Africa were devastated by a locust plague that began with unseasonably heavy rains in otherwise rather arid areas to the east, so ideal hatching conditions for grasshopper eggs were achieved. The UN Food and Agriculture Organization described the locust infestation as a "crisis" because it arrived at the time of the summer planting season. According to the UNFAO, locusts can move at up to sixty miles per day (thus making the more rapid, wind-assisted movement in the case of the Exodus story all the more miraculous and not merely "natural") and reach densities of two hundred thousand insects per acre. In the West African 2004 locust invasion, serious traffic accidents resulted from the blinding of drivers via locusts covering vehicle windshields or simply making general visibility on the roads difficult. The UNFAO states that locusts can travel in swarms containing billions of insects and that each locust can eat an amount of foliage equal to its own weight (0.07 oz.) each day. In modern times crop pesticides sprayed by aircraft can limit locust damage if national agriculture departments can react quickly enough to a locust onslaught; otherwise the recent damage from locusts continues to underscore the severity of such circumstances in Bible times when no chemical or mechanical techniques were available to ameliorate the severity of a locust plague.

10:16–17 In these verses Pharaoh admitted his guilt, asked for forgiveness, and requested prayer for the removal of the plague. None of these factors was new (cf. 9:27–28), and therefore the reader has reason to retain some skepticism about how long Pharaoh's apparent repentance would actually last and/or how genuine it actually was. On the other hand, there are indications in these verses of a somewhat greater intensity in Pharaoh's attitude: he *quickly* summoned Moses and Aaron, thus rapidly reversing himself publicly relative to his "final offer" in v. 11 and opening himself to the humiliation any ruler could experience at going back on a public stance originally designed to show toughness. Moreover, he now acknowledged sinning "against the LORD" in addition to sinning "against Moses and Aaron," whereas in the prior plague account he had merely acknowledged generally having sinned/been wrong (9:27). On top of this, he actually asked Moses and Aaron[168] to forgive him, which represents yet another way of acknowledging that he was wrong and they—and the true God—were right.

The NIV translation "[forgive my sin] once more" is somewhat misleading since it tends to suggest that Pharaoh was thinking of and calling attention to his prior sin (9:27) by using such language. In fact, a more accurate translation would be "[forgive my sin] this time,"[169] which shows that Pharaoh was either cleverly bargaining (I'm only asking just this once) or, more likely, that he realized events were now coming to a head and there would not occur a whole range of other plagues after this one. The NIV translation of the last clause of 10:17 ("to take this deadly plague away from me") is also unfortunate since the Hebrew literally says "so that he may take away from me at least this death."[170] Pharaoh's point was that he saw Egypt dying as a result of the combined effect of the hailstorm and the locust invasion, not merely that the plague was *deadly* in some sense. His words do not suggest a focus on a plague but rather on death. Pharaoh was beginning to get the point: he realized that the plagues were leading to death, not merely inconvenience or temporary hardships. Paul made the same kind of assertion in Rom 6:23 with his words, "The wages of sin is death." It is not that every sin leads instantly to death but rather that every sin does move the sinner further down the inevitable path to death; the ultimate punishment for sin in a universe created and sustained by a holy, omnipotent God is the extermination of evildoers. The king of Egypt, in his own limited way and according to the biases of his own culture and beliefs, was catching a glimpse of this truth.

---

[168] In the MT Pharaoh's request for forgiveness is in the singular (שָׂא נָא חַטָּאתִי), but in the majority of the other versions it is in the plural, representing the better reading (שְׂאוּ נָא חַטָּאתִי).

[169] Cf. NRSV, "Do forgive my sin just this once."

[170] Thus, e.g., NRSV, "that at the least he remove this deadly thing from me."

10:18–20 As in the case of earlier plagues (8:12,30; 9:33), Moses left Pharaoh to pray for the end of the plague. This overt mention of Moses' prayer functions in the overall narrative to remind the reader that it was always God who controlled events: Moses proposed but God disposed. God again used the wind, this time changing its direction ("changed the wind to a . . . west wind") and apparently also its intensity ("very strong"). Most of the English translations sound as if the original text meant to say that the east wind that brought the locusts in the first place was still blowing—thus perhaps suggesting that locusts were still arriving in Egypt—but the Hebrew does not support this interpretation. The Hebrew can be understood to mean "the LORD made a change to a very strong west[171] wind,"[172] leaving unspecified whether this change was simply a contrast to the previous wind's direction ("changed over to a . . . ") or a reversing of an east wind still blowing (i.e., "changed it [the wind] to . . . "). This strong wind bore up (NIV "caught up" is interpretive, making it sound as though the locusts left against their will) the locusts, speeding them away from Egypt, and blew them (*tqʿ;* not "carried them") to/toward ("into") the Red Sea, that is, the great body of water lying directly to the east of Egypt. The term here translated "Red Sea" is *yam sup,* rendered "Sea of Reeds" by many commentators,[173] a far too limited body of water for the scenario described here.[174] In other words, this is one of the passages that suggests *yam sup* really means "Red Sea," not "Sea of Reeds." God's special removal of the locusts resulted in the complete absence of locusts anywhere in Egypt. Note that the text does not say that the locusts drowned in the Red Sea—only that the wind blew them in that direction out of Egypt. Once they were gone, the plague was over, and we are in fact not told of their fate otherwise. With the plague over, Pharaoh again refused to let the Israelites leave Egypt, just as he had in every other instance, and just as Yahweh determined would be the case. It would have been smart for him to have obeyed the initial advice of his counselors (10:7) or at least after the plague had come about. But he was not able to do the smart thing. He was being manipulated and humiliated by the only wise God, made to look the fool that he was for having carried on the oppression of the Israelites in the first place.

[171] Lit., "sea wind," i.e., the wind that blows from the direction of the great sea, the Mediterranean. This is the standard way in Hebrew of expressing "west wind."

[172] וַיַּהֲפֹךְ יְהוָה רוּחַ־יָם חָזָק מְאֹד. The verb הפך can be either transitive or intransitive. The Hb. is somewhat elliptical, lacking an explicit direct object for the verb if it is transitive.

[173] So, e.g., Dunham, *Exodus*, 132.

[174] See the comments on 13:18; 15:4,22; 23:31.

10. Tenth Sign: Ninth Plague: Darkness (10:21–29)

To appreciate fully this plague account, one must understand how ominously darkness threatened ancient people. We travel easily at night with the aid of various forms of electric lighting; they were virtually immobilized by the darkness of nighttime[175] unless the night was cloudless and the moon relatively full. Although some ancient professional caravaneers could travel *partly* at night, they were able to do so mainly at times other than the dark of the moon but only because their animals could see better at night than they could and especially because they traveled on well-defined, well-remembered paths. Straying from those paths in darkness could be fatal.[176] We can be active at night because our homes and places of work can be cheaply illumined; they closed up their cities at night,[177] barred their courtyard gates, and locked their house doors. People abroad in the nighttime were assumed to be criminals and, typically, in fact were.[178] We feel relatively safe during the night, even away from home, with various means of communication to call for help readily available; they were at the mercy of common thieves and bandits when away from home at night,[179] and unless well-armed and in large groups, they were easy prey for those who used the nighttime as cover for evil. They understood that the darkness was essentially chaotic, a kind of enemy of the safe and the good;[180] we may think of it as just another phase of the day.[181] They considered confinement in darkness a grave punishment from God,[182] even a sort of sometimes purposeful force[183] and associated it with death;[184] we don't think much about it at all.

[175] Cf. the allusions to the terror of night in the following: Ps 121:6: "The sun will not harm you by day, nor the moon by night"; Isa 8:22: "Then they will look toward the earth and see only distress and darkness and fearful gloom, and they will be thrust into utter darkness"; Isa 50:10: "Let him who walks in the dark, who has no light, / trust in the name of the LORD and rely on his God."

[176] Jer 2:6; 13:16; Lam 3:2.

[177] Cf. Josh 2:5, "At dusk, when it was time to close the city gate . . ."; cf. Acts 9:25; Neh 13:9

[178] Job 24:16; 34:22; Ps 74:20; Isa 29:15.

[179] Ps 91:5, "You will not fear the terror of night"; cf. Song 3:8.

[180] And, indeed, darkness could itself function as a foe of those who might try to harm God's people (e.g., Exod 14:20; Josh 24:7). Cf. also the parallel pair pattern in Zeph 1:15 ("That day will be a day of wrath, a day of distress and anguish, a day of trouble and ruin, a day of darkness and gloom, a day of clouds and blackness") in which the association between various terms for darkness and various terms for disaster/harm/trouble shows the conceptual overlap between the two.

[181] The "Day of the LORD," when Yahweh will attack his foes, is consistently described as a time of darkness. Cf., e.g., Joel 2:31: "The sun will be turned to darkness and the moon to blood before the coming of the great and dreadful day of the LORD"; cf. Ezek 32:7; Amos 5:18.

[182] Cf. 1 Sam 2:9; Job 5:14; 15:30; 18:18; note the comparison of darkness with disaster in Isa 45:7; cf. Mark 15:33; Matt 25:30; Jude 6,13; Rev 16:10.

[183] E.g., Job 3:4–6; cf. John 1:5; Col 1:3.

[184] E.g., Job 24:17; Lam 3:6; Ezek 32:7; Matt 8:12.

Even so, were we in our day to have three days without light (v. 23), widespread panic would ensue. Everyone would realize that the natural order had been overturned and that a basic fact of life on the planet had been removed. Long before the three days were up, people would begin to understand the consequences: "If this keeps up, there will be no food because plants need sunlight to live; all animals will die because the food chain requires plants; we will die because everything we live on will be gone." Deep, total darkness of the sort God imposed on the Egyptians (v. 21) would also cause sensory deprivation, leading to disorientation and psychological distress. More than just those people inclined to light-deprivation depression would be severely depressed by the third day. A sense of doom would pervade all minds.

(1) Announcement, Plague, and Consequences (10:21–23)

[21]Then the LORD said to Moses, "Stretch out your hand toward the sky so that darkness will spread over Egypt—darkness that can be felt." [22]So Moses stretched out his hand toward the sky, and total darkness covered all Egypt for three days. [23]No one could see anyone else or leave his place for three days. Yet all the Israelites had light in the places where they lived.

Again in vv. 21 and 22 Moses is described as stretching out his hand toward heaven [NIV "the sky"], a synecdoche for raising God's staff symbolically toward heaven,[185] an action that would also play a prominent role in the later battle against the Amalekites in chap. 17.[186]

10:21 The NIV translation of v. 21 includes two unfortunate wordings. The words "will spread" are misleading since the Hebrew simply says "will be" and connotes nothing whatever about the process being gradual, as "spread" would imply. Indeed, in the context the onset of darkness appears to be instantaneous, unlike, say, the locusts' arrival in the prior plague. As for the translation "darkness that can be felt," this as well appears to be erroneous, although the Hebrew wording that engenders it is a hapax legomenon and therefore theoretically open to debate as to its precise meaning. If one wonders, however, "what sort of darkness can be felt?" one wonders reasonably. The absence of light cannot be felt. There is nothing in this passage or elsewhere in the Bible or in ancient Near Eastern literature in general to suggest that anyone ever thought there was such a thing as a darkness that could be felt. The proper translation, instead, is almost surely "a darkness that will require groping around." The Hebrew wording in question[187] employs the only attested *hiphil* of a root *(mšš)* that in the *piel* conjugation means "feel

---

[185] As already explicitly in 7:19; 8:5,16; 9:23; 10:13.

[186] See commentary on 17:8–16, esp. v. 16.

[187] וְיָמֵשׁ חֹשֶׁךְ.

around with one's hands," "grope," or "feel one's way" (thus used of the actions of blind persons in Deut 28:29; cf. Job 5:14; 12:25). In the construction used by Moses, the subject is quite obviously not the unexpressed indefinite "one/someone" but the noun "darkness." If the factitive-resultative *piel* means "feel around with one's hands," "grope," or "feel one's way," there is every likelihood that the causative *hiphil* would mean to *cause* these actions, that is, "to cause to feel around with one's hands," "to cause to grope," or "to cause to feel one's way."[188] Properly translated, then, into natural English, 10:21 should read, "Then the LORD said to Moses, "Stretch out your hand toward heaven so that darkness will be upon Egypt—a darkness that will require groping around."

10:22 We are told that the result of Moses' by now familiar symbolic action was just as predicted, with the added detail that the darkness plague lasted three days. The only other plague account that came close to specifying a duration was the first, which was over not more than seven days after it began (7:25). Some plagues sometimes sound as if they might have had their effect while lasting not more than a day (e.g. the hail) while some (e.g. the flies) seem, according to common sense, to have lasted at least several days. It is therefore possible that three days was roughly average for the duration of a plague, but, as we have argued above, three days of darkness would hardly have been considered an "average plague" by the Egyptians who had to experience it.

10:23 The darkness denied travel of any sort to the Egyptians. At this time in the ancient world, there was no way to project light over distances, as we can do with electric lights. Lamps were open bowls of clay pinched at one or more points on the rim so as to allow a channel for a wick or wicks, one end of the wick resting in the oil contained by the bowl, and the other burning to produce light. Reflectors and lenses were not yet known. The total candlepower of such lamps was roughly one per wick. One might light enough lamps to see a bit inside a house, but without the lights of the stars and moon, genuine travel was impossible. If one ventured outside and happened to bump into a neighbor who also had a lamp in hand, one might see the neighbor's face and vice versa; but the Egyptians were not naive about their situation—they knew that with nothing more than lamplight, they were essentially trapped in their homes until the plague ended. Again Moses mentioned the contrast between the circumstances of the Egyptians and those of the Israelites, as expected in this third "cycle" of plagues. Israel had day and

---

[188] Cf. *IBHS* §434, "Though both stems involve causation, the factitive-resultative *Piel* generally has to do with the bringing about of a state or condition, and the causative *Hiphil* with the causing of an event."

night; Egypt, neither since the Egyptian darkness was not merely a night, which always contains *some* light,[189] but a total darkness.

(2) Pharaoh's Most Substantial Concession So Far (10:24)

[24]Then Pharaoh summoned Moses and said, "Go, worship the LORD. Even your women and children may go with you; only leave your flocks and herds behind."

The plague had lasted three days. It apparently came to an end according to God's timing rather than by reason of special prayer from Moses, and with the return of daylight came also the opportunity for Pharaoh to summon Moses to his court, something that would have been impossible during the three days of darkness. Moses received another compromise offer from Pharaoh, one still calculated to keep the Israelites from leaving Egypt permanently but nevertheless an offer constituting evidence of a willingness to grant some of the Israelites' God's demands.

From Pharaoh's point of view, keeping the Israelite livestock behind in Egypt would have held hostage their primary agricultural enterprise,[190] as well as the number of Israelites required to stay and tend the flocks while the rest of the people were in the wilderness. He was, in other words, not offering anything that would actually be acceptable to the Israelites.

(3) Moses' Insistence on a Full Exodus (10:25–26)

[25]But Moses said, "You must allow us to have sacrifices and burnt offerings to present to the LORD our God. [26]Our livestock too must go with us; not a hoof is to be left behind. We have to use some of them in worshiping the LORD our God, and until we get there we will not know what we are to use to worship the LORD."

10:25 Although various sorts of sacrifices and burnt offerings were specified and regulated later in the Sinai Law (esp. Lev 1–7), it is apparent here that both Moses and Pharaoh understood what these terms meant. Sacrifices (animals killed and eaten "with" and before God according to the revealed concept that if you are to live, something alive must die in your place) and burnt offerings (animals burnt entirely as an exclusive gift to God rather than cooked and shared proportionately by God, priests, and worshipers) were both practiced at very early times in human history and in the religion of the Israelite patriarchs (Gen 8:20; 22:2–8,13; 31:54; 46:1).

10:26 Moses did, however, indicate rather unambiguously in his reply to Pharaoh that some aspects of the Israelite sacrificial system were still to be revealed. Moses and the Israelites could not presume that what they so far

[189] I.e., enough light for nocturnal animals to fare nicely.

[190] See Gen 46:31–34; 47:3–4; also comments on Exod 8:25–28.

understood about how, when, and why to provide sacrifices and burnt offerings to God would not be altered once all the nation had met with him formally in worship.[191] Moses could reasonably assume that the people would have to "use some of them [the animals] in worshiping the LORD," but he could not be sure how many or even whether or not entire categories (e.g., all lambs of a certain age) might not be needed. His answer was not stalling; it was a fully honest answer, which also served as a polite way of declining Pharaoh's inadequate offer, using factual, deferential language in service of the bargaining process. Note Moses' continuing emphatic use of the Hebrew word *ʿābad* ("serve/worship") twice here. He knew that Israel had been forced to serve *(ʿābad)* Pharaoh, but he longed for the time when the nation would with all its heart serve/worship *(ʿābad)* Yahweh.

(4) Pharaoh's Refusal and Moses' Prophetic Play on His Words (10:27–29)

27But the LORD hardened Pharaoh's heart, and he was not willing to let them go. 28Pharaoh said to Moses, "Get out of my sight! Make sure you do not appear before me again! The day you see my face you will die."

29"Just as you say," Moses replied, "I will never appear before you again."

10:27 There is nothing unexpected in Pharaoh's reaction. His refusal to allow the Israelites to leave was entirely consistent with God's plan as originally revealed to Moses in 3:19 and continued in 4:21 and thereafter. The careful reader knows that until the terms of 4:23 were fulfilled, that is, the tenth plague's death of the Egyptian firstborn, Pharaoh certainly would not let the Israelites leave Egypt.

10:28 Pharaoh then signaled verbally that all bargaining was over. He would not accede voluntarily to a complete exodus of Israelites. In spite of the pressure on him from his people and his court advisors, and in spite of the mounting severity of the plagues thus far, he could not bring himself to grant the demands of his enslaveds' God. So he addressed Moses with a threat containing three clauses that each said essentially the same thing: Don't let me see you again. It was not a modest threat but one that was underscored with the strongest possible warning, that Moses would be put to death if he came back again.

---

[191] In other words, though God had preliminarily met with Moses and Aaron (5:3: "Then they said, 'The God of the Hebrews has met with us'"), producing great changes in their outlooks and lives, he had not yet met with the nation as a whole; and there was every reason to believe that such an encounter would produce new relationships and expectations of the Israelites with respect to all sorts of things, including the sacrificial system. This anticipation proved correct, of course.

10:29 Moses' reply could be translated as follows: "You've said the very thing! I will not keep seeing your face!"[192] The force of his reply, in other words, was to tell Pharaoh that Pharaoh himself had essentially predicted the future.[193] Moses was getting out of Egypt for good (along with all Israel) and would never return. Moses would not be stuck in the land of oppression. He would not have to keep dealing with the recalcitrant Pharaoh. The Israelite people would not have to continue suffering under the cruel hands of the taskmasters and harsh conditions of their slavery. Soon all the miseries of bondage in Egypt would be history. The Israelites were about to leave, and therefore Moses could tell Pharaoh that his words had more significance than he realized. It was just about over; they would not deal with each other face to face much longer[194]—not because Pharaoh had won but because he was about to lose. In fact, Moses' words likely meant even more—that he and Pharaoh would literally never see each other again (see comments on 12:31–32).

Pharaoh's words contained a death threat ("the day you see my face you will die") that Moses could hardly ignore. These words presumably would have held a special repugnancy for him since he had already been sentenced to death by an earlier pharaoh (2:15) and had lived forty years in exile knowing that if he went back to Egypt and was in fact seen by that pharaoh (let alone by the relatives of the man he had killed[195]), he would be put to death.

---

[192] As Propp (*Exodus,* 341–42) points out, the Hb. expression here, עוֹד רְאוֹת פָּנֶיךָ, reflecting the idiom יסף + עוד + infinitive, can mean to do something one more time (the punctiliar sense), or it can mean to keep doing something (the durative sense). Pharaoh may have meant the punctiliar; but Moses played on his words by giving them a durative sense—"you won't still keep seeing me," as opposed to "you won't ever see me again, even once." Propp also draws attention to the opinion, first advanced by Isaac ben Judah Abarbanel, the fifteenth-century rabbinical commentator, that "see the face of" is actually an idiom for "have an official audience/meeting with" and does not mean simply "lay eyes upon" (cf. Gen 43:3,5; 2 Sam 3:13; 14:24,28,32; 2 Kgs 25:19; Jer 52:25). Thus the encounters in 11:10 and 12:31–32, not constituting official audiences with Pharaoh, could not be considered to be reporting anything contradictory to what Moses said in this passage.

[193] S. DeVries identifies this sort of phenomenon as a "regal self-judgment narrative: a story in which a king's word or act determines his own judgment, enhancing the belief that Yahweh's supreme authority comes to paradoxical expression in the responsible deeds of the institutional holders of political power" (*1 Kings,* WBC [Waco: Word, 1985], 207); cf. his *Prophet against Prophet: The Role of the Micaiah Narrative (1 Kings 22) in the Development of Early Prophetic Tradition* (Grand Rapids: Eerdmans, 1978).

[194] On the question of the proper understanding of the Hb. text of 11:10 and 12:31–32, either of which might be taken to confirm that Moses and Pharaoh did actually meet again, see the commentary on those passages.

[195] It is likely that the usual ANE blood vengeance culture prevailed in Egypt just as well as in Asia Minor proper. On the concept see W. T. Pitard ("Amarna *ekemu* and Hebrew *naqam,*" *Maarav* 3/1 [1982]: 5–25), who corrects the nonvengeance theory of G. Mendenhall (*The Tenth Generation* [Baltimore: Johns Hopkins, 1973], 69–104) and in so doing shows that the Egyptians understood the concept of retributive vengeance perfectly well. Blood vengeance was often a "family honor" phenomenon: members of the family of a person whose life was taken by some other person felt honor bound to take that other person's life (or at least the life of a member of his family) in retribution. To break this kind of extralegal personal vengeance, God provided various laws protecting the rights of accidental slayers and regulating due legal process in cases of manslaughter (e.g., Num 35:12–27; Deut 19:6–12; Josh 20:3–9).

Now another pharaoh[196] had made a remarkably parallel threat. Moses' anger at having to be subject to such "double jeopardy" would seem entirely understandable in the circumstances. Pharaoh's consistent refusal to bend his will under God's and to allow the Israelites their exodus had always been a certainty because God had so decreed it. Under such circumstances, Moses could hardly be expected to become angry when Pharaoh acted just as God had predicted he would and caused him to do. On the other hand, God had certainly not moved the king to make this death threat. It was Pharaoh's own idea and was outrageous in three ways. (1) It violated the immunity Moses should have enjoyed as a prophet of God. Since Moses spoke not on his own but was a spokesperson for God, Pharaoh's argument should have been with God, not Moses. This kind of violation of the immunity of a prophet in the ancient world represented a serious breach of religion and law.[197] (2) It was mean-spirited and vindictive. Pharaoh had been given chance after chance to allow the Israelite exodus, and even when he himself proposed terms for its happening, he had reversed himself when his terms had not been met in spite of clear warnings of the consequences. Now, instead of acknowledging his complicity and/or admitting his own inconsistency, he accused Moses of having done something worthy of death! (3) It was cowardly. Pharaoh rested his animosity toward the Israelites on the assumption that they were Egypt's potential enemies (1:10). The attempt to silence and intimidate Moses by a death threat was in fact a tactic, however poorly conceived, to try to silence and intimidate the Israelites in general. The various approaches of the past had failed (1:12,20); now telling Moses he could no longer represent his own people—disqualifying him from his calling under penalty of death—was a cheap end run around the abject failure of ill-conceived and paranoid pharaonic political policies. Pharaoh was trying to get rid of the problem of Yahweh's demands by preventing Yahweh's chosen messenger from bringing those demands to his attention.

11. The Great Sign of Sovereignty Announced: Tenth Plague Predicted: Death of Firstborn (11:1–10)

This pericope (11:1–10) has a three-part structure in which the announcement of the tenth plague, that of the death of the firstborn (11:4–8), is

---

[196] It could not have been the same pharaoh in light of 4:19.

[197] On the general concept of the inviolability of the prophet, cf. F. I. Andersen, "The Socio-Juridical Background of the Naboth Incident," *JBL* 85 (1966): 46–57; K. Baltzer, "Naboths Weinberg (1 Kön 21): Der Konflikt zwischen israelitischem und kanaanäischem Bodenrecht," *Wort und Dienst* 8 (1965): 73–88; id., "Considerations Regarding the Office and Calling of the Prophet," *HTR* 61 (1968): 567–81; G. E. Wright and R. H. Fuller, *The Book of the Acts of God* (New York: Doubleday, 1960), 149–51; J. Muilenberg, "The 'Office' of the Prophet in Ancient Israel," in *The Bible and Modern Scholarship: Papers Read at the 100th Meeting of the Society of Biblical Literature, December 28–30, 1964* (Nashville: Abingdon, 1965), 74–97.

carefully sandwiched between two reminders of what previously had been revealed: first, that the tenth plague would be effective at producing the exodus and that Israelites were to be financially prepared for it by obtaining wealth from the Egyptians (11:1–3); and second, that the whole series of prior plagues had not resulted in the exodus because that was the way Yahweh had planned things (11:9–10). This surrounding of "new" narrative material with "reminder" narrative material has the effect of helping orient the reader/listener to the fact that the plague of death on the firstborn and the resulting exodus of Israel from Egypt was not merely an event in itself but the culminating act of a long process controlled by God and brought to fruition exactly as he had predicted it before any of the process had started. Moses was writing this story not merely to help his fellow Israelites trust Yahweh *as* things happened but to help them learn to trust that Yahweh is the one who *makes* things happen in the first place, as part of a great redemptive plan for the benefit of his people.

(1) Review of the Plans for the Final Plague and the Enrichment of the Israelites by the Egyptians (11:1–3)

1Now the LORD had said to Moses, "I will bring one more plague on Pharaoh and on Egypt. After that, he will let you go from here, and when he does, he will drive you out completely. 2Tell the people that men and women alike are to ask their neighbors for articles of silver and gold." 3(The LORD made the Egyptians favorably disposed toward the people, and Moses himself was highly regarded in Egypt by Pharaoh's officials and by the people.)

11:1 The NIV is correct in taking the converted imperfect verb form that begins 11:1 as a pluperfect ("had said") rather than the simple past ("said") as most modern translations do.[198] Verses 1–3 are clearly resumptive, referring in summary fashion—not word for word but conceptually—to what God had told Moses in 3:19–22 and 7:3–5. Now at least Moses knew that the final plague was at hand; and the long series of announcements/warnings, plagues, refusals by Pharaoh, was coming to an end. Pharaoh and the Egyptians had indeed been humiliated many times over. God had shown them repeatedly that it was he who had true power and that their own gods

[198] Hb. does not have a separate, formal pluperfect. Grammarians recognize that the perfect verb form can have a pluperfect meaning but rarely recognize that the converted imperfect can also be pluperfect in meaning. The NIV translators, to their credit, were sophisticated enough to break with the unfortunate limiting "tradition" of recognizing a pluperfect sense only for the perfect. The evidence for a pluperfect sense within the range of meaning of the Hb. prefixed (imperfect) conjugations nicely summarized by *IBHS* §552–53, citing studies by both W. J. Martin ("'Dischronologized' Narrative in the Old Testament," *VTSup* 17 [Leiden: Brill, 1969], 179–86) and D. W. Baker ("The Consecutive Nonperfective as Pluperfect in the Historical Books of the Hebrew Old Testament" [Regent College Thesis, 1973]).

were ineffective nothings. Now was the time for the ultimate demonstration of his sovereignty, in the form of a punishment of such magnitude that Pharaoh would certainly not merely allow the Israelites to leave Egypt but would require that they do so. The latter part of the verse[199] may, in fact, be translated as follows: "After that, he will let you leave here. When he lets you leave, it will be complete[200]—he will actually drive you away from here."

11:2–3 These verses bring strongly to the reader's attention a sense of the psychological distance that had developed between Pharaoh and the rest of the Egyptians, something that a casual reader may not have fully appreciated previously, although evidences of it were certainly already mentioned in earlier portions of the story (e.g., 8:19; 9:20; 10:7). Anyone with an ounce of sense among the Egyptians had long since realized that resistance to the Israelites' God Yahweh was useless. Indeed, the Egyptians in general had come to respect[201] the Hebrews (presumably partly out of fear and partly out of pragmatism) and saw their pharaoh's policy of continued resistance to the exodus for what it was: a fanatical, destructive, hopeless stance that was doing nothing but harm. The virtually uniform consensus among Egyptians was that the Israelites were entitled to leave Egypt and that their God had shown himself fully capable of ruining the country if they were not allowed to do so. The only person who could not yet see this was Pharaoh because God had blinded him to reason as a punishment for his oppressions and as a means of demonstrating his divine power over the greatest human potentate of that era. The Egyptians' attitude toward the Israelites was not entirely a simple matter of normal human reasoning. God's plan was to provide his people with the financial wherewithal to survive as a nation on the move until they arrived at and settled in Canaan, so he supernaturally influenced the Israelites' Egyptian "neighbors"[202] to give them valuables simply for the

---

[199] אַחֲרֵי־כֵן יְשַׁלַּח אֶתְכֶם מִזֶּה כְּשַׁלְּחוֹ כָּלָה גָּרֵשׁ יְגָרֵשׁ אֶתְכֶם מִזֶּה.

[200] Or, "When he will have let you leave, it will have been complete"; cf. R. J. Williams, *Hebrew Syntax: An Outline,* 2d ed. (Toronto: University of Toronto Press, 1976), par 162, pp. 29–30.

[201] This is the sense of "favorably disposed" and "highly regarded" in the present statement: not that the Israelites and Moses were the sort of people everyone naturally wanted to associate with, but rather that the Israelites and Moses were held in awe by the general Egyptian population and by Pharaoh's officials because of the power their God had displayed on their behalf. The NRSV translation, e.g., is more to the point: "The LORD gave the people favor in the sight of the Egyptians. Moreover, Moses himself was a person of great importance in the land."

[202] The Hb. words employed here are the masculine and feminine forms of רֵעַ (not "neighbor" in the sense of someone who lives nearby but in the sense of a corresponding human being, just as in Jesus' parable of the Good Samaritan, Luke 10:29,36). In other words, the Israelites simply asked their counterparts in the land, the Egyptians, for valuables. There is no implication in these verses that Israelites lived side-by-side with Egyptians in Goshen or anywhere else.

asking and caused them to think highly of Moses as well, in direct opposition to the increasing bitterness Pharaoh was displaying toward him.

(2) Announcement of the Final, Decisive Plague to Pharaoh (11:4–8)

[4]So Moses said, "This is what the LORD says: 'About midnight I will go throughout Egypt. [5]Every firstborn son in Egypt will die, from the firstborn son of Pharaoh, who sits on the throne, to the firstborn son of the slave girl, who is at her hand mill, and all the firstborn of the cattle as well. [6]There will be loud wailing throughout Egypt—worse than there has ever been or ever will be again. [7]But among the Israelites not a dog will bark at any man or animal.' Then you will know that the LORD makes a distinction between Egypt and Israel. [8]All these officials of yours will come to me, bowing down before me and saying, 'Go, you and all the people who follow you!' After that I will leave." Then Moses, hot with anger, left Pharaoh.

11:4 At this point in the chapter the parenthetical retrospective review of vv. 1–3 has ended, and the reader's attention is once again drawn to the scene of Moses before Pharaoh. Moses introduced his words with a typical messenger formula ("this is what the LORD says") so that Pharaoh had no doubt that Moses was speaking as a prophet the words given to him by his God.[203] God announced here that he would personally move through Egypt to bring about the death of the Egyptian firstborn ("I will go throughout Egypt"). This personal involvement of Yahweh represents a further heightening of the severity of the plagues. Previously Yahweh had caused all the plagues, but in the case of those plagues caused by insects, Yahweh had produced the insects and *they* had gone throughout the land doing the intended harm. Now Yahweh himself was the immediate performer of the plague, the immediate visitor of the homes of the Egyptians. The further descriptions of the actual plague as it was carried out in chap. 12 emphasize God's direct role several more times, albeit with the addition of the somewhat enigmatic reference to the "destroyer" in 12:23.

Why did God announce that the deaths would occur at "about midnight"? The answer can have nothing to do with the modern concept of beginning a new day at midnight (which is calculated as the opposite of (twelve hours away from) high noon because the ancients tended to begin the day at either dawn or dusk. In the case of the Israelites the day began at dusk by reason of the creation order,[204] which was reinforced by the logical reckoning that

---

[203] As we have already noted, the messenger formula was a device used by people who memorized a speech given them by a superior and delivered it on behalf of that superior to an intended recipient. Any statement introduced by a messenger formula claims overtly not to be the composition of the speaker but verbatim what he was told to say by the one who had sent him (in Moses' case, by God).

[204] Thus the evening-morning sequence of Gen 1:5,8,13,19,23,31.

when one day was coming to an end another must therefore be starting. Rather, "midnight" in the sense of the concept in the ancient world was the deepest, darkest time of night, the point during the night when the most people were likely to be asleep (since people tended to retire to bed at dusk) and the time of greatest vulnerability and defenselessness. Thinking of the events of the plague from the point of view of the mercies of God, causing the death of so many Egyptians was indeed a severe punishment, but allowing them to die quietly in their sleep was an act of grace. The wailing predicted in v. 6 was not the wailing of pain during death but the wailing of grief at the morning's discovery of the dead in virtually every household.

11:5 Three questions arise naturally in connection with this verse: (1) Was God fair to kill the firstborn of families all over Egypt when by this time it was mainly the Egyptian king who was still resisting God's demands on behalf of Israel? Another way of stating this question would be: Why not kill Pharaoh rather than his firstborn and all the other firstborn—thus directly punishing the one person most guilty of sin against God? (2) Why kill the firstborn of cattle as well? (3) Would families with only girls escape the devastation of this plague since the NIV translation says explicitly "firstborn son"?

The answer to the first question is virtually impossible to state simply or briefly because it involves an understanding of the nature of God in relation to his wrath and justice and therefore requires a rather extensive survey of the full range of biblical data related to the topic. God does a great many things that remain beyond human understanding because human intellect is far too limited to allow for appreciation of the entire complexity of God's overall eternal plan for his universe and each individual in it. Nevertheless, it would seem reasonable to suggest that, first of all, Pharaoh was hardly the only guilty party in the oppression of the Israelites. His orders had to be carried out throughout the entire land, and this required the willing cooperation of his own court officials, regional administrators, military general officers and lesser officers, and civilians of all ranks and types.[205] Second, the judgment of God displayed in all the plagues was more than merely an act of retribution. It was also a definitive display of his superiority to all other gods, that is, false gods, for the benefit of all seekers of the truth throughout all subsequent history (12:12; cf. 12:14,24–27). Additionally, the fact that "innocent" people died in the general pattern of the implementation of this plague is not a unique sort of phenomenon. Consider specifically the very

[205] The statement in 1:22, "Then Pharaoh gave this order to all his people . . ." is surely to be taken at face value: an Egyptian pharaoh expected to be able to count on the cooperation and obedience of his population in general, and the lack of mention in the narrative of any opposition to the contrary, though it is an argument from silence, would appear to be in this case a legitimate argument from silence to the effect that the Egyptians found carrying out Pharaoh's orders to be to their own advantage.

young firstborn children, who presumably played no conscious, purposeful role in opposing or enslaving God's people. How is their situation materially different from innocents who die in natural disasters that happen often around the world today and throughout history? In other words, the mercy and fairness of God's actions in the case of the tenth plague on the Egyptians is a subset of the question of the mercy and fairness of God in all his dealings in a fallen world corrupted by original sin. Those who from our limited point of view tend to be regarded as "innocent" are regularly the victims of disastrous and even fatal circumstances and events. We trust a wise and loving God relative to their eternal destiny, but we certainly cannot deny that they suffer unfairly and unevenly in a world that is subject to such unfairness by reason of its subjection to futility as a result of human sin.[206]

The question of why the plague should involve killing the firstborn of cattle as well as of humans finds its answer in the fact that in most of human history there has been a close symbiotic relationship between cattle and humans, and therefore cattle, who shared the sixth-day creation order with humans,[207] were deeply appreciated in ancient times. Thus a full humiliation of Pharaoh and of the Egyptians would naturally be expected to include the death of the firstborn of cattle.

As to whether families with only female children escaped the effects of this plague, the answer is surely no, the NIV translation of *bekor* as "firstborn son" being potentially misleading.[208] This is confirmed by the statement in 12:30, "There was not a house without someone dead," a relatively unambiguous indication that daughters as well as sons were taken from their families. All sectors of society were to experience the plague, as indicated by the inclusion of the firstborn of Pharaoh, that is, the highest, then the firstborn of "the slave girl at her hand mill," that is, the servant girl who had the menial job of grinding the grain and was thus a representative of the lowest class in the society, to the cattle, who were surely not on the same scale of life value as the humans but whose inclusion showed that all humans no matter how high or low their estate *were* included.

11:6 The word used in the original for the NIV "wailing" (*ṣĕʿāqāh,* just as well translated "outcry" or the like) is the term used by God in 3:7,9 to describe the groaning/crying out of the Israelites from the misery of their hor-

---

[206] This is merely one of the implications of what is said in Rom 8:19–22.

[207] Cf. Gen 4:24–25 and the value attached to ownership of cattle in parallel to "ownership" of workers in Gen 20;14; Job 1:3.

[208] In Hb. the term *bĕkōr* as "firstborn" does not have a directly corresponding feminine form. The word that would seem to be its feminine counterpart, *bĕkōrāh*, means "rank" rather than "first to be born." The feminine word meaning "first to be born" reflects another nominal formation, *bĕkîrāh*. Thus, on the analogy of *ʾāb,* which can mean "father" but can also mean "ancestor" of either gender, *bĕkōr* means "firstborn" (of either gender) and not simply "firstborn son."

rific slave work. Here, then, is predicted a drastic turning of the tables so that it would be all Egyptians instead of all Israelites who would cry out—and for an even greater suffering. The term *ṣĕʿāqāh* could theoretically connote either wailing in the sense of an expression of grief on the part of those who have received bad news or the sound made by those dying from the plague.[209] In the present instance, however, it almost surely referred to the reaction of families to the discovery that during the night an oldest child had died in bed, as the parallel use of the term in 12:30 confirms ("loud wailing . . . for there was not a house without someone dead"). The prediction of worse wailing "than there has ever been or ever will be again" is a statement hard to refute: Egyptians might have participated in mass, national times of mourning for various reasons at prior times in their history,[210] but surely there would have been no parallel to the kind of sudden loss of life that God predicted here.

11:7 As in several preceding plague accounts,[211] Moses reported God's intention to differentiate completely between the Egyptians and the Israelites in the suffering. The NIV takes a translation liberty with the verse in its translation "but among the Israelites not a dog will bark at any man or animal." The actual literal meaning of the Hebrew is "but among the Israelites not a dog will stick out its tongue at any man or animal." In Bible times the dog was the least of the animals in terms of desirability or importance because it was a dirty, unwelcome scavenger animal—its reputation being somewhat akin to that of the rat in modern times (cf. 1 Sam 17:43; 2 Kgs 8:13; Eccl 9:4; Matt 7:6; Luke 16:26).[212] To say that not even a dog would stick out its tongue at an Israelite was a simple, graphically idiomatic way of saying that the Israelite humans and cattle would simply see no harm whatever from the tenth plague.

11:8 Moses then predicted to Pharaoh yet another—this time final—statement of distinction/reversal of roles between the Israelites and the Egyptians. The very people who had once bowed down to Pharaoh would bow down to Moses—not to acknowledge him as their sovereign as they did with Pharaoh but

---

[209] Passages such as Isa 5:7; Jer 49:21 appear to describe the crying out of people reacting to personally felt pain; most of the eighteen other uses of the noun are in contexts of crying out because of the sense of horror or affliction one has experienced.

[210] Compare the call to national mourning on the part of the Ninevites ordered by the king of Nineveh in Jonah 3:6–9 or by the prophet Joel to the Israelites in Joel 1:2–14.

[211] I.e., the accounts of a sufficient number of prior plagues (8:22; 9:4,26), as we have already argued, would seem surely designed to convey to the reader the impression that *all* the plagues distinguished between Israel and Egypt, the former enduring no suffering, and the latter always enduring nationwide suffering.

[212] D. W. Thomas, "KELEBH 'Dog': Its Origin and Some Usages of It in the Old Testament," *VT* 10 (1960): 410–27; F. C. Fensham, "The Dog in Ex. XI 7," *VT* 16 (1966): 504–7; E. L. Greenstein, "A Literary Solution to a Philological Crux: The Case of Exodus 11:7 [Hebrew]," in *The Bible in the Light of Its Interpreters* (Jerusalem: Magnes, 1994), 587–600.

to plead with him to leave Egypt and take the Israelites with him.[213] This prediction represents yet another humiliation of Pharaoh. Moses here stated that all Egyptians would disagree with the king's policy, a disagreement that had, of course, been progressively increasing at any rate. Now Moses announced that the time would come when in spite of Pharaoh's official position of resistance to the exodus, everyone else, as embodied in those who were supposedly most loyal to him (his own court officials), would want the exodus to happen and would beg for it "on their knees," as we might say metaphorically in modern English. When Moses said "all these officials of yours will come to me,"[214] he is referring to the idea of the officials' coming down off the royal platform where they usually stood next to the king. Moses' words paint an image of the royal officials abandoning their Pharaoh, an envisioned action consistent with the words that they will say requesting that the exodus commence ("Go, you and all the people"). That is when Moses would leave Egypt—when the king's policies had been proved worthless by their abandonment even at the hands of people supposedly the closest and most loyal to him.

Moses' anger in leaving Pharaoh related to the unwarranted, undeserved death threat Pharaoh had pronounced against him (10:28) and not to any intervening factors. The reader is expected to understand that all his words had presumably been delivered through his anger at the end of this encounter with Egypt's king.

(3) Review of Pharaoh's Prior History of Resistance to the Exodus (11:9–10)

[9]The LORD had said to Moses, "Pharaoh will refuse to listen to you—so that my wonders may be multiplied in Egypt." [10]Moses and Aaron performed all these wonders before Pharaoh, but the LORD hardened Pharaoh's heart, and he would not let the Israelites go out of his country.

11:9–10 Once again the narrative reverts to a retrospective, which the NIV, to its credit, recognizes with the use of the pluperfect "had said" at the outset of v. 9. The words of 11:9 are essentially a summary of 4:21–23, although the same themes are also found in part in such places as 3:19–20 and 6:1–8. Exodus 11:10 reminds the reader of what had been happening throughout the plague accounts,[215] always as predicted: God showed his wonders to the world, but Pharaoh, made a fool of by God, continued to resist the obvious conclusion (by now obvious to everyone but himself) that the best thing he could do was to let the Israelites leave Egypt permanently and totally.

---

[213] The NIV's "all the people who follow you" is a sensible conceptual rendering of what literally translates as "all the people at your feet." An alternate translation might be "all the people you lead."

[214] The NIV "will come to me" distorts the meaning of *yrd,* which always has the sense of "come down/descend," not merely "come."

[215] And certainly, therefore, not something that happened subsequent to Moses' prior prediction that he would not appear before Pharaoh again (10:29).

DIVISION OUTLINE

IV. THE PASSOVER AND THE EXODUS (12:1–13:16)
1. God's Instructions for Passover including the Use of the Blood (12:1–13)
   (1) Guidance for Preparing and Eating the Passover (12:1–11)
   (2) Description of Passover Death, Judgment on the Gods of Egypt, and the Protection of the Blood (12:12–13)
   Excursus: Judgment on the "Gods of Egypt"
2. God's Insructions for Passover Memorial of Unleavened Bread (12:14–20)
   Excursus: The Meaning of "Cut off From"
3. Moses and the Israelites Follow the Passover Instructions (12:21–28)
4. The Tenth Plague Strikes: Death of the Firstborn (12:29–30)
5. The Exodus Is Permitted, Under God's Vigil (12:31–36)
6. The Exodus Begins (12:37–42)
   Excursus: How Many Israelites Left Egypt?
7. Summation: The Passover Statute and Its Connection to the Exodus (12:43–51)
8. Exodus Memorials: Consecration/Redemption of Firstborn, Eating Unleavened Bread (13:1–16)
   (1) Introductory Statement of the Consecration/Redemption Regulation (13:1–2)
   (2) The Importance of Keeping the Feast of Unleavened Bread Annually in the Promised Land (13:3–10)
   (3) Basic Rules for Consecration/Redemption of Firstborn (13:11–13)
   (4) The Connection of Consecration/Redemption of Firstborn to the Exodus (13:14–16)

IV. THE PASSOVER AND THE EXODUS (12:1–13:16)

From a modern reader's point of view, the lengthy descriptions of how to prepare for and celebrate the annual ritual of the Passover (12:1–28,43–50; 13:2–10), coupled with instructions on consecrating/redeeming the firstborn of humans and animals (13:1,11–16) found in Exod 12 and 13 might seem to interfere with the flow of the narrative. After all, the story so far has been building plague by plague up to an expected final, climactic plague that the reader has been told would compel Pharaoh to release the Israelites from Egypt. The reader might be forgiven for not wanting to stop to read a rather lengthy section of instructions about how the Passover and firstborn consecration were to be undertaken. Indeed, anyone looking for uniformity of subject matter as a key to understanding the structure of the book might be puzzled at the introduction here of legal material, months prior to the Israelites' arrival at Sinai, where they presumably *should* have begun to receive the law. In other words, shouldn't all these words about the Passover and firstborn follow in their proper course somewhere, perhaps around chap. 23,[1] where the three annual festivals and their timing are formally announced to the Israelites as a covenant community? What could the writer have been thinking?[2]

The answer, we suggest, is that the writer, Moses, was thinking of the best interests of his audience. His immediate audience was the people of Israel at the time they were in the wilderness of Sinai, awaiting the opportunity to enter into and settle the promised land,[3] where they would actually need to follow these instructions carefully after a long hiatus of not having had any practice in following them at all.[4] His long-term audience was all

---

[1] I.e., 23:14–17, a section that could easily be followed by more detailed explanations of at least the Passover, if not all of the three great annual festivals.

[2] The scholar committed to a multisource documentary approach to Exodus will, of course, consider that the "intrusion" of this material is simply the result of the Priestly final redaction of the book with an eye to giving paramount attention to the ritual as opposed to the literary progress of the epic narrative that was the original interest of J or E (not a few assign the surrounding narrative, at least theoretically, to E).

[3] Cf. the arguments for the composition of Genesis, likewise, during the wilderness period in D. Garrett, *Rethinking Genesis: The Sources and Authorship of the First Book of the Bible* (Fearn: Mentor, 2000). As the Israelites were anticipating entry into the promised land, they needed their national purpose and history documented for a new generation that was growing up with only the experience of the wilderness years as their orientation and only the leadership of Moses and Aaron, now very elderly, to provide authoritative instruction. Written documents from the hand of Moses, documents we know as the Pentateuch, provided these necessary orientations for the Israelites of the conquest generation.

[4] Although it cannot be absolutely proven, it is likely that Josh 5:10–12 intends us to understand that the Israelites had not celebrated the Passover during the time they had lived mainly on manna, i.e., most of their thirty-nine years in the wilderness. By this reasoning, the celebration of the Passover under Joshua's leadership at Gilgal was the first such celebration since the original Passover, held the night of the exodus from Egypt as described in Exod 12, followed by the single memorial of it a year later while the Israelites were still encamped at Sinai (Num 9:1–14). Thus a whole generation may have grown up in the wilderness who had not known how the Passover was to be undertaken because they had no personal memory of seeing it done and participating in it year after year. See J. B. Segal, *The Hebrew Passover,* LOS 12 (London: Oxford University Press, 1963), esp. 3–4, 237. T. C. Butler provides a useful review of the critical approaches, most of which are skeptical of the historical authenticity of the Exodus texts (*Joshua*, WBC 7 [Waco: Word, 1983], 60–61). See also C. Brekelmans, "Joshua v 10–12: Another Approach," *OTS* 25 (1989): 89–95.

Israel throughout history—at the present time the church, an audience positioned to benefit from the real point of the exodus story: that God supernaturally delivers his people from bondage to bring them to a promised land and that they belong to him, not to themselves.[5] These features make the exodus event powerfully relevant to modern believers, and the fact that Moses was inspired to force the reader to take account of them at this stage in his five-chapter work is a literary blessing rather than evidence of literary awkwardness. For Christians, the fact that Jesus Christ is the true and ultimate Passover Lamb,[6] the firstborn of many brothers and sisters,[7] and the Redeemer of all of them[8] is a truth worthy of the powerful pause that draws it to our attention proleptically[9] in these chapters.

1. God's Instructions for Passover Including the Use of the Blood (12:1–13)

(1) Guidance for Preparing and Eating the Passover (12:1–11)

[1]The LORD said to Moses and Aaron in Egypt, [2]"This month is to be for you the first month, the first month of your year. [3]Tell the whole community of Israel that on the tenth day of this month each man is to take a lamb for his family, one for each household. [4]If any household is too small for a whole lamb, they must share one with their nearest neighbor, having taken into account the number of people there are. You are to determine the amount of lamb needed in accordance with what each person will eat. [5]The animals you choose must be year-old males without defect, and you may take them from the sheep or the goats. [6]Take care of them until the fourteenth day of the month, when all the people of the community of Israel must slaughter them at twilight. [7]Then they are to take some of the blood and put it on the sides and tops of the doorframes of the houses where they eat the lambs. [8]That same night they are to eat the meat roasted over the fire, along with bitter herbs, and bread made without yeast. [9]Do not eat the meat raw or cooked in water, but roast it over the fire—head, legs and inner parts. [10]Do not leave any of it till morning; if some is left till morning, you must burn it. [11]This is

---

[5] E.g., 1 Cor 6:19–20, "You are not your own; you were bought at a price"; cf. Ps 100:3; Acts 20:28; Rev 5:9; 14:4.

[6] John 1:29,36; 1 Cor 5:7; 1 Pet 1:9; Rev 5:16 *et passim.*

[7] Rom 8:29; Col 1:18; Heb 12:23.

[8] Luke 1:68; Rom 3:24; 1 Cor 1:30; Gal 4:5; Eph 1:14.

[9] It is not going too far to say that the great themes of Scripture are all introduced in the OT in one way or another, and then find fruition in the NT. That the Passover should have a memorial meaning under the old covenant and at the same time function to teach the Israelites – then and now – the concept of eternal deliverance in Christ is simply one illustration of this phenomenon. Likewise with the dedication/redemption of the firstborn: it helps teach the reader the essential concept of God's ownership of all life, and the fact that fallen life must be bought back from death by a payment to God, on the analogy of redeeming a firstborn child or animal.

how you are to eat it: with your cloak tucked into your belt, your sandals on your feet and your staff in your hand. Eat it in haste; it is the LORD's Passover.

12:1 The importance of this verse lies in its identification of Moses and Aaron, who were Levites and priests, as recipients of the legal instruction that follows. It was the responsibility of Levites and priests throughout the generations of Israel not only to keep the law themselves[10] but also to enforce it and teach it to the population as a whole.[11] Thus the nation's first two levitical priests are mentioned prominently as a paradigm for all later proper clergy, and the instruction assumes great importance, in as much as these legal instructions were given them already *in Egypt*, that is, even prior to Mount Sinai.

12:2 Why should God have to tell the Israelites when their year began, that is, which month was to be the first in their calendar? The answer has two aspects: one is that this was not at all a settled question for them, and they therefore needed a revealed guidance on the matter; the other is that God was teaching them to link even their measuring of time to his calling on their lives. Why was it not a settled question? The people groups of the ancient world varied in their sense of when the year should begin, with some cultures choosing a fall new year and some celebrating a spring new year. It is possible that most of the various Canaanite groups celebrated a fall new year and that one reason for this ruling from God was to be sure the Israelites differentiated themselves from the Canaanites, near whom they were eventually to live (indeed, *among* whom they *had to* live by reason of their eventual unfaithfulness in the conquest). Even so, the Israelites themselves held membership in a broad culture that, informally at least, regarded the transition from summer to fall as the "end of the year" and therefore the fall as the beginning of the calendar. This sense of calendar is sometimes known as the "agricultural calendar" because it pays special attention to the time of harvest as the conclusion of the agricultural year. Thus passages like Exod 23:16 ("Celebrate the Feast of Ingathering at the end of the year, when you gather in your crops from the field") and 34:22 ("Celebrate the Feast of Weeks with the firstfruits of the wheat harvest, and the Feast of Ingathering at the turn of the year") use the language of the agricultural calendar. This use of language should not be viewed as contradicting the present law establishing a spring new year. It is simply phenomenological, informal language, much as people today speak of the day "ending" with dusk or "beginning" at dawn, even though they well know that it technically ends/begins at midnight, or speak of the "weekend" as including Sunday, even though they are well aware that, in English-speaking tradition at least, the week actually

[10] E.g., Lev 22:9; Ezek 44:24.

[11] E.g., Deut 17:9,18; 24:8; 2 Chr 15:3; 31:14; 35:3; Neh 8:7,9; Jer 18:18; Ezek 7:26; Matt 2:4.

begins with Sunday.[12] It is clear that in terms of formal teaching in the Pentateuch, the new year is firmly established as commencing in the spring, the month of Nisan (what we would call March-April) being the first month, and that the *seventh* month was the one to which the *fall* festival was dated.[13]

Here we read that God has decided that history determines the calendar, and in particular, the history of God's saving act of the exodus does so.[14] Whatever might theoretically have been their previous thinking about a calendar, God decreed to his Old Covenant people that they would henceforth have a calendar designed to remind them of how they first became a people—it happened by reason of their deliverance by his mighty hand out of the bondage of the oppressor, an act so important that it was also to be memorialized by a special annual feast, the Passover.

12:3–4 At its heart, the Passover is a meal, a commemorative feast. Some modern American holidays are feasts (e.g., Thanksgiving and Christmas); others are not (e.g., Labor Day, July 4). Feast holidays have the special emphasis of careful preparation (thus the instruction in v. 3 that the sacrificial animal is chosen four days before the feast so that there be no last-minute arrangements and the possibility of haphazard celebration or lack of availability results) for gathering people together to share a common gratitude and/or remembrance as they share the common meal linked to that gratitude/remembrance. The gathering of an entire family of Israelites (or group of families eating one animal though in separate houses) together at a dinner table helped symbolize the general pattern throughout the nation, that is, the whole nation eating together, though of course at individual locations. In accordance with the feast nature of the Passover, Moses was told that the whole nation ("tell the whole community of Israel") must be instructed to eat the meal as households, not as individuals. Thus great emphasis is placed on *sharing* the meat of a *single* animal. The goal is to have one goat kid or lamb[15] for each full family, "one for each household." Therefore, if a household were composed of perhaps just one, two or three people, and they could not by themselves consume a whole goat kid or lamb at one sitting, v. 4 provides for sharing the meal with the next-door family, so that everyone at the two houses eats together from a single sacrificed animal and finishes the

---

[12] Of the many other examples of this sort of use of language, one prominent one is the tendency to speak of "sunset" and "sunrise" rather than "our portion of earth turning into the sun" or "our portion of earth turning away from the sun."

[13] Lev 23:6,23–25.

[14] J. W. McKay, "The Date of the Passover and Its Significance," *ZAW* 84 (1972): 435–47.

[15] The NIV has chosen, as do most modern Eng. translations, to render שֶׂה as "lamb" simply for brevity. The translators follow this convention even though they are fully aware that the term actually denotes the young of either goats or sheep (cf. v. 5) because the phrase "lamb or goat kid" is regarded as literarily too awkward to employ regularly.

meat of that animal during the meal. That is the meaning of "share one with their nearest neighbor, having taken into account the number of people there are." This might produce some situations in which a rather large number of people, consuming a goat kid or lamb, might each get only a relatively small portion of meat to eat. But the alternative – meat left over, or someone being forced to gorge himself in order to finish off all the meat in one sitting – was strictly to be avoided. Thus the statement at the end of v. 4, "You are to determine the amount of lamb needed in accordance with what each person will eat," or as it might be more clearly translated, "You must calculate the amount of goat kid or lamb (meat) each person will eat relative to the number of people." The principle was thus: Everyone had to eat the meat, and all the meat had to be eaten.

Why not allow leftovers? Why not allow gorging? Subsidiary answers to these questions could include the concept of sharing and its benefits for creating a sense of solidarity among the Israelites and a guarantee that no one would miss out on sharing the *understanding* of why the meat was being eaten because they ate it isolated from the group setting in which the memorializing words and actions were rehearsed and appreciated by all.[16] But the greater value is in preparation for the Messiah. The Messiah was to be *one* body, broken for all, symbolically eaten by all,[17] in order to help believers in the New Covenant keep aware of their unity as members of the *one* body. Partial consumption and fragments left over do not appropriately symbolize that body and that unity. The ultimate purpose of the Old Testament Passover instruction is to point forward to Christ, to the purpose of his death, memorialized in the ritual of the Lord's Supper that now replaces the Passover, and also to the unity of those accepted by him as his people, his body.

12:5 The Passover animal may be either a goat kid or a lamb, but it must be young ("year-old"), male, and perfect ("without defect"). A year-old goat kid or lamb is a virtually full-grown animal. Since lambing and goat kidding took place in the spring in ancient times (before modern artificial breeding allowed for other lambing/kidding schedules) and the Passover took place in the spring, there is every reason to take literally the language indicating that the animal to be eaten would be a year old, not merely within its first year of life. In animal husbandry of meat stock all but a few breeding

---

[16] In other words, the discipline of group instruction as opposed to the subjectivity of individual thought processes.

[17] Thus Luke 22:17, "Take this and divide it among you" and the inclusion of Judas as one of the group even though he was about to betray the Lord (Luke 22:20–21). Note also Paul's deep concern for the divisions present in the Corinthian church (1 Cor 11:18–19) specifically in connection with the Lord's Supper (vv. 20–22). As in the case of the Passover meal on which the Lord's Supper symbolic meal is based, the believers are to portray their unity visibly by the way they eat—together and in the same proportions (1 Cor 11:33–34).

males are culled and eaten, but virtually all of the females are kept for breeding, milking,[18] It therefore makes sense that the Passover animal would be a male. That it should be of perfect quality is, however, an element specially designed for inculcating spiritual values into the observance. Lame, spotted, off-colored animals are just as tasty as perfect ones. The meat of an animal with a split ear or a blind eye is not affected by the defect. Thus the reason for demanding perfection rested not in the quality of the meal but in the symbolic purpose: the animal served as a reminder of the eventual deliverance that a perfect God perfectly provided for his people as part of the process of making them holy like himself. Proper relating to God requires perfection.

How, then, could an animal help provide perfection for those who consumed it so that they could become acceptable to God? The answer is that it could not, except to the extent that the whole process of eating the animal in obedience to the Passover regulations was an act of faith and obedience, involving faith in God's gracious provision of the holiness that no human could himself or herself provide and obedience to a process that showed confidence in the true God's true promises and requirements. From the vantage point of the full overview of the plan of redemption designed by God before he even created human beings,[19] Jesus of Nazareth was to be young at the time of his death, male of course, and perfect—free from defect before God. His sinlessness qualified him and him alone to be the lamb of God, a human lamb rather than an animal of the flock, and yet a lamb in the sense of one meeting the criteria for the Passover meal.

12:6 The animals chosen four days in advance (12:3) would be properly distributed to every family and kept healthy[20] ("take care of them") until the time of slaughter. This was to take place "at twilight" so that there would be enough light for the process of slaughter, which also involved skinning, removing entrails, tying up for spit roasting, laying the proper fire. The eating itself took place later, after nightfall (v. 8), when the moon was full (the fourteenth day being the middle of the twenty-eight day lunar cycle, thus the exact time of the full moon). So there was maximal nighttime light for gathering together and eating, and, as well, the timing would function in commemoration of the coming full moon nighttime flight from Egypt that characterized the exodus (vv. 11–13). In New Testament times, of course, the Passover was celebrated at this same time of the month, during the night (e.g., John 13:30) as it has always been in Judaism. The New Testament's "last supper" with Jesus and his disciples was a Passover meal.[21]

[18] Few people may realize that, e.g., when they eat "chicken" they are usually eating neutered rooster.

[19] Cf. Rev 13:8.

[20] They had to be healthy or could not serve as proper sacrificial animals.

[21] Luke 22:1,7,13,15–23.

12:7 This verse is slightly elliptical because in mentioning only "the houses where they eat the lambs,"[22] it leaves to the reader's sense of logic to realize that this also included dwelling places such as tents and included people who lived alone but who may have celebrated the Passover with their families, and the like. Far more importantly, the verse specifies the power of the shed blood of a sacrificial animal to protect God's people from death. The purpose of the display of the blood on the doorframes of the houses—top and sides—is described further in v. 13 and vv. 22–23, but one should appreciate the fact that an omniscient God would hardly need a sign to know which people had been faithful to him and which had not. The sign therefore was presumably at least as much for the benefit of those who were to provide it, to require them to undertake an action that involved more than mere ideation, but one demonstrating their confidence in God's power to kill as well as to rescue. In this regard it is somewhat analogous to the action required in the plague of hail: those who believed enough to take preemptive measures kept their livestock; those who did not lost them (9:20–21). A dwelling's doorway is its interface with the outside world. There is nothing sacred or symbolic about the doorframe of a house, but there is also no better location to place a sign showing faith on the part of those who reside inside for the benefit of anyone outside who comes to check.[23] Note that the blood was smeared on the doorframe even before the Passover meal was eaten; this may be an instance of first things first, that is, that deliverance from death is the primary interest of these instructions and proper memorializing of the exodus the less crucial concern.

The Israelites were required to eat the Passover in a manner that demonstrated their readiness to leave Egypt immediately. All aspects of the cooking and eating were designed to minimize time and maximize preparedness for sudden departure. This was an issue of faith: did the families of the Israelites really trust God's promises for them? If so, were they willing to show that trust by arranging themselves so as to be fully prepared for departure, and by eating what was to be their last meal in Egypt in such a manner as not to impede their ability to gather together and start moving as soon as the command reached them? The willingness to go at a moment's notice and never to return cannot have been easy for most Israelites, even though they initially believed Moses' signs (4:31), had witnessed the nine plagues thus far, and had been treated so badly for so long. After all, they had lived in Egypt for 430 years—a long time to acclimate culturally and geographically—and were now being asked to leave behind everything they had ever

[22] The literal meaning of הַבָּתִּים אֲשֶׁר־יֹאכְלוּ אֹתוֹ בָּהֶם is "the houses in which they eat it."

[23] Cf. T. Friedman, "The Blood of the Paschal Sacrifice on the Doorpost," *BMik* 92 (1982): 21–28.

known: the place where they had lived all their lives, where their parents and grandparents had lived and died, and where they had prospered until the paranoia of the post-Hyksos pharaohs had taken over. They were leaving the houses they had built and raised families in. Added to this, some people are simply more psychologically "territorial" than others. For them, going elsewhere is almost always harder than staying put and trying to survive. But now their faith was to be shown; now they were to gather as families to eat a quick meal of quickly prepared ingredients and then to depart quickly in order to get a head start on any potential Egyptian pursuit.

12:8–9 Roasting over a fire required no setup or washup of pots and other utensils, no additional drawing of water, and no waiting time for the water to boil; thus it was the fastest, simplest way to cook meat. Bitter herbs were the easiest to find and harvest and were eaten as a side dish either raw or seared, as opposed to more elaborate ways of preparing, mixing, and cooking vegetables. Bread made without yeast could be rapidly mixed and heated: the usual multihour waiting time for the dough to rise and the loaf to bake was cut to just minutes. Eating raw meat would have been even faster but both distasteful and dangerous to health; boiling the meat would have been both slower and more cumbersome and therefore inconsistent with the emphasis on speed and readiness inherent in the Passover concept. The inclusion of "inner parts" in the roasting does not mean the goat kid or lamb was roasted whole—but merely that it was gutted very simply and then roasted rapidly, as opposed to the usual full butchering and separation of the various organ meats for consumption in various ways and at various times.

12:10–11 Although cooked meat rapidly putrefies without refrigeration or preservation by salting the only preservation method known in the ancient world), it could certainly last "fresh" a good many hours during the spring nighttime coolness in northern Egypt. Therefore many Israelites might have been tempted to save some for breakfast. But this would have violated the symbolic sense of the meal, indicating that those who saved the meat both distrusted that God would provide for them the next day as they were on the run out of the country and that God's deliverance was an immediate, once-for-all rescue and sparing of his people. Accordingly, any remains as a result of miscalculation (see comments on 12:4) had to be burned once the meal was over. It was, in other words, more a meal of religious observance than a meal to provide sustenance over time. Dressing for travel also was important as another indication of faith that the long-promised deliverance was truly at hand. People tucked cloaks into belts when they traveled; they kept cloaks on loose and full length at night for warmth and comfort.[24] Sandals normally were taken off at home; with this meal they were worn in the house,

[24] Cf. Exod 22:26–27; Deut 24:13. Note that both men and women wore cloaks (Deut 24:17).

because a trip was imminent. No one carried his staff around the house; it was a tool for protection and herding in the open (see "Excursus: Moses' Staff" at 4:14–17). A staff in the hand normally indicated readiness to be on the move, not a plan to stay at home. Thus the entire meal and its manner and posture of consumption were to indicate faithful readiness for a speedy departure. It was a meal eaten "in haste, . . . the Lord's Passover"—not a typical meal at all but God's specially assigned symbolic meal of exodus deliverance.

(2) Description of Passover Death, Judgment on the Gods of Egypt, and the Protection of the Blood (12:12–13)

12"On that same night I will pass through Egypt and strike down every firstborn—both men and animals—and I will bring judgment on all the gods of Egypt. I am the LORD. 13The blood will be a sign for you on the houses where you are; and when I see the blood, I will pass over you. No destructive plague will touch you when I strike Egypt.

12:12–13 This precise description of the tenth plague reveals that it would take place in a matter of hours at most ("on that same night"),[25] would affect the firstborn of all Egyptian humans and livestock, would be averted from homes that displayed the Passover blood on their doors as a sign of faithful obedience to God, would be a divine strike against Egypt, and—above all—would constitute "judgment on all the gods of Egypt." The blood on the doorposts showed acceptance of God's plan for rescue and trust in his word. After all, the sight of dried blood by itself had no power to deter death; it was only as the dried blood painted on the top and sides of the door was a testimony to the faith of the inhabitants in Yahweh that it had its efficacy. Thus the statement, "When I see the blood, I will pass over you"[26]—in other words, I will spare all those who show that they have placed their faith in me.

Excursus: Judgment on the "Gods of Egypt"

Who were the "gods of Egypt," and how did a plague that killed the firstborn of men and animals function as judgment against them? As we have already suggested at several points, Exod 12:12 makes clearest of all to the reader of the plague stories what the purpose of the plagues really was.[27] By the plagues God

---

[25] The Hb. says lit., "this night." In fact, the death of the firstborn was apparently virtually instantaneous, in light of 12:29, which says that it took place "at midnight."

[26] וּפָסַחְתִּי עֲלֵכֶם could also be translated "I will skip over you," using the common Eng. expression "skip," which can mean "to move around in a certain kind of hopping motion" and "to bypass"—a range of meaning similar to that of the Hb. verb פסח.

[27] Cf. B. Ramm, "A Theology of the Book of Exodus: A Reflection on Exodus 12:12," *SwJT* 20 (1977): 59–68.

demonstrated his superiority to all the supposed other gods, and by demonstrating that superiority in connection with the supposed gods of the greatest economic-political-military power of the day, God showed his sovereignty, *mutatis mutandis,* over all the nations of the earth and their "gods." This was an evangelistic enterprise. God's purpose was not to show off, as if he needed attention, or to prove himself to others, as if he were insecure. Rather, he is, as he has always been, a saving God who delights in rescuing human beings from captivity—sometimes captivity of a political, economic, or social sort but, far more importantly, from captivity to sin, which brings death. God desires all people to come to a saving knowledge of the truth,[28] and a large part of that truth is the fact that he is the only actual God and that faith in him is the only faith that accomplishes salvation and provides eternal life. The Egyptians were devoted to their gods and trusted them fully. The Israelites during their 430-year sojourn in Egypt probably had picked up much of that same attitude toward the Egyptian gods. Since such gods could not save, it was appropriate for God to dissuade those who would sincerely seek the truth from holding to a belief system that would guarantee their ultimate destruction. A good God therefore made sure that the belief system of the Egyptians, and for that matter all pagan cultures by logical extension, was exposed as fraudulent and foolish. Since trust in a variety of gods was at the heart of that belief system, exposing a variety of gods as nothings, unable to save, unable to grant life, and unable to defend Egypt and the Egyptians against the God of the Hebrews was a convincing method of forcing people to look elsewhere than their discredited gods for salvation. To evangelize is to turn people away from the bad news (no matter how attractive it might look) and toward the good news, and if that can be accomplished by dramatically and decisively exposing the bad news as truly bad and obviously false, the reality of the good news has opportunity to sink into the consciousness of those who witness the sort of events the Egyptians and Israelites did in the case of the plagues.

The Egyptians were pantheists, as most ancient and many modern people were/are as well. Pantheism is a belief system in which all nature is thought to partake of the divine: anything that exists is a manifestation of, or a part of, or an extension of, a god. To see, or touch, or hear, or taste is to come in contact with a god because all things are in some way *essentially* part of a god or goddess. Therefore, if something is *judged* anywhere in nature, that is a judgment on at least one god. And, by logical extension, ten or eleven supernatural acts of judgment showing control over ten or eleven different aspects of nature represent multiple judgment strikes against Egyptian religion (and ancient pagan religion as a whole).

The Egyptians were also polytheists, as were all ancient peoples other than the Israelites (i.e., the Israelites at those relatively rare times when they were actually orthodox and keeping the divine covenant). The Egyptian saw the universe as the habitation and expression of many gods and goddesses. Although from the point of view of a monotheist it might have been possible for a single, decisive plague to demonstrate Yahweh's superiority to all other gods, from the

[28] 1 Tim 2:4.

point of view of a polytheist this might not have been quite so clear. A polytheist might easily conclude that a single plague was in fact a judgment against one god, but ten plagues of different sorts could hardly be understood that way. Since polytheism envisions many gods performing a great variety of functions, ten different sorts of plagues showing God's control over a variety of functions within the natural realm serve to display the fact that the many gods *in general* do not have power against the one God in whose name Moses and Aaron spoke. Repeated exposures of various Egyptian gods as powerless makes rather clear that all such gods should be suspect as the mere product of human belief.

Moreover, consider the purpose of gods. What were the gods expected to do for those who worshiped them? What did the worshipers expect as the overall, basic, essential outcome of their devotion to the various gods and goddesses? The answer is that the worship of many gods had as its foremost goal to provide life. The gods were seen, above all, as the grantors of life and protectors of the living. To ignore the gods was to be in danger of ignoring the forces that provided life, the sustainers of existence. The gods, each in their particular ways, sustained the lives of those who worshiped them. The plagues, appropriately, were largely focused on death. Nearly all of them actually resulted in death (in the first nine, that of the plants or animals afflicted by or used by God as agents of the plague). The tenth and final plague was the ultimate one—and fittingly, it was the plague of death, showing that the gods, both severally and totally, of any sort and any status, could not save anyone or anything from death. If God can take the life of the firstborn, he can take the life of anyone regardless of birth order. If every household in Egypt was affected by the death that constituted this plague, then every household in Egypt should have been able to understand who held the power of life and death and who, by implication, did not. The gods did not. Yahweh did.

But false gods are false, are they not? The Egyptian gods were really figments of the imagination of those who thought them up and fashioned idols to represent them, were they not? How then could God speak of judging these gods? Was that not to give them a status in reality, to assert their existence?

Indeed, false gods do not exist. They are not demons by another name, fallen angels with real power, doing real things.[29] The consistent witness of Scripture is that they are nothings, nonbeings, imaginary deities from whom no response can ever be expected because they do not exist. Therefore, "judgment on the gods of Egypt" is practically speaking a judgment on *belief in those gods*, trusting in what cannot save as opposed to the only one who can. Exodus 12:12 is worded in a way designed to help capture the attention of those who actually thought, or might actually think, that what the Egyptians worshiped were real. In fact, judgment on the gods of Egypt, accompanied by their complete silence, is evidence

[29] Paul's statement in 1 Cor 10:20–21 is often wrongly read as if he were saying that false gods/idols had real power because they represented demons, something he directly said is not the case in 1 Cor 10:19, immediately preceding. Paul's point was that idol/false god worship plays directly into the hands of Satan and his fallen angels, honoring them and dishonoring the true God.

that they never existed. From one point of view, it is dismissal of their existence as nonsense.

Note how 12:2 concludes with the words "I am the LORD." This simple statement, found in many other places in the Old Testament, is part of the language of God's covenant with Israel. As it is used in a context like Exod 12:12, it is a reminder formula, intended to recall the language of the preamble of the covenant[30] and thus what would technically be called a reference by *incipit* to the covenant as a whole. God was in effect saying by these words: "I'm doing something here that is basic to my (soon to be fully revealed) covenant with you. I'm showing you whom you must pay sole attention to and who alone can save you and grant you blessing—if you keep my covenant. I'm making sure by dramatic and decisive means that you cannot miss the fact that I alone am life and truth for you. Pay attention to no other gods. I have powerfully demonstrated to you that they don't exist. I have also demonstrated to you what happens to people who think they do. Trust me alone and you'll have made the choice from which everything else important follows."

2. God's Instructions for Passover Memorial of Unleavened Bread (12:14–20)

14"This is a day you are to commemorate; for the generations to come you shall celebrate it as a festival to the LORD—a lasting ordinance. 15For seven days you are to eat bread made without yeast. On the first day remove the yeast from your houses, for whoever eats anything with yeast in it from the first day through the seventh must be cut off from Israel. 16On the first day hold a sacred assembly, and another one on the seventh day. Do no work at all on these days, except to prepare food for everyone to eat—that is all you may do.

17"Celebrate the Feast of Unleavened Bread, because it was on this very day that I brought your divisions out of Egypt. Celebrate this day as a lasting ordinance for the generations to come. 18In the first month you are to eat bread made without yeast, from the evening of the fourteenth day until the evening of the twenty-first day. 19For seven days no yeast is to be found in your houses. And whoever eats anything with yeast in it must be cut off from the community of Israel, whether he is an alien or native-born. 20Eat nothing made with yeast. Wherever you live, you must eat unleavened bread."

A considerable amount of repetition occurs in this passage, with the effect that the instructions of 12:14–16 are closely paralleled by the instructions of 12:17–20. The latter is not an exact repetition of the former, but it

[30] Thus "I am the LORD" occurs for the very first time in the OT at the point of the introductory preamble to the Abrahamic covenant in Gen 15:7 and for the second time at its reiteration in Gen 28:13, as well as in the preamble to the entire Sinai covenant (Exod 20:2) and in Deut 5:6, the parallel position in the Deuteronomy restatement. "I am the LORD" occurs 155 times in the OT, with virtually all occurrences functioning in one way or another to recall or allude to or anticipate God's divine covenant with his people.

contains many similarities. Thus the features of the Passover memorial of unleavened bread are stated twice, as a means of drilling into the mind of the hearer/reader the point: absolutely no yeasted bread could be eaten for the seven full days of the special Passover festival. To prevent even the slightest possibility that any sort of bread or breaded food in the house would become yeasted accidentally, all yeast had to be removed from all Israelite homes during the week-long festival.[31]

12:14 In saying "this is a day you are to commemorate" God did not slight the full seven-day festival as if it were not also to be commemorated equally; rather, the *starting* day was a crucial one. If the starting day was missed, then observing the rest of the days could not entirely make up for the loss of the one that specifically aligned with the day the Israelites actually left Egypt, the fourteenth of the first month at the full moon. The terms "for generations to come" and "as a lasting ordinance" provide two more supporting concepts linked to the concept of *commemorate*. It was very important that each subsequent generation renew for itself an awareness of the original Passover and its meaning.[32] It was "a festival to the LORD," thus a special and solemn religious celebration intended by its nonordinary character to focus attention on this memorable event every year. Why such an emphasis on commemoration? Because what is not carefully remembered by a community is very naturally and easily forgotten—and virtually completely forgotten as soon as the oldest members of that community who experienced the original event die. The full seven-day festival was not celebrated by the Israelites on the occasion of the first exodus as they actually fled from Egypt. They had experienced the exodus personally. It was clearly for generations to come, who had not been there to know God's salvation directly. Why did God want his people to remember the exodus so carefully? Because it was his supreme Old Covenant demonstration of deliverance, and he wanted his people to trust him as a delivering God. It was no accident that Moses, Elijah, and Jesus, on the Mount of Transfiguration, "spoke about his [Christ's] departure ["exodus"], which he was about to bring to fulfillment at Jerusalem" (Luke 9:31). The Old Covenant exodus was the paradigm of God's saving acts; the New Testament crucifixion was the ultimate exodus because it delivers not merely from bondage to human despotism but from bondage to sin itself, and thus it provides for life not merely in a promised earthly land but in an eternal promised land, the home of the Father.

12:15 Yeast (*śĕʾôr*, "leaven") in Bible times referred to the spores of yeast themselves, and, as well, what is now called "starter dough," that is, fermented

[31] Most yeasts can be airborne and can migrate to and grow within any dough not tightly sealed from the air, so this prohibition is not an example of excessive caution but of logical caution.

[32] Cf. P. R. Ackroyd, "The Meaning of Hebrew *DOR* Considered," *JSS* 13 (1968): 3–10.

dough. It was made in various ways. One was by airing out dough in the sun (to pick up the airborne yeast spores) after dipping it in wine or vinegar and storing it in a closed vessel until it went sour (fermented). Another method was to knead flour and water, add salt, boil the mix into a porridge, and then leave it until it went sour.[33] Because yeast spores can migrate easily, dough can easily become yeasted naturally, thus the need to cleanse the house of yeast so that what was intended to be unleavened bread doesn't turn out accidentally to be leavened. But why require eating unleavened bread as the special focus of the exodus memorial meal, the Passover? The answer is that unleavened bread was the unique food of the original exodus, the event God wanted his people to be sure not to forget. People everywhere normally eat leavened bread. It tastes better, is more pleasant to eat, is more filling. Leavened bread was the normal choice of the Israelites in Egypt too. But on the night they ran, there was no time for the usual niceties—a fast meal had to be eaten, and hastily made bread had to be consumed. The fact that a lamb or goat kid was roasted for the meat portion of the meal or that bitter herbs were eaten as a side dish was not nearly so special or unusual as the fact that the bread was unleavened, thus essentially forming sheets of cracker. Eating it at the memorial feast intentionally recalled the original departure in haste. Eating it for a solid week tended to fix the idea in one's consciousness. But was cheating—eating "anything with yeast in it from the first day through the seventh"—really worthy of such punishment that the offender "must be cut off from Israel"? The answer once again relates to the way actions indicate faith. God had declared that the action of smearing blood on doorframes was the sign of faith he would accept in order to avoid death in a household; now he declared that eating the Passover with its special, nonyeasted bread was the sign of faith that indicated a person was keeping the Passover as a believer in its meaning and therefore a true member of the covenant community of Israel.

Excursus: The Meaning of "Cut off From"

The expression found in Exod 12:15, "cut off from Israel," and its variants "cut off from the congregation of Israel" (12:19), "cut off from his people" (Exod 30:33,38), and "cut off from among his people" (31:14) has several dozen parallels throughout the Old Testament, a sizable percentage of them being found in Leviticus and Numbers. The wording sounds like a prescription for either banishment or execution, and the NIV translators obviously assumed that it was,[34] in

[33] Pliny the Elder provides a complete description of the various processes for producing yeast in his *Natural History* 18.26.

[34] The NIV translators have many allies in the assumption that וְנִכְרְתָה means "must be cut off [by the community via its legal process]." Most scholars do not seem to think that execution of the guilty person is actually intended. Among those suggesting that the penalty refers only to banishment are J. Morgenstern, "The Book of the Covenant, III," *HUCA* 8–9 (1931–32): 47–48; and G. von Rad, *Old Testament Theology* (New York: Harper & Row, 1962), 1:264.

light of their use of the modal verb "must be" instead of "shall be" in 12:15 and elsewhere. In other words, "must be cut off" as the translation of the Hebrew expression in question, *wĕnikrĕtāh*, tends to connote the idea that it was the responsibility of the community of Israel to get rid of the offender either by exile or by capital punishment. But if the proper contextual translation of *wĕnikrĕtāh* is simply "will be cut off," as we suggest, the expression would be more a statement of fact—this would be the eventual outcome for the person who committed this violation of God's law. An appropriate paraphrase might be: "God will see to it that this person is cut off." It was thus more of a divine curse than a legal guideline.

What then would "cut off from" Israel/the congregation/his people actually mean? The answer appears to be cut off from God's benefits to Israel in the near future and cut off from eternal life with them in the ultimate future.[35] It is somewhat a question of self-selection. The person who defies God's regulations shows that he has no interest in keeping covenant with him and therefore will eventually suffer the consequences of not obeying God. Refusing to keep the Passover regulation of unleavened bread for seven days (something that is not very hard to keep, after all) would show God that a person was not with him in faith because faith is demonstrated by faithfulness. Lack of faithfulness in trying to obey God's commands shows lack of saving faith in God. The proof of faith is a faithful life.

A rather wide variety of commands are accompanied by the warning that those who do not adhere to them will be "cut off." Propp[36] lists the following (here rearranged in canonical order): failure to practice circumcision (Gen 17:14); failure to eat unleavened bread during Passover (Exod 12:15,19); illegally manufacturing or using the sacred anointing oil (Exod 30:32–33,38); violating the Sabbath (Exod 31:14); eating sacrificed food while ritually impure (Lev 7:20–21); eating the fat or blood of a sacrifice (Lev 7:25,27); slaughter/sacrifice outside the tabernacle (Lev 17:4,9); forbidden sexual practices (Lev 18:29; 20:17–18); child sacrifice (Lev 20:2–5); necromancy (trying to divine the future by contact with the dead; Lev 20:6); worship function by a defiled priest (Lev 22:3); failure to observe the Day of Atonement (Lev 23:29–30); failure to commemorate Passover (Num 9:13); defiant, intentional sin (Num 15:30–31); and failure to purify oneself after contact with the dead (Num 19:13,20).[37] Of these the most telling is that of Num 15:30–31:

---

[35] According to C. Brichto ("Kin, Cult, Land and Afterlife—A Biblical Complex," *HUCA* 44 [1974]: 25, 37) being "cut off" means being "alienated" from the "kin-cult-land-afterlife complex." Cf. also S. A. Loewenstamm, "*Karet, hikkaret,*" *Ensiqlopia Miqra'it* 4.330–332 (Jerusalem: Bialik Institute, 1962), 330; J. Milgrom, *Leviticus 1–16*, AB (Garden City: Doubleday, 1991), 457–60; D. J. Wold, "The Meaning of the Biblical Penalty *Kareth* (Ph.D. diss., University of California, Berkeley, 1978).

[36] W. H. C. Propp, *Exodus 1–18,* AB (New York: Doubleday, 1998), 403–4.

[37] The concept of being cut off from one's people is not, however, limited to OT passages. It has a special sense in the OT, but the concept itself, related through various terminologies, is found widely in the ANE. See D. J. Wold, "The Meaning of the Biblical Penalty *Kareth* (Ph.D. diss., University of California, Berkeley, 1978), 4–7, 17–34.

> But anyone who sins defiantly, whether native-born or alien, blasphemes the LORD, and that person must be cut off from his people. Because he has despised the LORD's word and broken his commands, that person must surely be cut off; his guilt remains on him.

This is describing not an occasional intentional sin but what was at the heart of all abuses of the law that bring about being "cut off": a level of disobedience that constituted blasphemy, a defiance that indicates that the person despised God's word. That was the sort of person who could not be counted among the faithful in Israel, who had by his actions shown clearly that he did not desire to keep covenant with the true God. Such a person loses out on God's covenant benefits in this life and his eternal blessing as well. John words the matter this way in his Gospel: "This is the verdict: Light has come into the world, but men loved darkness instead of light because their deeds were evil" (John 3:19). One's choices have consequences relative to one's relationship to God. The covenant relationship does not overlook individual sin simply because it is a corporate covenant.

In summary: the statement that a person would be cut off from Israel was not juridical guidance for those enforcing laws but a prediction from God of the fate of the unfaithful. Not to be faithful is not to belong to God's people even if living among them (cf. Rom 2:28–29) and therefore not to enjoy their covenant blessings in the long run.

12:16 The two days at the beginning and end of the festival week were special; on them no work was done other than the most essential, which was food preparation so people could eat. These were days of "sacred assembly," in other words, days devoted to worship. The term here translated assembly is *miqrāʾ,* lit., "calling together," also translatable by the English word "convocation." The same term is used to describe the Sabbath in Lev 23:3, the Day of Trumpets in Lev 23:24, and both the New Moon and Sabbath festivals in Isa 1:13. Regular work is the antithesis of special worship. This is not because daily work is improper or ungodly but because the specialness of God cannot be honored sufficiently in the regularity of daily work. God seeks special attention from his people in ways that are not within the routine of their usual labors. Worship is intended to be a group enterprise conducted apart from the routine. The two special worship days, however, were *not* fast days. They were days of celebration and commemoration in worship, so food preparation and consumption were necessary in connection with them and must be provided for accordingly.

12:17 This verse reiterates the importance of celebrating the Passover feast properly and does so in two ways: first, by offering an alternative name for it: "The Feast of Unleavened Bread"; second, by emphasizing the timing of the feast: "It was on this very day that I brought your divisions [armies] out of Egypt." Elsewhere the name of the feast is usually the fuller *ḥag̱ hammaṣṣôt* ("Feast of Unleavened Bread"), but here it is titled only by its key word, *hammaṣṣôt,* [the] unleavened bread. Nevertheless, in light of the full formula *Observe* [NIV "celebrate"] *the Unleavened Bread*[38] and its parallels in Exodus laws commanding the observance of festivals and rites (12:24; 23:15; 31:13–4,16; 34:18), there can be little doubt that the festival, not merely the substance (unleavened bread), was to be *observed.*

The reference to the Israelites being organized into an army—God's army, implied in the words "your divisions" [armies][39]—is not new but harkens back to Exod 6:26 and 7:4. It reminds the hearer/reader that the Passover meal had overtones not only of haste in fleeing but of ready preparedness for battle. The Israelites were not merely leaving a place; they were also going to a place they would have to conquer militarily on God's behalf. The language at the end of the verse, "as a lasting ordinance for the generations to come," picks up the vocabulary of v. 14 as a further way of emphasizing how important the permanent memorializing of the exodus through the Passover had to be.

12:18 Lest there be any confusion in the mind of the hearer/reader as to the actual calendar dates for the seven days of observance of the Passover, the dates are here given for eating "bread made without yeast" as taking place "in the first month . . . from the evening of the fourteenth day until the evening of the twenty-first day." There is no new information here compared to v. 15 but simply a rewording with precise calendrical coordinates to reinforce the time of observance.[40]

12:19–20 These verses reword and expand slightly on v. 15, adding mainly the clarification that "whoever" applies to everyone "whether he is an alien or native-born" and that the law has no spatial or geographical limitation ("Wherever you live, you must eat unleavened bread"). Thus future generations of God's people were not to make the mistake of excluding relative newcomers who wanted to show their covenant loyalty to their (newly accepted) Lord merely because those persons were not yet accepted as Israelite citizens;[41] neither was anyone to feel entitled to an exemption from full observance because he or she was far away from the land of Israel proper or living in isolation from other Israelites.

---

[38] וּשְׁמַרְתֶּם אֶת־הַמַּצּוֹת.

[39] See note on 6:26.

[40] In Lev 23:5–6 and Num 28:16–17 the evening meal celebration is differentiated from the seven-day Feast of Unleavened Bread in the sense that the Passover meal is eaten on the night of the fourteenth of the month and the Feast of Unleavened Bread begins on the day of the fifteenth. This seems to be nothing more than a way of clarifying for priests and worshipers alike what happens when the first day off from work follows the evening of the eating the Passover meal and the seventh day, also off from work, comes in due sequence. Another way of saying this is that in the Leviticus and Numbers descriptions, the Passover meal is linked to the nighttime and the Feast of Unleavened Bread to the daytime. Thus "this day" in Exod 12:15 must refer to the daytime after the night on which the Passover is eaten.

[41] E.g., first- or second-generation converts from foreign people groups; cf. Deut 23:7–8.

3. Moses Teaches the Israelites to Follow the Passover Instructions (12:21–28)

[21]Then Moses summoned all the elders of Israel and said to them, "Go at once and select the animals for your families and slaughter the Passover lamb. [22]Take a bunch of hyssop, dip it into the blood in the basin and put some of the blood on the top and on both sides of the doorframe. Not one of you shall go out the door of his house until morning. [23]When the LORD goes through the land to strike down the Egyptians, he will see the blood on the top and sides of the doorframe and will pass over that doorway, and he will not permit the destroyer to enter your houses and strike you down.

[24]"Obey these instructions as a lasting ordinance for you and your descendants. [25]When you enter the land that the LORD will give you as he promised, observe this ceremony. [26]And when your children ask you, 'What does this ceremony mean to you?' [27]then tell them, 'It is the Passover sacrifice to the LORD, who passed over the houses of the Israelites in Egypt and spared our homes when he struck down the Egyptians.'" Then the people bowed down and worshiped. [28]The Israelites did just what the LORD commanded Moses and Aaron.

All the instructions in 12:1–20 were for the Israelites but had so far been announced only to Moses and Aaron (12:1). Now Moses repeated them for the Israelites by telling them to the elders, who would be expected to pass them on to the various clan leaders, and from them to the family heads, until everyone knew them and followed them. The instructions are therefore abbreviated here since the reader does not need a verbatim repetition of 12:1–20;[42] but Moses also added clarifying warnings and instructions to be sure the process would be followed carefully so that no one would die needlessly. As before, the instructions were intended both to direct the actions of the Israelites who were there on that first night of the exodus as well as for the benefit of all Israelites in all years thereafter who must carefully remember and identify with the significance of that first night when the tenth plague launched the exodus itself.

12:21 "Elder" *(zāqēn)* may also be translated "leader," for the term has little to do with age (that is only its original or root derivation rather than its functional usage) and everything to do with status as a leader. The last time the Israelite leaders were mentioned in the narrative was 4:29–31 when the *elders,* followed by the people in general, believed the miraculous signs Moses performed and thus believed in and worshiped the true God. A similar outcome is described here, particularly in vv. 27b–28. But what a great deal had happened in between! The Israelite foremen, presumably representing the views of many if not most Israelites, had denounced Moses and Aaron (5:19–21), and then the Israelites in

---

[42] Thus this is not the sort of context that requires complete or substantially complete repetition as a strict command-fulfillment context would (see comments on 35:4ff.).

general had joined them, refusing to listen to Moses because of the way their treatment had worsened once Moses began confronting Pharaoh with God's demands (6:9,12). What is not said thereafter, but may be safely assumed, is that this attitude gradually but definitely changed with each successive plague, as the Israelites were spared and the Egyptians humiliated. Now Israel was ready to obey because the alternative would be sheer folly: ignoring the commands of the God who had proved himself once for all not only real and not only interested in them but supreme over all forces that might prevent them from enjoying his blessing. Moses told them to round up[43] and "select" the animals appropriate for the Passover meal and then to slaughter them. These instructions probably were delivered on the tenth day of the month (cf. 12:3), that is, four days before the Passover so as to provide time for the whole process, but it is also possible that the time was now the actual day before the evening of departure in light of the way 12:29 seems to closely follow chronologically upon 12:28. If the Israelites were already gathered, ready for the exodus, and awaiting instructions, warning of a matter of hours would be sufficient for the community to act as instructed.

12:22 This verse repeats the essence of 12:7 with the added detail that a container ("basin") was to be used to collect the blood of the slaughtered lamb or goat kid, that a "hyssop" (marjoram) branch could be used for smearing the blood on the doorframe, and that once the blood was applied and the meal was over, no one was to go outside for the remainder of the night until dawn. These provisions were intended to make sure that an adequate supply of blood was collected (thus the basin), that it was well distributed on the tops and sides of the door (thus the use of a "brush"[44] as applicator; cf. the comparable use of hyssop in distributing blood in Lev 14:4; Num 19:6,18; Ps 51:7),[45] and that no one accidentally be at an Egyptian's house or anywhere among the Egyptians when the tenth plague struck (thus the confinement in the house).

12:23 Some of what is stated in this verse may seem enigmatic. Why should God himself "go through the land to strike down the Egyptians"? Did God need to get up close to a house before he could "see the blood on the top and sides of the doorframe and pass over that doorway"? And who or what was the "destroyer" that had to be told not "to enter your houses and strike you down"?

The answers to these questions may be understood as follows: First, God had already been identified as the direct cause of all the preceding plagues.

---

[43] The NIV translation "Go at once" is not consistent with any attested meaning of מָשַׁךְ, which normally means "seize, carry away, pull, drag, stretch out." Some lexicographers have thought that it could have the sense of "go" or "go off" in some contexts, but "go at once" is another sense entirely. "Round up" gives the sense in the present context.

[44] See G. Rinaldi, "Sull'uso di *ʾgdh (ʾaguddah)* nell'AT," *BeO* 27 (1985): 202–4.

[45] Cf. G. M. Crowfoot and L. Baldensperger, "Hyssop," *PEQ* 63 (1931): 89–98.

They were not merely events that he set in motion at some early stage or natural events generally subject to his control. So it was with the death of the wicked. In this world that God has created, human life does not just happen by accident, and no one's death is a random event. The Judge of all the earth always does right (Gen 18:25). And he is *the* Judge, the one directly and expressly involved. He personally saves every individual who places faith in him, and he personally oversees the ending of the existence of everyone whose life has not conformed to his will. He is not a deistic god but a personal God who relates personally, directly, and continually to his creation. Consistent with his nature and with the pattern already established in the plague accounts, God here personally oversaw the destruction of the Egyptian firstborn.

As to the matter of his seeing the blood on the doorframes, this is merely consistent with all the language used of God's perception of human activity.[46] He doesn't need to get up close; but he does see and deliver—personally—firstborn by firstborn, family by family. The "destroyer" could be none other than the Angel of the Lord, revealed as the angel that causes death in such contexts as 2 Sam 24:16 and Isa 37:36. This angel directly represents God and is thus "the Angel Yahweh"—Yahweh manifesting himself in angelic form.[47] God *personally* spared those who showed their trust in him by keeping the Passover regulations. He restrained the angel that would otherwise manifest his *personal* judgment against his enemies.

12:24–28 The Israelites were to understand the Passover regulations as permanent, binding requirements for all generations into the future (v. 24, "lasting ordinance for you and your descendants"), including all those who would eventually occupy the land of Canaan (v. 25). Each generation of parents also was expected to teach each generation of children the meaning of the ceremony that memorialized the deliverance from Egypt[48] (vv. 26–27). As

---

[46] See D. K. Stuart, "God's Cognition of Human Activity in the Deuteronomic History" (B.A. thesis, Harvard College, 1964). There is no good way to describe God's perception of events aside from using language associated with describing human perception of events. No culture has a separate perception vocabulary for the divine that is entirely distinct from that employed in connection with human cognition. To employ the kinds of terms that one would employ in speaking of mere humans in the fashion of an analogy when speaking of God represents "necessary anthropomorphism" or "unavoidable anthropomorphism." The alternative would be to speak of God as if he were a thing rather than a person since only language used of persons can convey the sense of God's personhood in a satisfactorily accurate manner.

[47] See the excursus at 3:2.

[48] Partly in contradiction to this evidence, G. dell'Orto argues that Moses' instructions in 12:1–13:16, esp. 12:23, do not contain the sort of definitive explanation about how the Passover was to function as an annual ritual slaughter that would suggest it was something new to the Israelites. In dell'Orto's opinion the Passover practice must have been a preexisting ritual slaughter the Israelites had grown up with in Egypt and were already well familiar with by the time of the exodus ("L'origine della pasqua," *Parole di Vita* 3 [1997]: 4–9). But the elaborate care with which the ceremony is described in chaps. 12–13 would suggest the opposite conclusion—that something already familiar to the people would hardly be given sixty-six verses of explanation, but a life-saving practice newly introduced to the people would indeed command such a large percentage of the text.

with other biblical law, the paradigmatic nature of the command automatically applies.[49] In other words, no Israelite parent could ever rightly say, "None of my children asked me about the point of the Passover ceremony, so I didn't tell them about what it means." Instead, the instruction to teach the upcoming generations the Passover tradition and law by responding to a child's question is simply a wording of *one instance* of how the teaching might occur; but occur it must. And the entire matter certainly was perceived as a command—not just the keeping of the Passover ceremony but the immediate instruction of children—as indicated by the observation in v. 27 that "the people bowed down and worshiped" as well as by the summation in v. 28 that "the Israelites did just what the LORD commanded Moses and Aaron."

From the point of view of the greater sweep of biblical revelation, the practice of teaching each new generation the meaning of the Passover helped guarantee the transmission of the *proto evangelium* throughout the historical continuum of the people of Israel until New Testament times, when the human-divine Lamb was slain once for all[50] as part of the divine plan of redemption set in place before the earth as we know it existed.[51] In other words, every Israelite properly instructed about the Passover should have been also partly prepared to expect a dying Messiah whose shed blood would provide a means of escape from death. It also contains something of a model of the biblical emphasis on the importance of parents' teaching children—a responsibility well understood before the advent of universal education but often neglected in present times in favor of professionalized education.[52]

The summation in v. 28 is the first of several (cf. 12:20; 39:32; Num 1:54; 8:3,20,22; 9:5) that relate to the establishment of ongoing worship practices (most of the others concern the construction and use of the tabernacle). The action of the people in v. 27 in bowing down and worshiping follows closely the similar act described in 4:31, where both the Israelite elders and the people in general indicated their belief in Yahweh's promise, their acceptance of Yahweh's rescue plan and a commitment to agree to participate in the exodus that would soon be taking place. Bowing and worshiping[53] says "I submit, I agree, I cooperate."

---

[49] See "Excursus: The Paradigmatic Nature of Biblical Law" at 20:1.

[50] Rom 6:10; Heb 7:27; 9:12,26; 10:10; 1 Pet 3:18.

[51] Rev 13:8; cf. 1 Pet 1:20.

[52] I.e., professionalized even in the church, where some parents delegate virtually all Christian education to Sunday School teachers, at the risk of not making sure personally that their children are properly and fully taught the essentials of the faith. Cf. Deut 11:19.

[53] The two Hb. verbs (השתחוה, קדד) normally occur together (fifteen times) and constitute a hendiadys, the sense of which is to "submit worshipfully" or the like. In fact, קדד never occurs by itself but always with השתחוה. But the latter occurs independently, without קדד, in some contexts.

4. The Tenth Plague Strikes: Death of the Firstborn (12:29–30)

[29]At midnight the LORD struck down all the firstborn in Egypt, from the firstborn of Pharaoh, who sat on the throne, to the firstborn of the prisoner, who was in the dungeon, and the firstborn of all the livestock as well. [30]Pharaoh and all his officials and all the Egyptians got up during the night, and there was loud wailing in Egypt, for there was not a house without someone dead.

The actual description of the tenth and most destructive plague is relatively brief, in keeping with the pattern established in the earlier plague accounts, where the description of what was to happen often is given more space than the description of what did happen. Verbatim command-fulfillment style was something Moses was well capable of using when appropriate,[54] but here, in two relatively simple verses, the horrible consequences of Egyptian resistance to God and abuse of his people over many years came to pass during a single night.

12:29 The firstborn died at midnight (or "in the middle of the night" as *ḥăṣî hallaylāh* could also be translated), apparently suddenly and all at once, stuck down directly by the Lord himself. The verse confirms what 12:12 predicted, in conformity with the overview of how the plagues would conclude that was revealed to Moses in 4:22–23 and consistent with the warning Moses had given to Pharaoh in 11:5. At that point in the story (11:5), Moses listed as sample deaths to come that of Pharaoh's firstborn, the slave/servant girl's firstborn, and the cattle's firstborn. Here the list is the same except that "the prisoner, who was in the dungeon" is substituted for "the slave [servant] girl who is at her hand mill." The difference has no significance beyond stylistic variation: both lists say, in effect, "from the greatest to the least to even the cattle."

The first oppressive pharaoh (1:8) had, with the complicity of his fellow Egyptians at all levels (see comments on 1:22) caused the death of all Israelite baby boys in every family (1:16,22), not because the boys had done anything to deserve death but because it was his brutal way of trying to suppress the power of the nation into which they had been born. Now the pharaoh of the plagues, his son/daughter or grandson/granddaughter,[55] and the children and/or grandchildren of the original oppressing generation experienced a corresponding disaster, the death of the firstborn in every family. This was not a case, however, of returning evil for evil. It was a case of divine retribution, justice meted out to those who deserved it, a judgment against an entire society and their absurd religious beliefs that led them to practice the horrible

[54] See the comments on the tabernacle construction guidelines and their verbatim fulfillment at 25:1–7 and 35:4–9 and thereafter.

[55] For a discussion of how "firstborn" need not mean firstborn son but can include female children as well, see comments on 11:5.

treatment they had given the Israelites in the past, thinking it appropriate. Evil for evil would have been accomplished if the Israelites themselves had figured out a way to kill Egyptian babies after having come to a position of power over their former oppressors. God, not Israelites, did this killing of the Egyptian firstborn, however, and did so within the bounds of his righteous judgment against evildoers.

12:30 This verse need not be interpreted to suggest that all the Egyptians from greatest to least were awakened by some sort of sounds of firstborn children dying. The deaths may have been very quiet, with many or all who died doing so in their sleep. The reason everyone (generally speaking, at least) got up during the night may simply have been because most had heard about the prediction that their firstborn would die at midnight. How many families who knew of the prediction would have planned to sleep through until morning and *then* check to see if their children were all well? A large percentage of parents probably did not sleep at all by reason of apprehension. Many probably checked on their children periodically. No clocks existed at this point in antiquity, so people could only have guessed the time, but soon enough after midnight people would have begun to find children dead and would have begun to wail. The wailing in one house would have alerted the inhabitants in another to check on the firstborn immediately; they would have found them dead too, and so the wailing would spread from house to house and intensify. "Wailing" *(ṣĕʿāqāh)* is the same term God used of the outcry of the Israelites under their bondage (3:7,9). Now it was the Egyptians' turn, in a full and dramatic reversal of fortunes.

In pantheistic Egyptian society, even the death of so many livestock would be mourned, in addition to the sense of economic loss.[56] We are not told whether the firstborn of Pharaoh was a daughter or a son. In either case, the sycophantic historiography of the Egyptians would not preserve record of any such humiliation, just as it did not preserve a record of anything else related to the exodus. The event was, however, sufficient to eliminate all resistance to the exodus on the part of the Egyptians, most notably, Pharaoh (12:31–33). The expression "there was not a house without someone dead" could as well or better be translated "there was not [an extended] family without someone dead." It would not be usual for a couple without children to live in their own home apart from the husband's parents or for an unmarried firstborn to live alone apart from his/her parents. Accordingly, virtually

[56] We note again that the use of כל in 9:6 ("*all* the cattle died") is better translated "all sorts of" ("*all sorts of* cattle died"), consistent with the usual range of meaning of the word כל. There were still cattle left when the tenth plague started, and since only the firstborn of the cattle died in the tenth plague, there were still cattle left after it ended as well.

all Egyptian families/households would have indeed experienced the tenth plague.

5. The Exodus Is Permitted Under God's Vigil (12:31–36)

31During the night Pharaoh summoned Moses and Aaron and said, "Up! Leave my people, you and the Israelites! Go, worship the LORD as you have requested. 32Take your flocks and herds, as you have said, and go. And also bless me."

33The Egyptians urged the people to hurry and leave the country. "For otherwise," they said, "we will all die!" 34So the people took their dough before the yeast was added, and carried it on their shoulders in kneading troughs wrapped in clothing. 35The Israelites did as Moses instructed and asked the Egyptians for articles of silver and gold and for clothing. 36The LORD had made the Egyptians favorably disposed toward the people, and they gave them what they asked for; so they plundered the Egyptians.

Israel left Egypt on sudden notice, freely, rapidly, and comparatively wealthy. In this section of the narrative Moses helps the reader understand four things: the suddenness of the exodus; why Pharaoh and the Egyptians finally gave full and even eager permission for the exodus; why the Passover observance so strongly emphasizes eating unyeasted bread; and how the Israelites financed their forty years in the wilderness, a fact that explains their eventual ability to contribute and/or purchase precious metals and other valuable materials for the tabernacle and its appurtenances.

12:31–32 The original strategy of the oppression of Israel had been based on the seemingly reasonable assumption that the Israelites, as Asian foreigners, must be kept under Egyptian control in Egyptian territory lest they join with other Asians, overwhelm the Egyptians, and take over the country by force (see comments on 1:10). That long-held strategy had endured approximately eighty years during the administrations of at least two pharaohs.[57] Yet now it was instantly overturned by the command of the pharaoh of the exodus. Why so total a reversal? Why would Pharaoh finally cave in to every demand made by Yahweh on behalf of his people so that he declared them free to "leave my people" (v. 31), that is, to separate from Egypt and the Egyptians, the very thing the official, long-term Egyptian governmental strategy had sought to prevent? Why would he now grant the "final" freedom that had been denied even after the horrendous plague of

[57] Moses was eighty when the exodus began (7:7), having been born during the early years of the oppression (1:8–2:2) under a different pharaoh from the one who began the oppression (4:19), so the oppression can be assumed to have lasted a minimum of eighty years and two pharaonic administrations.

darkness, that of taking "your flocks and herds, as you have said" (v. 32; cf. 10:24–27)?

The answer is implied in Pharaoh's request to Moses, quoted at the end of v. 32, "And also bless me." In Moses' carefully crafted narrative, the last time an Israelite blessed a pharaoh was when Jacob blessed the pharaoh whom Joseph served as prime minister (Gen 47:7,10). That was the last *recorded* time in Moses' story of the Israelites that the Egyptian king had accepted a blessing from an Israelite, an act that indicated appreciation and respect for the leader of the people who had come to live among the Egyptians. Now this pharaoh showed by his request that *he* had made the spiritual-psychological shift (however temporary it may in fact have been[58]) to the same sort of position of respect and appreciation for the Israelites as that embodied in their leader. Moses now stood in relation to Pharaoh in the position that Jacob himself had once stood. Of course, ultimately the death of the firstborn in his family and in all the Egyptian families was the obvious, decisive factor that changed all attitudes, a lethal divine display of power and judgment that could not be ignored. So now it was the Israelites who were to be feared and the Egyptians who found themselves in the position of supplication, via their Pharaoh.

Did Moses and Aaron appear that Passover night before Pharaoh? This is what would seem to be implied by most of the English translations, represented by the NIV's "During the night Pharaoh summoned Moses and Aaron and said." If he summoned them and spoke to them, it would seem obvious that Moses did indeed appear before him again, in contradiction to at least the apparent meaning of his words in 10:29, "Just as you say, . . . I will never appear before you again." The contradiction, however, is only apparent, the result of a translation choice. The Hebrew term here translated "summon" is *qārāʾ lĕ,* which does indeed sometimes mean "summon" (call to appear in one's presence) but often means "proclaim, send word to or inform by messenger."[59] The most likely scenario is that sometime after the exchange of words culminating in 10:29, Moses and Aaron returned to Goshen to organize the Israelites for the exodus (as much of the foregoing part of chap. 12 describes) and that Pharaoh's permission was sent to him there during the waning hours of the Passover night by mounted messengers.

12:33–34 A somewhat more literal translation of v. 33 would read: "The Egyptians pressured the people in order to get them to leave the land quickly because they said, 'We are all dead!' "[60] The point is that God used

[58] See comments on 14:5ff.

[59] As in, e.g., Num 16:12; Judg 21:13; Jer 1:15; Hos 11:1; Amos 7:4; 9:6; Job 12:4; and most demonstratively, Isa 61:1; Jer 35:17; Ps 57:3.

[60] A general woeful assertion of this sort is a way of a group's indicating that it has really encountered the living God and not just any old god or something merely supernatural. Cf. Exod 20:18–19 and see also comments on 33:20.

the Egyptians to help make the Israelites do what was still surely not an easy thing: to leave the country of their birth and the country their ancestors had occupied for 430 years. The Egyptian motive was clear enough—they wanted to avoid further fatal consequences of the policy of keeping the Israelites against their will in Egypt. Egyptians who lived anywhere near Israelites were begging them to depart at once because they feared the consequences of further delaying the will of the God who sought the release of his people. Without time to do the usual food preparation but wanting to have something to eat as they traveled, even in great haste, the Israelites took dough for bread. But since there was no time to mix in the leaven and then wait around for it to rise, they simply wrapped their freshly made dough in fabric (in this case clothing) to keep it from spoiling and carried the wrapped kneading troughs on their shoulders as they headed out.

12:35–36 God knew that his people had been impoverished by their years of slavery, but yet he was asking them to head off on a lengthy and costly journey. Even if their disobedience had not lengthened that journey to the span of a generation, that is, forty years (Num 14:34–35), it would still have been a journey lasting some months. How would thousands of people survive in the wilderness that lay between Egypt and Canaan during that time? They would need money to buy supplies from traders, caravaneers, and local settlements and (in the plan that he had for them but that they themselves could not necessarily yet comprehend) to make at his command a worship center and worship implements worthy of his greatness. Where would the money come from? The answer is: from the Egyptians—as plunder, in other words, the spoils of war.[61] This language ("so they plundered") represents yet another indication of the identity God was providing to the Israelites: that of his army, who would mostly go through the motions of fighting when he in fact fought for them in the Holy War (see comments on chaps. 14–15) but who needed to think of themselves as his fighting force, and organize and act like an army already in connection with leaving Egypt (cf. 6:26; 7:4; 12:17,51).[62] So the Israelites, emboldened by the moment and God's instruction, went around to Egyptian houses, where the shock of the death of the firstborn was still only hours old, and asked for valuables, money, and clothes (the meaning of "articles of silver and gold and . . . clothing"). They got whatever they asked, not merely because the Egyptians were now terrified of the Israelites but because God had supernaturally

---

[61] The Hb. verb used for "plunder" is the *piel* of נצל, which is used to refer to taking the booty of war, as in 2 Chr 20:25. R. Gradwohl has argued that the verb in question should rather be seen as referring to the proper payment released slaves receive as compensation for their service, but to do so he must rely partly on an arguable translation of Gen 31:9 in the *hiphil* rather than the *piel* as employed here ("Nissal and Hissil als Rechtsbegriffe im Sklavenrecht," *ZAW* 111 [1999]: 187–95).

[62] Cf. J. B. Moster, "Thus They Stripped the Egyptians," *Dor le Dor* 16 (1987): 41–44.

caused the Egyptians to think collectively along these lines ("The LORD had made the Egyptians favorably disposed toward the people"). Accordingly, previously weak little Israel came away from slavery to the greatest power of the day instantly enriched. People suddenly held in their pockets and bags more precious gems and metals than they would ever have had a chance to accumulate in a lifetime and all the clothes they would need for many years of living in the wilderness.[63]

6. The Exodus Begins (12:37–42)

[37]The Israelites journeyed from Rameses to Succoth. There were about six hundred thousand men on foot, besides women and children. [38]Many other people went up with them, as well as large droves of livestock, both flocks and herds. [39]With the dough they had brought from Egypt, they baked cakes of unleavened bread. The dough was without yeast because they had been driven out of Egypt and did not have time to prepare food for themselves.

[40]Now the length of time the Israelite people lived in Egypt was 430 years. [41]At the end of the 430 years, to the very day, all the LORD's divisions left Egypt. [42]Because the LORD kept vigil that night to bring them out of Egypt, on this night all the Israelites are to keep vigil to honor the LORD for the generations to come.

This section of the story describes the very beginning of the exodus travel, from the primary departure city to the first stopping point. It tells the approximate number of nascent soldiers involved and indicates that, already, many people had become Israelites by faith choice rather than by birth. It was a full exodus with nothing left behind, and the main food of the traveling nation was, of necessity, unleavened bread. The exodus brought to an end 430 years of resident alien status for Israel in Egypt, the last eighty years or so being years of slavery. God paid special attention to his people that night, and in response his people of all future generations were expected to come to pay special attention to him on its anniversary.

12:37 This verse asserts two things that surely made perfect sense to Moses' original audience and to most Israelites thereafter but which offer difficulties for modern readers because of our lack of knowledge of the ancient scene. The first is that of the location of the places named, Rameses and Succoth. We really cannot determine where these were located,[64] except that they were somewhere in northern Egypt, that Succoth was surely to the east of Rameses (since the Israelites started out going east before

[63] Having high quality Egyptian clothing conceivably may have been helpful to them at points since the same sort of respect given to the Egyptians could have come with recognition of their clothing (cf. 2:19), though no overt attention is given to this possibility in the narrative itself.

[64] See also comments on 1:11.

their later, special detour south), and that Rameses[65] may have been some kind of Egyptian delta capital city. Herrmann[66] argues that the official, full name of the city was "House of Ramesses, Beloved of Amun, Great in Victorious Might," usually abbreviated in Egyptian references to the simpler *pr-rʿ-ms-sw,* "House of Rameses." He considers it likely that Rameses was a large capital *area* (i.e., something like a district rather than merely a city as measured by the location of the city walls per se) that flourished during the nineteenth dynasty. We have already noted (1:11) that Rameses was apparently first built by Israelite slaves as a "store city," meaning a city intended to house war materials for fighting back potential Asian invaders. Sukkoth may well have been the city called in ancient Egyptian records *tkw.* Some scholars have suggested, however, that it may be another name for what 1:11 calls Pithom, that is, a city familiar to the Israelites because they had helped build it. Some believe it may not have been a city per se but a region to the east of Rameses. Others consider it likely that it represents what is now an eroded tel in the Wadi Tumilar, Tell el-Maskhuta.[67] The Israelites may have massed at Rameses in order to be grouped together (since it surely would have been located, as a defensive city, at or near a major road or crossroads), or it may simply be that this was the most prominent geographical point of reference near where their villages and settlements were located, and so its name was used to describe their point of departure from Egypt.

Excursus: How Many Israelites Left Egypt?[68]

The Hebrew of the Exod 12:37 says literally, "The Israelites traveled from Rameses to Succoth, about six hundred *ʾelephs* of foot-soldiers, besides women and children." The NIV translation, like most English translations, contains two arguable assumptions on the part of the translators: that *ʾeleph*[69] should be translated "thousand," and that *raḡlî* in the expression *raḡlî haggĕbārîm* should be

[65] Note that in 1:11 the name of the city (assuming it is the same city) is vocalized as רַעַמְסֵס *(raʿamses)* whereas in Gen 47:11; Num 33:3,5 and the present verse it is רַעְמְסֵס *(raʿmeses).* This represents simply a slight variation of the sort the Masoretes make regularly since medieval Hebrew was not entirely consistent in the resolution of short-vowel vocalized gutturals.

[66] S. Herrmann, *Israel in Egypt,* SBT, 2d series, no. 27 (London: SCM Press), 1973.

[67] So J. P. Hyatt, *Exodus,* NBC (London: Oliphants, 1971), 59–60; W. Helck, "*Tkw* und die Ramses-Stadt," *VT* 15 (1965): 35–48, esp. 41–48.

[68] In connection with this excursus, see also D. Fairman, "How Many Israelites Left Egypt?" *Dor le Dor* 18 (1990): 230–33; A. Lucas, "The Number of Israelites at the Exodus," *PEQ* 76 (1944): 164–68.

[69] The usual, traditional way to transliterate אֶלֶף into Eng. has been via the spelling *ʾeleph,* but the more strictly scholarly transliteration is *ʾelep*. Depending on the need for specificity of transliteration, we will use *ʾeleph* generally but *ʾelep* in cases where technical precision might better help the reader.

translated "men."[70] Both of these assumptions are, in our opinion, incorrect. The second, which assumes that *raḡlî* can mean "men," is not supportable in any Old Testament context.[71] Some lexicons go so far as to suggest that the term in the singular[72] might mean a "man on foot," but none could rightly suggest that it means simply "man." In the grammar of the verse, the addition of the appositional noun *haggĕbārîm* (lit., "[the] young men") simply clarifies the age of the man/men in question. Since *raḡlî* always occurs in contexts describing soldiers, including the present context (note the wording "all the LORD's divisions" in v. 41), and differs from any of the usual terms for "man" or "men," there really can be little doubt that it should be rendered "foot soldier" or, as some do, "infantryman" wherever it occurs in the Old Testament. The full expression *raḡlî haggĕbārîm*, then, means "young foot soldiers."[73]

Because the question of the meaning of *ʾeleph,* however, is so much greater an issue for people as it relates to the accuracy of the Scripture and the proper interpretation of various stories involving the Israelite exodus and conquest of Canaan, the discussion of this term requires a far more extensive review. The reader should bear in mind, however, that Moses did not refer to six hundred *ʾelephs* of "men" who left Egypt but to six hundred *ʾelephs* of foot soldiers. He was counting God's army, not all the people of Israel, and the following groupings of translations for *ʾeleph* must be considered in that light.

Here, from the NRSV, are the range of translations in English for Hebrew *ʾeleph*. We use the NRSV in order to provide a (hopefully, on this issue) neutral base of comparison to the NIV, especially in light of the fact that it is the most widely used major English translation in circulation after the NIV.[74]

---

[70] J. Wenham ("Large Numbers in the Bible," *JBQ* 21 [1993]: 116–20) has argued that the simplest way to understand *ʾeleph* all by itself is as "chieftain" (possibly vocalized incorrectly by the Medieval Masoretes, who should have rendered it as *ʾallûp* or the like), so that "soldier chieftains" would represent the six hundred who were counted. This ends up yielding the same count we propose below, and it is therefore a suggestion we feel must be taken seriously.

[71] Not even Jer 12:5 ("If you have raced with [armed] foot-runners and they have wearied you, how will you compete with horses?), in which the foot soldiers are armed guards who run before and after their masters' chariots (cf. 1 Sam 8:11; 1 Kgs 1:5). All other contexts are unmistakably military.

[72] The singular is in fact the form used in the Hb. of 12:37, but that is because in Hb. grammar a singular form of a noun is typically employed when modified by a plural number. In Hb. one typically says the equivalent of "ten tree" rather than "ten trees."

[73] "Young" would mean between twenty and fifty years of age. The lower number is established in Num 1, *passim.* The upper number is fixed by analogy with the priestly retirement age. If priests were required to retire at fifty (cf. Num 4, *passim,* and 8:25), it is hard to imagine that soldiers were expected to serve when even older.

[74] In other words, we use the NRSV somewhat for convenience in the role of a carefully-produced modern translation post-dating the NIV and providing a set of translations of the word *ʾeleph* against which the NIV translations can be compared, not because it is necessarily a superior translation to the NIV.

Eleph Translated "Thousand"

Exod 18:21: You should also look for able men among all the people, men who fear God, are trustworthy, and hate dishonest gain; set such men over them as officers over thousands, hundreds, fifties and tens.

Num 10:36: And whenever it came to rest, he would say, "Return, O LORD of the ten thousand thousands of Israel."

Num 31:4: You shall send a thousand from each of the tribes of Israel to the war."

Num 31:5: So out of the thousands of Israel, a thousand from each tribe were conscripted, twelve thousand armed for battle.

Josh 7:3: Then they returned to Joshua and said to him, "Not all the people need go up; about two or three thousand men should go up and attack Ai. Since they are so few, do not make the whole people toil up there."

1 Sam 23:23: Look around and learn all the hiding places where he lurks, and come back to me with sure information. Then I will go with you; and if he is in the land, I will search him out among all the thousands of Judah."

Eleph Translated "Cattle"

Deut 7:13: He will love you, bless you, and multiply you; he will bless the fruit of your womb and the fruit of your ground, your grain and your wine and your oil, the increase of your cattle and the issue of your flock, in the land that he swore to your ancestors to give you.

Deut 28:4: Blessed shall be the fruit of your womb, the fruit of your ground, and the fruit of your livestock, both the increase of your cattle and the issue of your flock.

Deut 28:18: Cursed shall be the fruit of your womb, the fruit of your ground, the increase of your cattle and the issue of your flock.

Deut 28:51: It shall consume the fruit of your livestock and the fruit of your ground until you are destroyed, leaving you neither grain, wine, and oil, nor the increase of your cattle and the issue of your flock, until it has made you perish.

Eleph Translated "Clan(s)"

Josh 22:14: And with him ten chiefs, one from each of the tribal families of Israel, every one of them the head of a family among the clans of Israel.

Judg 6:15: He responded, "But sir, how can I deliver Israel? My clan is the weakest in Manasseh, and I am the least in my family."

1 Sam 10:19: But today you have rejected your God, who saves you from all your calamities and your distresses; and you have said, 'No! but set a king over us.' Now therefore present yourselves before the LORD by your tribes and by your clans."

Isa 60:22: The least of them shall become a clan, / and the smallest one a mighty nation; / I am the LORD; / in its time I will accomplish it quickly.

Mic 5:2: But you, O Bethlehem of Ephrathah, / who are one of the little clans of Judah, / from you shall come forth for me / one who is to rule in Israel, / whose origin is from of old, / from ancient days.

Eleph Translated "Division(s)"

Num 1:16: These were the ones chosen from the congregation, the leaders of their ancestral tribes, the heads of the divisions of Israel.

Eleph Translated "Family(ies)"

Josh 22:21: Then the Reubenites, the Gadites, and the half-tribe of Manasseh said in answer to the heads of the families of Israel.

Josh 22:30: When the priest Phinehas and the chiefs of the congregation, the heads of the families of Israel who were with him, heard the words that the Reubenites and the Gadites and the Manassites spoke, they were satisfied.

Eleph Translated "Ox(en)"

Isa 30:24: And the oxen and donkeys that till the ground will eat silage, which has been winnowed with shovel and fork.

Ps 8:7: All sheep and oxen, and also the beasts of the field.

Eleph Translated "Tribe(s)"

Num 10:4: But if only one is blown, then the leaders, the heads of the tribes of Israel, shall assemble before you.

As the above sampling demonstrates, there is a considerable size to the semantic field or semantic domain or "range of meaning" of the word *ʾeleph* when viewed in terms of English translation equivalents. This probably results from the many semantic pathways that diverged from its original or "root" meaning, "ox." How could these meanings all derive from "ox," which denotes a full-grown (and usually but not always neutered) male bovine? The typically suggested route is as follows: Farmers would keep a herd of cows by letting them graze with one ox. The ox protected the whole herd, and the cows therefore tended instinctively not to stray far from him. Thus, wherever one saw a herd of large cattle in ancient times, one normally saw it arrayed around an ox. By simple economy of speech, "ox herd" or the like came to mean "herd *[ʾeleph]*." From there, because "herd" connotes a large group, variable in number, various definitions derived, ranging from "cattle" in general to "family" to "tribe" to "division." Then, for purposes of precise numerical counting (but not military unit description), the already widely used word was borrowed to indicate the quantity "thousand" in the decimal system. This modern reading back into the text of the mentality of the decimal system in all passages that contain descriptions of numbers of people is the reason that "thousand" is the word many translators have accordingly assumed must be the meaning in places like Exod 12:37.

But there is yet another use of *ʾeleph,* one that comes about in connection with the military system, a fact many translators have paid insufficient attention to. Israel's army was organized by units of size that are *called* by words that were all or mostly all borrowed originally from other meanings. These are usually found translated into English, in descending order, as the "tribe," the "thousand" *(ʾeleph),* the "hundred," the "fifty," and the "ten." An example of this way of referring to various military units is found at Deut 1:15: "So I took the leading men of your tribes, wise and respected men, and appointed them to have authority over you—as commanders of thousands, of hundreds, of fifties and of tens and as tribal officials."[75]

A helpful departure point for the analysis of how the words for military units are actually employed in the Hebrew Bible and what they ought to connote in English is that of Mendenhall,[76] who argues that the various military units were groups of varying sizes that served under a ranked leader. Thus, for example, the commander of an *ʾeleph* is called an *ʾallûp*, one charged with the responsibility of commanding an *ʾeleph*. Just how big was an *ʾeleph* then? Mendenhall suggests that it was the number of men of fighting age (above age twenty; cf. Num 1:3) that a single tribal subset (extended family) or village or district of a larger town could produce. What we do not know is the actual numbers of these extended families or village districts. In the case of a larger family or district, the number might be as many as twenty. A small village or district might produce just a handful. For general purposes of calculation, it may be assumed that most *ʾelephs* were not larger than fifteen and perhaps averaged a dozen.[77] The best term to translate *ʾeleph* in typical military contexts, such as Exod 12:37 (which specifically omits counting women and children because it is a count of the *fighting men* only), would be something like "platoon" or "squad," both of which are military terms familiar to English speakers. Accordingly, six hundred *ʾelephs,* the number mentioned in Exod 12:37, probably would contain not more than 7,200 fighting men, at an average of a dozen fighting men per *ʾeleph*. If one assumes that many of these were single,[78] but that most may have been married, that most who were

---

[75] We judge that all these names for military units are possibly subject to further analysis. In Deut 1:15 the pattern may be that of a chiasm, in which "commanders of thousands" *(ʾelephs)* might be intended as a parallel to the term *officials,* with the internal officers having different numbers of people under their jurisdiction. By this analysis the units do not appear in descending order of size. Alternatively, the meaning of some of the terms may have been misunderstood by the scribes who copied and updated the language Pentateuch (so that it could be understood by their own generation) as Humphreys and Rendsburg argue below.

[76] G. E. Mendenhall, "The Census Lists of Numbers 1 and 26," *JBL* 77 (1958): 52–66, esp. 60–66.

[77] These specific numbers (fifteen dozen) are ours, not necessarily Mendenhall's, though we think he would concur that they are reasonable guesses. Unit sizes vary in all armies—a wartime division in the US Army can reach thirty thousand soldiers; in peacetime it can drop below ten thousand—and so on for the smaller units.

[78] There is a popular notion that people used to marry when in their teens in ancient times and that marrying later, in one's twenties, is strictly a modern phenomenon. In fact, no one has demonstrated that this "trend" is true; most evidence supports the idea that people married in their twenties, on average, in Bible times as well as today.

married had children, and that there were many men who could not fight because they were either too old or too young or infirm, the total number of Israelites who left Egypt might in fact have been around 28,800–36,000 (assuming three or four nonfighters for every fighter). This is a large and formidable number[79] but by no means the two million or so that a misleading calculation based on taking *ʾeleph* unjustifiably as "thousand" would yield.

More recently, several careful analyses of the question of the number of Israelites who participated in the exodus have been offered. C. Humphreys and G. Rendsburg have both argued that a proper understanding of the original Hebrew text of Exodus yields counts of around 5,500 fighting men for Israel—just under five hundred per tribe on average.[80] Their arguments parallel generally what he have suggested above, though with a much greater focus on (and different way of analyzing unit strength of) the tribe-by-tribe and unit-by-unit calculations than we have given above. Under the approach they take to the question, their total numbers of Israelites who left Egypt perhaps would be roughly in the 22,000-27,500 range. Though they analyze the text's presentation of the numbers in a somewhat different way than we do, the results are remarkably similar. We have no evidence from ancient times that allows us to calculate precisely the number of nonfighting Israelites, so the exact number of the whole nation will presumably never be known. It was a few tens of thousands but almost surely not several million.

Twenty or thirty thousand people is a number that easily can fit into many modern sorts of venues, from small sports stadiums to beaches to public gatherings and rallies, a fact that may help modern readers of the book visualize the entire Israelite contingent, who were often in one place at one time. It is a number that fits the facts of the book of Exodus well. Such a number of Israelites is large enough to require the miraculous provisions of food and water that the book describes; it is small enough for the whole nation to gather encamped around the tabernacle at the various places listed on the Israelite wilderness itinerary. For most occasions of listening to speeches, the men only would have gathered,[81] several thousand or so in number, not too many to hear a speech shouted at them,

---

[79] That number would have represented a threat to the Egyptians in any case, but Pharaoh's expressions of Israelite size in 1:9 were in fact almost surely exaggerated, just as the Israelite spies' reports of the inhabitants of Canaan were in Num 13:26–33.

[80] C. J. Humphreys, "How Many People Were in the Exodus from Egypt?" *Science and Christian Belief* 12 (2000): 17–34; id., "The Number of People in the Exodus from Egypt: Decoding Mathematically the Very Large Numbers in Numbers i and xxvi," *VT* 48 (1998): 196–213; id., "The Numbers in the Exodus from Egypt: A Further Appraisal," *VT* 50 (2000): 323–28. G. A. Rendsburg, "An Additional Note to Two Recent Articles on the Number of People in the Exodus from Egypt and the Large Numbers in Numbers i and xxvi," *VT* 51 (2001): 392–96. Cf. M. McIntire, "A Response to Colin J. Humphrey's 'The Number of People in the Exodus from Egypt: Decoding Mathematically the Very Large Numbers in Numbers I and xxvi,'" *VT* 49 (1999): 262–64; and J. Milgrom, "On Decoding Very Large Numbers," *VT* 49 (1999): 131–32.

[81] Cp. the unusual situation of having women and older children present for a covenant renewal ceremony in Neh 8:2–3.

especially if its words were relayed.[82] Yet several thousand troops were formidable as a fighting force when directed at one place at a time.[83]

12:38 This verse confirms that the Israelites of the exodus (and thereafter) were actually a mixed people ethnically—something that most Christians are unaware of. The verse would best be translated as follows: "A huge ethnically diverse group also went up with them, and very many cattle, both flocks and herds."[84] To what was Moses referring? To the fact that many other persons who were not descended from Abraham or Israel joined the Israelites as they left Egypt. These people had observed the miraculous work of Yahweh, Israel's God, and had become convinced that conversion to him and life among his people would represent their best hope for the future. In this regard they were predecessors to Ruth, who declared to Naomi, "Your people will be my people and your God my God" (Ruth 1:16).[85] Among them were presumably a considerable number of Cushites, one of whom Moses ended up marrying as a second wife. The Cushites had relatively warm relationships with the Israelites long after the exodus as well.[86] There

---

[82] On the gathering of people to hear a speech in OT times, see the commentaries on Neh 8. G. Whitefield, the famous eighteenth century preacher in America, drew crowds of many thousands to hear his open-air preaching. Crowds in the tens of thousands heard presidential inaugurals and other public speeches long before the advent of electronic sound amplification.

[83] The small overall number of Israelites in respect to the size of the promised land of Canaan is acknowledged by God in his instructions to Moses in Exod 23:29–30 ("But I will not drive them out in a single year, because the land would become desolate and the wild animals too numerous for you. Little by little I will drive them out before you, until you have increased enough to take possession of the land"). Only with time could the Israelites be expected to multiply into a large enough nation to control Canaan fully; initially upon their entrance into the land they were too few in number to farm the land. In particular, they could not because of their relatively small size at first keep all of the land under cultivation that the Canaanite groups had been cultivating or keep out the wild animals who would eat their crops and herds. God therefore graciously granted them a gradual conquest of the promised land to allow them to grow into a nation large enough to keep the land properly husbanded.

[84] The עֵרֶב רַב in Hb. means, lit., "a great/huge mixed group," from the adjective רַב meaning "great/huge" and the noun עֵרֶב meaning "mixing" (often referring to the mixing of day and night, i.e., evening).

[85] Of note is the parallel language that the risen Jesus used to reassure his followers that they are in the same relationship to God as he is: "I am returning to my Father and your Father, to my God and your God" (John 20:17).

[86] See J. D. Hays, "Moses: The Private Man Behind the Public Leader," *BR* 16 (2000): 16–26, 60–63. Hays also suggests that Phinehas, mentioned in Exod 6:25, and a key figure in putting down the partly Midianite cultic immorality at Baal-Peor (Num 25) bore a name that was an Egyptian loan-word, meaning "the negro." If Hays is correct in this, it would mean that Moses' grandnephew Phinehas was also a Cushite and that therefore either Aaron had himself married a Cushite or, more likely, that his son Eleazar had (see 6:25)—or else that Eleazar had adopted a Cushite boy as his son. The circumstances behind the rebellion by Aaron and Miriam against Moses as described in Num 25 may have been more complex than mere racism, possibly not even involving any anti-Cushite feelings at all.

can be no certainty that Paul intended this verse to be considered as part of the background for his comments on the insignificance of ethnic origin for true Israelites in such places as Rom 2:28–29 and 4:11,16–17, though the concept is surely supported by the observations of the present passage. In Num 11:4 Moses also referred to the significant numbers of non-Israelites among the Israelites, after leaving Sinai and in the wilderness travels, by a term most modern English translators render as "the rabble" or the like.[87]

The problem with the NIV translation "large droves of livestock" is that it gives the impression, contrary to the original, that the Israelites had organized their cattle into huge, unified groups (which is what a drove is), whereas nothing supports such a notion. Moses simply used here a standard ancient literary style that mentions quantity of people first and quantity of animals second.[88] The livestock had constituted the last "hostage" group in Pharaoh's plan to keep the Israelites from leaving Egypt permanently, the last sticking point in the bargaining process that had played back and forth throughout the sequence of plagues (11:24–27). They are mentioned here, however, not merely because their presence among the departing Israelites indicated total victory over Pharaoh but as indication that the exodus constituted a complete emigration from Egypt of an entire people and their economic assets. The Israelites then made much use of their small and large cattle during the years in the wilderness, especially in connection with the sacrificial system (e.g., Exod 22:30; Lev and Num, *passim*).

12:39 This verse simply reports the fulfillment part of the command-fulfillment pattern related to the unleavened bread requirement (see 12:8,14–20). Bread was virtually everyone's main food in the ancient world; even the manna in the wilderness was characterized as "bread" from heaven (Exod 6:4ff.).[89] It is therefore natural that the Israelites would take bread dough with them—and appropriate that they could not take the time to let it become yeasted properly because of leaving Egypt in such a hurry. They thus ate the ancient equivalent of "hard tack" in the early days after the evening of the Passover because any other preparation of food for the journey was impossible in light of the pressure to leave (see also comments on

[87] וְהָאסַפְסֻף אֲשֶׁר בְּקִרְבּוֹ, "the rabble in their midst." R. R. Stieglitz ("The Lowdown on the Riffraff," *BR* 15 [1999]: 30–33, 54) argues that the references to these non-Israelites in the story represent a real historical memory and constitute some of the evidence of the general historicity of the account, as supported also by Egyptian literary references to "foreigners who lived amidst them" (i.e., amidst Asiatics like the Israelites).

[88] Cf. Exod 11:5; Jonah 4:11 also adds plants in the usual, commonsense order of worth (people, animals, plants); sometimes, however, the order is reversed for climactic effect (i.e., moving from lesser to greater), as in Gen 20:14 and Job 1:3.

[89] Meat was eaten sparingly, although the Israelites were allowed by law to eat meat at times other than at religious sacrifices, something many other ancient religious groups were not allowed to do (Deut 12:15).

12:31–32) and because the leftovers from the Passover meal could not be retained (cf. 12:10).

12:40–41 Here Moses reminded the reader of just how long the Israelite sojourn was: four centuries and three decades, a span of time that would cover perhaps fourteen or fifteen generations,[90] plenty of time for multiplication from the first seventy people (1:5) to the tens of thousands that departed on that spring day. If the early dating for the exodus (ca. 1440) is followed, the entrance of Jacob's family into Egypt dates to 1870 BC. If the later date (ca. 1260) is followed, the entrance occurred around 1690 BC. But the emphasis here is surely not on the chronology per se but on the way that Israel had been acclimated to Egypt for a very long time. When this long history of being settled in Egypt is compared to the history of the United States of America, for example (in America fewer than four hundred years have elapsed since the country was first settled permanently by Europeans), one can see the implications: it would be a radical change for people acclimated to one place and culture for so many generations to leave suddenly for a journey to a place none of them had ever even laid eyes on. Thus the Israelite departure in faith for a land of promise serves as an analogy for the pilgrimage of all God's saints from life in this world to their ultimate destination in the promised but as yet unexperienced next. [91]

Verse 41 should read, "At the end of four hundred and thirty years, on that same day, all the armies[92] of the LORD went out from the land of Egypt." The NIV translation of the middle adverbial phrase, "to the very day," is misleading because it suggests that the Israelites left Egypt 430 years precisely—not a day less or a day more—after they entered it, which

[90] I.e., if a generation is calculated conservatively at about thirty years. The usual Hb. term for "generation" is דּוֹר, which can admit of a number of different values, depending on context, in years. In the promise to Abraham of Gen 15, the "fourth generation" (v. 16) is said to occur after four hundred years (v. 13)! This surely reflects a meaning of דּוֹר as "lifetime," which for Abraham was 120 years—thus, indeed, 430 years was within the fourth 120-year generation after the Israelites entered Egypt. Elsewhere, דּוֹר seems to connote values of seventy years or forty years and yet elsewhere of twenty-five or thirty. Our calculation above is simply based on the way "generation" is used in modern English. On the interpretational challenges of this verse and the not infrequent skepticism expressed about its historicity, cf. *inter alia,* S. Kreuzer, "430 Jahre, 400 Jahre oder 4 Generationen—zu den Zeitangaben über den Agyptenaufenhalt der 'Israeliten,'" *ZAW* 98 (1996): 199–210; P. J. Ray, "The Duration of the Israelite Sojourn in Egypt," *AUSS* 24 (1986): 231–48; F. J. Neuberg, "An Unrecognized Meaning of the Hebrew *DOR*," *JNES* 9 (1950): 215–17; P Grelot, "Quatre cent trent ans (Exode 12:40): A propos de la chronologie sacerdotale du Pentateuque," *Studien zum Pentatuch: Fs. Walter Kornfeld zum 60* (Wien: Herder, 1977), 91–98; D. Luhrmann, "Die 430 Jahre zwischen den Verheissungen und dem Gesetz," *ZAW* 100 (1988): 420–23. A thoughtful defense of the historicity of the verse is provided by J. R. Riggs, "The Length of Israel's Sojourn in Egypt," *GTJ* 12 (1971): 18–35.

[91] Cf. Heb 11:11–16; 12:22–29.

[92] See note on 6:26.

is not the meaning of the original at all.[93] Moses' language draws attention to "that same day," that is, the day after the night of the Passover, making the point that there was no intervening delay between the Passover (the imposition of the tenth plague) and the first available opportunity to depart, which was the next day from our point of view and the same day (since the day began at sunset for the Israelites) from their point of view. Similar emphases on the dating of the beginning of the feast of unleavened bread to the daytime immediately after the Passover night are also found in Exod 12:17; 12:51; Josh 5:11. Note again the military language, "All the LORD's divisions [armies] left Egypt." They may not have fought yet, but they were his army. They were untested as a fighting force and surely no match for the Egyptians from a human point of view, but, then, when God is at the head of an army, how powerful does it need to be?[94]

12:42 A more literal translation of v. 42 would be: "It was a night of vigil by the LORD, to bring them out of the land of Egypt. This same night is a night of vigil for the LORD by all the Israelites throughout their generations." What God first did for Israel, a vigil or "watching,"[95] was to be remembered by a vigil on the part of his people for him—not because people can watch over God in a way comparable to his watching over them but because they can "stay on duty" during the night as a token of their appreciation for his original dutiful watch over them, sparing them from the tenth plague and preparing them for their liberation. A sort of "day – night" theme is worked into vv. 41–42. In parallel to the emphasis on "this same day" of v. 41 relative to the first day of the Feast of Unleavened Bread, v. 42 emphasizes "this night" (the immediately preceding night) as the time of the nighttime Passover memorial. Because God's people were to renew their all-important covenant relationship with God annually throughout the endurance of the Old Covenant with "this day" and "this night," these terms receive repetitive stress here in the narrative.

---

[93] The Hb. phrase in question, בְּעֶצֶם הַיּוֹם הַזֶּה, is a stock adverbial phrase that never means "to the very day" but always "on that same day" or the like, in all eighteen of its occurrences in the OT.

[94] The answer often is: the less powerful the better, so that God's power may be shown in contrast to the weakness of his human host; cf. Judg 7:4–8; Deut 20:5–8; 2 Cor 12:10.

[95] A review of the various ways the particular Hb. word (the in-verse hapax legomenon שִׁמֻּרִים) translated by the NIV as *vigil* has otherwise been rendered, has been provided by N. Ilan, "A Night of Watching," *BMik* 46 (2001): 97–114 [Hb.].

7. Summation: The Passover Statute and Its Connection to the Exodus (12:43–51)

[43]The LORD said to Moses and Aaron, "These are the regulations for the Passover:

"No foreigner is to eat of it. [44]Any slave you have bought may eat of it after you have circumcised him, [45]but a temporary resident and a hired worker may not eat of it.

[46]"It must be eaten inside one house; take none of the meat outside the house. Do not break any of the bones. [47]The whole community of Israel must celebrate it.

[48]"An alien living among you who wants to celebrate the LORD's Passover must have all the males in his household circumcised; then he may take part like one born in the land. No uncircumcised male may eat of it. [49]The same law applies to the native-born and to the alien living among you."

[50]All the Israelites did just what the LORD had commanded Moses and Aaron. [51]And on that very day the LORD brought the Israelites out of Egypt by their divisions.

Verses 40–42 laid special stress on *when* the Passover was to be observed. Now additional clarifying material for the strict observance of the Passover rite describes in greater detail than has heretofore appeared *who* may eat the Passover meal, *where* and *how* it must be eaten, and finally (v. 50) yet another reminder of *when* it is to be eaten. The Passover commemorates a crucial *event,* and therefore its observance must be event and process oriented, that is, who, where, when, and how oriented. The main emphasis of this section is clearly circumcision. It is circumcision that constitutes the external demonstration of acceptance into the covenant community and therefore circumcision that qualifies one and one's family to partake of the Passover meal.

12:43 God's Passover instruction appropriately addresses Moses and Aaron, the two priests[96] since the Passover is a religious rite and all subsequent priests and Levites would see themselves as heirs to the importance of keeping the statute[97] first delivered to Israel's levitical, priestly leaders. Included with this verse is the first injunction, "No foreigner is to eat of it." This does not mean that people who did not have a full genealogical pedigree as long-term Israelites could not eat the Passover and thus could not show by eating it that they were part of God's covenant people. The mixed ethnic group that was already blending into Israel (12:38) could partake, as

[96] On Moses' actual performance of priestly duties cf. Lev 8.

[97] The NIV's very loose translation "these are the regulations for the Passover" is not necessarily impossible but tends to obscure the point that there was a single rule, circumcision, that dominated. At any rate, the normal, literal translation of the text would be "this is the Passover statute."

could circumcised resident aliens, who might qualify as "foreigners" in the way the term is normally used in English. Here the original uses *nēkār,* a term for persons who are simply not part of the covenant community—"outsiders" might be a suitable translation. This does not constitute racial or ethnic discrimination. It represents proper religious discrimination. The improper kind hates and hurts simply because someone is of another religion. The proper kind recognizes that those who refuse to join by faith and practice the united community of believers set apart from all others precisely by faith and practice have no more right to claim membership in that community than a person without a driver's license has the right to operate an automobile on public roads.

12:44 But the Passover is decidedly not restricted by social status. All of Israel's laws were class free, in contrast to all the laws of their contemporaries. Therefore even a servant (NIV "slave")[98] of any sort including a servant purchased to work in a household may not be excluded from participation in the household's celebration of the Passover as long as he is circumcised, meaning as long as he is a member of the covenant community, a person who worships the only true God. The head of any household was responsible to see that the males within it who believed in Yahweh were circumcised, thus the language "after you have circumcised him," referring to the most likely scenario, that of an uncircumcised servant being brought into the household for a six-year period (cf. Exod 21:2) and needing circumcision. Like all laws, this one is paradigmatic; it does not list all possible situations but says enough that any reasonable person may extrapolate from it to know what to do in other related, but not identical, situations (e.g., that of the servant who grew up in one's household and therefore was already circumcised, that of the servant's male children—who must each be circumcised for themselves—that of the females whose relationship to their circumcised husbands or fathers suffices to credential them for the Passover, or that of widowed female slaves who once had a circumcised husband but now do not or of single female slaves). Common sense includes in the list of those who may and must partake of the Passover all those who have faith in Yahweh and excludes all who do not, with males showing it physically and females showing it by their formal relationships. In Old Testament law the examples cited are never intended to represent an exhaustive listing, but a sampling from which all instances can be addressed by analogy.

12:45 A "temporary resident" *(tôšāb)* would be excluded from the Passover because he or she would be someone without faith in Yahweh who was simply visiting or passing through or staying for a few days or weeks to

---

[98] The term עֶבֶד neutrally includes any sort of worker, from what Eng. might call "employee" to "hired hand" to [captured in war] "slave." See comments on 21:2ff.

help with some sort of project. A "hired worker" *(śakîr)* would be disqualified because he or she would be someone without faith in Yahweh who was merely doing some work on a household's property and staying on the property temporarily while doing so. Neither term refers to a permanent employee or permanent resident.

12:46–47 The Passover must be eaten in a single house, even when a group of families eat it, because it is a common meal consuming a single goat kid or lamb (see comments on 12:4). It must be eaten indoors because that best recalls to the worshipers' minds the need to stay indoors during the tenth plague, under the protection of the blood. As a secondary reason, eating indoors prevents nonqualified, noncircumcised people from helping themselves to the meal while it is left unattended outside, or dogs or other animals from doing the same, or the worshiper from simply dropping his or her portion in the dust after the meal was over and thus polluting what God intended to be a sacred symbol of salvation.[99] Here again God teaches his people concepts that will help them recognize the sacredness of the body of Christ as it is offered up on the cross for them as a substitutionary atonement in the future.

The prohibition against the breaking of bones is left unexplained. There appears to be nothing about eating a lamb or goat kid that makes the breaking of its bones intrinsically objectionable and nothing about breaking bones that would pollute the meat in any way. The concern apparently stems rather from God's desire that the lamb or goat kid adequately symbolize the body of Christ crucified (John 1:36) and, subsequently, the unity of the body of Christ in the sense of the church. Thus even the Old Testament covenant community was called to think of themselves as a unity, symbolized by a common meal that could not be divided except as portions of its flesh were eaten: the skeleton remained unified to indicate their unity, a present fact fully to be realized in the future by the work of the Savior on the cross.[100] Further symbolizing this unity, the whole community must eat

---

[99] Israelite tents and, later, houses had mostly dirt floors, but these were covered at key spots by carpets and the like, as far as we can discern; and, at any rate, discarding food indoors was not nearly as likely to be tempting as doing so outdoors.

[100] In other words, the OT covenant community learns to believe through this rite in a concept of a single, selected, sacrificial, unified lamb of God that would die for them as a symbol of their not having to die and through which they could rejoice for the deliverance God had granted them. Therefore, although they may not have known Christ personally through the indwelling of his Spirit, they could by faith generally understand the sorts of things he would one day do for them as they looked forward to God's future provision, particularly the idea that a single Savior would die for the whole people of God. For a very different understanding of the prohibition against breaking the bones of the Passover animal, cf. A. Scheiber, "'Ihr Sollt Ken Ben dran Zerbrechen,'" *VT* 13 (1963): 95–97; and F. J. Stendebach, "Das Verbot des Knochenzerbrechens bei den Semiten," *BZ* 17 (1973): 29–38.

the Passover as a common meal shared by every true Israelite on the same evening.[101]

12:48–49 Circumcision indicates membership in the covenant community of God. Since membership in that community is necessary for admission to the Passover rite, circumcision is necessary for admission to the Passover rite. It does not matter whether or not a person is a native-born Israelite; if he is not circumcised, no Passover for him; if he is circumcised,[102] it would be disobedient of him *not* to partake. Note Moses' anticipation of the entrance into the land ("then he may take part like one born in the land").[103] At this point, neither he nor the Israelites were aware that there would be a thirty-nine year hiatus between the Passover celebrated at Sinai (Num 9) and the one celebrated in the land of Canaan under Joshua (Josh 5:10) so that most of those in Moses' audience would actually celebrate only a single Passover, and would die off in the wilderness before entering the land. The long occupation of the land of Canaan, in fulfillment of the promises to Abraham, was, however, in view, so that the Passover rule linked Israelite legitimacy to "nativeness" in the land yet to be occupied. For the vast majority of Israelites ever able to celebrate a Passover, being "native" went together automatically with being circumcised and therefore being accepted as an Israelite.

12:50–51 Verses 50–51 constitute a brief fulfillment notice, of the sort already encountered in such places as Gen 6:22; 40:22; Exod 7:6,10,13, 20,22; 8:15,19; 9:12,35. Without fulfillment notices, readers of any age, but especially those in the ancient world where the prediction-fulfillment and command-fulfillment style was so prominent in stories, might wonder if what was prescribed to Moses and Aaron actually happened generally throughout the nation. In this case it certainly did. The Passover was celebrated, and Israel was thus united as a community of faith within God's protection and guidance because they "did just what the LORD had commanded Moses and Aaron." Then, "on that very day[104] the LORD brought the Israelites out of Egypt by their divisions [armies]." In other words, the morning after the Passover night was the time that the Israelites grouped together as

---

[101] The NIV translates v. 47 interpretively; the literal meaning is, "The whole congregation of Israel must do it."

[102] On the grammar of the wording (הִמּוֹל לוֹ) of the reference to circumcision in this instance, see R. Althann, "*MWL*, 'Circumcise' with *Lamedh* of Agency," *Bib* 62 (1981): 239–40.

[103] It is, however, possible that the phrase in question, אֶזְרַח הָאָרֶץ, usually translated either "native of the land" or "one born in the land," actually means only "citizen of the land" and refers to the confidence the Israelites already had that they were citizens of Canaan by reason of descendancy from Abraham, to whom Canaan had been promised by God. In other words, they may have regarded themselves as promised land citizens in advance, not unlike the way a child of US citizen parents is automatically a US citizen, even if born abroad and not having yet set foot in the US.

[104] See also comments on 12:41.

an army[105] and started on their exodus journey, evening and morning being a single day in the ancient calculation.[106]

8. Exodus Memorials: Consecration/Redemption of Firstborn, Eating Unleavened Bread (13:1–16)

At first glance it might seem that Exod 13:1–16 mixes together two unrelated topics: a set of new rules about consecrating and redeeming the firstborn of humans and animals and a somewhat expanded restatement of the rules for keeping the annual spring Feast of Unleavened Bread. In fact, these two topics were closely related. First, both of them had special applicability to the spring of the year. That was when the Israelites left Egypt in haste, so, as already noted repeatedly in chap. 12, it was the necessary and proper time for the Unleavened Bread memorial week of observance. What may be less obvious to the average modern reader, however, is that springtime was also the time when most domesticated animals gave birth, particularly the time of lambing and goat kidding, the primary interests of the Israelites, who were small cattle farmers par excellence.[107] Second, a special emphasis of Israelite religious learning focused on the transmittal of information from father to firstborn[108] and most commonly from father to firstborn son. It was assumed that if fathers would faithfully pass on to their firstborn the covenant commitments revealed through Moses, others in the family, both later-born sons and all daughters, would also be the beneficiaries. Part of this was simply cultural: fathers and their firstborn children carried special responsibilities for family leadership, which if exercised faithfully would include being sure the rest of the family members were both well informed and warmly encouraged and supported in keeping the terms of the covenant. The firstborn child occupied a position of honor at the dinner table and played a major role in the Passover meal. Third, both the Feast of Unleavened Bread and the consecration/redemption observance strongly relate to *settling into the promised land,* which Moses and the Israelites still assumed would be taking place within a matter of months. Those hearing these words were thinking about the very next spring, when instead of being on the run in the

---

[105] The plural in the text can be translated "armies" or "army," and this should not be considered confusing. Even in modern parlance one may speak of "army" as an entire branch of the armed services or as a group of fighting units therein. E.g., during WWII George Patton commanded "Third Army," within the "US Army," within the combined "Allied Armies."

[106] As in Gen 1, *passim.*

[107] Cf. Gen 47:3–6; Exod 10:24–26.

[108] Thus the standard teaching format uses father-son terminology as reflected regularly in the book of Proverbs, "My son," and also in Jesus' warning about receiving human teaching in place of the divine revelation ("Do not call anyone on earth 'father,'" Matt 23:9).

wilderness they would be handling the opportunities and responsibilities of springtime in a family-based farming society in the land of Abraham's sojourn. What links all the material of 13:1–16 together especially is this sense of preparation for inhabiting the land—and not forgetting once there to keep covenant with Yahweh, who had made it possible for his people to have all that they would enjoy in their new land.

(1) Introductory Statement of the Consecration/Redemption Regulation (13:1–2)

[1]The LORD said to Moses, [2]"Consecrate to me every firstborn male. The first offspring of every womb among the Israelites belongs to me, whether man or animal."

13:1–2 The Hebrew of the command here is technically gender neutral (lit., "Consecrate to me every firstborn. That which opens the womb among the Israelites, both human and animal, is mine"). The nouns for "firstborn" *(bĕkôr)* and "which opens" *(peṭer)* and the pronoun" that" *(hûʾ)* are all masculine, but their gender may be simply unavoidable "grammatical" gender rather than a wording intended to exclude female firstborn.[109] In practice, consecration/dedication of animal firstborn males was the norm, as v. 12 makes explicit, but for humans the wording seems more inclusive, or at least ambiguous, throughout this pericope. Laws such as this one are sometimes cited as precedent for the modern practice in many baptistic churches of "dedicating" babies, but in fact the ancient practice was limited to firstborn children and required the payment of a redemption price, factors conveniently ignored in the modern instance.[110] "Consecrate to me every firstborn" means "give over to me as holy *[qaddēš]*[111] every firstborn." God here and elsewhere[112] claims ownership of the firstborn of humans and animals, which their families were required to present to him as his property. Did he actually want to keep them? No, except in the rarest of instances (as in, e.g., the case of Samuel; 1 Sam 1:11). Thus the provision in vv. 13,15 for redeeming the firstborn back into the family by means of a buy-back payment. His desire was that the Israelites recognize his right to ownership of

---

[109] This would seem especially so in light of God's ruling in the case of the daughters of Zelophehad (Num 27:1–11; 36:1–13; Josh 17:1–4), a law dealing with precisely the sort of issues in which firstborn sons usually played the most significant role: inheritance.

[110] Those who "dedicate" babies in the New Covenant economy are actually practicing a form of "blessing" rather than biblical "dedication." Jesus' dedication at the Jerusalem temple by his parents was a fulfillment of Old Covenant Law, and not a New Covenant precedent.

[111] The basic meaning of "holy" is "belonging to God." Holiness is always derivative from God himself. The more humans are like him, the more they belong to him and are holy. The less they submit to him, the less holy they are.

[112] E.g., Num 3:13; 8:16–17; Deut 15:19.

the first and best, in whatever came to them in spoils of war, or harvests, or offspring. It is necessary and beneficial that human beings recognize that God is superior to them, and the requirement of a ritual that reminded every Israelite of this by insisting on "receiving" their firstborn from them helped create the spiritual attitude of submission so important for salvation, personal discipline, and blessing.

(2) The Importance of Keeping the Feast of Unleavened Bread Annually in the Promised Land (13:3–10)

[3]Then Moses said to the people, "Commemorate this day, the day you came out of Egypt, out of the land of slavery, because the LORD brought you out of it with a mighty hand. Eat nothing containing yeast. [4]Today, in the month of Abib, you are leaving. [5]When the LORD brings you into the land of the Canaanites, Hittites, Amorites, Hivites and Jebusites—the land he swore to your forefathers to give you, a land flowing with milk and honey—you are to observe this ceremony in this month: [6]For seven days eat bread made without yeast and on the seventh day hold a festival to the LORD. [7]Eat unleavened bread during those seven days; nothing with yeast in it is to be seen among you, nor shall any yeast be seen anywhere within your borders. [8]On that day tell your son, 'I do this because of what the LORD did for me when I came out of Egypt.' [9]This observance will be for you like a sign on your hand and a reminder on your forehead that the law of the LORD is to be on your lips. For the LORD brought you out of Egypt with his mighty hand. [10]You must keep this ordinance at the appointed time year after year.

13:3 The verse reads more accurately: "So Moses said to the people, 'Remember this day when you came out of Egypt, out of the house/place of slavery, for by strength of hand the LORD brought you out of here. Yeast may not be eaten.'" Especially significant is Moses' statement "brought you ought of here" since it reminds the reader that Moses was speaking these words to people who were still in Egypt proper and were only beginning to take the roads that would lead them out of it to freedom. Calling Egypt the house/place of slavery *(bēt ʿăbādîm)* has the effect of suggesting that the entire nation of Israel served the entire nation of Egypt just as an individual slave would serve in an individual house/place or family.[113] They had been the abused servants of a greater power; now they were being freed to be the happy servants of the Greatest Power.[114] The various parts of this verse do not contain new concepts[115] but the verse is somewhat unique in linking them together as it does.

---

[113] בֵּית translates as "place, family, house" in that order of frequency, in the OT.

[114] As noted earlier, עבד means "work," "serve," and "worship" depending on the context, so the Israelites were moving from *serving* Pharaoh and the Egyptians to *serving* God; their requests for exodus from Egypt were consistently phrased "so that we may serve/worship Yahweh."

[115] Cf. 6:1,7; 12:15–18; 39; 42; 51.

13:4–5 Just as modern Westerners learn as little children that Christmas comes only in the month of December, ancient Israelites learned early on, from this point in history forward, that the Feast of Unleavened Bread comes only in Abib. *Abib* is a collective noun that means "ears of grain," more loosely, "spring." It is the same month (March-April) that is later in the Old Testament called "Nisan," a term borrowed from Akkadian under Babylonian influence.[116] The Israelites were going to a foreign land from a foreign land—they were citizens of neither from the point of view of the Egyptians and Canaanite groups. Accordingly, they were not headed for a place that encouraged what was new to them as well: the observance of the Feast of Unleavened Bread; such a feast was completely unheard of in Canaan. The five people groups named here are representative of the rest (notably Perizzites and Gergashites).[117] God had promised their land to the Israelites, first on oath to Abraham (Gen 12:7), and then by renewal of that oath to his son (Gen 17:21,) and grandson (Gen 28:13,) and their descendants (Gen 15:16,18). On the spiritual rather than literal impact of the term "flowing with milk and honey" see comments on 3:8,17.

13:6–7 These verses restate and condense (with somewhat varied wording to help reinforce the concepts in the listener/reader's mind) what 12:14–20 have already covered: the Feast of unleavened bread must be a weeklong festival, culminating with a special celebration on the closing day, and requiring absence of yeast in all locations (13:7, "anywhere within your borders"; 12:20, "wherever you live").

13:8–10 Because Moses spoke these words to those who actually did participate personally in the exodus, he told them to make first-person statements such as "I do this" and "for me when I came out of Egypt." However, this does not exhaust the reason for the first person language. Another factor is also at play: Moses had in mind the pan-historical solidarity of the Israelite people. All generations of fathers are to say to their children[118] these

[116] The term appears only after the exile, in Neh 2:1 and Esth 3:7, whereas the term Abib appears exclusively in the Pentateuch. Were the supposed "P" materials actually postexilic as the classical version of the Documentary Hypothesis claims, one would not expect this differentiation. Note also the use of Abib in the place name "Tel Abib" ("Spring Hill") in Ezek 3:15.

[117] All sorts of combinations of the "seven" nations are found in the OT; Moses used a different list in 3:8,17 and would use others in Exod 23:28 (three people groups); Num 13:29 (five groups, including the Amalekites); Deut 7:1 (all the usual seven); Deut 20:17 (six groups). The Amorites (a name that can mean simply "westerners") suffices for all the native groups in Gen 15:16. The "Hittites" mentioned in the Bible are not the Anatolian nation also called "Hittites" but rather a local Canaanite group, the sons of Heth (Gen 23:3). Had the Anatolian nation appeared in the Bible, its people would have been called the Hattites (cf. Akk. *atti*).

[118] בֵּין is almost always translated "son," but on the analogy of the way that its plural (בָּנִים) means "children" and not necessarily "sons" (indeed, often "sons" would be quite misleading), the singular may mean "child" far more often than typical Eng. translations render it.

words, also in the first person, because all generations are part of the continuum that experienced the exodus. The community of faith at every age is supposed to identify fully with the original exodus generation, just as one gets "caught up" in a powerful story in book or movie form, or, more significantly, just as one identifies with various kinds of values and commitments learned from beloved grandparents and parents. A parade example of this sort of pan-generational teaching is found in Deut 4:3–40, in which Moses addressed his audience (who were in fact the generation that grew up in the wilderness) as if they had grown up in Egypt, as if they had also lived for many years already in the promised land (they weren't there yet), and, as well, as if they were about to be driven from it into Exile many centuries later, and then were the actual exile generation who had a chance to come back from that exile to new and greater blessings—in other words, as if one generation lived a thousand years. In God's economy *each* generation of his people is expected to cultivate an identification with all the experiences of *all* the generations, and all the generations must identify with the events that have happened or will happen to *any* generation.

The exodus story is to be repeated *on that day,* presumably the seventh, special day of the Feast of Unleavened Bread, regardless of how many other times in the year it may also be told. That way, at least annually, there will be a special focus on the Exodus for a week—at the beginning via the Passover rite and at the end with the seventh day's special testimonial. What was the point? Not a desire merely that an important memory be preserved but a desire that a life-saving covenant be kept! Verse 9 tells God's people that they are to take very seriously the responsibilities of the Feast of Unleavened Bread because its purpose is covenant renewal ("that the law of the LORD is to be on your lips"). For something to be *on your lips* is for it to be regularly thought of and talked about, something you know well and pay attention to (cf. 23:13; Deut 23:23; Ps 50:16). In an age when most people were not literate and those who were had very little writing material because it was so expensive, the ritual of that special spring week served in the same way that reminder messages on one's *hand* or *forehead*[119] would serve. It triggered remembrance of the covenant law by which the Israelites were kept in proper relationship with God and for which he had brought them out of Egypt in the first place (to *serve* him, not just to go to a nicer place to live). Keeping his covenant was the end goal because thereby Israel kept

[119] Here and in v. 16 the observance of the feast functions as a reminder that is compared to hand and forehead reminders. Actual hand and forehead reminders were indeed used by Israelites to keep cognizant of the divine law (Deut 6:8; 11:18), and the concept was used by John in his imagistic portrayal of the reminder marks required by the Beast (Rev 13:16; 14:9; 20:4). John's description of the practice helps us see that it was a way of demonstrating to whom one belonged in covenant relationship.

itself within God's salvation; keeping the feast was a means of being sure to be reminded to keep the covenant. God is ever an evangelist, who always seeks the rescue of his people from the penalty of sin and always seeks to keep them aware of their need to be rightly—dependently—related to him. Thus the feast must always be kept at the same time annually, never postponed, never rescheduled, never canceled, never abandoned ("you must keep this ordinance at the appointed time year after year," v. 10).

(3) Basic Rules for Consecration/Redemption of Firstborn (13:11–13)

11"After the LORD brings you into the land of the Canaanites and gives it to you, as he promised on oath to you and your forefathers, 12you are to give over to the LORD the first offspring of every womb. All the firstborn males of your livestock belong to the LORD. 13Redeem with a lamb every firstborn donkey, but if you do not redeem it, break its neck. Redeem every firstborn among your sons.

13:11–13 As is the case with the entire Pentateuch, this section comes from a time before the Israelites had entered the promised land and therefore anticipates what would happen once the land was settled. Accordingly, it begins with a temporal adverbial clause ("after the LORD brings you into the land of the Canaanites and gives it to you") that by implication makes the time of the wilderness wanderings an exception. Presumably the regular redemption of firstborn humans and animals did not occur with the same regularity during the wilderness period as it did later.[120] Verse 11's allusion to God's promise of the land to Abraham, Isaac, and Jacob ("as he promised on oath to you and your forefathers") echoes v. 4's, further reinforcing the idea that these regulations were for the promised land, not the wilderness.

"The first offspring of every womb" belongs to God, and in cattle it was specifically the "firstborn males" that were his. As we have already noted, God did not want to keep (and thus keep away from his people's homes and families) either the firstborn human babies or many of the firstborn animal babies. The criterion was that the firstborn males of normally edible animals (goat kids, lambs, oxen,—whatever was considered a proper food animal) were given to God as offerings, whereas the firstborn of humans and the firstborn of male animals used for work but not for eating (such as the donkey mentioned in v. 13) were redeemed by payment of a substitute. Thus the practical meaning of "give over to the LORD" in v. 12 is "bring to the tabernacle as a sacrifice."

[120] The special redemption related to the choice of the Levites in place of the firstborn in Num 3 is an exception; it seems to have occurred once only and is a mechanism for the incorporation of the Levites as the clergy tribe, rather than an outworking of the present general consecration/redemption regulation.

In the case of a donkey, a nonfirstborn lamb was an appropriate substitute (since all firstborn lambs must be given to God and none held back to serve as redemption substitutes). For children [NIV "sons," v. 13] the redemption price was five sanctuary shekels, just as it was for an unclean animal (a male work animal that one wanted to keep). The full explanation of the redemption pricing is found in Num 18:15–17.[121] The ruling in v. 13 about breaking the neck of an unredeemed donkey (used here as an example, not as the only instance of its type) may seem odd at first glance, but it was entirely within the principles of the redemption system. A firstborn animal could not simply be kept from God for one's own use—either for working or for eating. It belonged to God, so if it was not redeemed, it must be destroyed. God did not want people to waste the time of the priests and Levites at the central sanctuary by having people bring unneeded animals to them for destruction. The people could destroy the animals themselves. But by no means could anyone say, "Since God doesn't need this, I'll keep it and use it for myself." God decided what to use and what to destroy of what belonged to him. This regulation clarifies the process in the case of animals of no use to the sanctuary.

The ultimate purpose of this instruction was to prepare the Israelites for the death of Christ on their behalf. Though most generations of Israelites could anticipate this all-important event only vaguely, they certainly could grasp the basic concepts involved: if a life is to be restored, it must be *bought back* (redeemed) by a payment; and that payment is often the substitutionary death of something for something else. Paul's assertion in 1 Cor 6:20 and 7:23, "You were bought at a price," follows the logic of the Old Testament redemption system as it foreshadows the redemption price paid by Christ with his own blood.

(4) The Connection of Consecration/Redemption of Firstborn to the Exodus (13:14–16)

[14]"In days to come, when your son asks you, 'What does this mean?' say to him, 'With a mighty hand the LORD brought us out of Egypt, out of the land of slavery. [15]When Pharaoh stubbornly refused to let us go, the LORD killed every firstborn in Egypt, both man and animal. This is why I sacrifice to the LORD the first male offspring of every womb and redeem each of my firstborn sons.' [16]And

---

[121] "The first offspring of every womb, both man and animal, that is offered to the LORD is yours. But you must redeem every firstborn son and every firstborn male of unclean animals. When they are a month old, you must redeem them at the redemption price set at five shekels of silver, according to the sanctuary shekel, which weighs twenty gerahs. But you must not redeem the firstborn of an ox, a sheep or a goat; they are holy. Sprinkle their blood on the altar and burn their fat as an offering made by fire, an aroma pleasing to the LORD."

it will be like a sign on your hand and a symbol on your forehead that the LORD brought us out of Egypt with his mighty hand."

13:14–16 Children desire to learn the reasons for the practices they grow up observing. It was therefore to be expected that in their natural inquisitiveness Israelite children would ask their parents the meaning of the consecration/redemption of the firstborn. The parents were expected in replying to their children to link the practice to the exodus, which was triggered by the death of the Egyptian firstborn and the sparing of the Israelite firstborn. In effect the child was to be told, "Our identity is that of God's chosen people who were rescued from slavery in Egypt and rescued from the death of the firstborn by faith in Yahweh. We keep showing that faith by dedicating all firstborn children and all firstborn male livestock to God. But we buy back the children, and the livestock that are inappropriate for God's offerings because God is generous enough to allow us to do that. He still gets an offering, but it is a *substitute* offering for what he wants us to keep. When we do all this, we are doing something that reminds us of his powerful deliverance from Egypt."

Verse 14 repeats some of what vv. 3 and 9 have already said, and v. 16 restates much of what v. 9 contains. The slight differences (e.g., "a symbol [inscriptions] on your forehead"[122] in v. 16 as opposed to "reminder on your forehead" in v. 9) are, again, the sort of wording variations that help drive concepts permanently into one's memory.[123] Verse 15 provides the greatest amount of new material in the passage, even though none of it is new to the overall Exodus story. The Hebrew of vv. 14–16 contains nothing that definitively limits consecration/redemption of the firstborn to male children; the NIV translation is overly restrictive in using "first male offspring" and "firstborn sons" (better: "That is why I sacrifice to the LORD all the firstborn of the womb [i.e., animals] that are males and all the firstborn of my children I redeem").

[122] But the meaning of the object to be worn "between the eyes" (the literal meaning of the Hb. translated in the NIV as "on your forehead") may be somewhat debatable. The term is also found in Deut 6:8; 11:18. See E. H. Speiser, "TWTPT," *JQR* 48 (1957–58): 208–17; and H. Rand, "The Etymology of *Totafot*," *Jud* 42 (1993): 160–63. Rand suggests that the term *ṭôṭāpôt* comes from a combination of the names of two Egyptian gods, Thoth and Ptah (pronounced Phot). Since in Egyptian religion Ptah was a deity far superior to his divine scribe Thoth, Rand concludes that the word *ṭôṭāpôt* was coined by the Israelites as a purposeful mockery of the Egyptians—a highly speculative assertion on Rand's part but an indication of how difficult it is to pin down the precise meaning of the word.

[123] Because all learners retain new information better when it is in their own "fluent language," restating information with varying vocabulary increases the likelihood that greater numbers of people will hear/read the information in what to them seems language that makes sense. On the other hand, the language cannot be varied too often or too much since the greater the variation the greater the risk of communicating different concepts to different people. But within moderation variation in vocabulary in the restatement of information serves useful ends for teaching.

DIVISION OUTLINE

V. THE WILDERNESS JOURNEY TO SINAI (13:17–19:25)
  1. Reasons for an Irregular Route (13:17–14:4)
    (1) The Dangers of War for an Untested Army (13:17–18)
    (2) Special Transportation of the Bones of Joseph (13:19)
    (3) Early Destinations and the Pillar of Cloud/Fire (13:20–22)
    (4) Reversing Direction: God's Further Humiliation of Pharaoh (14:1–4)
  2. Attack of the Egyptian Army and Israelite Panic (14:5–14)
    (1) Egyptian Regret and Change of Mind (14:5)
    (2) Egyptian Chariot Pursuit of Israel (14:6–9)
    (3) Israelite Panic and Complaint (14:10–12)
    (4) Moses' Confident reassurance of God's Plan to Trap the Egyptians (14:13–14)
  3. Parting of the Red Sea and Drowning of the Egyptians (14:15–32)
    (1) God Sends Israel into the Sea to Gain Glory over Pharaoh and His Army (14:15–18)
    (2) The Divine Angel/Pillar Separates Israelites and Egyptians (14:19–20)
    (3) Israel Crosses the Red Sea on Dry Land (14:21–22)
    (4) God Confuses the Egyptian Army (14:23–25)
    (5) The Sea Drowns the Egyptian Army (14:26–28)
    (6) Summation: God's Deliverance and Resultant Faith (14:29–31)
  4. Victory Hymn of Moses (15:1–18)
    (1) Part I of Moses' Song: Praise to the Lord (15:1–3)
    (2) Part II of Moses' Song: Defeat of the Egyptians (15:4–10)
    (3) Part III of Moses' Song: Praise and Thanks to the Lord (15:11–13)
    (4) Part IV of Moses' Song: Reaction of Future Foes (15:14–16a)
    (5) Part V of Moses' Song: Israel, God's Sanctuary (15:16b–18)
  5. Prose Summation and Miriam's Reprise of the Hymn (15:19–21)
  6. Grumbling Begins: Water at Marah and Elim and God's Promise of Healing (15:22–27)
  7. More Grumbling: About Food (16:1–9)
  8. God Sends Quail and Manna from Heaven (16:10–36)
    (1) God Grants Manna in Response to the Grumbling about Food (16:10–15a)

(2) Manna Gathering and the First Disobedience in Connection with It (16:15b–20)
(3) Manna Gathering and the Sabbath (16:21–26)
(4) The Second Disobedience and the Sabbath Lesson Learned (16:27–30)
(5) Preserving the Manna for Generations to Come as a Testimony to God's Faithfulness (16:31–36)

9. More Grumbling and Water at Massah-Meribah (17:1–7)
10. Battle against the Amalekites at Rephidim and the Curse on Amalek (17:8–16)
    Excursus: Israelite Holy War
11. The Visit and Conversion of Jethro (18:1–12)
    Excursus: Was Moses Divorced from Zipporah?
12. Jethro Advises Implementing a Hierarchical Court System (18:13–27)
13. Arrival at Sinai and Call to Holiness (19:1–8)
    (1) Arrival at Sinai (19:1–2)
    (2) The Poetic Introduction to the Call to Covenant Holiness (19:3)
    (3) The Special Call to Covenant Holiness (19:4–6)
    (4) The Agreement of the People to Enter into Covenant with Yahweh (19:7–8)
14. Consecration in Preparation for Meeting God (19:9–15)
15. Meeting God on the Mountain (19:16–25)

V. THE WILDERNESS JOURNEY TO SINAI (13:17–19:25)

The Israelites had much to learn. They had just begun to leave Egypt, where they had been for so long leaderless and subjugated that their entire way of thinking tended to reflect that of people who owed their identity to their plight. They knew themselves as victims of the tyranny of the ancient world's greatest contemporary political-military-economic power. They knew one place to live: the Goshen area of northeast Egypt. They had never been allowed military arms or the knowledge of how to use them, even though God had just begun to organize them as his army. They were not used to direct guidance from God and understood little of the power of his presence among them. They operated with the usual assumptions of most people trying to understand the workings of God: a good and powerful god would hardly allow his people to go through troubles, dangers, griefs, and testings, would he? Their reasoning led them naturally to think: If God is all-powerful and can oppress the Egyptians through the plagues while sparing us, his people, entirely, we can now expect him to take care of all our wants and desires just as we define them, can't we?

This section of the Exodus narrative takes the reader from Egypt to Sinai, and in the process through various hardships the Israelites experienced. These included being pursued by Pharaoh's vastly superior army, a lack of water at various locations where God led them (what sort of God would tell his people to encamp where they couldn't even get a drink for themselves or water their flocks?), boredom with the same food day after day, being attacked and having to fight their first battle (against a fighting force experienced in projecting power in the very wilderness they were in), having disputes in such numbers that they needed a multitiered court system, and finding out that getting too close to a holy God was deadly. In all these events, however, God was at work to bring his people to a right relationship with him and to teach them dependence on his provision for them. He was shaping and educating them, allowing them to learn (frequently the hard way since that is all too often the only way people really learn a lesson) what it meant to trust him in all sorts of situations. In addition he was treating them in a way that has always been difficult for people to accept: he was not telling them everything they wanted to know. He told them what they *needed* to know in order to become his covenant people and in order to receive his salvation. They *wanted* to know much more, however: where to find water right away, how much longer this or that would last, how to be comfortable, how to avoid problems and dangers, and how to get out of unpleasant situations. Telling God how to do things and complaining about the things he does or doesn't do have always been rather popular enterprises. The Israelites on the way to Sinai did not hesitate to indulge in them.

1. Reasons for an Irregular Route (13:17–14:4)

(1) The Dangers of War for an Untested Army (13:17–18)

17 When Pharaoh let the people go, God did not lead them on the road through the Philistine country, though that was shorter. For God said, "If they face war, they might change their minds and return to Egypt." 18 So God led the people around by the desert road toward the Red Sea. The Israelites went up out of Egypt armed for battle.

13:17 The first reason for an irregular exodus route was the presence of the Philistines on the Asian coast of the Mediterranean, that is, virtually on Egypt's northeast border.[1] No definitive documentation of Philistine military

[1] That Philistia was considered to be right on the border between Canaan and Egypt is indicated by the wording of Gen 26:1–2, wherein God allowed Isaac to go only as far as "Abimelech, king of the Philistines," but not farther: "Do not go down to Egypt; . . . live in [this] land," implying that to go farther south past Philistia (Gerar, specifically) would be to enter Egyptian territory.

strength at the time of the exodus has survived from the ancient world. We know, however, that the Philistines were so daunting a fighting force at the time of the conquest, forty years later and beyond, that even at Joshua's death their territory remained unconquered (cf. Josh 13:1–5).[2] We also know that they were bold enough to attack Egypt proper in an effort to capture territory in the days of Ramses III, that is, about 1188 BC,[3] suggesting that they considered themselves at that time—considerably after the Israelites had entered Canaan—potentially able to defeat even the Egyptians, depending on the circumstances. Accordingly, God did not want his people to try to enter Canaan directly by the well-established coastal road from Egypt, the *Via Maris,* even though that was by far the shortest and easiest route from the point of view of travel time and theoretical convenience. The Via Maris led right through the heart of Philistine territory. Based on their behavior as recorded in Judges and 1 Samuel, the Philistines were looking to expand their territorial control and would hardly have been willing to let the Israelites enter Canaan, on which they themselves had designs, without an all-out fight.

By contrast, according to the Merneptah Stela,[4] Israel was not yet regarded as a nation but merely as a people group even as late as 1230 BC, a fact that may be taken as confirming the consistent biblical indications of their relative weakness militarily and politically. At least that is the sort of scenario that comports precisely with the picture painted here in Exodus and in the books of Judges and 1 Samuel. Could God have destroyed the Philistines on behalf of the Israelites? Of course. But the Philistines had so far

---

[2] Indeed, not until David's day did Israel dominate the Philistines. Thus it would hardly have been possible for the Israelites to beat them in a straight matchup a few weeks out of Egypt.

[3] In Ramses III's eighth year the Egyptians claimed to have turned back an onslaught of Philistine groups trying to invade Egypt proper, according to the Medinet Habu inscriptions at Thebes. Some came by sea; others, by land. According to the texts: "Their confederation was the Philistines, Tjeker, Shekelesh, Denyen, and Weshesh, land united. They laid their hands upon the lands as far as the circuit of the earth, their hearts confident and trusting: 'Our plans will succeed!'" (*ANET,* 262). In other words, the five groups known collectively by the name of their most prominent people group (the Philistines) constituted a formidable fighting force. In the same text is also found the statement: "No land could stand before their arms," a fairly clear assessment of Philistine military prowess.

[4] The Merneptah Stela is also sometimes called the "Israel Stela" because of its mention of Israel as a people living in Canaan but apparently not yet in full control of it. It is dated to the fifth year of Merneptah, which was about 1230 BC, and its claim that the Egyptians in some vague way pacified the Israelites is stylized in the sort of way that suggests little historical reliability. The actual statement about the Israelites is "Israel is laid waste, his seed is not" (*ANET,* 378). No actual military encounter with the Israelites is mentioned. Naturally, Pharaoh's claim to have subdued all of Canaan would be expected to include at least a pro forma boast that Israel was among the groups now under the Egyptian thumb. What is especially relevant to our discussion about the stela is its designation of Israel—alone among the national groups mentioned—as a people group rather than as a country/nation. This would seem to confirm its reputation, at least as far as the Egyptians were concerned, as a "small potatoes" foe.

done nothing to the Israelites and so were not in the same category as the Egyptians, who well deserved the punishment they had already received and were about to receive more of (i.e., their defeat at the Red Sea). Moreover, the Philistines were latecomers to Palestine, as compared to the Amorites/Canaanites, and therefore did not fall under the blanket condemnation of the "sin of the Amorites" that God had announced to Abraham in Gen 15:16 as the basis for the conquest of Canaan. So the Philistines were to be dealt with later[5] rather than immediately; it was not part of God's plan that they should be fought and subdued at this early stage. He therefore did not call Israel to try to conquer Philistine territory, and had they tried on their own to do so, they would surely have been defeated, just as happened when they tried later, on their own, to defeat the Canaanites (Num 14:44–45).

Without God's help, he knew that "if they face war, they might change their minds and return to Egypt." Would Israel really be so inconsistent as to give up the conquest and return to Egypt—of all places? And would they do so after all they had seen and experienced in the ten plagues? The answer is yes—decidedly yes. Not only did this very plan to return to Egypt actually occur less than two years later (Num 14:3,14), but one must not forget that the Israelites were accustomed only to Egypt; they had lived nowhere else for 430 years. A properly chastised Egypt, which had perhaps "learned its lesson" about mistreating the Israelites by force of the plagues, might have seemed to them the very place they would now be most safe and happy, especially if they had been beaten in war by the Philistines (as would be certain without divine aid) and therefore would feel justified in giving up on any plan to enter Canaan. God knew their limited perspectives and naïve expectations full well and thus led them away from Philistine territory.

God's compassionate words in the second sentence of this verse, "If they face war, they might change their minds and return to Egypt," demonstrate his concern for the unpreparedness of the Israelites to fight any other military force at this point. Thus, God made clear that the Egyptian army, far superior to that of the Philistines, would have crushed Israel in any normal military encounter. The reader is therefore prepared by this statement for the expectation that Israel would have little success in any future battle without special divine intervention—and, indeed, that is exactly what was required at the Red Sea (14:5ff.),[6] Rephidim (17:8ff.), and thereafter throughout

---

[5] Under David's leadership, ca. 1000 BC, the Philistines were permanently subdued (2 Sam 8:1; 21:15–22; cf. 1 Kgs 4:21).

[6] Indeed, B. Bachra points out that the entire unit of text from 13:17 through the end of chap. 14 is united by a number of concentric patterns that show that it is not an editorial composite from disparate sources but a coherent composition ("Structural Regularities in the Story of the Passage through the Sea (Exod 13,17–22 and Exod 14)," *SJOT* 16 [2002]: 246–63). Thus already what 13:16ff. is talking about prepares the reader for what chap. 14 describes.

virtually all of Israel's history. Accordingly, the divine defeat of the Egyptian army at the Red Sea will constitute an essential part of the deliverance of the people and a means of their encouragement to follow Yahweh from Egypt, and not back thereto.[7]

13:18 What, then, to do to avoid trying to go through Philistine-held territory into the promised land? The answer was for God to lead them in a different direction and on a different road, that is, "by the desert road toward the Red Sea."[8] Again Moses reminds us that the Israelites were God's army: "The Israelites went up out of Egypt armed for battle." The NIV translation is not correct. The Hebrew actually says, "The Israelites went up out of the land of Egypt organized by fifties." Fifties were one of the smallest fighting units, what might be called today "squads." The term does not literally refer to groups of fifty men but is part of the "thousand-hundreds-fifties-tens" language employed to delineate military units.[9] The Israelites were at this point not armed at all. Later they would carry mainly short swords (cf. Exod 32:27). The short sword was a common armament of the day, but the overall evidence suggests that the Israelites were less trained than other ancients at this point in their history in all war skills and were particularly deficient in archery, spear throwing, and slinging.[10] Formed up for battle they may have been—after a fashion. Trained for battle, however, they were not. There had been no permission or opportunity for learning martial arts under the Egyptians, and the fact that Israelite men could count themselves into (unarmed) squads did not mean they were in fact a capable fighting force on their own.

(2) Special Transportation of the Bones of Joseph (13:19)

[19]Moses took the bones of Joseph with him because Joseph had made the sons of Israel swear an oath. He had said, "God will surely come to your aid, and then you must carry my bones up with you from this place."

13:19 This verse might seem to a modern reader to introduce a side issue into the narrative, but the verse reminds the reader of an important hopeful practice in ancient Israel, relating to Israel's very identity as the chosen people and the typical Israelite's expectation of an afterlife. Joseph

---

[7] J. Derby, "The Miracle at the Red Sea," *JBQ* 20 (1991–92): 250–55.

[8] On this route see also vv. 20ff. F. Regalado suggests that the sea through which the Israelites passed was one of the lakes now incorporated into the Suez Canal district, i.e., either Lake Timsah or Lake Ballah, but not the Gulf of Suez in the Red Sea itself. Our position is that the sea was indeed the Red Sea, but it is not impossible that the lakes of the Suez region were loosely included in the Hb. term *yam sup* in Bible times ("The Location of the Sea the Israelites Passed Through," *Journal of the Adventist Theological Society* 13 [2002]: 115–34).

[9] As in Exod 18:21,25; Deut 1:15.

[10] Later archery was more frequently used (Josh 24:12; 1 Sam 18:4; 2 Chr 26:14); spear throwing remained rare (1 Sam 13:22), and slinging became more common (Judg 20:16; 2 Chr 26:14).

understood the promises of God to Abraham. He was well aware that someday the Israelites would leave Egypt and take their promised place "up"[11] in the promised land. So important to him was his identification in faith with the people of God and their eternal destiny that he exacted a deathbed promise from his brothers to the effect that they would be sure that his remains were brought out of Egypt and buried in Canaan (Gen 50:24–25). Since Joseph had been embalmed (Gen 50:26), his remains probably were more substantial than mere bones, that is, more like mummified remains that are eviscerated but still contain a full skeleton and skin, as well as desiccated flesh and hair. These the Israelites called "bones" in the Old Testament, just as they also referred to mere skeletal remains as "bones."[12]

The Israelites believed in life after death and took great care with their remains, or "bones." It was considered desirable for a whole family of as many generations as possible to be buried together in a common grave, not necessarily because grouped family burial made life after death more attainable but to show faith in the resurrection.[13] The wording "gathered to one's people/fathers" (e.g., Gen 49:29; Judg 2:10; 2 Kgs 22:20; 2 Chr 34:28) described an expectation of the intermediate state of paradise, from which one would be resurrected, with bodily remains (bones) rejoined and transformed by God's spirit (Ezek 37:1–14) into a spiritual body (1 Cor 15:44) with which to inhabit heaven forever. Burial in the same tomb with those who had gone on before symbolized faith in that outcome on the part of the deceased.

---

[11] Throughout the narrative, going from Egypt to Canaan is described as going *up,* not because Moses was thinking of north as "up" but because Egypt is largely lowland, near sea level, and Canaan is mostly highland, mountains and hills. Virtually throughout the Bible, people go "up" when they go higher in elevation (thus to Canaan, to Bethel, to Mount Zion and the temple) and "down" when they go lower in elevation (thus to Jericho, to Egypt, to the Dead Sea).

[12] On the deeply rooted concern for bone preservation, which is attested especially in the practice known as ossuary burial, see E. M. Meyers, *Jewish Ossuaries: Reburial and Rebirth. Secondary Burials in Their Ancient Near Eastern Setting* (Rome: Biblical Institute Press, 1971). Meyers explains the history and logic of secondary burials and resurrection expectation in the OT and ANE in this volume, which is not limited to ossuary analysis. Cf. A. Lemaire, "Burial Box of James the Brother of Jesus," *BAR* 28, no. 6 (2002): 24–33; D. Zlotnick, *The Tractate "Mourning" (Semahot): Regulations Relating to Death, Burial and Mourning* (New Haven: Yale University Press, 1966); L. Y. Rahmani, *A Catalogue of Jewish Ossuaries in the Collections of the State of Israel* (Jerusalem: Israel Antiquities Authority, 1994).

[13] Both life after death and resurrection are OT concepts and do not arise *de novo* in the NT. Much misunderstanding about this exists, to the extent that one still encounters misinformation to the effect that the OT reflects only a hazy notion of life after death. Although the NT provides many assurances in addition to the OT, from the OT alone a robust life after death understanding is easily demonstrated. Cf. P. S. Johnston, *Shades of Sheol: Death and Afterlife in the Old Testament* (Downers Grove: InterVarsity, 2002); also M. T. Kelsey, *Afterlife: The Other Side of Dying* (New York: Paulist Press, 1979).

For the Israelites leaving Egypt at the time of the exodus, as for Joseph centuries before, the promised land symbolized not merely an opportunity for freer, happier existence in this life, but it also symbolized eternal life with Abraham, Isaac, Jacob and the other great worthies of the past. There is no indication that Israelites assumed that if one died outside the promised land he or she could not have eternal life. Rather, they understood that for them to follow the plan of God in faith, including conscious inheritance of the land promised to Abraham on their behalf, was a part of the overall commitment to trust God for their present and future, including being buried where and with whom faithful Israelites would naturally want to be buried. The transportation of the bones of Joseph closed a chapter on Israelite history: just as elaborate care had been taken so that Jacob could be buried in the promised land rather than in Egypt (Gen 49:29–50:14), Joseph's remains deserved to be transported and reinterned there as well. Indeed, all the people alive at the time of the exodus were departing from the land of captivity to live and die in the land of promise and to be buried there. According to God's promises to Abraham, reiterated to his son and grandson, Israel belonged not in Egypt but in Canaan, and this verse reminds the reader that from the beginning it was the plan for this to be so.[14]

(3) Early Destinations and the Pillar of Cloud/Fire (13:20–22)

[20]After leaving Succoth they camped at Etham on the edge of the desert. [21]By day the LORD went ahead of them in a pillar of cloud to guide them on their way and by night in a pillar of fire to give them light, so that they could travel by day or night. [22]Neither the pillar of cloud by day nor the pillar of fire by night left its place in front of the people.

13:20 The second stage of the journey began. The location of neither Succoth (see 12:37) nor Etham[15] is certain, except that Etham was "on the edge of the desert," meaning that by reaching it, the Israelites were at the point of leaving inhabited Egypt, presumably continuing in their east-southeast direction. This does not mean that they were out of the range of Egyptian observation, as 14:3 makes clear. It is possible that we are to understand that the trip from Succoth to Etham took only a single day, but it is more

[14] The expectation of the departing exodus generation to die and be buried in the promised land was, of course, thwarted by their disobedience. Accordingly, they died and were buried neither in Egypt nor in the promised land but in the wilderness (Num 14:35; 26:65; Josh 5:4), an ignominy none would have chosen in advance.

[15] All three early LXX revisers, Aquila, Symmachus, and Theodotion, read "Ethan" instead of "Etham." This may reflect an assumption that the MT reading (the meaning of which is not clear) is a mistake for the word *ʾêtan,* which is well known and means "year-round" or "continuous" or "permanent." All three of them may have been reading from a Hb. *Vorlage* that contained the (probably erroneous) "correction."

likely that the language of the following two verses ("by day . . . by night") comports with a multiday (and perhaps multinight as well) journey to Etham and an encampment of more than one night there. This verse is of particular value when combined with 14:2–4. It helps show how the Israelite travels may have looked like a confused succession of attempts to leave Egypt that kept stopping when any given road reached the wilderness or the sea.

13:21–22 Moses introduced here the special visible symbol of God's presence to guide and protect the Israelites in the wilderness, the pillar of cloud/fire. The somewhat repetitious language of these verses in describing the pillar should not lead to the conclusion that there were two separate pillars. From Exod 14:24 ("the LORD looked down from the pillar of fire and cloud at the Egyptian army"), 14:19–20 ("the pillar of cloud also moved from in front and stood behind them, coming between the armies of Egypt and Israel. Throughout the night the cloud brought darkness to the one side and light to the other side"), 40:38 ("fire was in the cloud by night"), and Num 14:14 ("that your cloud stays over them, and that you go before them in a pillar of cloud by day and a pillar of fire by night") it is clear that there was only one cloudlike pillar, which represented God's presence, and that it appeared as a great column of dark cloud when viewed during the bright sunlit day but as a column of fire when viewed at night.[16] This is consistent with the descriptions of the cloud that covered the top of Mount Sinai as described in Exod 24:15–18. That cloud was dark to Moses, who was permitted to enter it, but appeared as a blazing fire to the other Israelites, who were not. It is common sense to assume that by day in the hot wilderness of Egypt and the Sinai peninsula, a cloud would seem welcome and comforting and that by night a fire would seem the same, providing light to see by and perhaps some warmth, as well as a terrifying barrier if it were positioned between the Israelites and a potential enemy.[17] The text, however, does not say that the cloud provided a shade over the heads of the Israelites. Rather, it went ahead of them to lead them—representing God's leadership as they moved through unknown territory.[18] Looking at a cloud ahead of one is

[16] M. Truper argues against the source-critical position that posits two separate cloud sources combined by a later editor in Exodus in his "Remarks on the Question of the Guidance in the Desert," *BMik* 39 (1994): 279–83. Cf. T. W. Mann, "The Pillar of Cloud in the Sea Narrative," *JBL* 90 (1971): 15–30; W. Gross, "Die Wolkensäule und die Feuersäule in Ex 13 + 14: Literarkritische, redaktiongeschichtliche und quellenkritische Erwägungen," in *Biblische Theologie und gesellschaftlicher Wandel: Für Norbert Lohfink* (Freiburg: Herder, 1993), 142–65.

[17] Barren wilderness such as those of the Sinai contain little that holds temperature. Accordingly, they warm up rapidly in the daytime and cool down rapidly after sunset. Temperature variations are thus typically greater between day and night in wilderness/desert areas than in other locales.

[18] The presence of the pillar did not obviate the need for a human guide. Hobab eventually served in this role (Num 10:29–32) since he knew the Sinai peninsula well. God's leadership may often be properly and necessarily supplemented by skilled human help.

pleasant and easy on a bright, hot day; looking at a comforting fire is similar at night. That was the main function of the pillar—a way of allowing the Israelites to look at God so as to be able to follow him without actually seeing him in his very person (33:20; cf. John 1:18; 1 John 4:12). The pillar-cloud was a manifestation of Yahweh himself, not merely something he sent them.

By reason of being guided by the pillar, the Israelites knew all day every day that God was present with them. Here was a supernatural, huge, and visible reminder that Yahweh was at the head of his people as they marched or encamped, whether by day or by night. Therefore, even the seemingly erratic route described by 13:20 in combination with 14:1–3 could be trusted because Yahweh was directing them on it. Yahweh chose the odd route—not they. Again, the pillar was not merely a sign from Yahweh—it *was* Yahweh ("The LORD went ahead of them in a pillar of cloud to guide them on their way and by night in a pillar of fire to give them light," 13:21). He manifested himself in the form of a pillar of cloud/fire for their benefit.[19]

(4) Reversing Direction: God's Further Humiliation of Pharaoh (14:1–4)

[1]Then the LORD said to Moses, [2]"Tell the Israelites to turn back and encamp near Pi Hahiroth, between Migdol and the sea. They are to encamp by the sea, directly opposite Baal Zephon. [3]Pharaoh will think, 'The Israelites are wandering around the land in confusion, hemmed in by the desert.' [4]And I will harden Pharaoh's heart, and he will pursue them. But I will gain glory for myself through Pharaoh and all his army, and the Egyptians will know that I am the LORD." So the Israelites did this.

14:1–2 The direction previously taken apparently headed east southeast (12:37; 13:20). Now comes a radical reversal of direction, presumably toward the north(east?) and a sea coast (either that of the Mediterranean or the Red Sea), where the Israelites were ordered to encamp for the third time since their initial departure. Surely such a route would look to anyone observing its contrast to the Israelites' previous direction as an indication of confusion. None of the locations mentioned in v. 2 can be identified with certainty today. They all probably were small, out-of-the-way places, allowing the thousands of Israelites to set up tents in an organized fashion near one another, with some sort of grazing places for their flocks and herds and adequate water for all—not the sort of locations that would have been well

[19] On the presence of God manifested in a divine fire, cf. also Gen 15:17; Exod 3:2; 19:18; Deut 4:24; 5:24; 9:3; J. K. Kuntz, *The Self-Revelation of God* (Philadelphia: Westminster, 1967), 96–100; S. Terrien, *The Elusive Presence* (San Francisco: Harper & Row, 1978), 109–12, 149–51); B. P. Robinson, "Moses at the Burning Bush," *JSOT* 75 (1997): 107–22; I. Wilson, *Out of the Midst of the Fire: Divine Presence in Deuteronomy* (Atlanta: Scholars Press, 1995).

populated by Egyptians. Accordingly, it is actually possible that none of them is mentioned in extant ancient texts, which list mainly large, populous cities and towns and entire regions. What had happened was that a complete reversal of direction had landed the Israelites somewhere along (as is most likely) the Red Sea coast,[20] looking as if they were afraid to head out into the actual wilderness.

All this constituted a divine ruse to trap Pharaoh one last time. Because the Israelites were still within the boundaries of Egypt throughout the time of these first three encampments (even though generally at the edges of the desert), there was ample opportunity for observation of their travels and activities by Egyptians in the vicinity. The Egyptians had a powerful and well-organized military with responsibility for keeping abreast of any activity on the nation's borders, and it is hard to imagine that regular reports of Israelite movements would not be promptly reported up the chain of command to Pharaoh's military advisors. The fact of the Israelite encampment at Pi-Hahiroth must have been known virtually immediately in the highest military circles.

Currid[21] suggests that Pi-Hahiroth could be a term that derives not from Egyptian but from Akkadian,[22] a Hebraized form of the Akkadian *pi-hiriti,* which means "the mouth/opening of the canal." This canal could have been the one that stretched from the Mediterranean to the area of the Great Bitter Lakes and perhaps even farther south, a defensive canal designed to inhibit an enemy's crossing into Egypt without great difficulty. But of course, such a canal would have had at least one major break or opening as a means of allowing traffic (controlled and guarded of course) to enter and exit Egypt for trade, military surveillance. In Currid's view this opening, over which the Israelites may have crossed, would have been located "near the Gulf of Suez."[23]

---

[20] This observation is based on conjecture, however, including the assumption that the "sea" mentioned in v. 2 is in fact the Red Sea and not any smaller body of water (cf. the designation "Sea of Galilee" for what to modern sensibilities would be a "lake" in Num 34:11; Josh 12:3; 13:27) and also not some part of the Mediterranean or Nile delta flowage further to the north.

[21] J. Currid, *Ancient Egypt and the Old Testament* (Grand Rapids: Baker, 1997), 134.

[22] As the Amarna letters (generally dated to about 1395–1365 BC) demonstrate, Akkadian was spoken and read in Egypt since it was the lingua franca of the ANE at the time of the exodus. The idea of the Egyptians using an Akkadian term as a loanword to identify a roadway over their prime defensive canal seems reasonable in light of the greater and earlier use of canals in Mesopotamia than in Egypt. As regards his use of the Egyptianized Akkadian term in his narrative, Moses would necessarily have spoken and read Akkadian as well as Egyptian and Hebrew on the basis of his training as a princeling prior to his siding with the Israelites.

[23] Ibid., 134. Part of Currid's argument is built on the way the name of this place is written in the travel itinerary list of Num 33. Further on the location of Pi-Hahiroth, see J. Simons, *The Geographical and Topographical Texts of the Old Testament* (Leiden: Brill, 1959), 249. See also K. Kitchen, "Exodus," *ZPEB* 2:430; D. Redford, "Pi-hahiroth," *ABD* 5:371; A. H. Gardiner, "The Geography of the Exodus," in Recueil d'études égyptologiques dediées a la mémoire de Jean-François Champollion (Paris: E. Champion, 1922), 13–214; M. A. Navon, "Pi-hahirot—The Mouth of Freedom," *JBQ* 27 (1999): 259–64.

The location of Migdol is a matter of speculation as is that of Baal Zephon.[24] Nevertheless, from the point of view of the value of the narrative to the reader, the ability to pinpoint sites on a map is not of major importance. What matters is the effect on Pharaoh that God was creating by leading the people on a seemingly erratic course: once again Pharaoh was being duped into a situation of humiliation, enticed to act in a manner that he thought would advantage himself and Egypt but would in fact further demonstrate his own and Egypt's impotency in the face of the awesome power of the only true God.

14:3–4 The theme of God's superiority to Pharaoh, seen repeatedly previously,[25] continues here. But how could Pharaoh be expected to conclude that the Israelites were suddenly unable to leave Egypt[26] after he had just been so severely taught the power of Israel's God in the ten plagues? What would give him the sense that suddenly he could gain victory over the Israelites when their God had just shown total superiority to him and his gods? The answer requires appreciating Egyptian religion in its ancient Near Eastern context. To all the ancients (except those Israelites who were beginning to understand the only true God) the gods and goddesses that controlled the world were arbitrary and capricious, quick to change their actions and attitudes, constantly vying with one another for power, not omnipresent but manifesting themselves at given locations and then leaving those locations unpredictably. James could say of Satan, "Resist the devil, and he will flee from you" (Jas 4:7) because Satan, who is finite and cannot be in all places at once, will soon lose interest in trying to tempt someone who resists him and will move on to someone else more likely to yield to temptation. Likewise, the Egyptians' gods were considered beings who might not always be present among their people. Accordingly, Yahweh knew that it would be natural for Pharaoh to think that he, Yahweh, after having expended great effort to demonstrate his power to the Egyptians, might now no longer be directly involved in helping the Israelites so that he, Pharaoh, could once again assert his power over them unhindered. Indeed, the Israelites themselves were not above assuming at times pessimistically that they had been abandoned by Yahweh.[27] Once again all of this was a plan of God announced in advance, so that Moses and the Israelites would not (if they could maintain their faith)

---

[24] Cf. W. F. Albright, "Baal-Zephon," in *Festschrift Alfred Bertholet* (Tübingen: Mohr-Siebeck, 1950), 1–14; H. Cazelles, "Les Localisations de L'Exode et la critique literaire," *RB* 62 (1955): 321–64; G. I. Davies, "The Wilderness Itineraries and the Composition of the Pentateuch," *VT* 33 (1983): 1–13.

[25] E.g., in 1:12,19–20; 2:9–10,15; 3:19–22; 4:21–23; 6:1,6; 7:1–5; 8–13; and all ten of the plagues.

[26] The NIV "hemmed in by the desert" is a conceptual rendering of what would be the more literal translation, "The wilderness has shut them."

[27] See Deut 31:17; Judg 6:13.

be surprised and discomfited by the coming Egyptian pursuit. The purpose of the plan was to "gain glory over[28] Pharaoh" as well as "all his army." Previously the vaunted Egyptian army[29] was not subject to the same sort of humiliation that Pharaoh, the Egyptians in general, their land, and their gods had endured. Now it was time in God's plan to include the army in the scheme of humiliation. Because the Israelites were already organized as an army and needed to think of themselves in terms of their upcoming military role, it hardly should come as a surprise that God would want them to see his sovereignty in a military encounter as a means of encouraging them toward the military challenges that lay ahead for them. A military defeat of the Egyptians also would demonstrate final proof of God's power to Egypt ("and the Egyptians will know that I am the LORD").[30]

The short sentence at the end of 14:4, "So the Israelites did this," refers strictly to their change of direction and encampment by the Sea—not their acceptance of the implied promise that the Egyptians would have no success in their pursuit of the Israelites (see v. 10).

2. Attack of the Egyptian Army and Israelite Panic (14:5–14)

(1) Egyptian Regret and Change of Mind (14:5)

5 When the king of Egypt was told that the people had fled, Pharaoh and his officials changed their minds about them and said, "What have we done? We have let the Israelites go and have lost their services!"

14:5 The appreciation of this verse depends partly on its linkage to v. 4 immediately preceding, in which God stated, "I will harden Pharaoh's heart, and he will pursue them." The Egyptians' reconsideration of their willingness to allow the exodus may have been partly, largely, or almost entirely a reasoned choice.[31] God was the one who made sure they actually took the

---

[28] The better translation is "gain glory over Pharaoh" rather than "gain glory through Pharaoh." The latter, in fact, is highly unlikely as a translation for וְאִכָּבְדָה בְּפַרְעֹה.

[29] The Amarna letters are full of references to the ability of the Egyptian army to overwhelm its enemies in a single day's war—views expressed by Canaanites in awe of Egyptian military might. See D. Stuart, "The Sovereign's Day of Conquest," *BASOR* 221 (1976): 159–64.

[30] On the use of this phrase specifically in reference to God's witness of himself to the Egyptians, see 7:5; 12:12.

[31] The older source-critical view that 14:5 preserves a separate tradition in Exodus of the Israelites' leaving Egypt via a "flight" in contrast to the dominant tradition throughout the book that it was an "expulsion" has been effectively challenged by M. Vervenne ("Exodus Expulsion and Exodus Flight: The Interpretation of a Crux Critically Examined," *JNSL* 22 [1996]: 45–58). Vervenne shows that a comparison of the language of 14:5–10 and of Gen 31:22–25 as well as influence of the immediate context of 14:5 (the narrative of the crossing of the Sea) makes it unlikely that the Hb. wording typically translated "that the people had fled" (כִּי בָרַח הָעָם) implies any separate or contradictory tradition about the nature of the exodus; i.e., that the text presents the story from a unified point of view.

decision to pursue the Israelites in an effort to reenslave them. The first clause of the verse is loosely coordinated with the remainder of the verse in terms of time. In other words, we should not assume that the meaning was "as soon as the king of Egypt was told . . ." but rather that having been told, Pharaoh and his advisors began gradually to wish they could have kept the Israelites in Egypt. The number of days or weeks that had transpired since the night of the Passover cannot be determined from the narrative.[32] Supposing that a week or two had gone by, it is not difficult to imagine that the leaders of Egypt were beginning to receive reports related to work stoppages of all sorts on important defensive building projects in the northeast delta,[33] by reason of the absence of Israelite brickmakers and construction workers. Moreover, this verse should not be read to infer that the only concern of the Egyptians was a minimized labor pool. The best translation of the original's final clause is, "We have let Israel go from serving us!"[34] The idea of *serving* included being under the subjection of the Egyptians and therefore not able to join with Asiatics in a war against Egypt, the scenario that had first engendered pharaonic policies of oppression (1:10).

(2) Egyptian Chariot Pursuit of Israel (14:6–9)

6So he had his chariot made ready and took his army with him. 7He took six hundred of the best chariots, along with all the other chariots of Egypt, with officers over all of them. 8The LORD hardened the heart of Pharaoh king of Egypt, so that he pursued the Israelites, who were marching out boldly. 9The Egyptians—all Pharaoh's horses and chariots, horsemen and troops—pursued the Israelites and overtook them as they camped by the sea near Pi Hahiroth, opposite Baal Zephon.

14:6 The translation should be, "So he got his chariot ready and took his people with him." In other words, there is no mention of "army" in the verse, a fact that is important for understanding Pharaoh's role in the pursuit of the Israelites. The army was caught in the Red Sea, as mentioned later in the chapter, but not Pharaoh and his advisors (i.e., his civilian retinue). He himself apparently did not actually go as far as the Red Sea but turned back—presumably with his advisors and other servants (some of "his officials")—after the divine cloud prevented him and his army from attacking the Israelites immediately at

[32] S. Spero suggests that the reason the Egyptians may not have been minded to pursue the Israelites any sooner than they did was that they were preoccupied with mummifying and burying all their dead, including all their sacred animals, which had to be mummified when buried ("'And Against All the Gods of Egypt I Will Execute Judgments,'" *JBQ* 27 [1999]: 83–88).

[33] Exod 1:11. It is, of course, highly likely that the mention of the building of Pithom and Rameses represents a listing of two prominent projects among many rather than the total of all the Israelites built for the Egyptians.

[34] The best way to construe the word כִּי at the beginning of this clause is as an asseverative, represented by the exclamation point in our suggested translation.

Pi-Hahiroth (see comments on 14:10ff.; 15:4). The army then made the attack on their own. Moreover, the use of the word *ʾam* ("people") functions as a reminder that the Egyptian *people* in general were of a mind to pursue and recapture the Israelites. Pharaoh's policy was, in other words, a popular one.

14:7 Chariots were formidable military weapons in ancient times and eventually thousands of them at once were employed in various important battles in the ancient Near East.[35] Solomon built up a large chariot force for defensive purposes. David, however, never used chariots. He disliked them because they had been used to oppress the Israelites, who were foot soldiers. Chariots, like cavalry, were useful primarily in flat terrain, and David's battles were for the taking and holding of the promised land, which is generally mountainous. David therefore seems to have had success against chariots mainly by choosing the ground on which he was willing to fight to his advantage.[36] Another sort of terrain that rendered chariots useless was wet, soft ground. Any ground that was muddy or swampy tended to allow chariots to become mired because the thin wheels of chariots, wooden with brass or iron bands around the circumference, penetrated soft ground easily and deeply. Most of the areas where Egyptians expected to fight were flat with hard ground—perfect for chariot warfare. Since the Israelites were still within Egypt proper when they were encamped at Pi-Hahiroth, they must have seemed easy prey for Pharaoh's chariot-based army. The total number of chariots is not given but must have numbered well over a thousand. The fact that six hundred were "choice" or "first-rate" *(baḥûr)* and that all of the chariots had chariot officers over them[37] indicates that the heart of

---

[35] At the battle of Qarqar in 854 BC. The earliest chariots were employed even prior to 3000 BC at such places as Kish and Ur in Mesopotamia, though these were rather clumsy four-wheeled fighting vehicles. By the time of the exodus the Egyptians had perfected the light, two-wheeled chariot, after losing their sovereignty to the Hyksos only a century or two before precisely because the Hyksos had mastered chariot warfare and the Egyptians had not. Accordingly, the Egyptians were now using chariots extensively and apparently were regularly modernizing their chariot corps with ever more updated models—thus the mention of the six hundred "choice" chariots as the newest and best in the army.

[36] As God had originally commanded Joshua (Josh 11:6,9), David hamstrung chariot horses when he captured chariots (2 Sam 8:4; 1 Chr 18:4) since chariots and even horses were generally useless to him. Solomon's development of chariot warfare in Israel was simply one more of his many violations of God's commands and standards.

[37] The plural noun here employed for "officers" is שָׁלִשִׁם, which some have argued means "third men on the chariots," i.e., referring to the fact that the best fighting chariots had a third man on them in addition to the driver and the bowman/spearman, a chariot commander who would also wield a bow and arrow and/or spear. But the wording Moses used here seems to refer to another issue: the chariot forces were well led by trained officers (one officer commanding each group of chariots) and were thus a formidable fighting force, not merely some sort of gathering of chariots that had been cobbled together in haste and incompetently supervised. On the possible meaning "warriors" for שָׁלִשִׁם, a more neutral rendering than "officers," see O. Margalith, "וְכֹל רֶכֶב מִצְרַיִם וְשָׁלִשִׁם עַל־כֻּלּוֹ," *BMik* 23 (1977): 68–72.

the well-trained, well-equipped army was engaged in pursuit of the Israelites, not merely a small contingent or token force.

14:8–9 Once again God "hardened the heart of Pharaoh king of Egypt," just as he had done in the case of each of the eleven signs, which included the ten plagues. Again, God's purpose was to humiliate Pharaoh and the Egyptians, to expose the nonsense of their religion, and to show himself the only true God. Pharaoh put in motion a full chariot pursuit of the Israelites, who had been going out confidently[38] ("marching out boldly") so far, buoyed in spirit by the favor God had shown them during all the plagues and by the fear God had placed in the hearts of the Egyptians after the Passover. The Israelites were an army[39] but one that traveled on foot with all dependents and possessions including cattle; the Egyptian army, on the other hand, was a professional military force able to move much faster with its horse-drawn chariots, so whatever time had elapsed between the Israelites' Passover morning departure and the Egyptians' decision to gather the chariot forces and pursue them, the Israelite lead had now been easily overcome.

It is not clear from the wording of v. 9 that Egyptian footsoldiers were used in the pursuit. The NIV translation ("all Pharaoh's horses and chariots, horsemen and troops") makes it seem so, especially by reason of rendering the Hebrew *ḥayil* as "troops" when in fact it is a collective noun that means "force" or "army." A more precise translation would be: "The Egyptians pursued them, all Pharaoh's horses and chariots and his chariot drivers—his force[40]—and caught up with them camped at the sea." The mention of the location of the Israelite encampment as "by the sea near Pi Hahiroth, opposite Baal Zephon" may seem redundant in light of how clearly the location had been established in v. 2, but this sort of repetition kept ancient audiences clear about details (they were mostly listening to the story read to them rather than reading it themselves from a scroll) and to remind even the most literate reader that the Israelites were attacked while encamped with their backs to the sea, that is, both unprepared and without a viable escape route.

(3) Israelite Panic and Complaint (14:10–12)

10 As Pharaoh approached, the Israelites looked up, and there were the Egyptians, marching after them. They were terrified and cried out to the LORD. 11 They said to Moses, "Was it because there were no graves in Egypt that you brought us to the desert to die? What have you done to us by bringing us out of

---

[38] The progressive verb in the concomitant temporal clause (וּבְנֵי יִשְׂרָאֵל יֹצְאִים בְּיָד רָמָה) refers to the overall progress of the Israelites that had been taking place since the Passover, not to what was currently happening, which was not a movement at all but the encampment at Pi-Hahiroth.

[39] Cf. 6:26; 7:4; 12:17,41,51.

[40] I.e., the *waw* in the construction וְחֵילוֹ may be taken as the *waw explicativum*.

Egypt? [12]Didn't we say to you in Egypt, 'Leave us alone; let us serve the Egyptians'? It would have been better for us to serve the Egyptians than to die in the desert!"

14:10–12 The sight of hundreds—perhaps thousands—of approaching chariots apparently drove all memory of God's assurances through Moses to the Israelites in 14:1–4 out of their minds. Those assurances were relatively generally worded, and it is possible that many or most Israelites had mistakenly regarded them as promises that Pharaoh's pursuit would not reach them but fail en route. Accordingly, when they actually saw the Egyptian chariotry coming at them and realized their helpless position (from a human point of view) as a poorly armed, untrained, unprepared army encamped with its back to the sea, they panicked. To their credit they at least "cried out to the LORD," showing that they regarded him as the one to save them.[41]

Verses 11–12 provide a summation of complaints spoken to Moses with the benefit of reconstructed hindsight—a classic instance of what is now called "recovered memory." The Israelites and those who joined them had hardly been forced to depart from Egypt. They had been only too glad to accept freedom from their bondage. In light of the bitter reproach of the Israelite foremen when Pharaoh had increased their workload as a result of Moses' demands (5:19–21), it is conceivable that some percentage of Israelites may have said at one time or another prior to the commencement of the plagues something like "Leave us alone; let us serve the Egyptians." But that had not been what anyone had consistently said, nor was it the prevailing attitude at any time. Now they suddenly "recalled" those words and the "fact" that they had all along thought the exodus was a bad idea. Faced with what they believed to be their imminent death, they redefined their recent history. Their pessimism was ill-founded entirely. The Egyptians were interested in capturing them and returning them to slavery rather than killing them (14:5), so their claim that "it would have been better for us to serve the Egyptians" was actually only a statement of the very thing the Egyptians had in mind for them. So they were wrong on two counts: they thought the Egyptians were coming to kill them, and they did not believe that God would rescue them. This was the first of the postexodus declarations by Israelites that they should have stayed where they came from. The others (e.g., Num 14:1–4;

[41] In the ancient world people usually had three kinds of gods: a personal god, who may have been one thought to have paid special attention to the individual on various occasions of supplication; a clan god, to whom all the clan prayed for matters relating to their common interest; and a national god, who was expected to deliver all his people in matters of war and other national crises (see H. Frankfort et al., *Before Philosophy: The Intellectual Adventure of Ancient Man* [Baltimore: Penguin, 1967]). The Israelites and those who had joined them (12:12) could at this point acknowledge Yahweh as their national God. We simply do not know what various individuals might have thought of him and whether or not they yet embraced monotheism, an otherwise new concept for most of them.

Josh 7:6–9) share considerably the theme of this one: when hardship is encountered, the miserable past suddenly looks like the good old days. The Israelites were simply thinking the way most people think of the past when the present seems unbearable.

(4) Moses' Confident Reassurance of God's Plan to Trap the Egyptians (14:13–14)

13Moses answered the people, "Do not be afraid. Stand firm and you will see the deliverance the LORD will bring you today. The Egyptians you see today you will never see again. 14The LORD will fight for you; you need only to be still."

14:13–14 In contrast to the majority of Israelites, Moses had understood the meaning of God's earlier promise of protection (14:2–4)—and had not only understood it but believed it. This speech of Moses represents perhaps his finest hour yet in the leadership of Israel. He urged calm, commanded simple, patient waiting (but not total inaction; see below), reassured the people that what seemed to them a certainty that they would die in the wilderness (v. 12) was in fact the last, hopeless gasp of Egyptian hubris, and explained to them the most basic tenet of Old Testament holy war:[42] God fights for his people and—no matter how undertrained, ill-equipped, poorly organized, or outclassed they might be—eliminated their foes.

From the point of view of God's attributes, Moses' speech alludes to five: (1) God is a dispeller of fear, a comforter of those who are afraid. (2) God is a deliverer from distress. (3) God invites and expects his people to trust in him ("Stand firm . . . you need only to be still"). (4) God removes danger. (5) God is a warrior against the forces of evil. The timing and application of these attributes are under God's control, not man's, but Moses could offer strong assurances to the Israelites in this instance because of what God had already said through him to them in regard to his plan to humiliate Egypt yet again, a last time.

A better translation of vv. 13–14 would be: "Don't be afraid. Stay where you are and see the LORD's salvation, which he will provide for you today. Because you have seen the Egyptians today, you will never see them again. The LORD will fight for you. You do not need to do anything."[43] Of particular note is the translation of the last sentence of v. 13. The modern English versions usually render this in the manner of the NIV, "The Egyptians you see today you will never see again," but that is not in fact the meaning. The meaning is that of our translation.[44] What Moses was saying was, in effect:

---

[42] See "Excursus: Israelite Holy War," after the commentary on 17:9.

[43] On the meaning of the *hiphil* of תַּחֲרִישׁוּן as "do nothing" rather than "keep still," compare 1 Sam 19:11 and Num 30:5. "Keep still" is often found as a translation here, but the Israelites were supposed to move (v. 15), not keep still.

[44] On the grammar see R. J. Williams, *Hebrew Syntax: An Outline,* 2d ed. (Toronto: University of Toronto Press, 1976) #468.

"You should be glad you are seeing the Egyptian army coming at you. Because you have seen the Egyptians, it means that God's prediction that he will trick them and trap them is about to be fulfilled. If you *didn't* see them, now *that* would be cause for worry because then God's prediction to us would *not* be coming true."

3. Parting of the Red Sea and Drowning of the Egyptians (14:15–31)

In this section of Exodus, Moses narrated one of the greatest stories of divine deliverance in all of Scripture, that of Israel's crossing the Red Sea on dry ground and the drowning of the Egyptian chariot army when they attempted to pursue them. This is the last story in the book involving direct contact with the Egyptians, and it provides one final and grand occasion for God to "gain glory through Pharaoh and all his army" (v. 17). It is looked back upon by many future Scripture authors as a moment of supreme demonstration of the power of God displayed for the benefit of those who place their faith in him. So significant is the event that Moses was inspired to follow his prose narrative account with a poetic one, that is, the hymn he wrote about the event (15:1–18). Thus the story is told twice—once in prose and once in poetry. The prose account, here, tells the story chronologically and with many of the usual sorts of details and descriptions. The poetic account is a hymn, a song of praise that not only looks back on the event but asserts future implications: if God could do this sort of thing to the Egyptians, he could certainly be trusted to bring to completion his whole plan to allow Israel to conquer and settle into the promised land and to reign over his people forever and ever. The reader must keep in mind that Moses, knowing the content of the hymn, left some of his points to be made by the hymn in the following chapter and therefore could provide a relatively concise overview of the events in the present chapter. Both the prose account and the poetic account must be read together to obtain the full story and its rich implications.

(1) God Sends Israel into the Sea to Gain Glory over Pharaoh and His Army (14:15–18)

15Then the LORD said to Moses, "Why are you crying out to me? Tell the Isra-
elites to move on. 16Raise your staff and stretch out your hand over the sea to
divide the water so that the Israelites can go through the sea on dry ground. 17I
will harden the hearts of the Egyptians so that they will go in after them. And I will gain glory through Pharaoh and all his army, through his chariots and his
horsemen. 18The Egyptians will know that I am the LORD when I gain glory through Pharaoh, his chariots and his horsemen."

14:15 The Israelites had assumed they were hopelessly trapped, with their backs to the sea and the Egyptians approaching them quickly by land (14:10–12). Where could they go? They couldn't possibly outrun the chariot-borne Egyptians even if they already had been moving on foot and not encamped. And they obviously couldn't just walk into the sea, could they? In fact the latter option, seemingly impossible and not having occurred to any of them, was exactly what God had in mind all along. His plan of deliverance for Israel and destruction for the Egyptian army involved something easy for the Creator of all things and all minds to imagine and execute—the parting of a body of water by wind (v. 21)—yet something previously outside of the realm of experience and therefore outside the realm of concept for either the Egyptians or Israelites.

No contradiction between v. 10 ("the Israelites . . . were terrified and cried out [plural] to the LORD") and v. 15 ("the LORD said to Moses, "Why are you [singular] crying out to me?") should be assumed. It was standard for the Israelites to speak to God using Moses as their intermediary and vice versa, a practice that eventually became "official" with the formal request of 20:18–19. Moreover, Moses was consistently identified with the character and fate of the people as a whole; as their leader he had to accept criticism leveled at them even if he himself was not responsible.[45] Moses knew that whatever God said to *him* was normally meant also for *them*. The first half of v. 15 is thus meant as a rebuke to the Israelites, not as a reference to some lack of faith on Moses' part that was not revealed in his words as quoted in vv. 13–14. Moses may not have known how God would deliver the Israelites, but he was certain they would be delivered.

In saying "Tell the Israelites to move on," God was asking for a breaking of camp, rounding up of animals, packing of belongings, an orderly departure by ranks. All this would take many hours, and, indeed, the remainder of that day and almost the entire evening were used in the process of getting the Israelites out of their encampment and into and across the sea (vv. 19–22).

14:16 Again the staff of God plays an important role in a miracle, symbolizing God's power and presence and reminding all concerned that it was not Moses but God who performed the supernatural. Again as well, the language of stretching out the hand refers to using the staff.[46] As the staff had affected the Nile in first plague, turning water to blood (esp. 7:17–20), and in the second, producing frogs from the Nile (8:1–15), now it would affect an even greater body of water, the Red Sea, causing it to divide. With God's

[45] This is one basis for the language of Isaiah's servant songs (the best known being that of chap. 53) in which the Messiah is a Moses figure who sometimes has distinct individual personal characteristics and sometimes embodies all of God's people at once. Paul's body-of-Christ conception of the church is yet another mirror of this biblical theme.

[46] "Excursus "Moses' Staff."

words in this verse Moses and the Israelites learned how it was that they could escape the Egyptians: they would take the direction they had assumed was the most impossible, away from the Egyptians, right into the ocean. Since nothing is impossible with God (Matt 19:26; Luke 1:37), what they had not been able to imagine as a direction in which to flee was now their escape route. God's promise to them did not merely offer an inconvenient but doable route of escape (as would be the case if they would have to float,[47] wade, or slosh their way out of danger) but would allow them actually to walk on dry ground—ground so dry that even chariot officers were willing to send their horses and chariots on it in pursuit of Israel. That sort of entirely dry path would make taking families, children, and animals along relatively easy and would also create a temptation for chariots, which would otherwise not be driven voluntarily into any sort of wet terrain.[48]

14:17–18 No sensible chariot commander would order chariots to go into a wet area. Later, in the days of the Judges, Canaanite charioteers found this out to their dismay. It was the mud in the Kishon River flood plain after a heavy rain that bogged down the chariot army of Sisera so that the Israelites under Deborah's general Barak could defeat them (Judg 4:1–16) and even forced Sisera to abandon his own chariot (Judg 4:15,17). God had in that situation also lured chariots to their destruction (Judg 4:7). They tried to fight near a rain-swollen river and lost.[49] Why, then, did the Egyptians follow the Israelites into the midst of the Red Sea, knowing full well that water and chariots don't mix? The answer is, similarly, that God lured them into it—made them stubborn enough to do it ("I will harden the hearts[50] of the

[47] The percentage of people in any society who are competent swimmers is low, and it was apparently much lower in ancient times. Competitive swimming and regular swimming instruction is an essentially modern phenomenon. The crawl, the most common swimming stroke in modern times, was introduced only in 1873 by J. A. Trudgen (and was called for a time "the trudgen"). The ancient Greeks were exceptional in teaching many of their naval sailors to swim, which served them well at the battle of Salamis in 480 BC, where their enemies, the Persians, drowned when their ships were destroyed because they did not know how to swim. Even the ancient Greeks, however, did not consider swimming so valuable a skill that they included it in their Olympic games. Swimming did not become an Olympic sport until 1896. The British navy introduced swimming instruction for sailors only in the 1900s. The relatively few ancient Egyptians who may have known how to swim would hardly have been inclined to teach the skill to the Israelites, and it may be safely assumed that few Israelites had learned it on their own in light of their lack of leisure time while in Egyptian bondage. Indeed, at a much later time Ezekiel describes a river deep enough that it must be swum as a river that "could not be crossed" (Ezek 47:5).

[48] See, e.g., A. F. Rainey, "Zertal's Woeful Linguistics," *BAR* 28, no. 5 (2002): 8–12.

[49] The Song of Deborah (Judg 5) makes clear that heavy rain was the special divine method of trapping the Canaanite chariotry in and around the Kishon (esp. v. 4, "the heavens poured, the clouds poured down water," and v. 21, "The river Kishon swept them away, the age-old river, the river Kishon").

[50] Meaning, "I will make the Egyptians stubborn." See "Excursus: The Hardening of Pharaoh's Heart" at comments on 4:19–31.

Egyptians so that they will go in after them," v. 17). The Egyptians were taking a huge risk to pursue into a body of water, but two factors must have gone into their divinely ordained stubborn thinking. First was the observation that a very wide dry path through the sea lay before them. ("If the Israelites can do it, are we going to be afraid to do it?") Second, they were under orders to recapture Israel, and what sort of excuse could they give Pharaoh and his advisors if they did not? ("Honest, they just walked right into the sea on this wide road of dry ground, and we didn't want to follow because we were on chariots and they were on foot.") Since God had determined to "gain glory through [over] Pharaoh and all his army, [over] his chariots and his horsemen," the Egyptians were doomed from the start. The revelation of Yahweh ("they will know that I am the LORD") in his greatness and sovereignty as the only true God was the goal of this final humiliation of Egypt.[51] The concluding phrase of vv. 17–18, "his chariots and his horsemen," does not necessarily refer to both chariotry and cavalry (as if "horsemen" referred to soldiers riding rather than driving horses).[52]

(2) The Divine Angel/Pillar Separates Israelites and Egyptians (14:19–20)

[19]Then the angel of God, who had been traveling in front of Israel's army, withdrew and went behind them. The pillar of cloud also moved from in front and stood behind them, [20]coming between the armies of Egypt and Israel. Throughout the night the cloud brought darkness to the one side and light to the other side; so neither went near the other all night long.

14:19–20 Verse 19 would better be translated: "Then the angel of God, who was traveling in front of Israel's army, moved and went behind them, so the pillar of cloud moved from in front of them and stood behind them." In other words, the angel of God and the pillar were the same thing: God's manifestation of himself in the visible presence of the Israelites.[53] In these verses God shows himself a protector of his people through the pillar, not merely a guide to them. That God should lead his people through the wilderness is important; that he should protect them from harm on the way is equally as important. Once the Israelites could see the Egyptian chariots

---

[51] On "I am Yahweh/the LORD" see 6:2,6–8,29: 7:5,17; 10:2; 12:2; 14:4, et al.

[52] Thus the NRSV translation, e.g., "his chariots, and his chariot drivers." The phrase is בְּרִכְבּוֹ וּבְפָרָשָׁיו and seems fairly unambiguous in context, although in other locations, פָּרָשׁ can have the sense of "horse rider." The phrase apparently is used in apposition to "his army" in v. 17, Pharaoh's army in this case being the rapid, chariot-borne force he had sent to catch up to and capture the Israelites.

[53] Accordingly, the NIV use of the term "also" in v. 17 not only adds an element to the text that is not found in the original but misleads the reader into the assumption that the angel and the pillar are two different things. On the identification of the angel of Yahweh/angel of God as God himself, see the excursus after the comments on 3:2–3.

approaching them, it was only a matter of minutes until they would be overtaken. Something therefore had to prevent the Egyptians from surrounding and reenslaving the Israelites, to allow God's people the many hours they needed to break camp, form ranks, and cross the Red Sea. The NIV interpretation of v. 20 may be correct, but the verse appears to suffer from ancient copying errors. The Hebrew reads, literally, "It came between the Egyptian camp and the Israelite camp, and the cloud was, and the darkness, and it lit up the night, and neither came near each other all night." The LXX reads the key portion differently still: "And there was darkness and blackness, and the night passed."[54] In other words, it is not possible from the state of the received text to be sure if the cloud lit up the night for both sides, gave light to one side and darkness to the other, or simply provided a dark barrier between the two opposing groups.[55] What *is* clear is that it kept the Egyptians from getting near the Israelites (and any Israelites from accidentally straying into the Egyptian encampment) and provided the Israelites with all the time they needed to escape into the sea. Just as events of the Passover night had differentiated Israel from Egypt to the disadvantage of Egyptians, the events of this night similarly worked against Egypt's interests.

(3) Israel Crosses the Red Sea on Dry Land (14:21–22)

[21]Then Moses stretched out his hand over the sea, and all that night the LORD drove the sea back with a strong east wind and turned it into dry land. The waters were divided, [22]and the Israelites went through the sea on dry ground, with a wall of water on their right and on their left.

It is always implied, though only sometimes stated, that when Moses "stretched out his hand," he did so with the staff of God in it.[56] In this instance the action provided, as it did so often in the plague stories, a visible motion to reassure him and those watching that the power of an invisible God was at work. A special *east wind* did the job of parting the waters of the sea here, in a manner somewhat akin to what a special *east wind* did in bringing the plague of locusts (10:13: "The LORD made an east wind blow across the land all that day and all that night. By morning the wind had

[54] καὶ ἐγένετο σκότος καὶ γνόφος καὶ διῆλθεν ἡ νύξ. The NRSV reads: "And so the cloud was there with the darkness, and it lit up the night." It is even theoretically possible that the statement "so neither went near the other" at the end of v. 20 refers to the light and the darkness, not the Egyptians and the Israelites, though this seems in context only possible rather than plausible.

[55] On the options and a proposed solution that relies plausibly on the LXX over the MT for certain parts of the verse, see M. Vervenne, "Exodus 14,20 MT-LXX: Textual or Literary Variation?" *Lectures et Relectures* (Leuven: Leuven University Press, 1999), 3–25.

[56] Cp. esp. 9:22–23 and 10:12–13, where the command from God to Moses reads, "Stretch out your hand," and then the description reads, "So Moses stretched out his staff," thus confirming the "hand"-"staff" equivalency.

brought the locusts"). An east wind is often seen as destructive or punishing, partly because east winds in Egypt, the Sinai, and Palestine are so often blisteringly dry and hot.[57] It is to be expected that some skeptics have argued that the mention of the east wind is the only fully historical element here—a wind that temporarily dried up some sort of small, normally marshy, and/or muddy area so that the Israelites could walk on it relatively easily and feel that if any Egyptians were to follow them (something that did not actually occur in the skeptical reconstruction) they would be harder to catch. The text, however, says that the wind actually pushed one part of the sea away from the other part ("drove the sea back . . . the waters were divided," v. 21) and created a "wall of water on their right and on their left."[58] The term used for "wall" here, *ḥōmāh,* connotes a very large wall—not a small stone wall or retaining wall but always a massively large (usually a city) wall,[59] towering above the Israelites, who marched on dry land with walls of water on either side of them.

It is clear from the descriptions given that the sea through which the Israelites walked was deep water, not something shallow. A city-wall sized wall of water on either side of them implies the division of a deep body of water, not merely the drying out of a shallow one or the drying out of wet terrain. Even the use of the term *yam* ("sea") here implies the depth of the water. *Yam* is never used for swamps or mud flats but is used consistently to describe large bodies of water (what we would call either lakes or oceans). On the identity of this body of water as the Red Sea, see below.

(4) God Confuses the Egyptian Army (14:23–25)

23The Egyptians pursued them, and all Pharaoh's horses and chariots and horsemen followed them into the sea. 24During the last watch of the night the LORD looked down from the pillar of fire and cloud at the Egyptian army and threw it into confusion. 25He made the wheels of their chariots come off so that they had difficulty driving. And the Egyptians said, "Let's get away from the Israelites! The LORD is fighting for them against Egypt."

Four difficulties thwarted the Egyptian army's attempt to capture the Israelites: they pursued into the sea, they suffered from God's direct debilitation

---

57 Cf. Gen 41:6,23–27; Job 15:2; 27:21; Pss 48:7; 78:26; Isa 27:8; Ezek 17:10; 19:12; 27:26; Hos 12:1; 13:15; Jonah 4:8.

58 Naturally, one can be as skeptical as one chooses about any of the component parts of the story, accepting those that fit a naturalistic theory and declaring all others either fictional or fictionalized.

59 There are 133 occurrences of חוֹמָה/חֹמָה in the Hb. OT, and without exception they indicate massive, high walls. This is the first occurrence of the 133. Since city walls were virtually always at least twenty feet high, the waves on either side of the Israelites made a deep channel through the water, not a shallow path through mud or ankle-deep brine.

of their minds, they had trouble with chariot wheels (possibly a synecdoche for any number of chariot failures), and they suffered a sense of defeatism. From the wording of vv. 23–24 we can assume that the entire Israelite contingent had either crossed through the sea onto dry land or were almost finished doing so by the time the pillar of cloud stopped being a barrier to the Egyptians. The Egyptians may have thought they had been stymied by a severe weather front, or fog, or an unusually cloudy night and felt that with the coming of dawn ("during the last watch of the night"; lit., "during the morning watch," i.e., the time when the night ends and morning arrives) things had obviously changed in their favor. Thus they did what was foolish—they drove chariots into the ocean. Of course, one could argue that it was foolish to *walk* into the ocean as well, as the Israelites had just done. But Israel knew it was responding to a command from God. The Egyptians knew only that their pharaoh had ordered them to capture the Israelites, and the dry land between the walls of water appeared to be the only way to go to do that.

The verb "looked down"[60] in v. 24 is not to be overinterpreted as if heaven must be understood as "up" or God must be understood as described here to be a very large humanlike being. The verb is regularly used simply to connote viewing something from a height, and as God towered over the Egyptians in his self-manifestation of the pillar of cloud, the verb is used in a rather routine manner in the context. Without God's help the Egyptians might easily have caught up with the Israelites, so he "threw [the Egyptian army] into confusion." Specifically, he bound their chariots' wheels so that they had difficulty driving them ("made the wheels of their chariots come off" v. 25, an interpretive translation of Hb. "he turned aside the wheels of their chariots").[61] The binding of chariot wheels would seem most naturally to refer to bogging down—most likely because the sea floor was soft and sandy/silty so that even though it was dry, it was not a suitable surface for narrow, metal-bound chariot wheels bearing the weight of a chariot and two or three armed men. The horses pulling the chariots, like the Israelite goats and sheep, would have been able to get through satisfactorily; the chariot wheels, however, effectively sliced deep into the soft ground and bound so

---

[60] וַיַּשְׁקֵף.

[61] The LXX, Syr., and SP all read "bound" their chariots' wheels, reflecting the verb אסר, while the Hb. MT seems to be the result of vocalizing a defective reading, as if the verb were the *hiphil* of סור, "turn aside." J. Stek ("What Happened to the Chariot Wheels of Exod 14:25?" *JBL* 105 [1986]: 293–94) argues for translating the MT Hb. as referring to the binding of the chariot wheels (by seaweed), and thus Stek favors the NIV marginal reading, "He jammed the wheels of their chariots." On narrow cartwheels bogging down, see also Amos 2:13 (translated mistakenly by the NIV to refer to a cart's "crushing" when in fact it is more likely the cart's "bogging down" that was intended in the original); cf. D. Stuart, *Hosea-Jonah,* WBC (Waco: Word, 1987), 306–7.

that the horses could not pull their own weight and that of the fully loaded chariots. This disaster, in turn, led to the psychological defeat of the Egyptian force. Their consensus attitude is worded by Moses as (lit.), "Let us flee from Israel because the LORD is fighting for them against Egypt."

This collective sentiment of the Egyptian army is noteworthy for its correct theology, not expected from a pagan group. God's purpose of revealing himself not merely to Israel but to Egypt as well had in fact been accomplished. The army, all of whom had experienced the plagues, now knew who Yahweh was, even if prior to the plagues his name would have meant nothing to them. The earlier statement "I am the LORD" had now become something they could understand.[62] What Moses had promised the people in 14:14 ("the LORD will fight for you") was apparent even to the enemy.

(5) The Sea Drowns the Egyptian Army (14:26–28)

[26]Then the LORD said to Moses, "Stretch out your hand over the sea so that the waters may flow back over the Egyptians and their chariots and horsemen." [27]Moses stretched out his hand over the sea, and at daybreak the sea went back to its place. The Egyptians were fleeing toward it, and the LORD swept them into the sea. [28]The water flowed back and covered the chariots and horsemen—the entire army of Pharaoh that had followed the Israelites into the sea. Not one of them survived.

14:26 Moses' second symbolic stretching forth of his hand with the staff in it initiates another miraculous movement of the sea, not to deliver Israel this time but to trap and drown the Egyptian army that had pursued them. God, of course, was the real leader in all these activities. It was he who commanded Moses' actions, and his staff (again implied rather than explicitly mentioned) represented his divine presence. Whatever Moses and the Israelites may have speculated previously about the form the Lord's deliverance of them would take, they now knew: he would drown their enemy. The Israelites knew how high the waters were piled on either side of the dry corridor and how deep the sea would be once the waters were back in place. It may not have been easy to walk between those walls of water, knowing what would happen if they collapsed. It cannot have been difficult to imagine the fate of the Egyptian army once God's words of instruction to Moses were known. Again the description of the enemy at the end of v. 26 is comprehensive, "the Egyptians and their chariots and horsemen." God assured his people of a total elimination of the enemy.

14:27 At daybreak, so that the Israelites could see the entire process clearly, the sea flowed into the former gap (the strong east wind presumably ceasing), and the Egyptians were caught in the midst of the water. In the NIV

[62] See comments on 14:18.

the final sentence reads as if the Egyptians somehow had passed through the sea entirely and had decided to head back toward it as they saw it going back to its usual place and depth (as if the Israelites were somehow heading somewhere the Egyptians were afraid to go or as if they thought they couldn't get back to Egypt if the waters returned to normal) but were not yet there when God swept them into the sea. All of this is obviated by the correct translation, which should be, "As the Egyptians were fleeing from it, the LORD shook the Egyptians off [more colloquially, dumped over the Egyptians] in the midst of the sea."[63] The language of the verse ("the sea went back to its place") seems to suggest not that the Israelites were still in the sea and only the part of it that the Egyptians were in returned to its place but rather that the Israelites were already fully across. Accordingly, 14:29 should not be read to suggest that the Israelites were still in the sea after the Egyptians had drowned; it is, rather, a summary statement that does not follow the current description chronologically but merely follows *narratively* because it is part of a summation.

14:28 The return of the water back to its usual place may have taken a few minutes or may have been virtually instantaneous; the text does not say. It was fast enough that no Egyptians could get back to shore, but all were killed. If they were typical of most ancients, virtually none of them could swim. If the distance of the corridor through the sea were several miles, even the best of swimmers caught miles from shore were without hope.[64] The Israelites were through the corridor and on dry ground; the Egyptians were in the corridor, and when the sea flowed over them, they were lost.

(6) Summation: God's Deliverance and Resultant Faith (14:29–31)

[29]But the Israelites went through the sea on dry ground, with a wall of water on their right and on their left. [30]That day the LORD saved Israel from the hands of the Egyptians, and Israel saw the Egyptians lying dead on the shore. [31]And when the Israelites saw the great power the LORD displayed against the Egyptians, the people feared the LORD and put their trust in him and in Moses his servant.

14:29–31 These verses sum up the great miracle of deliverance at the sea. Verse 29 repeats v. 22 almost verbatim. Verse 30 describes the event in

---

[63] Presumably the NIV translators were operating under the impression that לִקְרָאת cannot mean "from" or "before" or "in the face of" but can only mean "toward." In fact, all of the first three meanings are attested. Cf. NRSV: "As the Egyptians fled before it, the LORD tossed the Egyptians into the sea."

[64] Even modern long distance swimmers, such as those who swim the English Channel, are specially prepared, trained, and outfitted (bodies greased or protected by wet suits). Nothing of the sort existed in ancient times, though the warm waters of the Mediterranean would not have in themselves represented a threat to life from hypothermia.

general, emphasizing the great truth of God's deliverance of his people from their otherwise unbeatable foes and also presenting an aspect of its aftermath: as bodies began washing up on shore, the Israelites "saw the Egyptians lying dead on the shore." Presumably they also saw many horses and chariots washed up as well, but the human foes are the important topic. Once again God had differentiated his people from the Egyptians, just as had been the case in all the plagues, and once again death had been the result of Egyptian intransigence, just as in the case of the tenth plague. The NIV translation obscures a contrast quite visible in the Hebrew: In v. 30 Moses said, literally, that God saved the Israelites "from the hand [singular] of the Egyptians." Then in v. 31 he said, literally, that "Israel saw the great hand that Yahweh displayed against the Egyptians." The reader/hearer of the original catches the point: the hand of Yahweh is powerful; the hand of the Egyptians was weak. All of this fulfills just what was predicted by God to Moses in 6:1 ("[By] my mighty hand he will let them go; [by] . . . my mighty hand he will drive them out of his country."[65]

Verse 31 addresses this most important implication of all the events with attention to faith: the resultant faith of God's people in the Lord and their willingness to place their trust in him and in his representative, Moses. Not only does this verse thus identify the point of the story of the deliverance at the sea for all generations (all should learn from it that the Lord can be trusted to deliver his people, no matter what their plight) but adumbrates the New Testament emphasis on salvation by faith. What was important for Israel was not merely that they were safe and the Egyptians were not; what mattered was that faith saves, and God had shown them how faith in him could pay off to their lasting benefit. They were still new to good theology. Many of them at this early point understood very little of who Yahweh was and what he expected of them. But they had now seen one final, awesome act of deliverance from Egypt, and it prompted their fear[66] and trust.

4. Victory Hymn of Moses (15:1–18)

This "Song of the Sea" probably was the earliest-authored portion of the book of Exodus. Moses apparently composed it immediately after the deliverance that it describes (15:1), and Miriam, Moses' sister, taught it forthwith to the women of Israel (15:20–21). Later, in the process of writing the entire book of Exodus, Moses incorporated it into the narrative at this point, fol-

---

[65] Currid, *Exodus*, 306–7.

[66] "Fear" in the sense of fearing the consequence of disobedience and disloyalty to the one true God but real fear indeed, not just "respect" or "awe."

lowing his practice, already established in the composition of Genesis,[67] of including songs and poems that had become well known and popular among the Israelites at places in the narrative where such literary pieces naturally "belong." The advantage of this approach is that it combines for the reader/hearer the familiar musical/poetic lore of a people's heritage within a systematic narrative of their history and covenant. The result is an integration of beloved, familiar literary works within the whole of which they witness to parts, providing a connection of bits of revered musical poetry with the grand overview into which an organized mind wants them to fit. So even though Moses may have written the book of Exodus as late as the last year of his life, when he was one hundred and twenty, he wrote this great song when he was still eighty, even before Israel got to Mount Sinai. As Lord and Parry have amply demonstrated, folk poets can compose complex storytelling songs *instantaneously*.[68] There is no need to assume—indeed it would be incorrect to assume—that Moses (or anyone else) would have required weeks, months, years, or decades to put together such a song. The fact that it was inspired by God relates to its exact content, not to the ability of an ancient poet like Moses[69] to compose something of the song's length or form.

The song must have become instantly popular, judging from Miriam's decision (see comments on vv. 20–21) to teach it to the Israelite women. One can imagine groups of Israelites singing the song often on their way to Mount Sinai and during the wilderness wanderings after leaving Sinai as a new, replacement generation learned some of their history through music. So important did the song become to all generations of believers that it is described in John's great apocalyptic vision as a song to be sung even in heaven (Rev 15:3). In form the song is a victory hymn, a song sung to and

---

[67] The "prose poem" of Gen 1:1–26 may or may not have been already composed before Moses set to the task of writing Genesis. It is likely that 1:27 and 2:23 were poetic fragments of existing works that he excerpted, that Lamech's boastful song of 4:23–24 was preserved from long before Moses' time, that the poetic promise of 8:22 was likewise ancient in composition already by Moses' day, as was Noah's curse (9:25–27), the "Table of Nations" in chap. 10, the promise to Abraham in 12:2–3, and so on, as well as such larger units as the Edomite Genealogy (chap. 36) and the great Blessing of Jacob (49:1–27). Thus, although the Song of the Sea is the first epic poem to appear in Exodus, it is one of many in the whole Pentateuch that Moses worked into the overall narrative-covenant structure.

[68] For a full review of the process of oral epic/narrative composition and a bibliography of the relevant supportive studies, including the various studies by Lord and Parry of folk literature composition, see A. B. Lord, *The Singer of Tales* (1968; reprint, Cambridge: Harvard University Press, 1981).

[69] As a prophet and the paradigm for all subsequent prophets, Moses was a musical poet. It can even be argued that skill in musical poetry composition was part of the requisite "gifting" of an Israelite prophet.

about God in praise of his granting victory to his people over their foes.[70] The ingredients of Israelite hymns may almost always be summarized by the initials SRR: summons to praise, reasons to praise, recapitulation. All three elements are present in abundance in the Song of Moses.

(1) Part I of Moses' Song: Praise to the Lord (15:1–3)

[1]Then Moses and the Israelites sang this song to the LORD:

"I will sing to the LORD,
for he is highly exalted.
The horse and its rider
he has hurled into the sea.
[2]The LORD is my strength and my song;
he has become my salvation.
He is my God, and I will praise him,
my father's God, and I will exalt him.
[3]The LORD is a warrior;
the LORD is his name.

15:1 After the brief introduction that indicates that the song Moses composed became an instant expression of praise for what the Israelites had just experienced, the song itself begins with a summons to praise in the form of a first-person cohortative, which represents not merely Moses' personal intention to praise Yahweh but that of whoever sings the song. "I will sing" can also be translated "I must sing" or "Let me sing" or the like. The proper noun Yahweh ("the LORD") is used here and throughout the song, except when "God" or "god" is used of necessity in the identifying language of vv. 2,11, because although hymns may certainly be addressed to "God," the ambiguity of this term in the pluralistic, polytheistic world of the Old Testament yielded the result that "Yahweh" was the name of choice to denote specifically the only true, real God. Thus the vast majority of Israel's psalms and music about God uses the name Yahweh predominantly—as a safeguard and against misuse and misunderstanding and because there is a greater sense of personal identity to the name Yahweh than to the more generic title God. Both are proper; Old Testament hymnody leans to the side of caution, with Yahweh predominating.

---

[70] On the nature of Moses' song as a victory hymn, see, e.g., G. W. Coats, "The Song of the Sea," *CBQ* 31 (1969): 1–17; A. J. Hauser, "Two Songs of Victory: A Comparison of Exodus 15 and Judges 5," in *Directions in Biblical Hebrew Poetry* (Sheffield: JSOT Press, 1987), 265–84; M. Howell, "Exodus 15, 1b–18, A Poetic Analysis," *ETL* 65 (1989): 5–42; J. S. Kselman, "Psalm 77 and the Book of Exodus," *JANES* 15 (1983): 51–58; R. D. Patterson, "The Song of Redemption," *WTJ* 57 (1995): 453–61.

"For he is highly exalted" speaks to the result of the plagues and the victory at the Red Sea: Yahweh showed the Egyptians his greatness over all their gods (see comments on 12:12) and by implication—since the Egyptian gods were the greatest gods in the popular thinking of the day—over any "god" of any kind (see comments on 15:11). The second half (second poetic couplet) of the verse reflects the fate of the Egyptian chariot army. "The horse and its rider" does not refer to cavalry but to chariotry, and therefore the "rider" refers to the rider(s) on a chariot, not on horseback, as already noted on 14:9.

15:2 "The LORD is my strength and my song"[71] combines metaphors that convey the great truths that human strength is inadequate for the really important challenges of life (who on his own strength could defeat Satan or the various sorts of corrupt world systems that Satan has managed to bring into being?) and that true thoughts of God should inspire in us true expressions of the happiest, most joyous praise we can produce, which for most people is that of exuberant singing. The synonymous parallelism of the second couplet of the verse ("He is my God, and I will praise him, / my father's God, and I will exalt him") calls for heartfelt praise to Yahweh as one's own personal God as well as recognition that we are all in a grand lineage of his

[71] Is "song" the correct translation? Which root is in view here: *zmr* I or *zmr* II? The NIV has chosen to reflect "song," one option for the Hb. word that appears here as זִמְרָת. Most recently scholars have generally argued that the word (presumably reflecting a haplography of the expected final first person pronominal suffix *yodh* ["my"] by reason of confusion with the immediately following *yodh* of the hypocoristicon form *yah* for *yahweh*) really means "my strength/might." S. E. Loewenstamm ("'The Lord Is My Strength and My Glory,'" *VT* 19 [1969]: 464–70) understood the word in question to mean "glory" or the like, which seems to us somewhat less likely. Most lexicographers now recognize a *zimrāh* I, meaning "music," "instrumental sound," "song," or the like and a *zimrāh* II, meaning "strength" or "might" as found also in Isa 12:2 and Ps 118:14. In Moses' own writings, at Gen 43:11, Jacob is quoted as using the term in the expression *zimrat hā'āreṣ,* meaning "best [produce] of the land," which probably literally meant "strength of the land" in the sense of the highest quality produce. Indeed, the root *zmr* II is regularly used in the OT to mean "strengthen" in the context of "pruning" vines because pruning strengthens the fruit branches that remain. Because these meanings establish that *zimrāh* can mean "strength" or "might," and in light of its placement in Exod 15:2 in apparent parallel to the word עָזִּי ("my strength"), few recent commentators have doubted that it should be translated "my might" or the like rather than "my song" or the like. But the situation is not quite so open and shut. In a few other contexts the root *zmr* I, from which *zimrāh I* is derived, appears in close proximity to words for strength or might, so that "song" and "strength" are interwoven closely. Most notable among these are Ps 59:17 ("O my strength, I will sing praises to you") and Ps 21:13 ("Be exalted, O LORD, in your strength; we will sing and praise your might"). These might represent reasonable parallels to the situation in Exod 15:2 and support the NIV translation. On balance we think the evidence supports the translation "my strength and might" rather than "my strength and song." Cf. also J. D. W. Watts, "The Song of the Sea—Ex. XV," *VT* 7 (1957): 371–80; E. M. Good, "Exodus XV 2," *VT* 20 (1970): 358–59; S. B. Parker, "Exodus XV 2 Again," *VT* 21 (1971): 373–79; M. L. Barre, "'My Strength and My Song' in Exodus 15:2," *CBQ* 54 (1992): 623–37.

worshipers throughout the ages. With whatever we have inherited from a prior generation, nothing can be more important than our faith.[72]

15:3 In saying that "the LORD [Yahweh] is a warrior, the LORD [Yahweh] is his name," the song asserts God's willingness to fight for his people against their foes. Israel was being formed as a small people in a world used to wars of aggression by other small people, by coalitions of peoples large and small, and/or by great, imperialistic superpowers (the prime example of the latter being Egypt, as they all too well knew). Israel at Mount Sinai would be born by covenant into a world whose values would be almost entirely different from and usually opposed to their own.[73] Therefore they would have to fight and fight often. Indeed, they would have to fight their first real battle as an army in a matter of weeks, even before they reached Mount Sinai, against the Amalekites at Rephidim (17:8–16). On their own they could never hope to win against odds that were almost always stacked against them. Therefore it was important that they understood their God to be *a warrior,* one who would lead them into battle, who would fight for them during battles, and who would ensure their survival as his people. He was to define their battles for them, deciding when and where to go to war (cf. 17:16). They were to have no allies, no dependency on other foreign powers, no confidence in any earthly deliverer but only in the one true God, their God, Yahweh. In a fallen world hostile to his purposes, Yahweh must be a warrior. The same must be said, of course, for God's Son, who is of necessity a warrior on behalf of his people and will be the final destroyer of all things opposed to God (1 Cor 15:24–28; cf. Rev 19:11–16). The statement "the LORD [Yahweh] is his name" clarifies for the singer and audience of the song the identity of this one, supreme and highly exalted God: it is Yahweh, the God of the patriarchs, the creator of the world and all in it, and the sole God of the people of Israel. All other gods were distorted imitations of him fabricated in the minds and sculpting shops of those who worshipped them. "Name" conveys identity, and the song asserts the identity of the one who has delivered Israel as none other than Yahweh.

(2) Part II of Moses' Song: Defeat of the Egyptians (15:4–10)

4Pharaoh's chariots and his army

---

[72] Inherited faith is a fine thing as long as it is personalized and believed on its own and not merely as a formal outworking of loyalty to parents. From another perspective, parents who leave to their children all decisions about religion and make no effort to persuade them of the saving knowledge of God that they themselves have learned, have raised profoundly ignorant children—children who have been isolated from the most important of all truths by their own parents.

[73] See, e.g., G. E. Wright, *The Old Testament Against Its Environment* (London: SCM Press, 1950).

he has hurled into the sea.
The best of Pharaoh's officers
are drowned in the Red Sea.
5The deep waters have covered them;
they sank to the depths like a stone.

6"Your right hand, O LORD,
was majestic in power.
Your right hand, O LORD,
shattered the enemy.
7In the greatness of your majesty
you threw down those who opposed you.
You unleashed your burning anger;
it consumed them like stubble.
8By the blast of your nostrils
the waters piled up.
The surging waters stood firm like a wall;
the deep waters congealed in the heart of the sea.

9"The enemy boasted,
'I will pursue, I will overtake them.
I will divide the spoils;
I will gorge myself on them.
I will draw my sword
and my hand will destroy them.'
10But you blew with your breath,
and the sea covered them.
They sank like lead
in the mighty waters.

15:4–5 The beginning of v. 4 repeats what the end of v. 1 summarized in the introduction to the theme of the song: an awesomely powerful enemy military force was defeated by Yahweh, all on his own, as proof of his power and protection for his people. The second couplet reminds the singer or listener that the defeated, dead Egyptian troops were not a few reservists or second-rank fighters who made a big mistake and paid for it with their lives. They were the best Egypt had to offer; since Egypt's military was the best in the world of that day, they were the world's best troops, and their officers the best of the best. Neither 15:4 nor any other part of the overall narrative indicates that Pharaoh was with his troops when they drowned. As we have suggested earlier, it is likely that although he began the pursuit (14:6), he turned back when the pillar of cloud prevented immediate capture of the Israelites. Note the reference to "deep waters" in v. 5, waters that "covered them" so that "they sank into the depths." This is simply further evidence, preserved in the song, that what happened to the Egyptians was not some sort of bogging down in shallow water or muddy terrain but drowning in a large body of deep water.[74] Bodies do sink "like a stone" or other heavy object when they drown; later, when they have bloated, they can rise to the surface and wash to shore (14:30)—if they are near enough to shore for that to happen.

15:6 This verse combines observations about God's power and his victory over his and Israel's enemy ("majestic in power . . . shattered the enemy") with the idiomatic sense of "hand" as power, already seen in 3:19–20; 6:1; 7:4–5; 9:15; 13:3,9,14; and esp. 14:30–31. Nothing should be made of the term "right hand" as opposed to just "hand." The meter of the poetry called for another syllable, and "right hand" has one more syllable than "hand" in Hebrew as well as in English.[75]

15:7 These two couplets could also be translated: "In your great majesty / you smashed your foes, // You sent forth your fury, / it consumed them like stubble." An important theological truth is incorporated here, namely that God's eventual destruction of those who opposed him and his anger against evil are not opposed to God's majesty but are in fact inherent aspects of it. Modern sentimentalist thinking wants God to be ever-tolerant, always softhearted, and thus defines God's justice as something other than how the Bible defines it. In fact, the just God revealed in the Bible will not tolerate evil (though he is extremely patient in waiting for repentance, as he was for at least eighty years with the Egyptians) and plans for its eventual total elimination. People who insist on being part of the process of evil will be eliminated as well.

Those offended by these facts about God are wishing for a reality that has never existed. He does get mad; he does smash his foes, and he is majestic in doing so. Though the reference to "stubble" in the last line of the second couplet is not intended to recall the stubble gathered of hard necessity in 5:12, there can be no doubt that the first singers of the song knew all about stubble and how easily it burned up and disappeared when lit on fire. "Consumed" translates *ʾākal,* which can connote either "consume(d) by fire" or

[74] Some scholars who regard the song as an early composition fail to note the implications of its assertion of the drowning of the Egyptians in deep water when advancing the theory that the encounter at the "Reed Sea" was simply a case of Israelites getting away on foot in marshes where chariots could not follow, later embellished by centuries of tradition into the narrative of chap. 14. The arguments of B. F. Batto against the notion that there was a small body of water known as the Reed Sea (*yam sûp,* supposedly meaning "reed sea," that later became associated with the Red Sea are strong ("The Reed Sea: *Requiescat in Pace,*" *JBL* 102 [1983]: 27–35). Batto concludes that "at no point in Israelite history is there any evidence that *yam sûp* ever referred to a body of water other than the Red Sea. All occurrences of the tern *yam sûp* fit adequately . . . There is no reason whatever to posit the existence of a second *yam sûp*. In short, the hypothesis that the Israelites experienced deliverance from their Egyptian pursuers at some historical body of water whose name was dimly but accurately preserved as the "Reed Sea" should be laid to rest forever."

[75] For this reason and also for variety's sake, the more archaic-poetic "right hand" (יָמִין) is often found in poetry as an alternate to "hand" (יָד) with no difference in meaning.

"consume(d) by swallowing." Thus the one metaphor, swallowing, which was what the sea did to the Egyptians, suggests the other, which reflects the common theme of divine judgment by fire.[76]

15:8 This verse concentrates on the miraculous parting of the "surging" waters of the sea, which "piled up, stood firm like a wall," and "congealed in the heart of the sea." The Hebrew word used for "wall" here is *nēd,* which is perhaps better translated "dam" or "dyke,"[77] yet another indication of the deep-water nature of the phenomenon. The expression "in the heart of the sea" also connotes a deep-water deliverance[78] and not an event that took place in a reedy swamp or other shallow body of water.[79] The mention of Yahweh's "nostrils" represents a poetic metaphor, one of hundreds used in the Bible to describe God in terms intended not to suggest that he actually has physical body parts but to personalize his behavior since he is a person and not merely a force. Here the wind is described as coming specially from him as if he had blown it up with his nostrils—not just a wind that happened along. The last line of the triplet (the verse is actually a triplet rather than two couplets as suggested by the NIV formatting) could be better translated "the deeps churned in the heart of the sea," also tending to rule out a shallow-water event.[80] "Deeps" *(tĕhōmōt)* consistently refers to the ocean in the Old Testament.

15:9 This part of the song recreates the general attitude of the Egyptians and adds a detail the prose summary in chap. 14 does not contain: the army expected the usual reward of an ancient army, that is, plunder from those they captured. Even though the assignment was presumably to capture rather than to kill (implied in 14:5), the time-honored right of plunder and the knowledge that the Israelites had plenty with them (13:34–35) sparked the army's assault. The plan would have been to crush any Israelite resistance (which the militarily superior Egyptians would have assumed would be easily done) and resubjugate all survivors. This sort of "expectation of plunder" theme can be expressed in terms of an enemy's vain boasting (Judg 5:30) or a proper expectation when victory is truly assured (Isa 53:12). The

---

[76] E.g., Lev 21:9; Num 11:1–3; 16:35; Deut 4:24; 6:15; 9:3; 32:22; Isa 66:15; Amos 1:4,10.

[77] It occurs elsewhere only in Josh 3:13,16 and Ps 78:13.

[78] A different angle, one that we do not accept here because the dominant themes of the context seem to us to overrule the idea, is taken on this verse by A. Wolters, who regards the verse as changing the tone from that of deliverance to that of destruction ("Not Rescue but Destruction: Rereading Exodus 15:8," *CBQ* 52 [1990[: 223–40).

[79] בְּלֶב־יָם always has this sense, whether יָם is plural or singular in the expression. Cf. Ezek 27:4,25–27; 28:2,8; Ps 46:3; Prov 23:34; 30:19.

[80] The reader will forgive the many observations on deep vs. shallow water issues, necessitated by the fact that so many modern scholars have opted for a theory of shallow-water deliverance in a marshy area, an approach requiring a systematic evaluation of the likelihood of such a scenario in light of the testimony of the narrative's data.

Egyptians expected to catch up easily with the Israelites ("I will pursue, I will overtake them"), which did indeed happen until the intervention of God in the pillar of cloud, and to enrich themselves ("I will divide the spoils; / I will gorge myself on them") and then to defeat Israel in some sort of battle ("I will draw my sword / and my hand will destroy them"). In the final analysis they were thwarted in all these plans.

15:10 Combining concepts already encountered, especially in v. 8 (God's breath/wind and the massiveness of the waters involved) and v. 5 (the sea's covering the enemy and sinking like a heavy object), this verse serves the "recapitulation" purpose of this part of the hymn, bringing to a close what we have labeled Part II of Moses' Song of the Sea.

(3) Part III of Moses' Song: Praise and Thanks to the Lord (15:11–13)

11"Who among the gods is like you, O LORD?
Who is like you—
majestic in holiness,
awesome in glory,
working wonders?
12You stretched out your right hand
and the earth swallowed them.

13"In your unfailing love you will lead
the people you have redeemed.
In your strength you will guide them
to your holy dwelling.

15:11 An alternate translation of v. 11 would read as follows, understanding the verse to be a triplet rather than an unbalanced couplet (as apparently in the NIV format): "Who is like you among the gods, O LORD? / Who is like you, glorious among the holy ones / Awesome in praiseworthy acts, wonder worker." The emphasis of this verse is God's uniqueness. The mention of the gods should not be understood to suggest polytheism. The plural "gods" in Hebrew poetry (usually *ʾēlîm,* as here) includes in its range of meaning the various angels, authorities, and powers (1 Pet 3:22) that include heavenly angels as well as Satan and his fallen angels.[81] The prose/poetry plural *ʾĕlōhîm* is, of course, routinely used to refer to "their [other people's] gods,"[82] "other gods,"[83] "no gods,"[84] "foreign gods,"[85] and the like. If we

---

[81] Cf. Job 41:7 (אֵלִים); Isa 24:21; Dan 4:35; Matt 13:54; 14:2; Mark 6:14; Rom 8:38; 1 Cor 12:10; Eph 6:12; Col 1:16; 2:15; Heb 6:5. See also esp. Job 1:6 (בְּנֵי הָאֱלֹהִים) and Ps 82:1 (בַּעֲדַת־אֵל בְּקֶרֶב אֱלֹהִים).

[82] E.g., Exod 23:24.

[83] E.g., Exod 20:3.

[84] E.g., 2 Kgs 19:18.

[85] E.g., Gen 35:2.

were to put words in their mouths, Moses and those who sang this song would have meant by "who among the gods is like you": "You are infinitely superior to all real and false superhuman beings, including angels heavenly and fallen, and even to what the pagans think their nonexistent gods are." The repetition of "who is like you" emphasizes through rhetorical questioning the fact that God has no one like him.

Yahweh is then described as "glorious among the holy ones" (following the LXX) or "majestic in holiness" (following the MT). The merit of the LXX reading "among the holy ones" is its parallel to the opening words of the verse, "among the gods." The difference between "holy ones" and "holiness" was a single letter in the Hebrew spelling of that time period.[86] Holiness is the quality of belonging to/being like God; holy ones are heavenly beings (angels) that belong to God and are like him in the sense of doing his will and reflecting his values. God is also "awesome in praiseworthy acts" (NIV "awesome in glory"), meaning that what he does is always good and right and impressive at the same time. He is also a wonder-worker, one who does the supernatural and the amazing as easily as he does the typical and routine. He does regularly and constantly what no human or other being can do so that humans who trust in him and live in right relation to him can rejoice in his power to do what for them would be or seem impossible.

15:12 Again, as part of the necessary and appropriate sort of repetition that characterizes virtually all musical poetry (songs) in all cultures and times, the victory hymn mentions God's powerful "right hand" (cf. v. 6) and the death of the Egyptians ("the earth swallowed them"). Since the Egyptians drowned rather than being actually swallowed by the earth, one might wonder why this wording is present in the song. The answer is that "earth" *(ʾereṣ)* sometimes has the meaning "underworld" or "hell," as it almost surely does here.[87] Thus the meaning is, "They didn't just fail to catch us or fail to conquer us—they lost their lives in the process!" Although it was Moses who stretched out his hand with the staff of God in it to initiate the miracle at the sea (14:21), the song can properly attribute the whole thing to Yahweh ("You stretched out your right hand"). Thus the song confirms that what Moses did he did as Yahweh's "stand-in."

15:13 A grand theme of Scripture appears at this point in the song. Even though God has graciously come at various times and ways—most

---

[86] I.e., קְדֹשִׁים ("holy ones") as opposed to קֹדֶשׁ ("holiness"). The *yodh* found in the later orthography of the plural morpheme would not have been present in Moses' Bronze Age orthography.

[87] Unambiguous examples include Jer 17:13; Ps 63:9; Eccl 3:21; Ezek 26:20; 31:14,18; 32:18,24; Jonah 2:6. Cf. M. Dahood, *Psalms I–III,* AB (Garden City: Doubleday, 1968), *sub ʾereṣ* (e.g., in Vol. II, 72, 84, 176, 190, 232, 353; *TDOT, sub ʾereṣ; TWOT,* 74–75; F. M. Cross Jr. and D. N. Freedman, *JNES* 14 (1955): 247–48.

fully in Christ[88]—to the place where we live, it has always[89] been God's plan that his people should, because of the work of Christ, eventually join him where he lives.[90] The story of ancient Israel mirrors this.[91] God called them out of where they had been born and had been living (Egypt), bound them to himself in a covenant (at Sinai and again in Deuteronomy), and then led them to his holy dwelling (Israel/Jerusalem/the temple).[92] The same sort of thing happens in Christ, yet on a greater and more lasting scale. God calls those who believe in him out of where they have been born and are living (earth), binds them to himself in a (new) covenant (by believing in Jesus as Savior and Lord), and then leads them to his holy dwelling (heaven).

Those who first sang this song with Moses were not yet in Canaan/the land of Israel. They expected to get there soon, a hope that was dashed by their lack of confidence in God (Num 13–14); yet even though the arrival was delayed by forty years, it remained the exodus generation's great hope to settle where Yahweh himself had chosen to "dwell." It is obvious that an omnipresent God cannot be located only at one place.[93] But he can certainly manifest himself specially at one or more places, if he chooses, for the benefit of his people. In Deuteronomy and much of the Old Testament, relative to the dwelling of God in his "sanctuary" among his people (the tabernacle/temple), the place of God's choosing is called the place where he causes his *name* to dwell.[94] This part of the song continues in the Hebrew perfect tense/aspect that has dominated so far, but here the perfect may express the function sometimes called "prophetic perfect," by which a future seen prophetically is reported on as "having happened" because a prophet was, as it were, back from the past to report on what he saw (past tense) that happened (past tense) in the *future*—even though in actual fact from the point of view of his audience it has *not* yet happened. The term translated "unfailing love" in the NIV is *ḥesed,* a word that connotes mainly "loyalty" or "faithfulness" so that the first sentence of the verse could be translated, "You have lead/will lead faithfully the people you have redeemed."

The song's reference to God's redemption recalls 6:6 ("I will redeem you with an outstretched arm and with mighty acts of judgment"). Redeem *(gāʿal)* means to "reacquire" or "get back for oneself" or "buy back." The payment in a

[88] Cf. Heb 1:1–4; 3:3; 8:6.

[89] Eph 3:11.

[90] E.g., John 14:2–3.

[91] Sometimes the Scripture explicitly describes the way OT realities are intended as patterns for greater NT, heavenly realities (as Hebrews points out, e.g., Heb 8:5). At other times such things are mainly implicit

[92] Note that here in the song the promised land is termed God's *nĕwēh, dwelling* in the sense of "encampment," a place where one resides but which is not necessarily his ultimate home.

[93] 1 Kgs 8:27.

[94] Deut 1:25; 12:11; 14:23; 16:11; Ezra 6:12; Ps 74:7; Jer 7:12.

divine redemption is not always described as monetary; in the overall plan of redemption it is an ultimate payment in kind, that is, the person of Christ. When a thing is redeemed, its ownership changes. Israel had been from one point of view the property of Egypt and Pharaoh; now it was God's property, in the same sort of happy way a redeemed child is once again the property of its parents (cf. 13:13,15). Israelite obedience to God's covenant would logically, then, follow from their having been graciously redeemed (e.g., Deut 15:15: "Remember that you were slaves in Egypt and the LORD your God redeemed you. That is why I give you this command today"). The verse is a quatrain, two couplets closely parallel to each other and the topics somewhat interwoven as a result. Loyalty (NIV "unfailing love") is paralleled to "strength" as the divine resource that benefits Israel; God "will lead" his "people" who are "redeemed" to his "holy dwelling," for which that redemption qualifies them.

(4) Part IV of Moses' Song: Reaction of Future Foes (15:14–16a)

14 The nations will hear and tremble;
anguish will grip the people of Philistia.
15 The chiefs of Edom will be terrified,
the leaders of Moab will be seized with trembling,
the people of Canaan will melt away;
16 terror and dread will fall upon them.
By the power of your arm
they will be as still as a stone—

These verses address yet another aspect of the divine deliverance at the sea: its impact on the peoples/nations that the Israelites knew they would have to encounter as they proceeded to conquer the promised land. Because Moses grew up as an Egyptian princeling and spent the first forty years of his life exposed to royal concerns, he would have been well acquainted with political/military/economic events in Canaan and its environs. The Egyptians were obsessed with keeping Asia Minor from becoming a threat to their well being and thus kept constant tabs on what was happening in the four regions listed in these verses. The conquest of the promised land would of necessity involve the elimination of opposition from these regions. The predominant tense/aspect found in the Hebrew in these verses continues to that of the perfect so that the entire section could, if desired, be translated as if what is described were a foregone conclusion (again in the mode of the so-called prophetic perfect), thus:

14 The peoples heard, they trembled,
agony seized the inhabitants of Philistia.
15 Then were dismayed
the chieftains of Edom,
The nobles of Moab
Were seized with trembling.

The inhabitants of Canaan
melted utterly.
16 You brought down[95] upon them
terror and dread,
By your great power,
They were struck dumb as a stone.[96]

15:14 This couplet summarizes the general effect on the nations with which the Israelites had to be concerned: they would suffer anxiety at the thought of what the Israelite deliverance at the sea might mean for them if they were to opposed Israel's entrance to the promised land. Philistia is then mentioned first, as is appropriate. Not only were the Philistines closest and thus potentially the first foe to be encountered if God had not intervened (see comments on 13:17), they would eventually become Israel's most intransigent enemy until subjugated more or less permanently under David.[97] Superior to the Israelites technologically[98] and militarily,[99] the Philistines were a foe not beatable without divine help, part of which came in the form of the fear struck into the hearts of the Philistines by the loss of the Egyptian cavalry force at the sea.

15:15 Edom, Moab, and Canaan are mentioned in the same order that they were eventually encountered in the actual process of entering the promised land (Num 20–21; Josh 1–10). Neither Edom nor Moab were actually part of the promised land,[100] but access to the land required passage through those countries and their acquiescence for further Israelite activity. They were both emergent nations from all accounts, much like Israel at the time, that is, more in the nature of people groups trying to settle into an area than in the nature of established nations of long standing.[101] Note the hint in the

---

[95] Taking the *apparent* imperfect as a *yaqtul* preterite here and in the next verb, "were struck down," as well.

[96] Note that we are not arguing that this section of the song *must* be translated with past tenses into English, only that if one consistently applies the opportunity to attempt a "prophetic perfect" sort of translation, the results make sense within the context of the situation described at this point in Exodus, namely, a divine victory over Egypt by Yahweh on behalf of his people before, not after, his people had entered Canaan.

[97] See comments on 13:17.

[98] See 1 Sam 13:19–22.

[99] So by the time of the tragic events recorded in 1 Sam 31, the Philistines had so dominated Israel militarily that they had pushed them by a series of military victories all the way back to Mount Gilboa, not far from the Jordan river, and were at that point therefore actually or potentially controlling more "Israelite" territory than the Israelites were.

[100] Num 34:3–12; Josh 13:8–19:48.

[101] This observation is simply based on the references to these areas in Egyptian records and the evidence from archaeology at the relevant sites, as these compare with the biblical text. It is clear from Num 22:1–4 that the Moabites were so thinly represented in Moab and so outnumbered by the Israelites that they felt there was no chance of defeating them militarily, so they resorted to divination (Num 22:5–7). The Edomites were a more formidable fighting force, defending a smaller and more challenging territory, so they did not hesitate to oppose the Israelites militarily (Num 21:18–21). It is entirely possible that Israel could have beaten them, but war with Edom was not on the conquest agenda, so it was avoided.

terms "chiefs of Edom" and "leaders of Moab"[102] that these groups were not yet fully unified nations with kings. Likewise, "people of Canaan," paralleling "people of Philistia"[103] in v. 14, suggests at least a neutral position in the song relative to the political status of these areas. The terminology is poetic and does not prove the case, but it certainly comports with the inference sometimes drawn from the available archaeological data that Edom and Moab, as well as Canaan and what eventually became Philistia, were thinly populated and undergoing a continuing process of settlement rather than fully settled and politically established as nations at the time of the exodus.

These words were intended to hearten their first hearers. They also proved true in time. The Moabites were the most easily cowed (Num 22:2–3). The Edomites required more convincing, some of which was provided involuntarily by Balaam (Num 24:17–18) but most of which developed gradually over the years of Israel's wilderness wanderings (Deut 2:4) and still was not complete even in the days of Saul (1 Sam 14:47). Edomite and Philistine subjugation had to wait until the days of David (2 Sam 8:1,11–12), whereas Canaanite panic set in early (Josh 2:8–11).

15:16a Our suggested translation of this verse would be: "You will bring down upon them / terror and dread; // By your great power[104] / they will be struck dumb as a stone." In the holy war one of God's weapons is psychological affliction,[105] the creation of fear and cowardice in an enemy that might otherwise pose a formidable obstacle to the well-being of his people. This verse speaks of terror/dread (simple synonyms here) being brought by God on Israel's foes so that they are "dumb as a stone"—unable to talk and thus unable to organize as an army or take any other action to deny Israel its access to the promised land.

(5) Part V of Moses' Song: Israel, God's Sanctuary (15:16b–18)

until your people pass by, O LORD,
until the people you bought pass by.
[17]You will bring them in and plant them
on the mountain of your inheritance—
the place, O LORD, you made for your dwelling,
the sanctuary, O LORD, your hands established.
[18]The LORD will reign
for ever and ever."

---

[102] אַלּוּפֵי אֱדוֹם אֵילֵי מוֹאָב. A better translation would be "chieftains of Edom, nobles of Moab."

[103] V. 14: יֹשְׁבֵי פְּלָשֶׁת; v. 15: יֹשְׁבֵי כְנָעַן. A preferable translation might be "inhabitants of . . ." in each case.

[104] Lit., "by the greatness of your arm."

[105] I.e., getting people to think incorrectly about the strength of their position, not the causation of psychosis.

15:16b–18 The challenge of translating the Hebrew word *ʿad* in v. 16b is whether to take it as "until" (so NIV, quite reasonably) or as "when/as," a meaning it appears to have had in the older Bronze Age texts, at least in some contexts. Our preference is for "when" so that v. 16b is seen as introducing a new sentence and a new and final part of the song. This last section may be translated then as follows:

16bWhen your people will pass over,[106] O LORD,
When the people whom you created will pass over,
17You will bring them in and plant them
on the mountain of your possession,
The foundation of your dwelling place,
you have made, O LORD.
A sanctuary, O LORD,
your hands have created.
18The LORD will reign
for ever and ever!

Three great biblical themes conclude the song: God's creation of a people (v. 16b), God's eternal holy dwelling place as the home for that people (v. 17), and the eternal reign of God supreme over all things (v. 18).

With regard to creation of a people, it is important to remember that the Bible does not suggest that God finished his creation with the events described in the first chapters of Genesis. Rather, creation continues with the creation of Israel,[107] alluded to here in the song, the new creation that came about through the work of Christ[108] and the great re-creation at the end of the present age.[109] God's creation continues in stages, one of which was accomplished through the exodus and the subsequent incorporation of Israel as God's covenant people at Sinai. That is the stage of which the song speaks especially.

With regard to the theme of God's eternal holy dwelling as the proper and expected home for God's people, a topic already raised in part in v. 13, the song adds elements such as the idea that God "will bring them in and plant them" (thus making possible their entrance, which on their own they could not effect, and establishing them there permanently rather than merely help-

---

[106] Whether this is translated "pass over" or "pass by," it has the sense of getting past the barriers to entrance to the promised land, i.e., bypassing and not being deterred by the potential entanglements with those who wanted to block—militarily or otherwise—Israel's migration into and settlement within Canaan, i.e., the four groups mentioned in vv. 14–15.

[107] See esp. E. A. Martens, *God's Design,* 3d ed. (N. Richland Hills, Tex.: Bibal Press, 1998), 71–90, 169–92, 263–80. Cp. also Isa 43:1.

[108] 2 Cor 5:17 (properly translated, "If anyone is in Christ, it is a new creation; the old has gone, the new has come"); Gal 6:15; Rom 6:4; Eph 4:24; Col 1:15.

[109] So Isa 65:17; 66:22; Pet 3:13; Rev 21:16.

ing them to get into Canaan and leaving them to fend for themselves). It is clear from the song that Israel knew it was going to a mountainous land (in contrast to Egypt, which is in most of its topography very flat) and that God's sanctuary would be established on a *mountain* there. When God finally chose the threshing-floor-capped Mount Zion (2 Sam 24) as the place for a permanent sanctuary, it was in fulfillment of this expectation. Zion is envisioned here as the place of God's *inheritance,* that is, permanent personal real property. It is from this sort of language that one begins to trace the biblical theme of heaven as the ultimate Jerusalem.[110] It was not the case that Israelites chose Mount Zion to build a temple there, and God honored their choice. Just the opposite was the case—he chose the site,[111] and they merely responded according to what his "hands established."

The final verse of the song is a sort of recapitulation of the lessons it states throughout. God is supreme over all other beings and forces. And the Israelites, still in the process of getting to know him and about him and to use his newly rerevealed name, Yahweh, to distinguish him from all other gods and idols (see comments on v. 11), were expected to come increasingly to realize that he is eternal and that their association with him had eternal consequences. The New Testament develops this concept in greater detail, especially with the added emphasis on God's people sharing his reign (2 Tim 2:12; Rev 20:4,6; 22:5; cf. Dan 7:18). The unstoppable, uninterruptible, eternal reign of God is a widely represented topic within the Bible (e.g., Pss 10:16; 45:6; 48:14; Heb 1:8; Rev 1:18; 11:15) and an assurance to all who place their faith in him.

5. Prose Summation and Miriam's Reprise of the Hymn (15:19–21)

19 When Pharaoh's horses, chariots and horsemen went into the sea, the LORD brought the waters of the sea back over them, but the Israelites walked through the sea on dry ground. 20 Then Miriam the prophetess, Aaron's sister, took a tambourine in her hand, and all the women followed her, with tambourines and dancing. 21 Miriam sang to them:

"Sing to the LORD,
for he is highly exalted.
The horse and his rider
he has hurled into the sea."

15:19 This verse provides yet another bit of evidence that those who pursued the Israelites were chariot warriors exclusively. It mentions only

---

[110] Culminating in Rev 3:12 and 21:2 but developed in progression through such loci as Isa 52; Zech 12; 14; and Heb 12.

[111] Cf. Deut 12:9ff.

Pharaoh's "horses, chariots and horsemen," no foot soldiers. If there *were* any foot soldiers in the original contingent that pursued the Israelites as far as the edge of the sea, as some scholars have argued, they did not follow into the sea itself.[112] Otherwise, the verse contains no new information but provides a convenient summation of what happened to the Egyptians and the Israelites respectively when they each sought to enter the sea.

15:20–21 This is the first (and indeed only) mention of Miriam by name in the book. Although it is likely that she was the older sister who kept watch over Moses when he was in his special little ark and had the presence of mind to secure his own mother to nurse him for Pharaoh's daughter (2:4–8), there can be no absolute certainty of that identification (see comments on 2:4ff.). She is called here "Miriam the prophetess, Aaron's sister," a description that begs the question, Why not call her Moses' sister? The answer would appear to be that Moses used proper modesty in introducing her officially and culturally correctly here, linking her to the oldest living male in her family, Aaron, who was three years older than Moses and thus the proper person to be mentioned.[113] For Miriam to be called a prophetess[114] may mean that she had already distinguished herself in the faithful expression of God's verbal will to some group within, if not all of, the Israelites, unless it refers back from the point of Moses' writing Exodus specifically to Miriam's present function, that of conveying the word of God through song. Several other godly women bear this same title "prophetess" in the Old Testament (or its Greek equivalent in the NT): Deborah (Judg 4:4), Huldah (2 Kgs 22:14), Isaiah's wife (Isa 8:3), and Anna (Luke 2:36); a couple of not-so-godly women do as well (Noadiah in Neh 6:14 and "Jezebel" in Rev 2:20).[115]

---

[112] There is nothing at all to object to in the theory that foot soldiers were involved in the Egyptians' pursuit of the Israelites other than (1) what the text itself says, which never mentions any sorts of troops other than charioteers, and (2) the question of how effective a pursuit via an army on foot would be against another army on foot (Israel) that is actually on the move. Could trained troops move faster than untrained ones accompanied by family members and livestock? Probably so, but how much faster? The Egyptians would have had to bring with them all the sorts of shelter and armament and supplies and supply vehicles that corresponded to the Israelites' tents, household goods, and animals. Questions may also be asked as to whether the Egyptians would have been in better physical shape than the slavery-hardened Israelites and whether the Egyptian military would have been recently reorganized as a result of losing so many soldiers from the tenth plague. All in all, it would seem that a pursuit relying solely on chariotry was the most likely.

[113] Exod 7:6. Medieval rabbinic tradition speculated that Hur (see comments on 17:10) was Miriam's husband, but there is no evidence in the OT itself to support this.

[114] הַנְּבִיאָה.

[115] S. Ackerman has pointed out the parallel between Miriam's role as a prophetess here (rare for a woman in that day and culture) and Zipporah's role as a sort of surrogate priestess (likewise rare for a woman in that day and culture) in 4:24–26 ("Why Is Miriam Also among the Prophets? And Is Zipporah among the Priests?)," *JBL* 121 [2002]: 47–80).

Micah confirms Miriam's leadership role in the exodus (Mic 6:4), which, on the analogy of how Moses and Aaron exercised their leadership and how prophets in general do so, would have meant that she received instructive words from God to relay to the people as a way of guiding them. We do not know what these were apart from the present context any more than we know what sorts of prophetic oracles, say, Huldah may have uttered over time to make her the prophet of choice for King Josiah to consult in the crisis of 2 Kgs 22:11–20. Nevertheless, the leadership of the exodus was clearly a family affair, as confirmed also by the specific mention of the death and burial of Miriam (Num 20:1), an honorable sort of mention accorded otherwise only to Moses (Deut 34:5–6) and Aaron (Num 20:28; Deut 10:6; 32:50).

Miriam's role as leading musician-singer ("took a tambourine in her hand, and all the women followed her, with tambourines and dancing") comports with what we know of the role of women in the preservation and dissemination via music of the cultural values of the ancient world. Some Old Testament passages mention women singing and playing tambourines at occasions of victory over enemies (Judg 11:34; 1 Sam 18:6; cf. Jer 31:4) or other sorts of celebrations (Ps 68:25), but this also was something men could do just as commonly (1 Sam 10:5; 2 Sam 6:5) and that must as well have been done often by mixed groups (e.g., Judg 5:1; 2 Sam 19:35; 2 Chr 25:35; Ezra 2:65; Neh 7:67; Eccl; 2:8; Gen 31:27; Job 21:12; cf. Ps 68:25). The preservation of historical events through song was an expectation of ancient culture (Judg 5:1,11; Num 21:17; 1 Sam 21:11; 2 Sam 1:17–27; 3:33; 22:1). Miriam taught the song to "all the women" by singing it to them,[116] the way

[116] Some commentators have argued that Miriam sang the song to Moses and the men of Israel or led the women in doing so (thus singing antiphonally in response to the men) because the word "them" in the verse appears to be the masculine plural pronoun (לָהֶם) and because the verb in question (ענה) can mean "answer" rather than "sing" [a theory complicated by the fact that ענה in most contexts actually does not mean "answer" at all but rather "speak up." But the present context clearly suggests that it was the women to whom she sang. The old Bronze Age language that Exodus was originally written in has a variety of pronominal endings that are different from those of the later language (and specifically common "masculine" endings for either masculine or feminine), and ענה means "speak up" or "sing" much more often than it means "answer." Some think Miriam was the actual author of the song, though this conclusion requires ignoring what the text actually says in favor of an idealistic reconstruction of the facts. On the various points of view, see G. Janzen, "Song of Moses, Song of Miriam: Who Is Seconding Whom?" *CBQ* 54 (1992): 211–20; J. L. Kugel, "Is There But One Song?" *Bib* 63 (1982): 329–50; C. Meyers, "Miriam the Musician," in *A Feminist Companion to Exodus and Deuteronomy: A Feminist Companion to the Bible* 6 (Sheffield: Sheffield Academic Press, 1994), 207–30; A. F. van Dijk-Hemmes, "Some Recent Views on the Presentation of the Song of Miriam," in *A Feminist Companion to Exodus and Deuteronomy: A Feminist Companion to the Bible* 6 (Sheffield: Sheffield Academic Press, 1994), 200–206; G. J. Brooke, "A Lost Song of Miriam,' *BAR* 20 (1994): 62–65; P. Trible, "Bringing Miriam out of the Shadows," *BibRev* 5 (1989): 14–25, 34.

songs have always been taught in all cultures, even today when songs can also be learned by reading from written musical notation.

The quotation of 15:1 here in v. 21 by Miriam is simply a way of saying that she taught the Israelite women the *entire* song, not just the opening words cited in v. 21. Verse 21 contains the incipit title of the song—the first few words or the first couplet of the song. Citing the incipit apparently was the most common method of titling songs in ancient Israel,[117] as also in most of history until modern times.[118] Moses had authored this great victory song; Miriam now popularized it among all the women so that it would be known and sung in every family, every home. The result was that every Israelite, whether descended from Abraham or newly joined to the nation (12:38) would know by heart the story of the great divine deliverance of God's people at the sea.

6. Grumbling Begins: Water at Marah and Elim and God's Promise of Healing (15:22–27)

22Then Moses led Israel from the Red Sea and they went into the Desert of Shur. For three days they traveled in the desert without finding water. 23When they came to Marah, they could not drink its water because it was bitter. (That is why the place is called Marah.) 24So the people grumbled against Moses, saying, "What are we to drink?"

25Then Moses cried out to the LORD, and the LORD showed him a piece of wood. He threw it into the water, and the water became sweet.

There the LORD made a decree and a law for them, and there he tested them. 26He said, "If you listen carefully to the voice of the LORD your God and do what is right in his eyes, if you pay attention to his commands and keep all his decrees, I will not bring on you any of the diseases I brought on the Egyptians, for I am the LORD, who heals you."

27Then they came to Elim, where there were twelve springs and seventy palm trees, and they camped there near the water.

After the first great victory came the first big test. The Israelites did not pass it easily. When circumstances seemed threatening, they quickly forgot the significance of the deliverances they had recently experienced (ten plagues and the drowning of the Egyptians at the sea) and complained. God used the occasion of their complaining to test them and teach them about trusting him enough to obey him and thus enjoy his benefits. The degree to

---

117 An example of a repeatedly used incipit title can be found in 1 Chr 16:41; 2 Chr 5:13; 7:3,6; 20:21; Ezra 3:11.

118 It is still used today in hymnals and other music books. Cf. the uniform method of incipit titling in D. P. Hustad, ed., *Hymns for the Living Church* (Carol Stream, Ill.: Hope, 1984), a popular and widely used hymnal.

which they failed to accept and learn from that testing and teaching is not described in the present passage but has its outworking in the immediately following episodes in the narrative (16:1–30; 17:1–7).[119]

15:22–24 Once across the Red Sea, the Israelites went to Shur. This is a vast, rugged, and sparsely populated wilderness region in the northern Sinai, stretching from what in modern times is the eastern side of the Suez Canal to the Negev of Israel.[120] It was past the boundary fortifications the Egyptians had built to protect Egypt proper and thus represented freedom from the likelihood of any further Egyptian pursuit. One of the demands the Israelites had all along sought from the Egyptians, to go "into the wilderness,"[121] was now a reality. Much remained, however, before the second part of their demand, to serve Yahweh,[122] would be accomplished. They then traveled "for three days . . . without finding water." Presumably they were heading south, toward Sinai, along one of the ancient caravan routes that offered reasonable passage on foot for caravaneers who brought ample water supplies with them but that certainly was not laid out to get a large host of people to the nearest watering place.

From a human point of view, it is entirely understandable that the Israelites would have begun to worry about water by the third day without finding any. They and their animals probably had consumed nearly all the water they had carried with them in skins, and it is not inconceivable that as they approached Marah in expectation of being able to drink all they wanted, many of them drank their last water and/or gave it to the animals. Accordingly, finding foul water at Marah was not merely a disappointment but a cause of panic. "Bitter"

---

[119] Indeed, F. H. Polak regards Exod 15:22–17:16 as containing the key desert narratives that give the entire book its overarching narrative structure and theme ("Water, Rock and Wood: Structure and Thought Pattern in the Exodus Narrative," *JANES* 25 [1997]: 19–42).

[120] Crossing into Shur involved crossing the area that might be described as the "Red Sea-border lakes-Suez Canal depression" (what in modern times is the route of the Suez Canal) that formed the functional eastern border of ancient Egypt. Shur was the largely waterless region to which Hagar fled from Sarah's persecution, and was blessed to find a well (Gen 16:7) and one of the places associated with Abraham's sojourns (Gen 20:1). K. A. Kitchen emphasizes the relatively informal way boundaries and districts were identified and named as illustrated by the term "wilderness of Shur." He identifies the "wilderness of Shur/Etham" with the Isthmus of Suez as it extends from Timsah to the Suez Gulf: "Thus after crossing the lakes section of yam suph (be it Ballah, Timsah, or Bitter), the Hebrews (if headed south) would go through the Shur/Etham desert past the Etham (Ismailia) zone, on past the latitude of Suez, the three days' march (thirty-six to forty-five miles at twelve to fifteen miles per day) to Marah, Elim, then (again) to yam suph. This was simply a stop by the east (Sinai) shore of the Suez Gulf" (*On the Reliability of the Old Testament* [Grand Rapids: Eerdmans, 2003], 262–63). Some of the tribes David kept at bay by periodic preemptive raids were associated with the region of Shur as well (1 Sam 27:8) since the northeastern edge of that region bordered extreme southwestern Judah.

[121] E.g., 3:18; 5:1,3; 7:16; 8:27–28.

[122] Or to worship Yahweh. See comments on 7:16.

water (*mārāh* means "bitter" in Hb.) is often clear so that it looks potable but in fact contains large percentages of dissolved mineral salts that render it undrinkable. Thirsty people and animals will try to drink any water they find, but if they find it simply offensive, they will resist any consumption unless delirious with thirst. The Israelites may not yet have been at the delirious stage, but they certainly were not happy about what they encountered at Marah. This represented a test of faith of a sort they had not before experienced. It bore some resemblance to what the Egyptians had to deal with when the Nile was turned to blood (7:14–24), but that was a problem alleviated by digging temporary wells. Some Israelites may even have tried to dig around the edges of the water at Marah, presumably without success.

Their question, "What are we to drink?" was not in itself outrageous or even unfair. Their sin manifested itself rather in their *attitude,* which is suggested in the statement at the beginning of v. 24, "So the people grumbled[123] against Moses."[124] Moses was, of course, God's human representative among them and a likely target for blame. What is noteworthy, however, is that the people were following the pillar of cloud and therefore knew perfectly well that it was Yahweh who had led them to this location. But since Moses was the Lord's spokesman, they expected the answer to their complaint to come from him. The people did not have what they had expected and failed to trust God to provide it. Since the Garden of Eden that has been a formula for disobedience.

15:25a Yet another miraculous sign is described here, and in just half a verse. This supernatural demonstration of God's presence and provision is not notably different in kind from the demonstrations earlier used by Moses to convince the elders of Israel and then the people in general that he had been sent from God.[125] Moses needed something to assure the people that all was well; God told him what to do, and when he did it, God's care was demonstrated. Speculation about how a tree [NIV: *piece of wood*][126] could eliminate mineral salts from a large body of water is just as fruitless as speculation about how the Nile could turn to blood or how a staff could turn into a snake and back again: it was a supernatural, not a natural event; a miracle, not a prescientific application of a natural remedy. Nothing in the text suggests that the tree symbolized anything in particular (such as the tree of life or the like). Rather, Moses' faith in being willing to do what God com-

[123] "Complained" would be an equally satisfactory translation.

[124] D. J. Kline suggests that the name Marah (bitter) may also have preserved the sense of the Israelites' bitter attitudes that began with their bitter life in Egypt, and would be ameliorated by their acceptance of Yahweh's commands (see v. 26; "Proving and Provision at Marah," *Kerux* 15 [2000]: 24–29). In other words, obedience to God is an antidote to bitterness, not just in the taste of water but in personal and group attitudes.

[125] See comments on 4:1–9,29–30.

[126] The NIV translation of עֵץ as "piece of wood" is not impossible, just unlikely.

manded him, without understanding why or how it would work, is what is implicitly commended here.

15:25b–26 Verse 25b, "There the LORD made a decree and a law for them, and there he tested them," is both predictive of what was coming and resumptive of what had occurred. It could as well be translated: "There he made for them a statute, that is, a rule, because there he had tested them." In other words, the testing was already past—it was the leading of the people to a place where the water was no good. The statute/rule [NIV "decree . . . law"] would immediately follow as the content of v. 26.

The NIV wording "a decree and a law" does not refer to two things but to one; this is a classic case of hendiadys, the expression of a single concept by two or more words used in grammatical parallel.[127] As in a few other instances prior to the formal establishment of covenant law beginning in chap. 20, God gave a law intended to provide a general understanding for his people of his policies and principles.[128] What v. 26 called for was loyalty and obedience: loyalty in the sense of a willingness to pay close attention to what God's will was and to want above all else to please him by doing what he thinks is right ("listen carefully to the voice of the LORD your God and do what is right in his eyes"—also a hendiadys, a way of ensuring clarity by making the same point twice with different wordings) and obedience by not failing to "pay attention to all his commands and keep all his decrees" (another hendiadys—one concept stated with two different wordings). God's expectation was sweeping. His people must give him full, not partial, loyalty and obedience. If he wanted it, they were to do it.[129]

What advantage came from such loyalty and obedience? Perfect divine protection. The promise of v. 26, "I will not bring on you any of the diseases I brought on the Egyptians, for I am the LORD, who heals you," however, often has been misunderstood, taken as if it were a general guarantee that faithful believers cannot get sick or that if they do, they will always be healed in this life. Part of the tendency to misunderstanding comes from translation choices. The best translation of these sentences probably would be: "Any illness I brought on the Egyptians, I will not bring on you. For I am Yahweh, your doctor."[130] The promise here was not that Yahweh would

[127] Examples in Eng. include "kith and kin" for relative, "will and testament" for will, "up and around" for well.

[128] Other examples include Gen 1:28; 9:4–6; 17:9. Such laws tend to be so broadly applicable that they are not confined to the Mosaic covenant only.

[129] This is precisely the meaning of "your will be done on earth as it is in heaven" and of being in the image of God (essentially a job assignment to represent him faithfully on earth, not a description of human ontology).

[130] On the meaning "doctor" for the *qal* participle of רפא, cf. Gen 50:2; Jer 8:22; Job 13:4; 2 Chr 16:12. The NIV's "who heals you" sounds like some sort of declaration of universal fact; "your healer," or alternatively "your doctor," would be a lot less subject to misunderstanding. Cf. N. Lohfink, "'Ich bin Jahwe, dein Artz' (Ex 15, 26), Gott, Gesellschaft und menschliche Gesundheit in der Theologie einer nachexilischen Pentateuchbearbeitung (Ex 15, 25b. 26)," in *Ich will euer Gott werden,* SBS 100 (Stuttgart: Katholisches Bibelwerk, 1981), 11–73.

never allow those who place their faith in him to get sick. It was that the Israelites would be free from having to worry about the plagues. God averred that he would not become angry at them in such a way as to subject them to the miseries he had subjected the Egyptians to—if they were indeed loyal and obedient. His promise to serve as their doctor/healer also was not a promise that if anyone among them ever got sick he would immediately heal that person. It was instead an assertion that it was to him they must turn for healing if they found themselves afflicted as a result of sin. The story of the healing from snakebites in Num 21:1–9 is exactly the sort of situation envisioned in these words.

15:27 Marah was a place to drink but not to encamp. The Israelites actually camped further on, at Elim, which is described as having abundant water ("twelve springs") and being wooded ("seventy palm trees"). The location of Elim is, like so many other places mentioned in Moses' ancient narrative, uncertain; but assuming the people continued traveling southward toward Mount Sinai, a reasonable conjecture would be to associate the spot with the Wadi Gharandel, a riverbed in Shur that has plenty of water and trees in certain places.[131] Any groundwater source other than a dug well may be called a "spring" *('ayin),* so the twelve springs mentioned here may have been twelve separate "water holes" available for drinking and drawing water and watering herds at that time of year—even if all twelve holes were fed by one main source when the Israelites found the place over three thousand years ago. The number of trees may have been exactly seventy then, but the same number could hardly be expected all these years later. Accordingly, the identification of the spot cannot be made on the basis of a precise count of "springs" and trees in modern times.

7. More Grumbling: About Food (16:1–9)

[1]The whole Israelite community set out from Elim and came to the Desert of Sin, which is between Elim and Sinai, on the fifteenth day of the second month after they had come out of Egypt. [2]In the desert the whole community grumbled against Moses and Aaron. [3]The Israelites said to them, "If only we had died by the LORD's hand in Egypt! There we sat around pots of meat and ate all the food we wanted, but you have brought us out into this desert to starve this entire assembly to death." [4]Then the LORD said to Moses, "I will rain down bread from heaven for you. The people are to go out each day and gather enough for that day. In this way I will test them and see whether they will follow my instructions. [5]On the sixth day they are to prepare what they bring in, and that is to be twice as much as they gather on the other days." [6]So Moses and Aaron said to all the Isra-

[131] J. Simons, *The Geographical and Topographical Texts of the Old Testament* (Leiden: Brill, 1959), 252.

elites, "In the evening you will know that it was the LORD who brought you out of Egypt, 7and in the morning you will see the glory of the LORD, because he has heard your grumbling against him. Who are we, that you should grumble against us?" 8Moses also said, "You will know that it was the LORD when he gives you meat to eat in the evening and all the bread you want in the morning, because he has heard your grumbling against him. Who are we? You are not grumbling against us, but against the LORD." 9Then Moses told Aaron, "Say to the entire Israelite community, 'Come before the LORD, for he has heard your grumbling.'"

At Marah the grumbling had been about water. Now, a little farther along and after getting plenty of water at Elim, the grumbling was about food. And, again, from a human point of view the attitude of the Israelites is understandable. As they moved south toward Mount Sinai, they left one wilderness (Shur) for another (Sin), and an entire month had gone by. Buying or finding food in either wilderness would have been extremely difficult,[132] and the stores they had brought with them were surely depleted. It was, of course, another unannounced, unexplained test of their willingness to trust God. But they did not know that. How can human beings accurately figure out what is a test from God and what is just a circumstance they never should have gotten themselves into? In the case of the Israelites, they should have been able to say, "If God is visibly leading us in the form of the pillar of cloud, then we're supposed to be here, and our experience so far tells us that he'll provide for us this time too." But the newness of being without food, in a new location, the pain of hunger in their stomachs, the bleating of their animals, and the natural human tendency to be pessimistic when in pain all combined to cause them to grumble. A further factor may have been their success with grumbling at Marah. There a little grumbling had produced good water to drink. So now that food was needed, perhaps a little grumbling would again be in order. It was, however, a serious breach of faith to grumble against the living God, and that point Moses made eloquently in v. 8 by saying simply, "You are not grumbling against us, but against the LORD."

16:1 According to Num 33:10–11, part of the passage where Moses provided his most systematic review of the exodus and wilderness itinerary, the Israelites camped along the shore of the Red Sea between the time they left Elim and the time they entered the wilderness [NIV "desert"] of Sin. On their journey southward they were thus staying close to the east coast of the Red Sea and probably following rather consistently the old road that ran

---

[132] The same problems applied theoretically even at Mount Sinai, but at least there they were encamped for more than a year and had ample opportunity gradually to develop good sources of trade and supply, e.g., for some of the materials needed in the building of the tabernacle and its furnishings. Even there, however, both water and food had to be supplied miraculously.

southward along the eastern side of the Red Sea that the Egyptians had used for mining commerce.[133] Egyptian mining was seasonal, limited mainly to January–March. The Israelites were now using the road in mid to late April, so there was little risk of having their position betrayed by traveling Egyptian miners. At any rate, there was reason to assume the Egyptians would not have wanted to risk another debacle by launching a second pursuit of the Israelites—with virtually all conditions the same except that the Israelites were now merely on the opposite bank of the Red Sea—even if they did learn their location from travelers heading toward Egypt from the Sinai on the same road.[134] Since the Israelites left Egypt on the fifteenth day of the first month of the year (the day after the full-moon night when the tenth plague/Passover occurred) and arrived at this encampment "on the fifteenth day of the second month," Moses by this notation brings the reader to the awareness that exactly one month had passed since the exodus began. Moses' calendrical record keeping here is parallel to that already seen in 12:51.

16:2–3 Again grumbling took place, and Moses noted that "the whole community" took part, suggesting that the problem of not enough food to eat had been building steadily rather than having come about suddenly and that

[133] See I. Beit-Arieh, "Serabit el-Khadim: New Metallurgical and Chronological Aspects," *Levant* 17 (1985): 89–116. Currid (*Exodus,* 333) sums up the implication of the fact that this road had been used by the Egyptians during both the Middle Kingdom and the New Kingdom (i.e., from the twentieth to the twelfth century BC, thus covering the time of Israelite sojourn in Egypt as well as of the exodus) as follows: "We know that Semites participated in these [mining] expeditions. The Hebrews who had been in Egypt for four centuries would most certainly have known of this route." Additionally, Kitchen has commented on how the term *yam suph* (Red Sea or Sea of Reeds) was viewed territorially by the Israelites: "The term *yam suph* is also applied to the Gulf of Suez and to the Gulf of Aqabah, which flank the Sinai Peninsula. For the Gulf of Suez, cf. Num 33:10–11, south of Etham, Marah and Elim. For the Gulf of Aqaba, cf. Num 21:4; also Num 14:25, Deut 1:40, 2:1 and perhaps Jer 49:21. All other allusions are to the original *yam suph* of the Exodus at Pi-Hahiroth. In the case of the two gulfs, we have nothing more than extension of usage. Going from north to south, one passed a series of stretches of often salty water, and on arrival at the area of the later Suez, here was another long piece of water, stretching into the hazy distance. . . . So it was simply taken as being yet another installment of the collective *yam suph.* Across the Sinai, an analogous judgment was made; here was another long body of water stretching out south into the haze or horizon like Menzaleh or that of Suez. Nothing more sophisticated than that need be assumed. Compare the extension of the Greek term "Red Sea" to cover at one time the Perso-Arabian Gulf, Arabian Sea, and our present Red Sea. . . . Thus after crossing the lakes section of *yam suph* (be it Ballah, Timsah, or Bitter), the Hebrews (if headed south) would go through the Shur/Etham desert past the Etham (Ismailia) zone, on past the latitude of Suez, the three days march (thirty-six to forty-five miles at twelve to fifteen miles per day) to Marah, Elim, then (again) to *yam suph.* This was simply a stop by the east (Sinai) shore of the Suez Gulf" (*On the Reliability of the Old Testament*, 262–63).

[134] Cf. Currid, *Exodus,* 333–34, citing in part the conclusions of W. M. F. Petrie, *Researches in Sinai* (London: Murray, 1906), 169.

everyone was affected to some degree, perhaps most of them seriously. From time to time Moses reminded the reader that both he and Aaron were involved in many of the exodus incidents, and his inclusion of Aaron ("grumbled against Moses and Aaron") here overtly highlights that fact.[135] As the Israelites saw themselves, their families, and their flocks growing thinner and as they saw day after day no likely source of food in the wilderness in which they were traveling, it became obvious to them that they were going to die unless something dramatic happened to reverse their plight. Their month's journey had involved much care and effort, which now began to look to them as if it had all been expended in vain. So although their words were essentially rhetorical rather than literal (they didn't really wish they had died in Egypt and didn't want to die in the wilderness either but wanted something done to give them food to eat) they made a comparison in their complaint between the simplicity of dying where they were and the absurdity of going to all the trouble they had gone to in the past month and then dying anyway. This was the first time the Israelites made the "if only we had died in Egypt argument," but it would not be the last (see Num 11:4,18; 14:2; cf. 20:3; Josh 7:7). Their reference to dying "by the LORD's hand" recalls the plagues and the destruction of the Egyptians at the sea—they had been spared from all of those dangers but were now rhetorically arguing that perhaps they would have been better off eliminated by a plague or by drowning.[136]

They claimed that they had in Egypt "all the food" they wanted, which probably was an exaggeration, but not necessarily baseless. Nothing in the prior account of the Israelite suffering under Egyptian oppression suggested a lack of food. The "pots of meat" they sat around had been real, if not always a daily experience, since the Israelites, as small and large cattle farmers originally and right up through the time of the exodus, were routinely in a position to have meat to eat—perhaps considerably more than the average Egyptian.[137] Remembering now what they had convinced themselves were the good old days, the people viewed the past differently from how they viewed it when it was happening. The use of the word "assembly" *(qāhāl)* in v. 3 represents nothing more than a synonym of "community" *(ʿēdāh)* in v. 1.

16:4–5 God's provision for the Israelites immediately addressed both their short-term and their long-term need for food. Knowing that they would be spending a long time in the wilderness, he had prepared for them not just a means of getting enough of the food they were used to but something far

---

[135] Cf. 5:1,4,20; 6:26; 7:6–10,22; 8:8; 9:27; 10:3,11; 11:10; 12:1,28,31,43,50.

[136] On the *hand* of Yahweh see esp. 15:6.

[137] Gen 47:3–4; 50:8; Exod 9:4–7; 10:9,24; 12:5,12,21,32,38.

better: "bread from heaven." Moreover, God was teaching them a concept: that he was their ultimate provider, the one who from heaven gave them not necessarily what they expected but what they really needed. Thus his satisfying them with the bread of heaven becomes a theme of Scripture that not only refers to the manna described in this account (cf. Ps 105:40; Neh 9:15) but to the ultimate provision of eternal sustenance, Christ himself (John 6:31–58).

This great gift also involved a test. The NIV translation of the end of v. 4 obscures the point of God's statement. It should be translated "so that I can test them to see whether or not they will walk by my law." In other words, the people's willingness to obey the manna-gathering law *(tôrāh)* would show God whether or not they would be inclined to keep his covenant law *(tôrāh)* as revealed at Mount Sinai. It was not just a test to see if they could follow instructions but a test to see if their hearts were inclined to be his covenant people. The test itself required faith for an agricultural people. Farmers know that if one harvests only enough food in a day to meet the needs of that day, eventually one has no food because no crops or animals produce food every day.[138] Now they were being asked to restrain their natural tendency to gather as much as was available to gather in anticipation of the time when no gathering would be possible. God was teaching them to trust him every day afresh, and they were challenged to think about his provision in a way that had never before been part of their planning pattern.

Verse 5 should read, "On the sixth day, when they prepare what they bring in, it will be twice as much as they have been gathering each day." In other words, as they were out collecting their manna on the day before the Sabbath and made their preparations as to how much to bring back with them to their homes, they should plan on twice as much as would be usual on any of the other gathering days. This rule looks both forward and backward in *testing* Israel's faith in God's provision. It looks backward to the creation account, which specifies that God himself rested on the seventh day; it looks forward to the revelation of the fourth commandment, establishing Sabbath observance as part of the covenant, a commandment which itself looks back to the creation order.[139] The resulting arrangement provided a weekly opportunity for the emerging Israelite community to be tested by God and to learn about his faithful provision. Every sixth day they would have to discipline themselves to gather twice the usual amount of

---

[138] Not even cows and goats can be milked indefinitely; no common vegetable or fruit grows endlessly without a seed cycle; no fowl lay eggs every day.

[139] Exod 20:11: "For in six days the LORD made the heavens and the earth, the sea, and all that is in them, but he rested on the seventh day. Therefore the LORD blessed the Sabbath day and made it holy." Cf. W. A. M. Beuken, "Exodus 16.5,23: A Rule Regarding the Keeping of the Sabbath?" *JSOT* 32 (1985): 3–14; N. Negretti, *Il settimo giorno* (Rome: Biblical Institute Press, 1973).

manna but only that much. Every Sabbath they had to trust that when they woke up, there would be enough manna left to eat and that it would not have spoiled overnight as it might on other days.[140] Thus each week they would see how God provided for them, in a manner counterintuitive to their normal sense of how to gather and store food, and God could see how they were doing in learning to obey him in advance of his giving them his full covenant law over many months following the encampment at Sinai.[141]

16:6–8 Moses and Aaron were prophesying here, not merely making a prediction based on human reasoning. As in earlier instances and as would be common among the writing prophets, they referred to the concept of being reminded by the fulfillment of the divine word that the people should "know that it was the LORD who brought you out of Egypt."[142] This is the sort of thing that people living in a thoroughly polytheistic, syncretistic society needed to hear often, and it is no surprise that the exodus Israelites heard it often. There is only one Yahweh, he is the only real God, and it is he—not any other god or force or factor—who brought the Israelites out of Egypt. This, his miraculous provision of food for them *after* they left Egypt, should have reminded them of who he is and how he continued to provide for them. He is the same, the only God who brought them out of Egypt and now continued to be their (if they got the point, one and only) God.

In vv. 6–7 an evening-morning pattern is predicted, recalling again the Gen 1 creation account with its evening-morning format of the days of creation. As prophets, Moses and Aaron were representing God, speaking for him and not serving in their own authority, so they twice emphasized that the grumbling of the people represented the people's concern with God, not them ("Who are we, that you should grumble against us? v. 7; "Who are we? You are not grumbling against us, but against the LORD," v. 8).[143] In v. 8 the evening-morning pattern appears again, this time with more specificity as to what would happen at the respective times: at evening meat would come; at morning it would be bread.[144] The NIV translation of v. 8 can make the verse

---

[140] See comments on vv. 16–30.

[141] Num 10:11–12.

[142] Cf. the concept of knowing that I am/he is the Lord in prediction, in such places as Exod 6:7; 7:5,17; 10:2; 11:7; 14:4,18; and likewise in the prophets in such places as Isa 45:3; 49:23; Ezek 6:7 et passim (it is one of Ezekiel's most common formulae); Zech 2:9,11; 4:9.

[143] It is quite possible that the translation should actually be "What do we matter?" [i.e., with special emphasis on the pronoun]. In 16:7 and 16:8 occur the only two instances in the OT of an independent pronoun + *māh* in an apparent interrogative formation, which one presumes to be an idiom translatable as shown. But the fact that this apparent "idiom" occurs only in this context tempers our certainty about its meaning.

[144] It is also possible to translate לֶחֶם as "food," but here it seems especially appropriate to translate it as "bread" because of both the taste and feel (see v. 31) of the manna and because it is described as coming in contrast to "meat" (בָּשָׂר).

seem as if Moses were saying that although some meat would be supplied, only the bread would be truly abundant ("meat to eat in the evening and all the bread you want in the morning"). This is simply a mistranslation. Moses' statement should read, "When the LORD gives you meat to eat in the evening and bread in the morning, to satisfy you" (i.e., both the meat and the bread would satisfy the Israelite appetites).[145]

16:9 Moses continued speaking as a prophet and this time overtly spoke *through* Aaron to the people in the manner of the encouraging instruction of 4:15–16, which was intended especially for those occasions when Moses might be otherwise intimidated or reluctant to face the people's opposition. Since this encounter with the people represents the most serious opposition to Moses' and Aaron's leadership since the verbal attack by the Israelite foremen in 5:19–21, so it should be no surprise that Moses reverted to this "protective" communication style. Moses required "the entire Israelite community to come before the LORD," which suggests that all or virtually all the people had joined in the complaining about lack of food. To "come before the LORD" means to gather to whatever place or object represents Yahweh's presence among them. At this point in their history, it was the pillar of cloud. They must go right up to it and thus show they were ready for a meeting with Yahweh directly, not just through his intermediaries, Moses and Aaron. "He has heard your grumbling" does not refer to God's ability to perceive what the people were thinking and saying; in his omniscience he would always know that. It is, rather, an idiom for "paying attention to and planning to respond to" something.[146]

8. God Sends Quail and Manna from Heaven (16:10–36)

God was testing his people throughout the exodus events: leading them in odd directions without fully explaining why (14:1–4), surprising them with potentially destructive enemy attacks even after they had left Egypt (14:10ff.; cf. 17:8ff.), requiring them to walk into and through deep ocean water (14:15ff.), and taking them to locations that lacked the necessities of life (as in 15:23ff. and 16:2ff.). All of these challenges were part of a plan to develop a people's willingness to trust him. Explaining everything in advance would have run counter to that plan. It was necessary for Israel to learn faith while confused, while afraid, while desperate—not just in theory

---

[145] The NIV translation may have been influenced by v. 11, which does specifically link satiation with the bread and not the meat—but the reason for the distinction relates to the expected regularity of the manna as Israel's daily food in the wilderness and not to any notion that the quail failed to satiate the people's hunger.

[146] See comments on Exod 2:24; 3:7; 6:5; cf. Gen 16:11; 17:20; 21:26.

but under pressure of actual conditions where survival was uncertain and faith was tested to the limit.

The manna story represents yet another testing story: it is introduced as such (16:4) and features details that describe the way at least some Israelites failed the test at first (16:20,27–30). Because the schedule for gathering the manna seemed counterintuitive to ancient agrarians, it provided a way of testing Israel to see if they would obey not only those commandments that made perfect sense to them but also those that did not. The same sort of challenge exists today. If people think God demands a behavior that runs against their intuitive sense of what is right, or pleasurable, or reasonable, or just "not so bad" (sex outside of marriage, e.g.), it is easy for them not to take a commandment seriously, which (although few realize it) is the same as not taking God seriously. This correspondence of not respecting commandments and not respecting God explains the severity of God's reaction when his people do not do what he tells them to do (16:28).

The manna story here in chap. 16 is a rather long narrative account, but its length is appropriate when one considers that during the wilderness wanderings the Israelites saw the supernatural every day (the pillar of cloud) and also experienced the miraculous every day (manna as miraculous provision), with a double miracle every weekend (see comments on 16:22–26). Forty years of daily miracles earned the manna account a rightfully large place in the story of the wilderness, and it therefore should not be surprising that God required that a sample of the manna be placed in the ark, as one of its three sacred contents (16:33–34).

It is a shame that such a wonderful divine provision should have come about as a result of faithless grumbling on the part of the people. How much better it would have been had the Israelites prayed patiently and trustingly for God's answer to their lack of food a month into their exodus journey. Grumbling is hardly to be commended and is not in itself worthy of reward. God, however, still *heard* it and graciously responded—not in kind, that is, with a poor quality provision suitable for grumblers, but with a miraculous, tasty, nutritious, and sufficient food, exactly what he would have sent if they had prayed faithfully in the first place. His goodness to his people is not dependent on their willingness to respect him as they ought. This is not to say that respect for God's will is irrelevant to his rewards, only that his temporal, as opposed to eternal, rewards often do not correlate with our temporal behavior.[147]

[147] Cf. Matt 5:45; Jer 12:1; Job 21:7.

(1) God Grants Manna in Response to the Grumbling about Food (16:10–15a)

[10]While Aaron was speaking to the whole Israelite community, they looked toward the desert, and there was the glory of the LORD appearing in the cloud.

[11]The LORD said to Moses, [12]"I have heard the grumbling of the Israelites. Tell them, 'At twilight you will eat meat, and in the morning you will be filled with bread. Then you will know that I am the LORD your God.'"

[13]That evening quail came and covered the camp, and in the morning there was a layer of dew around the camp. [14]When the dew was gone, thin flakes like frost on the ground appeared on the desert floor. [15]When the Israelites saw it, they said to each other, "What is it?" For they did not know what it was.

16:10–12 God wasted no time in manifesting himself even more dramatically than through the pillar of cloud as a large visible object. He specially manifested his "glory" by immediately "appearing in the cloud" while Aaron was still giving them the instruction about drawing near to God. God's "glory" is his impressiveness/awesomeness, the sense of his divine greatness that may be difficult to describe in words but that is often felt in terms of fear, awe, amazement, and the sense that one is not in the presence of anything that is merely worldly but someone who is truly the essence of superiority and eternal authority, worthy of worship and adoration, and dangerous to oppose. While God cannot be seen, he often lets his glory be sensed.[148] In this case the cloud may have displayed a sort of blinding fiery brilliance (as in 24:16–17) and/or a smoky opaqueness (as in 40:35) that from the point of view of visibility at least overwhelmed those who encountered it. The Israelites apparently had no trouble sensing that God was right among them in real power and substantial presence. We possibly should understand the verse to imply that God's glory caused them to turn and look at the cloud even though they had been facing Aaron because it was so impressive that they sensed it even with their backs turned.[149] The Lord then spoke, almost surely from the cloud, although this was not stated explicitly, and graciously acknowledged that he had "heard" (was going to respond to) the grumbling of the Israelites and would give them in one twelve-hour period both meat and bread. As we have already suggested at 16:8, there was no skimping on either meat or bread. Rather, in v. 12, which locates the term *ṣābaʿ* (have one's fill of) with the bread but not the meat, it is the rhetorical balance of the sentence that indicates fullness in each case ("you will eat" is

---

[148] E.g., Exod 24:16–17; 40:34; 9:23; Num 14:10,21; 2 Chr 7:1–3; Luke 2:9.

[149] But one cannot prove this conjecture. It is also possible that someone in the crowd happened to turn around, saw how different the cloud looked with God's glory manifested from it, said the equivalent of, "Hey, look at the cloud!" and the word passed along to do so. The text simply does not say that it was a corporate sensing of the glory of God that made them turn or that they turned en masse instantly.

paralleled by "you will be filled with," the idea being that they didn't get filled without eating, and they didn't eat without getting filled). This provision would help them understand who they were dealing with (cf. v. 6).

16:13 The only mention of quail in the chapter comes in this verse. It is brief and obviously of secondary importance to the manna because the quail represented a one-evening supply of meat, whereas the manna was to be a daily occurrence for forty years and the more important food supply for that entire generation of Israelites. In ancient times meat was cooked and eaten immediately upon slaughtering because there was virtually no means of preserving it after the animal from which it came was killed. The quail would have provided a well-appreciated single evening meal for the people, relieving them of their hunger; but the manna was to be something that was always available for them and a food that, by contrast to any meat, could actually keep for two days when necessary (16:5,24) even though it normally melted away very fast if not collected (16:21). It also may be noted that God's plan was that the manna should constitute a morning food supply, which would have meant that the people would have to wait until the next day for food since it was still daytime when God gave them their answer.[150] Thus the quail represented a special one-time evening meal to give them immediate relief from hunger and tide them over until the permanent, daily food supply would begin.

Could God have supplied the manna before they even grumbled, before their food brought from Egypt had run out? Of course. But how would that have taught them the special sort of patience that he knew they would need to exercise in the future as his people when things got really hard?[151] That the quail arrived in abundance can be inferred from the statement that [the quail] "covered the camp." Most people may well have been able to catch as many as they desired. After they had eaten and gone to sleep, the regular nightly desert dew condensed on the ground, which remained the next morning. According to Num 11:9, the manna came down[152] as well during the night, so the description here and in the next verse need not be understood to mean that the manna followed the dew—only that it was visible when the dew lifted.

---

[150] If it had been nighttime, the gathering of the people would have been almost impossible unless the pillar would have been that of fire rather than cloud, and it is clearly designated as "cloud" in v. 10.

[151] Most people have some patience. Patience as a gift from God, however, is part of what distinguishes spiritual persons from mere human beings (Gal 5:22).

[152] Dew really does *come down* in that airborne moisture collects on the surface of the ground as air currents sweep past the cool surface of the ground and the water vapor that may have been very high in the air at a previous point is brought lower and condenses. "Dew" (טַל) also can refer to full-blown rain in some contexts (e.g., Hag 1:10; Prov 3:20).

16:14–15a Once the dew evaporated, the Israelites saw something they hadn't seen before and weren't expecting to find. The description can be best translated as follows: "There on the surface of the wilderness was a thin, crisp substance, thin like frost on the ground." In other words, it may not have appeared in "flake" form at all but perhaps in sheets. It may have been "flaky" in the way a pie crust is called "flaky" but not necessarily occurring in the form of separate, individual flakes. In old Hebrew/Canaanite at least one biform of the word for interrogative "what" was *mān* rather than the later and more common *māh,* so the Israelites' question "what is it?" *(mān hûʾ)* became eventually abbreviated into "what?" *(mān),* and the name stuck.[153] The usual "natural" explanation for manna is that it was the exudant of various kinds of plant lice that feed on the sap of the tamarisk trees that are abundant in the Sinai wilderness. This explanation assumes that the Israelites remembered the little bits[154] of sweet-tasting lice exudant found near tamarisk trees and as centuries went by built the memory through folklore into a whole food supply narrative. The text says nothing of the sort but describes a massive, collectable, permanent daily food source for thousands of people.

(2) Manna Gathering and the First Disobedience in Connection with It (16:15b–20)

Moses said to them, "It is the bread the LORD has given you to eat. [16]This is what the LORD has commanded: 'Each one is to gather as much as he needs. Take an omer for each person you have in your tent.'"

[17]The Israelites did as they were told; some gathered much, some little. [18]And when they measured it by the omer, he who gathered much did not have too much, and he who gathered little did not have too little. Each one gathered as much as he needed.

[19]Then Moses said to them, "No one is to keep any of it until morning."

[20]However, some of them paid no attention to Moses; they kept part of it until morning, but it was full of maggots and began to smell. So Moses was angry with them.

16:15b–16 The manna was God's bread, a divine gift for the sustenance of the people in the wilderness, not something that could be harvested at will in any quantity that happened to be desired. The amount of Passover goat or lamb meat was regulated so that no one could "pig out" on the meal and all

[153] The word for manna in Hb. is just the one-syllable *mān* (e.g., Neh 9:20) from which the later two-syllable form *manna* came into English via Latin. In Aramaic the interrogative *man* came to mean "who" rather than "what."

[154] And they are indeed little bits—available for the taking still today but hardly a sustaining food for a nation or for an individual, for that matter, and thus not the manna of which Exodus speaks.

would have a fair share appropriate to their needs (see on 12:3–4,10), and the Passover unleavened bread had to be prepared carefully in faithfulness to its symbolic value or dire consequences would result (12:14–20). The manna also could not be overgathered or overeaten without consequence. An omer[155] was the prescribed amount, set by God himself, for an average individual per day. The omer was equal to about two quarts,[156] just enough of relatively light, flaky food for a person per day, especially since sharing would occur in a household, allowing small children permission to eat less and larger adults to eat more as long as the average was an omer per person. The Israelites lived in tents during their constantly relocating time in the wilderness. Thus one's family were those "you have in your tent." But the references to tent continue long after, indicating that the first generation was seen as the paradigm generation of Israel, so the "natural" home for an Israelite was or was referred to as a tent even long after the Israelites were settled in permanent homes in the promised land (cf. Judg 4:17–20; 2 Sam 20:1; 2 Chr 10:16; Jer 30:18; Hos 9:6; Mal 2:12).[157]

16:17–18 These verses may seem to be telling a miracle story—that is, no matter what anyone tried to do (gathering a lot or a little), it all miraculously came out exactly to the amount required by his appetite that day, or the like. A more precise translation eliminates the possible misimpression: "The Israelites did so. Some gathered more, some less. Since they measured it by the omer, the person who had gathered more had nothing left over, and the person who gathered less had no shortage; each had gathered according to what he could eat." In other words, the opening statement that "the Israelites did so" meant that they obeyed the rule about not gathering too much but just enough, and the rest of the two verses confirms this by more detail, explaining how everyone was careful to use measuring containers so as not to break God's law.

16:19–20 A day's new manna had to be eaten that day, partly to prevent disease (since "when they kept part of it until morning . . . it was full of maggots"[158] and began to smell"), partly so that people could learn to trust

[155] On the use of "omer" here and "homer" elsewhere in the OT, see comments on v. 36 below.

[156] Archaeological evidence for the ephah (ten times the size of the omer) as holding twenty-two liters (about twenty quarts) comes from the so-called *lmlk* jars at Lachish, providing an actual objective measure for the ephah (also "bath") from which other measures, such as that of the omer/homer, may be extrapolated. See E. M. Cook, "Weights and Measures," *ISBE* 4.1046–55.

[157] "Tent" is merely a term for "home" in such passages. Promised-land Israel had settled into houses, not tents, made clear by the wording of Hos 12:9: "I am the LORD your God, [who brought you] out of Egypt; / I will make you live in tents again, as in the days of your appointed feasts." Tenting was necessary during the three great feasts (Passover, Pentecost, Tabernacles) because the city housing the central sanctuary (eventually Jerusalem) could not hold the whole population required to gather in one location for those feasts (Deut 12:4–28; cf. Exod 23:14–17).

[158] I. M. Ceccherelli actually suggests that the meaning of the word *manna* is to be derived from Akk. *munu,* "worm" ("La 'Manna,'" *BO* 39 [1997]: 56). This seems to us unlikely compared to the contextual explanation given in 16:15.

God's daily provision ("give us this day our daily bread" in the Lord's Prayer means "give us *today* the right amount of bread *for today*"), and partly to train the Israelites to observe other food consumption laws that forbade leftovers (e.g., Exod 12:10; 29:34; Deut 16:4). Thus overnight keeping of the manna was forbidden. In any large group there are always those inclined to test any rule, so it is not surprising that some of the people tried keeping uneaten manna until the next day. When they did so, they found it inedible, foiling their scheme to eat without doing the required daily gathering work. When the report of such disobedience reached Moses, he was understandably angry ("so Moses was angry with them"). He had a right and an inclination as God's representative among the people to be angry at their disobedience, but he also presumably had a fear of the consequences of a portion of the people disobeying an important test commandment. Presumably his being angry with them resulted in a tongue-lashing and whatever public humiliation went along with it, but not any further punishment since none is mentioned. With the incentive to keep manna overnight obviated by the putrid results, the people who had tried it may well have apologized and expressed contrition, enough so to convince Moses that they were repentant.

(3) Manna Gathering and the Sabbath (16:21–26)

21Each morning everyone gathered as much as he needed, and when the sun grew hot, it melted away. 22On the sixth day, they gathered twice as much—two omers for each person—and the leaders of the community came and reported this to Moses. 23He said to them, "This is what the LORD commanded: 'Tomorrow is to be a day of rest, a holy Sabbath to the LORD. So bake what you want to bake and boil what you want to boil. Save whatever is left and keep it until morning.'"

24So they saved it until morning, as Moses commanded, and it did not stink or get maggots in it. 25"Eat it today," Moses said, "because today is a Sabbath to the LORD. You will not find any of it on the ground today. 26Six days you are to gather it, but on the seventh day, the Sabbath, there will not be any."

16:21 God had worked out a simple, effective system for his people: new manna was available for gathering every morning, and old manna was gotten rid of by the heat of the sun. Lazy people were thus disciplined into getting up early enough to get their food for the day, and competitive types were unable to gain any advantage over others by gathering and keeping disproportionate amounts. In the shade of tents and kept under cloth cover in storage or during preparation outside the tents, the manna kept until evening.

16:22–23 Following instructions already given by God (16:5), the Israelites gathered double portions on the sixth day of the week, the day just prior to the Sabbath. The gathering must not have taken so long that this would be a problem once a week. It could have taken twice as long to gather two omers per person as to gather one, but more likely (though it cannot be proved) God supplied a greater abundance per unit of ground on the sixth day than on the others, making the gathering process of such a relatively light substance probably only marginally more time consuming. This new experience of getting twice the manna for approximately the same effort was sufficiently amazing and/or delightful as a proof of God's promise that "the leaders of the community came and reported this to Moses." The consistency of this experience—everybody everywhere had the same double results—may have been what they especially wanted him to hear and what he was hoping would be the case, for this was the first test of that part of the command involving the once-a-week sixth day special procedure. Their faith in obeying the testing of each day had now been supplemented by the reward of their faith for obeying the special provisions for the sixth-day's gathering.

Conveying to them God's word in his role as prophet, Moses began to teach the people about the Sabbath law, thus anticipating the fourth commandment (Exod 20:8–11). "Sabbath" means "stoppage," and under the old covenant it required discontinuation of all voluntary work. Gathering food was the most basic sort of work anyone did in the ancient world, so the gathering of manna could hardly be allowed to continue as usual on the Sabbath. Moses therefore instructed the people to cook the daily portion of manna as usual, but not to worry about keeping the remainder overnight since "tomorrow is to be a day of rest, a holy Sabbath to the LORD." The Sabbath, in other words, is not just a day of resting from work but a day of refocused service toward the holy, that is, toward God.[159] Note that the method of preparing manna for eating was either to bake it or to boil it.[160]

16:24–26 The daily provision of the manna was a miracle in itself. The provision of double manna every sixth day of the week was another. Now come two further, related miracles: the rotting process did not take place one day a week, and no manna appeared at all one day a week—both miracles taking place in the same sequence of days every week. Anyone who obeyed the earlier commands of God to harvest properly on the sixth day and save a day's worth for the Sabbath was rewarded by being able to comply with Moses' instruction the following, Sabbath day, "Eat it today" (v. 25). The time and energy normally spent gathering manna could now be spent on God's worship and, to some extent, not spent at all. The Creator of human beings, who had himself from the beginning of creation honored the Sabbath day and made it holy partly by resting on it, knew the nature of his creatures,

---

[159] See further comments on 20:8–11. At this point it may be noted simply that the concept may have been quite new to the Israelites, who presumably had been granted no Sabbaths in Egypt.

[160] By baking is meant the cooking in a covered pot or skillet over an outdoor fire, not oven baking, which was impossible in those days of constant travel. Boiling, i.e., cooking in an open or closed pot with water, was an alternative. Thus manna was cooked like bread or meal (e.g., oatmeal, cornmeal,) rather than eaten raw or otherwise prepared.

including the disadvantages of a lifestyle that allowed no real rest. He insisted that the people who were to be united with him in his covenant would rest weekly. This does not mean that they would do nothing but only that they would do as little as possible that would be *physically* hard, that is, the same sort of work they *had* to do on the other six days. By taking away the manna on the seventh day, God helped ensure that people would use that day for something other than the usual harvesting.[161]

(4) The Second Disobedience and the Sabbath Lesson Learned (16:27–30)

[27]Nevertheless, some of the people went out on the seventh day to gather it, but they found none. [28]Then the LORD said to Moses, "How long will you refuse to keep my commands and my instructions?

[29]Bear in mind that the LORD has given you the Sabbath; that is why on the sixth day he gives you bread for two days. Everyone is to stay where he is on the seventh day; no one is to go out." [30]So the people rested on the seventh day.

16:27–28 Again some people couldn't resist trying to get ahead, to advantage themselves, by disobedience to God's command. As some of them had tried to keep manna too long (16:20), some of them (perhaps some of the same people) now tried to get more on the Sabbath, probably fearing that what they had kept from the night before would never last through the whole day even if they saw that it had in fact lasted until the early morning. They found no manna and in the process showed themselves unwilling once again to trust God in the matter of a single commandment, not a promising sign in light of the fact that soon enough they would be expected to keep his entire covenant law as an indication of their trust in him. God's speech to Moses in vv. 28–29 ("then the LORD said to Moses") is, of course, a speech through him to all the people.[162] In asking, "How long will you refuse to keep my commands and my instructions?" God was not expecting an answer. This was a rhetorical way of saying, "I am counting on you to stop disobeying me."[163] As a divine rebuke for not showing a willingness to

[161] The question may also be raised as to whether or not the Israelite animals ate manna, or whether they had enough grazing land at all places in the wilderness (Moses had first gone to Sinai for good grazing land, after all, as 3:1 indicates). The text does not say, but it can hardly be doubted that cattle and flocks will eat bread gladly if it is offered to them (outdated bread is not wasted in farm areas) and sweetened bread (as manna in effect was) can be fed to small and large cattle alike to help fatten them up. Thus it is easy to imagine the Israelites feeding their flocks and herds some manna, or letting them sometimes graze on it, but also a reasonable presumption that the flocks and herds ate mainly grasses and other plants while with the Israelites in the wilderness. In light of the speed with which the Israelites were able to move about during these days, it is probable that their flocks and herds were limited mainly to milking and breeding animals, and were not nearly as extensive as they might have been in earlier days in Egypt or would be later once the people settled in Canaan.

[162] The pronominal forms are plural, not singular, making this entirely obvious in the Hebrew.

[163] On the rhetorical use of "how long" (here, עַד־אָנָה), cf. Num 14:11; Josh 18:3; Jer 47:6; Hab 1:2; Ps 13:1.

obey, it represents a serious threat to the purpose of the testing, that is, to find faith among the about-to-be covenant people.

16:29–30 Here Moses drew the lesson of the Sabbath for the Israelites, emphasizing that it represented a gift ("the LORD has given you the Sabbath"), as Jesus also taught.[164] Moses compared the gift of the Sabbath to the gift of the manna, two days' worth on the sixth day, for the sake of making the Sabbath rest possible. Moses' words, "Everyone is to stay where he is on the seventh day; no one is to go out," intended to restrict manna harvesting on the Sabbath, not to confine people inside their homes. They still needed to milk goats and cows, to feed all their animals, to relieve themselves outside the camp,[165] and so on. In other words, nothing in these verses justifies the later pharisaical insistence on the "Sabbath day's walk," a very limited number of steps allowed on the Sabbath.[166] Nor did Moses' instruction preclude grabbing a bite to eat on the run, something that is certainly not the same as full-blown harvesting of a crop, whether or not divinely provided.[167]

With no further incentive to try to gather manna on the Sabbath, "the people rested on the seventh day." As yet the entire set of formal methods of worship and religious instruction were not an issue. They were to come at Sinai. The first, most basic step had been teaching the Israelites to set aside the time for such things; how to do them would follow in the full presentation of the covenant beginning at Exod 20.

(5) Preserving the Manna for Generations to Come as a Testimony to God's Faithfulness (16:31–36)

[31]The people of Israel called the bread manna. It was white like coriander seed and tasted like wafers made with honey. [32]Moses said, "This is what the LORD has commanded: 'Take an omer of manna and keep it for the generations to come, so they can see the bread I gave you to eat in the desert when I brought you out of Egypt.'"

[33]So Moses said to Aaron, "Take a jar and put an omer of manna in it. Then place it before the LORD to be kept for the generations to come."

[34]As the LORD commanded Moses, Aaron put the manna in front of the Testimony, that it might be kept. [35]The Israelites ate manna forty years, until they came to a land that was settled; they ate manna until they reached the border of Canaan.

[36](An omer is one tenth of an ephah.)

---

[164] "Then he said to them, 'The Sabbath was made for man, not man for the Sabbath'" (Mark 2:27).

[165] See Deut 23:12–13.

[166] Cf. Acts 1:12, "Then they returned to Jerusalem from the hill called the Mount of Olives, a Sabbath day's walk from the city."

[167] Luke 6:1ff. and parallels.

16:31 In ancient times the refining of sugar had not been invented, and the only means of sweetening foods was to add either fruit compounds or honey to them. Honey is far sweeter than dried, crushed, or minced fruit, being approximately half sucrose and half fructose, and its taste in foods was the apex of ancient flavoring. Few Israelites ever had the luxury of making wafers (in effect, thin cookies) instead of bread, and honey was rare enough (since it had to be found in the wild rather than cultivated as today) that describing the manna as "like wafers made with honey" was tantamount to saying that it was "the most delicious food imaginable."

Manna was colored white, the comparison here to coriander seed (which is a pale white in color) intending nothing more than to establish a known color as the comparison point. The taste or texture of coriander seed, in other words, had nothing to do with the manna. Although it is possible that the term "manna" *(mān)* was already a known term (i.e., did not derive from the question of the Israelites in v. 14 but was conveniently remembered as a word that sounded like the wording of the question), the substance was not. The Israelites could have borrowed the name "manna" for it or else coined the name on the spot for this new food they encountered. Since "bread" *(leḥem)* is a common word for "food" in Hebrew, an alternate translation for the opening words of the verse would be, "The house/family of Israel [NIV "people of Israel"] called the food manna."

16:32–34 That a sample of manna should be kept with the ark, in the holy of holies of the tabernacle, was a major step of commemoration indeed. The holy of holies contained only one item of furniture: the ark, also called the ark of the testimony (e.g., Exod 25:21–22; 26:33–34) or perhaps even simply the Testimony[168] (e.g., Exod 27:21; 30:6), a box symbolizing the very presence of God himself. For a jar of manna to be kept there gave the manna prominence above many other objects, including the shewbread or lampstand or incense altar, which were excluded from the holy of holies by the tabernacle's inner curtain.[169] At this stage in the progress of the Israelites, the tabernacle had not yet been built or even prescribed, so God's command to them was simply that Aaron was to "place it before the LORD to be kept," a way of saying that it was to remain in God's presence—that is, in whatever place or object would symbolize God's presence. Once the ark was actually built, there being no provision for any separate table within the holy of holies to hold the manna, it was placed inside the ark, as Heb 9:4 confirms.[170]

---

[168] Interpreting the meaning of "testimony" in 27:21 and 30:6 is difficult since it could also be the case that "testimony" refers only to the tablets in these two verses and not to the ark that holds them. See the commentary on these verses.

[169] I.e., they were in the outer room, the holy place, but not in the holy of holies where God's presence was most deeply manifested. See comments on chaps. 25–26.

[170] Heb 9:4, "This ark contained the gold jar of manna, Aaron's staff that had budded, and the stone tablets of the covenant."

When the ark was inside the tabernacle, it was hidden by the curtain from the view even of the priests who ministered in the outer room. Layworshipers never entered the tabernacle at all but remained within its courtyard when engaged in worship. Moreover, the ark's contents were concealed by the atonement cover. How, then, could it be kept "for the generations to come, so they can see the bread I gave you to eat in the desert when I brought you out of Egypt"? The answer is that when the Israelites were invited to move from place to place by the actions of God's pillar of cloud/fire, they could see the ark plainly; and with its usual barriers to visibility removed, the chief priest was at such times presumably free to open the cover and display the contents. It may also have been the case that at festival times, the contents of the ark were removed and displayed for all worshipers to see. Certainly, however, the command was actually carried out, God's intent was for the manna to be visible (not just the jar but the manna inside it) regularly, as an encouragement to faith in God's continual provision for his people. Inasmuch as the ark itself was overlaid with gold inside and out (Exod 25:11), the large jar specified by Moses in v. 33 in the present passage ("take a jar and put an omer of manna in it"), whatever its composition at first, was eventually made of gold (Heb 9:4) since it was to function as a subcontainer within a pure gold container. The eventual contents themselves within the ark (the rod of wood, the tablets of stone, and the vegetable manna) were not gold, but the containers were. Of particular interest is the preservability of the manna sample: manna usually could not be kept overnight (16:20), but God would cause the manna in the jar in the ark to keep permanently—a miracle quietly implied but supernatural none the less.

Verse 34 describes the fulfillment of the command made in v. 33. This command-fulfillment style will come to dominate large portions of the later chapters of Exodus.[171] The "Testimony" mentioned here in v. 34 refers almost certainly to the tablets of stone on which the Ten Commandments would be written rather than the ark of the testimony that would hold them. Accordingly, the statement that "Aaron put the manna in front of the Testimony, that it might be kept" presumably means that he put it, in its jar, within the gold-covered chest that was called the ark. (The Hb. translated by the NIV and most other English versions as "in front of" can also be translated "right next to," "in the direct presence of," or the like.) Verse 34, however, may well describe the process in retrospect, after the ark was constructed and the tablets given to Moses by God for deposit therein. We cannot tell from these verses, in other words, whether Aaron put a sample of the very first manna in a (clay) jar, which eventually was transferred to the gold jar kept in the eventually constructed ark, or whether the fulfillment of

[171] See comments on 25:1ff.

this command was accomplished with some manna gathered months later, after the ark was built.[172]

16:35–36 The system of footnoting and endnoting was not invented until modern times, but these verses are the Bible's equivalent of a footnote or endnote—an explanatory note placed at the end of a portion of text. Moses may be the author of both verses, since he likely did not put the finishing touches on the Pentateuch until shortly before his death, roughly forty years later than the events described in most of chap. 16. Thus the statement that "the Israelites ate manna forty years, until they came to a land that was settled" brings the reader up to the point of the crossing of the Jordan by the Israelites under Joshua, when the end of the manna is explicitly mentioned (Josh 5:12). It is also possible that this footnote is an inspired compiler's later addition to Moses' work for the benefit especially of people who would search the Pentateuch itself in vain for any reference to the cessation of manna; there is none, other than here in v. 35, because at the time of Moses' death the manna was still being provided daily.

Verse 36 explains for a later generation or generations—either the one that grew up in the wilderness (and following) or the generations starting at some point after the Israelites had settled in Canaan—the meaning of the old word "omer." Moses used "omer" only here; in later passages he employed the slightly different term "homer[s]" (Lev 27:16; Num 11:32), which apparently became standard in later Hebrew.[173] Why the difference? The answer would seem to be that prior to the standardization of spelling and writing—a modern phenomenon—there was a tendency in good literature to use the various forms and/or spellings of a word at different places in a document so as to preserve the legitimate variations, each of which had essentially as much validity as the other. This practice did not prevent the virtual standardization of one form or spelling of a word over time (which is more a matter of mass interaction), but it did allow an individual writer to avoid trying on his own to effect any sort of standardization. At any rate, the note provided for the reader here indicates that an omer/homer was "one tenth of an ephah," meaning that it was about 2.2 liters, or about a half-gallon.[174]

9. More Grumbling and Water at Massah-Meribah (17:1–7)

[1]The whole Israelite community set out from the Desert of Sin, traveling from place to place as the LORD commanded. They camped at Rephidim, but there was no water for the people to drink. [2]So they quarreled with Moses and said, "Give us water to drink."

Moses replied, "Why do you quarrel with me? Why do you put the LORD to the test?"

[3]But the people were thirsty for water there, and they grumbled against Moses. They said, "Why did you bring us up out of Egypt to make us and our children and livestock die of thirst?"

---

[172] On the chronology see the comments on 40:2.

[173] Isa 5:10; Ezek 45:11,13; Hos 3:2.

[174] See also n. 141 above.

[4]Then Moses cried out to the LORD, "What am I to do with these people? They are almost ready to stone me."

[5]The LORD answered Moses, "Walk on ahead of the people. Take with you some of the elders of Israel and take in your hand the staff with which you struck the Nile, and go. [6]I will stand there before you by the rock at Horeb. Strike the rock, and water will come out of it for the people to drink." So Moses did this in the sight of the elders of Israel. [7]And he called the place Massah and Meribah because the Israelites quarreled and because they tested the LORD saying, "Is the LORD among us or not?"

17:1–2 In saying that "the whole Israelite community set out from the Desert of Sin," Moses meant, in effect, set out from within the wilderness of Sin. He did not mean that they left Sin, only that they were in it already (16:1) and continued to move further south within it, "traveling from place to place as the LORD commanded." As far as can be determined, Rephidim was located in the far southern Sinai, close to Mount Sinai, the modern Jebel Musa.[175] Accordingly, 17:1 brings the Israelites almost to Sinai, "The One of Sin."[176] The "traveling from place to place" apparently took several weeks, the exact amount of time being unspecified. But in light of the statement in 19:1 that the Israelites left Rephidim and made the short trip from it to Sinai exactly three months after setting out from Egypt and extrapolating from what has been said to this point about their wanderings, it seems that the bulk of those three months may have been taken up with travel in the wilderness of Sin, that is, the Sinai Peninsula south of the imaginary line from the northern end of the Gulf of Suez to the northern end of the Gulf of Aqabah. In each move God led them ("as the LORD commanded") by the pillar of fire/cloud so that they always could be sure of their itinerary.[177]

[175]This closeness is obvious in light of the indication in 17:5–6 that a whole group could walk from Rephidim to Sinai (Horeb) in part of a day. Rephidim's actual location is a matter of speculation, though the Wadi Rephayid in the southwest Sinai peninsula would seem to fit the data. Cf. B. Rogthenberg (with Y. Aharoni and A. Hashimshoni), *God's Wilderness: Discoveries in Sinai* (London: Thames & Hudson, 1961), 143, 168.

[176]The postpositive morpheme *–ay* in Hb./Canaanite commonly connotes "the one who" or "the one of."

[177]During this early stage of their wilderness wanderings, i.e., on the trip to Sinai, the Israelites did not have the formal advantage of Hobab's services as wilderness guide (see Num 10:29–32). But this does not mean that every Israelite was completely unfamiliar with the geography of the area in which they were commanded by God to travel. Hobab, Moses' son-in-law (not father-in-law as often translated in 10:29; see W. F. Albright, "Jethro, Hobab and Reuel in Early Hebrew Tradition," *CBQ* 25 [1963]: 1–11), may already have been offering informal travel guidance, and those Israelites who had presumably been pressed into service in the Sinai metal mines may have helped as well on the basis of their familiarity with the region. Of importance additionally may have been Moses' training as a princeling in the geography of territories of interest to the Egyptians. The human expertise involved did not in any way detract from the need to depend upon God for his leadership in the Israelites' travels (see Num 10:33). Rather, as the divine cloud pillar led them from place to place, they could benefit from human intelligence about a given area so as to know where best to encamp in terms of proximity to water, to grazing for their cattle, to safety from banditry, the weather, and to connection with traders in order to secure necessities not brought from Egypt. Remember also that Moses had driven Jethro's sheep already to Mount Sinai (Horeb), where he encountered the burning bush (3:1) before going back to Egypt, so Moses knew the destination of the Israelites at this time (3:12) and presumably at least some of the roads and features of the terrain as well.

The wording of 17:1 makes clear that the Israelites did not camp at Rephidim of their own volition but of God's, and therefore one is forced to conclude that once again God had led them directly to a place where there was no drinkable water (cf. 15:22–26).[178] Skeptical scholars sometimes have suggested that the present passage is a doublet of 15:22–26, but the details are quite different, the only similarities being the ones that would necessarily be likely to emerge in two stories about not finding water in a place people had expected to find it in light of who led them there.[179] Thus the event represents yet another test of Israel's faithfulness, a test that is again not easily passed and one with the added aspect of Israel's making the mistake of putting God to the test (see comments on v. 7, below).

The beginning of v. 2 probably would be better translated, "The people protested against Moses and said . . ." The NIV translation "quarreled with" tends to imply a heated argument back and forth between Moses and the people, whereas the narrative itself makes no mention of such an interchange. Moses' questions to the people at the end of the verse would, then, also best be translated: "Why do you protest against me? Why are you testing the LORD?"[180] As was his proper strategy in the case of the complaining about lack of food (16:6–8), Moses reminded the people that any complaint

---

[178] Rephidim may have been the site of the modern Wadi Rephayid, which often has water in its copious stream bed. But since the Israelites arrived at Rephidim at the beginning of summer, i.e., approximately mid-June (three lunar months after the spring full moon according to Exod 19:1), it is quite probable that the stream had already dried up; it was not a נַחַל אֵיתָן (*naḥal ʾētān*, year-round stream) but only a נַחַל (*naḥal*, a stream bed that is sometimes full of water, but not in the dry season).

[179] Those who find evidence of multiple authorship or inauthenticity commonly do so partly by reliance on an antipathy for variety and partly by reliance on an antipathy for consistency—inconsistently, as it suits their inclination. Passages that seem to resemble other passages in some particulars can be considered doublets, or inauthentic, by reason of similarity, i.e., lack of variety. Passages that contain material otherwise unexpected can be considered inauthentic by reason of not possessing enough similarity to the prevailing material of the overall context. In fact, ancient writers as well as modern ones sometimes related different events in relatively stereotyped ways (so that a great deal of similarity is obvious when accounts of two different events are compared) and sometimes with novel style and vocabulary (so that a portion of their work appears to be so different from their usual manner of writing as to seem plausibly the work of another person). Thus the more one studies both ancient and modern literature, the more leeway one has to give to authors to be at points similar to themselves and at other points dissimilar to themselves, without jumping to the conclusion that a "too similar" or "too dissimilar" passage's authorship has to be questioned. In the case of Exod 17:2–3 the wording is also paralleled rather closely by Num 20:2–5 (the rebellion at Meribah Kadesh); but this would seem highly likely if Moses wrote both passages. Why should he use entirely different vocabulary and phraseology when the events were to a considerable degree similar? See R. D. Cole, *Numbers*, NAC (Nashville: Broadman & Holman, 2000), 324–25.

[180] The verb ריב ("quarrel") can certainly mean "argue / quarrel / debate" but can as well have the sense "protest / bring a charge against" or the like. It does not need to involve an exchange of discourse between parties in the manner of an argument. Of course, "quarrel" in Eng. can have the sense simply of "disagree with" or "be critical of," but this is not its usual connotation.

against him was in fact a complaint against God since he was only following God's orders, and they were all following the pillar of cloud/fire to their various stopping places in the wilderness. Likewise, as was his proper direction in the previous story of complaining about lack of water as well (15:22–26), he would bring the people's complaint directly to God for resolution (v. 4).

In saying to the people, "Why do you put the LORD to the test," Moses showed that he knew that the protest represented an attempt to manipulate God. The people should have known by then that God would provide their needs. He had done so consistently throughout the plagues and their aftermath and most recently in providing both food and water supernaturally for them. The day of this current protest, after all, was one more day on which the people had been able to gather manna to feed themselves and their animals. What they were doing was refusing to wait for God to take care of them. Instead, soon after finding no drinkable water and having learned that their prior protests got results, they were launching a protest parallel to those of the past, thus testing God. "Testing God" is demanding or expecting him to do something special for you, something you haven't earned and don't per se deserve. Not all "testing," however, is sin. God's appropriate testing of Abraham's faith (Gen 22:1) or his testing of the Israelites' faith in chap. 15 ("there he tested them," 15:25) is described with exactly the same vocabulary (the *piel* of *nsh*) as is employed by Moses here. What is impermissible is any of testing of God (how could *his* faith be in doubt and need testing?) since it amounts not to a genuine attempt to assess loyalty but an attempt to get something out of him earlier or in greater quantity, or the like, than would otherwise happen. Testing God always involves some degree of doubt about whether or not one's present circumstances are all that one deserves and whether or not God could or should have done a better job of providing one's needs.

17:3–4 What the people did and said in v. 3 is conceptually similar to what they said in 16:2–3. Then it was grumbling against Moses and Aaron; here only Moses was mentioned, in keeping with the practice of mentioning Aaron periodically but not constantly.[181] There it was the starving of the people that they complained about; here it is death by thirst of whole families[182] as well as livestock because although the animals might still find

[181] See comments on 16:2–3. That Aaron was clearly involved in this event is explicitly asserted in Num 20:24: "Aaron will be gathered to his people. He will not enter the land I give the Israelites, because both of you rebelled against my command at the waters of Meribah."

[182] The term "us and our children" actually means "us and our families." Either *bānîm* (lit., "children") or *bānîm ûbānôt* (lit., "sons and daughters") is the standard way in Hb. to render Eng. "family." Note that Hb. does not normally include *ʾiššāh,* "wife," within the wording of this idiom, not as a discrimination against or slight of wives but as part of the efficiency of wording of the idiom. Logically, if one has children, one usually also has a spouse.

foraging food, they could not survive without water. So again the people grumbled (cf. 15:24; 16:2,7–9,12) against Moses, and again Moses knew that it was God to whom he must direct their grumbling. Judging from his words to God in v. 4, it may be concluded that either the people's rancor had reached a greater pitch than previously or else Moses, pained by the repeated attacks, had grown more sensitive to their criticism. Although a combination of both may be involved here, the latter is the more likely. Moses was not merely describing the people's attitude but was implying by referring to his own situation in such panicked terms that God must do something and quickly.

Even though God did not rebuke him, Moses had handled the people's protest incorrectly. Previously he had reassured them, taking God's side and asserting that God would provide for them (16:6–8) or simply acting as their intercessor in bringing their complaint to God (15:25). But here he took seriously the severity of the people's mind-set and paid special attention to his own welfare above God's will. Moses understandably feared being stoned because stoning was (and is) such a common way in the Near East of dealing with people seen to be a threat to the survival of a community or of a community's way of life. Recognized leaders were not above fear of stoning (e.g., Num 14:10; 1 Sam 30:6; John 8:59; Acts 5:26; 7:58; 14:19), and stoning was a legitimate form of legal punishment when one's crime was thought to be a capital crime against the community (Exod 19:13; Lev 20:2,27; 24:14). In other words, Moses looked here like a person afraid of losing his life for doing his job and showed a lack of confidence in God's provision for him that is parallel to and resultant from the people's lack of confidence in God's provision for them. Accordingly, this rebellion is remembered in Scripture not only as Israel's (Num 20:13,24; 27:14; Deut 6:16; 9:22; 33:8; Pss 81:7; 95:8; 106:32; Heb 3:8) but Moses' and Aaron's (Num 27:14; 20:24; Deut 32:51; Ps 106:32).

17:5 God was ready with a solution, just as he had been, of course, in the prior testings in which he also brought Israel to a circumstance where their confidence in him would be challenged by what they encountered relative to *their* expectations of what they should have been required to encounter. Moses symbolically took the position of the leader of the people in a manner that may indicate that he was given the honor before the people to substitute temporarily for the pillar of cloud/fire, in which form God presumably reappeared at Horeb in the next verse, or a manner that may indicate God's insistence that Moses lead the people rather than reflect the people's values.

Verse 5 is more literally translated: "The LORD said to Moses, 'Get out in front of the people. Take with you some of the elders of Israel, and take in your hand your rod with which you struck the Nile, and start walking.'" In other words, special emphasis is placed on Moses' getting "ahead of the people," the position that either the divine pillar or the "Angel of the LORD" held under the usual conditions.[183] "Some of the elders" (leaders) of the people as well as the *staff* of God[184] were required: the elders, to be witnesses of God's provision so as to quell the disturbance of the people, and the staff, to symbolize God's presence (which had been doubted by the people as v. 7 indicates) so that the miracle would properly be attributed to him rather than to Moses or anyone or anything else. Moses had used the staff to strike the Nile; now he would use it to strike water in a different sense, that is, by striking a rock.

17:6 God's presence and power represent the essentials for any miracle, and God explicitly promised Moses his presence in saying "I will stand there before you by the rock at Horeb." Horeb is the other name by which Mount Sinai is known.[185] The provision of water is a divine gift in many biblical contexts. Here, in association with the encampment at Rephidim near Sinai, God did not merely allow the Israelites to find water but showed them his provision for them by supplying that water in a place it was not otherwise available: from a rock at the base of the Mountain of God. Since the very location of Mount Sinai is in dispute, it can hardly be expected that the location of this rock could be easily recovered. There are a large number of rocks at the base of Mount Sinai (any rocky outcropping or large rock formation can be called a "rock" in Hb.), and one of these was indicated by God's presence (I will stand there"), almost surely through the pillar of cloud/fire.[186] Using the staff, Moses was to strike the rock so that it would yield water—hardly a normal means of finding water but in this case part of the plan to show Israel God's care for them and the importance of his presence at Mount Sinai. Moses carried out his assignment to strike the rock with God's staff "in the sight of the elders of Israel" so they could be witnesses for the sake of the nation as a whole to this revelation.

17:7 Moses named the location of the water at the base of Mount Sinai "Massah and Meribah," a name that in English could be rendered either in hyphenated form ("Massah-Meribah") or by an equivalency statement ("Massah, also known as Meribah"), but here it actually is more likely rendered meaningfully "both Massah and Meribah" since Moses apparently meant for both names to be used even if not necessarily always together.[187]

---

[183] Exod 13:21–22; 14:19.

[184] See "Excursus: Moses' Staff" at 4:14–17.

[185] Cf. 3:1, n. 13.

[186] This would seem to be confirmed by the reference to God's giving his answer to the people's complaining "out of a thundercloud" in Ps 81:7.

[187] The *waw* between the two names is presumably not the *waw explicativum,* which would mean, in a literal translation, something such as "Massah, i.e., Meribah" or "Massah = Meribah." But the name is not a compound of two different names representing two different identities as in [the College of] "William and Mary" or [the] "Eagle and Child" [inn]. It is a single place that Moses referred to in two different ways during the long time the Israelites were at Sinai. A more direct parallel would be Horeb and Sinai, two names for the same mountain.

In Hebrew, "Massah" means "testing/trial/temptation," and "Meribah" means "protest/contention/quarrel/strife." Only here is the location identified by both its names. The name occurs as Massah alone in Deut 6:16; 9:22; it is Meribah alone in Num 20:13,24; 27:14; Pss 81:7; 106:32. Both names are employed in poetic parallelism in the songs of Deut 33:8; Ps 95:8.

Does the fact that Moses chose two names for the site hint at the deep concern he had about the rebellion in which he had participated? Could it represent the result of roiling in his mind the events and their outcome—not merely the water but the fact that he had been complicit in the rebellion of the people by also complaining to Yahweh? The text does not say, but it may be reasonable to assume that the preservation of the two names and the repeated reference to the place and event in later biblical literature including his own writings in Numbers[188] and Deuteronomy suggest that Moses understood already the significance of what the Israelites had done and his acquiescence to it.[189]

The Israelites' inexcusable attitude becomes clear with Moses' concluding statement to the entire story: "They tested the LORD saying, 'Is the LORD among us or not?'" Had the people said something like, "Does the LORD intend for us to become weaker and weaker while we wait for him to supply us with water?" it would still have been an untrusting statement and evidence of lack of faith. But for the people actually to doubt God's *presence* among them was outrageously unfaithful. His presence was obviously manifest at all times, as it was at that very time through the pillar of cloud/fire, so the people's question must be seen as nothing other than a contempt of the Lord's leadership over them. It would be akin to asking a runner in the midst of running a marathon, "Do you intend to run in this race?" or asking a mother while she is in the kitchen working hard to get the family's meal ready, "Are we going to have any dinner tonight?" It is an insult. It looks at the obvious and implies by snidely denying it that it is no good. Israel thus incurred God's wrath and challenged God in a way he could not ignore.

---

[188] See L. T. Kok ("Parallel Scripts, Paradigm Shifts," *BZ* 42 [1998]: 81–90) for a discussion of how the separate incident described in Num 20:1–13 is not merely a doublet of the present story reworked editorially but a second, similar incident in which the people demanded water and in which several details are purposely selected for their usefulness within the literary form appropriate to the two incidents.

[189] Cf. W. Herrmann, "Ex 17.7bb und die Frage nach der Gegenwart Jahwes in Israel," in *Alttestamentlische Glaube und Biblische Theologie: Festschrift für Horst Dietrich Preuss* (Stuttgart: Kohlhammer, 1992), 46–55.

10. Battle against the Amalekites at Rephidim and the Curse on Amalek (17:8–16)

[8]The Amalekites came and attacked the Israelites at Rephidim. [9]Moses said to Joshua, "Choose some of our men and go out to fight the Amalekites. Tomorrow I will stand on top of the hill with the staff of God in my hands."

[10]So Joshua fought the Amalekites as Moses had ordered, and Moses, Aaron and Hur went to the top of the hill. [11]As long as Moses held up his hands, the Israelites were winning, but whenever he lowered his hands, the Amalekites were winning. [12]When Moses' hands grew tired, they took a stone and put it under him and he sat on it. Aaron and Hur held his hands up—one on one side, one on the other—so that his hands remained steady till sunset. [13]So Joshua overcame the Amalekite army with the sword.

[14]Then the LORD said to Moses, "Write this on a scroll as something to be remembered and make sure that Joshua hears it, because I will completely blot out the memory of Amalek from under heaven."

[15]Moses built an altar and called it The LORD is my Banner. [16]He said, "For hands were lifted up to the throne of the LORD. The LORD will be at war against the Amalekites from generation to generation."

17:8 Moses did not mention the reason for the Amalekites' attack on Israel, but even his very first readers would have known something of the history of enmity against Israel that carried on from the Esau-Jacob rivalry described in Genesis and something of the Amalekite modus operandi. Amalek was a grandson of Esau (Gen 36:12), and his descendants organized themselves into a very early national nomadic group ("first among the nations," in the words of Balaam, Num 24:20) that lived partly by attacking other population groups and plundering their wealth (cf. Judg 3:13). The Amalekites had domesticated the camel and used its swiftness effectively in surprise attacks.[190] Not only did the Amalekites attack Israel at Rephidim, but a year later they attacked them again at Hormah, when the Israelites had been driven out of southern Canaan and were on the run after their foolish attempt to enter the promised land in spite of God's command through Moses that they could not (Num 14:43–45).

The Amalekites may have traveled farther south on this occasion than was their usual habit in order to attack the Israelites[191] perhaps because they had heard that Israel was far from any population center and relatively

[190] Judg 6:3–5; 7:12; cf. 1 Sam 15:3. Over short distances camels can run forty-five miles per hour, considerably faster than a horse, and they were suited for transporting Amalekite raiding parties across desert/wilderness expanses to the outskirts of settlements, from which attacks on the settlements could be quickly accomplished.

[191] Various scholars have noted that all other extant historical records about the Amalekites place them normally in the northern Sinai or Midian or the Negev of Canaan, making the battle at Rephidim their most southerly foray on record.

defenseless. The fact that in the ensuing encounter the Israelites lost to the Amalekites except when Moses kept the staff of God elevated indicates the basic military superiority of the Amalekites to the Israelites, something they presumably were counting on in launching this raid in the first place.

17:9 Joshua appears here for the first time in the narrative, thus the first time in the Bible. He apparently had spent time during the days on the march from Egypt helping instruct the Israelites in martial skills and strategy, which would now see their first testing in actual combat. He was surely much younger than the eighty-year-old Moses since later he became Moses' successor. In 33:11 Moses referred to Joshua as his "young assistant," which suggests that he was a right-hand man to Moses in various ways, though at this point the ability to lead the people in battle appeared paramount.

The NIV translation "Choose some of our men" sounds potentially misleading since it may be understood to imply that there were many Israelites ready for battle and Joshua selected only some out of the entire army (as later at Ai, e.g., as described in Josh 7:3–4). In fact, an opposite sort of scenario probably presented itself: The text literally says, "Choose men for us and go out to fight against Amalek tomorrow." That is, Joshua probably had the challenge of finding men who *could* fight rather than paring down to a manageable amount the size of the group that would be needed from among all those who were qualified. Joshua may have approached this task of *choosing* on the basis of what later became regularized: the criterion that people who fought in battle should be healthy males between the ages of twenty and fifty.[192]

Of interest is that the Israelites had a day to prepare for battle. The Amalekites may have arrived gradually at Rephidim, signaling their presence early in the process, or else advance parties may have encountered the Israelites then gone north to get the main body of warriors with which to engage them, thus alerting the Israelites and allowing them time to prepare. Alternatively, the Amalekites may have announced to the Israelites that if they did not surrender their valuables, they would be attacked the next day. At any rate, Joshua had to pull together an army with a single day's notice, and part of the criteria he used for selecting fighters may well have been simply identifying those who had a sword. Many men may have begun to carry some sorts of knives or short swords, but it is hard to imagine that the Egyptians had allowed the Israelites much by way of armament while they were still in Egypt. Whatever arms the men now owned had probably been manufactured in the wilderness and may not have been of the highest quality—and almost surely not the greatest quantity.[193]

---

[192] On the assumptions behind these figures for the lower and upper age limits for fighting men, see "Excursus: How Many Israelites Left Egypt?" at the commentary on 12:37.

[193] The possibility cannot be ruled out that some or many Israelites obtained swords and other weapons of war directly from the Egyptians at the time of the Passover (see comments on 12:36, where "plundered the Egyptians" may be conjectured to include implicitly the taking of the enemy's weapons of war).

This is the first account in Exodus of Moses' making special use of the staff of God without being instructed by God to do so ("Tomorrow I will stand on top of the hill with the staff of God in my hands"). Does this wording mean that he was now confident of his own authority to use the staff as he saw fit? Almost surely not. By this time Moses expected his readers to realize that he would never use the staff unless commissioned by God to do so. In this relatively brief account of Israel's first warfare, many potentially supportive details are omitted, and one of them surely is the fact that God was behind the call to battle and the determination to use the divine staff as a symbol of God's presence with the people during the battle.

Excursus: Israelite Holy War

The Israelite encounter with the Amalekites at Rephidim represents an example of Old Testament holy war, an instance that anticipates the fuller delineation of the concept in later texts. The principles of holy war are codified in Deut 20:1–20, but important examples and supplemental aspects of the concept are found in many locations. Holy war may be summarized by twelve propositions:

1. No standing army was allowed. This meant that the battles were fought by amateurs, volunteers, who had to depend on God for their success and could not boast in their own accomplishments or claim special military prowess. A potential soldier was allowed—indeed invited—to give virtually any excuse for not serving in a battle[194] because God wanted only those who desired to be used by him as his warriors.[195]
2. No pay for soldiers was permitted. The entirely volunteer army could not seek personal reward by means of financial compensation for their efforts. Instead, they were to understand themselves as responding to God's call and not to any other incentives. They were going to war as his agents of justice, not as people seeking their own advantage.
3. No personal spoil/plunder could be taken. It was the standard practice in the ancient world for warriors to be attracted by the promise of spoil/plunder upon successfully conquering an enemy. The general rule was that a soldier could keep anything he could take from the enemy (or the enemy city or land) and carry off.[196]
4. Holy war could be fought only for the conquest or defense of the promised land. Israel had no right to any other land or to warfare for any other purpose.

---

[194] Accordingly, Deut 20:5–8 requires that the military leaders must openly invite those who may not have wanted to assert an excuse on their own behalf to go home and not participate in the battle on the basis of almost any sort of prior commitment, samples of which are announced to the assembled troops.

[195] David's Philistine mercenaries were, of course, an exception to the holy war provisions and thus, unfortunately, a violation of the principles of holy war. David's most egregious violation of the holy war rules took place as described in 2 Sam 24 (see below on point 4).

[196] Cf. the foiled expectation described in Deborah's Song, Judg 5:28–30, or the description of joy attending the division of spoils in Isa 9:3.

When David tried to build an empire and take a census in preparation for the wars that would be required to extend that empire beyond the boundaries of the promised land, he and Israel (the people had for the most part willingly participated) were severely punished (2 Sam 24:1–17).[197]

5. Only at Yahweh's call could holy war be launched. There was no opportunity to hold a national referendum or for a king or any other person, including the High Priest, to declare holy war. God alone was the arbiter of when such a war would be undertaken, if at all, and a true holy war was thus fought strictly and only at his call.[198]
6. Solely through a prophet could that divine call come. Prophets were spokespersons for God, who did not make up their messages but said what God had placed in their minds to say. Neither priest nor king nor nobles nor tribal leaders nor any other authorities except a prophet were in a position to declare a holy war. Moses was, of course, at all times a prophet.[199]
7. Yahweh did the real fighting in holy war because the war was always his. On the cosmic scale holy war was a war to defeat Satan and his angels, whose influence over earthly matters is invariably harmful. Israel was simply his human, earthly delegate to represent Yahweh's will, but he did the real fighting, with the Israelite people more or less conscious that they were "going through the motions."[200]
8. Holy war was a religious undertaking, involving fasting, abstinence from sex, and/or other forms of self denial.[201] It was an act of obedience to God and not of national pride or military strategy.
9. A goal of holy war was the total annihilation of an evil culture (the enemy, the Canaanites). This is based on Gen 15:12–16, in which God reveals to Abra-

---

[197] One might then ask how the battle at Rephidim, which was outside of the confines of the promised land of Canaan, could be considered properly an instance of holy war. The answer is that just as despoiling the Egyptians (3:21–22; 12:36) represented a first step in making it possible for the Israelites to get to the promised land, and the defeat of Pharaoh's army at the Red Sea represented a second step in the same progression, defeating the Amalekites was simply a third step in the process of getting to Canaan. Had Israel not been able to prevail against Amalek, the conquest and defense of the promised land would have been mooted.

[198] Thus when the Israelites decided to try to fight the Canaanites on their own, they lost miserably because the battle had not been called by Yahweh but was, rather, fought against his will (Num 14:41–45).

[199] Indeed, Moses is the paradigm prophet (Deut 18:15–22) whose ministry set the standards for all subsequent prophets.

[200] This is reflected, e.g., in Judg 5:20 ("from the heavens the stars fought") and in Paul's summation of our proper focus in our part of the ongoing holy war (Eph 6:12, "For our struggle is not against flesh and blood, but against the rulers, against the authorities, against the powers of this dark world and against the spiritual forces of evil in the heavenly realms."). The parade example of Israel's going through the motions of war in cognizance of the fact that the Lord actually does the fighting for them is found in Josh 6.

[201] On fasting in holy war, cf. 1 Sam 21:1–6, where David and his men were engaged in holy war and therefore were very hungry from their repeated fasting; or 1 Sam 14:24–45, a lengthy story resulting from Saul's oath requiring fasting during a campaign against the Philistines. On abstinence from sex, cf. 1 Sam 21:4–5 and 2 Sam 11:11–13.

ham the plan of conquest as a means of eliminating the "Amorites" (Canaanites) once their progressively evil culture had become so corrupt that God could do nothing other than to exterminate it. The total annihilation of the enemy and all that might have been taken as plunder followed logically from this commitment.[202]

10. The violator of the rules of holy war became an enemy. Those who violated the rules, such as by not practicing the required self-denial or the required disdain for spoils or the like, normally had to be punished with death, just as death is the due of the enemy being fought against.[203]
11. Exceptions and mutations were possible, especially in the case of combat with those who were not original inhabitants of the promised land, and therefore who were not automatically to be exterminated.[204] Accordingly, the Amalekites, as noninhabitants of the promised land, were added to the list of those who must be wiped out by special divine decree in 17:14 because otherwise the Israelites might not have been certain about whether or not to spare Amalekite lives.
12. Decisive, rapid victory characterized faithful holy war. It was the expectation that if God was behind a war, that war would essentially be concluded in a day, the "Day of Yahweh" or "Day of the LORD." In the ancient world there is a somewhat fuzzy distinction between a "battle" and a "war" because each military encounter with each new ethnic group or city state could be considered *either* a separate war or a separate battle within a protracted war of conquest. Nevertheless, God was regarded as capable of vanquishing all his foes in a single day.[205] That Moses should anticipate a battle against the Amalekites in a single day is consistent with this understanding of holy war.

17:10 The next day the battle began, with Joshua leading the Israelite army on the battleground and Moses "on top of the hill" with "Aaron and Hur" accompanying him. The identity of the hill in question remains uncertain since the region all around Sinai/Rephidim has plenty of hills, and anything from a small elevation to a mountain can be called a "hill" *(gibʿāh)* in Hebrew. Aaron is already well known as Moses' brother and the coleader of the Israelite exodus. But Hur is introduced here for the first time. His name seems to mean the equivalent of "Whitey" in Hebrew, in and of itself not

---

[202] For an example see Josh 6:17–19,21.

[203] On death for the person who breaks the fast, cf. 1 Sam 14:43–44; on death for the person taking plunder/spoil, cf. Josh 7:24–26.

[204] Cf. Deut 20:10–15; Josh 8:2,27.

[205] See D. Stuart, "The Sovereign's Day of Conquest," *BASOR* 221 (1976): 159–64, which argues that the origin of the phrase "the Day of the Lord" is to be found in the ANE notion that a truly great sovereign could win a war in a day, vanquishing all his foes and establishing full justice and order throughout his realm. Yahweh is the paramount great sovereign. His day of intervention, when it would come, would represent a decisive divine intervention in human history—joyously welcome to his allies and horrendously deadly for his foes.

special. More importantly, Josephus identifies him as the husband of Miriam.[206] Because of the prominence given to Hur as an appellate judge over the people in Moses' absence in 24:14, it would seem that he was one of the chief elders of the nation. Whether or not he was the Judahite Hur whose grandson was the supervising craftsman for the temple furnishings cannot be determined. The name is common enough (cf. the Midianite Hur mentioned in Num 31:8; Josh 13:21) that many people bore it.[207]

17:11 This verse does not teach the efficacy of "prayer without ceasing" but rather the fact that Israelite holy war was God's war. God reinforced this in the consciousness of Moses, Aaron, and Hur as well as the Israelite army by correlating the position of the staff with the fortunes of the army. It was important that the Israelites understand unmistakably that the only reason they could win against the Amalekites was that God was fighting for them, giving them the victory. The staff functioned in the case of this battle just as it had in the case of the plagues. As long as the staff of God was raised high, just as in the miraculous plagues and the miracle of the water from the rock immediately preceding, God's decisive role was properly acknowledged symbolically and the army prevailed. When the staff was lowered (because Moses grew tired, as v. 12 makes explicit), "the Amalekites were winning." Thus the staff portrayed God's sovereignty in the consequences of battle.[208]

17:12 The staff had to be above Moses' head—symbolizing God's superiority to all his people[209] as the leader in holy war—so when Moses became so tired that he could not keep it above his head long enough for the Israelites to succeed against the Amalekites, an intervention was necessary. The problem was not Moses' age or physical condition. He died a strong man.[210] The problem was the fact that human beings cannot keep their arms

---

[206] Whether this is nothing more than a speculation on Josephus's part or the preservation of a valid tradition cannot be discerned from the available evidence.

[207] Cf. also 1 Chr 2:50; Neh 3:9.

[208] This does not ignore the fact that in the ancient world the posture of prayer was with hands held up to heaven, as such passages as Pss 28:2; 63:4; Lam 3:41; 1 Tim 2:8 indicate. Ancient pictures of prayerful supplication do not generally suggest that the hands were held above the head or over the shoulders but rather in front of the chest or face, pointed upward in what we today think of as a typical posture of prayer with clasped hands or hands "kissing the mouth" (the language of worship in Job 31:27, properly translated). See Pritchard, *ANE,* plates 102, 123, 125, 130, 138. Moses was not simply praying however; he was serving as the representative of Yahweh, whose presence was manifested symbolically by the staff.

[209] As already in 9:29, "I will spread out my hands . . . to the LORD" and 9:33, "spread out his hands to the LORD." It is God whose power is symbolized by Moses' uplifted hands containing the staff of the Lord. Moses' hands had no power in themselves. Cf. B. D. Lerner, "Could Moses' Hands Make War?" *JBQ* 19 (1990–91): 114–19.

[210] Deut 34:7; cf. W. F. Albright, "The 'Natural Force' of Moses in the Light of Ugaritic," *BASOR* 94 (1944): 32–35.

above their heads indefinitely; anyone would eventually tire under the same circumstances. With Moses seated on a (low) stone and his hands held above his head by Aaron on the one side and Hur on the other, the staff could be above the height of his head because Aaron and Hur could keep their arms at a comfortable hanging height under Moses' elbows, probably with their fingers locked together cradling his elbows.

17:13 By nighttime this arrangement, fulfilling the purpose of having the staff along for the battle (v. 9), resulted in a total victory for Israel over Amalek. Note that the text says that "Joshua overcame the Amalekite army," not because he alone deserved credit but in keeping with standard ancient narrative style that identifies events with their leaders.[211]

17:14 Are God's words to Moses ("Write this on a scroll as something to be remembered") part of Moses' growing understanding that he was to become a preserver of this history? We cannot be sure because the mechanisms of God's leading Moses to write the Pentateuch are never described in the Pentateuch. We cannot know, either, whether the "scroll" on which the story of the entirely selfish, unwarranted Amalekite attack was written as "something to be remembered" was a separate scroll or the scroll of Exodus. The translation of the Hebrew could just as well be, "Write this as a memorial in the book," the book[212] being the one Moses already knew from God's inspiration that he was going to have to write (i.e., at least Exodus and perhaps the entire Pentateuch).

"Make sure that Joshua hears it" represents a way of saying that Joshua would have among his many assignments as Moses' successor to be on the lookout for Amalekites, who were hereafter as a result of their treachery to be considered in the same category as Canaanites—part of a culture fit for extermination. This is the earliest passage in the Pentateuch to imply that Joshua would succeed Moses as Israel's leader. A further assumption was that Joshua would pass on to his successor the obligation to exterminate the Amalekites. Indeed, Joshua himself had no opportunity to decimate Amalek during his lifetime, but left the task to his successors, with Saul and David actually finishing the job.

God's prediction, "I will completely blot out the memory of Amalek from under heaven," constitutes a very early "oracle against a foreign nation," a common form of oracle found later in the prophetical books. Such oracles

---

[211] This is, of course, hardly limited to the ancient world. It is perfectly natural in English to speak of "Roosevelt, Churchill, and Stalin" as having beaten "Hitler and Mussolini" in WWII even though the two groups had no direct contact, their respective armies having accomplished the victory. Similarly, General MacArthur is said to have "beaten the Japanese" or Alexander the Great to have "conquered the known world of his day."

[212] Hb. grammar includes the possibility that the article with "book" could be either the proleptic narrative article ("a, a certain, this,") or the simple article ("the").

predict the destruction or suppression of an enemy of Israel (and thus automatically an enemy of God) at some time of God's choosing in the future.[213]

17:15 Moses then built an altar there and named it. The practice of building an altar to commemorate a significant blessing from God (which can take the form of a rescue, a calling, a reassurance, or any other blessing) began already with Noah (Gen 8:20) and continued with Abraham (Gen 12:7–8) and the patriarchs (Gen 26:25; 35:7). Altars were for worshiping God, and worship always involves the expression of gratitude for blessing, whatever else it also properly includes. The patriarchs tended to build altars wherever they located because they understood their obligation to worship consistently. Moses was carrying on this tradition in building the altar at Rephidim to express thanksgiving to God for delivering the Israelites.

The patriarchs also sometimes named altars, particularly in the case of Jacob (Gen 33:20; 35:7). Moses here follows that example as well, by including a divine name in the name of the altar just as Jacob, for example, had done. Moses chose the name, lit., "Yahweh is my Signal Pole" (NIV "The LORD is my Banner"). The Hebrew word *nēs,* here translated "banner" in the NIV, does have that meaning in later Hebrew in the sense of a ship's ensign (Ezek 27:7), but in all earlier texts it refers not to something made of fabric or cloth but of a decorated pole held high and used as a signal marker or signal pole (Isa 5:26; 11:10,12; 13:2; 18:13; 30:17 [where it is parallel to a word meaning "flag staff"]; 31:9; 49:22; 62:10; Jer 4:6,21; 50:2; 51:12,27; Ps 60:4). It can also have the more generic sense of "sign/warning" (Num 26:10) and can as well mean just "pole" (Num 21:8) or "ship's mast" (Isa 33:23). Most often it is used in military contexts, where the *nēs* is a signal pole around which an army or army unit can rally, regroup, or return for instructions. Accordingly, Moses' name for the altar makes use of those connections. Because Yahweh had supplied the sign of his favor/presence/power by the staff—in effect a small military signal pole given to Moses—and had done so in the context of a military encounter, Moses stated by the name of the altar that the staff he had held high during the battle was the signal pole of Yahweh, a visible rallying point for the army of Israel in holy war.[214]

---

[213] All sixteen prophetical books contain some form of oracles against foreign nations, though in certain cases these are expressed very generally (e.g., Hag 2:7, "I will shake all nations"). Amos, the earliest of the writing prophets, has a substantial section of oracles against foreign nations as the first lengthy oracle in the book (Amos 1:3–2:16, with the interesting twist that Israel and Judah are included as "foreign nations" because their sins linked them with Yahweh's enemies and separated them from their former alliance with him).

[214] Various views on how to understand and how best to translate the words of vv. 15–16 have been offered. Well worth comparing among these are C. Houtman, "'YHWH Is My Banner'—'A Hand on the Throne of YH': Exodus xvii 15b, 16a and Their Interpretation," *OTS* 25 (1989): 110–20; R. Gradwohl, "Zum Verstandnis von Ex. XVII 15f," *VT* 12 (1962): 491–94; B. Couroyer, "Un egyptianisme en Exode, XVII, 15–16; YHWH-nissi," *RB* 88 (1981): 333–39; and D. Horowitz, "כִּי־יָד עַל־כֵּס יָהּ" *DD* 14 (1985): 56.

17:16 Moses then identified the staff as not merely a signal pole but as a symbol of Yahweh's throne. The key words (translated in the NIV "as hands were lifted up to the throne of the LORD") are preserved in the text in the old Bronze Age orthography, which did not indicate any vowel letters *(matres lectionis)* of any kind. Thus *yd; ʿālê,* "my hand," is spelled merely *yd; ʾal,* the old form of *ʿal* seen typically only in early poetry (which tends to preserve early orthography in some cases), is spelled just *ʿl*; *kissê,* the word for throne is spelled just *ks,* and the name Yahweh is represented by the common hypocoristicon yah.[215] What Moses said, then, was "My hand was at/on [i.e., touching] Yahweh's throne,"[216] a way of saying, "When I held up that staff, I was symbolizing the presence of Yahweh right with us, sitting on his throne, [ruling over the battle and helping us to win]." The verse, and thus the account of the battle against Amalek, ends with a summary of what God had told Moses to relay to Joshua: "Yahweh has war with Amalek in every generation," or as the NIV more idiomatically puts it, "The LORD will be at war against the Amalekites from generation to generation."

11. The Visit and Conversion of Jethro (18:1–12)

[1]Now Jethro, the priest of Midian and father-in-law of Moses, heard of everything God had done for Moses and for his people Israel, and how the LORD had brought Israel out of Egypt.

[2]After Moses had sent away his wife Zipporah, his father-in-law Jethro received her [3]and her two sons. One son was named Gershom, for Moses said, "I have become an alien in a foreign land"; [4]and the other was named Eliezer, for he said, "My father's God was my helper; he saved me from the sword of Pharaoh."

[5]Jethro, Moses' father-in-law, together with Moses' sons and wife, came to him in the desert, where he was camped near the mountain of God. [6]Jethro had sent word to him, "I, your father-in-law Jethro, am coming to you with your wife and her two sons."

[7]So Moses went out to meet his father-in-law and bowed down and kissed him. They greeted each other and then went into the tent. [8]Moses told his father-in-law about everything the LORD had done to Pharaoh and the Egyptians for Israel's sake and about all the hardships they had met along the way and how the LORD had saved them.

---

[215] The *heh* in *Yah* is not a *mater lectionis* but a consonant of the old verbal root *hwh*. The hypocoristicon *yah* is found in hundreds of Hb. names in the OT, such as Elijah, a compound name made up of the elements *ʾēlî* [my God] and *yah* [short for Yahweh].

[216] The NIV translation, "Hands were raised up to the throne of the LORD," cannot be sustained on the basis of the orthography. "Hands" would be written *ydm* in the Bronze Age, and although the plural of *ʿlh* ("to climb, go up, ascend") would indeed have been spelled just *ʿl* (for *ʿālû*) by Moses, the *qal* of *ʿlh* is consistently active, not passive. The ancient versions correctly took *ks* as an old spelling for *kissê*, except for the LXX, which interpreted it as a form of *ksh*, "to cover," and thus translated "by a secret [covered] hand."

[9]Jethro was delighted to hear about all the good things the LORD had done for Israel in rescuing them from the hand of the Egyptians. [10]He said, "Praise be to the LORD, who rescued you from the hand of the Egyptians and of Pharaoh, and who rescued the people from the hand of the Egyptians. [11]Now I know that the LORD is greater than all other gods, for he did this to those who had treated Israel arrogantly." [12]Then Jethro, Moses' father-in-law, brought a burnt offering and other sacrifices to God, and Aaron came with all the elders of Israel to eat bread with Moses' father-in-law in the presence of God.

This passage tells the story of the conversion of a relative, Moses' father-in-law, a development with personal meaning for many people since almost every believer can name a family member, close or distant, that he or she wants to come to faith. The placement of this story at this point in the book makes good sense in light of the fact that the Midianites and Amalekites were closely related; the defeat of the Amalekites (17:8–16), followed by the conversion of a Midianite (high?) priest (18:1–12) both demonstrate Yahweh's truth and power and his superiority over false gods and their adherents.[217]

The geographical placement of the Israelites also makes the narrative placement of this story logical: Jethro certainly knew where Mount Sinai was since in his employment under Jethro's authority Moses had driven his sheep there (3:1). Mount Sinai/Horeb may have been about the farthest reach of territory that Midianites had personal familiarity with, but since they did have knowledge of it, for Jethro to travel to it once the Israelites had reached it made perfect sense. This all may even have been prearranged: Moses had sent Zipporah and his sons back to Jethro when he came to the border of Egyptian-controlled territory, with the understanding that Jethro would bring them back to him at Sinai/Horeb since God had assured Moses that he would indeed return to Sinai, bringing the Israelites out of Egypt with him (3:12). The reader already knows that Moses took his formal leave from Jethro *after* he knew that he would be coming back to Sinai/Horeb (4:18).

---

[217] As might be expected, many source critics have opined that the Jethro story of Exodus 18 is a combination of relatively late source-specific material and even later editing designed to create a connection at this point between Moses and Jethro that did not in fact exist historically and would not have been likely to occur. Against this view, M. Weinfeld has argued rather persuasively that the chapter contains many elements that comport nicely with what we know of the situation in the Sinai peninsula in the late bronze age (fourteenth-thirteenth centuries BC). Weinfeld assumes (unnecessarily in our opinion) that the form of the story as it appear in Exod 18 may be from the early Iron Age (ninth century, according the Weinfeld's analysis) and that the people who actually worshiped Yahweh at Sinai may have been nomadic folk, but he adduces evidence in support of the historical plausibility of various parts of the overall story (M. Weinfeld, "The Traditions about Moses and Jethro at the Mountain of God," *Tarbiz* 56 [1987–1988]: 449–60 [Hebrew]).

The conversion of a priest bears little significance apologetically.[218] In this section of Exodus, Moses told how an important religious leader of the Midianites placed his faith in Yahweh, the God who had shown his glory in humbling Egypt and releasing Israel from bondage by supernatural means. Since Jethro may have held the title "the priest of Midian" (18:1 and see comments on 2:16) by reason of being a priest or the leading priest of the Midianites rather than merely one priest among many, his conversion to faith in the one true God must have resulted from the weight of overwhelming evidence. It may be assumed that Jethro would have been inclined to be skeptical of any questionable claims about Yahweh simply because believing in Yahweh would require abandoning the faith that he had not only held but led for so many years. An advocate of whatever faith the Midianites espoused, he reversed course and became a Yahwist upon seeing the entire nation of Israel free from the bondage of Egypt and brought safe by Moses to Sinai just as Moses had earlier told him Yahweh had predicted. The recent deliverance from the Amalekites must have had a powerful influence on Jethro's thinking as well since he would have been fully familiar with their fighting abilities vis-à-vis those of the Israelites. The stories of the plagues and the Red Sea deliverance would also have surely impressed him.

18:1 The news of Israel's dramatic departure from Egypt could hardly have been kept quiet; and from caravaneers, messengers, general gossip, and the like, Jethro had been learning of how Moses and the Israelites were faring during the plagues and the exodus itself. In his household, where Zipporah and Moses' sons were staying, any news of Moses, Aaron, and the Israelites must have been sought assiduously. One can imagine Jethro and Zipporah (and his employees, friends, and neighbors) asking any traveler from Egypt or the Sinai peninsula, "Have you any news of a man called Moses, or the people called Israel, or the Hebrews?"). As news was available, the household learned it.

Zipporah and her sisters readily recognized Moses as an Egyptian when they first encountered him at a well (3:19). This would hardly have been possible had they not been used to seeing Egyptians and hearing news about Egypt from time to time. Thus through the oral news network of the ancient world, Jethro eventually had "heard everything God had done for Moses and

[218] And in terms of exegesis, since not a few scholars have taken the position on humanist/history of religion grounds that Moses got his faith from Jethro and not vice versa. Cf. C. H. W. Brekelmans, "Exodus XVIII and the Origins of Yahwism in Israel," *OTS* 10 (1954): 215–44; B. P. Robinson, "Acknowledging One's Dependence: The Jethro Story of Exodus 18," *TNB* 69 (1988): 139–42; R. de Vaux, "Sur l'origine kenite ou madianite du Yahvisme," *Eretz-Israel* 9 (Jerusalem: Israel Exploration Society, 1969), 28–32; Weinfeld, "The Traditions about Moses and Jethro," 449–60; J. Van Seters, "Etiology in the Moses Tradition: The Case of Exodus 18," *HAR* 9 (1985): 355–61.

for his people Israel, and how the LORD had brought Israel out of Egypt." Moses may have prearranged for Jethro upon leaving Midian (4:18) to take Zipporah and their two sons into his home for safety after they had gone part of the way to Egypt with Moses (4:20–26) while he went about the dangerous business of confronting Pharaoh in Egypt, with the understanding that once the Israelites had left Egypt according to God's promise, they would reunite at Mount Sinai (3:12). If so, Jethro and Zipporah probably had been following Israelite progress and calculating when they should plan to leave for the prearranged rendezvous at the mountain of God.

18:2–4 Zipporah and her two sons with Moses play a prominent role in this narrative because the most basic reason for Jethro to bring them with him to Sinai/Horeb was to reunite Moses' family. As with major patriarchs in Genesis, the naming logic of the boys' names is provided here—a sign of the prominence of their father. Gershom's name probably was Egyptian, but it has some of the sound of "alien there" that would actually be *gēr šōm* [Gersham] in Hebrew rather than *gēr šōm* [Gershom] as vocalized by the medieval Masoretes. Since the LXX vocalizes the name as *gērsam* [=Gersham], however, it is quite possible that the original pronunciation was *gēr šām* and meant precisely "alien there" in Canaanite/Hebrew, whatever else it might also have meant by welcome coincidence in Egyptian. Hebrew names were often given at the time of birth on the basis of partial *similarity* to a meaningful statement made at that time rather than on the basis of actual etymology.[219] The name of the younger child, Eliezer, is fully Canaanite, meaning "God of help."[220] The sound of this name, too, was generally suggested by the sound of the vocabulary Moses used in connection with the naming.

Why was Zipporah living with Jethro and not with Moses since so many other Israelite women were traveling with their families? Had Moses been cautious about taking her with him to Egypt, or had their marriage fallen on hard times so that they had separated or, perhaps, even divorced, as some commentators have opined? The following excursus addresses this question.

Excursus: Was Moses Divorced from Zipporah?

Exodus 18:2–3 says literally, "Jethro, the father-in-law of Moses, took back Zipporah, Moses' wife, after her being sent away, along with her two sons." The

---

[219] Thus, e.g., if during a birth someone said, "This child is like his grandfather, who first dug a well here," the child might be named "Doug." For a full discussion of the process of homophonic naming, see D. Stuart, "Names, Proper," *ISBE* 3.483–88. Those scholars who point out that the naming explanations in the Pentateuch are not actually etymologically correct are simply stating the obvious. They weren't intended to be.

[220] The elements of the name are *ʾēl,* meaning "God"; *-i-,* a common way of rendering the epenthetic "neutral" vowel of the construct case ending, and *ʿēzer,* meaning "help."

word used in Exod 18:2 for "sending away" is a noun form, *šillûḥ,* which functions essentially as a gerund as used in the verse, a kind of verbal noun built from the *piel* verb stem. In medieval Hebrew it came to mean "divorce," so a number of rabbinical commentators, and a few moderns ones as well, concluded that Moses was divorced from Zipporah at least until this point in his life, if not permanently. For each of the reasons in favor of the conclusion that Moses and Zipporah had divorced, counter-arguments exist. First, the other two uses of *šillûḥ* in the OT are both in neutral/positive contexts (1 Kgs 9:16; Mic 1:14), suggesting no overtone of divorce, marital separation, or even marital friction. Second, the standard Hebrew word for divorce is not *šillûḥ* (which cannot be proved to mean "divorce" at all) but *kĕrîtut.*[221] Third, there is nothing untoward in Moses' marrying a second wife, i.e., the Cushite wife mentioned in Numbers. The Bible contains no specific law against polygamy, even in the NT, though it hardly endorses the practice, which is clearly inferior and not part of the creation design (cf. the monogamistic principle as enunciated in Gen 2:24 and Jesus' quotation of it as constituting the normative view of marriage in Matt 19:5). Old Testament leaders such as Abraham before Moses and David after him had more than one wife, so from one point of view it could be said that polygamy was not something that at least some Israelites felt obligated to avoid (though the fact that sinful characters in the OT did a thing hardly makes it right). Fourth, by the time of Moses' marriage to the Cushite woman, he and Zipporah were probably reunited (assuming that the second marriage took place after the arrival at Rephidim/Sinai, since a marriage prior to that time would be unlikely).

The NRSV, representing one legitimate way of reading the text, translates as follows: "After Moses had sent away his wife Zipporah, his father-in-law Jethro took her back, along with her two sons." In ancient Israel, as in most world cultures aside from that of the recent modern West, a woman who married was "sent away" from her father's family to become part of her husband's family.[222] If her husband later divorced her, he "sent away" his wife once again—this time back to her birth family and normally "sent away" her children with her as well. Thus "sending away" can connote a positive, happy event (leaving home to get married), but it can, conversely, connote divorce. Which kind of connotation does it have here?

In favor of the theory that Moses had divorced Zipporah sometime prior to this story of their reuniting are the following considerations. First, Moses was married to a black Cushite (Nubian) woman as of a point in time sometime after the Exodus according to Num 12:1. It is argued that he would not have felt free to marry this woman had he still been married to Zipporah, especially if he had merely sent Zipporah to Jethro for safety during the encounters with Pharaoh. In this line of reasoning a righteous man would not marry a second wife while his first was not present to be aware of the new marriage—at least formally if not by approval emotionally. Second, Exod 18:3 refers to "her children" (Zipporah's) rather than "his children" or "their children," as if the children were now legally

[221] E.g., Deut 24:1, 3; Isa 50:1; Jer 3:8.

[222] Cf. 1 Kgs 9:16; Mic 1:14.

assigned to her after the divorce rather than still being his own as well. Third, the "incident at the lodging place" recounted in 4:24–26 may be interpreted as evidence of marital friction between Moses and Zipporah, with her words, "Surely you are a bridegroom of blood to me" being taken as an angry, denunciatory attack on Moses, reflecting the extent of Zipporah's rage against him and perhaps marking the point of her being sent away from him back to her father's house.[223] Fourth (and possibly closely related to the third reason) is the fact that Zipporah did not continue to accompany Moses to Egypt even though that could be construed as their original intent as described in 4:20.[224] Marital discord would have ended the planned joint trip, with Moses going on alone to meet Aaron at Mount Sinai (4:27) and Zipporah being sent back to her father's home with the boys. Fifth, Zipporah was not living with Moses but with her father Jethro when Jethro came to see Moses at Rephidim/Sinai, creating at least the presumption of a marital separation. Sixth, it seems that Jethro mentioned having Zipporah and the boys with him in so overt and deferential a way (18:6) as to suggest that he was trying to effect a reconciliation. Jethro may be seen as virtually saying, "If you want to see me/accept me, you have to see/accept your wife and children too." Finally, from the overall perspective of the unity of Scripture, could not Jesus' statement in Matt 19:8 ("Moses permitted you to divorce your wives because your hearts were hard. But it was not this way from the beginning") be understood to associate Moses with divorce, disapprovingly, as if perhaps he were one of those whose hearts were "hard"?

For each of the reasons in favor of the conclusion that Moses and Zipporah had divorced, counterarguments exist. First, the other two uses of *šillûḥ* in the Old Testament are both in neutral/positive contexts (1 Kgs 9:16; Mic 1:14), suggesting no overtone of divorce, marital separation, or even marital friction. Second, the standard Hebrew word for divorce is not *šillûḥ* (which cannot be proved to mean "divorce" at all) but *kĕrîtut*.[225] Third, there is nothing untoward in Moses' marrying a second wife, that is, the Cushite wife mentioned in Numbers. The Bible never outlaws polygamy, even in the New Testament,[226] and Old Testament leaders such as Abraham before Moses and David after him had more than one wife. Polygamy was not something that a righteous Israelite would feel

---

[223] But see our analysis of the passage in the comments on 4:24–26.

[224] "So Moses took his wife and sons, put them on a donkey, and started back to Egypt."

[225] E.g., Deut 24:1,3; Isa 50:1; Jer 3:8.

[226] Thus the standard practice of Christian missionaries in parts of the world where polygamy is practiced is to require that married converts to Christian faith not add any wives to those they already have, nor divorce any. This does not mean that Christians should capitulate to an endorsement of polygamy. As G. P. Hugenberger (*Marriage as a Covenant* [Grand Rapids: Baker, 1998], 106-23) points out, "Nowhere do we find an express biblical permission for polygyny" (p. 111). See his argument there that no biblical texts "require the conclusion that polygyny was ethically approved," although it was "a legally valid form of marriage" (unlike "homosexual unions" or "marriage to a woman who was already another man's wife"; p. 113). He also proposes "the likelihood that the traditional interpretation of Lev. 18:18 is wrong and that this text, in fact, offers a general (ethical) prohibition of polygyny" (p. 115) and that "a number of texts appear to presuppose monogamy and perhaps even to advocate monogamy as desirable, if not normative" (p. 118).

obligated to avoid. Fourth, by the time of Moses' marriage to the Cushite woman, he and Zipporah probably were reunited (assuming the second marriage took place after the arrival at Rephidim/Sinai since a marriage prior to that time would be unlikely).[227] Thus Moses would not in fact have married the Cushite without Zipporah's awareness.[228] Fifth, the fact that the text mentions "her and her two sons" (18:2), "Moses' sons and wife" (18:5), and "your wife and her two sons" (18:6), that is, three different times in three different ways, gives them a prominence that appears positive and suggests approval on the part of the narrator, Moses. Indeed, it can be argued that Jethro was actually using the presence of Zipporah and the boys to ensure his own acceptance by Moses, whom he now encountered not as an escaped Egyptian alone but as the leader of a great nation of people that had just distinguished itself by beating the Amalekites in war, something Jethro and his Midianites could not expect to do.

Alternatively, it can be argued that Jethro seems to have been speaking proudly in his message in 18:6, as if he was bringing along a present for Moses that he knew Moses would be very happy to see because the marriage was not only intact but a happy one. Moreover, the terminology "her sons" does not suggest divorce. In a polygamous society, identifying children by connection to their specific mother is natural and often necessary.[229] Sixth, when Jethro came to Moses on these terms—as part of a "package deal" with Moses' wife and sons, Moses received him gladly, without any hint of rancor or disapproval at what Jethro had done. The fact that the story departs from the emphasis on Moses' wife and sons provided by the repeated mention of them in 18:1–6 and thereafter concentrates on the interaction of Moses and Jethro that begins in 18:7 reflects the typical economy of the narrative style rather than a slighting of Zipporah or the boys.Seventh, the boys' names are mentioned along with the reason for their names in vv. 3–4, a combination that happens elsewhere in the Old Testament only in cases of children who are proudly loved and accepted as

[227] The Israelites probably had less contact with non-Israelites before the exodus than after. The last-minute departure of the large ethnically mixed contingent that joined the Israelites in leaving Egypt meant that there were during the entire wilderness period many non-Israelite peoples among the Israelites (being incorporated into them), including a group of black Africans, from which Moses' Cushite [Nubian/Sudanese] wife would presumably have come (Exod 12:38).

[228] Although it is purely a speculative possibility, there is some reason to think that if the Cushite woman were serving as Zipporah's servant and Zipporah became unable to have further children, the servant might have been given to Moses as a substitute wife in the manner of Sarah's giving Hagar to Abraham in Gen 16:1–4. (Note that in that instance, Hagar was an Egyptian personal servant, and the custom of substitute marriage may have had Egyptian origins, as theoretically in the case of Moses as well.)

[229] For a parallel case cf. 1 Sam 1:4, which contrasts Peninnah's sons and daughters as "her sons and daughters" even though they are also Elkanah's, as opposed to Hannah's sons and daughters, a nul set at that point. Similarly, Caleb's sons by his wife Azubah are called "her sons" in contrast to those of his other wife. It may also be the case that when a woman was with her sons, even though their father was well known, they were identified as "her sons." This would seem to be the case in Matt 20:20 ("Then the mother of Zebedee's sons came to Jesus with her sons and, kneeling down, asked a favor of him").

part of a person's family line. Eighth, it may reasonably be assumed that 4:20–26 refers to a plan for Zipporah and the boys to accompany Moses only as far as the rendezvous with Aaron at Mount Sinai, the intent always having been for her to go back to her father's home with the boys in the interest of their safety because of the hostility of the Egyptians for Midianites, whose resistance against Egyptian attempts to subdue them had made them odious to the Egyptians.[230] Ninth, in 18:27 Moses "sends away" (*piel* of *šlḥ*)[231] Jethro but apparently keeps Zipporah and the boys with him, as if there were no thought of any other scenario. Tenth, Zipporah is called Moses' wife *(ʾiššāh)* three times. The Hebrew term for "first wife," *ʾēšet nĕʿûrîm,* usually is translated "wife of [one's] youth" (Prov 5:18; Mal 2:14–15). Notably, this term is not employed here to describe Zipporah. She was simply Moses' *ʾiššāh,* wife, happily returned to him by the escort of her father so Moses could be reunited with his family after protectively sending them away from him for the duration of his dangerous mission in Egypt.[232]

The evidence, then, suggests on balance that Moses was not divorced from Zipporah and that the Cushite woman he later married was a second wife, married either with Zipporah's knowledge and understanding or, possibly, after Zipporah's untimely death in the wilderness.

18:5–6 Presumably soon after he had heard that the Israelites had arrived at Rephidim/Sinai, Jethro sent a messenger to Moses, "I, your father-in-law Jethro, am coming to you with your wife and her two sons."[233] In order for a messenger to deliver this message, he would have had to be able to understand how to get from wherever in Midian Jethro lived to Mount Sinai/Horeb—another bit of evidence suggesting that the Midianites were familiar with the location of Sinai and how to get there. It was either a well-

---

[230] We must remember that the Egyptians were highly xenophobic, fearing war from Asiatics, and that Moses' appearance in Egypt married to an Asiatic from a warlike nation would tend to confirm the Egyptian suspicions that the Israelites, given the chance, would join in war with Asiatics against Egypt (Exod 1:9–10). Midianites may well have raided Egyptian settlements and caravans in the Sinai peninsula, earning Egyptian hostility.

[231] In other words, there is nothing at all negative and no overtone of divorce associated with the *piel* of *šlḥ;* it is, indeed, the verb form used in God's demand to Pharaoh "let my people go."

[232] None of this, of course, addresses the issue of whether or not Moses may have gotten married in Egypt during the first forty years of his life before he had to flee Egypt for Midian—something that would have been highly likely. If this were so, it is possible that upon the discovery of Moses' crime his original Egyptian wife would have been taken and given to another Egyptian, along with any children from that marriage, so that Moses could hardly have been reunited with that wife upon his return to Egypt, even if he had wanted to be.

[233] This quote is an example of a messenger speech, a memorized speech delivered by a messenger on behalf of the one who sent him, thus in the first person as if the sender were actually saying the words. It is a parade example of the first-person messenger speech form used extensively by the OT prophets, who indicated thereby that they were not making up what they said on the basis of general ideas planted in their minds by God but were saying the exact words he put in their minds and told them to say to their hearers on his behalf.

known mountain already or one whose location was, perhaps among many other mountains, easy enough to describe.[234] The purpose of the message quite possibly was to allow Moses time to reply, saying, "Yes, all is well, come ahead with Zipporah and the boys" or the like. This scenario in no way conflicts with the possibility that Moses had sent word on to Jethro as soon as he had arrived at Rephidim and that Jethro's message was simply a confirmatory reply indicating that he was about to get on his way with Moses' family in tow.

Moses, as narrator, here referred to Sinai/Horeb as the "Mountain of God" as already in 3:1; 4:27. In 3:1 he first mentioned Jethro by name,[235] almost as if to imply that Jethro had instructed Moses to take the flock to (the well-known location of) Mount Sinai, and in 4:27 he had described his meeting with Aaron there. The fact that Aaron could find his way to Mount Sinai from Egypt to meet Moses is a further indicator that the mountain was prominent enough to be well known.

18:7 No further mention is made of Zipporah in the Bible or of Gershom or Eliezer except as their names appear necessarily in genealogical references.[236] Moses presumably enjoyed a happy reunion with them, but his purpose in the narrative did not include dwelling on his own immediate family. Rather, he proceeded directly to the story of Jethro's conversion. A reader of Exodus might assume that Zipporah and Moses' sons placed their faith in Yahweh as a result of all they had heard already about Moses' call and the miracles he had experienced even before leaving Midian for Egypt. Indeed, in that society it might be expected that a man's wife and children would obediently honor his religious wishes, at least if they were strongly held. Jethro, on the other hand, was such a prominent public leader among his own people that the story of his conversion could serve as both an encouragement to the Israelites and an example to them of the importance of allowing faith in the only true God to spread to others.

---

[234] The traditional Mount Sinai in the southern Sinai peninsula certainly is an imposing mountain and must have served as a prominent landmark in the time of the exodus, regardless of what other associations it did or did not have at that time.

[235] Jethro could also be referred to by his clan name, Reuel; see comments on 2:18.

[236] An unfortunate aspect of the story of Moses' lineage occurs in Judg 18:30 and following, where a grandson of Moses through his son Gershom set himself up as a priest (thus the improper "Mushite" priesthood) and, along with his descendants led the tribe of Dan in ongoing heterodoxy. Cf. C. Hared, "Moise etat-il pretre?" *Bib* 40 (1959): 509–21; R. Nogah, "The Explanation of the Names 'Gershom' and 'Eliezer,'" *BMik* 35 (1989–90): 257–60 (Hebrew).

Moses showed proper, normal hospitality, deference, and family affection to Jethro by going out to meet him,[237] bowing to him,[238] and kissing him.[239] The statement translated by the NIV as "they greeted each other" would be better rendered in English, "They asked each other how they had been"[240] because that sort of inquiry is not quite the same as a greeting, although it conceivably could be considered part of the sequence of a full greeting. In saying "then went into the tent," Moses further indicated formal reception of his father-in-law as his guest. The Israelites were at that time, of course, living in tents, making appropriate comparable but symbolic dwelling of God in a tent—the tabernacle—as specified later in the book in great detail.

18:8 The testimony of God's people as to his actions in their lives on their behalf has always been an effective component of evangelism. Was Moses consciously seeking to convert his father-in-law to faith in the true and only God, Yahweh? Absolutely. He would surely have been a poor son-in-law and host not to have done otherwise since he now knew for sure that Yahweh was the supreme God and that the "gods" and men of the known world's superpower, Egypt, were entirely subject to his power. Moses probably spent a good many hours recounting to Jethro the entire story that we know in written form as Exod 4:27–17:16, and it is not at all improbable that

---

[237] Parallels are many: the host normally went out to meet his or her guest or family member arriving from a journey. This could occur in the case of a "superior" greeting an "inferior" (as in the king of Sodom coming out of the city to greet Abraham (Gen 14:17) or King Balak going out to welcome Balaam (Num 22:36); or in the case of an "inferior" greeting a superior (e.g., Jael going out to invite Sisera into her tent in Judg 4:18, or Jephthah's daughter coming out of the house to meet him upon his return from battle in Judg 11:34). A special kind of parallel is found in 1 Thess 4:16–17, where believers on the earth at the time of Christ's return rise to meet him in the air as a welcoming party, receiving him in honor as he comes to claim his kingship over all the earth. The details Paul provided of the eschatological greeting ceremony (the sounding of the trumpet, the shout of command, the voice announcing the monarch's arrival), are all consistent with what occurred in Roman times when a sovereign arrived at a city: the populace did not wait for him to have entered the city but assembled as a throng to greet him as he drew near.

[238] Examples of bowing to an arriving guest, whether friend or stranger, include Abraham's greeting of the angels in Gen 18:2; Lot's doing the same in Gen 19:1. It is normal for the "inferior" to bow first (or solely) to the "superior" in any encounter in the ancient world, as such instances as Gen 23:7,12; 24:26,48,52; 33:3, 6–7; 42:6; etc, demonstrate. Because an arriving guest is often the "superior" by the logic of hospitality, which generally treats a guest as the honoree in the relationship, it cannot be stated for certain whether Moses bowed to Jethro because Jethro was his guest or because Jethro was his "superior" generationally, as his father-in-law. Either reason would have sufficed.

[239] Examples of kissing one's parent or parent-in-law include Gen 27:27; 50:1; Ruth 1:14. But in many other instances, a kiss is simply a sign of affection among family members of whatever rank or relationship and does not indicate status per se, but rather tender love and affection (e.g., esp. Gen 29:13; 33:4; 45:15; Exod 4:27; Ruth 1:9; 1 Sam 20:41).

[240] וַיִּשְׁאֲלוּ אִישׁ־לְרֵעֵהוּ לְשָׁלוֹם.

such a full oral review may have been part of the process by which God prepared Moses to become the writer of the book of Exodus.[241] A tendency exists in the modern evangelical "testimony" to emphasize only victorious, successful parts of one's experience as a believer. Note how something of the opposite prevails in Moses' discussion with Jethro: he told him "about all the hardships they had met along the way," not to the exclusion of telling him "how the LORD had saved them" but with a proper balance of the difficulties and the deliverances, lest his potential convert wrongly think that God does not allow his people to face many dangers and trials in the process of their ultimate deliverance. "How the LORD had saved them" does not therefore refer specifically to salvation from sin in the present context but does help establish the character of Yahweh as a saving, rescuing God who acts to keep his people from being destroyed. Later in Exodus the focus will shift from God's saving his people from physical danger to his saving them from sin by teaching them how to be holy and preserve his holiness, but that is not yet the topic here.

18:9–11 Verse 9 actually says in the Hebrew: "Jethro was delighted for all the good things that the LORD had done for Israel."[242] In other words, he was not merely "delighted to hear about all the good things" but personally delighted by the facts themselves—because they answered questions he himself had about this God Yahweh who had appeared to his son-in-law and promised such great things for a certain enslaved people in Egypt. Thus his words in v. 11 suggest that he had been wondering about who this Yahweh really was and what he would be able to do in actual fact for the Israelites. Had Jethro, in other words, been at least somewhat skeptical of Moses' earlier report of his call and of his claims on behalf of Yahweh? Surely he had. It is difficult to imagine that he could ever have thrown over his own Midianite-Kenite theological life-long beliefs on the mere report by Moses of what had happened to him during his time grazing sheep near Sinai/Horeb.[243]

---

[241] In other words, to tell the story comprehensively to Jethro would have required Moses to formulate the outline of the story (scope and sequence) and to prioritize the inclusion of details (individual units of narrative) in a way that God could later use to make the writing of the story "natural" for a primarily aural audience. As a writer, Moses knew that his story would mainly be read to groups of people, so most would hear it rather than read it, and a first-time run-through orally with Jethro would certainly represent one helpful part of the preparation for that process, however strictly intentional it was at the time.

[242] וַיִּחַדְּ יִתְרוֹ עַל כָּל־הַטּוֹבָה אֲשֶׁר־עָשָׂה יְהוָה לְיִשְׂרָאֵל.

[243] Our line of reasoning here runs, of course, directly counter to the so-called Kenite Hypothesis, an old critical notion that Moses must have picked up his religious ideas (basic Yahwism) from the Kenite branch of the Midianites during his days living with Jethro and that Jethro was, therefore, far more of an influence on Moses than Moses was on Jethro. The data of the text show the influence going only one way, with Jethro converting to Yahwism rather than teaching it to Moses.

What convinced Jethro was God's rescue of Moses, whom he knew personally so well, and Israel, whom he had only heard about before this, "from the hand of the Egyptians" (v. 10). His words in v. 11, "Praise be to the LORD,[244] who rescued you from the hand of the Egyptians and of Pharaoh, and who rescued the people from the hand of the Egyptians," repeat the phrase "from the hands of the Egyptians" twice[245] because that was what really counted for Jethro. The defeat of a superpower and its gods, including the great Pharaoh of Egypt, was simply too great and inexplicable a victory other than by the involvement of a powerful supernatural being, the God Yahweh who had told Moses in advance that he would do just that. As a result, Yahweh became for Jethro at that moment the supreme God, "greater than all other gods"—the only supernatural being that in modern English usage would be called "God."[246]

The last clause in Jethro's speech ending in v. 11 is somewhat difficult to understand. The NIV translation "for he did this to those who had treated Israel arrogantly" may be correct, but the Hebrew seems rather to say something like, "Indeed, it is the reason why they acted arrogantly against them."[247] That is, the fact that the Egyptian gods were so arrogant against the Israelites was exactly what God intended in order to show his superiority over the Egyptian gods.[248] The final five Hebrew words in this verse are unusual, but not necessarily indecipherable; *kî* often means "indeed," as we have translated it; *baddābār ʾăšer* means "the reason why" (cf. 1 Kgs 11:27); and the *beth* that introduces it (blended phonically with the *heh*) could simply be the *beth essentiae* (already seen in v. 4; Moses probably used it regularly in his own speech). The final words, "acted arrogantly against them," fall in logically with the rest. By the last clause of v. 11 Jethro was, in other words, making the point that "it all happened just as God

---

[244] Or "Blessed by Yahweh," which is a standard way in Israelite history of pronouncing a benediction on Israel's God, as in Gen 24:27; 1 Sam 25:32; 2 Sam 18:28; (see W. S. Towner, "'Blessed Be YHWH' and 'Blessed Art Thou, Yahweh': The Modulation of a Biblical Formula," *CBQ* 30 [1968]: 386–99). For examples of other instances where non-Israelites pronounce a blessing on Israel's God, cf. Gen 26:28–29; Josh 2:9–11; 1 Kgs 5:2.

[245] I.e., as a semipoetic formulation and not as an awkward phrasing or dittography. The second half of the verse is omitted in the LXX, presumably by reason of haplography via homoioarchton.

[246] In Hb. אֱלֹהִים, here translated "gods," can refer to any supernatural beings, including angels, as well as false gods, who do not actually exist except in the imagination of their worshippers. Thus the "set" or semantic field of Hb. references for אֱלֹהִים includes the one true God, all false gods, all supernatural beings (angels, seraphim, cherubim), all demons, and even Satan. Jethro's words need not be understood to connote that he thought Yahweh was "greater than all other deities that actually exist" but rather "greater than all other supernatural beings or any of the supposedly supernatural beings that people think exist."

[247] כִּי בַדָּבָר אֲשֶׁר זָדוּ עֲלֵיהֶם.

[248] See the commentary on Exod 12:12; 15:11.

planned it—he even controlled the Egyptians' gods in their arrogance for Israel, humiliating them to show his greatness."[249]

18:12 How would someone show that he had converted to faith in Yahweh? (1) He would begin to worship Yahweh according to his best understanding of how that was to be done, and (2) he would eat a covenant meal with other worshipers of Yahweh in the presence of Yahweh. The Israelites had not yet received Yahweh's covenant with them as a people, so neither Jethro nor the Israelites yet understood all the exact ways to obey Yahweh and had to demonstrate conversion as well as they could. They all knew something about sacrificing as the heart of obedient worship since that concept had "trickled down" into the consciousness of peoples all over the earth from the days of the first family, who understood the basic concept of sacrifice: "something else must die so that I may live."[250]

A "burnt offering" was understood to atone for past sins and to appeal for forgiveness and acceptance.[251] "Other sacrifices" were offered by Jethro to be sure to cover for any inadequacies in approaching such a powerful and, indeed, omnipotent God as Yahweh was, to ensure that Jethro would be accepted in genuine fellowship with God himself.[252] Then "Aaron came with all the elders of Israel to eat bread with Moses' father-in-law in the presence of God," which signified the formal admission of Jethro into Israel. The religious leader of the nation, Aaron, and all the other leaders ("the elders") had a meal with him "in the presence of God," which can only mean before the altar that at that point most symbolized God's presence, that is, that altar that Moses had publicly built at Rephidim/Sinai (17:15–16)—inasmuch as the tabernacle/tent of meeting had not yet been constructed.[253]

12. Jethro Advises Implementing a Hierarchical Court System (18:13–27)

[13]The next day Moses took his seat to serve as judge for the people, and they stood around him from morning till evening. [14]When his father-in-law saw all that Moses was doing for the people, he said, "What is this you are doing for the

[249] Jethro thus anticipated the kind of theology found in Ps 82, where Satan's angels were influencing the various nations in evil ways, and God assumed authority over them to punish them.

[250] God introduced the concept of sacrifice as soon as the first family was expelled from Eden, so Cain and Abel grew up practicing it (Gen 4:4–5).

[251] Since already in the days of Abraham, God's people understood something of how the burnt offering functioned (Gen 22:2–13). For more on the concept, see comments on Exod 20:24–29; 29:18ff.

[252] See comments on Exod 20:24.

[253] The tabernacle/tent of meeting in which was housed the ark of the covenant would eventually take over the function of any mere altar as symbolizing the point of God's presence, but until that time, "in the presence of God" meant "in front of an altar built and dedicated to God."

people? Why do you alone sit as judge, while all these people stand around you from morning till evening?"

[15]Moses answered him, "Because the people come to me to seek God's will. [16]Whenever they have a dispute, it is brought to me, and I decide between the parties and inform them of God's decrees and laws."

[17]Moses' father-in-law replied, "What you are doing is not good. [18]You and these people who come to you will only wear yourselves out. The work is too heavy for you; you cannot handle it alone. [19]Listen now to me and I will give you some advice, and may God be with you. You must be the people's representative before God and bring their disputes to him. [20]Teach them the decrees and laws, and show them the way to live and the duties they are to perform. [21]But select capable men from all the people—men who fear God, trustworthy men who hate dishonest gain—and appoint them as officials over thousands, hundreds, fifties and tens. [22]Have them serve as judges for the people at all times, but have them bring every difficult case to you; the simple cases they can decide themselves. That will make your load lighter, because they will share it with you. [23]If you do this and God so commands, you will be able to stand the strain, and all these people will go home satisfied."

[24]Moses listened to his father-in-law and did everything he said. [25]He chose capable men from all Israel and made them leaders of the people, officials over thousands, hundreds, fifties and tens. [26]They served as judges for the people at all times. The difficult cases they brought to Moses, but the simple ones they decided themselves.

[27]Then Moses sent his father-in-law on his way, and Jethro returned to his own country.

Immediately after his conversion Jethro was able to play a helpful role in Israel by recommending the basic structure of the judicial system, a properly hierarchical arrangement that placed Moses at the top of the judicial pyramid as Israel's "supreme court" and established inferior courts/judges under him. As N. Sarna and others have pointed out, the attribution of Israel's judicial system structure to a Midianite's advice can hardly have served any late interpolator's purpose, and thus it may be considered one of the indicators of the passage's authenticity and antiquity.[254]

18:13 In the ancient Near East as in many parts of the world still today, the job of judging civil and criminal disputes goes along with a leadership

[254] "The judiciary is ascribed to the initiative and advice of a Midianite priest. This extraordinary fact testifies to the reliability of the tradition and to its antiquity. In light of the hostility that later characterized the relationships between the Midianites and the Israelites, it is hardly likely that anyone would invent such a story" (N. Sarna, *Exodus,* JPS Torah Commentary [Philadelphia: Jewish Publication Society, 1991], 100). From a different angle, cf. Robinson, "Acknowledging One's Dependence," 139–42; R. Knierim, "Exodus 18 und die Neuordung der Mosäischen Gerichtsbarkeit," *ZAW* 73 (1961): 146–71; H. Reviv, "The Traditions Concerning the Inception of the Legal System in Israel: Significance and Dating," *ZAW* 94 (1982): 566–75.

position.[255] To be a political or military leader was also to be a judicial leader, required to render decisions in cases of controversy.[256] Moses had presumably been judging the people regularly already, but a number of complicated cases had presumably continued unjudged because of the difficulty of holding court while on the move. Now came a day when Moses could wait no longer to address the caseload, and in spite of spending all the daylight hours hearing court cases, he had still apparently not finished when evening came (since people still "stood around him . . . till evening").[257] Moses took the traditional position of judge, sitting while the litigants stood before him, as remains the case in most courts around the world today. Clearly, if Moses was giving such a large proportion of his time to judging legal disputes, he could not do much else, at least on days he served as judge, and this threatened his leadership of the nation in other ways.

18:14 Jethro saw that this could not go on indefinitely. His own experience as a Midianite leader may have involved him in regular judging among the Midianites, and it was obvious to him that Moses had overcommitted his time to his judicial role. Nothing was wrong with Moses' serving as a judge; indeed it was clearly an obligation of his as leader of the people. What was wrong was his serving as the *only* judge, without any help, for simple cases as well as for complex ones ("Why do you alone sit as judge?"). In trying to do all the judging himself, Moses may not have been acting foolishly or overconfidently. He may simply have been waiting for God to reveal to Israel a proper, hierarchical judicial system and not trying to make one up on his own authority. Moreover, his only models would have been either the Egyptian system, where the pharaoh made himself available for any and all persons to see him in court, at least certain times during the year, or the Midianite model, where tribal leaders probably did something of the same.[258] But the most important reason for Moses' going it alone was that he

---

[255] This remains so even in modern Western nations with established judiciary systems, in such cases as crimes on board a ship (in which the captain acts as a judge) or in military units (where the commanding officer has a judicial role) or among embassy staffs in foreign countries (where the senior diplomat acts as judge). Aboard nuclear submarines, with their long, submerged voyages, the captain may render legal decisions that apply for months before any other military jurisdiction can be consulted.

[256] Part of the reason the military/political deliverers of Israel in the book of Judges were called *judges* (שֹׁפְטִים) was that they inevitably had to judge legal disputes even if that was not necessarily their primary purpose.

[257] It may also be inferred from Jethro's words about "all these people . . . will/may go home" in v. 23 that the caseload had gotten so large that people were having to wait days or weeks in line for a chance to have their case decided by Moses—i.e., that even after working all day judging cases, he still couldn't clear up the backlog and reduce the waiting line.

[258] The Amarna letters seem to confirm the availability of Pharaoh to be approached in his "court" by even the lowliest commoner, and it is hard to imagine how Moses and Aaron had access to Pharaoh unless by reason of his holding open court on occasion. See the note on 9:1–4.

functioned as a prophet, who dispensed God's revelation, and that was the reason for his answer in the next verse.

18:15–16 Moses was not merely a judge. He was a prophet who conveyed God's will when it was sought. The NIV translation, "the people come to me to seek God's will" can make it sound like Moses already knew God's will, but this was not the case. A better translation would be "the people come to me to inquire of God," which connotes better Moses' intermediary role.[259] Through him the people asked God for answers to their disputes, and thus Moses asserted that he did not really judge on his own but "decides between the parties and informs them of God's decrees and laws." In other words, the legal process involved the revelatory process in this case. That was almost certainly the reason Moses had felt obligated to do all the judging himself: the answers involved God's own decisions, and Moses understood himself to be the sole conduit for those to the people.[260]

But do not "God's decrees and laws" come only later, in chap. 20 and following, with the formal revelation of the covenant? The answer must be no; some of the decrees and laws of God were being proleptically revealed to the people for their benefit even before the unveiling of the Sinai covenant because answers were needed to important questions during the three months while the people were on their way to Sinai/Horeb and also because by dispensing decrees and laws in advance of Sinai, God was able to continue shaping his people's thinking in the direction of his eventual covenant relationship with them. Good education involves preparatory (propaedeutic) instruction as well as concomitant instruction and follow-up instruction.

18:17–18 Jethro did not find Moses' line of reasoning convincing (thus suggesting that Moses did not portray his method of doing all the nation's judging as divinely ordained but merely as logical) and countered with a simple but convincing argument: the method can't be right if it results in everyone's frustration and exhaustion. That the judicial workload must have been too much for one man is shown by the incontrovertible fact that both Moses and the people who waited for justice could not conclude business in a reasonable time span. In effect, Jethro's argument is an early version of the now popular legal saying "Justice delayed is justice denied."[261]

---

[259] "Inquire" (דרשׁ) tends in a context like this one to bear the technical sense of "seek a revelatory answer from God," as in Isa 8:19; 31;1; Jer 8:2; Ezek 14:3.

[260] This process may be seen in action in the book of Numbers. On a number of occasions a legal issue was brought before Moses, who then would bring it before God and get an answer that he then not only relayed to the people to satisfy the need for an answer at that point but which became part of the permanent covenant law thereafter, serving as statute law for guidance in any similar situations that might arise. Cp., e.g., Num 15:32–36; 27:1–11; 36:1–12.

[261] This maxim was formulated by William Gladstone, the British political leader (1809–1898).

How had such a heavy workload come about? The answer, it would seem, involves three facts. First, newly freed from having few legal rights under Egyptian oppression, the Israelites had a pent-up list of issues and complaints to settle properly as well as an eagerness to take advantage of their sudden freedom to function as free people function, including access by right to legal services. Second, the sheer size of the large group, including non-Israelites, under one visible leader surely meant that matters previously adjudicated by clan heads, village leaders, and the like were now considered by the people themselves to require adjudication by the nation's only divinely approved leader, Moses. Third, Moses' own eagerness both to help and please his people as well as to learn God's standards for the nation must have motivated him to spend much time and careful thought on every decision, including the time involved in waiting for an answer from God to his questions raised on behalf of the people.[262] He presumably treated no case lightly but threw himself into the work wholeheartedly and became entrapped by the caseload brought before him. Thus in spite of everyone's best intentions, the judging of disputes had bogged down, as was immediately obvious to someone new to the faith and the situation of Israel, such as Jethro was.

18:19–20 Jethro did not suggest that Moses discontinue judging, or that he stop serving as a representative of the people's problems to God, or that he leave off being God's spokesperson to teach the people God's decrees and laws. The people surely needed someone "to show them the way to live and the duties they are to perform," and Moses was indeed that person. Moreover, Jethro did not arrogate to himself divine wisdom but was careful to couch his words as suggestions subject to God's confirmation (the implication of the words "and may God be with you" in the first sentence of v. 19 and "if you do this and God so commands" in v. 23).

18:21–22 What Jethro believed to constitute God's will for Moses and the Israelites was a *trustworthy* judicial hierarchy—trustworthy in that the judges at the "inferior" level would be *selected* and would be "capable men . . . who hate dishonest gain."[263] These would lead the people as "officials"—people who were appointed to an actual societal office and did not take on a judging role merely as a task ancillary to their tribal rank or the

---

[262] Moses continued to bring difficult cases to God for a divine answer throughout the rest of his lifetime among the Israelites as the references given above from Numbers indicate. For examples of a prophet doing essentially the same thing, cf. Ezek 14:1–11; Zech 7:1–7.

[263] On the term used in the passage for "dishonest gain" (בֶּצַע, in this instance pointed pausally as בָּצַע) and its significance as an indicator of the familiarity of the Israelites with Egyptian legal standards, see C. Carmichael, "Joseph, Moses, and the Institution of the Israelite Judicature," *Go to the Land I Will Show You: Studies in Honor of Dwight S. Young* (Winona Lake: Eisenbrauns, 1996), 15–26.

like. Thus contrary to the Israelite priesthood or the ancient Near Eastern monarchy, the Israelite judiciary was to be appointed on the basis of honesty and ability rather than occupy an office automatically by reason of being born into a hereditary role. The various categories of society are here indicated by the division into "thousands, hundreds, fifties and tens." These terms are used elsewhere to denote military units, but here they delineate civilian groupings of various sizes. It is not any more likely that the terms are to be taken literally in this context than in a military context. The expression seems to have the sense of "all the various societal levels" rather than literally indicating that every ten people would have a judge; every fifty (five groups of ten), an appellate judge for that group; and every two appellate groups ("hundreds"), a higher appellate judge, and so on. In other words, the expression "thousands, hundreds, fifties and tens" seems to be essentially a figure of speech by which is meant "all the various population groupings."[264] By providing leaders for each population level, Moses could assure an adequate number of judges to handle all but the most complicated court cases.

These lower court judges would be available at virtually any time ("have them serve as judges for the people at all times"), taking uncomplicated cases ("the simple cases they can decide themselves") and adjudicating them regularly so that the people would have daily access to judges for most issues. This would leave most of Moses' time free of judicial responsibilities for him to lead the people in other ways, including his ministry of prayer and worship and his ministry of teaching and preaching all God's laws. But if a lower court could not make a decision, or if its decision was rejected and appealed by the litigant parties, Moses was available from time to time (perhaps one day a month or the like) for these cases that had already been heard in lower courts and were brought by the judges to him ("have them bring every difficult case to you"). Such cases were the sort that needed his intercessory function so the parties could have confidence that the decision represented divine authority (18:16). Moses thus became the court of last resort or supreme court of Israel. He remained a judge but delegated what would have been most of his caseload to subordinates.

---

[264] There was a blurry distinction between civil and military organization in ancient Israel. The neighborhood/extended family/clan civil leaders were also usually the persons chosen to gather up the fighting men and present them armed and ready for battle and to lead them into war if necessary. The same people these officials judged in peacetime they commanded (minus women and children and old men) in wartime. Accordingly, we should not be surprised to find the idiom "thousands, hundreds, fifties and tens" in military contexts (e.g., Deut 1:15; 1 Sam 8:12) as well. The use of part of the idiom, "hundreds and fifties," in Mark 6:40 in a strictly civil context seems to represent the same loose sort of usage (meaning essentially "various sized groups") as found here in Exod 18. On the general interchangeability of the civil and military units, see G. E. Mendenhall, "The Census Lists of Numbers 1 and 26," *JBL* 77 (1958): 52–66.

18:23 The first part of the verse could better be translated, "If you do this, that is, if God commands you to . . ." Jethro did not presume to tell Moses how to rearrange the Israelite judiciary on his own authority. But as a new worshiper of Yahweh and a concerned member of the community of faith, he ventured to formulate the plan he thought Moses ought to bring to Yahweh for approval. What he expected of Moses was the willingness to ask Yahweh if such an approach represented his divine will. Implied may be Jethro's presumption that Moses had earlier misinterpreted God's will about his role as judge, that is, that he had assumed he was to judge *every* case so God's will could be revealed in the verdicts rather than just the precedent-setting cases God had actually intended for him to limit himself to. Jethro's goal in this advice, which he assumed God would endorse, was that both Moses and the people would have relief: Moses from his huge workload ("you will be able to stand the strain") and the people's morale ("and all these people will go home satisfied").

18:24–26 These verses summarize the fulfillment of what was suggested, in typical repetitive command-fulfillment style.[265] Although it is not stated overtly, it may be assumed that Moses learned from God that Jethro's advice was either acceptable or even what God had intended all along and Moses had misunderstood. Thus already at Sinai/Horeb, three months after leaving Egypt, Israel had a hierarchical court system using chosen, not inherited, leaders as judges, with Moses as the supreme court.

18:27 In these few words little is said but much is implied. Moses' sending "his father-in-law on his way" does not connote any such overtone as "getting rid of Jethro" but suggests a warm, happy parting. Now Jethro, a convert to the true faith, could bring it back to Midian ("Jethro returned to his own country"). It would surely meet with hostility there (cf. Num 22:4ff.; 25:6ff.; esp. 25:17; 31:2), but at least among members of Jethro's household there may have been followers of Yahweh in due time.[266] Upon Jethro's earlier arrival at Sinai/Horeb, much had been made of his escorting Moses' wife and sons to be reunited with Moses (18:2–6). The absence of any mention of their returning to Midian with him suggests strongly that they stayed with Moses and joined the Israelite community, in which they remained thereafter. Finally, the verse adds its evidence to that of various earlier hints that travel between Mount Sinai and Midian was not a matter of trailblazing pioneering but something relatively uncomplicated to accomplish.

---

[265] On this style see "Excursus: Command-Fulfillment Repetition in Exodus" at 35:1.

[266] Surely it is likely that Moses' son-in-law Hobab, who may have been related in some way to Jethro (see Albright, "Jethro, Hobab and Reuel in Early Hebrew Tradition," 1–11) was a follower of Yahweh in light of his serving as Israel's guide in the wilderness (Num 10:19; cf. Judg 4:11 for the evidence that he was clearly a Kenite).

13. Arrival at Sinai and Call to Holiness (19:1–8)

(1) Arrival at Sinai (19:1–2)

[1]In the third month after the Israelites left Egypt—on the very day—they came to the Desert of Sinai. [2]After they set out from Rephidim, they entered the Desert of Sinai, and Israel camped there in the desert in front of the mountain.

19:1–2 Verse 1 may also be translated as follows: "Three months to the day after[267] the Israelites had left the land of Egypt they entered the wilderness of Sinai." The wilderness [NIV "Desert"] of Sinai was simply the wilderness area immediately around Mount Sinai, which in turn was within the much more vast Wilderness of Sin (cf. 16:1; 17:1; Num 33:11–12). Since neither Rephidim nor Sinai had a natural water supply (17:1,6), they were neither oases nor, presumably, known camping spots; thus the area around them was appropriately designated "wilderness" (NIV "desert"). The actual distance from Rephidim to Sinai may have been only a few miles (see comments on 7:5), so the Israelites could have made the journey described here, from one encampment to another, in a day. Indeed, the supernatural provision of water for the people described in 17:6 seems to suggest that while encamped at Rephidim the Israelites had to get their water at the base of Sinai/Horeb. Many people must have welcomed the move to the mountain since the daily round trip for water would have been enervating; and, in all probability, driving herds and flocks there for watering did not constitute enjoyable recreation. With the move described in v. 2, the Israelites now inhabited the base of the Mountain of God ("camped here in the desert in front of the mountain"), where they would stay put for ten months and nineteen days (see Num 10:11).[268] The divine promise of Exod 3:12 (in which the final "you" is plural) had now come to fulfillment, with the arrival of Moses and the people at Mount Sinai.

---

[267] Or "On the very day of the third new moon after . . ." Since they left Egypt on a full moon, the fact that they arrived on a full moon fixes the elapsed time as three (lunar) months.

[268] Another way to look at the timing of the encampment at Sinai is to trace its beginning to 16:1, which describes the Israelites as very near Sinai and which therefore indicates an encampment in the region of Sinai starting in the second month after the exodus. By simple arithmetic the Israelites then would have spent a full year "at" Sinai by the time they departed as described in Num 10:11. See B. J. Diebner, "Zum Afuenthalt 'Israels' am Sinai," *DBAT* 28 (1992/93): 58–67. Diebner regards the account of the duration of the encampment at Sinai as a fiction designed to show that the Israelites went through an entire ecclesiological year there; we would regard it as a fact pointing to God's gracious instruction of his people in the practice of worship throughout the months before they left Sinai in their new role of a covenant people ready to enter the promised land and live out the covenant responsibly.

(2) The Poetic Introduction to the Call to Covenant Holiness (19:3)

[3]Then Moses went up to God, and the LORD called to him from the mountain and said, "This is what you are to say to the house of Jacob and what you are to tell the people of Israel:

19:3 The verse appears to be poetical, displaying both metrical balance and parallelism throughout. This special poetic introduction gives vv. 4–6 a highlighted significance. Arranged stichometrically with explanation and translated precisely to show the poetic scheme, it lays out as follows:

Moses went up to God (ten Hb. syllables)
And Yahweh spoke aloud to him from the mountain (ten Hb. syllables)
    Saying (a two-syllable hinge connecting the two halves of the verse)
This you will say to the family of Jacob; (seven Hb. syllables)
You will tell the Israelites (seven Hb. syllables)[269]

By what is usually called synonymous parallelism, the first two clauses make the same essential point, namely, that Moses went up onto Mount Sinai[270] to listen to God's revelation; and the final two clauses make the same essential point as well, namely, that God told him what he was to say to the people of Israel. Note how "Yahweh" is paralleled to "God" *(ʾĕlōhîm)* just as "family of Jacob" (NIV "house of God") is paralleled by "Israelites" (*bĕnê yiśrāʾēl,* NIV "people of Israel"), so the second half of the verse is more overtly synonymous in its parallelism than is the first.

(3) The Special Call to Covenant Holiness (19:4–6)

[4]'You yourselves have seen what I did to Egypt, and how I carried you on eagles' wings and brought you to myself. [5]Now if you obey me fully and keep my covenant, then out of all nations you will be my treasured possession. Although the whole earth is mine, [6]you will be for me a kingdom of priests and a holy nation.' These are the words you are to speak to the Israelites."

This section summarizes the covenant, which will be spelled out more formally and in far greater measure in Exod 20–Lev 27.[271] It provides an opportunity for God to challenge the Israelites to enter into covenant with

---

[269] Assuming the *waw* introducing the final clause is a smoothing out of the poetry by scribes who did not realize it was actually a poem and not prose; otherwise, eight syllables.

[270] Throughout chaps. 19–33 Moses speaks with God only atop Mount Sinai; the transition in chap. 33 to the contact provided by the Tent of Meeting (33:7–11) represents both an opportunity and a compromise on the consistent previous pattern of locating all verbal encounters with Yahweh at the summit of the mountain. See D. Arichea, "Note: The Ups and Downs of Moses: Locating Moses in Exodus 19–33," *BT* 40 (1989): 244–46.

[271] On the terminology employed here (preamble, prologue, stipulations, sanctions) see "Excursus: The Exodus-Leviticus Covenant" at 20:1.

him. Their agreement would constitute a commitment in faith, in advance, to show their loyalty and gratitude by their obedience to his law.

19:4 This verse summarizes the preamble and prologue components of the Sinai covenant. It identifies the parties to the covenant ("I" and "you") as Yahweh and Israel and briefly reminds the recipients of how they came to be united with their God. The words "you yourselves have seen what I did to Egypt" encapsulate the entire story of the humiliation of Pharaoh and Egypt and the Egyptians through the plagues. "I carried you on eagles' wings" encapsulates the exodus itself, metaphorically describing the flight from Egypt as a soaring flight carried by an eagle. The words "and brought you to myself" express not merely the arrival at Sinai but the entering into covenant relationship (which is ultimately a family relationship)[272] with the only true God.

19:5–6 The stipulations component of the covenant format finds summary in the words "now if you obey me fully and keep my covenant," followed by a sanctions promise, "then out of all nations you will be my treasured possession."[273] "Although the whole earth is mine, you will be for me a kingdom of priests and a holy nation." Several important theological implications reside within the sanctions promises. First, although God is Creator and Father of all people and people groups, he announced here his intention to create for himself a particular people, a "treasured possession." This represents the separation of his chosen people from the general world population, or, stated in terms of the overall biblical plan of redemption, the beginning of the outworking of his intention to bring close to himself a people that will join him for all eternity as adopted members of his family. Second, full monotheism is expressed in the words "although the whole earth is mine." This is one of the clearest early statements of monotheism in the Bible[274] and certainly must have represented a sudden education for many

---

[272] On covenant relationship as kinship relationship, see F. M. Cross Jr., "Kinship and Covenant in Ancient Israel," in *From Epic to Canon: History and Literature in Ancient Israel* (Baltimore/London: Johns Hopkins University Press, 1998), 3–22.

[273] On the meaning of סְגֻלָּה (NIV, NRSV: "treasured possession"; HCSB: "own possession") and its derivation, see M. Greenberg, "Hebrew *segulla*: Akkadian *sikiltu*," *JAOS* 71 (1951): 172–74.

[274] Those still holding to the evolutionistic notion of a progression of biblical religion from polytheism to monotheism (full ethical monotheism emerging only during the Babylonian exile) will, of course, assume any such wording as this one to represent a late interpolation into the material. For a variety of views, some quite carefully nuanced, see: K. Baltzer, *The Covenant Formulary* (Philadelphia: Fortress, 1971); K. Galling, *Die Erwahlungstraditionen Israels,* BZAW 48 (Giessen: Verlag von Alfred Topelmann, 1928); E. Jacob, "Le peuple de Dieu (Ex 19,2–6a)," *AS* 42 (1970): 6–11; J. W. Klening, "On Eagles' Wing: An Exegetical Study of Exodus 19:2–8," *LTJ* 21 (1987): 18–27; R. Klopfer, "Zur Quellenscheidung in Exod. 19," *ZAW* 18 (1898): 197–235; R. Rendtorff, "Der Text in seiner Endgestalt: Uberlegungen zu Exodus 19," *Koch Festschrift,* 459–70; J. L. Ska, "Ex 19,3–8 et les pareneses deuteronomiques," *Biblische Theologie und gesellschaftlicher Wandel: Fur Norbert Lohfink* (Freiburg: Herder, 1993), 307–14.

of those present to hear Moses first relay these words to the people, since so many of them had grown up polytheists.[275]

Israel's assignment from God involved intermediation. They were not to be a people unto themselves, enjoying their special relationship with God and paying no attention to the rest of the world. Rather, they were to represent him to the rest of the world and attempt to bring the rest of the world to him.[276] In other words, the challenge to be "a kingdom of priests and a holy nation" represented the responsibility inherent in the original promise to Abraham in Gen 12:2–3: "You will be a blessing. I will bless those who bless you . . . and all peoples on earth will be blessed through you." Priests stand between God and humans to help bring the humans closer to God and to help dispense God's truth, justice, favor, discipline, and holiness to humans. Israel was called to such a function. How? The answer is not spelled out in the present context, but it surely was to take place in four ways: (1) Israel would be an example to the people of other nations, who would see its holy beliefs and actions and be impressed enough to want to know personally the same God the Israelites knew. (2) Israel would proclaim the truth of God and invite people from other nations to accept him in faith as shown by confession of belief in him and acceptance of his covenant, as Jethro had already done. (3) Israel would intercede for the rest of the world by offering acceptable offerings to God (both sacrifices and right behavior) and thus ameliorate the general distance between God and humankind.[277] (4) Israel would keep the promises of God, preserving his word already spoken and recording his word as it was revealed to them so that once the fullness of time had come, anyone in the whole world could promptly benefit from that great body of divinely revealed truth, that is, the Scriptures.[278]

---

[275] As far as can be determined, polytheism was the uniform religious viewpoint of ancient peoples, attempts to regard the religion of the Amarna pharaohs as monotheism notwithstanding (the Amarna religion was a modified type of henotheism, not monotheism). Thus the introduction of full-blown monotheism as part and parcel of the Sinai covenant was from a human point of view radically new to most of those gathered there.

[276] D. C. Van Zyl, "Exodus 19:3–6 and the Kerygmatic Perspective of the Pentateuch," *OTE* 5 (1992): 264–71. Cf. W. L. Moran, "A Kingdom of Priests," in *The Bible in Current Catholic Thought* (New York: Herder & Herder, 1962), 7–20; R. B. Y. Scott, "A Kingdom of Priests (Exodus xix 6)," *OTS* 8 (1950): 213–19; R. Martin-Achard, "Israel, peuple sacerdotal," *Verbum Caro* 18, no. 71–72 (1964): 11–28; G. Renaldi, "Un regno di sacerdoti," *BibOr* 7 (1965): 97–104; G. Barbiero, "*Mamleket kohanim* (Es 19:6a): i sacerdoti al potere?" *RivB* 37 (1989): 427–46.

[277] Cf. A. Wolff-Steger, "Auf Adlersflüglen—Die Erwählung Israels am Sinai: Exegese zu Exodus 19:1–6. It should be noted that election is always for a purpose; it represents a calling to a purposeful life of obedience, not merely the enjoyment of safety or comfort of some sort.

[278] Cf. Gal 3:29, "If you belong to Christ, then you are Abraham's seed, and heirs according to the promise." Further on the significance of the royal priesthood as described in v. 6, see J. A. Davies, "A Royal Priesthood: Literary and Intertextual Perspectives on an Image of Israel in Exodus 19:6," *TynBul* 63 (2002): 157–59.

Verse 6 ends with a command to Moses to be sure that the Israelites heard Yahweh's call to a covenant relationship ("these are the words you are to speak to the Israelites"), a command that found fulfillment immediately following.

(4) The Agreement of the People to Enter into Covenant with Yahweh (19:7–8)

[7]So Moses went back and summoned the elders of the people and set before them all the words the LORD had commanded him to speak. [8]The people all responded together, "We will do everything the LORD has said." So Moses brought their answer back to the LORD.

19:7 Establishing the pattern that would follow, Moses had gone up the mountain to hear from God (v. 3) and came down from the mountain to relay to the people God's will. He would go up again as v. 8 indicates.[279] Moses functioned as a faithful prophet, making up nothing on his own but simply relaying verbatim what God had given him to speak as his messenger ("summoned the elders of the people and set before them all the words the LORD had commanded him to speak"). This verse reminds the reader again of Israel's leadership structure, in which Moses did not typically deal with the people directly but with their leaders (elders), who represented the people in dealings with him (cf. 3:16,18; 4:29; 12:21; 17:5–6) or even with outsiders such as Jethro (18:12).[280]

19:8 But it was not merely the elders who agreed to enter into covenant with Yahweh. All the people did so ("The people all responded together, 'We will do everything the LORD has said'"), suggesting that the elders brought Moses' words throughout the congregation of Israel, required a response from everyone, and then brought the unanimously positive response back to Moses, who then brought it back up the mountain to God in preparation for actually saying the words in God's hearing ("So Moses brought their answer back to the LORD").[281] Was this sort of exercise necessary because Yahweh was a limited God who needed to wait to understand the thinking of his people or couldn't hear at a distance? Not at all. Rather, the formality of the process kept the people reminded that they were not dealing only with their elders or Moses or both but with the universe's only God, who was not approachable by just anyone, who was greater and more dangerous than any force they had ever

---

[279] The formal process of going up and down the mountain continues in the rest of the chapter.

[280] See, e.g., J. L. McKenzie, "The Elders in the Old Testament," *Bib* 48 (1959): 522–40.

[281] The NIV's loose translation obscures the intention, which was to show the reader that Moses conveyed verbatim the exact words of the people to God in the manner he also conveyed God's exact words to the people. The wording of the Hb. shows, in other words, in yet one more way how precisely Moses fulfilled the messenger role of a prophet.

otherwise known, and who was requiring of them in a patient, cadenced process their assent to the most important commitment they could make. Yahweh would hear their words of agreement only from his officially appointed spokesperson, Moses, so Moses brought those words to Yahweh.[282]

14. Consecration in Preparation for Meeting God (19:9–15)

[9]The LORD said to Moses, "I am going to come to you in a dense cloud, so that the people will hear me speaking with you and will always put their trust in you." Then Moses told the LORD what the people had said.

[10]And the LORD said to Moses, "Go to the people and consecrate them today and tomorrow. Have them wash their clothes [11]and be ready by the third day, because on that day the LORD will come down on Mount Sinai in the sight of all the people. [12]Put limits for the people around the mountain and tell them, 'Be careful that you do not go up the mountain or touch the foot of it. Whoever touches the mountain shall surely be put to death. [13]He shall surely be stoned or shot with arrows; not a hand is to be laid on him. Whether man or animal, he shall not be permitted to live.' Only when the ram's horn sounds a long blast may they go up to the mountain."

[14]After Moses had gone down the mountain to the people, he consecrated them, and they washed their clothes. [15]Then he said to the people, "Prepare yourselves for the third day. Abstain from sexual relations."

19:9 Moses learned of God's intention to make personal appearances to Moses in/by means of (or in the form of) a cloud, out of which the people could hear him speaking to Moses. Thus he would make plain to the people of Israel the fact of his communication to Moses, thus reducing the likelihood that the people would doubt Moses when he claimed to be delivering to them words from God. God wanted this confidence in Moses as his reliable prophet to be continuous and permanent ("so that the people will hear me speaking with you and will always put their trust in you"). Moses then told Yahweh the words the people had used in their agreement to enter into the covenant. Verse 8 mentioned his action in "bringing" the words to Yahweh. That referred to the process of going up the mountain with the message memorized. This verse refers to his actually saying the words of the people to Yahweh, that is, formally delivering their response to Yahweh's invitation to become his special covenant people.

19:10–11 Consecration means "making holy," which means "making acceptable to be close to God."[283] The consecration demanded of the Israelites

[282]This is, of course, not unlike prayer in general, which is not telling God anything he does not already know (Matt 6:8) but is responding to him according to a formal process of communication that he knows is appropriate and reminds humans of his sovereignty and their dependency.

[283]The most basic meaning of the word "holy" *(qādôš)* in Hb. is "belonging to God." In one way or another, anything that is correctly called holy is a thing that belongs specially to God.

in this instance involved becoming spiritually ready to get close to God (thus the two days of preparation indicated in the words "be ready by the third day") as well as eliminating that which was objectionable to God (thus the washing) and avoiding things that could distract from attention on God (thus the avoidance of sex required in v. 15). Does this verse, when coupled with v. 15, imply that getting dirty is evil or that having sex is evil? Not at all. Rather, it asserts that there are special occasions of prayerful preparation and worshipful activity that call for avoidance of the usual, nonsinful personal indulgences and demand special, focused, self-denying attention to God.[284] The common denominator is prayer: close focus upon God requires both time in prayer (three days in all, two of preparation and one of encounter) and an attitude of special attention to God (coming as clean and well dressed as one would in the case of appearing before anyone he or she wanted to honor) as well as a denial of things that focus on the self so that one can focus on God (v. 15, avoiding sex, which is intrinsically private and personal and not something properly done in connection with encounters with others outside of the marriage pair).

With proper warning of three days' notice, the people could expect a special revelation of God, a theophany on Mount Sinai ("The LORD will come down on Mount Sinai in the sight of all the people").[285] They had seen him regularly in the pillar of cloud/fire that went ahead of them during their wilderness travel so far, but these instructions suggest there would be something especially awesome about Yahweh's visible manifestation "in the sight of all the people" in the cloud at the top of the mountain.

19:12–13 Elaborate capital punishment rules kept the people from touching the mountain and even from touching anyone who ended up put to death for touching the mountain. Why? The answer is that God desired in this way to teach his people the seriousness of dealing with him. The mountain was his mountain, belonging to him, and thus was holy.[286] Although people specially prepared and consecrated to encounter God may approach him more closely than would otherwise be the case, no human in this world can get as close to him as any person in heaven can.[287] He has chosen to restrict his presence, manifesting it to a degree but not fully. One way to teach this to the Israelites so they would not foolishly think he was a human-

[284] OT holy war required temporary abstinence from sex (e.g., 1 Sam 21:4) and/or from food (1 Sam 14:28; 2 Sam 11:11); NT special times of prayer and/or prayer and fasting specify temporary avoidance of sex (1 Cor 7:5); and when fasting, obviously, of food.

[285] See "Excursus: The Theophany Structure of Exodus 3–4" at 3:1ff. for an introduction to the concept of OT theophany.

[286] Thus the standard term for Mount Sinai/Horeb was "Mountain of God" or, translated more simply, "God's Mountain" (Exod 3:1; 4:27; 18:5; 24:13; 1 Kgs 19:8).

[287] 1 Cor 13:12.

conceived god like an idol—who could be handled[288] or kissed[289] or otherwise manipulated physically or approached casually[290]—was to restrict access even to the mountain that God would touch in his theophany and to the "contagion" of touching anyone who had in fact touched the mountain. If a king required approaching with the greatest of care,[291] should not the King of Kings be honored even more carefully and respectfully? The boundary markers ("limits") placed around the base of the mountain served to prevent people in their daily course of grazing flocks and gathering manna and the like from straying thoughtlessly onto the actual edge ("foot") of the mountain.

Shooting to death (by arrows) or stoning to death served as penalties for trespass beyond the boundary markers. The latter was much more common than the former in ancient Israel.[292] Either penalty method kept those administering justice from even so much as touching the persons who had violated the command to stay back from the mountain; they could be put to death without contaminating those who had the responsibility to impose the penalty. An exception allowed for special invitation from God to his people to "go up to the mountain," meaning at and around its base but not further up the mountain, as a symbol of being allowed closer proximity to his holiness as he accepted his people into covenant with him and made them a more holy people. This was to be announced on the third day (19:16) by a sound like that of a horn ("ram's horn"), a divine signal not made by human lips on an actual horn/trumpet but made from the top of the mountain by God (19:16–19).

19:14–15 Having received the instructions to do so, Moses descended from the mountain and "consecrated" the people. As part of the two-day consecration in preparation for the third day, the people washed their clothes and abstained from sex.[293] Whatever else constituted the process of consecration in this case, we are not told. We may assume that Moses told the

---

[288] 2 Sam 6:6–7.

[289] 1 Kings 19:18; Hos 13:2.

[290] Cf. Exod 24:2; Lev 22:3; Num 17:13; note the description of the access to God of the Christian in Rom 5:2; Eph 2:18; 3:12, who nevertheless cannot approach him casually or disrespectfully.

[291] E.g., 2 Sam 14:33; 18:28; 24:20; 1 Kgs 1:16, 23, 31; Esth 4:11.

[292] On stoning to death as a punishment, cf. in the Pentateuch e.g., 21:28–29; Lev 20:2,27; 24:16; Num 15:36; 35:17; Deut 13:10; 17:5; 21:21; 22:21,24. Other examples of this punishment are described in the remainder of the OT. Shooting to death with arrows occurs almost exclusively as a divine punishment (2 Sam 22:15 = Pss 18:14; 64:7; 144:6; Ezek 5:16; indirectly through human agency, 2 Kgs 13:17; Jer 50:14). Both methods keep the punishers from actual physical contact with the trespasser in the situation of contact with the mountain in Exod 19.

[293] The Hb. lit. says "keep yourselves from women," worded this way because virtually all laws were addressed as if to men; the women understood that the laws applied to them as well, *mutatis mutandis*.

people to pray earnestly for their acceptance by God and to meditate upon the significance of the event they were about to take part in, but the *formal* signs of consecration were limited to getting clean and abstaining from physical indulgence.

For everyone to wash his or her clothes in a two-day period may have been a major undertaking. The water at Sinai was specially provided from the nearby cleft rock that Moses had named Massah and Meribah (17:1–7); how many people could gather around its pooling at once to wash their clothes is a matter of speculation. On the reasonable assumption that in the ancient world people did not wash clothes nearly so often as in the modern Western world, clothes washing may have been distributed over a period of weeks in the normal rotation at Sinai since obtaining water for animals and people could not be suspended but had to be maintained alongside any washing. Accordingly, the two-day clothes washing alone may have required long lines and a determined effort on everyone's part so that the whole people could be ready for their special covenantal encounter with Yahweh. In the arid desert climate, drying the clothes would have happened rapidly and without extensive effort. By the third day, the people were indeed consecrated (since the text explicitly says that Moses consecrated [past tense] them) and ready for one of the Bible's great encounters with the only true God and the awesomeness of his presence.

15. Meeting God on the Mountain (19:16–25)

**16On the morning of the third day there was thunder and lightning, with a
thick cloud over the mountain, and a very loud trumpet blast. Everyone in the
camp trembled. 17Then Moses led the people out of the camp to meet with God,
and they stood at the foot of the mountain. 18Mount Sinai was covered with
smoke, because the LORD descended on it in fire. The smoke billowed up from it
like smoke from a furnace, the whole mountain trembled violently, 19and the
sound of the trumpet grew louder and louder. Then Moses spoke and the voice of
God answered him.**

**20The LORD descended to the top of Mount Sinai and called Moses to the top
of the mountain. So Moses went up 21and the LORD said to him, "Go down and
warn the people so they do not force their way through to see the LORD and
many of them perish. 22Even the priests, who approach the LORD, must consecrate themselves, or the LORD will break out against them."**

23Moses said to the LORD, "The people cannot come up Mount Sinai, because you yourself warned us, 'Put limits around the mountain and set it apart as holy.'"

24The LORD replied, "Go down and bring Aaron up with you. But the priests and the people must not force their way through to come up to the LORD, or he will break out against them."

25So Moses went down to the people and told them.

19:16 From time to time speculation has been advanced to the effect that the phenomena described here on Mount Sinai indicate the eruption of a volcanic mountain, but little in the text supports such view, and the present verse counters it. The morning of the third day (lit., "on the third day, when morning came") dawned with thunder and lightning, neither of which need be characteristics of volcanic activity, as well as a "thick cloud over the mountain" (by which God manifested himself rather than a cloud that "hid" him) and a very loud trumpet sound. The cloud could certainly be thought appropriate to a volcanic eruption since huge smoke clouds are generated by active volcanoes, but not the trumpet sound.[294]

In fact, what Moses described here was a classic storm theophany, the manifestation of God in the form of a storm, something he first did in the Garden of Eden[295] and did on various occasions thereafter as described in Scripture.[296] This particular storm theophany took place on a mountain, thus giving rise to the volcano theory, but in fact there was no volcano involved. The fact that "everyone in the camp trembled" reflects not merely the combination of impressive sights and sounds (and perhaps already the impressive sensation of the earth trembling, if the mention of the mountain's trembling in v. 18 is intended as further description of what had been going on all morning, not just what happened subsequently) but the realization of God's impending presence and the dangers associated with it.

19:17 The trip from the Israelite encampment near the mountain to the foot of the mountain itself may have taken some hours, as the thousands of Israelites moved in organized fashion behind Moses. It is not clear whether they ringed the entire mountain or merely gathered around the base of one side, though the latter seems more probable. They were likely organized by tribes and families,[297] but otherwise may have been grouped in a large mass in preparation for watching Moses ascend the mountain and so that they

---

[294] Naturally, if one wishes to assume that what was in fact volcanic activity was later distorted in the telling into a divine encounter, one can also assume that the booming explosions associated with sudden eruptions within a volcanic crater could have been distorted in later telling into the sound of a horn/trumpet. But what is not consistent is that volcanic "booms" are short, and the biblical account describes long, generally continuous horn sounds (see on v. 19).

[295] On the erroneous translation "cool of the day" in Gen 3:8, which should be rendered "wind of the storm," see J. J. Niehaus, "In the Wind of the Storm: Another Look at Genesis iii 8," *VT* 44 (1994): 263–67; *God at Sinai* (Grand Rapids: Zondervan, 1995), 155–57.

[296] See comments on 9:13–35; cf. 1 Kgs 19:11ff.; Job 38:1; 40:6; Ps 83:15; Isa 29:6; 66:15; Jer 23:19; Ezek 1:4ff.; Nah 1:3.

[297] This assumption about the Israelite organization is based on the way the narrative itself seems to reflect a rather clear sense of tribe and family in various dealings. Cf. 1:1; 6:14ff.; 12:3,21. It also reflects the likelihood that the rigorous tribe/clan/family structure observed (still in the encampment at Sinai) in the census in Num 1 was not an entirely new development.

might hear his words all together as a group when he was speaking to them directly in the process of relaying messages between them and God, as implied in vv. 19,25 and in 20:19–20. Gathering together in one large body at the foot of the mountain may also have made it easier to keep the rule about not breaching the boundaries, since everyone was able to watch everyone else under such conditions, as opposed to having the people scattered around the entire base of the mountain where isolated groups or individuals might have been tempted in the absence of oversight to go partway up the slope for shade, a better view, or the like.

19:18–19 The text literally says, "As for Mount Sinai, smoke, all of it," suggesting that when the Israelites looked up the mountain, they saw virtually the whole engulfed in smoke rather than simply seeing smoke surrounding the pinnacle. The smoke also billowed upward as would be the case when smoke came out of the chimney/ceiling hole of a furnace, so the Israelites saw smoke surrounding the mountain as well as heading skyward from the top. God descended to the top of the mountain in the form of fire (not just "inside" some fire but "in fire" in the sense of "in the form of fire").[298] The language of "descending" here does not in itself support the view of a tiered universe in which heaven is above earth but rather is part of the necessarily spatial language of description of the intrusion of the divine into the spatial realm of earth (cf. Gen 11:5; Exod 34:5; Num 11:25; 12:5). "Come down" in this context thus means essentially "come from heaven to be specially present on earth" as with the angel in Matt 28:2.

The entire mountain quaked greatly, something all the Israelites would have felt and presumably have been terrified by.[299] This is a relatively typical part of the storm theophany as it takes place. Descriptions of other storm theophanies not uncommonly include earthquakes as well.[300] All this was accompanied by the sound of the horn/trumpet, apparently concomitant with the conversation of Moses and Yahweh (a better translation of v. 19 might be, "Then as the sound of the trumpet kept getting much louder, Moses was

---

[298] Cf. comments on 13:21–22, n. 16. Deut 4:24 provides the classic statement on this topic, "For Yahweh your God is a consuming fire." It is quite likely that the *beth* in the wording בָּאֵשׁ here in Exod 19:18 is the *beth essentiae,* to be translated here by "as" ("Yahweh descended on it as fire"). Once again the presence of God manifests itself through fire, as also in such contexts as Gen 15:17; Exod 3:2; 19:18; Deut 4:24; 5:24; 9:3; cf. J. K. Kuntz, *The Self-Revelation of God* (Philadelphia: Westminster, 1967), 96–100; S. Terrien, *The Elusive Presence* (San Francisco: Harper & Row, 1978), 109–12, 149–51; B. P. Robinson, "Moses at the Burning Bush," *JSOT* 75 (1997): 107–22; I. Wilson, *Out of the Midst of the Fire.*

[299] Cp. the way Matt 28:2 connects causally the arrival of the angel of the Lord at the garden tomb with the quaking of the earth.

[300] E.g., Judg 5:4; 2 Sam 22:8 = Ps 18:7; 1 Kgs 19:11; Pss 68:8; 77:18; 29:6; sometimes the theophany is not per se a storm theophany but still involves an earthquake, as in Zech 14:5.

speaking and God was answering him"). The Israelites saw all of this happening at once.

They also could hear and see that God was speaking to Moses and vice versa (i.e., they were conversing back and forth, something not made evident in the NIV translation), but the words spoken by God may not have been discernible since the proper translation of the last words of v. 19 may be "God was answering him by thunder" rather than the NIV's "the voice of God answered him." The Hebrew uses the expression *bĕqôl,* which could mean either "out loud" or "by thunder."[301] In the context the latter translation seems more likely. This is the beginning of the extended encounter with God at Sinai that Moses would experience, earning him the distinction of being the prophet with whom God spoke "face to face" (Exod 33:11; Deut 34:10).[302]

19:20 While the people stayed at the bottom of the mountain, Moses was called by God to meet with him at the top. God descended and Moses ascended to the point of contact. The summit of Mount Sinai thus became a temporary meeting place, a "sanctuary," where God and humans connected through the representation of Moses.[303]

19:21–22 Once again God instructed Moses to warn the people not to enter the holy area of the mountain itself. What might cause already-warned Israelites to try to get up the mountain? They may have been irresistibly attracted by the chance to see God (so they might think) and to know something of what "the gods know" (as in the appeal of Satan's temptation to Adam and Eve).[304] So many Israelites were naïve theologically, and so many in the group were new even to whatever Israelite traditions existed[305] that there was surely a real danger of people trying to follow Moses up the

---

[301] It is well established that the feminine plural form *qōlōt* can mean "thunder." On the masculine singular form *qôl* as thunder, cf. Job 37:2,4–5; 40:9; Ps 77:17–18. Note that it almost surely means thunder in Gen 3:8 as well (see J. J. Niehaus, *VT* 44 [1994]: 263–67; *God at Sinai*, 155–57).

[302] Israel also had the experience of dealing "face to face" with God ("The LORD spoke to you face to face out of the fire on the mountain," Deut 5:4), meaning "directly," and not implying that Israel (or Moses) actually saw God but rather saw a manifestation of his presence and knew they were dealing with him directly. See also the following note.

[303] That it was a sanctuary, a holy place where God's presence was specially manifested, is shown by the requirement that the people stay outside and be represented by a priest, Moses, as well as the obvious fact that God revealed himself there. The tabernacle and temple became more permanent sanctuaries, replaced eventually by the superior arrangement of the body of Christ (how can God not be present if his body is?) and ultimately and perfectly by heaven, where as Paul notes in 1 Cor 13:12, believers will see God "face to face" forever.

[304] Gen 3:5. In that original temptation the false promise was that good would come out of extensive knowledge. Instead, what happened was a greater level of intellectual faculty than human moral faculty could deal with. The merism "good and evil" in Gen 2 and 3 is a way of saying "everything"—not all knowledge but all sorts of knowledge, including knowledge in areas where humans are not equipped to deal morally with it.

[305] Again the implication of Exod 12:38 cannot be forgotten: most of the non-Israelites newly integrated into the nation would have known only pagan perspectives on connecting with the divine, i.e., the sort of thing exemplified in Gen 11:1–4.

mountain to satisfy their curiosity about things divine and to "get in on" the excitement of the moment. The fire, cloud, and thunder all served to help diminish this hubris by making frightening the thought of carrying out such a plan.

"Even the priests, who approach the LORD"[306] could not presume to go up the mountain or to even appear at its base without having consecrated themselves just as the rest of the people had (vv. 10,14–15). Except for Aaron the priests were in the same position as the people in being barred from going up the mountain (cf. v. 24). The threat that *many* would *perish* or that the Lord would "break out against them" is the same threat: the possibility of death as a penalty for trying to force one's way into God's presence.[307] God knew that not all the people would be so foolhardy to disobey the boundary rules, so he warns about *many* perishing rather than the people in general. The language implies nevertheless that there were many who, given the chance, might have failed to take the warning seriously enough—an indication of the need for the people further to develop their will to obey.

19:23 Moses' response to God ("the people cannot come up Mount Sinai") suggests one of two possibilities here, there being not enough data in the text to discern which is the more likely: either he was attempting to convey the attitude of the people as faithfully as he could, being the intercessor between them and God, or he was questioning the need to reinform the people of what they already knew, thus, in effect, protesting against the need to go back down the mountain to speak once again to the people.[308] If the latter option is correct, then just as in the case of 5:22–6:12, Moses was instructed to be sure to take God's message to the people after he had launched a protest to God: the protest was, in other words, ineffective in changing God's mind no matter how earnestly Moses may have made it. Note also that the prohibition against the people's coming up to Mount Sinai (not even starting up the base) is parallel to that given to Moses by God himself in 3:5 ("Do not come any closer"). At any rate, Moses properly alluded to God's words

---

[306] The phrase "who approach the LORD" may be used proleptically here in the sense of "who will approach the LORD," since the duties of the priests were not yet formally instituted, but it is more likely that the phrase reflects the fact that Aaron and his sons were already beginning to assume the roles of priests, something that will be confirmed later in Exodus. Alternatively, the warning may apply to individuals who to this point had been functioning as priests among the people, without the benefit of a regulated priesthood as established later.

[307] On "break out against" (פרץ ב) as an idiomatic way of connoting "attack," cf. 2 Sam 5:20; 6:8; 1 Chr 15:13; Jer 4:4; 21:2. Naturally, if God attacks someone, it is not likely that he will fail to inflict whatever punishment is inherent in the attack, including death. V. 21 uses the euphemism "fall" (נפל; NIV, interpretively, "perish"), and this verse uses the euphemism "break out against," but both rather clearly connote "put to death" in the context.

[308] On his former protests against something God called him to do, cf. 4:13; 5:22–23; 6:12,30; 17:4; and the implications as discussed in the commentary on 4:24–26.

as the basis for the prohibition and the recognition that there was no way the prohibition could be safely ignored. The words "put limits around the mountain and set it apart as holy" may be a direct quote of what Yahweh had earlier said to Moses but which Moses saved for this point in the narrative in the interests of efficiency, or they may simply summarize 19:10–15 without intending to suggest a verbatim quote of previous divine speech.

19:24–25 God's intention was that Moses hear the Ten Words[309] (the Ten Commandments) with the people since they would be audible to everyone and Moses would not be required to be at the summit to hear them. So he sent Moses back down to the people and priests who were stationed at the bottom of the mountain. The command to "go down and bring Aaron up with you" must not be understood to mean "bring Aaron up with you right away" but rather represents part of the plan for eventually bringing Aaron and others (the high priestly family and elders, 24:1–4; Joshua, 24:13) up the mountain on subsequent occasions. It was, in other words, a call for Aaron to ascend the mountain with Moses the next time Moses went back up rather than an indication that Aaron would either immediately or always be with Moses when he was atop Sinai.

Once again the warning to all others in Israel against trying to ascend the mountain carried the death penalty with it ("or he will break out against them," cf. comments on v. 22). In this way God effectively reminded the people of the significance of coming into his presence. Under normal conditions even specially sanctified people (19:10–11,14–15) can come only somewhat near his presence, but with God's own permission, some can more closely enter his presence. For God to be willing to enter *their* presence, dwelling within *them,* would be extraordinary under the terms of the Old Covenant relationship of God with his people but, *mirabile dictu,* is routine in the New Covenant.[310]

The wording of v. 25, "So Moses went down to the people and told them," is a simple, direct way to end the prelaw narrative portion of the book of Exodus on two themes: the awesomeness of God (since what he told them related to that awesomeness, to wit, the danger of trying to breach God's holiness) and the readiness of Moses and the people together at the bottom of Mount Sinai to hear God's Ten Words of covenant thundered at them from the top of the mountain—God's very words audible comprehensibly to all from the great height of the Mountain of God.

---

[309] On this term see comments on 20:1 in contrast to 21:1.

[310] Thus Jesus asserted that great as John the Baptist was among the Old Covenant worthies, the least individual in the kingdom of heaven is even greater because the indwelling of God through his Spirit is such a spiritual advantage for any person, an advantage uniformly granted in the New Covenant to all converts, not just those of distinction (Matt 11:11 and par). Possession of the Spirit and access to God are hallmarks of the superiority of the New Covenant to the Old.

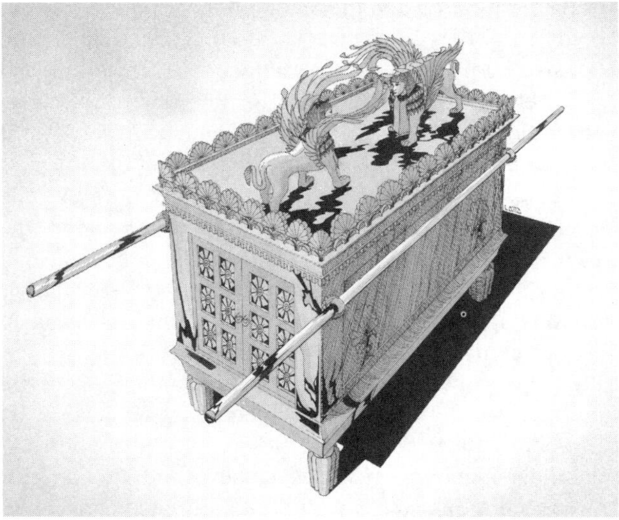

Reconstruction of the ark of the covenant drawn in the Egyptian style, reflecting 400 years of bondage in Egypt.

Reconstruction of the Israelite tabernacle and its court. The court was formed by curtains attached to erect poles. In front of the tent was placed the altar of burnt offerings and the laver. The tabernacle was always erected to face the east, so this view is from the northeast.

DIVISION OUTLINE

VI. COVENANT LAW (20:1–31:18) [CONTINUED IN THE BOOK OF LEVITICUS]

Excursus: The Exodus-Leviticus Covenant

1. The Ten Words and Their Significance (20:1–17)

   Excursus: The Paradigmatic Nature of Biblical Law

   (1) Preamble and Prologue (20:1–2)

   (2) The Ten Commandments (20:3–17)

      First Word/Commandment: No Gods other than Yahweh (20:3)

      Second Word/Commandment: No Idolatry (20:4–6)

   Excursus: The Attractions of Idolatry

      Third Word/Commandment: Speak Yahweh's Name Respectfully and Honestly (20:7)

      Fourth Word/Commandment: Observe the Sabbath in a Holy Way (20:8–11)

      Fifth Word/Commandment: Honor Father and Mother (20:12)

      Sixth Word/Commandment: You Must Not Murder (20:13)

      Seventh Word/Commandment: You Must Not Commit Adultery (20:14)

      Eighth Word/Commandment: You Must Not Steal (20:15)

      Ninth Word/Commandment: You Must Not Give False Testimony (20:16)

      Tenth Word/Commandment: You Must Not Covet Another's Possessions (20:17)

   (3) The People's Fear (20:18–21)

   (4) Response to God's Commands: Proper Worship (20:22–26)

2. The Covenant Code and Its Ratification (21:1–24:18)

   (1) Laws on Servants (21:1–11)

   Excursus: Slavery and Slave Laws in Ancient Israel

      Introductory Title for the Book of the Covenant (21:1)

      Time-Limited Service (21:2–4)

      Voluntary Permanent Service (21:5–6)

      Protections for Female Servants (21:7–11)

   (2) Laws on Injuries to People and Animals (21:12–36)

      Intentional and Unintentional Homicide Laws (21:12–14)

      Capital Punishment Laws against Assault on Parents, Kidnapping, and Cursing Parents (21:15–17)

      Laws on Life-Threatening Injury (21:18–21)

Laws Relating to Causing Permanent Injury (21:22–27)

Excursus: Talion Law *(lex talionis* or *ius telionis)*

Laws about Injuries Caused by or to Animals (21:28–36)

(3) Laws on Property (22:1–17)

Four Laws on Restitution for Theft, Along with a Note on Defense against Burglary (22:1–4)

Two Laws on Restitution for Damages from Neglect (22:5–6)

Laws Governing Property Responsibility Disputes (22:7–15)

Laws about Premarital Sex and the Bride Price (22:16–17)

(4) Social and Religious Requirements (22:18–23:9)

Three Characteristically Capital Crimes (22:18–20)

Laws against Not Loving One's Neighbor, with God as Enforcer (22:21–27)

Laws Requiring Respect for God's Holiness (22:28–31)

Laws on Honesty, Justice, and Fair Treatment with a Reminder That God Is Enforcer (23:1–9)

(5) Laws on Sabbaths and Annual Religious Festivals (23:10–19)

Two Six-Seven Laws on Sabbath Years and Days (23:10–12)

A General Warning to Keep the Covenant and Trust Yahweh Alone (23:13)

Laws on the Three Annual Festivals and Their Purpose (23:14–19)

(6) Instructions to Obey God during and after the Conquest (23:20–33)

Promise of the Angel of Yahweh to Lead the Way to the Promised Land (23:20–23)

Requirements and Promises Related to Worshiping the True God Exclusively (23:24–30)

Final Covenant Code Promises (of a Great Nation in a New Land) and Warnings (Against Idolatry/Polytheism) (23:31–33)

(7) Documentation of the Covenant and God's Confirming Glory (24:1–11)

(8) Introduction to Laws on the Tabernacle and Worship (24:12–18)

3. Laws on the Means of Worship (25:1–31:18)

(1) Laws on Donations for the Tabernacle Furnishings (25:1–9)

(2) Laws on Construction and Use of the Ark (25:10–22)

VI. COVENANT LAW (20:1–31:18)

Exodus has a classically bifid structure. Its first half (chaps. 1–19) tells the narrative of Israel's miraculous rescue from slavery in Egypt and successful flight to Mount Sinai, all in fulfillment of God's promise. Its second half introduces the Sinai Covenant (in 20:1–31:18), a formal, solemn expression of God's relationship to his people and theirs to him, and then continues on to describe Israel's rebellion against that covenant, subsequent renewal to it, and the fulfillment of its stipulations concerning the tabernacle (32:1–40:38). Thus the first half of Exodus is all about rescue from forced service to a pagan nation, and the second half is all about proper service for the one true God by keeping his covenant.

Excursus: The Exodus-Leviticus Covenant

The strictly covenant portion of the book (20:1–31:18) finds completion not in Exodus but in the book of Leviticus as indicated by the closing words of Leviticus, "These are the commands the LORD gave Moses on Mount Sinai for the Israelites" (Lev 27:34). In other words, Exodus gets the Sinai covenant underway but does not complete it. Indeed, the laws in Numbers continue the process of revelation of legal guidance under the covenant made at Sinai, as the Israelites experienced the need for divine guidance on matters not yet revealed even as of the end of Leviticus.[1]

The legal portion of Exodus is patterned after those of ancient covenants known as "suzerainty treaties," where a conqueror made a treaty with the conquered in which he "benefited" them with his protection and care as long as they would abide by the treaty stipulations.[2] Such covenants normally have six parts, summarized here with the coordinates that relate the structure to Exodus:

1. Preamble: which identifies the giver and recipients of the covenant ("the LORD your God," 20:2)
2. Prologue: a reminder of the relationship of the suzerain to the people ("who brought you out of Egypt," 20:2)
3. Stipulations: various laws/obligations on the part of the people (20:3–23:19; 25:1–31:18)
4. List of witnesses to the covenant ["I am Yahweh," Exod 29:46; 31:13; Lev 11:44][3]
5. Document clause: providing for writing down of the covenant so that periodic reading and relearning of the covenant can take place as time goes by (see Exod 24:4,7,12)
6. Sanctions: blessings and curses as incentives for obedience (see Exod 20:5–6,12,24; 23:20–31; cf. Lev 26:3–14 [blessings]; 26:14–39 [curses]; 26:40–45 [restoration blessings]).

---

[1] The supplemental instructions in Numbers are not secondary in importance; they are more like the various amendments to the Constitution of the United States, which include the famous Bill of Rights. Many of the laws in Numbers were indeed revealed by God after the Israelites left Sinai, but not as secondary "afterthoughts." They were, rather, a variety of statutes memorably imposed during the wilderness wanderings in response to specific needs as they arose. See, e.g., Num 15:32–36; 27:1–11; 36:1–12.

[2] This is precisely what Yahweh did for Israel: they were not on equal terms with him but took instead the role of vassals to a suzerain—a great king who rescued them and then gave (graciously dictated to) them the terms under which they could enjoy his benefits if they kept his commands.

[3] In the Deuteronomy covenant the primary witness to the covenant is Yahweh, but "heaven and earth" and "these words" and "you yourselves" are also found as secondary or backup witnesses. In Exodus-Leviticus, however, it is Yahweh who is the exclusive witness. Therefore, he is both the main character of the preamble as well as of the witness list, in contrast to the usual situation in other ANE covenants, where the king is the main character in the preamble, and various gods are the primary witnesses. Such a polytheistic approach would be completely out of place in Yahweh's covenant, which recognizes both explicitly and implicitly his sole divinity and ultimate kingship.

Only four of the six covenant ingredients are found in Exodus, mainly in what is usually called the Covenant Code (20:1–23:32). This is because Exodus is only the first portion of the full covenant that continues on in Leviticus and receives supplemental stipulations in Numbers.[4] Moreover, the Sinai Covenant is only the first statement of the full Pentateuchal or Mosaic Covenant, which finally concludes at the end of Deuteronomy. Nevertheless, already in Exodus the essential elements of the covenant are obvious: the revelation of who God is and what he wants of his people[5] and obedience to God as the path of covenant loyalty and thus of its blessings.[6]

1. The Ten Words and Their Significance (20:1–17)

Nothing in Exodus 20 is described as "commandment" or "law" or the like.[7] To be sure, the words presented here by God do indeed command his people most solemnly to act in ways that are basic to his covenant, but their significance goes beyond that of routine "laws." What the chapter contains—in particular, the Ten "Words" *(dĕbārîm)*—is more like the content of a national constitution than merely the content of one section of codified law or another. If the American legal corpus is used as an analogy, it could be said that the ten "words" of Exod 20 are somewhat like the Constitution of the

---

[4] Again in defense of the importance of the book of Numbers, the supplemental instructions in Numbers are not secondary in importance; they are more like the various amendments to the US Constitution, which include the Bill of Rights. Many of the laws in Numbers were indeed revealed by God after the Israelites left Sinai, but not as "afterthoughts." They were, rather, a variety of statutes memorably imposed during the wilderness wanderings in response to specific needs that arose.

[5] As E. Otto points out, one very distinct and obvious difference between the Israelite covenant law and the somewhat similar laws found among the Hittites and Mesopotamians is simply the way Israelite law consistently declared its origins in God, whereas the other laws took their authority from a king. This king was considered to be acting in the role of a mediator of the law on behalf of a divine figure but was nevertheless the promulgator of the law, which did not come directly from a god or goddess ("Korperverletzung in hethitischen und israelitischen Recht: Rechts- und religionhistorische Aspekte," *Religiongeschichtliche Beziehungen zwischen Kleinasien, Nordsyrien und dem Alten Testament,* OBO 129 [Freiburg: University Press, 1993], 391–425).

[6] A number of scholars have challenged the idea that the Exodus-Leviticus and/or Deuteronomic covenants reflect the structure of the second-millennium treaty covenants of the ANE, a connection that had been convincingly presented by G. E. Mendenhall (*Law and Covenant in Israel and the Ancient Near East* [Pittsburgh: Presbyterian Board of Colportage, 1955], also in *BA* 17 [1954]: 26–46, 49–76). Mendenhall has updated his conclusions in his article, coauthored with G. Herion in *ABD* ("Covenant") in which he suggests that the presentation of the form in the Bible is somewhat altered to reflect neo-Assyrian elements but still preserves elements that can only be second millennium in provenance. Our position holds that the elements thought to be neo-Assyrian (i.e., not exactly typical of second-millennium treaties) are simply the specific Israelite adaptations made by Yahweh through Moses, rather than having late extrabiblical origins at all. Cf. also R. D. Miller II, *Moses and Mendenhall in Traditio-Historical Perspective, IBS* 23 (2001): 146–66.

[7] Though it is possible that the Ten Commandments/Words are so described later by God himself. See comments on 24:12.

United States (legally binding in a most basic, foundational way but more than a mere set of individual laws) and the laws that follow (cf. 21:1, "These are the laws you are to set before them") somewhat analogous to the various sections of federal law dealing with all sorts of particular matters that have been enacted legislatively over time. The one group is absolutely "constitutional" or "foundational"; the other is specifically regulatory, following from the principles articulated in the more basic "constitution." It is both traditional and convenient to call them "the Ten Commandments," as long as their special nature is recognized. Indeed, in the comment Moses spoke following the repeat of the Ten Commandments in Deut 5:6–21, he explicitly again called them "words" (lit., "These are the words *[dĕbārîm];* NIV, inexplicably, "commandments"] the LORD proclaimed in a loud voice to your whole assembly there on the mountain," Deut 5:22).

The biblical commandments occur in three levels of specificity. At the most comprehensive level are the "two great commandments" of Deut 6:5 ("Love the LORD your God with all your heart and with all your soul and with all your strength") and Lev 19:18b ("love your neighbor as yourself"). The first of these commands requires in broad terms a loyal, covenantal obedience to God, who is put first above all other relationships.[8] The second requires loving (loyal) treatment of other human beings. Jesus gave his approval to what had

---

[8] From W. L. Moran's article "The Ancient Near Eastern Background of the Love of God in Deuteronomy" (*CBQ* 77 [1963]: 77–87) come the following citations demonstrating the idiomatic sense of "loving" God and "loving" neighbor as self. To love in such contexts does not refer primarily to emotional attachment but rather to active *loyalty,* to a commitment to be someone's ally and supporter regardless of how one might "feel" about that person.

1. (G. Dossin, *Archives royales de Mari* V 76:4): (To Yasmah-Adad, King of Mari, 18th c. BC [writer of the letter unknown]): "I am the king's servant and the one who <u>loves</u> you."

2. J. A. Knudtzon, *Die El-Amarna Tafeln* [=EA] 53:40–44 (Tushratta, king of Mitanni, to Pharaoh): "My lord, just as I <u>love</u> the king my lord, so do the king of Nuhashshe, the king of Ni'i . . .—all these kings are servants of my lord."

3. EA 114:68 (Rib-Addi of Byblos to Pharaoh): "Who will <u>love</u> if I die?"

4. EA 138:71–73 (Rib-Addi of Byblos to Pharaoh): "Behold the city! Half of it <u>loves</u> the sons of Abdi-Ashirta, half of it my lord."

5. EA 83: 47–51 (Rib-Addi of Byblos to Pharaoh): "If you send me no answer, I will leave the city and go away with the people who <u>love</u> me."

6. D. J. Wiseman, *Iraq* 20 (1958): 49, col. iv 266–68 (Esarhaddon to various vassal kings requiring them to be loyal to his son and successor Assurbanipal): "You will <u>love</u> Assurbanipal as yourselves."

7. L. Waterman, Royal Correspondence of the Assyrian Empire 266, 1105:32 (Oath imposed by Assurbanipal on his vassal kings just before going to war with Shamash-shum-ukin, his brother, in Babylon): "The king of Assyria, our lord, we will <u>love</u>."

8. 1 Kgs 5:15 [Eng. 5:1]: "Because Hiram had been a <u>lover</u> of David all his life" (כִּי אֹהֵב הָיָה הִירָם לְדָוִד כָּל־הַיָּמִים).

become in Judaism an understanding of the importance of the two great commandments as summations of all the others.[9]

He also specifically indicated that the rest of the commandments "hang on" these two (Matt 22:40). How so? The first four of the Ten Commandments hang on the command to love God since they describe ways to show covenant loyalty directly to him. The final six hang on the command to love neighbor as self, which Jesus also explained as doing to others as you would have them do to you (Matt 7:12). Thus the first four "vertical" commandments are balanced by the final six "horizontal commandments." Then, in order of hierarchy, follow all the others. The order is, then, the two, the ten, and the six hundred and one.[10] Some of the large group of six hundred and one remaining commandments address "vertical" concerns; others speak of the "horizontal."

Excursus: The Paradigmatic Nature of Biblical Law

Modern societies generally have opted for exhaustive law codes. That is, every action modern society wishes to regulate or prohibit must be specifically mentioned in a separate law. Under the expectations of this exhaustive law system, state and/or federal law codes run to thousands of pages and address thousands of individual actions by way of requirement or restriction or control or outright banning of those actions. By this approach, all actions are permitted that are not expressly forbidden or regulated. Thus it is not uncommon that criminals in modern Western societies evade prosecution because of a "technicality" or a "loophole" in the law—their undesirable actions are not *exactly* prohibited or regulated by a written law, so they cannot be convicted even though an objective observer may be convinced that what they did surely deserved punishment.

Ancient laws did not work this way. They were paradigmatic, giving models of behaviors and models of prohibitions/punishments relative to those behaviors, but they made no attempt to be exhaustive. Ancient laws gave guiding principles, or samples, rather than complete descriptions of all things regulated. Ancient people were expected to be able to extrapolate from what the sampling of laws did say to the *general* behavior the laws in their totality pointed toward. Ancient judges were expected to extrapolate from the wording provided in the laws that did exist to *all other* circumstances and not to be foiled in their jurisprudence by any such concepts as "technicalities" or "loopholes." When common sense told

[9] Luke 10:25–28; Mark 12:28–34; Matt 19:19 suggest that Jesus routinely taught the hierarchy of commandments, Deut 6:5 and Lev 19:18 being primary, and the Ten Words/Commandments following as explications of the two.

[10] Traditional Judaism counts six hundred and thirteen commandments in the rest of the Pentateuch. Following this enumeration, all the others are six hundred and one. This is merely a convenience; there is nothing especially meaningful, and certainly nothing sacred, about such a numbering.

judges[11] that a crime had been committed, they reasoned their way from whatever the most nearly applicable law specified to a decision as to how to administer proper justice in the case before them. Citizens of ancient Israel, and especially its judges, had to learn to extrapolate from whatever laws they had received from Yahweh to whatever justice-challenging situation they were dealing with. The number of laws dealing with any given application of justice might be few, but that would not prevent justice from being applied. It would simply have been the case that all parties were expected to appeal for guidance to those laws that did exist, whether or not expressed specifically in terms that dealt with the case under consideration. In other words, the Israelites had to learn to see the underlying principles in any law and not let the specifics of the individual casuistic citation mislead them into applying the law too narrowly.

God's revealed covenant law to Israel was paradigmatic. No Israelite could say: "The law says I must make restitution for stolen oxen or sheep [Exod 22:1], but I stole your goat. I don't have to pay you back," or "The law says that anyone who attacks his father or mother must be put to death [Exod 21:15], but I attacked my grandmother, so I shouldn't be punished," or "The law says that certain penalties apply for hitting someone with a fist or a stone [Exod 21:18], but I kicked my neighbor with my foot and hit him with a piece of wood, so I shouldn't be punished." Such arguments would have insulted the intelligence of all concerned and made no impact on those rendering judgments. It is in connection with the paradigmatic nature of Israel's covenant law that Jesus, following the established tradition in Judaism, could make so sweeping an assertion as that two laws sum up all the rest (see above). Properly understood, two laws do indeed sum up *everything* in the entire legal corpus of the Old Testament. So do ten laws (the Ten Words/Commandments); so do all six hundred and thirteen. The numbers go no higher, nor would they need to. If a reasonable number of comprehensive and comprehensible laws (as few as two, as many as six hundred and thirteen) are provided to a people as paradigms for proper living, there is no excuse for that people to claim ignorance of how to behave or to claim innocence when their sins are found out.

Most laws are expressed as commands in the masculine singular—the *you* of the laws is "you, a male person"—from a technical, grammatical point of view. But here again the reader/listener would not have the slightest ground to say, "It prohibits individual men from doing such and such, but I'm a woman/we're a group, so the wording of the law exempts me/us." Implicit in the wording is the need for paradigmatic extrapolation to all persons, singular or plural, male or female.

---

[11] It was no accident that judges were selected and in place already in Exod 18 before the covenant was even given to the Israelites. Without judges to extrapolate from the guiding principles of the law, the application of the covenant stipulations would have been impossible. Judges applied the principles found in the legal paradigms (laws) to the specific situations brought to them in court cases and rendered verdicts that were in accord with the guidelines of the laws, but not necessarily verdicts that were actually mentioned verbatim in the law since the cases themselves were not necessarily exactly those described in the samplings the law provides.

Within the New Covenant, the paradigm of the two great laws is summarized as the "Law of Christ" (Gal 6:2). Because of the help of the Holy Spirit, the need to memorize and remember six hundred and thirteen commandments is obviated. The law is no longer a matter of (paradigmatic) guidelines written externally on tablets of stone. It is now a matter of a clear sense of loving God and neighbor written on the mind by God's Spirit (Jer 31:31–34; cf. Rom 2:15) in accordance with the two commandments that always summed up God's will and/or the ten that in the Old Covenant were graciously given to clarify the two.

One may ask, "If the commands to love God with one's whole heart and to love neighbor as self are the two greatest, why weren't these the first commandments spoken at Sinai? Why did one of them ("love your neighbor as yourself," Lev 19:18) come later to the attention of the Israelites rather subtly, without fanfare, in the midst of the levitical "Holiness Code" (Lev 19–26) and the other ("love the LORD your God with all your heart," Deut 6:5) almost forty years later, in the new generation's law code, Deuteronomy? The answer is disarmingly simple: too many people could not appreciate the two great commandments except in reference to the others, including the ten principal expressions thereof, the Ten Words/Commandments of Exod 20. That is, without an awareness of all six hundred and thirteen commandments and seeing within them the high standards of God's holiness and his particular required and/or banned behaviors enumerated, a person corrupted by a fallen world does not easily get the point of what the two great commandments are intended to summarize. Once one has learned the breadth and depth of God's expectations for his holy people, however, the two greatest commandments serve brilliantly as comprehensive reminders of all that is expected of God's covenant people. This is the point of the law of Christ in the New Covenant. It is not an amorphous, contentless concept but a way of summarizing full obedience to everything Christ taught, demonstrated and reinforced from elsewhere in Scripture.

A final implication of paradigmatic law: not all laws will be equally comprehensive in scope. That is, some will be very broad in their applicability (love Yahweh your God) and some much more narrow (do not bear false witness). One might ask, "Why not say 'don't be dishonest in any way,' which would be broader and more comprehensive than 'don't bear false witness'?" But that would be missing the way paradigmatic law works: through a somewhat randomly presented admixture of rather specific examples of more general behaviors and very general regulations of broad categories of behavior, the reader/listener comes to understand that all sorts of situations not exactly specified (either because a law is so broad or so narrow) are also implicitly covered. In other words, when all the laws are considered together, one's impression is that both the very narrow, precise issues and the very broad, general issues fall under the purview of God's covenant. The wide variability of comprehensiveness is intended to help the person desiring to keep the covenant to say, "I now see that in the tiniest detail as well as in the widest, most general way, I am expected to try to keep this law—in all its implications, not just in terms of its exact wording." Some commandments are thus less broad in scope *in the way they are expressed* than is necessary to cover all the intended actions; others are so broad in scope *in the way they are expressed* that one could never think up all the ways they might be applied. This is just as it should be. The narrow and the broad taken together suggest the overall comprehensiveness of God's covenant will for his people.[12]

(1) Preamble and Prologue (20:1–2)

[1]And God spoke all these words:
[2]"I am the LORD your God, who brought you out of Egypt, out of the land of slavery.

20:1 This verse specially emphasizes that God[13] spoke the Ten Words/ Ten Commandments himself directly to Israel rather than through the intermediation of Moses. So frightening was this for the people to experience that as soon as God had finished, they demanded no further direct audition of God's commands (20:19). Part of their reason may have been their sense of sin and guilt once they heard the sort of standards to which they would be held by the covenant God was making with them, but the stated and therefore main reason was simply that hearing God's voice overwhelmed them (20:18) so that they feared they would die if they had to keep enduring it ("Do not have God speak to us or we will die," 20:19). The uniform witness of the Old Testament accounts of the revelation of the Ten Words at Mount Sinai (this and 20:18–19; Deut 4:10–14,32–40; 5:4,22–27; 9:10; Neh 9:13) includes the same sort of emphasis, that is, that the people heard the voice of God for themselves and thus could not doubt his presence among them,[14] a presence more directly manifest at Sinai than in any other mode previously since they had first learned of his interest in them (2:25; 4:31). All the people were hearing the voice of God just as Adam, Eve, Noah, Abraham, and the patriarchs had heard it and as Moses had heard it earlier at Mount Sinai when God first called him. And this time the voice of God was accompanied

---

[12] An obvious parallel in the NT is Paul's lists of gifts in Rom 12 and 1 Cor 12. Some gifts are narrow in scope; others are broad. Moreover, the two lists are not identical (any more than the laws of Exodus-Leviticus and Deuteronomy are identical). But as a paradigm for the entire corpus of gifts, Paul's lists eloquently tell the reader that any and all special abilities a person has been given by God that could help build up his church should be developed and employed to that end.

[13] The LXX uses κύριος (the normal equivalent of Yahweh) here rather than the expected θεός (God), something that is more likely to represent an inner-Greek translation choice or even corruption than a witness to a genuine variant in the Hebrew.

[14] J. I. Durham, *Exodus,* WBC (Waco: Word, 1987), 283; cf. R. Alter's analysis of the phenomena represented in chap. 20 in *The Art of Biblical Narrative* (New York: Basic, 1981), 131–54.

by such audio and visual displays (19:16–19; 20:18–21) as to leave no doubt in their minds as to both his presence and his uniqueness.[15]

20:2 The preamble and prologue to the Sinai Covenant appear here. The preamble, the portion of a covenant that identifies the parties to the agreement, occurs in the first clause and identifies Israel as the recipient, that is, "you," by the second-person singular pronouns (further identification being unnecessary; Israel knew very well who they were). "The LORD your God" is identified as the giver of the covenant.[16] This, then, is a two-party covenant, linking Yahweh and his people in formal legal relationship. Israel is represented by singular pronouns, not only because "singularity" is typical in the direct address of ancient legal material but because the entire nation is viewed as an entity, a united people responding as one to God's commands.[17]

The prologue, the part of a covenant that explains how the parties came to be related, is indicated in the second clause of the verse ("who brought you out of Egypt, out of the land of slavery").[18] By reason of having rescued Israel

---

[15] As might be anticipated, scholars who approach the material from a humanistic viewpoint would dismiss the text's claim that God actually spoke the words. An example of such skepticism is found in D. J. A. Clines, "The Ten Commandments, Reading from Left to Right," in *Words Remembered, Texts Renewed: Essays in Honor of John F. A. Sawyer,* JSOTSup 195 (Sheffield: Sheffield Academic Press, 1995), 97–112. Clines takes the approach that even though the Ten Words are presented as if they were God's, they probably were in fact rules made up by propertied Israelite elders, i.e., upper-class wealthy men who wanted to preserve their prerogatives as leaders and landowners in the society. Actual evidence for Clines' theory could not be more lacking, but the theory itself highlights the choice any reader has to make: either God spoke these commands or he didn't. If he did, they have enormous significance and are claims upon human belief and behavior than cannot be ignored or diminished. If he did not, they are merely human ideas masquerading as divine revelation, with no more validity than other human ideas.

[16] Thus it is especially noteworthy that he speaks here in the first person ("I," "me") because otherwise the covenantal nature of the law might be obscured. Later, beginning with the third commandment (20:7), he switches to referring to himself in the third person. Some scholars have taken this movement from first person to third person as significant for understanding the structure of the Decalogue (so R. G. Kratz, "Der Dekalog im Exodusbuch [Ex 20:1–17]," *VT* 44 [1994]: 205–38), but the reason appears to us to be linked much more to a need to establish covenant-style language ("I-you") at the beginning for a long enough span (five verses) that the suzerain-vassal relationship is placed clearly in the minds of the hearers.

[17] So with the concept of the body of Christ in the NT. A church is expected to function as a united people responding to the will of its head, not as a group of disparate individuals exercising their own personal preferences and governing themselves by mere human devices.

[18] The NIV wording may be justified if the literal Hb., which reads "out of the land of Egypt, out of the house of slavery," is understood to intend *bêt* ("place" rather than "house") as a parallel to *ʾereṣ* ("land") in what is certainly on the surface at least an apposition (land of Egypt//place of slavery). See also comments on 13:3,14. The expression "land of Egypt . . . house of slavery" is found widely in the OT, including regularly in Deuteronomy. If it provably had another connotation, such as "the status of servitude" or simply "bondage," the NIV translation would be obviated and the traditional translation ("out of the land of Egypt, out of the house of bondage") favored; but this does not seem supportable on the evidence.

from slavery in Egypt, Yahweh had a claim on his chosen people.[19] Such a claim is sometimes called a "*hesed* relationship," from the Hebrew/Semitic concept of *ḥesed,* or "loyalty required in response to loyalty shown."[20] Ancient Israelites/Semites believed, with much reason, that if person *A* had voluntarily rescued or aided person *B,* then person *B* had a true and lasting moral obligation to person *A*. One could not simply ignore significant good done on one's behalf by another; the doing of that good created an inescapable relationship of loyalty to one's benefactor—a sort of permanent gratitude writ large. What Yahweh had done for Israel was truly outstanding, not the least because of its uniqueness. What other god had ever rescued an entire people from bondage, leading them out of a superpower's oppression through miraculous means? If any ancient people believed that there existed even a remote parallel to the Israelite exodus, it is unknown from the extant literature.

(2) The Ten Commandments (20:3–17)

3"You shall have no other gods before me.

4"You shall not make for yourself an idol in the form of anything in heaven above or on the earth beneath or in the waters below. 5You shall not bow down to them or worship them; for I, the LORD your God, am a jealous God, punishing the children for the sin of the fathers to the third and fourth generation of those who hate me, 6but showing love to a thousand [generations] of those who love me and keep my commandments.

7"You shall not misuse the name of the LORD your God, for the LORD will not hold anyone guiltless who misuses his name.

8"Remember the Sabbath day by keeping it holy. 9Six days you shall labor and do all your work, 10but the seventh day is a Sabbath to the LORD your God. On it you shall not do any work, neither you, nor your son or daughter, nor your manservant or maidservant, nor your animals, nor the alien within your gates. 11For in six days the LORD made the heavens and the earth, the sea, and all that is in them, but he rested on the seventh day. Therefore the LORD blessed the Sabbath day and made it holy.

12"Honor your father and your mother, so that you may live long in the land the LORD your God is giving you.

13"You shall not murder.

14"You shall not commit adultery.

15"You shall not steal.

16"You shall not give false testimony against your neighbor.

---

[19] See F. C. Fensham, "Clauses of Protection in Hittite Vassal-Treaties and the Old Testament," *VT* 13 (1963) 133–43; id., "The Role of the Lord in the Legal Sections of the Covenant Code," *VT* 26 (1976): 262–74.

[20] On this important biblical concept, see K. D. Sakenfeld, *The Meaning of Hesed in the Hebrew Bible: A New Inquiry,* HSM 17 (Missoula, Mont.: Scholars Press, 1978); id., "Love (OT)," *ABD* 4.378–80.

[17]"You shall not covet your neighbor's house. You shall not covet your neighbor's wife, or his manservant or maidservant, his ox or donkey, or anything that belongs to your neighbor."

FIRST WORD/COMMANDMENT: NO GODS OTHER THAN YAHWEH[21] (20:3). **20:3** This first commandment presents a translation challenge. Does the Hebrew *ʿal-pānîm* mean "before me" or "other than me?" The difference is not insignificant because the former translation might suggest that the commandment calls only for Yahweh to be Israel's supreme God, and thus it is not a prohibition of polytheism but rather a hierarchicalizing of it, whereas the latter demands a monotheistic religion. Hebrew *ʿal-pānîm* (the form of the expression without the first-person singular pronoun) means lit., "at/to/before the face" and usually has the connotation of "against" or some derived sense therefrom. But does it have any special idiomatic meaning that can be discerned?

The evidence is not unambiguous. The basic compound preposition as it typically occurs (*ʿal-pĕnê* with a noun or pronoun functioning as the *nomen rectum* of the construct formation in which it is included) is found in Moses' writings. In Gen 49:30 it has the meaning "near [against] Mamre" in the sense of "next to [Mamre]." It occurs once again in Exod 20:20, where it means, construed with the second-person plural pronoun, "against you" or even "in your face," referring to the fear of God being taken personally and seriously. In Lev 9:24; Num 14:5; 16:22,45; 20:6 its literal meaning seems to be clearly in view in the wording "[the people] fell facedown." Deuteronomy 5:7 preserves the wording of the present verse in introducing the Ten Words/Commandments in their Deuteronomy context, whereas Deut 11:4 uses the expression with a third-person plural pronoun, "[He made the water of the Red Sea flow] against them" (NRSV "over them"; NIV "he overwhelmed them with the waters of the Red Sea").

Outside of the Pentateuch, *ʿal-pānîm* with a pronominal suffix usually means "against [me/you/them]" as in Isa 65:3; Jer 6:7; Nah 2:1, although various derived meanings such as "in my presence," can arguably be substituted. The LXX, Syriac, and the Targums translated the expression in Exod 20:3 with the equivalent of "in addition to me," in other words, as if the meaning from their point of view were that of exclusivity rather than hierarchy. We suggest that the balance of the linguistic evidence favors the judgment of these ancient translators, so a translation something like "You must have no other gods over

---

[21] On the issue of the enumeration of the Ten Words/Commandments, which has differed notably between Protestant and Roman Catholic traditions, see R. Youngblood, "Counting the Ten Commandments," *BR* 10 (1994): 30–35, 50, 52. We follow the Protestant tradition throughout in this commentary, not because it is a tradition but because we believe it reflects the better analysis of the structure of the Ten Words.

against me" or "You must have no other gods in distinction to me" would capture the idiomatic sense in the context. The text clearly prohibits *other* gods—so much so that some commentators have opined that the original form of the commandment might have been simply, "You must have no other gods," with the *ʿal-pānāy* ("before me") being added later.[22] There is in fact no evidence at all for this theory; it simply indicates the sense of such scholars that the commandment cannot mean merely that Yahweh is to have some sort of preeminence among many other actual divinities.

Why, then, did God not just say, "I am the only God. Don't believe in any others"? The answer is, as previously noted,[23] to be found in the range of meaning of the term *ʾelōhîm* (here "gods"). The word *ʾelōhîm* carries the connotation of "supernatural beings," including angels. Accordingly, this first word/commandment implicitly acknowledges that there are many "gods" (nonhuman, nonearthly beings) in the same sense that Ps 82 does (or that Jesus does in John 10:34–36) but at the same time demands that only Yahweh be worshiped as the sole divinity, or God. All other "gods" (supernatural beings such as angels) are to be understood and appreciated for their roles in the universe, but only Yahweh is divine.[24]

SECOND WORD/COMMANDMENT: NO IDOLATRY (20:4–6).[25] **20:4–5a** This word/commandment outlaws every sort of idolatry, in any form whatever. It also includes an explanation of how seriously God takes idolatry because of its ability to corrupt successive generations, keeping them from God's blessing and forcing him to mete out to them his wrath. Verses 4–5a provide the

---

[22] Durham, *Exodus,* 276, 284–85.

[23] See, e.g., comments on 15:11.

[24] Cf. O. Loretz, "Das 'Ahnen-und Gotterstatuen-Verbot' im Dekalog und die Einzigkeit Jahwes: Zum Begriff des Gottlichen in altorientalische und alttestamenlichen Qeullen," *Ein Gott allein? JHWH-Verehrung und biblischer Monotheismus im Kontext der israelitischen und altorientalischen Religionsgeschichte,* OBO 139 (Freiburg: University Press, 1994), 491–527. Loretz points out that the first word/commandment must also be considered a prohibition against ancestor worship, a practice that was widespread in the ANE. In typical ancestor worship, departed ancestors are thought to assume the status of gods, even though their identity was solely human during their lives in the flesh.

[25] Of some interest is the argument of N. Ararat that the commandments have traditionally been divided incorrectly and that the first five each contain two elements: an assertion that states a theological truth and a specific, practical command. The title of his article on the subject indicates what he regards as the proper content of the second commandment: "The Second Commandment: Thou Shalt Not Bow Down unto Them, Nor Serve Them, for I the Lord Thy God Am a Jealous God,'" *Shofar* 13 (1995): 44–57. Whatever merit this approach would have, it does not alter the content of the Decalog nor of any of its commands other than to try to enhance the logical consistency and orderliness of some of the commands themselves. In Ararat's theory, there would probably have been five commandments on one tablet and five on the other, something that we doubt strongly, since it is far more likely that the two tablets each contained all ten Words/Commandments and thus two tablets were appropriate because one represented the sovereign's copy and one the vassal's. See Youngblood, "Counting the Ten Commandments," 30–35, 50, 52.

wording of the prohibition itself, in language purposely repetitive and inclusivistic to be sure that the person willing to keep covenant with Yahweh understands that there can be no exception of any kind to the ban on idolatry.

The NIV renders this portion of the commandment rather loosely; a more precise translation would be: "You must not make for yourself an idol, or any likeness of anything that is in heaven above, or that is in the earth beneath, or that is in the water beneath the earth." Two common words for "idol" appear: *pesel* (here "idol") and *tĕmûnāh* (here "likeness"), the use of the two synonyms suggesting "any sort of idol." Similarly, "any sort of thing" is prohibited from being depicted—thus the somewhat elaborate and obviously comprehensive delineation of prohibited sources for copying: "heaven above, earth beneath, waters below." In other words, nothing from anywhere can be copied and used as an object of veneration.

The question might naturally be asked: Were not the tabernacle and its sacred objects, such as the ark (chaps. 25ff.), objects to be venerated? The answer is decidedly no. They were objects associated with Yahweh, things that surrounded his self-manifestation and gave a sense of localization to his presence, but they were not in themselves—even remotely—objects that partook of the divine nature, as idols were thought to do for the supposed gods they represented. And the Israelites certainly neither *bowed down* to nor *worshiped* them.

The nature of idolatry is usually misunderstood by modern people. Idolatry was not merely the practice of worshiping by means of statues and/or pictures as focal points for worship; it was rather an entire, elaborate religious system and lifestyle, all of it running counter to what God desired and desires true worship to be. The attractions of idolatry were very powerful and tended to draw even the Israelites away from true worship and covenant obedience to Yahweh in most generations. These attractions, or characteristics of idolatry, may be summarized as follows.

Excursus: The Attractions of Idolatry

1. *Guaranteed*: Ancients assumed that the presence of a god or goddess was guaranteed by the presence of an idol since the idol "partook" of the very essence of the divinity it was designed to represent. When, for example, a statue of a given god was carved and certain ritual incantations spoken over that statue to cause the essence of the god to enter it, the statue was then understood to become a functioning conduit for anything done in its presence from the worshiper to that god.[26] In the same way that a modern persons might speak to and look into a

---

[26] For a variety of data related to the *mis pi* or *mis pt* or *mrs pi* (all meaning "opening of the mouth") rituals the ancients thought gave a mere inanimate statue real life as a manifestation of a divine presence, see M. B. Dick, ed., *Born in Heaven, Made on Earth: The Making of the Cult Image in the Ancient Near East* (Winona Lake: Eisenbrauns, 1999); and esp. C. Walker and M. B. Dick, "The Induction of the Cult Image in Ancient Mesopotamia: The Mesopotamian *mrs pi* Ritual," which constitutes pp. 55–121 therein.

sound-equipped television camera knowing that their words and actions were being transmitted accurately to other locations, ancient people believed that the offerings they brought before an idol of a god and the prayers they said in the idol's presence were fully and unfailingly perceived by the god whom that idol represented.[27]

2. *Selfish*: Idolatry was an entire materialistic system of thinking and behavior, sometimes called the "fertility cult," built on the idea that the gods could do virtually anything but feed themselves. The one sort of "hold" or advantage humans had over the gods was the ability to feed them. Accordingly, it was felt that if one fed a given god, that god was in turn obligated to use his power on behalf of the feeder-worshiper. Not much else was required; if you fed a god adequately and regularly, that god would, in "quid pro quo" fashion, bless you in return with abundance of crops, fertility of cattle.

3. *Easy*: Frequency and generosity of worship (offering sacrifices) were the sole significant requirements of faithful idolatrous religion. Idolatry minimized the importance of ethical behavior. Ritual provision of food to the gods was important; keeping a divinely revealed covenant was not. At Sinai the Israelites took upon themselves the obligation to live as a holy people, subjecting themselves to obedience to hundreds of individual commandments so as to conform their lives ethically to Yahweh's will, including the faithful offering of sacrifices to the true God. By contrast, idolatry was easy, requiring sacrifices but little else.

4. *Convenient:* Deut 12:2 requires that the Israelites "destroy completely all the places on the high mountains and on the hills and under every spreading tree where the nations you are dispossessing worship their gods." Comparably, 1 Kgs 14:23 reports of Israelite idolaters that "they also set up for themselves high places, sacred stones and Asherah poles on every high hill and under every spreading tree." These ubiquitous idol shrines allowed worshipers to take a sacrifice to the god or goddess of their choice virtually any time of day, any day of the week, and at a location nearby any place they happened to be. By contrast, Yahweh's covenant required all Israelites to report to a single, central location three times a year, necessitating costly and time-consuming travel for many and prohibiting worship anywhere in the land but that single, approved sanctuary.[28]

5. *Normal:* Idolatry was the common way of religion—without exception outside Israel—in the ancient world. This made it seem entirely normal since no one could find any parallel to the Israelite covenant obligation to worship an invisible God outside of the area of Yahweh's special revelation to his people. Idolatry was, as well, the settled, experienced Canaanite way. When the Israelites

---

[27] A somewhat comparable notion stands behind "sympathetic magic," the notion that, e.g., whatever one does to a representative image that has been properly designed to represent another individual will in fact cause effects upon that individual. In West Indies voodoo, pins pushed into dolls representing one's enemy are considered effective to cause one's actual enemy's body to experience pain. The logic of sympathetic magic is partly behind the convictions idolaters held about the effectiveness of temple prostitution (see below, point 9).

[28] Exod 23:14–19; Deut 12:2–28. The central sanctuary eventually was constituted by the temple at Mount Zion but at first was wherever the ark and tabernacle were located.

entered Canaan, they could hardly help thinking that the successful farming methods of the Canaanites necessarily involved various idolatrous magical rituals used for generations, from boiling a goat kid in its mother's milk (see comments on 23:19) to sowing a crop in a special pattern with two different kinds of plant seeds (Lev 19:19; Deut 22:9). If an Israelite asked a Canaanite neighbor, "How do you farm around here?" the Canaanite neighbor probably would start his explanation with a description of how to make proper offerings to Baal and Asherah in advance of preparing the fields and planting (or other farm duties) in order to ensure the fertility of the farm. Moreover, idolatry was the way of the superpowers and the economically successful states, whose riches and prestige seemed to go hand in hand with their idolatrous rites.

6. *Logical:* Idolatry was polytheistic, syncretistic, and pantheistic. The ancients believed in a multiplicity of gods—every one being a specialist in some aspect of the world or nature; and therefore the ancients found it enormously attractive to think they could gain assured access to those gods through idols. It was unthinkable to most ancients that a single god could be the only God. The idea of a "general practitioner" having to be responsible for all the various divine duties was simply not part of the mind-set of ancient peoples, and it seems to have been, indeed, hard even for most Israelites to imagine as well, judging from the frequency to which they turned to polytheistic idolatry in their history.

Ancient people also believed in three categories of gods, all of which any individual was likely to differentiate by his or her own beliefs and worship: the personal god, the family god, and the national god. For most Israelites at most times, and for all other people who knew anything about Israel's God, Yahweh was merely a national god. Ancient Israelites might have, say, Dagon (Judg 16:23; 1 Sam 5; 1 Chr 10:10) as their personal god and perhaps Baal (e.g., Judg 2:13; 6:25,28,30–32; 1 Kgs 16:31–32) as their family god, but they would always have Yahweh as his national God. No Israelite, no matter how totally immersed in idolatry, would ever answer no to the question, "Do you believe in Yahweh?" But most, at most times in Israel's history, would, sadly, see him only as a national god (the one who had brought them out of Egypt or the one to whom they would appeal in times of war). Their greater day-by-day loyalty in worship would be directed toward the various idols representing their various categories of gods.[29]

7. *Pleasing to the senses:* 1 Kgs 19:18 describes the Israelite practice of worshiping the fertility-weather god Baal by, in part, bowing down to his idol and kissing it. Ezekiel 8:9ff. details some of the extensive depictions of various creatures in idolatrous form worshiped in Jerusalem. Idolatry provided worshipers with images of divinity pleasing to the eyes, spawned a whole, entrenched industry of image making (cf. Acts 19:24–27), and appealed to the sensual, even,

[29] On the three types of gods as worshiped by the ancients, see K. van der Toorn, *Family Religion in Babylonia, Syria and Israel* (Leiden: Brill, 1996); H. M. Gwatkin, "The Knowledge of God and Its Historical Development," Gifford Lectures #13 (www. giffordlectures.org); H. Frankfort et al., *Before Philosophy: The Intellectual Adventure of Ancient Man* (Baltimore: Penguin, 1949), 22, 87, 107, 123, 128–29, 218–33.

broadly speaking, to the "artistic" in the people. It was hard to appreciate the beauty or attractiveness of someone who refused to be seen, that is, Yahweh.

8. *Indulgent:* Although the Israelites were permitted by the covenant to eat meat whenever they chose (Deut 12:15), the usual pagan practice was to eat meat only as part of a worship sacrifice to an idol. That way, a portion of the sacrifice would go to the idol as a burnt offering, a portion to the priest representing the idol (and his family), and the remainder to the worshiper and his family, thus never "wasting" the effect of eating meat but rather getting double value from the meat: nutrition for oneself and favor with the idol god. Accordingly, the more frequently one ate meat (since it was always eaten in connection with worship) and the more meat one ate (since thereby the god's portion was increased), the more likely one could curry favor with the gods. "Pigging out" thus typified pagan sacrifices, in contrast to the more clearly symbolic value of an orthodox Israelite's worship.[30] Heavy drinking and drunkenness[31] also were considered proper in idol worship feasts because debauching oneself was simply part of being generous to a god.[32]

9. *Erotic:* Temple prostitution is described at various points in the Old Testament. Behind it lay the notion that all creation was in fact procreation, so everything that would exist had to be born into existence. When this was coupled with the "sympathetic magic" idea that things done symbolically in one location might cause certain behaviors in another, ritual worship sex performed in order to stimulate the gods to produce fertility on earth was the result. Ancient pagan worshipers were taught that if they, taking the symbolic role of, say, Baal, would have sex with a temple prostitute symbolically portraying, say, Asherah, this act would stimulate Baal and Asherah to have sex in heaven, which in turn would stimulate things to be born on earth: the young of flocks and herds, as well as the seedlings of all desired plants. Sex thus became a regular aspect of idol worship and was so widely practiced even at the Jerusalem temple in Israelite times that Josiah's reform had to pay special attention to its eradication (2 Kgs 23:6–7);

---

[30] NT believers were expected to recognize that the New Covenant sacrificial meal, the Lord's Supper, was symbolic and not intended to quench thirst or satisfy hunger (1 Cor 11:21–22,33–34). They were as well expected to keep strictly away from any sort of food sacrificed to idols (Acts 15:20,29; 21:25) because of the way that eating at a "temple restaurant" (every temple had at least one of what we would in modern times call a dining room) guaranteed that the meat one consumed had, in fact, already been dedicated in its entirety to an idol even though Christian believers might have regarded the whole business as without actual religious effect. First Corinthians 8:1–7 addresses the question of food offered to idols by indicating that although in theory the idol represented just a false belief, a "nothing at all" (v. 4), the practice of idol worship was so culturally ingrained that many believers would be unable to distance themselves emotionally and religiously from the assumption that the food was part of idol worship. Thus Paul ended up advising the Corinthians to stay away from temple restaurants even though idols don't represent real gods at all.

[31] Note the specific prohibition against drunkenness in 1 Cor 11:21–22, which occurred in the Corinthian church because new converts were so used to it in their prior pagan worship.

[32] A portion of the wine or other drink consumed was poured out to the god as a drink offering. On the consumption of wine at idol feasts, cf. Amos 2:8.

similarly, in northern Israel Amos noted the way father and son would visit the same temple prostitute (Amos 2:7–8).[33]

20:5b–6 This explanatory section of the second commandment, with its assertion that God is "jealous . . . punishing the children for the sins of the fathers," has been widely misunderstood. It does not represent an assertion that God actually punishes an innocent generation for sins of a predecessor generation, contrary to Deut 24:16 ("Fathers shall not be put to death for their children, nor children put to death for their fathers; each is to die for his own sin"; cf. 2 Kgs 14:6). Rather, this oft-repeated[34] theme speaks of God's determination to punish successive generations for committing the same sins they learned from their parents. In other words, God will not say, "I won't punish this generation for what they are doing to break my covenant because, after all, they merely learned it from their parents who did it too." Instead, God will indeed punish generation after generation ("to the third and fourth generation"[35]) if they keep doing the same sorts of sins that prior generations did. If the children continue to do the sins their parents did, they will receive the same punishments as their parents.

But to this is contrasted his real wish: to show "covenant loyalty" [NIV "love"] to "a thousand generations of those who love me and keep my commandments." By the greatest numerical contrast in the Bible (three//four to thousands), God identified eloquently his real desire: to have his people remain loyal forever so that he might in turn show them the rich blessings of his resulting loyalty to them. In vv. 5b–6 the terminology "love" and "hate" refers idiomatically to loyalty, not to emotional attitudes, feelings, or sentiment.[36]

THIRD WORD/COMMANDMENT: SPEAK YAHWEH'S NAME RESPECTFULLY AND HONESTLY (20:7). **20:7** This commandment is structured like the second in that it contains a prohibition followed by a threat of punishment for those who do not obey. It is expressed in third-person speech relative to its reference to Yahweh—a pattern that continues throughout the rest of the commandments.[37] The punishment does not specify particular results but indicates

---

[33] Note that the sex associated with idol worship accommodated homosexuals as well as heterosexuals (1 Kgs 14:24; 2 Kgs 23:7; Jer 5:7; cf. Deut 23:17; Job 36:14; Mic 1:7).

[34] E.g., Exod 34:7; Num 14:18; Deut 5:9; Jer 32:18.

[35] "Third and fourth" is idiomatic in Hb. for "whatever number" or "plenty of"; cf. Amos 1:3,6,11,13; 2:1,4,6; Prov 30:15,18,21,29. On the significance of the contrast between punishing for "three or four" generations out of necessity to enforce the covenant but being willing to bless for thousands, cf. S. Gevirtz, *Patterns in the Early Poetry of Israel* (Chicago: University of Chicago Press, 1963), esp. 18–21.

[36] See above, n. 3.

[37] This I/he me/him variation in divine speech occurs commonly in the prophetical books as well and elsewhere, somewhat less frequently, in the OT generally; it appears to be stylistic rather than semantically noteworthy since God can choose to speak for himself and about himself as he wishes.

the far more general and ominous danger of being held guilty by God, who may choose any way he desires to protect the holiness of his name from misuse.

Three sorts of questions arise in connection with this commandment: (1) What exactly is involved in taking God's name in vain/misusing his name? (2) Why is his name so important that protecting it is one of the ten foundational commandments to Israel? (3) What kind of punishment might ensue for breaking this commandment?

The primary meaning of "misuse the name of the LORD" (*nāśāh šēm yahweh,* lit., "raise up Yahweh's name for no good") would appear to be invoking his name as guarantor of one's words.[38] Examples would include promising someone something "by Yahweh," meaning: "I guarantee you that my promise is true, or Yahweh may kill me or otherwise punish me if I don't keep my promise," or giving legal testimony with the meaning of "I swear that my testimony in this legal matter/before this court is true with the guarantee that Yahweh may kill me or otherwise punish me if it isn't." In other words, the most basic, core idea behind this commandment is the prohibition of perjury.[39] We must remember, however, that the commandment is worded generally enough to encompass any misuse of Yahweh's name[40]—from making light of it or

[38] The seriousness with which such vows or oaths were taken is evident from the space allotted to them in the Mosaic covenant, namely, Num 30:1–16.

[39] T. Veijola provides a convincing parallel to the third word/commandment in the form of a Nineteenth Dynasty (i.e., as early as 1320 BC, remarkably close to the time of the giving of the law at Sinai) votive stela recording the words of Neferabu, who laments his own perjury: "I am the man who swore falsely by Ptah, the Lord of Maat. He has made me see darkness in the daylight [Neferabu was going blind]. . . . Preserve yourself from Ptah the Lord of Maat, because he will leave no crime [unpunished]. Fear to speak the name of Ptah wrongfully because whoever speaks of him wrongfully will come to grief" ("Das dritte Gebot (Namenverbot) im Lichte einer ägyptischen Paralleled," *ZAW* 103 [1991]: 1–17). Neferabu attributes his blindness to a cursing from the god Ptah, in whose name he dishonestly gave an oath. Veijola notes the striking parallel between the words "speak the name of Ptah wrongfully" (virtually a calque of "take the name of Yahweh in vain") and "swore falsely," indicating that the one is the definition of the other. T. Eissner, in *Das Namensmissbrauch-Verbot (Exodus 20,7/Dtn 5,11): Bedeutung, Entstehung und Frühe Wirkungsgeschichte* (Leipzig: St. Benno, 1999), also considers the third commandment a prohibition of perjury in the main and by implication any careless oath. He also suggests that it could conceivably encompass false prophecy and even magical practices done in the name of Yahweh (by invoking the divine name as a source of power in the magical act).

[40] This is argued well by H. B. Huffmon ("The Fundamental Code Illustrated: The Third Commandment," in *Pomegranates and Golden Bells* [Winona Lake: Eisenbrauns, 1995], 363–71), who suggests that a certain degree of ambiguity in a foundational law code is there by design and not accident: it allows wide application of the fundamental principles contained in the law over a long period of time within a culture. Nevertheless, Huffmon does not regard this law as so broad in its purview as to relate, e.g., to any prohibition on magical practices such as necromancy (i.e., using Yahweh's name to make contact with the dead). See also J. H. Tigay, *JPS Torah Commentary: Deuteronomy* (Philadelphia: Jewish Publication Society, 1996) on Deut 5:11.

overtly mocking it, to speaking about Yahweh in any way disrespectfully,[41] to using it as the theophoric element[42] in a personal name under social pressure to have one's family "look orthodox" when in fact their beliefs were pagan/ idolatrous.

Yahweh's name signified his essence. In any culture, modern or ancient, a name is a verbal symbol for a person or thing, and the ancients in particular obviously appreciated the way names connoted the very value, character, and influence of a person or thing. To speak Yahweh's name was to recognize his awesome power and holiness and even to invite his response to one's particular situation at the moment. Those who had not obeyed Yahweh might well fear even to mention his name out loud lest he respond by appearing in some fashion among them. Thus Amos 6:10 describes those wishing no contact with Yahweh's judgment against them as saying, "Hush! We must not mention the name of the LORD." Jesus reinforced and clarified this commandment with regard to making false promises (swearing falsely/uttering false oaths) that invoked God's name by banning the practice of invoking anything as a guarantor of honesty altogether, including any substitution for the divine name in an oath (Matt 5:33–37; 23:16–22; cf. Jas 5:12), thus virtually eliminating any kind of oathtaking and requiring one's word to be one's bond in any promise.[43]

The punishment for breaking this commandment remains unspecified and therefore could in theory take any form of God's choosing, from something relatively minor to death. Jeremiah provides examples of serious punishments when, for instance, a prophet speaks lies in Yahweh's name (a severe example of misusing Yahweh's name), including death for both the dishonest prophets and those who by believing their dishonest words also participate in the profanation of the divine name (Jer 14:14–16), banishment and death (Jer 27:15), or death at the hand of captors in exile (Jer 29:21).

---

[41] If one looks at all the uses of the expression לַשָּׁוְא (cf. Deut 5:11; Jer 2:30; 4:30; 6:29; 18:15; 47:11; Pss 24:4; 139:20), the sense of "speaking Yahweh's name for a bad purpose rather than a good one" can usually be substituted for "misuse Yahweh's name."

[42] A majority of first millennium BC personal names among Israelites mentioned in the Bible were "Yahweh" names, having some sort of reflex of the name Yahweh within the full name, such as *yah* or *yahu* or *yeho* or *yo*—all of which are ways that the hypocoristicon *yahw* (the one-syllable shortened form of the name Yahweh) would resolve in the Masoretic vocalization of these names, depending on phonetic context. See D. Stuart, "Names, Proper," *ISBE* 3.483–88; and the relevant sections of J. Tigay, *"You Shall Have No Other Gods": Israelite Religion in Light of Hebrew Inscriptions,* HSS 31 (Atlanta: Scholars Press, 1986); W. F. Albright, *Yahweh and the Gods of Canaan: A Historical Analysis of Two Contrasting Faiths* (Garden City: Doubleday, 1968); M. Noth, *Die Israelitischen Personennamen im Rahmen der gemeinsemitischen Namengebung* (1928; reprint, Hildesheim: Gg Olms, 1966).

[43] The phrase "so help me God" was designed not be understood as an oath invoking the name of God but a specialized type of prayer for assistance in telling the truth. The commandment against using God's name in vain need not be regarded as broken by such an oath in court.

To "hold guiltless" *(yĕnaqqeh)* connotes "letting someone get away without punishment."[44] That is expressly what Yahweh will not do if his name is misused.

FOURTH WORD/COMMANDMENT: OBSERVE THE SABBATH IN A HOLY WAY (20:8–11). This word/commandment is the longest of the ten (five words longer in the Hb. than the second commandment when both the commandments and the explanation-warnings accompanying them are considered together).[45] That does not mean that it is more important but only that it apparently was regarded as so basic and thus requiring sufficient clarification that it could not and would not be misunderstood and therefore misapplied or partially ignored. Throughout the expression of this commandment, a balance between "stopping" and "keeping holy" is struck: clearly the purpose of the Sabbath cannot be limited *either* to a break from work one day a week *or* to the setting aside of one day a week for special attention to godliness. Rather, both are to be done on every Sabbath.

Many ancient covenants had some sort of sign—something visible that would remind people of the covenant, lest they forget it.[46] The Sabbath functions as such a sign for the Mosaic or Sinai covenant, as 31:13,17 will specify. It provides a regular weekly reminder for everyone: as people keep the Sabbath, stopping their work and devoting themselves to worship, they demonstrate openly that they are keeping the covenant.[47]

---

[44] In the eighteen usages in the OT of the *piel* of *nqh*, a remarkable degree of consistency appears, so the concept behind the verb is relatively clear, with such generally synonymous definitions as "clear the guilty," "hold guiltless," "declare innocent," and "acquit" emerging logically from an inductive examination of the data.

[45] Y. Endo ("The Sabbath Law on Mount Sinai and in the Plains of Moab," *Exegetica* 6 [1995]: 59–75) suggests that the reason for the slight difference in wording between Exod 20:8–11 and Deut 5:12–15 is simply, as might be expected, the different settings of the two covenant statements—one a setting that emphasizes the *establishment* of the law on Mount Sinai (Exodus) and the other a setting that emphasizes the continuing *observance* of the already established Sabbath law. In other words, there is no difference in actual motive or requirement in either statement, and the wording differences are just what one would expect between an original covenant formulation and its renewal formulation a generation later.

[46] Two other biblical covenants are clearly described as having signs: the Noachic covenant, in which the rainbow became the sign-reminder of God's goodness in the covenant (Gen 9:12–13,17), and the Abrahamic covenant, in which circumcision of males was the sign-reminder (Gen 17:11). In the NT the Lord's Supper functions as a sign of the New Covenant; it has been argued by many that baptism serves as a sign of New Covenant initiation parallel to circumcision in the Abrahamic covenant, but baptism is not described per se as a sign in the NT.

[47] By parallel, in the New Covenant the person who claims to be a follower of Jesus but does not regularly set aside time to worship him is openly indicating that he is in fact not a follower and that his claim to be such is deceptive. A. Fersterer has argued forcefully against the idea that the Sabbath commandment was primarily designed to teach children to get in the habit of keeping the Sabbath or that its primary beneficiaries were servants, but he asserts instead that it is a commandment intended to shape the lives of all Israelites of every age, including especially "free adults" ("Exegetische Notizen zum Sabbatwort. Ex 20,8–11 bzw: Dtn 5, 12–15," *Protokolle zur Bibel* 3 [1994]: 41–63). Fersterer also links the liberating aspect of Sabbath keeping with the prologue to the Ten Words since the Sabbath was such a special indicator of Israel's covenant relationship to Yahweh.

20:8 "Sabbath" is the English reflex of a common Hebrew word *(šabbāṭ)* meaning "stopping/stoppage/cessation."[48] The Sabbath is the "stopping [day]", the day on which one's regular work ceases both for the sake of giving laborers a break from their daily routine and for the sake of providing a focus on God that is periodically (weekly) heightened. Most English translations render this verse as "Remember[49] the Sabbath day, to keep it holy," or "Remember the Sabbath day, and keep it holy," rather than the NIV's "remember the Sabbath day by keeping it holy." Which is correct, the traditional rendering that suggests that the *purpose* of remembering the Sabbath day is that it must be kept as a holy day—a day belonging to God—or the NIV, which suggests that the *means* of remembering the Sabbath day is by keeping it a holy day? Either translation is technically possible for the Hebrew wording (*lĕ* + infinitive construct with pronominal object suffix), but the choice made by the NIV translators represents the less likely option and the traditional translation the more likely, especially in light of the following explanatory material that describes the timing of the day as a weekly break (remember it each week, and don't keep working during it) as distinctly separate from its religious purpose (a day that God blessed and made holy, i.e., set aside for God).

20:9–10 These verses are best translated: "Six days you may work and do all your laboring, but the seventh day is a sabbath to the LORD your God. On it you must not do any laboring—you, or your son, or your daughter, your male worker, or your female worker,[50] or your animals, or the resident alien

---

[48] שַׁבָּת does not per se mean "rest" as has often wrongly been conjectured. Cf. G. Robinson, "The Idea of Rest in the Old Testament and the Search for the Basic Character of Sabbath," *ZAW* 92 (1980): 32–42. This does not mean, however, that the purpose of the Sabbath cessation did not include rest for laborers human and animal; it simply means that the point of the law is a cessation at the end of the work week that must be observed whether or not someone thinks he or his animal is tired enough to need it. The motivation should be that the worker must stop working because God's law says to stop working and to attend to worship, not because the worker thinks that he or his servant or his animal "needs" or "has earned" rest and relaxation.

[49] The imperative translation "remember" reflects a Hb. infinitive absolute, as is not infrequently the case in Hb. grammar; cf. J. D. W. Watts, "Infinitive Absolute as Imperative and the Interpretation of Exodus 20:8," *ZAW* 74 (1962): 141–45. Cf. also R. Yaron, "Stylistic Conceits II: The Absolute Infinitive in Biblical Law," in *Pomegranates and Golden Bells* (Winona Lake: Eisenbrauns, 1995), 449–60. Yaron demonstrates that the absolute infinitive does not convey a different or special legal sense when it is used in Exodus but often simply reflects common usage in normal Hb. grammar.

[50] For a rather speculative interpretation of the wording of this commandment as an antislavery polemic of the eighth century, BC, see J. Derby, "The Fourth Commandment," *JBQ* 22 (1994): 26–31. Derby takes the additional approach of speculating that the slightly different wording of the fourth commandment in Deut 5:12–15 came about because of the reforms of King Josiah in the late seventh century, particularly those that provided fairer regulations for the possession and treatment of slaves (in Derby's reconstruction) than had been the case earlier. As we have already argued above, the real reason for the difference in wordings is likely to be the difference in settings.

who is inside your gates." What this explanation portion of the word/commandment prohibits is not any sort of exertion, or the preparing of food, or the feeding or watering of animals, or anything else necessary to get through the day in an agrarian culture. Rather, it prohibits duplicating on the Sabbath any of the usual labors of the other six days that can possibly be stopped without actually causing someone or something harm. People and animals would still need to be fed; lactating animals would still need to be milked; priests would still work within the sanctuary.[51] But to the extent possible, all workers were to receive a day of rest.

How the Israelites might choose to distribute various sorts of minimal chores, such as feeding animals and preparing food, is not specified. Such necessities would have to take place at any rate, and those who truly tried to keep the covenant law would easily discover the fairest ways to make everyone's workload minimal on the day of rest and to provide compensatory rest for those who labored on the Sabbath out of necessity. The goal was no laboring at all; some unavoidable work would nevertheless have to be done by those who served food to people or took care of flocks and herds.[52]

The commandment specifically prohibits any Sabbath day shifting of laboring away from native Israelites to foreign workers ("nor the alien within your gates")[53] or from free Israelites to hired workers or servants ("nor your manservant or maidservant") or from adults to children ("nor your son or daughter"). Envisioned instead is an egalitarian work stoppage that benefits everyone and leaves everyone free and ready for worship and spiritual emphases.[54]

20:11 There could hardly be a stronger model for keeping the Sabbath than that of God himself. And there could hardly be a more impressive precedent

---

[51] Cf. Matt 2:5.

[52] The impossibility of actually doing nothing at all on the Sabbath was always obvious. In the NT, Jesus clarified this commandment by emphasizing its purpose, which is to give a break from work to human beings, not to restrict people from doing what is enjoyable (e.g., Matt 12:1–12 and par.; Luke 13:10–16; John 7:22–23). Paul helped New Covenant believers relate to the Sabbath by calling attention to its purpose of granting rest to workers, with the understanding that such a rest could come on virtually any day as long as it was not denied (Rom 14:5; cf. Col 2:16).

[53] Various attempts at restricting the definition of "alien" have not been convincing. Some Rabbinic traditions suggested that the alien spoken of in this law must have been what they called the *gēr ṣaddîq*, a converted alien who had been circumcised and was keeping the law. But surely the aliens are here protected because of the love of God for all people and not merely for his covenant people. Cf. H. R. Cole, "The Sabbath and the Alien," *AUSS* 38 (2000): 223–29.

[54] As a modern corollary, a believer today could not pretend to be keeping the spirit of the Sabbath commandment while shopping or eating at a restaurant on the Sabbath, thus causing others to work even though he or she were enjoying leisure. By this we do not mean to suggest that shopping or eating on the Sabbbath automatically violates this commandment, only that hypocrisy in the keeping of such a commandment would be easy to commit without care for its avoidance.

within history (and soon enough, within the Scripture itself)[55] than the creation account of Gen 1, which purposely describes creation in terms of six days[56] of labor and one day of rest.[57] God's model in this matter obviates all objections from anyone that he or she "doesn't need to take a day off" since God could hardly wear himself out. The Sabbath is not portrayed as a day of recuperation from those too weak to keep working day after day without rest. It is portrayed rather as a stoppage good for everyone, for the purpose of refocusing on holiness (all concerns that stem from *belonging to God*, which is what holiness is) in order to enjoy God's blessings of that day and its potential ("Therefore the LORD blessed the Sabbath day and made it holy"). The Sabbath, in other words, is designed to help people become spiritually stronger and closer to God; whatever it does by way of helping people recuperate from being physically tired (and it certainly can do this) is an incidental, rather than a primary, benefit.

The *change* the Sabbath brings about in one's weekly routine makes it a refreshing day rather than the absence of activity therein. Indeed, one whose weekly work was essentially sedentary (a "desk job") might be more active physically on the Sabbath than at any other time and still completely fulfill its obligations regarding the cessation of "labor." This does not mean that any activity on the Sabbath, as long as it would not be one's regular "work" activity, would be "holy." But if one were physically active in pursuit of service to God and/or godly service to others, it would be entirely consistent with the Sabbath law to work hard at such sorts of activities and be reasonably worn out by them at the end of the day. To love God is not to have a lazy day one day a week; rather it is to focus on doing his will specially on one day a week—to worship, learn, study, care, and strengthen the spirit.

---

[55] We must remember that as Moses was writing Exodus, he was in the process of a project that created the first Israelite Scriptures, and it cannot be discerned how much earlier he had already written Genesis. It is certainly possible that he "published" Genesis-Exodus (or Genesis-Leviticus or Genesis-Numbers or Genesis-Deuteronomy) as a unit so that readers of Exodus had no prior familiarity with Genesis except to the extent they had read it immediately before reading Exodus.

[56] The wording of the commandment, however, does not necessarily endorse a literal six-day creation any more than the wording of Gen 1 itself does.

[57] It can hardly be doubted that the Gen 1 creation account has among its purposes the reinforcement of the idea of the Sabbath. Critical scholars following the Documentary Hypothesis would assert that this format demonstrates that the Gen 1 account, at least in its present form, is entirely or mainly from the P(riestly) source. A simpler explanation is to say that Moses was inspired to write it in such a way as to demonstrate God's example to humanity of the process of working and then resting so that in this matter, like all others, humans are to take their examples of behavior from God himself. This is part of the meaning of humanity's creation "in the image of God" (i.e., as God's representatives on earth) and of the plea in the Lord's Prayer, "Your will be done on earth as it is in heaven."

At this point in the Ten Words, the focus shifts from what people must do to love God with their whole hearts to what people must do to love each other as they would want to be loved themselves.[58]

FIFTH WORD/COMMANDMENT: HONOR FATHER AND MOTHER (20:12). **20:12** The prior commandments were all concerned in one way or another with the necessity of honoring God as a basic means of keeping his covenant. Now comes a commandment that follows logically because it is concerned with honoring parents, who have the awesome role in the family of representing God to their children.[59] Although this word/commandment requires children to honor their parents in all sorts of ways large and small, there can be little doubt that its most basic insistence from the point of view of establishing a responsibility that might otherwise be shirked is to demand that children take care of their parents in their parents' old age, when they are no longer able to work for themselves, as well as to honor whatever their parents have prescribed by way of inheritance for their children. Thus the commandment is followed by the promise of living long in the promised land. Just as parents who have lived long in their own personal lives need to be cared for at the end of those long lives, so Israel as a nation (not every individual therein) would be able to enjoy a long life in the land God was giving them.[60]

This commandment is thus like the one that precedes it in linking the requirement to an action of God: As God rested on the creation Sabbath, so individual Israelites must do so each week in their own families; as God

---

[58] The expression "love *x* as yourself" is an idiomatic expression from ANE covenant enforcement language and does not endorse self-love (as would be contrary to 2 Tim 3:2). It is an elliptical way of saying "be loyal to *x* as you would want to be shown loyalty if you were *x*." It does not connote "love" in the sense of romantic or even emotional attachment but loyalty in keeping covenant. Cf. D. J. Wiseman, *Iraq* 20 (1958): 49, col. iv 266–68: "You will love Assurbanipal as yourselves" (a covenant stipulation of Esarhaddon to his vassal kings adjuring them to continue to be loyal to his son and successor Assurbanipal just as they would want the loyalty of others if the situation were reversed and they were Assurbanipal).

[59] So H. Jungbauer, *"Ehre Vater und Mutter": Der Weg des Elterngebots in der biblische Tradition* (Tübingen: Mohr Siebeck, 2002). Jungbauer argues that the commandment applies especially and generally to all adult sons, requiring them to care for the material needs of their aged parents and whatever other needs may be associated therewith. Cf. also M. Barre, "The Fourth Commandment: Is It Just for Kids?" *TBT* 29 (1991): 42–46.

[60] Cf. R. Albertz, "Hintergrund und Bedeutung des Elterngebots im Dekalog," *ZAW* 90 (1978): 348–74. Albertz sees a complex of responsibilities in the commandment, including that of children to understand that their parents, not they, are in charge of key aspects of their lives and have this charge *in loco dei;* this responsibility does not cease just because the children reach maturity of their own. Albertz argues that Akk. parallels are supportive of the biblical notion of the meaning of honoring parents, so the expectations were in fact general in the ancient world and not merely limited to Israel—something seen in Proverbs and other wisdom literature, where the expectation of honoring parents is hardly portrayed as only Israelite but rather as a basic human act of righteousness. Cf. J. Gamberoni, "Das Elterngebot im Alten Testament," *BZ* 8 (1964): 161–90; P. Green, "The Fifth Commandment," *ExpTim* 47 (1935–36): 504–7.

promises to take care of his dependents, Israel, for a long time in the promised land, so individual Israelites must take care of their dependent parents for a long time, as necessary, in their own families. The prior commandment looks back on the creation Sabbath, whereas the present commandment looks forward to the nation's tenure in the land of promise. There is not promise here of individually long life spans. Rather the promise refers to God's protection of his covenant people if and as long as they keep his covenant.

SIXTH WORD/COMMANDMENT: YOU MUST NOT MURDER (20:13).[61]

20:13 The commandment is expressed in just two words in the Hebrew, equivalent to "never murder" (see below). The KJV wording, "Thou shalt not kill," was always a deficient translation, though it could be more nearly defended in the early seventeenth century, when "put to death," "fall upon," "smite," and similar terms were commonly used for nonmurderous killing; so the word "kill" more often than it does today included the sense of murder.

The Hebrew term used here *(rṣḥ)* is, however, specific to putting to death improperly, for selfish reasons[62] rather than with authorization (as killing in the administration of justice or killing in divinely ordained holy war would be). God's Old Covenant people, being a theocratic community, were delegated the right to take human life by his command, either in the form of his capital punishment laws or his direct holy war call.[63] No Israelite acting on his own could decide that he had the right to end someone's life. Grammatically, the prohibition expressed in this and the following commandments, through the construction *lōʾ* + imperfect verb form, is perhaps most idiomat-

---

[61] Of interest is the order of the sixth, seventh, and eighth commandments in the LXX. The order of the Hb. (murder, adultery, stealing) is replaced in most traditions of the LXX of Exodus with the following order: adultery, stealing, murder. In most traditions of the LXX of Deuteronomy, the order is different still: adultery, murder, stealing. Various theories of how these altered sequences came about have been offered, but nothing survives from the ancient world to solve the riddle. We take the position that the Hb. order is original (it is, of course, the same in Exodus and Deuteronomy) and that the LXX orders are not. For a discussion of some of the possibilities and their theoretical implications, see A. Schenker, "Die Reihenfolge der Gebote auf der Zweiten Tafel: Zur Systematik des Dekalogs," *Das Gewicht der Gebote und die Möglichkeiten der Kunst* (Freiburg: Herder, 1993).

[62] Cf. L. Smith, "Original Sin as 'Envy': The Structure of the Biblical Decalogue," *Dialog* 30 (1991): 227–30. Smith considers the structure of the Decalog to be essentially chiastic, with the first commandment (against idolatry) and the tenth commandment (against covetousness) as the anchors, with the other commandments correspondingly paired (two and nine, three and eight) and the centerpiece to be the commandment against murder. Because the "anchoring" or "base commandments" against idolatry and covetousness prohibit what cannot be had properly and because murder is usually undertaken because someone wants something and kills its owner to get it (even if what one is willing to murder for is not a material thing but perhaps something like respect or prominence), Smith concludes that envy is the problem at the heart of most sin, including murder. Although his analysis has many disputable features, his assertion that murder is almost never an end in itself but the result of a sequence of sin that (we would say *often*) includes envy has merit.

[63] See "Excursus: Israelite Holy War" at 17:8–16.

ically rendered "you must not . . ." or "you cannot . . ." in modern English. This modal sense was once inherent in English in a wording such as "thou shalt not"/"you shall not," but it is no longer automatically recognizable therein so that "you shall not" or "you will not" sound almost like predictions rather than the firm prohibitions they are in Hebrew. Moreover, the prohibition here and in the following commandments is not expressed through the vetititive (e.g., *ʾal* + imperfect), which would represent a temporary injunction against a behavior, but through the permanent negative imperative (*lōʾ* + imperfect), which could be rendered "never murder" or the like.

Little difference separates the practical outworking of this command today from its original application in ancient Israel. In the New Covenant the state takes the roles of administration of justice and declaration of war; the church cannot do such things. But otherwise, and from the point of view of the individual believer, the prohibition works exactly the same way: no unauthorized "private" person or group has the right to end a human life. Moreover, the ban on murder has no modifying conditions: taking one's own life or ending someone else's for purposes of "mercy" do not qualify as allowable exceptions.

SEVENTH WORD/COMMANDMENT: YOU MUST NOT COMMIT ADULTERY (20:14).[64] **20:14** Other prohibitions of sexual immorality and regulations for sexual purity appear later in the covenant stipulations,[65] but the most important and basic of them is included in the Ten Words/Commandments: marital fidelity. No one is allowed to have sex with any married person except his or her spouse, and no married person is allowed to have sex with anyone other than his or her spouse.

Adultery was known in the ancient world as "the great sin."[66] Marriage is foundational to the creation order and to human society; husbands and wives can hardly function fully as one flesh if they do not trust each other. Sexual relations are the virtual seal of a marriage covenant, and adultery betrays the

---

[64] This is also a simple two-word commandment in the original, *lōʾ tinʾāp*, "never commit adultery."

[65] See esp. Lev 18; 20; Deut 27:21.

[66] See W. L. Moran, "The Scandal of the 'Great Sin' at Ugarit," *JNES* 18 (1959): 280–81. Moran points out that the term "the great sin" is used in Gen 20:9; Exod 32:21,30–31; 2 Kgs 17:21 to describe adultery and that Ugaritic and Egyptian texts support this terminological linkage. Of special note is Moran's view that since the biblical view of idolatry is that it is a sort of adultery, a kind of adultery of religious loyalty is expressed in the golden calf incidents of Exod 32 / 2 Kgs 17. Cf. also J. J. Rabinowitz, "The 'Great Sin' in Ancient Egyptian Marriage Contracts," *JNES* 18 (1959): 73.

emotional-psychological intimacy that specially connects adult men and women within marriage.[67]

This commandment does not explicitly condemn premarital sex, postmarital sex (as by a widow or widower), cohabitation without formal marriage, bestiality, or incest, all of which are dealt with elsewhere in various ways; but *by implication* it certainly does condemn all those practices.[68] These other forms of sex outside marriage are indeed violations of God's laws, but it is sex outside marriage involving married people that is especially threatening to basic family stability and thus receives special focus among the Ten Commandments. Again the principle of law as paradigmatic is essential for appreciating the implications of this command: reasonable and careful extrapolation from the paradigm of the adultery law yields the realization that all sex outside of marriage, whether before, during, after, or instead of a person's actual legal marriage would be a violation of the divine covenant.

Likewise, the commandment against adultery does not explicitly outlaw polygamy, a practice that, in fact, is not outlawed in the Bible. It is tolerated in the Old Testament (Deut 21:15–17) and denigrated in the New Testament (1 Tim 3:2,12; Titus 1:6) partly because ancient culture allowed it. Converts to Judaism or Christianity in the ancient world therefore often enough came from situations of polygamy, where a convert's divorcing all but one wife in order to achieve the desired monogamy would have represented an offense against marriage greater than polygamy. So polygamy was accordingly tolerated, but monogamy is everywhere in Scripture assumed as the ideal, as a creation ordinance (Gen 2:24) firmly reinforced by Jesus (Matt 19:5) and Paul (Eph 5:31).

The commandment also argues, implicitly, against divorce. If marriage is so important that it must be protected against adulteration—even the sort of

---

[67] By this representation we do not wish to suggest that the prohibition against adultery is a matter only of psychological pragmatism. Adultery is wrong because God does not like it. He is not required within the covenant stipulations to explain why he does not like certain things and does like others. Those who keep covenant with him do so primarily because they desire to obey his word out of love for him, not because they are convinced of the self-advantageous ramifications of each command or prohibition. As F. M. Cross Jr. has shown, the essence of covenant is kinship ("Kinship and Covenant in Ancient Israel," in *From Epic to Canon: History and Literature in Ancient Israel* [Baltimore: Johns Hopkins University Press, 2000], 3–21). One keeps covenant with someone because one desires to please that person whom one loves and is loyal to in a manner similar to the way one should love and be loyal to family members rather than because one can always see the pragmatic benefits for oneself of the actions required.

[68] Premarital sex and cohabitation without marriage are covered both directly and by implication in Exod 22:16–17; Lev 21:13–14; Deut 22:13–22. Incest is prohibited in Lev 18; 20:17–19. Bestiality is outlawed by Exod 22:19; Lev 18:23; 20:15–16; Deut 27:21. Widows and widowers could remarry under certain conditions but could not do so without restraint (Deut 22:30); having sex outside of marriage with a widow or widower would represent a type of exploitation encompassed by Exod 22:22–24; Lev 21:14; Deut 10:18; 24:17; 25:5–9; 27:19. All these laws would be interpreted by the usual required extrapolation from the paradigmatic statements themselves.

adulteration that might occur in brief interludes—it certainly is important enough to protect against dissolution altogether. Accordingly, divorce cannot be used as a mechanism to get around adultery (Deut 24:1–4; Jer 3:1), is condemned in the strongest divine terms in the Old Testament (Mal 2:16), and in Jesus' teaching represents the equivalent of adultery in any situation except where adultery itself is the justifiable reason for divorce (Matt 5:32; 19:9 and par.).

EIGHTH WORD/COMMANDMENT: YOU MUST NOT STEAL (20:15).[69] **20:15** Stealing is taking something that does not belong to you without permission.[70] Legal possession and personal ownership of things are permitted implicitly by this commandment, which assumes that stealing is possible, something that would technically not be possible in a completely communal society. There are, of course, no completely communal societies; ownership of things exists in all families and neighborhoods and entire societies, no matter what their economic organizational structure. But with ownership comes responsibility, and respect for ownership is a responsibility in itself as well. This command is reinforced by a variety of individual laws on stealing in Exodus (22:1–16), Leviticus (Lev 6:2–5; 19:11,13), and Deuteronomy (24:7). Stealing threatens the social order and causes pain to others by undermining the ability to possess with sure access things that are useful and needful. The food thief makes others go hungry; the work animal thief interrupts farming; the kidnapper tears apart a family; the clothing thief makes another suffer from the sun or the cold. This command against stealing is also reinforced repeatedly in the New Testament (Matt 19:18 and parallels; Rom 2:21; 13:9; 1 Cor 6:10; Eph 4:28; Titus 2:10; 1 Pet 4:15).

NINTH WORD/COMMANDMENT: YOU MUST NOT GIVE FALSE TESTIMONY (20:16).[71] **20:16** This commandment is also reinforced in Lev 5:1 (where false testimony appears to include refusing to divulge pertinent information at a trial, thus creating a false impression of what the facts really are) and Deut 19:18. A decent society requires a reliable court system and court

[69] This commandment, like the two that precede it, is formed in Hb. by two words, *lōʾ tignōb,* "never steal," or the like.

[70] For a working "theory of theft" as it applies to this commandment, see D. Little, "Exodus 20:15 'Thou shalt not steal,'" *Int* 34 (1980): 399–405. Little argues that the biblical assumption of theft is tied to the system of private property, so the commandment helps protect each individual's "sphere of moral self-supervision and self-determination against the threat of enslavement or exploitation" (p. 404).

[71] The Hb. term in use in this commandment refers specifically to words spoken by a witness or defendant in a court trial or other legal proceeding rather than any sort of false reporting at all. The grammar of the commandment (לֹא־תַעֲנֶה בְרֵעֲךָ עֵד שָׁקֶר) uses the verb *ʿnh* ("speak up"), with the preposition *b* in the sense of "against," and the term *ʿed šeqer* ("false testimony") as an accusative. It could also be translated, "You must not speak against your neighbor by way of a false testimony," taking the final two words as an adverbial accusative.

processes. Because crimes and disputes do occur, it must be the case that they can be adjudicated and the criminal behavior or unfairness thereby stopped. If witnesses in a trial, whether civil or criminal, do not tell the truth, it is extremely difficult for judges to render proper decisions. In other words, the court system of a nation depends on the honesty of its people.[72]

This is the first commandment to employ the word *rēaʿ*, "neighbor," in its general juridical sense of "anyone else you happen to come in contact with" rather than the more narrow sense of "someone living near you" (cf. Exod 3:22; 11:2; 12:4). In laws and formal rules, neighbor has nothing to do with proximity or familiarity; your "neighbor" connotes any other human being you may have dealings with, actually or potentially.

Does extrapolation from the paradigmatic principle of this law imply that dishonesty in general, not merely in court cases, is also forbidden? The answer must surely be yes, reasoning not merely from the general concept of paradigmatic law but from the way that stealing, false testimony, and dishonesty in general are linked together in Lev 19:11—not precisely in parallel to the way the eighth and ninth commandments occur together here in the Ten Words but in such a manner as to suggest that the concepts of false testimony and dishonesty per se overlap, just as common sense would imply.

TENTH WORD/COMMANDMENT: YOU MUST NOT COVET ANOTHER'S POSSESSIONS (20:17). **20:17** Coveting *(ḥmd)*[73] is desiring—wanting or craving something. The commandment does not say "do not covet," which would make no sense since much coveting is permissible or even commendable as long as the thing being coveted is something a person *should* desire and not something that already belongs to someone else exclusively (cf. e.g., coveting [desiring] something as perfectly proper as oak trees, Isa 1:29, or coveting [desiring] something as wonderfully proper as the Messiah, Isa 53:2; the verb is used of God's own coveting [desiring] of Mount Zion in Ps 68:16). Therefore the commandment is necessarily worded with objects for the verb "covet," these objects being things that one should not desire because they already belong to someone else.[74] "House" can as easily be translated "family

---

[72] See C. M. Swezey, "Exodus 20:16—'Thou shalt not bear false witness against thy neighbor,'" *Int* 34 (1980): 405–10. Swezey sees the need for honesty and morality because they represent a defense against both despair and indifference, which would otherwise result from the prevalence of evil. He also notes that three other parts of the covenant undergird honesty in court procedures: the requirement of two witnesses in criminal trials (Deut 17:6; 19:5); the general covenant instructions that relate to honesty (Exod 23:1–3; 6–9); and the holiness code's demands of honest behavior Lev 19:11–19).

[73] The root חמד carries the sense of "desiring" in all its forms and conjugations, although various synonyms may be found in translation, such as "crave," "find pleasure in," "love," "be precious."

[74] W. L. Moran, "The Conclusion of the Decalogue (Ex 20, 17=Dt 5,21)," *CBQ* 29 (1967): 543–54.

and property";[75] other objects forbidden to covet are someone else's spouse, servants, animals, or "anything that belongs to your neighbor." Although some traditions have separated this commandment into two (coveting a neighbor's "house" as separate from coveting a neighbor's wife), there appears to be no cogent reason for this division.[76] The entire verse is a prohibition against any sort of coveting of what someone else already rightfully has, with enough examples given as to leave no doubt that nothing properly owned by someone else can be coveted. Again the principle of paradigmatic law applies: from the list any reasonable person can extrapolate to all other instances of things that cannot be coveted. This commandment, like the prohibition against stealing, implies that God allows people to own things that belong to them and not to others.

Although it may seem to be belaboring the obvious to say so, the final commandment insists that God's covenant people realize that wishing to have good and proper things is good but that wishing to have the wrong things is bad. What people wish for has a major role to play in what kind of society they will create.[77] People able to curtail their wishing, so that it is limited to things they *should* desire, are people who contribute good to a society; those who want what they cannot properly have undermine a society's moral fiber. The commandment has no penalty attached; improper coveting is hardly enforceable by human beings. God here calls for his people to take an approach to their neighbors[78] that respects them and their possessions—an approach they must voluntarily agree to if they want to please him. Coveting is the starting

---

[75] In the OT the most common meaning statistically for בית is "place," followed by "family," and thereafter by "house" in the sense of "the building someone lives in."

[76] For reviews of the entire matter of which commandments are counted as the ten, see L. Hartman, "The Enumeration of the Ten Commandments," *CBQ* 7 (1945): 105–8 and more recently R. Youngblood, "Counting the Ten Commandments," 30–35, 50, 52.

[77] See L. Smith, "Original Sin as 'Envy,'" 227–230. Smith points out that some of the church fathers and also more recent scholars have opined that the essence of original sin is envy and that all the Ten Commandments in one way or another prohibit envy. (E.g., idolatry is attractive to people who think they can use its techniques to get what they don't yet have from God/the gods.) Smith suggests that the Decalogue should be taken chiastically so that idolatry ("theological envy") and covetousness ("anthropological envy") are actually the foundational stipulations of the covenant. In other words, the tenth word/commandment is not a small, quiet conclusion but a capstone for the entire Ten. In Smith's structuring of the Decalogue, the first word/commandment is comprehensive, but the remaining nine are ordered so as to concentrate chiastically on the prohibition against killing, because the violation of the others "finally attacks life itself." Even though much of his thesis is not convincing ultimately, the honor he gives to the final commandment in contrast to the way it is sometimes slighted deserves attention.

[78] This is the second and final time "neighbor" (רע) occurs in the Ten Words/Commandments (cf. 20:16). Again it has the meaning not of someone who lives nearby but the legal meaning of "anyone else/some other person."

point of stealing (forbidden by the eighth commandment) and, in the case of coveting someone else's spouse,[79] adultery (the seventh commandment).[80]

(3) The People's Fear (20:18–21)

[18]When the people saw the thunder and lightning and heard the trumpet and saw the mountain in smoke, they trembled with fear. They stayed at a distance [19]and said to Moses, "Speak to us yourself and we will listen. But do not have God speak to us or we will die."

[20]Moses said to the people, "Do not be afraid. God has come to test you, so that the fear of God will be with you to keep you from sinning."

[21]The people remained at a distance, while Moses approached the thick darkness where God was.

20:18–21 Hearing God speak audibly was frightening for the Israelites—so much so that they demanded that thereafter Moses should always relay God's words to them. This makes considerable sense in light of the consistent biblical witness to the ear-shattering volume of the voice of God. In all other cases where God is recorded as speaking audibly, the sound is described as deafeningly loud.[81] Moses was somehow able to endure God's voice, presumably by special divine grace, but the average Israelite found it so terrifying that he wanted nothing more of it. It was not merely the sound of God's words, of course, that had such an effect: "The people saw[82] the thunder and lightning and heard the trumpet and saw the mountain in smoke," and that combination of sensory data along with the voice of God itself was too much for them, so "they trembled with fear" and "stayed at a distance."

---

[79] Again we remind the reader that the paradigmatic nature of OT law requires extrapolating from the masculine singular, the form most laws are given in, to all persons, genders, and numbers. No thoughtful ancient Israelite would ever have said, e.g., "But what about a woman's coveting her neighbor's husband?" He or she would have known that legal language almost always used the second-person singular as an efficient way of stating a law rather than as a way of excluding anyone from having to obey it.

[80] In this connection B. Lang has argued that a special purpose of this commandment was "protecting the rights of Israelites who were absent for a protracted period to be secure in their marriages and possessions" ("'Du sollst nicht nach der Frau eines anderen verlangen': Eine neue Deutung des 9. und 10. Gebots," *ZAW* 93 [1981]: 216–24). He suggests that Exod 34:24 represents a promise of the same sort of security. This seems to us a limitation of this word/commandment to a sort of situation to which it surely applies but which is only one of many to which it applies.

[81] J. Lust, "Gentle Breeze or a Roaring, Thunderous Sound: Elijah at Horeb, 1 Kgs 19:12," *VT* 25:1 (1975): 110–15. Lust translates what traditionally has been rendered incorrectly as "a still small voice" as "a roaring and thunderous voice" or the like and shows that similar terminology is always used of God's audible voice. In other words, God never whispers or speaks quietly. He certainly may put ideas in people's minds (e.g., Neh 2:12; 7:5) but when he actually speaks audibly, his voice is overwhelmingly loud.

[82] The Hb. does indeed say "saw," but the verb in question *(raʿah)* can have the sense, as in Eng. "see," of "perceive" or "notice."

This was no mere choice of convenience for the people. They perceived that they could not repeatedly endure having to hear God speak directly to them ("Do not have God speak to us or we will die," v. 19). As an accommodation, Moses thereafter approached God closely, but the people "stood far away" (NIV "remained at a distance") as v. 21 states. What can be learned from this? Simply that the presence of God is so threatening to less than entirely holy people that his presence in this world, even among his own people, must be limited so as not to overwhelm humans.[83] This phenomenon is a reflection of the contrast between God's holiness and human sin. He cannot abide sin in his presence, so the closer he is to a sinner, the more difficult it is for the sinner to survive. Thus the full glory of personal contact with God that awaits believers in heaven is not yet manifest. Christ has shown the glory of God but in human dress; the indwelling Holy Spirit brings the person of God into the very spirit of every believer, but he arrives in a gentle, inviting manner, not a forcing, overpowering manner. Thus Paul could warn against quenching the Spirit[84] because human beings can, indeed, take negative advantage of the Sprit's limited, restricted presence and simply refuse to give active place to him at all.

The Israelite fear of dying, voiced by them in v. 19, may also have come from reasoning that if getting too close to God would result in death, as already announced in 19:12–13,20–24, then hearing the voice of God as if he were shouting in one's ear might suggest a similar sort of potentially fatal proximity. At any rate, Moses reassured the people with the assertion (v. 20) that God's closeness was a means of testing them to see if they really would be afraid of disobeying him by sinning ("God has come to test you, so that the fear of God will be with you to keep you from sinning"). In other words, it was an altogether good thing that the people were terrified of God—their reaction indicated that they would be afraid of offending him through sin, and thus their fear would function as a discipline to keep them from sin. This is, in fact, always the value of the much-encouraged fear of God in Scripture. Being afraid of the consequences of disobeying God is among the most helpful attitudes any believer can possibly have. Those who try to suggest that the various commands to fear God are merely encouragements to hold him in some sort of honor or awe completely miss the point that fear is a beneficial guiding mechanism for human behavior.[85]

---

[83] See also the commentary on 33:20.

[84] 1 Thess 5:19.

[85] Fear of death or injury helps people drive safely; fear of heart attacks helps people keep their cholesterol levels low; fear of academic failure helps people study and learn; fear of harming children helps keep marriages together. Fear is a basic motivator of human behavior, and attempts to deny that the Bible actually tells us that we should fear God are quite misplaced. See also M. Greenberg, "*NSH* in Exodus 20,20 and the Purpose of the Sinaitic Theophany," *JBL* 79 (1960): 273–76.

The point of v. 21 is that Moses kept climbing the mountain, getting closer and closer to the top where the dark cloud of God's glory was located (19:18–20) and where Moses had already been before he had descended to hear the Ten Words along with the people (19:21,24–25) whereas the people remained at the base of the mountain (19:17) as instructed in 19:12–13,21–22,24. Thus Moses (alone or with those allowed specially to accompany him such as Aaron; cf. 19:24) went genuinely close to the specially manifested presence of God. The others could not, by divine command and by their own recognition, and therefore they did not. This forms the pattern for future passages related to reception of the law at Sinai: Moses heard it directly, and the people heard it indirectly from him.

(4) Response to God's Commands: Proper Worship (20:22–26)

[22]Then the LORD said to Moses, "Tell the Israelites this: 'You have seen for yourselves that I have spoken to you from heaven: [23]Do not make any gods to be alongside me; do not make for yourselves gods of silver or gods of gold.

[24]" 'Make an altar of earth for me and sacrifice on it your burnt offerings and fellowship offerings, your sheep and goats and your cattle. Wherever I cause my name to be honored, I will come to you and bless you. [25]If you make an altar of stones for me, do not build it with dressed stones, for you will defile it if you use a tool on it. [26]And do not go up to my altar on steps, lest your nakedness be exposed on it.'

20:22–23 Proper worship involves a combination of things that must not be done and things that must be done. Paramount among things that must not be done in the biblical definition of worship are putting any other gods before Yahweh and practicing idolatry, that is, that which is found in the instruction of the first two of the Ten Words/Commandments. In light of their importance, these first two commandments are repeated immediately in vv. 22–23. But that is probably not the only reason for inclusion of the first two of the ten (with slightly modified wording). Rather, the first two function as an incipit (the first words of a piece used as a sort of title, or way of referring to the whole), suggesting the whole ten. This pattern is virtually identical to that seen already in 15:1–21, where the full text of the Song of Moses was presented (15:1–18); and then as part of a summary of the "response," the incipit was cited as a way of saying that Miriam taught the same song to the women of Israel (15:21).[86] In effect, then, the point God made to Moses may be paraphrased thus: "Tell the Israelites, 'You have seen for yourselves how I have spoken the Ten Words/Commandments to you from heaven.' "

[86] On how incipits functioned in Bible times, see W. F. Albright, "A Catalog of Early Hebrew Lyric Poems (Psalm 68)," *HUCA* 33 (1950–51): 1–39.

In this reminder to the Israelites of what they had just seen and heard, four factors are prominent. (1) Moses was now the intermediary, so God spoke through him instead of directly to the people ("the LORD said to Moses, "Tell the Israelites . . ."). (2) The Israelites were witnesses to their own obligation (cf. Josh 24:22; Matt 23:31) because they had *seen* (or perceived, i.e., seen and heard) for themselves the whole process. (3) God had "spoken . . . from heaven" to them; he was not merely some god who lived atop Mount Sinai, but his presence there was a localized manifestation of himself, whose real dwelling place is heaven. (4) They had to keep the Ten Words/Commandments, of which the first two are summarized as an incipit reference to all ten.

Verse 23 would more precisely be translated: "You must not make gods of silver or gods of gold along with me. You must not make them for yourselves." This "combined" way of summarizing the first two commandments is one of the reasons for their being treated as one in some traditions, but in fact it does not vitiate against their being separate commandments. Rather, this brief summary helps understand the first two commandments in another way: by using "along with me" *(ʾittî)* as a synonym for the earlier *ʿal-pānāy* (v. 3), it helps define the earlier term as a way of demanding monotheism rather than simply henotheism. Mentioning "gods of silver or gods of gold" represents a synecdoche and does not imply that these metals were the only materials from which idols were made. But since they were the most common, they stood for all materials and helped the Israelites remember that no idol—no matter how lovely in appearance or expensive in composition—could be worshiped as representing a god. Beautiful, expensive things cannot be excluded from the command against idolatry by the argument that they are "appropriate to God" or that they "call him to mind because their excellence suggests his excellence." That such a prohibition would need to be repeated virtually immediately after the Ten Commandments had been given is evidenced by Aaron's construction of the golden calf days or weeks later (chap. 32).

20:24–26 Worship is the first and most basic response of any believer to his or her Savior and Lord. Altars were necessary for sacrifices, which were in turn necessary for worship. At this early point in the covenant, God gave the Israelites a brief overview of altar construction in anticipation of their need to worship him properly. Now that he was becoming their covenant God, it was important that they be able to respond fully to him in worship, not merely repeating the practices of the past or simply borrowing from pagans the concepts and procedures of worship and sacrifice.

The Israelites had already experienced constructing and worshiping at an altar (Exod 17:15). The use of altars had shown itself very early, indeed was assumed from the start, in patriarchal tradition (Gen 8:20; 12:7; 13:4,18; 22:9;

26:25; 33:20; 35:1–7),[87] and Israel would eventually receive instructions for a far more elaborate altar to become a permanent, portable part of the tabernacle accoutrements (Exod 27:1–8). Meanwhile, however, there was need for an altar that could be built quickly and simply so that the Israelites could commence worshiping as a united covenant community. Moses built such an altar, as described here, and as soon as the Israelites had given their assent to the "Covenant Code," they began offerings on that altar, as narrated in 24:3–8.[88]

The initial altar God wanted was very simple: made of dirt ("an altar of earth," v. 24) or optionally of stone that was not cut, shaped stone but simply found stone crudely fitted together ("do not build it with dressed stones, for you will defile it if you use a tool on it"). The insistence on a simple—even primitive—altar relates to two factors: holiness and idolatry. Holiness is belonging to God; the altar must be his and his alone, a part of the means by which he accepts unholy people and makes them holy, through the transference of guilt from them to an animal.[89] Therefore the altar could not be something of which humans could take ownership because they shaped it and finished it with the same sorts of tools they might use for any mundane masonry project. Likewise, it must not be fancy enough to become like or to function as an idol, a thing that human hands had made yet was revered as possessing divine qualities. This altar must be so simple, made of natural elements that were simply assembled, that no one would make the mistake of identifying it as having in itself, intrinsically, numinous or theophoric character. The altar must be of the minimal sort of construction that would make it functional without becoming an object of appreciation or veneration in itself, something that in the mind of a worshiper might somehow rival or substitute for God. Additionally, it must not become in itself a threat to or pollution of Yahweh's own holiness, as things that are partial or dismembered or incomplete can sometimes do. In the same way that an animal that was sacrificed was to be full and complete (not maimed, sick, or already dismembered before

[87] D. Conrad, "Studien zum Altargesetz: Ex 20:24–26" (Diss., U. Marburg, 1968).

[88] Some scholars have seen a contradiction between the present altar command and that of Deut 12:4–7, as if the present verses envisioned a freedom for the Israelites to build altars wherever and whenever they wished in the future, and the Deuteronomy law forbade anything but one altar. The two supposedly divergent outlooks are typically said to be the product of different sources, which reflected different religious traditions within Israel. The weakness of such an approach is its failure to realize that the present command does not endorse multiple altars but simply regulates altar *design,* and the Deuteronomy command regulates altar *location*—to "the place the LORD your God will choose," i.e., ultimately Jerusalem. Another angle, following to a considerable extent the medieval Rabbi Ibn Ezra, is taken by J. Derby in his article, "A Pair of Contradictory Texts" (*JBQ* 27 [1999]: 125–29), in which the suggestion is made that the Exodus law regulates the altar up to the time of the building of the Solomonic temple in Jerusalem, and the Deuteronomy law regulates it thereafter.

[89] See comments on such passages as Exod 28; 29:1–34.

being brought for sacrifice), so the stones of a stone altar must be whole and complete.[90]

Moreover, it could not even have steps (v. 26). In ancient times most people did not wear what we could call underwear; so even though priests eventually wore undergarments (28:42), there would always be the risk, at this early stage particularly, that a worshiper's or a priest's genital-deficatory[91] area would be "exposed" to the altar, insulting God. Instead, the altar would be built of dirt just tamped together or crude stones fitted together into a waist-high rectangle upon which wood could be laid and fires built to cook the meat offered thereon—the simplest of outdoor grills or barbecues, as it were, for the simple purpose of cooking the meat of an animal to whom the guilt of the worshipers had been transferred.[92]

2. The Covenant Code and Its Ratification (21:1–24:18)

This foundational portion of the Sinai covenant continues without interruption from the Ten Commandments. Although God left off speaking directly to all the Israelites at their request after the Ten Commandments (20:19), he had not stopped revealing his covenant. Moses simply went directly to the top of the mountain (20:21) and the instructions continued, beginning with the reminder of the first two commandments (20:22–23) as an incipit of the Ten Commandments in general and with instructions about altar construction as an indication of the priority of worship (20:24–26). Now the divine discourse continues with what has come to be called the Covenant Code, a basic block of laws that guide the behavior of God's covenant people. After God finished speaking what could strictly be called the "laws" of the Covenant Code to Moses (ending at 23:33 with instructions that give both reassurance and warning), the covenant was formally accepted by the people and gloriously confirmed by God.

Agreement on the exact delineation in the text for the Covenant Code has not been easily obtained (e.g., many would suggest that it begins at 20:22 and others that it ends not with 23:33 but with the account of its ratification in chap. 24). Nevertheless, the Code shows all the earmarks of being highly unified and carefully structured in reference to the rest of Exodus.[93] After the Code, the book of Exodus moves on to describe God's instructions on the

---

[90] Cf. S. M. Olyan, "Why an Altar of Unfinished Stones? Some Thoughts on Exod 20,25 and Dtn 27, 5–6," *ZAW* 108 (1996): 161–71.

[91] The term used here, ערוה, can also be translated "genitals," though it seems within the context that the area of the genitalia rather than merely the genitalia themselves is referenced.

[92] See comments on 29:10,15,19.

[93] J. M. Sprinkle, *The Book of the Covenant: A Literary Approach,* JSOTSup 171 (Sheffield: Sheffield Academic Press, 1994).

means of worship (25:1 and thereafter), a separate block of revelation given during Moses' second great sojourn on Mount Sinai, one that lasted forty days (24:17).

(1) Laws on Servants (21:1–11)

1"These are the laws you are to set before them: 2"If you buy a Hebrew servant, he is to serve you for six years. But in the seventh year, he shall go free, without paying anything. 3If he comes alone, he is to go free alone; but if he has a wife when he comes, she is to go with him. 4If his master gives him a wife and she bears him sons or daughters, the woman and her children shall belong to her master, and only the man shall go free.

5"But if the servant declares, 'I love my master and my wife and children and do not want to go free,' 6then his master must take him before the judges. He shall take him to the door or the doorpost and pierce his ear with an awl. Then he will be his servant for life.

7"If a man sells his daughter as a servant, she is not to go free as menservants do. 8If she does not please the master who has selected her for himself, he must let her be redeemed. He has no right to sell her to foreigners, because he has broken faith with her. 9If he selects her for his son, he must grant her the rights of a daughter. 10If he marries another woman, he must not deprive the first one of her food, clothing and marital rights. 11If he does not provide her with these three things, she is to go free, without any payment of money.

Fittingly, the Covenant Code begins with a concentration on the treatment of human beings rather than animals, plants, or other things, and specifically with rules regulating the treatment of those human beings who might be most easily or most often mistreated or exploited, that is, servants/slaves.

Excursus: Slavery and Slave Laws in Ancient Israel

The various Hebrew terms translated by terms such as "servant," "slave," "maidservant," occur more than a thousand times in the Old Testament. The present passage reflects the broad semantic range encompassed by these terms and the concepts to which they refer. Although the laws in Exod 21:1–11 address primarily the circumstances of six-year contract servants, they do not *implicitly* distinguish among categories of employees. The most common vocabulary word used for the servant is *ʿebed,* which can mean "worker," "employee," "servant," or "slave." Anyone in any of these categories came under the protection of Yahweh's covenant law. The laws of this section also do not differentiate types of employers: the standard term used here, *baʿal,* can mean "boss," "employer," "master," or "owner." Similarly, the words translated "buy" in 21:2 *(qānâ)* and "sell" in 21:7–8 *(mākar)* can refer to any financial transaction related to a contract, much as in modern sports terminology a player can be described as being "bought" or "sold" from one team to another. Players are not actually the property of the team that "owns" them except as regards the exclusive right to their employment as players of that sport.

Much misunderstanding of Israelite law has arisen from failure to appreciate the analogous distinction that prevailed in ancient Israel. When the law was properly followed, persons who were servants/slaves/workers/employees held their positions by reason of a formal contract that related primarily to the job that they had "signed up" to perform, for a period of time, much as one enlists in the military today. In addition, some of the misunderstanding of biblical laws on service/slavery arises from unconscious analogy to modern Western hemisphere slavery, which involved the stealing of people of a different race from their homelands, transporting them in chains to a new land, selling them to an owner who possessed them for life without obligation to any restrictions and who could resell them someone else (although such did also occur in the ancient world). Whether one translates *ʿebed* as "servant," "slave," "employee," or "worker," it is clear that the biblical law allowed for no such practices in Israel. Indeed, the law reflects the fact that when obediently practiced by "boss/employer/owner" and "servant/slave/employee/worker" alike, Israelite service could be so beneficial to a worker that he or she would choose to enlist for a lifetime with the same employer (21:5–6).

What were the different categories of servant/slave? First, there were foreign-born servants whose lives were spared in war and who were allowed to live indefinitely, on the condition that they become permanent workers in Israel (Josh 9:23; 1 Sam 4:9). This is frequently referred to as "chattel slavery." Second, there were six-year servants who contracted to work for an employer for six years in return for wages and other benefits. Third, there were servants born in the boss's household who owed the boss something for the housing and food he had provided them until such time as they might choose to leave his property and/or employment. Fourth, there were various sorts of temporary employees and permanent employees who may have worked for a given individual under various sorts of arrangements, including day laboring.[94] These categories of slaves/servants/workers were employed in all sorts of ways: as personal servants, as farm workers, as conscript laborers (1 Kgs 9:21; 2 Chr 8:7–9), as temporary "hired hand," and the like.[95]

We should note also that virtually all industry in ancient times was "household" or "cottage" industry. Corporations or business partnerships as we know them in modern times did not exist. Almost all business was "small business" in the sense of family owned and family operated business, and someone who was in any sense an "employee," not the owner of his own business, worked for the head of a family, usually lived with or near that family on its property, and was paid according to a formal written or verbal "contract" that was somewhat more like the terms of enlistment used to enroll someone into military service today

[94] See Matt 20:1–12.

[95] Lev 22:10 speaks of the "hired worker" (*śākîr*, NIV "hired servant") working for a priest, and Lev 25:39–40 protects Israelites from being treated in the same way that foreign-born, war-captive slaves were treated, requiring instead that they be treated as if they were under the category of hired worker *(śākîr)*. In some cases the *śākîr* may have been someone who lived elsewhere than with his master/boss, whereas the *ʿebed* was (servant/slave/worker/employee) more often one who not only worked for financial compensation but also for housing and food, if not also clothing.

than a casual agreement expecting only certain hours to be worked at a place of employment.

Finally, Israel's service/slavery laws should be understood in terms of their own history of slavery in Egypt. The Egyptians made the Israelites slaves on the basis of their ethnicity,[96] forced them to serve as slaves for life, did not compensate them properly, if at all, and worked them unbearably hard as a means of keeping them weak and/or causing at least some to die under the burden of their slavery (1:9–14). Against this sort of historical experience, the Bible's laws protect all sorts of workers, guaranteeing them the right to gain their freedom after a set period of time (21:1–4) as against the Egyptian practice of permanently enslaving Israel. Biblical law allowed service out of love rather than out of necessity (21:5–6) as opposed to involuntary service under oppressive masters in Egypt. Biblical law also gave immediate freedom to those who had in any way been physically abused (21:26–27) as opposed to the severe abuse the Egyptians had imposed upon the Israelites. God's laws, then, provided divinely enforced covenant protections for those who worked for former slaves and made sure the former slaves did not return evil for evil once they had the opportunity to do so. Indeed, God's laws implicitly condemned the Egyptian treatment of the Israelites as illegal by prohibiting the very practices the Egyptians had used to suppress and weaken God's people in Egypt.[97]

INTRODUCTORY TITLE FOR THE BOOK OF THE COVENANT (21:11). **21:1** In saying, "These are the laws [*mišpāṭîm,* also translatable as "regulations," "statutes"] you are to set before them," God did not imply that what preceded—the Ten Words/Commandments and the reminders/implications of 20:22–26—were not also laws for Israel. Rather, the new term *mišpāṭîm* simply helped demarcate a corpus of law, the Book of the Covenant (21:1–23:33; cf. 24:7) that begins to provide greater specificity to the general sense of holy behavior required by the Ten Words/Commandments.

TIME-LIMITED SERVICE (21:2–4). **21:2** Type of law: casuistic (its specific circumstance does not apply to people who do not employ or are not employed as servants). Paradigmatic application: virtually any contractual work arrangement.

The normal contractual arrangement for an Israelite (or, more broadly, as here, *Hebrew*[98]) worker involved a service period of six years, which was

[96] I.e., the Asiatic origin of the Israelites was a basis for their being mistrusted to the point of being forced into slavery, lest they enjoy sufficient independence and resourcefulness to join with other Asiatics in war against the Egyptians should war break out. See comments on 1:9–12.

[97] See T. D. Alexander, "Exodus," NBC (Twenty-first Century Edition), 108–10.

[98] The use of the term "Hebrew" here reflects the early date of these laws, when the word referred to the Israelites as a social class rather than merely as an ethnic group. The mixed racial composition of the people receiving God's covenant law at this point (cf. 12:38) meant that there was a potential for Israelites to employ non-Israelites as slaves/servants. To protect any potential servants from exploitation, the term *Hebrew,* a broader socioeconomic term than *Israelite,* is used here appropriately. Cf. 1:15–19; 2:7–11.

"bought" by an employer who would normally be an individual with a large enough farm or other enterprise to be able to use the services of employees beyond the work his family members could do. There is no specification about how the money would be paid. Some servants may have agreed to a lump sum payment at the end of their six years of service, akin to what Jacob thought he was agreeing to when he obtained permission to marry Rachel (Gen 29:18–20). Others may have bargained for a lump sum payment at the very outset of their employment, which they then "worked off" over the next six years (akin to the arrangement Jacob was tricked into by Laban in Gen 29:23–30).[99] Still others must have agreed to periodic payments during the six years of their term of service.[100]

Women could also be employers (Prov 31:15), and female servants/slaves surely also fell under the purview of this law's statute of limitations for the length of a contract. To whom was the money paid to secure a worker? Most commonly to the worker himself, who "sold himself" into the service of another (Lev 25:48,50; Jer 34:14) for the money it would provide for him and/or his loved ones and who knew that along with the money would also come the promise of housing, food, and, depending on the contract, clothing. In the same way that military service, with its guaranteed pay, housing, food, clothing, and other benefits has always been a way out of poverty for many persons in many countries, so servanthood/slavery functioned similarly in ancient Israel.

This law would not necessarily apply to an enemy who was given the chance to live after being captured in war on the condition that he become a servant/slave to an Israelite family.[101] But it might. The paradigmatic nature of Israelite law would allow for the application of the six-year time limit in any situation where it might seem appropriate. For example, in the situation of a nation formerly at war with Israel and now at peace with them, the former enemy was now more or less an ally. Another situation would be one in which the captured servant decided to convert to faith in Yahweh and become a

[99] On the likelihood of a lump-sum payment at the outset of service as being at least one of the standard options, see the comments on 22:3.

[100] N. P. Lemche ("The Hebrew Slave," *VT* 25 [1975]: 129–44; "The Manumission of Slaves–the Fallow Year–the Sabbatical Year–the Jobel Year," *VT* 26 [1976]: 38–59) has argued (mainly via an argument from silence) that the laws requiring the release of Hebrew servants after a specified time probably were never actually followed, except briefly during the days of the Maccabees (second century BC) and then with disastrous consequences. Where Lemche is more convincing is in his contention that Israel did a poor job of keeping its covenant obligations, something the OT prophets certainly confirm. Establishing a negative assertion such as Lemche's contention that this law was not followed would require knowing how every Israelite with a servant treated that servant, and almost nothing from the ancient world has survived to give us enough data to even start such a process.

[101] Cf. Lev 25:44ff.; 1 Kgs 9:21.

worshiping Israelite. In such a case, as seemingly with Ruth, the usual rules of caution about accepting a foreigner into citizenship could be immediately waived.[102]

21:3–4 Type of law: casuistic (specific description does not apply except when a worker had a family). Paradigmatic range: protection of the rights of both worker and employer in virtually any situation of a worker who has dependents and (in much later tradition, not necessarily in the intent of the law) the establishment of matrilineal rights over children.[103] These verses give examples involving three situations: that of a single, unattached worker, that of a worker who starts his term of employment married already, and that of a worker who marries another worker under contract to the same boss and may have children during the time of contractual employment. The purpose of this compound-complex law is to ensure that neither worker nor boss loses what is rightfully his at the time of termination of the contracted service.

The first provision is simple enough: a worker who contracted for service while single and remained single during his[104] entire time of service presented no complication. Likewise, if he went into service married and came out married (implicitly whether or not children were born to him during the six years), there also was no problem. The complication came with the sort of scenario presented in v. 4. By way of background we note that all marriages in ancient Israel were arranged—someone "sold" the bride to the groom for a bride

---

[102] As a Moabite, Ruth would theoretically have had no chance to be fully accepted into Israel because she was a newcomer rather than a member of a Moabite family that had for at least ten generations been living in Israel (Deut 23:3). But because of her conversion (Ruth 1:16), she was immediately accepted as an Israelite herself and was free to marry a godly Israelite without any waiting period at all (Ruth 4:5–13).

[103] As M. Gruber points out, Exod 21:4 was extrapolated far enough that it became the basis in Judaism for the permanent and dominant idea that a child born to a Jewish parent and a non-Jewish parent would take the religious/ethnic identity of the mother rather than the father ("Matrilineal Determination of Jewishness: Biblical and Near Eastern Roots" in *Pomegranates and Golden Bells* [Winona Lake: Eisenbrauns, 1995], 437–43). He also demonstrates that it comports with the way the status of the mother rather than the father was inherited by the child in such second-millennium laws as the Code of Hammurabi (law no. 175) and the laws of Nuzi. Gruber considers attribution of inheritance via the father (where it occurs in the OT) to represent the result of a special act of adoption. As the footnote below indicates, we are not convinced that the law intended such an extrapolation, but there can be no doubt that the practice of matrilineal legitimacy certainly did occur eventually. Our view is that the law is in fact gender neutral and does not intend to establish matrilineal descendancy (or patrilineal descendancy either), even if many of Israel's neighbors had such laws.

[104] We must assume that the law would apply equally to men and women, so if one simply reverses the gender terms, the law still makes sense. In other words, if (only rarely) a woman servant was hired separately from consideration about her husband's status, this is the law the judges would look to for guidance. There are no laws separately detailing situations involving women in a parallel circumstance; the masculine singular terms are expected to suffice for both genders and for singular and plural.

price;[105] no dowry system existed, so the only payments went entirely to the bride's family. If a woman's parents were dead, some other person in the family made the arrangements and negotiated for the price. If a woman were already in contract service, her boss owned the rights to make arrangements for her marriage and to negotiate for her bride price, which was paid to him as employer. In other words, the family of her boss was now her "family" for purposes of marriage negotiation.[106]

With these factors in mind, the provisions of vv. 3-4 set the rules as follows: if an already married servant contracted for the usual six-year term of service, that servant should have built into the contract some provisions for the keeping of a spouse (i.e., the boss had to figure in the costs of housing, food, and clothing for the spouse as well). But if a boss allowed a woman already serving him to marry the servant he had hired while single, there had to be a compensation for the boss's costs incurred for that woman servant already serving him. Her potential to provide children was also an asset—considered part of her worth—and had to be compensated for as well in any marriage arrangement. Therefore, as a protection for the boss's investment in his female worker, a male worker could not simply "walk away with" his bride and children upon his own release from service after six years. He himself was certainly free from any further obligation at the end of his six years, but his wife and children still were under obligation to the boss ("only the man shall go free").

Does this mean that the wife and children stayed as slaves/servants for the rest of their lives? Not at all. If a servant wanted his wife and children to go free also, he seems to have had three main options: (a) He could simply wait for them all to finish their terms of service, while he himself worked somewhere else. The disadvantage of this arrangement is that he either could not live with his family or would have to pay for his own room and board at his former boss's farm. (b) He could find a good job somewhere and earn enough money to pay his former boss to get his wife and children out of their contractual obligation. The disadvantage of this arrangement is that it would have been difficult to find any job that would allow him to earn

---

105 For references to bride price payments see Gen 34:12; Exod 22:16; 1 Sam 18:25; 2 Sam 3:14; Hos 12:12). Hosea 3:2 describes what may have been a typical price for a second wife. It is a mistake to think that because husbands paid bride prices they owned their wives as if they were mere property. Rather, the bride price was a compensation to the bride's family (in the case of someone already a contract servant, to the bride's former boss).

106 On the concept of treating a servant as a member of the "family" or "household" (same word in Hb., i.e., בית), cf. the inclusion of female servants in the family responsibility of the godly woman in Prov 31:15; the inclusion of Abraham's servant as both member of household and potential heir (Gen 15:3); the use of a female servant to bear children on behalf of a wife (Gen 16:5); the power of the chief servant within the household of Abraham (Gen 24:2).

enough money to support himself and at the same time accumulate the sort of wealth that would cover the cost of compensating a boss for several years' worth of the labor of several full-time workers, which is what the wife and children represented to the boss. (c) He could agree to continue to work permanently for his boss. The disadvantage of this latter arrangement is that it would keep him a contract employee for the rest of his life. The advantage is that it would allow him to stay with his family, all of whom would have their basic needs met as well as having the spendable income they earned through the terms of their contracts and all of whom would have reasonably stable financial circumstances during their lifetimes. The attractiveness of such an arrangement on balance is presumably one factor that underlies the following law about the option of voluntary permanent service.

VOLUNTARY PERMANENT SERVICE (21:5–6). **21:5–6** Type of law: casuistic (specific description does not go beyond situations of servants who wanted to stay permanently in a boss's employ). Paradigmatic range: any situation where a person wished to enlist for life in the employ of someone else (i.e., would serve as guidance in such cases even if the servant in question were *not* married and/or did *not* have children). For the reasons discussed in the scenarios described above on v. 4, or for other reasons unspecified,[107] a servant might consider it to his disadvantage to go free and no longer be able to live with his family, losing the food, shelter, and clothing that had been provided for him. If he concluded that it was to his advantage to stay with his former employer for life, he could do so. But he could not enter into such a major commitment informally or impulsively. This law protects the worker from a rash decision or from being pressured by his employer into staying on permanently. It also protects an employer from the possibility of being charged with failing to honor the six-year time limit for a servant's contract

[107] Consider, e.g., that many people in modern times have chosen not merely to enlist in the military for a three- or four-year term of service but to make the military a career for life. Although modern militaries provide for a life career only through periodic reenlistments, these reenlistments are relatively automatically approved, so a person can confidently embark on a career in the military without serious fear of being denied reenlistment, subject to overall age and tenure limits that vary from nation to nation and service to service. In ancient Israel it was surely the case that a servant who had reached the point of age or health that he could no longer work might be given his freedom by an employer regardless of the fact that he had previously signed up for permanent service, or else might be retired from the responsibility of service while still allowed the benefits of living with the family of his employer until death. The laws need not specify such circumstances overtly; they would be understood by commonsense extrapolation from the laws that were actually spelled out.

labor. The protection comes in the form of a requirement that both boss and worker appear to enact a ritual before God (NIV "before the judges").[108]

Verse 6 should be translated: "Then his boss brings him to God and then brings him to a door or a door post, and his boss makes a hole in his ear with an awl, and he works for him thereafter." The process probably went something like this: boss and servant went to the tabernacle (later temple) and swore before the priests (who served as witnesses) while at the same time understanding that they were, far more importantly, swearing before God[109] (who served as the ultimate witness to any oath) that they both wanted to enter into a permanent employment arrangement. Then the boss bored a hole in the servant's ear, probably in the earlobe, which became a visible sign of permanent commitment to service. This prevented a servant from sneaking away from his boss, relocating elsewhere, and entering into a service contract with someone else. It also provided a permanent reminder to a boss that he had an obligation to employ the servant for life and could not renege on that obligation.[110] In the same way that the transfer of a shoe in the sight of witnesses reminded everyone involved of a contractual obligation related to the exchange of property (Ruth 4:7), making a hole in an ear served as a vivid event designed to help the recall, years later, of the contract made for permanent service. The use of the awl and doorpost was simply a way of ensuring a convenient and relatively painless public setting and means of boring the hole.

PROTECTIONS FOR FEMALE SERVANTS (21:7–11). **21:7–11** Type of law: casuistic (description limited to situations where a woman was sold into

---

[108] The NIV and some other versions have chosen to read "judges" for *ʾelōhîm,* "God." In support of their decision, the term *ʾelōhîm* is morphologically plural, so it can mean "gods" (not the only true God but lesser supernatural beings) in many contexts, including already Exod 12:2; 15:11; 18:11,15; 20:3,23. This could seem to lend credibility to the idea that by extension *ʾelōhîm* might mean "mighty people" or "persons of authority." The term is used as well in legal contexts in ways that might seem at first glance to refer more to human judges than God per se (mainly this verse and Exod 22:8–9). Seemingly convincing to some is the use of a plural verb with *ʾelōhîm* in Exod 22:9 (NIV "the one whom the judges declare guilty"), but see the commentary on 22:9. Against the decision to render the term "judges" is the logic of what "appearing before God" actually means as asserted in this commentary (and implicitly in most Eng. translations) and the fact that the Hb. text explicitly and routinely uses other words than *ʾelōhîm* for "judges" in Exodus (*pĕlilîm* in Exod 21:22; *šōpĕṭîm* or a form of the verb *špṭ* elsewhere). The idea that *ʾelōhîm* could mean "judges" or "leaders" at even a single place in the OT has always been conjectural and, in our opinion, unconvincing. Cf. C. H. Gordon, אלהים in Its Reputed Meaning of 'Rulers, Judges,'" *JBL* 54 (1935): 139–44.

[109] On examples of swearing before God, cf. Gen 21:23; Exod 22:11; 1 Sam 30:15; 2 Sam 21:7; and esp. 1 Kgs 8:31 // 2 Chr 6:22. In the overall context of 22:8–11 it is evident that appearing before *ʾelōhîm* (22:8) involves swearing an oath before Yahweh (22:11); this virtual equation of *ʾelōhîm* and Yahweh would tend to rule out a definition of *ʾelōhîm* as "judges."

[110] Cf. Ps 40:6 for the use of this practice as a metaphor for a relationship of lifelong obedience to God.

service, typically with the expectation of marriage). Paradigmatic range: any situation where a woman's rights might be endangered because she was a contract worker for a boss and no longer under her family's direct protection. Potential extended paradigmatic range: any situation where a woman's marital rights might be denied her, whether or not she was in service.

The same background of arranged marriage practices applies to this law as to 21:4 above. Although this law does not begin in v. 7 with the specification that it is describing a woman whose family makes a contract for her to become both a servant and a wife at the same time, the further wording of the law in vv. 8–11 makes clear that this is in fact the scenario under purview—a scenario from which extrapolation in the direction of protecting any rights of women in service or not could be made.[111]

Verse 8 does *not* say that women had no way to get out of service.[112] Indeed, v. 11 makes clear that they did, as does the paradigmatic application of the earlier law in vv. 2–3, with the gender switched, *mutatis mutandis*. The verse asserts, rather, that women had no automatic right to get out of marriage after a period of years—that is, that unlike service, marriage was not a term-limited matter but rather a commitment for life. This law assumes the payment to a head of a family of a *combined* contract labor *and* bride price, which would have been in all likelihood a larger sum of money than either payment separately. Why would a man "buy" a woman as servant and wife at the same time? There could be many reasons, He may already have had a first wife and wanted this second wife to have the status of servant, without inheritance rights, so that all of his inheritance would go to the children of the "wife of his youth"[113] as was expected by the arranged marriage terms of that earlier marriage. He may have been a widower who did not want to endanger the inheritance rights of his existing children who already had received their parcels of

[111] Citizens of ancient Israel, and especially its judges, had to extrapolate from whatever laws they had to whatever justice-challenging situation they were dealing with. Since the number of laws specifically dealing with protecting the rights of one gender as opposed to another was few, it would have been necessary to appeal for guidance to those laws that did exist, whether or not expressed relative to household service, in cases of denial of justice to a woman whether or not in household service. In other words, the Israelites were expected to become skilled at seeing the underlying principles in any law and not letting the specifics of the casuistic citation distract them into applying the law too narrowly.

[112] A better translation of v. 8 would be: "If her boss does not like her, although he designated her for himself, then he must let her be redeemed. He has no right to sell her to foreigners because of his dishonesty to her."

[113] I.e., one's first wife, the one married by arrangement when one was still a single young man. The phrase "wife of one's youth" (Prov 5:18; Mal 2:14–15) does not imply early age marriage. The evidence suggests that people married mainly in their twenties in ancient Israel and not usually in their teens as is often incorrectly assumed.

land to farm.[114] He may have had no land remaining to provide for heirs or simply no land at all in the first place (as would be the case if he were a Levite). He may also have had encumbrances on what he could do with his estate (e.g., if childless so far, he might have sold his property in advance to a next-of-kin, who would take it over upon his death). And so on. Whatever the scenario, it probably involved a man's desiring to marry a woman whose status as his wife would not also threaten the status of his estate.

Verse 9 would be better translated: "If he designates her for his son, he must deal with her according to the legal decree on daughters." The original Hebrew text brings out that a woman whose service contract is purchased along with her bride price is still a real wife, with all the protections that would accrue to anyone's daughter given in marriage in Israel under the provisions of the covenant. Verses 10–11 show that she must be treated as a regular, legal wife and could not be denied any wifely prerogatives simply because she was also technically a servant.[115] Three kinds of equalities are mentioned in typical paradigmatic fashion as standing for all the various ways a second wife had a right to be treated as equal to the first wife: equality with the first wife in food, clothing, and sexual relations ("marital rights"). Thus the covenant law tolerated second wives,[116] whether servants or not, but only if they were treated equally in the family to the way the first wives were treated. A second wife could not be a second-class wife. Failure to provide equal treatment *in every way* for a second wife was sufficient grounds for the wife to be freed from both her marriage (which had been profaned by the discrimination of her husband) and her service (since the original terms of the service-marriage had been violated in a *dishonest* way, as v. 8 says, therefore allowing the right to have one's service contract repurchased if the marriage obligations had not been lived up to).

The apostle Paul reiterated the principle behind the emphasis on marital rights (v. 10) in 1 Cor 7:3–5, in his reminder to married couples of the need for regular sexual activity in marriage. The Bible forbids sexual relations outside of marriage but requires it within marriage, demonstrating that marriage represents

---

[114] This would happen if, e.g., he had children by his new wife. He would be obligated to give the new children shares in his inheritance, thus reducing the shares of his other children.

[115] E. Levine ("On Exodus 21:10, *'Onah* and Biblical Marriage," *ZABR* 5 [1999]: 133–64) has shown that regardless of the meaning one assigns to עֹנָתָהּ in the context (in our judgment, justifiably rendered by the NIV as "marital rights"), the law is basic to the protection of married women in ancient Israel and to the stability of the society created by the Sinai covenant.

[116] This toleration comes within the context of toleration of human weakness in a considerable variety of areas. Jesus described the Mosaic covenant in these terms in Matt 19:8, as a covenant that included accommodation to sinfulness rather than a covenant that presumed only perfect behavior and motives. Without some means of accommodation to human frailty in any divine covenant, there can be no hope for humans to find acceptance with God, thus the importance of the forgiveness of sins in the preaching of the New Covenant.

a genuinely different state from singleness in God's eyes, with sexual intimacy serving as the covenant seal of marriage, and regular sexual relations functioning as a small-scale but important and required periodic marriage covenant renewal.[117]

(2) Laws on Injuries to People and Animals (21:12–36)

12"Anyone who strikes a man and kills him shall surely be put to death.
13However, if he does not do it intentionally, but God lets it happen, he is to flee to
a place I will designate. 14But if a man schemes and kills another man deliberately, take him away from my altar and put him to death.

15"Anyone who attacks his father or his mother must be put to death.

16"Anyone who kidnaps another and either sells him or still has him when he is caught must be put to death.

17"Anyone who curses his father or mother must be put to death.

18"If men quarrel and one hits the other with a stone or with his fist and he
does not die but is confined to bed, 19the one who struck the blow will not be held responsible if the other gets up and walks around outside with his staff; however, he must pay the injured man for the loss of his time and see that he is completely healed.

20"If a man beats his male or female slave with a rod and the slave dies as a
direct result, he must be punished, 21but he is not to be punished if the slave gets up after a day or two, since the slave is his property.

22"If men who are fighting hit a pregnant woman and she gives birth prematurely but there is no serious injury, the offender must be fined whatever the
woman's husband demands and the court allows. 23But if there is serious injury,
you are to take life for life, 24eye for eye, tooth for tooth, hand for hand, foot for
foot, 25burn for burn, wound for wound, bruise for bruise.

26"If a man hits a manservant or maidservant in the eye and destroys it, he
must let the servant go free to compensate for the eye. 27And if he knocks out the tooth of a manservant or maidservant, he must let the servant go free to compensate for the tooth.

28"If a bull gores a man or a woman to death, the bull must be stoned to death, and its meat must not be eaten. But the owner of the bull will not be held respon-
sible. 29If, however, the bull has had the habit of goring and the owner has been warned but has not kept it penned up and it kills a man or woman, the bull must
be stoned and the owner also must be put to death. 30However, if payment is demanded of him, he may redeem his life by paying whatever is demanded.
31This law also applies if the bull gores a son or daughter. 32If the bull gores a
male or female slave, the owner must pay thirty shekels of silver to the master of the slave, and the bull must be stoned.

---

[117] See G. P. Hugenberger, *Marriage as a Covenant: Biblical Law and Ethics as Developed from Malachi* (Grand Rapids: Baker, 1998).

[33]"If a man uncovers a pit or digs one and fails to cover it and an ox or a donkey falls into it, [34]the owner of the pit must pay for the loss; he must pay its owner, and the dead animal will be his.

[35]"If a man's bull injures the bull of another and it dies, they are to sell the live one and divide both the money and the dead animal equally. [36]However, if it was known that the bull had the habit of goring, yet the owner did not keep it penned up, the owner must pay, animal for animal, and the dead animal will be his.

INTENTIONAL AND UNINTENTIONAL HOMICIDE LAWS (21:12–14). Type of law: casuistic (situation cited limited to homicides). Paradigmatic range: homicide in general, with an interest in protecting society from murderers while protecting those who committed accidental homicide.[118]

This compound law is structured chiastically, with the first and last assertions dealing with murder and the required response to it (capital punishment) and the middle assertion dealing with accidental homicide and the required response to it (protection of the one at fault by means of temporary residence at a city of refuge). Verse 12 envisions purposeful homicide, that is, murder, and requires, as is consistently the case in all Old Testament law, the juridical death of the murderer. The subject is indefinite,[119] so no exemption is possible by reason of class or status or gender or age.[120]

Verse 13 addresses the exception to murder: unintentional/accidental homicide. Any sort of causation of another person's death without intent is encompassed by this law: fatally running over someone with a wagon, fatally hitting someone with a tool, unintentionally killing an ally in battle in what today would be called a "friendly fire incident," and the like. In much of the ancient world a mandatory vengeance system was built into the unwritten societal code of conduct. Under this system, you or someone in your family were expected to take the life of anyone who had taken the life of someone in your family, whether or not that person had done so purposefully. Virtually no distinction was made between purposeful and accidental homicide. In the logic of the vengeance system, the causing of a death required the parallel causing of a death to "satisfy" the grievance and make things equal. If family *A* had

---

[118] That this sort of law was indeed later interpreted in Israel as paradigmatic and was extrapolated from in identifying actions judged to be worthy of the death penalty is argued by B. Gosse, "Subversion de la législation du Pentateuque et symboliques respectives des lignées de David et de Saül dans les livres de Samuel et de Ruth," *ZAW* 110 (1998): 34–49.

[119] As indicated by the singular participle in Hb., a standard way of expressing "the one who" or "anyone who"; cf. R. J. Williams, *Hebrew Syntax: An Outline,* 2d ed. (Toronto: University of Toronto Press, 1976), #222.

[120] In other ANE law, murder was punished by death only when a person murdered someone of an equal or higher class. Murder of someone of a lower class was punished either by the payment of a fine or by putting to death someone in the murderer's household who was of the same class as the person murdered. This kind of class distinction is never allowed in biblical law, which represents a quantum leap in fairness over the prevailing attitudes in all societies outside Israel.

lost a member by reason of the actions of someone in family *B*, then family *B* ought to lose a member by reason of the actions of someone in family *A*. Intent was not considered in such cases.

To this way of thinking the true God responded with: "It is mine to avenge; I will repay" (Deut 32:35). The present law anticipates the system of cities of refuge with the wording "a place I will designate." These six cities, spread throughout Israel, would be controlled by Levites and would give sanctuary from the "avenger of blood" (the person who set out to avenge the death of a member of his family by seeking to kill the one who had taken his life) until such time as full, careful, patient legal processes could look into the fatality and rule fairly.[121] God's covenant thereby eliminated for obedient Israelites what had been a long-established but inherently unfair practice that dominated the way of life in the ancient Near East, blood vengeance.[122]

Verse 14 insists that there can be no protection, however, for the calculating murderer—not even the protection supposedly afforded by one's clinging to the horns (raised corners) of the tabernacle altar. The Israelites at Sinai were well aware of the ancient practice of seeking sanctuary at a sacrifice altar. The practice is not endorsed in the Bible, though it is twice described as taking place.[123] Its logic ran as follows: The altar represented God's acceptance of the transfer of sin from people to animals and was therefore a place of forgiveness as well as a specially sanctified, most holy object (cf. Exod 29:36–37; 30:10). Those seeking a fugitive criminal would not want to risk angering God by approaching it improperly, because of the prohibitions about approaching an altar casually.[124] A criminal who ran to it and seized hold of its horns and was not immediately struck down by God might conclude that he was at least temporarily safe from someone who might not be willing to take the same risk. In theory the ability to hold on to the horns of the altar without dying might even have represented a sort of proof of innocence in common thinking.

God rejects all this elaborately conceptualized nonsense and simply states in v. 14 that a murderer must be taken from the tabernacle altar ("my altar") and put to death. In other words, the Sinai covenant allowed no such thing as altar sanctuary. When Adonijah tried to make altar sanctuary work for him in 1 Kgs 1:50–51 and when Joab tried it again in 1 Kgs 2:29, they were doing so

---

[121] As the Israelites actually approached the promised land, the cities of refuge law was promulgated in Num 35:6–34. The cities were allotted by Joshua in the land distribution (Josh 21).

[122] Blood vengeance is still alive and well in the modern Near East. Entire villages can be decimated over time by ongoing blood feuds that spread beyond a single family (because of the intermarriage of extended families within villages). It remains, remarkably, an entrenched notion in some parts of Arab culture.

[123] E.g., 1 Kgs 1:50–51; 2:28.

[124] Cf. Exod 28:43; 30:20; 40:32; Lev 21:23; Num 18:3; Judg 6:30. Note also Jesus' condemnation of those who had the audacity to kill a prophet between two holy objects, the temple building and the altar within its courtyard (Matt 23:35; par Luke 11:51).

without warrant from the covenant. Likewise, the New Covenant makes no provision for any such practice, whether in churches or shrines or any other location. There is no location by which one can escape responsibility for one's civil or other crimes. Neither forgiveness nor freedom from prosecution is spatially connected. Such things are instead relational and in terms of their eternal dimension, dependent upon knowing Christ and his benefits, not where to hide or flee.

CAPITAL PUNISHMENT LAWS AGAINST ASSAULT ON PARENTS, KIDNAPPING, AND CURSING PARENTS (21:15–17). Just as the prior law on homicide (21:12–14) is actually a compound of three laws arranged chiastically in such a way that the first and third "sandwich" the second, so the present group of three laws appears to be constructed. All are capital crimes even though in each case the crime described does not involve the taking of life. The first and last crimes are related to each other because they both describe ways of "attacking" one's parents (and thus these laws help explain the meaning of "honor your father and mother," the fifth commandment, Exod 20:12). The second law (v. 16) deals with a nonhomicidal crime regarded as comparable in severity to the other two and thus requiring the death penalty, that is, kidnapping.

21:15 Type of law: casuistic (wording limited to cases of serious physical assault on parents). Paradigmatic range: any full-blown assault on one's parent(s) or other persons who might function as parents (grandparents, guardians, teachers *in loco parentis*). The format of this law is much like that of v. 12, with the exception that it lacks *wāmēt* ("so that he dies"); it begins with *makkēh* (*hiphil* participle, "the one attacking"), as does v. 12, and ends likewise with *môt yûmāt* ("must be put to death"). In other words, merely attacking one's parents physically is grounds for being put to death; it is not necessary that one's parents are killed in the attack for the death penalty to be applied.

This description does not envisage minor physical abuse (slapping, a single punch thrown in anger, or the like). The *hiphil* of *nkh* rather connotes at least the kind of physical attack designed to disable someone and leave him motionless on the floor or ground (i.e., the verb means at least to "beat down"). It is not uncommonly translated by "kill" (e.g., Gen 4:15) and can have the sense of "assault and leave for dead." But serious as the crime has to be for the death penalty to be applied, it does not have to result in the death of the parents. If someone attacks his parent(s) severely enough so that they might have died, he must lose his life. Parents are thus protected by this law above the general citizenry (21:18–19) or servants (21:20–21), whose actual murder must take place for the death penalty to apply. By contrast, the mere attack on parents itself is a capital crime, even if the parents should eventually recover.

21:16 Type of law: casuistic (description limited to a case of stealing another human being). Paradigmatic range: all kidnapping, without regard to class, gender, status, or age (*ʾîš* refers to any "individual"). The verse should be translated: "Whoever steals a person, whether he sells him or is found in possession of him, must be put to death." The verb for "steal" here *(gnb)* is the same as that of the eighth commandment, so to the alert Hebrew reader, there can be little doubt that this law is a particularized case of the apodictic "do not steal."[125]

Kidnapping is a capital crime. God regards taking someone away from home and family by force for relocation elsewhere (usually to be sold into slavery) as sufficiently horrendous that he requires kidnappers or slave traders to be put to death when apprehended. People's freedom from such oppression is important to God. Note that a slave trader cannot escape capital punishment by arguing that he was merely a "middle man," holding a kidnapped person whom he had not yet resold, that is, that he had not actually done much harm to the man kidnapped. The law condemns to death anyone trafficking in slaves, whether or not the original captor. The NIV rendering "still has him when he is caught" makes the law sound as if it applies only to kidnappers, an unfortunate implication not actually contained in the Hebrew wording (cp. Amos 1:6).

The situation of sparing the life of one's enemy in battle, in return for which he becomes a servant, is not encompassed under the notion of kidnapping, even though it also involves requiring someone to relocate to a new home and culture. The person who goes to war knows the risks and understands the "trade-offs" implied in taking up arms. Israelites therefore could and did exercise the option to force into service enemies not killed in battle (1 Kgs 9:20–22).[126]

21:17 Type of law: casuistic (wording limited to "cursing" parents). Paradigmatic range: any serious rejection of one's parent(s) or other persons who might function as parents (grandparents, guardians). The largest challenge to interpreting this law correctly is the ambiguity that surrounds the understanding of the meaning of *qll* in the *piel* stem. Brichto[127] has argued that the meaning here may not have to do with an actual spoken curse but with an act of "repudiation" of some sort. In two other places in the Old Testament the sever-

---

[125] But this law is not merely a restatement or slight expansion of the eighth commandment, as if the basic meaning of Exod 20:15 had to do with kidnapping, as both A. Alt (*Kleine Schriften I* [Munich: C. H. Beck'sche Verlagsbuchhandlung, 1953], 333–40) and A. Phillips (*Ancient Israel's Criminal Law: A New Approach to the Decalogue* [Oxford: Blackwell, 1970], 130–32) have, in fact, argued.

[126] The fact that such forced service was not necessarily lived out in a miserable life is illustrated by the positive situation and attitude of the captured servant girl in 2 Kgs 5, which passage also incidentally shows the independent freedom of action of Gehazi, Elisha's servant.

[127] H. C. Brichto, *The Problem of "Curse" in the Hebrew Bible,* JBLMS 13 (Philadelphia: SBL, 1963), 132–35.

ity of cursing one's parents is addressed, again with the notion of the action as a capital sort of offense (Lev 20:9; Prov 20:20; cf. 30:11). On the other hand, the *piel* of *qll* certainly can refer simply to what we would call "expressing the desire for harm to come to someone" or (verbally) "denouncing" someone (e.g., Exod 22:28; Deut 23:4). Cursing is not necessarily a sin per se since it can be done in the interests of godliness (cf. God's cursing those who curse Abraham's seed, Gen 12:3; Nehemiah's cursing those who had intermarried with pagans, Neh 13:25; Elisha's cursing the mocking youths, 2 Kgs 2:24—three of the forty occurrences of the *piel* of *qll*). It may also be undertaken in a manner that is essentially rhetorical (e.g., Job's cursing the day of his birth, Job 3:1).

Most likely this law envisions a situation in which someone would not merely in a moment of rage say to his parents something like "I wish you were dead!" but would publicly, perhaps by an oath spoken in the name of Yahweh, assert that he wanted never again to have anything to do with his parents and would not respect or serve them any longer as their child, wishing only harm for them. Thus the curser would, carrying out the curse, neither obey his parents nor care for them in their old age as was the expected duty[128] but would openly declare something to the effect that he wanted them "out of the way."[129] Such behavior was sufficiently outrageous that God would not tolerate its continuation within the covenant community, and he therefore declared it a capital crime.

LAWS ON LIFE-THREATENING INJURY (21:18–21). Again three closely related laws function together to present an overview of how people of any status are to be treated relative to inflicting serious harm that cripples someone.

Type of law in all three cases: casuistic (addressed circumstances wherein someone had inflicted fatal or potentially fatal blows to someone else, including in the case of disciplining a servant). Paradigmatic range: virtually any situation where one person inflicted an injury on another that did not result immediately in death or permanent injury.

21:18–19 This law employs—as a sample from which judges will extrapolate to make their rulings—a scenario of fighting, resulting from an argument, without concern for who started the fight. (If the judge in a case involving fighting actually could determine who started the fight, he might well use that information in his ruling, but the law allows for any situation, including those where it is impossible to determine who actually started the fight.) If one party is seriously injured in the fight, whether by hitting or

[128] See comments on 20:12.

[129] Wanting something or someone "out of the way" is in effect the sense of "curse" *(qll)* in at least the following contexts: Josh 24:9; 2 Sam 16:7; Job 3:1; Jer 15:10; Neh 13:2.

kicking ("fist" is the paradigm word for fighting without using anything as a weapon) or by something used as a weapon ("stone" is the paradigm word for any object used to inflict injury), the injured party could not claim more than the amount of money he lost from being out of work and whatever his costs were for recuperation. In other words, he could not claim, as modern Western laws often allow, special multiple "damages" for "pain and suffering" as long as he eventually recovers enough to be ambulatory ("walks around outside with his staff") and then finally fully well, without permanent injury ("completely healed"). Behind the logic of this law appears to be the assumption that people who choose to fight choose to take the risk of injury and cannot expect compensation beyond their actual out-of-pocket expenses for injuries they incur in fighting. There is no assumption of pre-meditation in this law.

21:20–21 A somewhat analogous situation must then be considered because a righteous Israelite might ask, on the basis of the previous verses, "Can I not, then, use corporal punishment ("a rod" being the paradigm word for any corporal punishment from slapping to caning) to discipline my servants, or my children, for that matter?" Without the present law this question could arise even though the situation of corporal punishment is not specifically a matter of fighting arising from an argument.[130] This law does not doubt the legitimate right of an employer to punish a servant physically.[131] But it addresses the question of how far any physical punishment could go by using the example of a "slave"—whether male or female—who was beaten, presumably for some sort of serious wrongdoing (e.g., stealing from his employer, but cp. Lev 6:2-4). What the employer could not do was beat the servant so severely as to cause either permanent injury or death, for both such eventualities are clearly forbidden by this law.

If the servant died, it was murder.[132] If the servant lost just a day or two at work, however, the owner was not obligated to do what the previous law required, that is, compensate the servant for time lost from work or for medical costs because "he is his money" (NIV "the slave is his property"). There was, in other words, no point in asking the servant's boss to compensate him-

[130] I.e., without the present law, the prior law would provide the closest situation from which to extrapolate about the kinds of situations envisioned in the present law. The judges are always forced to extrapolate their judgments on the basis of whatever law(s) comes closest to the situation about which they are asked to render a decision, so we assume that the reason for the inclusion of many laws in the code is precisely to cut down on the danger of incorrect extrapolation.

[131] Corporal punishment remains widely in use in the modern world, being built into the familial and even formal legal structures of many nations. It was virtually universally practiced in the ancient world and predominated in the modern Western world until the latter part of the twentieth century. Although many modern Westerners would today regard slapping, spanking, caning, to be forms of abuse, it should be noted that their opinions are not *historically* grounded.

[132] Note that there is no difference between "slave and free" in this case, in contrast to the explicit class differentiation made by all other extant OT-era law codes.

self for the loss of his own servant's labor. If the servant had been too severely punished, however, so that the servant took more than a couple of days to recover completely or was permanently injured, some combination of the terms of the prior law (vv. 18–19) and the law in vv. 26–27 would be used to make sure the employer did not get off without penalty.

LAWS RELATING TO CAUSING PERMANENT INJURY (21:22–27). Again three laws seem to be grouped together on the basis of a common issue, in this case the causing of permanent injury to someone, whether or not intentional. The first law (21:22–25) uses the example of injury to a pregnant woman and/or her unborn children; the second and third laws use the examples of body parts of a servant permanently injured by an employer, whether accidentally or purposely, and whether or not in the course of applying corporal punishment.

21:22 This verse contains some wording that is without parallel elsewhere in the Old Testament and thus challenging to translate.[133] The NIV rendering "and she gives birth prematurely" has not been accepted by most subsequent versions and commentators. The most likely translation for the disputed portion of the law would seem to be, "If men get in a fight and hurt a pregnant woman but she is still able to have children and there is no harm . . .," although other possible translations such as "so that her child/children are born" or "so that she has a miscarriage" have also been responsibly proposed.[134] In our view the law cites an instance in which a pregnant woman might or might not suffer some sort of permanent physical harm related especially to her ability to have children (i.e., she is made infertile by the injury), and/or her unborn child(ren)[135] might or might not suffer some sort of permanent physical harm.

---

[133] The literal meaning of וְיָצְאוּ יְלָדֶיהָ וְלֹא יִהְיֶה אָסוֹן would be "and her children come out but there is no harm." The NIV assumption that this refers to premature birth is by no means impossible but simply unlikely in the context.

[134] Further, as J. Ellington has proposed, the difference in the way the LXX and the MT take the meaning leaves uncertainty as to which is in view: miscarriage or premature birth. His translation of the LXX is: "And if two men struggle and they strike a woman with child, and her child go forth imperfectly formed, surely he shall be fined . . . But if it be perfectly formed, he shall give life for life" ("Miscarriage or Premature Birth?" *BT* 37 [1986]: 334–37). In other words, the LXX translation seems to envision that the penalty for causing the miscarriage of perfectly formed children warrants death, whereas the penalty for causing the miscarriage of imperfectly formed children warrants only a fine. U. Cassuto (*A Commentary on the Book of Exodus* [Jerusalem: Magnes Press, 1967]) on the other hand asserted that "the passage does not deal with miscarriage" (but is speaking of premature birth), thus assuming that the LXX rendering was conjectural and that the Hb. must and can be comprehended on its own. N. L. Collins points out that the verb used in 21:22 to refer to men fighting (יִנָּצוּ from *nṣh*) always conveys the sense of two people fighting and thus the specificity in the LXX and Syriac translations (*two* men) is simply proper ancient translation and not the addition of a concept by periphrastic translators ("Notes on the Text of Exodus XXI:22," *VT* 43 [1993]: 289–301).

[135] The use of the masculine plural, lit., "her children," is a standard grammatical device in Hb. to convey the abstract, i.e., "any child or children she might have."

The law insists that there should be a penalty for hitting a pregnant woman during a fight, even if she is not injured. It does not specify that penalty but leaves it to the woman's husband to suggest a penalty and to the judges (NIV "court") to impose one. Presumed in the logic of the law is that men are inexcusably out of control if they engage in a brawl so wild that a pregnant woman would be hurt in the process. If our suggested translation ("but she is still able to have children") or something similar ("if she has her child without harm") is correct, this is a law that would require waiting until after the woman gave birth to see what sort of penalty should be imposed against those who engaged in the fight. The husband could prosecute the case even if there was no harm to his wife or to his child(ren) since the mere risk and anxiety of facing the possibility of injury to the unborn or the infertility of his wife would warrant it.

21:23–25 However, if someone ends up permanently injured, whether the wife or the child(ren) or both, the penalty imposed must fit the severity of the damage. Here the Bible's first "talion" law penalty occurs.[136] Note that the wording of vv. 23–25 goes far beyond and does not even mention harm to the woman's fertility. And if it speaks as well of potential injuries to her unborn child(ren), it describes damage that could hardly have been the result of a blow to a pregnant woman while the unborn child was still in utero (e.g., "burn for burn").[137] Instead, the wording of these verses establishes a general principle for dealing with various permanent injuries; in other words, it uses the law of v. 22 as a jumping off point for the promulgation of a general approach to permanent injury, known as talion law.

Excursus: Talion Law (*lex talionis* or *ius talionis*)

The goal of laws that use the wording "life for life, eye for eye, tooth for tooth," is that the penalty imposed for causing physical injury must be appropriate to the nature of the injury. In other words, a mere monetary penalty (a fine) cannot be considered adequate justice when someone has been permanently

[136] "Talion" means "tooth" in Latin and is the shorthand way of referring to laws that specify penalties in the standardized language of "eye for eye, tooth for tooth," as in the current law.

[137] Here B. S. Jackson concludes that 21:22 is where the penalty for injury to the fetus is contained (so that injury to the fetus would be penalized only by a fine) and that penalty for injury to the pregnant woman is the injury actually covered by the talion law of vv. 23–25 ("The Problem of Exod xx1 22–25 (Ius Talionis)," *VT* 23 [1973]: 290–97). This approach assumes the Israelite law was basically following the sorts of penalties found in some contemporary ANE law codes, which called for a fine in the case of causing the loss of a fetus (e.g., Hammurabi's Law requires ten shekels to be paid for the loss of a fetus; see *ANET,* 175, line 275). The Middle Assyrian Laws, by contrast, require the exchange of a life for the loss of life in a fetus. Thus the picture is not consistent with regard to treatment of the fetus as a person or a thing in the ancient codes. By contrast, S. E. Loewenstamm argues that both fetus and mother are covered by talion law ("Exodus xxi 22–25," *VT* 27 [1977]: 352–60).

maimed by a person in a manner that clearly demands a punishment.[138] This kind of law represents an advance on the non-Israelite biblical-era laws, which routinely provided for fines as satisfying the legal requirement of justice in the case of a superior person's permanently injuring an inferior person.[139] By contrast to the laws of pagan nations, the law governing God's chosen people Israel required real equity at law and forbade people with money being able to buy their way out of criminal penalties.[140]

Talion laws are easily misunderstood if taken literalistically. They usually do not mean what they sound like they are saying to the modern ear. No evidence exists that any judges in the ancient world ever actually required a literal application of talion law beyond the first of its terms, "life for life." In cases of murder, the murderer was put to death as a "life for life" satisfaction of the law. But beyond that, there was no actual taking of someone's eye in exchange for his having ruined the eye of another person, nor was a tooth knocked out of a person in exchange for a tooth knocked out of someone else by that person and so on through the "bruise for bruise" penalty. Instead, expressions like "eye for eye" were understood idiomatically to mean "a penalty that hurts the person who ruined someone else's eye as much as he would be hurt if his own eye were actually ruined also." The precise penalty was left up to the judges by talion law; it might involve anything from banishment to loss of property (and/or property rights) to punitive confinement[141] to special financial penalties to corporal

[138] Cf. F. Crüsemann, "'Auge um Auge . . .' (Ex 21,24f) Zum sozialgeschichtlichen Sinn Talionsgesetzes im Bundesbuch," *EvT* 47 (1987): 411–26. Although Crüsemann regards talion law as a monarchy-period development, he rightly sees that it is not intended to be universal in its applicability but has as its primary function the prevention of powerful people using their money and influence to get their own way in the courts. "Eye for eye" therefore means, in effect, "completely fair without regard for wealth or status of the persons involved" and does not at all mean to authorize the destruction of an assailant's body part in compensation for the prior destruction of a victim's body part.

[139] Thus, once again, the biblical law is "no respecter of persons" and recognizes no class distinctions in the administration of justice. Though talion law sounds as though it might be "primitive" and thus early, those scholars who see biblical law as the amalgamation of laws representing an evolution of juridical ideas over centuries have more recently tended to argue that talion law is actually a very late development, archaistically included here as if from the time of Moses (see J. J. Finkelstein, "Ammisaduga's Edict and the Babylonian Law Codes," *JCS* 15 [1961]: 91–104, esp. 98–104; cf. A. S. Diamond, "An Eye for an Eye," *Iraq* 19 [1957]: 151–55; S. M. Paul, *Studies in the Book of the Covenant in Light of Cuneiform and Biblical Law,* VTSup 18 [Leiden: Brill, 1970], 70–79). The more empirical approach is simply to recognize that in this, as in many other facets of the Mosaic covenant, Israel was far ahead of its contemporaries and uniquely so.

[140] Here we differ with S. West ("The *Lex Talionis* in the Torah" *JBQ* 21 [1993]: 183–88), who argues that talion laws were never meant to be taken literally and that their purpose was, in fact, precisely to establish fair monetary compensations for physical injuries. West bases his argument in considerable measure on the parallels in Mesopotamian law, which certainly do set financial penalties for physical injuries but which we contend are ways of dealing with physical injuries that biblical law consciously rejects and is written *against*, not on the basis of. Nevertheless, as West rightly points out, many Jewish commentators as far back in time as the Talmud have argued, as he does, that "eye for eye" means more like "eye price for recognized eye value."

[141] But not confinement in a prison or penitentiary; these did not exist in ancient Israel.

punishment to public humiliation,[142] or to any combination of these. In support of this understanding of how talion laws were actually applied, an example of the nonliteralistic application of talion law follows immediately in vv. 26–27, in which the case of a servant's master damaging the eye or tooth of a servant required the loss of the servant's labor, not the gouging out of the master's eye or tooth.

The goal of talion law was always a simple one: to see that full justice was done.[143] Its unique wording ("*x* or *x*, *y* for *y*") conveyed to the ancient Israelites an important principle, namely, that someone who permanently injured another person ought to be fully punished in a way that really "hurt." Israel was not to accept a system of law that could allow one person to continue crippled for life and let the person who caused the crippling to continue merrily on, simply a bit less wealthy than he had originally been.

21:26–27 This law not only illustrates the nonliteralistic nature of talion law but also represents one of the covenant's most striking rejections of the sort of class-adjusted legal standards that prevailed elsewhere in the ancient Near East. Even though a servant was the "money" of his employer in the sense of being his contractually obligated "property" (see comments on v. 21), the right of a master to enforce his contract with his servant was not absolute. Human rights were more important. The servant's "owner" lost his ownership as soon as he physically abused his servant. Both the terms "male servant" and "female servant" (NIV "manservant or maidservant") are included in both vv. 26 and 27 as gender synecdoches, as a means of making sure the reader understands that this law applied to all servants. The "eye for eye" and "tooth for tooth" penalty in this case is understood, typically, nonliteralistically. Rather than any actual physical harm being done to the abusive employer to punish him for his crime, the employer simply lost the labor of his servant for the rest of the six-year tenure. Capable Israelite judges would have known how to extrapolate from the terms of this law to all the relevant situations to which it speaks. For example, if an employer permanently damaged the eye of a servant one day before the servant was to leave his service anyway, a judge might well declare that some other servant with a longer time remaining on his service contract should also go free, or that the servant's wife and/or children could go free with him, notwithstanding the usual terms for release of families already articulated in 21:3–4. Conversely, if an employer caused a permanent injury to a servant that was not debilitating (e.g., broke the servant's toe so that

[142] Cf. the examples in Jer 20:2–3; 29:26; Acts 16:24.

[143] So M. G. Kline, "*Lex Talionis* and the Human Fetus," *JETS* 20 (1977): 273–304. Kline addresses the issue of talion law specifically in reference to Exod 21:22–25 and argues that for the term "life for life" to be applied helps prove that fetuses are considered human, i.e., unborn children, and therefore not subject to remediation via fines, as opposed to "property," harm to which could indeed have been remediated by a financial penalty under OT law.

it healed crooked), a judge might require only that the servant would go free a week earlier than the date specified in his contract. This law is typically paradigmatic rather than exhaustive in its description of crime and punishment.

Under what circumstances would an employer maim a servant? Presumably, the answer has already been partly provided with the law in 21:20–21. Corporal punishment was intended to inflict disciplining pain, but if it got out of hand, it could inflict permanent injury as well. Thus the present law served as a curb to potential excesses in the law of 21:20–21.

LAWS ABOUT INJURIES CAUSED BY OR TO ANIMALS (21:28–36). The basic principle behinds these laws is that people are responsible for the animals they own, or for dangerous situations they create that end up harming someone else's animals. Almost everyone in the ancient world was a farmer. Even potters and masons typically planted crops and kept animals, though on a smaller scale than those who farmed full-time. Accordingly, laws governing circumstances of injury related to farm animals were needed and would have been referred to regularly by Israelite judges. If Moses had received the law in our day, these laws might have been replaced by some sample laws on motor vehicle homicide and accidents. In the same way that traffic accidents and crimes are common today, animal accidents and crimes were common in biblical times.

In the laws of this section concluding chap. 21, the *bull* is used as a sample animal. Sheep and some other animals were far more common, but the bull was the largest, strongest, and most dangerous of all the farm animals. So from the penalties imposed here related to bull behavior, a judge could reason "down the scale," as it were, to various situations involving injuries by or to animals of lesser size and lethality. Again the structure of this section appears to involve a simple chiasm, this time of the laws about bulls (vv. 28–32 and 35–36) surrounding a law about animals falling to their death in an uncovered pit (vv. 33–34). In our culture grouping things chiastically is not thought to be particularly useful; in ancient Israel, however, it served as a convenient way of ordering materials so that they could be memorized and remembered effectively. Ancient Israelites were so used to hearing concepts grouped concentrically or "sandwiched" within other concepts that they came to appreciate such patterns as mnemonic aids. Thus the law in vv. 33–34 is neither an afterthought nor an awkward interpolation into the midst of some laws on goring bulls; it is merely a conveniently inserted law within laws of roughly similar content producing a "bull-pit-bull pattern" of farm animal laws intended to be remembered by judges and general citizens alike as a sampling of how to handle incidents that involved death or injury to or from animals.

21:28–32 Type of law: casuistic (applied when someone had an animal that caused someone else harm). Paradigmatic range: virtually any situation of a farm animal doing damage or harm to someone other than its owner.

People who own animals are responsible for their behavior, except when that behavior could not have been predicted or reasonably expected in advance. In v. 28 the paradigm used to illustrate the legal principles intended to apply in such cases is that of a bull who killed someone, which was not what bulls usually or normally did. In such a situation, the bull's owner suffered loss of the bull (a considerable penalty in light of how expensive bulls were in any farm economy, even today) without even the chance to slaughter the bull and eat its meat (which would have been a means of partial recovery of the bull's value for its owner). Otherwise the owner had no further responsibility because there was presumably no way he or anyone else could have predicted such a thing from his bull. People worked with bulls/oxen[144] all the time on their farms; a fatal goring from a bull was an unusual event, not a common one. Stoning the bull represented a safe way for people to kill it without danger to themselves; any other means of safely putting it to death would have been acceptable presumably as well.

In v. 29 the situation shifts to that of a bull already known to its owner to be dangerous.[145] Here the owner who did not keep the bull properly confined had no excuse; if his bull killed someone, it was fully his fault that the person died, and the owner must be put to death for what today would be termed negligent homicide. The bull must also die since it would make little sense to keep it alive in light of the prospect of its killing someone else when given the chance.

How then could the law go on to say in v. 30, "However, if payment is demanded of him . . ."? Doesn't this undermine the whole point of the preceding penalty description requiring the death penalty? It does not. This second part of the verse gave necessary leeway to the judges in complicated cases. Suppose the bull had tried to gore someone only once, many years previously, and someone had borrowed the bull against the owner's advice and had mistreated the bull and *then* was gored to death. Under such circumstances a judge might well decide (and this law gave him the freedom so to do) that the death penalty for the bull's owner would not be fair—a fine being far more appropriate to the actual level of culpability.

The meaning of "he may redeem his life by paying whatever is demanded" is simply that if a compensation payment was demanded of him, then he had to pay a redemption price for his life in the full amount demanded of him by the judge, perhaps on the basis of an amount suggested by the family of the deceased (see comments on 21:22). The judge then either accepted the amount suggested or

---

[144] שׁוֹר can denote either a bull or an ox; indeed, the terms are not always distinguished even in modern Eng., though "ox" sometimes refers to any full-grown bovine male or female or any full-grown castrated bovine male, whereas "bull" is always masculine and usually not castrated.

[145] It could not actually have killed before because in that case it would have been itself put to death already. The presumptive scenario: it would presumably have tried to gore someone unsuccessfully in the past.

raised or lowered it to the final, official, redemption price. Note that the law did not call this price a fine. It was more than that—a redemption payment—because the penalty that lay behind the law was actually the death penalty. When it was not imposed, a fine was not substituted, but rather a buying back of one's life was allowed. There may be little visible difference between the two to a casual observer, but the concepts are in fact different. In the payment of a fine, someone was just providing for the value of a life (which in God's covenant is in fact priceless). In a redemption payment, someone was more or less symbolically acknowledging that his life, which God has a right to take, had been spared by divine will, and the money provided was more like an offering than a fine.[146]

Verses 31–32 take the paradigm further, to children and servants. Children's lives are as valuable as adult lives, so the law applied to them without further comment (v. 31). A servant, however, represented a different category in this kind of legal situation. This law envisioned a case of a servant working for person *X* being gored by a bull owned by person *Y*. Normally, servants were simply included implicitly in laws about people in general. But compensation for a servant's life was not always the same as in the case of the life of someone not a servant because of the way a servant functioned under the control of another person (the employer). Consider the analogy of a member of the military. If a lieutenant orders a private to go into harm's way in the course of military service and the private is killed, the lieutenant will not normally be put to death. Even if the lieutenant is found to have acted improperly, it is likely that he will be penalized short of the death penalty. The private's family may also sue for compensatory financial damages, but no one is put to death for the private's death. This does not mean that the private is considered less than fully human or mere property. Because the private was under the control of the military structure and was expected to do certain things by command that might involve risk, there is a different understanding of who must "pay" and how much must be paid in the case of the private's death.

A servant who was gored by a bull was presumably doing what his master told him to do by command. Typically, a servant told to work with or around a bull did not have the same freedom of independent decision making that someone else might have, and thus the servant's master had to share some of the responsibility for the servant's death with the owner of the bull that did the goring. This means that the owner of the bull was not *as guilty* in such a case as if the bull simply gored someone who happened to be walking along near its owner's property. The law in this case then provided a severe penalty (thirty shekels of silver[147] and the loss of the bull) to its owner but did not assume

---

[146] On the concept of redemption see 13:13–15; 15:3.

[147] I.e., he paid nearly a pound of silver. This law provided major compensation for injured workers, preventing them from being considered insignificant.

that he alone was fully responsible for the death of the servant. Naturally, the judges would have been free to impose the death penalty if it were decided that, for example, the bull's owner had intentionally let a goring bull loose against someone's servant who was, say, simply delivering a message to the bull's owner from his employer. That would be a case of murder, and that would make the status of the servant irrelevant.

21:33–34 Type of law: casuistic (applied when someone had done something that ended up causing the death of someone's farm animal). Paradigmatic range: almost any cause of loss to another person by reason of negligence. Verses 33–34, the middle element in the concentric pattern of animal laws, introduce the matter of liability for causing the death of an animal by negligence.[148] The example used is that of an animal fatality by reason of a deep pit into which a bull (NIV "ox")[149] or donkey fell and died. Since animals roamed a great deal and since a pit of the sort envisioned in this law was inherently dangerous and potentially fatal, the owner of the pit was properly liable for the death of the animal. But his liability was limited to the value of the animal, almost as if he had simply bought it for its meat. This was because of a relatively obvious, commonsense fact that stood behind the law but was not explicitly mentioned: *X*'s animal has no automatic right to be wandering around *Y*'s farm, near *Y*'s pit. Yes, animals could wander off; and yes, a deep pit was a dangerous thing to leave uncovered. But the owner of the wandering animal bore some responsibility for allowing it to wander off and therefore should be compensated at no greater a rate than the market value of the animal.

21:35–36 The final provision in this complex of laws about injury to and from farm animals is casuistic; that is, it takes up the sample instance of an animal causing the death of another animal essentially equal to it in value. Its paradigmatic range, however, covers virtually any situation where an animal harmed another animal. Verse 35 addresses a case of goring to death that could not be anticipated. The proper solution was a "liquidation" of the assets represented in the remaining live bull as well as the dead one by selling the live one (so that there could be no question of splitting the value equally: money divided easily) and splitting up the dead one for its meat. In the kind of case envisioned here, there was no easy way to tell which animal was really at fault and not enough evidence to make either owner obligated to compensate the other in terms of paying a penalty.

In v. 36, however, the situation changes to that of a bull known to its owner to be in the habit of goring. In such a case, it was the fault of the owner if his

---

[148] Purposely or accidentally causing the death of a farm animal was covered under the laws in 22:1 and 22:14–15.

[149] For some reason the NIV translators chose "ox" at this point for the same word, שׁוֹר, that they translate "bull" in the surrounding verses.

bull gored the bull of another person, and he had to pay for the dead animal at the market price, with the meat coming to him. Both these laws recognized that animal behavior was not totally predictable and controllable but also attempted to provide a fair and equitable solution when someone lost a valuable asset, a farm animal.[150]

(3) Laws on Property (22:1–17)

1"If a man steals an ox or a sheep and slaughters it or sells it, he must pay back five head of cattle for the ox and four sheep for the sheep.

2"If a thief is caught breaking in and is struck so that he dies, the defender is not guilty of bloodshed; 3 but if it happens after sunrise, he is guilty of bloodshed.

"A thief must certainly make restitution, but if he has nothing, he must be sold to pay for his theft.

4"If the stolen animal is found alive in his possession—whether ox or donkey or sheep—he must pay back double.

5"If a man grazes his livestock in a field or vineyard and lets them stray and they graze in another man's field, he must make restitution from the best of his own field or vineyard.

6"If a fire breaks out and spreads into thornbushes so that it burns shocks of grain or standing grain or the whole field, the one who started the fire must make restitution.

7"If a man gives his neighbor silver or goods for safekeeping and they are stolen from the neighbor's house, the thief, if he is caught, must pay back double.
8But if the thief is not found, the owner of the house must appear before the judges to determine whether he has laid his hands on the other man's property. In all cases of illegal possession of an ox, a donkey, a sheep, a garment, or any other lost property about which somebody says, 'This is mine,' both parties are to bring their cases before the judges. The one whom the judges declare guilty must pay back double to his neighbor.

10"If a man gives a donkey, an ox, a sheep or any other animal to his neighbor for safekeeping and it dies or is injured or is taken away while no one is looking,
11the issue between them will be settled by the taking of an oath before the LORD that the neighbor did not lay hands on the other person's property. The owner is to accept this, and no restitution is required. 12But if the animal was stolen from the neighbor, he must make restitution to the owner. 13If it was torn to pieces by a

---

[150] Some modern motor vehicle laws have a similar outlook and purpose: some assign no fault to either driver in certain kinds of accidents, and others assign a scale of penalties when fault can be determined, depending on the severity of the accident. But even when death results from negligent driving, virtually never is a person put to death or given life in prison as a penalty for motor vehicle homicide. The law recognizes that there is always present in a motor vehicle accident the uncontrollable and unpredictable element of human inability to guide a vehicle perfectly as well as the inability of any human to react perfectly in all traffic circumstances. Somewhat similarly, God's covenant law for his people Israel recognized that animals were not entirely predictable and provided a penalty and compensation structure accordingly.

wild animal, he shall bring in the remains as evidence and he will not be required to pay for the torn animal.

14"If a man borrows an animal from his neighbor and it is injured or dies while the owner is not present, he must make restitution. 15But if the owner is with the animal, the borrower will not have to pay. If the animal was hired, the money paid for the hire covers the loss.

16"If a man seduces a virgin who is not pledged to be married and sleeps with her, he must pay the bride-price, and she shall be his wife. 17If her father absolutely refuses to give her to him, he must still pay the bride-price for virgins.

RESTITUTION OR RESIDENCY? The laws in this section (22:1–17) of the Covenant Code reflect that God envisioned no jail or prison system for punishing crimes in Israel. Confinement in a penal institution is the primary way modern Western societies punish such crimes as theft or sexual exploitation, but Israel's law did not include confinement penalties at all. Sometimes this "omission" is treated only as the result of the fact that Israel was a people on the move, Sinai being only a temporary stopping place, and prisons being virtually impossible in a mobile society. But this cannot be the primary reason for the lack of confinement penalties in the law since the law looks forward in most places not merely to the immediate future in the wilderness but also to the time when Israel would be settled in the promised land and jails and prisons could certainly be constructed. There must therefore be another reason for the emphasis on restitution in cases of theft or property destruction or premarital sex without a payment of a bride price rather than residency (in a penal institution).

The advantage of restitution over residency is at least fourfold. (1) It compensates the victims of a crime more generously and more immediately than is the case in modern Western societies. (2) It requires the offender to deal directly with the person he has offended and to face the effects of his crime on that person. (3) It permits a repentant offender to continue a productive life immediately upon making restoration. (4) And it does not require society to provide housing, food, and clothing for the duration of the offender's imprisonment. In the logic of modern jurisprudence, however, potential disadvantages are also theoretically present in this system. In the main there are two: the richer the criminal, the easier it is for him to make restitution, so only poor criminals tend to end up punished by some other means than restitution for their failure to compensate the victim;[151] and imprisonment offers society the

[151] As in v. 3, where the court itself rather than the individual or his family sold a person into contract labor for six years (see comments on 21:2–11) and gave the money paid for his service to the person's victim. It is to be assumed that if the price paid for the service contract were greater than the compensation required, the balance would in fact go to the thief since his "debt to society" had been fully paid to the person he had stolen from. In other words, the law does not sanction giving the victim "whatever price the sale into service brings" but only the multiple of the loss required by the law.

protection of keeping out of circulation the person who, if fines alone were allowed to suffice for his penalty, could engage in criminal activity again immediately.[152]

Behind all the laws in this section is the simple principle that the person who causes someone else to lose something (whether personal property or real estate or money) by whatever means (from theft to mere neglect to bypassing the normal betrothal process) owes compensation to the person who has suffered the loss. The more intentional the means of deprivation (e.g., outright stealing), the higher the required restitution, normally calculated in multiples of the value of the loss suffered. Simple neglect was to be compensated on whatever level the judge in the case required. If no culpability was evident, however, no compensation was required. Some of these laws were intended to remind the Israelites that in God's providence, some things "just happened" and were no one's fault and therefore did not require restitution.

FOUR LAWS ON RESTITUTION FOR THEFT, ALONG WITH A NOTE ON DEFENSE AGAINST BURGLARY (22:1–4 [Hb. 21:37–22:3]). As in the previous chapter, in the present chapter are some instances of three or more laws being grouped in a concentric or chiastic pattern, and vv. 1–4 appear to be such a grouping. Verse 1 addresses victim compensation requirements for stealing livestock in the case of a thief who had actually been caught. Verses 2–3a address the difference between mere breaking and entering and actual burglary, indicating in the process the penalty meted out to a thief either on the spot by someone defending his farm or by a court. Verse 3b tells how to handle a situation in which a thief cannot make restitution for what he has stolen; and v. 4, completing the chiasm, again returns to the question of restitution for stolen animals but with the special qualification of reasonable doubt about the matter of intent on the part of the thief.[153]

22:1 [Hb. 21:37] Type of law: casuistic (applied to cases where restitution was needed after some sort of theft). Paradigmatic range: almost any theft

[152] Ultimately, the question of which of these approaches is most likely to be successful cannot be answered by sociological study. Israel's system of recompense for theft or property destruction was part of a whole covenant given to make a people holy, a nation of priests (Exod 19:5–6) *in contrast to* the rest of the world. It expected a different level of behavior and a different sort of motivation from what modern secular jurisprudence contemplates. And although a few theologians have actually argued that modern laws should be modeled as precisely as possible after OT biblical law (theonomy), most have recognized that the New Covenant is designed by God to permit believers to live and witness in any society in the world and leaves civil and criminal law to the individual nations (Rom 13:1–7), Christ's kingdom not being of this world at all (John 18:36; Rev 11:5).

[153] Both Cassuto (*Exodus,* 282) and B. S. Childs (*The Book of Exodus: A Critical-Theological Commentary* [Louisville: Westminster John Knox, 1974], 474) defend the ordering of these laws as logical and coherent. Daube (*Biblical Law,* 74–77, 85–89), followed by Durham, again here ascribes the order (i.e., his inability to discern an order) to "laziness, undeveloped legal technique, writing on stone or the like, oral transmission of the law and regard for tradition."

for which restitution could be made (a judge could extrapolate from this law to any situation where something valuable had been stolen and would not think of the law as being useful to him only in cases involving stolen animals). The situation described is that of intentional theft, the intent being established unmistakably by what the thief did with the animal after it was in his possession, that is, he ate it or sold it (which would prove intent). A significant multiple payback is required as the penalty, but the reader may reasonably ask, Why a fivefold payback for an ox and only a fourfold payback for a sheep?

A possible reason relates to the nature of sheep. They are inveterate wanderers, frequently going where they shouldn't; therefore they provide a more constant temptation for a person inclined to steal. They are easier to steal, being much smaller than an ox; they are more likely to show up in isolated locations away from their owner's property; and they can be much harder to drive home than an ox (who usually was trained and nose-ringed for easy handling in Bible times),[154] making returning them to your neighbor more of an annoyance than would, on average at least, be the case with an ox. In effect, then, sheep stealing is slightly more "understandable" than ox stealing. But there is yet another difference that probably accounts more precisely for the difference in penalty: a missing ox prevented work from being done on one's farm since oxen were so constantly used as work animals.[155] By contrast, a missing sheep may not do real harm for days at a time. Thus the loss of an ox was more substantial and required a more substantial penalty.[156]

From these examples, Israelite judges would extrapolate appropriate penalties for all sorts of animal (and even nonanimal) thefts. The judges would understand that a slightly less serious crime merits a slightly less severe resti-

---

[154] On the ease of taking care of oxen, see Zech 1:18–21, which is often translated confusingly but actually describes farmhands (NIV "craftsmen," Zech 1:20) herding horned oxen (symbolically representing the nations that had previously terrified Israel) back into their places so they could not harm Israel in the future.

[155] Cf. Exod 23:12; Num 7:3; Deut 5:14; 15:19; 22:10; 25:4; 1 Kgs 19:19.

[156] The NIV wording "five head of cattle for the ox" is defensible but not provable; it could as well be "five oxen for an ox" (e.g., NRSV) or the like, since the Hb. word translated by the NIV as "head of cattle" *(bāqār)* is used in various ways. Here it could signify five adult cattle of either gender, which would include the possibility of "five oxen" but not automatically require it. This relates to the consideration that there are two other, somewhat different, ways to think about the discrepancy in penalties. The first, and less likely, is that it could be quite hard for a thief to round up five adult males since adult females were much more abundant as a result of the usual farming selection in favor of females. So the law allowed for any five head of cattle, the mix of genders being less valuable as compared to adult male animals—if oxen only could even be found. The second and more likely is simply, as noted above, that sheep wander very easily, and people inclined to steal can steal sheep much more easily (sometimes just "taking" one that has wandered into one's own field) than oxen, so the crime of sheep stealing is actually somewhat less "deliberate" than oxen stealing would be. The slightly less serious crime merits the slightly less severe restitution.

tution. By this sort of penalty structure, God demonstrates his desire that punishments should be as precisely and carefully calculated as possible in any application of justice rather than mechanistically applied without regard for the actual circumstances of a crime.[157]

22:2–3a [Hb. 22:1-2a] Modern law statutes typically define burglary approximately as "breaking and entering in the nighttime with the intent to commit a felony." Modern case law has allowed homeowners to apply lethal force in defending their living quarters at nighttime, even if an intruder turns out to have been unarmed. The theory behind this day-night differentiation (i.e., between burglary and mere breaking and entering) relates to the decreased ability to see at night, especially in times and places where electric lighting may not be present or may not be sufficiently present.

There are four particular reasons for this. First, it may be assumed that a person who has legitimate business to do around someone else's house or property will do it in the daytime when visibility for working properly is good; thus, only a person with malicious intent would be entering and/or picking up and/or carrying things away from someone else's house during the night. Second, defending one's property at night, when the ability to see is limited, means that one cannot be as subtle in the application of force as might be possible during the daytime, especially because of the difficulty of seeing whether or not an intruder has a weapon. Third, a homeowner who has just been awakened from sleep by an intruder cannot be expected to react as calmly as could someone who is wide awake and will feel far more vulnerable to the sort of violence he may assume could be applied to him at any moment than would be the case in the daytime. Fourth, in the daytime one can call others to one's aid to subdue a thief; in the night this is much more difficult and could more easily result in the wrong person's being subdued.

Thus the present law allowed the use of deadly force against intruding thieves from sundown to sunup, but not during the daylight. The property owner could still defend against theft in the daytime but could not use lethal force in the process. The law, in other words, did not allow unlimited freedom to the victim of a crime to defend or retaliate. Even a criminal caught in the act of a serious crime had protections; conversely, even the victim of a serious crime could be prosecuted for murder if he resisted more violently than could be justified (thus the specific mention of being "guilty of bloodshed," v. 3a).

22:3b [Hb. 22:2b] Thievery has no excuse. Although it is true that a rich thief might suffer relatively less for his crime by paying back only a small percentage of his wealth in compensation/restitution, a poor thief could not

---

[157] Another way of saying this is to note that biblical law provides for a considerable degree of judicial discretion, within bounds, so that judges could and indeed were expected to take into consideration every aspect of a crime when rendering their judgments.

justify his actions by claiming that his poverty excused his crime. He must make restitution, and if he lacked the means to do so, he would have to earn it by selling himself into servitude, presumably for the usual six-year term (see comments on 21:2-4.). This law confirms that in a contractual sale into servitude the general practice may have been for the buyer to pay at least a major part of the money at the very beginning of the contract. Otherwise the wording "he must be sold to pay for his theft" would need modification since payment for the theft would be delayed by whatever number of years it would take for the thief to earn his payment. The presumption in the law is that of an immediate payment once the contract for servitude was agreed to.

22:4 [Hb. 22:3] Completing the chiasm of vv. 1–4 by reverting to the question of the amount of restitution (as was addressed in v. 1),[158] v. 4 provides for a reduced restitution penalty (double recompense rather than fourfold or fivefold) for a stolen animal found alive (and presumably well) in the possession of the thief. Why such leniency? Because God's law seeks to assess the amount of "harm done" rather than merely the sort of "crime committed." When a thief had not yet disposed of an animal, many outcomes were possible, including the possibility that he might have a change of heart and return the animal and beg for forgiveness. Moreover, the discovery of a theft without disposal of the stolen item usually would indicate a very recent theft, one that disadvantaged the actual owner in a more limited way than the situation envisioned in v. 1. Remembering that these laws are paradigmatic guidelines, we should at a minimum infer that God wants justice that takes into account all circumstances and motives and does not treat all acts of theft (or any other sort of crime) as if they were equal. Evaluation of the actual loss to the owner is a major consideration in a court's ruling on a theft.[159]

TWO LAWS ON RESTITUTION FOR DAMAGES FROM NEGLECT (22:5–6) [Hb. 22:4-5]. Type of law: casuistic (applied when someone had been neglectful so that damage to another's property had resulted). Paradigmatic range: virtually any situation where damages had been incurred by reason of another's neglect.

22:5 [Hb. 22:4] The paradigmatic example used in this law is that of a neglectful farmer whose grazing animals were not attended to well enough so that they eventually left his own land and grazed on someone else's. No intel-

---

[158] Note how some translations, notably the NRSV, place v. 4 immediately after v. 1 and then continue with vv. 2,3,5. This reordering of the verses represents a convenience for the modern reader but probably does not reflect an original order (i.e., an order that was garbled somewhere in the process of transmission) since the chiastic structuring of the verses is a far more likely explanation for their order than a theory that they became disordered in the process of copying and recopying over time.

[159] So in modern times law codes recognize the difference between "misdemeanor theft" and "felony theft" or, following another terminology, "petty larceny" and "grand larceny." How much the victim has lost is central to how severe the penalty imposed on the thief can be.

ligent farmer would allow his grazing cattle (sheep, goats, cows, bulls/oxen) anywhere near his planted fields or his vineyards without keeping them tethered.[160] But grazing cattle are instinctively driven to move to new pastures and will push through any but the strongest barrier (e.g., thick thornbushes used in OT times as field fencing),[161] and they cannot be left alone for long periods of time. At night many farmers brought their large cattle into the courtyards of their homes, where the large and thick stone/brick walls would confine them.[162] Smaller cattle (sheep and goats) were confined to specially built pens for the evening or at shearing time.[163] But they could not simply be left without attention, lest they wander off into someone's planted field or vineyard (or orchard) and ruin a portion of the crop by grazing and trampling. Should such neglect occur, the farmer responsible was required to supply restitution (an amount equal to what was eaten or trampled or otherwise ruined[164]) "from the best of his own" fields and vineyards/orchards. A farmer knew that if he were neglectful in the manner described in this law, he would lose not merely a certain amount of grain or fruit (or even whole fruit trees) but the very best of that grain or fruit—the quality factor serving as a serious deterrent in addition to the quantity factor.

22:6 [Hb. 22:5] This second law in the grouping is parallel to what preceded, though involving another instance of neglect as a paradigm for neglect of all sorts: letting a fire get out of control. The quality terms of the prior law ("the best of") may be assumed implicitly to apply here as well. It doesn't matter whether the grain was harvested already ("shocks of grain") or was still standing in the field ("standing grain") or both ("the whole field"); full, best-quality restitution must be made in kind by the negligent farmer.

LAWS GOVERNING PROPERTY RESPONSIBILITY DISPUTES (22:7–15) [Hb. 22:6-14] One of the most difficult challenges for any judge or arbiter is deciding between claims and counterclaims made by people who are supposed

---

[160] The purpose of grazing animals in fields or vineyards is to allow them to "clean up" ground cover and brush or stubble that provides food for the animals without hurting the crop planted there or one that had been harvested, leaving the stubble.

[161] Cf. Isa 5:5; Hos 2:6; Mic 7:4. Wood was so rare and expensive in ancient Israel that using it for a fence was virtually out of the question. Stone walls also were used to confine animals, but even so the barriers readily available to OT-era farmers were of limited strength; a farmer with grazing animals had to be vigilant, and animals generally had to be tethered, even in well-bounded fields (cf. Gen 49:11; 2 Kgs 7:10; Matt 21:2 par; Isa 37:29). At night or in cases of a large animal known to be dangerous, they were confined either to courtyards or to strong pens (Exod 21:29,36; 1 Sam 6:7).

[162] This is how it came to pass that the baby Jesus was laid in a manger in the courtyard of the inn at Bethlehem; biblical-era courtyards had animal feeding troughs. Jesus was not born in a "stable," in other words, but in the courtyard of the inn, where overflow guests were quartered.

[163] Cf. Num 32:24,36; 1 Sam 24:3; 2 Chr 32:28; Ps 78:70; Hab 3:17; John 10:1.

[164] The damage goats can do to fruit trees or vines is hardly limited to eating the fruit itself; eating the branches prevents future growth as well.

to be friends. It is possible for well-meaning individuals to disagree vehemently about who should take responsibility for a borrowed-but-lost item, or a borrowed-then-stolen item, or an item ruined while on loan. There is a natural tendency for the borrower or safekeeper of an item that did not actually belong to him permanently to take less interest in its preservation and to be psychologically and morally disinclined to feel fully responsible if the item is somehow lost, stolen, or damaged. Resentment over who is really to be held responsible in such cases can destroy not only friendships and neighborly[165] relations but can cause entire extended families to be at enmity,[166] something that could not be condoned in Yahweh's covenant community.

It was essential that Israelites understand and accept responsibility for the godly care of property, whether things or animals. Property entrusted by one person to another required acceptance of responsibility both by the giver and the receiver, and the laws that follow spell this out in a way that indicates its importance for keeping Yahweh's covenant in all aspects of life.

22:7–9 [Hb. 22:6-8] Type of law: casuistic (applied when a dispute arose over ownership or liability for safekeeping). Paradigmatic range: almost any situation where two parties disagreed over who should be responsible for some sort of property. Verse 7 addresses the easiest circumstance: theft of goods given to someone else for safekeeping was the responsibility of the thief as long as he was caught. He must repay double (the standard for nonanimal items), and the matter was closed between the person who entrusted his money (NIV "silver") or other goods to the neighbor.

Verse 8, however, introduces a more difficult issue: that of a neighbor's (fellow Israelite's or even fellow human's) claim that goods entrusted to his care were missing because they were stolen. How was the one who placed the goods with his neighbor to know whether they were stolen from the neighbor or by the neighbor? Or could they perhaps have been lost or ruined while in the neighbor's care, and now the neighbor was claiming theft as a way of avoiding responsibility for his negligence?[167] The only one who could know the answer is God.

In vv. 8–9 the NIV translators have chosen to render *ʾelōhîm*[168] as "judges," a translation that in our opinion cannot be sustained.[169] What the law calls for

---

[165] Remembering that "neighbor" means "fellow Israelite" or "anyone else you happen to come in contract with," not merely "nearby resident."

[166] These laws are promulgated in awareness of the way family feuds and hostilities in the Near East can grow from small disagreements and fester thereafter for centuries.

[167] Thus one reason for the inclusion of these laws immediately after the laws on negligence in vv. 5–6.

[168] Here in chap. 22 the expression is הָאֱלֹהִים, but this usage is standard for "the true God," or "the one and only God," and certainly need not mean "the gods" or "the judges" simply because it has the article (see Williams, *Hebrew Syntax,* #88).

[169] See comments on 21:6, note.

is a decision by God ("the owner of the house must appear before God," v. 8; "both parties are to bring their cases before God," v. 9).

How would this decision be accomplished? Verse 11 tells us: "The issue between them will be settled by the taking of an oath before the LORD." What if both parties swore that they were innocent? They and the court would simply have to leave the matter in God's hands for disposition, as Solomon envisioned in his prayer in 1 Kgs 8:31–32 ("When a man wrongs his neighbor and is required to take an oath and he comes and swears the oath before your altar in this temple, then hear from heaven and act. Judge between your servants, condemning the guilty and bringing down on his own head what he has done. Declare the innocent not guilty, and so establish his innocence"). But if both parties had (as the covenant expects) a proper fear of God (i.e., a fear of the consequence of disobeying him), it would normally be the case that, under oath, one of them would somehow and to some sufficient degree admit to being in the wrong in the dispute over the piece of property and would accept the requirement that he pay back double to his neighbor.

22:10–13 [Hb. 22:9-12] Type of law: casuistic (applied to situations of property given by one person to another for safekeeping). Paradigmatic range: any loss of anything while being kept by one person for another; a righteous judge would not consider its principles applicable only to lost animals. The provisions of these laws parallel for the most part those of 22:7–9 immediately preceding.

Various possibilities exist for the loss of a person's animal while it is being cared for by a neighbor. The law actually lists three that are fairly comprehensive in their coverage of possibilities ("it dies or is injured or is taken away"[170]), but any similar circumstance would fall under the purview of the law as well.[171] To avoid the inference that he was actually guilty of having disposed of the animal for his own profit or pleasure, the neighbor took an oath before God.[172] Note how seriously an oath of this sort was taken in ancient Israel (cf. 20:7,16): others must simply accept that the person taking the oath was telling the truth and leave the matter at that. Could the oath taker have been lying? Of course. But then he would have incurred God's enmity, a far worse matter than having incurred his neighbor's. If, however, the one who "lost" the animal could not or would not swear by formal oath in the presence of Yahweh (at the tabernacle or, later, temple) that he was innocent, he would be responsible to make the usual restitution.

---

[170] In this context "taken away" (נִשְׁבָּה) unquestionably means "carried off by a predatory animal" and does not mean "stolen by some" since the penalty for allowing an animal in one's care to be stolen is entirely different, as described in v. 12.

[171] E.g., an animal might be sold accidentally along with one's own animals brought to market or might simply wander off on its own and not be seen again.

[172] Here the text specifically uses the divine proper name Yahweh so that there can be no mistaking the auditor of the oath.

Verse 12, on the other hand, applies a standard that goes beyond the simple question of the innocence of the neighbor. Taking in an animal for safekeeping imposed a solemn responsibility on a person that required the person to preserve the animal from unobserved theft or pay restitution. One who agreed to keep an animal for another person for a time implicitly accepted this risk. The question might well be asked, "But since v. 13 exonerates the safekeeper from penalty if the animal could be proved to have been killed by a predator, why should the safekeeper be required to pay compensation for an animal that was stolen? The theft was no more his fault than the killing by the predator." The answer lies in the provability: only if the thief was caught was the safekeeper innocent (v. 7). Otherwise, he could not prove that a theft had occurred and thus presumptively was considered personally responsible for the loss of the animal. Claiming that "it must have been stolen" was no defense under the law.

22:14–15 [Hb. 22:13-14] Type of law: casuistic (applied in cases of borrowing or renting). Paradigmatic range: virtually any circumstance where someone who had borrowed or rented something could not return it whole or well. Borrowing or renting an animal represented a further extension of the sorts of laws already covered in vv. 7–13. To borrow (on renting, see below) was to take the risk that if one could not return the animal (animal being used here as a synecdoche for whatever might have been borrowed) in essentially the same condition it was in before being borrowed, one was obligated to pay damages. The restitution expected was surely along the lines of that specified in vv. 5–6, that is, a one-for-one substitute of as good or better quality. (One couldn't, e.g., return a twenty-year-old donkey as adequate compensation for a three-year-old donkey or a newborn buck goat for a breeding doe goat.)

Verse 15 clarifies the responsibility further in two facets: (1) If one borrowed or rented an animal along with the owner, it was the owner's job to look out for the welfare of his animal, not the borrower's. (2) If one rented an animal, the rental fee was expected to include "insurance" on the animal rented out. The owner must absorb the cost of an animal rented out that was then injured or killed while under the rental contract. As long as both parties knew that this was the arrangement (and the law was given to make sure that both would), then each knew where the risk lay.[173]

LAWS ABOUT PREMARITAL SEX AND THE BRIDE PRICE (22:16–17) [Hb. 22:15-16]. One might wonder what these regulations are doing here, at the end of a section clearly devoted to property responsibility disputes and crimes. Indeed, the NIV groups them with what follows rather than what precedes, as the

[173] This is not appreciably different from the situation with some rental automobiles today: the rental company insures the cars (though it may try to get the renter to assume some of the cost for the "deductible") and takes the risk that the renters may damage them.

first laws in a category they call simply "social responsibility" (vv. 16–31). The answer does not lie in the idea that women were regarded as property but in the idea that the institution of the bride price was an unwavering financial responsibility in ancient Israel that a man could not get out of paying by circumventing marriage vows and having premarital sex with a woman. Whether or not a man who had seduced a woman ended up being able to marry her, he had to pay the bride price[174] in either case. There are some significant implications to these laws relative to the way God regards sexual conduct in relation to marriage, as we discuss below.

22:16–17 [Hb. 22:15-16] Type of law: casuistic (applied when a man and a woman had had premarital sex without having made the proper betrothal and marriage arrangements, including the proper financial arrangements). Paradigmatic range: almost any bypassing of arranged marriage betrothal requirements that were designed not only to compensate the bride's family properly but to ensure a proper marriage and a proper start for a marriage). These verses, though they belong with what precedes, may be considered transitional in that they conclude the section on property responsibility/compensation and, as well, introduce the following section (vv. 16–31), which deals with various laws relating to social responsibility.

Biblically, marriage is understood to be a formal covenant, the most important of all *human* covenants. The sign of that covenant is sexual intercourse.[175] As Hugenberger has argued,[176] sexual intercourse functions as the sign of the covenant of marriage whether or not other formal, legal undertakings have been completed. In other words, sexual intercourse makes a couple "one flesh" or married *virtually* even if not legally and properly (as Paul contends in 1 Cor 6:16). Thus a couple who have engaged in sexual intercourse before marriage are "as if" married, and the bride price is due the woman's family whether or not they are actually allowed to get married.

Note, however, that neither here nor in 1 Cor 6:16 does the Bible direct that people who have had sexual intercourse without the benefit of marriage *must* go on to marry. Their virtual marriage is not regarded as an *actual* marriage in

---

[174] On the nature and purpose of a bride price in ancient Israel, see comments on 21:3–4. J. J. Finkelstein ("Sex Offences in Sumerian Laws," *JAOS* [1986]: 355–72, esp. 362–68) has argued on the basis of extrabiblical parallels that the reason for this law was that a woman who had sex with someone before her marriage could be arranged had seriously undermined her father's opportunity to arrange a marriage with anyone else, risking the complete forfeiture of the bride price, an important compensation to her family for the loss of her services once she moved, as was required by custom, to her husband's home. See also R. de Vaux, *Ancient Israel* 1:26–29, who suggests that a bride price may actually have been claimable by the bride herself if her father or her husband died.

[175] In biblical times a covenant usually had a reminder sign, which was some sort of symbol appropriate to the covenant's nature (for example, the rainbow was the sign of the covenant with Noah, circumcision of the Sinai covenant, baptism of the new covenant).

[176] G. P. Hugenberger, *Marriage as a Covenant* (Grand Rapids: Baker, 1998), passim.

God's sight, and no biblical ethic demands that they make their virtual marriage legal by actually marrying. The law is worded to describe the situation in which a man "seduces" a woman,[177] but it could be worded the other way around. No matter who seduces whom, the woman's potential bride price has been put at jeopardy, and the man's responsibility to pay it is therefore imposed.

Paying a price for a bride can seem a practice degrading to women, one that treats them as mere property. This was not the way it was understood in ancient Israel. In fact, it honored the value of a woman. Consider that the system does not allow one to think of price paid as an indicator of worth since the bride pays zero for her husband (there was no dowry system in ancient Israel), yet there is no doubt of the husband's worth. Part of the utility of a bride price was the way it forced a man to make a full and formal arrangement for marriage that properly involved both his interests and those of his bride-to-be, as well as the interests of his family and hers. The bride price requirement necessarily involved the families in substantial formal negotiations, and the price showed that something serious and important was at stake.[178] Taking a woman to oneself and taking away her virginity were honorable if the proper negotiations had been completed, and a proper indication of her worth had been paid to her family, and the couple were legally married. Simply having sexual relations with her, with or without her permission, devalued her and showed blatant disregard for her worth. It also showed that a person (or when the premarital sex was consensual, that the couple) viewed marriage or its covenant sign (sexual intercourse) as less than a formal, legal, lifelong contractual commitment. The betrothal/bride price system was designed to make marriage harder to come by than what could be achieved on whim or quick decision, and it elevated marriage accordingly because people instinctively value what is hard and costly to get.

Thus when a couple failed to go properly through the marriage negotiation process and had sexual relations anyway, the law required the man to pay the bride price. The father of the bride remained in the negotiator's position of being able to refuse to give his bride to her suitor (because if he loved his daughter, he would hardly want to see her married permanently to someone wrong for her just because she had been "seduced"). Since it would be much harder to marry her to someone else once she had been sexually compromised, he was still owed the bride price for her, lest no bride price ever be paid in the case that she was never, in fact, married thereafter. If he did allow her to marry

---

[177] The woman would have so much more to lose under the marriage laws and customs of Israel that it might be assumed she would have to be "seduced" more than the man, but laws are generally worded as applying to the singular male as a paradigm for all persons whether individual or plural.

[178] Here see also comments on 21:7.

the man she had already compromised herself with, whatever bride price was negotiated for the marriage prevailed.[179]

(4) Social and Religious Requirements (22:18–23:9)

18“Do not allow a sorceress to live.

19“Anyone who has sexual relations with an animal must be put to death.

20“Whoever sacrifices to any god other than the LORD must be destroyed.

21“Do not mistreat an alien or oppress him, for you were aliens in Egypt.

22“Do not take advantage of a widow or an orphan. 23If you do and they cry out to me, I will certainly hear their cry. 24My anger will be aroused, and I will kill you with the sword; your wives will become widows and your children fatherless.

25“If you lend money to one of my people among you who is needy, do not be like a moneylender; charge him no interest. 26If you take your neighbor’s cloak as a pledge, return it to him by sunset, 27because his cloak is the only covering he has for his body. What else will he sleep in? When he cries out to me, I will hear, for I am compassionate.

28“Do not blaspheme God or curse the ruler of your people. 29“Do not hold back offerings from your granaries or your vats. “You must give me the firstborn of your sons. 30Do the same with your cattle and your sheep. Let them stay with their mothers for seven days, but give them to me on the eighth day. 31“You are to be my holy people. So do not eat the meat of an animal torn by wild beasts; throw it to the dogs.

1“Do not spread false reports. Do not help a wicked man by being a malicious witness.

2“Do not follow the crowd in doing wrong. When you give testimony in a lawsuit, do not pervert justice by siding with the crowd, 3and do not show favoritism to a poor man in his lawsuit.

4“If you come across your enemy’s ox or donkey wandering off, be sure to take it back to him. 5If you see the donkey of someone who hates you fallen down under its load, do not leave it there; be sure you help him with it.

6“Do not deny justice to your poor people in their lawsuits. 7Have nothing to do with a false charge and do not put an innocent or honest person to death, for I will not acquit the guilty.

8“Do not accept a bribe, for a bribe blinds those who see and twists the words of the righteous.

9“Do not oppress an alien; you yourselves know how it feels to be aliens, because you were aliens in Egypt.

That we have entered in 22:18–23:9 a new section of the Covenant Code is signaled by the change of legal style: virtually this entire section is written in

---

[179] It may certainly be assumed that if the suitor tried to refuse to pay the bride price if he were denied the right to marry the woman by her father, the court would step in and force him to pay a price that it determined. He would not be allowed to get around his obligations to her and to her family.

apodictic legal wording, the alternative to the previously dominant casuistic legal style. In apodictic law the commands are given mostly in the second person, and the individual laws represent generally applicable legal instruction rather than the citation of cases designed to give a feel for particular situations and how to deal with them.

The noticeable change from casuistic to apodictic has led many scholars inclined toward atomistic analysis to identify this portion of the code, or even subportions of this portion, as a remnant of an original, independently composed code to which materials were eventually added to form the current code (or else a remnant that was incorporated into the current code) of chaps. 21–23. There are, however, a variety of compositional structural features that contribute to the coherence of the entire code, notwithstanding that it clearly has subsections, as any legal piece of its length would be expected to have. These apodictic laws pay special attention to crimes that should receive the death penalty (22:18–20, expressed paradigmatically by three capital punishment laws), laws forbidding the abuse of one's neighbor (22:21–27), laws that call attention to the importance of preserving God's holy honor (22:28–31), and a series of laws impressing on Israel the need for honesty in all relationships (23:1–8). Helping to unify this section of the Covenant Code is the twice-stated reminder that since the Israelites were themselves aliens in Egypt, they should remember the painful disadvantage of noncitizen status and be careful not to take advantage of anyone in an inferior social position (22:21; 23:9). This double reminder concludes both the opening set of laws (22:18–20) and the closing set (23:1–8) in the section and thus generally serves the function of an inclusio to surround and set off the remainder.

What should not be assumed is that this grouping of apodictic laws is somehow conceptually different or independent from the rest of the laws of the Covenant Code. In the composition of most Old Testament literature, materials of like nature tend to be grouped together.[180] It should not be surprising that within the code these laws, with their natural affinities for one another, would occur together. In ancient Israel's mainly oral-aural society, where writing and reading skills were less common than today, such affinity groupings made memorization and recall easier and thus served an important, user-friendly purpose.

---

[180] This tendency to group by similar genre, form, or the like is evident everywhere in the OT and was part of an ongoing tradition that culminated in the present organization of OT books into the fourfold Law-History-Poetry-Prophecy format found in English Bibles today. But within virtually any OT book such affinity grouping is evident already. Examples with which most readers may be familiar would include the way the prophetical books normally group woe prophecies, weal prophecies, oracles against foreign nations, each in their own "block" within the book; the way psalms of different literary forms tend to be grouped within the individual five books of the Psalter; the prologue-dialogue-monologue-epilogue structure of Job.

THREE CHARACTERISTICALLY CAPITAL CRIMES (22:18–20). **22:18–20** [Hb. 22:17-19] These three laws provide a paradigmatic overview of capital crimes. In other words, they were almost certainly intended to constitute a sampling of a broad range of offenses deserving the death penalty rather than to comprise the only three. Practicing occult magical arts ("do not allow a sorceress to live"), bestiality ("anyone who has sexual relations with an animal . . ."), and polytheism ("whoever sacrifices to any god other than the LORD . . .) represent very different topics brought together to suggest a wide panorama of criminal acts that could not be tolerated by the covenant community. The problem with these practices is not merely the abhorrent departure from decency they represent; their greater offense is in their attempt to substitute something in the place of the saving practices of Yahweh's covenant. God is always an evangelist, always seeking to rescue people from condemning sin. The types of sins that seriously deter people from accepting his salvation or that are patently contrary to living according to his covenant will are those that must be eradicated, even by such relatively drastic action as capital punishment. That these three laws are intended to be a sample triad of disparate capital punishment crimes is indicated by the three different ways the death penalty is stated: "do not allow . . . to live" (v. 18), "must be put to death" (v. 19), and "must be destroyed" (v. 20). If these laws had accidentally "fallen together" from originally independent collections, we might expect that they would not be worded with such variety; as it is, three different samples of capital crimes are worded three different ways to impress upon the reader that nothing less than the death penalty would do for such serious offenses. The message stated more colloquially is: You can put people who do these kinds of things to death in any of the several proper ways, but just be sure you don't let them live to pollute the covenant community with their practices.

But should sorcery, bestiality, and polytheism really be capital crimes? Aren't these laws barbaric examples of the primitive nature of ancient justice, of a value system inferior to our enlightened sense of right and wrong? On the one hand, it must surely be admitted that the Old Covenant law has been replaced by that of the New Covenant, with its emphasis on allowing the society in which one lives to administer the death penalty (even if unfairly) and not the church. This has the practical value of allowing different standards of justice among the different nations of the world because Christ's kingdom is not an earthly one. Thus for the Christian, capital punishment or any other punishment more severe than expulsion from the church is hardly an option. The basic answer from the point of view of the Old Testament covenant community, however, is that these capital punishment laws protected people from losing their chance for salvation. How so?

Sorcery led people astray from placing their faith in Yahweh alone by inviting them to think that with the help of a medium (as in the story of Saul and the medium at Endor, 1 Sam 28) or enchantress or the like, they could learn hidden information or gain power over their enemies, and so on. The term "sorceress" encompasses a range of occult practices,[181] any and all of which were forbidden to Israelites. Sorcery is condemned throughout the Old Testament (e.g., Lev 19:26; Deut 18:9–14; 2 Kgs 9:21–26; 17:17; Jer 27:8–11; Mic 5:10–15; Nah 3:1–4; Mal 3:5) and in the New Testament as well (e.g., Acts 8:9ff; 13:6–8; 19:19).

Bestiality ("sexual relations with an animal") is a relatively uncommon practice but stands paradigmatically as an example of the sorts of perversions Yahweh's covenant will not countenance. A person who practices bestiality shows himself to be someone who has no regard for godliness, but the practice goes beyond this in its significance. It also was apparently associated with various Canaanite fertility practices and thus was somewhat like the prohibition against boiling a goat kid in its mother's milk.[182] It represented the replacement of sexually based fertility religion for the saving truth of Yahweh's covenant.[183]

The third law in the opening group of three ("Whoever sacrifices to any god other than the LORD must be destroyed") prohibits polytheism or, to be precise, any religion except the worship of Yahweh. The covenant in process of being revealed here was for followers of Israel's God, the true God, and not for any other sorts of believers. "Whoever sacrifices to" is the virtual equivalent of "whoever worships." There was no religion in the ancient world that did not employ sacrifice (the offering of food) as a key part of worship, so "sacrifice" functions as a synecdoche for "worship."[184] Thus this command says, in effect, "Worship only Yahweh, and if you try to introduce any other worship into the covenant people, you must be put to death." Again the severity of the crime stems from its potential to keep people from the eternal salvation that was possible in the true God alone and therefore

---

[181] The term used in the text is מְכַשֵּׁפָה, referring to a woman who practices various occult arts including necromancy, the purported ability to be in contact with and learn from the spirits of the dead. It is never precisely defined in the OT, leading to the conclusion not that it is a term without meaning but that a variety of types of forbidden occult practices could be subsumed under the term. A parallel in terms of range of meaning would be the term "magician" in English, which can include many practices within its purview.

[182] See comments on 23:19; 34:26.

[183] So H. Cazelles, *Études sur le code de l'alliance* (Paris: Letouzy et Ané, 1946), esp. 76.

[184] Indeed, it may be argued that sacrifice was one of the religious universals of the ancient world, a reflection of a common memory, however imperfect otherwise, of what God had originally required of human beings (Gen 4:3–5; 8:20).

simply could not be achieved by fidelity to any other gods, whether by themselves or in syncretistic tandem with Yahweh.[185]

LAWS AGAINST NOT LOVING ONE'S NEIGHBOR, WITH GOD AS ENFORCER (22:21–27) [Hb. 22:20-26]. The terms "aliens," "widows," "orphans," "poor/needy" are not intended to be an exhaustive list of certain categories of people. Instead they are intended to be evocative of the entire range of disadvantaged, unprotected, and easily mistreated individuals and groups in ancient times, including those among the Israelites who were disadvantaged in any way. Any of these words or any group of these words in any combination can function as a synecdoche for "any or all unprotected people."[186] No government welfare system existed in Israel. It was the responsibility of the covenant community—each Israelite, assuming the covenant was actually kept faithfully—to contribute his share of the welfare burden personally (rather than through taxes), to avoid personally any discrimination against the needy in any way, and to treat all those in need or of limited resources as brothers and sisters, virtual family members. Yahweh himself was the enforcer of this demand for fair treatment of all the "little" people anywhere in Israel (vv. 23–24,27). He would not allow his people to act in a discriminatory manner, that is, in the manner of pagans. Their calling was to a higher standard, which reflected his own compassion for all.[187] If they obeyed his covenant fully, he would prosper them sufficiently that they could have enough for themselves and enough left over to take care of those who, for whatever reason, could not make a living (cf. Deut 15:4).

22:21–22 [Hb. 22:20-21] The Hebrew terms translated here "mistreat" (*ynh, hiphil*), "oppress" (*lḥṣ, qal*), and "take advantage of" (*ʾnh, piel*) are synonyms having broad semantic ranges, individually and together prohibiting

---

[185] Syncretism, the merging and blending of religious beliefs, was so common in the ancient world as to be virtually ubiquitous. A typical ancient person would not deny that Yahweh existed but might well deny that he was the only God or, indeed, that he was anything other than Israel's national god, i.e., one god among many gods of many nations. Israel's temptation was to follow this line of reasoning and to appreciate Yahweh as their national god (national deliverer and defender) but to find in Baal and Asherah the divine expertise for crop and animal fertility, in Dagon the divine expertise for grain abundance, in Molech the divine expertise for family prosperity. It can even be said that what the Israelites were tempted to do when they entered into idolatry was never to reject Yahweh outright but simply to reject his exclusivity.

[186] See comments on 6:4; 12:48–49; 20:10 for prior instances of the use of the term "alien" (גֵּר). "Widow" (אַלְמָנָה) and "orphan" (יָתוֹם) are commonly used together (the terms may be found in either the singular or plural, whether used together or separately) to denote any or all persons who need someone else to protect or to provide for them because of their disadvantaged position in ancient society. Cf. Job 24:3; Jer 49:11; Lam 5:3; Jas 1:27. Laws to be sure the poor were not taken advantage of or treated differently from the rich occur again in Exodus (23:6,11; 30:15) but were especially common in the continuation of the Sinai covenant in Leviticus (14:21; 19:10,15; 23:22; 25:25).

[187] Although all Israelites are God's people, there is a sense in which he specially identifies with the poor and needy as his "people" as over against the more well-to-do when the latter group attempts to exploit the former (e.g., Pss 14:6; 69:32; 112:9; Prov 14:31; Isa 14:30; 25:4).

any sort of misuse or unfair treatment of the needy. In v. 21 Israel is reminded of its history of mistreatment as aliens (noncitizens) in Egypt. The fact that Israel was in Egypt for 430 years before the exodus (Exod 12:20; Gal 3:17) confirms the definition of *gēr* used in v. 20 as "alien" or "resident alien" over against "nonresident" or "stranger." The Israelites lived in Egypt for over four centuries without the rights accorded to citizens, but they were certainly not *strangers* to Egypt. Because every member of the Israelite nation hearing these words for the first time had been in the situation of aliens in Egypt only months prior, it might be assumed that they would all automatically loathe any form of discrimination against aliens and would seek naturally to avoid the sorts of practices of which they themselves had painfully been victims. The law assumes nothing of the sort. Knowing human nature, God explicitly warned his people not to do what might have come naturally for them—seeking to enjoy the experience of lording it over someone else for once. Discrimination against noncitizens was so common in the ancient world, and the tendency to hypocrisy so natural for human beings, that Israel had to be warned against both at once in this law.[188] They could not rightly engage in what they so roundly condemned when it was done to them, and they could not fall into the easy patterns of the culture of which they were a part, but they had to break with temptation and tradition and act differently from others if they were to be Yahweh's holy covenant people.

In v. 22 the "widow" and "orphan" are added as examples of those who could easily be taken advantage of. How so? What made aliens (v. 21), widows and orphans, and the needy/poor (vv. 24–25) at risk for exploitation? The answer is simply that each of these types of persons lacked one or more types of protections otherwise afforded within the society in which they lived.[189]

Aliens lacked the guarantees of citizenship, which included the right to their own permanent land ownership among the tribes, the right to family, clan, and tribal support/backing in legal disputes, the right to direct involvement in the political process,[190] the right to freedom from exploitation by those with greater "clout" either politically or socially or monetarily than they possessed, and the right to resist noncriminal deportation. Widows lacked direct legal participatory rights (since women were represented by their hus-

---

[188] See also H. V. Bennett, *Injustice Made Legal: Deuteronomic Law and the Plight of Widows, Strangers and Orphans in Ancient Israel* (Grand Rapids: Eerdmans, 2002); and C. van Houten, *The Alien in Israelite Law* (Sheffield: JSOT Press, 1991).

[189] In addition to the reference in the note above, see also R. M. Price, *The Widow Traditions in Luke-Acts: A Feminist-Critical Scrutiny* (Atlanta: Scholars Press, 1997).

[190] Although ancient Israel was hardly a democracy, in both ancient and modern times opportunities for personal expression and the exercise of personal political rights flourish more fully as one goes "down" the ladder from the federal/national to the local level. One's rights in an individual village district, even within the context of an absolute monarchy, can be far more nearly "democratic" than one's rights relative to the power of the king.

bands in legal matters[191] and a widow had no husband) and could not own land in their own names under many conditions.[192] If too old to work, they would have no means of providing even for enough food to eat without other members of the family intervening on their behalf. A widow who had nothing otherwise to support herself could easily be made to work long hours for next to nothing as a virtual slave.

Orphans, if young enough, were similarly at the mercy of others. If they had no separate inheritance of their own and were not otherwise protected by older (extended) family members, they might have to work virtually endlessly for whatever anyone chose to pay them—perhaps just some food to get through each day. If there were no work and no one "took them in," they might actually starve to death or freeze to death.

22:23–24 [Hb. 22:22-23] Here God warned that social injustice could result in the unleashing of the covenant curses (the full listings of which are still to come, in Lev 26 and Deut 28–33) with the net effect of a general rejection of Israel and its consignment to destruction as a political entity. This represents a most serious sort of emphasis on the necessity for social justice if the people are to remain Yahweh's people and not be decimated and discarded by him. The wording here is something like the equivalent of saying, "I simply will not tolerate any exploitation of anyone! If it happens and is serious enough (partly the point of "they cry out to me"), I will ruin you in response!" The covenant curses cited in v. 24 are intended to function as examples, not as a complete list of the miseries that would come upon Israel as punishment for exploitation.

The first of these ("I will kill you with the sword") is of a type well attested in the Pentateuch (e.g., Lev 26:25, "I will bring the sword upon you," or Deut 32:42, "I will make my arrows drunk with blood, while my sword devours flesh"). The expression "the sword" is often used in the Old Testament and New Testament as a metonymy for "warfare" (cf. Exod 17:13; Lev 26:6; Deut 32:24; 2 Sam 1:12; 2:26). The threat implied here is that God would allow Israel's enemies to attack and exterminate them if they did not uphold social justice.

The second punishment sampled in the verse ("your wives will become widows") and the third ("your children fatherless") are examples of "loss of family" covenant curses (cf. Deut 28:30, "Another will take [your betrothed] and ravish her," or Deut 28:41, "You will have sons and daughters but will not keep them," or Deut 32:25, "The sword will make them childless," this last example combining both the warfare and loss of family curse types).[193]

---

[191] E.g., Prov 31:23; Ruth 4:1–11.

[192] The law that resulted from the case of the daughters of Zelophehad and their request for proper inheritance rights represented a great protection for women in Israel (Num 27:1–11; 36:1–12), but its benefits were limited to daughters, not to widowed wives.

[193] For an introduction to the covenant curses and blessings by category see D. Stuart, *Hosea-Jonah*, WBC (Waco: Word, 1987), xxi–xlii.

Two other examples of exploitation of the weak, firmly forbidden to Israelites, round out this section of laws: a prohibition against charging interest on a loan and a prohibition against taking any necessity as a surety on a loan.

22:25 [Hb. 22:24] Borrowing and lending are common practices in almost any society; they are not in themselves forbidden by this law. Indeed, during the revival of strict Israelite covenant law under Nehemiah almost a millennium later than Moses originally mediated it, lending and borrowing per se were allowed. It was charging interest (and presumably any other sort of exploitive practice) that were expressly prohibited, just as in this law.[194] Variations of this prohibition are found not only again in the Pentateuch (Lev 25:36–37; Deut 23:19–20) but also in a proverb that promises similar disaster for those who charge interest to the poor, interest that is by definition exorbitant (Prov 28:8: "He who increases his wealth by exorbitant interest amasses it for another, who will be kind to the poor"); and variations are found in the Prophets (notably Ezek 18:8,13,17; 22:12). The wording of v. 25 ("lend . . . to one of my people . . . who is needy") might seem at first glance to prohibit only lending at interest to the poor, allowing the charging of interest to those who can afford to pay it and merely prohibiting charging interest to those who are too indigent to add it to the repayment of their loan. But this is not the intent, as is shown by the parallels in Lev 25:36–37 ("Do not take interest of any kind from him, but fear your God, so that your countryman may continue to live among you. You must not lend him money at interest or sell him food at a profit") and Deut 23:19–20 ("Do not charge your brother interest, whether on money or food or anything else that may earn interest. You may charge a foreigner interest, but not a brother Israelite, so that the LORD your God may bless you in everything you put your hand to in the land you are entering to possess"). In other words, any charging of interest by Israelite to Israelite was *usury* (the charging of *excessive* interest) because zero interest was to be the norm for loan transactions.[195] The law cites the example of charging interest to the needy not because it was the only circumstance under which charging interest was forbidden but because it was an example of an illegal action that was especially unfair and exploitative.

This law contains the only reference to a "moneylender" (*nōšeh,* also translatable simply as "creditor" as in the NRSV here and NIV of 2 Kgs 4:1) in the Old Testament laws. It can be inferred from the prohibition against charging interest among Israelites that actual professional moneylenders would have had a chance to stay in business only in connection with business deals that

---

[194] Neh 5:1–13. Note that in the situation of that time, charging as little as one percent interest was defined as usury by Nehemiah (5:11).

[195] Cf. E. Neufeld, "The Prohibitions against Loans at Interest in Ancient Hebrew Laws," *HUCA* 26 (1955): 355–412.

involved foreigners (Deut 23:20); but it may also be the case that the primary referent in people's minds for this term would have been moneylenders in Egypt, who had exploited the Israelites when they were there.

22:26–27 [Hb. 22:25-26] This law addresses loan sureties, the properties that people put up as "collateral" for a loan to assure the lender that they will repay. Normally a lender's incentive to grant a loan is the confidence that if the borrower defaults, the lender can then take the property as his own in compensation for the unrecovered money. In the case of this law, as opposed to the law immediately preceding, a distinction is made between the way a poor person and a nonpoor person must be treated. The presumption of the law is that most people have property that does not represent their very survival or the continuance of their health and that if that sort of property is pledged as surety on a loan, such collateral is allowable.

By contrast, people who own so little that they would actually have to pledge an essential item to obtain a loan (the instance paradigmatically cited being a cloak needed to keep warm at night) must be exempted from the requirement of putting up a surety—or else have the essential surety returned to them nightly. Otherwise their health would be put at risk by the loan, and that is unacceptable to Yahweh. A law such as this is patently paradigmatic; for "cloak" one could substitute food, job, shelter, family member, or any other "essential" thing.[196]

The character of God ("I will hear, . . . I am compassionate"[197]) is cited as the guarantee of this loan. With such a guarantee, no exact penalty need be specified (how could God not know how best to punish someone who broke one of his laws?). Proper fear of Yahweh would motivate Israelites to respect these laws just as well as or better than some sort of fine or corporal punishment could.[198]

LAWS REQUIRING RESPECT FOR GOD'S HOLINESS (22:28–31) [Hb. 22:27-30]. Type of law: apodictic (second person direct command, with general applicability throughout the population). Paradigmatic range: requiring obedience and respect for what rightfully belongs to God or rightfully exalts

---

[196] Thus a modern equivalent might be "retirement plan" or "life savings" or "inheritance" or "house" depending on the circumstances. (In modern bankruptcy law, the principles inherent here are preserved: one can declare bankruptcy and be allowed to keep a house, a job, most of one's salary, and certain other essentials no matter how great one's debts or how many one's creditors.)

[197] On the compassion of God as an essential part of his nature, see Exod 34:6; Deut 13:17; 32:36; Neh 9:17; Ps 86:15.

[198] Additionally, it can be argued that disadvantaged people who were systematically discriminated against would suffer injustice at the hands of the court system as well as from individuals in a bigoted society. Accordingly, it is better to have Yahweh himself function as the guarantor of these laws than to leave them to the civil authorities, whose responsiveness and fairness might not be trustworthy because they would share the same discriminatory values as those whom the disadvantaged were accusing in court.

his holiness in all areas of life so that God's character, nature, claims, and possessions are neither challenged nor neglected.

22:28 [Hb. 22:27] The first of this group of laws requiring respect for God's holiness addresses the way a verbal attack can represent a serious sort of assault. Modern people used to the notion of virtually unlimited freedom of speech may not be fully aware of the power of words to do harm and to disrupt relationships, whereas ancients in some instances more clearly understood the dangers of unbridled free speech.[199] God's people could not curse either him or any legitimate leader in Israelite society. Paul's words before the Sanhedrin demonstrate his (and their) understanding that this applied even to those who may have been abusing their authority and that the law referred indeed to verbal attacks (Acts 23:5, "Do not speak evil about the ruler of your people").[200] The NIV translation "blaspheme" (show contempt for or revile God) for *qll* here therefore seems perfectly justified, although "curse" would also represent the Hebrew accurately. The law tells the Israelites that they had better respect God at all times and show full respect as well to any legitimate human leader of his people. The term translated "the ruler" in the NIV *(nāśîʾ)* refers to any leader with executive authority at any level in the society (lit., "a ruler among your people"), not just a national ruler.[201] It can also be translated "chief." The NIV use of the article is not justified; it should more safely be rendered *a* ruler/leader/chief. The term is indefinite in the original, both formally and logically. The requirement is not merely an Old Covenant expectation, as Rom 13:1–7 makes clear for the civil arena and as many New Testament instructions make

---

[199] Indeed, modern societies sometimes protect such things as sex shows and pornography/obscenity by arguing that these are forms of free speech, an idea that would have been laughable to ancients. On the risks of speaking freely without considering the potential of words to do great harm and cause lasting psychological damage, cf., e.g., Job 5:21; Pss 5:9; 12:3; 15:3; 52:2; Prov 6:17; 15:4; Jer 9:8; and esp. Prov 18:21; 25:15.

[200] In his extensive study *The Problem of Curse in the Hebrew Bible,* Brichto has argued that the first verb in this verse, קלל, *(piel)* translated by the NIV as "blaspheme," means merely "to make light of" and the like and is not in fact a synonym of the second verb in the verse, ארר (pp. 150–65), and this is accepted by Durham in his commentary (*Exodus,* 329). J. Scharbert (*Bib* 39 [1958]: 5–14) has also argued that while ארר means "curse," קלל *(piel)* means "show disrespect for" and that the two cannot be equated. We find these arguments unconvincing. The language of the present verse is highly parallelistic so that the two verbs are obviously intended to be generally interchangeable, and קלל *(piel)* is routinely recognized by lexicographers as meaning "curse" in the sense of "make a serious verbal attack on someone in the hope of harming them" or the like. Contexts such as Gen 12:3: Jer 15:10; Isa 8:21; would seem to be impossible to explain away as containing only the meaning "make light of" (or "neglect," "fail to appreciate") for קלל *(piel).* Indeed, the most basic sense of the verb is "to declare someone cursed" (W. Holladay, *A Concise Hebrew and Aramaic Lexicon of the Old Testament* [Grand Rapids: Eerdmans, 1971], 319). Cf. Exod 21:17.

[201] Thus so great a figure as the Messiah is a *nāśîʾ* in Ezek 44–48, but a mere clan leader can also be so titled (e.g., Num 25:14;1 Chr 7:40; 2 Chr 1:2).

clear in the arena of the church. Honor is to be shown to all who may warrant it, including in effect all one's brothers and sisters in Christ in a general sense and all church leaders in a specific sense.[202] Any legitimate leader in God's family, whether ancient Israel or the church, leads with God's authority and *in God's place* as his delegate. Therefore to curse such a leader is, indirectly but seriously, to curse God.

22:29–30 [Hb. 22:28-29] Respect for God's holiness also implies keeping basic rules such as the tithe and the firstborn offering because these are things that he rightfully owns and are thus due him automatically. Withholding[203] these from him represents a direct act of defiance, an open (to him even if not to others) refusal to cooperate with his covenant by keeping from him those things that directly show that he is the sovereign and that all things belong to him. Any Israelite might be tempted to keep back offerings or payments to God of any sort, just as people today tend to make religious and charitable offerings from what they regard as their discretionary (leftover) income rather than even placing such giving in the same category as mortgage or car payments—let alone giving them the highest priority of all. God can seem less demanding, less threatening, more "distant," more forgiving than the tax collector or the lending institution, and what is owed him can therefore end up being treated as secondary to what is owed to others. Note also the stern reminder in 30:15 relative to bringing tithes and offerings to the central sanctuary at the annual feast times. "No one is to appear before me empty-handed" (23:15).

The firstborn males of all humans and animals were God's. Did he actually expect that these would be given over to him in their infancy? Yes and no. Only those animals suitable for sacrificing (lambs, goat kids, calves, etc.) were actually received at the tabernacle and slaughtered, cooked, and eaten (or dedicated entirely to God as whole burnt offerings). The firstborn male offspring of all other animals and humans were to be redeemed instead, bought back from God by the payment of a price that substituted for their lives.[204]

Most sacrificial animals were slaughtered when young, but taking a newborn animal away from its mother before even a week had gone by would have

---

[202] E.g., Rom 13:8–10; 1 Cor 12:14–31; Eph 6:5; Phil 2:29; 1 Thess 5:12; 1 Tim 3:8–11; 5:17; 1 Pet 2:17.

[203] The term translated in the NIV by "hold back" (תְּאַחֵר) can also be translated "withhold" or "delay [in bringing]," but an intriguing suggestion, one that must remain, in our judgment, highly speculative, has been offered by A. Ahuviah in his Hb. article the title of which is simply a quote of the Hb. wording here, "*Mele'ateka wedim'aka lo' te'aher*," *BMik* 34 (1988/89): 24–26. He suggests that the Hb. verb employed here has sometimes been understood in Jewish/rabbinic history as having the meaning "to practice prostitution" in the metaphorical sense of dishonoring God publicly. Ahuviah connects this verse with the previous one logically and concludes that failure to bring sacrifices to God is a public disloyalty that goes hand in hand with cursing or blaspheming him.

[204] See comments on 13:13–15; 34:19–20; cf. Lev 27, passim.

been disadvantageous for several reasons. It would have denied Yahweh and the worshipers the benefit of a week of rapid growth, fattening the young animal and making it more desirable as a sacrifice. It would also have made the deprivation more shocking for the doe or ewe who gave birth, especially if the only young that happened to be born in a given birthing season were males.[205] Moreover, a newborn animal needs time to be cleaned up by its mother[206] and thus to be more presentable as a respectful gift to Yahweh.

Further, the command to "give them to me on the eighth day" makes very clear that the "seven days" of the preceding part of the sentence is not just a rough or "round" figure but a maximum/minimum limit—a precise length of time. Thereby no one can withhold his sacrifice from Yahweh for reasons of convenience; everyone has the same time requirement for promptness in bringing the sacrifice to the central sanctuary.

22:31 [Hb. 22:30] The covenant people were specially related to Yahweh as his own family by the covenant[207] and therefore were expected to reflect his standards in their own eating practices. The verse may also be translated: "You are a people consecrated to me. Therefore . . ." They might not have needed to be quite so strict as he is (e.g., they could eat lambs and goat kids that were less than the very best of the firstborn, i.e., the ones left over after they had given Yahweh in tithes the choice ones that he claimed),[208] but they could not let their standards drop so low as to eat carrion.

One reason for this prohibition was that the meat of an animal killed by other animals would still contain some of the blood and would thus violate the paradigmatic principle of the law in 23:18 (restated in 34:25).[209] Another reason was surely the concern for the people's health. Scavenged meat that had been dead for a time was subject to contamination from various sources, including bacteriological spread from the animal killed and/or the killer as

---

[205] Lambs and goats tend to have only one or two offspring at a time. The males were taken after a week for sacrifice, and the females were kept for milk and breeding, to increase the flock. The same basic approach is used nearly universally today relative to edible animal farming.

[206] As is now well understood, the mother's licking of the afterbirth stimulates hormonal changes that benefit the mother's milk production and physiological changes that strengthen the newborn animal.

[207] See "Covenant as Kinship" in Cross, *From Epic to Canon*.

[208] Cf. also Deut 12:15–20, where eating meat for the simple purpose of satisfying hunger is allowed, in contrast to the practice prevailing in much of the ancient world that saw all meat eating as yet another chance to get on good terms with the gods and so relegated the consumption of meat strictly to shrines as a matter of location and worship as a matter of purpose.

[209] Note also the fact that the Jerusalem Council regarded prohibition against eating meat with the blood in it ("the meat of strangled animals" rather than animals properly slaughtered so as to drain the blood from their bodies) as so basic that they made it one of their few requirements for Gentile converts to Christ (Acts 15:20,29; cf. 21:25).

well as from opportunistic parasites.[210] Similar laws to the present one are found in Lev 7:24; 17:15; 22:8. Such a pattern of reiteration—five times in all—for a single type of law shows its importance as a principle of covenant purity not to be ignored or practiced halfheartedly.

LAWS ON HONESTY, JUSTICE, AND FAIR TREATMENT WITH A REMINDER THAT GOD IS ENFORCER (23:1–9). The laws in this section appear to be grouped chiastically, with vv. 1–3 and vv. 6–9 employing apodictic legal style in addressing various sorts of potential violations of the legal system, including denial of justice to easily oppressable groups. Sandwiched between them are vv. 4–6, a small group of laws in casuistic format addressing the kind of attitude toward others in the community and basic moral behavior that should characterize God's covenant people even when no legal requirement per se is at issue.[211]

23:1–3 Type of law: apodictic (applied generally to everyone in the population). Paradigmatic range: any kind of false stating or reporting information about anyone. These laws expand slightly on the ninth commandment (Exod 20:16). The emphasis in these verses rests on the need for absolute honesty in speaking about others, from what one reports about others generally (the wording could even apply simply to gossip) to what one says in court when one is testifying as a witness in a criminal case.

"Do not spread false reports" (v. 1). Spreading[212] a false report could be damaging to the covenant community in several ways. It could influence what people thought about an individual so that they would relate differently to him than otherwise would have been the case; when the time came for people to testify in a court case about someone, their attitudes and even recollections could be prejudiced by the false "common knowledge" that the false report created. A false report could serve as the basis for improperly arresting and/or bringing to trial someone who was actually innocent or someone who was less responsible for a situation or crime than would rise to a prosecutable level; and

[210] While an animal is alive, its immune system fights with and suppresses a variety of diseases that are attempting to grow within its body. Once the animal dies, those diseases can move throughout the body, depending on temperature, chemical environment, and a variety of other factors, and contaminate tissue that previously was kept pure by the immune system. Animals suited to eat carrion (dogs, e.g.) are not likely to become sick from it; humans are more susceptible.

[211] An A B A′ pattern as a means of grouping some, but not all, laws was seen already in chaps. 21 and 22.

[212] לֹא תִשָּׂא שֵׁמַע שָׁוְא could also be translated, "Do not start a false report" or "Do not pass on a false report" or simply "Do not give a false report." The translation favored by many newer Eng. versions, "Do not spread a false report," is somewhat debatable in that it could be misunderstood to refer only to an elaborate attempt by someone to make a false accusation repeatedly and systematically in order to ensure that the false report traveled widely. This kind of action is comprehended by the law, but so are more limited kinds of actions, including something as limited as one person telling one other person something false about someone.

so forth. False reports could also create factionalism as one group believed the report about a member of another group, and the person's own group determined that the report had to have been started by the other group. False reports undermine the legal/judicial system by creating conditions that can lead to the conviction and punishment of an innocent person, robbing that person of the liberty that Yahweh's deliverance and protection of his people was intended to provide.

"Do not help[213] a wicked man by being a malicious witness" (v. 1). This part of the law envisions as one option the possibility of two or more people in collusion making a false charge against someone or falsely denying an accusation that was in fact correct. Because the law so strictly honored the testimony of two witnesses[214] against anyone accused of a crime (lest the case be based insufficiently merely on one person's word against another's), absolute honesty in giving testimony was essential to the correct functioning of the legal system. If two people could agree to falsify their testimony against someone whom they wished to harm, it would be extremely unlikely that a court would discover the falsehood and highly probable that an innocent person would be punished for something he or she did not in fact do. Conversely, the law equally encompassed the possibility that someone accused of a crime would be set free without penalty by reason of the false testimony of a friend who "helped [the] wicked man" avoid facing responsibility for his crime.

The NIV translation "crowd" (v. 2) is not the only option. A better translation might be "majority,"[215] and the temptation warned against here is that of being swayed in any action that would be wrong by the fear of looking foolish, incorrect, odd, or dishonest because of taking a position different from that taken by everyone—or virtually everyone—else. God has created human beings to be socially integrative and to try to cooperate with one another. As a result, it can be extremely difficult to take a stance in a difficult and emotionally charged situation or legal case against the majority (possibly including many of one's friends or even family) in favor of a person or cause that has no other advocates. An example would be the temptation—in a court case against a person who already has a long record of improper behavior and whom virtually everyone would like to see punished—to join the majority in accusing that person of some sort of impropriety even when one has no actual direct knowledge the person is guilty. This law calls for individual believers, who in so many other cases are expected to conform to the group (as in worship or in keeping any apodictic law applicable to everyone at all times) to be willing to

[213] Lit., "Do not join hands with . . .," an idiom for "cooperate with," "give aid to," "help."
[214] Deut 17:6; 19:5; Num 35:30; cf. Matt 18:16; John 8:17; 2 Cor 13:1; Heb 10:25.
[215] So the NRSV, ESV, GNB, NJB, REB.

think and act as individuals clearly enough and righteously enough that they can stand against all others in their actions or testimony.

The law in v. 3, coordinated with what precedes,[216] is cleverly worded. It might be thought that the usual temptation toward favoritism in a law case would be on behalf of a rich person, not a poor person (as the majority might do as envisioned in the previous verse). One might assume that testifying or returning a verdict on behalf of the rich might bring eventual reward or advantage to a witness or judge by reason of the rich person's gratitude. But the law, in an efficiency of expression, covers both the more likely temptation and the less likely temptation by citing the latter, "and do not show favoritism to a poor man." It has the effect of saying, "Do not show favoritism to anyone in any testimony you ever give or judgment you ever make—neither out of fear of the powerful or hope for personal gain nor out of sympathy for the suffering of the lowly." "His lawsuit"[217] is ambiguous; it could mean the lawsuit initiated by a poor person, but could also refer to virtually any involvement in a legal case of a poor person, either as plaintiff or defendant.

23:4–5 Type of law: casuistic (describes encountered situations involving the temptation not to act because to do so would be beneficial to one's enemy). Paradigmatic range: any chance to love your neighbor as yourself, including a neighbor with whom you are not on good terms. These requirements are neither about the legal system per se nor about oxen or donkeys only; they are expressions of Yahweh's expectations for his people that concentrate on general social attitudes using situations involving lost or stumbling animals as paradigmatic examples. By placing these sorts of laws in the midst of laws that concentrate on honest, godly behavior in cases of lawsuits, God in effect said to his people, "In the midst of giving you laws about lawsuit behavior, I want to insert a reminder that I expect you truly to love your neighbor in every situation, no matter how your selfish inclinations might cause you to feel."

The commands to catch and return to one's enemy his errant ox or donkey and to help one's enemy take care of his donkey in an accident represent serious challenges to normal selfish behavior and even to what might narrowly be regarded as prudent behavior. Most people would be disinclined to help an enemy (someone resented or troublesome or to whom one is motivated to be hostile for whatever reason) or would at least stay away from someone who showed hostility. Note that v. 5 provides as a parallel for "your enemy" in v. 4 the expression "someone who hates you" rather than "someone you hate," thus eliminating the possibility of arguing, "I'd be glad to help someone *I* hate, but it might not be safe to get involved with someone who hates *me*!" Comprehended in the law is virtually every situation of helping people. If one is

---

[216] So that it could also be translated "nor show favoritism to a poor person" or the like.

[217] רִיבוֹ.

required to help even those who have made themselves one's enemy, surely one would be required to help those who were more neutral on the scale of hostility, such as complete strangers or people who might merely be regarded as lazy in their care of their animals or the like. And, of course, friends and family and actual neighbors[218] would be included as well.

The present law addresses the need to love neighbor as self in somewhat the same way that Jesus' famous parable of the good Samaritan (Luke 10:29–37) does: by implication it defines neighbor broadly as anyone one may come in contact with and uses as an example of neighbor someone normally hated or despised (as in Jesus' parable, a Samaritan, hated by most Jews for heterodoxy, foreign practices).

The NIV translation of v. 5 could be misunderstood. The "it" at the end of the verse refers to the donkey, not the load, and "do not leave it there" is somewhat interpretive.[219] Most importantly, the law actually insists not merely that one be distantly civil to an enemy but that one actually become cooperatively involved with one's enemy in a complicated project (freeing a frightened and desperate animal from a harness around its body, righting the animal, removing the load from the backpack and/or side pack, reattaching the pack to the animal, repacking the pack, and perhaps carrying personally some of what was in it in order to lighten the load). The law does not assume that one's enemy mistreated the donkey; donkeys can fall for any of many reasons, not simply because they are overburdened, and they can't get back up easily with a load strapped to their body.

23:6–9 Type of law: apodictic (general applicability throughout the population). Paradigmatic range: not just court cases (explicit in vv. 6–7) but also fair and just treatment in or out of court and honest, even-handed dealings with all people, not just in cases where a bribe is offered or a resident alien is involved (these situations being used as examples, vv. 8–9). Verses 6–9 resume the thrust toward absolute integrity and fairness in all legal matters, but also include demands that are general enough that they involve all kinds of dealings between and among all the members of the people of Israel as well as those non-Israelites living among them.

This law repeats in apodictic format the essential point of 23:3, with somewhat contrasting language. The law in 23:3 used wording to eliminate favoritism toward the poor, whereas this law seeks to warn against favoritism against the poor. Together they prohibit any option but fairness and justice for the poor, in the same manner and degree as for any other person in the society. It

---

[218] Remembering that the term "neighbor" in legal contexts normally means "anyone else who lives in Israel" and has nothing to do with proximity of one's home to someone else. Cf. 20:16.

[219] The NRSV rendering, though more prosaic, is somewhat less ambiguous: "When you see the donkey of one who hates you lying under its burden and you would hold back from setting it free, you must help to set it free."

would have been easy to deny justice to poor people in lawsuits because the poor would lack the resources to insure justice for themselves. Moreover, the poor would be less likely than the rich to have friends on a jury, to be on good terms with the local judge, and so forth. They would also be less likely to have any sort of recourse if they lost a case—there would be less fear of reprisal or disadvantage on the part of those who denied justice to the poor or who even turned the poor away from being able to lodge a complaint in the first place because the poor have so little influence of any kind in a society.

No penalty specifically attaches to violation of this law. It is a basic covenant requirement, and its guarantor is Yahweh himself, as implied in the various first-person pronouns throughout the chapter (vv. 7,13,15,18,20,21–23,25–31,33) and in particular the statement in the following verse ("I will not acquit the guilty," v. *7*).

"Have nothing to do with [lit., "stay far away from"] a false charge" (v. 7) rings yet another change on the prevailing theme of absolute, uncorrupted justice as essential for the people who agree to Yahweh's covenant. What was implicit in several laws already stated now appears explicitly and specifically: no one should ever be involved in any way with a complaint against someone in a court case that is not entirely true. Honesty must prevail throughout the legal system or the system cannot function fairly. Neither a witness nor a defendant nor a judge nor a jury may contribute to a false charge.[220] By extrapolation, a law such as this warns against giving credence to any sort of false charges in the society as a whole, including, but not limited to, organizations, businesses, and schools where individuals or committees are responsible to investigate charges against members, employees, or students.

"Do not put an innocent or honest person [lit., "person in the right"] to death" (lit., "do not kill") is worded in such a way that it would apply to all sorts of situations in legal proceedings where capital punishment was potentially involved, but it also would potentially apply to any situation where someone or some group decided to take the law into their hands and kill someone. By saying "for I will not acquit the guilty" God makes clear that those who wrongly cause the death of an innocent person become themselves guilty by reason of their unjust action. Accordingly, this law calls for the greatest possible care in the legal process or in societal relationships to make sure that a rush to justice does not result in the death of someone whom everyone

[220] How might a defendant contribute to a false charge against himself? By accepting it as if it were true even though the crime he has committed is actually different and more serious. The common modern practice of "plea bargaining" does not necessarily violate this law as long as the crime admitted to in exchange for the sentence offered is a part of the total charge. However, when a defendant either voluntarily or under pressure agrees to plead guilty to a crime not actually encompassed within the original charges against him and not actually a crime he has committed, a modern plea bargain would indeed violate the letter and spirit of this law.

assumes is guilty but against whom overwhelming and unambiguous evidence cannot be found.

Paul reminded his readers that there is no action, no matter how evil, that people will resist doing if the financial reward is large enough.[221] Dismissing a lawsuit that actually has merit, rendering a guilty or innocent verdict when the opposite is actually reasonable, bringing a case against someone in order to harass rather than obtain justice are those things that have been and are being done in many places around the world on the basis of bribes.[222] The power of a bribe to make someone ignore evidence is here compared to the causation of blindness, and to speak a lie is here compared to a speech defect making it impossible for one to say what he wants to and should say. Bribery in effect cripples the normal, proper way of doing things and substitutes a perverted way. Even the person who normally can "see" (v. 8) matters clearly and who is normally "righteous" in all that he says may change dramatically under the power of a bribe.

Note here the general language of the command: it does not limit itself to court cases. Anyone who requires or accepts an extra, personal payment for his services in any area of society has been "bought" and will not act with proper neutrality and consistency.[223]

The wording of v. 9 differs modestly from that of 22:21 ("Do not mistreat an alien or oppress him, for you were aliens in Egypt") by letting "oppress" alone stand here for "mistreat . . . or oppress" in 22:21 and by adding "you yourselves know how it feels to be aliens" (lit., "you know the spirit[224] of the alien"). It is not the same law but essentially the same command, repeated for emphasis,[225] expanding on the expectation of natural sympathy for aliens that should have been manifest among Israelites, and appealing to the abhorrence of hypocrisy and inconsistency that the people *should* feel. The goal was to keep them from the natural human tendency to befriend those most like them

---

[221] See 1 Tim 6:10, which is properly translated to state that the love of money is "a root" of "all kinds of evil" or "every sort of evil," but not "the root of all evil."

[222] In many societies obtaining building or work permits or jobs or parking spaces or apartments or admission to school or police protection is based on one's ability and willingness to bribe an official who counts on bribes as a part of his or her expected income. And some people who could not imagine themselves doing such things will nevertheless actually try to hand a policeman a "payment" along with a driver's license when stopped for a traffic violation.

[223] Cf. also the teaching of John the Baptist that Roman occupation soldiers were not to accept or require personal payments (broadly subsumable under the category of bribe) for their services or as a means of supplementing their income but to be content to live on their (meager) wages (Luke 3:14).

[224] יְדַעְתֶּם אֶת־נֶפֶשׁ הַגֵּר, where נֶפֶשׁ has the sense of "spirit," "heart," or even "life."

[225] The parade example of repeated laws is the Ten Commandments, found in both Exodus and Deuteronomy. A comparable repetition of a single law is the thrice-stated law against cooking a goat kid in its mother's milk (23:19; 34:26; Deut 14:21). See comments on 23:19.

and discriminate against those thought to be somehow different. In many homogenous societies, aliens may be little different from natives. In ancient Israel the aliens were non-Israelites, but since Israel itself was composed of a mixed multitude ethnically (12:38) and spoke a language not unique but shared by many other groups including even those they were bound eventually to exterminate,[226] there is no reason to think they were any more or less prone to discriminate against aliens than most modern societies are.[227]

(5) Laws on Sabbaths and Annual Religious Festivals (23:10–19)

10"For six years you are to sow your fields and harvest the crops, 11but during the seventh year let the land lie unplowed and unused. Then the poor among your people may get food from it, and the wild animals may eat what they leave. Do the same with your vineyard and your olive grove.

12"Six days do your work, but on the seventh day do not work, so that your ox and your donkey may rest and the slave born in your household, and the alien as well, may be refreshed.

13"Be careful to do everything I have said to you. Do not invoke the names of other gods; do not let them be heard on your lips.

14"Three times a year you are to celebrate a festival to me.

15"Celebrate the Feast of Unleavened Bread; for seven days eat bread made without yeast, as I commanded you. Do this at the appointed time in the month of Abib, for in that month you came out of Egypt. No one is to appear before me empty-handed.

16"Celebrate the Feast of Harvest with the firstfruits of the crops you sow in your field. Celebrate the Feast of Ingathering at the end of the year, when you gather in your crops from the field.

17"Three times a year all the men are to appear before the Sovereign LORD.

18"Do not offer the blood of a sacrifice to me along with anything containing yeast. The fat of my festival offerings must not be kept until morning.

19"Bring the best of the firstfruits of your soil to the house of the LORD your God. Do not cook a young goat in its mother's milk."

In this portion of the book, a set of laws dealing with sabbaths (23:10–12) and a set of laws dealing with the three annual festivals (23:10–19) are placed so as to surround the special, overarching command in 23:13 demanding exclusive covenant obedience to and faith in Yahweh. This represents yet another instance of a three-unit legal pericope, as already seen in prior chapters and in the immediately preceding material of chap. 23 as well (23:1–9). By the system of sabbaths and annual festivals, God established for his people

[226] Hebrew is a branch of Canaanite, with only small differences between it and the various Canaanite dialects.

[227] Indeed, in the ancient world it would have been hard to find any more xenophobic, alien-hating people than the Egyptians, from whose behavior the Israelites were expected to have learned a lesson.

regular covenant reminders of their relationship to him as his worshiping people: the weekly Sabbath worship routine would provide a reminder-renewal every seventh day; the annual routine would provide three reminder-renewals coinciding with the natural agricultural times of rest and rejoicing with a focus on worship.

In addition to these there was to be every seven years a special concern for the land, animals, and people and every fifty years a major realignment of financial, land, personal, and social relationships (the Jubilee Year, Lev 25; 27; Num 36) intended to keep Israelites from losing touch with their basic values and social structures. The seven-year and fifty-year observances were different from the weekly and annual observances because they concentrated on the social-ecological order, whereas the weekly and annual observances concentrated on worship. In this chapter the near-term (weekly Sabbath), midterm (annual festivals), and long-term (sabbath year) laws are described. Further along in the Sinai covenant (Leviticus) they would be further detailed, and added to them would be the very long-term law about the Jubilee Year (Lev 25; 27). Instructions on the other two national holy days, the Day of Atonement and the Feast of Trumpets, are left entirely to Leviticus (16; 23:23–32) and Numbers (29:1–11).

TWO SIX-SEVEN LAWS ON SABBATH YEARS AND SABBATH DAYS (23:10–12). When Jesus said, "The Sabbath was made for man, not man for the Sabbath" (Mark 2:27), he summarized the point of these two laws, as well as others relating to the Sabbath. Both of them emphasize that the Sabbath, whether of years or days, was intended by God to provide restoration and well-being for God's people, not merely a cessation of all activity. This perspective is often missed by strict Sabbatarians in modern times, just as in ancient,[228] who stress doing nothing rather than doing what is relaxing and engaging in the least possible physical activity over doing things that produce refreshment and restoration.

23:10–11 Type of law: apodictic (second-person uniform command for all Israelites without limitation). Paradigmatic range: all productive land use without limit to type of crop. Here Israel learned that their farming practices must include a regular pattern of noncultivation. The purpose of such a practice every seventh year of letting the land lie fallow centered on the way such a routine helped the poor and wildlife. From an agri-science point of view, it also would allow the land some time for additional nitrogen fixing as natural grassing-over would occur on most of the surface of the uncultivated land, and this would be good for the land in the long run. The focus of the command, however, is ecological-humanitarian and not on improving productivity. This law reflects the "Sabbath" principle of the Gen 1 creation story (a cessation

[228] E.g., Matt 12:10–14; John 7:21–23; Mark 2:23–28.

after six out of seven periods of time have been completed), as also reflected in the weekly Sabbath command of 20:11 and the six/seven-year contract period for servants in 21:2.

At first glance it might seem that the law called for no intentional crop farming every seven years throughout Israel, so virtually all people[229] would take a year off from farming. But neither this expression of the farming sabbath nor that of Lev 25:1–7 actually states whether the expectation was a nationwide stoppage on all farms for all crops at the same time or a system of staggered seven-year cessations for individual crops in individual fields. The law on the Jubilee Year, which was to be celebrated every fifty years in Israel, clearly demanded full, nationwide compliance at the same time by all persons throughout Israel. In Lev 25:8–55 the statement of the Jubilee law follows with specificity[230] as to uniform, same-time compliance, directly after the law of the land sabbath (Lev 25:1–7, a command that provides no such specificity with regard to when a farmer would rest his crops as long as each field, grove, or vineyard was rested every seventh year). This suggests that farmers were given freedom to decide how to rotate or stagger the resting of their crops among their various fields, groves, and vineyards. In that way farmers were still actively farming each year, and roughly the same food volume would be produced every year throughout Israel.

It is difficult to imagine that the law would envision a system of total cessation of crop farming throughout Israel in light of the food shortages for humans and cattle that would result (but cp. Lev. 25:6-7,21). It seems that the law does not call for any cessation of animal farming every seven years, which would be tantamount to allowing most cattle and flocks to die if it were actually carried out.[231] Under the system envisioned in this law, poor people and wild animals would always have uncultivated fields in any given area in which to forage/harvest the spontaneous crop because farmers would always be rotating fields, vineyards, and groves in and out of cultivation.[232] If Israelites would follow this law faithfully, the presumed percentage of poor people in the land would not overwhelm the percentage of fallow land available for

[229] In an agrarian society such as Israel's, nearly all people farmed, whether as farm workers/servants or as family members of a farm family. Even tradespersons probably helped farm during key times such as plowing, planting, and harvesting, in addition to their trades (masonry, carpentry, pottery).

[230] Of particular interest is the command to have "the trumpet sounded . . . everywhere . . . throughout your land" (Lev 25:9) in the Jubilee law in contrast to a complete lack of any reminder system in connection with the farming sabbath laws.

[231] As noted already in connection with Exod 20:8–11, the word *šabbāt* has the sense not of "rest" (doing nothing) but of "cessation," i.e., cessation of normal activity in order to do something else: variety rather than inactivity.

[232] If the crop sabbath were not staggered/rotated, there would be no way the poor and the wild animals could survive the other six years beyond the year of the cessation.

them to live off. Note also the implied value system in the law: people are most important, animals next, and plants least important. This same hierarchy of value in life is reflected throughout the Old Testament, as, for example, in Jonah 4:5–11.

Note also that this law and the one that immediately follows it assume that the Israelites—forced laborers and small cattle farmers in Egypt—would be able to possess and farm the land of Canaan once they conquered it. Accordingly, the law implicitly promises them a fulfillment of God's plan originally announced to Abraham in Gen 12 and 15.

23:12 Type of law: apodictic (direct command to all Israelites). Paradigmatic range: a day of restoration each week for all people and animals. Observance of the Sabbath each week was important and essential not only as a benefit for people and animals but also because the Sabbath functioned as a covenant sign, that is, a weekly reminder that Yahweh had given Israel his covenant and they were to keep it solemnly. The sign aspect is delineated at 31:12–17 (with even the death penalty attached to its violation,[233] so important was the covenant and its weekly sign). Even though the issue of the day of stoppage/rest as a covenant sign does not yet surface at this point in the corpus of laws, this reminder of the importance of the Sabbath is part of the distributed package of emphases on the Sabbath that lead appropriately and inevitably to 31:12–17.

This law reiterates the fourth commandment (Exod 20:8–11), adding nothing by way of concept (cessation of work, animals, servants, and aliens are all mentioned in the fourth commandment already). In a culture based heavily on the written word, such a repeated law might (wrongly) not be thought entirely necessary; but in the ancient world as well as the modern, the repetition of a law so easily broken, in language slightly different from the original on which it is based, has the benefit of reinforcing the import of what is commanded and of showing as well its relevance to living out Yahweh's covenant in all its details.[234] It has sometimes been argued that the New Testament removes this law from being a requirement for Christians. In fact, the underlying principle remains, as indicated in Jesus' teaching[235] and Paul's.[236] The person who

---

[233] Exod 31:14–15.

[234] In an agrarian society the temptation to work seven days a week, at least during the intensely demanding seasons of plowing, planting, and harvesting, could become overwhelming. The repetition of this law helps make sure that no one can claim or even imagine that its importance was not great or that its interpretation was somehow flexible or subjective.

[235] Matt 19:17–19, where Jesus' sampling of laws from the Ten Words/Commandments is clearly representative of all ten rather than needlessly, explicitly exhaustive.

[236] Rom 14:5–6; Col 2:16, in which Paul subsumed Sabbath practice as well as holy day observance; he implied that as long as one keeps the spirit of the Sabbath law (so that ample time is in one's schedule for relaxation and worship), it need not be confined to a single day but could be distributed, at least in part, throughout the week.

works endlessly and/or makes others do so oppresses himself and/or others in violation of this law.[237]

A GENERAL WARNING TO KEEP THE COVENANT AND TRUST YAHWEH ALONE (23:13). **23:13** Type of law: apodictic (applied to all Israelites at all times). Paradigmatic range: the wording is comprehensive in demanding covenant obedience to everything commanded in the covenant and absolute monotheism as a focal point thereof. This general law is not merely a conclusion or merely an introduction but a summation of what precedes and follows. It is even possible that *ʾāmartî* (NIV and most versions, "I have said") could in this context bear the sense "I am saying" since the Hebrew perfect tense can refer to actions ongoing that began in the past, not merely actions completed in the past.[238]

The Sabbath law of the prior verse reiterated the timing of the weekly day of worship as established in the principial Ten Words/Commandments. The second sentence of this law clarifies the most important part of the community's worship, also reflecting the Ten Words/Commandments (Exod 20:3, "You shall have no other Gods before me"). It represents a slightly expansive restatement of that first word/commandment by adding the prohibition against even mentioning any other gods but Yahweh. He alone is to be worshiped, obeyed, believed in, honored. Calling on gods by name has always been essential to worshiping and obeying them. To prohibit saying a god's name is to prohibit all exercise of the religion associated with that god. Accordingly, this law represents an unmistakably clear assertion of monotheism within the Covenant Code from the time of Moses.[239]

LAWS ON THE THREE ANNUAL FESTIVALS AND THEIR PURPOSE (23:14–19). Type of laws: apodictic, applying without exception to all Israelites at all times (though the actual implementation would await arrival in the promised land). Paradigmatic range: hardly an issue since the festivals

[237] Thus the family that expects a wife/mother to prepare twenty-one meals per week without respite and serve the needs of the family equally on all days violates the command, as would the dairy farmer who never takes a break from the twice-daily milking, or the policeman who does special-duty shifts on days off from regular shifts, or the pastor who never sets for himself or herself a day off or its equivalent. People who do not observe a Sabbath, either in one day or its distributed equivalent, deny themselves or others the sort of life God intended.

[238] Common examples being the verbs of perception where the Hb. perfect tense normally indicates present rather than past action, e.g., *yādaʿtî*, typically meaning "I know" rather than "I knew."

[239] It was once popular in many circles and is still popular in some to theorize that true, full monotheism emerged only during and after the exile, i.e., in the sixth century BC at the earliest, as reflected in "Second Isaiah." By this theory the first commandment of Exod 20:3 was merely intended to make Yahweh the main God of the Israelites and to require them to worship other gods only secondarily. Since some of the scholars who have held that view actually date the Covenant Code earlier than the Ten Commandments and few date it as late at the exile, the present verse, properly understood, functions as a sharp piece of metal in the balloon of such a developmental theory about Israelite monotheism.

themselves were limited in number and quite specific, but the command relative to cooking goat kids in their mother's milk (v. 19) was certainly intended paradigmatically.

Full biblical worship is always corporate. Individuals can carry out a form of worship by themselves, using some of the elements of corporate worship, but they cannot alone worship in the normal manner enjoined in Scripture. From the point of view of comprehensive theology, this is because all proper worship on earth is a proleptic imitation of[240] and preparation for eventual worship in heaven, which is consistently portrayed as corporate.[241]

Thus all Israelite families were to gather three times a year (v. 14) in a single place (v. 17) and all together participate in festivals that had as their primary purpose worship, the adoration and praise of the true God. The three festivals are identified and described briefly in vv. 14–16; specific instructions of what to do and not to do in connection with such festivals are then delineated in vv. 17–19.

23:14 These words set out the basic overview: the nation must undertake to establish a system of three special annual festivals.[242] They were to be focused on Yahweh, not on the people themselves, and therefore by implication would be covenant worship festivals rather than mere celebrations of national history or harvest festivals. That each of them coincided with a point of "downtime" on the agricultural calendar does not suggest that they were originally Canaanite agricultural festivals that the Israelites borrowed and gradually sanctified by adding Yahweh worship. Rather, God in his concern for his people chose these breaks in their routine (the quiet days right after spring planting, the relaxed time after the early grain harvest, and the time following the fall harvest) as the time for their special religious observances. Thereby no one could claim that his job responsibilities prevented him from participating fully in worship, and everyone could associate worship with joy, a combination fulfilling the biblical ideal. Verse 17 complements this verse, somewhat in the manner of an inclusio, by adding the emphasis of total participation by every family, as represented by the male head of the family.

23:15 The first festival in the year[243] is named first, the "Feast of Unleavened Bread." The story behind this feast is recounted in chaps. 11–13, and its

---

[240] As comprehended within the words "your will be done on earth as it is in heaven," Matt 6:10.

[241] Rev 7:9; 19:1,6.

[242] The fact that the command is framed in the second-person singular (תָּחֹג) is merely consistent with legal expression, already regularly employed in the Covenant Code, which tends to put all typical imperatives in the masculine singular but does not thereby allow for individualistic fulfillment of the command.

[243] At this time in Israel's history the calendar year began in the spring, i.e., in mid-March, when the month of Abib occurred; considerably later and only for relatively brief periods was a fall new year dating system (also called Tishri dating) employed, under Mesopotamian influence.

initial observance was described in 12:1–28 and 13:6–10.[244] A full appreciation of what is stated here requires awareness of those passages. The command was therefore resumptive, given in preparing the Israelites for their existence in the promised land of Canaan, reinforcing what they had been told at least three months earlier as they prepared for the first Passover night—thus the statement "as I commanded you."

This further reinforcement of the Passover law may have proved additionally valuable to the non-Israelites who had aligned themselves with the Israelites in response to the plagues and left with them in the exodus (12:38). For many of these people, the whole idea of the Passover may have been entirely new. The law fixes the date for the festival in the minds of the covenant people, again repeating what was already commanded in 12:2ff. The festival commemorated a real historical event, with the purpose of keeping its memory, and therefore its message, alive throughout the generations of God's people. The concluding command, "No one is to appear before me empty-handed," states in a very slightly euphemistic, but absolutely unmistakable, manner that the festival involved giving an offering to Yahweh.[245] Not only would the worshipers eat specially during the week of the feast ("for seven days eat bread made without yeast") but they also would bring food to be dedicated to Yahweh and, by implication, partly eaten by the worshipers in his presence.[246] For the full background to the present command, see comments on 11:1–13:10. Passover coincided with the first grain harvest, that is, the barley harvest, being held immediately after it when otherwise the crop farming chores were minimal.

23:16 What is called the "Feast of Harvest" here is also known as the Feast of Weeks (e.g., Exod 34:22) and often is called the Feast of Pentecost or simply Pentecost in the New Testament because it was normally celebrated seven weeks or, "count off fifty days up to the day after the seventh Sabbath" (Lev 23:16), fifty days after the Passover was celebrated.[247] When the main

---

[244] A skeptical view of the festivals holds that they originated as Canaanite agricultural festivals, which were borrowed by the Israelites and gradually linked to past events in Israel's folklore history and also to Yahweh, the God the Israelites gradually tended to favor as their national god (cf. the excellent summary of this view by Durham, *Exodus,* 332–33). Not a bit of actual evidence exists for this theory, which is based entirely on naturalistic and evolution-of-religion premises.

[245] On the expression "appear before" see comments on v. 17.

[246] In all cases of offerings other than the whole burnt offering (Lev 1), a portion of what was offered was actually dedicated to Yahweh (normally burned to ash on the altar), a portion given to the priest for him and his family, and a portion received after preparation by the worshiper and his family for eating in the presence of the Lord. The tabernacle provided no special eating places other than the ground; the temple built by Solomon had a variety of dining rooms, called *liškôt*.

[247] The term "Pentecost," which became dominant once Greek became the lingua franca of Europe and the Mediterranean world, derives from the fem. sing. adjective *pentekostē,* meaning "fiftieth," modifying implicitly the fem. sing. noun *hēmera,* "day," thus, implicitly, "fiftieth day." In modern times Pentecost, remembering primarily the dramatic, initial New Covenant democratizing of the Holy Spirit as recorded in Acts 2, is celebrated on the seventh Sunday after Easter.

grain harvest, especially the wheat harvest, was completed, Israelites were expected to present to God a grain/cereal harvest offering with two loaves of salted and regularly leavened bread (not unleavened as in the case of the Passover festival) as well as a variety of animal sacrifices and whatever other freewill offerings the people chose to give (Lev 23:16–21; Num 28:26). The details of the process are left to the fuller explanation in Lev 23; here the one-day special festival is announced and the time for it set aside statutorily. Like the other two annual feasts, it celebrated primarily God's gracious deliverance and covenant faithfulness; secondarily it celebrated his provision of another year's grain harvest and the ability to continue to enjoy life, for which a successful harvest provided.

What is here called the "Feast of Ingathering" is also known as the Feast of Tabernacles, or Feast of Booths, or *Succoth* (Hb. for huts/booths). Described as well in Lev 23:33–43 and Deut 16:13–15, this festival coincided with the general fall harvest, not only of various second-crop grains but also of tree and vine crops such as olives and grapes. It followed by five days the Day of Atonement (Lev 16; 23:26–32) and required the Israelites to build temporary field huts (thus "booths" or in older Eng. "tabernacles"). The command to "observe the Feast of Ingathering at the end of the year" uses language some have suggested indicates a fall new year calendar in effect at this time. In light of 12:12,18, however, where the first month of spring, Abib, is clearly designated as the first month of the calendar year, the expression "end of the year" here more likely reflects the agricultural year.[248]

23:17 This command addresses worship. "Appear before the Sovereign LORD" (lit., "the Lord Yahweh") is simply a variation of "appear before the LORD" (the Hb. idiom *rā'āh* + *'el-pĕnê/lipê* + *yhwh*)[249] in the sense of "come to the tabernacle courtyard and stand facing the tabernacle tent entrance." Yahweh would soon enough represent his presence among his people symbolically through the ark of the covenant, housed in the tabernacle

[248] It is possible that either because it was standard throughout Egypt in general at this time—or at least in Goshen—the calendar used by the Israelites was a fall new-year calendar. But a more likely hypothesis sees the language relating to the farming year, which "ends" with harvest. Something akin to this kind of functional calendrical terminology dominates today in academic settings, where the "new year" (not calendrical, but academic) begins sometime in late August/early September following the extended "downtime" of summer, when fewer classes are offered and taken. The winter months were likewise downtime for the Israelites relative to their economy, which was agrarian. Thus in a manner similar to the way the modern academic year is said to "end" in May or June, prior to the summer academic hiatus, the Israelite agricultural year could be said to "end" in October, prior to the winter agricultural hiatus.

[249] The idiom can be worded with such variations as "appear before me" or "appear before *x*" when "*x*" (e.g., the altar) is representing Yahweh. Cf. v. 15; also 34:20,23–24; Lev 13:7 ("appear before the priest"); Deut 16:16; 19:17; 31:11; Isa 1:12.

(Exod 25:10–20; 26:1–37; 27:9–19); and there, within that courtyard, the heads of families (all the men) would stand to worship.

All worship involved an offering (v. 15) that was actually prepared and placed on the altar (if, e.g., in the form of meat to be cooked) or presented at the altar (if, e.g., a grain or drink offering) by a priest. Many believe that worshipers did not do their own sacrificing or presentation but watched as it was done for them by a priest properly consecrated for the task (Exod 29). The instruction in this verse is preliminary; the full explanation of how offerings were given to God comes later in the Sinai covenant at Lev 1–7 and at various other points throughout Leviticus.

23:18–19 Type of law: apodictic (unconditional, applying to all sacrifices by all Israelites at all times). Paradigmatic range: implicitly outlaw all sorts of other pagan rituals as well, not merely those specifically mentioned here because they represented some of the most common temptations for the Israelites. The four short laws in these two verses address pagan rituals that God would not allow his people to practice. Israel could not simply duplicate the religious rituals of the Canaanites or other ancient peoples and add a Yahwistic twist to them. God's nation was to live up to his high standards, reflecting the lofty truths that underlie his covenant, eschewing the approaches used by worshipers of other gods to currying divine favor or to attempt magically to lengthen or strengthen life.

The first command prohibited Israelites from offering "the blood of a sacrifice to me along with anything containing yeast."[250] Ancient peoples were well aware that when the blood was drained from an animal, the animal would die.[251] They thus rightly concluded that the life of an animal was in its blood.[252] In an attempt to strengthen or prolong their own lives, they started drinking or eating blood from animals sacrificed for worship or merely for eating, performing in effect an act of what is known as "sympathetic magic." This was strictly forbidden to the Israelites (Lev 3:17; 7:26; Deut 15:23) and even to the patriarchs long before there was an Israel (Gen 9:4).

Drinking blood is somewhat unappetizing, but using the blood as an ingredient in breads of various sorts (indicated here by the wording "anything containing yeast") was a method sometimes employed to enable people to

[250] Note also the repetition in 34:25, indicating the importance of this law.

[251] The main reason for their familiarity with this fact was their regular observation of the common practice of slaughtering an animal by first stunning it, then bleeding it while it was still alive so that its heart would pump out its blood, a process that greatly speeds the removal of blood from the animal.

[252] Cf. Gen 9:4; Lev 17:11,14; Deut 12:23. The life of an animal is, of course, in other things as well (ancients knew that you could beat an animal to death without drawing much blood), but the absence of blood does indeed bring about the absence of life in animals.

consume the blood in a palatable way.[253] Of special interest in this connection is the fact that Jesus did allow—even required—the drinking of blood *symbolically* in the observance of the Lord's Supper.[254] In this regard, the Lord's Supper is actually a purer symbol of the transfer of life from the sacrificial lamb (Christ) to the worshiper than any sacrifice in the Old Testament could be, in which the lamb's death was simply understood as a substitute for that of the worshiper, without the aspect of transfer of life per se.

The second command, "The fat of my festival offerings must not be kept until morning," mirrors the rule against attempted overnight preservation of the manna on any day except the Sabbath (see comments on 16:4–5,17–30), but has a more strongly prohibitive purpose here. The fuller statement of the principle comes in Lev 3:16–17: "The priest shall burn [the fat parts of a sacrificial animal] . . . on the altar as food, an offering by fire, for a pleasing aroma. All the fat is the LORD's. This is a lasting ordinance generations to come, wherever you live: You must not eat any fat or any blood." Though animal sacrifices could take place at various times of the day, a key time for making animal sacrifices was the evening.[255] The fat portions were separated from the muscle meats and were supposed to be presented as burnt offerings on the altar to God. Someone who tried to keep them for any other purpose—perhaps something as "minor" as keeping them overnight for use along with the morning offering, but perhaps for actual eating—was failing to sacrifice properly. At a minimum keeping the fat until morning would be "making God wait for his portion of the sacrifice," and could not be tolerated. Canaanites and other pagan peoples did not necessarily burn all the animal fat as a divine offering at the time of cooking animals on their altars: thus the temptation of the Israelites to imitate their neighbors instead of following God's decrees and the need specifically to obviate such an approach.

"Bring the best of the firstfruits of your soil to the house of the LORD your God"[256] moves the topic from possible abuse of animal offerings to possible abuse of crop offerings. With crop tithes and offerings, there was presumably less likelihood of the temptation to offer some and leave some for a later point

---

[253] Note that the wording of the prohibition in Hb. (לֹא־תִזְבַּח עַל־חָמֵץ דַּם־זִבְחִי) clearly speaks of mixing blood and yeast (to which flour and oil would be added) rather than simply consuming blood and yeast in the same meal or the like.

[254] John 6:53: "So Jesus said to them, "I tell you the truth, unless you eat the flesh of the Son of Man and drink his blood, you have no life in you"; John 6:55: "For my flesh is real food, and my blood is real drink"; 1 Cor 11:25: "This cup is the new covenant in my blood; do this, whenever you drink it, in remembrance of me."

[255] In fact, the two key times were morning and evening (Exod 29:38–42), thus the possible temptation to think that no harm would be done by keeping the evening's fat until morning and burning it then, under the most modest construal of the reach of this law.

[256] The fact that this verse repeats in 34:16 constitutes evidence of its basic importance in differentiating the Israelite covenant people from other people groups.

or for one's personal use at or around the tabernacle. Instead, the danger was that Israelites would be tempted not to bring the proper portion at all (if it were a tithe) or the proper quality (if it were either a tithe or any other grain/oil/wine offering). One could not leave at home a portion of a live lamb. The whole thing was brought to the tabernacle alive for slaughter there. But one could leave at home whatever portion of one's soil produce one wished—and perhaps in the absence of nosy neighbors one could hope that no one would be aware that the portion brought to the tabernacle was smaller and of poorer quality than it should have been compared to the portion retained at home for the family to enjoy. Such a practice would be comparable to the practice of denying God his portion of an animal sacrifice at the time the rest of the cooked animal was shared between the priests and worshipers. It would be cheating God, failing to honor him properly as the Lord of his people who deserved their best, not their leftovers.[257] Accordingly, both the first and the best of one's harvest was due to God—from any of the various harvests that the festivals followed.

The prohibition "Do not cook a young goat in its mother's milk" occurs three times in the Pentateuchal law (also in 34:26 and Deut 14:21). Canaanite fertility religion imitated the fertility practices generally found throughout the ancient world. These included "marrying" seeds when planting a field (Lev 19:19; Deut 22:9) on the theory that such a ritual would magically stimulate the powers of nature to procreate, producing more fertile crops. Since mother's milk (the milk of the goat doe) was what made the goat kids grow big and strong,[258] the folk theory developed that doe's milk employed in the process of a sacrifice (in this case by boiling rather than by roasting on an altar)[259] would somehow impart strength to the goat flock, making the whole flock more fertile. Such nonsense, if believed, could have led the Israelites to

[257] Note the comparable charge in Mal 1:14, applied to holding back the best for oneself and giving to God that which is inferior in an offering: "'Cursed is the cheat who has an acceptable male in his flock and vows to give it, but then sacrifices a blemished animal to the LORD; for I am a great King,' says the LORD of hosts, 'and my name is feared among the nations.'"

[258] As J. Milgrom notes, the depicting of a mother nursing its (or her) young was widely used in the ancient world as a symbol of fertility and, more specifically, of life ("'You Shall Not Boil a Kid in Its Mother's Milk,'" *BibRev* 1 [1985]: 48–55). In part because of this he concludes that the prohibition against boiling a goat kid in its mother's milk is more a call to reverence for life by a prohibition against commingling life and death. Milgrom acknowledges that this law, if observed, would help differentiate Israelites from their pagan neighbors, but he does not agree with the widely held view that the prohibition had as its main concern the prevention of a Canaanite magical fertility practice.

[259] Even Israelite sacrifices were boiled, although not exclusively when the law was properly enforced. The main way that most sacrificial meat was cooked was via boiling, after or before which it was placed on the sacrificial altar just briefly and in a token manner, since the altar was too small to cook fully all the meat that needed to come in contact with it in a day. Cf. Lev 6:28; 1 Sam 2:14; 2 Chr 35:13; Zech 14:20–21.

conclude that the power to shape their destiny and to live the abundant life was to be found in magical practices and fertility religion rather than in the only true, alive God.[260] Even if all other people groups known to them practiced these sorts of rituals, the Israelites could not. As Yahweh's people, they were to be above such things, attributing all life to the single Source thereof.[261]

(6) Instructions to Obey God during and after the Conquest (23:20–33)

[20]"See, I am sending an angel ahead of you to guard you along the way and to bring you to the place I have prepared. [21]Pay attention to him and listen to what he says. Do not rebel against him; he will not forgive your rebellion, since my Name is in him. [22]If you listen carefully to what he says and do all that I say, I will be an enemy to your enemies and will oppose those who oppose you. [23]My angel will go ahead of you and bring you into the land of the Amorites, Hittites, Perizzites, Canaanites, Hivites and Jebusites, and I will wipe them out. [24]Do not bow down before their gods or worship them or follow their practices. You must

---

[260] Cf. M. Haran, "Seething a Kid in Its Mother's Milk." *ErIs* 14 (1978): 12–18. C. J. Labuschagne takes a different approach, arguing that the prohibition is intended to prevent the eating of blood, a subject addressed immediately preceding, in 23:18 ("'You Shall Not Boil a Kid in Its Mother's Milk': A New Proposal for the Origin of Prohibition," in *The Scriptures and the Scrolls: Studies in Honor of A. S. van der Woude on the Occasion of His 65th Birthday* [Leiden: Brill, 1992], 6–17). He contends that the boiling in question would have involved cooking the kid along with its mother's colostrum and uterine remains, which would have contained blood. Thus to eliminate the possibility of consuming blood, the prohibition of this particular way of cooking goat kids was included in the Israelites' laws. Labuschagne's theory is surely worthy of careful consideration, but it is also possible that the reasons he cites would be more or less secondary to the basic reason, which we judge to be related more to imitation of the Canaanites and their fertility-cult mentality.

[261] The debate over the exact purpose of the prohibition about cooking a kid in its mother's milk has not been settled, and the view we espouse in this commentary has not been universally accepted. E.g., yet another, quite different direction has been taken by J. M. Sasson ("Ritual Wisdom?: On 'Seething a Kid in Its Mother's Milk,'" in *Kein Land für sich allein* [Göttingen: Vandenhoeck & Ruprecht, 2002], 294–308), who suggests that the actual vocalization of the command should reflect the Hb. word for "fat" (חֵלֶב) rather than "milk" (חָלָב). Sasson opines that the command could be wisdom advice presented in legal form: to cook a goat kid in its mother's fat would require killing the mother, a breeding doe, and thus foolishly reducing one's flock in the future by eliminating a doe that could continue to breed and produce many more goats for the flock. The strength of Sasson's case rests on the possible parallel in Deut 22:6–7, which requires sparing a female bird to lay more eggs rather than killing the bird along with her eggs. Its weakness, in my view as one who has raised goats for many years, is that I cannot imagine any goat farmer at any time, ancient or modern, so witless as to kill a breeding doe, thus losing not merely her future offspring but also all the milk she would have given for a year or more. At any rate, the rules for wild birds are bound to be very different from the rules for domesticated goats. Moreover, there is no indication in ancient literature that if the cooking were done in connection with a religious ritual (which Sasson does not suggest, of course) such a goat sacrifice would represent a proof of love/loyalty to a god that such shortsighted and/or self-denying butchering would be justified (this is not a parallel to child sacrifice, in other words). For an excellent review of the many disparate interpretations of this law already known in patristic times, see J. Moorhead, "Cooking a Kid in Its Mother's Milk: Patristic Exegesis of an Old Testament Command," *Aug* 37 (1997): 261–71.

demolish them and break their sacred stones to pieces. [25]Worship the LORD your God, and his blessing will be on your food and water. I will take away sickness from among you, [26]and none will miscarry or be barren in your land. I will give you a full life span.

[27]"I will send my terror ahead of you and throw into confusion every nation you encounter. I will make all your enemies turn their backs and run. [28]I will send the hornet ahead of you to drive the Hivites, Canaanites and Hittites out of your way. [29]But I will not drive them out in a single year, because the land would become desolate and the wild animals too numerous for you. [30]Little by little I will drive them out before you, until you have increased enough to take possession of the land.

[31]"I will establish your borders from the Red Sea to the Sea of the Philistines, and from the desert to the River. I will hand over to you the people who live in the land and you will drive them out before you. [32]Do not make a covenant with them or with their gods. [33]Do not let them live in your land, or they will cause you to sin against me, because the worship of their gods will certainly be a snare to you."

The Israelites had already been through much that was new to them in their exodus from Egypt and their travels in the Sinai wilderness, concluding at Mount Sinai, where God had so impressively—indeed, overwhelmingly[262]—appeared to them and begun to give them his law. Yet great adventures and risks lay ahead of them, not merely behind them, and they would face challenges to their faith in Yahweh from various directions. In the passage found here, God encouraged the Israelites to trust his generous and mighty provisions for them and at the same time warned them of some of the dangers they would encounter during the conquest of the promised land and their settling in to occupy it and build new lives there for themselves as his landed people.

A natural question that might arise from this material is: "What is it doing here?" After all, this is a passage of promise and warning, so how does it fit within typical legal material? Part of the answer comes in noting that all Old Testament law is promise and warning. Covenant laws are instructions for how to please the covenant Sovereign, with the implicit, and occasionally even explicit,[263] promise attached to each that keeping the law would bring the blessings promised in the sanctions portion of the covenant. Likewise they bear the implicit warning that failure to keep the law would lead to miseries of all sorts (the curses of the sanctions portions). Indeed, Israel's law was not

[262] E.g., 20: 18–19 (where the people ask Moses that they might never again hear the voice of God directly).

[263] E.g., Exod 20:12; cf. Paul's comments in Eph 6:2 and his discourse on the relationship of covenant to promise in general in Gal 3:17–19: "What I mean is this: The law, introduced 430 years later, does not set aside the covenant previously established by God and thus do away with the promise. For if the inheritance depends on the law, then it no longer depends on a promise; but God in his grace gave it to Abraham through a promise. What, then, was the purpose of the law? It was added because of transgressions until the Seed to whom the promise referred had come."

merely a law code but a covenant, a national agreement with Yahweh, whose purpose was to help people entrust themselves fully to him and live all of life under his gracious rule, not just a set of rules to control their behavior. The admixture of legal reminders, promises, and warnings in the prophetical books of the Old Testament provides a telling parallel to the purpose of the present passage: the prophets were covenant enforcement mediators, seeking to motivate the people to whom God had sent them to take his covenant seriously and embrace fully its guidance for their lives.

Motivation is what the present passage is especially about. It forms the conclusion to the Covenant Code, reminding the Israelites of who they were, where they were going, and how they were to get there. In that regard it may be considered something of an inclusio with the introduction to the covenant, especially the generally comparable words of encouragement and warning in 19:3–6. The special motivating force behind this concluding section of the Covenant Code is Yahweh himself. The angel he sent to guard and lead his people (vv. 20–22) was his angel ("my angel," v. 23), and God promised to oppose personally any who opposed themselves to his people (v. 22). The promise of abundant life he offered (vv. 25–26) came from his own grace, in response to his people's worshiping him exclusively (vv. 24–25). The terror he would send on the nations opposing Israel's conquest (v. 27) represented his own direct fighting for his people in a manner as irresistible as the flight of a hornet (vv. 28–30), so from the Israelite point of view he would simply have handed the land to them as a gift (v. 31) so little would have been their military contribution and so great his. Israel was a small and weak nation who would have to grow over time into the size and strength necessary to control all of Canaan (vv. 29–30). And the greatest danger of allowing the inhabitants of the promised land to live was not the threat they could do harm to Israel's peace but that they might keep Israel from being close and faithful to God, who was to be their exclusive focus (v. 33).

The Covenant Code is thus a means to an end: fidelity to the one on whom Israel's wellbeing entirely depended. Without Yahweh, they were nothing, could do nothing, and would end up as nothing. With him leading and them following obediently, however, all would fall properly into place, and their purpose as a people would come to fulfillment.

PROMISE OF THE ANGEL OF YAHWEH TO LEAD THE WAY TO THE PROMISED LAND (23:20–23). **23:20** The Lord's angel (the angel who is Yahweh[264]) would both "guard" the people on the way from Sinai to the promised land and "bring" them safely to their intended, promised destination. God's plan involved more than merely making Israel his people; it also involved giving them a place. Their identity as his people would in part be displayed by their

[264] See "Excursus: The Angel of the Lord" at 3:2–3.

having Canaan as a possession. On the way he would be with them; when they got there, he would dwell among them. His presence was assured by his promise, and they needed to learn to think in terms of his presence among them at all times. The angel would lead the way. He would go ahead, not merely go along. And he would be sent by God,[265] not merely arrive on his own.

23:21 Success requires obedience. The people could not hope to enjoy God's benefits, including his abiding protection, if they tried to make decisions on their own. Would they be so stupid and headstrong as to try to arrange for their own invasion of the promised land rather than following faithfully his leading? Absolutely. That was exactly what they eventually did after learning that they might not be able to enter the promised land as soon as they hoped by reason of their own lack of courage (Num 14:41–45). Knowing their capability to disobey, God reminded them sternly that only through obedience to his leadership and his word would they prosper in the conquest of Canaan. The angel had Yahweh's "Name . . . in him," a way of saying that "I will be with you, right there as you travel toward the promised land, right there as you begin the conquest, right there as you fight, right there as you settle in."[266] Accordingly, no rebellion against God's leadership (the angel bearing his "Name") could be tolerated. In the New Covenant the name of God was ultimately borne by his people, severally[267] and individually.[268]

23:22 It becomes clearer as the discourse progresses that the angel and Yahweh were one and the same. Here "what he says" and "all that I say" are treated syntactically as synonymous. (complete obedience meant keeping his covenant fully, including anything he might add to it after departure from Sinai.[269]) Careful listening to the law was required here, as was obedience to "all that I say." Then and only then would God "be an enemy to your enemies" and "oppose those who oppose you," that is, do their fighting for them according to the expectations of biblical holy war.[270] By reason of human imperfection, this kind of expectation is hard to follow, and it is not difficult to predict that Israel might fail to keep these commands fully. In effect, then, a need for divine grace was created implicitly by such demands, a grace that would allow

---

[265] The NIV translation, "See, I am sending . . ." is artificial. A normal way to indicate the future is by *hinnēh* plus the participle, as here. No special instruction to "see" anything is involved.

[266] On "name" as presence/identity, cf. Exod 20:24; Num 6:27; Deut 18:19–20; 2 Sam 7:13; I Kgs 8:16; 2 Kgs 21:7; Jer 7:10–12.

[267] E.g., Acts 15:17; 1 Pet 4:16; Rev 3:12.

[268] E.g., Acts 9:15–16; 19:5; 1 Cor 5:4; Rev 22:4.

[269] The laws in Num 10:11 and following, added as the Israelites moved through the wilderness after having left Sinai, were precisely the sort of thing this wording refers to. Of course, the paramount addition to the Sinai covenant is the Deuteronomy covenant, spoken to the Israelites at the last days before leaving the wilderness and crossing the Jordan into the promised land proper.

[270] A basic expectation of the doctrine of holy war is that Yahweh does the real fighting and his people fight in a more or less token manner. See "Excursus: Israelite Holy War" at 17:9.

for complete forgiveness and would provide for the complete presence of God among and within believers.

23:23 God, in the form of the angel manifesting his identity and presence, was willing to exterminate the various Canaanite groups whose doom was already announced in the judgment sentence spoken against them to Abraham in Gen 15:16. The six groups mentioned in this verse are a representative sample, but not the whole of the various ethnic subgroups more broadly called "Canaanite."[271] The dominant group was indeed the Canaanites, whose name could be used as a synecdoche generally for all native peoples in the region of the promised land. Earlier these had been more often called "Amorites" by the Mesopotamians, again using the name of one of the major groups as a convenient shorthand to encompass logically all the others. Paul referred to the "seven nations" (Acts 13:19) in Canaan (implicitly including also the Gergashites[272]), not because that was an exhaustive list but because it became slightly more common in Jewish tradition to speak of the seven than the six, even though six nations are more often listed than seven in Old Testament contexts describing the people groups of Canaan. The point is that God would wipe them out—the Israelites mainly would go through the motions of war rather than have to experience its terrors and ravages.[273] In the case of the repetition of the names of the nations in v. 28, only three names are used, still enough to suggest "all the people groups of Canaan."

The special emphasis here is on God's presence: the promises made are all ways of saying "I will be with you, right there as you travel toward the promised land, right there as you begin the conquest, right there as you fight, right there as you settle in." On the theme presented here of Israel's enemies becoming Yahweh's enemies, see Gen 12:3; 27:28–29; Deut 28:1–7; Josh 1:1–9; cf. also Acts 9:4; 22:7; 26:14. Indeed, all of the oracles against foreign nations in the prophetical books are predicated on the same underlying concept: those who opposed God's people opposed God himself.

REQUIREMENTS AND PROMISES RELATED TO WORSHIPING THE TRUE GOD EXCLUSIVELY (23:24–30). **23:24** Two demands were made upon the Israelites. The first was a prohibition of worship of the gods the Israelites would encounter once they reached the promised land, gods worshiped by the local Canaanites. The second was a demand for action: the people must destroy both idols and sacred stones, the means and reminders of worship.

[271] Cf. Gen 10:15–18; 15:19–21. The latter text mentions Kenites, Kenizzites, Kadmonites, and Rephaites, whose numbers and/or influence may have been greater in Abraham's day than in Moses', so they are mentioned to Abraham by God but not to Moses and the Israelites by God at Sinai.

[272] Cf. Deut 7:1; Josh 3:10; 24:11; Neh 9:8.

[273] See "Excursus: Israelite Holy War" at 17:9.

Why would Israel be tempted to worship local Canaanite deities? The answer is that once settled in Canaan, they would surely desire agricultural success, which in the ancient world was generally attributed to proper involvement of the deities in the agricultural process through worship. In general, ancient peoples believed that the gods could do anything but feed themselves. Humans therefore had the job of raising food for the gods, which was then "sent" to them through the offerings humans gave in the presence of the gods' idols. What part did the gods have in this process? They caused the crops to grow and the flocks and herds to multiply. The ancient farmer thought that the gods were absolutely essential to the agricultural process and that the way to involve the goodwill of the gods on behalf of one's farming was to worship them. The essence of worship was providing food for them in the form of sacrifices. When Israel would arrive in the promised land, the temptation to plant as the Canaanites planted, to cultivate as they cultivated, to harvest as they harvested, and to worship as they worshiped would be almost irresistible since all these were thought to go together as part and parcel of farming in any given locality.

To free his people from bondage to such attractive nonsense, dangerous because it could not save as only he could, Yahweh firmly forbade any involvement in pagan worship practices, just as he forbade any involvement in pagan planting or agricultural fertility rituals.[274] Likewise the Israelites were required to destroy any vestige of pagan worship, including not merely idols[275] but also "sacred stones." In this verse comes the first occurrence of the term "sacred stones" (NIV) in Exodus, often also translated as "pillars," and sometimes even simply partially transliterated (as *maṣṣēbôt* or the like) because the word is something of a *terminus technicus*. These were large stones erected as special reminders rather than small stones that could be carried. Jacob erected one at Bethel (Gen 28:18,22; 35:14–15), which he had anointed (Gen 31:13; 35:14) in recognition of God's revelation to him there, and another at Mizpah (Gen 31:45) as witness (along with a special stone heap that the whole family assembled) to the covenant he and Laban made. He also set one up to mark Rachel's tomb (Gen 35:20). Moses himself, at God's behest, would soon set up a sacred stone grouping, twelve such stones representing the number of the tribes of Israel (see comments on 24:4), suggesting that memorial stones or pillars were not per se illegal or heterodox when Israelites erected them as witnesses to some aspect of the one true God's relationship to them.

What could not be tolerated was the Canaanite pagan usage of sacred stones/pillars. These were routinely condemned in the Old Testament[276] because they marked pagan shrines and/or false religious locations of one sort

[274] See comments on 23:19; cf. Lev 19:19; Deut 22:9.

[275] On idols see comments on 20:4–6 and the accompanying excursus, "The Attractions of Idolatry."

[276] E.g., Exod 34:13; Lev 26:1; Deut 7:5; 12:3; 16:22; 1 Kgs 14:23.

or another. The Canaanite sacred stones probably were carved in most instances with idolatrous depictions and inscriptions (Lev 26:1, "Do not make idols or set up an image or a sacred stone for yourselves, and do not place a carved stone in your land to bow down before it"), and in many cases probably depicted in large sculpture of or at least a relief of the god they were intended to call attention to (e.g., 2 Kgs 10:27, "They demolished the sacred stone of Baal, and tore down the temple of Baal"). But carved or inscribed or not, such stones were forbidden to the Israelites if they were in any way associated with pagan idolatry. Merely moving them out of public view would not do; they might easily be found and reerected. Destruction was the only action appropriate for such symbols of paganism. Demolition of idols, which were mainly made of wood overlaid with gold or silver, could be accomplished by burning;[277] demolition of sacred stones was accomplished by smashing.

23:25–30 Verses 25–30 function as a sort of short blessings list, something of an adumbration of the blessings portion of the sanctions that would follow in greater abundance at the conclusion of the Sinai covenant (i.e., in Lev 26). The blessings and curses (the sanctions) of the covenant provided incentives for keeping it: curses as warnings of the disasters that would happen to the Israelites if they failed to keep the covenant and blessings as promises of good things that would happen to them if they succeeded in honoring their formal, legal relationship with their God. The curses are suggested in the wording of vv. 21 ("he will not forgive your rebellion") and 33 ("do not let them live in your land, or they will cause you to sin against me, because the worship of their gods will certainly be a snare to you") with wording that is relatively general; the blessings in vv. 25–30 are given with wording that is both more extensive and more specific. A proportionate reversal (more curses than blessings) provides a sort of balance in Lev 26.

23:25–26 As a result of proper worship (exclusively of Yahweh and exclusively according to his standards), there would ensue abundance of food and rain ("his blessing will be on your food and water"), health ("I will take away sickness from among you"), fertility ("none[278] will miscarry or be barren in your land"), and long life ("I will give you a full life span"[279]).

---

[277] E.g., Deut 7:5; 12:3.

[278] The gender forms in this statement are feminine and could apply to women or female animals or both, as is most likely in light of the general nature of the promise.

[279] The expression in Hb. used here, מִסְפַּר יָמֶיךָ אֲמַלֵּא, lit., "I will fill the number of your days," has no exact parallel elsewhere in the OT and is thus a hapax legomenon. Its meaning remains at least slightly speculative. The NRSV translates neutrally, "I will fulfill the number of your days." The closest parallel in Exodus would seem to be the statement in 20:12, "So that you may live long in the land," a promise not necessarily of long life for each Israelite but of a long habitation of the promised land by the Israelites in general, following the keeping of the fifth commandment ("honor your father and your mother"). But the context of the present promise certainly would allow for a promise of general health for all individuals in the sense of a full life span for everyone, so the NIV translation must be considered appropriate, if not ultimately provable.

These blessings can be considered reiterations of the original blessing to Abraham ("I will make you into a great nation and I will bless you," Gen 12:2). This sort of blessing is repeated often in the Mosaic corpus (e.g., Gen 26:3,24; Num 6:27; Deut 7:13; 15:6,10,18; 16:15; Deut 28:28) and is to be distinguished from the restoration (eschatological) blessings of the covenant, whose fulfillment follows the curse era of the exile. In other words, these are preexile blessings, promises for the first era of Israel's history, that of their life in the promised land prior to their rejection and exile. The restoration blessings (e.g., Lev 26:40–45; Deut 4:29–31; 28:1-13; 30:1-10) are commonly reflected in the prophetical promises of the new age as a future hope after the exile. These original promises for Israel in the land were, however, for the prophets something that was either coming to an end in their day or had ended already before the exile, depending on the time of the prophet.

23:27–30 God's assurance to his people included the promise of military victory in the campaign against the current holders of the promised land. This would not be accomplished merely by divine encouragement, divinely supplied insight or "intelligence" allowing the Israelites to outwit their enemies, or any other partial measure. Rather, it would happen because God would directly and personally overwhelm and defeat those who opposed Israel, in a measured and planned way designed to maximize the Israelites' opportunity to subdue the land over a period of time rather than all at once. The Israelites could, then, expect their conquest of Canaan to be, in effect, a rear guard action, a "mopping-up" after the destruction Yahweh would bring about in front of them as he led them into battle.

Four kinds of curses (predictions of disaster), known from the covenant curse collections in the covenant sanctions passages of Lev 26 and Deut 28–32, are mentioned here as God's methods of subduing the Canaanites in order to make possible Israel's conquest of the promised land. They are terror/fear,[280] confusion/helplessness,[281] defeat in battle,[282] and attack by wild animals/insects.[283] The principle we have noted before applies here as well: whenever a few of the dozens of types of covenant curses are mentioned, the reader is expected to understand them as samples of the full range of curses that will actually be unleashed.[284] We should therefore not take these four types of curses as the only or even as the primary sorts of afflictions God used to cow the Canaanites into submission, nor should we be surprised if no specific mention is made of them in the book of Joshua, where the actual conquest accounts are provided. Mentioning these four is a way of saying, "I will

---

[280] Cf. Lev 26:16–17,36–37; Deut 28:66–67; 32:25.

[281] Cf. Lev 26:37; Deut 28:20,28–29,32,34,65–67.

[282] Cf. Lev 26:17,25,37; Deut 28:35,49; 32:30.

[283] Cf. Lev 26:22; Deut 28:38–39,42; 32:24.

[284] Cf. Deut 28:16,20,45,61; 31:17; 32:23 and esp. Deut 29:20–21,27.

use whatever it takes to cause the Canaanites to be unable to resist your conquest of their land." Somewhat similarly, only three of the usual six or seven nations native to the land of Canaan[285] are mentioned in v. 28, in contrast to the six listed in v. 23. Again this is typical of the sort of synecdoche commonly seen throughout the Old Testament.

Farming is not just planting, cultivating, and harvesting crops on plots of land of one's choosing or raising flocks and herds in numbers convenient to one's time and energy. It also involves protection of those crops, flocks, and herds from pests, predators, and disease and proper preparation and rotation of crop land and grazing land. In much of Canaan—an area of the world almost entirely devoid of farmable flatland—the best way to grow crops was through terrace farming, which was labor-intensive not merely in the planting, tending, and harvesting but also in the preparation and maintenance of the terraces. Likewise, tree crops required extensive preparation and maintenance, and flocks and herds could not be left alone without proper protection or elaborate enclosure, lest they be easy prey for various meat-eating wild animals.

God had promised the Israelites that he would bless them with abundant farming results (vv. 23–26), and the combination of the large area available to farm (most of which had been cultivated over the centuries by the native Canaanites) and the great fertility in crops and herds meant that the small number of Israelites gathered at Mount Sinai would be insufficient to take, hold, and properly husband an area the size of the promised land (see v. 31). Thus under present conditions, the Israelites would be too few to keep the "land" (v. 29) from becoming "desolate," the "wild animals too numerous for you," and the need for time until the Israelites "increased enough to take possession of the land" (v. 30). Indeed, the present passage confirms that the Israelites were not a particularly large and impressive people group when they left Egypt (see "Excursus: How Many Israelites Left Egypt?" after 12:37). Because of their relatively small size, they could not be expected from the outset of their conquest of the promised territory to keep all of the land under cultivation that the Canaanite groups had been cultivating or keep out the wild animals that could eat their crops and herds. God therefore graciously granted them a gradual conquest of the promised land in order to allow them to grow into a nation large enough to keep the land properly husbanded. That gradual conquest is described partly in the book of Joshua, which outlines an occupation pattern that took place over many years, beginning with a central campaign, then eventuating in a southern campaign, and then finally a northern

---

[285] The Hittites mentioned here were not the great Anatolian nation (which would be pronounced *Hattites* were it in fact to occur in the Bible) but the local Canaanite subgroup also known as the "Sons of Heth." This is not to say that there were no cultural similarities between the Anatolian Hittites and Israel, particularly seen in laws and treaty formularies. See H. Hoffner, *The Laws of the Hittites: A Critical Edition* (Leiden: Brill, 1997).

campaign. Because the Israelites disobeyed God and were not entirely faithful to his commands for taking the promised land (the point of the paradigm story of Josh 7), the conquest was not merely gradual but actually partial (see, e.g., Josh 13:13; 23:13; Judg 1:27–36; 2:21–3:6), and the Israelites did not fully take possession of the promised land until the time of David—a date needlessly later, unfortunately, than God's offer in the present text.

FINAL COVENANT CODE PROMISES (OF A GREAT NATION IN A NEW LAND) AND WARNINGS (AGAINST IDOLATRY/POLYTHEISM) (23:31–33). **23:31–32** The traditional borders of the promised land are here described, beginning with the "Red Sea" (presumably the Gulf of Aqaba at its extreme northern shore)[286] on the southeast; and from there to the "Sea of the Philistines" (the Mediterranean) all along the west; and from the "desert" (the wilderness Negev of Judah, south and southwest) to the "River" (the Euphrates on the northeast). The promise to Abraham of this same land in Gen 15:18 uses only the wording "from the river of Egypt to the great River, the Euphrates," thus from the southwest to the northeast, including by implication everything in between and the borders intended by the other compass points as well. Deuteronomy 11:24 provides yet another wording, "from the desert to Lebanon, and from the Euphrates River to the western sea." These (and others also found in the OT) are all somewhat imprecise generalizations akin to "from Maine to California" or "from Canada to Mexico" as ways of describing the United States. The actual boundaries for Israel are described in final detail only in Josh 11–20, where the division of the land among the tribes takes place. Complete domination of all this territory would await the days of David[287]

Verse 31 establishes what God was willing to do: give Israel a vast, new land to occupy and purge it of its hostile inhabitants so that the land would be all theirs. It was a special gift not of a barren land that held no previous inhabitants because it was such a difficult place to live but of a fertile land that was occupied and had been farmed for centuries, which Israel could now claim for their own. Verses 32–33 state what Israel must do if this wonderful gift of God was to benefit them properly as his special covenant people. They must make no arrangements with any of the Canaanites or with any of their gods. The Canaanites were under God's judgment and due for extermination (Gen 15:16), so any agreement with any Canaanite group would represent a refusal on Israel's part to honor God's plan of judgment. The Canaanite gods could

---

[286] Doubts about the meaning of יַם־סוּף, traditionally translated "Red Sea" but often assumed to refer not to that body of water but to a smaller, tidal "Sea of Reeds," have been largely laid to rest by B. F. Batto in his article, "The Reed Sea: Resquiescat in Pace," *JBL* 102 (1983): 27–35. See also our comments on 13:17–18; 14:2; 15:5.

[287] See 1 Kgs 4:21–24 for the description as of the time of Solomon for the land David had placed under Israel's control through the military accomplishments summarized in 2 Sam 5; 7:1; 8:14–15.

not be tolerated because they were rivals to Yahweh's own exclusive claim on his people—not because he was a petty god whose ego was hurt by having other gods loved in addition to or instead of himself but because he, the only God, desired that his people be saved. Idols cannot save.

Thus both the people of Canaan and their religion had to be exterminated; eliminating one while keeping the other would not do. Both had to go lest they become sources of sin to the Israelites. That Israel allowed most Canaanites to live and embraced the worship of the very gods they were forbidden to have anything to do with (see Judg 2:10–23) forms the basis for the tragic history that was lived out in the land, finally resulting in expulsion from it into exile.[288]

23:33 This verse contains a small but informative part of the evidence for the Mosaic dating of the book of Exodus. If the book were a late (e.g., exilic or postexilic "P" source) fabrication intended to justify laws actually initiated first by Ezra, Nehemiah, or their ilk, it would surely describe ways to make accommodation with the local inhabitants of the land of Canaan. Instead, it demands something that actually did not happen (by reason of Israel's rebellion against God): extermination in holy war of the native population of Canaan as a punishment for the sinfulness of that culture (see above). The command here given anticipates a Canaan populated only by Israelites and those they brought by choice into the land (resident alien traders and workers, but not Canaanites). In reality, most of the local Canaanite population remained alive and well throughout the Israelite occupation of the land because the command given here was never adequately carried out. The discontinuity between what the law expected and what subsequently transpired argues against its after-the-fact fabrication in the postexilic period. The theory

---

[288] Here M. Weinfeld thinks that the wording about exterminating the Canaanites throughout this passage (23:20–33) is weaker than that of Numbers (33:50–56) and weaker still than that of Deut 7:2 and 20:16–17 ("The Ban on the Canaanites in the Biblical Codes and Its Historical Development," in *History and Tradition of Early Israel: Studies Presented to Eduard Nielsen* [Leiden: Brill, 1993], 142–60). He theorizes a progression of expectation, from expulsion to annihilation, the latter being a utopian concept never carried out. The weakness of this approach includes its failure to take seriously the bluntness of Yahweh's original annihilation promise in Exod 23:23 ("I will wipe them out") and the actual logic of the command in 23:33, "Do not let them live [in your land]" in the context of the Exodus situation, which orients the people against coexistence with the Canaanites in terms as strong as could be expected in such a setting when the people are still at Sinai. That Deuteronomy should use, forty years later, what Weinfeld judges to be somewhat more blunt, less compromising language reflects its setting: just days before the onset of a war of conquest, a setting in which people needed to understand without any confusion exactly what would be expected of them very soon, namely, a holy war of extermination. It could hardly be expected that Moses would simply repeat verbatim in Deuteronomy what he had conveyed from Yahweh to the people in Exodus as if the setting and the sense of immediacy were not different—and as if Deuteronomy were not being spoken to a new generation at the doorstep of a war of conquest.

that such laws read back into Israel's earlier history the conditions and expectations of the postexilic period is contradicted by the facts in this case.

(7) Documentation of the Covenant and God's Confirming Glory (24:1–11)

[1]Then he said to Moses, "Come up to the LORD, you and Aaron, Nadab and Abihu, and seventy of the elders of Israel. You are to worship at a distance, [2]but Moses alone is to approach the LORD; the others must not come near. And the people may not come up with him."

[3]When Moses went and told the people all the LORD's words and laws, they responded with one voice, "Everything the LORD has said we will do." [4]Moses then wrote down everything the LORD had said.

He got up early the next morning and built an altar at the foot of the mountain and set up twelve stone pillars representing the twelve tribes of Israel. [5]Then he sent young Israelite men, and they offered burnt offerings and sacrificed young bulls as fellowship offerings to the LORD. [6]Moses took half of the blood and put it in bowls, and the other half he sprinkled on the altar. [7]Then he took the Book of the Covenant and read it to the people. They responded, "We will do everything the LORD has said; we will obey."

[8]Moses then took the blood, sprinkled it on the people and said, "This is the blood of the covenant that the LORD has made with you in accordance with all these words."

[9]Moses and Aaron, Nadab and Abihu, and the seventy elders of Israel went up [10]and saw the God of Israel. Under his feet was something like a pavement made of sapphire, clear as the sky itself. [11]But God did not raise his hand against these leaders of the Israelites; they saw God, and they ate and drank.

24:1–2 Here begins the invitation from God to Moses to ascend Mount Sinai yet another time, for the special purpose of ratifying the Covenant Code. God's holiness must still be protected (see comments on 19:10–24); so only Moses, Aaron, Aaron's two oldest sons,[289] and the seventy elders of Israel[290] were allowed to form the ratification meal party, representing the rest of Israel through their leadership status. Everyone other than Moses in the leadership group (addressed as "you"—the Hb. is plural—in the statement in v. 1, "You

[289] Nadab and Abihu were introduced to the reader in the Moses-Aaron genealogy of chap. 6 (6:23), and their role as successors to Aaron received prominence further in the complete work of the Pentateuch (e.g., Exod 28:1; Lev 10:1ff.; Num 3:2–4; 26:60–61). Eleazar and Ithamar were surely also fully heirs of Aaron's priestly office from the start (see Exod 28:1), but even they were represented here by their two elder brothers in the representative group that actually were allowed to climb the mountain.

[290] Joshua would have been among the seventy, as indicated by his role in 17:9–14 and later in this chapter (v. 13). He was not always with Moses when Moses went up the mountain (see, e.g., 33:11) but was surely an elder. "Elder" (זָקֵן) in its typical actual usage means simply "leader" and does not necessarily imply anything about age, other than the fact that as common sense would dictate, elders were not children. See J. L. McKenzie, "The Elders in the Old Testament," *Bib* 48 (1959): 522–40.

are to worship at a distance") was required to stay away from the most direct contact with the presence of Yahweh. That nearest proximity was granted to Moses exclusively ("Moses alone is to approach the LORD," v. 2), as had been the pattern since the first encounter with Yahweh on Sinai in chap. 3.

In the ancient biblical world, covenants were normally concluded with a special covenant meal in which animals were symbolically cut in half (symbolizing the shared responsibility of the two parties as well as the severity of the penalty for breaking the covenant), then the parties to the covenant walked between the pieces, and then the meal was eaten together as a sign of friendship and alliance.[291] God's covenant with Israel, as represented through the now-completed Covenant Code, involved God as one party and the people as the other. Represented by the seventy-four leaders, the people were the other party. More than any other of the Israelite leaders, Moses stood directly between God and the people as a mediator, and although the text does not say so, he may well have eaten God's portion of the meal symbolically as God's representative at the ceremony.[292] The mass of the people could not "come up with him" (v. 2) but had to say below at the base of the mountain, kept back as before by the boundaries set there (19:12,23). By their acceptance of the covenant both in advance (see 19:8) and now, after hearing it (24:3,7), the people in general confirmed their willingness to abide by it, which was to be ritually symbolized by their elders' eating the covenant meal with Yahweh.[293]

After hearing the Covenant Code repeated to them by Moses just as he had heard it on the mountain, the people gave uniform assent to it, agreeing to keep it (v. 3). They did the same thing a second time, after Moses had written it down (v. 4) and then read it to them (v. 7). Thus they doubly confirmed the covenant with their vocal promise, in addition to the promise made in advance to keep it once they heard it (19:8). In each case the people committed themselves to obeying "everything" in the covenant. Such is the nature of any true covenant: keeping all of it is the only way to keep it; keeping only some of it and violating the rest is not keeping it at all.[294]

---

[291] See comments on 18:12, relative to Jethro's covenant meal with the Israelite elders.

[292] In the case of God's covenant with Abraham, a smoking firepot with a blazing flame served as a stand-in for God (Gen 15:17). In light of Moses' special invitation to come closer than any of the others to God, it would seem possible that he was chosen to represent God in the rituals at this larger covenant meal atop the mountain.

[293] Several helpful studies of covenant meals and the significance of the sacrifices and rituals that were conducted in connection with them have appeared, including that of R. Schmid, *Das Bundesopfer in Israel: Wesen, Ursprung und Bedeutung der alttestamenlichen Schelamim* (Munich: Kösel, 1964), 88–125; E. W. Nicholson, "The Covenant Ritual in Exodus XXIV 3–8," *VT* 32 (1982): 74–86; D. Doré, "Un repas d'alliance? Lecture d'Ex. 24, 1–2, 9–11," 147–71; R. S. Hendel, "Sacrifice as a Cultural System: The Ritual Symbolism of Exodus 24,3–8," *ZAW* 101 (1989): 366–90. A contrasting view may be seen in E. Kutsch's "Das sogennante 'Bundesblut' in Ex. XXIV 8 und Sach. IX 11," *VT* 23 (1973): 25–30.

[294] Cf. the way James summarized the well-known principle: "Whoever keeps the whole law and yet stumbles at just one point is guilty of breaking all of it" (Jas 2:10).

24:3 Grammatically, the expression "words and laws" could be a hendiadys expressing "every word of every law," but it is more likely a summary of the two major units of law thus far encountered, that is, the Ten Commandments (the Ten Words, see 20:1) and the rest of the "laws" (see 21:1), that is, all the stipulations and related statements of the covenant thus far—all the text from 20:1 to 23:33. At this point the people were united in their willingness to keep the covenant, something they did for the most part, however imperfectly, during the lifetimes of Moses and Joshua (Josh 24:31). Thereafter, unfortunately, Israel kept the covenant only sporadically. Covenants must be endorsed not merely by the generation with whom they are first concluded but must be reaffirmed through formal renewal commitments in each subsequent generation. The original assent so enthusiastically given here could not be expected to last without regular recommitment from generation to generation, and such recommitments were usually more lacking than not, judging from the infrequency with which they are mentioned in the text of 1, 2 Kings, for example.

24:4a Writing down the law was important if it were to be permanent and an accurate basis for continuing instruction of newer members of the community. Children would need to be instructed in the covenant as fully as their parents initially had been. Newcomers to the community from foreign places who accepted Yahweh's worship and integrated themselves properly into the Israelite nation needed to have the clearest possible understanding of everything the law required. Judges who would have to extrapolate from the covenant stipulations to decide difficult cases required precision in recalling exactly how God had given his commandments. Thus regular reading and rereading of the written covenant at appointed times served to keep it alive in the minds of the people as the basis for their life together with the one true God.[295] The first part of this verse thus makes reference to the concept of a "document clause" for the covenant.[296]

24:4b–6 Following the principles of worship and covenant-recognition already revealed in the Covenant Code itself, Moses carried out the actions appropriate to making the covenant an official, formally accepted commitment on Israel's part. Five elements centered the people's focus on their new relationship with God: an altar, twelve stone pillars, animal sacrifices, blood application, and the reading of the covenant. All this was to prepare the people for yet another—and this time the most "official"—verbal agreement to the newly revealed covenant with Yahweh.

The building of an altar reflected the teaching of 20:24–26, which, although worded primarily in terms of materials and construction design, had implicitly as its purpose to instruct the Israelites in proper worship. That

---

[295] Cf. Deut 31:11; 17:19; Josh 8:34; 2 Kgs 23:2; Neh 8:8,18.

[296] On the document clause see "Excursus: The Exodus-Leviticus Covenant" prior to 20:1.

worship involved the slaughtering and cooking of meat on the principle of substitutionary atonement (stated simply: "for me to live, something must die in my place"). The twelve stone pillars visibly represented the tribes of Israel, all of whom were committing themselves to keep the covenant both severally and together, and it also would function as a reminder to all who saw them that God had made a covenant at this place with a multifaceted people. The stone pillars *(maṣṣēbôt)* that he stood there at the base of Mount Sinai were the very sort of pillars prohibited in 23:24 if placed in connection with pagan religion. Placed as reminders of Yahweh's covenant with his people, they were welcome memorials to the saving grace of the only true God.[297]

The "young men" (v. 5) whom Moses sent to offer the sacrifices were not necessarily priests, since the priesthood at this early point was limited virtually to a single family (that of Aaron). The number of animals needed was large because of the pan-national nature of the occasion, requiring a large number of strong workers to handle the various offerings, including the "young bulls." It is likely that these young men worked under the supervision of Aaron and his sons, though Moses' own continuing priesthood would also legitimize their actions if they were done under his supervision. "Burnt offerings" are offerings dedicated entirely to God, burnt to ashes on the altar.[298] "Fellowship offerings" are offerings eaten by priests and worshipers alike, with a portion of fat from the animal being sacrificed symbolically dedicated to God and burnt to ashes on the altar.[299]

The portion of "blood" (v. 6) that Moses put in "bowls" was for sprinkling on the people, as a sign that they were recipients of the advantage that the shed blood provided.[300] The portion sprinkled on the altar was God's, signifying that he was the other party to the covenant, as represented in the ceremony of sacrifice by his altar.[301] Since without the shedding of blood there is no forgiveness (Heb 9:22), making a visible display of the blood from an animal killed for sacrificial purposes highlights for all to see the concept of atoning death. Such vivid reminders helped the Israelites keep in mind the source and nature of their forgiveness and acceptance: God and his grace (as he allows the slain animal to substitute for the sinner, based on the eventual perfect sacrifice of Christ to which all OT sacrifices point and upon which all OT sacrifices depend for their ultimate validity).

---

[297] A summary of the concepts involved in setting up *maṣṣēbôt* particularly of the way the twelve stones in this context represented a memorialization of a legal relationship between Yahweh and each tribe individually, and thus between the tribes themselves as well, can be found in C. F. Graesser, "Standing Stones in Ancient Palestine," *BA* 35 (1972): 34–63.

[298] See comments on 10:25; 18:12; 20:24.

[299] See comments on 20:24; cf. Lev 3; 7.

[300] See comments on 12:13–23; 29:20–21.

[301] See comments on 29:12,16,20; 30:10.

24:7 This final, formal reading of the "Book of the Covenant" (i.e., the Covenant Code of 20:1–23:33) by Moses, as God's representative, to the people, as recipients of the covenant, produced again the positive response of the people already indicated when prior opportunities presented themselves for making initial assents to it (19:8; 24:3). In the context of this solemn covenant ceremony at the base of the mountain of God, their words bound them by oath to obedience to the One who had redeemed them from slavery in Egypt and was about to deliver into their hands the land centuries before promised to them through Abraham. They knew the Giver of the words of the covenant: it was Yahweh ("We will do everything the LORD has said"); they thus also understood to whom they were bound and who would enforce the covenant if they broke it or ignored it.

24:8 Moses sprinkled[302] blood on the people in order to symbolize their being parties to the covenant. Some droplets would remain on their skin for days; some that fell on their clothing would be visible, if faded, for as long as the clothing lasted. The ceremony itself was so vivid and extraordinary as to be memorable, and its memory was intended to keep in the consciousness of the people the fact that God had joined with the people of Israel in a formal, official covenant to which both he and they were bound by oath.[303] The animal's blood recalled that oath (cf. v. 6), and therefore Moses commanded the people to take note of it and appreciate its meaning ("This is the blood of the covenant"; "See the blood of the covenant" [NRSV]). Moreover, the covenant was not merely a general concept. Rather, it was the sum of all its words, so Moses described it as "existing in accordance with all these words." Again the language emphasizes that Israelites were not free to keep only part of the covenant.

24:9–11 Seventy-four people ascended Mount Sinai to represent all Israel in the covenant meal (see comments on vv. 1–2), a special eating ceremony between parties to the covenant without which the covenant would not have been understood to make them allies/friends/kin. In the ancient world (and many places in the modern world) people would not eat together if they were not somehow allies or family. Eating was understood to convey acceptance, to declare approval of those with whom one dined. Just as Jesus' dining with tax collectors, nonpracticing Jews ("sinners"), and other such persons was regarded by many in his day as an act of approval of their

[302] Whether Moses used his fingers to do this sprinkling (as in Lev 4:6,17; 14:16,27: Num 19:4) or a hyssop branch as a sort of brush-applicator for the blood (as in Exod 12:22; Num 19:19ff.; cf. Heb 9:19) is not stated explicitly here or usually in passages that specify the sprinkling of blood.

[303] An oath was possible without a covenant (e.g., Exod 22:11; Lev 5:4; Num 5:19,21), but a covenant always involved an oath. God's oath was all the words of the covenant, especially the "I am Yahweh" (and similar) formulations. The people's oath is recorded in 19:8; 24:3,7.

behavior (Matt 9:10–11; 11:19; Mark 2:15–16; Luke 5:30; 15:2),[304] so eating a formal meal with others was understood to demonstrate mutual agreement, cooperation, acceptance, and respect.

What did the seventy-four humans actually see when they "saw the God of Israel"? They saw some sort of general shape that he allowed them to see vaguely; but they could see clearly and with true definition only one thing: "Under his feet was something like a pavement made of sapphire, clear as the sky itself" (v. 10; NRSV: "something like a pavement of sapphire stone, like the very heaven for clearness"). This is consistent with other visions of God in which viewers do not really see him (as 1 John 4:12 explicitly states) but see something that lets them know they are dealing with a person rather than a thing but who is otherwise glorious and brilliant, relatively indistinct, atop a platform of some sort that is indeed distinctly recognizable.[305] Such visions include, for example, that of Ezekiel (Ezek 1:26–28) and Amos (Amos 7:7, where the correct translation should be "standing on a wall of tin")[306] and Exod 33:23. Never do humans actually see God fully in his essence, but only something of a shape that God allows to be recognized as that of an actual (extremely huge) person, thus allowing some sort of focus on himself, something for the humans to look at and talk to.[307]

The area under God's feet, described as "something like a pavement made of sapphire," represents a unique description in the Old Testament. Hebrew *lĕbēnāh* (NIV, NRSV "pavement," also "paving stone" or especially "slab" the like; cf. Holladay) can refer to almost any flat stone surface, including the most common referent, a brick (e.g., Gen 11:3; Exod 1:14; Ezek 4:1). Sapphire as the composition of God's standing/sitting platform is paralleled only in Ezek 1:26 and 10:1, which may represent a conscious reference back to the present passage. The sapphire platform on which he stood appeared like the essence of the sky as regards clearness (NRSV "like the very heaven for clearness," v. 10)—which presumably gave the men on the mountain the impression that God was not actually standing on the mountain but was simply visible there in a personal sort of way, his glory so marvelous that normal footing such as the men themselves had would hardly be appropriate for him.[308]

---

[304] Cf. also Isa 11:7 ("The cow will feed with the bear, their young will lie down together, and the lion will eat straw like the ox") and 65:25 ("The wolf and the lamb will feed together, and the lion will eat straw like the ox"), which use eating together as a vivid way of portraying cooperation and mutual acceptance, thus perfect peace.

[305] But see T. C. Vriezen, "The Exegesis of Exodus xxiv 9–11," *OTS* 17 (1972): 100–133.

[306] See comments on Amos 7:7–8 in Stuart, *Hosea-Jonah* (new ed. forthcoming).

[307] Since otherwise God is invisible, there would hardly be the certitude that people had even been in his special presence. So a sort of corporealization serves the purpose of helping humans to understand that they are dealing with a person and not merely an idea in their own minds or a force or concept or numinous experience of some sort.

[308] Cf. F. Schnutenhaus, "Das Kommen und Erscheinen Gottes im Alten Testament," *ZAW* 76 (1964): 1–22. Cf. also P. Welten, "Die Vernichtung des Todes und die Königsherrschaft Gottes. Eine traditiongeschichtliche Studie zu Jes 25, 6–8; 24, 21–23 und Ex 24, 9–11," *TZ* 38 (1982): 129–46.

The statement "but God did not raise his hand[309] against these leaders" (v. 11) reflects the widespread assumption in the ancient world that to see God would be to die.[310] Nothing of the sort was God's intention; instead he showed himself, even though only vaguely and partially, so that the people's leaders would understand that he was a willing party to his covenant with them and so that they would remember that they had agreed to the keep his covenant in his actual, unmistakable, presence. "And they ate and drank" is a summation of the covenant meal.[311]

We do not know how covenant meals concluded; presumably, at a minimum, the parties rose, exchanged parting greetings, and departed. Perhaps in the case of this unique covenant meal, God disappeared from the sight of the others first, and they then understood that the formalities were over.[312] Inasmuch as the following pericope describes Moses and those who had been with him at this mountaintop covenant meal back again at the base of the mountain in conversation (24:14) and specifies that only Moses and Joshua made the next ascent (24:13), there is no doubt that 24:11 brings to a conclusion the account of the ascent of the seventy-four and their meal with Yahweh.

(8) Introduction to Laws on the Tabernacle and Worship (24:12–18)

[12]The LORD said to Moses, "Come up to me on the mountain and stay here, and I will give you the tablets of stone, with the law and commands I have written for their instruction."

[13]Then Moses set out with Joshua his aide, and Moses went up on the mountain of God. [14]He said to the elders, "Wait here for us until we come back to you. Aaron and Hur are with you, and anyone involved in a dispute can go to them."

[15]When Moses went up on the mountain, the cloud covered it, [16]and the glory of the LORD settled on Mount Sinai. For six days the cloud covered the mountain, and on the seventh day the LORD called to Moses from within the cloud. [17]To the Israelites the glory of the LORD looked like a consuming fire on top of the mountain.

---

[309] On the biblical idea of God's hand, see J. J. M. Roberts, "The Hand of Yahweh," *VT* 21 (1971): 244–51.

[310] See comments on 33:20; 20:19; cf. also Deut 18:16; and esp. Judg 13:22; Cf. D. Or, "And They Beheld God (Exod 24:11)," *BMik* 30 (1984/85): 257–58 (Hb.). Or suggests that the verb in 24:11, חזה, differs from the verb for "see" in v. 24 (ראה) precisely because it has a different, idiomatic meaning in the context: "to conclude a covenant." Accordingly, he understands the end of v. 11 to mean "they concluded a covenant with God and they ate and drank."

[311] See E. W. Nicholson, "The Antiquity of the Tradition in Exodus XXIV 9–11," *VT* 25 (1975): 68–79; "The Interpretation of Exodus XXIV 9–11," *VT* 24 (1974): 77–97; "The Origin of the Tradition in Exodus xxiv 9–11," *VT* 26 (1976): 148–60. Cf. J. L. Ska, "Le repas de Ex 24, 11," *Bib* 74 (1993): 305–27; D. Doré, "Un repas d'alliance? Lecture d'Ex. 24, 1–2, 9–11," in *L'Ancien Testament*. Le point théologique 24 (Paris: Beauchesne, 1977), 147–71.

[312] This would represent a presumptive analogy with, e.g., Judg 6:21; Ezek 10:18; Luke 24:31; Acts 1:9. In other words, the general pattern of divine/angelic departure is simply that of disappearing into the sky, leaving those in attendance watching but no longer seeing anything except the sky.

18Then Moses entered the cloud as he went on up the mountain. And he stayed on the mountain forty days and forty nights.

Yet another trip up to the top of Mount Sinai now commences. It may be assumed that Moses, Aaron, Aaron's two sons, and the seventy Israelite elders had descended the mountain once they finished the covenant meal described in 24:11. The present trip, involving only Moses and Joshua (v. 13), was of a very different nature from the previous one: it was for a lengthy stay atop the mountain (v. 18), with special attention to receiving God's own written guidelines for Israel's relationship to him (v. 12). This stay on the mountain continued through the events described in 32:1–16; Moses' sojourn atop the mountain would be cut short this time by God's own command (32:7).

24:12 Perhaps the best way to translate this verse would be: "Come up to me on the mountain and wait there; and I will give you the tablets of stone—as well as the law and the commandment—which I have written for their instruction." In other words, the verse intends to convey that it was the "tablets of stone" that God himself wrote, not all the laws of the covenant.[313] Consistently in Exodus, it was only the tablets of the Ten Words/Commandments that God actually wrote (see comments on 32:15–16; 34:1). All other commandments were written by Moses according to God's dictation (e.g., Exod 17:14; 24:4; 34:27; cf. Deut 27:3,8; 31:9). Indeed, Deuteronomy is even more specific as to God's personal writing being limited to the Ten Words/Commandments (Deut 4:13; 5:22; 10:2–4).

God invited Moses up the mountain with the clear instruction that he would be there a long time ("and stay here"). A special feature of this visit to the top is the promise of receiving the tablets of stone. These function effectively as the document clause[314] of the Sinai covenant—in part because the covenant's totality is reflected broadly in the Ten Commandments[315] and also because that which God himself wrote could surely be understood to symbolize his authorship of the whole, most of which was dictated to his amanuensis, Moses. For Moses to be able to receive these tablets personally and deliver them personally to the Israelites on God's behalf would parallel the personal experience of the leaders in eating the covenant meal with Yahweh as described in the passage immediately preceding the present context. That the tablets would eventually reside in the ark itself (25:21–22) as an indicator of

---

[313] It is also possible that the grammar of the verse is to be interpreted as containing two instances of *waw explicativum* (the *waw* that means "that is"), before הַתּוֹרָה and הַמִּצְוָה respectively. By this interpretation the Ten Commandments would simply be identified as "law" and "commandment" "for their instruction," and no other laws would be mentioned expressly in the verse.

[314] For an introduction to the concept of the document clause and its function within the covenant, see "Excursus: The Exodus-Leviticus Covenant" at 20:1.

[315] See under 1, "The Ten Words and Their Significance" (introductory comment to 20:1–17).

the permanent presence of God through his word shows their significance. But neither the tablets nor the rest of the law functions in a merely symbolic way. God's covenant is based on stipulations—rules that must be kept, requirements that if broken would condemn Israel to great pain and misfortune. God thus insisted that Moses understand that he himself had written the commandments "for their instruction."

From the ancient world outside of Israel, all surviving written evidence indicates that laws were understood to be given by a king to his people, not a god to his people. To be sure, the king could claim that a god or gods instructed him to promulgate the laws, but no claim close to the present one existed outside the biblical covenant—that God himself provided his laws directly to his covenant people and that he actually wrote the basic ones (the Ten Words/Commandments) personally on stone as a sign that all his laws came directly from him and are not the product of human invention. Israel's teacher was thus God himself, who gave them his covenant "for their instruction."[316] It cannot be escaped that when Jesus issued laws[317]—not merely as the one who wrote them down as dictated but as the actual author—he was staking a claim to divinity under the concept of Israelite covenant law, in which the author of the commands is also the divine Sovereign.

24:13–14 The anticipation of a long visit on the mountain is also evident in the way Moses took an assistant with him part way up the mountain[318] ("Moses set out with Joshua his aide") and the way he handed over his appeals court duties[319] temporarily to Aaron and Hur ("anyone involved in a dispute can go to them"). Being entirely alone on a very long visit probably seemed undesirable and unwise; Moses could always send Joshua away if God did not welcome his presence in the vicinity. Letting the Israelites go for weeks without resolution of important disputes could undermine the social peace among the newly merged[320] and newly responsible Israelites, who had until so very recently been ruled by and therefore thought in terms of Egyptian laws and legal procedures.

The choice of Aaron and Hur as temporary judges made perfect sense: they had already been seen publicly to be Moses' close associates (cf. 17:12), and

---

[316] לְהוֹרֹתָם.

[317] E.g., in Matt 5–7 and par. or John 13:34. Jesus was certainly a second Moses but far more than that at the same time.

[318] In light of 32:17 it is virtually certain that Joshua did not go all the way up the mountain to the top with Moses but waited for him at some point partway to the top. Indeed, this would appear to be a point made by the very structure of the verse, in which the wording of the second part, "and Moses went up on the mountain," purposely leaves out Joshua. Joshua shared some experiences with Moses but was hardly with him at all times and least likely at those times when Moses was specially in the presence of God within the glory cloud.

[319] See comments on 18:13–26.

[320] See comments on 12:38.

Aaron in particular had served with Moses from the beginning of the confrontations with Pharaoh in Egypt. Unlike Joshua,[321] they were both probably of about the same age as Moses[322] and thus commanded the respect that age and experience called forth in the ancient biblical world.

24:15–18 The cloud that covered the top of Mount Sinai and represented God's glory was similar to that which appeared during the daytime to be a pillar of dark cloud and during the night to be a pillar of fire as described in 13:21–22; 14:19–20,24. The cloud had already served as a protection and guide for the Israelites in their flight from the Egyptians. It was the same cloud previously indicated in 19:18. In Exodus as elsewhere in the Bible[323] it represented God's glorious presence: awesome, multifaceted, partly mysterious but also protective and encompassing.

Verse 15's statement, "When Moses went up on the mountain, the cloud covered it," indicates God's reception of Moses into his presence: the cloud standing for God physically met Moses and took him in, as it were, once he finally reached the top, where he could enter the cloud. That the reader is expected to remember that God represented himself on Mount Sinai through a cloud is evident in the usage "*the* cloud," which refers back to the last mention of cloud in the book (in 19:16), when Israel first encountered the power and awesomeness of Yahweh at Sinai as represented by a cloud. The cloud was, in other words, the glory cloud that represented God at Mount Sinai.

From v. 16 it is evident that Moses took six days to climb the mountain—waiting for almost a week outside the cloud for his audience with Yahweh. His traveling six days outside the cloud and then entering it may in some manner recall Yahweh's role as the six-day Creator of Genesis 1, but it may simply reflect a combination of facts: it took that long for Moses to climb the mountain once God had told Moses to do so and had shown himself to be at the top waiting for him, and Moses and Joshua may have traveled carefully and deliberately, stopping often and praying often in light of the awesomeness that yet another encounter with God on the mountain portended.

We are not told in any other account of people ascending Mount Sinai how long the trip to the summit took. For the seventy-four who went previously (24:9) the ascent may have been even slower, assuming advanced age and limited mobility for at least some of the elders. Moses was not unwelcome, however, at the summit, since God overtly invited him to enter the cloud ("called to Moses from within the cloud"). Thus when Moses finally reached the top, he was able to enter the cloud virtually immediately ("Moses entered the

[321] On Joshua's age see Josh 14:7,10; he was less than half the age of Moses or Aaron.

[322] Especially if Hur were indeed the husband of Miriam (something that is a speculation in Jewish tradition and not documented in the Bible); Aaron's being senior to Moses in age was already well established in 6:6–7.

[323] So, e.g., Exod 16:10; 40:34; Num 16:42; 1 Kgs 8:11; Isa 4:5; Ezek 1:28; 10:4; Luke 21:27.

cloud as he went on up," v. 18). This wording suggests by its silence about Joshua that he stayed near the top, but not at it—outside of the cloud but available to Moses as a dutiful aide.

Once again the cloud had a fiery aspect ("to the Israelites the glory of the LORD looked like a consuming fire," v. 17) so that from the base of the mountain Sinai's top seemed on fire ("fire on top of the mountain"). To many commentators and readers, this description has seemed irresistibly to suggest that Mount Sinai, wherever it was, must have been volcanic. The text, in fact, gives no warrant for such a conclusion; if Sinai was volcanic, so must the wilderness from Egypt to Sinai have been because God's glory cloud had appeared both as darkness and fire throughout the journey so far, changing every day and every night.[324]

"Forty days and forty nights" (v. 18) may not be intended as a literal description of the time Moses was on the mountain. "Forty" has an idiomatic usage in Hebrew, conveying the same sense that "dozens" or "a great many" can convey in English. Sometimes it is used literally to mean "forty" (one more than thirty-nine), but other times its more general meaning is apparent, as probably in the flood story (Gen 7:4,12,17; 8:6) or in the account of the scouting of the promised land in Num 13 (esp. 13:25) or other contexts (Judg 13:1; 1 Sam 4:18; 17:16). Could Moses have carried provisions with him that would have kept that long? Not easily, but the reader should suspect that he was fasting the entire time, as confirmed by Deut 9:9.[325]

3. Laws on the Means of Worship (25:1–31:18)

At the very outset of his covenant with Israel, immediately after the conclusion of the presentation of the Ten Commandments and Israel's response to them, God required his people to pay attention to proper worship (see comments on 20:22–26). Now, immediately after the conclusion of the presentation of the Covenant Code and Israel's response to it, God again required his people to pay attention to proper worship. Worship—where it is done, how it is done, by whom it is done, with whom is done, with what it is done—would

---

[324] The idea that Sinai must have been a volcanic mountain stems from a naturalistic view of the narrative, one that sees the Israelites as recording what they saw out of misunderstanding. By this way of thinking, they simply were overawed by the sort of phenomena that one sees when looking at an actively erupting volcano (smoke, explosions, the red glow of the molten rock spewing forth from the crater at the top) and interpreted such things as the manifestation of a god's glory. Even some modern evangelical Sinai hunters have made the mistake of limiting their search for the "real Sinai" to volcanic mountains, thus unwittingly giving support to a naturalistic interpretation of the data (e.g., R. Cornuke, D. Halbook, *In Search of the Mountain of God: The Discovery of the Real Mount Sinai* [Nashville: Broadman & Holman, 2000]).

[325] Jesus' fast in the wilderness for "forty" days followed this pattern, as one of the many indicators he was to be the sovereign and lawgiver of a new covenant, Moses-like but not merely so.

dominate the rest of the Sinai covenant, that is, the law through the rest of Exodus, through all of Leviticus, and up to Num 10:10. Not all of these materials are strictly legal in genre; some are narrative, some provide fulfillment descriptions relative to what had been commanded, and some partake of other genres and purposes. But the overwhelming emphasis of the rest of the covenant is worship.

Worship is the first, most basic response of a true believer to the true God. It should begin immediately upon conversion, continue with regularity and consistency throughout the rest of life, and will be continued forever in heaven. It is clear from the Scripture that God enjoys being worshiped and expects his people to find joy in worshiping him as well. Worship should bring pleasure and benefit both to the worshiper and to the true, divine object of his or her worship.

In the Old Covenant everything associated with worship had to partake of proper symbolism, so that the presence of God,[326] the purity of God, the superiority of God, and the nature of his salvation could be communicated visually and, at least sometimes, even tactilely, to his people. The tabernacle, its furnishings and implements, and those who facilitated worship were expected to reflect the only intelligent God in his covenant relationship to his specially chosen people.

(1) Laws on Donations for the Tabernacle Furnishings (25:1–9)

1The LORD said to Moses, 2"Tell the Israelites to bring me an offering. You are to receive the offering for me from each man whose heart prompts him to give. 3These are the offerings you are to receive from them: gold, silver and bronze; 4blue, purple and scarlet yarn and fine linen; goat hair; 5ram skins dyed red and hides of sea cows; acacia wood; 6olive oil for the light; spices for the anointing oil and for the fragrant incense; 7and onyx stones and other gems to be mounted on the ephod and breastpiece. 8Then have them make a sanctuary for me, and I will dwell among them. 9Make this tabernacle and all its furnishings exactly like the pattern I will show you."

Preparations for worship must begin at the beginning, with a place to gather and the kinds of things that will represent Yahweh's covenant presence among his people. The very first step of all this requires the assembling of materials out of which the worship accoutrements can be constructed. But

[326] As J. Cohen asserts, the presence of God through the tabernacle to be built according to the instructions that follow here represents a remarkably awesome and potentially terrifying manifestation of the divine among a people who so recently had found it impossible to tolerate even his voice from afar (20:18–19); J. Cohen, "The Dilemma of the Sanctuary," *JBQ* 25 (1997): 185–87; cf. also his "The Tabernacle—A Psycho-Theological Enterprise," *DD* 18 (1989–1990): 81–83, 116.

where to find everything since the Israelites were camped in the wilderness of Sinai, far from any civilization?

Some materials, mainly wood, were available in the vicinity—most notably acacia wood, from the acacia trees that grow so abundantly and hardily in both Africa and Asia Minor and specifically the Sinai peninsula. Even so, the harvesting and rough shaping of the wood would have to be done by individuals in preparation for their donating it as requested in v. 5. Other materials would have been found already in the possession of the people themselves. Thus was the appropriateness of a general call to all willing Israelites to surrender some of their valuables, most of which they had taken as spoil from the Egyptians a few months earlier,[327] so that out of these items and what they found locally could be made the tabernacle and its furnishings.

This passage speaks of the need for voluntary contributions, setting a pattern for worship that has always characterized biblical religion. Although God himself could provide anything ever needed for his purposes, including his worship, he delegated to his people the opportunity to do so and thereby gave to them the gift of experiencing generosity and self-sacrifice, as well as a sense of direct involvement in their essential ongoing relationship with him.

25:1–2 "The LORD said to Moses" is a standard statement that will be repeated, with minor variations, at other points in this section of the book (e.g., 30:11,17,22,24; 31:1). It is not a new statement but one that has been encountered many times already (starting with 4:21; cf. 6:1,10; 7:1,8,14,19). Most people who formed the audience for Exodus, until modern times, were listeners rather than readers, and such an introduction reminded the listener that Moses dutifully repeated what he was told rather than composing anything on his own authority.

The "offering" was invited from everyone but required only from those who were willing to give ("from each man whose heart prompts him to give"). Like many later provisions in the law that invite but do not require some sort of gift or service,[328] this one sought contributions from those who willingly made them available for the tabernacle and the worship that would take place therein. In the new covenant this principle was reaffirmed by Paul in 2 Cor 9:7 ("Each man should give what he has decided in his heart to give, not reluctantly or under compulsion, for God loves a cheerful giver"). Note that the offering is "for me," that is, for God, and not merely for a thing, that is, the tabernacle. The tabernacle was symbolically God's house, intrinsically his property, and not merely a place he and the Israelites would conveniently use.

25:3–7 God gave Moses an overview of the construction/fabrication materials. The materials required for the tabernacle and worship therein will be

[327] See comments on 3:22; 11:2.

[328] E.g., Deut 20:5–9, which requires that holy war participation had to be absolutely voluntary.

described further as they appear in the subsequent instructions, that is, chaps. 25–30. They are grouped here according to type. First come the metals (v. 3), then the fabrics (v. 4), then the skins and the wood (v. 5), followed by the lamp oil, the fragrant anointing oil ingredients and the incense ingredients (v. 6), and finally by the gemstones to be used on the high priest's special breastpiece (v. 7). The metals would be needed for covering the wooden framework of the tabernacle structure and for covering the various altars, the table, and the ark. Some would be used purely, without forming overlays over wood, as in the case of the solid gold rings that held the ark poles (v. 12), the sold gold plates, dishes, bowls, and pitchers (v. 29), the solid gold lampstand (vv. 31ff.), and most notably the ark's atonement cover/mercy seat (vv. 17–22).

The fabrics were for various sorts of tabernacle curtains (26:1ff.) as well as for the priestly garments (28:2ff.). The skins were for the tabernacle outer weather shields (26:14). The wood provided the framework of anything that needed to have strong spans—from tabernacle rafters to table and altar surfaces and legs (e.g., the ark, 25:10ff.; the table, 25:23ff.; and the altar, 27:1ff.). The oil fueled the oil lamps of the tabernacle lampstand (25:3ff.; see esp. 27:20–21) and as well was the base and main ingredient of the anointing oil (to which fragrances were added) for use regularly by the priests (30:22ff.). The incense was compounded into a formula especially for tabernacle use only (30:34ff.) from the ingredients donated. The gemstones adorned part of the ephod (28:6ff.) but were especially needed for the high priest's breastpiece (28:15ff.) to represent the tribes of Israel as they were symbolically brought into the presence of the Lord regularly by the high priest, over his heart (see comments on 28:29).

25:8 Just five words comprise the Hebrew of this verse, which could be translated, "They will make me a holy place[329] and I will locate among them"; or "They must make me a holy place so that I can dwell among them";[330] or "If they build me a holy place, I will locate in their midst" or the like.[331] This

---

[329] Durham (*Exodus,* 354–55) reminds us that the term employed for "Sanctuary" is not limited to the Tabernacle: "The 'holy place' (מִקְדָּשׁ) which Israel is to make has a wider reference than just the Tabernacle (מִשְׁכָּן), mentioned specifically in v. 9. מִקְדָּשׁ includes the Tabernacle, of course, but its broader reference is to any and every place of Yahweh's theophany (cf. Josh 24:25; Exod 15:17; Amos 7:9; Ezek 11:16). Any place where Yahweh comes to dwell is in that coming and residence an holy place, and any place so designated is to be respected as such by the people in covenant with Yahweh."

[330] Here the LXX has as the second clause, "and I will be visible among you," which seems more likely to represent an interpretive translation of *šākantî* than an actually different *Vorlage*.

[331] The interrelationship of the two clauses in this verse (וְעָשׂוּ לִי מִקְדָּשׁ וְשָׁכַנְתִּי בְּתוֹכָם) is not formally marked except by typical prostaxis with *waw,* so that the manner in which the one subordinates to the other must be inferred from the context. In each of the examples of possible translation above, "holy place" is substituted for the more common "sanctuary" to be sure that the reader does not understand "sanctuary" in the modern English sense of "the large room a church where the worship services are held" since the Israelites actually worshiped outdoors, in the courtyard of Yahweh's house.

verse is the simplest and perhaps also the strongest statement in Exodus—a book often described as specially reflecting the theme of the presence of God[332]—of God's concern to center himself among his people and to have them organize themselves around him.

Almost surely a measure of contingency is present here: God would not dwell among his people unless they invited him by properly preparing a house for him to inhabit/dwell in/locate in (*šākan* thus indicating their willingness to live within the stipulations of his covenant and to honor him as their covenant sovereign by serving him there). It was not that God required a building with a courtyard in order to dwell somewhere; it was that he desired that the people make a home for him and then locate their houses/tents around his house/tent and join him regularly at his courtyard for covenant meals, confirming their ongoing relationship and receiving the blessings inherent therein.[333]

25:9 God had a "pattern," or plan, for the tabernacle and the things that were to go in it (ark, altars, table, lampstand, priestly garments worn by those who attended him in his tabernacle) that he would specially reveal to Moses and that must be followed exactly. What was the point of such a demand for precise adherence to a revealed design? It was to create a longing for and hope of heaven in the hearts of God's people—a desire to live in his presence forever. Hebrews 8:5 refers to the tabernacle as "a sanctuary that is a copy and shadow of what is in heaven," adding, "This is why Moses was warned when he was about to build the tabernacle: 'See to it that you make everything according to the pattern shown you on the mountain.' "

Does this therefore mean that there is another tabernacle, a heavenly one, of which the earthly one was a symbol? Indeed, one must surely understand Heb 9:11–12 in such a way ("When Christ came . . ., he went through the greater and more perfect tabernacle that is not man-made, that is to say, not a part of this creation. He did not enter by means of the blood of goats and calves; but he entered the Most Holy Place once for all by his own blood, having obtained eternal redemption"). What one must be careful *not* to do, however, is to assume that the Mosaic tabernacle was intended to be an exact copy,

---

[332] This idea can, however, be overstated—as if Exodus were the virtually the key to the concept of the presence of God among the books of the Bible and the primary basis for the doctrine of the presence of God. Many other parts of Scripture comparably address the topic of or reflect the reality of the presence of God (notably, but not exclusively: Numbers, Psalms, Isaiah, Jeremiah, Ezekiel, the Gospels, Acts, Revelation).

[333] Cf. Exod 20:24: "'Make an altar of earth for me and sacrifice on it your burnt offerings and fellowship offerings, your sheep and goats and your cattle. Wherever I cause my name to be honored, I will come to you and bless you;" Deut 12:7: "There, in the presence of the LORD your God, you and your families shall eat and shall rejoice in everything you have put your hand to, because the LORD your God has blessed you."

if perhaps a small version, of a tabernacle in heaven.[334] Instead, the tabernacle was a symbolic *representation* of the realities of heaven, a relatively simple earthly reflection of God's actual dwelling place, designed to point to the greater and more eternal opportunity to live with God and not merely to create an expectation for a comparable but nondegradable tent structure in heaven. Finally, the tabernacle was a real thing—not a fiction of the postexilic period that "priestly" writers created to provide a background for their program of temple restoration in the Persian era; it was a buildable, transportable, worship structure that provided the newly constituted Israel with a sense of the presence of its covenant Lord.[335]

(2) Laws on Construction and Use of the Ark (25:10–22)

[10]"Have them make a chest of acacia wood—two and a half cubits long, a cubit and a half wide, and a cubit and a half high. [11]Overlay it with pure gold, both inside and out, and make a gold molding around it. [12]Cast four gold rings for it and fasten them to its four feet, with two rings on one side and two rings on

[334] For considerations of how the earthly tabernacle or temple might have reflected a heavenly temple, cf. O. Keel, *The Symbolism of the Biblical World* (New York: Seabury, 1978), esp. 171–76; *TDNT* 8:256–57 (τύπος).

[335] K. A. Kitchen, "The Desert Tabernacle: Pure Fiction or Plausible Account?" *BR* 16 (2000): 14–21. Kitchen compares the design and purpose of the tabernacle to purification shrines, burial shrines, and war shrines known from ancient Egypt and suggests the tabernacle as described in Exodus accurately reflects Bronze Age Egyptian-Semitic religious and cultural institutions. What God gave the Israelites through Moses by way of design for the place at which he would be worshiped was thus something they could understand at least generally, build at least satisfactorily to his standards (see comments on 39:32–43), and use at least until he caused a more permanent and substantial temple to be built to replace it. The tabernacle was a condescension of sorts to human limitations but at the same time a symbol of a relationship and a future eternal dwelling. Further on the design of the tabernacle from Egyptian parallels, see M. M. Homan, "The Divine Warrior in His Tent: A Military Model for Yahweh's Tabernacle," *BR* 16 (2000): 22–33, 55. Homan likens the tabernacle to the layout of ancient Egyptian war camps, with the closest parallel being that of the camp of Rameses II at the Battle of Kadesh on the Orontes River (ca.1290 BC) as known from the various monuments of Rameses II (on the walls of the Ramesseum). The many references to Yahweh as a warrior and his people as an army fit well with this background overtone to the tabernacle. Additionally, D. Fleming has shown that large tent structures of the sort that the tabernacle constituted were known as far back as the Mari period (early second millennium BC) and were used for public functions, with frames and covering fabric just as described in the Exodus account and with terminology that connects with the biblical tabernacle ("Mari's Large Public Tent and the Priestly Tent Sanctuary," *VT* 50 [2000]: 484–98). All of this is consistent with the nature of biblical revelation in general: God usually reveals things to people graciously, in a way they can comprehend and identify with (often only after considerable effort), and not usually in a way that makes no sense to them. People learn by comparing what they know and are familiar with to whatever new thing(s) they are being asked to understand. By revealing the tabernacle in a design that was not incomprehensible but rather had analogies to things they understood from their culture, God gave his people a new thing—not merely another military camp shrine but a new thing—that nevertheless bore some resemblance to things they knew and thus could be comprehended, *mutatis mutandis*.

the other. [13]Then make poles of acacia wood and overlay them with gold. [14]Insert
the poles into the rings on the sides of the chest to carry it. [15]The poles are to
remain in the rings of this ark; they are not to be removed. [16]Then put in the ark
the Testimony, which I will give you. [17]"Make an atonement cover of pure gold—
two and a half cubits long and a cubit and a half wide. [18]And make two cherubim
out of hammered gold at the ends of the cover. [19]Make one cherub on one end
and the second cherub on the other; make the cherubim of one piece with the
cover, at the two ends. [20]The cherubim are to have their wings spread upward,
overshadowing the cover with them. The cherubim are to face each other, looking
toward the cover. [21]Place the cover on top of the ark and put in the ark the Testi-
mony, which I will give you. [22]There, above the cover between the two cherubim
that are over the ark of the Testimony, I will meet with you and give you all my
commands for the Israelites.

Although it might seem more systematic to begin with a description of the design of the tabernacle and then to address the particular furnishings that fit within it, the importance of the ark as *the* item that would symbolize God's presence among his people far outweighs such considerations, and its design therefore was described first, even before that of the tabernacle that would house it.

The passage reveals the two special purposes of the gilded chest known as the ark. First, this ornate portable box/chest would house the "Testimony," the two tablets of the Ten Words/Commandments written by God himself, one copy as his and one copy as Israel's, stored together as a symbol of their covenant agreement (see also comments on 24:12; 31:18; 34:1–4,29). Second, the lid of the ark would serve as the so-called "mercy seat" (v. 17 NRSV), an elaborate pure gold sculpture that symbolized a place for God to stand (rather than to sit; see comments on v. 17) as a contact point for the Lord of Glory and his earthly people and a location from which to continue to reveal divine truth to the Israelites (v. 22).

THE BASIC DESIGN OF THE ARK (25:10–15). **25:10–15** The ark/chest was to measure two and a half cubits by one and a half by one and a half cubits. A cubit was the distance from the tip of a man's middle finger to the end of his elbow when his hand was held flat and straight in the plane of his forearm, that is, about eighteen inches. It has been speculated that there existed also a so-called "royal cubit" of twenty-one inches rather than eighteen inches, and the Bible refers to changes in cubit standards that may have taken place as the monarchy introduced standardized measuring systems over time (2 Chr 3:3). Nothing in the present description, however, suggests that the cubit was anything but about eighteen inches long, so the ark was forty-five inches long, twenty-seven inches wide, and twenty-seven inches high—presumably in its exterior dimensions.

Not very large in size, its impressiveness was to be found in its appearance—an object so large made of pure gold façade (all the surfaces were gold overlaid or solid gold) would surely have been stunning to the eye. The overall structure, including the carrying poles, was acacia wood, the strong, enduring, easily worked[336] wood abundant in the Sinai and so many other parts of the ancient Near East.

Verse 11 emphasizes the importance of having all visible surfaces, inside and out, gilded. In addition there must be a gold trim ("molding") at the edges so that the ark was not merely a plain box but something more elegant. The exact nature and size of this molding trim is nowhere specified, but moldings have the effect of "dressing up" stark, straight structures. The moldings around the ark probably protruded from the edges, as moldings of boxes typically do, on a plane medial to the planes formed by the sides meeting to make the edges. Thus the ark was a small but very elegant (fancy) chest.

From v. 12 we learn that it was to have "feet," the dimensions of which are not stated, so that the main body of the ark rested above the ground. The underside of the ark was not to touch the ground (or floor), but only the bottoms of the feet would do so. Such is the construction of almost any sort of chest more substantial than a mere storage container. These feet had rings attached to them, one ring protruding to the side from each of the feet, so a gilded acacia wood pole could be run through the rings on each side (vv. 13–14) and the ark lifted by the ends of the poles and transported. By having the rings in the feet and not in any other part of the box proper, the special quality of the ark would be protected: any scratching, bending, marring, would be limited to the feet. To minimize the possibility of damage and even wear to the poles, the rings, and the feet, the poles were "to remain in the rings" of the ark (v. 15). In that way, though the poles were truly removable technically, they would in fact be treated as a permanent part of the ark structure and the portability of the ark with minimal damage would be ensured.[337] Had the poles been removed each time the ark was set down along a journey and reinserted

[336] Some woods are very strong but can splinter or crack easily or may have grain that raises away from the smooth surface in places; a wood that is easily worked is one that can be cut, shaped, sanded, and still maintain its integrity.

[337] Num 4:5–6 indicates that the poles were indeed removed for one special purpose: to make possible the careful wrapping of the ark in the special dividing curtain (dividing the most holy place where the ark resided when the tabernacle was set up from the rest of the tabernacle space) and then in a layer of sea cow hides and then in a final layer of blue cloth. Once all the proper wrapping was completed, so that the entire body of the ark was wrapped and, presumably, the legs as well, only the carrying rings would be visible. The poles were then reinserted and used for carrying the ark. Therefore, no nonpriestly Israelite, and only a few priests at most, would ever be able to see the ark. It would always remain hidden from their sight either by the dividing curtain (veil) of the tabernacle or by its elaborate wrapper when transported. What the average Israelite could see, at most, were the rings and poles. In all likelihood the ark was wrapped and the poles reinserted before the outer curtains of the tabernacle were taken down, so no typical Israelite would ever see the ark without its poles. See also "Excursus: The Invisible God of the Old Covenant" after the commentary on 26:33.

each time the ark was lifted and moved again, the amount of wear and tear would have been increased, and the possibility that one of the Levites carrying the ark would fall against it or cause it to be damaged would have been greatly increased.[338]

The ark symbolized God's presence, his purity, his superiority, and his covenant blessing. Anything that damaged, or even threatened potentially to damage the ark, however slightly, was in itself a sort of symbolic threat to these important divine realities. The Israelites were to respect the symbols of the realities as a way of showing respect for the realities themselves. A comparable New Covenant requirement of respect in connection with a symbol of a reality applies in the case of the Lord's Supper. The supper itself is only a symbol of a reality, but disrespect for the symbol leads to serious consequences (1 Cor 11:20–34).

THE ARK AS CONTAINER (25:16). **25:16** Although it had powerful symbolic value, the ark also had functional value. It was a container, a chest (the meaning of *ărōn*) to hold something very important, "the Testimony" (NRSV "covenant"), that is, the tablets of the Ten Words/Commandments. The Hebrew word[339] translated "Testimony" by the NIV can also mean "decree" or "command" or "[collection of] decrees/commands" since it is used often as a collective noun. A case can be made for the NIV translation since the tablets were in fact a witness/testimony to the covenant, a relationship that the tablets described in writing. The NRSV translation "covenant" can also be defended because the tablets were the written version of the covenant, the visible "covenant" document. Regardless of which translation is preferred, the tablets were a means of preserving in writing the formative terms of a covenant that was itself not merely a piece of writing but a reality that the writing described. In saying "which I will give you" (see also v. 21), God predicted that he himself would initially take care of fulfilling the document clause responsibility of his covenant.[340]

---

[338] One can imagine the following scenario as reason for forbidding removing the ark poles: A group of Levites were preparing to move the ark. A couple of them were holding one end of a carrying pole while another was crouched next to the ark with his hands near one of the rings, waiting to help guide the pole through the ring as the others "fed" it to him. Those feeding the pole were also either crouched down or bent far over, since the poles had to be inserted just inches from the ground at ankle height. The honor of carrying the ark would have been given not necessarily to the youngest, most physically fit Levites but quite probably to the oldest, most honorable Levites who had earned this special privilege by years of faithful service and general seniority. If one of those holding the pole teetered, or the one with his hands ready to guide the pole into the ring teetered, the suddenly askew pole could bang into the ark or can push the Levite next to the ring against the ark, or he lose his balance and fall against the ark, or the like. Would this sort of thing usually have happened? No, but the possibility that it would eventually happen, with resulting damage or desecration of the ark, was what the rule against removal obviated. The death of Uzzah as described in 2 Sam 6:3–8 is a vivid reminder of the importance of protecting the ark's holiness.

[339] עֵדוּת.

[340] See "Excursus: The Exodus-Leviticus Covenant" prior to the commentary on 20:1.

THE ARK'S ATONEMENT COVER (25:17–22). **25:17–22** The Hebrew word employed here for the special gold slab adorned with cherubim statuary that was placed atop the ark is *kappōret,* from the *piel* of the root *kpr,* a root that refers in various ways to the concept of atonement or reconciliation—the process of causing people to be true friends, allies, or kin and not to be distant, hostile, or at odds. The word *kappōret,* a *qattult* patterned noun in Hebrew, intrinsically means something like "accomplishment of reconciliation" or "fact of atonement." Because the *qal* stem meaning of *kpr* is literally "to cover over," it is not impossible that some sort of original root sense of "covering" would have been understood by native speakers of Moses' day to attend to the usage of the *piel* of the root as well, and the NIV's "atonement cover" provides for that possibility nicely.

The atonement cover was not merely the lid of the ark. It was a special, solid gold appurtenance that fitted on top of the lid and represented a paramount happy and sacred fact of Israel's existence: their God, the only true God, had in his eternal kindness and love arranged for them to enjoy reconciliation with him as the key provision of his covenant. They were not strangers or enemies; they were his covenant family. He was close to them, not far away. They had a familial connection with him and could even sense that connection spatially in the fact of the ark's atonement cover, where his divine presence was graciously manifested on their behalf.

The older traditional name "mercy seat" conveyed this important reality to some extent, though considerably less perfectly than "atonement cover" in our estimation. A weakness inherent in the connotation of the term "mercy seat," however, occurs in connection with the functional nature of the *kappōret:* it was more likely a pedestal or standing platform than a seat, a reflection of the dazzling slab that appeared under the feet of Yahweh when the elders saw him on Mount Sinai (24:10)—not a throne or chair or the like. Although it is true that God is elsewhere described in some English translations, including the NIV, as "enthroned between the cherubim," this English translation may be suspect; a more literal translation would be "cherubim dweller" since the Hebrew wording makes no mention of a "throne" or any "enthronement."[341]

---

[341] In all of the passages in the OT (1 Sam 4:4; 2 Sam 6:2; 2 Kgs 19:15; 1 Chr 13:6; Pss 80:2; 99:1; Isa 37:16) where Yahweh is supposedly described as "enthroned between the cherubim" (in, e.g., the NIV), the Hb. expression employed is either יֹשֵׁב הַכְּרֻבִים or (once, in Ps 99:1) יֹשֵׁב כְּרוּבִים. Either of these virtually identical expressions would mean "the dweller of the cherubim" or more naturally "the cherubim dweller." The NRSV translates the Hb. phrase as "enthroned on/upon/above the cherubim," which has the advantage for the reader of not suggesting that the atonement cover itself is a throne as the NIV translation would tend to imply, but rather that it is a platform for Yahweh's throne, which is in the logic of this translation (above the cherubim, not between them). One cannot overlook the fact that the first word in the phrase in question, יֹשֵׁב, could possibly be translated "sitter" so that the phrase could theoretically mean "the cherubim sitter," from which one could (erroneously in our opinion) derive the sense of "the one who sits with the cherubim" or the like. But there is no warrant in the Hb. expression for employing the word "between" in Eng. translation, so the NIV's "who is enthroned between the cherubim" cannot be regarded as anything but a rather interpretive rendering.

The dimensions of the atonement cover are exactly those of the lid of the ark (see 25:10) it was designed to fit over precisely.[342] It was to be made of pure gold, not a slab of wood overlaid with gold as the rest of the major surfaces of the ark were. At its ends were two pure "hammered gold" statues of uncertain height (but probably not more than a cubit high at the very most and more likely only a few inches high in light of the overall proportions of the ark) that portrayed cherubim. The only prior mention of cherubim in the Bible was Gen 3:24, which says nothing about their appearance but indicates that they were powerful beings, of the sort that a human would hardly be able to overcome and thus fully able to keep God's garden from being invaded by humans.

That cherubim were winged—at least as they appeared when visible to the human eye—is evident from 2 Sam 22:11 and the description given of them in 1 Kgs 6:24–29; 8:6–7. Ezekiel's descriptions of cherubim are the most revealing, but it is not certain whether or not this is because he had a special purpose to embellish their descriptions (as in his comparison of the city of Tyre to a cherub that guarded the Garden of Eden in Ezek 28:14–16, which is a metaphorical way of stating how splendid and powerful Tyre had once been, not a literal description of anything related to cherubim). At any rate, Ezek 10:7–8 indicates that cherubim had hands, and Ezek 10:14 indicates that they had four faces to their heads. Various examples of ancient iconography presumably intended to represent cherubim show three characteristic elements: the body of a lion, the face of a human, and wings.[343] The most we can say for certain is that cherubs were some sort of intelligent, powerful angelic being depicted as winged. Perhaps on the atonement cover they were represented as winged lionlike figures with human faces, but we cannot be sure. One faced the center of the atonement cover from one end, the other from the other end. Their wings were raised, so as to *overshadow* the atonement cover, providing a kind of symbolic partial enclosure that protected the surface.

The tablets of the Testimony (the Ten Words/Commandments) were to be placed inside the ark once it was completed and the tablets were given to Moses by God (see comments on chap. 32), and the atonement cover itself was to become a site where God would "meet with" Moses (the pronoun

---

[342] This might imply that at least a portion of the lid fitted down into the sides of the ark onto a shelving near the top of the sides on which it rested. It might also mean that if it had a lip all around that overlapped the top of the sides, this lip was small enough that it would not be regarded as adding appreciably to the dimensions of the lid. Nothing in the text allows us to understand precisely how the lid was designed relative to the four sides of the open top of the ark, exactly how high up on the sides the decorative molding was, or how the lid fit near or within or around the molding.

[343] Thus a cherub is sometimes referred to as a winged sphinx. But the accuracy of these non-Israelite depictions can hardly be taken as definitive for true biblical cherubs any more than pagan idols can be taken as accurate depictions of proper worship devices.

"you" is singular in the Hb.) and through him (and his successors) deliver "all my commands for the Israelites." In other words, once the tabernacle was set up and the ark properly placed within it and the tablets within it, the top of the ark would be where Moses would look. And, though seeing nothing, he would understand in faith that he was facing Yahweh and as confirmation would certainly hear the voice of Yahweh from that direction.

(3) Laws on Construction and Use of the Table (25:23–30)

23"Make a table of acacia wood—two cubits long, a cubit wide and a cubit and a half high. 24Overlay it with pure gold and make a gold molding around it. 25Also make around it a rim a handbreadth wide and put a gold molding on the rim. 26Make four gold rings for the table and fasten them to the four corners, where the four legs are. 27The rings are to be close to the rim to hold the poles used in carrying the table. 28Make the poles of acacia wood, overlay them with gold and carry the table with them. 29And make its plates and dishes of pure gold, as well as its pitchers and bowls for the pouring out of offerings. 30Put the bread of the Presence on this table to be before me at all times.

25:23–30 The tabernacle represented Yahweh's house among the Israelites—he would soon encamp in his large house in their midst, and they would encamp around his house according to their tribes in concentric circles (Num 2). He himself was symbolically represented as dwelling in the "back room" of his house by means of the ark. In the tabernacle's "front room" were several pieces of furniture, the sorts of things that represented the furniture of a home, though on a grander scale. The first of these pieces of household-style furniture to be described is the table. It was primarily for food—a dining table of sorts, symbolizing the fact that Yahweh really did live among his people and inhabit his house in much the same way that they inhabited theirs.

There were several physical similarities between the table and the ark, as the descriptions of each show. Both were rectangular objects made of wood overlaid with gold, both had a decorative-functional molding around the top, the tops of both were the same height above the ground (one and a half cubits, or twenty-seven inches), and both had rings protruding from their four legs, through which wooden poles also overlaid with gold were inserted as a means of carrying the object without touching it directly—a way of preserving its sacredness.

There were also differences. Whereas the dimensions of the ark were two and a half cubits (forty-five inches) by one and a half cubits (twenty-seven inches) as seen from above, the table was smaller: two cubits (thirty-six inches) by one cubit (eighteen inches) as seen from above. Moreover, the ark was a chest, having greater body depth and shorter legs, whereas the table was an object on which—rather than in which—things were placed, with longer legs and no body depth other than that provided by the thickness of its top and the moldings that surrounded the top. The moldings not only decorated the table but provided, in the case of the upper molding, a barrier against items accidentally slipping off one of the edges.

The most likely reading of vv. 24–25 is that the table had two moldings: one at the bottom edge of the top structure and the other just inches above that, at the top edge of the top. It may be assumed that the top had a thickness of perhaps three or four inches, which may have been provided by the thickness of the solid wood used for the top, or alternatively by side pieces extending down from the top between the legs all around, giving the appearance of thickness as viewed from the side. These side pieces or "rails" would not likely have extended down from the actual top surface more than a few inches, and at their bottom edges they would have had molding added as prescribed.

Verse 25 requires "a rim a handbreadth wide" with "a gold molding on the rim." Although we know that a handbreadth is about four inches wide, we cannot discern from this description whether the four-inch rim was (1) a decorative edging around the circumference of the table lying in the same plane as the top of the table and thus simply having the effect of widening the top; (2) a four-inch decorated barrier extending straight up from the edges of the table all around so as to provide an open-topped four-inch deep box at the top of the table, thus allowing things to be stacked tightly on the table without risk that they would fall off the edge; (3) a four-inch decorated barrier extending diagonally out from the top edge of the table, providing less depth to the top "box" but actually greater length and width to the area of containment, if things were placed in such a way to overlap the top proper; (4) four-inch side rails extending down from the top, either between the legs or inside or outside of the legs, providing stability to but not actually extending the dimensions or holding capacity of the top.

Although we cannot discern which of these options represented God's intent for his table, the description was undoubtedly sufficient for Bezalel to construct it (see comments on 31:1ff.) because of the standards for tables extant at the time and/or God's knowledge of Bezalel's inclinations. Some freedom may have been intended for Bezalel to interpret the general order according to his own artistry since nothing is said about a number of matters, including the thickness of the legs or the top, the means of joining the wood pieces, the thickness of the gold overlay, the dimensions of the carrying rings, the thickness and length of the carrying poles.[344]

Verses 26–28 give the same sort of information as provided about the rings and carrying poles for the ark in vv. 12–14 except that the poles used for carrying the table probably were removable, in contrast to the poles used to carry

[344] This is consistent with the lack of specificity in many important commands in Scripture. Something as central as the Great Commission of Christ comes to his church in appropriately general terms: *make disciples* does not specify exactly how in various circumstances conversion and follow-up study must take place; *going into all the world* does not specify methods, distances, times, numbers. The details are left to *illumination* (the individual guidance of persons by God in response to prayer) in the process of carrying out *revelation* (the general message of God to all people).

the ark, which were to remain fixed in the carrying rings attached to the legs (25:15). But v. 27 does specify something that must be assumed as well in the case of the location of the rings of the ark: the carrying rings must not be too low on the legs. That would have given the table a high center of gravity and would have made it difficult to carry upright. By having the rings high on the table legs—"close to the rim"—most of the height of the table would be carried below the poles, hanging, a configuration that would use gravity to stabilize the table in an always upright position as it traveled. Proper, safe portability was important since the entire tabernacle was to travel with the Israelites throughout their wilderness journeys.

A great king such as Yahweh deserved to dine and to be served his meals in proper style, and eating directly off the top of the table would not constitute such style. His table therefore required "plates and dishes of pure gold, as well as pitchers and bowls," as v. 29 indicates—although these implements were not solely for his personal symbolic use but were actually employed in the rituals of the tabernacle at which both priests and worshipers also took part. The NIV word order unfortunately makes the text sound as if the pitchers and bowls were not necessarily made out of gold. As a better alternative, the HCSB follows the Hebrew word order more correctly: "You are also to make its plates and cups, as well as its pitchers and bowls for pouring drink offerings. Make them out of pure gold." Similarly, the NRSV: "You shall make its plates and dishes for incense, and its flagons and bowls with which to pour drink offerings; you shall make them of pure gold." The NRSV rendering "plates and dishes for incense" is, however, interpretive—no specific mention is made of incense in the vocabulary of the verse, and the term used for NRSV "dishes" does not necessarily mean "dishes for incense."[345] Utensils for solid foods, for liquids, and for symbolic offerings such as incense were all included potentially in this listing.

As v. 30 indicates, the main food placed on the tabernacle table was to be bread, a special bread symbolically offered to Yahweh as his food.[346] No other type of food was actually placed on the table, even though the utensils that went with the table were used for other meal ingredients including the drink offerings. The "bread of the Presence" derives its name from its function: it was bread that was set in Yahweh's presence, that is, inside his house (tabernacle) for him to enjoy along with the other foodstuffs that constituted the sacrifices of his people. Most of the food given to Yahweh was given outside, in the tabernacle courtyard, where it was burned on the altar and symbolically sent to

---

[345] In our judgment the most literal translation of the part of the verse mentioning the four implements would be: "its dishes, its basins, its jars, and its bowls." Such a listing would possibly be suggestive of all sorts of vessels and need not be considered a complete list of types of vessels that could have been placed on the table. Cf. Exod 37:16; Num 4:7.

[346] The bread of the Presence is also mentioned in 35:13 and 39:36, in contexts that add little to our information about it.

him through the rising of its smoke. The bread of the Presence was, by contrast, provided to him inside the tabernacle structure, closer to the ark, and therefore even more obviously directly in his presence than food cooked on the altar or drink offerings poured out at the altar.[347]

Those were also offered in his presence,[348] but the inside of the tabernacle was simply closer to the very presence of God than the outside. Moreover—and this aspect is surely also inherent in the name "bread of the Presence"—the bread was there on the table "before me [in my presence] at all times." It even traveled with the table when the Israelites were in transit from place to place (Num 4:7–8). When new bread had been baked for setting on the table, the old bread was removed, but not before the new bread was ready for placement on the table (1 Sam 21:6). Though it is not explicitly stated in any biblical text, the high priest probably replaced the twelve[349] old loaves with the twelve new ones loaf by loaf rather than by clearing all the old loaves away and then putting down all the new ones, so there was never an instant when the top of the table was entirely bare. All other offerings were periodic, being presented in various rituals at certain times of the day, week, month, or year. This offering was continual—never ceasing, representing the endless adoration, appreciation, and intercession of the Israelites day and night throughout the years and ages. A token of their covenant obeisance was always in the presence of Yahweh.[350]

---

[347] In the ancient world religious practices sometimes reflected, though in a distorted, occasionally even debauched manner, the true, revealed religious practices that had once been shared by all (in the time of the first family or immediately after the flood). Thus much pagan religion contains degenerations of true religion. The offering of bread to God appears to be such a phenomenon. In Mesopotamian religion it was common to offer bread to gods on food tables located in their temples. But these bread/food tables were located immediately in front of the idol of the god or goddess and were understood to be food the god needed (following the ancient pagan notion that the one thing the gods could not do for themselves was feed themselves). This represents a degeneration of the true practice, reflected here: God does not need food. It is offered to him symbolically, not to satisfy his hunger. Thus it is placed outside his personal room (the holy of holies) and separated from the ark, which represented him personally) by the curtain dividing the holy place from the holy of holies. The commentary to the *Jewish Study Bible* ([New York: Oxford, 2004]) cogently expresses the difference: "This partition between God and the table makes it clear that the bread of display is not actually consumed by God but is only a token gift—this is also underlined by the fact that it was eaten by priests. That its purpose was display, not consumption, is also indicated by the fact that it is replaced weekly, not daily as elsewhere in the ancient Near East."

[348] See comments on 29:2–26,42; 40:6; Lev 1:3; 3:1,7–8,12.

[349] Twelve loaves were baked each week for the bread of the Presence (Lev 24:5–9), which stayed for a full week in Yahweh's presence, i.e., the holy place or outer room of the tabernacle, and then were removed and eaten by the priests (1 Sam 21:4–6). The actual baking was the responsibility of the Kohathite branch of the Levites (1 Chr 9:32), a logical assignment in light of their having responsibility for transporting the table itself and its implements (Num 4:15; cf. Num 7:9).

[350] One might compare this to the way the prayers of the saints are always before God (e.g., Eph 5:20; 6:18; 1 Thess 5:17; Heb 13:15; cf. Luke 24:53; Acts 1:14) or the way Christ's intercession for his people is always underway before God the Father (Heb 7:25) or the way God is praised by those in his presence continually in heaven (Rev 4:8; 7:15).

Numbers 4:7–8 specifies how the utensils were to be specially wrapped with the shewbread on top of the table, then covered with protective hides and carried along with the table as a unit by the Kohathite branch of the Levites when the Israelites moved from place to place. Properly handled, a portion of bread of the Presence never ceased being in general contact with the top of the table.

First Kings 7:48 indicates that the Solomonic temple retained the practice of a bread of the Presence table, which apparently was remanufactured for the temple rather than simply imported from the tabernacle. Second Chronicles 4:19 refers to "the tables on which was the bread of the Presence," indicating that there may have been more than one. In fact, from the Chronicler's descriptions there likely were ten bronze lavers (2 Chr 4:6), ten lampstands (2 Chr 4:7), and ten tables (2 Chr 4:8,18) in Solomon's temple. What is not clear from the Chronicler's description, however, is whether all ten of the tables were used for the bread of the Presence. Nine may have been used for supporting shorter lampstands as opposed to the self-standing "floor" lampstand and only one used for the bread. Thus "on them" in the Chronicler's language (v. 18) "on them" would mean "on them considered as a group but not on every one of them individually." Alternatively, Solomon's expanded priesthood and temple worship may have required a greater quantity of bread than was required of the Israelites starting at their sojourn at Sinai, necessitating more table space. We judge that the most likely scenario is that Solomon put one special table for the bread in his temple and nine lesser tables, but this can hardly be proved.[351]

(4) Laws on Construction and Use of the Lampstand (25:31–40)

[31]"Make a lampstand of pure gold and hammer it out, base and shaft; its flower-like cups, buds and blossoms shall be of one piece with it. [32]Six branches are to extend from the sides of the lampstand—three on one side and three on the other. [33]Three cups shaped like almond flowers with buds and blossoms are to be on one branch, three on the next branch, and the same for all six branches extending from the lampstand. [34]And on the lampstand there are to be four cups shaped like

[351] R. Dillard (*2 Chronicles*, WBC [Waco: Word], 1987) analyzes the options as follows: "[Option] (1) Since the ten lampstands are similarly distributed five on the north and five on the south (4:7), the lampstands may have stood on these tables which should be distinguished from the table used for the Bread of the Presence. (2) The tables may have been used for the Bread of the Presence. Although the tabernacle accounts (Exod 25:23–40; Lev 24:5–9) and Ezekiel's temple vision (Ezek 41:22) mention only one table for this purpose, the temple design may have multiplied the number of tables as it had the number of lamps. Cf. the plural in 1 Chr 28:16 and 2 Chr 4:19, but contrast the singular in the parallel passage in 1 Kgs 7:48. Other passages suggest that the Chronicler knew of only one table for the Bread of the Presence (2 Chr 13:11; 29:18; cf. 1 Chr 9:32; 23:29). Josephus (*Ant.* 8.88–90) does speak of more than one table, but also distinguishes the one table for the Bread of the Presence from the rest."

almond flowers with buds and blossoms. [35]One bud shall be under the first pair of branches extending from the lampstand, a second bud under the second pair, and a third bud under the third pair—six branches in all. [36]The buds and branches shall all be of one piece with the lampstand, hammered out of pure gold.

[37]"Then make its seven lamps and set them up on it so that they light the space in front of it. [38]Its wick trimmers and trays are to be of pure gold. [39]A talent of pure gold is to be used for the lampstand and all these accessories. [40]See that you make them according to the pattern shown you on the mountain.

Yahweh's house needed light since Yahweh lived there symbolically and allowed humans to minister to him there. It made sense that Yahweh's house should be lit by lamplight, though on a grander scale by far than that of the individual family homes of the people. He himself had no trouble seeing indoors in a windowless structure at night, but the humans who served him needed the light. (We must keep in mind, however, that only priests and/or Levites would truly *need* the light from the lampstand; no nonlevitical worshipers ever set foot inside the tabernacle.)

Lamplight was used routinely throughout the tents of the Israelites. Once the tabernacle and its furnishings were actually built and set in place, the average worshiper did indeed get to see such things as the lampstand and therefore could become quite familiar with their appearance because the doorway tent curtains were pulled back during the daytime, and anyone could peer from the courtyard into the outer room of the tabernacle (not the holy of holies, which was cut off from general view by its special entrance curtain). At night the light from the seven oil lamps that the lampstand held would have made the tabernacle the brightest thing in the Israelite encampment, aside from some of the cooking fires, and certainly the brightest lit "living quarters" in the entire encampment since no individual family would have chosen to use the large amount of oil necessary to keep seven lamps lit in a single tent. In all probability, having the lights on meant then much the same thing that it means now: someone's home. In this case, symbolically, "Yahweh was home" among his people.

DESIGN OF THE LAMPSTAND (25:31–36). The lampstand was a floor-standing (as opposed to table-standing), candelabra-like golden structure with six branches and a "trunk" made to resemble an olive (!) tree but with certain almond (!) tree features and intended almost certainly not merely to provide light for the tabernacle but also to symbolize the tree of life (!), that is, Yahweh's gift of life to his people.[352] This passage provides an overall look at the general design. From such passages as Zech 4; Ps 52; and Rev 11 other characteristics are also discernable.

---

[352] It was thus a special tree, unlike no single tree in nature but having several characteristics from more than one of them as a way of representing the idea of a tree of life.

25:31–32 The lampstand was made of shaped (beaten/hammered) solid gold all joined into a single piece with a base of some sort (not described in detail in any passage) that gave it stability on the floor of the tabernacle and a shaft/trunk that rose vertically from the base to the desired height (probably several cubits, that is, perhaps five or six feet high, but the height is never specified). Off of the shaft/trunk came decorated branches made to resemble tree branches. With three branches heading off to one side and three to the other side and including the main shaft or center trunk, there were a total of seven different supports for oil lamps.

25:33–36 Cups were needed to support the actual lamps that would hold the oil. The lamps were to sit cradled in each cup. The cups were to be made to resemble almond flowers, each one having a calyx ("buds")[353] and, emerging from the calyx, the blossom. In this way the oil lamps would sit artistically in a gold flower on a gold tree—an appropriately lovely setting for Yahweh's special light. Since each branch had three flower-shaped cups and the shaft/trunk had four cups (v. 34), there may have been a total of twenty-two places where oil lamps could be placed. Alternatively, there may only have been seven specific places for oil lamps, with the other fifteen simply made to "match" so that the viewer would see what looked like a lovely tree with many flowers, some of which held lamps and most of which did not.

The buds described in v. 35 are those that were attached not to one of the branches but to the shaft/trunk. They were spaced so that they fitted nicely at different heights from the branches, with one bud almost surely near or at the top of the shaft/trunk (thus higher than the branches) and the other three below the pairs of branches successively. Even if the various parts of the lampstand were first made separately (a strong likelihood), they were all joined together seamlessly, probably by heating and beating, as has been the means of shaping and joining gold for millennia, so the tree-shaped lampstand was a single thing in somewhat the same way that a tree is a single thing.

Because the lampstand clearly had almond flower motifs, it is entirely understandable that many commentators have assumed that it was intended to resemble an almond tree. There is some reason to conclude, however, that it more nearly resembled an olive tree, albeit an olive tree with twenty-two almond flowers on it. Such a conclusion depends partly on two assumptions: first, that both Zechariah and Revelation refer to the Solomonic and second temple lampstands respectively, and, second, that both of these lampstands reflected the design of the original tabernacle lampstand. These assumptions are, in the final analysis, not provable.[354] If they are correct, however, the information Zechariah and Revelation provide, perhaps supported also by

---

[353] The calyx is the green supporting outer base and containing structure from which a flower's petals actually emerge. In the case of the lampstand, the calyxes were gold, not green, of course.

Ps 52, suggest olive tree motifs for the trunk and branches of the treelike lampstand. In Zechariah's vision of the Solomonic temple[355] lampstand, he reported that he saw "a solid gold lampstand with a bowl at the top and seven lights on it, with seven channels to the lights. Also there are two olive trees by it, one on the right of the bowl and the other on its left" (Zech 4:2–3). It would appear that these "olive trees" were intended to be not separate trees (see below) but the olive treelike branches on either side of the treelike temple lampstand.

In Zech 4:11–12, Zechariah further describes the lampstand as he sees it in his vision as having "two olive trees on the right and the left of the lampstand . . . two olive branches beside the two gold pipes that pour out golden oil."[356] In both Hebrew and Greek, part of a tree can be called a "tree" as is apparently the usage in Zech 4.[357] Revelation 11:4 employs comparable imagery, in the context of a temple vision:[358] "These are the two olive trees and the two lampstands that stand before the Lord of the earth." In Zechariah the two parts of the olive treelike lampstand (as we understand his meaning) symbolize Zerubbabel and Jeshua, the Judean governor and high priest in 520 BC; in Revelation the two parts of the olive treelike lampstand symbolize (as we understand it) the church in its dangerous but faithful witness to the world. It is not necessary to decide with final certainty, however, what the olive tree images symbolize to appreciate that in both these visions it is olive tree imagery, not almond tree imagery, that predominates to describe the branches to the right and left of the lampstand. Psalm 52:8 may contribute to this issue by

---

[354] We simply lack the evidence to confirm or deny whether or not Solomon's temple lampstand was a copy of the tabernacle lampstand (or perhaps even that very lampstand transferred from the tabernacle to the temple and then supplemented with nine other lampstands). We also cannot be certain whether or not Zechariah's vision and John's vision (Revelation) describe precisely the actual lampstand of the first and second temple, respectively, rather than describing modified, symbolic lampstands of a sort that never actually existed in the OT tabernacle or temple.

[355] His vision would logically have described the original (Solomonic) temple lampstand since the second temple, whose construction he encouraged, was not yet built in 520 BC when he saw his visions.

[356] The temple-based olive tree-styled lampstand that Zechariah saw may have differed from the one used earlier in the days of the tabernacle by reason of having an oil bowl at the top and a system of oil feeder tubes supplying oil to the lamps wicks located on the trunk and the branches, but it is also possible that Zechariah's actual meaning has been mistranslated and therefore misunderstood. See D. Stuart, "Zechariah," in *Micah-Malachi*, WBC (forthcoming).

[357] Thus עֵץ means either "wood" or "piece of wood" or "tree" or "part of a tree"; similarly, at least some of the words for "tree" in Greek have comparable ranges of meaning.

[358] That the chapter concerns a temple vision is evident both from Rev 11:1 ("I was given a reed like a measuring rod and was told, 'Go and measure the temple of God'") and Rev 11:19 ("Then God's temple in heaven was opened, and within his temple was seen the ark of his covenant"). The temple John knew was, of course, the second temple, though his vision is of its true model in heaven.

reason of the connection of the olive tree and the temple ("I am like an olive tree flourishing in the house of God; I trust in God's unfailing love for ever and ever"), though it may also merely be making reference to the olive trees that presumably grew in the temple courtyard.[359]

Why should anyone care whether the lampstand was designed to look like an olive tree with almond flowers or like an almond tree only or neither? The answer is that a lampstand made to resemble an olive tree with almond blossoms would symbolize three things at once: God's provision, Israel's nationhood, and miraculous divine deliverance. Since olive oil was the fuel for the seven lamps that sat on the lampstand, an olive tree design for the lampstand itself might have been considered common sense. Beyond this, however, the God who began creation with the words "let there be light" could be considered as symbolized in a fashion through the olive oil, which kept the lamps of the tabernacle burning continually as a reminder of his constant watchfulness over Israel (Exod 27:20; Lev 24:2; cf. Exod 25:6; 35:8,28). Olive trees or branches tended also to represent the nation of Israel itself (Jer 11:16; cf. Judg 9:8; Hos 14:6) as Paul also indicated in his comments in Rom 11:24 and according to 2 Chr 11:11,17. Olive oil was one of Israel's most abundant products and was exported in large quantities (e.g., 1 Kgs 5:11), and the olive branch symbolized peace and God's favor (e.g., Gen 8:11). The almond, on the other hand, was specifically associated with the exodus provisions of miraculous deliverance because Aaron's/God's/Moses' staff[360] was an almond wood staff. That staff was so important to the history of Israel's faithfulness in its covenant relationship with God (through its use in the plagues or at the Battle of Rephidim) that it was eventually included in the contents of the ark (Num 17:1–11; Heb 9:4)

DESIGN OF THE LAMPS AND ACCESSORIES FOR THE LAMPSTAND (25:37–40). **25:37–40** The seven lamps themselves were also made of gold (Exod 37:23) as were the wick trimmers (devices used to keep the flax wicks shaped for maximum flame with minimal smoke output and thus maximum light output without smudging the interior of the tabernacle) and trays to hold wicks, wick trimmers, filler flasks. The orientation of the lamps had to be "so that they light the space in front of it." This is not mere common sense: the Israelites might have assumed they should orient the lamps (which were oil bowls with a pinched edge out of which hung a saturated wick so as to cast the most light) in the direction of the holy of holies, the room containing the ark. But God wanted the lamps to light the holy place more for the benefit of the priests who ministered there as for himself, in other words. Again this is evidence of the fact that

[359] But were such trees in the temple courtyard precisely because that seemed appropriate in light of the presence of the olive "tree" lampstand inside the holy place?

[360] See comments on 4:14–17, "Excursus: Moses' Staff."

the Israelites were being informed that God did not *need* the lampstand to see; it was for his servants primarily. The lampstand and all that went with it were to be made from a full talent[361] of gold: God did not have in mind a spindly, delicate lampstand but a solid one that could endure travel and hold heavy lamps for generations.

Note the command in v. 40 that the lampstand and its accessories were to be constructed "according to the pattern shown you on the mountain" (HCSB more explicitly bring out the present progressive tense, "according to the model [NRSV "pattern"] of them you have been shown on the mountain"). This implies two considerations. First, the verbal description given here and supplemented elsewhere in the Old Testament of the lampstand is only a summation. The actual *pattern* was being shown to Moses and was later surely communicated by him to Bezalel and the other craftsmen who built the lampstand.[362] We cannot therefore know exactly what the lampstand was to be like; what we can know is generally its structure and motifs. The particulars were in the oral "blueprints" Moses conveyed to the craftsmen from images revealed to him by God.

Second, the lampstand, like the rest of the tabernacle, was intended to reflect precisely God's design, not merely a human design from general guidelines (25:9; cf. Num 8:4). This theme receives considerable emphasis in the New Testament (Acts 7:44; and esp. Heb 8:5[363]). The tabernacle, in other words, pointed to heaven—to the eternal home of God in which his redeemed people were intended eventually to dwell without distance from him (Rev 11:19) and as members of his own household (John 14:1–6). The tabernacle was, in other words, a training device for orienting the Old Covenant people toward their New Covenant heavenly home.[364]

(5) Laws on Construction and Use of the Tabernacle (26:1–37)

[1]"Make the tabernacle with ten curtains of finely twisted linen and blue, purple and scarlet yarn, with cherubim worked into them by a skilled craftsman. [2]All the curtains are to be the same size—twenty-eight cubits long and four cubits wide. [3]Join five of the curtains together, and do the same with the other five. [4]Make loops of blue material along the edge of the end curtain in one set, and do the same with the end curtain in the other set. [5]Make fifty loops on one curtain and fifty loops on the end curtain of the other set, with the loops opposite each

[361] A talent represented approximately seventy-five pounds.

[362] See comments on Exod 31:2; 35:50; 36:1; 37:1; 38:22; cf. 2 Chr 1:5.

[363] "They serve at a sanctuary that is a copy and shadow of what is in heaven. This is why Moses was warned when he was about to build the tabernacle: 'See to it that you make everything according to the pattern shown you on the mountain.' "

[364] In this connection, John's Revelation regularly portrays the elders in heaven as numbering twenty-four, twelve representing the tribes of Israel (who in turn represent all Israel) and twelve for the disciples of Jesus (who represent all the church) so that the Old Covenant and New Covenant people of God are united in heaven, reigning with Christ (e.g., Rev 4:4,10; 5:8; 11:16; 19:4).

other. [6]Then make fifty gold clasps and use them to fasten the curtains together so that the tabernacle is a unit.

[7]"Make curtains of goat hair for the tent over the tabernacle—eleven altogether. [8]All eleven curtains are to be the same size—thirty cubits long and four cubits wide. [9]Join five of the curtains together into one set and the other six into another set. Fold the sixth curtain double at the front of the tent. [10]Make fifty loops along the edge of the end curtain in one set and also along the edge of the end curtain in the other set. [11]Then make fifty bronze clasps and put them in the loops to fasten the tent together as a unit. [12]As for the additional length of the tent curtains, the half curtain that is left over is to hang down at the rear of the tabernacle. [13]The tent curtains will be a cubit longer on both sides; what is left will hang over the sides of the tabernacle so as to cover it. [14]Make for the tent a covering of ram skins dyed red, and over that a covering of hides of sea cows.

[15]"Make upright frames of acacia wood for the tabernacle. [16]Each frame is to be ten cubits long and a cubit and a half wide, [17]with two projections set parallel to each other. Make all the frames of the tabernacle in this way. [18]Make twenty frames for the south side of the tabernacle [19]and make forty silver bases to go under them—two bases for each frame, one under each projection. [20]For the other side, the north side of the tabernacle, make twenty frames [21]and forty silver bases—two under each frame. [22]Make six frames for the far end, that is, the west end of the tabernacle, [23]and make two frames for the corners at the far end. [24]At these two corners they must be double from the bottom all the way to the top, and fitted into a single ring; both shall be like that. [25]So there will be eight frames and sixteen silver bases—two under each frame.

[26]"Also make crossbars of acacia wood: five for the frames on one side of the tabernacle, [27]five for those on the other side, and five for the frames on the west, at the far end of the tabernacle. [28]The center crossbar is to extend from end to end at the middle of the frames. [29]Overlay the frames with gold and make gold rings to hold the crossbars. Also overlay the crossbars with gold.

[30]"Set up the tabernacle according to the plan shown you on the mountain.

[31]"Make a curtain of blue, purple and scarlet yarn and finely twisted linen, with cherubim worked into it by a skilled craftsman. [32]Hang it with gold hooks on four posts of acacia wood overlaid with gold and standing on four silver bases. [33] Hang the curtain from the clasps and place the ark of the Testimony behind the curtain. The curtain will separate the Holy Place from the Most Holy Place. [34]Put the atonement cover on the ark of the Testimony in the Most Holy Place. [35]Place the table outside the curtain on the north side of the tabernacle and put the lampstand opposite it on the south side.

[36]"For the entrance to the tent make a curtain of blue, purple and scarlet yarn and finely twisted linen—the work of an embroiderer. [37]Make gold hooks for this curtain and five posts of acacia wood overlaid with gold. And cast five bronze bases for them.

GENERAL SUMMARY OF THE TABERNACLE AND ITS COURTYARD. The following summary is intended to orient the reader to the material contained in this chapter and some of the next chapter. The particulars will then be discussed in connection with the individual verses of the text.

The Hebrew word for tabernacle is *miškān,* which means in Hebrew "living place" or "dwelling place." The tabernacle was a fancy rectangular tent in which God lived symbolically in the presence of his people. After being built, it was set up in the middle of the entire Israelite encampment so that all the individual small, simple Israelite tents surrounded the one big fancy tent of Yahweh in concentric circles. When he led them in traveling or in going into war, he went out in front of them in the form of his angel or the pillar of cloud/fire. But when they encamped, his home was in their very midst, and they gathered their homes around his.

His dwelling place faced east and had two rooms. The east room was an outer room or entrance room called the holy place that was thirty feet (twenty cubits) long, fifteen feet (ten cubits) wide, and fifteen (ten cubits) feet high. In it were three pieces of furniture: a food/utensil table, a lampstand, and an incense altar. On the west was an inner or "back room" called the most holy place that was dimensionally a cube: fifteen feet (ten cubits) long, fifteen feet (ten cubits) wide, and fifteen feet (ten cubits) high. In it was the ark of the covenant—an ornate box with a special platform on its lid that symbolized God's presence. This room was divided from the outer room by a special woven curtain of blue, red, and gold with cherubim motifs.

The tabernacle was made of three layers of fabric that were spread, stretched, and/or hung over a framework resembling interconnected ladders made of gilded wood. The inner layer (the layer visible to anyone inside) was, similarly to the curtain mentioned above, also a beautiful curtain cloth elaborately woven of blue, red, and gold colors with cherubim motifs patterned into the weaving. Over that was a middle layer of goat hair, giving thickness and protection. The outer layer was of dugong (sea cow) hides, providing a waterproof side to the elements.[365] Only priests, specially prepared by rituals, could enter the tabernacle itself. The other Israelites had to remain in the courtyard to worship.

The tabernacle was located at the western end of a rectangular courtyard that was made of linen curtains seven and one-half feet high, hung from poles, going all around to form the boundary. The courtyard was one hundred and fifty feet (one hundred cubits) long and seventy-five feet (fifty cubits) wide, with a thirty foot (twenty cubits) wide entrance on the eastern end that usually was open but had a curtain of blue, purple, and scarlet that could be used to close off the courtyard entirely. In the eastern end of the courtyard stood two items: an altar for grilling sacrificial meat and a laver for the priests to wash up before entering the tabernacle.

[365] At least this would seem to the most likely translation of the Hb. But cf. P. Cooper, "Of Badger Skins and Dugong Hides: A Translator's Guide to Tabernacle Covers," *BR* 16 (2000): 30–31.

Understandably, such an important symbolic structure was referred to by more than one term in the original. The most common is *miškān,* "dwelling place." But others are used, including *miškān Yahweh* ("Yahweh's dwelling place"; e.g., 25:9), or *miškān hāʿēdût* ("the Testimony's dwelling place," e.g., 38:21, so called because the tabernacle housed the ark that held the Ten Words/Commandments, which were the "testimony" to the whole covenant), and *miškān ʾōhel môʿēd* ("the dwelling place that is the Tent of Meeting,"[366] e.g., 39:32, referring to the way the tabernacle replaced the earlier "Tent of Meeting"[367]), or simply *ʾōhel môʿrēd* ("Tent of Meeting," e.g., 28:43), or *bêt yahweh* ("Yahweh's house," as in 34:26), or *qōdeš* ("Holy Place/Sanctuary," e.g., 38:24), or *miqdāš* ("Holy Place/Sanctuary" as in 25:8).

Everything making up the tabernacle and its courtyard could be rather quickly disassembled, wrapped or bundled up, and transported as the Israelites moved from place to place before settling in Canaan. It also could be reassembled rather quickly whenever they set up camp. Thus as the Israelites moved, God moved with them. Wherever they went, he lived in their midst.

DESIGN OF THE INNER CURTAINS (26:1–6). **26:1–6** Ten curtains, each measuring forty-two feet (twenty-eight cubits) long and six feet (four cubits) high/wide were used to line the tabernacle walls and ceiling. They were woven of high-quality, twisted linen, strong and fine, mixed with yarns dyed three different colors. The color names translated "blue, purple and scarlet" may have been hues generally in these color ranges,[368] based on assumptions from modern dyeing practices using dye sources presumed to be those employed in the wilderness of Sinai and/or Egypt;[369] but regardless of the actual hue, the translations can be considered roughly accurate. The linen was surely dyed as well.

The curtains were connected into two sets of five, by means not specified in the verbal description given here—probably by sewing so that each of the two sets of curtains measured forty-two by thirty feet. These two curtain groups were then joined temporarily whenever the ark was set up by connecting loops of blue material at their edges (fifty loops along the forty-two foot edge, or one loop about every ten inches) with special gold joining rings.[370] All joined up, the curtain mass that formed the tabernacle roof and

---

[366] The Hb. construct here appears to be an example of the appositional genitive, in which the *nomen regens (miškān)* is equivalent to the *nomen rectum* (*ʾōhel môʿēd,* itself a construct).

[367] See comments on 28:43.

[368] See A. Brenner, *Colour Terms in the Old Testament,* JSOT 21 (Sheffield: JSOT Press, 1982).

[369] Much of the thread and yarn used may have come from Egypt, part of the spoils taken by the Israelites from their neighbors as they departed. See comments on 25:1–7 and 12:35–36. Whether any or all of it already had been dyed in the colors represented here or how much of it may have been dyed or redyed in response to the need at Sinai cannot be known.

[370] It is fairly obvious that these gold joining rings were not solid circles but had some sort of opening in their circumference to allow the curtain loops to be slipped within the rings, perhaps vaguely in the manner of a modern key chain connecting ring.

sides measured forty-two by sixty feet.[371] Some of this was draped to form side walls and the back wall, so the actual floor space of the tabernacle was forty-five feet by fifteen feet (six hundred and seventy-five square feet). As later described, this floor space was divided in a two-thirds and one-third split into two rooms, the holy place (two-thirds of the floor space, or thirty feet by fifteen feet) and the most holy place (one-third of the floor space, or fifteen feet by fifteen feet).[372]

DESIGN OF THE PROTECTIVE CURTAINS AND WEATHER COVERINGS (26:7–14). **26:7–14** The ornate inner curtains were ten in number, and each measured forty-two feet (twenty-eight cubits) long and six feet (four cubits) wide (26:1–2). Thus in total the inner curtains provided 2,520 square feet of lovely inner wall and ceiling surfacing. The second layer of curtains that also went over the top and sides of the tabernacle and thus protected the beautiful inner curtains, lying right over them, was made of goat hair,[373] probably a single dull color. There were eleven middle curtains in number, and although the same width—four cubits (six feet)—as the inner curtains, they were slightly longer, thirty cubits (forty-five feet). In all these second-layer protective curtains provided 2,970 square feet of surface or 450 square feet more than the inner curtains. The larger size and number of the protective goat hair curtains made it possible for them to cover completely the inner curtains on all outer surfaces of the tabernacle so as to preserve the delicate beauty of the inner surface and to screen the inner curtains from casual view by outsiders. Worshipers could look into the tabernacle from the courtyard as they brought their sacrifices to Yahweh and might have been able to see at a distance something of the beautiful workmanship and color of the inner curtains. From the outside, however, the inner curtains were invisible. Of course, the middle layer of curtains also buffered the more delicate inner curtains from the heavier outer layer of hides as well.

---

[371] It is, of course, theoretically possible that the slightly ambiguous description given here means to say that the curtain sets were joined at their shorter edges, in which case the result would be a dimension of thirty by eighty-four feet for the fully joined curtain mass. Given the height of the tabernacle (ten cubits or fifteen feet), this would be unlikely since the side drapes would then not be long enough to reach to the ground to enclose the tabernacle interior from public view.

[372] This can be calculated by figuring the amount of draping over the back wall required to reach from the top to the ground and counting the width of the individual curtains to the point of the clasps (v. 6) from which the dividing veil curtain hung (v. 33).

[373] Here we side with the NIV, HCSB, NRSV, JPS over against an alternative theory, i.e., that the second layer was made not of goat hair but goat skin, i.e., goat hides with the hair still on them, not tanned (so Durham, *Exodus,* 371). That עִזִּים, lit., "goats," would also logically mean "goat hair" is consistent with the phenomenon of the use in Hb. grammar of the masculine plural to denote natural products in an unnatural state—in this case the goat hair shorn from the goat skin.

The goat hair curtains were joined into two sets—one of these sets was made up of five curtains just as the inner curtains were joined into sets of five, but the other set was comprised of six curtains, with the last of the group at the front edge of the tabernacle kept as a protective curtain for closing off the front of the tabernacle as needed. It could be folded and unfolded as appropriate, just as the fancy curtain it covered could so that when entrance to and egress from the tabernacle were desired, it could be folded back. But when the tabernacle was shut up, it could be unfolded and let down to cover the entire front (26:9). Just as the two sets of inner curtains were joined by fifty gold rings connecting fifty loops on each set, the goat hair curtains were joined similarly by fifty bronze rings.[374]

The second, goat-hair layer, viewed as a single covering (when all joined), was both wider and longer than the inner layer—longer because it contained an extra curtain[375] and wider because each curtain was made to have additional length.[376] Accordingly, as vv. 12–13 indicate, there could be an overlap of this middle layer on top of the inner layer, both at the back of the tabernacle as well as at the sides. Based on the wording of these verses, it is fairly certain that the curtains lay in the opposite plane to that of the length of the tabernacle. In other words, since the front of the tabernacle faced east and its back was to the west, the curtains were draped from the south side to the north side (thinking of draping them "left" to "right" as one faced the front of the tabernacle).

Verse 14 describes two other layers of tabernacle covering. The third layer was made of "rams skins dyed red" (NIV, HCSB) or simply "tanned rams' skins" (NRSV). The latter may be the more likely translation since the tanning process gives a reddish-brown hue to rams skins, and it is the tanned nature of those skins (pliable, soft, thick, protective without being bumpy) and not their color that is the focus of the description. The fourth, or outer layer was made from the "hides of sea cows" (HCSB "manatee skins," NRSV "fine leather," NJPS "dolphin skins").[377] This final layer was the one people would see most of the time, the layer exposed to the weather. The thick, durable leather hides of sea cows would protect from the hot sun, rain, snow, dew, frost, dust, and

---

[374] Because the same Hb. word can designate either bronze (a copper and tin alloy) or copper, it is not always possible to tell whether something like the clasps for the second layer of (goat hair) curtains of the tabernacle were actually bronze or simply copper. Because Egyptian technology (which the Israelites had most recently been familiar with) was as advanced as that of any other place, and because bronze production had begun fully long before the time of Moses, and in light of the desire for the tabernacle to be as ornate as possible, it is likely that the tabernacle metals described in most translations were really bronze, not merely the simpler and less durable copper.

[375] I.e., eleven curtains from front to back rather than ten as in the case of the inner set.

[376] That is, as compared to the ornate curtain immediately underneath it.

sand and would withstand setup and teardown repeatedly as the Israelites moved from place to place.

The curtains and covering layers had no symbolic value in themselves. They were mainly functional, providing enclosure for Yahweh's house. The grand, exquisite nature of that house fitted its purpose, the housing of the symbols of loving and protective divine presence among the chosen people. Though God kept himself invisible, the symbols of his presence helped his people remember that he dwelt among them, watched over them, set their agenda for life, and offered constantly to them the blessings of his covenant, even in the hostile environs of the wilderness.

DESIGN OF THE FRAMING UPRIGHTS THAT SUPPORTED THE CURTAINS (26:15–25). **26:15–25** These verses describe a simple but effective method of forming rigid wall supports for the tabernacle. A total of forty-eight ladder-like frames sat on silver bases of some sort.[378] The front, or east end, of the tabernacle had none of these supports because it was designed to be open for entrance and egress by the priests during a day's worship. Twenty of the frames supported the north wall, twenty supported the south wall, six supported the back wall, and two others were used to double the strength at the back corners. These extra back corner frames were separate at the bottom but joined at the top by a ring or rings—thus possibly forming a sort of A-frame at the back corners, adding stability.[379] It seems possible that the frames were not erected so as to stand fully vertical but were spread so that the curtains were slightly wider apart at the bottom than at the top as viewed from either the east or the west. As a result, the tabernacle with its "floor" included had the shape—as viewed from the outside—of what would technically be called a

[377] The Hb. word in question here, תְּחָשִׁים, is not fully understood. The translation "fine leather" follows Cross's suggestion that the outer covering was made of high quality *imported* leather, which would comport with his understanding that the description contained here is that of the P source's fifth-century projection of appropriate building materials back into the time of Moses (F. M. Cross Jr., "The Priestly Tabernacle," *BAR* 1 (Garden City: Doubleday), 201–28, esp. 220, n. 21). The more likely material used was, however, specifically the hide of aquatic creatures, for which "sea cows" is acceptable, though other, more specific translations such as "dolphin skins" or "dugong skins" or "manatee skins" may be considered. In another sense "fine leather" could be considered to provide a neutral translation since such aquatic hides do indeed constitute a leather of high quality, providing both beauty and weather protection.

[378] We are told nothing about the design of the silver frame bases. They may have been round, square, or rectangular. They may have had some sort of legs that projected from them. Moses knew from the plan God showed him how they were to be made, but that part of the plan does not find actual verbal description here.

[379] The greatest danger to the tabernacle's integrity was surely high wind. The weight of the four layers of covering would have helped keep the tabernacle from being blown over, but the bracing provided by the doubled corner frames would also have been a factor in helping the tabernacle withstand gusts of wind.

solid isosceles trapezoid, not strictly a solid rectangle, as one looked at it from either the east or the west.[380]

The upright frames were made from acacia wood, the abundant and durable wood of the wilderness and many other parts of the holy land, just as the other wooden objects of the tabernacle all were, and overlaid with gold (v. 29) as were also the ark, the table, the ark poles.[381] These frames had two poles side by side, twenty-seven inches (a cubit and a half) apart, connected to one another by cross pieces so that they resembled ladders. We are not told how many cross pieces there were on each frame but only that the length of each frame was fifteen feet (ten cubits). Since the tabernacle floor space was forty-five feet by fifteen feet, the twenty frames on each side would have been set every two feet three inches (every twenty-seven inches) on center. And since they were twenty-seven inches wide, it can be deduced that they butted against one another. If they were also lashed together or otherwise fastened to one another when the tabernacle was erected—as is very likely—they would provide a continuous framework, strong and rigid, for the horizontal frames and the curtains. Verses 22–24 describe the back (west) wall frames in the same way, undoubtedly butted against and connected to one another, with the added strength provided by an A-frame structure produced by putting another frame at each back corner and interlocking that frame with the one under it at the top. Thus forty-eight ladderlike acacia wood gilded frames and ninety-six silver bases formed the side supports for the tabernacle.

Again there is nothing especially symbolic about this account. The frames and their bases were functional, utilitarian, but also beautiful, as befits Yahweh's house. His house reflected his glory, and even its frames were required to be lovely in accordance with that glory.

DESIGN OF THE FRAMING CROSSBARS THAT FURTHER SUPPORTED THE CURTAINS (26:26–29). **26:26–29** This description of the horizontal crossbars is relatively laconic. We do not know if they were single poles or more elaborate structures—perhaps ladderlike frames on the analogy of the upright framing members. There were fifteen of them, but how they were attached to the

---

380 There is, in other words, a possibility that the inside *side* curtains were draped down (vertically) to form the interior space of the holy place and the holy of holies, so these two inner rooms of the tabernacle would not have been technically a cubic rectangle and a cube, respectively. Of course, the other layers of curtains were *draped* over the inner ones and did not simply hang vertically. Presumably all or nearly all of the gilded framing braces would have been visible from the inside of the tabernacle, and since the curtains were on the outside of these framing braces, it was gold—not fabric—that was in every case closest to Yahweh's symbolized presence, the ark.

381 To the novice it might seem that a huge amount of gold would be required for the gold overlay of all these wooden pieces, but we remind the reader that a single ounce of gold can be beaten into gold leaf covering nearly one hundred square feet in modern times. How closely Bezalel and his associates could come to such a spreading of their gold is hard to know, but with patience they probably could make their gold coverings stretch nearly as widely.

sides and back end, other than at least in part by rings (v. 29), we do not know. The language "five for the frames on one side" may not refer to placement at all but rather to the symmetry of the overall count—reminding the craftsmen to think in terms of five crossbars for each of the three framed sides of the tabernacle. If these crossbars were in fact simple bars a few inches in width at most, stretching from side to side (as viewed from the front), they would be spaced every three feet (every two cubits since there were fifteen bars for forty-five feet of "roof" length). They may also have been composite frames three feet wide, placed so as to butt up against one another in the manner of the uprights. We simply do not know.

A center crossbar or ridge pole extended from the frontmost of these crossbars at the east end to the rearmost of the crossbars, at the west end, thus stretching forty-five feet in all from front to back (v. 28). The center ridge pole united all the crossbars and kept them spaced properly and added rigidity.[382] All these roof supports were made of acacia wood, as expected, and also overlaid with gold, as expected, in consistency with the rest of the gold-overlaid wooden materials of the tabernacle.

REFERENCE TO THE ACTUAL PLAN AS OPPOSED TO THE TEXT SUMMARY (26:30). **26:30** Moses did not just hear words. He saw pictures. The words he heard from Yahweh, or at least his précis of them, are what we find in the text of Exodus as it describes the tabernacle design. But Moses actually saw what we might call the "blueprints" as well. Thus when he came back from the mountain and passed on God's instructions to Bezalel, Oholiab, and their coworkers,[383] he not only told them what to make and how to make it, but he also knew how to recognize its finished look because he had been shown what the various tabernacle components were to look like. The partial information provided in the written text represented no problem to them, even though it can be confusing at places to us, because Moses had seen a visual supplementation of the spoken words and knew exactly what Yahweh wanted for his house.

---

[382] The principle of cross bracing on modern floor and ceiling joists is exactly the same, and the added rigidity is remarkable since the cross braces do not merely link one joist to another but all joists to all other joists so as to make a unit out of what would otherwise be essentially independent timbers. This is accomplished by the addition of very light cross braces to the much heavier joists. What is important to note theologically here is that the cross bracing was simply a construction technique and has no symbolic meaning of any kind. The lightweight framework of the tabernacle made it portable, and it was its portability that *was* symbolic, i.e., of Yahweh's traveling with his people—not unlike the indwelling of the Spirit in the New Covenant, whereby the believer can always and in every place be assured of the abiding presence of God in his or her life. We must be sure that we appreciate the significance of the tabernacle without adding to it false interpretations of the meaning of its component parts—as if none were simply functional and all were theologically typological.

[383] See comments on 31:1–11.

Thus the tabernacle was not merely an *interpretation* of a general concept. It was a precise build-out of a *revealed* design. Yahweh therefore, in effect, built his own house among the Israelites, though he did it through the workmanship of Israelite craftsmen. It was his design they followed precisely. They did not think up a house and offer it to him, but rather he revealed what his house was to be like and graciously allowed them to build it for him.

Hebrews 8:5, referring to the priests of the Old Covenant and the Jerusalem temple, states: "They serve at a sanctuary that is a copy and shadow of what is in heaven. This is why Moses was warned when he was about to build the tabernacle: 'See to it that you make everything according to the pattern shown you on the mountain.'" Insisting on exact design plans and building precisely to those plans, God ensured that his house would be respected not merely as a lovely building but as a "copy and shadow"—in other words, a *replica* on a small scale and in earthly material—of his heavenly temple. What is the point of this? Simply that God wanted his people to understand that their ultimate purpose was to dwell with him in heaven, not on earth. He gave them a small sample of what his heavenly home is like, required them to locate themselves and their homes around his (see Num 2), and thus taught them the principle that they belonged in proximity to him. He projected his presence symbolically among them on earth in this way so that they could learn to long for and live for the time when they would actually dwell in his presence permanently.

DESIGN OF THE SPECIAL CURTAIN/VEIL IN FRONT OF THE HOLY OF HOLIES (26:31–35). **26:31–35** The curtain that closed off the most holy place ("Holy of Holies") from the front room of the tabernacle (the "Holy Place") was manufactured to match the curtains that lined the inside of the tabernacle (26:1) and the entrance curtain (26:36), so everything in the interior of the tabernacle shared the same general appearance of blue, purple, and scarlet yarn and finely twisted linen curtains with cherubim motifs worked into them, supported by gilded frames and poles with silver bases.

The special veiling curtain hung from four gold-covered poles that had silver bases, so with the support of these poles at intermediate points, the veil stretched from one side to the other of the interior of the tabernacle, that is, from south to north. It hung with the gold clasps mentioned in v. 6 from the top of the tabernacle and may as well have been supported at the tops of and probably at least also at the bottoms of the support poles. It was one long, single curtain, not a divided curtain that could be opened easily. To get past it, one would have to move at least one of the poles at either side and go around it because it was not designed to be gotten past under normal conditions; rather, it provided a barrier past which people could not normally go.

Behind it in the most holy place was set the ark; in front of it in the holy place stood the table and lampstand. As one faced toward the back (west end) of the tabernacle, the table stood to the right (or north side) and the lampstand to the left (or south side). There is nothing symbolic about these placements other than that they suggest the accoutrements of a tent-house with a back room. The veiling curtain divided the tabernacle into two unequal spaces, with the most holy place being nominally cubic (ten by ten by ten cubits, i.e., fifteen by fifteen by fifteen feet) and the larger holy place being nominally a cubic rectangle, with double the floor space, twenty by ten by ten cubits (thirty feet by fifteen feet by fifteen feet). Because the sides may have slanted in rather than standing strictly vertical, the actual ceiling height may not have been a full ten cubits but more like, perhaps, eight cubits (twelve feet).

The dimensions of the veiling curtain are not given. It must have been at least twelve feet high and fifteen feet wide to isolate the most holy place from the rest of the tabernacle since if it did not reach from floor to ceiling, someone at a distance on higher ground might be able to see the ark over its top edge. The elaborate precautions taken to be sure that the ark was never seen except by the high priest annually would suggest that such a possibility would be foreclosed by the simple expediency of making the curtain stretch from wall to wall and floor to ceiling.

Excursus: The Invisible God of the Old Covenant

The ark of the covenant must have been a stunningly beautiful object. All its surfaces presented pure gold to the viewer, and the ornate solid gold cherubim statuettes with outstretched wings that adorned the atonement cover were surely lovely complements to the careful craftsmanship that went into every aspect of the ark itself, extending even to its relatively utilitarian legs, rings, and carrying poles. Would it not have made sense that God would therefore want his people to see his ark at any and all times and in seeing it to be reminded of his greatness, glory, superiority, and presence among them? Indeed, would it not also have made sense regularly to take out the contents of the ark—the stone tablets of the Testimony (the Ten Commandments), the sample of manna, and the rod Aaron and Moses had used both in Egypt and the wilderness—and show them to the people as reminders of God's covenant faithfulness and as encouragements to continue to trust both his commands and his provisions?

In fact, God kept the ark and everything in it hidden from view all the time. Most Israelites, including most Levites, never, *ever* saw the ark. Whenever the people were encamped and the tabernacle erected, the ark was hidden from view (even from the view of the priests, with the sole exception of the high priest once a year) by the dividing curtain/veil in the tabernacle, behind which the ark resided, totally blocked from the sight of anyone in the holy place. Before the ark was transported, while the curtains of the tabernacle still surrounded it and kept it from public view, the high priest, assisted by a small number of other priests, wrapped the ark in three layers of protective fabric (see Num 4:5–6).[384] The

[384] It is possible the high priest personally performed the first wrapping alone so that the other priests did not actually see the ark until it had been wrapped once, but it is also possible to imagine that several priests took down the dividing curtain (veil) and approached the ark with the veil between themselves and the ark to keep from gazing upon the ark and placed the curtain as covering over the ark in that fashion, somewhat in the manner of Shem and Japheth as described in Gen 9:23.

innermost of these layers was the special dividing curtain/veil of the tabernacle; the second was made up of specially prepared sea cow hides, and then a third, outer layer was made of blue cloth. Once all this rather elaborate wrapping was completed, including in all probability the ark's legs, the entire ark was completely invisible to public view other than its carrying rings and carrying poles. Accordingly, no nonpriestly Israelite and only a few priests at the very most[385] would ever be able to see the ark itself, and then only if they happened to be assigned to help the high priest wrap it for transport. It would always remain hidden from most priests either by the dividing curtain (veil) of the tabernacle or by its elaborate protective wrapping when transported. What the average Israelite could see—at most, at a distance, and only when the ark was being transported—were rings and poles.[386]

Moreover, the contents of the ark were never put on public display. Indeed, it is not clear they were ever seen by anyone after they were placed in the ark. There is no textual information to the effect that the inside of the ark was ever opened for cleaning or anything else. When the ark was set in its place behind the curtain/veil of the erected tabernacle, only the high priest had access to it, and that only once a year for the sole purpose of applying blood to the atonement cover of the ark as a propitiation for the sins of the people (Heb 9:7), not for doing anything to or with the contents themselves. It is even possible that the lid of the ark could be sealed in some way to the sides so that it could not be opened either casually or accidentally.[387]

Why would God have his people go to such lengths to manufacture the most holy symbol of his presence among them and place within it the crucial indicators of his covenant provision and then not allow any of it to be seen by almost anyone ever again? A partial answer would be that he did not want them to treat any of these objects as an idol.[388] This answer would be true but would go only some of the way toward revealing his real purpose. The fuller answer, we suggest, comes in many places in Scripture but especially succinctly in Heb 11:6:

---

[385] If, indeed, they were privileged to help the high priest wrap it. Conversely, the high priest alone might have placed the curtain/veil over the ark and then was assisted by others in the wrapping of it, or at least some of them could have closed their eyes or were blindfolded as they helped carry the curtain/veil to the ark. We are given no information in the text to help us know the answers to these speculations since having the answers surely would not provide any better appreciation of the process and its significance than the few details we do have.

[386] And once the ark was placed in Solomon's completed temple (1 Kgs 8:6) and the veil of the temple closed in place, the ark would thereafter have been seen only by the high priest and only once a year (Heb 9:7). No one else would see it again, under normal conditions, not even wrapped because transport of the ark would have ceased permanently.

[387] The Hb. text of 1 Sam 6:19 is misleadingly translated in the NIV and many other modern English versions as suggesting that the people of Beth Shemesh actually took the top off and looked into the ark. The Hb. idiom used is *rā'āh bě,* which means simply "look at" or "see" and does not normally mean" look into." It is possible that the people of Beth-Shemesh did any number of things to the ark, but the passage does not say anything other than that they "saw" the ark, which could mean that they saw it up close, still covered, or that they saw it uncovered (assuming that it had not been transported properly covered to Beth-Shemesh).

"Without faith it is impossible to please God, because anyone who comes to him must believe that he exists and that he rewards those who earnestly seek him."

In the Old Covenant just as in the New, God saved people from their sins on the basis of their faith, not their sight or certainty. He has always asked for people to trust in him, even to the extent of believing that he exists and that if he does exist, he is a God well worth seeking and knowing, as Heb 11:6 says. He has always limited his exposure to people so that no one can say, "I had no choice but to believe in God—he was there, right in front of me all the time, so how could I not?"[389] Israelites in the Old Covenant knew there was an ark to symbolize the presence of God among them, but they knew it only by faith, not by sight. None could touch it, only a few had ever seen it, and even when it was out in the open in transport, all anyone could really see was a blue-wrapped object carried by golden poles. They *believed* that it contained the Ten Commandment tablets, the manna, and Aaron's rod, but no one ever *saw* them. They knew God's symbols of covenant provision by faith, not by sight.

The New Covenant believer knows by faith that Jesus lived among us, died on the cross for the remission of our sins, and was resurrected to glory thereafter. But no modern person saw any of it, and no pictures exist. All we have is the written report. It was the same for the Old Covenant saints. They had the oral and then written report about the ark and its contents, but they could not see either the ark or the contents. By faith they believed that there was an ark behind that curtain in the tabernacle, and by faith they believed that the Ten Commandments and other objects were inside that ark. This pleased God, who has always delighted in being trusted and who has in fact always *required* that he be trusted for his benefits to be known.[390]

DESIGN OF THE ENTRANCE CURTAIN AND ITS SUPPORT POSTS (26:36–37). **26:36–37** Yet another ornate curtain, not part of the ten that constituted the interior sides and ceiling and distinct from the dividing veil in front of the holy of holies/most holy place, hung at the front of the tabernacle and functioned as an entrance curtain. It was designed and made of the same fabrics and colors but without any cherubim motifs woven into it. Thus the

---

[388] Indeed, the Israelites at a later point acted virtually as if they regarded the ark as an idol (1 Sam 4:3–5); and the Philistines, for their part thoroughly idolatrous, assumed without hesitation that the ark was an idol and that it and its contents were representatives of divinities (1 Sam 4:6–80).

[389] To this observation one might raise the objection that Jesus Christ could be seen and touched and was not hidden from public contact. This is certainly true. The fact that he was God in the flesh was not obvious, however, and still had to be received as a fact by faith. No obvious glory or irresistible divinity surrounded Jesus to make him seem to be God to those who came in contact with him. It is what he said and did that convinced those willing to be convinced.

[390] On the question of whether anyone in any scriptural account actually is described as having fully seen God, see the commentary on 24:11 and the references there. As to the interconnection between knowing Christ by faith and not sight and the benefits of Christ, Melanchthon's famous epigram remains instructive: "Hoc est Christum cognoscere—beneficia eius cognoscere" ("to know Christ is to know his benefits").

cherubim motifs would be visible when this curtain was closed only to those who actually went inside the tabernacle. Five unique vertical columns (different from the other vertical framing pieces) helped support this curtain, though it may also have been hung from the top of the frontmost crossbar with gold hooks, the same method of hanging or joining as was used for the interior curtains. We are not told how the five columns of acacia wood overlaid with gold that helped hold this curtain were spaced. If two were at the very edges and three spaced equally along the front, the distance from column to column at the fifteen-foot-wide front of the tabernacle would have been about three feet, nine inches. How this curtain was to be pulled or draped back (or up) is likewise not specified.

It is no accident that the bases for the five columns at the front of the sanctuary were bronze rather than silver as all other bases in the tabernacle (not the courtyard) were. This entranceway was the farthest point in the tabernacle from the most holy place and its ark. The use of the cheaper metal conformed to the principle that the closer one was to Yahweh's presence, as symbolized by the ark, the closer one was to holiness and glory; the farther away one was, the less direct was the impact of the holiness and glory. Thus objects in the courtyard of the tabernacle need not be composed either of gold or of silver. The entranceway, at the very border of the tabernacle and the courtyard, helped make the transition from tabernacle to courtyard by the simple symbolism of its metallic supports.

(6) Laws on Construction and Use of the Main Altar (27:1–8)

1"Build an altar of acacia wood, three cubits high; it is to be square, five cubits long and five cubits wide. 2Make a horn at each of the four corners, so that the horns and the altar are of one piece, and overlay the altar with bronze. 3Make all its utensils of bronze—its pots to remove the ashes, and its shovels, sprinkling bowls, meat forks and firepans. 4Make a grating for it, a bronze network, and make a bronze ring at each of the four corners of the network. 5Put it under the ledge of the altar so that it is halfway up the altar. 6Make poles of acacia wood for the altar and overlay them with bronze. 7The poles are to be inserted into the rings so they will be on two sides of the altar when it is carried. 8Make the altar hollow, out of boards. It is to be made just as you were shown on the mountain.

In various ways during Old Covenant times, God taught his people the basic principle of salvation from sin: *something that God considers a substitute must die in my place so that I may live*. Altar sacrifice was the primary way for this substitution to happen. In preparation for Christ's death on the cross, which was the ultimate sacrifice to which all others pointed, animal sacrifice was required of all Israelites. Since it is dangerous to eat raw animal meat, God required that it be cooked, and to accomplish this a large outdoor grill was required. By killing an animal, then cooking it on that grill in God's presence (i.e., in front of the entrance to the tabernacle), and then eating it in God's presence (symbolically sharing the meal with him), the Israelite worshiper learned over and over again the concept of substitutionary atonement and of covenant renewal.[391] The sacrificial meal always included a portion of a formerly living thing (sacrificial animal) that had been put to death in the place of the worshiper. It was prepared and cooked at God's house (the courtyard of the tabernacle, on the altar described in this passage) in God's presence, and it renewed the worshiper's commitment to his or her covenant with Yahweh each time it was eaten.

God also taught his people in many ways during Old Covenant times that he loved corporate worship. Individuals were not to worship him separately at their own homes or in mere family groups at convenient locations as the pagans did. Instead they were to come together as an entire people, bring their sacrifices to one place, cook them all on a single altar, and eat them all at a single location, his tabernacle. Accordingly, the altar had to be fairly large to accommodate the constant flow of sacrificial meat placed upon it for grilling.[392]

27:1–8 Its top surface was thus four and a half feet high ("three cubits high") off the ground and was a square seven and a half feet on each side ("five cubits long and five cubits wide"), providing a total of fifty-six and one-quarter square feet of grilling area (minus whatever was taken up by the corner "horns" and any rim that may have surrounded the top, if either of these imposed upon the total surface of the top). Like other tabernacle furniture, the altar was composed of acacia wood (v. 1) and overlaid with metal, in this case bronze rather than gold, bronze being the "outdoor" or courtyard metal of choice for things of metal at the tabernacle and gold being the "indoor" or internal tabernacle metal.

The altar had horns at the corners (v. 2), which were curving protrusions upward from the flat plane of the main surface of the altar[393] that helped hold anything on the altar from falling over the edge. The implements used to service the purpose of the altar were also made of bronze (v. 3). These included ash pots (to receive and store ashes from the surface temporarily before dumping), fire pots (pots holding live coals for getting new fires going each morning), shovels to remove the ashes and reconfigure the live coals that cooked the meat, sprinkling bowls (bowls that held liquids used for any purpose, from

---

[391] See comments on 24:11.

[392] We have already noted that, at least on major feast occasions, most meat was probably cooked mainly in pots and then placed only briefly on the sacrifice altar, since otherwise the amount of meat available for cooking would have been far greater than the amount of space available on the tabernacle altar to cook it adequately. A token duration on the sacrificial altar of any given sacrifice was therefore all that could probably be managed at festival times, when all Israel was actually putting the altar to use constantly through the agency of the priests.

[393] Because animal horns are also curved protrusions upward from the (vaguely) flat plane of an animal's head, the term for animal horns was borrowed in Hb. to refer to the horns of the altar as well. See also on 34:29 for another sense of the root *qrn* in Hb.

sprinkling water on the flames to moderate them to sprinkling cooking oil on the food or on the surface of the altar[394]), and meat forks for handling the meat as it was put on, taken off, or moved around the surface of the altar. These pieces of equipment had no symbolic value but served the needs of the cooks (priests) in the various parts of the cooking process.

Verses 4–5 appear to describe very generally two features of the altar: its bronze grilling surface ("grating") and a bronze net/strainer/grillwork ("network," but the Hb. can mean any of these) that hung below the surface, halfway from the surface to the ground. It cannot be proved from the short descriptive wording employed, but the net/strainer/grillwork may well have held the burning wood (and after burning for a time, mainly coals) that sent the heat up through the surface grating to cook the meat on the grill surface. Verses 6–7 specify a transportation method much like that used in the case of the ark, that is, acacia wood poles overlaid with metal, in this case bronze, that were inserted through rings fixed on two sides of the altar so that it could be carried by a group of priests/Levites, probably at least eight of them (two at the front and two at the back of each pole). Obviously these poles may have been longer than those used for the much smaller ark and were not to be fixed in the rings at all times but rather were taken out whenever the altar was used for cooking because of the need for access at all sides of the altar to tend to the meat, the coals, the ashes.

Verse 8 indicates that the altar was to be lightweight, not a solid box but a framework of wood with bronze overlay and bronze top grating and wood net/strainer/grillwork. By repeating the essence of the wording already used in 25:9,40; 26:30 ("It is to be made just as you were shown on the mountain"), the last half of the verse again reminds the reader that there were many more details to the altar than are provided through the verbal description. Once more, Moses heard God tell him to conform the tabernacle and its furniture to a divine "blueprint" that God allowed him to see, and not merely to what craftsmen would construct from a general verbal description, filling in from their imagination what the words did not cover. The tabernacle and all things within it and immediately surrounding it constituted a replica, a mirroring microcosm of the heavenly sanctuary of God, symbolically portraying the fact that he had graciously chosen to project his heavenly presence to earth among his covenant people, reminding them in a visible way that he was with them, leading them, caring for them, and receiving their regular worship gladly.

---

[394] In many or most instances, liquefied fat melted from the burnt fat portions of offerings (e.g., Lev 3:3,9,14,16) would have greased the grilling surface, but there may have been oiling of meats in some cases as well.

(7) Laws on Construction and Use of the Courtyard (27:9–19)

[9]"Make a courtyard for the tabernacle. The south side shall be a hundred cubits long and is to have curtains of finely twisted linen, [10]with twenty posts and twenty bronze bases and with silver hooks and bands on the posts. [11]The north side shall also be a hundred cubits long and is to have curtains, with twenty posts and twenty bronze bases and with silver hooks and bands on the posts.

[12]"The west end of the courtyard shall be fifty cubits wide and have curtains, with ten posts and ten bases. [13]On the east end, toward the sunrise, the courtyard shall also be fifty cubits wide. [14]Curtains fifteen cubits long are to be on one side of the entrance, with three posts and three bases, [15]and curtains fifteen cubits long are to be on the other side, with three posts and three bases.

[16]"For the entrance to the courtyard, provide a curtain twenty cubits long, of blue, purple and scarlet yarn and finely twisted linen—the work of an embroiderer—with four posts and four bases. [17]All the posts around the courtyard are to have silver bands and hooks, and bronze bases. [18]The courtyard shall be a hundred cubits long and fifty cubits wide, with curtains of finely twisted linen five cubits high, and with bronze bases. [19]All the other articles used in the service of the tabernacle, whatever their function, including all the tent pegs for it and those for the courtyard, are to be of bronze.

In ancient Israel one worshiped *at* Yahweh's house, but not *in* Yahweh's house. People who live in tents do not cook inside but outside, and they typically eat their meals outside as well. Since the tabernacle was a tent, a portable home for Yahweh, it is only logical that he would expect his invited guests (Israelite worshipers) to join him at but not in his tent-home. His personal servants (the priests) might enter his home and come and go from it for certain purposes, but all others met with him outdoors. To make a special area for worship, God insisted that his tabernacle have a courtyard within which worship would take place. The area outside the courtyard would simply constitute normal space like any other in the Israelite encampment, but inside would constitute holy ground.

The courtyard would need to be large enough to accommodate hundreds of worshipers at a time as well as the priests who served Yahweh on their behalf and the animals that were being prepared or cooked and, of course, the tabernacle itself. Since worshipers ate their portion of sacrificial meals "in Yahweh's presence,"[395] which means in the tabernacle (and later temple) courtyard, there was a constant stream of people during times of sacrifice entering the courtyard, watching their sacrifice prepared, receiving it from the priests, sitting and eating as households, and then departing for their own homes. But the courtyard would also need to be small enough and made of

---

[395] Cp., e.g., Deut 12:18, "You are to eat them in the presence of the LORD your God at the place the LORD your God will choose—you, your sons and daughters, your menservants and maidservants, and the Levites from your towns"; cf. Deut 12:7; 14:23,26; 15:20.

lightweight and portable materials so that it could be easily broken down for transportation yet rapidly set up for use as a worship center once the Israelites, following Yahweh's lead through the pillar of cloud/fire, encamped at a given location.

The tabernacle measured at least fifteen feet (ten cubits) wide and forty-five feet (thirty cubits) long and may in fact have taken up somewhat more ground space than that because of the diagonal slant of the sides downward from the top toward the base.[396] At any rate, its footprint within the courtyard would have required no less than 675 square feet, not counting whatever ropes and tent pegs may also have been used to help secure the tabernacle, if any. The courtyard was, by comparison, 150 feet (100 cubits) long and 75 feet (50 cubits) wide, or 11,250 square feet. There is nothing sacred or symbolic about the dimensions of the courtyard, other than the fact that its size provided for corporate worship, signifying in the Old Covenant that God accepted and delighted in the group adoration of his people, together at a single location—a model of heaven, where all the grand, historic assembly of the people of God from all places and ages will together praise his magnificent name forever.

27:9–11 The description of the courtyard starts with the two longest sides, the south and the north, each of which had one hundred and fifty feet (one hundred cubits) of curtains made of twisted linen supported by twenty posts (one every seven and a half feet, or every five cubits). These posts probably were made of acacia wood, though the text does not specify their construction. They also probably were not overlaid with any metal, though they had bronze bases like the bases of the special pillars at the entrance to the tabernacle and had silver bands around them from which were hung the curtains all around by means of silver hooks. God's words at this point do not indicate whether or not rings were used to fasten the curtains to these hooks, whether hanging loops were attached to the curtains, or whether some sort of "buttonholes" sewed into the curtains' edges (and at other points as well if the curtains were larger than seven and a half feet wide) were used for attaching the curtains to the hooks. There is also no indication of how long the curtains used at the sides of the tabernacle were. One likely scenario is that the courtyard side curtains were square, seven and a half feet (five cubits) by seven and a half feet (five cubits). Clearly, the curtains were of that height (v. 18), and since the spacing of the posts would average that width (see above), a system of square curtains might have proved simple and effective. These would have

[396] It is theoretically possible that only two or three of the three outermost layers slanted in this way and that the fancy innermost curtains, those woven of scarlet, blue, and blue yarn (26:1ff.), hung straight down to form vertical sides for the interior. By this scenario the inner curtains would have been inside the plane of the golden side supports, something that we judge less likely than that the gold side support frames were always inside the curtains rather than between them and the protective layers outside them.

been attached at their edges to the poles at several points, providing a solid curtain wall on the south and north sides of the courtyard.

27:12–15 The west end of the courtyard, only half the length of the south and north sides, was curtained in the same manner as they were. The dimensions given suggest the possibility, once again, of square curtains seven and a half feet (five cubits) on each side, attached to poles spaced just as was the case at the longer sides.[397] The east side, however, which was the place of entrance and exit, had to be treated differently. It was seventy-five feet (fifty cubits) wide. Two curtains came from each corner toward the center, stretching twenty-two and a half feet (fifteen cubits) each, leaving a gap in the center of the east side of thirty feet (twenty cubits). These curtains probably were of the same sort as the others used on the south, west, and north sides, though no specification is given. Their supporting posts were spaced just as the others were, although clearly these curtains were rectangular, not square, since their length of twenty-two and a half feet (fifteen cubits) was three times their height (seven and a half feet, or five cubits).

27:16–18 A special entrance curtain hung in the center of the east side. It was thirty feet (twenty cubits) wide and made exactly (at least as far as the description given goes) like the inner curtains of the tabernacle, except for lacking any cherubim motifs. Again the spaces of the supporting posts for this entrance curtain were the same (seven and a half feet, or five cubits) on average as all the others around the courtyard. Indeed, as v. 17 indicates, all the posts around the courtyard were the same—as were probably all the curtains in texture and fabric, if not dimension—except for the special entrance curtain. The fact that this curtain was one piece meant that it was used more for closing up the courtyard at night than as the equivalent of a doorway for going through; during the day it would have been gathered to one side to allow access through virtually all of the entrance opening.

One could easily see the top of the tabernacle, which was nearly fifteen feet high (depending on the degree of angle of the side frames and curtains) over the tops of the curtains all around since they were only seven and a half feet high. That is all an observer standing outside the tabernacle could see, however, except during the daytime when the special entrance curtain was open—allowing and indeed inviting God's covenant people into his sacred ground, set off from the common ground of the camp by a simple but effective courtyard

[397] The obvious alternative scenario is that these side curtains were in fact like the two curtains that hung at each side of the special entrance curtain and were three times as wide as high. The advantage of fewer curtains would be better coverage of "gaps," meaning that the casual observer could not so easily find a break in the line of curtains (say, around a pole, where the curtains may have been pulled tight away from the pole by the wind) and look into the courtyard. But the ability to view the courtyard was hardly an issue since it could be entered readily by worshipers who could view it to their hearts' content.

within which worship occurred. Thus, from the point of view of height, the tabernacle itself was dominant rather than its courtyard, whereas from the point of view of commodiousness, the courtyard was obviously the place where most people could assemble. The tabernacle was exclusive; the courtyard, relatively more inclusive; and the two together constituted what could simply be called "Yahweh's house."

27:19 Ropes and tent pegs were needed to stabilize the courtyard curtain and keep it from blowing over in the wind. Other incidental metal articles used in the courtyard (basins, jugs, tools for repairing things, accessory implements for the restraint of animals.) were to be of bronze because this was the Bronze Age, that is, prior to the introduction of normal iron use in about 1200 BC when bronze was the standard, common metal. The courtyard was not of the same degree of closeness to pure holiness as was the tabernacle proper. Tent pegs probably were also used in securing the tabernacle proper, and since these would stand in the ground outside the tabernacle, they too would have been of bronze rather than gold or silver.

(8) Laws on Keeping the Lamps Lit (27:20–21)

[20]"Command the Israelites to bring you clear oil of pressed olives for the light so that the lamps may be kept burning. [21]In the Tent of Meeting, outside the curtain that is in front of the Testimony, Aaron and his sons are to keep the lamps burning before the LORD from evening till morning. This is to be a lasting ordinance among the Israelites for the generations to come.

27:20–21 Since the tabernacle was a symbolic house for Yahweh to dwell within, it would not have been polite for the Israelites, who had oil lamps lit in their own tents during the evening hours, to have denied Yahweh the same courtesy. Most of their lamps almost surely would have been extinguished, except for one, when the last member of the family went to bed, and in many homes all lamps would have been put out at that time.[398] But Yahweh did not sleep. Therefore it would have been entirely inappropriate to allow his lamp to go out during the night hours because that could be interpreted to mean symbolically that he had "gone to bed."[399] Therefore one of the types of contributions the people could be make for the maintenance of the tabernacle and proper worship therein was olive oil—pressed and filtered through fabrics to produce clear oil that would burn brightly in the beautiful seven gold lamps of the lampstand that stood just outside the curtained entrance to the most holy place (25:31–40).

---

[398] An emergency need for light in the wee hours would have required going outside to find still-live coals to light the wick of a lamp or to a neighbor's house for the use of a still-lit lamp to ignite the wick.

[399] We have already noted, however, that *functionally* the light in the tabernacle was for the benefit of the Lord's servants, not him, because he needed no light to see.

The priests ("Aaron and his sons") had a solemn duty assigned them with these words to be sure that there was enough oil in the tabernacle lamps each evening (and adequate wicks, it goes without saying) so that the lamps would remain burning brightly through the night until dawn, when they could be extinguished. The priests' responsibilities for lamp tending and the peoples' responsibilities for oil donation constituted "a lasting ordinance among the Israelites for the generations to come." This was no more lasting an ordinance than any other related to the tabernacle, but by stating such a severe wording in connection with what might be regarded as a simple, minor, commonsense responsibility, God impressed, *a fortiori*, all the other worship responsibilities on his people and priests as well.

Of interest is the use of the term "Tent of Meeting" in v. 21. Moses explained later (in 33:7) the origin of this term, which at first referred to a sort of temporary pretabernacle tent for divine contact used by Moses until the tabernacle itself could be constructed. This verse represents the first occurrence of the term in the Old Testament. It probably was used in distinction to the tabernacle when the one was in use and the other being built; but as soon as the tabernacle was actually put into use, the original Tent of Meeting was discontinued, and the term Tent of Meeting was transferred to the tabernacle, becoming yet another way to connote "tabernacle." Moses used "Tent of Meeting" here for an audience that already worshiped at the tabernacle and already had made the transfer of terminology since he wrote Exodus after the tabernacle was constructed.[400]

(9) Laws on Priests' Clothing (28:1–43)

[1]"Have Aaron your brother brought to you from among the Israelites, along with his sons Nadab and Abihu, Eleazar and Ithamar, so they may serve me as priests. [2]Make sacred garments for your brother Aaron, to give him dignity and honor. [3]Tell all the skilled men to whom I have given wisdom in such matters that they are to make garments for Aaron, for his consecration, so he may serve me as priest. [4]These are the garments they are to make: a breastpiece, an ephod, a robe, a woven tunic, a turban and a sash. They are to make these sacred garments for

[400] In other words, the idea that "tabernacle" (almost always with the article, as הַמִּשְׁכָּן) also called just "the tent" (הָאֹהֶל as in 26:12, e.g.) and "Tent of Meeting" (אֹהֶל מוֹעֵד) are terms that reflect different literary sources that have somehow been (poorly) harmonized in the text of Exodus seems to us to violate Ockham's Razor, by positing an evolutionary source-critical scenario far more complicated than the simple historical explanation that Moses himself offered openly in 33:7. Note also that אֹהֶל מוֹעֵד, a construct without the article on the *nomen rectum,* represents a formation in current use before the article had become normalized in Hb. (in the beginning of Iron II, or around 1000 BC), and not a late usage at all. On the timing of the introduction of the article into Hb. usage, see T. Lambdin, "The Junctural Origin of the West Semitic Definite Article," in *Near Eastern Studies in Honor of William Foxwell Albright* (Baltimore: Johns Hopkins Press, 1971), 315–33.

your brother Aaron and his sons, so they may serve me as priests. 5Have them use gold, and blue, purple and scarlet yarn, and fine linen.

6"Make the ephod of gold, and of blue, purple and scarlet yarn, and of finely twisted linen—the work of a skilled craftsman. 7It is to have two shoulder pieces attached to two of its corners, so it can be fastened. 8Its skillfully woven waistband is to be like it—of one piece with the ephod and made with gold, and with blue, purple and scarlet yarn, and with finely twisted linen.

9"Take two onyx stones and engrave on them the names of the sons of Israel 10in the order of their birth—six names on one stone and the remaining six on the other. 11Engrave the names of the sons of Israel on the two stones the way a gem cutter engraves a seal. Then mount the stones in gold filigree settings 12and fasten them on the shoulder pieces of the ephod as memorial stones for the sons of Israel. Aaron is to bear the names on his shoulders as a memorial before the LORD. 13Make gold filigree settings 14and two braided chains of pure gold, like a rope, and attach the chains to the settings.

15"Fashion a breastpiece for making decisions—the work of a skilled craftsman. Make it like the ephod: of gold, and of blue, purple and scarlet yarn, and of finely twisted linen. 16It is to be square—a span long and a span wide—and folded double. 17Then mount four rows of precious stones on it. In the first row there shall be a ruby, a topaz and a beryl; 18in the second row a turquoise, a sapphire and an emerald; 19in the third row a jacinth, an agate and an amethyst; 20in the fourth row a chrysolite, an onyx and a jasper. Mount them in gold filigree settings. 21There are to be twelve stones, one for each of the names of the sons of Israel, each engraved like a seal with the name of one of the twelve tribes.

22"For the breastpiece make braided chains of pure gold, like a rope. 23Make two gold rings for it and fasten them to two corners of the breastpiece. 24Fasten the two gold chains to the rings at the corners of the breastpiece, 25and the other ends of the chains to the two settings, attaching them to the shoulder pieces of the ephod at the front. 26Make two gold rings and attach them to the other two corners of the breastpiece on the inside edge next to the ephod. 27Make two more gold rings and attach them to the bottom of the shoulder pieces on the front of the ephod, close to the seam just above the waistband of the ephod. 28The rings of the breastpiece are to be tied to the rings of the ephod with blue cord, connecting it to the waistband, so that the breastpiece will not swing out from the ephod.

29"Whenever Aaron enters the Holy Place, he will bear the names of the sons of Israel over his heart on the breastpiece of decision as a continuing memorial before the LORD. 30Also put the Urim and the Thummim in the breastpiece, so they may be over Aaron's heart whenever he enters the presence of the LORD. Thus Aaron will always bear the means of making decisions for the Israelites over his heart before the LORD.

31"Make the robe of the ephod entirely of blue cloth, 32with an opening for the head in its center. There shall be a woven edge like a collar around this opening, so that it will not tear. 33Make pomegranates of blue, purple and scarlet yarn around the hem of the robe, with gold bells between them. 34The gold bells and the pomegranates are to alternate around the hem of the robe. 35Aaron must

**wear it when he ministers. The sound of the bells will be heard when he enters the
Holy Place before the LORD and when he comes out, so that he will not die.**
**[36]"Make a plate of pure gold and engrave on it as on a seal: HOLY TO THE
LORD. [37]Fasten a blue cord to it to attach it to the turban; it is to be on the front
of the turban. [38]It will be on Aaron's forehead, and he will bear the guilt involved
in the sacred gifts the Israelites consecrate, whatever their gifts may be. It will be
on Aaron's forehead continually so that they will be acceptable to the LORD.**
**[39]"Weave the tunic of fine linen and make the turban of fine linen. The sash is
to be the work of an embroiderer. [40]Make tunics, sashes and headbands for
Aaron's sons, to give them dignity and honor. [41]After you put these clothes on
your brother Aaron and his sons, anoint and ordain them. Consecrate them so
they may serve me as priests.**
**[42]"Make linen undergarments as a covering for the body, reaching from the
waist to the thigh. [43]Aaron and his sons must wear them whenever they enter the
Tent of Meeting or approach the altar to minister in the Holy Place, so that they
will not incur guilt and die.**
"This is to be a lasting ordinance for Aaron and his descendants.

INTRODUCTORY SUMMARY (28:1–5). **28:1** This verse represents yet another way in which God taught the Israelites about the inherited nature of the priesthood: "Aaron your brother" (i.e., the Aaron who is part of your family[401] and therefore one of the Levites) and "his sons" (i.e., his heirs)[402] must be brought to Moses for proper investiture, "so they may serve me as priests." Thus God declared the priesthood an office that is passed down from generation to generation within a family that is within a tribe of Israel—not an office that can be purchased (cf. 2 Chr 13:9–10) or taken by reason of power or influence (2 Chr 26:16–21) or by popular election or any other means. Only God could make someone a priest; it was not a human choice.[403] This chapter appears to concentrate on the things appropriate to the high priesthood rather than the priesthood in general. As D. Fleming has argued, it is Lev 8 that

[401] Aaron is almost surely an Egyptian name. (Moses, Aaron, and Miriam all had what appear to be Egyptian names, i.e., names that do not seem to have any specific meaning in Hb./Canaanite.) Other Israelites and non-Israelites who were part of the exodus people (12:38) may have borne the name Aaron as well, and therefore the specifications "your brother" and "from among the Israelites" informed the people, once Moses reported this to them, of God's choice for high priest and patriarch of the priesthood that would follow. This information was undoubtedly less for Moses' benefit than for the benefit of the people in general. Although some scholars have suggested that the supposedly redacted text makes Aaron Moses' brother even though he actually was not, no evidence exists that he was anything but Moses' brother, referred to in the text in ways always appropriate and not artificial.

[402] "Sons/children" (בָּנִים) is the standard term for heirs/descendants in the OT, being employed to connote that sense far more frequently than "seed" (זֶרַע) or "children's children" (בְּנֵי בָנִים).

[403] So in the New Covenant the gifts and calling of God are recognized by ordination of one evidently gifted and called; strictly speaking, it was not an office for which one could apply or "try out."

appears to be the chapter more specifically devoted to regulations related to priests in general; but both chapters share common elements because high priests were not so different from ordinary priests that information about their roles, ordination, and equipment would be without overlap.[404]

Vestments signified authority in the ancient world.[405] In the absence of a monarchy in Israel, these vestments made the high priest the leader of the people. Evidence of a specially vested high priest as leader of Israel appears in many places in Israel's history, including the restoration after the Babylonian captivity (Zech 3:5–7) as well as the organization of the Jewish people in New Testament times (Matt 26:65). Because Israel was begun as a theocracy rather than a monarchy, the sort of vestments that conferred dignity and authority that a king might have worn in other cultures were worn by God's high priest in Israel as a way of confirming the high priest's role as representative of Yahweh for purposes of worship.[406]

A guest does not prepare the food at another's home—the homeowner does the preparation of the food and the guests join in eating it. Thus in the logic symbolized by the meal-based sacrificial system, worshipers at the tabernacle were Yahweh's guests and the priests were Yahweh's servants, serving both the host and the guests. In the case of tabernacle worship, the guests brought the food not because it was theirs and they wanted to honor their host by contributing to the meal; it was not theirs, but they were bringing that portion of their harvest that had belonged to Yahweh from the beginning. By reason of having a meal together they were showing covenant relationship since it was not normal in ancient times for people to eat together unless they were allies.

---

[404] D. Fleming, "The Biblical Tradition of Anointing Priests," *JBL* 117 (1998): 401–14.

[405] So David's wife Michal was offended when he did not wear the signs of royalty but rather wore what might be described as the ancient equivalent in terms of clothing of shorts and a T-shirt as he celebrated the ark's entrance to Jerusalem (2 Sam 6:14–16,20). Likewise, Joseph's long-sleeved robe (not a coat of many colors; see the commentaries) represented inheritance rights and thus a special favoritism to him by his father Jacob (Gen 37:3). Similarly, the renewal of Joshua's priestly garments signify his favor with God (Zech 3). Dress functions to indicate identity and formal function in all cultures and is not irrelevant to position or office or intention—as in worship.

[406] Pace Durham (*Exodus,* 385), who reflects a relatively common critical view that the present passage is from the sixth/fifth-century P source in saying "thus at least some of the ornate vestments described here probably began as vestments for the sacral king, performing his duties as Yahweh's own anointed one. As time passed, the kings turned over some of these duties to the priests; then with the successive Assyrian and Babylonian destructions of the two monarchies, the priest took over the royal vestments, and by the postexilic period, many of the royal functions as well." This view fails to recognize how the high priest served as Yahweh's agent in worship and thus represented him during the early, theocratic days before the monarchy and received recognition in this role partly by reason of his vestments. There have been many attempts to prove the existence of a sacral kingship in Israel, but the fatal problem with each of them is the remarkable lack of evidence.

Already the priestly succession is identified specifically in God's personally naming Nadab, Abihu, Eleazar, and Ithamar to the priesthood along with Aaron.[407]

28:2–5 Here God simply gave the names of the six most important of the eight priestly garments he would require and describe in more detail later in the course of the chapter. Later, as well, the special flower-like medallion worn at the front of the turban (vv. 36–38) and the linen undergarments (vv. 42–43) are also mentioned. The present passage grants, therefore, a brief, orienting overview to the reader/hearer upon which specific details would follow.

No special order applies to the vestments named in v. 4; that is, at least the order does not correspond to the order of vestments detailed in the rest of the chapter, suggesting that there would be no requirement for the priest to don these garments in exactly the same order every time or that when not worn they should be stored in some certain order, or any such thing.[408] As long as they were all worn in their proper, logical position, which was generally a matter of common sense, the garments would identify the high priest and correctly (and symbolically)[409] represent Israel before God and God before Israel thereby.

One notes immediately that the fabrics and colors of the materials for the garments (v. 5) were the same as those also used for the lovely inner curtains and entrance curtain of the tabernacle itself.[410] The description given clearly makes the vestments similar to and reflective of the "dignity and honor"[411] (v. 2) of the tabernacle. One also notes that they are called "sacred garments" (v. 4), to be manufactured by the same men, or at least the same sorts of men, who would

---

[407] Nadab has already been mentioned in 6:23 and 24:1. He appears as well in the story of his death in Lev 10, partly retold in Num 3; 26. Cf. also Num 3:2; 26:60; 1 Chr 6:3 for additional genealogical citation. Abihu is always mentioned in connection with Nadab. Eleazar and Ithamar figure as the replacements for Nadab and Abihu after their judgment death in Lev 10 and the partial retelling of that story in Num 3. Eleazar and his descendants also had special tabernacle maintenance responsibilities (Num 4:16) not distributed to descendants of Aaron in general. Otherwise, Eleazar and Ithamar appear in the same passages as do Nadab and Abihu.

[408] "Their curious mingling of repetition and terseness suggests that these instructions were set down for people who knew what was being described, who had seen the vestments, in various combinations, in use; thus the instructions omit what would have been, for such persons, too obvious to require statement, but would have made the descriptions clearer to us" (Durham, *Exodus,* 384–85).

[409] Cf. the suggestions of C. F. Keil on the symbolism associated with the high priest's vestments in *Manual of Biblical Archaeology I* (Edinburgh: T&T Clark, 1887), 216ff.

[410] See comments on 26:1,31,36.

[411] "Essentially a uniform draws attention to the office or function of a person, as opposed to his individual personality. It emphasizes his job rather than his name . . . Furthermore, we can see that, in general, the more prestigious the office, the more splendid the uniform . . . In putting on these clothes [Aaron] took to himself all the honor and glory of the high-priesthood. In a religion the principal doctrine of which was the holiness of God, the high priest, who mediated atonement between God and man, was an extremely important person. His glorious clothing symbolized the significance of his office" (G. Wenham, *Leviticus,* NICOT [Grand Rapids: Eerdmans, 1979], 138–39).

eventually be assigned the task of constructing the tabernacle ("skilled men to whom I have given wisdom in such matters," v. 3; cf. 31:2–6; 35:30–34; 36:1–2; 37:1; 38:22–23; 2 Chr 1:5). The tabernacle would not function properly without its priests; the priests could not function properly apart from the tabernacle. The high priest, for whom the garments described in this chapter were specifically intended, was the leader of all the priests; and even though the focus is, naturally, upon his garments first, the principle of (general) priesthood-tabernacle interdependence finds establishment already in the present passage.

THE EPHOD (28:6–14). The word "ephod" refers to a torso garment, that is, a piece of clothing that covers the body from thigh to shoulder, normally without covering either arms or legs.[412] The linen ephod typically worn by priests or temple servants (e.g., 1 Sam 2:18; 22:18) was a simple garment. Indeed, when David wore just a linen ephod in order to dance in front of the ark, it seemed to his wife Michal that he was dressed too commonly and possibly even immodestly—and did not look like a king (2 Sam 6:5,14,16,20–22). This suggests that the ephod alone was not regarded as the only garment one would normally wear.

The ephod described in the present passage and throughout the Pentateuch was, by contrast, nothing simple and was not worn alone. It was, rather, a very elaborate and impressive sort of ceremonial vest worn over other garments and used to clothe its wearer symbolically so as to represent God among his people.[413] Indeed the ephod became eventually such a symbol of the divine presence that "forged" ephods—modeled on the proper, legitimate one—could actually be worshiped as if they were idols.[414]

In the divine instructions given to Moses in this chapter, the ephod is distinguished from the breastpiece that was attached to it for the purpose of divining God's will through the Urim and Thummim. The term ephod, however, came to include automatically the notion of "ephod with breastpiece attached" since the two pieces were not used separately, and after the book of Exodus one encounters the term "ephod" rather consistently for the ephod-breastpiece assembly.[415]

28:6–8 The ephod had the same fabric base and the same colors as the rest of Aaron's garments and as the tabernacle inner curtains, and it had to be

[412] Cf. W. R. Arnold, *Ephod and Ark,* HTS 3 (Cambridge: Harvard University Press, 1917); K. Elliger, "Ephod und Chosen," in *Festschrift Friederich Baumgartel,* EF 10 (Erlangen: Universitätsbund, 1959), 9–23. Also in *VT* 8 (1958): 19–35.

[413] Cf. M. Haran, "The Form of the Ephod in the Biblical Sources," *Tarbiz* 24 (1955): 380–91.

[414] This was the case with the ephods mentioned in the book of Judges. Gideon, the originally reluctant but eventually brave Israelite judge whose theology was far from orthodox, made a gold-laden ephod for his hometown of Ophrah that came to be regarded and used as an idol by people from all over Israel (all over Israel being the meaning of "all Israel" in Judg 8:27 and elsewhere). Later, in Judg 17–18, one reads of Israelites, including heterodox priests, also using an ephod as if it were a representation of divinity, i.e., an idol. Cf. M. Noth, "The Background of Judges 17–18," in *Israel's Prophetic Heritage* (New York: Harper & Brothers, 1962), 68–85. It is not necessary to conclude that all ephods were alike. The three common features may have been construction from valuable materials, housing for something akin to the Urim and Thummim, and use in divination. Cf. G. Wenham, *Leviticus,* 139, esp. n. 6. The later models, such as that created by Gideon, probably were all bastardizations of the real thing used at the tabernacle.

specially made by a skilled craftsman so that it would be a truly high-quality garment.[416] Its two "shoulder pieces" (v. 7) were either loops or straps or cords that allowed the front and the back of the garment to be tied together once the ephod was placed on the high priest. We cannot tell from this description whether the ephod was somewhat like a rectangle with a neck hole in the middle that was put over his head and then attached at the sides by these "shoulder pieces" or whether it was essentially a two-part garment, with a front piece and a back piece, the two pieces hanging on the shoulders of the high priest by straps designated as shoulder pieces.[417]

The ephod also had to be secured around the high priest's waist, lest it hang loosely in the manner of a signboard. For this purpose a special, elaborate "waistband" (v. 8) of the same fabric and coloring as the rest of the ephod was attached to it, perhaps at the edges of the back piece and wrapped around the wearer's body and tied—somewhat in the manner of tying the waistband of a modern-day bathrobe that has an attached waistband that ties at the front, or any sort of jacket or vest that has a integrated waistband or "belt" that hangs down to the side when not fastened but is otherwise worn fastened at the front.

28:9–10 Although what we read here is a general verbal description much less detailed than the actual visual plans Moses saw on the mountain (25:40; 26:30; 27:8), we can discern from the description given that the special feature of the ephod per se (leaving aside the breastpiece) was its shoulder stones. These two stones, one for each shoulder, were made of onyx and engraved with the names of the sons/tribes of Israel (v. 9), six names on each stone in order of the births of Jacob's twelve sons (v. 10). We cannot be certain, however, that we actually know the birth order of those children.

The accounts in Gen 29–30 and Gen 35 are organized in such a way as to suggest the order of the various sons, but the order may be more thematic than chronological.[418] If the naming order given in Gen 29–30; 35 is

---

[415] The sole exception is Lev 8:8, where the breastpiece is mentioned as part of the ceremony of ordination of Aaron and his sons since in that ceremony the donning of all the various priestly garments and following of various processes for ordination are all specifically and individually described as a model for future generations. Such specificity never again occurs, however, and the term *ephod* thereafter covers the notion of both the ephod and its attached breastpiece.

[416] Cf. vv. 5,15; 26:1,31,36; 36:35; 39:3,8.

[417] The NIV translates the Hb. of v. 7 as calling for shoulder pieces that attach at the *corners,* but with the HCSB, NRSV, and other versions, these can be understood as attaching at the "edges." Either translation is defensible in light of the ambiguity of the wording.

[418] In other words, as one reads the accounts in those chapters, linked as they are to the various wives of Jacob/Israel, one observes that the accounts do not shift back and forth from birth to birth, as we might expect, but tend mainly to shift from the various births of one wife to the various births of another. There are slight exceptions to this, as in Gen 30:22, when Joseph's birth to Rachel is separately recorded after a series of births to Leah, with language related to the timing that seems to require the conclusion that Joseph was born after all of Leah's and all of Bilhah's children were already born. But fixed as that chronological point in the order may be, the exact birth order of Leah's children relative to Bilhah's children is not so evident.

followed and the names engraved on the onyx stones started on the right shoulder's stone[419] and continued in order, the right shoulder stone would have borne the names of Reuben (Gen 29:32), Simeon (Gen 29:33), Levi (Gen 29:34), Judah (Gen 29:35), Dan (Gen 30:5), Naphtali (Gen 30:8). The left shoulder stone would have been inscribed with the names of Gad (Gen 30:11), Asher (Gen 30:13), Issachar (Gen 30:18), Zebulun (Gen 30:20), Joseph (Gen 30:24), and Benjamin (Gen 35:18). If this understanding of what is meant by the listing order in Gen 29–35 is correct, namely that it represents the actual birth order, then this was indeed the likely order of delineating the sons/tribes of Israel in *this* case. It is not, however, the way the sons/tribes are necessarily always listed. In fact, the names are almost never listed in the same order, giving pause to the assumption that we can actually know for certain the correct chronological order. Here is a summary of just some of the relevant passages:

Gen 29–35	Reuben, Simeon, Levi, Judah, Dan, Naphtali, Gad, Asher, Issachar, Zebulun, Joseph, Benjamin
Gen 46:8–27	Reuben, Simeon, Levi, Judah, Issachar, Zebulun, Gad, Asher, Joseph, Benjamin, Dan, Naphtali
Gen 49	Reuben, Simeon, Levi, Judah, Zebulun, Issachar, Dan, Gad, Asher, Naphtali, Joseph, Benjamin
Exod 1:2–6	Reuben, Simeon, Levi, Judah, Issachar, Zebulun, Benjamin, Dan, Naphtali, Gad, Asher (Joseph is necessarily mentioned out of order as already in Egypt, in 1:6.)
Num 1:5–15	Reuben, Simeon, Judah, Issachar, Zebulun, Joseph, Benjamin, Dan, Asher, Gad, Naphtali
Num 1:20–42	Reuben, Simeon, Gad, Judah, Issachar, Zebulun, Joseph, Benjamin, Dan, Asher, Naphtali (Levi is omitted from this list because Joseph's sons Ephraim and Manasseh combine to compensate for Levi's choice as the clergy tribe in this context.)

Because the biblical text does not give us a list of the sons of Israel that is unambiguously identified as being in birth order, we cannot be certain of the actual birth order of the sons of Israel. We can, however, be sure of two things: (1) Moses and the Israelites did know that order; and (2) it wasn't an order that was usually regarded as important enough to use in most of the listings of those sons, so we cannot infer from the command to list the names in order in this context that it was anything beyond a logical or natural way to group the names. In other words, no evidence exists to suggest that the birth order was the *preferential* order. Rather, listing the names in

[419] We assume that the names would start at the right because alphabetical Semitic languages such as Hebrew read from right to left.

birth order probably had no further significance than to suggest that just as Jacob's sons were born in order to him and became the "sons [*family*] of Israel" (usually translated "house of Israel"), so the high priest represented the whole *family* of Israel in God's presence as symbolized by the ephod shoulder stones.

28:11–14 The valuable stones were to be carefully engraved, with the names cut deeply and permanently into the onyx ("the way a gem cutter engraves a seal"),[420] mounted in fancy gold settings to enhance their dignity, fastened permanently to the shoulders of the ephod by braided gold chains, and thus borne by Aaron with him whenever he ministered in the presence of Yahweh, "as a memorial before [Yahweh]"—a reminder to all that Aaron represented not merely himself but the whole people and that the whole people were important to God. The stones were not hidden or a minor embellishment on the ephod. They hung by their special gold chains and swung noticeably as Aaron moved, an easily visible reminder of the people's corporate solidarity with Aaron before the Lord of Glory.

THE BREASTPIECE (28:15–30). The breastpiece was a square fabric pouch used for divination. We can think of it as a huge (eighteen inches square), fancy pocket worn over the high priest's chest as part of the ephod that held stones used for discernment of the will of God. These stones, called Urim and Thummim ("lights" and "darks"; see the excursus below), were used in faith (but in a manner not ever described exactly in the Bible) to get answers to questions the Israelites had for God. The breastpiece was, however, not merely a storage place for these important stones. It was also a place where yet another representation of the twelve tribes of the Israelites could be borne by the high priest as he ministered in the presence of Yahweh. Already the reader is aware that the two onyx shoulder stones of the ephod held the engraved names of the twelve tribes, six to a shoulder stone (vv. 9–12). Now the reader learns that there would be yet another means of representing those twelve tribes—this time by twelve individual precious stones, one for each tribe, with the name of a single tribe engraved on a single stone. By means of the combination of the shoulder stones and the breastpiece stones, the Israelite tribes were represented both as groups and individually by the high priest. In

---

[420] Seals had to be inscribed deeply so as to be able to make a clear and legible impression in the clay (later wax) to which they were applied. Merely scratching the names into the onyx would not even have come close: the names were cut deeply and precisely into the gemstone.

that way both the entire family and the individual families were "listed" before God at all times of worship.[421]

28:15 Like the ephod and other materials associated with the tabernacle, the breastpiece had to reflect the royal colors, fabric, and precious metal of the inner part of the tabernacle and had to be made to exacting standards by a fabricator of the highest ability ("the work of a skilled craftsman"; cf. 26:1,31; 28:3,6; 31:5; 35:33). This emphasizes once again the integrated way that tabernacle and priesthood worked together and that the purpose of that work was to represent the great king Yahweh to his people and vice versa.

28:16 This description of the dimensions of the breastpiece could be misunderstood as suggesting that it started as a square eighteen by eighteen inches ("a span long and a span wide"), which was then folded over into a rectangle ("folded double") measuring eighteen by nine inches. More probably, the final dimension after folding is intended, so that the cloth *before* being sewn into a big pocket/pouch was actually thirty-six inches by eighteen inches (two spans by one span) in addition to the gold chains that attached it to the ephod proper (see below). Although we do not know Aaron's size and weight, the fact that the average adult male Israelite of that time was about five feet two inches tall and weighed about one hundred and thirty pounds suggests that the average high priest would have this breastpiece stretched over his full chest—from under his armpits to his waist and from the middle of one side to the middle of the other side of his torso—covering his whole chest and belly area. In other words, the breastpiece was not merely a patch on his ephod but a square frontal vest, a very prominent, central, expansive, symbolic display of the covenant relation of God to his people.

28:17–21 Twelve stones arranged three to a row in a total of four rows, engraved and mounted comparably to the ephod shoulder stones (v. 11), represented the tribes of Israel. The text provides no grounds to think that the particular kinds of stones had any special value except that they were all valuable gems, indicating how precious the Israelites were to Yahweh. Indeed, no little diversity exists as to the actual identification of these gems, as the following comparison on page 611 indicates.[422]

---

[421] Psychologically, this sort of "listing" may have been encouraging even to Israelites *as individuals*. Full worship is always corporate in the Bible, so no Israelite who properly understood the nature of worship would resent the fact that the stones represented him or her through his or her tribe. But consider the extrapolation that can be made on the basis of the comparison of "size of group" from the shoulder stones to the breastpiece stones: i.e., from six tribes per stone to one tribe per stone. If that pattern is extrapolated to its logical conclusion, the individual could realize that eventually it would go to clans, families, and individuals so that as different sized units were represented by the gem stones worn by the high priest, God was aware of different sized units of his people, and concerned for all of them, right down to the individual (and for that matter, to the individual parts of his or her body: Matt 10:30).

	NIV	NRSV	HCSB
v. 17	ruby, topaz, beryl	carnelian, chrysolite, emerald	carnelian, topaz, emerald
v. 18	turquoise, sapphire, emerald	turquoise, sapphire, moonstone	turquoise, sapphire, diamond
v. 19	jacinth, agate, amethyst	jacinth, agate, amethyst	jacinth, agate, amethyst
v. 20	chrysolite, onyx, jasper	beryl, onyx, jasper	beryl, onyx, jasper

28:22–28 The breastpiece was clearly a separate item from the ephod and was not sewn to it but attached by gold chains at the shoulders and gold rings at the waist, as described rather clearly in these verses. It needed attachment so that it would function as a real garment and not as a swinging appendage (v. 28). Why would it not have been simply made as a frontpiece to the ephod—a pocket sewn on the ephod as it were? The simple answer may be that it was desirable to be able to clean/launder the two garments separately. The high priest handled blood regularly, splashing it and dabbing it and sprinkling it in a variety of worship practices.[423] Although we are not told explicitly how these garments were cleaned, they must have been regularly rinsed/washed in some way so as to keep them from becoming foul smelling, encrusted, and blackened from dried blood.

28:29–30 These two verses indicate the two special purposes of the breastpiece: representation and divination. With regard to representation, the high priest (Aaron stood for himself and all his successors) "will bear the names of the sons of Israel over his heart." Why? "As a continuing memorial before the LORD," that is, as a symbol of the fact that whatever he did, he did as the people's representative, and his actions would have the same essential effect they would have if all of them, one by one, had done the same thing. The high priest symbolized all Israel.

[422] One could engage in a thorough discussion of the evidence and options for identifying these gems, but its value would be virtually counterproductive, suggesting that knowing the exact gems was the key to something about the meaning of the passage or the breastpiece, when the text makes no hint of such. Any twelve gems, as long as they were truly valuable, would have symbolized the value of the tribes to their God. No faithful Israelite or tribal group would have said any such thing as "Shucks—all we got was the jasper!" Cf. J. S. Harris, "The Stones of the High Priest's Breastplate," *AnLeeds* 5 (1966): 40–62.

[423] Cf. 24:6,8; 29:12,16,20–21; 30:1ff.; Lev 1:5,11 passim.

Excursus: The Urim and Thummim

As regards divination (seeking the will of God by some sort of physical action), the breastpiece's pocket was the holding place for the divination stones, the Urim and Thummim ("lights" and "darks"[424]). How were these used? There are three strong possibilities: (1) A number of light and dark stones were contained in the pouch. When, in faith and with prayer, the high priest asked God questions, he would then pull out stones one by one to give answers, a light stone perhaps indicating yes and a dark one indicating no (or vice versa). (2) Only two large stones were in the pouch. Each time the high priest had a question for God on behalf of the people, he reached in and found one. Its color told him, as above, the answer. Then he replaced the stone and reached again for a new answer. This seems unlikely since it would have been all too easy for the priest to have a fairly good sense of which of the two stones was where in the pouch. (3) Two or more stones were in the pouch, shaped something like dice, with alternating sides or faces colored light and dark. These were pulled from the pouch, "thrown" as dice are thrown, and examined to see which colors came "up."[425]

We have no indication from biblical material that allows us to sort among these options and understand what the Urim and Thummim looked like and how they actually were employed physically. What we do know is that God sometimes chose to reveal his will in this manner rather than by speaking directly to the people. No less an important decision than the choosing of a replacement for Judas for the inner core of the church's apostolic witness was reached in a similar manner in the New Covenant (Acts 1:26), suggesting that God may honor a nonverbal means of choice or discernment of his will from among options or in response to questions posed. It should be obvious to the reader of the Pentateuch and the Bible in general, however, that God did not and does not normally use "divination" methods as his primary mode of revelation.

The term "over his heart" is used twice in these verses (once in the form "over Aaron's heart")—referring in turn to the position of the names of the Israelite tribes as well as to the Urim and Thummim stones used to discern the will of God. The Bible does not teach that the heart was the center of the emotions or of the spirit or of the mind, but all these concepts were alive and well in the culture in which the Bible was revealed and were part of the idiomatic language and conceptual framework reflected in the Bible's language (much like the expressions "learn it by heart" or "I haven't the heart for . . ." in today's English). Accordingly, having the breastpiece and its contents "over Aaron's heart" helped Israel-

---

[424] Because of the similarity of *tummîm* to *tāmîm* ("truth," a noun in the usual masculine plural form used for abstract concepts), some commentators over the years concluded that the names of the stones were "Light" (*ʾûrîm,* also a singular abstract in the masculine plural formation) and "Truth." The original meaning appears, however, to have been "lights" and "darks."

[425] Our summary is hardly the only way to think of the options. For different angles on the question see E. Lipinski, "'Urim and Tummim," *VT* 20 (1970): 495–96; E. Robertson, "The 'Urim and Tummim': What Were They?" *VT* 14 (1964): 67–74; cf. E. Reiner, "Fortune-Telling in Mesopotamia," *JNES* 19 (1960): 22–35.

ites understand the value of these objects and the corresponding value to God of his covenant people and of his desire to reveal himself to them.

Theologically, the Urim and Thummim represented something on the order of last resort appeals to God for guidance—not individual guidance but national guidance on matters that would require the agreement and concerted effort of the whole people.[426] The people's first resort was supposed to be obedience to the written covenant since the written covenant constituted the most basic or foundational guidance, generally and perpetually applicable, that they possessed. The second resort would be to listen for direct divine guidance through the word of God from a prophet, something that God occasionally, but not necessarily regularly, gave them. The third resort would be prayer, and Urim and Thummim use fall under this category. With prayer, seeking to understand how best to take a national direction of some sort, the Urim and Thummim would be drawn from the breastpiece pouch and examined for God's answer to the people's prayer. It may be assumed that they understood or should have understood that if they had faithfully tried the first two resorts and received no word from the Lord, they might in faith try the third resort, not as a matter of right but as allowed by and guided by an orthodox high priest ministering properly "before the Lord." It may also be assumed that since the Israelites were drawn more often to heterodoxy than orthodoxy and usually preferred idol worship to keeping Yahweh's covenant, their use of the Urim and Thummim would most often have failed—and that they and/or the high priest at any given time may not have known the difference, blinded as they were by their disobedience. The Urim and Thummim were mechanical devices of divination that had validity in certain limited contexts and only as God chose to guide the hand of the high priest in response to faithful prayer from an obedient people. In themselves they were simply colored stones that possessed no intrinsic powers.

THE HIGH PRIEST'S ROBE (28:31–35). **28:31–35** By contrast to the multicolored ephod with its multicolored breastpiece, the robe worn under the ephod was of one color, blue (v. 31). Thus it coordinated in color with the ephod but did not rival it in beauty. It appears to have been a large rectangle, about eight feet long, with a hole in the middle for the high priest's head (v. 32) that was finished all around with a bound collar (NIV "woven edge like a collar"; NRSV "woven binding around the opening, like the opening in a coat of mail"; HCSB "a woven collar with an opening like that for body armor"). The robe would then hang front and back of the high priest, presumably down to about his ankles, with the sides overlapping each other or else actually sewn together. If they were simply overlapped or if the robe was ample enough that

[426] In this connection the NRSV translation of 28:30, "Thus Aaron shall bear the judgment of the Israelites on his heart before the LORD continually," would seem considerably less likely than that of the NIV ("Aaron will always bear the means of making decisions for the Israelites over his heart") or the HCSB ("Aaron will continually carry the means of decisions for the Israelites over his heart before the LORD").

it needed to be gathered to the high priest's body, they would be secured with the sash of the ephod so that the robe provided full coverage of the priest's body. All around the hem (the bottom circumference) of the robe pomegranate-shaped yarn tassels in the dominant colors of the tabernacle and ephod (blue purple and scarlet, v. 33) were interspersed with small gold bells (vv. 33–34).

The pomegranate was a prized fruit of the ancient Near Eastern world, denoting abundance and beauty but without theological significance otherwise.[427] The pomegranate tassels added decorative beauty to the robe but had no special function otherwise, unless they were so closely spaced in connection with the bells that they actually functioned as mufflers for the bells—something that cannot be either proved or disproved from the general descriptions given in the text.[428]

The gold bells at the lower hem of the robe (v. 34) had a most important function: preventing the high priest's death (v. 35). This part of the description implies that the high priest led the other priests into the holy place (the outer room) of the tabernacle in those cases where other priests accompanied him, so whether he was alone or accompanied, he was the first to enter or exit. Yahweh's privacy and dignity were thus further symbolized by the ruling that his house could not be invaded without proper warning. A house that could be entered and exited casually would hardly constitute a royal domicile for the Lord of Glory.[429] Did God actually need to hear the bells to know that the high priest, with or without other priests accompanying him, had entered the tabernacle? Hardly. Once again the value of a part of the vestments resided not

---

[427] In Deut 8:8 the Israelites were promised pomegranates as among the desired fruits of the land of Canaan, and the Israelite spies brought back to the people pomegranates as samples of the abundance of the land they were supposedly about to enter (Num 13:23). Indeed, the complainers in the wilderness remembered the pomegranates of Egypt as part of the greatness of life in that land, which they were foolishly beginning to view wistfully (Num 20:5). The pomegranate flower is regarded as lovely, and the juice was made in ancient times into a sweetened wine (Song 8:2). Generally, the pomegranate was seen as an example of the good life (Joel 1:11; Hag 2:19; Song 4:23; 7:12). Solomon caused pomegranate motifs to be cast in bronze for his temple (1 Kgs 7:18–20; 2 Kgs 25:12 and par). The pomegranate motif was one of many used in decorations in the ancient world.

[428] The (secondary) purpose of muffling would be to keep the bells from hitting each other and therefore scratching, nicking, or denting each other, but simple spacing would have the same effect, so one is forced to conclude that decoration was the sole provable function of the pomegranate tassels.

[429] Cf., e.g., the offense done to Noah by Ham (Gen 9:21–25), a sort of invasion of privacy, apparently motivated by incestual lust. Otherwise, by analogy, since the tabernacle represents heaven generally, the restriction on access to the tabernacle and the death penalty attendant for violation thereof reminded the alert covenant keeper that heaven required permission to enter and could not be invaded or casually entered or accessed by all equally. It was a king's dwelling and open only to those to whom the king chose to grant entry. The alternative was death.

in its actual required function but in the symbolism of that function relative to the covenant reality established by God for the benefit of his people.

THE TURBAN FOREHEAD PLATE (28:36–38). **28:36–38** Although the turban itself has not yet been described (see v. 39), its dominant feature would be the special gold forehead "plate" (NRSV "rosette") that is therefore mentioned first, on the analogy of the way the ark is mentioned before the tabernacle in general or the ephod before the vestments that were actually donned first. The forehead plate was to bear the engraved inscription "HOLY TO THE LORD [Yahweh]" "as on a seal" (thus deeply cut into the gold and of permanent quality; cf. vv. 9,11,21). The "blue cord" that attached it to the turban (v. 37) presumably was colored the same hue of blue as was the robe (v. 31).

The gold forehead plate was not primarily decorative but apparently symbolized Aaron's role as representative of the people in the process of atonement (v. 38). The grammar of v. 38 seems to link the plate with his bearing the people's guilt, so much so that it might be better to translate the verse: "It should be on Aaron's forehead so that Aaron may bear the iniquity of the holy things [i.e., their sacrificial gifts] that the Israelites make holy [i.e., offer as holy offerings] with regard to any of their holy gifts; it must be on Aaron's forehead continually so that they [the people] will have favor with Yahweh." In other words, without the forehead piece on the turban, Aaron's representative role on behalf of the people in seeking forgiveness from sin through offerings might have been nullified or at least endangered.

How could a simple gold plate with a simple inscription on it such as HOLY TO YAHWEH[430] play such an important role in "bearing guilt" and making the Israelites "acceptable to the LORD"? The answer is that conscious faith is central to religious ritual. The person who takes communion thinking that it is a snack during a worship service does not renew in covenant obedience Christ's "death until he comes again" but rather just eats some food (in violation, of course, of the purpose of the ritual; cf. 1 Cor 11:20–22,34). The person who participates in a ceremony of baptism regarding it as a refreshing dip in a body of water has not signified conversion to Christ or the reception of the Spirit but has merely had an extremely truncated bath. The person who attends church merely to look pious has not truly worshiped but has simply been present when other people did. In other words, a person's belief about what he or she is doing in a religious act is essential to the validity of that act.

[430] The term קֹדֶשׁ לַיהוָה, "Holy to Yahweh" [NIV HOLY TO THE LORD], occurs commonly hereafter in Exodus, Leviticus, and Deuteronomy and the Prophets—in a distribution pattern that runs directly counter to the Documentary Hypothesis separative assignment of legal material to P and D respectively. Once the wording was introduced here, it is natural that it would become a "theme" term within Israel's religion, and that is exactly what an empirical survey of the data would suggest. So-called "P" and so-called "D" use the term comparably and indistinguishably.

The forehead piece was merely a *reminder,* to Aaron and the Israelites, that Aaron's actions on their behalf were done in *faith* for a purpose: to receive God's gracious forgiveness of sins that they might be holy, in accordance with his command that they serve him as "a kingdom of priests and a holy nation" (19:6). It was their faith that Aaron's actions were done faithfully and in faith on their behalf that saved them from their sins, not the gold forehead piece worn on the turban. The gold piece and its inscription merely symbolized the meaning behind Aaron's actions.

One of Zechariah's prophecies of the great latter days in Christ takes the wording "HOLY TO THE LORD" and uses it within his depiction of a coming time of generalized holiness (Zech 14:20–21: "On that day HOLY TO THE LORD will be inscribed on the bells of the horses, and the cooking pots in the LORD's house will be like the sacred bowls in front of the altar. Every pot in Jerusalem and Judah will be holy to the LORD Almighty, and all who come to sacrifice will take some of the pots and cook in them"). Zechariah depicts the democratization of holiness with the wording of the inscription (as originally only on Aaron's forehead but in the latter days on every horse), bells (as originally on Aaron's robe but in the latter days adorning even horses as an expansion on the function of their usual bells), and cooking pots (as originally used for secular purposes but in the latter days used for holy sacrifices because so many people will worship the true God in spirit and truth that every pot in Jerusalem will be needed). Zechariah's reuse of the present passage's content confirms its meaning: the inscription signifies the holiness that results from obedience in faith, which in the new covenant becomes so widespread that it surpasses what could ever be accomplished by a human high priest, no matter how many sacrifices he might try to make on behalf of the people.

THE HIGH PRIEST'S TUNIC, TURBAN, AND SASH (28:39). **28:39** Here no special symbolism is intended, other than that of the quality of the materials and manufacture as they show appropriateness for service to the great King, Yahweh. The tunic was something like a shirt, and it was almost surely worn under, not over, the robe, though the means of wearing it is never described in the Old Testament. It and the turban were made of linen, with the tunic having a checkered weave—visible perhaps as the sleeves and part of the collar protruded from under the robe.[431] The sash, for tying the robe and inner garments around the high priest's waist, was to be "the work of an embroiderer," a description that uses the same language found already in 26:36 and 27:16 in connection with the tabernacle's inner curtains, thus suggesting that it was to be made to resemble

[431] The NIV translation is not impossible but probably obscures the fact that the tunic was woven in a checkered pattern—decorative, not symbolic. וְשִׁבַּצְתָּ ("you must weave in a checkered pattern") is more overtly rendered by the NRSV, which reads "the checkered tunic of fine linen."

them or "pick up" their motif as part of the high priest's garment, just as the ephod and breastpiece did.

GARMENTS FOR THE OTHER PRIESTS (28:40–43). **28:40–43** The term "Aaron's sons" functions as the standard wording in the Pentateuch to refer to priests in general. For the priests, "tunics, sashes and headbands" [NRSV "headdresses]" were required, undoubtedly specially made but also undoubtedly not exactly the same as those worn by the high priest. As if to underscore this, the word for "headbands" in Hebrew is entirely different from the word for the "turban" worn by the high priest. However these vestments were made, they were of sufficient quality and beauty as "to give them dignity and honor" (v. 40; cf. 28:2) so that the regular priests, who served under the high priest, would still be worthy of service at the house of the Lord of Glory.

Since only "tunics, sashes and headbands" are mentioned among outer garments, it is likely that the regular priests did not always—or ever—wear robes. This would seem to be the point of the wording in 29:7–8 as well. In light of the work at least some of them had—butchering, lifting hunks of meat on and off the altar, separating innards from cookable flesh, carrying coals, cleaning up ashes—the wearing of a robe may not have been appropriate in any case, so the tunics, sashes, and headbands may have been the sole outer garments actually required. It is also possible that these three garments are simply mentioned in the fashion of a synecdoche for all the garments, including a robe, perhaps because the wearing of a robe may have been optional, even weather-dependent. The present text does not unambiguously indicate either option. All priests, however, whether high priest or regular priest, wore linen underpants, "reaching from the waist to the thigh," in accordance with the prohibition against accidentally exposing one's private parts to anything holy to Yahweh (cf. 20:26). In virtually all cultures, public exposure of the area from thigh to waist is considered vulgar, regardless of wherever other bodily "modesty zones" may or may not be identified.

Verse 41 describes an order to be followed for three separate actions: the vesting, anointing, and consecration/ordination of the high priests (and, except for the anointing,[432] of other priests), an order that apparently was not deviated from, judging from allusions elsewhere to the three-part sequence, including the following chapter of Exodus.[433] Its wording should not be construed to imply that "these clothes" were only those mentioned in v. 40; rather the point is that "these clothes" (those required of the high priest and, comparably, those

[432] See comments on 29:8–9.

[433] See esp. Ps 133:2 ("It is like precious oil poured on the head, running down on the beard, running down on Aaron's beard, down upon the collar of his robes.") and Lev 8:12 ("He poured some of the anointing oil on Aaron's head and anointed him to consecrate him.") In the logical context of both passages, the high priest has been vested, is then anointed and then consecrated/ordained.

required of the regular priests) would be donned prior to anointing with oil and consecration/ordination. Similarly, the final sentence of v. 43 ("This is to be a lasting ordinance for Aaron and his descendants") almost surely refers to all of the regulations in chap. 28 rather than merely the rule about linen undergarments immediately preceding. Accordingly, it is properly set out as a separate paragraph in the NIV.

(10) Laws on Ordination of the Priests (29:1–46)

1"This is what you are to do to consecrate them, so they may serve me as priests: Take a young bull and two rams without defect. 2And from fine wheat flour, without yeast, make bread, and cakes mixed with oil, and wafers spread with oil. 3Put them in a basket and present them in it—along with the bull and the two rams. 4Then bring Aaron and his sons to the entrance to the Tent of Meeting and wash them with water. 5Take the garments and dress Aaron with the tunic, the robe of the ephod, the ephod itself and the breastpiece. Fasten the ephod on him by its skillfully woven waistband. 6Put the turban on his head and attach the sacred diadem to the turban. 7Take the anointing oil and anoint him by pouring it on his head. 8Bring his sons and dress them in tunics 9and put headbands on them. Then tie sashes on Aaron and his sons. The priesthood is theirs by a lasting ordinance. In this way you shall ordain Aaron and his sons.

10"Bring the bull to the front of the Tent of Meeting, and Aaron and his sons shall lay their hands on its head. 11Slaughter it in the LORD's presence at the entrance to the Tent of Meeting. 12Take some of the bull's blood and put it on the horns of the altar with your finger, and pour out the rest of it at the base of the altar. 13Then take all the fat around the inner parts, the covering of the liver, and both kidneys with the fat on them, and burn them on the altar. 14But burn the bull's flesh and its hide and its offal outside the camp. It is a sin offering.

15"Take one of the rams, and Aaron and his sons shall lay their hands on its head. 16Slaughter it and take the blood and sprinkle it against the altar on all sides. 17Cut the ram into pieces and wash the inner parts and the legs, putting them with the head and the other pieces. 18Then burn the entire ram on the altar. It is a burnt offering to the LORD, a pleasing aroma, an offering made to the LORD by fire.

19"Take the other ram, and Aaron and his sons shall lay their hands on its head. 20Slaughter it, take some of its blood and put it on the lobes of the right ears of Aaron and his sons, on the thumbs of their right hands, and on the big toes of their right feet. Then sprinkle blood against the altar on all sides. 21And take some of the blood on the altar and some of the anointing oil and sprinkle it on Aaron and his garments and on his sons and their garments. Then he and his sons and their garments will be consecrated.

22"Take from this ram the fat, the fat tail, the fat around the inner parts, the covering of the liver, both kidneys with the fat on them, and the right thigh. (This is the ram for the ordination.) 23From the basket of bread made without yeast, which is before the LORD, take a loaf, and a cake made with oil, and a wafer. 24Put all these in the hands of Aaron and his sons and wave them before the

LORD as a wave offering. [25]Then take them from their hands and burn them on the altar along with the burnt offering for a pleasing aroma to the LORD, an offering made to the LORD by fire. [26]After you take the breast of the ram for Aaron's ordination, wave it before the LORD as a wave offering, and it will be your share.

[27]"Consecrate those parts of the ordination ram that belong to Aaron and his sons: the breast that was waved and the thigh that was presented. [28]This is always to be the regular share from the Israelites for Aaron and his sons. It is the contribution the Israelites are to make to the LORD from their fellowship offerings.

[29]"Aaron's sacred garments will belong to his descendants so that they can be anointed and ordained in them. [30]The son who succeeds him as priest and comes to the Tent of Meeting to minister in the Holy Place is to wear them seven days.

[31]"Take the ram for the ordination and cook the meat in a sacred place. [32]At the entrance to the Tent of Meeting, Aaron and his sons are to eat the meat of the ram and the bread that is in the basket. [33]They are to eat these offerings by which atonement was made for their ordination and consecration. But no one else may eat them, because they are sacred. [34]And if any of the meat of the ordination ram or any bread is left over till morning, burn it up. It must not be eaten, because it is sacred.

[35]"Do for Aaron and his sons everything I have commanded you, taking seven days to ordain them. [36]Sacrifice a bull each day as a sin offering to make atonement. Purify the altar by making atonement for it, and anoint it to consecrate it. [37]For seven days make atonement for the altar and consecrate it. Then the altar will be most holy, and whatever touches it will be holy.

[38]"This is what you are to offer on the altar regularly each day: two lambs a year old. [39]Offer one in the morning and the other at twilight. [40]With the first lamb offer a tenth of an ephah of fine flour mixed with a quarter of a hin of oil from pressed olives, and a quarter of a hin of wine as a drink offering. [41]Sacrifice the other lamb at twilight with the same grain offering and its drink offering as in the morning—a pleasing aroma, an offering made to the LORD by fire.

[42]"For the generations to come this burnt offering is to be made regularly at the entrance to the Tent of Meeting before the LORD. There I will meet you and speak to you; [43]there also I will meet with the Israelites, and the place will be consecrated by my glory.

[44]"So I will consecrate the Tent of Meeting and the altar and will consecrate Aaron and his sons to serve me as priests. [45]Then I will dwell among the Israelites and be their God. [46]They will know that I am the LORD their God, who brought them out of Egypt so that I might dwell among them. I am the LORD their God.

This chapter prescribes the regulations for proper consecration/ordination of priests in Israel from the time of Moses onward (vv. 1–37), as well as the permanent daily consecration offering for the tabernacle (vv. 38–43). Properly consecrated/ordained priests serving at a properly consecrated house of God would help provide for the presence and blessing of God (vv. 44–46).

The consecration/ordination ceremony described in vv. 1–37 had a total of six steps, three of which were washing, clothing, and anointing the priests, and the other three of which involved preparation and execution of sacrifices. The washing ritual (v. 4) and the first two sacrifices (the bread/cakes/wafers offering of vv. 2–3,23–25 accompany the first two actual sacrifices, that of the bull and the first ram, vv. 10–18) are not particularly unique to priestly consecrations/ordinations and must be considered as functioning to prepare for the ordination and make everything holy. The actual ordination/consecration involves the unique three steps of clothing the priests, anointing them, and specially offering an ordination ram as a sacrifice.

Because of the similarities of Exod 29 and Lev 8–9 (esp. 8), it is not surprising that source critics have tried to identify separate provenances for each and also to determine which is the earlier source. No consensus has emerged, and as Durham states, "The question remains insoluble," but not because, as he suggests, there is a need for "additional information."[434] We would suggest that it remains insoluble because the attempt itself is futile by reason of the fact that there were never two sources but one, and the sources did not originate at different times but at a single time, that of Moses and the Israelites at Sinai. Exodus 29 and Lev 8–9 simply complement one another within the overall structure of the Sinai covenant, with such repetitions as occur being minor in comparison to the large blocks of command-fulfillment repetition within Exodus itself, those differences being a function of the way Leviticus addresses priestly responsibilities in a considerably more focused manner than does Exodus and, specifically, that Lev 8–9 in particular narrates the actual performance of the ordination/consecration ceremony.

OVERVIEW OF THE ORDINATION/CONSECRATION OF PRIESTS (29:1–9). **29:1–9** In parallel to his pattern of presentation in several prior passages, God here first names the materials needed for the process (vv. 1–3) and then begins to describe the process as it would logically unfold. This order has a simple logic to it since the materials would have to be collected considerably prior to the ordination itself. Moses would do the first ordination/consecration, so these commands were addressed to him (in the second-person singular) initially, but in time others would follow this process—presumably the high priest at any given time being responsible to ordain all other priests and even his successors since they would be his son(s).[435]

Note again the explicit language in v. 1 identifying priests as servants of Yahweh. Since the tabernacle was his house, those who worked there on his behalf were his servants. They helped the guests, but they clearly worked for

---

[434] Durham, *Exodus*, 393–94.

[435] There is no evidence in the OT that Israelite kings ever properly ordained/consecrated priests. Moses was not here acting in the role of a king but of a priest since he was, like Aaron, a priest and fully qualified to conduct any priestly business.

Yahweh, not for the people who came to visit Yahweh. The sacrificial food to be gathered included a young bull (ideal for eating, not an old, tough animal) and two perfect rams (it would be easy and not much of a sacrifice to get imperfect ones since farmers cull all but the best males, which they keep for breeding) as well as a variety of wheat flour bread, cakes, and wafers, the latter being unleavened but of high quality, made with plenty of oil. All these represent the ingredients of a special meal.[436] The presentation of the breads in a basket (v. 3) simply reinforced the formality of the meal.

Ritual washing was required for priests (v. 4)—and this in an era when no humans understood anything about germs and the health value of cleanliness. Washing after sacrifice may have been a common-sense sort of convenience in light of the residue of blood, animal parts, and other food a priest might have on his hands. Washing before sacrifice, however, represented obedience to a divine command that came from a divine understanding of the correlation between purity, health, and holiness, even if priests may have thought it was simply so that the holy things would not get dirty. The priests in this instance were washed before being robed, suggesting also respect for the priestly garments that washing would help keep clean (v. 4), and then dressed (vv. 5–6) in the sorts of garments described in chap. 28, here focusing on the high priest's garments. No mention is made of the linen undergarments, which probably were already on the priests when they were brought into the tabernacle for the washing ceremony. In other words, the washing included most parts, but not all of their bodies lest the linen underwear become wet.

Having been washed and dressed, Aaron and the other priests, his "sons" (lit. in this case since his own sons would succeed him as priests and soon enough figuratively applying to his descendants who would serve in that office), were then consecrated (with the special notation that Aaron, as high priest, was also anointed, v. 7). Verse 7 should not be taken as if it described what took place in actual chronological order without interruption after v. 6. In other words, we must assume that the high priest's turban was removed from his head when he was anointed, the oil being poured on his hair and not

[436] Various vegetable and milk-based foods may have been eaten routinely in ancient Israel once the people occupied the promised land, but this unleavened bread/meat combination represents a special wilderness meal that probably was an unusual and noteworthy break from the daily diet of manna. When such a meal was eaten years later, it may have in fact been accompanied by other foodstuffs not mentioned here, for there is no suggestion that they would necessarily have been prohibited or unwelcome. Meat meals were always very special in the ancient world, celebratory and ceremonial. Israelites could eat meat whenever or wherever they chose (Deut 12:15), but most pagans thought that eating meat that was not offered to an idol at a worship shrine was a waste of a chance to get on the good side of a god or goddess.

on his hat.[437] Once the high priest had been properly consecrated/ordained, the other priests were to follow (vv. 8–9), with their vestments donned as appropriate to their status and role, thus differentiated from the high priest both by the nature of their vestments and by their not being anointed as he was.[438] High priest and other priests being washed and dressed in a ritual that was always to be followed, they were ready for the consecration ceremony. It is noteworthy that the priests themselves did not provide the animals for their consecration/ordination. Pagan priests did so (cf. 2 Chr 13:9), but true Israelite priests were born into their role and did not have to buy their office.

THE USE OF A BULL AS A SIN OFFERING (29:10–14). **29:10–14** The sacrifice of the bull in this instance appears to have constituted a sort of preparatory "sin offering," designed to atone for any unforgiven sin the priests may have previously committed and, as it were, brought with them into their ordination ceremony, as well as any uncleanness or holiness that might have somehow defiled the altar of the tabernacle. The instruction "Aaron and his sons shall lay their hands on its head" (v. 10) provides a symbolic means of transferring their guilt to the body of the animal.[439] They could not actually do this transferring but rather were symbolically acceding to the basic principle of sacrifice: something must die in my place if I am to live—here specifically focused on "living" in the manner of a holy priest acceptable to God.

The bull having been slaughtered "in the LORD's presence" (inside the tabernacle enclosure, at least generally before the front curtain of the tabernacle,

---

[437] The purpose of the oil was akin to the purpose of the washing—to effect ritual purity that would symbolize true holiness before God. Oil killed lice, which were otherwise endemic in Bible times, and the high priest could not properly appear before God lousy. The application of plenty of oil to the high priest's head and proper laundering of the vestments would guarantee the absence of lice. (Head lice and "body" lice, the latter being in fact clothes lice and not body lice at all, were thus respectively killed. Cf. H. Zinsser, *Rats, Lice and History* [New York: Black Dog & Leventhal Publishers, 1996]). On the way that anointing oil was accordingly prized, cf. Ps 133:2, which also apparently indicates that the oil was not applied to the high priest's turban but to the head hair, as also confirmed by Lev 21:10.

[438] That anointing did not apply to all priests but only to the high priest. Those passages that refer to the anointing of Aaron and "his sons" do not mean "sons" in the sense of all priests (since all priests were descendants of Aaron, the distinction must be specially noted). From Lev 4:3,5,16; 6:22; 16:32 and esp. 21:10 it seems clear that only the high priest was actually ritually anointed for being properly able to assume office.

[439] It has also been argued by some scholars that the placing of hands on the head of the sacrificial animal signified transfer of ownership, i.e., from the worshiper to Yahweh. Even if this were in part the connotation, it could not have been the full connotation because the worshiper's sin would still not have been transferred. But if one argues that the transfer of ownership takes with it the sin, so that God "receives" the sin and then annihilates it, that would at least preserve the atoning value of the transfer. The simpler and more comprehensive outlook is that laying hands on the animal signified that the worshiper's sin was what transferred to the animal to be put to death. In general, laying on hands is a symbol of the transfer of something: in the NT often a special spiritual gift was what was transferred, as in ordination to a teaching-preaching ministry.

so as to be "at the entrance to the Tent of Meeting,"[440] v. 11), its blood was used to "cleanse" the altar's horns and otherwise poured out at the altar's base, but not with a sense of inclusio (as if applying blood to the top and the bottom of the entire altar would "cleanse" the whole). Rather, the rest of the altar would be cleansed by the blood of the first ram (v. 16), yet to be sacrificed.

In a manner typical of most sacrifices, the fatty parts of various internal organs were offered symbolically to Yahweh as his portion (v. 13),[441] and the useless[442] parts (flesh, hide, offal) were burned outside the camp, completely away from the tabernacle or even any Israelite dwellings. Thus only the blood was used for cleansing the area at the top of and around the base of the altar and a small part of the animal for an offering to God—the vast majority of the bull being simply disposed of by burning. Why? Because no one was to "enjoy" eating this bull. Its death was an atoning, sin-cleansing death rather than any sort of basis for a fellowship meal.[443]

THE FIRST RAM, AS A WHOLE BURNT OFFERING (29:15–18). **29:15–18** Again the priests lay their hands on an animal to symbolize the transference of sin from them to it before it was killed (v. 15). Already a bull had been sacrificed, but only its blood and some fat portions had been employed in a sin-atoning ritual (vv. 10–14). This time the first of the two rams was used, and all of it would be burned on the altar except for its blood, which was sprinkled on the altar on all sides. The blood of the bull was applied to the horns and base of the altar (v. 12), and the rest of the altar was ritually cleansed through the sprinkling of the sacrificial animal's blood on its sides, which were previously not touched by the blood (v. 16). This ram was cut in pieces and its inner parts cleansed of offal and blood by washing (v. 17) so that it constituted properly prepared symbolic "food" for Yahweh. In most sacrifices parts of the animal were thrown away, parts were offered to Yahweh by burning to ashes on the altar, and the rest were cooked and eaten by the worshipers and priests, who each got a share.[444] In this case the entire animal was offered to Yahweh by being burnt to ashes, so all the parts were placed on the altar, and nothing was thrown away or kept by the worshipers or priests (v. 18).

In the vocabulary of offering, God "smells" a sacrifice through its "pleasing aroma." This does not mean that Israelites actually thought he "inhaled" it or the like or that it was food for him as if he actually could get hungry. Rather it was a way of describing the fact that the rising smoke of the sacrifice as it

---

[440] On the term Tent of Meeting for the tabernacle, see comments on 27:21; 28:43.

[441] See Lev 3:3–4 and passim in Lev 3–9.

[442] I.e., useless for this ceremony, though not always useless. Indeed, the meat of bulls was rarely "wasted" in the unusual manner called for here.

[443] For comparable requirements relative to the disposal of the animal outside the camp, cf. Lev 6:23; 10:16–20.

[444] Cf. the descriptions in Lev 1–7.

burned up on the altar wafted up into the sky and therefore symbolically was given to God and to no one else "by fire."[445]

USING THE BLOOD OF THE SECOND (ORDINATION) RAM (29:19–21). **29:19–21** In the prior two instances of using blood from a sacrificial animal—the bull and the first ram—the blood was employed for ritual cleansing from sin, applied to the altar and its surrounding ground. Its purpose was to cleanse the *place* and the *process*, but not yet the *persons*. Now, however, the blood of the second ram, the ordination ram (see v. 22), was applied to "Aaron and his sons," that is, to the priests. First, the priests to be ordained lay their hands on the ram, once again to transfer their sins from it as they gave it over to Yahweh (v. 19). Then, having properly slaughtered it, the high priest (Moses as the officiant in this initial instance but later whoever was high priest) took some blood collected in the process of slaughter and touched it to the right[446] earlobe, right thumb, and right big toe[447] of each priest being ordained. There was no desire in this ceremony to make the priest all bloody but merely to apply to him a small token of the blood of atonement (v. 20) on exposed flesh at the top,[448] middle,[449] and bottom[450] of his body, suggesting by that distribution that the blood carried out its symbolic function on his entire person.[451] That which remained of the blood after its application to the extremities of the priests the officiant must then "sprinkle . . . against the altar on all sides."

---

[445] All terms related to God's cognition of human activity are essentially "necessary anthropomorphisms." They do not really portray God as merely having the characteristics of a human being on a large scale, but rather credit God with being able to do anything a human being can do and infinitely more. See D. Stuart, "God's Cognition of Human Activity in the Deuteronomic History," B. A. honors thesis, Harvard University, 1964.

[446] Nothing in biblical teaching exhibits a prejudice against the left side of the body, but since the right side is that side used most skillfully by most people because they are right-handed, the application of the blood to the right ear, thumb, and big toe would have seemed appropriate and common sense. Therefore in God's gracious concern to have the ordination/consecration make sense symbolically, the right side was the side that received the blood.

[447] We noted earlier that the lack of specification for shoes or sandals anywhere in the priestly garment prescriptions suggested that priests ministered barefoot. While the current regulation could conceivably have been carried out satisfactorily if a priest were wearing some sort of sandals that were open-toed, it was obviously not intended to be carried out in the case of a priest wearing shoes. On balance the present context suggests as well that the priests ministered barefoot.

[448] His ears were essentially the topmost exposed skin on his body since the turban was right above them.

[449] His thumbs appeared at about the middle height of his body. Because his hands may have been the only uncovered parts of his body at the middle height (assuming the possibility of long sleeves, at least on the high priest's vestments), one of them was appropriately the spot for applying the blood to the middle area as considered from top to bottom.

[450] If the priests did indeed not wear shoes or sandals but served barefoot, the toe was surely at the lowest part of the body.

[451] Since merism (the expression of totality via polarity) is so common in Semitic logic, as demonstrated by the frequency of meristic expressions in the OT (e.g., the expression "good and evil" meaning "all knowledge" numerous times in the OT), it would seem reasonable that this meristic application of the ram's blood to what today are commonly called the "extremities" of the body would likewise convey to the priest and the observers alike a sense of "full coverage" of the blood.

What happened next (v. 21) had yet another symbolism attached to it. Moses retrieved some of the blood that was already applied "against the altar" (v. 20), meaning on its sides (vv. 16,20) and/or its horns (v. 12), mixed it into the anointing oil (a compounded oil that will be described in detail in 30:23–32), and sprinkled that on the priests, with the result that in consequence of all of the process—not just the anointing—"he and his sons and their garments will be consecrated." The text does not state explicitly that the blood taken from the altar was mixed with the special anointing oil, but such a conclusion follows from the facts of the situation. The amount of blood available from the altar would be very small since the smooth bronze metallic surface on the sides and horns (the grill top was not sprinkled or touched with blood) would contain just token amounts of blood—so little that it would be a matter mainly of dabbing at the bits of blood residue after virtually all of it had simply run down the sides onto the ground. What few grams (or more likely milligrams) of blood would be salvaged from the altar in this way would then under no conditions be enough to sprinkle the priests and their clothing. Only by mixing of the tiny bit of blood into the ample supply of anointing oil would Moses or the successive officiant high priests have had enough liquid for the blood actually to reach the bodies and clothing of the priests being ordained.

But blood there must be, no matter how small and token the amount. Why? Because it is the death of Christ that qualifies his servants to be holy enough to enter into the work of his ministry because that death can be signified only by blood, not oil, and because all Old Testament sacrifices point to the ultimate sacrifice of Christ, the sacrifice that actually provides the atonement, to which all other previous sacrifices look for their derived validity. In the logic of the Old Testament's revealed sacrificial system, oil helps signify purity and cleanness, but not forgiveness. The combination of the oil and the blood signify purity of service and forgiveness of sin respectively. Purity and forgiveness made the priests acceptable to God—"consecrated,"[452] meaning "holy."

OFFERING THE REST OF THE SECOND (ORDINATION) RAM (29:22–26). **29:22–26** The selection and distribution of various parts of this second ram were only slightly unique practices; for the most part, they were common to the Old Testament sacrificial system. Giving "the fat, the fat tail, the fat around the inner parts, the covering of the liver," and "both kidneys with the fat on them" to God through burning to ashes on the altar was not unusual but normal (see also below, vv. 27–28). Nor was adding the "right thigh" unique to this particular sacrifice,[453] although the inclusion of a sample of the bread, the cakes made with oil

---

[452] Rendered by the HCSB and NRSV, e.g., as "holy," since the original is simply the adjective קָדֹשׁ most commonly translated by the word "holy."

[453] Cf. the right thigh as the standard allotment for the priests out of a fellowship offering (Lev 7:32–33; 8:25–26; Num 18:18).

and the wafers (v. 23), was special,[454] these ingredients already having been placed near the altar and thus "before the LORD," to be burned on the altar along with the meat. Before being burned, however, both meat and bread were placed in the hands of the priests so they could hold them up before Yahweh as a special symbolic offering—not one they had themselves provided per se but one they symbolically offered to God as their own before it was all put on the altar to be burned up. This symbolic offering is called a "wave offering,"[455] literally worded in the original: "You (masculine singular, still referring to Moses as the officiant) shall wave them as a waving,"[456] a wording that does not negate the fact that the priests would actually be involved in doing the waving but merely emphasized that Moses must see to it that this happened (see also v. 26). On "pleasing aroma to the LORD," see comments on v. 18 above. Verse 26 adds the requirement that the breast meat of the second ram also be presented as a symbolic (wave) offering before being cooked and then consumed by the priests as their share[457] of the ordination ram.[458]

MAKING THE OFFERING PORTIONS AND GARMENTS PERMANENT FEATURES OF ISRAEL'S SACRIFICIAL SYSTEM (29:27–30). **29:27–30** In saying "consecrate those parts of the ordination ram that belong to Aaron and his sons" (v. 27), God did not imply that the breast and right thigh were not already holy for the ordination offering; rather he demanded that they be treated always as holy,[459] to be given only to the priests and never to layworshipers or otherwise

---

[454] But not so special that it was not also included in a somewhat comparable special ordination/consecration, that of the Nazirite, as described in Num 6, esp. vv. 15–17,20. But note that the animals used in a Nazirite consecration ceremony were quite different from those used in the ceremony described here and that there are many other ways animals can be sacrificed (Lev 1–7).

[455] Cf. the many wave offering references in Exod 25:2–3; 35:22; 38:24,29; Lev 7:30; 8:27–29; 9:21; 10:15; 14:12,24; 23:15,17,20; Num 6:20; 8:11–21; 18:18. Other references to the wave offering occur in Ezekiel, Ezra-Nehemiah. Here and elsewhere the terms and are used virtually as synonyms though they may somehow have referred to slightly different motions. Traditional rabbinic Judaism recognized the תְּרוּמָה as implying the raising and lowering of an offering before the altar (the NRSV translated it "elevation offering") and the תְּרוּמָה as implying the moving forward and backward of an offering with respect to the position of the altar. But either of them may also have been used synecdochically as a term encompassing the idea of any altar offering, as appears to be the case in Mal 3:8. See R. Clendenen and R. Taylor, *Haggai, Malachi,* NAC (Nashville: Broadman & Holman, 2004), 416–17.

[456] וְהֵנַפְתָּ אֹתָם תְּנוּפָה. Even though we do not know the exact motions that may have constituted the waving, it is likely that they were at least simply lifting the offered item up in the air in front of the altar and perhaps moving it around or back and forth, then bringing it back down to waist height and placing it on the altar (or not, depending on what type of wave offering it was).

[457] Again "your share" is in the singular in the original but logically does not refer to Moses or his successor officiant only. The singular language allows for a single person, or any greater number as well, to be ordained/consecrated.

[458] The breast meat, like that of the right thigh, was properly the priests' portion of those sacrifices, particularly fellowship offerings, where most of the meat was eaten by the priests and worshipers rather than being burnt on the altar to Yahweh. Cf. Lev 10:14–15; Num 6:20; 18:18.

[459] The basic sense of "holy" is "belonging to God." In this case God delegated this portion of what was his—the offering animal—to be eaten by his servants the priests in future fellowship offering meals.

disposed of. This use of the *piel* of *qdš* reflects the sense of "set aside for my use/the use that I specify." Thus the worshipers were to understand that whenever they offered a fellowship offering, [460]they made a "contribution" (v. 28) to the priests: worshipers could not expect to get the whole animal back, cooked, that they brought in for offering but rather the selectively butchered animal minus the parts that were not already offered to God or given to the priests.

Likewise, vv. 29–30 specify that the high priestly vestments described in chap. 28 (here summarized with mention only of the high priest's vestments but not necessarily ruling out the possibility that a regular priest could inherit his father's vestments as well) would be inherited, so successive generations would not need to make new garments as long as the old ones remained intact and serviceable. To wear the robes of office from one's great forebears would presumably help encourage a new high priest (or any priest) to think of his role as keeping the sacred traditions of the past. Wearing vestments for seven (straight) days (v. 30) was on the one hand necessary since the ordination process was a week-long affair (v. 35). But another purpose may be in view here as well: having the new ordinand dress the part for a full week upon taking office allowed for all to see and get used to the idea that the new successor to the high priesthood had taken over and would now be the one to carry out the high priest's functions. After the seven-day transition period, people would be used enough to the concept that a new person had taken over as high priest, and the vestments could be worn only as needed thereafter.

RESPECTFULLY COOKING AND EATING THE ORDINATION RAM (29:31–34). **29:31–34** The ram had to be cooked within the tabernacle courtyard ("a sacred place") by a means not here specified. Based on information contained in other details (e.g., Exod 27:3; 38:3; Lev 6:28; 1 Sam 2:13–15), however, we can speculate that the meat was mainly boiled in large pots and then "finished" or "browned" ceremonially on the bronze sacrifice altar of the tabernacle. The priests then sat in the courtyard, in front of the entrance to the tabernacle tent itself, to eat their portion of the ram and the remainder of the bread that had not been given to Yahweh symbolically by fire. As befit the ordination apportionment of meat as well as that which would become the standard apportionment in fellowship offerings, only the priests could eat the breast and right thigh, as portions sacred to God and designed for them specifically to eat.

Because this meat and bread had all been consecrated, it was now considered holy, and any remainder of it could not be disposed of in a profane manner, as "leftovers" in a regular home meal could. It could not be kept for later snacking or given away to others or anything of the sort. Therefore anything

[460] The fellowship offering had complexities and subprocedures that are not entirely well understood (cf. commentaries on Lev 3; 7) but in general can be described as an offering designed to provide forgiveness from sin (thus in part analogous to the whole burnt offering) and also to celebrate the covenant fellowship of Yahweh and his people.

remaining after the evening ordination/consecration ceremony could not be eaten even as soon as the next morning but had to be burned—presumably by a fire somewhere within the tabernacle courtyard, but this is not stated. The statement "it must not be eaten, because it is sacred" refers to what it had become" once it was not eaten in the first place, that is, right after being cooked. It changed from the category that we might label "consumable sacred" into the category we might label "too late be consumable sacred." In other words, it had always been sacred/holy (set aside for Yahweh's special use) ever since being offered in the first place, so it belonged to Yahweh and could not be treated as if anyone else had control over it. Since leftovers were not what he had designated his sacred meat to become (though it was consumable when it was first consecrated), now that it was no longer within the time limit for consumption, it was sacred and nonconsumable; what belonged to Yahweh he could treat as he pleased according to his sense of what constituted proper timing for eating food offerings.

SUMMATION OF THE ORDINATION/CONSECRATION OF PRIESTS (29:35). **29:35** Here God concluded the ordination/consecration regulations with a summary statement that said, in effect, that "the preceding is how you are to ordain priests, and the process is to take a full week."

CONSECRATING THE ALTAR (29:36–37). **29:36–37** The paragraphing in the NIV, HCSB, and a number of other English versions indicates that the translators of those versions assumed vv. 36–37 to be part of the ceremony for the ordination of the priests. Although it is certainly possible that the same week was originally used for the consecration of the altar as for the consecration/ordination of Aaron and his sons,[461] these verses almost surely address a separate and distinct ceremony, in which seven bulls, other than those used for the ordination of the priests, were sacrificed, once each day, "as a sin offering to make atonement." By this means the altar was, as a unit, made fit for the use to which it would ever after be put: accepting the offerings placed upon it as gifts to Yahweh symbolizing his acceptance of the death of animals (as they point to the eventual death of Christ) for the forgiveness of sin. No mention is made here of the process of using the blood of a bull to bloody (only) the horns of the altar as was done in the ordination of the priests, the main portion of the bull being burned up outside the camp. The seven bulls used in that ceremony were strictly for the ordination of priests.

These other seven bulls were strictly for the purification of the altar, so any sin that might attend to it from any source (it was, after all, constructed by craftsmen using materials that were not originally sacred) would be expiated. Moreover, the altar was then to be anointed daily for seven days (v. 36), in

---

[461] I.e., the week in which these orders were actually carried out there at Sinai (the first week of the second year after the Israelites had left Egypt; Exod 40).

connection with the special tabernacle anointing that will be described in 30:22–33. Although there are some parallels, as would be expected, between what was done to make the altar holy and what was done to make the priests holy, the differences are also obvious. In the altar consecration as opposed to the priest consecration, no blood was sprinkled on the sides of the altar or dabbed on its horns, no rams or breads were involved, no meal was eaten from the sacrificed animal, and the bulls were offered differently.[462]

The final sentence of v. 37 as it appears in the NIV (and nearly all other English versions) is mistranslated. There is no automatic transfer of holiness by mere contact with a holy object in the Old Covenant, as the translation "whatever touches it will be holy" would infer. Indeed, the opening point of Haggai's third oracle (Hag 2:10–19) is based squarely on the fact that while defilement is transferable, holiness is *not*. What most English translators have failed to recognize is the modal meaning of the imperfect verb form usually (mis-)translated here "will be holy."[463] It should be rendered gerundively, that is, "whatever touches it must be holy." This is a *prescription* rather than a *description,* a requirement that unholy things not be brought into contact with the consecrated altar so as to deconsecrate it and require it to be consecrated all over again.

REQUIRED DAILY GENERAL OFFERINGS (29:38–42a). **29:38–42a** Twice daily on behalf of all the people of Israel, yearling rams and accompanying offerings were made on the tabernacle altar, in the morning and the evening.[464] These rams, cakes, and wine were offered as whole burnt offerings ("offering made by to the LORD by fire," v. 41), which means that they were sin offerings, intended to appeal for forgiveness on the part of the people to their God. Most recent English versions including the NIV and HCSB read "lambs" instead of "rams" here, partly as a concession to modern unfamiliarity with flock animals and partly because it is thought that "lamb" can cover for both lambs and rams, but *kebeś* clearly refers to a ram, that is, a male lamb, as opposed to *kibśāh* (ewe-)lamb. Under only the rarest of conditions would anyone offer a female lamb; they were

[462] Since a "sin offering" was usually a whole burnt offering, it is almost certain that v. 36 requires burning the whole bull on the altar, with no priests or worshipers consuming any part and no disposal of the bull by burning outside the camp (29:11–14).

[463] יִקְדָּשׁ, assuming the "simple" *qal* imperfect. The most common modal meanings of the Hb. imperfect are may, might, should, must, could, can, and would. Any of them may potentially be the preferred translation of the "helping" or "auxiliary" verb used to render the Hb. imperfect since there is no formal/visible difference between a modal imperfect and a simple imperfect in Hb.

[464] Note that these offerings were made at "morning" (not exactly dawn) and twilight (not exactly sundown), so they would be roughly spaced evenly, i.e., what we would think of as about twelve hours apart. In those days before clocks, it was impossible to find a more precise guide to dividing the twenty-four hour day than the sun's rhythms, variable though these were. But surely this spacing of the offerings was intended to cover Israel under God's forgiveness "night and day," as it were.

kept for breeding, milking. It is the rams that were offered, and since the term used here specifies the male,[465] it seems reasonable to render "ram" as the best translation.

The rams were to be a year old; newborns would not do. Since sheep lambing (birthing) takes place in the springtime, the Israelites were required to wait a year or more in many instances before they could offer a ram, which meant they were virtually always offering a fully grown, valuable animal, as opposed to a very young one, as in the case of the Passover lamb/goat kid (see comments on chap. 12). Every day two of these valuable animals died as a reminder of the need for an eventual once-for-everyone and all-time atoning death to cover the sins of the Israelites.

The accompanying offerings rounded out a sort of meal for Yahweh: "A tenth of an ephah" (v. 40; roughly two quarts/two liters) of "fine flour" (milled and sifted flour) was compounded with "a quarter of a hin" (about a quart/liter) of olive oil to make a very rich cake/biscuit dough to accompany each ram, and additionally "a quarter of a hin of wine" (about a quart/liter of wine) was also poured out on the altar as a drink offering. As the meat, dough, and wine sizzled and burned to smoke/ashes, this "consumption" symbolized Yahweh's acceptance of his people's covenant meal.[466] The "pleasing aroma" was in the smoke sent up into the sky to represent the conveyance of the offering to him. Although other offerings were occasional, such as for ordinations or for one of the three annual festivals (23:14–17), these offerings were daily, year-in and year-out offerings, sent up to God from the bronze altar located "at the entrance to the Tent of Meeting before the LORD."

REMINDER AND PROMISE OF THE PRESENCE OF GOD AMONG HIS PEOPLE (29:42b–46). **29:42b–46** The Israelites had clearly seen the presence of God among them in the form of the pillar of cloud/fire that accompanied and led them from Egypt to Sinai. That manifestation of his presence among them would not continue forever. Instead, once the tabernacle was fully built and in use, God's presence would be specially manifest there—still a visible indicator of his living among his people but now in the form of his "house." Thus he promised that "there I will meet you and speak to you" (Moses and presumably anyone who was his proper successor), and "there also I will meet with the Israelites" (v. 43). Eventually Moses would not have to go up to Mount Sinai or seek to speak with God at the older tent of meeting; he would encounter God at the tabernacle, the new tent of meeting, enthroned between the cherubim on the cover of the ark (25:22; cf. Num 7:89).

---

[465] As opposed, e.g., to the more generic *śeh*, which refers to any lamb or goat kid.

[466] The fact that in Hb. fire is said to "eat" (אכל) what it consumes makes the consumption of the food by the fire an appropriate symbol for Yahweh's "consuming" the offering.

In saying "the place will be consecrated [made holy] by my glory," God indicated the real means of sanctification—to which various sacrifices and rituals merely pointed—as his own presence. Where he is, he takes possession, and thus things near him become his and are holy.[467] Nevertheless, the rituals were important, as v. 44 states. The ultimate means of sanctification is God's presence, but the proximate means was obediently carrying out the ritual consecration actions for the "Tent of Meeting" (tabernacle), "altar," and "priests" as the chapter earlier describes. With the tabernacle, as well as its place of expiation through sacrifice (altar) as well as God's servants (priests) to help the people benefit from that expiation, all in place, God could properly "dwell among the Israelites and be their God"—protecting them, blessing them, receiving their worship, and bringing them along toward their eternal salvation. This is the meaning of "I will . . . be their God."

Verses 45–46 reiterate much of the language of promise initiated in Exod 6:7 ("I will take you as my own people, and I will be your God. Then you will know that I am the LORD your God, who brought you out from under the yoke of the Egyptians"). The question might be asked, "Why would the Israelites need to know that their God was Yahweh and that he was the one who had brought them up out of Egypt? How could there be any doubt in their minds?" And the answer is: Indeed, there was doubt, confusion, and a powerful cultural predisposition against the kind of faith in Yahweh that he was trying to teach them to have. While Moses was hearing these very words, directly from God on Mount Sinai in fact, the Israelites at the bottom of the mountain were already grumbling that he had disappeared and that they would need new gods (see comments on chap. 32).

Virtually all those gathered at Sinai had grown up as polytheists, pantheists, and syncretists in Egypt—just as they would have if they had grown up anywhere else in the ancient world for that matter. They had little difficulty in believing that there could be a god named Yahweh who was one of many gods and goddesses. But to believe that he was the *only* God, superior to the most powerful gods they had once believed in,[468] the Creator of the world and their Creator through many miracles as a people—that was harder for them. Sixty-eight times in the Old Testament God told his people that he wanted them to "know that I am Yahweh."[469] This was a different concept from knowing that Yahweh existed; it was a sort of semantically "loaded" shorthand for the assertion: "Know that I, who created and control all things, and have all power, and have been providing all these supernatural blessings for you that you have

---

[467] Again keeping in mind that the essence of holiness is belonging to God.

[468] See comments on 12:12.

[469] In the prophets, e.g., the theme "know that I am Yahweh" often has exactly the same sort of purpose as in the present context: to assert Yahweh's sole sovereignty in the world and reject any sort of polytheism.

been witnessing, am Yahweh—there is no other god doing these things but only me, Yahweh. Give up your polytheism, pantheism, and syncretism and believe that I am the only God and place your full faith in me, obeying my covenant."

What is especially important about the current expression of this theme is its assurance that the Israelites could know Yahweh in their *worship* of him.[470] That worship was the only true, correct, spiritual worship taking place anywhere on the planet. Its implementation through the instructions given in this chapter fulfilled God's original calling promise to Moses in 3:12, "This will be the sign to you that it is I who have sent you: When you [singular, i.e., Moses] have brought the people out of Egypt, you [plural, i.e., Israel] will worship God on this mountain." Now he in fact was proposing to dwell among them and was saying overtly "I am their God." If they would properly and consistently worship him, with all the covenant obedience that proper and consistent worship implied, they would be a people who knew the only true God as *their* God.

(11) Laws on Construction and Use of the Incense Altar (30:1–10)

1"Make an altar of acacia wood for burning incense. 2It is to be square, a cubit long and a cubit wide, and two cubits high—its horns of one piece with it. 3Overlay the top and all the sides and the horns with pure gold, and make a gold molding around it. 4Make two gold rings for the altar below the molding—two on opposite sides—to hold the poles used to carry it. 5Make the poles of acacia wood and overlay them with gold. 6Put the altar in front of the curtain that is before the ark of the Testimony—before the atonement cover that is over the Testimony—where I will meet with you.

7"Aaron must burn fragrant incense on the altar every morning when he tends the lamps. 8He must burn incense again when he lights the lamps at twilight so incense will burn regularly before the LORD for the generations to come. 9Do not offer on this altar any other incense or any burnt offering or grain offering, and do not pour a drink offering on it. 10Once a year Aaron shall make atonement on its horns. This annual atonement must be made with the blood of the atoning sin offering for the generations to come. It is most holy to the LORD."

The fragrant smoke from burning incense symbolized prayer in the biblical world. This connection may be seen somewhat tenuously through the simile in a synonymous parallelism in Ps 141:2 ("May my prayer be set before you like incense; may the lifting up of my hands be like the evening sacrifice") and

---

470 "Thus, as the chapters leading up to Yahweh's Advent on Mount Sinai demonstrate Yahweh's Presence by what *Yahweh* does, the chapters that follow that Advent are here interpreted as chapters that demonstrate that Yahweh is present by what *Israel* does, first of all in the way they are to live, and second, in the places, the symbols and the acts of their worship" (Durham, *Exodus,* 397).

may possibly be reflected in Luke 1:10 ("And when the time for the burning of incense came, all the assembled worshipers were praying outside"). It appears overtly, however, in Rev 5:8 ("They were holding golden bowls full of incense, which are the prayers of the saints") and is confirmed in Rev 8:3 in wording that relates closely to the present passage in Exodus ("Another angel, who had a golden censer, came and stood at the altar. He was given much incense to offer, with the prayers of all the saints, on the golden altar before the throne") and 8:4 ("The smoke of the incense, together with the prayers of the saints, went up before God from the angel's hand").

Because of the way the earthly tabernacle reflected God's heavenly sanctuary (Heb 8:2–5; 9:24), it may be assumed that Moses and the Israelites understood that the incense altar had as its purpose the symbolizing of the prayers of Israel as they were made throughout the land and that the perpetual burning of incense reflected the way people pray at all times of day and night.[471] Inasmuch as the high priest always consciously represented the people in his actions in the tabernacle (see comments on 28:9–12,21,29–30,36–38), his offering of incense was a means of portraying the prayers of the whole people. After Aaron only legitimate, Aaronic priests could offer incense,[472] and only the high priest could do so on the actual golden incense altar that was located in the holy place as described in this passage.

DESCRIPTION AND PLACEMENT OF THE INCENSE ALTAR (30:1–6).

30:1–6 The incense altar was smaller than the bronze sacrifice altar, being eighteen inches ("a cubit") square and thirty-six inches ("two cubits") high. Like the ark (25:10–20), and more particularly like the table (cf. 25:23–28), it was made of acacia wood surfaced with gold, but like the bronze altar (27:1–8) it had rounded corner protuberances extended upward from its top, known as "horns." In a manner akin to the table, it had a decorative molding of gold around the edge of its top, giving it something of a "lip" that would help hold incense on the surface, and it had gold rings through which poles of acacia wood overlaid with gold could be inserted to carry it.

---

[471] It is likely that passages such as 1 Chr 6:49 ("Aaron and his descendants were the ones who presented offerings on the altar of burnt offering and on the altar of incense in connection with all that was done in the Most Holy Place, making atonement for Israel, in accordance with all that Moses the servant of God had commanded") do not actually assert that the offering of incense provided atonement, in the sense of forgiveness of sins, but that the whole process of obedient worship as it centered on the offering of sacrifices on the bronze altar, and included incense offerings, could be referred to as having an atoning purpose. Prayers for forgiveness, which the burning incense symbolized, were indeed a part of the process of forgiveness. Pagan worship also involved incense offerings, with a given incense altar devoted to a given god (2 Chr 30:14; 34:4).

[472] Cf. Num 16:40, "This was to remind the Israelites that no one except a descendant of Aaron should come to burn incense before the LORD." Priests could add incense to offerings on the bronze altar of the courtyard (e.g., Lev 2:2; 6:15; Deut 33:10), but only the high priest could offer incense on the golden altar within the tabernacle itself (e.g., Lev 16:12–13).

The incense altar stood in the holy place and more specifically "in front of the curtain that is before the ark of the Testimony." This description of its placement finds no exact parallel in the placement descriptions of the other holy place furniture (table and lampstand), and the fact that it is followed by an apposition mentioning the atonement cover of the ark ("before [or "in front of"][473] the atonement cover that is over the Testimony") suggests that it was "front and center"[474] directly before the curtain, or in the middle between the table and the lampstand. This would fit the symbolism of the incense as representing prayer before God since the fragrant smoke could be expected to reach into the holy of holies, there to offer its sweet aroma to God, whose presence is represented by the ark in its entirely and more narrowly, by the "atonement cover that is over the Testimony."

PROPER USE OF THE INCENSE ALTAR (30:7–10). **30:7–10** The timing of the offering of incense coincided with that of the morning and evening sacrifices described in 29:38–42. Likewise, it took place at the times when the high priest dealt with the seven lamps on the lampstand (25:31–39), putting them out in the morning and preparing them for lighting again once evening arrived. Once again a twice-daily regimen, spaced as far apart as the seasons would allow so as to be roughly every twelve hours on average, suggested by its symmetry an around-the-clock vigil, in this case a vigil of prayer. The altar

---

[473] The very same Hb. preposition, לִפְנֵי, is translated "in front of" by the NIV earlier in the verse and "before" here simply for variety; but no such variety appears in the original.

[474] It has often been suggested that there is something odd about the way the incense altar is described in this passage since it seems isolated—it isn't mentioned in connection with the other holy place furniture in chaps. 25–26 but comes up for the first time here in chap. 30. Most scholars have tended to assume that the reason for its isolation is that it was somehow left out of the early traditions and was only later added, in this unlikely location, by the "Priestly" (P) writer. Y. Muchiki ("Why the Description of the Altar of Incense Was Postponed (Exod 30:1–10)," *Exeg* 10 [1999]: 19–31) suggests that the placement of the incense altar description is intended to form an inclusio with the descriptions of other tabernacle furniture that begin in chap. 25, so Exod 25:1–30:10 constitutes an obvious unit related directly to the tabernacle and its accompaniments. C. Meyers offers yet another plausible explanation: According to Lev 16; 1 Kgs 7; and Zech 14, the incense altar was used not only inside the holy place but also in the courtyard of the tabernacle. Since the altar could be used outside the actual physical enclosure of the tabernacle proper, the placement of its description here properly fits the idea of the gradations of holiness we have noted already, beginning with the most holy (holy of holies and its one piece of furniture, the ark) and ending with the least holy, the courtyard. Meyers suggests that when the incense altar was used in the courtyard, its position directly in front of the opening curtains made possible the drifting of the incense smoke into the tabernacle proper, in parallel to the way its placement front and center in the holy place allowed its smoke to drift into the holy of holies as well, when the interior of the tabernacle was its location ("Realms of Sanctity: The Case of the 'Misplaced' Incense Altar in the Tabernacle Texts of Exodus," in *Texts, Temples and Traditions: A Tribute to Mehachem Haran* [Winona Lake: Eisenbrauns, 1996], 33–46). Both reasons (that suggested by Muchiki and that suggested by Meyers) may be correct, the two of them combining to make the placement of the incense altar description here instead of earlier in Exodus a "no-brainer" for Moses.

inside the tabernacle holy place was strictly an incense altar, using the special incense that will be described later in the chapter (30:34–38). The prohibition against "any other incense" (v. 9; better: "any foreign/strange incense" or, with HCSB, "unauthorized incense") or food offerings was required by the fact that on the bronze altar, food mixed with incense *could* be offered (Lev 2:1–2,15–16; 6:15). In the absence of this explicit prohibition, priests might eventually have assumed that mixed offerings could, by analogy, be offered on the incense altar as well.

For this altar too a sin-removal ceremony was required, on the analogy of the sanctification of the bronze altar (29:36–37). It was done annually, by way of blood from the Day of Atonement offering, the details of which are described in Lev 16, where the cleansing of the incense altar is not specifically mentioned but is included in the overall description of using blood from a bull and a goat to "cleanse" the furniture of the tabernacle. The statement at the end of v. 10, "It [masculine singular] is most holy to the LORD," refers in all likelihood to the incense altar itself (masculine singular) rather than to the process of cleansing it annually since the process was simply the means to making and keeping the altar "most holy," that is, fully belonging to God and fit for the use he prescribed for it.[475]

(12) Laws on Census Atonement Payments (30:11–16)

[11]Then the LORD said to Moses, [12]"When you take a census of the Israelites to count them, each one must pay the LORD a ransom for his life at the time he is counted. Then no plague will come on them when you number them. [13]Each one who crosses over to those already counted is to give a half shekel, according to the sanctuary shekel, which weighs twenty gerahs. This half shekel is an offering to the LORD. [14]All who cross over, those twenty years old or more, are to give an offering to the LORD. [15]The rich are not to give more than a half shekel and the poor are not to give less when you make the offering to the LORD to atone for your lives. [16]Receive the atonement money from the Israelites and use it for the service of the Tent of Meeting. It will be a memorial for the Israelites before the LORD, making atonement for your lives."

This instruction requires the Israelites to enter into a census only with great caution and under potentially great penalty. Why? What was wrong with

---

[475] Durham (*Exodus,* 400) reviews the history of skepticism about the antiquity of the use of incense and incense altars in Israelite worship. Partly based on his own dissertation ("The Senses Touch, Taste and Smell in Old Testament Religion" [D. Phil. Thesis, Oxford, 1953], 373–77) and published works of W. F. Albright (*The Archaeology of Palestine and the Bible* [New York: Revell, 1933], 108–9), G. E. Wright (*Biblical Archaeology* [Philadelphia: Westminster, 1962], 114–15), K. Galling ("Incense Altar," *IDB* 2:699), N. Glueck ("Incense Altars," in *Translating and Understanding the Old Testament* [Nashville: Abingdon, 1970], 325–42), and others, he concludes that the archaeological evidence for the early use of incense and incense altars in Israel is compelling.

taking a census? Isn't it useful to know the population figures? The answer is that in the ancient world, as far as we know, a census was taken for one of only two purposes: to prepare for war or to impose some sort of taxation. In ancient Israel there was technically only one purpose: to prepare for war. Because the Israelites had no right to go to war except for the taking and holding of the promised land by holy war[476] as called explicitly by Yahweh through a prophet and because they had no right to impose taxes beyond the contribution system revealed in the law by God himself, the taking of a census would constitute in most cases an act of direct covenant disobedience.

King David himself ran afoul of this law. In 2 Sam 24 one reads the account of his insistence on a census, even though he was opposed vigorously by his military commander-in-chief, Joab, because David had decided to go beyond his divinely assigned task of taking and holding the promised land to form an empire incorporating territories outside of the promised land. This action by David resulted in a severe plague, just as v. 12 of the present passage warns would happen. In light of the severity and risk of census taking, Israelites were instructed by this passage to regard their lives as in danger and to pay a ransom for themselves whenever they entered into a census.

30:11–12 The opening words of this set of laws assume there will be occasions when the Israelites are properly to take a census but at the same time sternly inform them that they must never get used to the idea as if it could be done at whim or in any way as a matter of their own discretion. The reason that each person had to pay a ransom for his[477] own life, even though he was simply being counted rather than doing the counting, was that the voluntary nature of Israel's army meant that each person counted was deliberately and cooperatively allowing himself to be counted. This is, in fact, the meaning of the term "crosses over" employed in v. 13. People willing to fight had to be reminded that they could not choose when, where, against whom, or anything else related to that fighting. They could choose to fight or not, but that only; all other aspects of the holy war process was God's decision, not theirs. God announced that a plague would be the penalty for breaking this law, including conducting a census without the ransom payments. Since a plague was, by definition, a judgment on the corporate rather than the individual, it would be imposed by reason of a general failure to have a ransom system in place rather than any isolated instances of individuals' not coming up with the ransom money or failing to provide the full amount or the like.

What was "a ransom for [one's] life" (v. 12)? It was a payment through which one symbolically bought his [or in special cases another's] life back from God. It was not a penalty for being willing to go to war or a bribe paid to

---

[476] See "Excursus: Israelite Holy War" at 17:9.

[477] In the case of being counted for a census, only men were involved.

God in order to escape death in war. Rather, it recognized two important facts: (1) God owns the lives of his people, and (2) although he would have the right to require his people to lose their lives in battle, he generously gave them back their lives so they could enjoy the abundant life he had for them within his covenant protection. These two principles are seen in the ransom/redemption[478] laws found already in Exodus[479] as well as being related to the concept of *atonement* (see below). In 13:13, for example, we read: "Redeem with a lamb every firstborn donkey, but if you do not redeem it, break its neck. Redeem every firstborn among your sons." What was the point of this sort of law? It was that something that rightfully belongs to God (e.g., firstborn animal, firstborn son) may be given back to its owner (e.g., one's life) rather than taken by God as long as his rightful claim to it is recognized by the payment of the appropriate ransom/redemption/atonement fee in substitution for the thing itself. Thus if the Israelites were not capable of being ransomed, it would mean that they were in fact destined for death in war, on the principle enunciated in Lev 27:29, "No person devoted to destruction may be ransomed; he must be put to death."[480]

The conceptual interconnection of ransoming and redeeming is confirmed by the New Testament's use of these terms for the same act of Christ on our behalf: that he *ransomed* us from death or *redeemed*[481] us from death is one and the same assertion. If we compare such statements using the language of "ransom" as Matt 20:28 ("just as the Son of Man did not come to be served, but to serve, and to give his life as a ransom for many"), or 1 Tim 2:6 ("who gave himself as a ransom for all men"), or Heb 9:15 ("now that he has died as a ransom to set them free from the sins committed under the first covenant") with such passages as Gal 3:13 ("Christ redeemed us from the curse of the law by becoming a curse for us"), or Gal 4:5 ("to redeem those under law, that we might receive the full rights of sons"), or Titus 2:14 ("who gave himself for us

[478] The reader will note that we are following here a line of reasoning that takes "ransom" (כֹּפֶר) in the present context as a virtual synonym for "redemption" (פִּדְיֹן) because of the similarity of usages of the two terms/roots. E.g., in 21:30 the language of "paying a redemption for one's life" (נָתַן פִּדְיֹן נַפְשׁוֹ) is not significantly different conceptually from the expression here in 30:12, נָתְנוּ אִישׁ כֹּפֶר נַפְשׁוֹ.

[479] And as well in those that follow the present passage. Of special relevance are Exod 13:15, "When Pharaoh stubbornly refused to let us go, the LORD killed every firstborn in Egypt, both man and animal. This is why I sacrifice to the LORD the first male offspring of every womb and redeem each of my firstborn sons"; Exod 21:30, "However, if payment is demanded of him, he may redeem his life by paying whatever is demanded"; Exod 34:20, "Redeem the firstborn donkey with a lamb, but if you do not redeem it, break its neck. Redeem all your firstborn sons."

[480] Since in holy war the spoils were forbidden but became "devoted to destruction," the law of Lev 27:29, while addressing a different matter from holy war, nevertheless actually addressed the principle of *ḥrm* (devotion to destruction) in an informative manner.

[481] Indeed, in most Eng. versions of the NT, both terms, "redeem" and "ransom," can be found as translations of the same Gk. verb, λυτροῦσθαι, or its noun, λῦτρον.

to redeem us from all wickedness and to purify for himself a people"), it becomes evident that the two ideas are comparable metaphors for describing the same phenomenon.[482] Although the concept of atonement is yet another concept, it overlaps with these two to describe the same phenomenon as well.[483]

30:13–15 Israel's all-volunteer holy war army was made up of men aged twenty years and older[484] (there was no automatic upper age limit). No matter how wealthy or poor anyone was, the same price of a half shekel was to be paid as the ransom/redemption price upon volunteering for duty. This indicates the classless nature of Israelite society under God's covenant: everyone had the same value, and no one could claim to be special or privileged when serving in God's army as his agents of judgment on corrupt cultures.[485] The process of volunteering involved, as the term "cross[es] over" implies, having potential volunteers grouped facing a recruiting leader, who would call for all men twenty years or older who were fit and willing to join in battle to cross over to him, that is, to walk from where they were standing to where he was standing so their enlistment could be visible to all.[486] A half shekel (about a fifth of an ounce of silver) was not a fortune[487] but was sufficiently demanding so that the ransom/redemption was costly enough that it could not be regarded by anyone as trivial.[488] In v. 15 note that the expression "to atone for your lives"[489] is also used to describe the process of ransom/redemption, providing yet another angle on the concept of substituting something for one's life so that one may have one's life back. In v. 16 the payment is termed "the atonement money" (or, very literally, "the atonement silver" since at this point

---

[482] This phenomenon can also be described with such terms as "atonement" and "reconciliation" and "propitiation." Even though each of these terms has a distinctive nuance, each is also appropriate to denote the achievement of Christ's sacrifice in winning back sinners from the penalty of death.

[483] See below in reference to the vocabulary employed in vv. 15–16, and cf. the "atonement/atone" vocabulary of Rom 3:25; Heb 2:17; 1 John 2:2; 4:10.

[484] Cf., e.g., Exod 38:26; Num 1:3,18,20,22; 26:4; 32:11; 1 Chr 27:23; 2 Chr 25:5.

[485] For further explanation see "Excursus: Israelite Holy War" at 17:9.

[486] In all likelihood a recruiter or messenger/recruiter would arrive at a tribal encampment, or later in Israel's history village or section of a city, and ask that all men twenty years and older would assemble in a square or other appropriate location, give a speech describing the nature of the impending war/battle for which he was recruiting soldiers and reminding all present that no one had to serve, and then ask for volunteers to fight symbolically as Yahweh's army. The process finds substantial description in such passages as Deut 17; Judg 19–20; and passim within the historical books.

[487] Cp. the valuations of Lev 27:3–7 or Num 3:47.

[488] In terms of buying power at that time, it would have had the equivalent of what several hundred dollars would mean to a modern American.

[489] לְכַפֵּר עַל־נַפְשֹׁתֵיכֶם.

the Israelites probably did not possess coins in abundance but did have precious metals that could be weighed out).

30:16 This verse explains why God gave the present instruction about census ransom/redemption/atonement payments at this point in Exodus. The money collected was to be used for the "service" (upkeep, general expenses, related to proper worship, the exact expenditures presumably determined according to the decision of the high priest at any time as he was sensitive to the leading of God) "of the Tent of Meeting,"[490] that is, given to Yahweh for his house (tabernacle).[491] Moses may have been the person to receive the collected payments prior to the conquest; thereafter it would have been one of the successors of Aaron, but they were only intermediaries. Each payment was directed to Yahweh for his service/worship.

The money given thus functioned as "a memorial for the Israelites before the LORD," a visible token or indicator of the fact that Yahweh knew that the volunteers belonged to him and thus were holy.[492] They had made "atonement" for their lives and knew that Yahweh regarded them as his own.[493] Since such a practice has its ultimate analogy in the death of Christ as a payment for atonement for sins, one should not forget that this divine substitutionary death causes all who believe in it by faith to be remembered by God as his own.[494]

(13) Laws on Construction and Use of the Washing Basin (30:17–21)

[17]Then the LORD said to Moses, [18]"Make a bronze basin, with its bronze stand, for washing. Place it between the Tent of Meeting and the altar, and put water in it. [19]Aaron and his sons are to wash their hands and feet with water from it. [20]Whenever they enter the Tent of Meeting, they shall wash with water so that they will not die. Also, when they approach the altar to minister by presenting an offering made to the LORD by fire, [21]they shall wash their hands and feet so that they will not die. This is to be a lasting ordinance for Aaron and his descendants for the generations to come."

---

[490] On the term "Tent of Meeting" see also "General Summary of the Tabernacle and Its Courtyard at 26:1.

[491] In other words, the money collected probably was put into a fund from which expenditures could be made from time to time (as for replacement curtains or regilding of poles or the like) rather than spent as soon as received. Since the Israelites did not go to war constantly, there would be times when the fund was low and other times when the fund was flush with money.

[492] Again we remind the reader that the essence of holiness was belonging to God.

[493] Thus this memorial (זִכָּרוֹן) compares with the symbolism of the Passover (cf. the use of זִכָּרוֹן in Exod 12:14; 13:9 and in 28:12 that of the high priest's shoulder stones and in 28:29 that of the breastpiece's twelve jewels).

[494] Cp. also the allusion to the redeemed belonging to God as holy warriors in Rev 14:1–5. There the 144,000 who are the "firstfruits" (the first believers throughout the Roman Empire representing twelve thousand believers for each of the first twelve disciples and thus symbolizing the unstoppable growth of God's kingdom in counterdistinction to the Roman kingdom) have "kept themselves from women" just as David's holy warriors had done according to 1 Sam 21:4–5. Cf. also 2 Sam 11:8–11.

30:17–21 Certain laws in the Old Testament reflect God's concern for the health and/or safety of his people, in addition to his concern to teach them by the symbolism of those laws how to be a holy people and to respect his holiness as they approach the symbols of his presence. The law in this passage concerning construction and use of a bronze wash basin is one of these dual-purpose laws.[495] The basin itself is not described except for its composition (bronze),[496] its general shape (a basin), and the fact that it must be placed upon a stand, also to be made of bronze.[497] The emphasis of the passage is, in fact, not on the design of the basin at all but on its purpose: to provide a water supply for washing hands and feet in connection with any holy purpose in the tabernacle or tabernacle courtyard.

Most modern people know because of discoveries that are for them now more than a century old that washing hands and feet helps prevent the contraction and spread of disease. Even in modern times, however, washing is not taken seriously enough by many people.[498] In Bible times there was no understanding of germs or of the fact that washing skin could remove nearly all infectious microbes from skin. God, however, understood the process entirely and benefited his people by teaching them the value of washing both hands/arms[499] (the need for which is obvious since people use their hands to "han-

---

[495] Others would include the Levitical food laws, virtually all of which protected the Israelites from pathogens and allergens, especially since these would have been dangerous in the Sino-Palestinian climate of Bible times before refrigeration or any knowledge of other means of safe food preparation and diet rotation to avoid allergen loading. Included as well would be the sexual purity laws that helped prevent the communication of sexually transmittable diseases.

[496] Note that once again the "common" metal was bronze; these instructions date from the Bronze Age, from a time before fine iron working was known, at least among the Israelites, so that an item as complicated to craft as a wash basin would not even be thinkable as a possibility for production in iron.

[497] Not even the dimensions of the stand are given, either here or in the parallel fulfillment description (38:8). It probably was fairly small, perhaps holding several gallons of water, in light of the need for all the tabernacle furniture to be portable. The huge bronze lavers Solomon built for the temple could be much larger because they were fixed structures. Each of the ten Solomonic lavers held about two hundred and fifty gallons and was about eight feet high (1 Kgs 7:27–39), requiring a priest to climb to the edge for washing. One gets the impression that the tabernacle basin on its stand may have reached perhaps three or four feet high, by contrast.

[498] Perhaps the most classic example is the way hepatitis A is spread in most cases by food preparers or handlers who are themselves infected but have not taken the trouble to wash their hands (or feet or shoes in the case of persons spreading the disease in farm fields) before coming in contact with food. Repeatedly, these and similar outbreaks are traced to individuals who did not bother to wash before handling food.

[499] In all likelihood the priests washed their "hands and feet" in such a way as to make their forearms and forelegs clean as well and would not have washed only their hands if their wrists and ankles (or higher on each limb) were also dirty. The Ugaritic description of Baal's cleaning up for sacrifice with the synonymous parallel couplet "he washed his hands to the elbow, his fingers to the shoulder" has sometimes been taken as a humorous exaggeration but may also represent something of the sense of how *yād* can refer to an area greater than merely the extremity of the arm beyond the wrist. Moses had already used it to mean forearm in Exod 17:11. Cf. also 1 Kgs 10:19 (the arm rests on the throne described, lit., as "hand rests"); 2 Kgs 5:18.

dle" things) and feet/lower legs (the need for which was also acute in tabernacle service, which was undertaken by priests, as we have noted, barefoot).[500]

But the cleansing of priests' hands and feet required by this law had for them its greatest value in teaching the importance of purity. Dirt represents a visible indication of adulteration of a clean thing. Dirt in food mars the taste; dirt in clothing changes both the appearance and potentially even the comfort of the clothing. Dirt looks bad/wrong/out of place on any surface where it does not normally belong, and most people regard the feel of dirt (when there is enough of it to feel) as objectionable. From this common sense about dirt, God taught his people, through these commands that related directly to the priests who served in the tabernacle and/or its courtyard, that his holiness demands purity. Things and people brought close to his presence could not be sloppy, imperfect, common, adulterated, or otherwise "dirty." Accordingly, the hands that touched the sacrifices or the feet that walked into the tabernacle had to be washed to remove dirt and to make the priest of Yahweh symbolically pure before him so as to be able to serve worthily in his house.

The importance of this rule for all priests is underscored both by repetition and by the addition of the death penalty for violation. In v. 20 the text says "they shall wash with water so that they will not die" in connection with preparing to enter the tabernacle tent itself (called here again the Tent of Meeting; cf. 30:16); in v. 21 the text says "they shall wash their hands and feet so that they will not die" in connection with approaching the altar to make a sacrifice thereon.[501] By means of the two slightly different wordings—almost in the manner of a synonymous parallelism—the full concept is conveyed, that is, "they must wash both hands and feet with water before either entering the Tent or approaching the altar." It is likely that all priests may have washed upon starting their service in the tabernacle courtyard, but some may have been assigned mainly to animal care, slaughtering, butchering, and may not have been required to wash regularly throughout the day. Any priest bringing a sacrifice to the altar or entering the holy place for any reason, however, would have had to wash each time—not just at the beginning of a day's service but throughout the day, each separate time he ministered at the altar or within the Tent.

Nothing is said about how often the water was to be changed, whether towels for drying were used, whether hands and feet were ever to be dipped into the basin, or whether the basin was simply a source for water that was ladled onto hands and feet. These matters were left to the common sense of the Israelite priests and may even have been accomplished somewhat differently at different times or according to the individual preferences of various high

---

[500] See comments on 29:19–21.

[501] The wording in the original, לְהַקְטִיר אִשֶּׁה לַיהוָה, translated in the NIV as "by presenting an offering made to the LORD by fire," refers to any sacrifice cooked on the altar, not merely to whole burnt offerings.

priests.[502] What counted was the ritual washing for all visits to the Tent or the altar and the need to keep these rules as "a lasting ordinance for Aaron and his descendants." Each generation needed to understand purity: that God's holiness was not a thing to be trifled with and that a holy God demanded that those approaching him be pure. In the New Covenant it is the "pure in heart" who meet this standard, as Jesus taught (Matt 5:8; cf. 1 Tim 1:5; 2 Tim 2:22; Ps 73:1,13). Baptism signifies this achievement of purity through the forgiveness of sins (Heb 10:22; Acts 22:6).

(14) Laws on Formulation and Use of Anointing Oil (30:22–33)

[22]Then the LORD said to Moses, [23]"Take the following fine spices: 500 shekels of liquid myrrh, half as much (that is, 250 shekels) of fragrant cinnamon, 250 shekels of fragrant cane, [24]500 shekels of cassia—all according to the sanctuary shekel—and a hin of olive oil. [25]Make these into a sacred anointing oil, a fragrant blend, the work of a perfumer. It will be the sacred anointing oil. [26]Then use it to anoint the Tent of Meeting, the ark of the Testimony, [27]the table and all its articles, the lampstand and its accessories, the altar of incense, [28]the altar of burnt offering and all its utensils, and the basin with its stand. [29]You shall consecrate them so they will be most holy, and whatever touches them will be holy. [30]"Anoint Aaron and his sons and consecrate them so they may serve me as priests. [31]Say to the Israelites, 'This is to be my sacred anointing oil for the generations to come. [32]Do not pour it on men's bodies and do not make any oil with the same formula. It is sacred, and you are to consider it sacred. [33]Whoever makes perfume like it and whoever puts it on anyone other than a priest must be cut off from his people.'"

Anointing related to cleanness and purity as symbols of holiness. God demanded that his priests, the servants of his house, be clean and pure. But lice were endemic in biblical times, and to be "lousy" was hardly to be clean and pure. The solution was regular use of oil, which kills lice.[503] Only the high priest was ritually anointed ("oiled") as a condition of being installed in office (chap. 29), but all priests were required to use a perfumed sacred oil, described in this passage, not only on their own heads but also on the tabernacle furnishings. Oiling the furnishings did not imply that they were capable of supporting lice in the same way that a living body can, but oiling would help protect the furnishings from any lice accidentally transmitted by an imperfectly oiled priest or by priests' clothing as it received lice from contact with lice-bearing worshipers bringing their offerings to the tabernacle. As v. 29 states, "Whatever touches them [must be] holy." Lice are not holy.

---

[502] Following the logic that the high priest was the chief administrative officer over the tabernacle, in addition to his sacral duties. Cf. 2 Kgs 12:10; 22:4; 23:4; Neh 3:1; Hag 1:14; Mark 14:53 and par.

[503] See comments on 29:7.

THE FORMULA FOR THE TABERNACLE ANOINTING OIL (30:22–25). **30:22–25** The amount of the ingredients listed here would add up to a sizeable quantity of anointing oil. A "hin of olive oil" (v. 24) was about a gallon in modern measurement. The quantity of fifteen hundred shekels of fragrance (five hundred of myrrh, two hundred and fifty of cinnamon, two hundred and fifty of cane, and five hundred of cassia) was about thirty-eight pounds in modern measurement. The cinnamon may have been a dry measure, unless cinnamon sap is meant. It is less certain which of the other fragrances were liquid in form, but whether or not they all were, their proportions relative to the oil were such that when everything was blended with the olive oil the result would still be a liquid. Thus the whole mixture would be both fragrant and pourable/daubable. If the fragrances were all in dry/powder form, as some have suggested in light of their being described according to weight (i.e., "dry measure"), it would seem that mixing them with only a gallon of oil would produce something more akin to a paste than an oil. But it is hard to doubt from the text that the desired compound was an oil to be poured, not a paste to be smeared; so how did the combination of ingredients listed produce an oil?

Several solutions have been proposed, all of which are to some extent speculative, but none of which is unreasonable: (a) the spices were to be cooked with water until they became distilled into liquids that then were blended with the oil;[504] (b) the paste mixture of oil and spices was pressed through filtering cloths leaving behind the relatively dry fragrance residue but yielding an oil that now had the essence of the fragrances strongly present within it;[505] (c) the paste was later diluted with as much olive oil as was needed to make it adequately liquid, so the paste served as the fragrant "base" from which whatever amount necessary for perfuming the anointing oil was taken as needed. Of these options the second has the advantage of fitting best with the implications of the wording "the work of a perfumer" (v. 25). In general perfumes are made by forcing essences of fragrant materials into oils rather than simply by adding ground up or otherwise powdered plant material to oil in order to make a slurry. Thus the NIV carefully translates "formula" where some other versions translate "mixture." Verse 25 clearly restricts the formula to sacred applications in saying, "It will be the sacred anointing oil."

Note that the anointing oil is also described explicitly as a "perfume" mixture (v. 33) and "the work of a perfumer"[506] (v. 25). Sweaty bodies were to be avoided in the tabernacle among God's servants the priests (thus the linen

---

[504] This is a view that some medieval rabbis held of how the anointing oil fragrances were liquefied; cf. Cassuto, *Exodus*, 397–98.

[505] Cf. A. Lucas, *Ancient Egyptian Materials and Industries*, 3d ed., rev. (London: Arnold & Co., 1948), 104–10.

[506] רֹקֵחַ.

garments, as explained by Ezek 44:17–18), and likewise the odor of smelly bodies was to be offset by perfume, at least symbolically.

USE AND MISUSE OF THE SACRED ANOINTING OIL (30:26–33). **30:26–33** The tabernacle and everything in it had to be anointed with the special holy anointing oil. Verses 26–30 describe how everything mentioned in chaps. 25–30 required anointing, with the exception of the high priest's clothing, including the ephod and its breastpiece, which were considered for anointing purposes all of a piece within the process of anointing Aaron (as is clear from 29:7,21). The anointing process had as its purpose to make everything associated with the tabernacle holy (30:29, "so they will be most holy"). Logically, this meant making everything "fitting to belong to God" and therefore to be placed in his presence. Anointing accomplished this purpose by symbolizing the killing of that which produced impurity (vermin), leaving behind a purified person or object. In effect the Israelites understood that the anointing of the tabernacle and its furniture, and Aaron and his sons and their clothing (29:21), showed that they were setting aside these things for God, consigning them to his realm and special possession.[507] Jacob had long prior anointed a crude stone pillar at Bethel (Gen 28:18; 31:13; 35:14)[508] as a way of indicating that he understood it to be a thing special to God. The Israelites were now to follow this general concept of anointing the place where God's presence was specially manifest.

And they were to do so permanently,[509] "for the generations to come" (v. 31). No one could decide to change the anointing oil formula or to stop using it in consecration/ordination ceremonies. Verse 32 also prohibits allowing nonpriests at some later point to copy the formula and make oil to anoint themselves for nonpriestly purposes (keeping away lice and smelling good in the process or else trying to get special blessing for cleansing from a skin dis-

---

[507] Lev 21:10 delineates the difference between the anointing of Aaron and the anointing of the priests in general. Aaron's head was anointed specially and separately; the other priests got their anointing through the general sprinkling of oil described in 29:21 and Lev 8:30.

[508] It is possible that the verbs in Gen 35:14 should be translated with the Eng. pluperfect: "Jacob *had* set up a stone pillar at the place where God had talked with him and he *had* poured out . . ." but even more likely is that the incident described in 35:14 is a second anointing or reanointing of the pillar, with perhaps only the first verb being appropriately translated in the pluperfect, unless more than one stone pillar actually stood at Bethel after the action described in 35:14.

[509] But the wording of God's command does not specify frequency, the reason for which should be obvious. He had not revealed to the Israelites in advance how many times they would set up and take down the tabernacle as they traveled from Sinai to Canaan (and certainly, at this point, they had no idea they would spend almost forty years doing so rather than just a few months) and within their journeys in Canaan as they conquered the land city by city and region by region. On the assumption that a full reanointing would take place each time the tabernacle was unpacked and set up as a worship center, the frequency of reanointing could only remain unspecified. The minimum frequency for reanointing would be once a year (30:10), but the maximum could be much more often.

ease by using special oil[510]). This is consistent with the proper translation of v. 29, "You shall consecrate them so they will be most holy, and whatever touches them must be holy." Holiness cannot be transmitted by touching (Hag 2:11–12, summarizing the Levitical law), but corruption can indeed be transmitted by touching (Hag 2:13, again summarizing the Levitical law). Thus all who served in the courtyard or tent had to be careful themselves to be holy, properly consecrated, so that they could then avoid contamination of anything at God's house.[511] The prohibition "do not pour it on men's bodies" would have applied to nonpriestly use, of course, but also to wrongful use on priests. Only the high priest could have oil poured on him and only on his head. All other pouring of the sacred oil on a person was improper. The penalty for misuse—whether copying the formula or using the sacred oil for a common purpose—was being "cut off from his people" (v. 33).[512]

(15) Laws on Formulation and Use of Incense (30:34–38)

34Then the LORD said to Moses, "Take fragrant spices—gum resin, onycha and galbanum—and pure frankincense, all in equal amounts, 35and make a fragrant blend of incense, the work of a perfumer. It is to be salted and pure and sacred. 36Grind some of it to powder and place it in front of the Testimony in the Tent of Meeting, where I will meet with you. It shall be most holy to you. 37Do not make any incense with this formula for yourselves; consider it holy to the LORD. 38Whoever makes any like it to enjoy its fragrance must be cut off from his people."

30:34–38 The purpose of the sacred incense, the procedure for its employment, and the twice-daily incense burning pattern within the tabernacle have already been indicated in the law requiring an incense altar within the holy place of the tabernacle (30:1–10). The spices themselves cannot be confidently identified except for frankincense, which is mentioned here first and will be mentioned frequently hereafter in the Old Testament, most often in connection with its role as an ingredient in the cereal offerings.[513]

Note that the instructions for the sacred incense make no mention of quantities. The calculation of quantity would become obvious in time. Since the

---

[510] As Lev 14:10ff. indicates, a sort of anointing was used as part of the process of declaring any person free from an infectious skin disease (cf. also the shaving of all head hair, vv. 8–9)—again demonstrating the logical association of oil with purification, deriving ultimately from its ability to kill lice. On the symbolic extension of this in NT times, cf. Jas 5:14.

[511] Cf. Lev 21:1–22:16; Num 19:6–7,11ff.; Ezek 44:15–31.

[512] On the meaning of this term, see comments on 12:15,19.

[513] Of the twenty-two occurrences of "frankincense" (לְבֹנָה) in the OT, seventeen concern the use of this fragrance as a sort of garnish for grain offerings (e.g., Lev 2:1–2; 2:15–16; cf. 5:11, where its use with sin offerings is explicitly disallowed). Frankincense was obtained from a whitish plant resin of the tree known as Boswellia Carteri et Frereana, widely available and prized in the ANE and most often imported from either Hadramaut or Somalia in north Africa.

incense was to be offered daily, there would be a regular, periodic, predictable need for more to be compounded, at least during any time that the tabernacle was set up and functioning, that is, when the Israelites were not actually on the road in transit from one location to another. This would contrast with the more unpredictable frequency of usage of the perfumed anointing oil, which would be required annually (30:10) and thereafter as often as the tabernacle was set up after being transported to a new location as the Israelites traveled, or as often as a new set of priests were ordained—and as rarely as a new high priest would be ordained. One setting-up of the tabernacle would require only one application of anointing oil, no matter how long the tabernacle might stay set up in that location. But regardless of length of location, the erected tabernacle would require a standard quantity of incense per day.

The identification of the four ingredients that made up the incense is generally not doubted. The first two ingredients, however, have often been referred to by various names.[514] Using the NIV terminology, which is as good as any, we can identify the ingredients. "Gum resin" was a powder obtained from the hardened drops of fragrant resin found in the bark of the Myrrh bush. The word used to refer to it in Hebrew means simply "a drop."

"Onycha" was a powder obtained by scraping the horny shell cover of certain clamlike mollusks found in the Red Sea. When burnt, this powder emits a strong aroma. The Hebrew word used here means, literally, "aromatic shell." As an isolated warm water section of the otherwise colder water Indian Ocean, the Red Sea supports a considerable variety of unique subspecies of mollusks.

"Galbanum" was a brownish, very strong-smelling resin taken from the lower part of the stem of a Ferula plant, where it is naturally exuded. From the point of view of geographic availability, the Ferula, a thick-stalked plant with yellow flowers and fernlike green foliage, is a Mediterranean Sea coastal plant. Galbanum acts in the manner of a scent preservative, so when mixed with other ingredients in a perfume, it tends to allow the distribution of the scent over a long period of time.

"Frankincense," a resin from Boswellia trees,[515] provides a lovely balsam fragrance to anything it is added to. Although gum resin might be obtained from a variety of locations where the Israelites traveled, onycha came from the Red Sea, galbanum from the Mediterranean coast, and frankincense from north Africa. The Israelites may have had such a supply of these materials

---

[514] E.g., what the NIV calls "gum resin," the HCSB and NRSV call "stacte," and Durham (*Exodus*, 406, 408) calls more generically "resin droplets." What the NIV, HCSB, and NRSV call "onycha," Durham calls more generically "mollusk scent."

[515] See also note above.

with them from despoiling the Egyptians[516] that they could assemble satisfactory quantities for mixing the incense at Sinai. But eventually they would have to trade for them, purchasing them from the spice caravans that crisscrossed the Near East in ancient times (Gen 37:25; 1 Kgs 10:2,10,25; Song 3:6; Ezek 27:22; Rev 18:13).

But why was salt to be added to the incense (v. 35, "it is to be salted")? Various explanations have been offered,[517] but the most likely derives from the fact that salt was the only preservative known in ancient times. By reason of its powerful antibacterial properties (though these were not understood at the time, of course), salt was observed to preserve foods that would otherwise putrefy rapidly, especially in the hot climate in which most Israelites lived. Accordingly, salt became important both as an actual preservative and as a symbolic preservative,[518] and terms such as "of salt" became equivalent in meaning to "permanent."[519] At a minimum, adding salt to the incense symbolized the desire that it remain always pure and preserved and not old or rancid. Beyond this it probably also symbolized the fact that the sacred incense represented a part of the ritual remembrance of the covenant of Yahweh with his people.[520] Thus the requirement of v. 35 that "it is to be salted and pure and sacred" means something like "it must be understood as a permanent symbol of my covenant, which is pure and holy with my people, who are to reflect the fact that I make promises that are permanent and that I myself am absolutely pure and holy."

---

[516] Spices were unquestionably regarded as treasures in the ancient world (cf. 1 Kgs 10:2; 2 Kgs 20:13), so it is hard to imagine that when the Israelites solicited wealth from the terrified Egyptians as they left Egypt (12:35–26) they would not have obtained spices among other valuables. Note the fact that the Magi who brought gifts to the newborn Jesus included the spices "frankincense" and "myrrh" among their precious presents (Matt 2:11).

[517] Cassuto takes an entirely different tack, identifying מְמֻלָּח not as "of salt" but an idiom for "pure" (*Exodus,* 400). He, like many other commentators, is obviously concerned that the various spices mentioned in the formula do not require preserving; but this concern should be obviated by the fact that the use of the salt is symbolic rather than technically being an "active ingredient."

[518] E.g., Num 18:19: "Whatever is set aside from the holy offerings the Israelites present to the LORD I give to you and your sons and daughters as your regular share. It is an everlasting covenant of salt before the LORD for both you and your offspring." Note also the words of Elisha in 2 Kgs 2:20–21: "'Bring me a new bowl,' he said, 'and put salt in it.' So they brought it to him. Then he went out to the spring and threw the salt into it, saying, 'This is what the LORD says: "I have healed this water. Never again will it cause death or make the land unproductive."'"

[519] As in the term "covenant of salt," 2 Chr 13:5; Num 18:19.

[520] Thus the requirement of Lev 2:13: "Season all your grain offerings with salt. Do not leave the salt of the covenant of your God out of your grain offerings; add salt to all your offerings." Note also the way that having eaten salt can be used as a synecdoche for having concluded a covenant: "Now because we share the salt of the palace and it is not fitting for us to witness the king's dishonor, therefore we send and inform the king" (Ezra 4:14, NRSV).

The mixture of spices, properly salted, was then ground to powder and placed on the incense altar, which was located "in front of the Testimony in the Tent of Meeting" (see also 30:6). As the powder burned, it gave off a beautiful fragrant smoke, honoring God and symbolizing the prayers of his people.[521] Twice the Israelites were reminded of the holiness of this incense with the wording "it shall be most holy to you" in v. 36 and "consider it holy to [Yahweh]" in v. 37. This holiness was to be enforced by a banishment/death penalty (v. 38),[522] the wording of which indicates why people might try to imitate the tabernacle incense: to "enjoy its fragrance,"[523] that is, to obtain selfishly in their own homes the same high-quality scent of burning spices that glorified God in the tabernacle holy place.[524]

With this final command, the description of the tabernacle and its furnishings is complete.

(16) Appointment of Bezalel and Oholiab and Other Craftsmen (31:1–11)

1Then the LORD said to Moses, 2"See, I have chosen Bezalel son of Uri, the son of Hur, of the tribe of Judah, 3and I have filled him with the Spirit of God, with skill, ability and knowledge in all kinds of crafts—4to make artistic designs for work in gold, silver and bronze, 5to cut and set stones, to work in wood, and to engage in all kinds of craftsmanship. 6Moreover, I have appointed Oholiab son of Ahisamach, of the tribe of Dan, to help him. Also I have given skill to all the craftsmen to make everything I have commanded you: 7the Tent of Meeting, the ark of the Testimony with the atonement cover on it, and all the other furnishings of the tent—8the table and its articles, the pure gold lampstand and all its accessories, the altar of incense, 9the altar of burnt offering and all its utensils, the basin with its stand—10and also the woven garments, both the sacred garments for Aaron the priest and the garments for his sons when they serve as priests, 11and the anointing oil and fragrant incense for the Holy Place. They are to make them just as I commanded you."

---

[521] See comments on 30:1–10.

[522] See comments on 12:15,19.

[523] The Hb., לְהָרִיחַ בָּהּ, can also be translated simply "to produce a nice smell with it" or "to use it as incense," but the NIV's interpretive translation is justifiable as expressing explicitly what is implicit in the prohibition as the motive for copying the formula.

[524] People who selfishly want the best for themselves are often wont to define the best by some external standard, such as what is found at the best place they've had a chance to visit. To be able to say something like, "Yes, it's the same recipe they use at the White House" or "We got it in Paris—they just don't have anything like it around here" would be a modern equivalent of an ancient Israelite's saying, "Do you enjoy that scent? It's exactly the same as the tabernacle's." Of course, the most objectionable sort of imitative use of the tabernacle incense would have been to use it for a pagan shrine in honor of an idol god, but we have no evidence that this sort of religious forgery was ever actually undertaken.

Only the best materials were to be used in the manufacture of the tabernacle and its furnishings, according to the instructions of chaps. 25–30. Here in 31:1–11 God insists as well that only the best workmanship be assigned to the actual task of construction. The process begins with the appointment of people who are already skilled, gifted artisans. To this is added the special spiritual filling of Yahweh, with the result that the completed tabernacle and everything in it will be of top quality, an exact fulfillment of what Yahweh wanted, rather than any mere approximation. Worshipers of all succeeding generations could be sure that the tabernacle at which they worshiped was in fact built exactly as Moses had seen it in the divinely revealed plan. Indeed, when Moses carefully inspected the tabernacle and all its accoutrements, he found it "just as the LORD had commanded" (39:32).

With this passage we come to the penultimate pericope of the long Sinai legal discourse, the verbatim record of God's covenant instructions to Moses. There remains only one more section, 31:12–18, which concludes with God's personal presentation of the tablets of the Ten Words/Commandments. Since *aural* reception of the Ten began the whole process of legal revelation on Sinai in the first place (20:1), it becomes obvious that 20:1–31:18, concluding with a description of *written* reception of the Ten, forms a coherent unit and that that unit is nearing its end with the present commands. These verses provide two sorts of information. They identify the artisans selected by divine appointment and also provide a concise yet remarkably comprehensive summary of what has already been said in chaps. 25–30.

31:1–3 Bezalel is identified by his descendancy from Judah, which came through Judah's son Perez (1 Chr 2:4), Perez's son Hezron (1 Chr 2:5), Hezron's son Caleb (1 Chr 2:18), and then in continuing succession Hur and Uri, Bezalel's grandfather and father, respectively (1 Chr 2:19–20).

It is not necessary to assume that the Hur mentioned as Bezalel's grandfather was the Hur who helped Moses keep his hands aloft in prayer during the battle with the Amalekites at Rephidim (17:10–13) since that Hur may have been a relative of Moses' and Aaron's, thus a Levite, and the name Hur (meaning "Whitey") probably was common.[525] What is perhaps most significant about Bezalel's family lineage is his being a Judahite. In all aspects of tabernacle service and maintenance, Levites were the only persons allowed responsibility. They alone could set up, take down, transport, maintain, or utilize anything pertaining to the tabernacle. But the original construction was another matter. The servants in God's house were chosen for their duty by reason of birth lineage; but those who actually built it were chosen because of spiritual gifting. No Judahite would be able to touch anything in the tabernacle

[525] Cf. Neh 3:9 and as well Num 31:8; Josh 13:21, where the name was also known among Midianites.

once it was constructed and sanctified, but until then the best craftsmen, regardless of tribe, would handle every part of it as they made it into a beautiful, portable divine dwelling for Israel's God. Note also that Oholiab's tribe is identified as Dan (v. 6); moreover, Joshua, Moses' aide and successor as leader of the people, was an Ephraimite (1 Chr 7:27). Clergy service was restricted by tribe; no other leadership was.

The NIV translation of v. 2, "I have chosen Bezalel," somewhat obscures the meaning of the original (lit., "I have called by name Bezalel). The idiom employed in the Hebrew connotes specifically selecting a single individual, that is, *naming* that individual to a job. In this case Bezalel, and no one else, was to head the tabernacle construction project; no substitute could be employed in his place, and his specific background and skills were the ones God planned to enhance with the filling of his Spirit. Appropriately, he was mentioned early on in the fulfillment portion of the tabernacle construction descriptions as was Oholiab (see 35:30–36:2) because when the work got underway it was the key workers who started everything in train.

Verse 3 does not say that God gave Bezalel four things ("Spirit of God,[526] . . . skill, ability and knowledge") but correctly translated says that he gave Bezalel mainly one thing: his Spirit, which then perfected Bezalel's wisdom, insight, knowledge, and work performance in general. The clearest translation of the Hebrew might be: "I have filled him with God's Spirit in [regard to] wisdom, in insight, in knowledge, and in every sort of work." In other words, the way the filling of the Spirit of God affected Bezalel was to enable him to be wiser, more insightful, more knowledgeable, and more capable of any sort of work to which God assigned him. The wording cannot be understood to mean that he would receive the Spirit of God and, then, other things in addition but rather the Spirit of God in a way that provided the amounts of the other things needed so that Bezalel's tabernacle work would be up to God's standards.

Excursus: The Meaning of Being "Filled with the Spirit"

The concept of being filled with the Spirit of God is often misunderstood and sometimes grossly so, as compared to its actual biblical usage. Some have assumed that being filled with the Spirit must represent a powerful emotional

[526] For רוּחַ אֱלֹהִים the NRSV reads "divine spirit" as if a pagan were speaking and as if the actual expression were not the Hb. construct but the genitival expressed with a preposition, i.e., רוּחַ לֵאלֹהִים. Because the Hb. construct requires the translation "the Spirit of God" or "God's Spirit" in light of having a proper noun as the *nomen rectum,* it appears that the NRSV translation is tendentious. In the NRSV as a matter of course, רוּחַ אֱלֹהִים is rendered "spirit of God" (small *s*) throughout the OT so that the idea of the Holy Spirit is tacitly eliminated from the OT and sequestered within the NT, where "Spirit of God" (capital s) is the rendering. Even so, the NRSV renders רוּחַ אֱלֹהִים normally in other contexts as "the spirit of God" rather than "divine spirit," the latter perhaps being a solipsism of the Exodus translator. Cf. 35:31.

experience that produces sensations and feelings that are otherworldly, with the result that the person filled receives an emotive impetus to enjoy life more richly or experience living on a higher plane. Others have opined that being filled with the Spirit equates to having a second specific work of grace in one's life, subsequent to and deeper than mere salvation/conversion, whereby God takes over more of one's life than would be possible if one were simply a forgiven believer. Yet others have concluded that "speaking in tongues" (by which they mean engaging in paratactic vocalization not associated with any earthly language) is the requisite sign of being filled with the Spirit and that apart from speaking in tongues the filling of the Spirit does not occur. Still others, reasoning erroneously from Paul's contrast of being filled with the Spirit and being drunk (Eph 5:18), assume that being filled with the Spirit must be like drunkenness, in other words, characterized by a blissful loss of self-control,[527] as if Paul were asserting that the two phenomena are analogous instead of in fact asserting that they are polar opposites: being filled with the Spirit should result in complete self-control.

In fact, "being filled with the Spirit" is a biblical idiom for "having from God the ability to do or say exactly what God wants done or said." In the case of Bezalel in Exod 31:3; 35:31, his being filled with the Spirit meant that he could correctly construct the tabernacle and its furnishings exactly as God wanted them made—which is in fact what both verses say was the effect of his being so filled. In Mic 3:8, Micah describes being filled with the Sprit "to declare to Jacob his transgression, to Israel his sin," in other words, to speak God's word forcefully and effectively—to say what God wanted said. The angel's assurance to Zechariah that Jesus would be filled with the Holy Spirit even from birth (Luke 1:15) goes on to describe the effect thereof as empowering him to be persuasive: "Many of the people of Israel will he bring back to the Lord their God. And he will . . . turn the hearts . . . to make ready a people prepared for the Lord" (Luke 1:16–17). Likewise, in Luke 1:67 when Zechariah was filled with the Spirit, the result was his ability to prophecy accurately. When Elizabeth was filled with the Spirit (Luke 1:41), the result was an inspired speech to Mary (vv. 41–45).

In Acts each account of being filled with the Holy Spirit includes overt reference to its result: a speaker's ability to speak God's word as God wants it spoken (Acts 2:4; 4:31; 9:17;[528] 13:9,52[529]). Indeed, the case is well supported by a negative: in Acts 5:3 Peter assets that "Satan" had "filled" Ananias, with the result that he "lied to the Holy Spirit." Thus the filling of the Spirit brings true, godly assertions from the mouth of the speaker because the speaker says what God wants said; the filling of Satan, on the other hand, brings lies, which is what the father of lies" (John 8:44) produces. In Ephesians, Paul's command to be filled

[527] Paul's teaching could not be clearer as to the fact that losing self-control could never be spiritual in light of his emphasis on self-control as a basic part of spirituality; cf. Gal 5:23; cf. Acts 24:25; 1 Cor 7:5; 1 Tim 3:2; 2 Pet 1:6.

[528] The result of Paul's own being filled with the Spirit in 9:17 is described in Acts 9:20–22, "At once he began to preach in the synagogues . . . proving that Jesus is the Christ."

[529] The result of the filling of the Spirit mentioned in 13:52 is immediately described in 14:1, namely, effective preaching.

with the Spirit (5:18) is followed immediately by the expected result: "Speak to one another . . ." (5:19).

Understanding the idiomatic meaning of "being filled with the Spirit" obviates any notion that Bezalel experienced the New Covenant phenomenon of the indwelling of the Holy Spirit far earlier than anyone else. In fact, he was not a New Covenant convert fourteen hundred years early but was simply a man aided by God's Spirit to do exactly what God wanted him to do, so the product of his craftsmanship was fully to God's high standards, essentially as if God had done it himself.

31:4–5 The tabernacle and all its furnishings (chaps. 25–30) consisted of acacia wood, metal (gold, silver, bronze, gems), and fabric. Bezalel may not have possessed skills in the area of spinning, weaving, or dyeing (i.e., fabric work) because these are not mentioned specifically here, but he clearly understood a great deal about artistic metal working, wood working, and the cutting and setting of gems. Both at the end of v. 3 and again at the end of v. 5 his abilities relative to "all kinds of craftsmanship"[530] are praised, so whether or not he would personally fashion a particular part of the tabernacle, he understood how to assess the quality of others' work.

31:6 Aside from his mention here and in the fulfillment passages of 35:34; 36:1–2; 38:23, Oholiab's name is not otherwise found in the Bible, but the wording here suggests that he was the number two in command on the tabernacle project and perhaps even a coleader.[531] But an unnamed number of persons also helped make the tabernacle just as it was designed by God to be, persons to whom God gave special wisdom to augment their own. The Hebrew misleadingly translated by the NIV as "I have given skill to all the craftsmen to make everything I have commanded you" actually says, "In the mind of all who have wise minds I have put wisdom so that they can make everything I commanded you." In other words, the emphasis is more on being in tune with God's desires by always making the right choices among the construction and design options being constantly presented than simply giving skill to craftsmen. Moreover, the NIV translation choice "craftsmen" could be understood to suggest that only men would have been involved in the tabernacle construction. In fact, women were explicitly responsible for much of the fabric manufacture (35:25–26), and both men and women were involved together in locating and contributing materials (35:29; cf. also 36:6).

31:7–11 These verses review succinctly everything mentioned in chaps. 25–30, with the final command, "they are to make them just as I commanded

[530] Inexplicably, the NIV translates בְּכָל־מְלָאכָה "in all kinds of crafts" in v. 3 and "in all kinds of craftsmanship" in v. 5 even though the context displays no hint of a shift in nuance of meaning between the two verses.

[531] What the NIV renders "I have appointed . . . to help him" would be more precisely translated "I have personally appointed . . . along with him," a considerably stronger statement of coresponsibility than "to help him" would suggest. Cf. HCSB, "I have selected Oholiab . . . to be with him."

you" (v. 11), reiterating for the benefit of the workmen the insistence on exact replication that God had already given to Moses (25:9,40; 26:30; 27:8).

(17) Laws on the Sabbath (31:12–17)

[12]Then the LORD said to Moses, [13]"Say to the Israelites, 'You must observe my Sabbaths. This will be a sign between me and you for the generations to come, so you may know that I am the LORD, who makes you holy.

[14]"'Observe the Sabbath, because it is holy to you. Anyone who desecrates it must be put to death; whoever does any work on that day must be cut off from his people. [15]For six days, work is to be done, but the seventh day is a Sabbath of rest, holy to the LORD. Whoever does any work on the Sabbath day must be put to death. [16]The Israelites are to observe the Sabbath, celebrating it for the generations to come as a lasting covenant. [17]It will be a sign between me and the Israelites forever, for in six days the LORD made the heavens and the earth, and on the seventh day he abstained from work and rested.'"

31:12–17 Why make mention of the Sabbath at this point, within the section of Exodus that deals with the tabernacle? Had the Sabbath not already been dealt with satisfactorily in 16:23–19 and especially in the Ten Words/ Commandments, that is, Exod 20:8–11? The answer is that the tabernacle was for worship; worship occurred weekly, on the Sabbath; and if the Sabbath were not properly observed, worship would not properly take place; so therefore the tabernacle would not be properly used.

There are both similarities and differences between the relatively lengthy commandment in Exod 20:8–11 and the restatement here in 31:12–17. The following table shows generally how these comparisons (here of key wording rather than of exact wording, ignoring conjunctions and other less important vocabulary) demonstrate that the present commands reflect all the essentials of the Ten Words/Commandments Sabbath law, while adding reminders of its perpetual observance and the penalty of being cut off/put to death for dishonoring the Sabbath.

The structure of the pericope is repetitious, especially in the way vv. 16–17a echo vv. 13–14a. This can be seen in the table on page 655, which demonstrates that the repetition is not absolute or dittographic but stresses internally the lasting nature of the Sabbath requirement and the fact that failure to keep this important covenant sign would represent a very serious breach of covenant relationship between Yahweh and his people.

God is the guarantor of his own covenant with his people, and his example forms the basis for their behavior.[532] Accordingly, in 31:17, the concluding

[532] Perhaps the parade example of God's expecting imitation of his own character from his own people is found in Lev 11:45; 19:2, "Be holy because I am holy," cited prominently by Peter in 1 Pet 1:16.

Exod 20	Exod 31
Remember the Sabbath	Observe my Sabbaths/Observe the Sabbath
Keep it holy	It is holy to you
Six days you shall labor	For six days work is to be done
Seventh day is a Sabbath	Seventh day is a Sabbath of rest
On it you shall do no work	Whoever does any work on that day
-0-	must be cut off
Not you, son, daughter, manservant, maidservant, animals, alien within gates	-0- -0-
Six days the Lord made heavens, earth, sea	Six days Lord made heavens, earth
and all that is in them	-0-
He rested on the seventh day	On the seventh day he abstained from work and rested
Lord blessed the Sabbath day	-0-
Made it holy	Holy to the Lord
-0-	Sign between me and you for generations to come
-0-	So that you may know I am the Lord
-0-	Anyone who desecrates it put to death
-0-	etc.

statement of the Sabbath law draws the attention of the people to his own work of seven days, as described in Gen 1, and his resting/abstaining from work on the seventh day. Hebrews 3 and 4 develop this theme relative to an overview of all history: God's creation rest occurred once, not every week. The weekly Sabbath is in part a reminder of that divine, eternal rest. Our opportunity to enter that same rest (the joy of heaven forever with God) requires obedience through Christ (Heb 4:3–6) lest the curse of Ps 95:11 ("they shall never enter my rest") be the result.

The Sabbath is a sign of obedience to the covenant. Those who keep no Sabbath (who neither rest the equivalent of one day per week nor worship weekly) are by their very actions indicating openly to all that they are not partners to the covenant. Those who faithfully keep the Sabbath, on the other

31:13–14a	31:16–17a
[Say to] the Israelites	The Israelites
You must observe my Sabbaths	are to observe the Sabbath
Will be sign between me and you	This will be a sign between me and the Israelites
for generations to come	forever/for generations to come
so that you may know that I am the Lord	-0-
who makes you holy	-0-
Observe the Sabbath	The Israelites . . . observe the Sabbath (also above)
-0-	(celebrating it . . .) as a lasting covenant
Because it is holy to you	-0-

hand, make a public declaration of their covenant loyalty to the "LORD of the Sabbath."[533]

(18) Conclusion: Presentation of the Ten Commandments to Moses (31:18)

[18]When the LORD finished speaking to Moses on Mount Sinai, he gave him the two tablets of the Testimony, the tablets of stone inscribed by the finger of God.

31:18 The text of Exod 24:12 reads: "The LORD said to Moses, 'Come up to me on the mountain and stay here, and I will give you the tablets of stone, with the law and commands I have written for their instruction.'" From the moment he ascended the mountain, Moses was to anticipate receiving the special tablets of stone that would represent a permanent record of the Ten Words/Commandments of God as spoken directly by him to the people, and as recorded in chap. 20, in addition to the other laws that he himself would write down on paper or parchment, a temporary surface compared to the stone. But nothing in 24:12 speaks of the tablets being written by God's finger, even though the NIV wording of the present verse would seem to refer to something already well known, that is, "*the* tablets of stone inscribed by the finger of God." In fact, the verse would better be translated: "Then he gave to Moses when he had finished talking to him on Mount Sinai the two tablets of the testimony, stone tablets written by God's finger."[534] There is no article in the

[533] Matt 12:8; Luke 6:5.

[534] The HCSB has it essentially this way ("the two tablets of the testimony, stone tablets inscribed by the finger of God").

original attaching to "stone tablets written . . ." It is at *this* point, not earlier, that the reader first learns that God would personally inscribe on a permanent medium the words he audibly[535] spoke to the people earlier from atop the mountain. Not only does the present verse bring to a conclusion one more segment of the Mount Sinai legal revelation, but it also further endorses the Ten Words/Commandments as the premier legal formulation for Israel. All other laws are important and not to be ignored, but the Ten Words are so foundational, so principial, that they have a status and personal divine "endorsement" all their own.

This is also the first place in the narrative where the number of the tablets of stone—two—is specified. The reason for the two tablets has nothing to do with the length of the commandments as opposed to the size of the tablets (as if it were necessary to employ two tablets to fit all the commandments onto them, half on one and half on the other). The full text of the Ten Words/Commandments was written on each tablet, one copy being God's and one copy being Israel's.[536] This reflects the standard ancient Near Eastern treaty covenant practice of providing a copy of the covenant both to the vassal and to the sovereign. The fact that the two tablets were eventually placed together in the ark (Deut 10:5; 1 Kgs 8:9; Heb 9:4) further symbolized the ark's role as a point of contact for God and his people, the place where his covenant relationship with them was symbolized by, among other things, the law, obedience to which linked Israel to Yahweh and Yahweh to Israel.

[535] And terrifyingly; see comments on 20:15–18.

[536] See also comments on 20:3.

DIVISION OUTLINE

VII. REBELLION, RENEWAL, AND FULFILLMENT OF GOD'S INSTRUCTIONS FOR THE TABERNACLE (32:1–40:38)

Note on Exodus 32–34

1. Rebellion, Covenant Breaking, God's Mercy, and Covenant Renewal (32:1–34:35)
   - (1) Israel's Idolatry with the Golden Young Bull (32:1–6)
   - (2) God's Anger and Moses' Intercession (32:7–14)
   - (3) Moses' Anger and the Levite Punishment (32:15–29)
   - (4) Second Intercession and Plague (32:30–35)

   Excursus: The Book of Life
   - (5) Reiteration of Laws on God's Angel and Holy War Conquest (33:1–6)
   - (6) The Tent of Meeting (33:7–11)
   - (7) The Need for and Promise of God's Glory (33:12–23)
   - (8) Renewal of the Stone Tablets and the Covenant (34:1–28)
     - The Replacement Tablets (34:1–4)
     - God Shows Moses His Glory (34:5–7)
     - Moses Again Raises His Great Concern: Will God Go with Israel? (34:8–9)
     - God's Answer: Keep My Covenant and I Will Go with You (34:10–11)
     - Warnings against Covenants/Treaties with the Inhabitants of the Promised Land (34:12–16)
     - Renewal of the Covenant with a "Decalogue" of Sample Laws (34:17–26)
     - Document Clause: Putting the Covenant in Writing (34:27–28)
   - (9) Moses' Face Reflecting God's Glory (34:29–35)
2. Fulfillment of the Laws on the Means of Worship (35:1–40:38)

   Excursus: Command-Fulfillment Repetition in Exodus
   - (1) The Importance of the Sabbath (35:1–3)
   - (2) Offerings of Tabernacle Materials (35:4–29) [Fulfillment of 25:1–7]
     - God's Call for Materials (35:4–9)
     - God's Call for Skilled Worker (35:10–19) [Summarizes parts of 26–28; 30 with Further Fulfillment Especially in 37; 39; 40]

The People Respond to the Call for Materials (35:20–29) [Fulfillment of 25:1–7]

(3) The Work of Bezalel, Oholiab, and the Other Skilled Craftsmen (35:30–36:7)

Moses Appoints and Endorses the Craftsmen and Designers (35:30–36:1) [Fulfillment of 31:2–6]

The People's Oversubscription to the Call for Donations (36:2–7)

(4) Construction of the Tabernacle (36:8–38) [Fulfillment of 26:1–27]

(5) Construction of the Ark (37:1–9) [Fulfillment of 25:10–20]

(6) Construction of the Tabernacle Table (37:10–16) [Fulfillment of 25:23–29]

(7) Construction of the Lampstand (37:17–24) [Fulfillment of 25:31–39]

(8) Construction of the Incense Altar (37:25–28) [Fulfillment of 30:1–5]

(9) Composition of the Anointing Oil and the Incense (37:29) [Fulfillment of 30:22–25 and 30:34–36]

(10) Construction of the Main Altar (38:1–7) [Fulfillment of 27:1–8a]

(11) Construction of the Bronze Basin and Stand (38:8) [Fulfillment of 30:17–21]

(12) Construction of the Courtyard (38:9–20) [Fulfillment of 27:9–19]

(13) Amounts of the Materials Used for the Tabernacle and Its Furnishings (38:21–31) [General Fulfillment of 25:1–3a]

(14) Construction of The Priestly Garments (39:1–31) [Fulfillment of 28:2–43]

Overview (39:1) [Fulfillment of 28:2–5]

Construction of the Ephod (39:2–7) [Fulfillment of 28:6–14]

Construction of the Breastpiece (39:8–21) [Fulfillment of 28:15–28]

Construction of the Robe (39:22–26) [Fulfillment of 28:31–35]

Construction of the Tunics and Turban (39:27–31) [Fulfillment of 28:36–43]

(15) Moses' Inspection Finds All Materials Made as Commanded by God (39:32–43) [Fulfillment of 35:10–19]

(16) Moses' Sets Up the Tabernacle, Priestly Investment, and Placement of All Furnishings (40:1–33)

IV. REBELLION, RENEWAL, AND FULFILLMENT OF GOD'S INSTRUCTIONS FOR THE TABERNACLE (32:1–40:38)

Note on Exodus 32–34

These three chapters "interrupt" by reason of the chronology of events[1] the account of the tabernacle (its design, purpose, construction), but they do so in a way that has great significance for appreciating the book of Exodus as a whole[2] and for understanding the challenges to Israel's faith posed by the dominance of idolatry and idolatrous thinking still very much alive in the minds of the people of Israel while they were at Mount Sinai. In chap. 32 we see Israel turn against the Ten Words/Commandments through idolatry (even helped by Aaron, of all people) and Moses' recognition of this terrible betrayal of Yahweh by publicly breaking the tablets of the covenant. What then would become of Israel? Having unquestionably and even eagerly broken the divine covenant that held their only promise of divine blessing and presence, would they simply be left to die in the wilderness by the God they rejected—or would they perhaps wander off into the promised land on their own, to face whatever fate might be theirs without the leading of Yahweh, including, possibly, annihilation at the hands of the Canaanites?

Chapters 33–34 answer these questions. Yahweh, in response to the intercession of Israel's human leader Moses, was indeed willing to forgive his people and reinstitute his covenant with them, once again writing on the tablets his law that granted them the blessing of covenant relationship He also graciously promised to accompany them all the way through the wilderness and into the promised land. He would even go so far as to grant Moses a kind of encounter with himself that would "show" his goodness to Moses and reassure him, and through him Israel, that they were back in his covenant love and looking toward a great future as his special possession. What could have destroyed Israel's favored relationship with Yahweh (open, flagrant idolatry) was dealt with decisively and thoroughly, and what might have been lost (Yahweh's guiding, protecting presence

---

[1] And not at all, we would argue, merely as a stylistic device in the narrative.

[2] Indeed, E. G. Newing goes so far as to say that these three chapters form the "pivot" of the entire Hexateuch (Genesis–Joshua). He contends that the various individual narratives housed within chaps. 32–34 are highly ordered and balanced one with another—so much so that the progressions of themes and events can be schematized through a series of charts that Newing produces in demonstration of the unifying patterns ("Up and Down—In and Out: Moses on Mount Sinai: The Literary Unity of Exodus 32–24," *ABR* 41 [1993]: 18–34).

for his little, recently liberated people) returned in abundance. These chapters show Yahweh's goodness (33:19) in rich measure and lead into the accounts of the construction of the tabernacle in a way that makes those accounts not chronicles of futility but descriptions of the means of worship of a God who was willing to come close, even closer than he ever had before, to his fully forgiven people.

1. Rebellion, Covenant Breaking, God's Mercy, and Covenant Renewal (32:1–34:35)

(1) Israel's Idolatry with the Golden Young Bull[3] *(32:1–6)*

1When the people saw that Moses was so long in coming down from the mountain, they gathered around Aaron and said, "Come, make us gods who will go before us. As for this fellow Moses who brought us up out of Egypt, we don't know what has happened to him."

2Aaron answered them, "Take off the gold earrings that your wives, your sons and your daughters are wearing, and bring them to me." 3So all the people took off their earrings and brought them to Aaron. 4He took what they handed him and made it into an idol cast in the shape of a calf, fashioning it with a tool. Then they said, "These are your gods, O Israel, who brought you up out of Egypt."

5When Aaron saw this, he built an altar in front of the calf and announced, "Tomorrow there will be a festival to the LORD." 6So the next day the people rose early and sacrificed burnt offerings and presented fellowship offerings. Afterward they sat down to eat and drink and got up to indulge in revelry.

The famous incident of idolatry described in this passage and the way Moses admirably dealt with it are hymned in Ps 106:19–23, indicating especially through the wording of v. 21 of that psalm ("they forgot the God who saved them") how outrageous was their turning to idol worship:

At Horeb they made a calf
  and worshiped an idol cast from metal.
They exchanged their Glory
  for an image of a bull, which eats grass.
They forgot the God who saved them,
  who had done great things in Egypt,
miracles in the land of Ham
  and awesome deeds by the Red Sea.
So he said he would destroy them—
  had not Moses, his chosen one,

[3] It is common to translate *ʿēgel* (עֵגֶל) as "calf" in 32:4,5,8,19,20,24 and elsewhere, but the term actually refers to the strongest of domesticated animals, the full-grown but still young bull, thus simply "young bull." In Eng. the term "calf" tends to connote a small bull or cow not yet full-grown, which is not, as far as we know, what Aaron made for the Israelites as described in this passage. We will use the translation "young bull" in our references to the idol.

stood in the breach before him
to keep his wrath from destroying them.

We should remember that just a few months prior to this incident, the Israelites and the other ethnic groups among them[4] were still living in Egypt, deeply influenced by its pagan culture, just as they had been for hundreds of years. They had all grown up in a society devoted to the religious system and way of life known as idolatry, and they were understandably, though by no means excusably, not yet used to the rigorous anti-idolatry demands of Yahweh's covenant with them. Because the attractions of idolatry for them were so strong[5] and their recent stance against it so derivative and new, they were, in fact, not at all genuinely committed to its eradication in their beliefs and practices, as the present passage demonstrates all too clearly.

Added to the frailty of their commitment to the newly established covenant with Yahweh was Moses' long absence, ongoing as chap. 32 opens. There is no evidence that in his previous trips to the top of Mount Sinai he had ever stayed overnight. Thus he probably had been with his people every day since long before the exodus began, was seen constantly among them, and made himself at least theoretically available without fail to any and all of them virtually every day (see, e.g., 18:13–26). Now, however, he had been gone for "forty"[6] days, and the sudden complete lack of contact with him surely took its toll on their entire outlook relative to everything he had been relaying to them from God. After all, if the primary spokesperson, representative, and delegated leader of a movement seemingly disappears indefinitely from sight, would it be surprising that large numbers of people would begin to doubt the purpose or value of the movement itself?

Moreover, the people had not been told how long Moses would be gone. Exodus 24:18 indicates for the reader that Moses ended up staying on the mountain for forty days, but nothing there or elsewhere in the narrative indicates that either he or any other Israelite knew in advance how long he would be gone. Not only so, but Aaron had specifically been left in charge (24:14).[7] The fact that the people of Israel would turn to Aaron for help in

---

[4] See comments on 12:38. It must have been especially hard for the nonethnic Israelites who were now accepting the Israelite covenant and converting to Yahwism to keep everything straight, but the ethnic Israelites themselves were hardly much better, in light of the eagerness with which they went back into the idolatry of their dominant life experience.

[5] See "Excursus: The Attractions of Idolatry" at 20:6.

[6] See comments on 24:18.

[7] That verse also mentions Hur, but Hur may have been to Aaron as Joshua was to Moses: not an equal but an assistant, so the people would not have thought of Hur as someone to turn to for leadership in the same way they thought of Aaron in the present circumstances. In the story of the battle against the Amalekites in chap. 17, we possibly are to understand Hur as present (17:10–13) to assist Aaron, which he did in holding up Moses' arms, while Moses' own assistant, Joshua, was preoccupied with the battle itself (17:9,13).

returning to idolatry can hardly be surprising. He was already designated as their leader pro tempore and in light of the length of Moses' absence would have seemed to many the logical choice to be their new permanent leader.[8]

32:1 The question may be raised as to whether Moses' intent as narrator of this material was to convey the idea that the people "gathered *around* Aaron" or that they "gathered *against* Aaron." The Hebrew expression employed, *qāhal niphal* + *ʿal,* is used by Moses only three other times, all in Numbers and all in contexts of opposition and hostility, where the proper translation is "gather against" or the like.[9] The only other usage of this same compound term is found in Ezek 38:7, where it clearly does not mean "gather against" but in fact means "gather around" in support.[10] Alternatively, it may be that the expression *qāhal niphal* + *ʿal* had a large enough range of meaning that it was always technically ambiguous in itself and required contextual definition.[11] Since Ezekiel's Hebrew is centuries later than that of Moses' and may reflect semantic drift over time for this particular compound, it is safest to assume that Moses' own usage would be consistent and that he intended his readers to understand that the people gathered in hostility *against* Aaron to pressure him into helping them return to idolatry (cf NJPS). This does not excuse Aaron, who should have been willing to resist such pressure but who instead caved in to it. Yet it does tell us that Aaron may have acted partly out of fear for his own popularity/wellbeing/acceptance or the like.

But why did the people want "gods[12] who can go before us"?[13] Were they not satisfied with Yahweh's leadership during the past months, as he went

---

[8] Aaron was also older than Moses (see comments on 7:6) and thus in a culture that often prized firstborn males would have seemed a more logical choice *a priori* for national leader even than Moses was (cf., e.g., 1 Sam 16:6-13.). In addition, priestly functions were already being considered by the Israelites hadn't heard about the priestly instructions in Exod 25–31 yet because Moses had not come back down from Sinai after having been given those chapters of instruction, but they already understood Aaron to be a leader of some sort of priests (see 19:22–24), and his credentials in this area made him a logical candidate to lead them religiously in their foray into national idolatry.

[9] So Num 16:3: "They came as a group to oppose Moses and Aaron" (NRSV, "They assembled against Moses and Aaron"; Num 16:42: "When the assembly gathered in opposition to Moses and Aaron" (NRSV, "When the congregation had assembled against them;" Num 20:2: "The people gathered in opposition to Moses and Aaron" (NRSV, "so they gathered together against Moses and against Aaron"). Similarly HCSB.

[10] So NIV, "all the hordes gathered about you;" similarly NRSV, HCSB.

[11] Many expressions are similarly ambiguous and depend on context for specific definition. Consider two partially parallel Eng. compound expressions: "pin down," which can mean "get a specific answer" (as in "I couldn't pin him down as to the time") or "keep under hostile fire" (as in "we were pinned down for hours before help came"); and "roll over," which can mean "acquiesce" (as in "he rolled over once we pressed him") or "dominate" (as in "we rolled over him without any trouble"). An expression perhaps most akin in ambiguity to the Hb. expression under discussion, especially in light of its having a noun as object of its preposition, is the phrasal verb "go at it." This can have the sense "work together" (as in "they went at it and solved the problem in no time") or of "fight one another" (as in "they went at it until neither of them could stand up any longer").

before them day and night?[14] The answer was partly a matter of the strong attractions of idolatry, partly a matter of the absence of Moses, who was so closely associated with Yahweh's presence,[15] partly a matter of the passage of time during which the obvious presence of Yahweh in the pillar of cloud and fire was lacking, partly a matter of the attractiveness of the idea of a syncretism of Yahwism with the Egyptian bull cult (see below), but mostly a matter of something that continues to plague even Christian people today: an inability to see that the spiritual world is primary to and in control of the physical and visible world. In order to help his people understand the truth, Yahweh insisted on being believed in rather than being seen. It was so much easier to believe in something that could actually be seen. The Israelites were powerfully attracted to the latter option.

The reference to Moses as "this fellow Moses[16] who brought us up out of Egypt" is not an attempt to avoid thinking of Yahweh as the one who rescued the people from their slavery; rather, it is consistent with God's own characterization of Moses as the deliverer. In Exodus sometimes Moses is described as the one who brought Israel out of Egypt and other times it is Yahweh who is so described.[17]

---

[12] Although a few commentators (notably L. R. Bailey, "The Golden Calf," *HUCA* 42 [1971]; J. P. Hyatt, *Exodus,* 304; R. W. L Moberly, *At the Mountain of God: Story and Theology in Exodus 32–34,* JSOTSup 22 [Sheffield: JSOT Press, 1983]) have suggested that אֱלֹהִים should be translated by the singular, "god," here, the plural verb obviates this possibility without unwarranted textual revision. And the context itself indicates a dissatisfaction with one God, who is represented by only one man and who therefore in the absence of that man was not able (so the people thought in their folly) to protect Israel adequately. Against the singular translation see, e.g., J. N. Oswalt, "The Golden Calves and the Egyptian Concept of Deity," *EvQ* 45 (1973): 13–20; J. M. Sasson, "Bovine Symbolism in the Exodus Narrative," *VT* 18 (1968): 380–87; H. C. Brichto, "The Worship of the Golden Calf: A Literary Analysis of a Fable on Idolatry," *HUCA* 54 (1983): 1–44.

[13] The meaning of this idiom, הָלַךְ לִפְנֵי, is essentially "to lead," with special emphasis on protecting against enemies by leading in battle; cf. Exod 32:34; Num 14:14; Isa 45:2; 58:8; Ps 59:10.

[14] Indeed, Exod 13:21 uses the exact Hb. expression (*hlk qal + lipnê*) also employed in the present context: "By day the LORD went ahead of them in a pillar of cloud to guide them on their way and by night in a pillar of fire to give them light, so that they could travel by day or night."

[15] As G. W. Coats points out, the problem of the Israelites was not with Moses' lack of leadership because it was of poor quality, which is not an issue in the current text, but with his lack of leadership at the time because he simply wasn't present to lead (*Rebellion in the Wilderness* [Nashville: Abingdon, 1968], 188–90).

[16] On the meaning in the context of זֶה מֹשֶׁה ("this fellow Moses") see J. Joosten, "The Syntax of *zeh Mōšeh* (Ex 32,1.23)," *ZAW* 103 (1991): 412–15.

[17] Moses was the one who "brought Israel out of Egypt" in 3:12; 33:1; Deut 9:12. Yahweh was the one in 12:17,51; 20:2; Num 20:6. But no contradiction of any sort is implied with this varying focus on leadership. Note especially Mic 6:4, which is the most inclusive verse in the OT relative to the leadership of the exodus, identifying Moses, Aaron, Miriam, and God as the leaders of the exodus and helping the reader understand God's delegation of the exodus leadership as no denigration of God's primary and ultimate leadership. God did it, but he did it partly through intermediaries, not limited simply to Moses.

In saying "we don't know what has happened to him," the people were reflecting not just a genuine confusion but also a lack of faith at the same time. Had they been willing to trust God fully, they would have been willing to wait as long as necessary for Moses to return.[18] But their assumptions got the best of them: it appeared after "a very long time" (the meaning of "forty days and forty nights" in 24:18 and of "so long"[19] in 32:1) that Moses might not be coming back at all. The people had manna and water, so they were not panicked for food; but they wanted to get on with their journey and not stay in the wilderness of Sinai forever, a place where they had recently suffered an unprovoked attack by Amalekites. They needed, in their opinion, guidance, protection, and divine power backing them in their conquest of the promised land. They needed, they thought, real, tangible gods. When one remembers what a closely won military contest the battle at Rephidim had been (17:8–16), it is not so surprising that they would not have wanted again to experience that sort of uncertainty.

32:2–4 Acceding to the pressure he felt from the people, Aaron helped them revert to idolatry. Seeking the appropriate material (gold), he asked for earrings from the women and children, but not the men. This could reflect his estimation that more than enough earrings would be produced that way to have sufficient gold for an idol, leaving the men still resplendent in their own earrings. Or it could reflect the fact that only women and children—not men—wore earrings among the Israelites, perhaps because earrings were a visible sign that only a man's "dependents" wore, either in Egypt or generally among Israelites.[20]

The statement "so all the people took off their earrings and brought them to Aaron" does not imply in the original that every single Israelite had agreed to the idolatry. Hebrew *kōl* is often used to connote "all sorts of" as well as "every last one of," and there may have been many people, especially

[18] It is also possible that at least some of the people had begun to think of their leadership as too human and wanted divine leadership, via idols, from then on. They may have thought Moses had been limited as a leader since he was now gone, demonstrating that reliance on their (merely human) leader had failed them. Perhaps many had begun to discount the past signs of God's direct leadership such as the pillar of cloud/fire and the signs of Yahweh's presence on Mount Sinai. Since many of the Israelite leaders had actually been in God's special presence atop Mount Sinai (24:9–11), it is hard to imagine that the people would not have been deeply impressed by that—impressed enough not to fall for the idea that bull idols could substitute for Yahweh. Thus the rebellion toward idolatry could have been led by others, now asserting their influence. One notes that the text does not identify those who pressured Aaron to give them new gods.

[19] בֹּשֵׁשׁ, having something of the nuance of "be kept from" as if Moses actually had been unable to get back to the Israelites.

[20] Certainly in many cultures the dress of women and children differs from that of men. Consider the past practice in North America of dressing young boys in dresses, thus aligning them with their mothers and sisters until they were older.

Levites (see below) who resisted the folly that Aaron and others had gotten into. Exactly how Aaron built the golden young bull idol is difficult to decipher. What the NIV translates as "made it into an idol cast in the shape of a calf, fashioning it with a tool" the NRSV, for example, translates as "formed it in a mold, and cast an image of a calf."[21] Particularly in doubt is the exact meaning of *massēkû,* usually translated "molten image" or the like but not well understood in fact.[22] Nevertheless, it was indeed Aaron, of all people, who cooperated in the crafting of an idol!

Collecting the earrings, melting them into gold, and shaping the gold around a wooden form to make an idol may have taken more than a day. This, indeed, could have built the suspense. The result was full approbation, unfortunately. Not only had Aaron made an idol, but he apparently had made a good one—so the reaction of people (an indefinite but large group described simply as "they") was to recognize Aaron's work as an idol fit for them to follow and indeed to have followed. That is, they recognized the calf as the embodiment of the divinity that had led them in their exodus and so told each other, "These are your gods, O Israel, who brought you up out of Egypt." Such an announcement sounds much like that made by Jeroboam I when he introduced to the northern Israelites his countercultus golden young bulls ("Here are your gods, O Israel, who brought you up out of Egypt," 1 Kgs 12:28), the only difference being that Jeroboam said "Here are . . ." and the people surrounding Aaron said "These are . . ." In all likelihood Jeroboam knew of or was informed of the tradition stemming from this passage and capitalized on its continuing popularity in his own day. In either case, there is little doubt that Israelites of all times believed that it was Yahweh, and no other god, who had delivered them from Egypt. In other words, Yahweh was now being represented by an idol, the very sort of thing forbidden clearly by the second word/commandment.

32:5 Just as Jeroboam in his day was trying to modify the true religion of Yahweh into an idolatrous version, so Aaron attempted something of the

[21] The Hb., וַיָּצַר אֹתוֹ בַּחֶרֶט וַיַּעֲשֵׂהוּ עֵגֶל מַסֵּכָה, is worded somewhat ambiguously, being translated literally as something like "he shaped it with a stylus and made it into a young bull metal-cast idol" (cf. HCSB, "fashioned it with an engraving tool, and made it into an image of a calf"). Probably the Hb. wording intends us to understand that he melted down the gold, put it into a mold or molded it around a wooden form, got the general shape of a young bull from it, and then did the finishing detail with a stylus-type tool (cf. LXX ἐν τῇ γραφίδι). The somewhat related passage in Judg 17:1–4 indicates that two hundred shekels of silver (roughly five pounds) would suffice for a cast idol (the proper translation of the comparable part of 17:4 being "he made it into a shaped idol, i.e., a cast-metal idol" rather than the NIV's "who made them into the image and the idol."

[22] See the review of various suggestions for the meaning of *massēkû* in J. I. Durham, *Exodus,* WBC (Waco: Word, 1987), 416, 419–20. He tends toward the translation "overlaid image" (referring to an image of wood overlaid with gold or silver). For the same phenomenon I would suggest the translation "plated idol."

reverse: to salvage worship of Yahweh by associating the idolatrous version squarely with Yahweh, building an altar in front of the calf, and declaring a "festival" (worship-feast day)[23] to Yahweh for the following day. Building an altar in front of a god/idol conformed to the expected positioning of sacrifices in idolatry; it guaranteed that the god would see the offerings made to him and accept them. By contrast the orthodox biblical positioning of the altar in the courtyard of the tabernacle, and later temple, so that there was no direct line of sight from the ark in the holy of holies to the altar because of the curtain/veil hiding the ark was actually a positioning that required Israelites to have the faith to understand that the one true God actually saw what they did for him without having his idol right behind and facing the altar on which they did it.

32:6 Again imitating orthodoxy through idolatry, the people "sacrificed burnt offerings and presented fellowship offerings," which were forms of offering otherwise appropriate for Yahweh (on burnt offerings see Exod 10:25; 18:12; 20:24; 24:5; 29:18,25,42; 30:9,28; 31:9; on fellowship offerings see 20:24–25; 29:28). "Burnt offerings," also known as "whole burnt offerings," sought atonement for the worshiper's sin.[24] "Fellowship offerings," also known as "sacrifices/offerings of well-being" celebrated the worshiper's ongoing covenant relationship with Yahweh.[25] Had they been worshiping Yahweh correctly at his tabernacle, they would have been doing a good thing; but here they were worshiping exactly as forbidden in the second word/commandment (Exod 20:4–6,23) and were ignoring a law they had solemnly agreed to keep (24:3,7).

Further copying the worship styles of idolatry after eating and drinking the idol-worship meal prepared from their fellowship offerings,[26] the people began to engage in "having fun" (NIV "revelry," HCSB "to revel").[27] If any overtone of sexual debauchery is intended here, it is not followed through in

[23] Aaron used orthodox language in referring to the heterodox festival day he was proclaiming. The term translated here "festival to the LORD" (חַג לַיהוָה) was already used in 12:14; 13:6 to refer to the Passover and occurs again in Lev 23:41; Num 29:12 in reference to the feast of Tabernacles. The essentially comparable phrase חַג־יְהוָה ("Yahweh's festival") also occurred in 10:9 (cf. Lev 23:39; Judg 21:19; Hos 9:5).

[24] See Lev 1 et passim.

[25] See Lev 3–6 and esp. Lev 7 et passim.

[26] Burnt offerings would have been entirely consumed on the altar, so they would not have provided any sort of meal for the people. The fellowship (wellbeing) offerings, however, were to be distributed by a token portion to the god, a small portion to the priest, and the rest to the worshiper and his family, who would then eat their portion at or around the shrine—similar to but still a distortion of the proper mode of eating a fellowship offering in Yahweh's presence, i.e., in the courtyard of his tabernacle.

[27] Hb. צחק *piel;* one of seven uses in the OT (cf. Gen 19:14; 21:9; 26:8; 39:14,17; Judg 16:25). It can certainly connote sexual activity (Gen 26:8; 39:17) but can also mean simply to have fun (Judg 16:25) or "play" (Gen 21:9).

the rest of the narrative: Moses later described shouting (v. 17), singing (v. 18), and dancing[28] (v. 19), but not the sort of cultic prostitution the Israelites later indulged in at another location (Num 25), and identified the people's sin as idolatry per se (vv. 31–32; 34–35). The revelry of the occasion was apparently singing and dancing with abandon, bad enough as a means of celebration of the people's newfound relationship with an idol.

(2) God's Anger and Moses' Intercession (32:7–14)

7Then the LORD said to Moses, "Go down, because your people, whom you brought up out of Egypt, have become corrupt. 8They have been quick to turn away from what I commanded them and have made themselves an idol cast in the shape of a calf. They have bowed down to it and sacrificed to it and have said, 'These are your gods, O Israel, who brought you up out of Egypt.'

9"I have seen these people," the LORD said to Moses, "and they are a stiff-necked people. 10Now leave me alone so that my anger may burn against them and that I may destroy them. Then I will make you into a great nation."

11But Moses sought the favor of the LORD his God. "O LORD," he said, "why should your anger burn against your people, whom you brought out of Egypt with great power and a mighty hand? 12Why should the Egyptians say, 'It was with evil intent that he brought them out, to kill them in the mountains and to wipe them off the face of the earth'? Turn from your fierce anger; relent and do not bring disaster on your people. 13Remember your servants Abraham, Isaac and Israel, to whom you swore by your own self: 'I will make your descendants as numerous as the stars in the sky and I will give your descendants all this land I promised them, and it will be their inheritance forever.'" 14Then the LORD relented and did not bring on his people the disaster he had threatened.

Although Moses and Yahweh were conversing on Mount Sinai, the purpose was not further revelation of laws but consideration of whether or not the people deserved to continue under Yahweh's covenant blessing. In this part of the story, God laid a challenge before Moses in the form of a rhetorical proposal ("leave me alone so that . . . I may destroy them," v. 10). Moses creditably took up this challenge and unselfishly appealed for God to preserve his relationship with his people, even though the alternative might have been attractive to Moses' own ego ("I will make you into a great nation").

32:7 In saying to Moses, "Go down . . .," God was not bringing his time with Moses on Mount Sinai to a hasty conclusion. The tabernacle instructions, which were the purpose of this particular time with God on the mountain, had been completed, as their fulfillment narrative (chaps. 35–40) confirms, and the next forty days and nights on the mountain were soon to

[28] It is possible that "dancing" (מְחֹלֹת) is intended as a euphemism for more overtly sexual debauchery, but no proof of such a use of the term exists.

come at any rate (34:1–28). Although the people's idolatrous rebellion against Yahweh's covenant could conceivably be regarded as an interruption of the process of revealing the law to Moses, it was neither a long-term nor an insurmountable interruption.

The fact that God used second-person speech of Moses' role in the exodus ("your people, whom you brought up out of Egypt") does not represent God's shifting of blame or responsibility away from himself to Moses but is consistent with the way attribution of leadership for the exodus varies according to context (see note on 32:1). God here assigned Moses the responsibility to deal with the sin of the people with whom he had become so closely identified. The NIV translation "[the people] have become corrupt" is doubtful. Such a meaning is possible for the verb in question here, *šḥt,* if it were used in the *niphal* (e.g., Gen 6:11; 8:20), but the *piel,* the verb stem actually employed here, has more the meaning "to ruin, to act ruinously, to do a corrupt thing." In other words, God was not saying to Moses that the Israelites were no longer capable of doing good (i.e., had become corrupt in the sense of being spoiled/polluted or the like) but that they had done something so wrong that it constituted acting corruptly. Thus, for example, the NRSV "have acted perversely" or the HCSB "have acted corruptly" more nearly capture the sense that the situation, while very serious, was not one of no hope whatever for Israel's redemption.

32:8 However, God's summary for Moses of what had happened in the camp while he had been on the mountain indicates how much the nation had already turned from its promise to follow Yahweh's covenant. Even if every single person had not participated,[29] many had eagerly done so, and the rest had not acted to repudiate them, with the result that the nation as a whole, the nation on balance, can be described simply as "they": "They have been quick to turn away from what I commanded them" indicates the divine assessment of Israel's propensities to covenant infidelity.

God then defined this sin clearly, leaving no doubt that the second commandment had been violated utterly. They made for "themselves" a metal-plated idol (rather than merely being camped near where one existed already or rather than having a few people try to make a crude clay idol) "in the shape of a bull" (see below), bowed down to it ("worshiped it," clearly indicating their belief that it was a god), "sacrificed to it" (further proving their belief that it had the power to bless and save them), openly stated that it represented the gods they now had chosen to believe in (thus also potentially violating the first commandment against worshiping any god but Yahweh), and attributed to the idol their rescue from Egypt, thus associating Yahweh syncretistically with the young bull, as if now, finally, Yahweh could be

[29] See comments above on 32:2–4.

properly worshiped and his presence properly represented among them in contrast to the inferior ways it had been previously manifest. Since God himself had chosen his ways of personal manifestation in the past (fire, smoke, pillar, overpowering voice), the people's choice of a dumb idol who could do none of these things over the living God was also a rejection of his methods of demonstrating his presence. What they could see and touch at their convenience was what they wanted—a god who would let them live as they wished and have a good time when they wanted to and who would not impose his covenant requirements on them. Theirs was a foolish choice reflecting badly on any people so self-absorbed and self-destructive as to make it.

In this verse God referred to the idol with the same definitive term already seen in v. 4, *massēkā,* lit., "metal-plated young bull idol" (NIV "idol cast in the shape of a calf"). What made this particular kind of idol seem so "right" to the Israelites that when they saw it they proclaimed, "These are your gods"? Indeed, what caused Aaron—to the extent that he felt he had an easy choice in the matter[30]—to select this design to represent Yahweh idolatrously, as opposed to any other of the many designs that may have been theoretically within his range of options? The answer may provide insight into the thinking of the people. Substantial evidence exists to suggest that an idol in the shape of a young bull fit with the Egyptian concept of how deity was to be envisioned.

A vigorous young bull seemed to the Egyptians an appropriate way to represent a truly powerful god.[31] In other words, by their actions Aaron and the people showed themselves still to be "Egyptian Israelites" rather than "Yahweh's Israelites." They demonstrated that they were not really at home away from home but were beginning already to long for a reversion to the ways of living and thinking they grew up with and that in retrospect seemed comfortable and, indeed, better than what they were now experiencing (cf. the overt expression of this a year later in Num 14 and the similar challenge of Yahweh to Moses relative to destroying the Israelites in that context). The people were, in other words, so wedded to their old culture that they could manage to justify in their minds its false religion, even to the point of the

[30] The fact that Aaron probably felt himself under pressure and afraid of the consequences of opposing the people does not exonerate his actions, though it may have helped him to rationalize his actions. In fact, he willingly committed a severe sin and helped the people to do so as well.

[31] See esp. Oswalt, "The Golden Calves and the Egyptian Concept of Deity," 13–20; cf. M. Aberbach and L. Smolar, "Aaron, Jeroboam and the Golden Calves," *JBL* 86 (1967): 129–40; L. R. Bailey, "The Golden Calf," *HUCA* 42 (1971): 97–115; G. A. Wainwright, "The Bull Standards of Egypt," *JEA* 19 (1933): 42–52. A different theory of the origins of the calf/bull idol worship is found in the approach of A. F. Key, "Traces of the Worship of the Moon God Sin among the Early Israelites," *JBL* 84 (1965): 20–26; cf. J. Lewy, "The Assyro-Babylonian Cult of the Moon and its Culmination in the Time of Nabonidus," *HUCA* 19 (1945–46): 405–89.

type of animals used to represent a god, even though that religion had been proved false over and over again by Yahweh's mighty acts on their behalf right up to the present time (so esp. 12:12). Old habits and ways of thinking die hard; in times of stress people often revert to them even though they are useless or destructive. Such are the limits of reliance on human wisdom in a fallen world.

32:9–10 In Hebrew the idiom "I have seen this people" means "I am fully aware of what this people is like" or "I know all about this nation."[32] It does not suggest that God would have to pay special attention to a group in order to know what they were doing. In other words, it does not suggest him to be less than omniscient as if he hadn't been seeing them at all times.[33] "Stiff-necked" is a compound adjective meaning "stubborn and oppositional."[34]

In saying "Now leave me alone" God made a rhetorical demand. He was challenging Moses rather than commanding him. Moses had no power to stop God from doing anything, so there would have been no need whatever for God to ask permission of Moses to do something through the statement "leave me alone." Rather, it was a rhetorical way of saying to Moses: "Here is what I will do unless you intervene." For God to announce to a prophet (Moses being the paradigm for all future prophets) his intention to do something as a way of inviting intercession has many parallels, the most famous perhaps being those of Amos 7:1–6, where God showed Amos things he was planning to do by way of judgment upon Israel and then, in response to Amos' intercession, relented. In that context he was clearly inviting Amos to intercede so that he (God) might relent. A similarly prominent example is found in Jonah's required announcement that Nineveh would be destroyed in "forty days" (Jonah 3:4), a message Jonah reluctantly gave because he knew that it represented an invitation to repent and not an irreversible condemnation.[35]

In v. 10 God rhetorically proposed three things: to unleash his anger ("so that my anger may burn against them"),[36] to destroy the current Israel ("that I may destroy them"), and to make a new nation from Moses' descendants ("then I will make you into a great nation"), thus effectively replacing the

---

[32] Cf. Gen 7:1; 31:12; Exod 3:7,9; Deut 9:13.

[33] Cf. Gen 31:2; Exod 3:9; Deut 9:13; Eccl 1:14.

[34] Cf. 33:3,5; 34:9; Deut 9:6,13; 10:16; 31:27.

[35] "Yet forty days" is a way of saying, "If you don't repent even after I have given you plenty of time to do so, I will destroy you." On the idiomatic nuance of אַרְבָּעִים, "forty," see comments on 24:18.

[36] To "burn with anger" (חרה אף) usually carries the sense of being sufficiently angry to do something major about the anger or against the object of the anger, i.e., to get mad enough to take serious action. Moses used the expression often in his writing (Gen 39:19; Exod 4:14; 15:7; here and in 32:11,19; Num 11:1,33; 12:9; 24:10; 25:3; 32:13; Deut 6:5; 7:4; 11:17; 29:23,27).

promises to make Abraham into a great nation (e.g., Gen 12:2; renewed in Gen 18:18; 21:18; 35:11; 46:23) with new promises to do the same for Moses. This tested Moses' commitment to God's original plan, the plan to make a great people out of Abraham. Would the test proposal appeal to Moses? It certainly might have since it might have flattered him to think himself worthy of being the patriarch of a great new nation and of having the regularly troublesome Israelites eliminated by divine fiat so that his own future would be brighter and more successful.

32:11–14 Much to his credit, Moses revealed no desire to replace Abraham and no interest in easing his own problems by seeing the recalcitrant Israelites obliterated. Indeed, as the reader will learn in v. 32, Moses was willing to offer the loss of his eternal life rather than see the nation of Israel eliminated from the earth. He appealed to God (just as God expected him to by inviting him through the rhetorical "leave me alone . . ." in v. 10) with three arguments, all of which appealed to God's character of consistency and faithfulness.[37] The first is: Why should God nullify the result of his demonstration of divine power? ("whom you brought out of Egypt with great power and a mighty hand"). The second is: Why should God grant the Egyptians delight in seeing the Israelites crushed—and by their own God? ("Why should the Egyptians say, 'It was with evil intent that he brought them out, to kill them in the mountains and to wipe them off the face of the earth"). The third is: Why should God go back on his promises to the patriarchs? ("Remember your servants Abraham, Isaac and Israel, to whom you swore by your own self: 'I will make your descendants as numerous as the stars in the sky and I will give your descendants all this land I promised them, and it will be their inheritance forever"). This sort of appeal to God appears again, though not in exactly the same form or wording, in Num 14:13–19 (in connection with the rebellion in the wilderness) and in Deut 9:26–29 (a reminder of the present context). Abraham himself had appealed to God's character and past faithfulness in Gen 18:22–32 on behalf of the city of Sodom.

Moses' intercessory prayer was not more eloquent or more convincing in its arguments than many prayers in the Bible. Would it work? Moses surely

[37] A very different analysis is provided by Durham (*Exodus,* 429) with his comment that "Moses' whole concern is with the people; he seems not to have realized the gravity of the actions, that they have themselves negated their privileged relationship with Yahweh." It is hard to imagine that Moses would not take seriously Yahweh's word for what the people had done or that his unselfish, prophetic intercessory advocacy for the people could be dismissed by the suggestion that it was simply the expression of an unbalanced concern for the people and not for Yahweh's will as well. By appealing to Yahweh's promises, character, and past actions, Moses showed that his whole concern was not just for the people but for the fulfillment of Yahweh's plan of redemption involving the people.

hoped that it would and may have had a confidence that it would, but if so, his confidence may have been based more on his relationship with Yahweh than on his skill in prayer. In other words, because of who he was, rather than how he prayed, Moses could expect his prayer to be treated with compassion.[38] He was the one Yahweh had chosen to bring the people out of Egypt and into Canaan. To reach only half the goal would hardly fulfill the expectation of faith that God had put within him. Reminding God of his promises was hardly needed from the point of view of God's memory; it was, rather, a means of showing his faith in who God was, something he also continued to pursue further in the aftermath of the people's sin (see comments on 33:12–18).

Of course, God never desired to destroy his people in the first place, so he was willing to relent[39] in response to Moses' appeal (v. 14). Nevertheless, the threat was genuine rather than theoretical, and the response of God reveals his willingness to respond to prayer. Indeed, this is one of many passages in Scripture that demonstrate God's responsiveness to the prayer of a righteous person prayed not for selfish reasons but out of a desire to see God's will accomplished.[40] It is important to remember that Moses here stated that God "relented and did not bring on his people the disaster he had threatened"—which is not at all the same as saying that God agreed to do nothing. What he had threatened was to destroy Israel; what he ended up doing was to punish them with a plague (32:34–35), a lesser punishment but by no means an acquittal.[41]

In v. 12 the Egyptians are portrayed as saying that God would kill the Israelites in the mountains. This is entirely in concert with the Egyptian mentality that the foreign lands outside of Egypt were "the mountains." The middle Egyptian terms for "foreigners" usually involved some form of the plural Egyptian word *ḫ3swt,* "mountains"/"mountainous lands" (as in "ruling foreigners," *ḥk3w ḫ3swt,* literally "rulers of the mountains," the term from which *Hyksos* is derived.

In v. 13 God is described as swearing by himself ("you swore by your own self"), a way of saying that he formally, solemnly gave his promise[42] to

---

[38] See M. D. Spencer, "Moses as Intercessor," *ScrB* 19 (1999): 79–86.

[39] The Hb. verb, וַיִּנָּחֶם *niphal* of נחם, translated by the NIV as "relented" can more simply be rendered in Eng. as "changed his mind" (so, e.g., NRSV). The idea that God would not shift direction or adjust his plans in response to prayer is foreign to the Bible but unfortunately at home with some forms of deterministic theology. Opposition to "open theism" need not lead to a rejection of God's flexibility and responsiveness as if he cannot change direction in accord with his own purposes.

[40] Cf., e.g., Prov 15:29; Jas 5:16; 1 Pet 3:12.

[41] Note that later, in 34:7, Moses would specially acknowledge God's consistency in giving punishment where it is deserved rather than in arbitrarily overlooking sin ("he does not leave the guilty unpunished").

[42] Cf. Gen 22:16; Isa 45:23; Jer 22:5; 49:13; Ezek 20:5; Heb 6:13.

create and maintain Abraham's descendants as a great people. Humans swear by something greater than themselves; God swore by himself because there was nothing greater.[43]

In v. 14 the wording concluding the verse is of great importance: Yahweh changed his mind about the disaster he planned to bring on "his people." They would not have been a people at all had he carried out what he threatened; instead this part of the narrative concludes with a reminder that he remained their God and they his people, his special possession, the kingdom of priests and holy nation—however deeply corrupted they may have been at this point—that he had created them to be (19:6).

(3) Moses' Anger and the Levite Punishment (32:15–29)

15Moses turned and went down the mountain with the two tablets of the Testimony in his hands. They were inscribed on both sides, front and back. 16The tablets were the work of God; the writing was the writing of God, engraved on the tablets.

17When Joshua heard the noise of the people shouting, he said to Moses, "There is the sound of war in the camp."

18Moses replied:

"It is not the sound of victory,
it is not the sound of defeat;
it is the sound of singing that I hear."

19When Moses approached the camp and saw the calf and the dancing, his anger burned and he threw the tablets out of his hands, breaking them to pieces at the foot of the mountain. 20And he took the calf they had made and burned it in the fire; then he ground it to powder, scattered it on the water and made the Israelites drink it.

21He said to Aaron, "What did these people do to you, that you led them into such great sin?"

22"Do not be angry, my lord," Aaron answered. "You know how prone these people are to evil. 23They said to me, 'Make us gods who will go before us. As for this fellow Moses who brought us up out of Egypt, we don't know what has happened to him.' 24So I told them, 'Whoever has any gold jewelry, take it off.' Then they gave me the gold, and I threw it into the fire, and out came this calf!"

25Moses saw that the people were running wild and that Aaron had let them get out of control and so become a laughingstock to their enemies. 26So he stood

---

[43] God's taking an oath, essentially an idiomatic way of referring to a divine promise, is not to be followed exemplaristically, as Jesus' teaching in the Sermon on the Mount makes clear: "Again, you have heard that it was said to the people long ago, 'Do not break your oath, but keep the oaths you have made to the Lord.' But I tell you, Do not swear at all: either by heaven, for it is God's throne; or by the earth, for it is his footstool; or by Jerusalem, for it is the city of the Great King. And do not swear by your head, for you cannot make even one hair white or black. Simply let your 'Yes' be 'Yes,' and your 'No,' 'No'; anything beyond this comes from the evil one" (Matt 5:33–37).

at the entrance to the camp and said, "Whoever is for the LORD, come to me." And all the Levites rallied to him. [27]Then he said to them, "This is what the LORD, the God of Israel, says: 'Each man strap a sword to his side. Go back and forth through the camp from one end to the other, each killing his brother and friend and neighbor.' " [28]The Levites did as Moses commanded, and that day about three thousand of the people died. [29]Then Moses said, "You have been set apart to the LORD today, for you were against your own sons and brothers, and he has blessed you this day."

32:15–16 "Moses turned" refers to his departure from his usual position of looking up at God—who was majestically manifest in glory, clouded from the view of all others, above the summit of Mount Sinai[44]—and facing down the mountain to descend from it. Most of vv. 15–16 reminds the reader that the tablets of the Ten Words/Commandments were unique in that God wrote them himself, as opposed to laws Moses wrote on other tablets or papyrus or leather[45] at God's dictation. The tablets were not divided among the commandments, but each tablet contained all ten, so that one tablet represented the suzerain's copy and one the vassal's, in accordance with standard ancient Near Eastern document preservation practices.[46] These two tablets were the most valuable material thing on earth at that time, as the reader is now informed clearly, so that later when Moses breaks them, the reader can appreciate the severity of the sin that would have caused him to do something so destructive to something so precious.[47]

The fact that the tablets were written on both sides is not unique in itself—most tablets from the ancient world are two-sided. In light of the relatively short length of the total wording of the Ten Words/Commandments, however, the mentioning of both sides' being written on suggests that the writing was relatively large, big enough that more than one person could view the writing, as a group stood and looked together at it. Moreover, and presumably even more important, the tablets had no space left for additions.

---

[44] See, e.g., 19:16–20; 20:18–21; 24:10.

[45] Four writing surfaces were used at this time in history: stone (for the most official, royal sorts of inscriptions), clay tablets (mainly for cuneiform Babylonian and Assyrian), leather (various animal skins including calfskin, goatskin, sheepskin), and papyrus (the least permanent of all but increasingly employed for writing at this time). That the tablets of the Ten Words/Commandments were on stone comports with the use of stone for the highest-level, most enduring communications throughout history. Cf. the modern phrase "it's not chiseled in stone" to describe things less than permanent.

[46] See also comments on 24:12; 31:18. The "document clause" part of the covenant structure was fulfilled thereby (cf. "Excursus: The Exodus-Leviticus Covenant" prior to 20:1).

[47] The Bible never draws an explicit parallel between the breaking of the tablets and the breaking of Christ's body on the cross, but the concept that God would cause harm to something precious to himself because of the severity of the sin of his people is in a general sense shared by the incident of the breaking of the covenant tablets and the punishment of Christ on the cross. There is here, in other words, a circumstantial comparability rather than a doctrinal connection.

The Ten Words/Commandments were designed to be a primary and fully sufficient locus of covenant expectation, lasting and settled, to which the rest of the laws were explanatory rather than strictly supplemental or substitutionary.[48]

32:17 As Moses came down the mountain, he met up with Joshua, who was waiting for him at a prearranged place partway between the top and the bottom.[49] Continuing toward the Israelite encampment at the foot of the mountain, they heard the noise of the pagan revelry in which the people were indulging (v. 6), a sound so loud, and perhaps disorderly as well, that Joshua mistook it for the sound of battle. As Israel's military general, he well knew the sound of war (cf. 17:8–10)—the yelling, screaming, cacophonous din combined from the organized war shouts,[50] calls of fighters to one another, the screams of pain, the shouts of fury, and so on. That sounds similar enough to those of war should have come from the Israelites' pagan carousing indicates the degree to which the loss of self-control[51] was generalized among the population. What Joshua and Moses heard probably was a mixture of sounds[52] from such things as drunken singing, wild dancing, men shouting as they chased women and women screaming as they were being chased, people fighting over food and drink, women fighting over men and men fighting over women, and the sort of shrieking that pagans thought appropriate to rousing the gods.

32:18–19 But it was not a war sound—neither "the sound of victory" nor "the sound of defeat." What Moses knew both from being forewarned

---

[48] In other words, if a person truly and fully understood the Ten Commandments, he or she would understand the remaining 611 commandments. This is parallel to Jesus' teaching that on the two great commandments hang all the Law and the Prophets (Matt 22:37–40). From the two great commandments, loving God and loving neighbor, stem the Ten Commandments, and from them in turn stem the others. One might wonder at the need for the Ten Commandments at all in light of Jesus' emphasis on the two. The key to understanding the issue is the Holy Spirit. Without the indwelling of God's Spirit as granted exclusively in the New Covenant, the two great commandments can be easily interpreted subjectively and self-servingly (as when people, even today, think that loving your neighbor as yourself means that you must first love yourself—the very opposite of what it actually means, as 2 Tim 3:2 confirms). Thus in the Old Covenant the Ten and the other 611 were very much needed. In the New Covenant, when the Spirit is not quenched by the believer's sin, however, the two will do very nicely as "the law of Christ" (e.g., Gal 6:2; cf. Jas 2:8).

[49] See comments on 24:13.

[50] Cf. Josh 6:10; 1 Sam 17:20; Isa 8:9; 13:4; Jer 4:16; 49:2; 2 Chr 13:15; Ezek 21:22.

[51] Loss of self-control is a serious sin (cf. Prov 25:28; 1 Cor 7:5; Gal 5:22–23; 2 Tim 3:3; 2 Pet 1:6). Note that self-control was considered a basic fruit of belief in Christ in the preaching of the apostles (e.g., Acts 24:25). The fact that some religious groups, ancient and modern, have actually glorified loss of self-control as "spiritual" is an indication of how remarkably people can fool themselves in contrast to biblical teaching.

[52] The NIV translation "the noise of the people shouting" is in fact only one possibility for the Hb. קוֹל הָעָם בְּרֵעֹה. Perhaps more likely is the NJPS "the sound of the people in its boisterousness." In other words, the text does not limit the noise to mere shouting.

(vv. 7–8) and what he could discern among the din of the revelry was some other sort of sound—perhaps, though not for certain, including loud, raucous singing that was a major component (though almost surely not the sole component) of the noise Joshua had mistaken for the sound of war. In the Hebrew text this verse appears to have the characteristics of a poetic triplet and is thus typically rendered stichometrically, as in the following example:

Moses replied:
"It is not the sound of victory,
 it is not the sound of defeat;
  it is the sound of singing that I hear."

But does the Hebrew actually say this? A neutral, very literal rendering of the original might be: "He said, 'The sound of noise going back and forth that I hear is not the sound of noise going back and forth of victory, and it is not the sound of noise going back and forth of defeat." In other words, Moses apparently did not refer to singing at all.[53] He said he did not discern the noise of war (either the kind of noise a victorious army might make or the kind of noise a defeated army might make or both together), but it is not in fact clear that he heard singing.

The revelry of the Israelites did involve adoration of the young bull and the dancing that accompanied it, both of which told Moses that the people

---

[53] Certainly some major translations do not think so, as evidenced, e.g., by the NRSV's rendering: "But he said, 'It is not the sound made by victors, / or the sound made by losers; / it is the sound of revelers that I hear.'" Cp. the HCSB, "It's not the sound of a victory cry / and not the sound of a cry of defeat; / I hear the sound of singing!" But the challenge of translating this verse goes well beyond merely the vocabulary. The syntax may be understood in more than one way. Here, e.g., is a translation that reads the final four word of the Hb. as resumptive and appositional:

He said: וַיֹּאמֶר
It is not the noise of victory אֵין קוֹל עֲנוֹת גְּבוּרָה
And it is not the noise of defeat—וְאֵין קוֹל עֲנוֹת חֲלוּשָׁה
The noise that I hear. קוֹל עַנּוֹת אָנֹכִי שֹׁמֵעַ

A key question for the translator is how best to render Hb. עֲנוֹת (construct) twice and whether or not to give any notice to the unusual Masoretic pointing עַנּוֹת in Moses' final usage of this term. All three would seem to be forms of the *qal* infinitive construct of one of the four separate verbs involving the consonants ענה, i.e., either ענה I or II or III or IV. ענה I can refer to speech/noise going "back and forth." ענה II carries of the sense of humiliation/degradation, which probably is not relevant here. ענה III deals with worry and preoccupation, also not likely appropriate to the context. ענה IV has the sense of singing/making noise/howling and the like and is most likely the verb we are to understand as being used by Moses in the context—but because it does not necessarily refer to singing per se, it can simply be used of "noise" or "noisemaking." If it is in fact a kind of biform of ענה I (noise/speech going back and forth), it could have the derived meaning of "song/singing" as a derivative of the way singing is often a group function ("back and forth") and often even antiphonal (structured in a back-and-forth pattern). But we simply cannot be sure Moses is to be understood as referring to singing at all. The wording may be intended to describe a hubbub or din or "crowd noise" in general and nothing particularly musical.

had indeed gone into pagan idolatry, and he became enraged. In his anger he threw the tablets to the (rocky) ground at the base of the mountain and broke them to pieces. Was this action simply a hasty, angry, impulsive move on Moses' part—one that he might have regretted at a later time of greater personal calm? We suggest that such an explanation is unlikely. Instead, Moses' breaking of the tablets was an important symbolic act done carefully, deliberately, and openly for the benefit of the Israelites because of the way violation of a covenant is routinely described in the ancient Semitic world as a "breaking" of that "covenant."[54] In a striking parallel, Zechariah broke a staff he had identified as representing God's covenant with the nations as a means of demonstrating the breaking of that divinely granted covenant (Zech 11:10).

We should remember that the "foot of the mountain" mentioned in this verse is not simply an incidental description of where Moses happened to be at the time he smashed the tablets. "The foot of the mountain" holds a special place in the narrative as the people's official gathering place and worship arena (19:12), thus their place of meeting with God (19:17) as well as the location of the only proper worship altar (not the one Aaron built) as described already in 24:4. In Deut 4:11 Moses reminded the people: "You came near and stood at the foot of the mountain while it blazed with fire to the very heavens, with black clouds and deep darkness." Moses broke the tablets at the proper place, where the Israelites could see him do it, as a public act, signifying the breach of the covenant and the impending imposition of the consequences thereof, that is, punishment for the violators. Was Moses capable of impulsive acts? Certainly. But nowhere in the Exodus narrative or anywhere else in the Scripture is his breaking of the tablets described as impulsive. It was a reasoned, overt act demonstrating a fact (the covenant had been broken) and warning of a consequence (divine wrath—far worse than the anger of Moses). The expression used to describe Moses' anger is a common one *(ḥārāh + ʾāp)* and does not indicate that he lost control of himself or was "blind with rage" or the like.[55]

32:20 Moses did everything he could to destroy the bull idol permanently and desecrate it fully. Because the idol was made primarily of wood

---

[54] Cf. the "breaking" language in Gen 17:14; Lev 26:25,44; Deut 31:16,20; Judg 2:1–2; Isa 24:5; Jer 11:10; 14:21; 31:32; 33:20; Ezek 16:59; 17:18; Hos 6:7; 8:1; Mal 2:10. Cf. also R. N. Whybray, "*ʿannôt* in Exodus XXXII 18," *VT* 17 (1967): 122.

[55] The expression is used fifty-two times in the OT, most commonly of God, who certainly cannot be accused of losing control of himself. Anger is often an appropriate emotion, is not automatically a sin or flaw (or otherwise God would be sinful and flawed), and is not always to be concealed or suppressed.

overlaid with gold, it could be burned.[56] So Moses burned it in a fire[57] and then ground up the resulting charcoal and gold slag into a powder (presumably with a group of mortars and pestles used by people to whom he delegated this task) and then threw the powder into the drinking water supply (the flow of water at the base of Mount Horeb known as Massah and Meribah; cf. 17:6–7; Deut 9:21).

The statement that he "made the Israelites drink it" may not be the best translation of the Hebrew and at any rate probably does not mean he had them all line up and drink some as an organized group punishment. Rather it means that by putting the powder into their water supply, he saw to it that eventually the powder was drunk along with the water[58] and thus went through the Israelites' bodies, came out as waste, corrupted and defiled, and therefore was ruined permanently as material fit for an idol.[59] Burning, grinding, and scattering were actions commonly employed in the ancient world to get rid of an idol permanently so that it could never be reconstituted from its scavenged elements and be thought again worthy of worship.[60] Thus Josiah did a similar sort of thing with the Asherah idol he removed from the Jerusalem temple ("He took the Asherah pole from the temple of the LORD to the Kidron Valley outside Jerusalem and burned it there. He ground it to powder and scattered the dust over the graves of the common people," 2 Kgs 23:6) and with the high place idol and altar from Bethel (2 Kgs 23:15; cf. 2 Chr 34:4), and a king of Moab burned the bones of a king of Edom to powder in order to try to deny him a reconstituted body in the resurrection (Amos 2:1).[61]

32:21 Moses' opening question to Aaron ("What did these people do to you . . .?") allows for the possibility that the people had somehow pressured Aaron into crafting the bull idol and supervising their pagan revelry. This

[56] S. E. Loewenstamm, "The Making and Destruction of the Golden Calf," *Bib* 48 (1967): 481–90; esp. 481–82; F. C. Fensham, "The Burning of the Golden Calf and Ugarit," *IEJ* 16 (1966): 191–93; Durham, *Exodus,* 431. But contrast L. G. Perdue, "The Making and Destruction of the Golden Calf—A Reply," *Bib* 54 (1973): 237–46.

[57] The usual translation "the fire" reflects the occasional use of the article in Hb. to designate an item being introduced into the narrative—i.e., "a certain fire that he made." Cf. 2:15.

[58] Thus suggesting the superior translation "and so the Israelites had to drink it."

[59] Cf. *Jewish Study Bible,* 185., n. 20. This would seem to be the implication of Moses' description of the event in Deut 9:21.

[60] To the objection that metal cannot be "crushed" (טחן) and would not "burn (שׂרף), H. Rand offers evidence that these terms are indeed appropriate ways in biblical Hb. to convey the notion of smelting the gold and then grinding it into powder ("The Destruction of the Golden Calf: A Reply," *JBQ* 23 [1995]: 242–47).

[61] A Ugaritic text describing the goddess Anat's destruction of the death god Mot also involves burning, grinding, and scattering as the natural sequence of determined permanent destruction (*ANET* 140:ii); cf. U. Cassuto's discussion in "Baal and Mot in the Ugaritic Texts," *IEJ* 12 (1962): 77–86.

does not necessarily suggest any uncertainty on Moses' part as to whether Aaron could possibly have a good excuse for his actions in spite of whatever pressure he felt, but it more likely resulted from Moses' cultural deference to his older brother and—previously—great ally in the exodus leadership. In other words, Moses should not be understood as assuming that Aaron was not actually at fault. Not only so, but his words "such great sin" and his attribution of leadership into that sin ("you led them") make abundantly clear that Aaron deliberately committed a serious wrong against God.

32:22–24 Aaron's response was both self-serving and unconvincing. It thus was dishonest and indefensible. By his inability to provide a reasonable account of why he would have agreed to the people's request for idolatry, he condemned himself.[62] His virtual "I was just a bystander" defense would be laughable if he were not so prominent a leader among the Israelites, one whom Moses had trusted to act properly in his absence (24:14). One notes in this instance Aaron's deferential speech to the leader of the people even though Moses was his younger brother ("do not be angry, my lord") as well as his attempt at deflecting the blame from himself to the people ("you know how prone these people are to evil").

Going even further, Aaron sought to shunt some of the blame toward Moses himself, with his quote of the people's remark about how they had been virtually abandoned by Moses through his long absence, thus again emphasizing the sense that the people felt leaderless (needing gods who could "go before" them) and betrayed ("as for this fellow Moses . . . we don't know what has happened to him"). Least convincing of all is Aaron's absurd claim that forces beyond his control made the bull idol out of the gold of the peoples' jewelry ("I threw it into the fire, and out came this calf!").

On occasion commentators have suggested that Aaron's comments in his own defense were part of a way of thinking about idols in the ancient world—that they emerged supernaturally as an extension of the god they represented and were not in fact created by humans. This sort of mythopoeic thinking could conceivably have been employed by Aaron in desperation ("I've got to think of something to say to Moses when he gets back"). But it

[62] D. H. ha-Cohen tries to let Aaron off the hook a bit by suggesting that the second-to-last word in the verse (בְרָע) means "had contributed," based on an Arabic cognate, and that the second part of the verse should be taken as a question translated something like [our translation], "Did you know that the people had [actually] contributed?" In other words, by ha-Cohen's reasoning, Aaron had not expected them to contribute anything when he asked them for their gold in v. 2, so he was taken off guard by their contribution and forced into making the calf for the people by the way they called his bluff ("אַתָּה יָדַעְתָּ אֶת־הָעָם כִּי בְרָע הוּא" ["You Know That the People Were Evil (Exod 32:22)"], *BMik* 37 [1991–92]: 131–36). Resting any semantic study on an Arabic cognate is tenuous, and positing an interrogative nuance to the end of the verse is conjectural, so ha-Cohen's approach remains speculative in our opinion.

wouldn't have fooled the other Israelites, and it didn't fool Moses, as v. 25 makes abundantly clear. Most importantly, it didn't fool God, who already had informed Moses of the sin (32:7–8) and had already pronounced his condemnation of it (32:9–14).

32:25 This verse may be translated otherwise than in the NIV. For example, the JPSV renders it: "Moses saw that the people were out of control—since Aaron had let them get out of control—so that they were a menace to any who might oppose them." The word translated by the JPSV as "menace" and by the NIV as "laughingstock" *(šimṣâh)* occurs only here;[63] and because it is a hapax legomenon, its meaning cannot be definitively established. More often than not, some sort of root definition of "whisper" or "derisive whisper" or "insignificance" (in the sense of "pushover [to their enemies]") is proposed for it. So we are faced with two possible concepts for what it was that Moses saw as a problem: the idea that the Israelites' being out of control would make them easy prey for potential enemies"[64] (who would regard them as a joke/a fighting force so embarrassing that out of concern for politeness they should only be whispered about), or the idea that the Israelites' being out of control would mean that anyone who tried to oppose them (i.e., to get them under control) would have a difficult time of it. Either of these concepts could be correct; our knowledge of the meaning of the Hebrew term in question does not allow us to choose between the two with confidence.

32:26–28 God made it clear to Moses (v. 27, "this is what the LORD . . . says") that those who were committed to the idolatry had to be "cut off" from Israel. A modern person accustomed to the sentimentalism of Western liberal thinking might find the idea of killing idolaters impossible to justify. Moses, on the other hand, understood that leaving idolaters in the midst of Israel to influence others away from the opportunity for eternal life was impossible to justify. God revealed to him that a fight was underway over saving truth. If the idolatry were allowed to continue, many people in ancient Israel would turn from saving truth to condemning falsehood, from the promise of eternal life with God to destruction in hell—and since Israel was the repository of God's saving truth at this time, allowing the idolatry to continue might have affected the potential for eternal life of countless future generations of Israelites and Gentiles alike.

Moses' actions as described in this passage are not to be copied exemplaristically; the New Covenant does not allow for killing as a means of preservation of orthodoxy. But here was an Old Covenant watershed

[63] Though a possibly related form occurs in Job 4:12; 26:14, but the meaning in those contexts is equally puzzling to translators.

[64] Cf. HCSB, "so that they would be vulnerable to their enemies."

instance of being "for Yahweh" (the only God who could save) or for an idol (that cannot save and can only distract from saving truth). So Moses positioned himself at the entrance (Hb. "gate" or "gateway") to the camp (on its spatial organization, see Num 2) so as to symbolize standing at the dividing point between Israel and non-Israel and said, "Whoever for Yahweh, to me!" (there is no verb "is" and no verb "come" in the verbless clause of the original).

Immediately, all Levites rallied to him. Since Aaron was a Levite and had led the move toward idolatry, it can hardly be doubted that other Levites had also succumbed to its attractions. But now everyone was being given a chance to repent and reestablish loyalty to Yahweh's covenant. All the Levites did so decisively—including, surely, a chagrined and probably openly embarrassed Aaron. Some of the Levites' motivation may have come from tribal loyalty to their fellow tribesman Moses, especially now that they had seen Aaron publicly rebuked and had seen the bull idol so decisively destroyed. But to their credit they all seized the occasion to align themselves with Yahweh and against the idolatry that many of them had so recently embraced.

The command to kill idolaters was not Moses' idea but Yahweh's, and Moses introduced it in v. 27 with a full messenger speech formula ("This is what the LORD, the God of Israel says") in authenticating it.[65] At first glance it might seem that God was ordering the Levites to kill everyone else, but the wording is actually not intended to imply that. What the Levites were to do was to "go back and forth through the camp from one end to the other," which means carefully and systematically approaching everyone and finding out whether or not they intend to return to Yahweh, abandoning their idolatry. Those found to be committed to idolatry must be killed. Those sorry for being caught up in it but now actively repenting must be spared.

A parallel situation occurred later, at Baal-Peor, as described in Num 25. There, as Num 25:2 states, the Israelites once again sacrificed to false gods (thus necessarily having built altars for the purpose), ate, and bowed down before those gods (the gods in this case being various manifestations of Baal). What is more explicitly brought to the attention of the reader in Num 25 as opposed to the present passage, however, is that the revelry involved was overtly sexual, as Num 25:1,6–8 reveals. Again the remedy was the

---

[65] The primary purpose of a messenger speech formula (e.g., "thus says . . ."; "the word of . . .") is to remind an audience that the speaker is not making up anything but simply repeating a memorized message given him by his master. The prophets used messenger speech formulas especially when they were faced with hostility or opposition to their preaching and needed to remind their audience that it was Yahweh who sent the message and therefore Yahweh to whom the audience's hostility was directed (and who would deal with that hostility). See D. Stuart, "The Old Testament Prophets' Self-Understanding of their Prophecy," *Themelios* 6.1 (1980): 9–14.

same: death to idolaters. As directed by God (Num 25:5), Moses ordered that "each of you must put to death those of your men who have joined in worshiping the Baal of Peor." The imposition of the death penalty is vividly illustrated by the action of a prominent Levite, Phinehas, who killed a man and woman in the midst of pagan religious prostitutional "revelry" (Num 25:8). As the Num 25 passage makes clear, only those who engaged committedly in idolatry were put to death, not everyone indiscriminately. It was surely the same in the present context.

After killing about three thousand (or three companies)[66] of people, the Levites succeeded in ending the idolatry at Sinai (v. 28). Their willingness to kill all the committed idolaters, regardless of whether or not they were Levites or family members or friends (vv. 27,29) was evidence of their own devotion to Yahweh and further confirmation of their appropriateness as the clergy tribe of Israel ("today you have ordained yourselves for the service of the LORD"). The Hebrew of the verse can be literally translated "consecrate yourselves today to Yahweh" since the verb involved *(milʾû)* is an imperative. Whatever the Levites may have been expecting about their role as the clergy/priestly tribe prior to this point, they now knew that through Moses' instruction God was setting them aside for that special purpose.[67] What they did in killing friends and family members must have been agonizingly difficult for most of them; but it was faithful to God's will and therefore earned them his blessing. Israel was once again—however tentatively—free of idolatry, and Yahweh was once again Israel's sole focus of worship.

(4) Second Intercession and Plague (32:30–35)

30The next day Moses said to the people, "You have committed a great sin. But now I will go up to the LORD; perhaps I can make atonement for your sin." 31So Moses went back to the LORD and said, "Oh, what a great sin these people have committed! They have made themselves gods of gold. 32But now, please forgive their sin—but if not, then blot me out of the book you have written." 33The LORD

---

[66] See comments on 12:37.

[67] It is not necessary to read these verses as suggesting that the idea had suddenly occurred to God that he could make the Levites his special religious leadership tribe. In fact, the priesthood had already been assigned within the tribe of Levi by being restricted to Aaron's descendants (27:21; 28:1—though only Moses knew it up to this point since it had been revealed to him on the mountain immediately prior to these events), so there already existed the presumption that the Levites would be the clergy tribe of Israel. What this account does is to show further the correctness of God's already partially revealed choice. Parallels may be found in the assignment of special meaning to rainbows (which probably occurred already before the flood and not only after it) in Gen 9:13–17 or the special recognition that name changes gave to persons God had already chosen for a special purpose in his plan (Abram-Abraham, Jacob-Israel). Indeed, the prophets often identify an action as confirming that something done much earlier was in fact the choice of God (see comments on 3:12).

replied to Moses, "Whoever has sinned against me I will blot out of my book.
[34]Now go, lead the people to the place I spoke of, and my angel will go before you.
However, when the time comes for me to punish, I will punish them for their sin."
[35]And the LORD struck the people with a plague because of what they did with
the calf Aaron had made.

Throughout history plagues—meaning epidemics of illness—have been instinctively interpreted by people as dramatic evidence of widespread judgment or divinely imposed national tragedy.[68] Jeremiah included plagues among his famous triad of great disasters ("sword, famine and plague"; i.e., war, food shortages so severe as to cause starvation, and disease epidemic).[69] A plague could be the means of application of divine wrath in the Old Testament, as the Israelites had observed personally in the case of the ten plagues (only some of which involved illness, of course[70]) that struck the Egyptians and brought about the exodus. Now in this passage Israel experienced a plague and therefore a dramatic reminder of the severity of the sin they had just fallen into and a severe warning not to do it again.

32:30 The reference to the events of "the next day" does not necessarily mean that everything described in the earlier part of chap. 32 took place in a single day. Indeed, vv. 5–6 show that more than one day was involved. We can say for certain that the killing described in v. 28 lasted just a day because of the way vv. 28–29 are worded. Additionally, we should take seriously the possibility that most or all of the action mentioned from v. 9 onward (when God informed Moses of the idolatry going on at the base of the mountain) happened in one day (the same day described in vv. 28–29), since it is hard to imagine that Moses would have taken his time dealing with the idolatry he found upon arriving at the base of Sinai.

Now that Moses had done what he could to correct the people, the rest was up to God. Moses thus proposed in this verse to fulfill the point of his earlier prayer (vv. 11–13) that God would spare the people and remake them into his holy nation. To accomplish this, Moses needed to go back atop Mount Sinai ("up to the LORD") for yet another audience with Yahweh, to whom he would make intercession on behalf of the people. He hoped that

---

[68] By no means should any outbreak of disease be interpreted as evidence of a specially sent divine judgment for a particular sin. Most disease is indeed the result of divine judgment, but the judgment in question is simply part of the overall subjection of all creation to futility (Rom 8:20), i.e., disease as one consequence of living in a fallen world. Nevertheless, the natural tendency of people to interpret plagues as signs of divine disfavor is something God sometimes has chosen to utilize in bringing his people to repentance.

[69] Jer 14:12; 21:7,9; 24:10; 27:8,13; 29:1–18; 32:24,36; 34:17; 38:2; 42:17,22; 44:13; Cf. the triad common in Ezekiel as well (5:12,17; 6:11–12; 7:15; 12:16; 14:21) and its dramatic concluding occurrence in Rev 6:8.

[70] See comments on 5:3; 9:14.

perhaps *(ʾûlay)* he could "make atonement for" the people's sin, a concept that could also be translated literally as "get your sins covered/forgiven." What the people had done was a very serious sin indeed; it would take direct appeal to Yahweh in the Sinai glory cloud (19:9; 24:15,18) by Yahweh's own appointed intercessor to try to make things right. The covenant had been broken, as symbolized by Moses' own actions the prior day in smashing the precious tablets of testimony; a major sort of appeal was now Israel's only hope for restoration. In other words, the killing of the three thousand by the Levites was only the beginning of the process of regaining God's favor and blessing. That action went only as far as to identify and eliminate those who resisted correction. The punishment of the general population who had originally gone along with the idolatry and now were presumably sorry they had awaited resolution at the summit of the mountain.

32:31 It is instructive that Moses did not try to minimize the people's sin in the process of trying to gain forgiveness of it. Biblically, confession of sin (being entirely honest with God in stating its nature and extent) is part of true repentance; the person who understates his sin is not really demonstrating repentance to God. So Moses bluntly described the people's sin both in the prior verse in addressing the people, and now to God directly, as a "great sin" and as idolatry ("they have made for themselves gods of gold"), a violation of the first two commandments.[71] The wording "gods of gold" recalls the language of the second commandment in 20:23, "Do not make any gods to be alongside me; do not make for yourselves gods of silver or gods of gold." As Moses later taught in Deuteronomy, the gold on an idol (the gold surface of a carved wooden idol) is detestable to God (Deut 7:5)—its beauty can never be construed as something God would enjoy, and its value can never be redeemed by salvaging the gold when an idol is discarded (so Moses' actions earlier, v. 20).

32:32–33 In these verses Moses linked his appeal for forgiveness for Israel's sin to an offer to lose his own eternal life if the people's sin could not be forgiven. God replied that he would not give eternal life to sinners, implying both that Moses was not at fault and that he, God, was fully in charge of judging between the righteous and the wicked and would make the determination of who obtained eternal life. Thus "Whoever has sinned against me I will blot out of my book" (v. 33) represents a statement of

[71] Since there could be no proper Yahwistic idolatry, any form of idolatry that supposedly involved Yahweh, however honorifically the intent of the idolaters, not only represented Yahweh by means of idols (breaking the first commandment) but also placed some other god before him to some degree (even if that god were a distortion of Yahweh, a quasi-Yahweh of some sort), thus breaking both of the first two Words/Commandments. From another angle: to put other gods before Yahweh in the ancient world was done *always* via idolatry; no one conceived of any other way to do so. Thus the first two commandments were, in practice, normally broken together if broken at all.

divine practice, a standard of justice that God maintains—as well as a strict warning that eternal life is not automatic and that a person who tries to enter it without his sins being forgiven could not succeed. Verse 33 is, then, one of the Bible's stronger statements about the absolute necessity for the forgiveness of sins, and therefore, for a savior. It can be regarded as implicitly messianic even if not overtly so.

Moses' offer to be blotted out of the Book of Life (along with, not instead of, the Israelites)[72] was selfless and noble, showing his deep identification with the people. He was willing to go beyond even what he had said earlier in vv. 11–13 and give up on his own future lest the people he had led would have no future by reason of their "great sin."

Excursus: The Book of Life

In speaking of "the book you have written" (Exod 32:32), Moses made reference to a concept that God himself directly confirmed in response to Moses by employing the term "my book" (32:33). Moses and God both seemed to indicate that sinful behavior can cause a person or persons to be blotted out (erased/expunged, *mḥh*) of a special book kept in God's possession. What book were they referring to? What was its nature? Why did they talk of sin and its consequences with a term like "book"?

In the ancient world both governments and individuals kept records of populations. These records were used for many of the same sorts of purposes that official records are used for in modern times—taxation, military duty, establishing property ownership. Once a given population (e.g., of a clan, a town, a region, a flock, or the like) became so great that no person or small group of persons could maintain in his or her head a full, accurate list of the inhabitants, a listing (book/scroll)[73] of inhabitants was required to be prepared in writing. Of course, this "book" had to be updated as the actual population changed. When someone was born into or moved into a clan/town/region, it was necessary to add the name of that person to the listing/census (book) kept for that group. When someone died or moved away, it was necessary to remove his or her name from the book. Thus the listing was always a current listing of those who were alive in that clan/town/region at any given time. In other words, the book that held their names was a "book of life." Only the names of the living were found in it. The dead's names were removed ("blotted out") periodically as needed.

---

[72] One must note that Moses did not offer here to die instead of the people but rather with them. He had already been honored by God with the rhetorical offer of a nation of his own in place of the nation of Israel (32:10), and his appeal in this instance may be seen as saying, in effect, "Well, if you kill them, you ought to kill me too, even though you've already supported me so strongly." In other words, Moses *could* be understood at most here to mean, "If you do kill off Israel, you'll lose me too by rights. But that is not the same as saying, "Let me die in their place, so only one person will die and all the rest may go on as your people."

[73] The same Hb. word, סֵפֶר, is translated either "book" or "scroll" or "record," depending on the context.

Books of the living had a long history. Behind them lay the need for accurate counting and record keeping, even among illiterate people. In many relatively primitive societies something of the same sort of record keeping prevails even today. In certain cultures an illiterate shepherd will keep in a bag or bundle of some sort a small pebble representing each of his sheep. When he acquires a new sheep by birth or purchase, he will add a pebble to the bundle. When he loses a sheep, he will remove a pebble and throw it away. Thus, even though the shepherd may not be skilled at counting larger numbers, and even if he may lack the knowledge of how to keep a written record of his total number of sheep, and even if he might at any given time (especially during lambing season) have trouble remembering the exact number of sheep under his control, he can always refer to the bundle to find one pebble for each sheep alive in his flock. This same sort of simple census system was widely enough used in ancient Israel that Abigail could refer to it metaphorically in her statement to David about her confidence that God would preserve his life (1 Sam 25:29): "Even though someone is pursuing you to take your life, the life of my master will be bound securely in the bundle of the living by the LORD your God. But the lives of your enemies he will hurl away as from the pocket of a sling." The "bundle of the living" to which Abigail referred was a metaphorical one: an imaginary bag that held the symbols of the lives of the living. To remain in the bag was to be alive still; to be hurled from it was to lose one's life. Metaphorically, she was speaking about David's potential death versus his potential ongoing life.

Far more common in Scripture than Abigail's "bundle of the living" is the term "book of life" and its various paraphrases (Book/Scroll of the Living, My Book, Lamb's Book of Life). Consider, for example, the plea in Ps 69:28 against oppressive enemies: "May they be blotted out of the book of life[74] and not be listed with the righteous." This expression parallels Moses' words in Exod 32:32 in that it imagines a book in which the living are listed, but not necessarily listed permanently. If people displease God by their sins, he can blot them out of his book, that is, see to it that they do not continue to live (i.e., to have eternal life) after the "first death" and instead experience the "second death" (eternal destruction) after the first (cf. Rev 2:11; 20:6,14; 21:8).

Because of the commonness of the concept, Paul could, without further explanation, refer to fellow believers, whose eternal destiny was certain by reason of their having trusted Christ for salvation, "as fellow workers, whose names are in the book of life" (Phil 4:3). In Revelation, John used the term "book of life" six times, once with reference to the possibility (or not) of being blotted out of the Book of life (Rev 3:5) and five times with reference to having one's name found in the Book of Life at the great final judgment of all the earth (Rev 13:8; 17:8; 20:12,15; 21:27). In other words, if your name is in the Book of Life at the judgment, you will live forever in heaven. If it is not, you will be destroyed in hell—you are not *listed* among the living and cannot therefore live on. It is useful to note that John also called the Book of Life the "book of life belonging to the

[74] The NIV does not capitalize Book of Life, so the reader will notice that it is written "book of life" whenever the NIV is quoted directly.

Lamb that was slain from the creation of the world" (Rev 13:8) as a way of indicating that it is through Christ alone that eternal life is obtained.

Already in Exod 17:14 the general idea of blotting out people's names (i.e., being sure they die and do not live on) was applied to the Amalekites ("Then the LORD said to Moses, 'Write this on a scroll as something to be remembered and make sure that Joshua hears it, because I will completely blot out the memory of Amalek from under heaven' "; cf. Deut 25:19). But the threat to blot out the name of the Israelites, related to their idolatry at Sinai as described in the present context, is also expressed and/or recalled (e.g., Deut 9:14, "Let me alone, so that I may destroy them and blot out their name from under heaven. And I will make you into a nation stronger and more numerous than they"). The danger of being erased from the Book of Life can apply as well to the individual who breaks the covenant even if most Israelites did not (Deut 29:20, "All the curses written in this book will fall upon him, and the LORD will blot out his name from under heaven").[75] Fortunately, God's promise to Moses in Exod 32:33 was that only those who sinned against him by flouting his covenant would be blotted out, a theme picked up in both Deut 32:26 ("I considered scattering them and blotting out their memory from mankind"[76] [NIV, "I said I would scatter them and blot out their memory from mankind"]) and 2 Kgs 14:27 ("And since the LORD had not said he would blot out the name of Israel from under heaven, he saved them by the hand of Jeroboam son of Jehoash").

Malachi 3:16 appears to reflect the general concept of a book/scroll of the living: people in Malachi's postexilic Judean community put together a book/scroll of those committed to keeping God's covenant and thus who could be presumed to be on their way to eternal life rather than to being blotted out of God's book.[77] Daniel 12:1 unambiguously reflects the concept: "At that time Michael, the great prince who protects your people, will arise. There will be a time of distress such as has not happened from the beginning of nations until then. But at that time your people—everyone whose name is found written in the book—will be delivered."

What conclusions can be drawn from this brief survey of the concept? First, the Book of Life is a record of those going on to eternal life as opposed to those who by their own decisions have rejected God and his salvation (cf. John 3:19–20). To have one's name in the Book of Life is to have persevered in faith and obedience to God until the final judgment of the earth. To have one's name

[75] Note the full wording of the context (vv. 18-20), which makes abundantly clear that the final sentence in v. 20 is speaking about exceptional Israelites who broke the covenant willingly, not the general population who might sin from time to time. The person who wishes to go his own way and not accept responsibility to keep the covenant loses its blessings and receives its curses.

[76] In the context, Deut 32:27–31 goes on to say that God decided against that option for the sake of preserving his people against their enemies.

[77] It is also possible that what Malachi referred to was simply a covenant renewal document that everyone agreeing to keep the covenant signed. But Malachi's meaning may well go beyond such a witness document to imply the creation of a symbolic Book of Life.

blotted out is to have offended God by lack of faith and, accordingly, by disobedience so that one cannot continue to live, that is, have eternal life.

Moreover, important for understanding God's purposes in judgment is to appreciate that everyone starts out in the Book of Life. It is a book of the living, and all who are born originally appear in it. God does not arbitrarily put some names in it and not others. All who come into the world have the potential for eternal life, according to God's will (1 Tim 2:3–4; 2 Pet 3:9) but most ignore, reject, disdain, put off, or otherwise forfeit that potential—and so their names are eventually blotted out of the Book of Life.[78] When they appear at the judgment and the books are opened (Dan 7:10; Rev 20:12), their names will not appear in the Lamb's Book of Life because they chose a different direction during their lives on earth from the direction God prescribed. Their rejection of him eventually earns them rejection from being listed among the living. Their fate is then destruction, the second death (Rev 2:11; 20:6,14; 21:18).

32:34–35 The connection between vv. 34 and 35 can easily be misunderstood. It can seem that the final sentence of v. 34 ("However, when the time comes for me to punish, I will punish them for their sin") is a prediction of what follows immediately in v. 35 ("And the LORD struck the people with a plague"). But this is not at all the point of the text. Verse 34 represents God's command to Moses to continue on in the exodus plan. Thus he told him to "lead the people to the place I spoke of," that is, take them to the promised land (referring back to the original command to do so in 3:8,17)[79] and of his promise to lead the way with the angel of the Lord (a reiteration of 23:20–23). In other words, it is now completely clear that the idolatry of the people at Sinai had not resulted in their destruction, but God had been faithful to his original intent, just as Moses prayed he would be (32:11–14) and had spared the nation for its original purpose, to conquer and occupy the promised land. The second sentence of v. 34 therefore is just as the NIV translates it, a contrasting thought referring to a future time (which in hindsight can easily be identified as the Babylonian exile) "when the time comes" for Yahweh "to punish" his people, a time when he then indeed "will punish" them for their sin. That punishment brought Israel's tenure on the land as an independent nation to a conclusion. The various curses described in Lev 26 and Deut 28–32 were unleashed, and Israel thereafter, until the time of Christ's transformation of true Israel into the church, was in captivity: physically relocated to Babylon in 586 BC but always politically incorporated into one empire or another even after the exile for the rest of its history as a single people group.

---

[78] One could argue that the time of blotting out would be when they died, once they no longer had any opportunity to retain their names in the Book by trusting Christ for their eternal life, but the Bible does not speak to the question of when blotting out occurs.

[79] Cf. the reminder of this in Deut 10:11.

The plague described in 32:35, in other words, was a small-scale warning, a sample of God's wrath,[80] but by no means the actual full punishment for abandoning the covenant as indicated in the covenant sanctions of Lev 26 and Deut 28–32 and as delineated in Lamentations or any other of the other passages describing the fall of Jerusalem and the aftermath of captivity. We are not told how many people died in this warning plague, if any. The three thousand deaths described in vv. 27–29 may well have been the extent of the taking of life; this plague may have made many sick but none fatally. It was a divine punishment of "the people with a plague because of what they did with the calf Aaron had made"—in other words, a one-time, ad hoc punishment for what had happened at one point at Sinai on the way to the promised land. It was not the full-scale covenant imposition of curses that brought to an end the benefits of the covenant to Israel. That would come many centuries later.

(5) Reiteration of Laws on God's Angel and Holy War Conquest (33:1–6)

[1]Then the LORD said to Moses, "Leave this place, you and the people you brought up out of Egypt, and go up to the land I promised on oath to Abraham, Isaac and Jacob, saying, 'I will give it to your descendants.' [2]I will send an angel before you and drive out the Canaanites, Amorites, Hittites, Perizzites, Hivites and Jebusites. [3]Go up to the land flowing with milk and honey. But I will not go with you, because you are a stiff-necked people and I might destroy you on the way."

[4]When the people heard these distressing words, they began to mourn and no one put on any ornaments. [5]For the LORD had said to Moses, "Tell the Israelites, 'You are a stiff-necked people. If I were to go with you even for a moment, I might destroy you. Now take off your ornaments and I will decide what to do with you.'" [6]So the Israelites stripped off their ornaments at Mount Horeb.

33:1–2 Most of the content of these verses functions as a reminder of what has been said before. If the plague described in 32:35 took the nature of a disease epidemic, it would have required days or weeks to run its course. Thus a reminder of the big picture—the general purpose of the exodus—was much in order once the plague was over. Such a reminder would keep Moses and the people focused on God's plan for them, which they might have been tempted to doubt in light of the plague's severity, and also would be an encouragement to Moses that God's provision and support had not ended but had merely been interrupted, as it were, by the people's idolatry. In saying "leave this place," God reiterated the fact that the stopover at Sinai, important as it was and lengthy as it turned out to be (roughly ten

[80] God does many things as small samples of bigger things to come; cf. 2 Pet 2:6; Jude 7; Matt 24:8; 1 Cor 15:8; 1 Tim 1:16.

months), was only temporary. The Israelites belonged in the land originally promised to Abraham, that is, Canaan, and not in the Sinai wilderness.[81]

Carefully repeated themes in these verses include the idea that Sinai was a place the Israelites did not belong in permanently but rather must eventually "leave" (cf. 23:20; 32:34): "the people you brought up out of Egypt" (cf. 3:12; 12:51; 13:3,9,14,16; 14:11; 16:3,6,32; 18:1; 19:4; 20:2; 29:46; 32:1,7,11,23; sometimes with Moses but more often with God as the one who brought them to Sinai); "the land I promised on oath" (3:17; 12:25; 13:11; 32:13); the land of promises made to "Abraham, Isaac and Jacob" (3:6,15–16; 4:5; 6:3,8; 32:13); the inheritance promised to their "descendants" (32:13); the encouragement of God's "sending an angel ahead of you" (23:20,23; 32:34) "to drive . . . out" (23:28–31)[82] the "Canaanites, Amorites" (cf. 3:8,17; 13:5,11; 23:23,28).[83]

33:3 The expectation of "going up into the land flowing with milk and honey" has also been mentioned earlier in Exodus (3:8,17; 13:5; there are many other references especially in Numbers and Deuteronomy), but the warning that ends v. 3 is something new. Now comes a kind of rhetorical proposal to limit the presence of God with his people, a proposed limitation that is later removed in response to Moses' intercession (33:12-23): God's statement "I will not go with you" represents what would be a mercifully necessary restriction of the divine presence that is further elaborated in v. 5. The Israelites were already described as "a stiff-necked people" by God in 32:9, and his potential to "destroy" them already was raised in 32:10. God obviously did *not* want to destroy his people, however, so here he indicated that his rhetorical offer at the present time to them was that he would not directly accompany them in the same degree that he had spoken personally to them from Sinai (20:1–19) or appeared personally to Moses several times at the top of the mountain. The close divine presence at Sinai under this scenario would be moderated after the Israelites left Sinai. God would be more indirectly present with them in the future for their own benefit, lest his intol-

---

[81] Some scholars have assumed that the command to leave Sinai overrode the command to build the tabernacle, which would require considerable time at a fixed location (Sinai), so this passage in effect represents at least a temporary suspension of all that has gone before in terms of the instructions for completion of the tabernacle. But the actual picture is much more positive than this: the conquest of the promised land was a great and ancient patriarchal promise at the heart of the exodus plan (see comments on chap. 3), and a call to leave Sinai was a divine reiteration of that promise, not a sudden interruption of the tabernacle program. Cf. W. Rudolph, "Der Aufbau von Exodus 19–34," in *Werden und Wesen des Alten Testaments,* BZAW 66 (Berlin: Töpelmann, 1936), 41–48; R. E. Hendrix, "A Literary Structural Analysis of the Golden-Calf Episode in Exodus 32:1–33:6," *AUSS* 28 (1990): 211–17.

[82] For "drive out" the *piel* of *grš* is employed, just as in Pharaoh's driving out the Israelites from Egypt (6:1; 10:11; 11:1).

[83] As we have noted earlier, the listing of the native Canaanite/Amorite groups can vary; there was no set number or order to the names (see comments on 3:8,17).

erance of sin should require him to "destroy them on the way," that is, before they reached the promised land. To keep his plan of redemption on course, God had to limit his contact with Israel (see comments on v. 5).

33:4–6 The mood of the Israelites in this passage contrasts dramatically with their idolatrous revelry as described in the prior chapter. More importantly, the nature of Yahweh's presence among them had shifted greatly. The people had shown by their idolatry that they craved a direct and obvious divine presence to lead them in their journeys. Indeed, the golden young bull was to their way of thinking a means of capturing the presence of some gods (gods that represented a distorted understanding of Yahweh), and the people rejoiced finally to be able to see the gods who had been—they thought—helping them on the exodus so far (32:4). Now as part of their punishment for that folly they would have to live with *less* then they had before. Instead of a God who directly communed with Moses and whose presence could be seen on the mountain, they would have to live with a much more elusive representation of God's presence, an angel, and therefore they realized that they had been demoted from people who dealt with Yahweh directly through Moses to people who now would have an angel added to the chain of command.[84]

God had said bluntly (even if it was only a rhetorical threat he would eventually not carry out) that he himself would not go with them (v. 3), and they now mourned because what they had so craved and had tried to manufacture—direct divine presence—was now even further removed from them than it had been. The rest of the journey would require even more faith, not less, and would be even more frightening because the people would be more on their own than they had been.

Disappointed, afraid, ashamed, rebuked, at "these distressing words" (v. 4), the people mourned. God himself, speaking through Moses, commanded them to mourn in saying "now take off your ornaments" (v. 5, following the initial, temporary action to do so described in v. 4); and he also let them know in no uncertain terms that their future might involve unknown hardships or further punishments ("and I will decide what to do with you"). By reason of God's words they knew that their God had partially rejected them, and they felt the impact of this rejection.

In the ancient Near East, mourning tended to involve appearance,[85] not just attitude, so that what one wore was a part of the appearance aspect of

---

[84] See also W. Baumgartner, "Zum Problem des 'Jahwe-Engels,'" in *Zum Alten Testament und Seiner Umwelt* (Leiden: Brill, 1959), 240–46.

[85] Cf. the many biblical references to wearing sackcloth as a sign of mourning (e.g., Gen 37:34; 2 Sam 3:31; Esth 4:1–4); the use of ashes and dust to add a feeling of misery (the opposite of cheerfulness) to one's head and skin (e.g., Job 42:6; Ezek 27:30) and wearing a frown in public (e.g., Matt 6:16) attest to the desire in ancient times to show oneself in mourning. In extreme cases even animals were made to look as if in mourning (Jonah 3:8; for historical parallels see D. Stuart, *Hosea-Jonah*, WBC [Waco: Word, 1987], 493).

mourning. Nothing fancy could adorn a mourner because fancy dress was associated with cheerfulness and might contradict the desired pattern, which was thoroughgoing mourning behavior designed to appeal to a god (or the true God) for relief of suffering (including in this case relief from the unknown miseries that might be subsumed under "and I will decide what to do with you"). Therefore they removed all adornment and made their appearance "plain" as a sign of mourning.

Withholding of divine presence is a severe covenant punishment. To be denied access to the presence of God (usually meaning to be expelled from the covenant community and therefore to be unable to worship and sacrifice, which means to be unable to have one's sins forgiven) constituted a sort of ultimate penalty for heterodox practice. An example of such a severe penalty is found in Lev 22:3: "Say to them: 'For the generations to come, if any of your descendants is ceremonially unclean and yet comes near the sacred offerings that the Israelites consecrate to the LORD, that person must be cut off from my presence. I am the LORD' "). Often the prohibition of Yahweh's presence is simply predicted directly by God; no Israelite court would be needed to impose such a penalty. In these instances terms such as "set my face against" or "hide my face from" convey the idea of divine removal of presence from an individual (e.g., Lev 20:3).

But the punishment of a limited divine presence carries with it an element of mercy as well. This is the reason for the statement in Exod 33:3, "Because . . . I might destroy you on the way." God admits no one on earth into his full presence because he does not tolerate sin in proximity to himself. The closer a sinful being would get to the true God, the greater the danger of that person's destruction. Instead, God mercifully limits his presence among human beings on earth so as not to have to destroy them because of their sinfulness. The present warning of the withholding of divine presence does not mean that God would not in fact help the Israelites to get to Canaan nor that he would have no further contact with them. It does mean, however, that because of their sin and therefore also for their own sakes, he would not directly accompany them on their journey to Canaan in the same degree of presence he had manifested himself among them at Sinai[86] and accompanied them from Egypt to Sinai through the pillar of cloud/fire (e.g., 13:21–22; 17:1–6).

What were the Israelites wearing that seemed inappropriate for the mourning attitude they now chose? The Hebrew word translated by the NIV

---

[86] The merciful limitation of divine presence continues today. Were we in our present sinful condition to be ushered into the direct presence of God in heaven, we would be destroyed. This is part, though only a part, of the reason for the expected resurrection transformation into a "spiritual body" (1 Cor 15:44) that no longer will be capable of the lusts of the flesh and therefore will be suitable for habitation of heaven, where sin is not tolerated as it is on earth.

(and, e.g., NRSV) as "ornaments"[87] seems to refer to jewelry of all sorts, the sort of decorative wear a mourner would not choose to be seen in. Such "ornaments" were often made of gold (2 Sam 1:24; Jer 4:30), and therefore the present removal of all jewelry, including gold, parallels the removal of gold earrings required by the call for gold that Aaron announced in seeking material for the Sinai idol (32:2–4).[88] What they had once taken off in a sinful action they must now again take off as a reminder that they were in mourning because of the results of that sinful action. Ezekiel 7:20 appears to echo the former event ("From their beautiful ornament, in which they took pride, they made their abominable images, their detestable things; therefore I will make of it an unclean thing to them," NRSV) and possibly even the latter prohibition of jewelry ("I will make of it an unclean thing") though in a context that reflects knowledge of rather than directly describes Exod 32–33.[89]

In Exod 33:6 the NIV inexplicably translates simply, "So the Israelites stripped off their ornaments at Mount Horeb." This does not reflect the wording of the Hebrew,[90] which should be rendered (as, e.g., NRSV and HCSB) "from Mount Horeb onward." In other words, for the rest of the exodus and wilderness wandering, the Israelites dressed as if in mourning. They did not merely take off their jewelry while at Horeb (Sinai) but kept it off for the next forty years. God's threat, "I will decide what to do with you," hung over them all that time, and some of their actions in that long period of wilderness wandering may well reflect their resultant anxiety.

(6) The "Tent of Meeting" (33:7–11)

7Now Moses used to take a tent and pitch it outside the camp some distance away, calling it the "tent of meeting." Anyone inquiring of the LORD would go to the tent of meeting outside the camp. 8And whenever Moses went out to the tent, all the people rose and stood at the entrances to their tents, watching Moses until he entered the tent. 9As Moses went into the tent, the pillar of cloud would come down and stay at the entrance, while the LORD spoke with Moses. 10Whenever the people saw the pillar of cloud standing at the entrance to the tent, they all stood and worshiped, each at the entrance to his tent. 11The LORD would speak to Moses face to face, as a man speaks with his friend. Then Moses would return to the camp, but his young aide Joshua son of Nun did not leave the tent.

---

87 HCSB "jewelry"; עֲדִי.

88 These ornaments were presumably all originally part of the spoils taken from the Egyptians as the Israelites departed Egypt (11:2; 12:35). Accordingly, they were signs of victory and triumph, which could hardly be worn appropriately now that the people were being punished by their own God.

89 Cf. R. E. Hendrix, "A Literary Structural Analysis of the Golden-Calf Episode in Exodus 32:1–33:6." *AUSS* 28 (1990): 211–17.

90 מֵהַר חוֹרֵב.

In this passage Moses explained to the reader what sort of relationship God established with Israel (and with himself, Moses, and his aide, Joshua) after his announcement that he would no longer accompany them closely. What he so far granted to them was a more distant presence, not an utter abandonment. In contrast to the elaborate tabernacle and its many symbols of the presence of God, the Israelites would now deal (for a time) with a small, simple "meeting tent"[91] (or as tradition words it "tent of meeting").

The differences and limitations are important. Instead of the community's being organized around the tabernacle (Num 2), the tent of meeting would reside "outside" the camp.[92] Instead of worshiping at the tabernacle in their midst, the people would worship from afar, from their homes looking toward the tent of meeting. Instead of a cadre of priests led by Aaron manning the tabernacle, the tent of meeting would be manned by one person, Joshua, so that in the absence of priests and sacrifices, there stood only a non-Levitical assistant, a caretaker.[93] God's presence would now be both distant and non-continuous (v. 10), a diminished presence.

But God's love, protection and care for his people, however mitigated, did not cease. Indeed, he still spoke to individuals, through Moses, in response to special inquiries (v. 7).[94] Fortunately, this arrangement was not permanent. Eventually the Israelites were to be able to benefit from a greater measure of the presence of God, as originally contemplated in the tabernacle instructions (Num 2–10), even though this presence was still considerably short of what might have been theirs (and would eventually be theirs again) had they not rejected him by their idolatry at Sinai (Exod 32).

33:7 The "tent of meeting" (lowercase, not capitalized in the NIV) described here is simply a kind of substitute for the tabernacle, which already was designated "Tent of Meeting" (uppercase in the NIV) in Exodus 27:21; 28:43; 29:4,10,30,32,42,44; 30:16,18,20,26,36; 31:7. The term used for "tent of meeting" is exactly the same in the Hebrew[95] for both the tabernacle and

[91] The form of the phrase אֹהֶל מוֹעֵד is that of the adjectival construct, in which the second element ("meeting," the *nomen rectum*) functions as an attributive adjective to the first element ("tent [of]," the *nomen regens*).

[92] Cf. C. Dohmen, "'Nicht sieht mich der Mensch und lebt' (Ex 33:20): Aspekte der Gotteschau im Alten Testament," *Jahrbuch für Biblische Theologie* 13 (1998): 31–51.

[93] Joshua was an Ephraimite (Num 13:8,16).

[94] The Hb. term used here, בִּקֵּשׁ, refers not just to "looking for" but when employed in reference to Yahweh has the sense of "desiring guidance from" or "seeking an oracle from." Cf. *THAT* 1:335.

[95] אֹהֶל מוֹעֵד. The NIV wisely renders this term as "tent of meeting" (lowercase and quotes) when it is referring to (echoing terminologically) the tabernacle and as Tent of Meeting (caps and no quotes) when it refers to the actual tabernacle. This is surely the way Moses intended his use of the term, though in his Hb. neither quotation marks nor capitalization were available to help make such a distinction for the reader.

this simple tent set up outside the camp, and it is obvious that Moses, desiring to preserve whatever opportunity he could for direct communication with Yahweh, kept the communication function of the tabernacle alive in the terminology he used for the tent. There is no evidence that this "tent of meeting" played any other role than that of a communication point—it never held the ark or any other sacred furniture,[96] and it never was employed as a site for sacrifices.[97] The tabernacle was designed for a great range of purposes, only one of which was communication with God (29:42). This latter role was the only one intended for the "tent of meeting."[98]

This is the first mention of the small, substitute "tent of meeting"[99] outside the camp, as opposed to the tabernacle. We may assume that this tent would never have been invented or needed had not the idolatry of chap. 32 taken place and the close presence of God been withdrawn from Israel as a

---

[96] Contra J. Wellhausen (*Die Composition des Hexateuchs und der Historishchen Bücher des Alten Testaments* [Berlin: Walter deGruyter, 1963]), 93), who contended, without supportive evidence, that the "tent of meeting" held the ark of the covenant, which had been made from Israelites' discarded gold jewelry mentioned in 33:6. Wellhausen's reasoning involved both the idea that the same term was used of the two structures as well as the idea that the ark was the touch point of divine-human contact and therefore must have been built already at this point in the story and housed in the tent where Yahweh met with Moses so directly. It is an idealized reconstruction of history from data that contain nothing per se that would actually support the reconstruction.

[97] Cf. M. Haran, *Temples and Temple-Service in Ancient Israel* (Oxford: Clarendon, 1978), esp. 265–69. Haran rightly insists that the interaction between Moses and Yahweh always took place at the entrance to (i.e., outside) the "tent of meeting" and not inside. Yahweh was represented by the pillar of cloud *outside* the tent. The inside remained completely empty because the "tent of meeting" was simply a symbol of the real Tent of Meeting, the tabernacle, and not a full functional substitute for it. Yahweh withheld many aspects of himself from his people during the time between the Exod 32 idolatry fiasco and the completion of the actual tabernacle, but not his truth—it was something they could still access by inquiry with Moses as the mediator.

[98] Cf. G. von Rad, "The Tent and the Ark," in *The Problem of the Hexateuch and Other Essays* (Edinburgh: Oliver & Boyd, 1966), 103–24; von Rad also argues for an occupancy connection between the "tent of meeting" and the ark of the covenant (i.e., that the "tent of meeting" in fact housed the ark at one point, as does R. de Vaux, "Ark of the Covenant and Tent of Reunion," in *The Bible and the Ancient Near East* [Garden City: Doubleday, 1971], 136–51).

[99] Later this tent is mentioned in Num 11:16–17,24–26; 12:1–8; Deut 31:14–15, in contexts or with wordings that make clear it was the simple small tent rather than the tabernacle that was being referred to, whereas the term Tent of Meeting (capitalized helpfully in the NIV) is used far more frequently, i.e., scores of times to refer to the tabernacle, so "tent of meeting" is mentioned rather rarely compared to Tent of Meeting (tabernacle). In seventeen places (e.g., Exod 39:32,40; 40:2,6,22,24,29,34) the appositional construction "the tabernacle, the Tent of Meeting" is employed to be sure the reader realizes that it is the tabernacle that is being talked about since the term in the Hb., which does not employ capitalization, can be ambiguous as to its referent.

result.[100] The wording "Moses used to take a tent" (past durative use of the imperfect verb form) does not mean that he used to take a certain[101] tent prior to the timing of 33:7 but rather that *starting* with the timing of 33:7, Moses regularly *thereafter* employed a certain tent as a symbolic substitute for the actual Tent of Meeting, the tabernacle.

By pitching this tent used for *meeting* God outside the camp "some distance away" (or better, "far off from the camp," NRSV), Moses reminded all the people how relatively distant God had become at that point from his people. Presumably, to pitch the tent any closer to the camp would have been impossible, a violation of God's warning that he would not closely accompany his people on their journey to the promised land (v. 3).[102] Since tents were what the Israelites lived in at that time, this one symbolized God's dwelling just as the grander Tent of Meeting (tabernacle) was designed to do; but this one always stood empty—just a tent to indicate that God still had a "place" somewhat distant from and not for the time being *among* his people—but still a place where he could be consulted. "Anyone inquiring of the LORD would go to the tent of meeting outside the camp" means simply that any Israelite who needed guidance from God would go there and through Moses—not independently of him—ask God for the guidance he or she needed.[103] God certainly had been disappointed in and angry at his people after the golden calf incident, but he had not gone so far in distancing

---

[100] Some scholars have argued that this entire passage on the "tent of meeting" (33:7–11) is inappropriate (e.g., Durham: "The five verses of Exodus 33:7–11 . . . are . . . completely out of place," *Exodus,* 443) in the context of the imposition of divine absence (33:1–6)—since it is about divine presence, not absence. We would contend, however, with what we judge to be a majority of scholars, that the threat of divine absence is exactly what makes the present passage necessary. This is a passage about God's merciful amelioration of his judgment. Without it one could hardly understand how Moses and the Israelites knew where to go and what to do during the next period of time. Thus the "tent of meeting" existed *in spite of* but not in opposition to Yahweh's judgment. Cf. U. Cassuto, *A Commentary on the Book of Exodus* (Jerusalem: Magnes, 1967), 429–32; Moberly, *At the Mountain of God,* 63–64; and, from another angle, R. E. Clements, *God and Temple* (Philadelphia: Fortress, 1965), 36–38.

[101] The Hb. article preceding אֹהֶל represents an instance of the proleptic article used to introduce a topic into the narrative; cf. comments on 2:15.

[102] Cf. L. Rost, "Die Wohnstätte des Zeugnisses," in *Festschrift Friedrich Baumgärtel* (Erlangen: Verlag Universitätsbund Erlangen, 1959), 158–65.

[103] The process likely worked as follows: an inquirer would explain to Moses what guidance he or she sought from Yahweh, and Moses would enter the tent to ask Yahweh for guidance. After returning from inside the tent, he would report, as Yahweh's messenger ("Thus says Yahweh . . ."), to the inquirer. This sort of prophetically mediated guidance is seen commonly enough in the later prophets (e.g., Ezek 20:1ff.; Zech 7:2ff.) even though they did not have a tent or other place to enter physically/visibly into God's presence.

himself from them that he would refuse to guide them as a group in the wilderness (33:2) or refuse to help individuals understand his will.[104]

Two particular ancillary benefits may also have accrued to this "tent of meeting." One would have been the way it forced individual Israelites to show their dependence on Yahweh, in contrast to their prior infidelity in the incident of idolatry described in the previous chapter. To inquire of the Lord, an Israelite had to separate himself spatially from the other Israelites in the camp and openly walk the considerable distance to the tent of meeting. He thus would not be able to blend into a crowd of orthodox worshipers without identifying his own personal commitment to Yahweh. In virtually all other situations, the Israelites en masse had agreed to or disobeyed the covenant.[105] Now the individual would have to show his loyalty to Yahweh publicly, at least if he wanted to know something from Yahweh.

A second benefit may have been the credentializing of Moses. Previously, he was always far distant from the people on top of Mount Sinai, not visible to them and, to their thinking, simply gone away without certainty of return (see their comment in 32:1, "We don't know what has happened to him"). They never actually heard Yahweh give Moses the laws and never actually saw Moses in close proximity to Yahweh. Now, with the tent of meeting pitched outside the camp but still within sight of it, they could not fail to see that every time Moses entered the tent of meeting the glory of God also entered it. Time and again, therefore, Moses was shown to be God's chosen, special person among them.[106] Though the tent of meeting was far off from the camp, it was far less far off than the top of Mount Sinai; what used to happen out of their sight now happened in full view.[107]

33:8–10 Verse 8 indicates that the people's respect for Moses[108] had fully returned, and their disregard of him (32:1) had, rightly, disappeared. To rise and stand was the standard action of respect in the ancient world, as

---

[104] So today we would still argue that even the worst sinner is not denied the opportunity to understand what God would want him or her to do and to become. In other words, saving truth is not withheld from people because of their sin; their sin might keep them from seeking it or acting on it, but God does not hide knowledge of salvation from them in order to punish them. God is always an evangelist. See D. Wells, *God the Evangelist* (Grand Rapids: Eerdmans, 1987).

[105] As in the case of 20:8; 24:7.

[106] This probably was a factor in God's locating the credentializing of the elders of Israel via his Spirit at the tent of meeting (Num 11:16–17), which is described as being "outside" the camp in Num 11:24–30, indicating at least the possibility that the tent of meeting was still used occasionally when the tabernacle was being transported and there was neither a proper location nor time enough to set it up fully.

[107] The implication of vv. 8–10 is that the tent of meeting was not so far away that it was difficult to see from the camp, and therefore Moses must have chosen a spot to pitch it that he knew was visible from the area where the people were encamped.

[108] Childs, *Exodus*, 592–93.

also, generally, in the modern. The Israelites were a fickle people, but at this point at least they no longer doubted Moses as their leader. Indeed, since his purpose in going to the "tent of meeting" outside the camp was to converse with God, they especially respected his trips there since they had no other conduit to God's guidance for them. In v. 9 God's presence, symbolized in the "pillar of cloud," arrived at the entrance[109] to the tent just as Moses arrived there, thus indicating divine approbation of and an obvious divine encounter ("meeting") with Moses. As long as Yahweh spoke with his prophet, the pillar of cloud stayed there at the entrance. The wording implies that when it departed, Moses and all the other Israelites knew that God had concluded the meeting. As v. 10 indicates, the people could see the pillar of cloud, a symbol they already knew represented Yahweh among them (13:21–22; 14:9,24), and so they gave proper respect to this distant (far outside the camp) indication of Yahweh's presence by worshiping (bowing to the ground, probably prostrate).[110]

33:11 Although God's presence among the Israelites in general was currently greatly curtailed, this distancing did not apply to Moses. The same close conversational relationship he enjoyed with God atop Sinai was also available to him at the entrance to the little "tent of meeting," a face-to-face encounter as someone "speaks with his friend."[111] Because the reader might wonder what would happen to the "tent of meeting" when Moses was not there, he added the detail that Joshua guarded it at all times ("Joshua son of Nun did not leave the tent"). This fact does not automatically elevate Joshua above the other Israelites, as if to a par with Moses, since any Israelite could go to the tent with an inquiry for God; access to it was not especially restricted for individuals or small groups. But it does show the trust Moses (and God) placed in Joshua and his continuing importance as a leader (see already comments on 17:9–14; 24:13; 32:17).

Joshua's not leaving the tent is not intended to imply that he lived *in* it—only that his own tent was nearby so that he could serve as its custodian. Joshua thus lived outside the concentrated Israelite encampment. Joshua was called Moses' "young aide" not because he was immature but because he

---

[109] The entrance was the intended point of contact; cf. 29:4,11,42; relative to the entrance of the tabernacle, which the entrance to the "tent of meeting" stood for in the absence of an erected tabernacle.

[110] The NIV translation "stood and worshiped" is unfortunate because it implies to the reader that the people worshiped while standing, perhaps via the raising of hands. (Interestingly, the few depictions of hands raised in worship in the ancient world show them raised to the mouth, not above the head as is favored in modern Western worship.) The Hb. construction וְקָם כָּל־הָעָם is part of a hendiadys in which the first element וְקָם does not literally connote "stand" but "stop whatever else you're doing and . . ." A better translation would be simply "bowed in worship" or the like. Durham takes וְקָם to be a separate act and translates accordingly: "All the people would stand up: then each man would prostrate himself in worship" (*Exodus,* 439).

was so much younger than Moses, who was eighty at this point.[112] Forty years later, Joshua may himself have been eighty years old (or more) when he led the Israelites in the conquest of Canaan.[113]

(7) The Need for and Promise of God's Glory (33:12–23)

[12]Moses said to the LORD, "You have been telling me, 'Lead these people,' but you have not let me know whom you will send with me. You have said, 'I know you by name and you have found favor with me.' [13]If you are pleased with me, teach me your ways so I may know you and continue to find favor with you. Remember that this nation is your people."

[14]The LORD replied, "My Presence will go with you, and I will give you rest."

[15]Then Moses said to him, "If your Presence does not go with us, do not send us up from here. [16]How will anyone know that you are pleased with me and with your people unless you go with us? What else will distinguish me and your people from all the other people on the face of the earth?"

[17]And the LORD said to Moses, "I will do the very thing you have asked, because I am pleased with you and I know you by name."

[18]Then Moses said, "Now show me your glory."

[19]And the LORD said, "I will cause all my goodness to pass in front of you, and I will proclaim my name, the LORD, in your presence. I will have mercy on whom

---

[111] In all likelihood, the kind of encounter Moses had with God at the entrance to the "tent of meeting" was the same as he had when on top of Mount Sinai (20:18–21; 24:9–11; 15–18), even though this is the first place in the narrative that mentions speaking with God "face to face." In other words, Moses probably did not intend here to suggest by the wording "face to face as a person talks with his friend" that he now had an even closer relationship with Yahweh than in those encounters on the mountain but rather to remind them that he still had *just as close* a relationship as he had previously. The expression "face to face" (פָּנִים אֶל־פָּנִים) is an idiom. It does not mean "looking at each other" or the like as if Moses actually saw God when Moses stood in the "tent of meeting" and Yahweh stood in front of it in the form of the glory cloud. (This could hardly be so in light of the explicit statement of God later in v. 20, "You cannot see my face, for no one may see me and live." Its sense is more that of the Eng. expression "up close and personal." The Eng. idiom "person to person" is relatively similar as well (because it does not imply visual perception), and the idiom "heart to heart" is also analogous (because, likewise, it emphasizes the quality of intimacy of the conversation rather than any visual perception). The exact expression פָּנִים אֶל־פָּנִים ("face to face") occurs three other times in the OT: in Gen 32:30, where Jacob saw an angel and believed he had been in the very presence of God, in Deut 34:10, which refers essentially to the present passage, and Ezek 20:35, where God said to the Israelites: "I will bring you into the desert of the nations and there, face to face, I will execute judgment upon you." As an illustration, here is how the Hb. expression פָּנִים אֶל־פָּנִים (rendered in the following examples as "face to face") might be used idiomatically if it were used in Eng. as it is used in Hb.: "He called me long distance and we spoke face to face even though I didn't think he knew me that well" or "Her emails are always face to face—never impersonal."

[112] See comments on 7:7. Cf. also F. Dumermuth, "Josua in Ex. 33, 7–11," *TZ* 19 (1963): 161–68.

[113] A reasonable inference from Josh 13:1; 23:1.

I will have mercy, and I will have compassion on whom I will have compassion. [20]But," he said, "you cannot see my face, for no one may see me and live."

[21]Then the LORD said, "There is a place near me where you may stand on a rock. [22]When my glory passes by, I will put you in a cleft in the rock and cover you with my hand until I have passed by. [23]Then I will remove my hand and you will see my back; but my face must not be seen."

For Moses the presence of God was confirmed again and again[114]—most fully by an actual theophany, an appearance of God in some sort of visible manifestation. We have already argued that what happened in these theophanies was not that Moses actually saw God in the same way believers will see him in heaven but that God manifest himself by producing for Moses' benefit some sort of shape that was visible and therefore gave a sense of closeness and locality to his contact with Moses.

At this point in the story of the exodus, Moses very much needed the reassurance God now proposed to give him. The exodus assignment—to bring the people not just from Egypt to Sinai but now from Sinai to the promised land, was complicated by the vivid evidence of the people's idolatry in chap. 32 that they were a recalcitrant lot, suggesting that Moses' task would not be a light one. Moreover, God's refusal so far to grant his direct presence any longer in accompanying the people means that Moses would, as it were, be more on his own in leading Israel hereafter than he had been before—and the job had proved hard enough already.

The theophany promised here would reassure him. It would strengthen his resolve and build his confidence. His assignment was daunting and his resources few. If he knew, however, that God's glory abode with him and that therefore God's favor and care attended his actions, he could endure and prevail.

33:12 How could Moses say to God, "You have not let me know whom you will send with me" when God had just said (v. 2) "I will send an angel before you"? The answer comes partly with the realization that delayed response is a stylistic technique in the narrative that Moses employed regularly,[115] as well as the recognition that the difference between "before" and "with" was very large in Moses' mind. For God to "be with" someone represents an idea expressed repeatedly in Moses' Genesis narrative, especially in such passages as Gen 21:20; 26:3; 31:3; 39:2,23, carrying the sense of "to guide/protect/take care of" (cf. also Deut 32:12, "The LORD alone led him; no foreign god was with him").

---

[114] We are at this point in Exodus on the verge of the fifth theophany in the book, which comes in 34:5–7. This section prepares Moses for it, encouragingly. Some theophanies came more by surprise (e.g., that of chap. 3).

[115] See comments on 34:6. Cf. W. Irwin, "The Course of the Dialog between Moses and Yahweh," *CBQ* 59 (1997): 629–36.

33:13 For a second time (cf. vv. 12,17) Moses used the expression *māṣāʾ* + *ḥēn* + *bĕʿênê* (be pleased with/find favor), in this instance as the protasis of a conditional sentence ("If you are pleased with me" also translatable as "If I have found favor with you" or "If I have found favor in your sight") because he had a request to make of Yahweh that was based on Yahweh's declaration that he had found favor with him (vv. 12,17). Moses' request was to know God better.

What is especially instructive to us is Moses' understanding of how that would be accomplished: by being "taught" God's "ways." As Luther's friend Melanchthon once eloquently stated, *hoc est Christum cognoscere: beneficia euis cognoscere* ("To know Christ is to know his benefits"). There is little room for mysticism in biblical religion; we do not know God by having some sort of inexplicable ethereal communion with him, in which our feelings are used as the evidence for our closeness to him. We know him by learning his ways (i.e., his revealed standards, revealed methods, and revealed benefits)—in other words by objective, rather than subjective, emotional, means.

Moses continued with the sound approach he had already taken in 32:11–13 by saying, "Remember that this nation is your people." In so doing Moses showed himself once again the servant of God's revealed, clearly established purposes rather than someone who just wanted to be in charge or someone who wanted his job for its inherent prestige. Although he had a right to claim favor with God because God had so declared it (vv. 12,17), the focus of his request for a continuation of that favor (the third of four uses in this passage of *māṣāʾ* + *ḥēn* + *bĕʿên*, be pleased with/find favor) was not himself but God's people. Thus Moses' actions here have long been regarded as instructive and exemplary for all those in leadership in God's service. Other biblical examples include the attitude of Jesus (e.g., John 17:9,15,20,24) and of Paul (e.g., Rom 10:1; 2 Cor 13:9).

33:14 God made here a further, huge and wonderful, concession relative to the degree to which he would be present with Moses and the Israelites when they left Sinai. This was clearly a quantum gain (from the point of view of Moses and the people) on the prior promise of an "angel" to lead them (33:2). It was a full restoration of the original idea of God's promise to bring the Israelites out of Egypt and into the promised land *personally* as stated in 3:8,12,17. It shows that Moses' prayerful appeal had in fact been entirely successful—not because Moses could get anything he wanted from God but because of God's character of "goodness" and "mercy" and "compassion" (v. 19 below) and his nature as the God who is "compassionate . . . gracious . . . slow to anger, abounding in love and faithfulness, maintaining love . . ., forgiving wickedness, rebellion and sin" (34:6–7).

This was only one stage in the bargaining process, however. Moses would continue to ask for more and more assurance of God's presence to guide him and the people (see comments on 34:9). But already God's statement "my Presence will go[116] with you" is a far greater reassurance than that of 33:3. It promises something the Israelites desperately wanted—the same sort of full, personal presence of God that existed at Sinai and was effectively, though not permanently, withdrawn with the words of 33:3. Now Israel would have the "presence" of God in the sense of what the Hebrew literally calls his "face."[117] This is a guarantee of accompaniment by God during Israel's journey to the promised land.[118]

The accompanying promise, "I will give you rest," could be taken to mean that Moses' job would be easier if God went with him,[119] but the audience for this statement was more likely Israel as a whole,[120] and the "rest" envisaged was that which had already been promised in 15:13,17, that is, Canaan, the promised land of *rest* for God's people.[121] Jesus' great promise in Matt 11:28 may contain a conscious paraphrase of the present wording.

33:15–16 So important to Moses was the need for God's constant presence, hopefully as direct and complete as it had been there at Sinai, that he pleaded with God not to ask him and the people to leave Sinai without it. His

---

[116] Since Moses and the Israelites had already been told to "go" *(hlk)* in 33:1, this promise of Yahweh to "go" *(hlk)* as well is a genuinely significant comfort because it committed Yahweh to the same action as that required of his people, even if it involved his presence with them on the journey in a somewhat more limited way than was encountered at Sinai.

[117] The difference between this statement and that of 33:3 is not, however, the result of a focus on Moses here as compared to Israel there; the second-person singular is used in both places, consistent with God's treatment of Israel as a unity and of standard legal style, in which covenant commands and promises are normally made in the second-person singular so that they apply both to each individual and also to the whole nation as a unit.

[118] As opposed to what is envisioned in a translation such as that of the JPSV, which seems to impoverish the concept by rendering it as God's being "in the lead." In our opinion the JPSV is not convincing. For פָּנַי יֵלֵכוּ to be rendered as "I will go in the lead," when its literal meaning is "my face will go," would seem to stretch the meaning too far. The question in the context is whether or not Moses and the Israelites would have God's presence in some form with them to guide and protect them on the next stage of the journey, not where in the procession God would be in relation to the bulk of the people.

[119] So the JPSV rendering, "[I] will lighten your burden."

[120] The problem of deciding whether Moses or all the people is the referent for "you" arises because the Hb. pronoun is in the singular. Since God addressed his people often as "you" singular throughout the Bible both as a way of emphasizing their corporate identity and as a way of emphasizing each individual's responsibility to do his part among the whole, there is not any formal way to differentiate when singular pronouns refer to Israel corporately or to one individual within Israel in contexts like the present one.

[121] Cf. Deut 12:10; 25:19; Josh 1:13–15; 21:44; 22:4; 23:1; and compare the extension of the theme in Heb 3–4, with special reference to the events of Num 13–14, as esp. summarized in Num 14:20–23.

language was not brusque, and he was not commanding God; it was the language of prayerful appeal, which can be voiced normally in the Hebrew with the imperative,[122] as here. He based his appeal especially on God's concern for God's own glory/reputation, an approach Moses would also use again in such contexts as Num 14:13–16, making clear that God's desire for glory was not petty or vain but evangelistic: he was always at work providing for the possibility of the Gentiles' hearing and believing.[123]

Note also that Moses included the people in God's favor ("you are pleased with me and your people") but understood that God's favor on his people was an aspect of his display of his greatness to the nations. Moses here followed his previously seen admirable commitment to gaining nothing for himself alone but making sure the Israelites saw God's blessing (cf. 32:11–14). For Moses to go ahead alone in the leadership of the Israelites would surely result in mistakes, losses, and failures of various kinds, not the least being the likelihood of military defeat of the Israelites at the hands of their enemies (cf. Num 14:42). So again Moses emphasized how essential God's presence was to the entire remaining exodus enterprise. Unless Israel succeeded where other nations would expect them to fail, no one would infer that their God was great ("What . . . will distinguish me and your people from all the other people?"). The success of Israel versus their enemies was, in the old covenant, a witness to the world.[124] When their enemies prevailed against them, they were shamed and disgraced to the world, indeed, cursed,[125] and their special nature as the one people of the one true God was blurred to the vision of others. The lesson is clearly put by Moses: it was God's presence with his people, and all that that implied, that made his people special—they did not have within themselves any particular intrinsic characteristics to "distinguish" them. God's distinction was what they received derivatively but did not possess innately.

33:17 For the fifth and final time in the passage the idiom *māṣāʾ* + *ḥēn* + *bĕʿênê* (find favor/be pleased with) appears, referring to God's being pleased with Israel and Moses, almost in the manner of an inclusio with the occurrence in v. 12, especially since major parts of the two verses are so similar in wording (see comments on 33:12). In vv. 12–16 Moses had pleaded with God to the effect that "if you are pleased with me, please give me and the people your presence." Now God indicated his positive reply almost as if he were saying: "Since your appeal for my presence is based on

[122] Technically, the vetitive, i.e., the negative of the imperfect, and in this case the special time-limited negative of the imperfect with *ʿal*.

[123] On this theological concept of God's evangelism of the nations, see Wells's *God the Evangelist*.

[124] Cf. Gen 14:20; Exod 23:22,27; Lev 26:7; Num 10:9.

[125] Cf. Lev 26:37–38; Deut 28:25,31,68.

my being pleased with you—and that is a convincing ground, indeed, since I am the one who declared it so—I will honor your request." The fact that he knew Moses "by name" (see comments on v. 12) reinforced his pleasure with him. He did not merely like Moses. They had a special relationship to each other ("I know you by name") upon which God's mercy to him and the people was partly based. The combination of God's loving mercy and Moses' faithful persistent prayer (cf. Luke 18:2–8) was paying off. God would now send more than just an angel; he would personally come with the Israelites, as will be defined in the coming verses.

33:18 Why did Moses ask God to show him his glory?[126] Had he not seen God's glory already in the cloud that protected the Israelites as they escaped from the Egyptians?[127] Had the glory of Yahweh not appeared on Sinai for all to see,[128] and had not Moses entered inside that glory cloud repeatedly?[129] The answer is that Moses had indeed seen God's glory in the past and therefore wanted to see it again, in as full a way as God might choose to show it, in order to know that just as God's glory had reassuringly accompanied him and the Israelites on such occasions in the past, Moses could count on it to be with them again once they finally set forth from Sinai. That would convince him that God was indeed still close, still protective, and still interested in him and the Israelites as his people. In other words, the glory of God was something Moses directly associated with the approbation of God on his leadership of the Israelites; and if he could again see it, he could again be certain that his leadership would once again be blessed by the great King of heaven. Previously, the glory of God had always been provided at God's initiation and witnessed corporately (e.g., 16:7–10; 24:16–17), but this time Moses took the initiative to ask for a personal audience with God. That God responded favorably indicates Moses' acceptance with God based on his faithfulness at all prior points of testing.[130]

---

[126] Again the phrasing of the Hb. original is not dictatorial but petitionary—properly polite and respectful.

[127] Exod 16:7, "In the morning you shall see the glory of the LORD, because he has heard your grumbling"; Exod 16:10, "While Aaron was speaking . . ., they looked toward the desert, and there was the glory of the LORD appearing in the cloud."

[128] Exod 24:16–17: "The glory of the LORD settled on Mount Sinai. For six days the cloud covered the mountain, and on the seventh day the LORD called to Moses from within the cloud. To the Israelites the glory of the LORD looked like a consuming fire on top of the mountain."

[129] Exod 19:9,16; 24:15,18; 33:9.

[130] Sarna (*Exodus,* 214) notes that the previous experiences of God's glory were characterized by three components: (1) the glory was seen corporately, (2) it was seen at a distance, and (3) it took place at God's initiation ([God] "freely chooses the time and place," in Sarna's words). By contrast, this time Moses, as Sarna says, "pleads for an exclusively individual experience, one that is close at hand and that occurs in response to his personal request there and then."

In v. 13 he had asked to know God's "ways"—an important request and one that would gain him much benefit. Then he went further: he wanted an experiential sensory perception of God. Such things were rarely granted to humans, as Moses would have been well aware, but Moses understood that if God were willing to grant his request for this kind of personal familiarity, he would be all the more strongly reassured of God's favor on the forthcoming expedition away from Sinai and on to the promised land of Canaan.

33:19–20 In these verses Yahweh, the only true and living God, responded to Moses' request for knowing God's ways (v. 13) with a promise to "proclaim his name" (his character and essence, thus his ways; i.e., what he is like and what he expects his people to be like). Furthermore, to the request for a vision of his "glory" (v. 18) Yahweh responded with a promise to have "all [his] goodness" pass before Moses. These things would happen "in his presence," but he would not let Moses "see [his] face," lest he die from doing so.[131] In other words, God would "show" Moses things that would convince him of God's presence yet would stop short of actually letting Moses look at him. In fact, this sort of limited exposure—enough for human perception to be truly aware of the divine presence but not enough for humans to have an early experience of the sort of direct perception of God that only heaven would allow—had already taken place in the theophanies described in 3:6; 24:11 and earlier in this chapter in vv. 8–11.[132] Therefore the reader would be mistaken to assume that what Moses actually *saw* would be significantly revelatory; it was rather what he *learned* through God's words that would most help him to understand that his request to be taught God's ways (v. 13) and to be shown God's glory (v. 18) had indeed been granted.

Especially important in all of this is the purpose: Moses and the Israelites had been separated from Yahweh's covenant blessing by the great sin of idolatry as

[131] In the same way that merely *hearing* the voice of God directly was too much for the Israelites to endure (20:18–19), *seeing* him in any way—even seeing an obviously limited manifestation of his glory granted for the sake of reassurance—would represent an overwhelming challenge for a mere human. God knew how to make it happen short of killing Moses, as he did already in 24:9–11; this is what vv. 21–23 are about.

[132] Here we repeat an assertion made in connection with 24:9–11. Since otherwise God is invisible, how can people ever have the certitude that they have been in his special presence? The answer is that sometimes, rarely in history, God has produced for them a sort of corporealization that serves the purpose of helping them understand that they are dealing with a *person* and not merely an *idea* in their own minds or a force or concept or numinous experience of some sort that would not represent the same thing to them as understanding that they were really in the presence of a personal God. Different people need different levels of confidence for different tasks. Having a vision of God is not normally needed for serving him and will not normally be something God will grant upon request. He will grant faith, and he will grant guidance, but theophanies are few and far between.

described in chap. 32. They eagerly desired restoration to Yahweh's favor. Could they be sure it would be granted them? Moses wanted some sort of absolutely incontrovertible evidence that Yahweh had again accepted his people and would go with them into the promised land, continuing to be their beneficent covenant sovereign. He needed a sign that would convince him that God was with him and the Israelites—and "seeing was believing."

But what exactly did God mean by "all my goodness," and how could such goodness "pass in front of" Moses? Perhaps the answer is to be found in a different translation of *ṭûb* than the NIV's "goodness." In this line of reasoning, the noun *ṭûb* connotes more the sense of "[the] best" (Gen 24:10) or in the case of something visible, "loveliness/splendor" (Hos 10:11) so that the translation could actually read, "I will cause my full splendor to pass in front of you." What God would then be promising Moses accordingly would be a chance to sense God's glory visually—to see something so *splendid* to behold—the *best* thing he could possibly see as a human—that he would know without a doubt that it represented/manifest God's presence passing before him. He wouldn't actually see God as if God were like a human whose entirety could be seen in one place, and he wouldn't have any worry about dying from what he saw because v. 20 warns about something God was, in fact, not going to let happen to Moses.[133]

This might have been what God would have chosen to do for Moses, but a problem with such an interpretation is that it ignores the point made in vv. 21–22, namely that Moses actually did not get to see much of *anything* at all (see the comment on those verses).[134] He was hidden in a rock crevice that was covered by Yahweh's corporealized "hand"—meaning almost surely that he could not see God at all except, after God had passed by, his "back" (see comments on vv. 21–22). Therefore the sensing of Yahweh's goodness must have occurred mainly in a nonvisual way.

Preliminarily, two considerations may be expressed about God's causing his "goodness" to pass in front of Moses. The first of these, simply put, is "what else could God show him?" God has no badness. Therefore "all my goodness" would have to convey something like "an even fuller sense of who I am than you have thus far been able to grasp." Second, the actual fulfillment of Moses' request would not occur until it could take place in a covenant context, that is, in 34:4–7. Then and only then would things make sense because it was through his covenant relationship with Israel that God's full goodness would be experienced. God's goodness was, in other words, not so much a thing to be seen at a certain time by looking in a certain direc-

[133] Cf. Deut 5:24; 18:16; 1 Tim 6:16; 1 John 4:12.

[134] The situation might be likened to having a conversation standing opposite someone in a completely dark or smoke-filled room or the like. There is no question that the conversation is "face to face," but there is also no actual visual contact with the other person. One knows that the other person is really there—truly present—but one sees nothing per se.

tion but an ongoing experience of the nature of God as he manifest his nature for the benefit of his people through his beneficent covenant.[135]

Also important is that God would cause "all my goodness"[136] to pass in front of Moses. Does this mean that Moses would actually be able to perceive "all" of God—to somehow comprehend the fullness of the Godhead? Hardly. Rather, the meaning of "all" in this case is more likely "nothing but." An analogy presents itself in the way light may be said to banish darkness. In a room full of light one would not say that there was a mixture of light and darkness but "all light" or "nothing but light." While in theory darkness might be said to exist in places where the light was blocked from penetrating, it could certainly not be said that among those surfaces where the light struck, some areas were dark and some were not. All would be perceived as nothing but light. So God's goodness as revealed to Moses would be total ("all") in the sense of nothing but goodness.

Far more important than what Moses would see was what he would hear: Yahweh invoking his own name. Through the idiom *qārāh* + *bĕ*+ *šēm* (usually translated "call on the name of"), which can mean "to speak out loud the name of" (and therefore "invoke") or "call out to" in the sense of pray to/ask for help from/worship, God promised Moses that he would speak his own name so Moses would know for certain with whom he was dealing and would not be subject to doubt that his eyes had played tricks on him, or any such thing. This is an instance of God's giving to a person the special reassurance he needed in a special situation, providing powerfully convincing evidence of his presence to that person in an *aural* way, parallel to the *visual* way his splendor could do the same thing.

Such divine evidences are exceptions, not the rule. A few biblical characters to hear God's voice; the vast majority do not. A few are allowed to see some sort of visible manifestation of his presence; most never do. Jesus, who ultimately represented God among humans in this world, was seen and heard by thousands of people, but their number is relatively small compared to the number of all those who have neither seen nor heard him personally.[137] Theophanies are exceptions, not the rule. They strengthen the

---

[135] This is also how we understand the nature of God in the New Covenant. We do not know God merely by reason of being able to state accurately a list of his attributes, i.e., things we know about him, useful as such a list can be. Rather, we know him by his involvement in our lives as Lord, as we interact with his Lordship through covenant obedience and the willingness to be led by his Spirit that indwells us. Knowing God personally happens to some degree, though on a more important and eternal scale, as knowing anyone else happens: by spending time with him—true, obedient time—in all the various ways that is possible and becoming closer to him as time goes by.

[136] כָּל־טוּבִי.

[137] Note Jesus' commendation of the faith of those who would come after him without a chance to see him as did those while he was in the flesh: "Because you have seen me, you have believed; blessed are those who have not seen and yet have believed" (John 20:29; cf. John 6:36; 1 Pet 1:8).

confidence of those to whom they are given, in highly exceptional circumstances where such strengthening is needed and where less sensory encouragement would not suffice. Most people must rely on reports of theophanies rather than participation in one, and to seek a theophany as Moses did here would have no warrant unless one were on a par with Moses in job assignment and closeness to Yahweh and in an old covenant setting, neither of which is possible now. Fortunately, having the Holy Spirit dwelling in us is far better and far more permanent an asset.[138]

God's assertion, translated traditionally, "I will have mercy on whom I will have mercy, and I will have compassion on whom I will have compassion," addresses Moses' special relationship with him; but more broadly it speaks to his name, that is, his character and ways. A better translation of this part of the verse would be: "I will invoke my name Yahweh before you, that is, I show grace in being gracious and I show mercy in being merciful."[139] The characteristics of Yahweh, namely his grace and mercy, are placed here in grammatical apposition to the *name* of Yahweh. Moses did indeed enjoy God's special mercy and compassion in one way at one time, but in other ways and at other times, God's mercy and compassion would take different forms with other people.

Thus a general principle is stated rather than merely a personal word to Moses. God's "mercy" and "compassion" were granted to all his covenant people (Deut 13:17; cf. Jas 5:11) and should in turn characterize the behavior of all his covenant people (e.g., Zech 7:9), but they are not automatically available to all other people unless they join in covenant with God. God's assertion, then, is a general statement of his covenant blessings, which are special incentives for those who know his name (i.e., seek to keep his covenant). The promise concerning mercy and compassion is therefore not so much a divisive statement (as if "on whom . . ." were intended to be merely discriminatory) as a part of the reassurance God gave Moses, saying in effect: You won't just receive my common grace; you (my people) will receive my covenant mercy and compassion.

Verse 20 takes the form of a restrictive clause followed by an explanatory clause. Moses could expect a great manifestation of God's presence to commence shortly but could not expect actually to see him fully—as fully as, for example, angels see God in heaven[140] or as the redeemed will one day see him.[141] Such full proximity to the holiness of God would require the death

[138] As Jesus clearly taught in Matt 11:11. The nature of the indwelling of the Spirit under the New Covenant eclipses any experience of God in the Old, including that of Moses. In other words, Moses had nothing on us.

[139] A slightly different but essentially comparable translation is provided in the JPSV: "I will proclaim before you the name LORD, and the grace that I grant and the compassion that I show."

[140] Matt 18:10.

[141] 1 John 3:2.

of someone like Moses, a sinful human still on earth, not yet transformed into the likeness of Christ and therefore not yet fit to experience a higher level of the presence of God than he was about to experience here. Similarly, in Num 12:6–8 God explained to Miriam and Aaron that what Moses saw when he "saw" God was his *těmūnāh,* his "likeness" or "depiction" (NIV, unconvincingly, "form").[142]

33:21–23 Here God helped Moses to understand that his theophany, however extraordinary and impressive, would nevertheless be limited, in accordance to what he had just explained in vv. 19–20. Moses would receive some sense of the glory of God departing, moving away from him ("you will see my back") so that he would realize he had actually perceived something of God's true, visible manifestation of himself (even if not of his full essence)—but only the back, that is, not much at all. This provides something of an analogy for Moses. In the same way that we do not see much of a person when we see only his or her back walking away from us, but can still tell who it is if we know that person well enough, Moses was allowed to sense what God caused him to recognize as the "back" of God's visibly manifested glory moving away from him and could therefore understand that he had perceived God's true—though not at all complete—presence as a reassurance for his great task ahead, that of leading the people from Sinai to the promised land. In the Hebrew idiom, however, to see only the back and not to see the face means, in effect, "to see nothing" or "to see virtually nothing."[143]

The "rock" on which Moses stood waiting for God's glory to pass by, the "cleft" in that rock in which God put Moses, and that he personally put Moses in it all indicate the location as the top of Mount Sinai once again. God's words, "There is a place right here where I am" (NIV "There is a place near me") could hardly designate any other site than Mount Sinai because Sinai was his temporary dwelling place throughout Exod 20:1–40:33. The

142 Cf. the parallel pairing of *těmūnāh,* "likeness," with *pānayim,* "face," in Ps 17:15. The context in that psalm may conceivably be that of seeing God in heaven, but this is less than clear. Nevertheless, Moses' seeing God "face to face" and seeing his "likeness" are presumably one in the same, both ways of speaking of a limited-scale but *personal* encounter of the presence of God.

143 In the Hb. idiom, if you do not "see the face" of someone, you do not have actual contact with him at all. E.g., when David said that Absalom could not have any further contact with him, David said, "He must go to his own house; he must not see my face," and the text confirms, "So Absalom went to his own house and did not see the face of the king" (2 Sam 14:24). The same idiom appears in Gen 43:3,5; 44:23; Exod 10:28. Accordingly, to "see [only] the back" is idiomatic for seeing virtually nothing: as God says in Jer 18:17, "Like a wind from the east, I will scatter them before their enemies; I will show them my back and not my face in the day of their disaster." This does not mean the Israelites would look at Yahweh and actually see him turned in another direction from them but that they would not find him around when they needed him; in other words, they would not see him at all.

NIV's "where you may stand on a rock" is a possible translation,[144] but the Hebrew for rock has the definite article,[145] so "where you may stand on the rock" is a more likely translation, "the rock" meaning Mount Sinai.[146] The actual fulfillment of this promised encounter took place on Mount Sinai, as expected and as described in the next chapter (34:4–7 and following).

The statement "my face must not be seen" reflects not merely God's protection of his presence but a gracious act of protection of Moses' life. Were he to see God fully, it would be beyond his capacity to endure as a sinful human, and he would die as God already warned him in v. 20. This is yet another reference to the beneficent partial withholding of God's presence.[147] The descriptions "cover you with my hand" and "remove my hand" do not mean that God is a very large human-shaped being with a giant but human sort of hand capable of sheltering a person's entire body; rather, these are the kinds of necessary anthropomorphisms without which little of God can be described.[148] To Moses the hand of God would seem a gentle, caring thing as opposed to, say, a lightning bolt, as the means of placing him in the rock's cleft. It was a way of saying to Moses not that God has a huge hand but that he would personally protect Moses from what otherwise would kill him.[149]

(8) Renewal of the Stone Tablets and the Covenant (34:1–28)

[1]The LORD said to Moses, "Chisel out two stone tablets like the first ones, and I will write on them the words that were on the first tablets, which you broke. [2]Be ready in the morning, and then come up on Mount Sinai. Present yourself to me there on top of the mountain. [3]No one is to come with you or be seen anywhere on the mountain; not even the flocks and herds may graze in front of the mountain."

[4]So Moses chiseled out two stone tablets like the first ones and went up Mount Sinai early in the morning, as the LORD had commanded him; and he carried the two stone tablets in his hands.

[5]Then the LORD came down in the cloud and stood there with him and proclaimed his name, the LORD. [6]And he passed in front of Moses, proclaiming,

---

[144] Taking the article with rock as the proleptic article of narrative introduction, i.e., "a certain rock."

[145] הַצּוּר.

[146] Indeed, the Hb. term used here for rock, צוּר, was already used of Horeb/Sinai in 17:6. Cf. HCSB "the rock."

[147] See also in the Introduction, "Theology of Exodus: The Limited Presence of God in Israel's Midst."

[148] Cf. D. Stuart, "God's Cognition of Human Activity in the Deuteronomic History," A.B. diss., Harvard College, 1964.

[149] Cp. "my right arm" and similar expressions used idiomatically and without any anthropomorphic presupposition. As F. Hartenstein has argued, if Moses with his privileged access to God really couldn't see God in this passage, surely humans in general cannot, just as 3:20 states ("Das 'Angesicht Gottes' in Exodus 32–34," in *Gottes Volk am Sinai* [Gütersloh: Gütersloher Verlagshaus, 2001], 157–83).

"The LORD, the LORD, the compassionate and gracious God, slow to anger,
abounding in love and faithfulness, [7]maintaining love to thousands, and forgiving
wickedness, rebellion and sin. Yet he does not leave the guilty unpunished; he
punishes the children and their children for the sin of the fathers to the third and
fourth generation."

[8]Moses bowed to the ground at once and worshiped. [9]"O Lord, if I have found
favor in your eyes," he said, "then let the Lord go with us. Although this is a stiff-
necked people, forgive our wickedness and our sin, and take us as your inherit-
ance."

[10]Then the LORD said: "I am making a covenant with you. Before all your
people I will do wonders never before done in any nation in all the world. The
people you live among will see how awesome is the work that I, the LORD, will do
for you. [11]Obey what I command you today. I will drive out before you the Amor-
ites, Canaanites, Hittites, Perizzites, Hivites and Jebusites.

[12]Be careful not to make a treaty with those who live in the land where you are
going, or they will be a snare among you. [13]Break down their altars, smash their
sacred stones and cut down their Asherah poles. [14]Do not worship any other god,
for the LORD, whose name is Jealous, is a jealous God.

[15]"Be careful not to make a treaty with those who live in the land; for when
they prostitute themselves to their gods and sacrifice to them, they will invite you
and you will eat their sacrifices. [16]And when you choose some of their daughters
as wives for your sons and those daughters prostitute themselves to their gods,
they will lead your sons to do the same.

[17]"Do not make cast idols.

[18]"Celebrate the Feast of Unleavened Bread. For seven days eat bread made
without yeast, as I commanded you. Do this at the appointed time in the month of
Abib, for in that month you came out of Egypt.

[19]"The first offspring of every womb belongs to me, including all the firstborn
males of your livestock, whether from herd or flock. [20]Redeem the firstborn don-
key with a lamb, but if you do not redeem it, break its neck. Redeem all your first-
born sons.

"No one is to appear before me empty-handed.

[21]"Six days you shall labor, but on the seventh day you shall rest; even during
the plowing season and harvest you must rest.

[22]"Celebrate the Feast of Weeks with the firstfruits of the wheat harvest, and
the Feast of Ingathering at the turn of the year. [23]Three times a year all your men
are to appear before the Sovereign LORD, the God of Israel. [24]I will drive out
nations before you and enlarge your territory, and no one will covet your land
when you go up three times each year to appear before the LORD your God.

[25]"Do not offer the blood of a sacrifice to me along with anything containing
yeast, and do not let any of the sacrifice from the Passover Feast remain until
morning.

[26]"Bring the best of the firstfruits of your soil to the house of the LORD your
God.

"Do not cook a young goat in its mother's milk."

[27]Then the LORD said to Moses, "Write down these words, for in accordance with these words I have made a covenant with you and with Israel." [28]Moses was there with the LORD forty days and forty nights without eating bread or drinking water. And he wrote on the tablets the words of the covenant—the Ten Commandments.

THE REPLACEMENT TABLETS (34:1–4). God's instruction to Moses to prepare two new stone tablets and his promise to write the Ten Words/Commandments on these new tablets just as he had on the former ones conveys a most welcome message: God had decided to forgive the Israelites and accept them once again as his covenant people, and he would renew his covenant with them, through which all sorts of blessings would once again be theirs. Like an employer saying to a previously dismissed employee, "Welcome back to the company. Let me show you your work station" or a judge saying to a person whose punishment had been completed, "You're free to go and resume your former life," God said to Moses and through him to Israel, in effect: "Bring some new tablets. Let's put the covenant back in force."

34:1 The new tablets were to be exactly like the old: stone tablets written on personally by God and containing the same wording as the originals (cf. 20:2–17; 24:12; 31:18; 32:15–16). In the narrative about the original tablets, God personally provided the tablets (32:16). Here Moses would chisel them out of stone, so he was assigned the job of providing the tablets. God took upon himself only the job of writing on them.[150] As 34:28 confirms, the Ten Words/Commandments would be the content of these,[151] and as logic dictates from our understanding of how covenants worked, the tablets were again both complete copies of the Ten Words/Commandments (not five on one tablet and five on the other), with one tablet representing the sov-

---

[150] There is no hint in the text that this was a way of indicating that God had not completely forgiven the Israelites. Whether Moses supplied the tablets or God supplied them, no message about forgiveness is conveyed. More likely the requirement that Moses supply the tablets hints at the fact that after the original covenant, which was initiated entirely by God, all subsequent covenant arrangements were renewals thereof and thus required human initiation lest humans do nothing about broken covenants and simply wait for God to forgive them and reinstate his covenant. Thus the imperative "chisel out two stone tablets like the first ones" may be a way of implying that from now on Israel would be expected to start the process of covenant restoration whenever it was needed. This is, of course, exactly what had to happen: Israel's leaders had to take responsibility to initiate covenant renewal as they became aware that the covenant was broken with the preaching of the prophets and/or by what they personally witnessed (e.g., Josh 24; 25; 2 Kgs 11:17; 23:3; Neh 8). Another possibility, overlapping somewhat in concept, may be added to this one: that the requirement for producing the tablets represents a way of reminding the Israelites that "it won't be quite so easy this time. You need to show your commitment." A simplistic comparison might be: "Yes, you can be on the team again this year, but this time you'll have to supply your own uniform"—something new is added as a reminder that the participant has to show a commitment—a proper level of responsibility—the second time around.

ereign's (God's) copy and the other representing the vassal's (Israel's) copy.[152] God again referred to Moses' breaking the first pair of tablets ("the first tablets, which you broke") as a reminder that the prior covenant had actually been not just violated in some limited way but *broken,* making this offer of covenant reinstatement all the more timely and an evidence of gracious divine willingness to forgive and restore.

34:2 Most people traveled in the ancient Near East by starting out on a journey at first light when the temperature was better for the effort of traveling and because departing at dawn enabled the traveler to cover the maximum distance. Thus the idiom for starting on a journey is usually worded "got up early and . . ." Accordingly, there was nothing unusual about God's command to Moses to "be ready in the morning, and then come up" in light of the time and effort involved in climbing to the top of Mount Sinai.[153] "Present yourself to me there on top of the mountain" would imply that Moses was to go where he usually went and wait for the cloud of Yahweh's glory to appear to him and envelop him as it had done in the past (19:9; 24:15–18) and would do again (34:5).

34:3 God's holiness is a threat to the unholy, so nothing and no one he does not specifically declare acceptable may safely approach him. Accordingly, to protect his holiness and to protect those who might be struck dead by coming too close to him, he once again issued a warning against people and animals going anywhere on Mount Sinai.[154] The special mention of "flocks

---

[151] This view has not always prevailed among critical scholars. Starting with J. Wellhausen (*Die Composition des Hexateuchs,* 93), various scholars have taken the position that the present passage presents an alternative decalogue to that of 20:2–17, one that has been most often called "the ritual decalogue." This is based partly on the fact that one can identify ten commandments in 34:17–28, and partly on the presupposition that the Pentateuch is merely a human book that was composed from many sources over a long period of time, so one should generally try to find the sources and documents behind the final form rather than taking the final form at face value. Many in a prior generation of scholars suggested that the "decalogue" in 34:17–28 is earlier than that of 20:2–17 (so J. Morgenstern, "The Oldest Document of the Hexateuch," *HUCA* 4 [1927]: 54–98; S. Mowinckel, *Le décalogue* [Paris: Felix Alcan, 1927], 19–55; H. H. Rowley, "Moses and the Decalogue," in *Men of God* [London: Thomas Nelson & Sons, 1963], 7–36). Some placed it much later (i.e., not even remotely in the same time period that the book of Exodus places it, which is just a matter of weeks younger than the decalogue of 20:1–17) regardless of its relationship to the decalogue of 20:1–17. These include R. H. Pfeiffer, "The Oldest Decalogue," *JBL* 43 (1924): 294–310; and F. V. Winnett, *The Mosaic Tradition* (Toronto: Toronto University Press, 1949), 30–56, 155–71. For a more complete discussion of the various views and their problems, see Durham, *Exodus,* 458–60.

[152] See comments on 31:18.

[153] It is also possible that the command establishes a sense of importance: what one does first thing in the morning can be what is most important, above other commitments and responsibilities. Thus, e.g., the Jewish Sanhedrin met first thing in the morning in NT times, its business being given at least symbolic priority by reason of the meeting time.

[154] See 19:10–13,21–24, describing the first encounter on Mount Sinai, in which even after having gone through three days of ritual purification the people could go only as far as the base of the mountain; cf. 24:2.

and herds" is necessary because Sinai contained grassy grazing areas the people might find irresistible without specific warning.[155] The prohibition of access to the mountain is part of the anticipatory preparation appropriate to the eventual arrival (34:5) of Yahweh.[156] What the NIV renders as "in front of the mountain" would better be translated "toward/in the vicinity of the mountain."[157] In other words, the flocks and herds could not graze around the back, as opposed to the *front* of the mountain, nor in fact anywhere at the base.

34:4 This verse records the fulfillment of what was commanded in the prior three verses. (The command-fulfillment pattern will become very important and prominent in the following chapters.) There is nothing unusual in any of the language of this verse. The statement that Moses carried the two stone tablets in his hands is merely a way of pointing out that he was prepared with them as he was supposed to be and obediently brought them personally with him as he had been commanded to do. Moses may certainly have sought the help of a skilled stonemason[158] in preparing the tablets; if so, it is the sort of obvious detail he chose not to include in the narrative.

GOD SHOWS MOSES HIS GLORY (34:5–7). Here God graciously responded favorably to both of Moses' earlier appeals: the desire that he could see God's glory (33:18), to which God responded as promised in 33:19 by "passing in front of Moses" (v. 6), and the desire that he would teach Moses his ways (33:13), to which God responded with the proclamation of his name and what it stands for (vv. 6–7), including both compassion and justice.

34:5 The language "came down . . . and stood" represents a standard way of describing what otherwise is not easily comprehended by humans, that is, that God manifested himself specially and personally in Moses' presence. Thereby Moses could perceive that a real personal being had come to him and not just a concept, or a feeling, or a numinous impression. As before, he employed a cloud (not just any but the cloud of his glory[159]) as the visible part of the manifestation.

He then "proclaimed[160] his name, the LORD [Yahweh]." Although the basic meaning of the verbal form *yahweh* is well enough understood,[161] that

---

[155] It was, after all, at Mount Sinai that Moses, while grazing flocks and herds there, first encountered Yahweh in the burning bush (Exod 3:1–2).

[156] Being ready for and properly preparing the way for the divine sovereign's arrival is a repeated biblical theme. Cf. Isa 40:3; Amos 4:12; Mal 3:1; Luke 1:76; Rev 16:12.

[157] The Hb. here is אֶל־מוּל, not the more common term לִפְנֵי for "in front of." Although אֶל־מוּל can sometimes mean "in front of," it clearly means "toward/in the vicinity of" in many contexts (cf. 1 Sam 17:30; 1 Kgs 7:39) and should so be translated here.

[158] Cf. 1 Kgs 5:18, suggesting that even much later the Israelites were not renowned as stone cutters.

[159] Cf. 13:21–22; 14:19–20,24;16:10; 19:9,16; 24:15–18; 33:9–10; 40:34–38.

[160] See comments on 33:19.

[161] See comments on 3:15–16.

is not what Yahweh was concerned with here, any more than one who invokes the name of Jesus would do so only to think about the fact that it comes from a Hebrew word meaning "salvation." It is the (divine) person behind the name that one seeks when invoking a divine name. Moses had sought to know that Yahweh would be with him and Israel as they left Sinai to head toward the promised land, and knowing Yahweh—knowing who he really was and what he would be like in reference to his people—was what Moses craved. Yahweh's self-proclamation would provide that.

34:6 As promised in 33:21–23, which contains the prediction of how Yahweh would "pass in front of" Moses, Yahweh fulfilled his promise and in so doing began revealing himself by stating his name twice.[162] The repeating of the name was certainly for the purpose of emphasis but also could have had some of the overtones associated with the pattern called repetition of such that Yahweh was in effect saying to Moses, "I am your dear Yahweh" or "to you I am your dearest friend, Yahweh" or something of the sort. But this cannot be proved since here Yahweh was stating his own name. In all other possible contexts of the repetition of endearment phenomenon, the repetition occurs with direct address, so someone is calling the name of another twice—and not his own name.

In this verse God cited five attributes that characterize him—all of which would be welcome to Moses and the Israelites, who needed very much to count on his compassion toward them in light of their having previously angered him by their behavior. The first attribute of Yahweh listed is that he is a "compassionate" God,[163] meaning that he genuinely cares about humans and holds toward them a tender attitude of concern and mercy.[164] Second, he called himself "gracious,"[165] meaning that he does things for people they do not deserve and goes beyond what might be expected to grant truly kind favor toward people, favor of which they are not necessarily worthy.[166] Third, he described himself as "slow to anger,"[167] meaning that his patience with people's less-than-satisfactory behavior and/or failures in any

[162] This delayed response (the fulfillment of the promise made by God in 33:19 has been delayed until now) is one of the techniques of Moses' narrative style. Cf. W. Irwin, "The Course of the Dialog between Moses and Yahweh," *CBQ* 59 (1997): 629–36.

[163] אֵל רַחוּם.

[164] On all of these terms used to connote attributes of Yahweh, see *TWOT, TDOT, NIDOTTE, ad loc.*

[165] חַנּוּן.

[166] Grace is always beyond what can be expected; cf. the repeated use of *ḥēn* to connote the idea of "better than we could have expected" in the shout of the people at the completion of the temple in Zech 4:7.

[167] אֶרֶךְ אַפַּיִם, meaning, lit., "long-nosed," with its probable origin as an idiomatic expression in the idea of anger being seen in some larger animals by the way that they snort.

realm, including the moral, is very great. Fourth, he declared himself to be "abounding" (lit,. great) in covenant "love [loyalty]."[168] Careful studies of the Hebrew word, *ḥesed,* translated as "love" by the NIV here demonstrate that it connotes long-term, reliable loyalty of one member of a covenant relationship to another.[169] However fickle and unreliable humans may be in their relationship to God, he is nothing of the sort but can be counted on in every situation and at all times to be completely faithful to his promises for his people.

Next he described himself as "[abounding in] truth," meaning that whatever he says is correct and reliable and may be trusted even to the extent of life and death issues, or indeed *eternal* life and death issues.

34:7 The list of divine attributes continues. First comes "maintaining covenant loyalty[170] to thousands" (NIV "maintaining love to thousands") which, in light of the fuller wording of this attribute in 20:5–6, must be understood to be a slightly elliptical wording of the great promise that God will continue his covenant blessings to his people indefinitely—to thousands of generations, not merely thousands of people—as long as they do not break his covenant and thereby force him to unleash its sanctions. "Forgiving wickedness, rebellion and sin" refers to the forgiveness of evils and sins of all sorts, something God alone can accomplish and indicates that it is a characteristic of his nature to do so.

Thus the New Testament doctrine of the forgiveness of sins, on which the promise of eternal life so decidedly depends, flows from the very nature of God. He does not reluctantly forgive sins against himself and others; he does so eagerly, as a manifestation of his character, by which he delights in doing so. In the list "wickedness, rebellion and sin," the final term, "sin," is the most inclusive. These are not three distinct kinds of behaviors but three vocabulary words used together to indicate what any of them might convey; and since they are used together, they combine to indicate what Jesus meant when he said, "Every sin and blasphemy will be forgiven" (Matt 12:31).[171]

---

[168] חֶסֶד.

[169] K. D. Sakenfeld, *The Meaning of Hesed in the Hebrew Bible: A New Inquiry,* HSM 17 (Missoula: Scholars Press, 1978); id., "Love (OT)," *ABD* 4.378–80; J. S. Kselman, "Grace (OT)," *ABD* 2.1085–86; G. R. Clark, *The Word Hesed in the Hebrew Bible,* JSOTSup 157 (Sheffield: Sheffield Academic Press, 1993).

[170] Again the Hb. word here is חֶסֶד, which refers more to loyalty than love, although it can sometimes be translated "love" as long as it is understood that "love" in such a sense would be that sort of love that causes one to remain loyal and faithful, keeping up one's obligations and consistent, steady favorable relations with another.

[171] Jesus went on, of course, to explain that such forgiveness requires faith and that lack thereof—which he labels "blasphemy against the Spirit [the convicter of sin]"—necessarily interferes with forgiveness taking place. He does not otherwise limit God's readiness to forgive sin upon the request of the penitent sinner.

God then issued a corrective against the natural human tendency to accept grace on the assumption that because an infinite God can produce an infinite amount of grace, sin has no significant consequence.[172] This corrective is introduced simply by the normal Hebrew word for "and," which the NIV justifiably translates "yet" but which is not a strong adversative word. Perhaps an even more revealing, even if tendentious, translation would be something like: "[Forgiving wickedness, rebellion and sin] and at the same time not letting anybody off [i.e., making sure that the guilty get what they deserve]."[173]

In connection with the wording "he punishes the children and their children for the sin of the fathers to the third and fourth generation," see comments on 20:5–6. As already suggested there, this wording means something quite different from what it might seem to mean to the casual reader. It does not mean that God would punish children and grandchildren for something their ancestors did but that they themselves did not do. Rather, it describes God's just punishment of a given type of sin in each new generation as that sin *continues* to be repeated down through the generations. In other words, God here reminded his people that they could not rightly think something like "we can probably get away with doing this in our generation because God punished an earlier generation for doing it, so the punishment for it has already been given, and *we* don't have to worry about it."

MOSES AGAIN RAISES HIS GREAT CONCERN: WILL GOD GO WITH ISRAEL? (34:8–9). **34:8** Three instructive points may be taken from this brief verse. First, note that Moses' natural and immediate ("at once") response to being in the presence of God was to worship ("bowed to the ground . . . and worshiped").[174] When human beings are where God is, they ought to honor him by their thoughts and actions. In the Old Covenant his special presence was localized from the point of view of human perception, so people worshiped him where they understood him to have shown himself approachable: either at his visible sanctuary (Sinai, tabernacle, tent of meeting, temple) or where he manifested his glory through a cloud (as here).[175] In the New Covenant he promises to be present wherever people gather for worship,[176] something akin to the Old Covenant promise to inhabit the tabernacle when it was

---

[172] Paul, of course, addressed the problem of sinning so that grace may abound as well (e.g., Rom 6:12ff.).

[173] The *piel* of נקה, "to declare innocent/let off from any penalty," is also used in the decalogue (20:7) in connection with the commandment against using the divine name in vain, another instance of the way vocabulary and themes repeat from Exod 20 to the present context, just as might be expected since we are dealing in the present context with a renewal of the covenant first instated in Exod 20.

[174] Cf. also 4:31.

[175] Cf. esp. 24:9–11.

[176] Matt 18:20.

properly erected and furnished but much democratized because gathering for worship can take place at millions of locations at once, whereas in the Old Covenant it took place legally only at one. Moreover, in the New Covenant God actually indwells believers through his Spirit, thus making a worshipful approach to all of life appropriate.[177] This worshipful approach is not the same as full-blown corporate worship but an elevation of the significance of daily life for the obedient believer as opposed to the nonbeliever.

Second, note that for Moses worship preceded appeal. He would certainly again press his deep desire for God's presence on the journey to Canaan, but first he showed God his priorities: adoration ahead of supplication.

Third, worship is an act that exalts the one being worshiped but seeks to draw no favorable attention to the worshiper. Moses "bowed to the ground" following the standard way of his culture: reducing his profile and placing himself at the mercy of the one above him, that is, indicating his unworthiness and submission. Worship that draws attention to self, in either the Old or the New Covenant, is flawed.

34:9 Counting on the merciful characteristics that God described of himself in vv. 6–7, especially the willingness of forgive, and also counting on those qualities to absolve the Israelites of the danger of the (just) punishments God might well have imposed upon them as described in v. 7, Moses continued the appeal for the presence of God that he began in earnest already in 32:11–13 (with the prayer to spare Israel from death) and had reiterated several times already (e.g., 32:31–32; 33:12–16,18). In his favor in this appeal was God's record of reassurance already well established (32:33–34; 33:2,14,17,19–23). In other words, each time so far since the incident of the golden bull, God had responded favorably to Moses' intercession on behalf of Israel. As Moses had asked for a little more certainty of God's full presence each time, God had responded favorably—much in the nature of ancient Near Eastern bargaining style, where the final goal in mind is reached by small steps rather than by an outright request from the start for what is sought.[178] He now pressed the case to its final full level: he asked God for two guarantees of grace: (1) that he would go in Israel's very midst without restriction on the degree of his presence ("let the LORD go with us") and (2) that he would forgive the people's sin so that they would no longer be under danger of judgment and covenant rejection ("forgive our wickedness and our sin").[179]

---

[177] So Rom 12:1.

[178] Of course we have already seen this sort of "bargaining" style in the negotiations between Moses and Pharaoh for the right to leave Egypt (5:1ff.).

[179] Note the repeat of the sort of vocabulary already used in v. 7, i.e., עָוֹן, "wickedness," and חַטָּאת, "sin." The use of two of the three terms for sin that God himself promised to forgive in 34:7 is more than adequate to show that Moses was taking God up on his offer to forgive Israel all their transgressions.

Moses thus asked for nothing less than complete acceptance of the nation ("take us as your inheritance"). The verb used here for "take as inheritance" is *nāḥal,* which has already appeared in 23:30 and 32:13 in reference to Israel's possession/inheritance of the land of Canaan as a fulfillment of the promises to the Patriarchs and in its noun form *naḥălāh* as the promised land of inheritance in the song of Moses (15:17). But here the emphasis is not on the land Israel would inherit but on Israel as the inheritor of Yahweh's favor and protection—Israel as the firstborn son, the prime heir of the blessings of the father.[180]

This is an example of the way covenant relationships have as their backdrop kinship relationships so that covenant loyalty *(ḥesed)* is equivalent to family membership.[181] Moses could make this request in spite of the fact that he acknowledged Israel as a "stiff-necked" (stubborn and inclined to rebellion[182]) people. How? Because of God's forgiving nature, which can dismiss the guilt of even the most rebellious sinners.

GOD'S ANSWER: KEEP MY COVENANT AND I WILL GO WITH YOU (34:10–11). **34:10** The assertions of this verse are generally parallel to those of 19:4–6. Mercifully, God agreed to full covenant restoration by means of a remaking of the Sinai covenant—a reinstitution, not a revision. This was decidedly not a new covenant, as God had already made clear in v. 1 by referring to "the words that were on the first tablets," This is also clear in v. 28 by his reference to "the words [commandments]" and in the ten sample commandments that are quoted in vv. 14–26, as sample repetitions of commandments already given in the original covenant statement of chaps. 20–23.[183]

But this was not merely the sort of covenant *renewal* that would take place at various future times in Israel's history either. This was, rather, a divine *restoration* of a broken covenant, one that had been made temporarily null and void by Israel's corporate return to idolatry (and therefore automatically polytheism, since there was no monotheistic idolatry in the ancient world) as described in chap. 32. The covenant needed to be reinstated if it was to be of help to Israel, and Yahweh showed his merciful and patient nature as described by himself so magisterially in vv. 6–7 by taking the responsibility upon himself to reinstitute it for the benefit of his once and

---

[180] Cf. Gen 21:10; 24:7; Hos 11:1; but esp. Exod 4:23, where Israel is called "my firstborn son" by Yahweh.

[181] F. M. Cross Jr., "Kinship and Covenant in Ancient Israel," in *From Epic to Canon: History and Literature in Ancient Israel* (Baltimore: Johns Hopkins University Press, 1998), 3–22.

[182] Note that the third member, rebellion, of the "sin" trilogy from v. 7 (wickedness, rebellion, sin) is here picked up implicitly; whereas the other two, wickedness and sin, are mentioned explicitly by Moses.

[183] In particular, 34:14–26 restates much of what was contained in 23:12–33. See below.

now again covenant people. Therefore God used the present tense statement, "I am making a covenant with you."[184] He was making the same Sinai covenant once again, but he was indeed *making* it anew, remaking it, not just reminding the people of the content of it.

As might be expected in the case of a covenant reinstitution, all of the expected features of the covenant structure[185] are represented in some fashion in this chapter.

In keeping with the sort of identification of parties to the covenant normally found in a covenant preamble, God identified himself in v. 6 ("the LORD, the LORD" ["Yahweh, Yahweh"]) and also identified Israel explicitly as the other party ("your people . . . the people you live among," v. 10; also "God of Israel," v. 23; "covenant with Israel," v. 27).

As regards the prologue (a brief accounting of the relationship of the parties to each other), God's description of himself in vv. 6–7 constitutes the sort of thing found in a covenant prologue, as does Moses' description of Israel in vv. 8–9. The stipulations are represented by the ten key sample laws in vv. 14–26, and these are introduced as well by summary commands to obey the covenant in vv. 11–12.

The sanctions are indicated by such promises of blessing as that of v. 10 ("I will do wonders . . . awesome is the work that I . . . will do for you"),[186] the driving out of the Canaanites (vv. 11,24), and the enlargement of territory and protection from enemies (v. 24). Implied curses appear within v. 12 ("they will be a snare among you"), v. 14 ("a jealous God" [meaning one who will punish if disobeyed]), and v. 15 ("they will invite you and you will eat . . .").

There is no specific list of witnesses here to the covenant, but the promise of blessing offers witnesses to the blessings that the Israelites would enjoy (v. 10). The reason for this arrangement as regards the usual inclusion of formal witnesses in a covenant description is presumably that in this as in most biblical covenant contexts, God himself is the ultimate witness to his own

[184] The Hb., הִנֵּה אָנֹכִי כֹּרֵת בְּרִית, lit. says, simply, "I am hereby cutting a covenant" [the words "with you" being an addition by the NIV translators]. Thus the original uses the language for establishing a covenant by the ceremony of cutting an animal as a symbol both of a shared meal uniting the parties as if in a family (since meat is normally cut up to be served to more than one person), as well as of the dismembering/death that would be deserved by the party that breaks the covenant.

[185] See "Excursus: The Exodus-Leviticus Covenant" prior to the commentary on 20:1ff.

[186] The language of 34:10 reflects to a considerable degree the prologue emphases of 19:4–6: "You yourselves have seen what I did to Egypt, and how I carried you on eagles' wings and brought you to myself. Now if you obey me fully and keep my covenant, then out of all nations you will be my treasured possession. Although the whole earth is mine, you will be for me a kingdom of priests and a holy nation." The wording is not the same, but the concept of Israel as a display of God's greatness to the nations shines brightly in both passages.

covenant; he needs no other witness, whether divine or human or material.[187]

The last of the six covenant structural elements, that of the document clause, is indeed well represented in this passage, in vv. 1,4 by way of description of the preparation of the tablets for the writing of the covenant so that the parties might each have copies, and also in v. 27 ("Write down these words, for in accordance with these words I have made a covenant with you and with Israel").

This verse describes as well God's special concern for the witness of his people to his sovereign nature as they live for him by keeping his covenant in the midst of nonbelievers. This concern takes the form of a willingness to do great things for his people as an evidence of his greatness ("Before all your people I will do wonders never before done in any nation in all the world. The people you live among will see how awesome is the work that I, the LORD, will do for you"). The people could not, however, find a ground for *self*-confidence in this promise; what God would do was honor himself through the great things he did for Israel rather than through the great things Israel did by which other people were impressed.

34:11 A requirement precedes a promise in this verse. The requirement is that of covenant obedience—the *sine qua non* of any expectation for divine blessing in the long term. "Obey what I command you today" is nothing less than a demand for complete adherence to the complete Sinai covenant as it is reinstated by a merciful God on this occasion. What Moses and the Israelites would especially desire as a first sort of blessing once they reached the promised land was then added as a promise: the expulsion of the groups currently occupying the promised land, in accordance with the original covenant guarantees to Abraham.[188]

This verse picks up much of the language of 23:23 ("My angel will go ahead of you and bring you into the land of the Amorites, Hittites,

---

[187] The covenant itself can be seen as the witness between the two parties as well, as in Gen 31:44 ("Come now, let's make a covenant, you and I, and let it serve as a witness between us") or Deut 31:26 ("Take this Book of the Law and place it beside the ark of the covenant of the LORD your God. There it will remain as a witness against you"). Likewise, memorial objects, usually stones or stone structures, can serve as witnesses (e.g., Gen 31:46–48,52; Josh 22:34; 24:27; 1 Sam 6:8). On God as the explicitly named witness to a covenant, see Gen 31:50; Judg 11:10; 1 Sam 12:5; 20:42; Jer 42:5; Mic 1:2; Mal 2:14.

[188] Gen 15:16–21. On the people groups mentioned here as representative of the local population of Canaan, see comments on 3:8,17; 13:5; 23:23; 33:2. Once again the listing of the people groups is not a rigid one but varies both as to which exact groups are named and in the order of their being named. As might be expected in light of the fact that the present passage repeats many of the themes near the end of the Covenant Code (chaps. 21–23), the present listing is quite close to that of 23:23, containing the same six local groups in Canaan, although in a slightly different order.

Perizzites, Canaanites, Hivites and Jebusites, and I will wipe them out") and 23:28 ("I will send the hornet ahead of you to drive the Hivites, Canaanites and Hittites out of your way"), since it is part of the introduction to the restatement of the covenant through various samplings from or restatements of selected verses in 20:2–23:33.

WARNINGS AGAINST COVENANTS/TREATIES WITH THE INHABITANTS OF THE PROMISED LAND (34:12–16). This section (34:12–16) and the one that follows (34:17–26) represent the stipulations, blessings, and warnings in the reinstituted covenant. Since the original covenant text was stated in chaps. 20–23 (followed by the ratification ceremony in chap. 24 and thereafter tabernacle/worship plans), it is natural to regard the Ten Words (20:2–17) as the opening of the text of the covenant proper and the ending of the Covenant Code (23:12–33) as its closing. The Ten Words/Commandments will be repeated on the new tablets (34:1,4), and the ending of the Covenant Code is repeated here, though not with exactly the same wording. Thus through an inclusio[189] the entire original covenant formulation of chaps. 20–24 is renewed—leaving aside, of course, the instructions for formulating the tabernacle/worship implements (chaps. 25–31) since these refer to things not yet constructed or put into practice and therefore not breakable as part of the covenant breaking that took place with the golden bull/calf incident of chap. 32.[190]

34:12 The warning here follows closely the theme of 23:32–33, which reads, "Do not make a covenant with them or with their gods. Do not let them live in your land, or they will cause you to sin against me, because the worship of their gods will certainly be a snare to you." The present verse likewise warns against making a covenant ("treaty"; see below) with those "who live in the land" and the danger that doing so would end up being a "snare"—a means of entrapment into sinful covenant breaking—that would

[189] There are various types of inclusios with various functions, but all of them share generally the same format, in which a block of material is both set off from its surrounding context and united by being placed (or "sandwiched') between two prominent and related literary elements of some sort. In this case the inclusio pattern serves to sample from the beginning and end of chaps. 20–24 and thereby to suggest the renewal of the entire five chapters of covenant without having to repeat the whole tediously. In the case of the reuse here in chap. 34 of covenant elements found originally in chaps. 20–23, the inclusio represents a general pattern, but not a rigidly applied one. There are also elements repeated from outside of chaps. 20–23—e.g., 34:19–20 picks up on Exod 13:13—and some elements have no parallel from earlier covenant language (e.g., 34:16, "When you choose some of their daughters as wives for your sons and those daughters prostitute themselves to their gods, they will lead your sons to do the same" has no specific parallel in chaps. 20–23 or anywhere earlier in Exodus.

[190] The sampling of chaps. 20–23 by means of this inclusio is the real reason for the inclusion of a "decalogue" of commandments here in chap. 34; the theory that the "ritual decalogue" of 34:17–26 predates the Ten Words/Commandments of 20:2–17 or rivals them for significance fails to take account of this simple organizational scheme in Exodus.

lead to disaster. In other words, 34:12 may be regarded as a somewhat abbreviated restatement of 23:32–33.

The word "treaty" is used here misleadingly by the NIV to translate the same Hebrew word[191] rendered as "covenant" in the NIV of 23:32. Both verses, in fact, are prohibiting the same thing: any sort of covenant with either the people of the land of Canaan or their false gods. No covenant other than the one Yahweh was giving his people could be entered into by them; their reliance upon him for blessing and benefit must be absolute and exclusive.[192]

34:13–14 These two commands, to destroy everything connected with idolatry and to worship no other gods but Yahweh, are chiastically rephrased restatements of 23:24, "Do not bow down before their gods or worship them or follow their practices. You must demolish them and break their sacred stones to pieces." Here occurs the first mention[193] in the Old Testament of "Asherah poles" or sacred poles/posts [NRSV and other versions]. In this context, as in Deut 7:5; 12:3; 16:21, the masculine plural of *ăšēr* probably refers to any sort of carved wooden structure that was used as a divine symbol of some sort in pagan religion in that day rather than being limited only to Asherah poles, that is, pole-based carved representations of the goddess Asherah, the consort of the Canaanite weather-god Baal and a fertility benefactress according to local Canaanite thinking.[194]

---

[191] בְּרִית. This inconsistency of translation on the part of the NIV is most unfortunate because it denies to the NIV reader the opportunity to see that God contrasted the great benefits of his own proper covenant (בְּרִית) with the absolutely inevitable dangers of any other covenant (בְּרִית) with anyone else. Yahweh's covenant with his people was exclusive; it always prohibited his people from making other covenants, including the sort that could be described (not entirely accurately) as "treaties." This was because in the ancient world that Israel inhabited, any binding arrangement with pagans involved either legitimizing pagan gods (in whose name the other nation would be acting in making a treaty with Israel) and in demoting Yahweh to the level of other gods (since most such covenant-treaties were parity covenants, in which the parties related to each other and implicitly to their gods on equal terms). In addition, such covenants with foreigners would inevitably allow the pagans involved to regard Yahweh as a weak god unable to protect his people by himself and needing to have his people protect themselves by making covenants with those who might otherwise (or should otherwise) be their enemies. Such an impression takes away the incentive for foreigners to join with Israel in its true, saving covenant with Yahweh.

[192] And so, in the New Covenant, any existential reliance on person or thing other than on the one true God is bound to bring harm and to distract from the desired relationship of God with his people (cf. Matt 6:24; Heb 13:5; 2 Pet 1:4; 1 John 2:15–17).

[193] Via the suffixed plural אֲשֵׁרָיו.

[194] On Asherah, which we suggest is not exclusively in view here, see M. Jastrow Jr. and G. Barton, "Asherah," in *JewishEncyclopedia.com*; R. Kletter, *The Judean Pillar-Figurines and the Archaeology of Asherah* (Oxford: Tempus Reparatum, 1996); S. A. Wiggins, *A Reassessment of 'Asherah': A Study according to the Textual Sources of the First Two Millennia B.C.E.* (Neukirchen-Vluyn: Neukirchener Verlag, 1993); J. Hadley, *The Cult of Asherah in Ancient Israel and Judah* (Cambridge: Cambridge University Press, 2000); P. Torge, *Aschera und Astarte* (Leipzig, 1902).

What Israel had to do if they were to keep the covenant was not again to have any of the accoutrements of idolatry—altars, sacred stones, sacred poles/posts[195]—or any other god than Yahweh. The NIV translation of v. 14 ("Do not worship any other god, for the LORD, whose name is Jealous, is a jealous God") may be correct and certainly reflects the way the language of the verse usually has been understood by translators. Nevertheless, we suggest that the grammar of the Hebrew would more likely yield the following translation for this verse: "You must worship no other god, because Yahweh is jealous for his name. He is a jealous God."[196] Regarding the concept of Yahweh's being a jealous God, see comments on 20:5, where the language first appears in the Old Testament.[197] This is the only verse in the Old Testament in which mention is made of his being jealous for his name, the meaning of which expression is simply that he guards his name's significance—it points to his nature, character, and uniqueness as the only true God—and will not allow it to be profaned by idolatry or any other misuse.

34:15 This command reflects 23:32 ("Do not make a covenant with them or with their gods") in a shortened and simplified form but with the same essential message: the Israelites had to regard Yahweh's covenant with them as absolutely exclusive if they were to benefit from his salvation. If they made any sort of covenant relationship with other gods or with the Canaanites, who worshiped other gods, they would violate the terms of his covenant and suffer the terrible consequences.

Some individuals choose to follow a given religious path by reason of careful, systematic investigation of the evidence and an evaluation of all other options. But most people do not do any such thing. Rather, they imitate what others do, responding to invitations, formal or informal, to join others around them in whatever religious practices seem dominant. If the Israelites made the mistake of binding themselves in any sort of covenant with any Canaanite group, or all the Canaanite groups, they could expect the natural consequence: a comfortable social and political interaction, followed by a comfortable will-

[195] These three main sorts of idol furnishings are almost surely not meant to be exhaustive but rather a sampling, representative of anything whatever that would be used or displayed in connection with idol worship.

[196] Since *qn'* can take an object, as in Prov 23:17 (אַל־יְקַנֵּא לִבְּךָ בַּחַטָּאִים "Do not be jealous of/about sinners"), there is no reason to suppose that the predicate adjectival usage here ("is jealous") could not function similarly so that שְׁמוֹ, "his name," would function syntactically as an adverbial accusative of specification ("jealous as regards his name" or simply "jealous for his name").

[197] We would especially remind the reader that God's jealousy, including the demand that he be exclusively worshiped, does not arise from petty motives but from beneficent ones. The problem with idols is not that they make God feel bad but that they cannot save, thus keeping from salvation those he wants to see gain eternal life. His hatred of idols reflects his love for us, not any insecurity with regard to himself.

ingness to consider the validity and efficacy of the Canaanite lifestyle, including its worship practices, followed by an embracing of Canaanite religion.

Such things happened again and again in ancient Israel, in fact. One needs only to look at the religious situation in the days of the Judges or in Josiah's time (2 Kgs 22–23) or in Ezekiel's (Ezek 8:9ff.) to see how frequently and thoroughly the Israelites turned away from orthodox faith and toward Canaanite idolatry.[198]

Worship of other gods is here called prostitution *(znh),* a metaphorical way of describing infidelity to God's covenant. Since prostitutes are by definition flagrantly unfaithful to any one person but sell themselves to various people for gain, a people that seeks blessing through various gods and is not religiously pure and devoted to one God can be likened to a prostitute. Thus the Scripture often employs this metaphor for covenant infidelity through idolatry and/or the various practices associated with idolatry.[199]

One of the strong attractions of idolatry for Israelites was the feasting and revelry associated with pagan idolatry.[200] They had already shown themselves enamored of such activities (32:5–6) and would surely find it hard to resist joining the Canaanites in what was otherwise forbidden. Indeed, the story of Israelite idolatry at Baal-Peor (Num 25) is further proof that even the generation born in the wilderness would fall easy prey to such temptations. Being invited to eat at a sacrifice was like being invited out in modern times to dine at a fine restaurant: the invitation would be hard to turn down, and refusing probably would even be thought somewhat impolite. So God warned the Israelites strictly against the whole orbit of idolatry, knowing how desirous his people would naturally be of accepting such invitations.

34:16 Intermarriage in the Bible is never discouraged on ethnic grounds, but religious intermarriage is consistently discouraged on religious grounds. In other words, there is nothing negative associated with the mixing of races,[201] but great danger attends the mixing of religions. What eventually became a severe problem blocking progress in the Judean restoration[202] was a risk already for the Israelites at this early stage in their history as a people

---

[198] See also Judg 2:10–19.

[199] E.g., Lev 17:7; 20:5–6; Num 25:1; Deut 31:16; Judg 2:17; 8:27 (in all of which contexts the key word is *znh,* whether or not typically translated in the modern Eng. versions as "engage in prostitution" or the like). English translations of this root as "adultery" or the like are incorrect. It always connotes prostitution. On all Israel as characterized by prostitution because the whole nation was failing to keep the Mosaic covenant, see Hos 1:2 (which should be translated, "Marry a woman of prostitution and have children of prostitution because the whole land has gone thoroughly into prostitution"—a way of indicting everyone, young and old, as covenant breakers and not referring at any point to anyone's sex life. Cf. Stuart, *Hosea-Jonah*, 22–23, 26–27.

[200] See "Excursus: The Attractions of Idolatry" after 20:4–6.

[201] See., e.g., Num 12:1; Jer 39:16–18.

[202] See Ezra 10; Neh 13.

because they had grown up among varied ethnic groups in Egypt, were camping at Mount Sinai with varies ethnic groups in their midst,[203] and could easily assume that there were few hazards attendant to mixing with other national groups. Over time young men and young women would meet each other and ask their parents to arrange their marriages (as in the prominent example of Sampson in Judg 14:1–10), so it would be almost inevitable that as international marriages then took place, those marriages would bring idolatry into Israel. It happened that way with Solomon (1 Kgs 11:3–4) because marriages in Bible times, as today, were rarely blocked and often not even much discouraged for reasons of religious incompatibility. But Yahweh insisted otherwise here, knowing the inclinations of his people and the power of romantic attraction to overcome inadequate religious conviction.

Of particular significance was that throughout the biblical world, marriage usually involved a woman's leaving her home and family and moving to her husband's ancestral home to become a member of his family.[204] If the religious convictions and habits of a non-Israelite woman were, as would be expected by the time she reached marriageable age, well established, she would import them into Israel upon getting married to an Israelite and going into Israel to live within his household.[205] This explains the wording of the warning in this verse, "When you choose . . . daughters as wives for your sons . . . they will lead your sons . . ." It was normally the women coming into Israel through marriage that brought idolatry with them. The women leaving Israel to marry into non-Israelite nations posed little threat to the purity of Israel's religion. Since Israelite men stayed put when they married, they were not normally the source of the threat either.[206] Again in this verse we find a second use of the metaphor of prostitution for covenant infidelity (cf. v. 15). These two verses begin the metaphor in the biblical corpus, where it appears repeatedly until Rev 19:2. This verse has no specific paral-

[203] Exod 12:38.

[204] The routine paying of the "bride price" in which a groom symbolically purchased his wife reflected this (cf. John 3:29, "The bride belongs to the bridegroom"), as he took her from her family (to which the "bride price" was paid) and bought/brought her into his. That bride prices were essentially symbolic rather than a real purchase of property is evidenced by such factors as the low amount Hosea paid for his second wife (Hos 3:2 compared with Deut 22:29), with whom he never consummated the marriage (see Stuart, *Hosea-Jonah*, 63–64, 66–67), and Saul's request for a bride price in Philistine foreskins rather than currency (1 Sam 18:25).

[205] Ruth's conversion to faith in Israel's true God upon moving from Moab to Judah (Ruth 1:16) represented an exception, not the rule. It is a testimony to Naomi's strong faith, which Ruth had amply witnessed, but also constitutes an example of marriage-based conversion, even if a rare positive one.

[206] Thus this warning was not aimed at women as if they were weaker religiously or more prone to idolatry than men; it was aimed at the fact that women were usually very strong in their faith and that given a chance would share it willingly within their families and neighborhoods.

lels earlier in Exodus, even in chap. 23 other than continuing the themes of 23:32. It may therefore be considered somewhat special to the present context, explaining how idolatry made inroads into Israel if intentional efforts to stop it were not diligently undertaken at all times.

RENEWAL OF THE COVENANT WITH A "DECALOGUE" OF SAMPLE LAWS (34:17–26). These commandments sample from the Covenant Code of Exod 20–23, particularly from chap. 23, as noted above. There are ten of them (in the manner they are most naturally and thus most usually counted, i.e., with two commandments in v. 25),[207] and they are all worded in apodictic[208] style, just as are the original Ten Words/Commandments of chap. 20.

34:17 "Do not make cast idols" is an abbreviated reiteration of the commandment in Exod 20:4, "You shall not make for yourself an idol in the form of anything in heaven above or on the earth beneath or in the waters below." The golden young bull Aaron made in chap. 32 was the first instance of a "cast idol," so the prohibition against idolatry in the present context logically emphasizes that sort of idol since it would be the kind to which the Israelites would be especially attracted from this point forward. Indeed, the precedent of the incident in chap. 32 surely influenced Jeroboam I's decision to copy what Aaron had first made in the wilderness at Sinai and make two such cast idols that caused northern Israel to sin institutionally ever after (1 Kgs 12:28).[209]

34:18 This verse repeats Exod 23:15 almost word-for-word. The differences are just enough to show that the commandment is being stated freshly rather than being merely a literary copying from 23:15.[210] Why include this

---

[207] A detail ignored by the NIV paragraphing.

[208] I.e., general, all-situation, second-person commands rather than *casuistic* style, which involves sample situations that may or may not apply to everyone in the same way.

[209] It is noteworthy that 1 Kgs 12:28 states that Jeroboam I made his two cast idols in the form of golden young bulls—one for Bethel and one for Dan—*after seeking advice,* which suggests that the linkage with the Exod 32 incident was entirely intentional according to that advice, with the words "here are your gods, O Israel, who brought you up out of Egypt" (which parrot Exod 32:4,8). The conclusion cannot be escaped that the prohibition against "cast idols" is worded here so as to prohibit not only what Aaron and the Israelites had done at Sinai but also to try to prohibit the sort of thing that the great and influential "sin of Jeroboam" (1 Kgs 13:34) would inevitably create and make permanent later. God knew well not just what his people *had* been capable of but what they *would* be capable of.

[210] Indeed the two differences (אֲשֶׁר here instead of כַּאֲשֶׁר in 23:15; בְּחֹדֶשׁ הָאָבִיב here instead of the reference to the month through a pronoun, בוֹ, in 23:15) have actually served to give some source critics pause in their inclination to see the present passage as merely a later, intentional, dittograph of the earlier commandment—those, that is, that do not actually take the present "decalogue" as in fact more original than that of chap. 20. Since Moses was writing these words at Yahweh's dictation, the differences can be attributed to divine intent and not merely a bad memory on Moses' part—and the parallel situation raised by comparing wordings of the same laws in Deuteronomy and Exodus confirms in many cases that a slight differentiation in wording probably indicated the sort of newness or freshness that was thought appropriate to a new promulgation of an existing or previous covenant.

particular emphasis again—restating yet one more time[211] the schedule for the exodus-commemorating Passover (and later in the present context for the other main festivals)? The answer is simply that what the Israelites had done in the case of the cast idol of the young bull would tend to constitute—for some at least—a precedent as a festival. In order to obviate any possibility that the people might end up thinking they had a right to hold a "golden bull festival" annually, any legitimate chance to do so is here denied. Again the need for such a specifically worded prohibition was shown eventually in the fact that, despite this kind of law, the golden bull incident of chap. 32 had indeed formed a precedent in the common consciousness for the "sin of Jeroboam." The covenant anticipated the sin and outlawed it; the later nation showed its outlaw sinfulness by doing just what the covenant had long banned.

34:19–20a The statements in these verses expand somewhat on the more succinct law in 13:13, "Redeem with a lamb every firstborn donkey, but if you do not redeem it, break its neck. Redeem every firstborn among your sons." Thus, just as the prior law (34:18) references commandments from chap. 12, this one references a command from chap. 13—showing that while the new "decalogue" derives mainly from material earlier in chaps. 20–23 and especially chap. 23, it is not limited to that corpus but seeks to reiterate, through sampling, any and all divine covenant requirements from earlier in the book.

Redemption laws represent God's kindness to his people. By rights he owned everything that was born first among any group, whether animal or human, just as the firstfruits of what was grown were also his. But although he did insist on receiving the first of all that was harvested from crops, he did not in fact want his people to give away to him every person or animal that was born first. Some of these were best kept by their families or their owners. So although they technically belonged to God and ought in theory simply to be given to him, he would allow them to be "repurchased" from him by a payment, and he would receive the payment in lieu of the animal or person. Such was the basic idea behind redemption laws, as indicated by the language of v. 19.

In the case of the present law, three instances of how to handle redemption situations are then indicated paradigmatically in v. 20, as sufficient to represent all similar cases. Since donkeys were not needed at the tabernacle/temple but were beasts of burden that would be much better put to use by individual families on their farms, God allowed them to be redeemed through a substituted lamb or goat kid.[212] Female donkeys would be kept for

---

[211] The timing of the Passover was not introduced de novo in 23:15 but reiterated there, following on the comprehensive instructions of Exod 12.

[212] Most Eng. versions translate שֶׂה here as elsewhere in the OT with "lamb" for convenience and brevity, but the term refers to either a lamb or a goat kid.

breeding, but since only one male stud would usually be needed for a herd of donkeys, an Israelite with a large number of newborn male donkeys might choose simply to euthanize some of them quickly, by breaking their necks, rather than go to the expense of substituting a lamb or goat kid for them. This God allowed since in either case he did not want or need donkeys at the tabernacle, either as sacrificial animals or as work animals, and the taking of animal life was simply not a sin as the taking of human life would be.

The final redemption command, "Redeem all your firstborn sons," leaves no option for euthanasia in the case of humans. God does not want child sacrifice, nor does he want the forcible taking of children from their families for tabernacle/temple service.[213] Therefore all firstborn humans must be redeemed so that they could remain alive and with their families, even though from a theoretical point of view they would be Yahweh's property from birth.[214]

34:20b The command "No one is to appear before me empty-handed" restates a principal of worship, verbatim from 23:15: believers show their loyalty to God by coming to worship him with a gift rather than with nothing to offer. In the New Covenant the gift is typically monetary, but in the Old it was something that could be eaten, according to the prescriptions of the covenant law, because all worship involved eating a covenant renewal meal, the ingredients of which were provided by the worshipers to be prepared and then shared with the priests and with God.[215] At the times of the three annual festivals (Passover, Pentecost, Tabernacles) as well as any other times, the worshiper was responsible not merely to "show up" for worship but to "put up" evidence of covenant loyalty to God. Leviticus 1–7 details the nature of the various types of sacrificial offerings that were to correspond to worship needs.

34:21 The beginning of this verse summarizes what is found in 20:9–11 and reiterates as well what was taught at length about the Sabbath in Exod 16. But the ending, "even during the plowing season and harvest you must rest," adds an explanation not found elsewhere, one appropriate for people looking forward to occupying the promised land and being able to farm that land for crops. As the prior command was about participation in worship by providing elements of the worship meal, the present is about participating in

---

[213] Note that Samuel was presented to the tabernacle voluntarily as a vowed gift and not in lieu of a redemption payment (1 Sam 1:11).

[214] In the case of humans, the redemption was accomplished with a monetary payment of five shekels, as indicated in Num 18:15–16. A sacrifice was also made on the occasion of the dedication circumcision on the eighth day, but that is not the same as the redemption price (Lev 12:3; cf. Luke 1:59; 2:21; Phil 3:5).

[215] See comments on 32:6.

worship by taking the time throughout the year to observe the Sabbath and its purposes.

Plowing/planting and harvesting/reaping are the two most intense times in a farmer's life.[216] The temptation to work seven-day weeks is very strong during these seasons since plowing and harvesting at the right time can be essential to crop productivity, and "beating the weather" can seem to necessitate taking no time off during these crucial periods, that is, working through Sabbath days. But the combination of worship and rest provided by the Sabbath was more important to God—and should have been more important to the worshiper—than farm productivity. In other words, the concept of responding to an emergency, such as is constituted by the need to rescue an animal from a pit on the Sabbath (e.g., Luke 14:5), cannot be extrapolated to suggest that maximizing one's potential for a good crop constitutes a similar emergency and therefore could justify working on the Sabbath day. In the life of the New Covenant believer, worship, prayer, Scripture study, and Christian service must likewise take precedence over making money, lest gaining the temporal world result in losing one's eternal soul (Mark 8:36; Luke 9:25).

34:22–23 The remaining two festival times are now addressed, albeit a few verses later than the law covering the Passover (v. 18). This divided presentation allows for the in-context treatment of the issues of offering in general, including the sacrifice of the firstborn (v. 19), redemption of things not intended for sacrifice (v. 20a), the requirement of participation in provision of the worship covenant meal (v. 20b), and the requirement of observance of the Sabbath (v. 21), all topics that quite naturally fit among and are therefore here fitted within—rather than listed before or after—the festival laws. The festival laws thus form an inclusio around the sacrifice/redemption requirements so that timing commands surround method commands in a way that suggests to the Israelites that they must pay attention to both equally: when to worship and how to worship.[217]

It has sometimes been opined that the Israelite festivals were borrowed from the Canaanites, as harvest celebrations that evolved into religious festivals. No evidence for such an approach is found in the Old Testament. What the Bible describes is a divinely revealed set of special pan-Israel worship times linked theologically to the exodus, the nation's defining moment, but generously scheduled by God to coincide with harvest times so that the Israelites would not be prohibited from successful farming and could offer to God in worship the firstfruits of their farming labors at the natural time to do

[216] Cf. the plowing/harvesting parallels in 1 Sam 8:12; Prov 20:4; 1 Cor 9:10.

[217] In the New Covenant these issues are also of parallel importance. A person who worshiped correctly but rarely would be disobedient, just as would a person who worshiped frequently but incorrectly.

so, after a harvest. Thus the major worship times followed the major harvest times. Passover followed the harvest of lambs and goat kids (born in the early spring), Pentecost followed the wheat harvest fifty days later; and Tabernacles followed the olive and grape harvest in the fall.

The wording "all your men are to appear" does not prohibit women and children from worship but assigns the representation of families to fathers/husbands in appearing before the tabernacle altar to present to God the sacrifice on behalf of their families.[218]

34:24 The first part of this verse reiterates the divine promise to drive out the inhabitants of Canaan, as had been stated in 23:27–30.[219] Moreover, the overt first-person promise "I will drive out" represents yet another reassurance that as a result of Moses' pleading on behalf of the people in chaps. 33–34, Yahweh himself would accompany the people to the promised land and settle them there—not merely sending an angel (33:2) to do the job and not merely accompanying them under some sort of hyper-limited divine presence devoid of its usual power or glory (33:12–19). "[I will] enlarge your territory" presumably predicts the creation of the promised land as an Israelite possession by the process of its conquest (described in Josh 1–11) rather than a promise that God would keep enlarging the borders of Israel thereafter.[220]

The second part of the verse continues the theme of the three annual festivals, with a reassurance that must surely have been important for Israelites potentially worried about what would happen to their farms and homes whenever they would have to leave them three times each year to go to the central sanctuary (see esp. Deut 12). Would enemies, such as seasonally raiding nomadic groups (cf., e.g., Judg 6:3) take advantage of this requirement that people leave home periodically? Would ill-intentioned neighbors or outright enemies move boundary stones (cf. Deut 19:14; 27:17; Prov 22:28; 23:10) and take land away from its former owners while they were

[218] Neh 8:1–12 makes obvious the involvement of both men and women rather equally in worship; 1 Sam 9 also provides an instance of how women participated in worship through the covenant meal. The father/husband in a family would be the one actually to take the sacrifice to the priest at the altar before the tabernacle/temple, but he did so on behalf of the rest of the family (much in the same way that a father/husband might today be the one who would place the family's tithe or offering in an offering plate in church on behalf of the rest of the family).

[219] Exod 23:27–30: "I will send my terror ahead of you and throw into confusion every nation you encounter. I will make all your enemies turn their backs and run. I will send the hornet ahead of you to drive the Hivites, Canaanites and Hittites out of your way. But I will not drive them out in a single year, because the land would become desolate and the wild animals too numerous for you. Little by little I will drive them out before you, until you have increased enough to take possession of the land.

[220] David's sin in seeking to establish an empire that exceeded the set boundaries (Num 34:2–12) of the promised land got him—and Israel—in great trouble (2 Sam 24).

busy worshiping at another location—one that for many of them was several days distant? Leaving home in Bible times could be a frightening matter, but here God reassured his people that if they were faithful in worshiping him, he would be faithful in protecting their homes and lands while they did so. Conversely, the covenant sanctions also warn elsewhere[221] that this sort of thing was exactly what could happen if the Israelites did *not* keep the covenant.

34:25 These two commands repeat those of 23:18, requiring two separate things: (1) no eating of blood (a Canaanite/pagan practice) and (2) no delay in consumption of the sacrificial meal. In addition, the Israelites are prohibited from the eating of bread made with yeast, which would undermine the symbolism of unleavened/unyeasted bread as a reminder of the Passover.[222] This verse offers only a slight change of wording from that of 23:18 (again giving by means of a wording adjustment the flavor of freshness to this new statement of the covenant but not materially altering the command). The concept of not trying to sacrifice or eat offering leftovers, which was stated in 23:18 with the words "the fat of my festival offerings must not be kept until morning" is her rendered with the words "do not let any of the sacrifice from the Passover Feast remain until morning." In fact, it was the fat portions that would have most likely been kept and not fully offered to Yahweh by someone trying to get a second meal out of a single offering;[223] but as "fat" serves as a synecdoche for any part of the offering in 23:18, the wording here simply makes more explicit that no part may be retained overnight for consumption when hungry the next day.

The wording here "from the Passover Feast" is likewise a synecdoche in which one feast offering stands for all three as opposed to 23:18, where "my festival offerings" automatically includes all three. Thus 34:25 contains one shortening of a concept spelled out in the corresponding verse (23:18) through synecdoche and one lengthening of a concept not spelled out in 23:18 with comprehensive language but suggested there through synecdo-

---

[221] E.g., Lev 26:16; Deut 28:30–31,33,38–40.

[222] Cf. 12:8,15,18,34,39; 13:3,6 and the reiterations in 23:15,18 as well as, by logical consequence, 29:2,23. In general the Israelite bread sacrifices were to be yeastless (Lev 2:4,11; 6:16–17; 7:12–13; 8:2,26). The NIV reads as if the prohibition against drinking blood might have applied only when yeasted bread was offered, but the point was in fact that neither blood nor anything with yeast in it could be offered as a sacrifice or consumed in connection therewith. A better translation might therefore be simply, "Do not offer the blood of a sacrifice to me, nor, likewise, anything containing yeast."

[223] Thus exposing the real motive of the insincere worshiper: to get more meat to eat rather than to honor and praise Yahweh. This is yet another way the Scripture reminds the reader that all sacrifices/offerings, including the Lord's Supper, are symbolic acts of worship and not occasions for satisfying one's appetite (cf. 1 Cor 11:22, where Paul condemned Christians for using the occasion of the Lord's Supper to slake their thirst and/or satiate their hunger).

che. The many parallels in Deuteronomy to this sort of practice (lengthening some statements from Exodus-Numbers and shortening others) as well as those already cited in the present context suggest that this pattern is actually a standard, if not virtually uniform, practice and not accidental in the citation of covenant laws in different contexts.

34:26a "Bring the best of the firstfruits . . ." repeats verbatim what 23:19a said, but 23:19a was preceded by a more lengthy set of instructions about the firstfruits of various crops constituting the offering.[224] The point here, once again, is that the crop farmer could not do less than the animal farmer: both must bring God the best and nothing less, and both must bring the best of the first—not the best of what may later be harvested after the worshiper has had first choice at the best. From the point of view of the new covenant in modern times, this requires a tithe from the moment the paycheck is received (and so regularly thereafter), presented to God gladly, yet as a prime obligation to be met *before* other bills are paid, and not an offering of spare change or a few dollars left over after all other financial obligations have been satisfied, as is more usually the practice. What one offers to God reveals tellingly where one places God in one's hierarchy of importance. "No other gods before me" (20:3) encompasses a great deal, including financial priorities.[225]

34:26b "Do not cook a young goat in its mother's milk" repeats 23:19 verbatim and is also found in Deut 14:21.[226] The repeated reminders suggested that such a practice was widespread in the world of the Israelites and represented what would be a strong temptation for them once they reached Canaan and saw the local inhabitants relying on this magical technique as a means of increasing the fertility of their flocks. It also probably served as a paradigmatic reminder against all fertility religion techniques in general, such as sowing a field or planting a vineyard with two kinds of seed as a means of getting them to "mate" and thus be fertile (Lev 19:19; Deut 22:9).[227]

DOCUMENT CLAUSE: PUTTING THE COVENANT IN WRITING (34:27–28). **34:27** By means of this divine proclamation of its document clause,[228] the renewed covenant is strongly endorsed. That the sovereign

---

[224] 23:16: Celebrate the Feast of Harvest with the firstfruits of the crops you sow in your field. Celebrate the Feast of Ingathering at the end of the year, when you gather in your crops from the field.

[225] In other words, the command to tithe the firstfruits can be understood as a logical inference from the command to have no other gods before Yahweh (20:3), which can itself be regarded as a logical inference from the command to love God with one's whole heart (Deut 6:5).

[226] See E. H. Merrill, *Deuteronomy,* NAC (Nashville: Broadman & Holman, 1994), 238.

[227] One is almost tempted to translate it, "Do not cook a goat kid in its mother's milk, and the like" with the sense, "Do not cook a goat kid in its mother's milk or attempt any other magical fertility rite."

[228] See "Excursus: The Exodus-Leviticus Covenant" prior to 20:1.

and vassal should each receive their copy indicates the arrival at the conclusion of the covenant and its formal approval. Making permanent the covenant by reducing it to writing constituted a sign of its reinstitution, the very thing Moses had been appealing to God for throughout the last two chapters, ever since he had to acknowledge the abrogation of the first covenant by his destruction of its symbolic tablets[229] (32:19).

So Moses had to write down all the words[230] of the covenant, not just the Ten Words/Commandments, which would be recorded separately and personally on the two tablets by God himself (34:1). What did Moses write? Everything from 20:18 to the present point in the narrative that constitutes covenant commands that he had not written down already, specifically the content of chaps. 25–31 minus strictly narrative portions thereof and at least 34:10– 26.[231]

34:28 Three points are made here: that Moses was in God's presence for forty[232] days and nights, that he fasted completely during that time, and that God personally (not Moses) wrote the Ten Words/Commandments on the tablets once again.

This was Moses' second occasion of being atop Mount Sinai in the special presence of God for such a period of time, the first having been described in chaps. 24–32 and summarized in 24:18.[233] Deuteronomy 9:9–25 and 10:10 reinforce this scenario, both indicating that Moses spent two forty-day periods in God's presence receiving the law. Was this length of time necessary because of all that he had to write down? Hardly. That could have been done in a few hours. Rather, he undertook his long fasting out of his deep identification with the people of Israel and his desire for God's blessing on them. Deuteronomy 9:9 reminds the Israelites of Moses' forty-day fast in the context of their rebelliousness (9:4–8), and Deut 9:18 states explicitly that the second occasion of fasting was for Israel's sin, especially the idolatry described in chap. 32 ("I ate no bread and drank no water,

---

[229] Symbolic in that they contained only the Ten Words/Commandments but represented the whole.

[230] Note the repeated use of the phrase "these words" corresponding to the earlier terminology "all the LORD's words and laws" (24:3) and "all these words" (24:8) in an overtly covenant context, in which what was written down was not a sample but clearly the full text of all that was dictated to Moses by God.

[231] Our question concerns what Moses wrote at the point in time that 34:27 describes, i.e., written material that was covenant content per se. Since he wrote all of Exodus eventually, the issue of what he wrote becomes less significant once the whole book has been produced, except as the content of the covenant might otherwise be misunderstood.

[232] We have already argued that "forty" was an idiomatic term connoting generally "a great many" or "dozens of." Cf. 24:18.

[233] "Then Moses entered the cloud as he went on up the mountain. And he stayed on the mountain forty days and forty nights."

because of all the sin you had committed, doing what was evil in the LORD's sight and so provoking him to anger").[234] Since Deut 10:10 says, "Now I had stayed on the mountain forty days and nights, as I did the first time, and the LORD listened to me at this time also. It was not his will to destroy you," it would seem evident that Moses fasted both times out of concern for the possibility of God's judgment on the people and that each time his earnest appeal was honored by a gracious God ("listened to me at this time also").

The antecedent for "he wrote" is not Moses but Yahweh, the nearest grammatical antecedent in the verse. Moses had already made clear that it was God, not he, who wrote the Ten Words/Commandments on these tablets (34:1); so from the point of view of the narrative, there is no ambiguity about who "he" refers to in the statement. Note also that the term used for what God wrote is, once again, literally "the Ten Words,"[235] since these were of a different rank of significance from the other commandments/statutes/laws.

(9) Moses' Face Reflecting God's Glory (34:29–35)

29When Moses came down from Mount Sinai with the two tablets of the Testimony in his hands, he was not aware that his face was radiant because he had spoken with the LORD. 30When Aaron and all the Israelites saw Moses, his face was radiant, and they were afraid to come near him. 31But Moses called to them; so Aaron and all the leaders of the community came back to him, and he spoke to them. 32Afterward all the Israelites came near him, and he gave them all the commands the LORD had given him on Mount Sinai.

33When Moses finished speaking to them, he put a veil over his face. 34But whenever he entered the LORD's presence to speak with him, he removed the veil until he came out. And when he came out and told the Israelites what he had been commanded, 35they saw that his face was radiant. Then Moses would put the veil back over his face until he went in to speak with the LORD.

Any reader of Exodus at any time in history might justifiably ask, "What's the point of all this attention to how much Moses' face shone? Why does it conclude such an important narrative as that of chaps. 32–34?" In fact, Moses reviewed the story of his radiant face here in considerable detail because it had important implications.

First, it confirmed—even reestablished—his leadership and role as intermediary with God on behalf of the people: Moses really did meet with God,

---

[234] This is confirmed by Deut 9:25, where Moses said, "I lay prostrate before the LORD those forty days and forty nights because the LORD had said he would destroy you," the threat of destruction being what followed the idolatry incident of chap. 32 (cf. 33:1–5).

[235] עֲשֶׂרֶת הַדְּבָרִים; cf. Exod 20:1, where they had been called "words," but note that the full phrase "the Ten Words" occurs for the first time in the present context. They are never called "commandments" in the OT but always "words."

whose glory was so awesome (even when restricted by the cloud in which the meeting took place and even though Moses could only see God's "back") that it left an effect upon Moses that everyone else could not fail to attribute to his having been in God's (limited) presence and therefore to have been confirmed by God as Israel's human leader.

Second, it confirmed Yahweh's presence, the very thing sought so assiduously by Moses in his various appeals in chaps. 33–34 and so missed by the people when they thought they might have lost it (33:1–5). If people couldn't even bear to look at Moses because his face was powerfully affected, however residually and partially, by Yahweh's glory, then that glory, not at all residual in Yahweh himself, was back among Israel!

Third, it confirmed Yahweh's greatness. What pagan worshiper ever glowed with the reflection of an idol's glory? What other nation could claim that its god was so awesome that one who had spent time with him terrified all others in that nation by the mere retained reflection of the divinity's glory?

Fourth, it reminded all those who seek constantly for an ever-closer relationship with God that one can actually have so close a connection with the only true and living God that one may not even notice the extent of the effect ("he was not aware that his face was radiant," v. 29)—though, to be sure, the kind of reflected glory Moses experienced would be expected in heaven rather than on earth.

Fifth, as Paul explained in his discussion of this passage in 2 Cor 3:7–18, the "glory that lasts" from the New Covenant was in fact much greater than the Old Covenant glory on Moses' face that faded over time. Consistent with this emphasis, Jesus taught that any person who knows God through Christ in the New Covenant has gone far beyond even the remarkable glory of Moses after coming down from Sinai because of the significance of the indwelling of the Holy Spirit and what it means in terms of the presence of God in one's life in Christ (Matt 11:11). All who know Christ as Savior and live for him reflect his glory—even more powerfully than Moses did, though without the visible frightening effect—by reason of living the transforming life of the Spirit (2 Cor 3:18).

34:29 Descending from Mount Sinai, Moses had in his hands the two very special tablets, here called the two tablets of the Testimony[236]—each

---

[236] On the term "tablets of the Testimony" see comments on 31:18; 32:15; on the term "Testimony" as indicating by synecdoche the ark, see comments on 16:34; 27:21; 30:6; on "Testimony" as referring to the tablets themselves by ellipsis, see comments on 25:16,21. The fullest and most common related term is "ark of the Testimony" (when the ark itself is the focus) in 25:22; 26:33–34; 30:6,26; 31:7; 39:35; 40:3,5,21. Note, however, that some modern translations consider עֵדָה as nothing more than a synonym for בְּרִית, "covenant," and so translate "ark of the covenant" or tablets of the covenant" in all these contexts.

containing the Ten Words/Commandments representing the sovereign's and the vassals' copies of the covenant—that would eventually be placed, according to God's command, in the ark of the testimony/covenant[237] as symbolic documents confirming the covenant between Yahweh and his only special people on earth.

"He was not aware that his face was radiant because he had spoken with the LORD" [Yahweh] indicates that the glory of God is not a painful or harmful thing when borne by one upon whom God's favor rests. This was partly Paul's point in 2 Cor 3:17–18. It was a joyous and delightful experience to reflect God by living in his Spirit, something that one doesn't feel physically but something that nevertheless projects God's powerful presence in one's life and upon the lives of others.[238] That Moses should after the fact, when he was no longer in God's presence directly, still retain a very impressive effect of God's presence proves the presence of Yahweh among the people, just as they so desired (33:1–5 and thereafter). The presence was obviously there if Moses' face so obviously reflected it, and that means that God had not withdrawn from Israel as represented by his not having withdrawn from Israel's mediator with him, Moses.

To this point it could be said that the covenant had certainly been reaffirmed and God's presence among his people reestablished, but what about Moses' authority among the people? He had been rejected as their leader during his first long absence (32:1). Though they increasingly showed him respect (as in their posture of worship whenever he would go to the little tent of meeting, 33:7–11),[239] they had not yet otherwise formally acknowledged their mistake in rejecting him as leader and as Yahweh's representative among them. Yahweh took care of all that by giving Moses an unmistakable credential: radiant glory, residual to an obvious divine encounter, that no one could doubt established him as a favorite of God.[240]

There has been some debate about what Moses' face actually put forth. Whatever it was, it came from "the skin of his face"[241] (NIV, inexplicably,

---

[237] 25:15,21; cf. Deut 10:5; 1 Kgs 8:9; Heb 9:4.

[238] On the concept, see G. D. Fee, *God's Empowering Presence: The Holy Spirit in the Letters of Paul* (Peabody, Mass.: Hendrickson, 1994), passim.

[239] Of course, 33:7–11 describes a pattern that pertained mainly in the future compared to what is described in the present passage, which speaks of what was visible just as soon as Moses came down from the covenant reaffirmation meeting on Mount Sinai. Thus we do not know how many times the honoring of Moses as described in 33:7–11 had actually taken place by *this* point.

[240] As Durham (*Exodus,* 466) puts it, "If Moses should remain discredited, both the repetition of Yahweh's revelation and instruction given already, and also the continuing revelation and instruction to be given through him would be compromised. Moses' authority must therefore be reestablished in the eyes of the very people who have rejected him and by none other than Yahweh himself."

[241] עוֹר פָּנָיו.

just "his face"] rather than out of his mouth or from within his cupped hands or his famous staff or any other source. In Hebrew the usual way to indicate that something has "shined" is through the *hiphil* conjugation of the verb *'wr*. But the text here uses the simple *qal* of the verb *qrn*, a root normally associated with "horn." Many attempted explanations of the implication of this choice of verb have been forthcoming,[242] and most commentators have concluded that the force of the Hebrew is to indicate that the skin of his face "sent forth rays" or "radiated" rather than merely shining brightly or the like. The NIV translation "was radiant" is sound, although the adjective "radiant" has come to mean merely "cheerful in appearance" or "obviously happy" (as with "glowing"), so something like "sent forth rays" would seem a less ambiguous rendering of the Hebrew.

34:30 It is likely that something other than mere bright light radiated from Moses' skin because the text never says that anyone was blinded by looking at him or forced to look away or to shield their eyes. Rather, it indicates that people were frightened by what they saw when they looked at his face ("they were afraid to come near him").[243] Perhaps it pulsed with an odd light; perhaps it gave the impression of brilliance radiating out in various planes; perhaps it looked like it was on fire (see 24:17). Probably it appeared, on a smaller scale, as frightening as God's glory cloud on top of Mount Sinai was to the Israelites (19:16; 24:16–17) or the pillar of cloud had been to the Egyptians in the wilderness (14:24). Just as the people had been warned not to come near Mount Sinai when God's glory settled on it (19:12) and found themselves indeed horrified by that glory (20:18–19), now it continued to strike fear into them, even though reduced to a reflected state, when it was as near to them as Moses was upon his return among them after descending the mountain.

---

[242] See, e.g., M. Agmon, "The Radiance of the Skin of Moses' Face and the Veil (Exod 34:29–35)," *BMik* 31 (1985/86): 186–88 (Hb.); F. Dumermuth, "Moses strahlendes Gesicht," *TZ* 17 (1961): 241–48; Y. Gil, "*ki qaran 'or pene moseh*," *BMik* 30 (1984/85): 341–44 (Hb.); A. T. Hanson, "John i 14–18 and Exodus xxxiv," *NTS* 23 (1977): 90–101; C. Houtman, "Het verheerlijkte gezich van Moses [The Glorified Face of Moses]," *NTT* 43 (1989): 1–10; K. Jaros, "Der Mose 'strahlende Haut,'" *ZAW* 88 (1976): 275–80; A. Jirku, "Die Gesichtsmaske des Mose," *ZDPV* 67 (1944–45): 43–45; J. Morgenstern, "Moses with the Shining Face," *HUCA* 2 (1925): 1–27; M. Tsevat, "The Skin of His Face Was Radiant (Ex. 34:29)," *ErIs* 16 (1982): 163–67; W. H. Propp takes a rather different view of the effect of Yahweh's glory on the skin of Moses' face in his article "The Skin of Moses' Face—Transfigured or Disfigured?" *CBQ* 49 (1987): 375–86, arguing that what the Israelites found difficult to look at was the disfigurement of Moses' face as it bore the effects of close exposure to divine glory. (It didn't hurt Moses, but it was terrible to look at.) Propp has also reviewed the meaning of the literal connotation of *qrn* in the narrative ("Did Moses Have Horns?" *BibRev* 4 [1988]: 30–37). Sasson has taken a very different approach in his "Bovine Symbolism in the Exodus Narrative," 380–87, by suggesting a link between the terminology of "horns" (rather than merely "rays") and the golden young bull idolatry of chap. 32.

The wording of the verse specifically includes Aaron along with everyone else as unable to bear coming too close to Moses, thus pointing out that the leader of the people at the time of the idolatrous rebellion described in chap. 32 now can see for himself Moses' authenticating divine glory. The people who had once dismissed Moses' leadership by saying, "As for this fellow Moses who brought us up out of Egypt, we don't know what has happened to him" (32:1) now could see for themselves that what had happened to him was that he had been with and had been accepted by the very God they needed to fear. Moses here carried a small amount of what in larger measure would kill anyone who got too close (cf. 33:20).[244]

34:31 Aaron is again mentioned, since his willingness to accept Moses as leader was partly at stake, and the leaders of the people as a whole are mentioned, also suggesting their role in confirming Moses' leadership over them. Aaron and the elders were now no longer fleeing from Moses (implied in the wording "came back to him") but were approaching him again at his call to them, which must have included eventually some sort of reassurance that he was not coming to them in judgment and that his face would not kill them or harm them in any way. "He spoke to them" presumably indicates that he explained where he had been, what God had said about being willing to be close to them once again, and other reassurances of the good results of his encounter with Yahweh on the mountain.

34:32 Consequently, all the people eventually gathered around Moses (presumably rounded up and brought there by the leaders) to listen to him formally preach the instructions he had received for them in his most recent forty-day stay with God on the mountain. At this time they still were all

---

[243] So Propp's speculation ("The Skin of Moses' Face," 375–86) that the text could be read to suggest that he was actually disfigured by his encounter with Yahweh's glory. The Hb. is ambiguous as to whether his skin itself had "horns" (i.e., had become misshapen with pointy lumps of some sort) or whether it gave off "rays"(i.e., something visual appeared to protrude from his face). Our problem in resolving the challenge is simply that the actual meaning of the Hb. verb *qrn* is not well understood, being used here in what amounts to a hapax legomenon. In the three verses where *qrn* occurs as a *qal* verb (34:29,30,35), it is in the same basic syntactical pattern: either קָרַן עוֹר פָּנָיו "the skin of his face radiated," or קָרַן עוֹר פְּנֵי מֹשֶׁה, "the skin of Moses' face radiated"; so even though the expression is found three times in the passage, it is essentially the same expression all three times, without the sort of differentiation that might help us better understand its meaning. The meaning "ray" for the segholate noun form from the same root (as in Hab 3:4) is surely relevant in some way to the meaning of the verb but provides insufficient specificity to help define the verb's meaning decisively. Accordingly, nearly all translators render *qrn* as either "was radiant" or "shone" or a wording consistent with one of these two options.

[244] See S. L. Sanders, "Old Light on Moses' Shining Face," *VT* 52 (2002): 400–406. Sanders presents evidence that what made Moses' face difficult to tolerate was indeed light, but he goes on to suggest that by radiating the glory of God after being with God, Moses was no longer simply and only human but had become imbued with something of the divine—a conclusion not actually supported by the wording of the text.

looking at his radiating face, which must have continued to terrify and amaze them, even though it actually bore no danger for them. Here was God's prophet speaking the very words of God to them, with a face so terrifyingly glorious that few could manage to doubt that what he was relaying to them was absolutely true and that he had been personally sent by God to make sure they knew it. In light of what is stated in the verses immediately following, it might have been so hard for the people to look directly at him that they listened with their faces turned away or perhaps bowed to the ground.

34:33–35 Moses surely did not need a veil[245] for his own comfort (see comments on v. 29), and he certainly didn't need to protect God from God's own reflected glory, so he didn't wear the veil when he was in God's presence. Indeed, he had already sought the most direct possible exposure to God's glory (33:18) and would hardly wish to have a diminished experience thereof afterwards. Therefore the veil he donned when neither atop Sinai nor at the tent of meeting was undoubtedly for the people's sake—not because his unveiled face would physically harm them but because it apparently scared them so much psychologically that they found it hard to be near him.

The people presumably were distracted and unnerved by whatever came from Moses' face. It must have looked terrible in both senses of that word—causing terror and unpleasant to view. Of course he needed to be near them routinely as their leader and teacher, so use of the veil provided a way for him to deal with them, including in his ongoing role as supreme judge.[246] Verses 34–35 suggest that there were many times that Moses spoke with God directly and closely, a reprise of the implications of the tent of meeting narrative in 33:7–10, with its emphasis on their common face-to-face encounters (33:11). In other words, he was in the very presence of Yahweh when inside the tent of meeting, and later inside the tabernacle, just as much as he was in the very presence of Yahweh when he was in the glory could on top of Mount Sinai. That meant that whatever instructions he received from

---

[245] It should be noted that this veil (מַסְוֶה) had nothing to do with the "veil" of the tabernacle/temple, which was a thick woven curtain (פָּרֹכֶת), in spite of J. Janzen's attempt to link the two, on the basis of the fact that both in a sense shield or provide containment for God's glory (*Exodus* [Louisville: Westminster John Knox, 1997], 262). The (now archaic) use of the word "veil" for the tabernacle/temple curtain as well as Moses' face veil is mostly a phenomenon of King James era English. Moses was not making any connection between what he wore over his face and the tabernacle curtain. The tabernacle curtain blocked any view from any direction; Moses' veil allowed him to see out but kept his face from scaring those who looked directly at it. If it were a typical Near Eastern face veil, it would have revealed his eyes and forehead, much in contrast to the tabernacle curtain, that went from floor to ceiling and side to side so that nothing whatever could be seen through it or around or over it or under it.

[246] See comments on 18:13–26.

God from within the tent of meeting or tabernacle were just as authoritative for the people of Israel as instructions he received while on the mountain.[247]

Excursus: Command-Fulfillment Repetition in Exodus[248]

A large percentage of the material found in Exod 35–40 repeats—often either verbatim or virtually verbatim for many consecutive verses—what Exod 25–31 has already stated. In light of the usual terseness and economy of expression in the biblical text of Exodus, as well as generally in the Bible (do we not often wish the writer had provided *more* detail so we could understand something better?), this degree of repetition is extraordinary. What purpose does it serve?

We are not here concerned with any sort of repetition at all that may be found in the Bible. For example, the material extensively shared among the Gospels, or between Samuel-Kings and 1, 2 Chronicles, involves repetition but owes its existence to a necessity: if different books by different inspired authors take at least partially unique perspectives on how to tell an important story, it will be necessary for the common elements of that story to be told in each of those accounts. An author cannot leave out essential information simply because some other author has already included that information in his or her separate book. Likewise, the several psalms repeated in the Psalter with wording changes limited mainly to presentation of the divine name as "God" *(ʾĕlōhîm)* in most primary poetic positions in Pss 40–81 in contrast to "the LORD" *(yahweh)* in primary poetic positions[249] elsewhere simply reflect a wording targeted to a different audience. Some scholars assume the different preferences for the divine name result from geographical patterns (thus a preference for *ʾĕlōhîm* in the north of Israel and *yahweh* in the south at times), but virtually no evidence exists to prove or disprove this theory. Similarly, Israel's need for a new statement of the covenant for a new generation of Israelites resulted happily, due to God's

[247] This equality of authority for God's instructions, wherever issued, should not be overlooked, and becomes especially important for Leviticus-Deuteronomy. See Houtman, "Het verheerlijkte gezich van Moses [The Glorified Face of Moses]," 1–10.

[248] The approach taken here differs substantially from that in the following fine studies: A. Aejmelaeus, "Septuagintal Translation Techniques—A Solution to the Problem of the Tabernacle Account," in *Septuagint, Scrolls and Cognate Studies,* SBLSCS 33 (Atlanta: Scholars Press, 1992), 381–402; G. J. Brooke, "The Temple Scroll and LXX Exodus 35–40," in *Septuagint, Scrolls and Cognate Studies,* SBLSCS 33 (Atlanta: Scholars Press, 1992), 81–106; C. Houtman, "Wee fiktiv ist das Zeltheiligtum von Exodus 25–40?" *ZAW* 1106 (1994): 107–13. Each of these studies discusses the fact that the LXX translation of Exod 35–40 differs in various ways from the LXX translation of the same wording in chaps. 25–31 and regard that difference in the Greek as significant. We regard it as insignificant, however—simply an inner-Greek translation decision made by the original LXX translator of the Old Greek in order to modify the tedium posed by the extensive repetitions. In effect, the original LXX Old Greek translator chose style over consistency but did not provide any reason to doubt the originality of the material in either chaps. 35–40 or 25–31. He is visibly translating the MT *Urtext*, not fabricating anything or hinting about the origin or authenticity of any part of Exodus.

[249] This is often expressed with the language of "A and B words." In Hb. poetic parallelisms if the "A word" is *yahweh*, the "B word" used in parallel to it will be *ʾĕlōhîm*, and vice versa.

mercy through Moses, in what we now call the book of Deuteronomy, with its extensive repetitions from Exodus-Numbers, because an entirely new audience at a new time and place would benefit from a newly formulated restatement of covenant essentials.[250]

None of the above represents the sort of repetition we see in Exod 35–40. Here a single author, Moses, closely within his own book reported in considerable detail and involving extensive repetition the fact that what God told him and the Israelites to do (build and furnish the tabernacle), he and they definitely did. He was not repeating what some other inspired author said in another biblical book covering the same basic story and thus being required out of fairness to his reader to say many of the same things. Instead, Moses provided us not only with a lengthy account of what he and the Israelites were supposed to do (chaps. 25–31) but also *at length,* with remarkably little change in wording, descriptions of the fact that they did it.

This level of repetition has always made working through Exod 35–40 a challenge for modern readers unused to such large-scale repetitions. Would it not have been enough to say simply that "everything God commanded Moses and the Israelites to do to build and furnish the tabernacle they did"? After all, statements of that general nature are actually employed a number of times earlier in Exodus without difficulty or confusion as to what was commanded and what was done.[251]

Several reasons for the extensive reiteration of previously stated material at the conclusion of the book of Exodus are apparent. First, it follows the rules of an honored literary genre found elsewhere in the ancient Near East, most notably illustrated in the lengthy command-fulfillment repetition of the Keret epic. In

---

[250] This is especially significant in light of the way their parents had failed to keep key provisions of the original Sinai covenant (Exodus-Numbers). The reformulated covenant (Deuteronomy) gives a true immediacy and freshness to the relationship between God and Israel as the people entered the promised land—but it is not a new covenant; it is a restatement in overtly six-part covenant form of the same covenant God had revealed at Sinai.

[251] The following are examples of statements indicating that something that had been commanded or stated was carried out or heard, without including a repetition of either the statement/command or the fulfillment/hearing: 4:28: "Then Moses told Aaron everything the LORD had sent him to say"; 4:30: "Aaron told them everything the LORD had said to Moses. He also performed the signs before the people"; 6:29: "Tell Pharaoh king of Egypt everything I tell you"; 7:2: "You are to say everything I command you"; 7:6: "Moses and Aaron did just as the LORD commanded them"; 7:10: "So Moses and Aaron went to Pharaoh and did just as the LORD commanded"; 18:1: "Now Jethro, the priest of Midian and father-in-law of Moses, heard of everything God had done for Moses and for his people Israel, and how the LORD had brought Israel out of Egypt"; 18:8: "Moses told his father-in-law about everything the LORD had done to Pharaoh and the Egyptians for Israel's sake and about all the hardships they had met along the way and how the LORD had saved them"; 18:24: "Moses listened to his father-in-law and did everything he said"; 19:8: "The people all responded together, 'We will do everything the LORD has said.' So Moses brought their answer back to the LORD"; 24:3: "When Moses went and told the people all the LORD's words and laws, they responded with one voice, 'Everything the LORD has said we will do"; 24:7: Then he took the Book of the Covenant and read it to the people. They responded, 'We will do everything the LORD has said; we will obey.' "

that famous Ugaritic myth, the god El commands King Keret in a dream to do a considerable number of things. Instead of simply stating something like, "So Keret did everything El had commanded him," the text repeats more than ninety lines of instruction almost but not entirely verbatim, with the most important and obvious change being in the verb tenses. In other words, El repeatedly says to Keret, *Do xyz,* and eventually the fulfillment repetition reports repeatedly that Keret *did xyz,* saying all the same things and leaving virtually nothing to the imagination. This is precisely the phenomenon that occurs in Exod 25–31 and 35–40.[252] The ancient extrabiblical command-fulfillment accounts like that of the Keret epic thus furnish us with something of a "control" against which to evaluate what is happening in this sort of genre when we find it in a biblical setting. The reason for the genre is in fact easy enough to see: elaborate, even tedious repetition forces the reader/listener to agree that a set of important instructions was unquestionably carried out to the letter. In other words, the command-fulfillment repetition pattern is a way of highlighting the *importance* of what is commanded and the *precision* with which it was obeyed. By implication the things produced in obedience to the original command must be considered important—they were commanded in great detail and produced in rigorous complicity with the command. In other words, things over which such a great "fuss" have been made in the text can only be seen as of paramount significance, things neither to be ignored nor treated lightly nor taken for granted.

Second, it is not accidental that this genre is employed to describe God's longest set of commands in all of Exodus—greater in volume than even the Decalogue (chap. 20) and Covenant Code (chaps. 21–24) put together. But why not do the same with those commands? The answer, again, is simple enough: the command-fulfillment pattern is useful mainly in situations where what has been commanded is easily measurable and can be verified as to whether or not a set of commands was carried out as commanded (and usually rather promptly). By contrast, the various laws of the Decalogue and Covenant Code regulate the whole life of the Israelite community from the time they were revealed and forward to all generations. Only God himself would know if those laws were being

[252] D. Garrett summarizes the phenomenon helpfully: "Simple repetition . . . is common in ancient Near Eastern literature. In the Ugaritic Epic of Keret, for example, King Keret is in distress because his entire family has been killed in a series of disasters. In a dream, he receives instructions from El concerning what he should do. El's instructions, which occupy lines 60–153, say that he should make a sacrifice, muster his people for a military campaign, and go to the land of Udum, ruled by King Pabil. There he is to demand the daughter of Pabil, Hurriya, for his wife. Keret awakens and carries out the instructions. In describing how Keret obeyed El's command, lines 156 ff. are for the most part a verbatim repetition of lines 60–153 (albeit from a different perspective). This narrative technique is employed in the Bible as well. In Genesis 24 the text tells how Abraham's servant, after a prayer for divine guidance, meets the future wife of Isaac at a well (vv. 12–27). Then it gives the servant's account of all this to Laban, but again quotes almost verbatim the previous material (vv. 34–48; with adjustments for the difference of perspective). Acts, similarly, gives three complete accounts of Paul's vision on the way to Damascus (9:1–19; 22:3–16; 26:9–18)" (*Rethinking Genesis: The Sources and Authorship of the First Book of the Pentateuch* [Fearn: Christian Focus/Mentor, 2000], 22–23).

obeyed fully because so many human behaviors are private and cannot be known generally or measured accurately by humans. On the other hand, a building and its furnishings can be built or not built, furnished or not furnished, according to the instructions. Indeed, Moses himself eventually had the task of inspecting the tabernacle and its furnishings to determine whether or not all had been provided according to divine specification (39:33–43) and of being sure as well that the tabernacle was erected and its furnishings properly placed as commanded (40:1–33).

Third, command-fulfillment repetition was both instructive and regulatory for its primary original audience—Israel's priests, Aaron, and his sons. They had the profound responsibility of making sure the people worshiped properly, when, where, and as they should. This was not because having his people go through certain motions was important to God per se. Rather, God desired to have his people as close to him as his holiness would allow and regularly reminded of their dependency on him, lest they stray into behaviors and beliefs that could not save from sin. The tabernacle provided the locus of that closeness and the place of renewal of covenant fidelity in worship. Priests were reminded by the repetition of tabernacle instructions in Exodus of the fact that they led worship at a place God himself had clearly ordained and through a structure and its furnishings that God himself had approved. The command-fulfillment pattern legitimized their service, representing God to the people and the people to God.

Finally, the command-fulfillment pattern was, at least potentially, preventive. Idolatry, to which the Israelites were always inclined, made worship very easy and very convenient: any high hill and any green tree would provide a site for a simple altar and a place to eat the sacrificed meal (1 Kgs 14:23; 2 Kgs 17:10; Jer 2:20; 3:6; Ezek 6:13; 20:28). By contrast, God required his people to worship him in a far more noble and, indeed, elaborate way and to house his symbol, the ark, in a moveable house/tent so he could always reside as their monarch in the midst of his people. The Israelites might well have degenerated into idolatry even more often than most of them did were it not for the undoubtable, unassailable clarity of the tabernacle instructions as conveyed by the degree of repetition inherent in the command-fulfillment structure of the end of Exodus. No Israelite who truly desired to please Yahweh and worship him properly could ever claim to have been unaware of how to worship him at one central location at the properly furnished house of divine design, not of human devising.

2. Fulfillment of the Laws on the Means of Worship (35:1–40:38)

Exodus 35–40 contains a high proportion of the same material already revealed in chaps. 25–31, but not in the same order. Several factors account for this reordering, most of which will be addressed in detail below in the commentary on specific passages. Foremost among these factors is the need to portray in chaps. 35–40 how the various objects were actually constructed in order. In chaps. 25–31 the call for Israelites to bring as donations materials out of which the tabernacle and its furnishings can be made is followed by a description of the objects themselves in the order of their importance and holiness, that is, moving from the most sacred (the ark, a direct representation of Yahweh and the place of his contact with his people) to the least sacred (the courtyard perimeter).

In chaps. 35–40 by contrast the objects are described in the order they were actually constructed, an order dictated by common sense and necessity. A modern analogy might be found in the difference between how a church might be described before being built and the order in which it would actually be built. If a church building committee were describing what they wanted their new church to be like, they might well start by describing the sanctuary, then perhaps certain other interior rooms, then perhaps the general external appearance, what sort of steeple (or not) might be desired, furnishings, lighting, and other décor. But a builder could not build the church in that order. He would start with clearing the site, then pouring footings, and then a foundation, and then sills, then the framing. The building committee's ordering of its desires would be completely appropriate, but so would the builder's ordering of the building process. The two orders are not the same, and no one who really understands the building process from conception to construction would expect them to be. The vision comes in one order, the implementation in another.

Additionally, there are places where something stated in detail in chaps. 25–31 is more succinctly summarized in chaps. 35–40 and other cases where something stated in chaps. 25–31 is expanded upon in chaps. 35–40. We will examine these as they occur in the text. The general reasons for such differences appear to be twofold.

First, in an oral society some differences between command wording and fulfillment wording were needed in order to help the listener keep aware of which section of the literary work he or she was listening to. Much can be repeated verbatim, but if everything is, then the long stretch of completely identical material actually confuses, rather than helps, the listener.

Second, the fulfillment section (chaps. 35–40) is intended to complement, not merely to repeat, the first without differentiation (chaps. 25–31). It reinforces and builds upon what has already been stated and does this by variations that although modest in number and scope compared to the repetitions are still welcome as "fresh." Psychologically, the hearer/reader recognizes that this new material is not just prior material but information that has been reshaped and repackaged so that it comes across with sufficient novelty as to be of interest and to seem worthy of careful attention. Another way to put it is this: the bits and pieces of different material keep the hearer/reader attentive and willing to listen to the repetitions of the bulk of the same material once again.

The following table lists the main comparisons between chaps. 25–31 and 35–40, with occasional references to fulfillments or repetitions of commands in Leviticus or Numbers, where these are also useful for comparison.[253]

Command		Fulfillment
25:1–7	call for offerings of various materials	35:4–9; 35:21–29
25:10–22	the ark	37:1–9
25:23–30	the table	37:10–16
25:31–39	the lampstand	37:17–24
26:1–37	the tabernacle proper	36:8–38
27:1–8	bronze altar for burnt offerings	38:1–7
27:20–21	oil for the lampstand	command renewed in Lev 24:1–3
28:1–5	priests' dress summary	command renewed in 35:19; fulfilled in 39:1,41; cf. 40:13–14; Lev 8:7–8
28:6–14	ephod	39:2–7
28:15–30	breastpiece	39:8–21; Lev 8:8
28:31–43	remaining priests' garments	39:22–31
29:1–37	consecrating priests	Lev 8:1–36
29:38–43	daily offerings	command renewed in Num 28:1–8
29:44	consecration of tabernacle consecration of altar	command renewed in 40:9 command renewed in 40:10 fulfilled in Lev 8:11

[253] Some of the Exodus commands are actually repeated or fulfilled in Leviticus or Numbers, and some are reviewed or alluded to as past events in Deuteronomy. We must remember that Exodus is not a self-contained work but part of the entire five-book Pentateuch, and many of its themes and narrative details find their outworking further on in the Pentateuch, just as some depend on what happens earlier, in Genesis, by way of background.

Command		Fulfillment
29:44	consecration of priests	command renewed in 40:13
30:1–5	incense altar	37:25–28
30:6	incense altar placement	command renewed in 40:6 fulfilled in 40:26
30:7–9	rules for incense burning	40:27
30:10	atonement for incense altar	command renewed in Lev 4:7
30:17–21	bronze washing basin	38:8; 40:30
30:22–33	anointing oil for objects, priests	35:28; 37:29; 40:9; Lev 8:10–12,30
30:34–38	incense	35:28; 37:29; 39:38; 40:27
31:1–11	Bezalel and Oholiab/work overview	35:30–35; 36:1–7
31:12–17	Sabbath	command renewed in 35:1–3; Lev 23:3; cf. Num 15:32–36; Deut 5:12–15

(1) The Importance of the Sabbath (35:1–3) [Fulfillment of 31:12–18]

**1 Moses assembled the whole Israelite community and said to them, "These are
the things the LORD has commanded you to do: 2 For six days, work is to be done,
but the seventh day shall be your holy day, a Sabbath of rest to the LORD. Who-
ever does any work on it must be put to death. 3 Do not light a fire in any of your
dwellings on the Sabbath day."**

35:1 The essential prerequisites for the construction of the tabernacle are now in place: God has reiterated the covenant, the nation has been cleansed of those who refused to repent from idolatry, the covenant has been written down and taught to the people, and they have accepted the covenant and Moses' leadership once again. It is now time for the fulfillment of what God commanded to be made and used for properly worshiping him so that the first response of the believer (worship) can begin as it should.

Why, then, does the story of the fulfillment of the tabernacle construction commands begin with a repeat of Sabbath law? The primary reason is surely that the Sabbath was the sign of the covenant, the visible weekly proof that the people of Israel were keeping their part of the great divinely revealed legal obligation through which came their protection and blessings (see comments on 20:8–11; 31:13,17).[254] In a certain sense Israel's *formal* starting point for keeping Yahweh's covenant was keeping the Sabbath, that is, the fourth word/commandment, not because doing so was more important than fulfilling the first three words/commandments but because obedience to the Sabbath requirement was the most obviously measurable of them—either in the keeping or in the disobeying. By the fact that he kept (or did not keep) the Sabbath each week, an Israelite showed without ambiguity whether or not he was committed to keeping the covenant. Merely keeping the Sabbath did not confer righteousness if other commandments were violated, but it was an openly visible essential—a *sine qua non*—of covenant loyalty. Not to keep it would be to say publicly to the world "I am not in covenant relationship with the Lord of the Sabbath."[255]

In addition, by the placement of the Sabbath law here, God also linked chaps. 25–31, which are mostly dedicated to the topic of worship, with what follows in the rest of chaps. 35–40, which are as well mostly dedicated to worship. A brief summary of the laws about the weekly day of worship, the Sabbath, thus functions like a hinge to connect the command and fulfillment sections. The worship that was to occur every week honored with praise and adoration the giver of the covenant so recently renewed in chap. 34.

A third and somewhat temporal reason for the reiteration of Sabbath teaching at this point in the sequence of events may have been to keep Israelites from violating the Sabbath in the construction of the tabernacle. It might have been readily assumed by the people and perhaps even some of their priests that building something so holy as the tabernacle would trump any concern about the nonholiness of breaking the Sabbath law. In fact, the sign of the covenant can never be denigrated even for a purpose so positive.[256]

35:2 The prohibition against working on the Sabbath day and the death penalty attached to its violation are reiterations of what has already been commanded in 20:8–11 (which, like all the Ten Words/Commandments has no *expressed* death penalty clause) and 31:13–17, where the death penalty for violating the Sabbath does, in fact, explicitly appear (31:14–15). The wording

---

[254] In general it would be appropriate to consider 35:1–3 as a fulfillment parallel to all of 31:12–18 (so, e.g., Durham, *Exodus,* 470).

[255] On this title for Jesus see Matt 12:8; Luke 6:5—yet another way in which Jesus subtly but unmistakably showed himself to be Yahweh in the flesh.

[256] Note that none of Jesus' exceptions to what legalists had declared as prohibited on the Sabbath actually constitute normal work. Helping an animal in an emergency (Matt 12:10–14) and eating uncooked food (Matt 12:1–8 par) were both allowed by the original Sabbath regulations of the Mosaic covenant. Jesus was not loosening the actual rules for covenant keeping in his teaching on these matters but clarifying them. Likewise, his illustration involving the right to water animals on the Sabbath (Luke 13:13–17) was a demonstration of the inconsistency of legalistic teaching about doing good on the Sabbath, not a new, weaker standard.

here has some variations that allow for summation of what was stated earlier (e.g., the wording "Sabbath of rest to the LORD," which combines the concepts of "Sabbath to the LORD" from 20:10 and "rested on the seventh day" from 20:11 and "Sabbath of rest, holy to the LORD" from 31:15).

35:3 The command "do not light a fire in any of your dwellings on the Sabbath day" is also a summational statement, a way of stating briefly that no work can be done on the Sabbath, as is clearly spelled out not only in the prior verse but in the prior passages on the Sabbath in chaps. 20 and 31. But what does lighting a fire have to do with working? The answer is that the simplest sort of work that anyone might be tempted to do on the Sabbath (within the category of prohibited work, work that must *not* be done, in fact[257]) was cooking meals. It would be easy for any Israelite to rationalize that cooking a meal would clearly be allowed since eating was not itself prohibited as work; indeed, eating on the Sabbath had been divinely provided for already through the double supply of manna each sixth day (see comments on 16:14–35).

But the Sabbath law recognized that either allowing or requiring the cooking of meals on the Sabbath would undeniably represent work for the women and/or servants of the family and thus represent a clear violation of the law. So the command against lighting a fire is, by the principle of synecdoche, a command to eat cold food on the Sabbath, that which has been prepared (whether cooked or not) the previous day, so the women and/or servants of the household could have their day of rest and not just the householding men. The prohibition does not mention all fires but only those in private homes since those on the tabernacle altar were entirely appropriate for the Sabbath offerings (Num 28:9). Even so much as gathering firewood, when not a matter of emergency, was considered work and thus merited the death penalty (Num 15:32–36).[258]

[257] The Israelites, like all farmers throughout history, milked their goats and cows twice a day, seven days a week and almost surely fed and watered their animals on the Sabbath in essentially the same manner as they did on any other day of the week. This represented work on the Sabbath but a sanctioned work because, among other things, not to do so would have caused great pain to the animals.

[258] To the objection, "But what if the man's family were sick and he needed the wood to make them a fire to keep them warm?" the answer would be, "He should have borrowed wood from a neighbor and not gone out collecting it or sought refuge from a neighbor for his sick dependents" or "a sick person might need to get cooled off in the sweltering Sinai wilderness but would hardly need to get warm beyond what blankets would provide." In the story in Num 15 it is fairly obvious that the investigation revealed that the man was doing far more than merely gathering enough wood to meet an emergency need but was in fact engaged in work he could and should have done on other days of the week. The story of the Sabbath wood gatherer follows the ruling in Num 15:30 that sins done "with a high hand" (in open and knowledgeable defiance of the covenant) merit the death penalty. Gather wood on the Sabbath is a prelude to lighting a fire on the Sabbath, as forbidden in Exod 35:3. Recent studies of the story in Num 15 suggest that the man's actions represented preparation for further covenant breaking. Cf. J. Weingreen, "The Case of the Woodgatherer (Numbers xv 32–36)," *VT* 16 (1966): 361–64; A. Philips, "The Case of the Woodgatherer Reconsidered," *VT* 19 (1969): 125–28.

(2) Offerings of Tabernacle Materials (35:4–29) [Fulfillment of 25:1–7]

[4]Moses said to the whole Israelite community, "This is what the LORD has commanded: [5]From what you have, take an offering for the LORD. Everyone who is willing is to bring to the LORD an offering of gold, silver and bronze; [6]blue, purple and scarlet yarn and fine linen; goat hair; [7]ram skins dyed red and hides of sea cows; acacia wood; [8]olive oil for the light; spices for the anointing oil and for the fragrant incense; [9]and onyx stones and other gems to be mounted on the ephod and breastpiece.

[10]"All who are skilled among you are to come and make everything the LORD has commanded: [11]the tabernacle with its tent and its covering, clasps, frames, crossbars, posts and bases; [12]the ark with its poles and the atonement cover and the curtain that shields it; [13]the table with its poles and all its articles and the bread of the Presence; [14]the lampstand that is for light with its accessories, lamps and oil for the light; [15]the altar of incense with its poles, the anointing oil and the fragrant incense; the curtain for the doorway at the entrance to the tabernacle; [16]the altar of burnt offering with its bronze grating, its poles and all its utensils; the bronze basin with its stand; [17]the curtains of the courtyard with its posts and bases, and the curtain for the entrance to the courtyard; [18]the tent pegs for the tabernacle and for the courtyard, and their ropes; [19]the woven garments worn for ministering in the sanctuary—both the sacred garments for Aaron the priest and the garments for his sons when they serve as priests."

[20]Then the whole Israelite community withdrew from Moses' presence, [21]and everyone who was willing and whose heart moved him came and brought an offering to the LORD for the work on the Tent of Meeting, for all its service, and for the sacred garments. [22]All who were willing, men and women alike, came and brought gold jewelry of all kinds: brooches, earrings, rings and ornaments. They all presented their gold as a wave offering to the LORD. [23]Everyone who had blue, purple or scarlet yarn or fine linen, or goat hair, ram skins dyed red or hides of sea cows brought them. [24]Those presenting an offering of silver or bronze brought it as an offering to the LORD, and everyone who had acacia wood for any part of the work brought it. [25]Every skilled woman spun with her hands and brought what she had spun—blue, purple or scarlet yarn or fine linen. [26]And all the women who were willing and had the skill spun the goat hair. [27]The leaders brought onyx stones and other gems to be mounted on the ephod and breastpiece. [28]They also brought spices and olive oil for the light and for the anointing oil and for the fragrant incense. [29]All the Israelite men and women who were willing brought to the LORD freewill offerings for all the work the LORD through Moses had commanded them to do.

GOD'S CALL FOR MATERIALS (35:4–9). **35:4** Since God had said in 25:1, "Tell the Israelites to bring me an offering. You are to receive the offering for me from each man whose heart prompts him to give," Moses took the command seriously and did not merely pass the word among the people or assemble only the leadership and ask them to relay the command throughout the people. He assembled the whole community (fulfilling the command for each person to be invited to respond),[259] comprised of all those old enough and well enough to gather in one spot, and told them all directly about God's desire that they respond willingly to his call for the donation of materials. He reminded them that the call for materials came from God as a command and was not something either he or other Israelites had decided on their own was necessary. Everything about the tabernacle was of divine design and origination. Humans were graciously allowed to participate in its construction, but they could not claim any credit otherwise. It was God who told humans how he wished to be worshiped, not humans who told God what they had decided to do by way of worship.

35:5–9 The language here duplicates 25:3–7 verbatim, starting with the words "gold, silver and bronze" (v. 5). In 25:1 God had commanded, "Tell the Israelites to bring me an offering," which is paraphrased here appropriately as "From what you have, take an offering for the LORD" (v. 5). The statement in 25:1, "You are to receive the offering for me from each man whose heart prompts him to give" is here fulfilled by Moses' declaration, "Everyone who is willing is to bring to the LORD an offering." Moses thus fulfilled God's command to tell the people to offer the materials by doing just as God had said.

This passage stands as a model for the way things of God are provided for by humans.[260] The covenant community[261] responds to what they perceive as a divine call and give freely, without coercion, until the need is met. They give of their own possessions so that each person participates through personal sacrifice. Part of the privilege of serving God is to be found in the opportunity to donate to his purposes things that in his common grace he has already entrusted to the possession of his people. The highest honor a person can have in connection with anything he or she owns and might otherwise have used for self is seeing it given over to and incorporated into that which God thereafter owns and uses for his honor. The story of the donations of the people ends in 36:4–7, with the report that the donations far exceeded the need, thus confirming that the people took Moses' call seriously. Having been chastened by the terrible results of their rebellion against Yahweh in

---

[259] From the fulfillments of 25:1 in 35:22 ("All who were willing, men and women alike"), 35:25–26 ("Every skilled woman spun with her hands and brought what she had spun . . . And all the women who were willing and had the skill spun"), and 35:29 ("All the Israelite men and women"), it is clear that in this instance (25:1) as in many others, אִישׁ must be translated "person" and not "man."

[260] Cf., e.g., 1 Chr 29:9; 17; 2 Chr 31:5; Neh 11:2; 1 Cor 9:5–6; 2 Cor 8:3-5.

[261] Note how important it was that the covenant community and not merely the geographical community should rebuild the temple after the exile (Ezra 4:1–3).

the past,[262] they now wholeheartedly responded to an opportunity to show their loyalty.

GOD'S CALL FOR SKILLED WORKERS (35:10–19) [Summarizes Parts of 26–28; 30 with Further Fulfillment Especially in 37; 39–40]. This listing of component parts of the tabernacle, its furnishings, and its courtyard reflects systematically various descriptions of these articles in the command sections of chaps. 26–28 and chap. 30, but it also finds many parallels in 39:32–41, where the original command to provide the tabernacle can also be considered to have been fulfilled as Moses inspected the tabernacle and found it fully in compliance with the design he was given by God on Sinai.

35:10 "All who are skilled among you" summarizes the earlier instructions that various tabernacle parts were to be constructed by "a skilled craftsman" (26:1,31) or "all the skilled men" (28:3) or "the work of a skilled craftsman" (28:6,15). The wording "everything the LORD has commanded" (35:10) reflects particularly the language of 31:6 ("I have given skill to all the craftsmen to make everything I have commanded you"). This concept will also be reiterated in 39:32 ("The Israelites did everything just as the LORD commanded Moses"). In this situation the biblical theme of God's use of human beings to accomplish his will is further developed. The emphasis of "Let us make man in our image" (Gen 1:26) is not ontological but vocational. It refers to humans being heaven's representatives[263] on earth to do what God wants done on earth (cf. "as it is in heaven," Matt 6:10), as the remainder of Gen 1:26 goes on to clarify ("let them rule over . . . all the earth"). God's genius in creation is demonstrated partly in his delegation of important assignments to humans—assignments of divine design but of human fulfillment.[264]

35:11 Building the "tabernacle" (the symbolic house-tent for Yahweh) was commanded as a general, overall requirement in 26:1 and will be summarized in general in 39:32-33 as well. This was followed in the original tabernacle commandments given to Moses by instructions concerning the various component parts of the tabernacle, including the "covering" in 26:14 (cf. 39:34); the "clasps" in 26:6,11,33 (cf. 39:34); the "frames" in 26:15–23,25 (cf. 39:34); the "crossbars" in 26:26,28–29 (cf. 39:34); the "posts" in 26:32,37 (cf. 39:33 [note that these are different from the posts used to hang the courtyard curtains mentioned in 27:10–12,14–17; cf. 39:40)]; and the "bases" for the posts in 26:19,21,25,32,37 (cf. 39:40 [these

---

[262] See esp. 32:27–28; 33:4–6; and the evidence of repentance shown in the people's posture and attitude in 33:8–10.

[263] The term used for "image" in Gen 1:26 is צֶלֶם, a standard Semitic vocable for "idol," i.e., something that represents a god in a specific location. Cf. Gen 1:27; 5:3; 9:6.

[264] Durham refers in this connection to the "partnership of human genius and dexterity with divine design" (*Exodus,* 476).

bases, again, were just for the tabernacle posts and were separate from the base for the lampstand (25:31) or the bases for the courtyard posts]; 27:10ff.; cf. 39:40).

35:12 The "ark" was described in 25:10–12 (cf. 39:35); its carrying "poles" were depicted in 25:13–16 (cf. 39:35); its "atonement cover" in 25:17–22 (cf. 26:34; 39:35); and the "curtain" dividing the holy of holies from the holy place, used as a wrapping for the ark as it traveled[265] ("the curtain that shields it" was described in 26:31–33; cf. 39:34). These important items are simply listed here without description or elaboration because this listing is part of a brief speech reminding people of what constituted the tabernacle and its furnishings so that they could go home and find or make appropriate materials to donate. The fulfillment of the original ark command of chap. 25 is found in 37:1–9, and the original curtain command is in 36:35; 39:34. The ark was the only object that occupied the holy of holies, the back room of the tabernacle that represented God's private room.[266]

The table, lampstand, and altar of incense described in 35:13–15 constituted the three pieces of furniture in the spare but elegant holy place, the front room of the tabernacle.

35:13 The "table" that stood in the holy place, the larger of the two rooms of the tabernacle, was described in 25:23–27 (cf. 39:36); its "poles," in 23:27–28; its "articles" (plates, dishes, pitchers, bowls), in 25:29 (cf. 39:36). The table will be described again as fulfilled through its actual construction in 37:10–16 (leaving out in that context any mention of the bread, which was a temporary substance, not a piece of furniture, chaps. 36–38 being devoted to hardware rather than to perishable substances). The "bread of the Presence" that was to be placed upon it constantly as a symbolic offering to God for his personal use in his house was originally described in 25:30 and will be mentioned again as precisely provided in 39:36.

35:14 The "lampstand" was described in 25:31–36,39–40; its "accessories," in 25:38–39; its "lamps," in 25:37; and its "oil," in 27:10–21. All these are again summarized as fulfilled in 39:37. The lampstand is also described as constructed in 37:17–23 but without the mention of oil per se because, as we have already noted, the bread was a perishable substance, and the descriptions in chaps. 36–38 are limited to tabernacle hardware.

35:15 The "altar of incense" was commanded by an overall description in 30:1–10 (a further fulfillment description will occur in 37:25–28); its "poles," specifically in 30:4–5 (cf. 37:27–28); the tabernacle's priestly "anointing oil," in 30:22–33 (cf. 37:29); and its "incense," in 30:34–38 (cf.

---

[265] Num 4:5–6.

[266] For discussion of the purpose and symbolism of the ark, table, lampstand, and incense altar see the comments on these items in chs 25–30, *ad loc*.

37:29). In addition, these are summarized in 39:38 with the exception that that brief inspection summary does not specifically mention the altar's poles. The "curtain for the doorway at the entrance to the tabernacle" was ordered in 26:36–37 and will be further described as constructed in fulfillment of that order in 36:37. It will also be mentioned in the summary of the inspection of the completed tabernacle in 39:38,40 as well as 40:28. This curtain is distinct from the one used to provide an entrance gateway to the courtyard (27:16).

35:16 The "altar of burnt offering" was commanded in 27:1–8; its "bronze grating" specifically in 27:4–5; its "poles" in 27:6–7; its "utensils" in 27:3. The fulfillment of the command to make the altar is described further in 38:1, and its being set up for use in 40:6,10,29. Note the mention specifically of its bronze grating in the further fulfillment descriptions of 38:4–5,30 and 39:39; its poles in 38:5 and 39:39; and its utensils in 38:30,39.

The "bronze basin" was commanded in 30:17–21, with mention specifically of its "stand" in 30:18. The fulfillment of this command for the basin and its stand will be also addressed in 39:8,39 as well as in the description of the setting up of the tabernacle in 40:7,11,30. Note that the "altar of burnt offering" and the "bronze basin" were the two pieces of tabernacle courtyard furniture; otherwise the courtyard was mainly a gathering place for priests, people, and animals for worship, which involved sacrifice on the altar and the proper ritual cleansing of the priests with the water in the basin, as noted in 29:4; 30:18–20 (cf. 40:7,12,30).

35:17 Here the mention of the "curtains of the courtyard" reprises the commands in 27:9,12,16,18, and the curtains will be addressed as well in the fulfillment descriptions of 38:9,15–18; 39:40. The actual erection of these curtains is described in 40:8,33.[267] The "posts" and "bases" for them were described in 27:10–17. Further fulfillment descriptions occur in 38:9–19,30 and 39:40. The erection of the posts and bases occurs in 40:18. The "curtain for the entrance to the courtyard" was commanded in 26:36; 27:14,16 and will be mentioned again in the fulfillment passages of 38:14–18; 39:38–40; as well as in the tabernacle erection description in 40:5,8,28,33.

35:18 In 27:19 God specified bronze as the material for the "tent pegs" in both tabernacle and courtyard. This is further fulfilled in 38:20,31 and 39:40 (cf. Num 3:37; 4:32). Although it is obvious earlier in Exodus that between the tent poles and the tent pegs ropes would be strung to carry the tension, the term "rope"[268] does not occur in connection with the tent and courtyard curtain support system until this verse. Mention of the ropes recurs, however, in 39:40 (cf. Num 3:26,37; 4:26,32).

---

[267] Note also the further description in Num 3:26; 4:26.

[268] מֵיתָר.

35:19 The wording of this verse duplicates that of 31:10 and will be duplicated by 39:41 as well. The command to prepare priestly garments was given in detail in chaps. 28–29 (reprised in chap. 39), but also summarized in 31:10 as quoted here. In 40:13–16 Moses is described as fulfilling the command via the actual investiture of the priests.[269]

THE PEOPLE RESPOND TO THE CALL FOR MATERIALS (35:20–29) [Fulfillment of 25:1–7]. **35:20–21** Again the term "the whole Israelite community," already employed in vv. 1,4, reminds the reader that everyone, and not merely representatives, leaders, or some particularly equipped group was called upon to respond. In all likelihood, virtually everyone did so.[270] The tabernacle project was a nationwide effort. The whole people had been summoned, so now, having heard the instructions, they "withdrew from Moses' presence" in order to go home and to work on the project. Virtually every family probably was involved in some fashion. Proper biblical worship is always corporate, which means that everyone in the covenant community not physically prevented from participation should attend and take part.

The term "Tent of Meeting" summarizes the tabernacle and all its furniture as commanded in chaps. 25–27 (and 30:1–10,17–21); the term "all its service" speaks of what chap. 29 and 30:22–37 covered; the term "the sacred garments" refers to the garments described in chap. 28. The different listing order of these items reflects, as already noted, a style that adds a modicum of freshness and thereby helps keep command-fulfillment texts from being tedious.

These verses follow v. 5 earlier in the chapter in identifying those who responded as those who were "willing"; the participation in providing materials was not forced but voluntary, a model in Scripture of the proper attitude of people in connection with any chance to support the purposes of God (see note 262).

35:22 Moses clearly indicated that both genders were involved in the work by placing "men and women alike" in apposition to "all who were willing."[271] Some vocations, such as the priesthood, were limited by gender; worship and preparation for it through contributing materials for the tabernacle and the worship that occurred within its courtyard were not.

---

[269] Cf. Lev 8; 16.

[270] In 36:5–6 those who contributed are called generally "the people" located "throughout the camp," whether "man or woman." This suggests that anyone who contributed in any way—not just by working directly on the tabernacle or its furniture, but by donating goods, time, or talent, was officially regarded as included in the effort. This should hardly be surprising. Successful community projects require participation of many people at many levels of involvement.

[271] The word order is reversed in the Hb. (הָאֲנָשִׁים עַל־הַנָּשִׁים כֹּל נְדִיב לֵב), but this does not affect the grammatical analysis of the phrases in apposition.

The "gold jewelry" described here by means of some examples may have been worn almost exclusively by women, though some may have been from children (see comments on 32:2). If 33:6 is to be understood as implying that the Israelites never donned jewelry again at Sinai after taking it off in mourning for the consequences of their idolatry as described in chap. 32, the no-longer-worn gold baubles would not really be useful for much else, at least in the short run, and therefore would constitute a ready source of the gold needed for the tabernacle furniture.

In presenting these as "a wave offering to the LORD," the people presumably appeared before the most visible symbol of Yahweh at the moment, which would have been the small, symbolic tent of meeting (33:7–11). There they presumably held up the items to "show" Yahweh that they were being donated (an act more helpful psychologically to the worshiper than to the omniscient God) and waved them back and forth.[272] This is something of a necessary anthropomorphism: when humans want to be sure that someone else won't fail to see something, they wave it back and forth. Here the Israelites wanted to be sure that Yahweh saw their offering, so they waved it just as they would if he were a human being standing there in front of them. This does not suggest that they didn't think he could see well or was distant; it suggests that they understood very well that he was indeed in front of them (at least) and that they were indeed in his presence when they brought their offerings. The way they showed this faith was by doing what one does when one *knows* that another *is* present and *can* see, even though they could not in see Yahweh.

35:23 On this list of fabrics see 25:4–5; 26:1,7,14,31,36; 27:16; 28:5,8, 15,33,39 (cf. 35:6–7).

35:24 On "silver" and "bronze," the other two metals used in the tabernacle and its courtyard in addition to gold—for various objects, especially posts and bases—see 25:3; 26:11,19,21,25,32,37; 27:2,6,10,17; 30:18; 31:4; 35:5. On "acacia wood" as the structural ingredient for various furniture items and tabernacle curtain supports, see 25:5,10,13,23,28; 26:15,26,32,37; 27:1,6; 30:1,5; 35:7.

35:25 This verse suggests that, as in most known cultures, women in ancient Israel handled the important task of spinning yarns and linen thread. The task is indeed crucial and delicate; if yarn or thread is improperly spun, a fabric made from it cannot be neat and even and will not be as strong or as durable.[273] Though it is not stated here, we also can assume that the women

---

[272] See comments on 29:24,26–27. The Hb. terminology clearly indicates waving back and forth, and not merely holding something up (*nwp*).

[273] Consistency in the spinning makes possible the greatest number of threads per inch, and as well the greatest possible symmetry for purposes of joining sections of fabric together.

may have had a hand in dyeing at least some of the fabric in the colors mentioned.[274] On the fabrics and colors see v. 23 above.

35:26 Various wools, hairs, and furs present different characteristics and challenges for the spinner. Spinning goat hair is not generally regarded as harder than other sorts of spinning,[275] so the verse probably does not intend to suggest that the women who spun the goat hair yarn were specialists but simply that the large number of goat hair curtains used as protective coverings for the tabernacle proper meant that many women saw fit to dedicate their skills specifically to spinning goat hair. On the eleven goat hair curtains see 25:4 and especially 26:7–13; 36:14–18.

35:27 The "onyx stones" mentioned here were introduced in the commands of 25:7; 28:9,20. On the "other gems" see 25:7 and especially 28:17–21. Further fulfillment of the command is found in 39:10–14.

35:28 On the "spices" see 30:23,34; 35:8; on the lamp "oil," 25:6; 27:20; 35:8,14; and with regard to further fulfillment, 39:37; on the "anointing oil," 25:6; 29:7,21; 30:24–25,31–32; 31:11; 25:14; for further fulfillment, 37:29; 39:37; 40:9 and on the "incense," which was burned on the special altar dedicated to its use, 25:6; 30:1,7–9,27,35,37; 31:8,11; 35:8,15; and for further fulfillment, 37:25,29; 39:38; 40:5,27.

35:29 This summary verse reminds the reader of several things: (1) that both men and women contributed, (2) that everything they brought from home to contribute was brought entirely voluntarily, (3) that the work for which their contributions were made was God's work, and (4) that God himself, through the intermediation of Moses, had issued the command that it be done. Accordingly, the tabernacle, as well as what was used by and worn by the priests who served there to represent the people to God, had divine sanction; and the materials used in it and for it were gifts to God that once freely given, belonged entirely to him. What was once common and even profane became transformed by God's loving design and command into what was now perfectly and beautifully holy.

"All the Israelite men and women" reiterates the both-genders emphasis already seen in 11:2 (where some of the materials eventually used in the ark were first gathered) and v. 22 earlier in this chapter. "Were willing" reiterates vv. 5,21–22. "Freewill offerings" reprises in part 25:2–3 and 35:5,21–22,24. On Moses as the vehicle for God's commands about the materials and

[274] Based on modern analogies, fabric can be dyed before it is spun or after; there is little difference in the results. In the case of hides, the dyeing takes place after curing.

[275] Presuming that the Israelites' goats were long-haired goats. Some modern varieties of goats (e.g., Saanens) have rather short hair that can be harder to spin successfully than long goat hair, but the varieties of goats presumed to have lived in ancient times in north Africa and the Near East were long-haired.

tabernacle work in general, cf. vv. 1,4; 36:5; 39:1,5,7,21,26,29,31–32,42–43; 40:16,32.

(3) The Work of Bezalel, Oholiab, and the Other Skilled Craftsmen (35:30–36:7)

30Then Moses said to the Israelites, "See, the LORD has chosen Bezalel son of Uri, the son of Hur, of the tribe of Judah, 31and he has filled him with the Spirit of God, with skill, ability and knowledge in all kinds of crafts—32to make artistic designs for work in gold, silver and bronze, 33to cut and set stones, to work in wood and to engage in all kinds of artistic craftsmanship. 34And he has given both him and Oholiab son of Ahisamach, of the tribe of Dan, the ability to teach others. 35He has filled them with skill to do all kinds of work as craftsmen, designers, embroiderers in blue, purple and scarlet yarn and fine linen, and weavers—all of them master craftsmen and designers.

1So Bezalel, Oholiab and every skilled person to whom the LORD has given skill and ability to know how to carry out all the work of constructing the sanctuary are to do the work just as the LORD has commanded."

2Then Moses summoned Bezalel and Oholiab and every skilled person to whom the LORD had given ability and who was willing to come and do the work. 3They received from Moses all the offerings the Israelites had brought to carry out the work of constructing the sanctuary. And the people continued to bring freewill offerings morning after morning. 4So all the skilled craftsmen who were doing all the work on the sanctuary left their work 5and said to Moses, "The people are bringing more than enough for doing the work the LORD commanded to be done."

6Then Moses gave an order and they sent this word throughout the camp: "No man or woman is to make anything else as an offering for the sanctuary." And so the people were restrained from bringing more, 7because what they already had was more than enough to do all the work.

MOSES APPOINTS AND ENDORSES THE CRAFSTMEN AND DESIGNERS (35:30–36:1) [Fulfillment of 31:2–6]. **35:30–35** These verses contain much of the same wording seen already in their original command context (31:2–6). Some differences exist, including those that are necessary to the present context, in which Moses reminded the people of what God had earlier said to him on Mount Sinai (e.g., here in v. 30 Moses told the Israelites that "the LORD has chosen . . ." compared to 31:2, where God spoke in the first person, "See, I have chosen . . ."; or also in v. 34 here, "[God] has given both him and Oholiab" as opposed to the original divine statement in 31:6, "I have appointed Oholiab . . . to help him").

Other differences are present here because they help the audience (all Israel, once again summoned all together after some time had gone by and the people had gathered and/or produced the materials called for) to appreciate the way the construction would be ordered. For example, the mention at the end of v. 34 of Bezalel's and Oholiab's "ability to teach others" is something implicit in 31:6 but made explicit here so that no one would fail to understand that the process by which God would "have given skill to all the craftsmen" (31:6) would include the learning process generally known as apprenticeship. Nothing in the earlier command context or here in the fulfillment context should be understood to suggest that the various craftsmen were suddenly given all the knowledge and skill they needed for constructing the tabernacle by divine fiat. Instead, just as prevails today in God's work, some skills are the result of a lifetime of study, training, and experience, some are the result of special divine intervention and guidance, and some are learned from others in the process of carrying out a given assignment for the Lord. Thus Paul's discussion of spiritual gifts (Rom 12; 1 Cor 12) never denies the idea that gifts can be gradually obtained and/or improved with practice over time.[276]

Verse 35 of the present context also elaborates slightly on 31:6 in its listing of jobs done by both men and women, tasks already described in earlier contexts but here reprised as a way of reminding everyone of two things: (1) Bezalel and Oholiab were in charge of the work overall, but (2) they needed all sorts of help from experts so that the result would be one of excellence. This is also the force of the closing words of v. 35, "all of them master craftsmen and designers"—implying that no part of the tabernacle would be the work of mere amateurs but that all would be the best that human beings could make it, operating under divine design and giftedness.

The tabernacle building project thus parallels what the work of God at its best has always entailed: an opportunity for everyone to contribute in some way, even if mainly by donation, and also an expectation that everything would be to the fullest and best extent and quality possible, by the people best qualified to do it, called for and guided by God.

36:1 This statement continues and completes by way of summary the divine endorsement of Oholiab and those who would work under his leadership, with the caveat that all the actual builders must be gifted by God ("to whom the LORD has given skill and ability to know how to carry out all the work") and that everything must be accomplished strictly according to the revealed divine plan ("just as the LORD has commanded"; cf. Exod 26:30). It was not a democratic undertaking: no one could demand to be allowed to work on the building, courtyard, or furniture to satisfy a desire to be involved or merely out of a casual desire to help. It was an expert task. Nor was it a project that humans could modify in any way; no one would be

---

[276] Indeed, he indicates this in the case of the "greater gifts" by encouraging that they be sought (1 Cor 12:31) and developed (1 Cor 14:12).

allowed to suggest making the tabernacle bigger, or more elaborate, or differently furnished.[277]

THE PEOPLE'S OVERSUBCRIPTION TO THE CALL FOR DONATIONS (36:2–7). With this passage Moses augmented the command-fulfillment pattern with a heartwarming story about how enthusiastically the people responded to the call for donations of materials needed for the tabernacle. This is just the sort of account that takes away much of the tedium of reading the fulfillment chapters. The fulfillment takes on special meaning when it is understood that it happened in abundance, from willing hearts gladly giving, and that nothing needed for the tabernacle construction was ever lacking. When a community is asked to back something as major as the tabernacle project was and does so fully and rapidly, it speaks volumes about that community's unity of purpose, its solidarity in responding to the divine call.[278] The people who some weeks earlier had been defiant and degenerate in their faith (chap. 32) now joined together to make sure that what God had asked them to do would not fail to happen. This constitutes further evidence of their repentance for their earlier involvement in the golden young bull idolatry and their present confidence in Moses and his mediation of God's instructions for covenantally faithful worship.

36:2–3 The holy project swung rapidly into motion. "Bezalel and Oholiab" (see 31:2) and "every skilled person" (see 26:1) went to work, under a process that saw Moses receiving the people's offerings and immediately passing them on to the builders. (This ensured that Moses could inspect everything donated, for appropriateness and quality, before it went to any of the constructors.) The fact that the people "continued to bring freewill offerings morning after morning" demonstrates that they were not perfunctorily fulfilling the call for offerings but were eagerly and cheerfully doing whatever they could to be sure that enough supplies for the work would be in the hands of the craftsmen. It would not be going too far to suggest that the people were here described as highly enthusiastic about the project, recognizing in it the opportunity to begin keeping the covenant correctly as opposed to their prior gross disobedience (chap. 32).

---

[277] In the present Western hemisphere church (at least), what the Bible teaches about churches, church growth, and preaching has in many instances been largely or virtually entirely eclipsed by supposedly superior insights gained from the disciplines of marketing, management, advertising, and psychology. Clearly, many in the church think there's room for improvement on the original divine plan.

[278] Compare the situation described in Ezra 3–5, in which discouragement after a good start at rebuilding the temple once the Israelites had returned from the Exile led to an eighteen-year hiatus in building, during which inertia threatened to continue unabated. Yet, as the book of Zechariah also describes, the people eventually got behind the second temple construction project and finished it by 516 BC, just in time to meet the deadline established by Jeremiah's prediction of a seventy-year exile (586–516 BC; Jer 25:11–12; 29:10; cf. Dan 9:2; Zech 1:12; 7:5).

36:4–7 Moses was eventually required to insist rather forcefully to all the people ("throughout the camp") that no more material could be donated, since all required supplies had reached full levels. Some men and women gathered or spun or wove or dyed or otherwise prepared tabernacle contributions that never were used for the tabernacle? Such overages probably were put to some other use by families and clans, but they were not used at the tabernacle.[279]

(4) Construction of the Tabernacle Proper (36:8–38) [Fulfillment of 26:1–27]

[8]All the skilled men among the workmen made the tabernacle with ten curtains of finely twisted linen and blue, purple and scarlet yarn, with cherubim worked into them by a skilled craftsman. [9]All the curtains were the same size—twenty-eight cubits long and four cubits wide. [10]They joined five of the curtains together and did the same with the other five. [11]Then they made loops of blue material along the edge of the end curtain in one set, and the same was done with the end curtain in the other set. [12]They also made fifty loops on one curtain and fifty loops on the end curtain of the other set, with the loops opposite each other. [13]Then they made fifty gold clasps and used them to fasten the two sets of curtains together so that the tabernacle was a unit.

[14]They made curtains of goat hair for the tent over the tabernacle—eleven altogether. [15]All eleven curtains were the same size—thirty cubits long and four cubits wide. [16]They joined five of the curtains into one set and the other six into another set. [17]Then they made fifty loops along the edge of the end curtain in one set and also along the edge of the end curtain in the other set. [18]They made fifty bronze clasps to fasten the tent together as a unit. [19]Then they made for the tent a covering of ram skins dyed red, and over that a covering of hides of sea cows.

[20]They made upright frames of acacia wood for the tabernacle. [21]Each frame was ten cubits long and a cubit and a half wide, [22]with two projections set parallel to each other. They made all the frames of the tabernacle in this way. [23]They made twenty frames for the south side of the tabernacle [24]and made forty silver bases to go under them—two bases for each frame, one under each projection. [25]For the other side, the north side of the tabernacle, they made twenty frames [26]and forty silver bases—two under each frame. [27]They made six frames for the far end, that is, the west end of the tabernacle, [28]and two frames were made for the corners of the tabernacle at the far end. [29]At these two corners the frames were double from the bottom all the way to the top and fitted into a single ring; both were made alike. [30]So there were eight frames and sixteen silver bases—two under each frame.

[31]They also made crossbars of acacia wood: five for the frames on one side of the tabernacle, [32]five for those on the other side, and five for the frames on the

[279] Specifically, however, certain mixtures that were already prohibited for private use could not be put to private use and would have had to be destroyed if mixed already (e.g., Exod 30:31–32,37).

west, at the far end of the tabernacle. [33]They made the center crossbar so that it extended from end to end at the middle of the frames. [34]They overlaid the frames with gold and made gold rings to hold the crossbars. They also overlaid the crossbars with gold.

[35]They made the curtain of blue, purple and scarlet yarn and finely twisted linen, with cherubim worked into it by a skilled craftsman. [36]They made four posts of acacia wood for it and overlaid them with gold. They made gold hooks for them and cast their four silver bases. [37]For the entrance to the tent they made a curtain of blue, purple and scarlet yarn and finely twisted linen—the work of an embroiderer; [38]and they made five posts with hooks for them. They overlaid the tops of the posts and their bands with gold and made their five bases of bronze.

36:8–13 This paragraph duplicates in past tense fulfillment ("then they made . . . they also made") what 26:1–6 commanded in the imperative ("make, then make"). By starting this way, that is, with a virtually verbatim fulfillment description, the passage suggests that all other original commands were fulfilled precisely and that it would not be necessary for Moses to use the same level of detail in all his subsequent fulfillment descriptions. He sometimes would repeat all the details and sometimes would not, thus obviating mere mindless repetition.

36:14–19 This paragraph describes the fulfillment of what was commanded in 26:7–14 but shortens the description with summations at various points. A typical example is that of 26:9, "Fold the sixth curtain double at the front of the tent," which is omitted here, as are a number of other details from the original instructions in chap. 26. After an initial paragraph that does repeat the language of the original command virtually verbatim (36:8–13), he holds the reader's attention by some judicious condensation. The condensations occur in v. 9 and after v. 12 (so that 26:12–13 is essentially skipped—a simple but effective way to shorten the passage).

36:20–30 Note that in this description of the fulfillment of the commands of 26:15–25, Moses reverted to virtual verbatim correspondence between what was done as compared to what had originally been ordered, as he did in the case in 36:8–13. Thus we observe him alternating between full duplication of the original command wording and the sort of précis he employed in 36:14–19.

36:31–34 This short paragraph also leaves out nothing of the detail of the original command in 26:26–29—all is described as fulfilled, without condensing any wording.

36:35–38 These verses shorten in a rather obvious way certain details of the original commands in 26:31–37, of which they describe the fulfillment.[280] Thus, as in the case of 36:14–19, Moses again varied the style in a

[280] In addition, Moses did not repeat 26:30, one of the several reminders in the original tabernacle proper command section to construct the tabernacle strictly according to divine revelation.

modest way to break up monotony, but he left no doubt in the reader's mind that everything commanded in chap. 26 was in fact accomplished as required. Verses 33–35 of chap. 26 are simply skipped in this summary, and 26:37 is slightly reworded in 36:38.

(5) Construction of the Ark (37:1–9) [Fulfillment of 25:10–20]

[1]Bezalel made the ark of acacia wood—two and a half cubits long, a cubit and a half wide, and a cubit and a half high. [2]He overlaid it with pure gold, both inside and out, and made a gold molding around it. [3]He cast four gold rings for it and fastened them to its four feet, with two rings on one side and two rings on the other. [4]Then he made poles of acacia wood and overlaid them with gold. [5]And he inserted the poles into the rings on the sides of the ark to carry it.

[6]He made the atonement cover of pure gold—two and a half cubits long and a cubit and a half wide. [7]Then he made two cherubim out of hammered gold at the ends of the cover. [8]He made one cherub on one end and the second cherub on the other; at the two ends he made them of one piece with the cover. [9]The cherubim had their wings spread upward, overshadowing the cover with them. The cherubim faced each other, looking toward the cover.

37:1–5 These verses describe the fulfillment of 25:10–15 virtually verbatim—differing mainly in adding the important detail in 37:1 that "Bezalel made the ark." The chief of all the builders, specially filled with the Spirit of God for these tasks (31:2–3), was entrusted with this most precious object of all, as was fitting.

In chaps. 25–26 the command to build the ark precedes the command to build the tabernacle proper. Here the fulfillment of the command to build the ark follows that of the fulfillment description related to the tabernacle proper. Why the different order? The answer probably is quite simple: The ark was protected by the curtains of the tabernacle; it was wrapped for travel in the curtain that divided the holy place from the holy of holies, and it was also protected when the tabernacle was set up in place by the various layers of external tabernacle surfacing. Therefore Bezalel chose (perhaps at Moses' suggestion or even instruction) to ready the protective material first so that the ark would not sit out exposed to the elements for all to see—either type of exposure potentially constituting profanation.[281]

37:6–9 These verses describe the fulfillment of 25:17–20 also virtually verbatim, with changes limited almost entirely to verb tenses (even the difference in the Hb. between 25:19 and 37:8 is more minute than the NIV's

[281] The ark was never seen by the Israelites in general or even by the priests in general (i.e., by anyone except the high priest, and that only annually) because it was always hidden from view by the curtain/veil when the tabernacle was erected and always wrapped tightly and hidden from view when being transported. Thus people believed in the ark by faith—it was for all practical purposes invisible to them, just as was their God, whose presence it symbolized. Cf. Num 4:4–6.

adjusted word order would suggest, being limited to a change in the verb tense and a preposition). Note that Bezalel may have been the sole worker on the ark; nothing in the language of this passage can be interpreted to mean that any other persons were involved, in contrast to the more general "they" references to unnamed workers on other parts of the tabernacle furnishings. The paramount symbol of the invisible God was made by the one he chose and specially guided to make it.[282]

(6) Construction of the Tabernacle Table (37:10–16) [Fulfillment of 25:23–29]

10They made the table of acacia wood—two cubits long, a cubit wide, and a cubit and a half high. 11Then they overlaid it with pure gold and made a gold molding around it. 12They also made around it a rim a handbreadth wide and put a gold molding on the rim. 13They cast four gold rings for the table and fastened them to the four corners, where the four legs were. 14The rings were put close to the rim to hold the poles used in carrying the table. 15The poles for carrying the table were made of acacia wood and were overlaid with gold. 16And they made from pure gold the articles for the table—its plates and dishes and bowls and its pitchers for the pouring out of drink offerings.

37:10–16 Aside from some necessary changes in verb tense and some very slight adjustments in word order to prevent repetition monotony, this paragraph duplicates what has been seen already in 25:23–29, so the construction order of ark-table-lampstand continues in the fulfillment phase of the tabernacle account just as it did in the command phase. Note that here the indefinite "they" describes the workers. Whoever they were and how many they were is never identified.

(7) Construction of the Lampstand (37:17–24) [Fulfillment of 25:31–39]

17They made the lampstand of pure gold and hammered it out, base and shaft; its flowerlike cups, buds and blossoms were of one piece with it. 18Six branches extended from the sides of the lampstand—three on one side and three on the other. 19Three cups shaped like almond flowers with buds and blossoms were on one branch, three on the next branch and the same for all six branches extending from the lampstand. 20And on the lampstand were four cups shaped like almond flowers with buds and blossoms. 21One bud was under the first pair of branches extending from the lampstand, a second bud under the second pair, and a third bud under the third pair—six branches in all. 22The buds and the branches were all of one piece with the lampstand, hammered out of pure gold.

---

282 Thus, other than Moses and the high priests after him, Bezalel may have been the last Israelite to see the ark uncovered until its capture by the Philistines in the days of the Judges (1 Sam 4:17; 5:1ff.).

[23]They made its seven lamps, as well as its wick trimmers and trays, of pure gold. [24]They made the lampstand and all its accessories from one talent of pure gold.

37:17–24 In these verses that which was commanded in 25:31–39 is reiterated, with the expected changes in verb tense and two modest exceptions: 25:37–38 is condensed into 37:23, and the word order of 25:39 is adjusted in 37:24. Again the names and numbers of workers are not mentioned here, so we do not know who and how many were the "they" that made the lampstand. With this lampstand description, the ark-table-lampstand order of the command phase (chap. 25) is again duplicated, but that pattern ends here since the incense altar was not commanded until chap. 30, even though its construction description follows immediately here. This would appear to be yet one more way Moses headed off monotony in the fulfillment section, but it may also relate to the actual construction decision-making process, no reason to delay getting at the building of the incense altar along with the ark, table, and lampstand.

(8) Construction of the Incense Altar (37:25–28) [Fulfillment of 30:1–5]

[25]They made the altar of incense out of acacia wood. It was square, a cubit long and a cubit wide, and two cubits high—its horns of one piece with it. [26]They overlaid the top and all the sides and the horns with pure gold, and made a gold molding around it. [27]They made two gold rings below the molding—two on opposite sides—to hold the poles used to carry it. [28]They made the poles of acacia wood and overlaid them with gold.

37:25–28 This paragraph follows 30:1–5 closely—essentially verbatim—with a slight wording order change in 37:25 as opposed to the wording order of 30:1 in the interests of stylistic variation and the expected verb tense changes. The original incense altar command was linked in chap. 30 with instructions for the use of incense and the atonement process for the incense altar. Those instructions (30:7–10) are not construction commands per se, and therefore we would not expect to find, and do not find, them repeated here in the fulfillment phase where construction descriptions are the focus.

(9) Composition of the Anointing Oil and the Incense (37:29) [Fulfillment of 30:22–25,34–36]

[29]They also made the sacred anointing oil and the pure, fragrant incense—the work of a perfumer.

37:29 Here the formula for the special anointing oil (30:22–25) used for priests and tabernacle objects (28:41; 29:7,21,29,36; 30:30–33; 31:11) is not repeated or described in any particulars, but Moses merely noted that "they" obeyed the command to make it. Likewise, the original, detailed description of the fragrant incense (30:34–36) and how and when it was to be used

(30:7–9,37–38) are not repeated here. This verse thus condenses in the fulfillment section a considerable amount of language from the command section. The most likely reason for this high degree of abbreviation is that the materials in question were not permanent pieces of furniture but substances intended to be used up over time, requiring reformulation periodically. The formulation descriptions thus functioned regularly as guidelines in a way that the fulfillment descriptions needed not.

(10) Construction of the Main Altar (38:1–7) [Fulfillment of 27:1–8a]

1They built the altar of burnt offering of acacia wood, three cubits high; it was square, five cubits long and five cubits wide. 2They made a horn at each of the four corners, so that the horns and the altar were of one piece, and they overlaid the altar with bronze. 3They made all its utensils of bronze—its pots, shovels, sprinkling bowls, meat forks and firepans. 4They made a grating for the altar, a bronze network, to be under its ledge, halfway up the altar. 5They cast bronze rings to hold the poles for the four corners of the bronze grating. 6They made the poles of acacia wood and overlaid them with bronze. 7They inserted the poles into the rings so they would be on the sides of the altar for carrying it. They made it hollow, out of boards.

38:1–7 Aside from the expected changes in verb tense and a modest style adjustment through word reordering (e.g., 38:4–5 reorders 27:4–5) for the sake of variety, this passage reprises 27:1–8a. The builders were now moving out from the tabernacle proper to the courtyard in their building plan. The main altar (altar of burnt offering) was one of the two courtyard objects, the other being the washing basin that will be referred to in the next verse. Moses reported that in every detail the sacrifice altar (main altar, altar of burnt offering) was built just as ordered.

(11) Construction of the Bronze Basin and Stand (38:8) [Fulfillment of 30:17–21]

8They made the bronze basin and its bronze stand from the mirrors of the women who served at the entrance to the Tent of Meeting.

38:8 Moses here concentrated mainly on the fulfillment of 30:17–18, where the basin's physical characteristics are described, and not on 30:19–21, where the proper use of the basin is described. This is to be expected since we are in a section dealing with construction of what had been ordered built, not usage—usage instructions needing no repetition here. Moses had done so with a simple summation, especially since the original command itself was not very detailed, describing simply "a bronze basin, with its bronze stand" (30:18), essentially the language repeated here.

In the original command there was no anticipation of where the bronze for this basin would come from, but since the basin was obviously a more prominent object than the other brass objects (mainly tent poles) in the courtyard, one could have anticipated that its bronze (an alloy of tin and copper) might have been of special origin if possible. Here we learn indeed that it was not just any bronze brought by donors from any source, which might have involved the possibility of slightly uneven quality. Instead, it appears to have been a very high quality bronze—polished bronze from mirrors donated by women responding to the earlier donation call (37:4). Such bronze probably was as flaw-free as any that could be found since it would have been rejected for mirror use if it were not a successful, visibly consistent alloy of pure tin and copper.

But another, quite fascinating detail is also included here: one that presumes some common knowledge that Moses and his audience shared, but that we do not.[283] At some point after the tabernacle was built, certain women were employed to serve at its entrance—a practice that probably continued as long as the tabernacle was in use, judging from the mention of it in 1 Sam 2:22, hundreds of years after the time of the present description. How were these women chosen, and what exactly did they do? We have no firm information. They quite possibly volunteered—or were paid with a portion of the sacrifices—to help with utensil cleanup,[284] general courtyard cleanup,[285] water resupply,[286] ancillary food preparation, guiding and assisting other women worshipers,[287] washing priests' clothes,[288] and the like. The first such group

[283] Moses was writing Exodus for the wilderness generation, to remind them and the new generation (those who were growing up in the wilderness and who would be the ones to enter the promised land) of what they had been through and what God's will was for them. Thus he was writing to contemporaries after the tabernacle had been completed and put into use and after the arrangements were made for women to serve at its entrance. Thus the fact that certain women eventually served at its entrance was common knowledge to him and his audience even if such an arrangement were not yet in place when the women originally donated their mirrors.

[284] See, e.g., Lev 6:28.

[285] Sacrificial animals were not housebroken. Not only so, but many body parts had to be disposed of in the process of preparing and cooking animals. Cf. 29:14; Lev 4:12,21; 6:11; 8:17; 9:11; 13:46; 16:27. Priests may have done most of the disposal work (note the masculine pronouns in many of the commands), but women may have helped in various ways.

[286] In most cultures it has primarily been a woman's job to provide water for a home, and Israelite women probably supplied the water for use in the bronze laver at the tabernacle. Cf. Gen 24:11; Exod 2:16.

[287] E.g., Lev 12. It is highly unlikely that OT priests would ever have touched women worshipers because of the sense of distance that was maintained between the genders in Bible times and because of the possibility that the woman (or man) worshiper was defiled by undisclosed contact with a dead body and therefore would ruin the priest's holiness for service. So in those cases where women required being held or led by the hand or the like (because of age or infirmity, e.g.), a trained woman worker at the entrance to the tabernacle would naturally have been the ideal person to handle the task (e.g., Num 5:16–18,24–25).

[288] Lev 6:27. Nothing explicitly tells us that women did the washing, and many passages in Leviticus sound in English as if they describe men washing their own clothes (e.g., Lev 17:15), but it would certainly be surprising if men actually did a significant proportion of clothes washing in any ancient culture at any time.

of women may have been chosen from among those who donated their mirrors, precisely because such a gift of something normally valued by a woman would tend to demonstrate her devotion to God.

(12) Construction of the Courtyard (38:9–20) [Fulfillment of 27:9–19]

9Next they made the courtyard. The south side was a hundred cubits long and had curtains of finely twisted linen, 10with twenty posts and twenty bronze bases, and with silver hooks and bands on the posts. 11The north side was also a hundred cubits long and had twenty posts and twenty bronze bases, with silver hooks and bands on the posts.

12The west end was fifty cubits wide and had curtains, with ten posts and ten bases, with silver hooks and bands on the posts. 13The east end, toward the sunrise, was also fifty cubits wide. 14Curtains fifteen cubits long were on one side of the entrance, with three posts and three bases, 15and curtains fifteen cubits long were on the other side of the entrance to the courtyard, with three posts and three bases. 16All the curtains around the courtyard were of finely twisted linen. 17The bases for the posts were bronze. The hooks and bands on the posts were silver, and their tops were overlaid with silver; so all the posts of the courtyard had silver bands.

18The curtain for the entrance to the courtyard was of blue, purple and scarlet yarn and finely twisted linen—the work of an embroiderer. It was twenty cubits long and, like the curtains of the courtyard, five cubits high, 19with four posts and four bronze bases. Their hooks and bands were silver, and their tops were overlaid with silver. 20All the tent pegs of the tabernacle and of the surrounding courtyard were bronze.

Nothing asserted in 27:9–19 is left out here, although enough variety of order and slight additions or subtractions keep the present fulfillment passage from being a mere repetition of the command on which it is based.

38:9–11 This part of the passage is virtually a verbatim reprise of 27:9–11 with the necessary verb tense changes being made and the phrase "for the tabernacle" of 27:9 being omitted.[289] Likewise, some space is saved in 38:11 with the omission of the clause "is to have curtains" from 27:11.

38:12–17 Most of these verses repeat 27:12ff., with the usual and expected changes in order to bring the description to the present context, but the content of 27:16 is delayed until 38:18, with some reordering of the wording. Additionally, 27:17 is actually expanded slightly in explicit detail in 38:17 in regard to the "tops" of the posts being "overlaid with silver," something implicit but not stated in 27:17.

38:18–20 The remainder of what has not yet been covered from chap. 27 is here addressed as completed, with the content of 27:19 somewhat rearranged and distributed throughout vv. 19–20.

---

[289] In the Hb. it is simply a single word, הַמִּשְׁכָּן, "the tabernacle." By this point in Exodus, no other courtyard is conceivably in view, but in chap. 27 the idea of the courtyard was new.

(13) Amounts of the Materials Used for the Tabernacle and Its Furnishings (38:21–31) [General Fulfillment of 25:1–3a]

[21]These are the amounts of the materials used for the tabernacle, the tabernacle of the Testimony, which were recorded at Moses' command by the Levites under the direction of Ithamar son of Aaron, the priest. [22](Bezalel son of Uri, the son of Hur, of the tribe of Judah, made everything the LORD commanded Moses; [23]with him was Oholiab son of Ahisamach, of the tribe of Dan—a craftsman and designer, and an embroiderer in blue, purple and scarlet yarn and fine linen.) [24]The total amount of the gold from the wave offering used for all the work on the sanctuary was 29 talents and 730 shekels, according to the sanctuary shekel.

[25]The silver obtained from those of the community who were counted in the census was 100 talents and 1,775 shekels, according to the sanctuary shekel— [26]one beka per person, that is, half a shekel, according to the sanctuary shekel, from everyone who had crossed over to those counted, twenty years old or more, a total of 603,550 men. [27]The 100 talents of silver were used to cast the bases for the sanctuary and for the curtain—100 bases from the 100 talents, one talent for each base. [28]They used the 1,775 shekels to make the hooks for the posts, to overlay the tops of the posts, and to make their bands.

[29]The bronze from the wave offering was 70 talents and 2,400 shekels. [30]They used it to make the bases for the entrance to the Tent of Meeting, the bronze altar with its bronze grating and all its utensils, [31]the bases for the surrounding courtyard and those for its entrance and all the tent pegs for the tabernacle and those for the surrounding courtyard.

38:21–31 This passage is somewhat unique in the present fulfillment context because it refers only obliquely to what God had commanded earlier, in 25:1–3a, at the very outset of the tabernacle design instructions rather than replicating closely the detailed word order of any of the earlier command passages. The reason is simple enough: the donations for the tabernacle were to be truly, unquestionably voluntary and therefore could not be predicted in advance, and this passage is mainly a catalog of quantities of metal donations. The other kinds of materials donated will be taken up in chap. 39.

Does this mean that the passage offers new information about the tabernacle design or construction? No, but it certainly does portray the complete success of the voluntary donation effort in terms that are hard to downplay. The Israelites did not just come up with a bit of gold, silver or bronze here or there; they gave a huge amount,[290] fulfilling every possible need and providing the

[290]The quantities of the three metals are large but by no means impossible for that time in the ancient world, especially because of the way the Israelites had despoiled the Egyptians upon leaving hastily at the time of the tenth plague (12:35–36; note the specific mention of precious metals among the things requested of and received from the Egyptians). As A. Lucas has documented, the Egyptians had by the time of the exodus established a highly productive precious metals industry capable of providing more than enough gold, silver, and bronze to equip the tabernacle in the amounts described here (*Ancient Egyptian Materials and Industries,* 3d ed., rev. [London: Edward Arnold, 1948], esp. 222–91).

tabernacle with a wealth of metallic beauty. This constitutes yet one more way of demonstrating that (a) the tabernacle was built just as it should have been—no corners had to be cut anywhere because there weren't enough materials for some of the components; and (b) the people were right with their God—they gave all that could have been expected of them because of their desire to please Yahweh (cf. 36:2–7).

38:21 The statement "these are the amounts of the materials used . . ." introduces and leads logically to the remainder of chap. 38, in which "amounts" actually refers to metal amounts—nothing else is quantified specifically. What follows in 39:1–31, however, is also concerned with describing materials used, and in a few cases within that block of verses, quantities are also indicated (e.g., vv. 10–14). Moreover, since the metal amounts in the remainder of chap. 38 are relevant to the metal objects described in chap. 39 (especially the gold mentioned throughout 39:1–31), the first words of 38:21 probably should be considered introductory to everything in 38:21–39:31.

Moses had long been alternating between the synonyms "tabernacle" and "Tent of Meeting,"[291] but here he introduced a new two-term combination, an instructive apposition, "tabernacle, the tabernacle of the Testimony."[292] This is yet another way Moses made sure his audience understood that the tabernacle was not the housing for an idol or for the actual presence of a god but was the housing for a symbol of the only God, Yahweh, and his means of grace for his people—his covenant ("the Testimony"). People were not brought to God under the Old Covenant primarily by performing rituals, including rituals at the tabernacle, important as these were. They were made part of God's family by keeping his covenant, through the obedience that comes by faith. The tablets placed in the ark were the witness/Testimony[293] to that covenant and thus to God's ongoing desire and determination to save his people and see them through to eternal life.[294]

---

[291] See comments on 33:7–11.

[292] הַמִּשְׁכָּן מִשְׁכַּן הָעֵדֻת, an obvious semantically-repetitive apposition by which he makes sure that his audience knows that the tabernacle was not merely any tent (the basic meaning of "tabernacle") but a special one that held as its most significant content the two copies on tablets of the Ten Words/Commandments.

[293] עֵדֻת can be translated by either "witness" or "testimony" as well as by "covenant" (the latter being the more common choice in many modern translations). Indeed, עֵדֻת can be understood as a straightforward synonym in the Pentateuch for בְּרִית, the word that the NIV rather consistently translates via "covenant" in contexts like the present one.

[294] A simple slogan for the essence of a covenant would be: No rules, no relationship. One of the obvious flaws of the current widespread ethos in many Western manifestations of evangelical Christianity that emphasizes the need for a relationship with God but deemphasizes the need for obedience to biblical rules is that the one cannot exist without the other. The proof of a covenant relationship is the keeping of the covenant; the proof of conversion to Christ is living a converted life.

We learn here for the first time that Moses, as one of the many checks and balances he probably imposed to do everything possible to meet perfectly the demands God had originally given him for the tabernacle, had worked out a system of recording material quantities, employing Levites in this work ("recorded at Moses' command by the Levites"). Not all scribes were Levites, and not all Levites were scribes, but some were both (cf. 1 Chr 24:6; 2 Chr 34:13; Neh 8:9; 13:13) and for good reason. As Moses trained and assigned responsibilities to the Levites, it would have become clear that one of their duties would be the proper organizing and recording of worship donations—not just those given to build the tabernacle as in the present instance but also those brought as the years went by, the various worship sacrifices at the tabernacle and later temple.[295] Likewise, since Levites were to be teachers of the law in their support role undergirding the priests, literacy among them would be called for and encouraged. At this point the Israelites were still only months away from having left Egypt; but we nevertheless see here some of the beginnings of the Levitical role as it will be developed and widened in time. Levites worked under the leadership and direction of priests, so the choice of "Ithamar," the fourth son of Aaron and therefore a person in the lineage to become high priest,[296] was logical for the leadership of such a major task as checking the materials used in the tabernacle.[297]

38:22–23 It is by now no surprise to the reader that Bezalel (see comments on 31:2; 35:30; 36:1–2; 37:1) and Oholiab (see comments on 31:6; 35:34; 36:1–2) played important oversight roles and used their personal

---

[295] Who, other than Levites, were likely to have recorded the quantities of animals offered on various occasions at the tabernacle and later temple (e.g.,1 Kgs 8:63; 1 Chr 29:21; 2 Chr 29:32; Ezra 6:17)? It was their job to assist the priests at such times in ensuring that what was prescribed was carried out.

[296] We have already encountered Ithamar briefly in 6:23 and 28:1. His role becomes prominent in Lev 10:6ff. and thereafter in Num 3–4; 7. His role as a supervisor of Levites is again evident in Num 4:28,33; 7:8. Num 3:4 indicates his prominence by noting that after the death of Nadab and Abihu, the first two sons of Aaron, Ithamar was one of only two remaining sons who "served as priests during the lifetime of their father Aaron." One gets the impression, once all the material on him and his older brother Eleazar is analyzed, that Eleazar functioned somewhat more as the actual executive high priest and Ithamar somewhat more as the administrative high priest, but the materials are scanty, and we cannot be sure if this pattern prevailed generally.

[297] Grammatically it is impossible to decide with certainty which of the following translations is superior: (1) "Ithamar, son of the priest Aaron," (2) "Ithamar, the priest, son of Aaron," or (3) the slightly (perhaps purposely) ambiguous translation used by the NIV, "Ithamar son of Aaron, the priest." But considered contextually, אִיתָמָר בֶּן־אַהֲרֹן הַכֹּהֵן is almost surely worded here (i.e., with הַכֹּהֵן, "the priest," coming last in the compound of words) to draw attention to *Ithamar's* priestly identity rather than that of Aaron and therefore to remind the reader that Ithamar functioned as a priest (eventually high priest) in his tallying role supervising Levites, and not merely as a family member (he was, after all, Moses' nephew) Moses could trust.

skills in constructing things related to the tabernacle. So why bring up one more time the fact that these two gave leadership to the project?[298] By mentioning once again Bezalel, a Judahite, along with Oholiab, a Danite, Moses very effectively reminded the reader that the tabernacle was a pan-Israelite project, not run by or overly influenced by any tribe but contributed to by any and all individuals from all tribes, as their gifts and calling dictated. These verses, as they follow v. 1, also tend to suggest that the craftsmen from the various tribes must have worked closely and harmoniously with the overseers/tallyers, who were Levites, as they in turn answered to a priest, Ithamar. Finally, it provides one more opportunity, with some variety of wording compared to prior contexts, for the assertion that the fulfillment of the tabernacle construction occurred at the base of Mount Sinai just as it had been originally commanded by God at the top of it.

38:24–25 Now Moses relayed what the Levites under Ithamar's direction learned through their careful inventorying of donations and usages: that the people had donated through the gold wave offering[299] a grand total of "29 talents and 730 shekels" of gold, which in modern terms would be at least a ton (2,000 pounds) and perhaps as much as 2,200 hundred pounds.[300] The "shekels" mentioned indicate a rather precise count for the total donation, even to the point of tallying a fraction of a talent (730 shekels add up to about 18 pounds, i.e., about a quarter of a talent) that the count showed had come in above what amounted to an even number of 29 talents (about 2,175 pounds).

We do not know for sure what a "sanctuary shekel" was. It probably was nothing more than an official measure against which others were checked, so the mention of it here is a way of pointing out that these figures on the gold donations are absolutely accurate against the official standard of measuring. It is also possible that it was heavier or lighter than other shekel standards, but no evidence exists to confirm such a second standard. Presumably what Moses intended to convey at this point was that the gold measurement could be completely trusted because it was not just estimated or roughly weighed

---

[298] Indeed, the choice by the NIV to put these verses in parentheses (a device that did not exist in Bible times) can be justified by the fact that the information per se provided about these two men is not new and would not have been required to help the reader understand that the tabernacle was built with all the metals needed. These verses stand in the narrative at this point not because the identifying details in them are required to understand who Bezalel and Oholiab were but because of the way the mention of what are by now two "old friends" to the readers, along with Ithamar, a much less well-known character, highlights effectively the cooperation between clergy and laity.

[299] See comments on 29:24; 29:26–27; 35:22.

[300] Various equivalencies are used that differ somewhat because we cannot know for sure what exact weights and measures were employed at any given ancient time and place, but it is generally thought that a talent of gold was equal to about 75 pounds and a shekel to about 2/5 of an ounce at most periods of time. When the math is done, this yields about 2,193 pounds for the amounts of gold listed in v. 24.

by someone's homemade set of weights but measured against the official standard for the nation, the one already in use to calculate proportions for sacrifices.[301]

38:26 The silver offering brought in more metal than the total of the gold and bronze combined. The total of "100 talents" (7,500 pounds) plus a fraction of a talent (1,775 shekels, i.e., about 44.4 pounds) was not, however, merely the happy but accidental result of mere voluntarism combined with a nice supply of silver throughout the populace. Instead, it came directly from the requirement of the payment of atonement money equivalent to one-half shekel per person when the census was taken (see comments on 30:11–17). Here we learn that by the time the silver was actually used, a census had already been taken,[302] that 603,550 were counted through it, and therefore the resulting amount of money came to what was raised when 603,550 was multiplied by one-half shekel and converted to talents with the fractional remainder expressed in shekels.[303]

---

[301] See 30:13,24. One reasonable conjecture is that Moses established the sanctuary shekel at Sinai sometime after arriving there to be used as the basis for measurements thereafter.

[302] The census described in Num 1 could hardly have been the first count of the people, based on the date given in Num 1, which describes a census that follows rather than precedes the date indicated for the completion of the tabernacle (Exod 40:1) by one month. The implication of this information would be that a census earlier than that of Num 1 had produced the silver in the quantity described here. But another scenario must be considered. Since the amount of the silver here described is exactly what would have been collected in connection with the Num 1 census, we could regard the census of Num 1 as actually having taken place prior to the completion of the tabernacle. This would mean that Moses had either arranged some of the material of Exodus, Leviticus, and Numbers thematically rather than strictly chronologically or that any assumption about the passage of time between the latter chapters of Exodus and the first chapters of Numbers is at best speculative. At the very most fifty days transpired in total between the setting up of the tabernacle and the departure from Sinai, in light of the dates indicated by a comparison of Exod 40:1 and Num 10:11. But nothing in the Pentateuch requires assuming that the Num 1 census was the only one taken formally at Sinai. More likely a census taken at the time of the donations for the tabernacle yielded the results described here and then was confirmed by the census a few weeks later as described in Num 1, so there was no need to describe both censuses (indeed, had Moses taken the trouble to describe both of them, skeptics would dismiss one of them as a doublet of the other). What Moses seems to have done (and quite efficiently from a narrative style point of view) was to describe one census overtly (Num 1) and let the slightly earlier census that yielded the same result remain implicit rather than explicit since he already had "covered" the topic in 30:11–16 in a context implying a census and silver collection from all Israelites prior to the actual tabernacle construction.

[303] Squaring this count with the lower numbers of Israelite fighting men arrived at by other means of analysis (see "Excursus: How Many Israelites Left Egypt?" at 12:37) remains problematic. Merely assuming that the amount of money collected has been exaggerated, as many have done, can hardly be regarded as a methodologically desirable solution. A more likely explanation might be found by starting with the assumption that the count given for shekels was based on the same sort of meaning for *ʾelep* used in the case of counting the troops, and therefore the actual amount of silver was considerably lower than what a strict modern decimal system reading of the numbers would seem to suggest.

Several facts are worth noting here. First, silver was most often used in the ancient world for small coinage or the equivalent thereof—not unlike coins in the coinage of America today, where most coins are "silver" (in appearance if not actually in fact), and higher amounts of money are not. Second, the number of Israelites indicated here is exactly the number given in the later census list summation of Num 1:46—indicating that the two passages are referring to the same event, a single census and not two. This is confirmed by the descriptions in the early chapters of Numbers of the setting up of the tabernacle, its dedication, and putting into use its implements. It is possible that the atonement money was collected well before the actual census, but it is also possible that the silvering of the tabernacle poles, bases, and hooks was one of the later tasks in the whole tabernacle construction process and therefore that the silver donation was not completed until later in the process than the gold or even bronze donation. The text does not provide enough information for us to sort this out definitively. Third, the amount indicates that everyone had complied with the goal of receiving a half shekel from each person—no matter what his societal rank—who was ready to fight and therefore was counted in the census (see 30:15). "Beka" means "split" or "half" in Hebrew and was a term used colloquially to indicate a half shekel. On "crossing over" as a way of participating in a census count, see comments on 30:13–14.[304]

38:27–28 The uses of the silver here mentioned are just as originally indicated in 26:19–25,32; 27:10–17 and the later fulfillment parallels in 36:24–36. We also learn by simple division that each silver post base weighed about seventy-five pounds and that the remainder of the silver (about 44.4 pounds) was used for hooks, bands, and tops—inside the tabernacle rather than outside (in the courtyard) where bronze was used. Most of what was visible above the floor inside the tabernacle itself had all gold surfacing decoration (cf., e.g., 36:38).

38:29–31 The bronze amounts finish the list, following the gold-silver-bronze order of metals depending on how close one was spatially to the center symbol of holiness, the ark. No details are given as to exactly what portion/poundage of the bronze was used per tent pole base in the courtyard, how much the bronze altar weighed, or how large each tent peg was. We know only the total for all bronze donated and used (other than that made from the donated mirrors as described in v. 8) as 70 talents, 2,400 shekels, or 5,310 pounds. Again we are told it was used just as commanded, that is, for

[304] I.e., the wording "crossed over" does not refer to the crossing of the Red Sea (as assumed, e.g., by P. Enns, *Exodus,* in The NIV Application Commentary [Grand Rapids: Zondervan, 2000], 549, n. 55) but to crossing over from the group of potential volunteers to the group of actual volunteers for holy war, at the invitation of the officer mustering the troops in a given location. See comments on 30:13–14.

the objects already described for us as required to be made of bronze (26:11,37; 27:2–6; 27:10–19).

With the end of chap. 38 the tabernacle itself is not yet completed (see 39:32), but its materials are in hand and its component parts are described as fashioned. There still remains for completion the matter of the priestly garments for use at the tabernacle (39:1–31). After that the next thing to be covered for the sake of completeness in the fulfillment of the tabernacle building commands was Moses' inspection of its parts—again not the assembled tabernacle but the completed parts that would be put together to set it up (chap. 40) and, for that matter, taken apart for transportation whenever the Israelites moved at Yahweh's direction.

A question remains: Why did Moses give the reader the measured amounts of the three metals but nothing else? After all, he did not tell what quantity of acacia wood was used, or how much yarn, or how many sea cow hides, or the like. Only the gold, silver, and bronze are inventoried for the reader. The answer must be found in two considerations: (1) the three metals were by far the most costly—most precious—ingredients in the tabernacle construction; and (2) the three metals had a special significance because of their splendor, used as indicators of proximity to the symbols of Yahweh's presence.

As regards the first of these considerations, the cost/preciousness of the metals, listing the large amounts received from the Israelites of each of the three of them was a way of showing the people's dedication to Yahweh and their desire to honor him by making his symbolic dwelling place all that it should be—a grand residence for the greatest Being, the God above all gods. As regards the second of these considerations, the proximity indication with the type of metal used, the fact that the silver and gold far outweighed the bronze, shows how splendid (solid gold) was the ark and its immediate surroundings (the interior of the tabernacle, where gold never touched the ground and silver was never visible above the bases of the frames), which was the inaccessible part of the tabernacle, the part never even seen by the average Israelite. The use of bronze for the more accessible area, the courtyard, indicated a degree of holiness because of the relative value of bronze. But it also indicated its relatively diminished holiness because a courtyard was a space where virtually anyone could enter, as opposed to a house, where only the servants were admitted, and then only to the outer room in the case of the two-room tabernacle.

(14) Construction of the Priestly Garments (39:1–31) [Fulfillment of 28:2–43][305]

[1]From the blue, purple and scarlet yarn they made woven garments for ministering in the sanctuary. They also made sacred garments for Aaron, as the LORD commanded Moses.

[2]They made the ephod of gold, and of blue, purple and scarlet yarn, and of finely twisted linen. [3]They hammered out thin sheets of gold and cut strands to be worked into the blue, purple and scarlet yarn and fine linen—the work of a skilled craftsman. [4]They made shoulder pieces for the ephod, which were attached to two of its corners, so it could be fastened. [5]Its skillfully woven waistband was like it—of one piece with the ephod and made with gold, and with blue, purple and scarlet yarn, and with finely twisted linen, as the LORD commanded Moses.

[6]They mounted the onyx stones in gold filigree settings and engraved them like a seal with the names of the sons of Israel. [7]Then they fastened them on the shoulder pieces of the ephod as memorial stones for the sons of Israel, as the LORD commanded Moses.

[8]They fashioned the breastpiece—the work of a skilled craftsman. They made it like the ephod: of gold, and of blue, purple and scarlet yarn, and of finely twisted linen. [9]It was square—a span long and a span wide—and folded double. [10] Then they mounted four rows of precious stones on it. In the first row there was a ruby, a topaz and a beryl; [11]in the second row a turquoise, a sapphire and an emerald; [12]in the third row a jacinth, an agate and an amethyst; [13]in the fourth row a chrysolite, an onyx and a jasper. They were mounted in gold filigree settings. [14]There were twelve stones, one for each of the names of the sons of Israel, each engraved like a seal with the name of one of the twelve tribes.

[15]For the breastpiece they made braided chains of pure gold, like a rope. [16]They made two gold filigree settings and two gold rings, and fastened the rings to two of the corners of the breastpiece. [17]They fastened the two gold chains to the rings at the corners of the breastpiece, [18]and the other ends of the chains to the two settings, attaching them to the shoulder pieces of the ephod at the front. [19]They made two gold rings and attached them to the other two corners of the breastpiece on the inside edge next to the ephod. [20]Then they made two more gold rings and attached them to the bottom of the shoulder pieces on the front of the ephod, close to the seam just above the waistband of the ephod. [21]They tied the rings of the breastpiece to the rings of the ephod with blue cord, connecting it to the waistband so that the breastpiece would not swing out from the ephod—as the LORD commanded Moses.

---

[305] This section has eleven verses fewer than the instructions section that parallels it in chap. 28. The condensations are of various sorts, though mainly limited to fewer details in the descriptions of the apparel items mentioned and the general omission of wording related to the purpose and function of that apparel. As we have already noted, purpose and function descriptions were not given fulfillment descriptions because the purpose of the fulfillment descriptions was to demonstrate the actual manufacture of material things, not their employment.

[22]They made the robe of the ephod entirely of blue cloth—the work of a weaver—[23]with an opening in the center of the robe like the opening of a collar, and a band around this opening, so that it would not tear. [24]They made pomegranates of blue, purple and scarlet yarn and finely twisted linen around the hem of the robe. [25]And they made bells of pure gold and attached them around the hem between the pomegranates. [26]The bells and pomegranates alternated around the hem of the robe to be worn for ministering, as the LORD commanded Moses.

[27]For Aaron and his sons, they made tunics of fine linen—the work of a weaver—[28]and the turban of fine linen, the linen headbands and the undergarments of finely twisted linen. [29]The sash was of finely twisted linen and blue, purple and scarlet yarn—the work of an embroiderer—as the LORD commanded Moses.

[30]They made the plate, the sacred diadem, out of pure gold and engraved on it, like an inscription on a seal: HOLY TO THE LORD. [31]Then they fastened a blue cord to it to attach it to the turban, as the LORD commanded Moses.

OVERVIEW (39:1) [Fulfillment of 28:2–5]. **39:1** Repeatedly in the command portions and also in the earlier fulfillment portions of the tabernacle texts in Exodus the phrase "blue, purple and scarlet yarn" has appeared (see comments on 25:4; 26:1,31,36; 27:16; 28:5–6,8,15,33; cf. 35:6,35; 36:8,35,37; 38:18,23). These reds and blues were associated with royalty and conveyed sovereignty and greatness—thus being appropriate for a Great King's tabernacle and for the vestments of those who served as his servants in it (the priests). Here the fulfillment section concentrates on the priests' vestments: those of the high priest primarily ("the sacred garments for Aaron"; cf. 28:2) but as well the priestly robes, referred to here as "the woven garments."

CONSTRUCTION OF THE EPHOD (39:2–7) [Fulfillment of 28:6–14]. **39:2–7** In the present passage 39:2 ("gold . . . yarn . . . linen") reprises most of 28:6 verbatim, with the phrase at the end of 28:6, "the work of a skilled craftsman," being placed at the end of 39:3 in the fulfillment description.[306] Verse 3 explains how the command of 28:6–8, which required that the gold be blended with the yarn and linen, was accomplished: the gold was hammered into sheets and then cut[307] into thin strands so that it

---

[306] For this verse (39:2) the MT reads "he," referring to Bezalel as the sole crafter of the ephod. The NIV has either obscured this with a stylistic harmonization ("they") or decided to read the plural, "they," with the SP and the Peshitta, both of which probably used the plural more for translation consistency than because they actually had a plural in their respective Hb. *Vorlagen*.

[307] The MT indicates again with the singular ("he") that Bezalel was the one who cut the thin strips of gold, although a number of other ancient text witnesses employ some form of plural here (SP, Tgs., Peshitta). The plurals are more likely to be the result of a translation decision for the sake of consistency than because of an actual Hb. plural in the text being looked at by those translators (cf. note above).

could be interwoven with the yarn and linen.[308] This produced a patterned cloth that must have sparkled brightly yet would have been entirely flexible and wearable as a fabric. Thereafter, 39:4 reprises 28:7; 39:5 reprises 28:8; 39:6 condenses and thereby summarizes 28:9–11; and 39:7 condenses and summarizes 28:12–14.

CONSTRUCTION OF THE BREASTPIECE (39:8–21) [Fulfillment of 28:15–28]. **39:8–21** These verses reprise 28:15–28 verbatim except for the usual and necessary changes of verb tenses expected in the fulfillment part of the book as opposed to the command part and the following small differences: 28:23 is modified slightly in 39:16 by adding specific mention of the "two gold filigree settings,"[309] and at the end of 39:21 Moses added the wording "as Yahweh commanded Moses," thus providing convenient reference back to the command section and making the point once again that what was produced was what was designed by God. In the original command context, 28:29–30, the explanation for the symbolism of the breastpiece was provided; that is not necessary here, in a context that concentrates on what was manufactured rather than how it was used. Indeed, virtually nothing in the present context is concerned with how anything was actually used in worship (or in the case of the Urim and Thummim, omitted here,[310] in worshipful divination). So no parallel to 28:29–30 is found located between the description of the breastpiece and that of the robe. These slight variations maintain a degree of welcome stylistic novelty without actually changing anything significant from the command to its fulfillment in the manufacture of the breastpiece.

---

[308] Metalworkers can hammer gold into sheets as thin as a thousandth of an inch since gold has such a high malleability and tensile strength; but the thickness of the gold "fabric" used in the ephod can only be guessed at—perhaps a few thousandths of an inch for durability and flexibility combined. Lucas confirms that the present description of making gold thread/lace was already developed by the Egyptians and therefore, by implication, would have been known to a person such as Bezalel from his training in Egypt (*Ancient Egyptian Materials and Industries,* 263–65).

[309] At this point the SP (alone) adds the wording "and they made the Urim and Thummim just as Yahweh had commanded Moses," which seems likely to be more a translator's harmonization for the sake of what he regarded as completeness than a preservation of wording lost in all other traditions.

[310] The Urim and Thummim are perhaps the most notable items described in chap. 28 (vv. 30-31) that are not mentioned at all in the fulfillment parallel of the present context. Not a few scholars have commented on this omission, some taking the approach that the whole concept of the Urim and Thummim must have been secondary to the tabernacle narrative if their manufacture could actually be left out of a major fulfillment section like this. But the lack of mention of the Urim and Thummim is simply consistent with Moses' purpose in this part of Exodus: to describe what was made and omit what it was made for. The Urim and Thummim, being in all probability simply light and dark stones, would have been more or less found objects and not things to be manufactured (though they may have been shaped or finished in some way) and thus are omitted here in concert with the standard practice of omitting virtually any mention of purpose and use for anything.

CONSTRUCTION OF THE ROBE (39:22–26) [Fulfillment of 28:31–35]. **39:22–26** In this section of fulfillment description, 39:22 repeats 28:31 with the words "the work of a weaver" added (an expression not found anywhere in the command materials, although the need for people with the skill of a weaver was mentioned 35:35). Common sense would indicate that looms operated by skillful weavers were thus required for the making of the cloth for the extraordinary priestly robes.[311]

Thereafter, 39:23 slightly rewords but does not change the sense of 28:32, and 39:24 reprises 28:33 with the addition of "and finely twisted linen," leaving out the words in 28:33 "with gold bells between" them since this idea is picked up instead by 39:25–26. Indeed, 39:25–26 rewords 28:33b–34 and adds "to be worn for ministering" as a description of the purpose of the robe, a summation of the fuller purpose description in 28:35. This purpose description, short as it is, is relatively unusual. As noted above, purpose descriptions are either omitted in the fulfillment context or shortened to the minimum since accuracy of fulfillment was the issue, not the purpose of the thing being constructed. The purpose will be addressed in the stories and instructions about use and action, as described in Leviticus and Numbers.

CONSTRUCTION OF THE TUNICS AND TURBAN (39:27–31) [Fulfillment of 28:36–43]. **39:27–31** The most important words in this section of the fulfillment description, as in so many other places in the present general context, are "as Yahweh commanded Moses," found here twice, in v. 29 and v. 31, following their earlier occurrences in vv. 1,5,7,21,26. The Hebrew for this clause could also be translated "just as Yahweh had commanded Moses."[312] It reminds the reader that the tabernacle and everything made for it, here specifically priestly vestments, were designed by Yahweh (not Moses or Aaron or anyone else), revealed to the Israelites through the very words of God delivered to Moses on Mount Sinai, and then manufactured by people so obedient to and under the control of Yahweh that what they made was just exactly, precisely, specifically what he wanted made. It all turned out perfectly to his specification and therefore to his liking—so it could then function as it was supposed to, to provide for proper, approved worship acceptable to the one being worshiped.

Worship is absolutely basic to a proper relationship to God, and if that worship can take place properly, then the relationship can begin properly with a reasonable hope of growing to maturity and productivity. Skewed worship would undermine one's relationship to God from the very start and likely lead

---

[311] Since weaving is a skill that takes years to master, the emphasis on the requirement that the best fabric, that of the priests' robes, be woven by an expert weaver makes perfect sense; trusting the assignment to anyone but an expert would potentially result in inferior fabrics.

[312] כַּאֲשֶׁר צִוָּה יְהוָה אֶת־מֹשֶׁה, translated by Durham "exactly as Yahweh had commanded Moses" (*Exodus*, 493).

to an odd, distorted, and ineffective relationship with the one to whom a worshiper's praise and adoration should be directed as soundly and joyfully as possible. It would have been a tragedy for the Israelites to have undermined their chances for a right relationship with Yahweh by disobeying, even unintentionally, his will regarding the place of, and manner of, worship. By his grace, however, there was no tragedy; Israel worshiped with a high degree of consistency where and as they should, at least while Moses remained alive.

What 28:36–43 required is reprised here but in a different order and with the wording often considerably condensed. Here 39:27 rewords 28:39 (e.g., the imperative "weave the tunic of fine linen" of 28:39 appears as the indicative "they made tunics of fine linen—the work of a weaver"). Exodus 39:28 picks up and condenses or in some cases slightly expands various parts of 28:37 ("turban"), 28:39 ("turban of fine linen"), 28:40 ("headbands"), and 28:42 (linen undergarments). Also 39:29 connects to 28:39–40 ("sash") as well as to 28:39 ("fine linen, the work of an embroiderer") and even to some extent to 28:29 (with its general specification of "blue, purple and scarlet yarn"). The mention of the turban "plate" and its inscription in 39:30 recalls 28:36, though with modified wording, and the reference to the attaching "cord" for the turban plate (39:31) repeats the essence of 28:38.

(15) Moses' Inspection Finds All Materials Made as Commanded by God (39:32–43) [Fulfillment of 35:10–19]

[32]So all the work on the tabernacle, the Tent of Meeting, was completed. The Israelites did everything just as the LORD commanded Moses. [33]Then they brought the tabernacle to Moses: the tent and all its furnishings, its clasps, frames, crossbars, posts and bases; [34]the covering of ram skins dyed red, the covering of hides of sea cows and the shielding curtain; [35]the ark of the Testimony with its poles and the atonement cover; [36]the table with all its articles and the bread of the Presence; [37]the pure gold lampstand with its row of lamps and all its accessories, and the oil for the light; [38]the gold altar, the anointing oil, the fragrant incense, and the curtain for the entrance to the tent; [39]the bronze altar with its bronze grating, its poles and all its utensils; the basin with its stand; [40]the curtains of the courtyard with its posts and bases, and the curtain for the entrance to the courtyard; the ropes and tent pegs for the courtyard; all the furnishings for the tabernacle, the Tent of Meeting; [41]and the woven garments worn for ministering in the sanctuary, both the sacred garments for Aaron the priest and the garments for his sons when serving as priests.

[42]The Israelites had done all the work just as the LORD had commanded Moses. [43]Moses inspected the work and saw that they had done it just as the LORD had commanded. So Moses blessed them.

From an accomodationist, human point of view, one might be tempted to forgive the Israelites if they encountered difficulty completing the tabernacle in all facets and therefore had to start worshiping at it when it was not yet fully furnished, or perhaps before all of its surfaces were completely overlaid with the precious metals required in the instructions. After all, they were working in a wilderness on this project, relying solely on donated materials, using at least some tools that might have had to be manufactured after leaving Egypt—so who could blame them if they didn't completely finish the tabernacle and do a perfect job on every detail the first time around? But that was not the case because it was not what God would have allowed. "All the work . . . was completed (v. 32); they "did everything just as the LORD [had] commanded Moses" (vv. 32,42); "Moses inspected the work and saw that they had done it just as the LORD had commanded" (v. 43). So full had been the participation of the people, so generous their donations, so skilled the workmen, so diligent the experts assigned to the work, so high in quality the materials, and so precisely inspected the final product that the tabernacle was just right—a perfect fulfillment of the divinely revealed ideal and a flawless place at which to worship the only true God. The present passage reassures the reader of these facts. Israel was off to a proper start in its covenant relationship with God: it had the place and means of worship exactly as it should have had them.[313]

Many things related to the tabernacle remain to be addressed, however—even things that impinge directly on the tabernacle. For example, in Leviticus and Numbers the reader finds that Moses recorded extensive divine guidance (including oversight and approval) on such matters as how and why sacrifices were to be offered at the tabernacle,[314] how and why priests were to be consecrated/ordained for service at the tabernacle,[315] how the

---

[313] The text contains no indication of how much time it took for the Israelites to construct all the tabernacle components. Since the Israelites were at Sinai slightly less than a year (comparing Exod 19:1 with Num 10:11 and observing that the tabernacle was finished at the turn of the year according to 40:17) and Moses gave the people the tabernacle instructions after a variety of events including the golden young bull idolatry, the forty days on Mount Sinai, earlier sojourns on the mountain, and teaching the populace following those sojourns, we can estimate that not more than seven or eight months at the most were available for the construction of the tabernacle. But this was not important for Moses to relay; what he cared about was the quality of the product, not the time it took to produce it. Indeed, the story gives the impression that the Israelites were under no time pressure at all to produce the tabernacle but rather were expected to take all the time they would needed to be sure that it fully met the design God revealed to Moses. Timing didn't matter as much as did precise conformity to design.

[314] Lev 1–7, as well as most of Lev 8–9. The topics of Lev 1–7 (or 1–9, depending on how one views the structure of Leviticus), do not so much "interrupt" the tabernacle narrative (as some scholars have tried to suggest) as to round out the necessary instructions on worship—being logically supplemented by the ordination and priestly service narratives of Lev 8–9—that are absolutely essential prerequisites to putting the tabernacle finally into use and receiving visible divine acceptance of the tabernacle as a place Yahweh approves of and at which he will manifest his glorious presence (Lev 9:23–24).

[315] I.e., Lev 8–9, following on such passages in Exod as 29:1–46 and some of the shorter passages alluding to priestly duties such as 30;30–33 or 34:25.

tabernacle was to be set up and taken down, and where it was to be placed within the Israelite encampment,[316] and so on. In other words, the end of Exodus was not the end of the tabernacle story, nor was the narrative of the completion of the tabernacle materials to be equated to the completion of what Moses would have to say about the purpose and function of the tabernacle.

39:32 This verse introduces the summational statement of tabernacle completion that follows, with a comprehensive overview, in five ways: (1) it employs both common terms for the tabernacle ("tabernacle, the Tent of Meeting") so that even the most casual reader, or someone entirely new to the book of Exodus, would not be confused about which structure was in mind; (2) it uses the past tense, "was completed," as a way of indicating the finality of the work; (3) it reminds the reader that the project was a national/community project simply by saying "the Israelites did";[317] (4) it establishes that the total project was complete by saying "everything"; and (5) it confirms that all was properly done with the common clause "just as the LORD commanded Moses." Whenever God's people carry out an assignment correctly and fully, it is a source of great delight, as it certainly should be. What could be more important on earth than to do the will of heaven (Matt 6:10)?

39:33a "Then they brought the tabernacle to Moses" signals three important points. (1) The tabernacle was something moveable—something that could be broken down into its component parts and transported. This was important because its location symbolized God's nearness to his people. Had there been difficulty in bringing it to Moses, there would certainly have been the possibility of difficulty in transporting it from place to place along with everything else the Israelites had to carry with them on their journeys in the years ahead.[318] (2) The inspection process was now about to begin, conducted by the only person truly qualified among all Israelites to do the task. Neither Aaron nor any of his sons nor Bezalel nor Oholiab nor any other human had seen the tabernacle design revealed on Mount Sinai as Moses had. It fell to Moses to inspect everything, and once the people were in the process of bringing the tabernacle components to him for his inspection, the construction project was coming to an end. (3) The work had to be perfect. Moses held the right and responsibility to reject any aspect of the construction that did not meet the standards revealed to him within the divine glory cloud of Sinai. That he did not need to reject anything, but found all in order,

[316] Esp. Num 1; 3–4; 7; 9–10; 31.

[317] The Hb. wording can also be translated "the Israelites made . . ."

[318] Of course, at this point they did not yet know they would be moving through the wilderness for thirty-nine additional years. The portability and durability of the tabernacle would turn out to be even more essential than the Israelites themselves might yet have assumed necessary.

is testimony to the fidelity of the people to the whole process—donations, prefabrications, final fabrications, weaving, carpentry, metalworking—and therefore testimony by implication to the desire to obey God that prevailed, at least at that time and location, throughout the nation.

39:33b–41 These verses cover essentially the same ground as did 35:11–19, which called for these materials and component parts of the tabernacle to be constructed. Present here are some of the sorts of differences that by now in the tabernacle narrative we have come to expect as routine in the fulfillment part of the book: slight expansions, slight contractions, and word order adjustments to provide a modicum of variation and obviate tedium.[319] But nothing here ignores what is in 35:11–19, so the present passage makes clear that every individual part of the tabernacle and its furnishings was produced and brought to Moses just as expected by God.

39:42–43 Of special import here is the comment that Moses "inspected the work,"[320] which would hardly have been limited to a cursory look to be sure everything was present and accounted for but presumably included examining closely the quality of the expert labor or workmanship. When he checked the ark, he was not looking merely for an ark covered with gold; he was looking for what would correspond exactly, in every detail, to what he had seen on Mount Sinai when God revealed the ark plan to him. And so his inspection was a matter of quality control and not merely a determination of completion of required objects.

After confirming by inspecting it that all the work was done "just as the LORD had commanded" him (see above), Moses then "blessed" the Israelites. What exactly does this mean? What did Moses do to bless the Israelites? The answer is that he said a kind of prayer,[321] probably a relatively brief one, probably worded in the third person—a precative (wish) expression of desire that God would bring benefit to his people.

Blessing someone or some group was a common practice in biblical times. Earlier in Exodus even Pharaoh had asked Moses for a blessing, that is, a prayer expressed as a benediction asking God to benefit him (Exod

[319] Examples include the way 39:34 uses the wording "the covering of ram skins dyed red, the covering of hides of sea cows" to expand with specificity on what was summarized simply by the two words "its covering" (one word in Hb.) in 35:11; "the ark" of 35:12 is called "the ark of the Testimony" here in 39:35; "the lampstand" in 35:14 is described as "the pure gold lampstand" in 39:37, and the wording "that is for light with its accessories" in 35:14 becomes "with its row of lamps and all its accessories" in 39:37; and so on. Note that some apparent differences between the present passage and 35:10–19 are due simply to the NIV translation inconsistency. E.g., the same Hb. phrase, פָּרֹכֶת הַמָּסָךְ, is rendered by the NIV "the shielding curtain" in 39:34 but "the curtain that shields it" in 35:12.

[320] מְלָאכָה, which tends to include not just "work" but "labor," "workmanship."

[321] For an extensive discussion of the topic, see C. Westermann, *Blessing* (Philadelphia: Fortress, 1978).

12:32). When God blesses someone or something, he declares that person or thing to be blessed, that is, fortunate because that person or thing will receive benefit from God.[322] The parade example in all of Moses' writings of an occasion where the people were blessed by one of their leaders—that is, a situation at least generally comparable to the present one—is that of the Aaronic blessing of Num 6:22–27.[323] That blessing is especially instructive for us because of its divine definition of what a blessing consists of. God instructed Moses on how a blessing should be delivered in saying: "This is how you are to bless the Israelites. Say to them . . ." What follows is a type of prayer in which a priest (at least in the case of Num 6:22–27) asks God through a precative[324] to give benefit to the people:

May Yahweh bless you and keep you;
may Yahweh make his face shine upon you
and be gracious to you;
may Yahweh turn his face toward you and give you peace.[325]

There is an assumption of divine approval inherent in such a blessing. The person giving the blessing cannot control God and cannot speak for him without permission. He cannot *make* God bless someone or something just by saying the right words. But if he "has the mind of" God—that is, if he correctly understands God's will—then his prayer said in the form of a wish can be assumed to have a certain force, to be more than a pure wish (i.e., merely a type of hope) and, in fact, a true declaration of God's intention to provide benefit for the person or thing being blessed. The Num 6 blessing looks forward to the following benefits from God: keeping (God's watching

---

[322] Examples already encountered in Exodus include 20:11, blessing the Sabbath, i.e., making it a day with divine benefits; 20:24, blessing the people as a result of their proper worship; 23:25, blessing what people eat and drink so that it would not do them harm; and 32:29, blessing the Levites for their faithfulness in helping root out idolatry from among the people.

[323] The event in Lev 9:23, where "Moses and Aaron . . . blessed the people" after coming out of the newly erected tabernacle (there called Tent of Meeting) surely is also parallel, but it does not give any hint of the content of the blessing, i.e., what words might have been said, any more than does the present account.

[324] The precatives in Hb. are usually distinguishable by their third-person form and sometimes even by their apocopated, specially accented morphology (especially in what are called "weak" verbs). They are usually translated by such terms as may/may it be that/I wish that/let it be as follows, or the like. The terms "jussive" and "volitive" are also employed by Hb. grammarians as synonyms of "precative."

[325] The precatives (or jussives or volitives) of the Hb. text are not simple indicatives but are verb forms that connote a wish or desire and therefore may also be translated more obviously than the NIV does ("the LORD bless you"), as, e.g., "May Yahweh bless you." Alternatively, the Hb. could perfectly well be translated in such a way as to make explicit what is implicit in blessing prayers: "It is my prayer that Yahweh should bless you and keep you; that Yahweh should make his face shine upon you and be gracious to you; that Yahweh should turn his face toward you and give you peace."

over people for good—caring for them and guiding them through life's dangers), a shining face (general favor and benefit),[326] being gracious (giving things that weren't earned but that will be much appreciated), turning the face toward (paying special favorable attention to), and giving peace (wellness, wholeness, full-orbed good fortune). A blessing does not imply a promise that nothing negative will ever happen to the person being blessed, but it does imply a desire that much good will happen to that person.

What specifically did Moses say to the people by way of a blessing? We do not know. It may well have been something brief and generally applicable like the Aaronic blessing of Num 6, but its exact content was not important enough in the narrative for Moses to quote it. He said only that he blessed the people in response to their nationwide holy construction effort, thus reassuring them that what they had done was approved and that they were in the favor of their covenant Lord, Yahweh.

(16) Moses Sets Up of the Tabernacle (40:1–33)

[1]Then the LORD said to Moses: [2]"Set up the tabernacle, the Tent of Meeting, on the first day of the first month. [3]Place the ark of the Testimony in it and shield the ark with the curtain. [4]Bring in the table and set out what belongs on it. Then bring in the lampstand and set up its lamps. [5]Place the gold altar of incense in front of the ark of the Testimony and put the curtain at the entrance to the tabernacle.

[6]"Place the altar of burnt offering in front of the entrance to the tabernacle, the Tent of Meeting; [7]place the basin between the Tent of Meeting and the altar and put water in it. [8]Set up the courtyard around it and put the curtain at the entrance to the courtyard.

[9]"Take the anointing oil and anoint the tabernacle and everything in it; consecrate it and all its furnishings, and it will be holy. [10]Then anoint the altar of burnt offering and all its utensils; consecrate the altar, and it will be most holy. [11]Anoint the basin and its stand and consecrate them.

[12]"Bring Aaron and his sons to the entrance to the Tent of Meeting and wash them with water. [13]Then dress Aaron in the sacred garments, anoint him and consecrate him so he may serve me as priest. [14]Bring his sons and dress them in tunics. [15]Anoint them just as you anointed their father, so they may serve me as priests. Their anointing will be to a priesthood that will continue for all generations to come." [16]Moses did everything just as the LORD commanded him.

[17]So the tabernacle was set up on the first day of the first month in the second year. [18]When Moses set up the tabernacle, he put the bases in place, erected the frames, inserted the crossbars and set up the posts. [19]Then he spread the tent over the tabernacle and put the covering over the tent, as the LORD commanded him.

---

[326] On the whole concept of the face of a deity imparting life-giving, beneficial light, see J. J. Niehaus, *God at Sinai*, 226–29.

[20]He took the Testimony and placed it in the ark, attached the poles to the ark and put the atonement cover over it. [21]Then he brought the ark into the tabernacle and hung the shielding curtain and shielded the ark of the Testimony, as the LORD commanded him.

[22]Moses placed the table in the Tent of Meeting on the north side of the tabernacle outside the curtain [23]and set out the bread on it before the LORD, as the LORD commanded him.

[24]He placed the lampstand in the Tent of Meeting opposite the table on the south side of the tabernacle [25]and set up the lamps before the LORD, as the LORD commanded him.

[26]Moses placed the gold altar in the Tent of Meeting in front of the curtain [27]and burned fragrant incense on it, as the LORD commanded him. [28]Then he put up the curtain at the entrance to the tabernacle.

[29]He set the altar of burnt offering near the entrance to the tabernacle, the Tent of Meeting, and offered on it burnt offerings and grain offerings, as the LORD commanded him.

[30]He placed the basin between the Tent of Meeting and the altar and put water in it for washing, [31]and Moses and Aaron and his sons used it to wash their hands and feet. [32]They washed whenever they entered the Tent of Meeting or approached the altar, as the LORD commanded Moses.

[33]Then Moses set up the courtyard around the tabernacle and altar and put up the curtain at the entrance to the courtyard. And so Moses finished the work.

GOD'S COMMAND TO SET UP THE TABERNACLE (40:1–16). **40:1** In Exodus "the first month" refers to mid-March to mid-April, as already defined in 12:2,18. The Israelites, along with many other ancient peoples, regarded the turn of the year as taking place at the end of winter and the beginning of spring rather than sometime after the start of winter, as is the modern tendency. The tabernacle had been finished in just under a year from the time the Israelites had left Egypt.[327] For it to be set up on the first day of the first month of the year represented a way of celebrating the new year—in effect a way of linking the new year with worship.[328]

By commanding Moses to set up the tabernacle "on the first day of the first month," God was also indicating that the whole job could be done in a day. The tabernacle was intended to be highly portable, and its portability would be tested with the first setup. Worship was so important to the travel-

[327] Comparing Exod 12:17 with 40:2.

[328] Even though the tabernacle was only a building set up on the first day of the first month, its purpose was worship, and it is significant that this first erection of the tabernacle was undertaken at God's command on a special day in the year. The modern practice in many churches of recognizing the advent of a new year by a worship service or prayer vigil thus has a kind of OT precedent, though one to be sure that did not actually involve a worship service per se on the new year but rather an erection of a building. By implication, a celebration of the new year would have been included, however, in each year's calendar rather automatically with the celebration of the new moon (Num 10:10; 28:14; Ps 81:3).

ing Israelites that had they required more than a few hours to set up their tabernacle, it would potentially have hindered their ability to move quickly, at God's command, in the wilderness.

40:2–8 Here Moses was required to set up the tabernacle itself, that is, the tent structure (v. 2), then to set up the ark, the single piece of furniture in the holy of holies, being sure it was not visible to anyone outside the holy of holies by shielding it with the floor-to-ceiling curtain (v. 3). He then set up the furniture in the holy place, also shielded from general view by a curtain (vv. 4–5), the furniture for the courtyard (vv. 6–7), and the enclosure curtains for the courtyard (v. 8). These items, their construction, and their placement have been reviewed several times already in Exod 25–27; 30–31; 35–39, so the summary of the erection of them is appropriately brief, without much supporting detail.

40:9–11 The need to anoint and the process of anointing the tabernacle and its furniture was already adumbrated in 29:36; 30 and especially 30:25–29, so the fulfillment of that command can be reviewed here succinctly as finally completed at the occasion of the first erection of the tabernacle. Anointing symbolizes cleanness and purity, as discussed already in chap. 29. These items of furniture had a sacred purpose; their proximity to Yahweh's symbolized presence in the holy of holies reflected that sacredness and required recognition by the anointing ceremony that they were part of the holiest place in the nation.

40:12–15 These verses represent the outcome of what was ordered in chaps. 28–29. But there is an important significance in the wording here: it is partly predictive in saying that "their anointing will be to a priesthood that will continue . . ." In fact, that anointing would take place some days later, in the event described in Lev 8, when the actual ordination[329] through the prescribed anointing and offering of sacrifices is recorded in the biblical record.[330]

40:16 The reassurance that "*Moses did everything just as the LORD commanded him*" is a type of summary statement that begins a sequence of such summaries (usually via the shorter wording "*as the LORD commanded him*") that strongly support the concept of precision of fulfillment characterizing the chapter (vv. 19,21,23,25,27,29,32). Moses was not the maker of the tabernacle, but he was its quality control supervisor, who saw by personal inspection that it conformed to all that Yahweh had directed on Mt. Sinai. He had the authority to reject any part of it should it fail to meet divinely-revealed

---

[329] This was indeed a formal instruction to ordain Aaron and his sons in spite of the fact that the context's brevity does not include any of the usual Hb. terms for ordination.

[330] The NIV translation of the parts of v. 9 ("and it will be holy") and v. 10 ("and it will be most holy") also contain future tenses, of course, but the future orientation of vv. 12–15 is even more overt.

standards, but by reason of God's merciful involvement in the whole process, he found no flaws at all.

MOSES SETS UP THE TABERNACLE (40:17–33). **40:17** Did the erection of the tabernacle just happen to fall on New Year's Day, or was it put together that day as a further indication of its importance? The text does not overtly tell us, but it is hard to argue against the likelihood that such an auspicious day was chosen for the first tabernacle setup because it fit with the fact that the tabernacle itself was so auspicious as a sign of God's presence among the Israelites. In other words, when the tabernacle component parts were all ready to assemble, they probably were not assembled immediately but rather were kept ready by Moses (for several days? several weeks?) for the first day of the new year when he would put everything together and thus symbolically house Yahweh in the midst of his people.

The first month was an important time in the Israelite calendar, not only because it was the time established for the Exodus-honoring Passover festival (12:12ff.) but also because it was apparently God's intention that it be closely connected with the tabernacle (see Num 9:15–23). Thus the first Passover celebrated in the wilderness—that of the first month of the second year—required the erection of and availability of the tabernacle for the presentation of the appropriate Passover offering there by all Israelites (Num 9:7,12–13; cf. Exod 23:15, "No one is to appear before me empty-handed"). The exact chronology of the events described in Exod 40, Leviticus, and Num 1–9 is hard to establish definitively, but much of that entire block of Scripture revolves around the first month of the second year the Israelites came out of Egypt and during which they were camped at Sinai.[331]

40:18–19 These verses describe in summary fashion the actual assembly of the tabernacle framework, curtains, and covering, as commanded in detail originally in chap. 26, ending with what might be called the "theme statement" of this chapter, "as the LORD commanded him."

40:20–21 These verses sum up the placement of the tablets of the Ten Words/Commandments (the "testimony") in the ark and covering those tablets with the ark's special cover and then setting the ark within the holy of holies with the floor-to-ceiling dividing curtain that separated it from the

---

[331] Further on the significance of the first day of the month, see Num 9:1,5 and Josh 4:19. Note also that the new moon festival each month provided a natural sort of, culturally expected, setting for solemn religious celebrations (see esp. Num 29:6). Indeed, what the NIV routinely translates "month" could often be more precisely rendered "new moon," as in, e.g., Exod 19:1, "On the third new moon after the Israelites had gone out of the land of Egypt, on that very day, they came into the wilderness of Sinai" (NRSV). If the Israelites arrived at Sinai on a new moon, there to receive the covenant from Yahweh their God, it makes sense that God would also link the tabernacle to the covenant in yet one more way, by causing its setting up to occur on the new moon—in this case at the turn of the year as well.

holy place (25:10–22; 26:33–34). Again the chapter's theme statement, "as the LORD commanded him," concludes this paragraph.

40:22–23 This short paragraph summarizes the placement of the table in the holy place of the tabernacle with the bread of the presence on it, as originally required by the instructions of 25:23–30; it too concludes with the (by now expected) characteristic theme words "as the LORD commanded him."

40:24–25 Moses placed the lampstand and lamps within the holy place as well, "as the LORD commanded him" originally in 25:31–40; 26:35, on the south side of the holy place or left side as one faced toward the holy of holies (the tabernacle being oriented with its opening curtains to the east (27:13–16).

40:26–28 The gold incense altar went into the holy place as well, right in front of the special curtain that created the barrier to the holy of holies, thus finishing the placement of furnishings (table, lampstand, altar) for the holy place of the tabernacle. Earlier in Exodus no specific instruction to Moses required that he burn the incense at this point, so one may ask why he did it here. The answer is that he was functioning as God's priest prior to the actual consecration of the Aaronic priests, which would take place in Lev 8. Eventually the priests would take over the assignment of burning the incense,[332] but for now Moses alone was unquestionably qualified. Moses thus fulfilled the commands of Exod 30:1–9, again, "as the LORD commanded him," followed by the erection of the entrance curtain on the east end of the tabernacle proper (26:36–37).

40:29 The bronze altar on which offerings were cooked was set up by Moses in the courtyard in front of the entrance to the tabernacle proper, "as the LORD commanded him" in 27:1–8.

40:30–32 Moses then placed the bronze washing basin in the courtyard "as the LORD commanded Moses" in 30:17–21. The NIV wording of v. 31, "Moses and Aaron and his sons used it to wash their hands and feet," could seem to suggest that then and there Moses, Aaron, and Aaron's sons washed their hands and feet, that is, on the occasion of the erection of the tabernacle on the first day of the first month of the second year.

A better translation of the Hebrew,[333] one that would make clear that such a washing was in the future—not necessarily immediately upon the assembling of the tabernacle—would be "Moses, Aaron, and Aaron's sons were to wash their hands and feet from it." Verse 32 continues that future perspective with its main verb in the imperfect, thus anticipating the washing actions

[332] Lev 2:1–2; 15–16; 6:15; and esp. 16:12–13.

[333] וְרָחֲצוּ מִמֶּנּוּ מֹשֶׁה וְאַהֲרֹן וּבָנָיו אֶת־יְדֵיהֶם וְאֶת־רַגְלֵיהֶם. Note that the main verb (וְרָחֲצוּ) is a converted perfect beginning the sentence, indicating future habitual rather than past action.

described in the ordination of the priests (Lev 8:6). Just as 40:12 was predicting what Moses would eventually do once the tabernacle was entirely set up, so the present paragraph also looked forward to Lev 8, the upcoming consecration/ordination of Israel's priests. This is shown in the NIV's wording in v. 32, "whenever they . . . ," describing recurring actions not yet initiated.

40:33 The courtyard and its entrance curtain were the last items Moses assembled in place, consistent with the original command to do so in 27:9–19 and the recent reminder of that command in 40:8. This final step was not necessarily undertaken as an example of the chronological order of setting up and/or disassembling the tabernacle. Even though when Moses set it up this time he set up the tabernacle proper first and the courtyard last, there is no evidence that the tabernacle proper was set up first and the courtyard set up last *each* time the Israelites arrived at a new location in their journeys in the wilderness. In Num 3–4 the impression given about tabernacle setup and breakdown is that of a joint venture on the part of the workers, with various subdivisions of the Levites working together at the same time to set up or break down various parts of the tabernacle rather than waiting for one part to be taken care of before moving on to the next.

"And so Moses finished the work." He surely didn't do it all himself,[334] but in all likelihood at this juncture he was already training Levites for the work they would eventually do (Lev 3–4). Nevertheless, in biblical Hebrew as in modern English, one can describe the leader of a project as its doer; mentioning the actual hands-on workers is not required because their involvement would be assumed by any thoughtful reader.

(17) The Cloud of Yahweh's Glory Covering the Tabernacle (40:34–38)

34Then the cloud covered the Tent of Meeting, and the glory of the LORD filled the tabernacle. 35Moses could not enter the Tent of Meeting because the cloud had settled upon it, and the glory of the LORD filled the tabernacle. 36In all the travels of the Israelites, whenever the cloud lifted from above the tabernacle, they would set out; 37but if the cloud did not lift, they did not set out—until the day it lifted. 38So the cloud of the LORD was over the tabernacle by day, and fire was in the cloud by night, in the sight of all the house of Israel during all their travels.

In the Masoretic tradition, Exod 40:33 is separated from 40:34 by a formal paragraphing division. However, it is possible that vv. 33b and 34 are to

---

[334] Indeed, it would seem impossible for a single person to do certain of the tasks associated with the setting up of the tabernacle, such as the erection of the large frames and the pulling of the lengthy curtains and coverings over the top of the frames. Likewise, how could Moses possibly put the ark in place by himself since the only proper way to transport it was with the two poles that had to be carried on either end?

be linked syntactically so that the combination would read, "When Moses finished the work, the cloud covered the Tent of Meeting."[335] Either way the presence of the cloud was the result of the successful, obedient completion of the tabernacle, which was therefore ready for the presence of Yahweh to inhabit it symbolically through his glory cloud. The cloud came because the tabernacle was complete, whether or not the grammar per se supports that sequencing.

40:34 The "cloud" was none other than that which first appeared in 12:21–22 and guided and protected the Israelites thereafter in the wilderness as described in 14:19–20,24; 16:10. It was the same cloud the Israelites had seen atop Mount Sinai since their arrival at the mountain (19:9,16; 24:15–18) and the same cloud that had indicated the presence of Yahweh at the entrance to the little tent of meeting Moses had set up outside the camp (33:9–10; 34:5). It was a way God chose to manifest himself—a visible presence—indicating symbol of an invisible God. In the hot, arid wilderness of Sinai, where the sun beat down mercilessly upon people, plants, and animals, a cloud during the day represented a cool, beneficent, shade-giving divine kindness. But the cloud was much more than that. It displayed Yahweh's glory, which was an awesome and frightening thing the closer one got to it. Accordingly, as the Israelites saw the cloud, they understood it to be a potentially overwhelming manifestation of the presence of their God, to be avoided carefully and not infringed upon.[336] The cloud had thus progressed in location from Mount Sinai to the little, temporary tent of meeting to the tabernacle. Presumably since it was only sometimes seen at the tent of meeting, it usually was still seen on Mount Sinai from which it "came down" (33:9) when Moses arrived there (and to which it presumably returned when he left the tent).

"And the glory of the LORD filled the tabernacle." How would an invisible God show his people that he had indeed come to dwell among them as they so earnestly desired[337] and that thereby he was fully in covenant relationship with them, willing to go with them wherever he led them[338] that is, that the rift between Yahweh and his people had been fully healed by reason of God's gracious love for his people and in consequence of Moses' faithful intervention with Yahweh[339] on behalf of the people? The answer is that he visibly went into his house! He left Mount Sinai and came to dwell among the encampment of his people, just as he had promised he would (33:14–17). His people had built his house for him just as he commissioned it, and he

[335] Cf. JPSV.

[336] See comments on 19:16 passim.

[337] See comments on 33:4–6.

[338] See comments on 34:9ff.; and esp. 33:14–17.

[339] As recounted in 32:31–32 and passim in chaps. 33–34.

showed his approval of their efforts and, more importantly, his desire to dwell among them by symbolically entering his house through the glory cloud that covered the house ("Tent of Meeting" now in the sense of tabernacle) and also filled its inside spaces.

The cloud was not the glory but a visible envelopment of the divine glory. God's glory per se might or might not be visible in all manifestations, but when he caused it to be visible, at least through its piercing of the darkness of the cloud, its brilliance was contained in part within the cloud so as not to be impossible to look upon.[340] A similar filling with divine glory showed God's acceptance of the Solomonic temple as his symbolic dwelling place[341] and his heavenly temple likewise.[342]

40:35 Most of this verse restates in slightly different wording what v. 34 said, but with one very important addition: Moses could not enter the tent of meeting precisely because it was filled with Yahweh's glory. Why was this so? Had not Moses earlier entered right into the glory cloud at the top of Mount Sinai?[343] Had he not been inside the little symbolic tent of meeting that served as a contact point between him and Yahweh until the tabernacle had been built, with God's glory descending upon the entrance just a few feet away?[344] And had he not stood right next to Yahweh's glory on other occasions?[345] Of course. All of these former encounters with God's glory had indeed occurred, but now Moses was barred from the tabernacle—the one he had just inspected and set up, thus having been all around its component parts and surely inside it when the furniture was placed there. Why, then, could he not enter once God had entered?

The answer is that the tabernacle was now Yahweh's house and no one else's. It was no more appropriate now for Moses to enter the tabernacle, even though he had been all through it as its building supervisor, than it

---

[340] If something as modest in its proportion of divine glory as the reflected glory of God on Moses' face was difficult for people to look at (see comments on 34:29–35), surely the direct glory of God would be virtually impossible to behold. But since God made it possible for Moses to see it, there can be little doubt that he did so specially, gently, so Moses himself was not even aware of what otherwise might have been impossible to endure (34:29). Consider also that the cloud glowed so brightly with the glory of God that at night it appeared as a pillar/column of fire (13:21–22; 14:24; v. 38). This may have meant that what Moses and the Israelites saw as they looked into the tabernacle from the entrance curtains—even during the daytime—was an awesome glow, perhaps pulsating or flashing (20:18; cf. 2 Sam 22:13 // Ps 18:2), in light of the fact that the interior of the tabernacle was lit only by the single lampstand, and the holy of holies was not lit at all—unless by divine glory.

[341] 1 Kgs 8:11 // 2 Chr 5:14; cf. 2 Chr 7 7:1–2; Ezek 10:4; 43:5.

[342] Rev 15:8, where again the idea of the glory of God filling the temple prevents anyone else from entering.

[343] Exod 24:18.

[344] Exod 33:9–10.

[345] E.g., Exod 34:5.

would be for a house builder in modern times to retain a key and enter at will a house that he had built once it was sold to its occupying owner. When the new owner enters, the new house is exclusively his—not the builder's. Later Moses and Aaron would be able to enter the tabernacle, and provision would be made for the high priest to enter it, even the holy of holies, periodically. This was possible because the glory cloud did not continue to stay inside the tabernacle but mainly hovered on top of it, as vv. 36–38 state overtly.[346] But by the present act of occupying his house through his glory and temporarily keeping all others out, God showed Moses and all Israel that the house was now his and his alone and indeed his truly and entirely, the very thing they had built it to become.

40:36–38 These verses are also repeated, largely verbatim, in Num 9:15–22 in a way that links the present context with the story of the eventual travels of the Israelites and that of Yahweh's tabernacle (and thus far more importantly, Yahweh) with them. In between the two contexts there remains a period of about forty-eight days (from the first day of the first month of the second year, when the tabernacle was erected, as stated in 40:1, to the twentieth day of the second month of the second year, when the Israelites left Sinai, as stated in Num 10:11). During those forty-eight days, the instructions and activities described in all of Leviticus and in Num 1:1–10:11 take place.

The tabernacle usually had the cloud hovering over it; but "whenever the cloud lifted from above the tabernacle," the Israelites knew to set out from wherever they were encamped. They had learned the basics of being led by the cloud prior to arriving at Sinai (13:1–2; 16:10). They knew that if the cloud did not move, they were not to move either but to stay encamped at the last location to which God had led them (v. 37). Just as it had appeared as a dark cloud in the daytime and a fire in the nighttime prior to Sinai (13:21), so it now also changed appearance from day to night and back again as it hovered over the tabernacle (v. 38). The once relatively distant cloud (either far above them in the wilderness or on Mount Sinai or at the entrance to the little tent of meeting outside the camp) was now in the center of their encampment,[347] right above the dwelling place of their God, who "lived" inside his tabernacle. They could see the cloud at all times, so it could at all times guide them in their travels (v. 38).

Once built, the tabernacle became the symbol of Yahweh's presence among his people; and his glory cloud atop the tabernacle, a further symbol of his presence and also of his guidance. The book of Exodus comes to an end here, with the reader implicitly invited to appreciate that a new grand

[346] And as Num 9:15ff. and 10:11ff. confirm.
[347] Num 1:50–53; 2:2ff.

chapter in the history of the Israelites was about to get underway—their travels toward Sinai as their God would lead them. Moses' very next words in the Pentateuch continue the tabernacle story (Lev 1:1, "The LORD called to Moses and spoke to him from the Tent of Meeting"), confirming that the tabernacle was the place from which God would communicate with him and through him to Israel from then on. The invisible, only true God no longer spoke at a distance, on Sinai, but now to Moses, the people's honored and accepted representative,[348] from within their very midst.

Wonderful as this was, it was but a shadow of the closeness to God available now to his corporate people known as the church[349] and his direct indwelling available to every individual who repents of sin and trusts in God's gift of salvation through Christ[350]—his New Covenant's new Moses and his for-all-time honored and accepted representative,[351] rescuer,[352] lawgiver,[353] law ender,[354] and heavenly Temple.[355]

[348] See comments on 33:8–11.
[349] Matt 11:11.
[350] Eph 2:22; Col 1:27.
[351] John 1:14.
[352] Matt 1:21; 2 Tim 1:9.
[353] Gal 6:2.
[354] Rom 10:4.
[355] Rev 21:22.

Selected Bibliography[1]

Ackerman, J. "The Literary Context of the Moses Birth Story." In *Literary Interpretations of Biblical Narratives*. Nashville: Abingdon, 1974, 74–119.

Aejmelaeus, A. "Septuagintal Translation Techniques: A Solution to the Problem of the Tabernacle Account." In *Septuagint, Scrolls and Cognate Studies*. SBLSCS 33. Atlanta: Scholars Press, 1992, 381–402.

Albright, W. F. "Jethro, Hobab and Reuel in Early Hebrew Tradition." *CBQ* 25 (1963): 1–11.

_____. "Northwest-Semitic Names in a List of Egyptian Slaves from the Eighteenth Century B.C." *JAOS* 74 (1954): 222–33.

Andreasen, N.-E. A. *The Old Testament Sabbath*. SBLDS 7. Missoula, Mont.: Society of Biblical Literature, 1972.

Ararat, N. "The Second Commandment: 'Thou Shalt Not Bow Down Unto Them, Nor Serve Them, For I the Lord Thy God Am a Jealous God.'" *Shofar* 13 (1995): 44–57.

Auffret, P. "Essai sur la structure litteraire d'Ex 14." *EstBib* 41 (1983): 53–82.

Baltzer, K. *The Covenant Formulary*. Philadelphia: Fortress, 1971.

Barre, M. "The Fourth Commandment: Is It Just for Kids?" *TBT* 29 (1991): 42–46.

Barrett, M. P. V. "Tests, Tests, and More Tests: Theme Through Several Chapters. Exodus 5,14–17, 32." *BV* 25 (1991): 29–40.

Batto, B. F. "The Reed Sea: Requiescat in Pace." *JBL* 102 (1983): 27–35.

Baumgartner, W. "Zum Problem des Jahwe-Engels." In *Zum Alten Testament und Seiner Umwelt*. Leiden: Brill, 1959, 240–46.

Beale, G. K. "An Exegetical and Theological Consideration of the Hardening of Pharaoh's Heart in Exodus 4–14 and Romans 9." *TJ* 5 (1984): 129–54.

Boecker, H. J. *Law and the Administration of Justice in the Old Testament and Ancient East*. Minneapolis: Augsburg, 1980.

Brenner, M. L. *The Song of the Sea: Ex 15:1–21*. BZAW 195. Berlin: de Gruyter, 1991.

Branden, A. van den. "Le Decalogue." *BeO* 33 (1991): 93–124.

Brueggemann, W. "Pharaoh as Vassal: A Study of Political Metaphor." *CBQ* 57 (1995): 27–51.

Cassuto, U. *A Commentary on the Book of Exodus*. Jerusalem: Magnes Press, 1967.

Childs, B. S. "The Birth of Moses." *JBL* 84 (1965): 109–22.

_____. *The Book of Exodus: A Critical-Theological Commentary*. Louisville: Westminster John Knox, 1974.

Clark, G. R. *The Word* Hesed *in the Hebrew Bible*. JSOTSup 157. Sheffield: Sheffield Academic Press, 1993.

Clifford, R. J. "The Exodus in the Christian Bible: The Case for 'Figural' Reading." *Theological Studies* 63 (2002): 345–62.

Clines, D. J. A. "The Ten Commandments, Reading from Left to Right." In *Interested Parties: The Ideology of Writers and Readers of the Hebrew Bible*. JSOTSup 205.

[1] Here, following the NAC series format, I have provided a sampling for the benefit of the reader from among the more than seventeen hundred books, articles, and commentaries on Exodus in my personal listings. Inclusion here does not intend to suggest that these works are of better quality than those I have not listed but simply to give some sense of the range of literature on various sections and issues of Exodus.

Sheffield: Sheffield Academic Press, 1995, 26–45.
Coats, G. W. "Despoiling the Egyptians." *VT* 18 (1968): 450–57.
_____. *Rebellion in the Wilderness*. Nashville: Abingdon, 1968.
Cole, H. R. "The Sabbath and the Alien." *AUSS* 38 (2000): 223–29.
Collins, N. L. "Notes on the Text of Exodus XXI:22." *VT* 43 (1993): 289–301.
Cross, F. M. Jr. "Kinship and Covenant in Ancient Israel." In *From Epic to Canon: History and Literature in Ancient Israel*. Baltimore/London: Johns Hopkins University Press, 1998, 3–22.
_____. "The Song of the Sea and Canaanite Myth." In *Canaanite Myth and Hebrew Epic*. Cambridge: Harvard University Press, 1973, 112–44.
_____. and D. N. Freedman. "The Song of Miriam." In *Studies in Ancient Yahwistic Poetry*. SBLDS 21. Missoula, Mont.: Scholars Press, 1975, 45–65.
_____. "Yahweh and the God of the Patriarchs." *HTR* 55 (1962): 225–59.
Couroyer, L. P. "L'Exode et la bataille de Qadesh." *RB* 97 (1990): 321–58.
Currid, J. E. *Ancient Egypt and the Old Testament*. Grand Rapids: Baker, 1997.
_____. *A Study Commentary on Exodus*. Vol. 1 (Chapters 1–18); Vol. 2 (Chapters 19–40). Auburn, Mass.: Evangelical Press, 2000–2001.
_____. "The Rod of Moses." *BurH* 33 (1997): 107–14.
_____. "Why Did God Harden Pharaoh's Heart?" *BibRev* 9 (1993): 46–51.
Curtis, E. M. "The Theological Basis for the Prohibition of Images in the Old Testament." *JETS* 28 (1985): 277–87.
Davies, J. A. "A Royal Priesthood: Literary and Intertextual Perspectives on an Image of Israel in Exodus 19:6." *TynBul* 63 (2002): 157–59.
Derby, J. "The Fourth Commandment." *JBQ* 22 (1994): 26–31.
_____. "The Two Tablets of the Covenant." *JBQ* 21 (1993): 73–79.
Dohmen, C. "Der Sinaibund als Neuer Bund nach Ex 19–34." In *Der neue Bund im Alten: Studien zur Bundestheologie der beiden Testamente*. QD 146. Freiburg: Herder, 1993, 51–83.
_____. "'Nicht sieht mich der Mensch und lebt' (Ex 33:20): Aspekte der Gotteschau im Alten Testament." *JBT* 13 (1998): 31–51.
Dozeman, T. B. *God on the Mountain: A Study of Redaction, Theology and Canon in Exodus 19–24*. SBLMS 37. Atlanta: Scholars Press, 1989.
Dumbrell, W. "Exodus 4:24–26: A Textual Re-examination." *HTR* 65 (1972): 285–90.
Durham, J. I. *Exodus*. Word Biblical Commentary. Waco: Word, 1987.
Enns, P. *Exodus*. The NIV Application Commentary. Grand Rapids: Zondervan, 2000.
Esslinger, L. "Freedom or Knowledge? Perspective and Purpose in the Exodus Narrative (Exodus 1–15)." *JSOT* 52 (1991): 43–60.
Exum, J. C. "'You Shall Let Every Daughter Live': A Study of Exodus 1:8–2:10." *Semeia* 28 (1983): 63–82.
Fensham, F. C. "Transgression and Penalty in the Book of the Covenant Code." *JNSL* 5 (1977): 23–41.
Fersterer, A. "Exegetische Notizen zum Sabbatwort. Ex 20,8–11 bzw. Dtn 5, 12–15." *PzB* 3 (1994): 41–63.
Fleming, D. "Mari's Large Public Tent and the Priestly Tent Sanctuary." *VT* 50 (2000): 484–98.
_____. "The Biblical Tradition of Anointing Priests." *JBL* 117 (1998): 401–14.
Frankfort, H. *Ancient Egyptian Religion*. New York: Harper & Brothers, 1961.
Freedman, D. N. "Strophe and Meter in Exodus 15." In *Pottery, Poetry, and Prophecy*. Winona Lake: Eisenbrauns, 1980, 187–227.
Fretheim, T. E. *Exodus*. Interpretation: A Bible Commentary for Teaching and Preaching. Louisville: Westminster John Knox, 1991.

_____. "The Plagues as Ecological Signs of Historical Disaster." *JBL* 110 (1991): 385–96.

Fuller, R. "Exodus 21:22: The Miscarriage Interpretation and the Personhood of the Fetus." *JETS* 37 (1994): 169–84.

Garrett, D. *Rethinking Genesis: The Sources and Authorship of the First Book of the Pentateuch.* Fearn: Christian Focus/Mentor, 2000.

Gosse, B. "L'expiation-racon d'Ex 30, 11–16." *BN* 63 (1992): 26–29.

Hamiel, H. Y. "The Lord Has a War against Amalek." *BMik* 35 (1989–90): 32–46 (Hebrew).

Haran, M. "Seething a Kid in Its Mother's Milk." *ErIsr* 14 (1978): 12–18.

Hillers, D. R. *Covenant: The History of a Biblical Idea.* Baltimore: Johns Hopkins Press, 1969.

Homan, M. M. "The Divine Warrior in His Tent: A Military Model for Yahweh's Tabernacle." *BR* 16 (2000): 22–33, 55.

Hoffmeier, J. K. *Ancient Israel in Sinai: The Evidence for the Authenticity of the Wilderness Tradition.* Oxford/New York: Oxford University Press, 2005.

_____. *Israel in Egypt: The Evidence for the Authenticity of the Exodus Tradition.* Oxford: Oxford University Press, 1997.

Hort, G. "The Plagues of Egypt." *ZAW* 69 (1957): 84–103; *ZAW* 70 (1958): 48–59.

Houtman, C. *Exodus, Vol 1 (1:1–7:13); Vol 2 (7:13–19:25); Vol 3 (20–40).* Leuven: Peeters, 1993–2000.

Huffmonn, H. B. "The Fundamental Code Illustrated: The Third Commandment." In *Pomegranates and Golden Bells.* Winona Lake: Eisenbrauns, 1995, 363–71.

Humphreys, C. J. "The Number of People in the Exodus from Egypt: Decoding Mathematically the Very Large Numbers in Numbers I and xxvi." *VT* 48 (1998): 196–213.

_____. "The Numbers in the Exodus from Egypt: A Further Appraisal." *VT* 50 (2000): 323–28.

Isbell, C. "Exodus 1–2 in the Context of Exodus 1–14: Story Lines and Key Words." In *Art and Meaning: Rhetoric in Biblical Literature.* Sheffield: JSOT Press, 1982, 37–61.

Isser, S. "Two Traditions: The Law of Exodus 21:22–23 Revisited." *CBQ* 52 (1990): 30–45.

Janzen, J. G. "The Character of the Calf and Its Cult in Exodus 32." *CBQ* 52 (1990): 597–607.

_____. "Song of Moses, Song of Miriam: Who Is Seconding Whom?" *CBQ* 54 (1992): 211–20.

Joosten, J. "The Syntax of *zeh Moseh* (Ex 32.1.23)." *ZAW* 103 (1991): 412–15.

Jungbauer, H. *"Ehre Vater und Mutter": Der Weg des Elterngebots in der biblische Tradition.* Tübingen: Mohr Siebeck, 2002.

Kaiser, W. C. Jr. *Exodus.* Expositor's Bible Commentary. Grand Rapids: Zondervan, 1990.

Kitchen, K. A. "Egyptians and Hebrews, from Raamses to Jericho." In *The Origin of Early Israel—Current Debate, Beer-Sheva XII.* Beer-Sheva: Ben Gurion University, 1998, 65–131.

_____. "From the Brickfields of Egypt." *TynBul* 27 (1976): 137–47.

_____. "The Desert Tabernacle: Pure Fiction or Plausible Account?" *BR* 16 (2000): 14–21.

Kline, M. G. "*Lex Talionis* and the Human Fetus." *JETS* 20 (1977): 273–304.

Koch, R. "Le sixieme (cinquieme) commandment (Ex 20, 13; Dt 5, 17)." *StMor* 16 (1978): 9–30.

Kosmala, H. "The So-Called Ritual Decalogue." *ASTI* 1 (1962): 31–61.

Labuschagne, C. J. "'You Shall Not Boil a Kid in Its Mother's Milk': A New Proposal for the Origin of Prohibition." In *The Scriptures and the Scrolls: Studies in Honor of A. S. van der Woude on the Occasion of His 65th Birthday*. Leiden: Brill, 1992, 6–17.

Lohfink, N. *Das Hauptgebot*. AnBib 20. Rome: Istituto Biblico e Pontificio, 1963.

_____. "The Song of Victory at the Red Sea." In *The Christian Meaning of the Old Testament*. Milwaukee: Bruce, 1968, 67–86.

Loretz, O. "Das 'Ahnen-und Götterstatuen-Verbot' im Dekalog und die Einzigkeit Jahwes. Zum Begriff des Gottlichen in altorientalische und alttestamenlichen Qeullen." In *Ein Gott allein? JHWH-Verehrung und biblischer Monotheismus im Kontext der israelitischen und altorientalischen Religionsgeschichte*. OBO 139. Freiburg: University Press, 1994, 491–527.

Marshall, J. W. *Israel and the Book of the Covenant: An Anthropological Approach to Biblical Law*. SBLDS 140. Atlanta: Scholars Press, 1993.

McCarthy, D. J. *Old Testament Covenant: A Survey of Current Opinions*. Richmond: John Knox, 1972.

McKenzie, J. L. "The Elders in the Old Testament." *Bib* 48 (1959): 522–40.

Meek, T. J. *Hebrew Origins*. TB 69. New York: Harper & Brothers, 1960.

Mendenhall, G. E. "The Census Lists of Numbers 1 and 26." *JBL* 77 (1958): 52–66.

Milgrom, J. "'You Shall Not Boil a Kid in Its Mother's Milk.'" *BibRev* 1 (1985): 48–55.

Miscall, P. D. "Hear and Believe Forever." *TBT* 25 (1987): 381–85.

Moberly, R. W. L. *At the Mountain of God: Story and Theology in Exodus 32–34*. JSOTSup 22. Sheffield: JSOT Press, 1983.

Moran, W. L. "A Kingdom of Priests." In *The Bible in Current Catholic Thought*. New York: Herder & Herder, 1962, 7–20.

_____. "The Ancient Near Eastern Background of the Love of God in Deuteronomy." *CBQ* 25 (1963): 77–87.

Muchiki, Y. "Why the Description of the Altar of Incense Was Postponed (Exod 30:1–10)." *Exegetica* 10 (1999): 19–31 [Japanese].

Muilenburg, J. "The Form and Structure of the Covenantal Formulations." *VT* 9 (1959): 347–65.

Nagano, S. "The Elders of Israel in Exodus 24: 9–11." *AJBI* 19 (1993): 3–33.

Negretti, N. *Il settimo giorno*. Rome: Biblical Institute Press, 1973.

Niccacci, A. "Sullo sfondo egiziano di Esodo 1–15." *LASBF* 36 (1986): 7–43.

_____. "Yahweh e il Faraone. Teologia biblica ed egiziana a confronto." *BN* 38/39 (1987): 85–102.

Niehaus, J. J. *God at Sinai*. Grand Rapids: Zondervan, 1995.

Olyan, S. M. "Why an Altar of Unfinished Stones? Some Thoughts on Exod 20,25 and Dtn 27, 5–6." *ZAW* 108 (1996): 161–71.

Osborn, N. D. "Tent or Tabernacle? Translating Two Traditions." *BT* 41 (1990): 214–21.

Oswalt, J. N. "The Golden Calves and the Egyptian Concept of Deity." *EvQ* 45 (1973): 13–20.

Otto, E. "De Dekalog als Brennspiegel israelitischer Rechtsgeschichte." In *Alttestamentlische Glaube und Biblische Theologie: Festschrift fur Horst Dietrich Preuss*. Stuttgart: Kohlhammer, 1992, 59–68.

Patrick, D. "The First Commandment in the Structure of the Pentateuch." *VT* 45 (1995): 107–18.

Paul, S. M. *Studies in the Book of the Covenant in the Light of Cuneiform and Biblical Law*. VTSup 18. Leiden: Brill, 1970.

Polak, F. H. "Water, Rock and Wood: Structure and Thought Pattern in the Exodus Narrative." *JANES* 25 (1997): 19–42.

Plaut, W. G. "The Israelites in Pharaoh's Egypt—A Historical Reconstruction." *Judaism* 27 (1978): 40–46.

Preuss, H. D. "'Ich will mit dir sein.'" *ZAW* 80 (1968): 139–73.
Propp, W. H. C. *Exodus 1–18*. AB. New York: Doubleday, 1998.
_____. "The Skin of Moses' Face: Transfigured or Disfigured?" *CBQ* 49 (1987): 375–86.
Ray, P. J. "The Duration of the Israelite Sojourn in Egypt." *AUSS* 24 (1986): 231–48.
Regalado, F. "The Location of the Sea the Israelites Passed Through." *Journal of the Adventist Theological Society* 13 (2002): 115–34.
Rendtorff, R. "Der Text in seiner Endgestalt. Uberlegungen zu Exodus 19." In *Ernten was man sat. Festschrift fur Klaus Koch zu seinem 65*. Neukirchen-Vluyn: Neukirchener Verlag, 1991, 459–79.
Riggs, J. R. "The Length of Israel's Sojourn in Egypt." *Grace Journal* 12 (1971): 18–35.
Robinson, B. P. "Zipporah to the Rescue: A Contextual Study of Exodus IV 24–26." *VT* 36 (1986): 447–62.
Sakenfeld, K. D. *The Meaning of Hesed in the Hebrew Bible: A New Inquiry*. HSM 17. Missoula, Mont.: Scholars Press, 1978.
Sasson, J. M. "Ritual Wisdom?: On 'Seething a Kid in Its Mother's Milk.'" In *Kein Land für sich allein*. Göttingen: Vandenhoeck & Ruprecht, 2002, 294–308.
Sheriffs, D. "Moving on with God: Key Motifs in Exodus 13–20." *Themelios* 15 (1990): 49–59.
Ska, J. L. *Le passage de la mer: étude de la construction, du style et de la symbolisme d'Ex 14, 1–31*. AnBib 109. Rome: Biblical Institute Press, 1986.
Speiser, E. A. "Census and Ritual Expiation in Mari and Israel." In *Oriental and Biblical Studies*. Philadelphia: University of Pennsylvania Press, 1967, 171–86.
Spencer, M. D. "Moses as Intercessor." *ScrB* 19 (1999): 79–86.
Sprinkle, J. M. "The Interpretation of Exodus 21:22–25 *(lex talionis)* and Abortion." *WTJ* 55 (1993): 233–53.
_____. *The Book of the Covenant: A Literary Approach*. JSOTSup 171. Sheffield: Sheffield Academic Press, 1994.
Stolz, F. "Exodus als Kriegstat Jahwes." In *Jahwes und Israels Kriege: Kriegstheorien und Kriegserfahrungen im Glauben des alten Israels*. Zurich: Theologischer Verlag, 1972, 90–97.
Tomes, R. "Exodus 14: The Mighty Acts of God." *SJTh* 22 (1969): 455–78.
Tigay, J. H. "'Heavy of Mouth' and 'Heavy of Tongue': On Moses' Speech Difficulty." *BASOR* 231 (1978): 57–67.
Trible, P. "Bringing Miriam out of the Shadows." *BibRev* 5 (1989): 14–25, 34.
Vaux, R. de. "La mission de Moise." In *Histoire ancienne d'Israel, Vol. 1: Des origins a l'installation en Canaan*. Paris: Gabalda, 1971, 305–37.
Vervenne, M. "Exodus Expulsion and Exodus Flight: The Interpretation of a Crux Critically Examined." *JNSL* 22 (1996): 45–58.
Watts, J. D. W. "The Song of the Sea—Ex. XV." *VT* 7 (1957): 371–80.
Weimar, P and E. Zenger. *Exodus*. Geschichten und Geschichte der Befreiung Israels. Stuttgart Bibelstudien 75. Stuttgart: KBW Verlag, 1975.
Weinfeld, M. "What Makes the Ten Commandments Different?" *BibRev* 7 (1991): 34–41.
Wenham, J. "Large Numbers in the Bible." *JBQ* 21 (1993): 116–20.
West, S. "The *Lex Talionis* in the Torah." *JBQ* 21 (1993): 183–88.
Wilson, R. R. "The Hardening of Pharaoh's Heart." *CBQ* 41 (1979): 18–36.
Yaron, R. "Stylistic Conceits II: The Absolute Infinitive in Biblical Law." In *Pomegranates and Golden Bells*. Winona Lake: Eisenbrauns, 1995, 449–60.
Youngblood, R. "Counting the Ten Commandments." *BR* 10 (1994): 30–35, 50, 52.
Zyl, D. C. van. "Exodus 19:3–6 and the Kerygmatic Perspective of the Pentateuch." *OTE* 5 (1992): 264–71.

Selected Subject Index

Person Index

Selected Scripture Index

Leviticus

Numbers

Deuteronomy

Joshua

Judges

Jeremiah

Lamentations

Ezekiel

Daniel

1 Corinthians

2 Corinthians

Galatians

Ephesians

Philippians

Colossians

1 Thessalonians

1 Timothy

2 Timothy

Titus

Hebrews

James

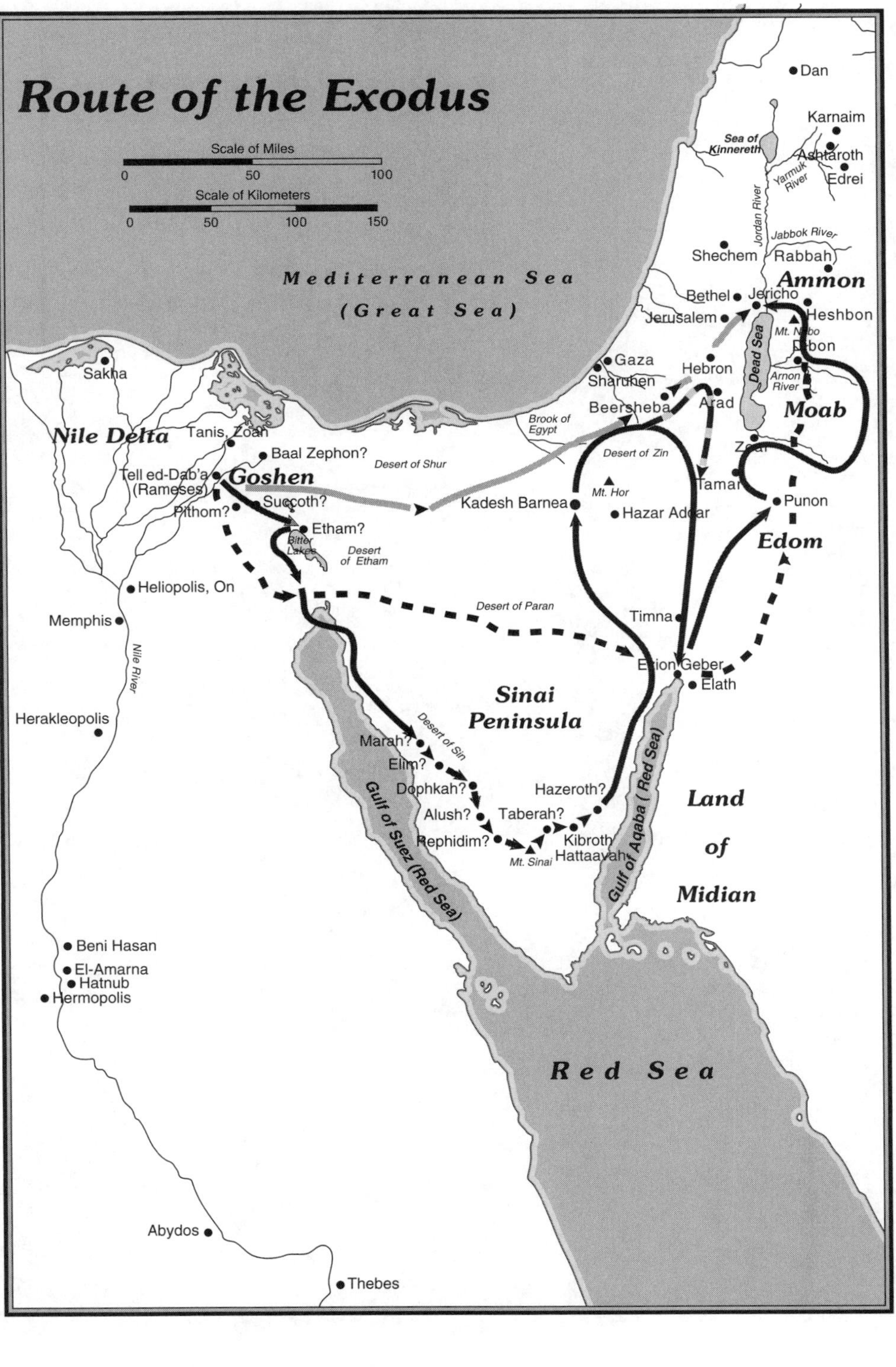
Route of the Exodus
Scale of Miles
0
50
100
Scale of Kilometers
0
50
100
150
Mediterranean Sea
(Great Sea)
Dan
Karnaim
Sea of Kinnereth
Ashtaroth
Yarmuk River
Edrei
Jordan River
Jabbok River
Shechem
Rabbah
Ammon
Bethel
Jericho
Jerusalem
Heshbon
Mt. Nebo
Dibon
Dead Sea
Gaza
Sharuhen
Hebron
Arnon River
Arad
Beersheba
Moab
Brook of Egypt
Zoar
Desert of Zin
Tamar
Mt. Hor
Kadesh Barnea
Hazar Addar
Punon
Edom
Sakha
Nile Delta
Tanis, Zoan
Baal Zephon?
Desert of Shur
Tell ed-Dab'a (Rameses)
Goshen
Succoth?
Pithom?
Etham?
Bitter Lakes
Desert of Etham
Heliopolis, On
Memphis
Desert of Paran
Nile River
Timna
Ezion Geber
Elath
Sinai Peninsula
Herakleopolis
Desert of Sin
Marah?
Elim?
Dophkah?
Hazeroth?
Alush?
Taberah?
Rephidim?
Mt. Sinai
Kibroth Hattaavah
Gulf of Suez (Red Sea)
Gulf of Aqaba (Red Sea)
Land of Midian
Beni Hasan
El-Amarna
Hatnub
Hermopolis
Red Sea
Abydos
Thebes